Handbook of Research on Promoting Economic and Social Development Through Serious Games

Oscar Bernardes
ISCAP, ISEP, Polytechnic Institute of Porto, Portugal & University of Aveiro, Portugal

Vanessa Amorim
Porto Accounting and Business School, Polytechnic Institute of Porto, Portugal

A volume in the Advances in Human and Social
Aspects of Technology (AHSAT) Book Series

Published in the United States of America by
IGI Global
Information Science Reference (an imprint of IGI Global)
701 E. Chocolate Avenue
Hershey PA, USA 17033
Tel: 717-533-8845
Fax: 717-533-8661
E-mail: cust@igi-global.com
Web site: http://www.igi-global.com

Library of Congress Cataloging-in-Publication Data

Names: Bernardes, Oscar, 1978- editor. | Amorim, Vanessa, 1992- editor.
Title: Handbook of research on promoting economic and social development
  through serious games / Oscar Bernardes, and Vanessa Amorim, editor.
Description: Hershey PA : Engineering Science Reference, [2022] | Includes
  bibliographical references and index. | Summary: "With technological
  novelty a growing basis for innovative change in many kinds of
  environments such as in education, commerce, marketing, work, health,
  governance, and sustainability, this publication will contribute to the
  serious games field by investigating original contributions and methods
  that use serious games in various domains and areas"-- Provided by
  publisher.
Identifiers: LCCN 2021037993 (print) | LCCN 2021037994 (ebook) | ISBN
  9781799897323 (hardcover) | ISBN 9781799897347 (ebook)
Subjects: LCSH: Video games--Social aspects. | Serious games. |
  Gamification. | Simulation games in education.
Classification: LCC GV1202.S47 H36 2022 (print) | LCC GV1202.S47 (ebook)
  | DDC 794.8--dc23/eng/20211109
LC record available at https://lccn.loc.gov/2021037993
LC ebook record available at https://lccn.loc.gov/2021037994

This book is published in the IGI Global book series Advances in Human and Social Aspects of Technology (AHSAT) (ISSN: 2328-1316; eISSN: 2328-1324)

British Cataloguing in Publication Data
A Cataloguing in Publication record for this book is available from the British Library.

All work contributed to this book is new, previously-unpublished material. The views expressed in this book are those of the authors, but not necessarily of the publisher.

For electronic access to this publication, please contact: eresources@igi-global.com.

Advances in Human and Social Aspects of Technology (AHSAT) Book Series

Mehdi Khosrow-Pour, D.B.A.
Information Resources Management Association, USA

ISSN:2328-1316
EISSN:2328-1324

MISSION

In recent years, the societal impact of technology has been noted as we become increasingly more connected and are presented with more digital tools and devices. With the popularity of digital devices such as cell phones and tablets, it is crucial to consider the implications of our digital dependence and the presence of technology in our everyday lives.

The **Advances in Human and Social Aspects of Technology (AHSAT) Book Series** seeks to explore the ways in which society and human beings have been affected by technology and how the technological revolution has changed the way we conduct our lives as well as our behavior. The AHSAT book series aims to publish the most cutting-edge research on human behavior and interaction with technology and the ways in which the digital age is changing society.

COVERAGE

- Digital Identity
- Computer-Mediated Communication
- End-User Computing
- Technology Dependence
- Technology Adoption
- ICTs and human empowerment
- Technology and Social Change
- Cyber Bullying
- Cyber Behavior
- Cultural Influence of ICTs

IGI Global is currently accepting manuscripts for publication within this series. To submit a proposal for a volume in this series, please contact our Acquisition Editors at Acquisitions@igi-global.com or visit: http://www.igi-global.com/publish/.

Titles in this Series

For a list of additional titles in this series, please visit: http://www.igi-global.com/book-series/advances-human-social-aspects-technology/37145

Handbook of Research on Applying Emerging Technologies Across Multiple Disciplines
Emiliano Marchisio ("Giustino Fortunato" University of Benevento, Italy)
Information Science Reference • © 2022 • 405pp • H/C (ISBN: 9781799884767) • US $245.00

Impact and Role of Digital Technologies in Adolescent Lives
Shaveta Malik (Terna Engineering College, India) Rohit Bansal (Department of Management Studies, Vaish College of Engineering, Rohtak, India) and Amit Kumar Tyagi (Vellore Institute of Technology, Chennai, India)
Information Science Reference • © 2022 • 313pp • H/C (ISBN: 9781799883180) • US $195.00

Applied Ethics in a Digital World
Ingrid Vasiliu-Feltes (University of Miami, USA) and Jane Thomason (University College London, UK)
Information Science Reference • © 2022 • 316pp • H/C (ISBN: 9781799884675) • US $195.00

Multidisciplinary Perspectives on Diversity and Equity in a Virtual World
Emily K. Reeves (Midwestern State University, USA) and Christina Janise McIntyre (Midwestern State University, USA)
Information Science Reference • © 2022 • 317pp • H/C (ISBN: 9781799880288) • US $195.00

Next-Generation Applications and Implementations of Gamification Systems
Filipe Portela (University of Minho, Portugal) and Ricardo Queirós (ESMAD, Polytechnic Institute of Porto, Portugal)
Engineering Science Reference • © 2022 • 281pp • H/C (ISBN: 9781799880899) • US $245.00

Philosophical Issues of Human Cyborgization and the Necessity of Prolegomena on Cyborg Ethics
Ivana Greguric (Faculty of Croatian Studies, University of Zagreb, Croatia)
Information Science Reference • © 2022 • 352pp • H/C (ISBN: 9781799892311) • US $195.00

Technological Influences on Creativity and User Experience
Joshua Fairchild (Creighton University, USA)
Information Science Reference • © 2022 • 305pp • H/C (ISBN: 9781799843542) • US $195.00

Human Factors Issues and the Impact of Technology on Society
Heather Lum (Embry-Riddle Aeronautical University, USA)
Information Science Reference • © 2021 • 333pp • H/C (ISBN: 9781799864530) • US $195.00

701 East Chocolate Avenue, Hershey, PA 17033, USA
Tel: 717-533-8845 x100 • Fax: 717-533-8661
E-Mail: cust@igi-global.com • www.igi-global.com

EDITORIAL ADVISORY BOARD

List of Contributors

Table of Contents

Detailed Table of Contents

Chapter 1

Arthur Stofella, Universidade Federal de Santa Catarina, Brazil
Luciane Maria Fadel, Universidade Federal de Santa Catarina, Brazil

Serious games need to reflect reality to achieve their purpose, whether learning, training, or provoking a behavioral change. At the same time, serious games employ features that make gaming a self-motivating, engaging, and fantastic activity. This chapter presents a conceptual model to support the design of serious games that deals with the balance between fidelity and play. Design science research guided the model development. Fidelity was conceived as a field force that attracts fun, motivation, and engagement. The model arranged the game elements into three major groups: the Game-World, the Interaction-World, and the Player's-World. Fidelity can assume different levels in each of these worlds. The Fidelity and Play model (FP) allows a holistic view of the relationship and balance between fidelity and play in a serious game.

Chapter 2

Jose A. Ruipérez Valiente, University of Murcia, Spain

The exponential growth of technology is transforming most existing sectors in the world. One of the technologies that is significantly impacting our society is video games, which have become a new cultural form of expression. Moreover, research suggests that, especially within educational contexts, they present great learning opportunities. However, little is known in serious games about the interplay of the in-game activity, learning gains, and enjoyment with the game. Therefore, in this chapter, the authors use data from a pilot study conducted with a STEM inquiry-learning serious game to compute behavioral metrics and analyze their relationship with the learning gains and enjoyment of students based on survey responses. The author reports on the exploratory results of the different metrics and correlation analysis to analyze the interplay between these three sets of metrics. This work will exemplify the potential that learning analytics approaches and serious games have to transform education and training across contexts.

Chapter 3

Kun Wang, The University of Manchester, UK
Ian Stewart, The University of Manchester, UK

To address the learning, teaching, and functional issues in a pandemic, large-sized class, and virtual learning environment, a two-week-long serious game was designed to act as the main welcome activity. Three hundred twenty students played through four scenarios with the pandemic as their background, and a narrative device contributed to an immersive learning environment. The game was deployed over two weeks, using a range of reports, video content, online collaborative platforms, and novelty applied mass communication theory, which effectively enhanced inter- and intra-team interaction and prepared the students for their project management team-based experiential learning. This case study will walk readers through the processes and theories used to create the game and ensure its operational, social, and pedagogic benefits.

Chapter 4

Adnan Ahmad, COMSATS University Islamabad, Lahore, Pakistan
Furkh Zeshan, COMSATS University Islamabad, Lahore, Pakistan
Muhammad Hamid, University of Veterinary and Animal Sciences, Lahore, Pakistan
Rutab Marriam, COMSATS University Islamabad, Lahore, Pakistan
Alia Samreen, COMSATS University Islamabad, Lahore, Pakistan

When game elements are used in other domains, it is referred to as "gamification," which is used to improve the engagement and motivation level of users. These benefits encourage its use in education to enhance student engagement, motivation, and learning outcomes. This chapter highlights the historical advent of gamification, its blending into the educational domain, an overview of various platforms to aid this blending, and an exploration of studies signifying its benefits in education. This chapter also outlines a case study to investigate its effectiveness and provides some practical considerations for the educational industry. The analysis suggests that gamification can be considered as a complementary tool to be integrated into the traditional classroom environment.

Chapter 5

Pierluigi Muoio, University of Calabria, Italy
Lorella Gabriele, University of Calabria, Italy

This chapter presents an experience of university distance education carried out during the COVID-19 emergency, using gamification to make teaching more engaging and motivating for students. In particular, the proposed work is aimed at addressing two different needs: 1) to proactively deal with the exceptional consequences due to COVID-19 in the educational field and 2) to innovate teaching practices by promoting an active learning approach. Hence, game elements and game design techniques were used to design a course program aimed at fostering a high degree of involvement among students to increase both personal satisfaction and student performance. Results confirm that the set educational path, giving greater emphasis to the social, emotional, and experiential dimensions, actively engaged students in the learning process, recording a high percentage of appreciation for the course.

Chapter 6

Héctor Cardona-Reyes, Center for Research in Mathematics, Mexico
Miguel Angel Ortiz Esparza, Universidad Autónoma de Aguascalientes, Mexico

Derived from the current situation, in which physical contact and closeness between people must be taken care of due to COVID-19, emerging technologies such as virtual reality have taken a fundamental role in continuing with activities in various areas of society. This chapter proposes the use of virtual reality environments as an alternative for the acquisition of learning skills for children in an immersive and interactive way with user-centered content. The design elements of the software, the user-centered aspects, and the involved actors considered for the production of the proposed interactive virtual reality environments are presented. As a result, the evaluation of the user experience resulting from the use of the proposed interactive environments with elementary school children is presented. Virtual reality is a technology that nowadays can be an effective support for the acquisition of learning skills through the execution of various tasks designed by a multidisciplinary group and above all encourages the user to continue acquiring learning skills in a friendly and fun way.

Chapter 7

Kartheka Bojan, BrainBerry Ltd., UK
Aikaterini Christogianni, Brainberry Ltd., UK
Elizabeta Mukaetova-Ladinska, Leicester University, UK

Serious gaming (SG) is an emerging field that has a unique role in healthcare. With big data and continuous monitoring becoming a new trend in healthcare, SG is evolving faster in the medical field due to its fit into psychology and neuroscience. The SG multi-perspective and multi-functioning framework has the potential to add new dimensions to current treatment pathways and make a significant contribution to healthcare big data. SG data will add more perspective and value to clinical data both from psychological and neurological perspectives, which are still underplayed fields. SG research directed into intensive scientific and clinical pathways is critical for the next level of evolution of health data and health systems. This chapter addresses the importance of psychological data being implemented into health data and SG's role and its future in contributing to new treatment pathways for any disease condition.

Chapter 8

Ana Maria Gonzaga, Hospital Magalhães Lemos, Portugal
Maria Céu Lamas, Escola Superior Saúde, Instituto Politécnico do Porto, Portugal

With the increase in average life expectancy and the demographic ageing of the worldwide population, several challenges have emerged at the social, economic, and health are levels. To improve this process, the WHO advocates active ageing, where cognitive stimulation is one of the important aspects to consider for the adoption of a healthy lifestyle and the care of one's mental health. In this framework, serious games can bring more benefits to older people and caregivers. In order to assess the contribution of serious games, a bibliographic research was carried out in the Web of Science database, using the terms "serious game" and "elderly." It is found that the use of serious games has benefits in several domains. Within the scope of cognitive stimulation, there are several games, although they do not value the difficulties that individuals have in their IADLs. In this context, it is important to stimulate skills related to money management. This intervention will help to maintain daily living skills and optimize responses to functional losses, resulting in active aging.

Chapter 9

Patricia Quiroz-Palma, Universitat Politècnica de València, Spain & University "Eloy
Alfaro" of Manabi, Ecuador
M. Carmen Penadés, Universitat Politècnica de València, Spain
Ana Gabriela Núñez, University of Cuenca, Ecuador & Universitat Politècnica de València,
Spain

As serious games are nowadays more frequently used for learning purposes in different domains, the success of the tasks in the organization depends on the stakeholders' training and capabilities, and in the emergency management domain, this is no exception. Accordingly, stakeholders in emergency management need adequate training to respond effectively to an incident. Their perception of safety is a goal for organizations, and proper training could ensure their adequate participation in the activities of emergency plan management. This chapter presents a serious game for training stakeholders to respond to emergency incidents designed to optimize the costs involved. For this purpose, a tool was developed that allowed the learning process to be evaluated through an experiment with a group of workers in an organization. The results obtained were found to be valuable assessments of the learning objectives and showed that serious games contributed to improving continuous training in organizations.

Chapter 10

Lucas Antonio Oliveira Rodrigues, Federal University of Uberlândia, Brazil
Leonardo Assis Gaspar, Federal University of Uberlândia, Brazil
Rogério Sales Gonçalves, Federal University of Uberlândia, Brazil

The video game market has been experiencing constant growth throughout the last decade, especially after 2008 with the rise of mobile gaming and after 2016 with virtual and augmented reality technologies. As a result of the ever-growing applications of games, the rehabilitation process of disabilities caused by stroke, cerebral palsy, and other neurological diseases has incorporated games designed to assist recovery. Based on these facts, this chapter deals with the development of two serious games designed to be integrated with two structures: ReGear, a new design for interlimb rehabilitation mechanisms, and HOPE-G, a novel gait rehabilitation structure capable of balance training. Both systems apply assist-as-needed control techniques to improve the outcomes of the treatment. The first clinical trials in one of the structures were conducted on a group of healthy volunteers and another with post-stroke patients, showing encouraging results regarding the serious game and the mechanical design.

    Maria Cutumisu, University of Alberta, Canada
    Simran K. Ghoman, University of Alberta, Canada
    Georg M. Schmölzer, University of Alberta, Canada

Resuscitation Training for healthcare professionals (RETAIN) is an immersive simulation-based platform that aims to improve access for neonatal resuscitation providers. This review of the research that measures the educational outcomes of training with RETAIN identified nine original research papers, two review papers, and one case study. Findings show that RETAIN is clinically relevant, engaging, improves short-and long-term knowledge and transfer of the key steps of neonatal resuscitation, and may be used as a formative or summative assessment. Further, performance on the RETAIN digital simulator was moderated by healthcare professional (HCP) attitudes, including growth mindset, and was compared across clusters obtained based on HCPs' attitudes towards technology. This simulator presents an attractive and accessible immersive learning approach towards training and assessing neonatal resuscitation competence. By improving the knowledge and skills of neonatal resuscitation providers, immersive media such as RETAIN may ultimately improve health outcomes for our smallest patients.

    Richard Chen Li, The Hong Kong Polytechnic University, Hong Kong
    Meike Belter, HIT Lab NZ, University of Canterbury, New Zealand
    Zoë Platt-Young, HIT Lab NZ, University of Canterbury, New Zealand
    Heide Karen Lukosch, HIT Lab NZ, University of Canterbury, New Zealand

Mental health and neurodevelopmental disorders are common among children and young adults. They can negatively affect children's social behaviour, development, and performance in school. This chapter discusses three common mental health and neurodevelopmental disorders and how serious immersive games could support this group. Serious immersive games are games that are designed with a certain purpose in mind and make use of immersive technologies like virtual or augmented reality. As games are a vital element of youth culture, the authors claim that immersive game elements could be utilized to engage a larger group with the health system and offer safe and motivating environments. This chapter shows that work exists to explore the use of games or immersive technologies in mental health support. However, the authors also show that there are shortcomings in the current research and propose research directions to address those.

    Nicholas Kun Lie Goh, Institute of Mental Health, Singapore
    Tze Jui Goh, Institute of Mental Health, Singapore
    Choon Guan Lim, Institute of Mental Health, Singapore
    Daniel Shuen Sheng Fung, Institute of Mental Health, Singapore

A key ingredient in successful psychological therapies is found in patients' motivation and willingness to engage in and follow through with the therapy program. Engaging children is challenging for various reasons, such as their role in their presentation for treatment and differences in parent and child motivations. This chapter explores the utility of serious games as a potential option that offers an engaging and effective approach to psychiatric treatment for children and adolescents with mental health difficulties. The authors review research projects utilizing the serious games methodology at the Child Guidance Clinic, an outpatient psychiatric clinic for children and adolescents in Singapore, in the management of various mental health concerns. The utility and feasibility of gamified interventions for autism spectrum disorders, attention-deficit hyperactive disorder, anxiety disorders, and anger management issues are discussed, along with practical implications for the application of serious games in mental healthcare.

Chapter 14

The present work focuses on the issue of serious game design (SGD) through the lens of sociocultural theory. First, the main challenges that the field of SGD faces are briefly outlined. Second, Vygotsky's sociocultural theory is introduced and explored as a means to address these challenges. Third, a rationale for SGD that is informed by Vygotsky's ideas is introduced. This rationale is based on (1) viewing concepts as psychological tools and (2) conceptualizing two types of resources for SGD: exploration and application. According to this rationale, SGD needs to include a problem, exploration resources, and application resources. The chapter concludes with a discussion of the major implications of the proposed rationale for SGD.

Chapter 15

The chapter aims to explore how serious games can provide cultural organizations with opportunities to attract audiences. In the first part, main terms (games, serious games, gamification, meaningful gamification) are defined, along with some features of players as well as game-related aspects, like dynamics and mechanics, that are identified and described. The chapter presents the main features of an effective design of serious games for cultural heritage. This part is supported by the application of gamification literature concepts and models to cultural heritage and by evidence from applications in the field. In the last part, some controversial aspects connected to the use of gamification for cultural heritage are presented. Some problems in implementing, mostly connected to the lack of resources, and some possible solutions are outlined.

Chapter 16

Queens Game explores the potential of creating a serious game for cultural heritage through collaborative intersectorial research and production. Popular neo-medieval entertainment-games lack correct historical content and the appeal of modern character-based screen period drama, which often focuses on female protagonists: princesses attract large followings. Female player-characters in games usually act and dress like males – though studies show that female gamers prefer atmospheric exploration, interactive drama, and gathering and crafting to defeating enemies. The Queens Game incorporates well-researched history and features exploration and gathering, utilizing period-drama and musical approaches to characterization and staging. The player-character, based on a real medieval princess, lives in a virtual, populated, explorable version of her real castle, now built over. Medieval visual, musical, and storytelling modes in a historically accurate setting immerse visitors in the Middle Ages, potentially attracting players who don't normally enjoy games as well as those who do.

Serious games are analyzed through the principles of New Humanism, the humanization of computer games for training. The chapter defined the types of serious games for Western and Japanese management. Based on this, the characteristics and criteria that serious next-generation games must meet are described. In particular, hard-skills serious games are focused on Western management; emphasize gameplay on formalization, logic, clear rules, and work functionality; and have the aesthetics of a challenge aimed at academic training and practice of skills. The core of soft-skills serious games are creativity, innovation, research, personal qualities, and implicit knowledge aimed at solving cognitive and social problems, so they best embody the principles of the Japanese approach to management. The threats and shortcomings of such games have been clarified. The trends in the development of serious games in automated recruiting systems are revealed. It is emphasized that in the "education-recruitment-spirituality" system, serious games play a connecting and integrating role.

Chapter 18

The circular economy has gained attention in recent years as a sustainable alternative to the current linear economic model. Supply chains have an essential role in the transition towards a circular economy. However, the transition towards circular supply chains is challenging for companies due to the lack of knowledge and awareness among the supply chain members. In order to overcome this barrier, the CircuSChain Game was developed based on the well-known Beer Distribution Game. The CircuSChain Game is a multi-player board game supported by a calculation sheet. The game considers reuse, refurbishing, remanufacturing, and recycling activities within closed-and open-loops, as well as CO_2 emissions and material scarcity concepts. An experiment was conducted with industrial engineering students in order to test the CircuSChain Game and assess its educational value, game pace, entertainment value, and simplicity.

Nadeem Ahmed Khan, Dr. B. R. Ambedkar National Institute of Technology, Jalandhar,
India
Arun Khosla, Dr. B. R. Ambedkar National Institute of Technology, Jalandhar, India
Girish S. Pujar, National Remote Sensing Centre, Hyderabad, India
Parampreet Singh, Dr. B. R. Ambedkar National Institute of Technology, Jalandhar, India

Agroforestry is a type of land management in which trees or shrubs are planted around or amid crops or pastureland. It integrates agriculture and forestry technology to create land-use systems. This approach aids farmers in raising production, managing nutrient cycling, and enhancing their socio-economic standing. However, well-managed systems have several advantages over monocultures, although this approach is not widely used in the country. Agroforestry is hampered by a lack of competent management, a lack of technological help, a rigorous regulation of tree harvesting, and an irregular, unorganized market. As a result of these factors, farmers are hesitant to plant trees on their land, leading to the notion of agroforestry not being widely used in the world. Through this chapter, the authors attempt to understand the reasons for the lack of knowledge about agroforestry and help in designing solutions using serious gaming to alter farmers' behavior and propose a method in the form of a serious game to promote agroforestry practices among the farmers.

Sonali Beri, Dr. B. R. Ambedkar National Institute of Technology, Jalandhar, India
Arun Khosla, Dr. B. R. Ambedkar National Institute of Technology, Jalandhar, India
Girish S. Pujar, National Remote Sensing Centre, India
Parampreet Singh, Dr. B. R. Ambedkar National Institute of Technology, Jalandhar, India

Serious games are potential providers of education and are in trend nowadays as they are a combination of education and fun. There are various applications for it, and one of those is in the context of natural resource management. Water scarcity is an issue that is being witnessed nowadays all over the world. Annual water consumption is much more than that of groundwater recharge. To overcome such issues, a watershed can be an efficient approach leading towards groundwater replenishment and improving the quality of water, along with other benefits like preventing soil erosion, floods, etc. A GIS-based serious game for watershed management will be a good way to increase stakeholder participation in water resource conservation and management. Adding an extra element to this project can be beneficial. It is to make the game GIS or geospatially adaptive (i.e., a framework to be implemented to replicate the game to different locations without human intervention).

Sam Redfern, Newby Chinese Ltd., Ireland
Richard McCurry, Newby Chinese Ltd., Ireland

In this chapter, the authors discuss the Newby Chinese game-based learning (GBL) platform for group-based teaching of beginners Mandarin Chinese as a second language. Details are provided on the design of games within the platform, the pedagogical theories which they support, and the ways that theories of fun and teaching intersect to produce an effective learning experience which students actually enjoy.

While aspects of the games within the platform have been designed to specifically support modern Chinese-learning pedagogy, the approaches taken and lessons learned should be useful for a range of GBL content. Newby Chinese has been used by thousands of students over the last three years, and its continued development has been informed by this practical experience.

The chapter explores disruptive uses of serious games to achieve radical urban visions through the presentation and critical discussion of three recent case studies developed in graduate and postgraduate university courses. The chapter addresses the underpinnings of game-based design practices and discusses their untapped potential to spark imagination and bring about new urban visions. The focus is on subverting the expectations of the aims, methods, and results of spatial design projects in the context of higher educational institutions. Most importantly, games and play are used to radically address pressing technical, societal, and environmental topics in a disruptive way, generating new urban visions that push the limits of what is considered probable, desirable, and even imaginable.

Due to technological advancement, the authors see a huge change in the way of teaching and learning. Game-based learning (GBL) is applied in order to motivate students, improve their knowledge, and make the process of education more enjoyable. This chapter will focus on explaining the process of learning analytics (LA) in the context of GBL, which can play a meaningful role in transforming learning pathways in games into interpretable information for teachers. Respectively, the overarching aim of this work is to verify the potential of GBL and LA applied to the educational process through four case studies, each of which presents an important metric in the geometry game Shadowspect, developed in order to train geometry and spatial reasoning skills by solving a series of geometry puzzles. The case studies will be focused on data-driven game design, learner modelling and adaptive learning, game-based assessment (GBA) of 21st-century skills, and teacher-oriented visualization dashboards.

Chapter 24

Technology has garnered attention as a successful tool for second language learning that could help improve immigrant integration and inclusion. More specifically, digital learning games have been identified as an effective tool for enhancing a variety of outcomes related to second language learning, including language acquisition, motivation, and confidence. Digital learning games differentiate instruction, provide immediate feedback, situate the learning, and offer a safe and engaging environment to practice the target language. However, it is important that digital learning games are designed with the end-users in mind. For that reason, this study outlines how researchers and game developers can utilize user-centered design to develop a context-specific digital language learning game for immigrants. As an example, the authors present the four-phase process of an ongoing game design project in Finland, including general findings from interviews with teachers.

Preface

Recent years have seen a surge in the popularity of serious games. The number of peer-reviewed scientific articles devoted to serious games (SG's) has grown, reinforcing this trend. Serious games have gained traction in various fields, including health, education, business, and technology.

There is a debate about "games" and "serious games". This book examines the extensive literature on the economic and social impact of serious games through various scenarios. However, before discussing the literature, it is necessary to review what a game is and a serious game.

Gaming is becoming increasingly prevalent in our culture and everyday lives as a type of leisure activity, and we play in a variety of contexts and scenarios with the goal of acquiring pleasant and unique experiences for ourselves and other people. There are many different definitions of the "game" concept, and there is a great deal of debate over it. Game definitions frequently lump together games and video games, as the majority of definitions were created after video games established themselves as a symbol of cultural strength and an innovative sector seeing rapid expansion. However, according to the Oxford Dictionary, a game is "a form of competitive activity or sport played by rules". A game can also be thought of as the sum of the following characteristics: fictitious activity, unpredictability, rules, time and space limits, and no mandatory character. In addition, games have their own set of advantages, providing higher levels of engagement and intrinsic motivation in their users, contributing to the achievement of cognitive, emotional, and social benefits.

The gamification field is still growing, so many theories are related to the gamification definition. Gamification is considered a concept whose origin is associated with the digital industry, and its first use was in 2008; however, it has only started to be widely used from 2010. Gamification is represented by specific criteria, through the concepts: (1) gamefulness - which represents the quality of experience and behavior; (2) gameful interaction - resources that provide a certain quality; and (3) gameful design - design of the elements presented in the games.

The concept consists of implementing and developing game design elements, namely: components, mechanics (internal and external), and game dynamics. The game components represent the furthermost directly observable and tangible form of gamification through systems that include points, badges, content unlocking, progress bars, teams, levels, or missions. The gaming components are responsible for executing the respective gaming mechanics through incentive-like mechanisms such as challenges, competition, cooperation, feedback, rewards, or virtual goods. In this way, motivational dynamics are created, corresponding to a more intangible form of gamification.

Its distinction from the serious game's concept is fundamental in defining the gamification concept. In this sense, it is necessary to consider first the differences between the elements of gamification and the design of games that compose each of these typologies. While gamification uses game elements in non-game contexts, SG's use various game elements to build a game for purposes unrelated to fun or entertainment, such as educational learning, human resources management, or other fields. However, according to the literature, SG's and gamification jointly seek changes in their users' behaviors to offer the best overall experience to their users through pleasant interactions using different levels of motivation.

Because games have been proven to teach knowledge or skills that will be useful in life, serious games can also increase engagement and target behavior in many areas. In this sense, this book covers many topics related to serious games that fit into today's world. Therefore, it is suitable for anyone interested in learning more about serious games and their application in various fields.

The book comprises 24 chapters, where every chapter explains different implementations of serious games from a multidisciplinary view. It covers all the necessary information about serious games, starting from fidelity and play model: balancing seriousness. An interesting point of view where serious games in the educational context could be more beneficial during the COVID-19 pandemic is also presented in this book. In the health domain, the contributions of serious games are described, namely from the perspective of money management by the elderly, emergency management training, neonatal resuscitation education, and in the context of mental health. It also discusses the role of serious games in sociocultural theories, cultural heritage, new humanism recruitment, agroforestry, and watershed management. Contributions on how game-based techniques might be applied in radical urban visions and educational contexts are also included in this book.

The first chapter, "Fidelity and Play Model: Balancing Seriousness," proposes a conceptual model for serious game creation that addresses the balance of fidelity and play. This chapter's Fidelity & Play model provides a comprehensive understanding of the relationship and balance between fidelity and plays in a serious game.

Gaming is a new cultural form of expression that has a tremendous impact on our culture. Moreover, studies show that games are excellent teaching tools in school settings. Nevertheless, little is known about how in-game activities, learning, and game enjoyment interact in serious games. In this context, Chapter 2, "The Interplay Between In-Game Activity, Learning Gains, and Enjoyment in a Serious Game on STEM," purports to analyze data from a pilot study conducted with a STEM inquiry-learning serious game to compute behavioral metrics and analyze their relationship with the learning gains and enjoyment of students based on survey responses.

The next chapter, " The Case of a Serious Game to Prepare 320 International Students for Virtual Learning in Project Management During a Pandemic," seeks to analyze the learning, teaching, and functional issues in a pandemic, large-sized class and virtual learning environment. This case study will take readers through the methods and theories that developed the game and ensured its operational, social, and pedagogical benefits.

"Application of Gamification in Modern Education" highlights the historical advent of gamification. It is blending into the educational domain, an overview of various platforms to aid this blending and an exploration of studies signifying its benefits in education. Additionally, this chapter details a case study to demonstrate its efficacy and discusses some practical implications for the educational world.

The chapter "Gamification as an Engaging Approach for University Students in Distance Education" covers an experience of university distance education carried out during the COVID-19 emergency, using gamification to make teaching more engaging and motivating for students. The proposed study addresses two distinct needs: 1) proactive response to the extraordinary implications of COVID-19 in the educational setting, and 2) innovation in teaching practices through the promotion of an active learning approach.

As a result of the current circumstance, in which physical contact and proximity between people must be maintained due to COVID-19, developing technologies such as virtual reality has played a critical role in allowing many sectors of society to continue operating. "User-Centered Virtual Reality Environments for Elementary School Children in Times of COVID-19," Chapter 6, proposes the use of virtual reality environments as an alternative for the acquisition of learning skills for children in an immersive and interactive way with user-centered content.

Serious games are an emerging field that has a unique role in healthcare. The following chapter, "The Role of Serious Games in Healthcare and Its Contribution to the Healthcare Ecosystem: Serious Games vs. Wearables," discusses the necessity of incorporating psychological data into health records, as well as the relevance and future of serious games in developing novel treatment approaches for any chronic condition.

"Money Management: Serious Games for the Elderly" is the title of Chapter 8, which highlights that serious games can bring more benefits to older people and caregivers. There are several games within the scope of cognitive stimulation, although they do not value the difficulties that individuals have in their Instrumental Activities of Daily Living. In this context, it is crucial to stimulate skills related to money management. This intervention will help maintain daily living skills and optimize responses to functional losses, resulting in active aging.

Chapter 9, "Improving Emergency Management Training Within Organizations: TiER-Tool – A Serious Game," presents a serious game for training stakeholders to respond to emergency incidents designed to optimize the costs involved. For this purpose, a tool was developed which allowed the learning process to be evaluated through an experiment with a group of workers in an organization.

As a result of the ever-growing applications of games, the rehabilitation process for disabilities caused by stroke, cerebral palsy, and other neurological diseases now includes games that aid in recovery. In this context, the chapter "Serious Games Integrated With Rehabilitation Structures and Assist-as-Need Techniques" explores the development of two serious games designed to be integrated with two structures: ReGear, a new design for interlimb rehabilitation mechanisms, and HOPE-G, a novel gait rehabilitation structure capable of balance training.

"Immersive Learning in Neonatal Resuscitation Education: An Overview of the RETAIN Project," presented in Chapter 11, introduces the REsuscitation TrAINing for healthcare professionals (RETAIN). It is an immersive simulation-based platform that aims to improve access for neonatal resuscitation providers. Findings shows that RETAIN is clinically relevant engaging, improves short-and long-term knowledge and transfer of the critical steps of neonatal resuscitation, and may be used as a formative or summative assessment.

Mental health and neurodevelopmental disorders are getting common amongst children and young adults. Chapter 12, "Immersive Games for Neurodiversity and Mental Health in Children and Young Adults," discusses three joint mental health and neurodevelopmental disorders and how serious immersive games could support this group.

The next chapter, "Gamifying Interventions: Sweetening Mental Health Interventions for Children," explores the utility of serious games as a potential option that offers an engaging and practical approach to psychiatric treatment for children and adolescents with mental health difficulties. The utility and feasibility of gamified interventions for Autism Spectrum Disorders, Attention-Deficit Hyperactive Disorder, Anxiety Disorders, and Anger Management issues are discussed, along with practical implications for the application of serious games in Mental Healthcare.

Chapter 14, "A Rationale for Leveraging Serious Game Design Through Sociocultural Theory," focuses on the issue of Serious Game Design (SGD) through the lens of Sociocultural Theory. First, the main challenges that the field of SGD faces are briefly outlined. Second, Vygotsky's sociocultural theory is introduced and explored to address these challenges. Third, a rationale for SGD informed by Vygotsky's ideas is introduced.

"Serious Games Applications for Cultural Heritage: Benefits and Main Design Issues" aims to explore how serious games can provide cultural organizations with opportunities to attract audiences. The chapter presents the main features of an effective design of serious games for cultural heritage, supported by the application of gamification literature concepts and models to cultural heritage and evidence from applications in the field.

"A Serious Game for Cultural Heritage?" Chapter 16, presents the Queen's Game that explores the potential of creating a serious game for cultural heritage through collaborative intersectoral research and production. Queens Game incorporates well-researched history and features exploration and gathering, utilizing period-drama and musical approaches to characterization and staging.

Serious games may be analyzed through the principles of New Humanism. In this context, the chapter "Serious Games for Recruitment in the New Humanism" presents the trends in the development of serious games in automated recruiting systems. In the "education - recruitment - spirituality" system, serious games play a connecting and integrating role.

Chapter 18, "CircuSChain Game: A Serious Game to Explore Circular Supply Chains," reinforces that supply chains have an essential role in transitioning towards a Circular Economy. The CircuSChain Game is a multi-player board game supported by a calculation sheet. The game considers reuse, refurbishing, remanufacturing, and recycling activities within closed-and open-loops, as well as CO^2 emissions and material scarcity concepts.

Agroforestry is land management in which trees or shrubs are planted around or amid crops or pastureland. It integrates agriculture and forestry technology to create land-use systems. In this perspective, the chapter "Promoting Agroforestry Using Geo-Spatially Enabled Serious Gaming" aims to understand the reasons for the lack of knowledge about agroforestry and help in designing solutions using serious gaming to alter farmers' behavior and propose a method in the form of a serious game to promote agroforestry practices among the farmers.

"A Framework for Location-Specific Self-Adaptive Serious Game for Watershed Management" highlights that annual water consumption is much more than that of groundwater recharge. To overcome such issues, the authors propose that a watershed can be an efficient approach leading towards groundwater replenishment and improving water quality and other benefits.

In Chapter 21, "Multiplayer Game-Based Language Learning," the authors discuss the Newby Chinese game-based learning (GBL) platform for group-based teaching of beginners Mandarin Chinese as a second language. Thousands of students have used Newby Chinese over the last three years, and this practical experience has informed its continued development.

"Game-Based Practices for Radical Urban Visions" explores disruptive uses of serious games to achieve radical urban visions through the presentation and critical discussion of three recent case studies developed in graduate and postgraduate university courses. The chapter addresses the underpinnings of game-based design practices and discusses their untapped potential to spark imagination and bring about new urban visions.

Game-based learning is applied to motivate students, improve their knowledge, and make the process of education more enjoyable. "Unveiling the Potential of Learning Analytics in Game-Based Learning:

Case Studies With a Geometry Game" focuses on explaining the process of Learning Analytics (LA) in the context of GBL, which can play a meaningful role in transforming learning pathways in games into interpretable information for teachers.

The last chapter, "Improving Immigrant Inclusion Through the Design of a Digital Language Learning Game," highlights that technology has garnered attention as a successful tool for second language learning, which could help improve immigrant integration and inclusion. In this context, the chapter outlines how researchers and game developers can utilize user-centered design to develop a context-specific digital language learning game for immigrants.

Chapter 1
Fidelity and Play Model:
Balancing Seriousness

Arthur Stofella
Universidade Federal de Santa Catarina, Brazil

Luciane Maria Fadel
Universidade Federal de Santa Catarina, Brazil

ABSTRACT

Serious games need to reflect reality to achieve their purpose, whether learning, training, or provoking a behavioral change. At the same time, serious games employ features that make gaming a self-motivating, engaging, and fantastic activity. This chapter presents a conceptual model to support the design of serious games that deals with the balance between fidelity and play. Design science research guided the model development. Fidelity was conceived as a field force that attracts fun, motivation, and engagement. The model arranged the game elements into three major groups: the Game-World, the Interaction-World, and the Player's-World. Fidelity can assume different levels in each of these worlds. The Fidelity and Play model (FP) allows a holistic view of the relationship and balance between fidelity and play in a serious game.

INTRODUCTION

The continued development of the digital games industry has allowed the influence of games to expand beyond personal entertainment. Indeed, serious games have a purpose beyond fun, related to learning, teaching, training, or changing players' behavior (Blumberg et al., 2012; Dörner et al., 2016). Serious games present a relatively safe environment to improve knowledge and skills (Haoran et al., 2019). Therefore, professional training considers games great value (Maheu-Cadotte et al., 2018; Ricciardi & Paolis, 2014).

In this context, Bergeron (2006) indicates the importance of content accuracy within serious games, understanding that the game's theme's material must be coherent with reality. Bergeron (2006) argues that serious games require a different level of fidelity than entertainment-focused games. Franzwa et al.

DOI: 10.4018/978-1-7998-9732-3.ch001

(2014) suggest that educational content could be inserted into narratives, scenarios, and mechanics that allow players to participate in a space different from the real world. However, space must be similar when the environment or context is crucial to the educational topic. Thus, the serious games' content needs to reflect reality to achieve the purpose, whether learning, training, or provoking a behavior change. Attributes and behaviors of objects, characters, or phenomena within the storyworld should have a certain level of fidelity. At the same time, serious gaming uses features that make gaming a self-motivating, engaging and fantastic activity.

Fidelity is the extent or level that the virtual environment emulates real-world situations, phenomena, objects, and sensations (Alexander et al., 2005). Therefore, fidelity is a feature of serious gaming related to impersonating and representing a part of reality with a certain level of realism.

The literature presents few game models that deal directly and explicitly with the interplay between fun and fidelity, such as Harteveld's Triadic Game Design (2011) and Rooney's Theoretical Framework for Serious Game Design (2012). Rooney (2012) points out that the logic behind fidelity in serious games is based on two factors: (i) pedagogical objectives: providing an effective learning experience, and (ii) game objectives: engaging and influencing players' immersion. Therefore, it is possible to imagine that play is influenced and directly related to the proximity to the reality that designers seek to attribute to serious gaming. Both models situate fidelity with a certain degree of independence from play.

Rooney's model considers three types of fidelity: Physical fidelity, such as similarity to a level of visual, audio, controls, and physics aspects with reality. Functional fidelity or the degree to which the in-game equipment acts following its real-world counterpart. Finally, Psychological fidelity represents the level at which the game replicates the psychological factors of the real task.

Belloti, Berta, and De Gloria (2010) point out that methods and instruments direct the design and development of serious games. Mendonça (2015, p. 29) corroborates by stating that models "are entities of scientific practice indispensable for the advancement of science, as they function as human instruments to achieve the approximate understanding of the reality of the world," serving for the description and scientific explanation to generate knowledge.

This chapter presents a conceptual model to support developers and designers during the development process of serious games that deals with the balance between the game elements and fidelity. The aim is not necessarily to make in-depth criticisms of other models developed to create serious games but to present an approach that highlights the concept of fidelity in making this type of game.

The Fidelity-Play model (FP model) conceives the game elements in three major groups: the Game-World, the Interaction-World, and the Player-World. Fidelity can assume different levels in each of these worlds.

The Game-World presents the elements that can be designed to create a game that presents itself uniquely to the player. The Interaction-World is accountable for representing the characteristics that arise from the player's interaction with the game. The Player's-World is inhabited by elements related to the player's involvement.

The conceptual model clarifies the inherent problem of games with a purpose beyond fun: the balance between game elements that prioritize fun and 'serious' content, understood as an approximation of game content towards its counterpart, fidelity. The model serves as a tool to help game developers and researchers understand and craft serious games.

This approach to reality is examined concerning game elements such as fun, motivation, and engagement during the development process of serious games. The level of fidelity is related to the game characteristics, which can be manipulated according to those elements. The models consider that the storyworld should extrapolate reality. For example, in a game to train doctors, the players can make mistakes without placing their safety or the patient at risk. However, just as each player's gaming experience is unique, the very perception of the degree of fidelity may depend on each player's experience. Therefore, the real situation, the content, and the goal should serve as guidelines for the decisions made during the game development process related to narrative, choices, contexts, and interaction possibilities.

Therefore, it is admissible to question the relationship between the level of fidelity and the state of flow (Csikszentmihalyi, 1990), both being related to the level of skill, abstraction, and reasoning the player when faced with the challenges presented by the serious game. The level of fidelity brings the game closer or further from reality, while it is also an activity that takes place in a magic circle with its own rules (Huizinga, 2008).

The FP model allows a holistic view of the relationship and the balance between play and fidelity sought for the serious game. The model is constructed starting with a literature review on game theories and exploring the limits between fidelity and fun.

BACKGROUND

Game is a complex concept defined by many authors. Stenros (2017) assessed the fundamental differences between 60 different definitions and highlighted that the understanding of games changes over time.

Even before games turned to be a common activity in digital format, their unique characteristics were introduced by Huizinga (2008). The author argued that games predate human culture, associated with animals' activities. Games have entertainment and educational goals for developing and improving skills valuable to players throughout life, hunting, and living. Huizinga connects the game with playful characteristics, such as order, tension, movement, change, solemnity, rhythm, and enthusiasm. This connection reinforces the playful purpose of a game. Indeed, Huizinga (2008) highlights the fun purpose of games by establishing that games are non-mandatory and non-serious activities.

Salen and Zimmerman (2003) complement these qualities by placing the game as a system in which players participate in an artificial conflict, defined by rules that has quantifiable results. Rules can be understood as conditions, pre-determinations, norms, principles, sets of instructions, or formulations. These rules give meaning to the operating structure of a game, regulating and governing behavior and articulating, to a certain extent, the players' experience within the created space and time by the game itself.

Games are commonly interpreted as fun activities, usually focusing on the intention to entertain. For the most part, the fun experience provided by engaging in this activity is the very reason people play (Kirriemuir & Mcfarlane, 2004). However, the continuous growth of the digital games industry has allowed games to have a wider reach than just the entertainment field, as they promote technological development and innovation in other sectors as well (Fleury et al., 2014). Thus, the training sector uses serious games based on the properties, characteristics, elements, factors, mechanics, and dynamics of games to help players transfer and retain knowledge.

There is no universally accepted definition of serious games (Dörner et al., 2016), which may vary depending on its application and personal opinion (Blumberg et al., 2012; Breuer & Bente, 2010; Dörner et al., 2016; Susi et al., 2007). When considering the term 'serious game,' the fun aspect may be restricted by the idea of seriousness due to the stereotype of games designed for educational purposes (Wang et al., 2009).

Connoly et al. (2012) carried out a systematic review of empirical evidence on computer games' positive impacts and outcomes and serious games concerning learning and engagement. The results found follow these dimensions:

1. Acquisition of knowledge and understanding of the content;
2. Perceptual and cognitive skills – players of digital entertainment games demonstrate a range of advantages related to attention and visual perception compared to non-players. Findings showed that games could support real-world decision making;
3. Motor skills - improvements such as depth perception and operative performance; (d) behavior change;
4. Social and interpersonal skills;
5. Affective and motivational results;
6. Physiological results – change in systolic blood pressure during the game and in the anxiety state;
7. Expected and unexpected results – as something unforeseen.

For Blumberg et al. (2012), serious games take advantage of computer technology and have an educational, instructional, training purpose or seek to encourage attitude change and, at the same time, have a certain level of entertainment. Therefore, it is essential to determine the level of entertainment and the 'serious' part of a game to preserve the motivational power of games (Kirriemuir & Mcfarlane, 2004).

Prensky (2001) built a relationship between fun and learning through games, questioning learning as suffering, while fun promotes relaxation and motivation. According to Sauvé (2010), motivation is the effort or energy that a person is prepared to spend to carry out a learning task. It allows players to find pleasure in the activity, regardless of the learning gains they can achieve, distinguishing games from other educational forms that the student sees as monotonous or tiring. The incentive to learn depends on the student's importance on the final objective, interest in the task, and perception of the difficulty (Sauvé, 2010). The author also presents conditions for encouraging students in educational games, which would be related to challenge and competition, active participation in learning, teamwork, and interaction.

In addition, Laamarti et al. (2014) believe that the seriousness is within the message or idea the game transmits to the player. Exposing the player to an environment that delivers content from a 'know-how' or previous experience would be linked to a specific context or discipline. Thus, the 'serious game' can generate motivation and engagement, offering fun and entertainment and having a purpose of learning or training. Several researchers approach the balance between these elements as one of the biggest challenges in developing serious games (Belloti et al., 2010; Franzwa et al., 2014; Giessen, 2015; Gloria et al., 2014; Laamarti et al., 2014).

Considering that fun has a high priority, a player can get distracted or interrupt the progress entirely, searching for a reward (Franzwa et al., 2014). Based on tests and feedback carried out with students, Franzwa et al. (2014) recommends three concepts to increase fun and minimize frustration while trying to maintain a balance between fun and learning:

1. Educational content must be incorporated into a fantastical narrative, except when the environment is an essential component of the education topic;
2. Player orientation is implemented to present slowly rather than providing all instructions at once
3. Supplemental feedback can be obtained by extrinsically rewarding the player with some type of expendable virtual currency or "points."

Laamarti et al. (2014) point out that the entertainment offered by the game should not be sacrificed to achieve the purpose of learning, training, or education. The game's serious objective would not be reached for these researchers if its players did not see it as fun. Complementarily, Haring (2011) understands that if entertainment elements are prioritized in a game, the educational content may be lost. However, if the importance is placed on education, there may not be space for fun. The goal is to achieve an optimal level between these two elements that complement each other (Blackburn, 2021).

Becker and Parker (2012) understand that all serious games can be understood as a type of simulation, but not every simulation is a game. Positioning simulations and games as opposites severely limit the advantage of using simulation technology for game design since much of the technology that supports computer simulations (hardware and software) is the same used for digital game development (Becker & Parker, 2012).

Tobias and Fletcher (2007) suggest a framework for differentiating between simulations and games that use computer technology to function effectively. For the authors, simulations emphasize reality, are concerned with scenarios and tasks, focus on task completion, and are not necessarily interactive. While entertainment is more critical for games, narrative and missions are necessarily interactive.

Several games contain a simulation engine, even if the simulations do not use key game elements such as fantasy (Charsky, 2010). A fantasy world game could be thought of as an abstraction of the simulation of a reality-like society. A simulation of a real situation, on the other hand, can reflect some behavior in the real world and can use fantastic elements seeking learning that can be useful in the reality of the individual who is playing.

Table 1. Difference between simulations and games

Simulations	Games
Emphasis on reality over entertainment	Emphasis on entertainment over reality
Concern with scenarios and tasks	Concern with storylines and quests
Emphasis on task completion	Emphasis on competition
It may not be interactive	Necessarily interactive
Not all simulations are games	All games are simulations

Source: (Tobias and Fletcher, 2007, p.21).

Both serious games and educational simulations conceive the real world as a core constituent, represented as information or through a dependence between two relevant variables within the system (Imlig-Iten & Petko, 2018). It is possible to imagine, for example, that the characteristics or behavior of an object, character, or phenomenon within the serious game must reflect its counterpart in the real world (Plecher et al., 2020).

Machado et al. (2009) argued that serious games for healthcare professional training can minimize the difficulty of obtaining materials, personnel training, and product validation. Interactive learning made it possible for students and professionals to constantly improve their knowledge and skills while safeguarding the safety of both patients and professionals before performing an actual procedure (Bergeron, 2006; Graafland et al., 2012; Ricciardi & Paolis, 2014; Maheu-Cadotte et al., 2018).

Graafland and Schijven (2018) stated that much effort was put into developing simulations focused on the realism of the physical appearance of the environment, understanding it as responsible for conducting learning. However, the authors suggest that the similarity of activities and procedures performed within the game concerning real-world situations is essential. Therefore, the narrative, scenario, rules, and other game characteristics should reflect the natural environment.

The advantage of the serious games approach relies on creating games with content dedicated to learning instead of adapting entertainment games for educational practice (Freitas, 2006). The players engage with the educational content in an object that brings together the simulation and game worlds, leverages the educational value of technology-enhanced simulation to teach students specific technical or cognitive skills, and the motivational, interactive, and immersive aspects inherent in games (Ribaupierre et al., 2014).

The challenge comes from immersive situations providing concrete and compelling contexts to engage players. Furthermore, serious games can support a context to acquire and test knowledge and skills, and they provide a barrier-free environment where new knowledge, practices, and solutions can be developed (Belloti et al., 2010).

De Freitas (2018) corroborates games as learning tools, helping students' motivation, engagement, and being associated with a behavior change, proving to be a more practical approach when used in a hybrid way with traditional methods. Thus, serious games' content should reflect reality to achieve their purpose, whether learning, training, or a behavior change. Attributes and behaviors of objects, characters, or phenomena within the digital world must portray the real world. At the same time, serious gaming uses features that make gaming a self-motivating, engaging and fantastic activity. However, to develop serious games that succeed in their objective, it is essential to balance these antagonistic features.

BALANCING FUN AND SERIOUSNESS

Design and Characteristics of Serious Games

Game design enables players to create meaning through interactions (Salen & Zimmerman, 2003). For Salen and Zimmerman, this meaningful play interaction emerges from the player's discernible, integrated actions and reaction process.

Hence, the team of experts, designers, and educators must cooperate to make the game more meaningful. The team should work for 'serious' content and coherent implementation and discussion within the game (Bergeron, 2006; Dörner et al., 2016). Thus, a narrativized interface (Bizzocchi, Lin, & Tanenbaum, 2011) can support fun while serious, and the interface incorporates some of the content supporting immersion and meaning-making. The ecology of the game should prioritize voluntary participation, which supports intrinsic motivation (Holliday, 2021).

The design team creates a game based on a series of motivational, engagement, and fun elements. Table 2 summarizes the findings of a systematic literature review on these elements. Even though there is no consensus in the literature on all the characteristics that support motivation, engagement, and fun, it was possible to highlight the most cited and the overlapping concepts, such as narrative and fantasy or agency and control.

The review listed many elements, which were arranged in categories. The design category gathered elements that the designer could manipulate, and the interaction category gathered elements conceived as interaction qualities. Finally, the player category figured out the elements manifested during the user experience. These categories formed the Game-World, the Interaction-World, and the Player's-World.

The Game-World is divided into the **mechanism** and **storyworld** elements. Mechanism elements determine what the player can or cannot do within the game. The storyworld elements are responsible for assisting the player in understanding the purpose of the game and the creation of meaning.

The Interaction World represents the elements that arise from the player's interaction with the game.

The Player's-World is inhabited by elements related to the player's involvement. Both the Game-World and the Interaction-World are designed. However, the Player's-World is indirectly designed or instigated as it depends on the player's experience when interacting with the game.

Table 2. A summary of the motivational, engagement, and fun elements

	Game-World	Interaction-World	Player's-World
Game Features	**Mechanisms** Rules Rewards States of Victory Adaptability Artificial intelligence Goals **Storyworld** Narrative Fantasy Challenge/Conflict Environment Mystery Discovery	Action Language Choices Sociability Assessment Control Feedback Interactivity Instructional	Agency Submission Concentration Player Skills Sensory Stimulus Value Identity Immersion Fun Curiosity Expression

Source: The authors.

Fidelity in Serious Games

All training, whether in games, simulations, or real scenarios, implies the transfer of knowledge within a structured environment to the relatively unstructured atmosphere of real-world applications (Alexander et al., 2005). Bergeron (2006) argues that serious games for healthcare training must have precision in content, and the content must be consistent with reality, referring to visual graphics, audio, objects, and characters' behavior. Graafland and Schijven (2018) point out that the transfer of knowledge will occur if the challenges and actions within the games correspond adequately and cohesively to reality.

Like simulators, games can emulate the real world with a certain level of realism, providing training opportunities without the same risks as in the real world (Alexander et al., 2005). Thus, the level of fidelity of the game becomes an essential attribute for serious games. The level of fidelity is also crucial to present the results in choosing different and even misguided strategies for an in-game task compared to its real-world counterpart (Chalmers & Debattista, 2009; Chalmers et al., 2009).

The definition of the term fidelity is entirely associated with the study and performance of simulations. For Hays and Singer (1989), fidelity is about a training situation's level of similarity to carry out more efficient training. For Feinstein and Cannon (2002), fidelity is the level of realism that a simulation presents to the student.

Therefore, this chapter appropriates the definition of Alexander et al. (2005), in which fidelity is described as the extent to which the virtual environment emulates real-world situations, phenomena, objects, and sensations. Considering the complexity of the conceptual definition of the term fidelity, this study accounts for three components: (a) Physical, (b) Functional, and (c) Psychological fidelity.

Alexander et al. (2005) explain that physical fidelity applies to the similarity of visual, audio, displays, controls, and physics. Hence, it is about how much the virtual simulation emulates the physical properties of the real environment. Thus, it can cover a variety of dimensions: visual, sound, olfactory, tactile, etc.

Functional fidelity relies on the operational equipment within the game compared to real-world equipment. Psychological fidelity replicates psychological factors, such as stress, fear, motivation, and relief experienced while performing a particular task.

It is possible to postulate that the appropriate level of fidelity for a training system depends on the skills or behaviors that must be trained. Fidelity is a feature developers can manipulate and determine (Alexander et al., 2005). Thus, a game or simulation might contain different levels of each fidelity component. For example, a game can present low physical and functional fidelity but high psychological fidelity (Kuipers et al., 2017). Wherefore, if serious games and the operating environment share properties related to training goals, certain aspects of the serious game can have lower levels of fidelity without compromising training effectiveness. So, designers need to prioritize components that require a more realistic representation of features.

Brydges (2010) suggests that the level of fidelity should follow the students' progress. Lower fidelity for beginners and higher fidelity as students become more advanced. A high level of fidelity, especially physical, in combination with a highly complex task is likely to cause a cognitive overload for beginners, making learning difficult (Dankbaar et al., 2016). For Dankbaar et al. (2016), the fidelity and complexity of the cases presented in a simulation must be aligned with the student's level of proficiency.

Research tends to describe physical fidelity (Harteveld, 2011). However, Graafland and Schijven (2018) say that, as long as problem-solving follows the same rules as the real-life situation, physical fidelity might be secondary to the learning outcome. Thus, a high level of graphical realism does not necessarily enhance learning (Alexander et al., 2005; Graafland et al., 2015; Lukosch et al., 2019).

Rooney (2012) points out that the logic behind fidelity in serious games is based on two factors: (i) pedagogical objective providing an effective learning experience, and (ii) game objectives for engaging and influencing players' immersion. Therefore, it is possible to imagine that game qualities are designed and directly related to the fidelity designers attribute to serious gaming. Furthermore, enhancing reality is recommended considering relevant aspects such as educational intent and design, disciplinary content, and simulation (Barton & Maharg, 2007; Irshad & Perkis, 2020).

However, the relationship between fidelity and game qualities can also occur in a conceptual approach, not necessarily abstract, such as mythological creatures. Thus, it is possible to expect all three fidelity components to influence the game characteristics that provide entertainment.

FP Model

A model for fidelity and play in a serious game was designed to conceptually formalize the topics reviewed in this chapter with the intention of understanding and communicating. Figure 1 shows the model that delivers a suggestion for designing serious games, serving as a guide for making and justifying decisions related to fidelity and play. The FP model represents the three worlds, their static and dynamic relationships and constructs (Japiassú & Marcondes, 2001; March & Smith, 1995; Shehabuddeen et al., 1999; Mendonça & Almeida, 2012).

Figure 1. The Fidelity x Play model
Source: The authors.

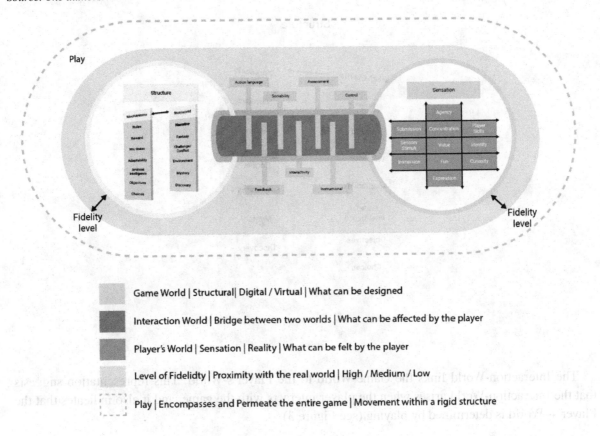

The Game-World is responsible for structuring the game and exists without the player's intervention. It is composed of elements that are subdivided into two groups: (1) Mechanisms: formed by rules, reward, victory state, adaptability, artificial Intelligence, goal and choices; and (2) Storyworld: consisting of narrative, fantasy, challenge/conflict, environment, and mystery (see Figure 2).

These two groups perform possibilities. They also contextualize the events connected by the cause-and-effect relationship and structure the game's purpose.

Figure 2. The Game-World
Source: The authors.

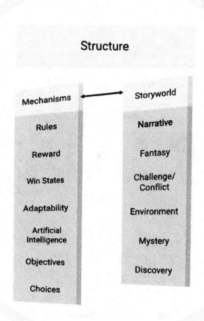

The Interaction-World links the Game-World to the Player's-World. This representation suggests that the Interaction-World arises when the player interacts with the game, and it also indicates that the Player's- World is determined by playing (see Figure 3).

Figure 3. The interplay among the worlds
Source: The authors.

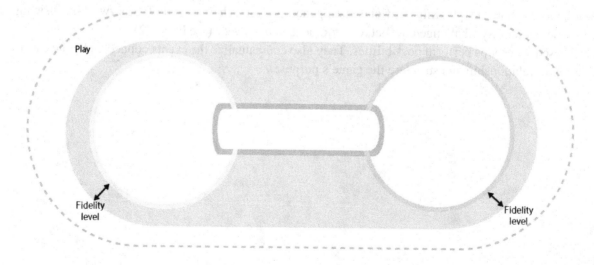

Serious game's core content relates to the real world, and the development team can control the level of fidelity, bringing the digital world closer to the real world. Fidelity is understood as a field force that embraces and accounts for the three existing worlds of serious games. This field force filters the information passed to the player from the other components. For example, a real medical case narrative and the player's interaction with non-playable characters or tools can establish a level of fidelity.

The field force can expand or contract, causing the level of fidelity to be closer to reality as it shrinks.

Intended to represent a connection between the Game-World and the Player's world, the Interaction-World is constituted by the game elements: action language, feedback, sociability, interactivity, evaluation, instructional, and control (see Figure 4). These elements have a dual characteristic: they were designed to influence the player, but they need interaction to come to life. For example, some feedback may have been projected into the game, but it will only occur in the presence of a player. This world provides a bridge between the virtual environment, through the actions performed by the player, and reality represented here as the sensations that the player experience during the act of playing.

Figure 4. The Interaction-World
Source: The authors.

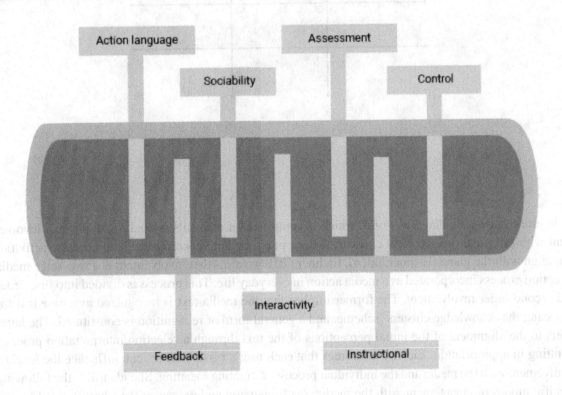

The Interaction-World highlights the interplay between what was designed for the game and the actions performed by the player. The elements' "T" format intends to portray a greater or lesser presence of these characteristics in the game and the intensity of the player's interaction within the game environment.

Figure 5. The Player's-World
Source: The authors.

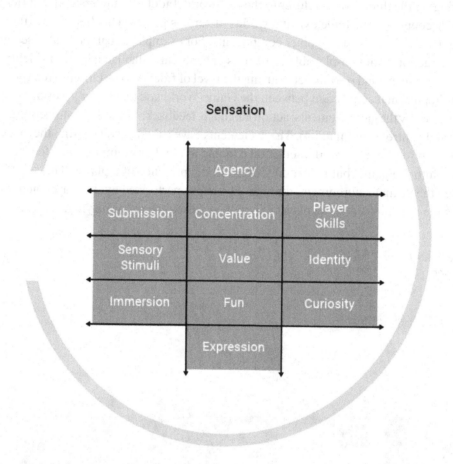

Figure 5 shows the Player's-World, which is comprised of elements related to the player's involvement with the game. Involvement consists of perceptual, cognitive, emotional, and conative activities that align with the game (Eichner, 2014). Eichner (2014) claims that involvement is a two-stage media reception process incorporated as a media action in everyday life. This process is divided into first-order and second-order involvement. The former implies that the media text is recognized as a base text for accessing the 'knowledge clusters' scheme, and a general form of recognition is constituted. The latter refers to the alignment of the initial perceptions of the text through a selection/interpretation process, resulting in appropriation. Eichner reinforces that each user's particularities can influence the level of involvement with the media and the individual process of creating meaning. She identifies the following specific modes of engagement with the media: (a) Immersion and presence; (b) Character; (c) Ludic; (d) Excitement; (e) Spectacle; (f) Analysis; (g) Inspiration; (h) Habitual involvement; and (i) Agency.

Therefore, Player's-World's components cannot be directly designed by the development team but stimulated or encouraged as they emerge from the playing.

Agency, immersion, sensory stimulus, value, player skills, concentration, fun, expression, submission, identity, and curiosity forms the Player's world. These attributes are interdependent. For example, a higher sensory stimulation might affect players' immersion, and consequently, their concentration when playing.

Therefore, the model might help professionals and researchers understand the interplay of different elements during serious game development. The FP model also highlights the need for a certain level of proximity to reality in a serious game. Therefore, physical, functional, and psychological fidelity must be designed within all game elements.

SOLUTIONS AND RECOMMENDATIONS

Digital media became an ordinary object in everyday and professional contexts, both as entertainment and to help with daily activities. Likewise, serious digital games have conquered a more expansive space within the academy and a platform for training. The availability of serious games developed for training has increased in the last decade. This context urges game developers and researchers to use tools for creating serious games. These tools emphasize the conflict between principles and characteristics essential to entertainment-oriented games and a purpose with 'serious' content.

The FP model allows a holistic view of the relationship and balance between play and fidelity of a serious game. It considers the inherent problem of games with a purpose beyond fun: the balance between game elements that prioritize fun and 'serious' content, understood as fidelity. The model might be used as an instrument for consultation throughout the game development process, mainly during the conceptualization and definition phase. The model can also guide the analysis of the pre-existing serious game to understand the interplay between fidelity and play.

The FP model can understand the interplay between fidelity and play in greater depth. It also characterizes topics related to serious gaming and fidelity to communicate and share the knowledge acquired.

To develop the FP model, we examined the main features that constitute games and the particularities of serious games. We also identified little consensus in the literature about motivating, engaging, and promoting fun. The nomenclature overlaps concepts, such as narrative and fantasy or agency and control. Due to many different terms, we grouped them based on their function and concept. Three worlds hold these groups: the Game-World, the Interaction-World, and the Player's-World.

This arrangement allowed separating the elements that are designed (Game-World); the elements designed but also influenced by the player (Interaction-World); and the elements that arise from the player's involvement with the game (Player's-World).

The model allows us to observe the elements' interdependency within their worlds and concerning each other. This organization is intended to facilitate understanding the serious game and its premises, allowing inferences about desirable technical characteristics.

The model also highlights serious games complexity, qualifying to discuss each world and making explicit the multidisciplinary nature of the game. Considering that each player perceives a different experience, the boundaries among the worlds are not obvious, assuming a continuous field force between them.

The concept of fidelity also has little consensus in the academic community. Several papers deal with different terms with overlapping meanings, generating inevitable confusion. Fidelity was analyzed as a force that attracts fun, motivation, and engagement. Therefore, the real space, the content, and training should serve as a baseline to the narrative elements, choices, contexts, interaction, and all game elements.

For example, designers can manipulate fidelity following narrative to enhance reality. Thus, the game allows doctors to make mistakes without putting their safety and the patient at risk. However, just as each player's gaming experience is unique, the very perception of the degree of fidelity may depend on each player's experience. In addition, the literature points out that the degree of fidelity should follow the level of complexity of the content and students' knowledge. More straightforward and more abstract content is aligned with low fidelity, and as the content becomes more complex, the degree of fidelity becomes higher. Therefore, fidelity is a continuum between low and high levels.

The conceptual model development followed the Design Science Research methodology, comprising the problem awareness, suggestion, development, and conclusion phases. The problem awareness was built by analyzing different models to understand the impacts of the representation on their purpose.

The analysis suggested a difference between model and framework. Models have an abstract and dynamic nature towards propositions and statements that express the relationships between the elements but do not present specific guidelines or practices for their implementation. In comparison, frameworks make explicit the fundamental bases and objectives of a system and expose an orientation to be implemented. Thus, a framework can encompass the goals and definitions of more than one model.

The problem awareness also indicates that the formal component's representation can present different levels of abstraction. When the level of abstraction is low, the model comes closer to a step-by-step system, not necessarily demonstrating the possible relationships between the components but rather phases and stages of production. Thus, the formal representation of the model itself may be responsible for configuring different meanings for the reader. Therefore, we suggest that narrativizing the model could promote meaning-making.

In addition, different graphical representations of the models were proposed, suggesting other relationships between their components: the play and fidelity. This iterative process allowed insights to create a model, and the development phase proposed the final conceptual model.

The conclusion presented the results and summarized the findings. The final model might contribute to the research of serious games.

FUTURE RESEARCH IDEAS

Future research intends to validate the model by game developers and designers creating a serious game. In addition, pedagogical or educational theories can analyze the model filtering by theoretical and practical evolution.

Future research will also establish a consensus on the term 'fidelity' in serious games. The very concept of 'fidelity' should be reconsidered, and research should examine other terms such as 'similarity' to better represent the translation between reality and representation.

ACKNOWLEDGMENT

This research was supported by the Coordenação de Aperfeiçoamento de Pessoal de Nível Superior – Brasil (CAPES) – Código de Financiamento 001.

REFERENCES

Alexander, A. L., Brunyé, T., Sidman, J., & Weil, S. A. (2005). *From Gaming to Training: A Review of Studies on Fidelity, Immersion, Presence, and Buy-in and Their Effects on Transfer in PC-Based Simulations and Games*. DARWARS Training Impact Group.

Barton, K., & Maharg, P. (2007). E-Simulations in the wild: interdisciplinary research, design, and implementation. In D. Gibson, C. Aldrich, & M. Prensky (Eds.), Games and simulations in online learning: Research and development frameworks. Academic Press.

Baum, D. R., Riedel, S., & Hays, R. T. (1982). *Training Effectiveness as a Function of Training Device Fidelity*. Alexandria, VA: U.S. Army Research Institute: ARI Technical Report 593.

Becker, K., & Parker, J. (2012). *The Guide to Computer Simulations and Games*. Wiley.

Belloti, F., Berta, R., & De Gloria, A. (2010). Designing Effective Serious Games: Opportunities and Challenges for Research. *International Journal of Emerging Technologies in Learning (iJET), 5*(SI 3), 22-35.

Bergeron, B. (2006). *Developing Serious Games (Game Development Series)*. Charles River Media.

Bizzocchi, J., Lin, M. B., & Tanenbaum, J. (2011). Game, narrative, and the design of interface. *International Journal of Art and Technology, 4*(4), 460–479. doi:10.1504/IJART.2011.043445

Blackburn, N. N. (2021). *OGrES Welcome! Toward a Systematic Theory for Serious Game Design. In CHI PLAY '21*. ACM.

Blumberg, F. C., Almonte, D. E., Anthony, J. S., & Hashimoto, N. (2012). Serious Games: What Are They? What Do They Do? Why Should We Play Them? In K. E. Dill (Ed.), *The Oxford Handbook of Media Psychology*. Oxford University Press. doi:10.1093/oxfordhb/9780195398809.013.0019

Boyle, E. A., Hainey, T., Connolly, T. M., Gray, G., Earp, J., Ott, M., Lim, T., Ninaus, M., Ribeiro, C., & Pereira, J. (2016). An update to the systematic literature review of empirical evidence of the impacts and outcomes of computer games and serious games. *Computers & Education, 94*, 178–192. doi:10.1016/j.compedu.2015.11.003

Breuer, J., & Bente, G. (2010). Why so serious? On the Relation of Serious Games and Learning. *Eludamos (Göttingen), 4*(1), 7–24.

Brydges, R., Carnahan, H., Rose, D., Rose, L., & Dubrowski, A. (2010). Coordinating Progressive Levels of Simulation Fidelity to Maximize Educational Benefit. *Academic Medicine, 85*(5), 806–812. doi:10.1097/ACM.0b013e3181d7aabd PMID:20520031

Chalmers, A., & Debattista, K. (2009). Level of Realism for Serious Games. In 2009 Conference in Games and Virtual Worlds for Serious Applications (pp. 225-232). Coventry.

Chalmers, A., Debattista, K., & Ramic-Brkic, B. (2009). Towards high-fidelity multi-sensory virtual environments. *The Visual Computer, 25*(12), 1101–1108. doi:10.100700371-009-0389-2

Charsky, D. (2010). From Edutainment to Serious Games: A Change in the Use of Game Characteristics. *Games and Culture*, *5*(2), 177–198. doi:10.1177/1555412009354727

Connolly, T. M., Boyle, E. A., MacArthur, E., Hainey, T., & Boyle, J. M. (2012). A systematic literature review of empirical evidence on computer games and serious games. *Computers & Education*, *59*(2), 661–686. doi:10.1016/j.compedu.2012.03.004

Csikszentmihalyi, M. (1990). *Flow: the psychology of optimal experience*. Harper & Row.

Dankbaar, M. E., Alsma, J., Jansen, E. E., van Merrienboer, J. J., van Sasse, J. L., & Schuit, S. C. (2016). An experimental study on the effects of a simulation game on students' clinical cognitive skills and motivation. *Advances in Health Sciences Education: Theory and Practice*, *21*(3), 505–521. doi:10.100710459-015-9641-x PMID:26433730

Dörner, R., Göbel, S., Effelsberg, W., & Wiemeyer, J. (2016). *Serious Games: Foundations, Concepts and Practice*. Springer International. doi:10.1007/978-3-319-40612-1

Eichner, S. (2014). *Agency and Media Reception: Experiencing Video Games, Film, and Television*. Springer VS. doi:10.1007/978-3-658-04673-6

Feinstein, A. H., & Cannon, H. M. (2002). Constructs of simulation evaluation. *Simulation & Gaming*, *33*(4), 425–440. doi:10.1177/1046878102238606

Fleury, A., Nakano, D., & Cordeiro, J. H. (2014). *Mapeamento da Indústria Brasileira e Global de Jogos Digitais*. BNDES.

Franzwa, C., Tang, Y., Johnson, A., & Bielefeldt, T. (2014). Balancing Fun and Learning in a Serious Game Design. *International Journal of Game-Based Learning*, *4*(4), 37–57. doi:10.4018/ijgbl.2014100103

Freitas, S. (2006). Using games and simulations for supporting learning. *Learning, Media and Technology*, *31*(4), 343–358. doi:10.1080/17439880601021967

Freitas, S. d. (2018). Are Games Effective Learning Tools? A Review of Educational Games. *Journal of Educational Technology & Society*, *21*(2), 74–84.

Garris, R., Ahlers, R., & Driskell, J. E. (2002). Games, motivation, and learning: A research and practice model. *Simulation & Gaming*, *33*(4), 441–467. doi:10.1177/1046878102238607

Giessen, H. (2015). Serious games effects: An Overview. *Procedia: Social and Behavioral Sciences*, *17*, 2240–2244. doi:10.1016/j.sbspro.2015.01.881

Gloria, A., Belloti, F., Berta, R., & Lavagnino, E. (2014, January). Serious Games for education and training. *International Journal of Serious Games*, *1*(1). Advance online publication. doi:10.17083/ijsg.v1i1.11

Graafland, M., Bemelman, W. A., & Schijven, M. P. (2015). Appraisal of Face and Content Validity of a Serious Game Improving Situational Awareness in Surgical Training. *Journal of Laparoendoscopic & Advanced Surgical Techniques. Part A.*, *25*(1), 1–7. doi:10.1089/lap.2014.0043 PMID:25607899

Graafland, M., & Schijven, M. (2018). How Serious Games Will Improve Healthcare. In H. Rivas & K. Wac (Eds.), Digital health: scaling healthcare to the world (pp. 137-157). Springer International Publishing. doi:10.1007/978-3-319-61446-5_10

Graafland, M., Schraagen, J., & Schijven, M. (2012). Systematic review of serious games for medical education and surgical skills training. *British Journal of Surgery*, *99*(10), 1322–1330. doi:10.1002/bjs.8819 PMID:22961509

Hamstra, S. J., Brydges, R., Hatala, R., Zendejas, B., & Cook, D. A. (2014). Reconsidering Fidelity in Simulation-Based Training. *Academic Medicine*, *89*(3), 387–392. doi:10.1097/ACM.0000000000000130 PMID:24448038

Haring, P., Chakinska, D., & Ritterfeld, U. (2011). Understanding serious gaming. A psychological perspective. In P. Felicia (Ed.), *Handbook of Research on Improving Learning and Motivation through Educational Games: Multidisciplinary Approaches* (pp. 29–50). IGI Global. doi:10.4018/978-1-60960-495-0.ch020

Harteveld, C. (2011). Triadic Game Design: Balancing Reality, Meaning, and Play. Springer. doi:10.1007/978-1-84996-157-8

Hays, R. T., & Singer, M. J. (1989). Simulation fidelity in training system design: Bridging the gap between reality and training. Springer-Verlag. doi:10.1007/978-1-4612-3564-4

Holliday, E. L. (2021). *Breaking the Magic Circle: Using a Persuasive Game to Build Empathy For Nursing Staff and Increase Citizen Responsibility During a Pandemic. In CHI PLAY '21*. ACM. doi:10.1145/3450337.3483511

Huizinga, J. (2008). *Homo Ludens: O Jogo como Elemento na Cultura*. Perspectiva.

Imlig-Iten, N., & Petko, D. (2018). Comparing Serious Games and Educational Simulations: Effects on Enjoyment, Deep Thinking, Interest and Cognitive Learning Gains. *Simulation & Gaming*, *49*(4), 401–422. doi:10.1177/1046878118779088

Irshad, S., & Perkis, A. (2020). *Serious Storytelling in Virtual Reality: The Role of Digital Narrative to Trigger Mediated Presence and Behavioral Responses. In CHI PLAY '20 EA*. ACM. doi:10.1145/3383668.3419908

Japiassú, P., & Marcondes, D. (2001). Dicionário Básico de Filosofia (3rd ed.). Rio de Janeiro: Zahar.

Ker, J., & Bradley, P. (2010). Simulation in medical education. Understanding Medical Education: Evidence, Theory, and Practice, 164-180.

Kirriemuir, J., & Mcfarlane, A. (2004). *Literature Review in Games and Learning*. Futurelab.

Kuipers, D. A., Terlow, G., Wartena, B. O., Veer, J. T., Prins, J. T., & Pierie, J. P. (2017). The Role of Transfer in Designing Games and Simulations for Health: Systematic Review. *JMIR Serious Games*, *5*(4), 1–9. doi:10.2196/games.7880 PMID:29175812

Laamarti, F., Eid, M., & Saddik, A. E. (2014). An Overview of Serious Games. *International Journal of Computer Games Technology*, *2014*, 1–15. doi:10.1155/2014/358152

Lukosch, H., Lukosch, S., Hoermann, S., & Lindeman, R. W. (2019). Conceptualizing Fidelity for HCI in Applied Gaming. In *HCI in Games - 1st International Conference, HCI-Games 2019, Held as part of the 21st HCI International Conference, HCII 2019, Proceedings* (pp. 165-179). Springer.

Machado, L. d., Moraes, R. M., & Nunes, F. L. (2009). Serious Games para Saúde e Treinamento Imersivo. In Abordagens Práticas de Realidade Virtual e Aumentada (Vol. 1, pp. 31-60). Porto Alegre.

Maheu-Cadotte, M.-A., Cossette, S., Dubé, V., Fontaine, G., Mailhot, T., Lavoie, P., Cournoyer, A., Balli, F., & Mathieu-Dupuis, G. (2018, March). Effectiveness of serious games and impact of design elements on engagement and educational outcomes in healthcare professionals and students: A systematic review and meta-analysis protocol. *BMJ Open*, 8(3), 1–7. doi:10.1136/bmjopen-2017-019871 PMID:29549206

Maran, J. N., & Glavin, R. J. (2003). Low- to high-fidelity simulation - a continuum of medical education? *Medical Education*, 37(1), 22–28. doi:10.1046/j.1365-2923.37.s1.9.x PMID:14641635

March, S. T., & Smith, G. F. (1995). Design and natural science research on information technology. *Decision Support Systems*, 15(4), 251–266. doi:10.1016/0167-9236(94)00041-2

Mendonça, F. M. (2015). *Ontoforinfoscience: metodologia para construção de ontologias pelos cientistas da informação - Uma aplicação prática no desenvolvimento da ontologia sobre componentes do sangue humano (HEMONTO)*. Tese de Doutorado.

Mendonça, F. M., & Almeida, M. B. (2012). *Modelos e Teorias para Representação: Uma Teoria Ontológica Sobre o Sangue Humano*. Anais do XIII Encontro Nacional de Pesquisa em Ciência da Informação - XIII ENANCIB.

Muchinsky, P. M. (2006). Psychology Applied to Work: An Introduction to Industrial and Organizational Psychology (8th ed.). Belmont, CA: Thomson Wadsworth.

Mylopoulos, J. (1992). Conceptual modeling and telos. In P. Loucopoulos & R. Zicari (Eds.), Conceptual modeling, databases and case: An integrated view of information systems development. John Wiley and Sons.

Plecher, D. A., Herber, F., Eichhorn, C., Pongratz, A., Tanson, G., & Klinker, G. (2020, December 4). HieroQuest - A Serious Game for Learning Egyptian Hieroglyphs. *Journal on Computing and Cultural Heritage*, 1-20.

Prensky, M. (2001). Fun, Play and Games: What Makes Games Engaging. In Digital Game-Based Learning (pp. 1-31). McGraw-Hill.

Ravyse, W. S., Blignaut, A. S., Leendertz, V., & Woolner, A. (2017). Success factors for serious games to enhance learning: A systematic review. *Virtual Reality (Waltham Cross)*, 21(1), 31–58. doi:10.100710055-016-0298-4

Ribaupierre, S. d., Kapralos, B., Haji, F., & Stroulia, E. Dubrowski, & Eagleson, R. (2014). Healthcare training enhancement through virtual reality and serious games. In C. Lakhmi, L. Jain, & P. Anderson (Eds.), Virtual, augmented reality and serious games for healthcare (pp. 9-27). Berlin: Springer.

Ricciardi, F., & Paolis, L. T. (2014). A Comprehensive Review of Serious Games in Health Professions. *International Journal of Computer Games Technology*, 2014, 1–11. doi:10.1155/2014/787968

Rieber, L. P. (1996). Seriously considering play: Designing interactive learning environments based on the blending of microworlds, simulations, and games. *Educational Technology Research and Development*, *44*(2), 43–58. doi:10.1007/BF02300540

Rooney, P. (2012). A Theoretical Framework for Serious Game Design: Exploring Pedagogy, Play and Fidelity and their Implications for the Design Process. *International Journal of Game-Based Learning*, *2*(4), 41–60. doi:10.4018/ijgbl.2012100103

Roungas, B. (2016). A model-driven framework for educational game design. *International Journal of Serious Games*, *3*(3), 19–37. doi:10.17083/ijsg.v3i3.126

Salen, K., & Zimmerman, E. (2003). *Rules of Play: Game design fundamentals*. MIT Press.

Sauvé, L. (2010). Effective Educational Games. In D. Kaufman & L. Sauvé (Eds.), Educational Gameplay and Simulation Environments: Case Studies and Lessons Learned (pp. 27-50). Information Science Reference. doi:10.4018/978-1-61520-731-2.ch002

Shehabuddeen, N., Probert, D., Phaal, R., & Platts, K. (1999). *Representing and approaching complex management issues: part 1 - role and definition*. Centre for Technology Management (CTM).

Stenros, J. (2017). The Game Definition Game: A Review. *Games and Culture*, *12*(6), 499–520. doi:10.1177/1555412016655679

Susi, T., Johannesson, M., & Backlund, P. (2007). *Serious Games - An Overview*. School of Humanities and Informatics, University of Sköde, Sköde, Suécia.

Tobias, S., & Fletcher, J. D. (2007). What Research Has to Say About Designing Computer Games for Learning. *Educational Technology*, 20–29.

Vaishnavi, V., Kuechler, W., & Petter, S. (2004). *Design Science Research in Information Systems*. Retrieved Última atualização 30 de Junho de 2019, from http://www.desrist.org/design-research-in-information-systems/

Wang, H., Shen, C., & Ritterfeld, U. (2009). Enjoyment of Digital Games What Makes Them "Seriously" Fun? Enjoyment: At the Heart of Digital Gaming. In U. Ritterfeld, M. Cody, & P. Vorderer (Eds.), *Serious games: Mechanisms and effects*. Routledge.

Xexéo, G., Carmo, A., Acioli, A., Taucei, B., Dipolitto, C., Mangeli, E., & Azevedo, V. (2017). *O que são Jogos: Uma ntrodução ao Objeto de Estudo do LUDES*. Universidade Federal do Rio de Janeiro.

ADDITIONAL READING

Boyle, E. A., Hainey, T., Connolly, T. M., Gray, G., Earp, J., Ott, M., Lim, T., Ninaus, M., Ribeiro, C., & Pereira, J. (2016). An update to the systematic literature review of empirical evidence of the impacts and outcomes of computer games and serious games. *Computers & Education*, *94*, 178–192. doi:10.1016/j.compedu.2015.11.003

Costikyan, G. (2002). I Have No Words & I Must Design: Toward a Critical Vocabulary for Games. In M. Frans (Ed.), *Proceedings of Computer Games and Digital Cultures Conference* (pp. 9-33). Tampere: Tampere University Press.

Denholm, J., & Lee-Davies, L. (2018). *Enhancing Education and Training Initiatives Through Serious Games*. IGI Global. doi:10.4018/978-1-5225-3689-5

Hamstra, S. J., Brydges, R., Hatala, R., Zendejas, B., & Cook, D. A. (2014). Reconsidering Fidelity in Simulation-Based Training. *Academic Medicine*, *89*(3), 387–392. doi:10.1097/ACM.0000000000000130 PMID:24448038

Ker, J., & Bradley, P. (2010). Simulation in medical education. Understanding Medical Education: Evidence, Theory, and Practice, 164-180.

Ravyse, W. S., Blignaut, A. S., & Botha-Ravyse, C. R. (2020). Codebook Co-Development to Understand Fidelity and Initiate Artificial Intelligence in Serious Games. *International Journal of Game-Based Learning*, *10*(1), 37–53. doi:10.4018/IJGBL.2020010103

Westera, W. (2019). Why and how serious games can become far more effective: Accommodating productive learning experiences, learner motivation and the monitoring of learning gains. *Journal of Educational Technology & Society*, *22*(1), 59–69.

KEY TERMS AND DEFINITIONS

Design Science: Part of science that deals with phenomena and artifacts created by humanity.

Fidelity: In the context of serious games, it is a characteristic that represents the level of proximity that the physical, functional, and psychological components within the digital world have with the real world.

Game Features: Particularities that give quality to games.

Model: A graphical representation with more outstanding dynamics among the components that build the structure of the system it aims to represent, having an abstract nature and not being decisive to guide the implementation or operation of the specific design actively.

Play: Experience of performing activities within a context governed by rules.

Serious Games: Games that use its elements of motivation, engagement, and fun for teaching, learning, training, or positive behavior change.

Simulation: Representation of a part of reality, whether graphically or not, that knows the real world at its core.

Chapter 2
The Interplay Between In-Game Activity, Learning Gains, and Enjoyment in a Serious Game on STEM

Jose A. Ruipérez Valiente

https://orcid.org/0000-0002-2304-6365

University of Murcia, Spain

ABSTRACT

The exponential growth of technology is transforming most existing sectors in the world. One of the technologies that is significantly impacting our society is video games, which have become a new cultural form of expression. Moreover, research suggests that, especially within educational contexts, they present great learning opportunities. However, little is known in serious games about the interplay of the in-game activity, learning gains, and enjoyment with the game. Therefore, in this chapter, the authors use data from a pilot study conducted with a STEM inquiry-learning serious game to compute behavioral metrics and analyze their relationship with the learning gains and enjoyment of students based on survey responses. The author reports on the exploratory results of the different metrics and correlation analysis to analyze the interplay between these three sets of metrics. This work will exemplify the potential that learning analytics approaches and serious games have to transform education and training across contexts.

INTRODUCTION

The exponential growth of technology is transforming most existing sectors in the world, increasing the performance and potential applications that in the past no one thought could be real (L. M., Madhushree and R., Revathi and Aithal, 2019). One of the sectors that is being importantly impacted is the educational one, where the incorporation educational technologies is helping improve the quality of the learning process, facilitating the work of instructors and enhancing the education received by students (Dabbagh

DOI: 10.4018/978-1-7998-9732-3.ch002

et al., 2016; Thomas, 2016). Within these educational technologies, there are multiple directions in the literature, and within this chapter, we focus on the potential of video games within educational contexts (Squire, 2011).

The importance of video games in our society has also raised significantly during the last decade. Video games have become a new cultural form of expression and are impacting everyday life such as consumption, communities and the identities of the individuals that belong to a society (Daniel & Garry, 2018). Moreover, they are becoming very widespread, and all kids are growing up playing video games, with will change the future generations where video games will become a native medium. Also, the perceptions regarding video games are changing, as 74% of American parents believe that video games can be educational for their children, and 57% also play video games with them (ESA, 2019). Therefore, video games are going further beyond mere entertainment purposes and are deeply penetrating society at different scales and for multiple purposes (Muriel & Crawford, 2020).

Within educational contexts, video games have been one of those educational technologies that have become trendier over the last decade. Several authors have addressed the benefits of game-based learning, as games can represent more interactive scenarios that players can inhabit, adapting to a set of rules and constraints, to accomplish an established objective after surpassing a series of challenges (Gee, 2003, 2008; Prensky, 2006); this resembles much more realistically real-life situations than other more passive mediums like the ones that learners are usually exposed during traditional education. In fact, several literature reviews have shared very positive insights about the use of games for education, for example for the acquisition of 21st century skills (Qian & Clark, 2016) or for learning math (Divjak & Tomić, 2011). However, games are still scarcely used for educational purposes, and little is known yet about why games work and in which cases they might not be good options.

Specifically within the context of STEM education, teachers acknowledge that STEM education can help promote 21st century skills, but that STEM teaching needs to link the curriculum with real life situations to inspire students (El-Deghaidy & Mansour, 2015). In this sense, game-based learning can help to provide such environments facilitating these realistic environments where children can learn by experimenting in a virtual game world (Eichler, Perry, Lucchesi, & Melendez, 2018). However, a recent systematic literature review on game-based learning in STEM education revealed that still more research is needed to address the fundamental question on when games can be good for STEM education and when not (Gao, Li, & Sun, 2020). Therefore, in this chapter, we want to better understand the relationship between the activity that students perform within the game based on in-game metrics, the learning gains that students experience after playing the game, and the enjoyment during this activity. This can help better understand the interplay between these three important cornerstones of the implementation of games in the classroom (Wang, Nguyen, Harpstead, Stamper, & McLaren, 2019). To do so, we use data from a pilot study conducted with Radix, an inquiry-learning STEM game that was tested across US schools. We will use in-game data from this game to compute behavioral metrics and analyze their relationship with the learning gains and enjoyment of students based on survey responses before and after interacting with Radix as part of their algebra sessions in their school. More specifically, this chapter has the following two objectives:

1. To perform an exploratory analysis of the results of a pilot study with Radix on algebra contents with several classes across the US.
2. To perform a correlational analysis to analyze the interplay between the in-game metrics, the learning gains, and the levels of enjoyment.

The rest of the chapter is organized as follows: Section 2 presents a background on educational technologies, serious games, and learning analytics. Section 3 depicts the methodology that we have pursued to reach our objectives and Section 4 describes the results for each one of the objectives. We finalize the paper with discussion and future work directions, and a conclusion in Sections 5 and 6 respectively.

BACKGROUND

We can find in the literature a broad spectrum of studies that can be categorized within the scope of technology-enhanced learning. First, we have specific educational software, such as learning management systems that have become the norm during the last decade (Muñoz Merino, Delgado Kloos, Seepold, & Crespo García, 2006), intelligent tutoring systems that provide smart environments to learn specific topics (Anderson, Boyle, & Reiser, 1985), simulations (Dameff, Selzer, Fisher, Killeen, & Tully, 2019), virtual (Pan, Cheok, Yang, Zhu, & Shi, 2006) or augmented reality (Ke & Hsu, 2015), and many other types of interactive learning environments that can take very diverse forms (Renkl & Atkinson, 2007), and where we can include video games, which is our focus (De Freitas, 2006). Moreover, there have also been several hardware trends that are attempting to perform a boost in the devices used for educational purposes, such as mobile devices (Ke & Hsu, 2015), wearables (Cain & Lee, 2016), smart glasses (Holstein, McLaren, & Aleven, 2017), or sensorized smart classrooms (Prieto, Rodríguez-Triana, Kusmin, & Laanpere, 2017) across others cutting-edge technologies.

Finally, one of the most notorious research directions in technology-enhanced learning has been on the development of data-intensive applications for different purposes, such as adaptive learning to personalize the contents based on the current status of a student (Magnisalis, Demetriadis, & Karakostas, 2011), data visualization dashboards that can be used by instructors to track the progress of the students or used by students for self-awareness purposes (Charleer, Santos, Klerkx, & Duval, 2014; Park & Jo, 2015), automatic actuators that can include early warning systems to detect students at risk (Delen, 2010) or recommendations systems that can send suggestions to students (Dwivedi & Bharadwaj, 2015), or student behavioral modeling in order to understand how are the students interacting with the learning environment (Muñoz-Merino, Ruipérez Valiente, & Kloos, 2013), which is the kind of analysis that we conduct. These are only some examples of the new advances in this domain.

In terms of interactive learning environments, we focus on video games. There have been numerous advocates of game-based learning, some of them indicating that the foundations are quite different from other forms of learning and they should be conceptualized with different frameworks and design approaches (Plass, Homer, & Kinzer, 2015). Multiple authors have performed meta-reviews on game-based learning concluding that even though, the benefits are notorious, one needs to pay careful attention to the design, the motivation of the learners, and the many contextual factors (De Freitas, 2006; Divjak & Tomić, 2011; Qian & Clark, 2016). However, serious games might also have other purposes than learning, for example motivating users to take care of their health (Baranowski et al., 2016). Therefore, the purposes that serious games can are broader than those of educational games. One of the key features of all these games is that they can increase the engagement and enjoyment that users experience during the activities when compared to other more traditional settings (Callaghan, McShane, & Eguiluz, 2014). However, little is known regarding the relationship of this enjoyment with what users do within the game, and in this chapter, we go beyond the state of the art by analyzing the interplay between ingame metrics and enjoyment.

A common approach to analyze the impact that these educational technologies can have on the learning process is the implementation of learning gains, which are often computed based on the difference between a pre-test performed before conducting the interactive activity and a post-test after finishing the activity (Vermunt, Ilie, & Vignoles, 2018). This is a common approach in the literature, and researchers have measured learning gains after playing a game (Wang et al., 2019), interacting with a Khan Academy course (Ruipérez-Valiente, Muñoz-Merino, & Kloos, 2018), or conducting tasks within an intelligent tutoring system (Kochmar et al., 2020), among many other examples. In our study we also perform this approach by computing the learning gains after playing with Radix, moreover, we go beyond the state of the art by connecting these learning gains with the in-game behavioral metrics.

Finally, our work can be framed within the area of learning analytics, which was previously defined as the "measurement, collection, analysis, and reporting of data about learners and their contexts, for purposes of understanding and optimizing learning and the environments in which it occurs" in the First International Conference on Learning Analytics & Knowledge in 2011. Our work draws from techniques in this field in order to model the behavior of the learners with the game. For example, other studies have also used learning analytics in games to build visualization dashboards to support the instructors in the classroom (Jose A. Ruiperez-Valiente, Gomez, Martinez, & Kim, 2021), to perform a game-based assessment of creativity (Yoon J Kim & Shute, 2015), or other content constructs like first aid and resuscitation skills (Charlier, 2011), to adapt a game based on the previous behavior of the users (Peirce, Conlan, & Wade, 2008), or to detect sequences of errors in a geometry game (Gomez, Ruipérez-Valiente, Martínez, & Kim, 2021), among many other potential examples. However, to the best of our knowledge, this is the first study in games that combines learning analytics in-game metrics with enjoyment and learning gains to analyze the interplay between these three cornerstones. Here lies the main contribution of this chapter with respect to the current literature.

METHODOLOGY

In this section of the chapter, we describe the methodology that we have pursued to analyze the interplay between in-game metrics, enjoyment and learning gains. Figure 1 shows an overview of the methodology that we will describe in detail in the following different subsections.

Figure 1. Overview of the methodology pursued in this study

The Radix Endeavor Serious Game

The Radix Endeavor is an inquiry-based, multidisciplinary, MMO-style online game for STEM learning that includes a balance of guided tasks and open-ended exploration. It is inquiry-based in the sense that in it, players solve problems by exploring a topic, figuring out what questions need to be asked, and determining a pathway to answer those questions. It is an MMOG-style in that it involves players controlling an avatar in a third person perspective, is set in a virtual multiplayer world that is open-ended and includes set sequences of tasks for players to work through as they explore the world and build conceptual understanding. It was developed at the MIT Education Arcade (see videos in the YouTube channel[1]), was launched in January 2014, and was free to play. Radix is aligned with the Next Generation Science Standards for biology and the Common Core State Standards for math, incorporates STEM practices, and encourages students to develop 21st century skills (e.g., critical thinking, collaboration) inside and outside of the game. It is meant to be played over the course of a semester and revisited during each relevant curricular unit.

When players enter the game for the first time, they begin a sequence of tutorial quests designed to get players used to moving around the world, using tools, and collecting data about their environment. Upon completion of the tutorial quest line, an array of topical quest lines is unlocked. The game contains several quest lines including genetics, ecology, evolution, human body systems, geometry, algebra, and statistics. In this study, we will focus on the quest line of algebra. While the quests are sequenced within a topic area, players are free to switch between quest lines according to their interests throughout their play sessions. Each quest line may have anywhere from four to ten quests within it, and each quest is made up of multiple smaller tasks which provide some scaffolding to players. The quest content is aligned with curriculum standards, and the tasks are specific to the domain.

Figure 2 shows an example of the interface of Radix where the avatar of the player, called Tyrion, is situated in the middle of the screen. On the right side, we see the tools that the player has available; these are the tools that are used as part of the inquiry-based learning process to solve the quests. Moreover, on the bottom-right part of the interface, we observe the mini-map, that students use to travel through the world and reach the places needed to solve the different quests. On the bottom-left part of the interface we see the chat area, which is one of the main features enabling social interaction between the learners, with a general chat that anyone can write in and read, but also the possibility to send private messages to specific users to maintain communications that others cannot read. Moreover, students can also create groups to solve quests in a collaborative way. On the left side of the interface, we can see the inventory of the character, which contains the items that they can take from the Radix world, such as seeds, crystals, rocks, and plants among many other things. Finally, on the upper-left part of the interface, we see other available options in the menu panel such as the diary, the letters, the quest menu, and some other configuration tabs. Students need to interact with all these features to solve the quests.

Figure 2. Example of the interface of Radix

Pilot Study

Radix was used across numerous schools in the US and in other international countries. In this study, we focus on using the data from a controlled pilot study that ran from January 2014 through August 2015. While the game was designed with high school math and biology teachers in mind, Radix has been used by upper elementary, middle, and high school teachers as well as by a few instructors at community colleges and universities. During the pilot period, informal marketing and outreach was done to recruit teachers to participate in the pilot at various levels. Participating teachers were provided with professional development opportunities and implementation resources, which included in-person sessions, monthly webinars, an online forum, information on alignment with standards, and suggestions for bridging curriculum. Teachers were encouraged to tailor their implementations and use the game as they saw fit in their classroom; most had their students play relevant quest lines at the time they were covering a given topic area in their class. However, we did not have a tight control of the way teachers implemented Radix in their classes. Radix remained accessible to be played by anyone, and to be used by teachers in their classes until late 2019. However, the game is not available any more on the web.

Several participating teachers implemented Radix in their classes. They were asked to align the quests selected for their students with the curriculum that they were teaching and use both sets of contents (traditional and the ones provided by Radix) at the same time. From the several sets of contents that we explained previously, in this study we focus on algebra. Therefore, we use the data of those teachers that implemented Radix quest line on algebra while they were teaching algebra in their classes. Therefore, the pre- and post-tests that we utilize are also on algebra contents.

Pre-Test, Post-Test, and Enjoyment Survey

The pre-test and post-test were the same identical test that focused on core algebra elements and was designed collaboratively with math teachers. The main difference is that the pre-test was taken by the students before interacting with Radix, and the post-test was taken by the students after finishing the sessions where they would be interacting with Radix. The procedure was designed so that we could guarantee a proper inference of the learning gains of students. In the case of the algebra test, there were 18 questions ranging across the different common core standards of algebra.

The enjoyment survey was taken after playing Radix game with the objective of measuring the levels of enjoyment that students experienced while playing the game. It had a total of 12 items that had to be responded in a 6-points Likert scale with the following categories: 'Completely False', 'Mostly False', 'Somewhat False', 'Somewhat True', 'Mostly True', 'Completely True'. These items were collected from previous validated instruments (Fang, Chan, Brzezinski, & Nair, 2010; Myers, Nichols, & White, 2003), and adapted to our game environment and pilot study with Radix. There has been in the literature multiple other instruments to measure engagement with learning environments, for example to measure enjoyment with e-learning games (Fu, Su, & Yu, 2009) or to measure flow in learning with MOOCs (Heutte, Fenouillet, Kaplan, Martin-Krumm, & Bachelet, 2016). However, these were multifaceted instruments with multiple sub-constructs, and given that we were working with children and teenagers, we designed a straightforward questionnaire with a limited number of items focused on enjoyment. Find below in Table 1 with each one of the items that were responded to as part of this survey.

Table 1. Items of the enjoyment survey

Item	Statement
1	I would be willing to play "Radix" again because I think it is a fun game.
2	If I have trouble understanding a problem, I go over it again until I understand it.
3	When I run into a difficult homework problem, I keep working at it until I think I have solved it.
4	I would describe "Radix" as very interesting.
5	If I have trouble solving a problem, I am more likely to guess at the answer than to look at examples in the book to try to figure things out.
6	"Radix" let me do interesting things.
7	If I have trouble solving a problem, I will try to get someone else to help me.
8	I thought "Radix" was quite enjoyable.
9	I try to complete homework assignments as fast as possible without checking it.
10	When I run into a difficult homework problem, I usually give up and go on to the next problem.
11	When I read something for class that does not make sense, I skip it and hope that the teacher explains it in class.
12	I enjoyed participating in "Radix."

We want to clarify that the use of Radix was the only intervention that was solicited to the teachers implementing this case study across the US. We did not perform any debriefing between the sessions using Radix and the completion of the post-tests.

Metrics

In this subsection we describe the metrics that we computed. The in-game metrics were based on previous work that generated a multi-dimensional model of engagement in Radix based on four dimensions: the general activity, the exploration activity, social activity, and quest activity (Ruiperez-Valiente, Gaydos, Rosenheck, Kim, & Klopfer, 2020). We decided to use these granular metrics to provide the maximum information possible for the exploratory and correlational analysis, so that we avoid losing information by using the higher-level models of engagement from previous work; therefore, these previous models of engagement in four dimensions are not used for any purposes in this work. Find below the specific definition of each one of the in-game metrics that we used:

- *active_time*: The number of active minutes in the game.
- *number_events*: The total number of actions (events in the logging system) generated by the student in Radix.
- *n_unique_zones*: Number of zones that the student visited in Radix.
- *n_different_explore_events*: There are 19 different tools or actions that a player can experiment with within the Radix world in order to solve quests and learn STEM content. This metrics provides a percentage of tools used by this student.
- *n_total_explore_events*: Number of events that are related to the use of experimental tools in the game.
- *p_completed_algebra_quests*: Percentage of completed questions by the student that belong to the algebra quest line.
- *p_correct_algebra_quests*: Percentage of correct attempts with respect to the total of the attempts performed within the algebra quest line.
- *p_change_quest_chain:* Since Radix does not force students to complete quest chains in a linear sequence, that means they can jump from one quest chain to another one, for example, from a biology quest to an algebra quest. This item measures how frequently the student changes from one quest to another. Therefore, if the value is very small, it means that the student tends to advance linearly in Radix, and if the number is high, it means that the student tends to jump from one quest line to another with high frequency.
- *n_chats*: Total number of chats sent by this student, taking into account both private messages between students to a single user and also zone chats that can be read by all users.
- *chars_per_chat_msg*: This metrics is calculated by dividing the number of total messages of a student by the number of alphanumeric characters of those messages, to provide an average value of the length of each chat message.
- *party_joined*: Total number of parties joined by the student. The parties in Radix allow students to group together to perform collaborative task solving.

In addition to the previous in-game metrics, we also use the following metrics obtained through the surveys:

- *pre_test*: Score obtained by the student in the pre-test taken before interacting with Radix, in order to understand the initial knowledge of the student.
- *learning_gain*: The learning gain of the student calculated by computing the difference between the post-test and the pre-test. Learning gains can range from -1 to 1.
- *avg_enjoyment*: This metric is an average measure of the 12 items from the enjoyment survey. Since there were six survey categories, we transformed them into an integer range from 0 to 6.

In order to measure the relationship between the variables, we compute the Pearson correlation coefficient, as a linear correlation between two sets of data as follows:

$$r = \frac{n\sum xy - (\sum x)(\sum y)}{\sqrt{n(\sum x^2) - (\sum x)^2}\sqrt{n(\sum y^2) - (\sum y)^2}}$$

Final Data Collection

Since the in-game metrics are computed based on the tracking logs, and the rest of the metrics are computed based on the surveys, we had to link both sources of data together. This is done via the information provided in the survey by the student, which indicated the name of their character in Radix, and this allows us to properly merge both sources of data to perform this analysis. Moreover, for the final data collection, we had the following requisites to include a user account as part of the study:

- Teacher, staff, and research accounts were removed, leaving only accounts from students.
- We eliminated accounts that had not reached a minimum interaction of two hours, which is the estimation from designers for learners to getting familiar with Radix game mechanics.
- We kept only the accounts that had completed the first three quests of the tutorial, since the two first quests do not require any specific interaction with the environment– just speaking with the non-player characters (NPCs)–and the third task is the first one where they need to use a tool to correctly finish the quest.
- We kept only those accounts that completely responded to the pre-test, the post-test and the enjoyment surveys.

From the entire data sample, a cohort of 164 students met all the aforementioned criteria and are included in the study, 53% of the learners were male and 47% female. The majority of the learners were part of 6th and 7th grade classes (43% and 54% respectively), and the rest were in 8th grade. We would like to highlight that this is a good sample size considering all the instrumental work to organize the sessions and gather this data.

RESULTS

The results of this book chapter are organized into two subsections. The first one depicts an exploratory analysis of the different in-game metrics and survey ones to understand its distribution and results of the pilot study. The second one performs a correlational analysis to better understand the relationship between in-game activity, learning gains, and enjoyment.

Exploratory Analysis of the Metrics

The exploratory visualizations presented in this section will help to understand how the different metrics are distributed to better comprehend the interaction that students did with Radix as well as the survey results in terms of learning gains and the levels of enjoyment experienced by the students. In that sense, Figure 3 shows a violin plot that includes all the previously defined metrics, which are grouped based on the category and filled with different colors. The three horizontal lines represent the 25%, 50%, and 75% quantiles from bottom to top respectively. We have the in-game metrics, that are colored differently depending on their dimension (general activity, exploration, quests, and social) and we also have the survey metrics with a different color.

Regarding the activity metrics, the *active_time* is depicted in hours; therefore we see that the average user invested five hours playing with Radix, but there are multiple users as outliers that invested more than 20 hours, which is a significant amount of time. Moreover, we see a similar pattern with *number_events*, where the average user generated around 400 events, but some users did more than 2000 events. Therefore, this conveys that the degree of global interaction with the game varied greatly from one student to another, with a majority of students that invested between 2.5 and 7.5 hours, but a nice cohort of users that invested between 15 and 20 hours. The number of events might be affected by the kind of play that they developed.

Regarding the metrics for the in-game exploration, the average user explored seven unique zones (*n_unique_zones*) of the Radix world, did six different exploration tool events (*n_different_explore_events*), and performed around 150 different exploration events (*n_total_explore_events*). These metrics depict how much each student explored the Radix world, without taking into account if they were able to advance with the algebra quest line (or with any other quest lines). We note that there might be some users that invested a lot of time or explored heavily the world of Radix but did not progress with the quest system or performed badly in the survey post-tests. We see a similar form in the shape of the violin subplots for the metrics *n_unique_zones* and *n_different_explore_events,* indicating the relationship between the global in-game activity and the in-game exploration.

Regarding the quest metrics, we first see based on *p_change_quest_chain* that the average user approximately tended to change between quest chains 20% of the times. This number is not so high, and therefore, most students tended to act in a more linear way. However, we do see some students with high numbers, above 40% and 50%, which would be students that perform frequent quest chain changes. The distribution of the metric is clearly normal, with a rather thin upper tail. We will see the impact that this can have in the next subsection. In terms of the two metrics on algebra quests, we see that the average user completed around 25% of the algebra quests, with the distribution clearly varying from 0 to 100% of algebra question completion (*p_completed_algebra_quests*). Therefore, there are important differences between how many quests the different students solved. Some of the users struggle to resolve questions correctly, but others just invested more time on other aspects of Radix, such as the social ones or the exploration. Moreover, the percentage of correct responses in these quests (p_*correct_algebra_quests*) is around 70%, which is a high ratio that denotes that the difficulty was not too high, and most of the students that attempted to solve a quest, were able to complete it correctly. The distribution of the metric clearly shows bell curve that is not too abrupt, so the difficulty of the quests can be considered as appropriate.

In regard to the social metrics, we also see a great variability that denotes a key feature of Radix, which is the possibility for users to collaborate between them, generating a lot of social activity and interaction between peers. More exactly, we see that the average user sent around 80 chat messages (n_*chats*), which had around 10 chars per chat message (*chars_per_chat_msg*). These two indicators signal that the students did write many messages but also most of them were quite short messages. This of course changes importantly between users. In addition, the metric *party_joined* shows that the creation of parties to jointly solve quests was a common activity, as most users participated in at least three parties. We see a similar distribution in the three social metrics, where most students are clustered in the lower bound of the distribution; however, we do see a small proportion of users located in the upper tail in the three metrics denoting high interesting for the social side of Radix.

Figure 3. Violin plot of the different in-game and survey metrics. The three horizontal lines represent the 25%, 50%, and 75% quantiles from bottom to top respectively

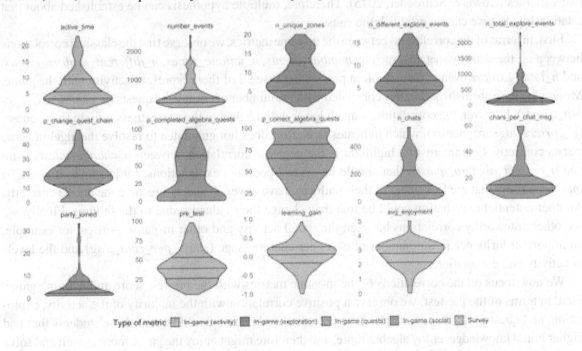

Finally, we have the survey metrics, where the *pre_test* indicates that the average user obtained a score of around 45 points from a maximum of 100. Therefore, we see that students started with an activity with a borderline knowledge on algebra. The pre-test score is widely distributed between this range, with users obtaining almost perfect scores and others failing almost all responses, as usual in K12 settings with a wide spectrum of kids. The results in terms of *learning_gain* is not very positive, since we see that the average learning gain was around 0 points, meaning that on average, the score in the pre-test and post-test was quite similar. It is also important to note that the distribution of the learning gains is also broad, so we have multiple cases of students that scored in the post-test much higher and lower than in the pre-test. There might be multiple reasons to explain this. At last, the *avg_enjoyment* metric shows a value close to 3 points over the maximum of 5 points. We believe this is a good number that denotes that the majority of students enjoyed the experienced of combining Radix algebra quests with the normal curriculum of algebra that their teacher was providing in their classes.

Correlations and Interplay between the Metrics

After presenting an overview of the metrics in the previous subsection, we now conduct a correlation analysis to see the interplay between the metrics. Figure 4 shows a correlation diagonal matrix that includes all the in-game and survey metrics considered in the study. Each cell indicates the correlation between the variable in the *x*-axis and the variable in the *y*-axis, where all the cells in the diagonal have a value of 1. Correlations range from -1 to 1, with a 0 indicating no relationship at all between the two variables. The color intensity and the number on the cell encode the value of the correlation with blue for positive ones and red for negative ones. Before sharing the correlational results, we would like to remind the reader that correlation does not imply causation, but just an observed association between two variables (Cowls & Schroeder, 2015). Therefore, multiple hypothesis can be established about that relationship, but we cannot establish the cause.

First, in terms of the correlations between the in-game metrics, we observe first the classical correlations between all the activity metrics, such as *number_events*, *n_unique_zones*, *n_different_explore_events*, and *n_total_explore* events, that are often present because all of them represent activity with the game. Moreover, these are also moderately correlated with the number of completed quests (*p_completed_algebra_quests*), however, the correlation is much lower with respect to the correctness ratio in those quests (*p_correct_algebra_quests*), which indicates that effort does not guarantee to resolve the algebra game quests correctly. One interesting highlight is the negative correlation between *p_change_quest_chain* and *p_correct_algebra_quests*; there could be several potential explanations, for example, it could be that those users that are less linear in their pathway, have lower chances to resolve the quests correctly. Another potential explanation could be that they change their behavior due to the failures. Finally, we see other noteworthy correlations between the social activity and other in-game metrics, for example, an important influence in the number of chars per chat message (*chars_per_chat_msg*) and the levels of activity and exploration.

We now focus on the correlations of the in-game metrics with the pre-test score and learning gains. First, in terms of the pre-test, we observe a positive correlation with the majority of the activity, exploration, and quest performance metrics; one potential explanation could be that those students that had higher initial knowledge, enjoy algebra more, and therefore might enjoy the game more as well and solve more tasks. Another potential explanation could be that the game is just easier and therefore find it more amusing, or that they are motivated by math and use Radix just as practice. We do see also especially high correlations for the *party_joined* and *n_chats* social metrics, which might also be in relationship with a motivation with the game. Then, in terms of the learning gain, we observe a positive correlation with most of the activity and exploration metrics, which could mean that those students that interacted more with Radix, were able to improve their knowledge. Moreover, we also see a positive correlation with *p_correct_algebra_quests*, which indicates that the ones that achieved a better performance in Radix algebra tasks, also achieved a higher learning gain. Finally, we find a negative correlation with *n_chats*, indicating that students that texted less might have a higher learning gain.

Finally, one important correlation of 0.32 is the one emerging between the *learning_gain* of the student and *avg_enjoyment*, which indicates that those students that enjoyed the time spent playing Radix tended to learn more than their peers.

Figure 4. Correlation analysis of the in-game and survey metrics displayed in a diagonal grid. The color of the cell encodes the strength of the correlation

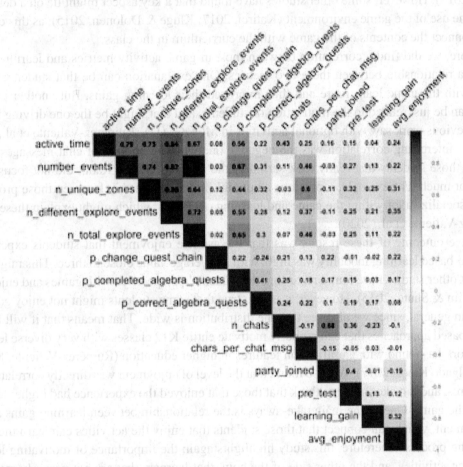

DISCUSSION AND FUTURE RESEARCH DIRECTIONS

After presenting these results in this section we will provide potential explanations, discussion, as well as future research directions. First, in terms of the learning gains results, one of the first highlights was the low level of learning gains, with an average value close to 0. There are multiple interpretations that can come out of this. In the first instance, the teachers did not provide any encouragement to perform better in the external tests. Therefore, some students might have not taken them too seriously, and that might have affected the learning gains. Moreover, the algebra quest lines were designed to foster inquiry-based learning, and they were not directly connected with the contents of the administered external measures on algebra. If we compare these results with other studies implementing learning gains before and after interactive learning environments have reported much higher learning gains (Corbett, Kauffman, Maclaren, Wagner, & Jones, 2010; Kochmar et al., 2020), but these were more controlled cases studies, and the contents of the system were directly related with the test items. Another study using the algebra learning game called DragonBox also found that students did not improve significantly their learning gains after using this environment, when compared to the use of a specialized tutoring system (Long, Yanjin and Aleven, 2014). However, some other studies have found that a key aspect might lie on a debriefing period after the use of the game environment (Katirci, 2017; Kluge & Dolonen, 2015), as this can help students to connect the contents of the game with the curriculum in the class.

Furthermore, we did find a correlation between most in-game activity metrics and learning gains, which raises a relationship between these two metrics. One explanation can be that students that interact more with the game learn more and thus improved their learning gains. But another potential explanation can be just related to the motivation of students, and that might be the one driving them to improve as previous work saw with optional activities in MOOCs (J.A. Ruiperez-Valiente et al., 2016). Moreover, one interesting correlation was the negative one with the number of chat messages, which might be that those students that really took seriously the interaction with Radix did not focus on the social side that much. For example, a previous study did find a relationship between those profiles of students that socialize a lot within the game and learning outcomes, which might explain these results (J.A. Ruiperez-Valiente et al., 2020).

One positive outcome of these results was that the average enjoyment that students experienced with this game-based learning modality was high, with an average value close to three. This might be in line with what other studies have found regarding the students' perspectives with games and enjoyment (Yoon Jeon Kim & Shute, 2015). However, it is also true that some students might not enjoy games or gamification in general, since we also see that the distribution is wide. That means that it will be hard to find game-based approaches that can properly motivate entire K12 classes with very diverse learners, as previous work has found with gamification features in higher education (Ruipérez-Valiente, Muñoz-Merino, & Delgado Kloos, 2017). We also found that the level of enjoyment was directly correlated with in-game features, and it makes sense to think that those that enjoyed the experience had higher levels of activity with the game. One of the main take-aways is the relationship between learning gains and the level of enjoyment, which can connect that those students that enjoy the activities can learn more during the learning process. Therefore, this study highlights again the importance of motivating learners with the proper activities, and the other side of the coin, that learners that are not properly motivated will perform worse.

This book focuses on promoting economic and social development through serious games. Therefore, one of the most direct conclusions is that game-based learning approaches can suppose a significant improvement to increase the motivation of students, and that can help improve the overall learning that students achieve. Moreover, in Radix students were able to develop inquiry-based learning, exploring a virtual world and trying to understand algebra based on interacting with different features, learning by doing, without being passively exposed to the contents like is usually done in lectures. This has been depicted by several authors as one of the greatest assets of games for learning, which is the possibility to inhabit virtual worlds, in a way that resembles much more realistically the kind of challenges that they will face in real life (Gee, 2008; Prensky, 2006). In this work, we have depicted the potential of learning analytics in games to compute a set of in-game metrics that we were able to use to model the behavior of the students with the game. Therefore, these analytics also represent an important opportunity to perform game-based assessment, either for formative or summative purposes (Yoon Jeon Kim, Almond, & Shute, 2016). These assessments can be performed unobtrusively without impacting the game flow of students in what is known as stealth assessment (Shute, 2005), and then can be used to provide students with personalized feedback that can help them improve certain aspects. This can be done by developing teacher-facing dashboards in games that provide detailed information regarding the in-game activity of students with the game (Jose A. Ruiperez-Valiente et al., 2021).

Our work also has some limitations. For example, this analysis has been focused on a single quest line of Radix, and we will also aim to replicate this analysis in other quest lines. Moreover, even though Radix site was maintained for more than five years and used widely, the technology became obsolete and is no longer available for the public. However, we think that these findings might generalize well to other STEM games that support inquiry-based activities to experiment and learn by doing, and there are multiple examples in the literature about these kind of games, for example IT-Adventures that is focused on teaching information technology concepts using inquiry-based learning (Rursch, Luse, & Jacobson, 2010) or the Factory Game, that focuses on macroscopic-microscopic concepts of the properties of liquid in chemistry (Srisawasdi & Panjaburee, 2019). We would encourage current researchers in this area to replicate these experiments to further analyze the relationship between in-game activity, learning gains, and enjoyment.

Future work should focus on addressing approaches to address those learners that might not be motivated by games, for example by better understanding the reasons so that these lessons learned can be looped back to the design of new serious games. Moreover, the learning analytics modeling in serious games also represents great opportunities, therefore future work should continue the development of these models, perhaps using more complex artificial intelligence techniques, or even developing new specific algorithms for the context of games. A clear challenge in this aspect is the scalability of these analytics across different serious games, an issue that needs to be tackled without a doubt if we want to systematically implement them (Alonso-Fernandez, Calvo, Freire, Martinez-Ortiz, & Fernandez-Manjon, 2017). Finally, another potential research opportunity within the context of serious games and learning analytics lies in the use of multimodal approaches using biometrics or audiovisual information, in order to augment the level of analysis and inferences that can be drawn (Blikstein & Worsley, 2016). All of these future directions can help serious games to make an extraordinary impact on society across diverse contexts.

CONCLUSION

This chapter has tackled a novel topic which was the interplay between in-game metrics, learning gains, and the levels of enjoyment. We have done so by presenting a novel methodology utilizing learning analytics to compute several behavioral indicators, and then we linked those to survey responses generated before and after playing with Radix game. Our main findings suggest a clear relationship between the learning games and the levels of enjoyment. However, while most of the learners enjoyed the experience, not all of them improved their knowledge. Both learning gains and enjoyment were in general positively correlated with in-game metrics, and those learners engaged much more with the platform than the rest. An issue that remains open regarding how to motivate those learners that did not find this game-based learning activity with Radix engaging, as this is something that has been frequently raised by other gamification and serious games case studies. This work has exemplified the potential that analytics approaches, and serious games have to transform education and training across contexts.

REFERENCES

Alonso-Fernandez, C., Calvo, A., Freire, M., Martinez-Ortiz, I., & Fernandez-Manjon, B. (2017). Systematizing game learning analytics for serious games. *IEEE Global Engineering Education Conference, EDUCON*, (April), 1111–1118. 10.1109/EDUCON.2017.7942988

Anderson, J. R., Boyle, C. F., & Reiser, B. J. (1985). Intelligent tutoring systems. *Science, 228*(4698), 456–462. doi:10.1126cience.228.4698.456 PMID:17746875

Baranowski, T., Blumberg, F., Buday, R., DeSmet, A., Fiellin, L. E., Green, C. S., Kato, P. M., Lu, A. S., Maloney, A. E., Mellecker, R., Morrill, B. A., Peng, W., Shegog, R., Simons, M., Staiano, A. E., Thompson, D., & Young, K. (2016). Games for Health for Children-Current Status and Needed Research. *Games for Health Journal, 5*(1), 1–12. doi:10.1089/g4h.2015.0026 PMID:26262772

Blikstein, P., & Worsley, M. (2016). Multimodal learning analytics and education data mining : Using computational technologies to measure complex learning tasks. *Journal of Learning Analytics, 3*(2), 220–238. doi:10.18608/jla.2016.32.11

Cain, R., & Lee, V. R. (2016). Measuring Electrodermal Activity to Capture Engagement in an After-school Maker Program. *Proceedings of the 6th Annual Conference on Creativity and Fabrication in Education - FabLearn '16, 1*(718), 78–81. 10.1145/3003397.3003409

Callaghan, M. J., McShane, N., & Eguiluz, A. G. (2014). Using game analytics to measure student engagement/retention for engineering education. *Proceedings of 2014 11th International Conference on Remote Engineering and Virtual Instrumentation, REV 2014*, (February), 297–302. 10.1109/REV.2014.6784174

Charleer, S., Santos, J. L., Klerkx, J., & Duval, E. (2014). Improving teacher awareness through activity, badge and content visualizations. In New Horizons in Web Based Learning (pp. 143–152). doi:10.1007/978-3-319-13296-9_16

Charlier, N. (2011). Game-based assessment of first aid and resuscitation skills. *Resuscitation, 82*(4), 442–446. doi:10.1016/j.resuscitation.2010.12.003 PMID:21277070

Corbett, A., Kauffman, L., Maclaren, B., Wagner, A., & Jones, E. (2010). A Cognitive Tutor for Genetics Problem Solving: Learning Gains and Student Modeling. *Journal of Educational Computing Research, 42*(2), 219–239. doi:10.2190/EC.42.2.e

Cowls, J., & Schroeder, R. (2015). Causation, Correlation, and Big Data in Social Science Research. *Policy and Internet, 7*(4), 447–472. doi:10.1002/poi3.100

Dabbagh, N., Benson, A. D., Denham, A., Joseph, R., Al-Freih, M., Zgheib, G., ... Guo, Z. (2016). *Learning Technologies and Globalization*. Springer International Publishing., doi:10.1007/978-3-319-22963-8

Dameff, C. J., Selzer, J. A., Fisher, J., Killeen, J. P., & Tully, J. L. (2019). Clinical Cybersecurity Training Through Novel High-Fidelity Simulations. *The Journal of Emergency Medicine*, *56*(2), 233–238. doi:10.1016/j.jemermed.2018.10.029 PMID:30553562

Daniel, M., & Garry, C. (2018). *Video Games As Culture*. Routledge. doi:10.4324/9781315622743

De Freitas, S. (2006). Learning in Immersive worlds A review of game-based learning. *JISC ELearning Innovation, 3*(October), 73. doi:10.1111/j.1467-8535.2009.01024.x

Delen, D. (2010). A comparative analysis of machine learning techniques for student retention management. *Decision Support Systems*, *49*(4), 498–506. doi:10.1016/j.dss.2010.06.003

Divjak, B., & Tomić, D. (2011). The impact of Game-based learning on the achievement of learning goals and motivation for learning mathematics - literature review. *Journal of Information and Organizational Sciences*, *35*(1). jios.foi.hr/index.php/jios/article/view/182

Dwivedi, P., & Bharadwaj, K. K. (2015). E-Learning recommender system for a group of learners based on the unified learner profile approach. *Expert Systems: International Journal of Knowledge Engineering and Neural Networks*, *32*(2), 264–276. doi:10.1111/exsy.12061

Eichler, M. L., Perry, G. T., Lucchesi, I. L., & Melendez, T. T. (2018). Mobile game-based learning in STEM subjects. In *Encyclopedia of Information Science and Technology* (4th ed., pp. 6376–6387). IGI Global.

El-Deghaidy, H., & Mansour, N. (2015). Science Teachers' Perceptions of STEM Education: Possibilities and Challenges. *International Journal of Learning*, *1*(1), 51–54. doi:10.18178/ijlt.1.1.51-54

ESA. (2019). *2019 Essential Facts About the Computer and Video Game Industry*. Retrieved from https://www.theesa.com/resource/essential-facts-about-the-computer-and-video-game-industry-2019/

Fang, X., Chan, S., Brzezinski, J., & Nair, C. (2010). Development of an instrument to measure enjoyment of computer game play. *International Journal of Human-Computer Interaction*, *26*(9), 868–886. doi:10.1080/10447318.2010.496337

Fu, F. L., Su, R. C., & Yu, S. C. (2009). EGameFlow: A scale to measure learners' enjoyment of e-learning games. *Computers & Education*, *52*(1), 101–112. doi:10.1016/j.compedu.2008.07.004

Gao, F., Li, L., & Sun, Y. (2020). A systematic review of mobile game-based learning in STEM education. *Educational Technology Research and Development*, *68*(4), 1791–1827. doi:10.100711423-020-09787-0

Gee, J. P. (2003). What video games have to teach us about learning and literacy. *Computers in Entertainment*, *1*(1), 20. doi:10.1145/950566.950595

Gee, J. P. (2008). Learning and games. *The Ecology of Games: Connecting Youth, Games, and Learning*, 21–40. doi:10.1162/dmal.9780262693646.021

Gomez, M. J., Ruipérez-Valiente, J. A., Martínez, P. A., & Kim, Y. J. (2021). Applying Learning Analytics to Detect Sequences of Actions and Common Errors in a Geometry Game. *Sensors (Basel)*, *21*(4), 1025. doi:10.339021041025 PMID:33546167

Heutte, J., Fenouillet, F., Kaplan, J., Martin-Krumm, C., & Bachelet, R. (2016). The EduFlow Model: A Contribution Toward the Study of Optimal Learning Environments. In L. Harmat, F. Ø. Andersen, F. Ullén, J. Wright, & G. Sadlo (Eds.), *Flow Experience: Empirical Research and Applications* (pp. 127–143). doi:10.1007/978-3-319-28634-1_9

Holstein, K., McLaren, B. M., & Aleven, V. (2017). Intelligent tutors as teachers' aides: Exploring teacher needs for real-time analytics in blended classrooms. *ACM International Conference Proceeding Series*, 257–266. 10.1145/3027385.3027451

Katirci, N. (2017). *The Influence of DragonBox on Student Attitudes and Understanding in 7th Grade Mathematics Classroom*. University at Albany, State University of New York. Retrieved from https://search.proquest.com/openview/967700b0c633db144a461e8fff33347d/1?pq-origsite=gscholar&cbl=18750&diss=y

Ke, F., & Hsu, Y.-C. (2015). Mobile augmented-reality artifact creation as a component of mobile computer-supported collaborative learning. *The Internet and Higher Education*, *26*, 33–41. doi:10.1016/j.iheduc.2015.04.003

Kim, Y. J. (2015). Opportunities and Challenges in Assessing and Supporting Creativity in Video Games. *Video Games and Creativity*.

Kim, Y. J., Almond, R. G., & Shute, V. J. (2016). Applying Evidence-Centered Design for the Development of Game-Based Assessments in Physics Playground. *International Journal of Testing*, *16*(2), 142–163. doi:10.1080/15305058.2015.1108322

Kim, Y. J., & Shute, V. J. (2015). The interplay of game elements with psychometric qualities, learning, and enjoyment in game-based assessment. *Computers & Education*, *87*, 340–356. doi:10.1016/j.compedu.2015.07.009

Kluge, A., & Dolonen, J. (2015). Using Mobile Games in the Classroom. In H. Crompton & J. Traxler (Eds.), *Mobile Learning and Mathematics: Foundations, Design, and Case Studies* (pp. 106–121). Taylor & Francis.

Kochmar, E., Do Vu, D., Belfer, R., Gupta, V., Serban, I. V., & Pineau, J. (2020). Automated Personalized Feedback Improves Learning Gains in An Intelligent Tutoring System. In I. I. Bittencourt, M. Cukurova, K. Muldner, R. Luckin, & E. Millán (Eds.), *Artificial Intelligence in Education* (pp. 140–146). Springer International Publishing. doi:10.1007/978-3-030-52240-7_26

Long, Y., & Aleven, V. (2014). Gamification of Joint Student/System Control Over Problem Selection in a Linear Equation Tutor. In *International conference on intelligent tutoring systems* (Vol. 8474 LNCS, pp. 378–387). doi:10.1007/978-3-319-07221-0

Madhushree, Revathi, & Aithal. (2019). A Review on Impact of Information Communication & Computation Technology (ICCT) on Selected Primary, Secondary, and Tertiary Industrial Sectors. *Saudi Journal of Business and Management Studies, 4*(1), 106–127. Retrieved from https://econpapers.repec.org/RePEc:pra:mprapa:95150

Magnisalis, I., Demetriadis, S., & Karakostas, A. (2011). Adaptive and intelligent systems for collaborative learning support: A review of the field. *IEEE Transactions on Learning Technologies*, *4*(1), 5–20. doi:10.1109/TLT.2011.2

Muñoz Merino, P. J., Delgado Kloos, C., Seepold, R., & Crespo García, R. M. (2006). Rating the importance of different LMS functionalities. In *Proceedings - Frontiers in Education Conference, FIE* (pp. 13–18). 10.1109/FIE.2006.322715

Muñoz-Merino, P. J., Ruipérez Valiente, J. A., & Kloos, C. D. (2013). Inferring higher level learning information from low level data for the Khan Academy platform. In *Proceedings of the Third International Conference on Learning Analytics and Knowledge - LAK '13* (pp. 112–116). ACM Press. 10.1145/2460296.2460318

Muriel, D., & Crawford, G. (2020). Video Games and Agency in Contemporary Society. *Games and Culture*, *15*(2), 138–157. doi:10.1177/1555412017750448

Myers, M. D., Nichols, J. D., & White, J. (2003). Teacher and Student Incremental and Entity Views of Intelligence: The Effect of Self-Regulation and Persistence Activities. *International Journal of Educational Reform*, *12*(2), 97–116. doi:10.1177/105678790301200202

Pan, Z., Cheok, A. D., Yang, H., Zhu, J., & Shi, J. (2006). Virtual reality and mixed reality for virtual learning environments. *Computers & Graphics*, *30*(1), 20–28. doi:10.1016/j.cag.2005.10.004

Park, Y., & Jo, I. (2015). Development of the Learning Analytics Dashboard to Support Students' Learning Performance Learning Analytics Dashboards (LADs). *Journal of Universal Computer Science*, *21*(1), 110–133.

Peirce, N., Conlan, O., & Wade, V. (2008). Adaptive educational games: Providing non-invasive personalised learning experiences. In *Proceedings - 2nd IEEE International Conference on Digital Game and Intelligent Toy Enhanced Learning, DIGITEL 2008* (pp. 28–35). 10.1109/DIGITEL.2008.30

Plass, J. L., Homer, B. D., & Kinzer, C. K. (2015). Foundations of Game-Based Learning. *Educational Psychologist*, *50*(4), 258–283. doi:10.1080/00461520.2015.1122533

Prensky, M. (2006). Don't bother me, Mom, I'm learning! How computer and video games are preparing your kids for 21st century success and how you can help! Paragon House.

Prieto, L. P., Rodríguez-Triana, M. J., Kusmin, M., & Laanpere, M. (2017). Smart school multimodal dataset and challenges. *CEUR Workshop Proceedings*, *1828*, 53–59. doi:10.1145/1235

Qian, M., & Clark, K. R. (2016). Game-based Learning and 21st century skills: A review of recent research. *Computers in Human Behavior*, *63*, 50–58. doi:10.1016/j.chb.2016.05.023

Renkl, A., & Atkinson, R. K. (2007). Interactive Learning Environments: Contemporary Issues and Trends. An Introduction to the Special Issue. *Educational Psychology Review*, *19*(3), 235–238. doi:10.100710648-007-9052-5

Ruiperez-Valiente, J. A., Gaydos, M., Rosenheck, L., Kim, Y. J., & Klopfer, E. (2020). Patterns of Engagement in an Educational Massively Multiplayer Online Game: A Multidimensional View. *IEEE Transactions on Learning Technologies*, 13(4), 648–661. Advance online publication. doi:10.1109/TLT.2020.2968234

Ruiperez-Valiente, J. A., Gomez, M. J., Martinez, P. A., & Kim, Y. J. (2021). Ideating and Developing a Visualization Dashboard to Support Teachers Using Educational Games in the Classroom. *IEEE Access: Practical Innovations, Open Solutions*, 9, 83467–83481. doi:10.1109/ACCESS.2021.3086703

Ruipérez-Valiente, J. A., Muñoz-Merino, P. J., & Delgado Kloos, C. (2017). Detecting and Clustering Students by their Gamification Behavior with Badges: A Case Study in Engineering Education. *International Journal of Engineering Education*, 33(2-B), 816–830.

Ruipérez-Valiente, J. A., Muñoz-Merino, P. J., & Kloos, C. D. (2018). Improving the prediction of learning outcomes in educational platforms including higher level interaction indicators. *Expert Systems: International Journal of Knowledge Engineering and Neural Networks*, 35(6), e12298. Advance online publication. doi:10.1111/exsy.12298

Ruiperez-Valiente, J. A., Munoz-Merino, P. J., Kloos, C. D., Niemann, K., Scheffel, M., & Wolpers, M. (2016). Analyzing the Impact of Using Optional Activities in Self-Regulated Learning. *IEEE Transactions on Learning Technologies*, 9(3), 231–243. Advance online publication. doi:10.1109/TLT.2016.2518172

Rursch, J. A., Luse, A., & Jacobson, D. (2010). IT-adventures: A program to spark IT interest in high school students using inquiry-based learning with cyber defense, game design, and robotics. *IEEE Transactions on Education*, 53(1), 71–79. doi:10.1109/TE.2009.2024080

Shute, V. J. (2005). Stealth Assessment in Computer-Based Games to Support Learning. In S. Tobias & J. D. Fletcher (Eds.), *Computer Games and Instruction* (pp. 503–524). Information Age Publishers.

Squire, K. (2011). *Video Games and Learning: Teaching and Participatory Culture in the Digital Age. Technology, Education—Connections (the TEC Series)*. ERIC.

Srisawasdi, N., & Panjaburee, P. (2019). Implementation of Game-transformed Inquiry-based Learning to Promote the Understanding of and Motivation to Learn Chemistry. *Journal of Science Education and Technology*, 28(2), 152–164. doi:10.100710956-018-9754-0

Thomas, S. (2016). *Future Ready Learning. Reimagining the Role of Technology in Education. Office of Educational Technology, US Department of Education*.

Vermunt, J. D., Ilie, S., & Vignoles, A. (2018). Building the foundations for measuring learning gain in higher education: A conceptual framework and measurement instrument. *Higher Education Pedagogies*, 3(1), 266–301. doi:10.1080/23752696.2018.1484672

Wang, Y., Nguyen, H., Harpstead, E., Stamper, J., & McLaren, B. M. (2019). How Does Order of Gameplay Impact Learning and Enjoyment in a Digital Learning Game? In S. Isotani, E. Millán, A. Ogan, P. Hastings, B. McLaren, & R. Luckin (Eds.), *Artificial Intelligence in Education* (pp. 518–531). Springer International Publishing. doi:10.1007/978-3-030-23204-7_43

ADDITIONAL READING

Dörner, R., Göbel, S., Effelsberg, W., & Wiemeyer, J. (2016). *Serious games*. Springer International Publishing. doi:10.1007/978-3-319-40612-1

Ifenthaler, D., & Kim, Y. J. (Eds.). (2019). *Game-Based Assessment Revisited*. Springer. doi:10.1007/978-3-030-15569-8

Klopfer, E., Haas, J., Osterweil, S., & Rosenheck, L. (2018). *Resonant games: Design principles for learning games that connect hearts, minds, and the everyday*. MIT Press. doi:10.7551/mitpress/10887.001.0001

Lang, C., Siemens, G., Wise, A., & Gasevic, D. (Eds.). (2017). *Handbook of learning analytics*. SOLAR, Society for Learning Analytics and Research. doi:10.18608/hla17

Loh, C. S., Sheng, Y., & Ifenthaler, D. (2015). *Serious games analytics* (C. S. Loh, Y. Sheng, & D. Ifenthaler, Eds.). Springer International Publishing. doi:10.1007/978-3-319-05834-4

Reich, J. (2020). *Failure to disrupt: Why technology alone can't transform education*. Harvard University Press. doi:10.4159/9780674249684

Shaffer, D. W., & Gee, J. P. (2006). *How computer games help children learn*. Palgrave Macmillan. doi:10.1057/9780230601994

Spector, J. M. (2015). *Foundations of educational technology: Integrative approaches and interdisciplinary perspectives*. Routledge. doi:10.4324/9781315764269

KEY TERMS AND DEFINITIONS

Educational Technology: This term englobes technologies, software, and hardware that are used as part of the educational and training process of learners.

Game-Based Learning: This is the field that addresses how to use games as a medium to learn, either in informal or in formal contexts.

In-Game Metrics: When players interact with the game, they generate tracking logs which are raw data containing a detailed record of the actions that they performed during the game. This term refers to using quantitative approaches to transform the raw data in metrics that can reconstruct the behavior of players with the game.

Learning Analytics: This field of research collects data from the learners and the educational context where the education is taking place and applies quantitative and qualitative methods to understand and improve the learning process and the context where it is happening.

Learning Gains: This metric is computed by calculating the difference between a post-test and a pre-test. The pre-test usually takes places before developing a learning activity and the post-test after the activity is finished. It helps understand if students are learning or not.

Serious Games: These are games that have as main purpose one beyond entertainment, for example learning, training a user to change their habits, or health rehabilitation.

STEM Education: This term refers broadly to education on science, technology, engineering, and math topics, which is often considered as a specific branch of education to the specific nature and pedagogical approaches of these knowledge areas.

Technology-Enhanced Learning: This term refers specifically to improve learning with the use of technology, and therefore it needs to justify how the technology has improved the previous learning setup.

ENDNOTE

[1] Radix trailer: https://www.youtube.com/watch?v=2fzphUwa6Lc

Chapter 3
The Case of a Serious Game to Prepare 320 International Students for Virtual Learning in Project Management During a Pandemic

Kun Wang
The University of Manchester, UK

Ian Stewart
https://orcid.org/0000-0002-4968-527X
The University of Manchester, UK

ABSTRACT

To address the learning, teaching, and functional issues in a pandemic, large-sized class, and virtual learning environment, a two-week-long serious game was designed to act as the main welcome activity. Three hundred twenty students played through four scenarios with the pandemic as their background, and a narrative device contributed to an immersive learning environment. The game was deployed over two weeks, using a range of reports, video content, online collaborative platforms, and novelty applied mass communication theory, which effectively enhanced inter- and intra-team interaction and prepared the students for their project management team-based experiential learning. This case study will walk readers through the processes and theories used to create the game and ensure its operational, social, and pedagogic benefits.

INTRODUCTION

2020/21 was the first academic year that the students of UK Higher Education Institutions (HEIs) had to start their learning during a pandemic. The University of Manchester MSc Management of Projects

DOI: 10.4018/978-1-7998-9732-3.ch003

(MoP) degree enrolled 320 students, 80% of them were international students. International students on our programme were going to have no chance to get into the campus to study or go through the vital supporting processes that make learning more efficient and enjoyable, such as negotiating new relationships with fellow students and lecturers. They faced the challenge of studying the course purely online, across fourteen hours of time zones. The teaching staff had to deal with the fact that their students were also dealing with the pandemic, creating new challenges for the administration and lecturers to simultaneously handle never-before-experienced emergent crisis issues as well as deliver the intended teaching and learning material.

Most of the teaching materials in our project management degree are based around experiential learning and team-based learning. In such a learning environment, to complete the assessments and gain credit, students need to be able to obtain experience of management in project-based teamwork (Jeong and Bozkurt, 2014); as well as be able to adapt to work with students from diverse cultural or educational backgrounds. Most students are without previous experience in working in large-sized, international teams. The nature of very large size cohort environments makes some students feel lost and lack a sense of belonging to the cohort (Stewart and Wang, 2019). Entering this context unprepared can directly impact students' emotional status, mental health and learning experience.

At the beginning of each year, due to the large class size, issues such as students not knowing how to find team members, different preferences in communication platforms and taking too long to do ice-breaking, regularly occur. These cause an inefficient start to our teaching activities. These are common problems in a normal year, but this is even more serious in a situation where students will never occupy the same physical space. Not occupying the same space causes the vital team formation stages of 'forming' and 'storming' to be more unpredictable as normal channels for resolving early conflict are unavailable. Good relationships are also vital for the good mental health of students, which was under particular threat due to the isolating effects of distance learning and the crises of Covid (Grubic, Badovinac and Johri, 2020).

Due to this, the University extended the length of 'welcome week', from one to three weeks, which gave more time to prepare the lecturers and students to handle the challenges of this teaching and learning environment. The main purpose of a welcome week is to lead the students to engage with the administrative, technical, and social aspects of the teaching & learning environment. Such engagement and preparation helps the transition from previous undergraduate education to postgraduate to lead the students to engage with the technical and social aspects of the teaching and learning environment (Leese, 2010). In a normal year, there would be several activities to get students into groups, to discover each other and the university campus, as well as begin to establish working relationships that would carry them through the coming year. None of this would be possible now. A meaningful welcome activity for students was needed, something to simultaneously deliver the needed social gains especially in starting the social integration that is vital for a successful, motivated cohort as well as build some pedagogically useful skills.

The following is presented as a case study of a Serious Game in production, which was designed to satisfy these needs. The objectives of this case study are to:

- Present the contextual drivers behind the decision to develop a serious game and subsequently shape its design
- Identify the processes and theories used to create the game and ensure its operational, social, and pedagogic benefits.

- Present the game mechanism and how it made the students a part of the game function, materials, and the overall user experience of the game.
- Present the game's strengths and weaknesses in operation and what the academics learned regarding the use of team-based, mixed-media Serious Games at a high scale.

By playing the game, the students naturally obtained a high scale of interaction with each other, which was vital for the success of our large-scale learning, especially, in a Covid-era blended learning context. Following the advice presented here, this game or similar could be applied in the welcome activities for any other academic programme or even new staff onboarding programmes in work organisations.

Main Game Features

- An interesting, timely storyline with sufficient verisimilitude to reflect pandemic situations and engage students.
- Low human and economic cost for the institution as it was free of the need to use specific software or devices and students provided most of the labour to move the game forward.
- Capitalises on virtual nature to be highly scalable, further teams could be added with little extra labour for academics managing it.
- The development of project management competencies to be effective in the experiential learning programme, also in employment.
- Demonstration of online platforms to students and freedom to develop online teamworking systems around the infrastructure provided.
- Making students aware of the community of peers despite large-class global setting and the realities of being in large teams.
- A debrief that connects students' gameplay to the elective modules in the teaching & learning programme.

BACKGROUND

Although there are a range of necessary academic and administrative matters to be covered in a Welcome Week, there is also a need for 'fun', which is especially useful in initiating the social integration of the students. A decision was made to evaluate the possibility of using a team-based Serious Game to support the social functions of the welcome week. Gamification is defined as using game mechanisms in non-game systems to motivate and engage learning, to increase user's motivation, experience and engagement (Strmečki, Bernik and Radošević, 2016). Motivation and engagement were useful and highly desirable outcomes for a welcome week activity, therefore this direction made sense. Gamification principles are also reflected in the design of an activity or simulation, by adding such things as achievements (badges), points, shops, leader boards and a motivating spirit of competition (Easley and Ghosh, 2016).

There is also an established practise of using games and simulations in Project Management education (e.g. Stewart & Wang, 2019; Denholm and Davies, 2017; Stewart et. al, 2016; Denholm et al, 2015). Our work was inspired by the award-winning Harvard leadership simulation 'Patient Zero', which features the exciting scenario of a spreading Zombie pathology in major cities and where leaders need to make decisions to save the population and the reputation and morale of the country. However, it insufficient for our needs given the sheer size of the cohort, our need to engage students in large groups and also encourage discovery and interaction between the groups. It lacked the 'motivating spirit of competition'. There were also cost factors. A set of licences for a Harvard simulation were too costly at our scale, given the financial uncertainty at the University and restrictions on all cash spend. Any teaching innovation that requires the labour of academics also comes at a human cost to the academics. Therefore, we needed an activity that students could drive forward themselves, instead of requiring the labour of an academic.

O'Connor et al. (2021) summarized the challenges of large-size classes in virtual and experiential learning, which are:

a. coordinating communication with a large number of teams,
b. managing teams and facilitating team communication and trust,
c. managing virtual team performance and instructor feedback throughout the experiential exercise, and
d. managing and evaluating student engagement.

The nature of large size class environments also makes some students feel lost and lack an emotional bond to the cohort (Stewart and Wang, 2019). According to Geithner and Menzel (2016), team-based activities can effectively enhance the rate of engagement. This requires carefully designed activities and team structure design. These challenges were to be met through a development that was to follow the sequence of the widely accepted Robson et al. (2015) game design framework of mechanics, dynamics, and emotions/aesthetics.

Our work also featured two novel applications of theory from outside of Serious Game design. Firstly, the Australian Immersive Education Academy (AIEA), model of immersive learning experiences provides the following principles when developing immersive learning experiences:

1. Autonomy: the learning experience needs to be highly interactive and learner-directed;
2. Presence: students need to be highly engaged by using multisensory inputs and strong emotional attachments to the learning materials;
3. Realism: The learning environment needs to be 'real' enough;
4. Subject: lecturers need to take an instructive and constructive role, and provide situated and timely feedback.

Secondly, as the game would have to rely extensively on mixed digital media, understanding the reasons why individuals are motivated to take an active role in consuming and acting on informational media of different kinds is important (Kisekka, Han and Sharman, 2014). The Uses and Gratification Theory (UGT) of Blumler and Katz (1974) emanating from the study of mass communication, summarized four needs of individuals that must be satisfied to engage them in consuming media, which are, the need to relax (diversion); the need for making friends and become a part of a social group (personal relationship); the need to find more about themselves, from the media (personality of identity) and the need to use media to find out what is going on around themselves (surveillance).

DESIGN OF THE 'KINGDOM OF MOP' GAME

To address the learning, teaching and functional issues above, a two-week-long serious game was designed to act as the main welcome activity alongside introduction lectures in the welcome programme. Robson et al. (2015)'s first aspect of serious game design is 'Mechanics' specifying the goals, rules, the context, interactions and boundaries of the game situation. These are subdivided in setup, rule mechanics, and progression mechanics. Following the inspiration of Harvard's 'Patient Zero', we decided from the start to make the game scenario-based. It was decided to use the Covid pandemic as a background to the game and a narrative device to contribute to an immersive learning environment. Further inspiration came from a Chinese documentary drama about finding 'Patient Zero' in a Covid-affected city. There were also several news stories in the UK around the pandemic response that acted as further ideas for scenarios within the game and for creating a degree of verisimilitude. The game would be entitled 'The Kingdom of MoP'. 'MoP' is a reference to the name of our MSc programme 'Management of Projects'. MoP is a young nation, recovering from a war for independence, facing the outbreak of a deadly virus of unknown aetiology. The game would be played though scenarios. Each scenario was designed to incorporate/require certain project management competencies and also be aligned to modules within our master's degree. This is shown below in table 1.

Table 1. Scenarios and their relation to the programme and project management competencies

Scenario	Project Management Competency	Related Programme Module	Inspirations for the Scenario
1. National day	Conflict management Change management Resource allocation People and organisation	Conflict Management & Dispute Resolution People & Organisation Project Planning & Control Risk Management	News items on many events that had been cancelled after Covid-19 Harvard Leadership serious game
2. Student Protest	Conflict management Change management Resource allocation People and organisation	Conflict Management & Dispute Resolution People & Organisation Project Planning & Control Risk Management	News report from China and the UK on student protests at major universities during quarantine
3. Patient Zero	Data collection Communication Data visualisation Covid 19 Health & safety	Project Management Research methods Risk Management	Chinese epidemiological investigation TV docudrama
4. Personal Protective Equipment (PPE) Supply Chain	Data collection Commercial management / communication Data visualisation Covid 19 Health & safety	Project Management Research methods Commercial Management Contract Management Risk Management	News reports on UK response to Covid and emergency supply chains for PPE

The rule and progression mechanics were determined by our context. The game had to be large team-based, delivered by digital mixed-media. There were more than 300 hundred students in the cohort, hence in each team there would 10 or more students. The cohort would be divided into dyads of teams, 15x 'A' and 15x 'B' teams. Also, as the largest impact of the large-size class setting on academics is the labor cost of supporting assessment and feedback, this required the design of game mechanism to move from lecturer-centered labor to student-centered. In each scenario one team in the dyad would be the 'actor' in the role of the crisis management group of Kingdom of MoP, working to develop a solution. The other team would play a facilitative/assessing role, acting according to the information given to them, delivering key parts of the game experience, and acting as an assessor of the solutions. Team As would be the actor teams in scenarios one and three, Team Bs the actor teams in scenarios two and four.

Acting teams allocate their members to military, administration or medical roles using points, the weighting of which, affects the range of possible actions available in the scenario. This allocation cannot be changed in later rounds, so the 'tone' of the team has real risks and unknowable consequences.

- Administration affects the team's ability to gather information and the allowable format for its presentation/data visualization, the ability of the team to ask the lecturer questions, interact with other teams and submit their solutions.
- Military creates inter-team powers such as the ability to seize information without interview and either improves or reduces the soft skills of soldiers in the scenarios.
- Medical affects the supply of health information available to the teams such as the test outcomes in scenario three as well as health-related interventions.

The crisis management functions of the roles needed to be simple enough to be understood to avoid students spending too much effort on studying medical or military situations, creating financial systems or preparing for war with other teams.

Set One: Scenario One and Two

Communication skills are referred as one of the most important competences of project managers (Starkweather and Stevenson, 2011). There are often knowledge and information asymmetries between the project team and stakeholders (Butt, Naaranoja and Savolainen, 2016; Müller and Turner, 2005). This set of scenarios creates information gaps, between people looking forward to a gala and a government concerned about the public health; students suffering from poor quarantine environment and a military that needs to maintain social stability. This forces students, in both Team As and Bs, to consider the other side's situations and reasons for behaviour and communicate to overcome asymmetry.

Scenario One – National Day

A grand national parade is planned to celebrate National Independence Day. People from all over the nation will be expected to flood to the capital for a day of celebrations and displays of military, artistic and cultural value. There will be amusements and entertainments or families and food from all regions of the nation and at night, the largest firework display ever seen. Millions have been spent on preparations; the whole thing is 'too big to fail'. Facilitating patriotic Team Bs are told the story of the difficulties upon which the kingdom was founded, the struggles of the common men and women and how these had paid hard-earned money to be at the celebration in the capital, they represent these ones. However, Team As are told there is a virus called Covid-60061 (60061 is the code number of a core module on their programme) in a neighbouring kingdom that shares a long land border with the Kingdom of MoP and that there have already been hospitalisations for severe respiratory symptoms which may or may not be this virus. They need to decide about whether they still want the celebration to go ahead and in what format and what exactly they want to tell B Teams. The A team's solution will be a report on the format for the National Day gala.

Actor Team As were given the points allocation description as in table 2, and they need to submit the allocation to the lecturer after reading the instruction:

Table 2. Scenario One points allocation system

	1 point	2 points	3 points
Military	Soldiers cannot be sent to the places you need them to, but they can provide warning functions such as publishing military warnings regarding security actions and military maneuvers	Soldiers can be sent to the place you want but they will act aggressively. If you use this level, you must describe in your proposal what level of force will be used, to what effect and the possible consequences to the public	Soldiers can be sent to the place and behave in a disciplined manner and be effective. Soldiers can also be used in other departments to help their people in the Kingdom of MoP.
Administration	You can only describe what you will do without any explanation	In this case, only text can be used in your proposal, but you can add explanations of why you made such a policy, to convince and comfort your people.	In this case, your team can make higher-value proposals including supporting evidence such as videos, figures or tables in your proposals.
Medical	There might not be enough hospital places for patients. There is insufficient PPE for your country. The research success rate is very low. Only 10% of the people in your country can be tested	There are enough hospital places for patients but there are risks that the cure rate is low. You do some basic research if the virus is not re-generating too quickly. Key workers can be tested in your country.	There are enough hospital places for patients. The cure rate is medium. You have a world-leading research ability, however this time Covid 60061 is new to you. Your test equipment is sufficient.

Scenario Two – Student Protest

The Grand University of MoP has had an outbreak of Covid60061 in the student body and so has had to sterilise some of its buildings and put students in quarantine to protect them and limit the spread of the virus on campus. The University of MoP asked for help from the Government Crisis Team (B Teams) as the students seem to be preparing a large protest march against the quarantine and the University handling of the situation. Team Bs are aware that social media will take the student's message around the world, and they are very good at using it. Team Bs know that the University would like the protest stopped. The problem is the students have some very valid concerns. In this scenario, Team As play the role of the Student Union and are given information describing the poor situation that students are in -their building has an old and badly maintained air conditioning system that increases the danger of infection. Due to local lockdowns, students are facing food shortages, in addition to being surrounded by ill colleagues and mounting anxiety and other mental illness. B teams are not aware of what that the students are suffering from. If B teams have sufficient points allocated to their 'administration' function, they could get a chance to interview their A team partners. In this scenario, B teams need to submit their role point allocation. The function of the points can be seen in table 3.

Table 3. Scenario Two points allocation system

	1 point	2 points	3 points
Military	Soldiers cannot be sent to the places you need them to, but they can provide warning functions such as publishing military warnings regarding security actions and military maneuvers	Soldiers can be sent to the place you want but they will act aggressively. If you use this level, you must describe in your proposal a level of force will be used to what effect and the possible conflicts to the public	Soldiers can be sent to the place and behave in a disciplined manner and be effective. Soldiers can also be used in other departments to help their people in the Kingdom of MoP.
Administration	You can only have text in your proposal.	You can add figure or table explanations of why you made such a policy, you can also have a video speech together with your proposal to convince and comfort your people.	You have a strong administration team, the team can be sent out to interview team As, so your proposal can target their needs (You can post in blackboard discussion board and ask for A teams' comments). You can add figure or table as well as your explanations of why you made such a policy, to convince and comfort your people. You can also have a video speech together with your proposal to convince and comfort your people.
Medical	There might not be enough hospital places for patients. There is insufficient PPE for your country. The research success rate is very low. Only 10% of the people in your country can be tested	There are enough hospital places for patients but there are risks that the cure rate is low. You can do some basic research if the virus is not re-generating too quickly. Key workers can be tested in your country. So, you can only state the staff infection rate here. You have PPE for university staff and soldiers.	There are enough hospital places for patients. The cure rate is medium. You have a world-leading research ability, however this time Covid 60061 is new to you. Your test equipment is sufficient. You can use data in your report to support your decisions with both student and university infection rates. (You can ask the lecturer for support data or research yourself). You have PPE for everyone, university staff, soldiers, and students.

Set Two: Scenario Three and Four

Often unlike their undergraduate education, postgraduate students are expected to have qualitative and quantitative research skills, involving data collection and analysis. Our degree teaches project management research methods throughout semester one and two, and the dissertation module is 1/3 of the overall course credit. It is vital to acquire such research skills as quickly as possible. In scenario three and four, apart from working within the project team, students need to research their scenario problems and collect data from other teams by interview, as well visualising data and writing up their reports.

Scenario Three – Patient Zero

It cannot be hidden any longer, Covid60061 is now an epidemic. There is a need to find out who the 'patient zero' is in the Kingdom of MoP, to begin to be able to model the movement of the virus through the population. Team A is tasked with finding this person, who will be in one of the 15 B teams in the cohort. Administration and Medical points allocation can impact how many B teams they can interview. Each B team was given materials about their footpath and symptoms including times, places, and health status that the team has had in the recent week (to simplify the epidemiological chain, each team had the same footpath rather than every single team-member getting a footpath). A teams need to trace B teams one by one, to infer whether the team been infected as well as where and when the team got the virus. A Team's medical points can determine how many 'covid test outcomes' they can obtain directly from the academic, with the outcome they do not have to infer the infections by symptoms described by B. High military points can allow an A team to 'seize' other teams' outcome or cooperate with other A teams by sharing the covid-test outcomes and B teams' information. B teams will wait for the A side report to tell them who is the one that brought the virus to the Kingdom. The effects of earlier role points allocation are in table 4.

Table 4. Scenario Three points allocation system

	1 point	**2 points**	**3 points**
Military	Your team has less power, so you need to share whatever raw data you have obtained or investigated with the team who has higher military points than you. Your soldiers cannot be sent out to investigate.	You can send your military teams out to investigate the cases and you can ask for other A teams to share the data with you, but they can reject your request if they have the same or higher military points than you.	You can send your military teams out to investigate the cases. As you have a strong military, you can 'force' any teams to joint-investigate the covid 60061 case or share their data with you.
Administration	Due to the limited resource you gave to administration, you can only speak to up to 10 B teams. In this case, only text and tables can be used in your proposal.	In this case, text, figure and tables can be used in your proposal, but you can add explanations of why you made such a policy, to convince and comfort your people. You can speak to all B teams.	Your team can make higher-value proposals including supporting evidence such as videos, figures, or tables in your proposals. You have skillful administration people so you can easily get all the footpath of B teams. You can simply ask the lecturer for the footpath data
Medical	You can only diagnose B teams from the symptoms	You can ask the lecturer for 7 B teams covid test outcome	You can ask the lecturer for all B teams covid test outcome

Scenario Four - Personal Protective Equipment (PPE) Supply Chain

The Kingdom of MoP response to the spread of the virus has been slow. It has been proven that Personal Protective Equipment (PPE) can inhibit the spread of the virus and keep key workers safe. This is especially important for the hospitals. B Teams are given the task of initiating a ramp-up of PPE production. They need to research and plan what needs to be done for production. A Teams were given the roles of different suppliers who own either raw materials, labour or machines that are essential for production of PPE. A teams have different financial status which might require B teams to investigate and provide sufficient money. They await the call by the government (B teams). Again, to simplify the process, there is no best supply chain, B teams just to need to engage three A teams that can make a whole chain. However, if Bs cannot convince As that they understand their concerns and have a solution for them, As could reject the request to join the supply chain. The points allocation of B teams can impact how much PPE knowledge they can obtain from the academic, how many A teams they can interview and negotiate for price and supply quantity, and whether can they coerce participation. The effect of earlier team role points can be seen in table 5.

Table 5. Scenario Four points allocation system

	1 point	2 points	3 points
Military	Your soldiers cannot assist the mask production.	You can send your military teams out to ask A team to shift their product line, but they can reject.	As you have a strong military, you can 'force' one other A teams to produce the equipment you want. Your soldiers can be trained to be workers.
Administration	Due to the limited resource you gave to administration, you cannot negotiate with A teams.	In this case, text, figure, and tables can be used in your proposal, you can add explanations of why you made such a policy, to convince and comfort your people. You can speak to up to 7 A teams.	You have skillful administration team so you can speak to and negotiate with all A teams. In this case, text, figure, and tables can be used in your proposal, but you can add explanations of why you made such a policy, to convince and comfort your people. You can ask an A team to co-produce the report.
Medical	You need to find out which team is producing what. You do not have sufficient funding to help the industry to do the research, development, and transformation.	You have $1 million funding for helping business to do the research, development, and transformation.	You have $1 billion for helping business to do the research, development, and transformation.

Next came determining the 'win' conditions and the means of creating competition. In a given scenario, the acting team takes the information that they are given by the facilitating team and develops a solution to the scenario problem, according to their assessment of the situation, the actions that are permitted according to their team points allocation and any proprietary information that they have been able to generate or obtain by other methods. The acting teams write their solution to the scenario in a report and post it on an online discussion board allocated to that scenario. This is summarised in figure 1.

Figure 1. The Game mechanism

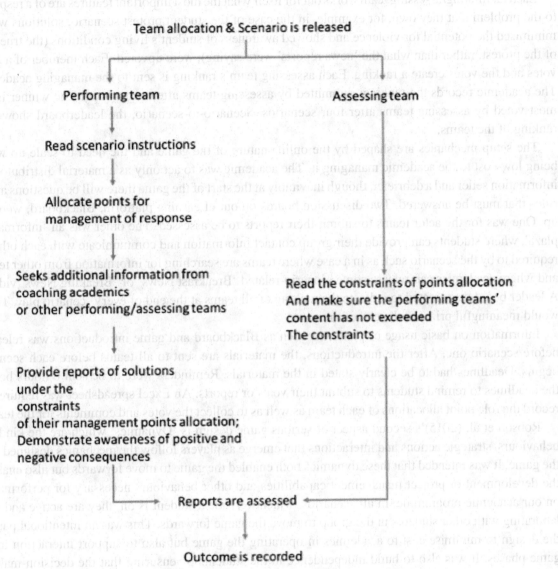

The winning report for each scenario is decided by peer assessment. The largest impact of the large-size class setting is the labour cost of supporting assessment and feedback. Asikainen (2014) proposed peer assessment as a solution, however, students lack of experience of assessing the work of other students is a threat to the quality of this. In our game, the materials were carefully designed in each scenario for the non-acting, assessing teams, to give them a good understanding of the scenario background and aspects to assess. The facilitating teams in the dyads know the full range of the scenario and are in the best position to critically evaluate the solution. At time for assessment, all the acting team solutions are compared and assessed by every facilitating team. A decision was made not to use formal assessment criteria. The view taken was that this was still a game, we did not want students bogged down in forensic analysis of solutions to match to an assessment rubric.

Each facilitating/assessing team works out for itself what the most important features are of a response to the problem that they own, for example, in the case of the student protest scenario, solutions which minimised the potential for violence and showed awareness of student's living conditions (the true root of the protest, rather than what the 'news reports' were saying), were upvoted. Each member of a team votes and the votes create a ranking. Each assessing team's ranking is sent to the managing academic. The academic records the rankings submitted by assessing teams after each round. The winner is the most voted by assessing teams after four scenarios. Scenario-to-scenario, the leaderboard shows the ranking of the teams.

The setup mechanics are shaped by the online nature of the game and the need to scale up while being low-cost to the academic managing it. The academic was to act only as a material distributor, an information seller and a debriefer, though inevitably at the start of the game there will be questions about rules that must be answered. Two discussion boards on our eLearning platform, Blackboard, were set up. One was for the actor teams to submit their reports to be assessed. The other was an 'information plaza', where students can provide their group contact information and communicate with each other if required to by the scenario such as in a case where teams are searching for information from other teams and where academics can release some scenario-related 'Breakfast News' or 'Breaking News' videos. A leader board was created to indicate the ranking of all teams at the end of every scenario play. There would meaningful prizes at the end of the game.

Information on basic usage of platforms such as Blackboard and game introductions was released before scenario one. After the introductions, the materials are sent to all teams before each scenario begins. Deadlines had to be clearly stated in the materials. Reminders were to be sent 6 hours before the deadlines to remind students to submit their votes or reports. An Excel spreadsheet was required to record the role point allocations of each team as well as to collect the votes and comments for the teams.

Robson et al. (2015)'s second aspect of serious game design is 'Dynamics' which are the kinds of behaviours, strategic actions and interactions that emerge as players follow the mechanics designed into the game. It was intended that these dynamics both enabled the game to move forwards but also enabled the development of project management capabilities and other behaviours necessary for performance on our academic programme. In all scenarios, whichever side a student is on, they are active and collaborating with other students in the group to move the game forwards. This was an intentional part of the design to minimise cost to academics in operating the game but also to support interaction in all game phases. It was also to build independence in the students by ensuring that the decision-making rights rest with the students.

The teams would be working on tasks with constrained resources and information asymmetry. This aligns with the behaviours and characteristics of project work, as in a project, people need to work in a temporary team to bring together different types of expertise (Gillard, 2009). Project management requires practitioners to work with limited resources (Morris, Pinto and Söderlund, 2011). Students would also have to develop negotiation and conflict management skills. The unchangeable allocation of team role points would lead students to consider risk management. Research methods, particularly qualitative methods, would be unfamiliar to the majority of our students but would be required for the game and their Master's dissertations. The report writing practice in the game would have obvious applications for their academic work.

Robson et al. (2015)'s third aspect of serious game design is emotions/aesthetics, the desirable emotional responses evoked in players when they interact with game elements (the 'aesthetics') the point systems, progress, or achievement markers. An important element of this design aspect is sensitising the designer to the possibility of negative emotions from gameplay – from the process and the outcomes e.g., being on a losing team. We were certain that a combination of peer pressure and a desire to build connections with fellow students in the cohort would be motivating, as would the satisfaction of creating solutions as a team validated by the recognition of peers. We hoped that this would overcome any possible negative feelings towards playing a game, allow forgiveness of any unexpected problems with the game and compensate for any negative emotions from being in a non-winning team.

Students need to be psychologically charged to be engaged to learn. A storyline of crisis can engage students with its emotional impact. Using the pandemic as a background to the game and a narrative device had potential problems. Robichaud (2020), the author of the 'Patient Zero' Harvard simulation, warned that there needed to be a balance between the educational trigger and perhaps controversial or shocking things being used as triggers. Given our global setting, it was also necessary to avoid the risks of games that might contain factors or imagery that were distasteful to other cultures.

The Debrief

Although the game was designed to teach and develop useful skills for our experiential-based learning programme, some types of learning cannot take place unless there is a systematic debrief. One problem with experiential learning models, such as Kolb Learning Cycle (Kolb, 2006), is that students have to be instructed before applying the knowledge through practice. In the welcome week, there was no time for instruction in project management. Therefore, after experiencing the game, some students would need help understanding how this game taught them about project management and how this would help them in the coming academic programme and the actual workplace. This was very simple and was designed to be conducted via Zoom on the final day of the game for approximately one hour.

1. Show the different information available to A and B sides for each scenario
2. Display the points allocation of all teams and let students discuss their reflections on their resource management, the cause-and-effect between their available information, their decisions, and the assessments of the assessing teams.
3. Display artefacts such as a 'word cloud' analytic of students' comments on the winning reports. This can make the qualities of winning communication clearer
4. Let the winning team share the experience of how they approached each scenario and why they think they were the winner in each scenario.
5. Discuss the link between the events and academic programme modules.

DISCUSSION AND LESSONS LEARNED

The main theoretical impact of this case study is that in the course of meeting O'Connor et al. (2021)'s large online class challenges this activity integrated gamification principles and game and media design theory into learning activities in an online and large-size class context. Constraints that we designed under forced innovation, for example, institutional financial restrictions in the pandemic forced us not to rely on purchasing external software and to build around students own devices (Ranieri, Raffaghelli and Bruni, 2018). In operation, the game performed as expected, with also some unexpected benefits. At the beginning of each year, due to the large class size, issues such as students not knowing how to find team members, different preferences in communication platforms and taking too long to do ice-breaking, regularly occur. These cause an inefficient start to our teaching activities. Our initiative created a more efficient start to the year, initiating students into ways of finding each other. Compared to years without starting with this game, the team forming issues in the formal semesters, such as changes of coursework team leaders, were much reduced. Problems to do with the student registration create further inefficiency in starting the new academic year. Having to use university resources to participate in our game forced those with incomplete or defective registration to become apparent, which also improved the postgraduate administration process.

We knew that students were going to create their own communication infrastructures around our 'official' provision, that would effectively lock us out, so we allowed this. There could be a concern in that incorrect information could be exchanged, or information that could 'break' the game, such as assessing teams giving their acting partner team 'information from the future'. However, there was no evidence of this occurring. Teams seemed keen to keep each other honest which we theorise was due to the authentic sense of competition between the groups. Although there were no leaks, it did not stop some individuals from trying, as was reported to us. Teams can develop proprietary information, however, there could be a danger of 'friends' sharing information across teams in a way that short-circuits the game. Adding stamps such as 'Secret' or 'Do Not Copy' to materials can enhance the imperative to compete against the forces in the scenario and the other teams.

There were more enquiries about the rules and operations than expected, which made us critically evaluate our instruction sets. There was a tendency for some students to waste time on elaborating their roles, conducting pointless medical or military research. Many times, the rules and what was expected or permissible needed to be repeated. Clear instructions are vital in the global, distance learning context as students are sometimes inexperienced English readers and have fewer possibilities to raise questions and seek explanations. As we became the face of the institution during the welcome programme, we dealt with a large number of questions about other university departments, mostly around enrolment. It might have been better to give students more signposting to the different departments of the university they might need before the game begins. Early team progress was affected by latecomers. We did not realise how many of the cohort had not enrolled when we created the teams. In future, we would allocate teams at the last possible minute before the game has to begin.

Ideally, more lecturers should have been involved in the operation and debrief, especially the module co-ordinators to help trigger the students' interests in the programme modules. This would require stronger leadership or senior management support for the game implementors. Using the University eLearning platform helped students to become familiar with what would become their principal channel for learning. At the beginning of the pandemic, our university primarily promoted 'Blackboard Collaborate' as the main teaching platform. During this game, we found out that in some countries, Blackboard Collaborate was unstable. Despite these problems, most students were quite forgiving of any gaps or variable performance. However, some students refused to participate, thinking the game was below their status as MSc students.

Evaluating our design by AIEA principles, its strengths are:

Autonomy: The students are fully autonomous in the game. Their interactions are channelled by the game mechanics, but within these, they are free to create proprietary information and act on it. The lecturer role in this game is a 'shop' – part of the game mechanics rather than instructing the students in the activities.

Realism: The game was adapted from the real Covid-19 stories that students were aware of or had experienced in their real life. Appropriate terminology was used for military, administrative and medical aspects

Presence: Even though this is a large-size class teaching and the team size is large – 10 students per group, due to each group having three departments and multiple missions (performing their role in the scenario, assessing the other side's reports, managing the team, communicating with other teams or the lecturer, report writing), there were many ways for students to be present and engaged.

Subject: Instructive feedback is provided only after the activities are finished to help students understand which knowledge points from the game are associated with their future academic programme. Feedback is mainly from the dyadic team in a constructive mode that fully reflects the game context

According to the 'Uses and Gratification Theory (UGT) of Blumler and Katz (1974) the strengths of our design are:

Diversion: some fun news videos and hot topics in recent news fulfil the needs of the students to be relaxed, with such real-world and fun facts in learning materials, students were willing to read the materials.

Personal relationship: students need to interact with actual peers to find the information required by scenarios, by doing so, they were playing active roles and getting to know their peers within and beyond their teams, as scenarios 3 and 4 required students investigate matters or resources beyond their dyad.

Personality of identity: students can learn from feedbacks and get to know their ranking after the scenario is complete. Their identify in the game is also manifest through debates on points allocation. Students must clarify their positions in the game regarding roles and decisions and so they assert their identity in their teams.

Surveillance: students are able to actively engage in the discussion boards to see the updated news about the scenarios, the updated leader board and the responses from others when negotiation is required.

Finally, due to Covid-19, there was a restriction of available funding for our welcome week. We calculated that our design saved $4500 against purchasing an approximate serious game from Harvard Business School. Using dyads of teams to assess each other's proposals saved around £1500 labour cost versus using lecturers or teaching assistants to do this. However, the labour cost of administrating this game also needs to be considered. Lecturers need to allocate groups, drop the personalized game materials team by team, answer students' questions and run the game data analysis. We have not been able to calculate the cost of these aspects of the game operation, but it is a worthy research question for all serious games – what is the real human cost to the creators and operators?

In the future, even though the pandemic will slip into our history, the underpinning design and mechanism of this game is still transferable as to other management education contexts as crisis management is core in project or operation management.

CONCLUSION

This serious game was successful in creating a more efficient start to the academic year, but not without cost to or work from the game creators. Many students raise concerns at the start of the course that they would not be able to make friends with peers due the large-size, distance learning cohort. Our game-initiated students into ways of finding each other, ice-breaking and collaborating. The game helped build cooperative relationships with others that persisted beyond the game. They experienced teamwork in large teams as well as other project management competencies vital for performance on our course and in demand from employers. They also got a feel for how large-size experiential learning would look in the upcoming academic year.

This case study has presented readers with the rationale, decision-making, processes, and theories used to create the game, specifically Robson et al. (2015) and ensure its operational, social and pedagogic benefits. This included a novel application of the 'Uses and Gratification Theory (UGT) of Blumler and Katz (1974). It has been shown how the game was our response to a specific set of circumstances and constraints during the time of Covid 19, such as distance learning, a global student body, financial uncertainty at the University. Through our design, the students participated as a part of the learning experience. Making the students a part of the game's function as well as being recipients, created pedagogic, social, and even economic benefits. We hope that what has been presented here will be useful and inspirational in helping colleagues to create similar serious games.

REFERENCES

Asikainen, H. (2014). *Successful learning and studying in Biosciences: Exploring how students conceptions of learning, approaches to learning, motivation and their experiences of the teaching-learning environment are related to study success* [Unpublished doctoral dissertation] University of Helsinki.

Blumler, J. G., & Katz, E. (1974). The Uses of Mass Communications: Current Perspectives on Gratifications Research. Sage Annual Reviews of Communication Research, 3.

Butt, A., Naaranoja, M., & Savolainen, J. (2016). Project change stakeholder communication. *International Journal of Project Management*, 34(8), 1579–1595. doi:10.1016/j.ijproman.2016.08.010

Easley, D., & Ghosh, A. (2016). Incentives, Gamification, and Game Theory: An Economic Approach to Badge Design. *ACM Transactions on Economics and Computation (TEAC), 4*(3).

Geithner, S., & Menzel, D. (2016). Effectiveness of Learning Through Experience and Reflection in a Project Management Simulation. *Simulation & Gaming, 47*(2), 228–256. doi:10.1177/1046878115624312

Gillard, S. (2009). Soft Skills and Technical Expertise of Effective Project Managers. *Proceedings of the 2009 InSITE Conference.* 10.28945/3378

Grubic, N., Badovinac, S., & Johri, A. (2020). Student mental health in the midst of the COVID-19 pandemic: A call for further research and immediate solutions. *The International Journal of Social Psychiatry, 66*(5), 517–518. doi:10.1177/0020764020925108 PMID:32364039

Jeong, K. Y., & Bozkurt, I. (2014). Evaluating a Project Management Simulation Training Exercise. *Simulation & Gaming, 45*(2), 183–203. doi:10.1177/1046878113518481

Kisekka, V., Han, W., & Sharman, R. (2014). Utilizing the Uses and Gratification Theory to Understand Patients Use of Online Support Groups. *AMCIS 2014 Proceedings*. Available at: https://aisel.aisnet.org/amcis2014/Posters/HealthIS/11

Kolb, D. A. (2006). *Experiential learning: Experience as the source of learning and development.* Prentice Hall, Inc.

Leese, M. (2010). Bridging the gap: Supporting student transitions into higher education. *Journal of Further and Higher Education, 34*(2), 239–251. doi:10.1080/03098771003695494

Morris, P., Pinto, J., & Söderlund, J. (2011). *The Oxford Handbook of Project Management.* Oxford University Press. doi:10.1093/oxfordhb/9780199563142.001.0001

Müller, R., & Turner, J. (2005). The impact of principal–agent relationship and contract type on communication between project owner and manager. *International Journal of Project Management, 23*(5), 398–403. doi:10.1016/j.ijproman.2005.03.001

O'Connor, C., Mullane, K., & Luethge, D. (2021). The Management and Coordination of Virtual Teams in Large Classes: Facilitating Experiential Learning. *Journal of Management Education, 5*(4), 739–759. doi:10.1177/1052562921995550

Ranieri, M., Raffaghelli, J., & Bruni, I. (2018). Game-based student response system: Revisiting its potentials and criticalities in large-size classes. *Active Learning in Higher Education, 22*(2), 95–96.

Robichaud, C. (2020). *Leadership Simulation: Patient Zero.* Harvard Business Publishing Education. https://hbsp.harvard.edu/product/7215-HTM-ENG?Ntt=Leadership

Robson, K., Plangger, K., Kietzmann, J., McCarthy, I., & Pitt, L. (2015). Is it all a game? Understanding the principles of gamification. *Business Horizons, 58*(4), 411–420. doi:10.1016/j.bushor.2015.03.006

Starkweather, J., & Stevenson, D. (2011). PMP® Certification as a Core Competency: Necessary But Not Sufficient. *Project Management Journal, 42*(1), 32–41. doi:10.1002/pmj.20174

Stewart, I., Denholm, J., & Blackwell, P. (2016). *Simulations in Project Management - Unexpected Events, Human Costs: Initiating an Autoethnographic Inquiry. European Conference on Game Based Learning*, Paisley, UK.

Stewart, I., & Wang, K. (2019). Simulations and Games in Management Education – The human costs of creating and participating in 'useful illusions'. *Proceedings of the British Academy of Management.*

Strmečki, D., Bernik, A., & Radošević, D. (2016). Gamification in E-Learning: Introducing Gamified Design Elements into E-Learning Systems. *Journal of Computational Science, 11*(12), 1108–1117. doi:10.3844/jcssp.2015.1108.1117

Chapter 4
Application of Gamification in Modern Education

Adnan Ahmad
COMSATS University Islamabad, Lahore, Pakistan

Furkh Zeshan
ⓘ https://orcid.org/0000-0002-2960-9632
COMSATS University Islamabad, Lahore, Pakistan

Muhammad Hamid
University of Veterinary and Animal Sciences, Lahore, Pakistan

Rutab Marriam
COMSATS University Islamabad, Lahore, Pakistan

Alia Samreen
COMSATS University Islamabad, Lahore, Pakistan

ABSTRACT

When game elements are used in other domains, it is referred to as "gamification," which is used to improve the engagement and motivation level of users. These benefits encourage its use in education to enhance student engagement, motivation, and learning outcomes. This chapter highlights the historical advent of gamification, its blending into the educational domain, an overview of various platforms to aid this blending, and an exploration of studies signifying its benefits in education. This chapter also outlines a case study to investigate its effectiveness and provides some practical considerations for the educational industry. The analysis suggests that gamification can be considered as a complementary tool to be integrated into the traditional classroom environment.

DOI: 10.4018/978-1-7998-9732-3.ch004

INTRODUCTION

Throughout the history, games have always been seen as a mean of entertainment and different types of trainings (McGonigal, 2011) due to their inherit tendency of engaging the user. Such advantages have encouraged researchers to adapt various game elements in other areas. One such endeavor is the concept of gamification, where multiple gaming elements are incorporated in a non-gaming context (Koivisto & Hamari, 2014). This adoption is done to serve several purposes other than entertainment such as job hiring, critical situational thinking and even character building (Deterding, 2012). This is because it engages users and motivates them to solve difficult problems (Zichermann & Cunningham, 2011). It is used in diverse contexts and for a lot of different purposes. For example, it is often proposed as an efficient technique to promote learning, engagement of customers and employees' performance (Seaborn & Fels, 2015). It is also often proposed that by inculcating any general activity with various engagement and motivation principles through game design elements, some desired behavioral changes can be attained (Nah et al., 2013). Various gamification tools and methodologies have been designed covering multiple domains to enhance the users' engagement and motivation. Moreover, multiple experiment setups have been devised to explore how this amazing technique can be used to direct users' behaviors in a particular direction and its long-time effects on them (Seaborn & Fels, 2015).

Gamification has not emerged recently, but has some successful history in business and marketing to maintain users' engagement, social interactions and the quality and quantity of actions (Hamari, 2013). This is often achieved through membership benefits, promotions and other reward points (Nelson, 2012). A large pool of recent empirical research studies can be seen as an evidence of numerous benefits of applying gamification in diverse domains including politics, business, marketing and public health (Lee & Hammer, 2011; Seaborn & Fels, 2015). Also in recent times, a new strategy, advergames, is used by some marketing agencies to promote their products. These advergames are simple video games containing advertisements for different products and are designed to promote a company, their products, or their services (Lee & Hammer, 2011). Similarly, airlines offering frequent flyer packages, Starbucks, a coffee franchise having partnership with Foursquare – a location based social network, to provide points to its 'loyal' customers, Nike+ attracting their costumers to set personalized goals as well as challenges for friends, and even Fiat, an automobile company, allowing its customers to play FiatDrive and earn points (Martínez-López et al., 2016), show how gamification and gaming elements are effectively used by major business companies to engage and motivate users.

These and other similar endeavors encouraged the researchers to apply different elements of gamification in the field of education to enhance students' learning behaviors. Gamification has the ability to enhance the users' engagement in an activity which, if coupled with effective teaching, can improve the learning experience of students (Kapp, 2012; McGonigal, 2011). Keeping this in view, many researchers have integrated multiple gamification elements in classrooms and observed an improvement in students' overall motivation and engagement. This chapter explores the historical advent of gamification, existing theories present in this domain, their blending in the classroom teaching, and the effect of different gamification elements on students' learning behaviors. It further presents an overview of various platforms to aid the blending of gamification in the education domain, and an exploration of studies signifying its merits and demerits. The analysis suggests that gamification can be considered as a complementary tool to be integrated in the traditional classroom environment but careful consideration is required to reduce its negative impacts.

GAMIFICATION PLATFORMS

Various gamification theories are presented in the literature to signify how each of the gamification elements enhances different dimensions of users' behaviors (AlJarrah, Thomas, & Shehab, 2018). Gamification environment is usually designed to enhance either of the two motivation types, a) extrinsic motivation or b) intrinsic motivation. The first type is termed as reward-based gamification while the second is called meaningful gamification. To achieve the former, a reward based activity is usually designed which utilizes external rewards to enhance the users' behaviors. Most commonly used external rewards are badges, levels/leaderboards, achievements, and points commonly referred as BLAP (Nicholson, 2012). Badges signify achievements. Levels are environment with increasing difficulty and reflect one's overall progress. Leaderboards display ranks according to one's achievements for social comparison. Achievements are bonuses that are given to a user after they complete some challenging task. Points are scores indicating one's performance. Reward-based gamification is more focused on short-term benefits by triggering the extrinsic motivation through external rewards.

In the meaningful gamification, the main focus is on the long-term benefits through invoking the users' intrinsic motivation (Nicholson, 2015). It is founded on the self-determination theory and tries to invoke autonomy, competence, and relatedness in the users (Ryan & Deci, 2000). Autonomy is about freedom to prefer certain action against another. Competency is the possession of required knowledge, skill or ability. Relatedness is the social relationship between users. During the last decade, gamification and its elements have been ubiquitously adapted in various fields including marketing, business, education, and security etc. due to its potential to drive the users' behavior in the desired direction.

Multiple studies have explored the adaption of gamification constructs and its elements in the education domain and reported their experience, challenges, and findings. Recently, Ahmad et al. (2020a) presented that a gamification framework, when applied to education, has at least three components, namely: gamification constructs, game design elements, and gamification assessments, as shown in figure 1. Gamification constructs provide recommendations on how to design the gamification environment and consist of goal orientation, achievements, reinforcements, competition, and fun orientation. These goals are then achieved through the second component of the framework, i.e., game design elements which comprise of points, badges, rewards, levels, ranks, and leaderboards. Once a gamification environment is designed and applied, its benefits are assessed through the third component, assessments. These assessments can be horizontal, where different groups having diverse exposures can be compared, and/or vertical, where one group can be observed over time. These assessments can further evaluate the impact of gamification on the learning outcomes and/or learning behaviors of students.

Figure 1. Gamification framework
(adapted from Ahmad et al., 2020a)

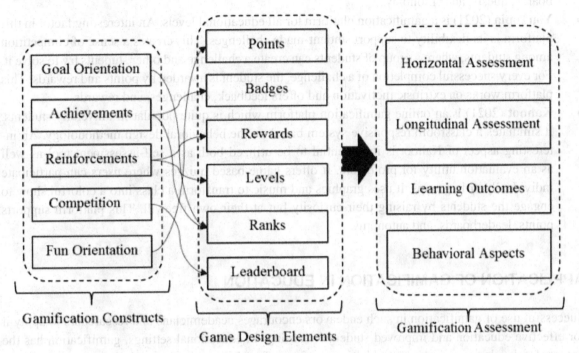

Moreover, some research studies have presented the platforms for gamification that can be used to embed gamification constructs in the education settings. Some of the most famous platforms include ClassCraft, Kahoot!, Rezzly, Seppo and Youtopia. It will be interesting to explore these frameworks to understand gamification and the exploratory efforts presented in the next section. Below is a brief introduction of these platforms.

- **Classcraft** (2021) is a gamification platform for web, android, and IOS. Its main objective is to transform a classroom into a collaborative learning environment. Usually, small teams are formed which can acquire one of the three roles: warriors, mages, or healers. Each role has different set of attributes which encourages collaboration instead of competition among students. The platform has incorporated achievements, badges, levels, and relatedness.
- **Rezzly** (2021) is a web based gamification platform for diverse levels of education, i.e., from preschool to university. Its core functionality is the completion of quests, where each quest is an educational task provided by the course instructor. The quests can be accepted or rejected by the instructor and specific hidden quests can also be explored after acquiring a particular rank. The students get points and badges on successful completion of different quests. This platform is equipped with points, badges, leaderboard, autonomy, and relatedness.
- **Seppo** (2021) is another gamification platform for students from preschool to university. It supports assignment oriented learning where each assignment is regarded as one game that incorporates multiple tasks. Students compete with each other to win a game but the order of challenges is selected by them. This platform also provides location based learning so the students can take

local specific challenges and the instructor can track them. This platform offers points, leader-boards, quests, and autonomy.

- **YouTopia** (2021) is a gamification platform for all educational levels. An interesting factor in this platform is its flexibility to support student-made challenges. This creates a sense of competition among students, where a group of students can create a challenge and other students try to solve it. For every successful completion of a challenge, the student is awarded by points and rewards. This platform works on extrinsic motivation and offers feedback, challenges, and rewards.

- **Kahoot** (2021) is an online gamification platform which is quite popular in university students. It simulates a classroom responsive system based on the behavioral design methodology. An interesting aspect of Kahoot is its potential to be utilized both as a self-assessment tool as well as an evaluation utility for professors. It offers game-based quizzes where users can participate individually or in groups. It uses graphics and music to transform a class into a colorful show to engage the students by raising their curiosity but at their own freewill. This platform supports points, leaderboards, and autonomy.

APPLICATION OF GAMIFICATION IN EDUCATION

Successful use of gamification in such endeavors encourages academicians and researchers to apply it for effective education and improved students' learning. In educational settings, gamification has the potential to develop an environment which is engaging and motivating to enhance the learning experiences of students (McGonigal, 2011). It is also interestingly notable that the concept of gamification naturally aligns with education as the notions of points, grades, scholastic levels and degrees are historically core components for measuring success in education (Seaborn & Fels, 2015). Also, it is thoroughly explained by Nah et al. (2013) as well as Lee and Hammer (2011) that the structure of educational institutes has inherited several elements of gamification. For example, students get marks for completing assignments, quizzes, performing in various exams and other classroom activities which are then converted into grades. Later on, the students get promoted if have shown desired behaviors throughout the academic year.

Gamification strategy appears to have more influence in education due to its inherited reward structure (Domínguez, et al., 2013) and its ability to support motivation. Therefore, if gamification is applied in education it can enhance learning process and improve learning outcomes (Kapp, 2012). Gamification has already begin to flourishing in education in the form of its various applications in science (Rouse, 2013), maths (Goehle, 2013), health education (Gabarron et al., 2012), business (Reiners, et al., 2012), foreign languages (Danowska-Florczyk & Mostowski, 2012), security (Yonemura et al., 2017), and programming (Sprint & Cook, 2015). Moreover, gamification has also been used to motivate peers collaboration (Li et al., 2013), making effective assessments (Moccozet et al., 2013), realizing exploratory learning (Gordillo et al., 2013), and to enhance the students' creativity level (Barata et al., 2013).

The traditional education settings provide feedback to students, but it has several constraints of time, teacher-to-student interactions, and grades (Kapp, 2012). Gamification when blends with education present a number of benefits.

a)   Gamification has signified its role to support positive patterns by using game elements in serious tasks (Hamari, Koivisto and Sarsa, 2014). Traditional learning is often criticized as less interesting while on the contrary, games are 'fun' and have the potential to keep users engaged even if the task is difficult (Lee & Hammer, 2011). Thus introducing game-elements in inherently dull learning activities can transform them into somewhat interesting ones (Ahmad et al., 2020b), and motivate students to work towards educational tasks in a more enjoying manner (Hanus & Fox, 2015).

b) Gamification experience can support students to have clear understanding of an actionable task as they get immediate reward if performed well. This environment allows the students to experiment, have mistakes, and learn from their errors. It has the potential to use failure as an integral part of students' learning without the fear of failure, peer pressure, embarrassment or any effect on grading (Lee & Hammer, 2011). These advantages cannot be exercised in an actual classroom environment, and can help the student to utilize their mistakes in a positive manner.

c) In traditional educational settings, teachers usually use scaffolding instructional techniques – information delivered by levels of difficulty, which cannot accommodate each student's requirements. Gamification presents an individual solution to this where difficulty is only increased when the student demonstrates a significant level of mastery (Beed, Hawkins, & Roller, 1991).

d) Gamification environments can work as autonomous applications that can be used in classrooms as well as in e-learning environments. Gamification applications have the potential to change how students learn, and how they perceive education. Moreover, gamification applications are highly effective for shy students, especially females, who can work privately on their lacking concepts without needing any help from their peers or from the course teacher.

By exploring the literature, it was observed that gamification is applied on diverse audience. Figure 2 exhibits a distribution of gamification literature based on its audience.

Figure 2. Distribution of gamification literature based on audience

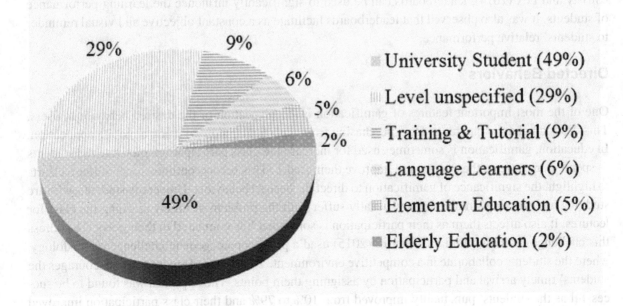

Various research efforts have integrated the gaming elements in the education domain to develop a gamification environment that can be used to enhance the learning outcomes and learning behaviors of the students. Following is an overview of the research efforts related to gamification in the field of education after classification in different domains.

Teaching Methodologies

Gamification has been explored through multiple teaching methodologies from two aspects: 1) how it can be blended with different teaching methods to provide the most satisfactory results; and 2) which elements of gamification have the most crucial impact on enhancing the desired learning behaviors in the students. Several researchers have investigated diverse teaching methods and their blending with the gamification elements. For instance, different gamified elements were explored by Sanmugam et al. (2016), where students were allowed to work with multiple elements including leaderboard, badges, and points. From the result, it was shown that most of the students preferred leaderboards on other gamification elements. It was also observed that badges can help the students to improve themselves. Furthermore, points were more preferred in the online mode to enhance the learning behaviors of the students compared to the traditional physical settings. In another research, Velázquez-Iturbide et al. (2016), with the help of eMadrid project, collected several research efforts about gamification and its quality as compared to different methodologies of learning. They particularly explored the advantages of social media learning and blended learning. The proposed methodology allows the designing, deployment, and evaluation of gamified environments in collaborative settings. In another research, Denny (2013) measured the effect of embedding a badge-based gamification tool within an online education system. The experiments on 1031 students discovered that students were motivated to contribute more without compromising on the quality of their contribution. Also the results reflected that gamification has enhanced the motivation of students as they spent more time on the tool. Another attempt to gamifying an e-learning environment by various gamification elements of trophies, leaderboards and competition resulted in higher grades and more motivated students (Dominguez et al., 2013). Also, as observed by Christy and Fox (2014), leaderboards can be used to significantly influence the learning performance of students. It was also observed that leaderboards facilitate as a constant objective and visual reminder to students' relative performance.

Directed Behaviors

One of the most important features of gamification is the invocation of the desired behavior in users. This desired behavior can range from purchasing from a particular store to using a mobile application. In education, gamification is sometimes used for increase the class participation, motivate the students to spend more time on the course, and improve their grades. This section outlines some of these efforts to highlight the significance of gamification to direct the desired behaviors. University students, who are studying and working simultaneously, usually suffer with the problem of timely reaching the class for lectures. It also affects them as their participation is somewhat low compared to their peers. To address this challenge, Lambruschini and Pizarro (2015) used a process management challenge methodology, where the students collaborate in a competitive environment. The gamified environment encourages the students' timely arrival and participation by assigning them points. The approach was found to be successful as the students' punctuality improved from 10% to 79% and their class participation improved from 15% to 47%. In another research, Grant, Shankararaman, and Loong (2014) documented the use of gamification for influencing the attendance of the students and their engagement in the class. They introduced a reward-based system for students that gives them points for completing a task. The results reflected that the response of students was more positive compared to the responses from the previous semesters. Similarly, Barata et al. (2013) invested how gamification and virtual environments can be used to improve the sense of autonomy in students and to enhance their creativity. To achieve this, they integrated a virtual environment with gamification. Preliminary results suggested that the students in the virtual gamification settings remained motivated throughout the course and perform course assignment after acquiring the required knowledge. Moreover, a gamified tool for black-board learning system was implemented by Domínguez et al. (2013). The empirical study divided the sample into control and experiment group, where the latter was exposed to various gamification features including challenges, trophies, leaderboard and badges. The results reflected that the performance for the experimented group was better than the control group.

Programming

Computer programming is considered as a difficult yet important skill for students. Various gamification applications have been developed to teach this complicated science to the students in a more interesting way in an engaging environment. In order to increase the retention of students, Sprint and Cook (2015) presented a classroom game to teach computer programming to students. Their results reflected that the gamified environment improved the learning outcomes of the students and most of them (83.33%) preferred it over to the traditional classroom teaching approach. In another research, Isaac and Babu (2016) applied gamification in a programming course to increase logical thinking, engagement, and motivation of the students. It was observed that the students in the gamified settings learned more programming concepts than the students in the non-gamified settings. It was observed by Abidin and Zaman (2017) that students at the undergraduate level face difficulty to learn the programming concepts which demotivates them to master this important skill. So, the authors designed a gamified environment based on Kahoot in a programming class. The experimental results, conducted over 120 students, showed that a majority of students (90%) enjoyed the gamified environment and improved their understanding of programming concepts. Similarly, Tretinjak, Bednjanec, and Tretinjak (2014) investigated multiple teaching methodologies to figure out how students can achieve good results with respect to grades and learning outcomes and how can they be more interested in a course. They developed a gamified environment to gain the desired outcomes in different computer based courses. The results reflect that 76% students enjoyed the gamified environment. Also, the students reported that gamification has helped them improve their comprehension of the concepts and enhance their logical thinking. Likewise, Ristov, Ackovska, and Kirandziska (2015) gamified computer hardware based courses with the aid of programming where the students were asked to develop a game by changing their low-level hardware terminologies with the high-level programming terminologies. The results suggested that students acquired sufficient knowledge of hardware control and more of them enrolled in hardware-based courses in the later semesters. Moreover, Maia and Graeml, (2015) used gamification to teach computer science courses to undergraduate students. During this activity, they observed an increase in students' interest and improvement in students' learning effectiveness. Also, the students claimed an improvement in their perceived competence in the gamified environment compared to the traditional settings. A major problem faced by the software industry is the training of their employees in recent programming courses. To address this, Butgereit (2016) developed a gamified environment approach to promote ubiquitous learning. The gameplay initiates as a treasure hunt where participants cover lessons and explore clues. The experimental results reflect an attitudinal change in employees as they wanted to learn new things after the experiment.

Computer Security

Security is an important domain and basic understanding of key security concepts is a basic skill for most of the curriculum. In order to teach some basic concepts of security, several researchers have explored the advantages of gamification. In one such initiative, Yonemura et al. (2017) developed a gamified environment to educate college students about operational technology security. They performed an experiment with two hundred students and with two scenarios. The results suggest that most of the students got a good understanding of general security measures and liked the gamified environment. In another research, Alami and Dalpiaz (2017) introduced the STS-Tool trials, a gamified environment to teach core security concepts. They outlined the design of their system along with the embedded gamification elements. Their results found that the students successfully acquired most of the course content and their learning outcomes were easily achieved. Similarly, Cornel, Rowe, and Cornel (2017) aimed to enhance the interest and awareness of key concepts of cybersecurity among students. The authors proposed a methodology to test whether their method is effective for teaching cybersecurity concepts. They also designed a framework for effective educational platforms and compared it with existing methods. For this research the selected gamification elements were scores, points and challenges, which resulted in an increase in students' skills, capabilities, effort and interest.

Miscellaneous Subjects

Gamification has been used in a number of subjects to improve the engagement of students and to keep them motivated. This section outlines a few of these initiatives to highlight the research efforts in this direction. Usually, text editors integrate punctuation and dictionaries but do not have a writing assistance function. To address this limitation, Lee and Lim (2014) showed a way to use rewards, compensation and scores in an application for practicing phrase building. To gamify an algorithm course, Yohannis and Prabowo (2015) integrated algorithm visualization, game elements, and instructional design. They developed a conceptual model on the learning instructions of various algorithms and their visualization. They also measured the learning outcomes of students based on their intervention. The experimental results reflected that the students working in the gamification settings performed better compared to those students who remained in the traditional educational settings. In another research, Bellotti et al. (2013) presented the gamification of an entrepreneurship course. The course was gamified through a game-like approach to challenge the students and engage them in difficult tasks. The students were assigned points on the basis of their activities which further lead them to a final challenge. The results showed that the approach improved the students' skill in the course and their perceived competences. In another initiative, the importance of reasoning in traditional learning environment is explored (Elorriaga, Antúnez, and Nicolino, 2016). They suggested that the students are required to learn destructuring of their traditional learning environment in order to enhance reasoning. The proposed gamification environment consisted of feedback, badges, and rewards. The results showed that the students achieved all the important skills to take university level courses. Moreover, Holman, Aguilar, and Fishman (2013) developed an educational system to highlight the significance of gamification and to improve the learning experience for students. The system supports various types of assignments, where students can assign different percentages to their assignments. It also keeps record of their accuracy in multiple assignments to calculate their course grades. An online quiz application, developed by Snyder and Hartig (2013), for medical residents was aided with gamification elements. Results metrics revealed significantly higher participation and correct responses. A post-test showed that more than 95% users appreciated the setup, while 30% desired more questions.

Early Education

Gamification is not only proven to be an important tool for adults but younger students can also get various benefits from this amazing tool. In order to integrate electronic gadgets in schools of rural areas, Botra, Rerselman and Ford (2014) used gamification for teachers' engagement and motivation. The authors performed this exercise in three iterations: a) a single school, b) 11 schools and c) 14 schools. The feedback of this activity was found to be positive. It was observed that the integration of technology in classroom is facilitation however it can only be meaningful if it is well-planned. In another research, Kekuluthotuwage and Fernando (2017) proposed an interactive system for early education. Their designed educational system used a gamified methodology to teach core concepts to children. It was concluded that most of the children provided positive feedback about the gamified prototype. Likewise, an interactive application to teach letter writing to children was proposed by Rinnert et al. (2017). They also find that many positive learning traits were increased by applying gamification e.g. effort, motivation, enjoyment (fun), engagement, competitiveness, skills, learning outcome, dedication, interactivity, satisfaction, encouragement.

Negative Aspects

As with almost everything, gamification also has a downside. Some studies have explored negative aspects associated with the use of gamification in education domain. For instance, it was observed by Andrade, Mizoguchi, and Isotani (2016) that the game features introduced in the educational settings can cause a distraction to the students. Even when they are spending time using the system, their core goal deviates from learning to game elements. In some gamification systems, the time a student spends exploring the system or customizing it according to his/her requirements is considered as enhancing the engagement. However, it usually turns out to be just spending time on the system in order to get the rewards rather than focusing on the learning. Moreover, students having low performance get discouraged when exposed to competitive leaderboards, which reduces their sense of competence and interest in the system. Another side effect of gamification is its potential addiction that can cause dependency on the platform (Jeong & Lee, 2015), where the student may not learn much in other scenarios without gamification elements. This problem relates to more exposure to the elements causing extrinsic motivation and less focus on the intrinsic motivation over an extended period of time. To address this, keen observation is required to design the gamification system that gives particular attention to the relationship of each student with different gamification elements. Also, monitoring the students' interactions with peers, with the gamification elements, and with the system can reduce these possible negative aspects. Gamification has the potential to enhance the learning behaviors and learning outcomes of students if applied in a controlled environment with careful consideration.

CONCLUSION

This chapter highlighted the impact of integrating serious games in education. It explored the historical advent of serious games, its blending with education, various frameworks used for this blending, and a rich set of studies already explored this blending. This exploration highlighted that gamification can be integrated in future classroom as a complementary technique to enhance students' interest in the course content and increase their learning outcomes. However, some aspects of this blending of gamification in education require more exploration from the research community. In the future, more personalized gamification environments can be developed keeping in view the user's personality and behavioral traits. Moreover, some gameplay can be incorporated in the gamification environment to increase users' engagement and interest. Gamification has proved its potential from exploratory, observational, and experimental research methodologies. Now it is the time when its integration in the traditional classroom settings should be visualized not only as an experiment but as a complementary component.

REFERENCES

Abidin, H. Z., & Zaman, F. K. (2017, November). Students' perceptions on game-based classroom response system in a computer programming course. In *2017 IEEE 9th International Conference on Engineering Education (ICEED)* (pp. 254-259). IEEE.

Ahmad, A., Zeeshan, F., Marriam, R., Samreen, A., & Ahmed, S. (2020b). Does one size fit all? Investigating the effect of group size and gamification on learners' behaviors in higher education. *Journal of Computing in Higher Education*, 1–32.

Ahmad, A., Zeshan, F., Khan, M. S., Marriam, R., Ali, A., & Samreen, A. (2020a). The impact of gamification on learning outcomes of computer science majors. *ACM Transactions on Computing Education*, *20*(2), 1–25. doi:10.1145/3383456

Alami, D., & Dalpiaz, F. (2017, September). A gamified tutorial for learning about security requirements engineering. In *2017 IEEE 25th International Requirements Engineering Conference (RE)* (pp. 418-423). IEEE. 10.1109/RE.2017.67

AlJarrah, A., Thomas, M. K., & Shehab, M. (2018). Investigating temporal access in a flipped classroom: Procrastination persists. *International Journal of Educational Technology in Higher Education*, *15*(1), 1–18. doi:10.118641239-017-0083-9

Andrade, F. R., Mizoguchi, R., & Isotani, S. (2016, June). The bright and dark sides of gamification. In *International conference on intelligent tutoring systems* (pp. 176-186). Springer. 10.1007/978-3-319-39583-8_17

Barata, G., Gama, S., Fonseca, M. J., & Gonçalves, D. (2013, October). Improving student creativity with gamification and virtual worlds. In *Proceedings of the First International Conference on Gameful Design, Research, and Applications* (pp. 95-98). 10.1145/2583008.2583023

Beed, P. L., Hawkins, E. M., & Roller, C. M. (1991). Moving learners toward independence: the power of scaffolded instruction. *The Reading Teacher, 44*, 648-655. doi:10.2307/20200767

Bellotti, F., Berta, R., De Gloria, A., Lavagnino, E., Antonaci, A., Dagnino, F. M., & Ott, M. (2013, July). A gamified short course for promoting entrepreneurship among ICT engineering students. In *2013 IEEE 13th International Conference on Advanced Learning Technologies* (pp. 31-32). IEEE. 10.1109/ICALT.2013.14

Botra, A., Rerselman, M., & Ford, M. (2014, May). Gamification beyond badges. In *2014 IST-Africa Conference Proceedings* (pp. 1-10). IEEE. 10.1109/ISTAFRICA.2014.6880651

Butgereit, L. (2016, May). Gamifying mobile micro-learning for continuing education in a corporate IT environment. In *2016 IST-Africa Week Conference* (pp. 1-7). IEEE.

Christy, K. R., & Fox, J. (2014). Leaderboards in academic contexts: A test of stereotype threat and social comparison explanations for women's math performance. *Computers & Education, 78,* 66-77. . doi:10.106/j.compedu.2014.05.005

Classcraft. (2021). Available at https://www.classcraft.com/

Cornel, C. J., Rowe, D. C., & Cornel, C. M. (2017, September). Starships and cybersecurity: Teaching security concepts through immersive gaming experiences. In *Proceedings of the 18th Annual Conference on Information Technology Education* (pp. 27-32). 10.1145/3125659.3125696

Danowska-Florczyk, E., & Mostowski, P. (2012). *Gamification as a new direction in teaching Polish as a foreign language.* ICT for Language Learning.

Denny, P. (2013, April). The effect of virtual achievements on student engagement. In *Proceedings of the SIGCHI conference on human factors in computing systems* (pp. 763-772). 10.1145/2470654.2470763

Deterding, S. (2012). Gamification: Designing for motivation. *Interactions, 19*(4), 14-17.

Domínguez, A., Saenz-de-Navarrete, J., De-Marcos, L., Fernández-Sanz, L., Pagés, C., & Martínez-Herráiz, J. J. (2013). Gamifying learning experiences: Practical implications and outcomes. *Computers & Education, 63,* 380–392. doi:10.1016/j.compedu.2012.12.020

Elorriaga, M., Antúnez, M. E., & Nicolino, M. S. (2016, October). The game as a way to destructuration: Learning to reason through game. In *2016 International Conference on Interactive Mobile Communication, Technologies and Learning (IMCL)* (pp. 43-45). IEEE. 10.1109/IMCTL.2016.7753768

Gabarron, E., Schopf, T., Serrano, J. A., Fernandez-Luque, L., & Dorronzoro, E. (2012). Gamification Strategy on Prevention of STDs for Youth. *Studies in Health Technology and Informatics, 192,* 1066–1066. PMID:23920840

Goehle, G. (2013). Gamification and Web-based Homework. *PRIMUS (Terre Haute, Ind.), 23*(3), 234–246. doi:10.1080/10511970.2012.736451

Gordillo, A., Gallego, D., Barra, E., & Quemada, J. (2013). The city as a learning gamified platform. In *Frontiers in Education Conference* (pp. 372-378). IEEE. 10.1109/FIE.2013.6684850

Grant, E. S., Shankararaman, V., & Loong, J. L. K. (2014, December). Experimenting with Gamification in the Classroom. In *2014 IEEE 6th Conference on Engineering Education (ICEED)* (pp. 79-83). IEEE. 10.1109/ICEED.2014.7194692

Hamari, J. (2013). Transforming homo economicus into homo ludens: A field experiment on gamification in a utilitarian peer-to-peer trading service. *Electronic Commerce Research and Applications, 12*(4), 236–245. doi:10.1016/j.elerap.2013.01.004

Hamari, J., Koivisto, J., & Sarsa, H. (2014, January). Does gamification work? A literature review of empirical studies on gamification. In *2014 47th Hawaii international conference on system sciences* (pp. 3025-3034). IEEE.

Hanus, M. D., & Fox, J. (2015). Assessing the effects of gamification in the classroom: A longitudinal study on intrinsic motivation, social comparison, satisfaction, effort, and academic performance. *Computers & Education, 80*, 152–161. doi:10.1016/j.compedu.2014.08.019

Holman, C., Aguilar, S., & Fishman, B. (2013, April). GradeCraft: What can we learn from a game-inspired learning management system? In *Proceedings of the third international conference on learning analytics and knowledge* (pp. 260-264). 10.1145/2460296.2460350

Isaac, J., & Babu, S. V. (2016, March). Supporting computational thinking through gamification. In *2016 IEEE Symposium on 3D User Interfaces (3DUI)* (pp. 245-246). IEEE. 10.1109/3DUI.2016.7460062

Jeong, E. J., & Lee, H. R. (2015). Addictive use due to personality: Focused on big five personality traits and game addiction. *International Journal of Psychology and Behavioral Sciences, 9*(6), 2032–2036.

Kahoot. (2021). Available at https://kahoot.com/

Kapp, K. M. (2012). *The gamification of learning and instruction: Game-based methods and strategies for training and education.* Pfieffer.

Kekuluthotuwage, P., & Fernando, P. (2017, September). HomeSchool: An interactive educational tool for child education. In *2017 National Information Technology Conference (NITC)* (pp. 34-39). IEEE. 10.1109/NITC.2017.8285652

Koivisto, J., & Hamari, J. (2014). Demographic differences in perceived benefits from gamification. *Computers in Human Behavior, 35*, 179–188. doi:10.1016/j.chb.2014.03.007

Lambruschini, B. B., & Pizarro, W. G. (2015, July). Tech—Gamification in university engineering education: Captivating students, generating knowledge. In *2015 10th International Conference on Computer Science & Education (ICCSE)* (pp. 295-299). IEEE.

Lee, J. J., & Hammer, J. (2011). Gamification in education: What, how, why bother? *Academic Exchange Quarterly, 15*(2), 146.

Lee, S., & Lim, S. (2014, December). Considerations on gamification of e-learning application: Case study with phrase building training application. In *2014 6th International Conference on Multimedia, Computer Graphics and Broadcasting* (pp. 55-58). IEEE.

Li, C., Dong, Z., Untch, R. H., & Chasteen, M. (2013). Engaging Computer Science Collaborative Learning Environment. *International Journal of Information and Education Technology (IJIET), 3*(1), 72–77. doi:10.7763/IJIET.2013.V3.237

Maia, R. F., & Graeml, F. R. (2015, October). Playing and learning with gamification: An in-class concurrent and distributed programming activity. In *2015 IEEE Frontiers in Education Conference (FIE)* (pp. 1-6). IEEE.

Martínez-López, F. J., Anaya-Sánchez, R., & Aguilar-Illescas, R. (2016). *Online brand communities: Using the social web for branding and marketing*. Springer. doi:10.1007/978-3-319-24826-4

McGonigal, J. (2011). *Reality is broken: Why games make us better and how they can change the world*. Penguin.

Moccozet, L., Tardy, C., Opprecht, W., & Léonard, M. (2013). Interactive collaborative learning (ICL). In *2013 International Conference on. Interactive Collaborative Learning (ICL), 2013 International Conference on* (pp. 171-179). 10.1109/ICL.2013.6644565

Nah, F. F. H., Telaprolu, V. R., Rallapalli, S., & Venkata, P. R. (2013, July). Gamification of education using computer games. In *International Conference on Human Interface and the Management of Information* (pp. 99-107). Springer.

Nelson, M. J. (2012, October). Soviet and American precursors to the gamification of work. In *Proceeding of the 16th international academic MindTrek conference* (pp. 23-26). 10.1145/2393132.2393138

Nicholson, S. (2012). *A user-Centered theoretical framework for meaningful gamification*. Paper presented at the Games+ Learning+ Society 8.0, Madison, WI.

Nicholson, S. (2015). A recipe for meaningful gamification. In *Gamification in education and business* (pp. 1–20). Springer.

Reiners, T., Wood, L. C., Chang, V., Gütl, C. H., Teräs, H., & Gregory, S. (2012). Operationalising gamification in an educational authentic environment. In *IADIS Internet Technologies and Society* (pp. 93-100). Academic Press.

Rezzly. (2021). Available at https://www.rezzly.com/

Rinnert, G. C., Martens, M., Mooney, A., Talbott, J. A., & Rinnert, B. (2017, June). Energetic alpha, playful handwriting practice for children. In *Proceedings of the 2017 Conference on Interaction Design and Children* (pp. 687-691). 10.1145/3078072.3091981

Ristov, S., Ackovska, N., & Kirandziska, V. (2015, March). Positive experience of the project gamification in the microprocessors and microcontrollers course. In *2015 IEEE Global Engineering Education Conference (EDUCON)* (pp. 511-517). IEEE. 10.1109/EDUCON.2015.7096018

Rouse, K. (2013). *Gamification in science education: The relationship of educational games to motivation and achievement*. The University Of Southern Mississippi.

Ryan, R. M., & Deci, E. L. (2000). Self-determination theory and the facilitation of intrinsic motivation, social development, and well-being. *The American Psychologist*, 55(1), 68–78. doi:10.1037/0003-066X.55.1.68 PMID:11392867

Sanmugam, M., Zaid, N. M., Abdullah, Z., Aris, B., Mohamed, H., & van der Meijden, H. (2016, December). The impacts of infusing game elements and gamification in learning. In *2016 IEEE 8th international conference on engineering education (ICEED)* (pp. 131-136). IEEE. 10.1109/ICEED.2016.7856058

Seaborn, K., & Fels, D. I. (2015). Gamification in theory and action: A survey. *International Journal of Human-Computer Studies, 74*, 14–31. doi:10.1016/j.ijhcs.2014.09.006

Seppo. (2021). Available at https://seppo.io/

Snyder, E., & Hartig, J. R. (2013). Gamification of board review: A residency curricular innovation. *Medical Education, 5*(47), 524–525. doi:10.1111/medu.12190 PMID:23574079

Sprint, G., & Cook, D. (2015, March). Enhancing the CS1 student experience with gamification. In *2015 IEEE integrated STEM education conference* (pp. 94-99). IEEE.

Tretinjak, M. F., Bednjanec, A., & Tretinjak, M. (2014, May). Application of modern teaching techniques in the educational process. In *2014 37th International Convention on Information and Communication Technology, Electronics and Microelectronics (MIPRO)* (pp. 628-632). IEEE. 10.1109/MIPRO.2014.6859643

Velázquez-Iturbide, J. Á., Robles-Martínez, G., Cobos, R., Echeverría, L., Claros, I., Fernández-Panadero, M. C., ... Delgado-Kloos, C. (2016, September). Project eMadrid: Learning methodologies, gamification and quality. In *2016 International Symposium on Computers in Education (SIIE)* (pp. 1-5). IEEE. 10.1109/SIIE.2016.7751874

Yohannis, A., & Prabowo, Y. (2015, September). Sort attack: Visualization and gamification of sorting algorithm learning. In *2015 7th international conference on games and virtual worlds for serious applications (vs-games)* (pp. 1-8). IEEE.

Yonemura, K., Yajima, K., Komura, R., Sato, J., & Takeichi, Y. (2017, November). Practical security education on operational technology using gamification method. In *2017 7th IEEE International Conference on Control System, Computing and Engineering (ICCSCE)* (pp. 284-288). IEEE. 10.1109/ICCSCE.2017.8284420

Youtopia. (2021). Available at https://youtopia.com/

Zichermann, G., & Cunningham, C. (2011). *Gamification by design: Implementing game mechanics in web and mobile apps*. O'Reilly Media, Inc.

KEY TERMS AND DEFINITIONS

Advergames: Simple video games that contain advertisements for different products and are designed to promote a company, their products, or their services.

Gamification: Incorporation of gaming elements in a non-gaming context.

Gamification Platforms: Used to embed gamification constructs in the non-gaming environment.

Horizontal Assessments: Assessment of different groups having diverse exposures.

Meaningful Gamification: Focuses on the long-term benefits through invoking the users' intrinsic motivation.

Reward-Based Gamification: Utilizes external rewards to enhance the users' behaviors.

Vertical Assessments: Assessment of one group over time.

Chapter 5

Gamification as an Engaging Approach for University Students in Distance Education

Pierluigi Muoio
University of Calabria, Italy

Lorella Gabriele
https://orcid.org/0000-0001-6812-1595
University of Calabria, Italy

ABSTRACT

This chapter presents an experience of university distance education carried out during the COVID-19 emergency, using gamification to make teaching more engaging and motivating for students. In particular, the proposed work is aimed at addressing two different needs: 1) to proactively deal with the exceptional consequences due to COVID-19 in the educational field and 2) to innovate teaching practices by promoting an active learning approach. Hence, game elements and game design techniques were used to design a course program aimed at fostering a high degree of involvement among students to increase both personal satisfaction and student performance. Results confirm that the set educational path, giving greater emphasis to the social, emotional, and experiential dimensions, actively engaged students in the learning process, recording a high percentage of appreciation for the course.

INTRODUCTION

The dramatic health emergency caused by the spread of COVID-19 in the early months of 2020 has shocked the world, producing serious consequences in various aspects of daily life. Most of the countries declared a state of total lockdown, they have stopped the educational activities or moved part of them or all, via the web, adopting Distance Education. For the first time, schools, universities, and other educational institutions were confronted with a series of problems that were not at all easy to solve.

DOI: 10.4018/978-1-7998-9732-3.ch005

The need to carry out teaching activities exclusively at distance implies both looking differently at the educational relationship between teachers, students and knowledge, and rethinking space, time, and tools.

However, distance education cannot just be thought of as a transposition of the real classroom with the virtual one.

Thus, the emergency led to a series of experimentation in which digital technologies and tools were extensively used to ensure continuity in teaching and learning.

Due the stopping of face-to-face teaching, and the consequent starting of distance education "experimentations" teachers of all levels had to use tools and technologies, including Open Source (Muoio, 2018), originally designed for collaborative work in the corporate environment.

In recent years, Information and Communication Technologies (ICTs) brought a radical change in different areas of knowledge. Different authors (Edmonds et al., 2005; Ott, Pozzi, 2010; Aqda et al., 2011; Daud and Zakaria, 2012) highlight how their pervasive use in any field of the society, can be exploited to learn in new ways, to develop individuality and initiative, but at the same time, the collaborative and cooperative learning, and creativity.

The use of technologies in educational context refers to the constructivist perspective (Piaget, 1967; Papert, 1984, 1986, 1991) according to which learners have an active role in the knowledge acquisition process. Teachers guide subjects in these processes, and students "learn by doing" through real experiences. Different studies (Šimonová and Bílek, 2012; Cárdenas et al., 2016; Gabriele et al., 2017; Gabriele et al., 2019; Bilotta et al., 2020) underline how ICTs, if well integrated in the didactic context, can be really motivating and engaging tools; they can promote an active, collaborative, participative and problem-based learning; they can support the acquisition of workgroup skills and can foster creativity and self-reflection. ICTs, multimedia environments combining images, sounds and animations, emotionally involve the user in the learning processes (Psomos, Kordaki, 2015; Hartsell, 2017).

Taking into account these perspectives, in the COVID-19 educational emergency, many software applications have been adapted to support educational processes, although, in some cases, not suitable to replace face-to-face teaching activities.

This complex phase based on distance learning has been animated by discussions, doubts, difficulties and questions about the relationship between digital media and teaching.

This framework invites us to consider two issues: the concrete ways in which technologies are currently used in educational contexts; the need to integrate them into an overall project that takes into account the organisation of the activities, teaching and learning methodologies and strategies.

The distance learning introduced in this period is a direct consequence of emergence and not of careful work on the teaching approach. In most cases, in the absence of valid pre-existing strategies, face-to-face lessons, with their specific dynamics, were replicated online.

For several years, digital technologies and competences have been the subject of recommendations, documents and indications from various national and international bodies.

These documents have emphasised that the use of ICT in everyday teaching does not automatically produce positive results. Instead, it is necessary to start methodically with a process of integration of ICT so they can really enhance the teaching-learning process.

Today's society is defined as fluid, collective (Levy, 1996), liquid (Bauman& Lyon, 2015), in which everything can be transformed and redefined, and every field is pervaded by technologies.

Technologies influence the way to access the information, which is no longer described by the 'one-to-many' model; hence, they open to a process of negotiation and co-construction of contents (Biondi,

2007). For example, adolescents and students come into contact with many sources of knowledge and develop habits and attitudes towards learning long before they arrive in school and university classrooms.

They become protagonists of their own growth and educational process, taking an active role in their own choices, in a life-long learning perspective. They are aware that, today, the task of education is no longer exclusively delegated to the traditional educational agencies in charge.

This scenario highlights the need to rethink education in the knowledge society, promoting with appropriate actions a new idea of school and university.

Hence, every real context can be an opportunity for education and cultural enrichment, therefore formal, informal and non-formal learning must be integrated and 'stitched together' so as to enhance the variety of experiences.

The frontal lesson based on a transmissive model where contents have a central role in comparison to the individual, cannot be an effective teaching method. The dynamic and complex society described highlights the need to change perspective, placing the individual at the centre of the educational process, with his originality, fostering his ability to think, collaborate, create, and elaborate.

In this perspective, technology cannot be a goal of the educational process, instead it has to be integrated in the education,where ICTs become useful tools to enhance the experience of knowledge, making the educational offer more effective and congruent with the characteristics of digital natives (Prensky, 2001).

In our opinion, distance education has to provide both pedagogical and technological tools; it should not be limited to formal "academic" teaching, but has to include practice sections and new tools/models to build and transfer meaningful experiences to the learners.

This chapter presents an experience of university distance education during which the researchers used gamification to make teaching more engaging and motivating for students. In particular, the proposed work is aimed to address two different needs: 1) to proactively deal with the exceptional consequences due to COVID-19 in the educational field; 2) to innovate teaching practices by promoting an active learning approach.

BACKGROUND

The game has very ancient origins, it accompanied the evolution of human being over the millennia and it has a great importance from an ontogenetic point of view. For instance, during play, children try new things, solve problems, invent, create, test and explore ideas. For this reason, the game is considered by scholars as an innate biological need and is indicated as a universal principle of the cultural evolution of the human being (Frissen et al., 2015).

However, when the game is used in non-playful contexts, it becomes gamification (Deterding et al., 2011), and it has the task of placing individuals at the centre of system, enabling to stimulate positive and constructive elements, such as intrinsic motivation, generosity, teamwork, joy, passion (Sassoon, Maestri &Polsinelli, 2019; Zainuddin et al., 2020).

Nowadays, gaming is considered an engaging and motivating teaching tool and a set of methodologies efficacy adopted also in university contexts and in adult education (Raju, Ahmed &Anumba, 2011; Nordby et al., 2016; Nesti, 2017; Gómez-Carrasco et al., 2019; Nieto-Escamez&Roldán-Tapia, 2021). In particular, in educational contexts, gamification can successfully support the strategies adopted by the teacher to facilitate and promote learning. According to Nakamura &Csikszentmihalyi (2014), gaming stimulates and feeds the willingness to learning, leading the subject to reach a condition of flow, that is a total immersion feeling in an activity, perceived as completely satisfying, where the actions are performed without any effort, in a perfect balance between anxiety and boredom.

During the Covid-19 period, gamification has been used and integrated in different educational contexts, as shown by the literature review outlined in Table 1.

Articles were collected using the sciencedirect platform, according to the criterion "publication date" set "2020 to present", "COVID-19 or Pandemic", "gamification approach".

Table 1. Application of gamification in educational context

Study	Study design, duration, and participants	Application context and Results
Azar & Tan (2020)	The study investigated the University Interns' perceptions of ICT Techs application in teaching the English Language during this Covid-19 Pandemic in Malaysia. ICT Techs the University Interns' prefer to enhance secondary school students' English.	Findings indicate that the use of gamification in second language learning has significant benefits to enhance students' learning process and to improve motivation. Moreover, the authors stress some gamification aspects, which are the capability to create a relaxed, fun, and comfortable learning environment for students.
Legaki et al. (2020)	Legaki et al. (2020) designed and implemented a web based gamified application. They tested the application with 279 undergraduate and MBA students at the School of Electrical and Computer Engineering of the National Technical University of Athens, Greece (hereafter ECE, NTUA) and 86 undergraduate students at the Business Administration Department in the School of Business and Economics of the University of Thessaly, Greece (hereafter Business Administration).	The findings highlight that gamification improves students' learning performance. Its impact is even more important in the case of engineering students, where no gender differences emerge. Otherwise, in the case of gamified groups at the ECE, NTUA, female participants have achieved the highest performances and the highest improvement.
Oe, Takemoto & Ridwan (2020).	24 students that participated in a business class during the pandemic period were interviewed to measure learning.	The qualitative analysis of the interviews was used to define a conceptual framework and to provide recommendations for pedagogy stakeholders on how to implement and improve the effectiveness of gamification in business education.
Pérez-Serrano, Fernández-Sande & Pallares (2020)	The authors used the simulation game to educate students enrolled at the first-year Media Business course of the Bachelor's Degree in Journalism at the Complutense University of Madrid.	Students positively rated the gamification tools as highly motivating, visually appealing, useful to work on entrepreneurship skills and to consolidate knowledge.
Zain et al. (2020)	Gamification model has been used with the aim to drive people behaviour change in domain health awareness campaigns.	Authors develop a conceptual Model (GAMEBC) based on Self-Determination Theory (Ryan, Rigby & Przybylski, 2006) to develop a gamification software able to ensure the behaviour change in the health domain. According to the GAMEBC model, both intrinsic and extrinsic motivation elements need to be correctly balanced. They individuated the following key motivational features: Autonomy, Competence, Relatedness, and Engagement
de Las Heras et al. (2021)	The authors developed a digital platform prototype (BioVL), proposing a framework for the systematic development and conceptual design of educational process simulators. BioVL includes the learning perspective; the motivational strategy by using gamification; the educational resources.	The BioVL platform was developed to prepare engineering students and trainees to have an active role in the transition versus Industry 4.0 skills and knowledge, to meet the demand for a more efficient and higher quality bio-manufacturing education, as well as flexibility and creativity.

Continued on following page

Table 1. Continued

Study	Study design, duration, and participants	Application context and Results
Nieto-Escamez&Roldán-Tapia (2021)	The authors identified and analysed 11 papers to deepen how gamification strategies have been used during the COVID-19 pandemic to assess student's learning and motivation.	The analysis featured that gamification especially fit whenever carried out along with traditional lectures and can be a useful educational tool during COVID times. Students perceived gamification as creative, innovative, able to aid them to interface with their schoolmates during isolation time. However, some of them asserted that they did not feel entangled in the proposed activities.
Taladriz (2021)	Flipped learning methodologies and gamification strategies were used to teach computer networks in a cybersecurity engineering degree (Universidad Rey Juan Carlos in Spain).	Gamification appeared to be a very promising complement to flipped mastery, as it is able to engage students in working on the materials provided. The results were found to be particularly suitable for university teacher training programmes, so this approach was extended to all disciplines across the university.
XU et al. (2021)	A literature review of current studies published between 1999 and 2020 aimed to investigate the effect of gamification on intrinsic motivation.	The analysis of the collected articles shows that gamification is generally associated with: an increase of intrinsic motivation; a reinforcement of extrinsic motivation. Both positively affect the willingness of the student to complete the assigned tasks. Moreover, the key elements of gamification, points, badges, trophies, increase the perceived effectiveness of the students.

Therefore, taking into account as the literature highlights, game elements and game design techniques were used to innovate the course program. Integrating these engaging methodologies in the traditional teaching-learning process, the researchers aimed to promote: a) high degree of involvement of students and b) active participation, generating a virtuous circle (between motivation, involvement, and flow) able to increase both personal satisfaction and performance.

METHODOLOGY

Course Program

The experimental work program was given in the academic year of 2019–2020, in the *Basic Computer Science Laboratory class*, Course Degree in Business Economics (University of Calabria, Italy), involving 120 students.

The didactic activities lasted three months, starting in the second half of March until the end of May. They were all carried out remotely, as required by the health situation and in compliance with the relevant measures regarding the containment and management of the epidemiological emergency.

For remote lessons, the University of Calabria provided teaching staff and students with Microsoft Teams platform, that includes tools for streaming, screen sharing, virtual whiteboards, allowing also real-time communication, sharing of different kinds of digital documents and other functions.

Therefore, the lessons of the course were carried out entirely in distance, in synchronous mode. Videoconferencing was planned weekly by the lecturer within the virtual community (Team) of the course. Lessons were held twice a week for two hours for a total of 22 hours.

Microsoft Teams platform allowed students to use different tools to interact during the lessons and ask questions as the real classroom. Lessons were recorded, in this way participants had the possibility to review the synchronous lessons also in the following days.

The course lecturer was available for questions, explanations or feedback by setting up an email appointment or using a web chat service Teams.

The main objective of the course was to provide students with digital skills useful for their degree professional profile. Hence, contents were assembled in four learning units. The first learning unit was devoted to deepening the fundamental concepts of Computer Science, Information and Communication Technologies and its applications in modern society.

The second learning unit was focused on the functioning of telematics networks, Internet and its main services, and deepened the concepts of World Wide Web, hypertext and hypermedia. In the third learning unit students learned how to manage folders and documents on their own PC, to recognize the different file extensions, to search for information and specific documents on the browser, copyrighted materials and open resources.

The fourth learning unit was focused on the use of spreadsheets: how to manage and to analyse data in both personal and professional contexts. In particular, this unit aimed to develop students' analytical and computational skills. Hence, they learned both basic and advanced formulas and functions to increase productivity and develop complex reports useful in the accounting, economic and administrative fields.

The teaching methodology foresaw a strong integration between theory and practice. During the course, gamification methods and tools were applied through the LabG@me environment, with the aim of encouraging the use of the teaching materials and making learning more enjoyable, fun and more effective. A detailed description of the activities, and the kind (i.e. presentation or video) and quantity of didactic materials given during the course, is sketched in Table 2.

Table 2. Course contents details

Learning Unit	Details	Didactic materials	Game developed
Basic concepts	To know the fundamental concepts of Computer Science, Information and Communication Technologies (ICT) and its applications in modern society	N° 1 Presentation N° 1 Booklet N° 3 video clips N° 5 educational games	Memory game Millionaire game Hangman game Association game Multiple-choice quiz
Networks and Web	To understand the functioning of telematics networks, Internet network and its services including the Web service.	N° 1 Presentation N° 1 Timeline N° 1 video clip N° 6 educational games	Timeline Crossword Millionaire game Memory game N° 2 Multiple-choice quizzes
File management and Web search	To learn how to manage folders and documents on own PC, to recognize the different file extensions, to learn how to search for information and specific documents on browser	N° 3 Presentations N° 4 educational games	Memory game Hangman game N° 2 Multiple-choice quizzes
Spreadsheets	To learn basic and advanced functions of a spreadsheet.	N° 3 Presentations N° 4 educational games	Madboy game Missing Word Cloze N° 2 Multiple-choice quizzes

Source: authors' elaboration

LabG@me: The Gaming Platform

LabG@me is a gamification-oriented learning environment implemented with PHP and Mysql Database. The tools and functionalities have a strong 2.0 connotation and are able to promote interaction and communication (De Pietro, De Rose &Muoio, 2010). In LabG@me, users can find and use Learning Objects provided by the teacher and linked to each Learning Unit (LU). Each participant can register a personal profile in which to add a personal description, interests, contact addresses, and other elements useful to sign up its own digital identity.

The *personal profile* is an autonomous operational workspace in which users can publish text messages, documents, images, and links to Web resources. Another social-oriented feature of LabG@me is the possibility to add comments to the posts of other participants and to mark them as important and significant.

Figure 1. A screenshot of a personal profile from the Italian version of LabG@me

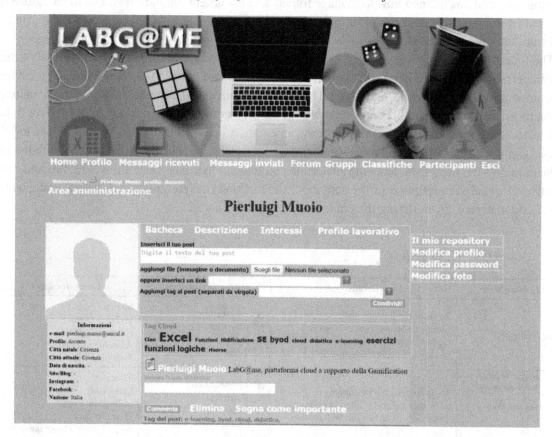

The gamification activity carried out via LabG@me accompanied the whole course, involving students in a workgroup competition. The play-based contents were organized into four LUs of the course programme. Each LU was made available to students after each lesson and was composed of the didactic materials (references materials, presentations, films), quizzes and games (Memory game, Millionaire game, Hangman game, Crossword puzzle, Madboys). These latter were designed to reinforce the contents of the learning presented by the teacher during the lessons and were implemented according to different levels of complexity, requiring an increasing skill level. This choice was due to avoid that the rapid achievement of objectives could cause boredom and reduce the students' involvement (Lister, 2015). The adopted approach in the implementation of gamification activities, the intrinsic motivation was stimulated (Chan, Nah, Liu & Lu, 2018; Xu et al., 2021), a high degrees of involvement were promoted and an active participation of the students was developed.

At the end of each game, the score obtained by the student was added to the one obtained in the previous game sessions, thus increasing the total score of the team.

The activities concerning the learning unit on spreadsheets, quizzes and didactic games were also accompanied by some "challenges" based on speed in solving some exercises introduced by the teacher and then proposed within LabG@me. The student who was quickest to deliver the correct solution accumulated points each time, after the teacher had checked that it was correct, which increased their personal score.

The student who completed the task most quickly and most correctly accumulated points which increased his or her personal score.

One of the games proposed on learning unit number four is "Madboy" (see Figure 1), inspired by platform-type video games and with three levels.

Each player had to choose an avatar with which to avoid obstacles, defeat monsters and answer multiple choice questions inserted during the path game. The questions, related to the concepts on the spreadsheets and with increasing difficulty according to the level of the game, were aimed at reinforcing notions and meanings acquired during the lessons.

The correct answer earned points, while the wrong answer was penalised. The contact of the avatar with monsters and dangerous objects resulted in the loss of one of the three 'lives' provided at the start. The loss of all lives obliged each player to start the game over by starting a new "game". At the end of each game, the points obtained were added to the personal score shown in the general classification. According to these dynamics, a community ranking was created, which was always updated and could be consulted by everyone in a special section of LabG@me, which made learning more fun and exciting, as it was immersed in a competitive, playful and completely different context from the serious and formal one of traditional university teaching.

Figure 2. A screenshot of the Madboy game, used to deepen some spreadsheet concepts

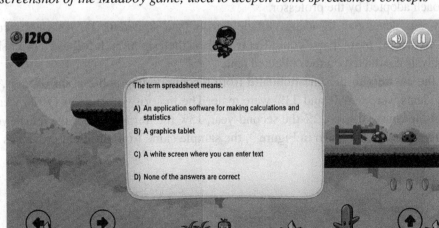

The last LU of the course, foresaw quizzes, educational games and speed challenges in solving the different tasks. Doubts and errors arising at the end of each challenge were analysed and discussed together with the professor in the LabG@me discussion forum. Moreover, in the last LU, a more sophisticated game was proposed, inspired by the video games platform and with three levels. Each player had to choose an avatar useful to move towards each level, avoiding obstacles, defeating monsters and answering multiple-choice questions scattered along the way. The questions of each LU had an increasing difficulty according to the level of play, and had the aim of reinforcing knowledge and meanings acquired during the streaming lessons. The correct answer allowed to earn a point, while a penalty was assigned for each wrong answer.

According to these dynamics, a community ranking was developed, which was updated after each game session and could be visited by each student. This made learning more fun and exciting, as it was immersed in a competitive, playful and completely different environment from the serious and formal one of traditional university teaching.

The students' performances were collected for each LU and a final mark was assigned. Moreover, at the end of the course, an online questionnaire was administered on the gamification activity, the LabG@ me environment and its main functionalities, in order to understand the students' opinion, their point of view and obtain useful feedback for further courses.

RESULTS

Students' Course Questionnaire

At the end of the course, students evaluated the academic course they attended by answering a questionnaire in order to collect useful information also on the students' satisfaction. The questionnaire was subdivided in two sections, twenty questions in mixed modality: open-ended questions, multiple choices and agreement scale. The first section is related to understanding students' experience with distance learning, their needs and moods. The second section was related to the teaching approach adopted by the lecturer, the LabG@me environment and its main functions, in order to understand the students' opinion, their point of view and to obtain useful feedback for future developments.

Students responded to the questionnaire items based on Likert scale by choosing one of the suitable answers, indicating the level of agreement that mostly reflected their opinions about the course and the teaching approach adopted by the professor.

The survey was developed by using Google Forms (see Appendix 1). Answers were collected anonymously, so that the participants could freely express their opinion. It follows a brief sketch of the descriptive analysis conducted on the collected data.

Analysing the answers to the questionnaire from a socio-demographic point of view, it emerged that 67% of students were female and 33% were male. The majority of students (79%) were attending the first year of the course degree, 2% the second-year, 15% the third-year, 3% the fourth-year, and 1% were off-course students. As shown in Figure 3, the sample came from different provinces of Calabria region (South of Italy).

Figure 3. Province of origin of the students

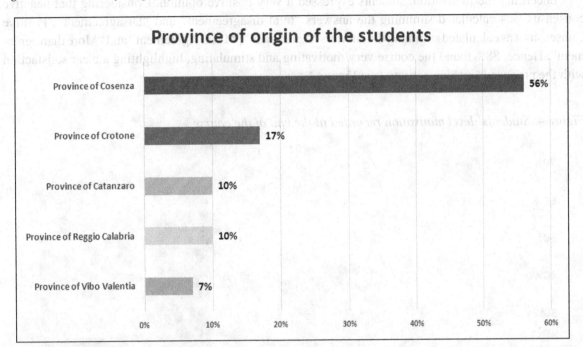

The main devices that students used for distance learning was the notebook (61%), followed by the desktop PC (21%), the smartphone (13%) and the tablet (5%). The platform used for the video lessons, Microsoft Teams, was assessed as quite adequate by the majority of the sample (72%).

Only 7% of the students did not rate the platform positively.

77% of the students rated the teachers as fairly competent in the use of distance learning tools, 18% rated the teachers as very competent and only 5% of the teachers were considered to be little or not at all competent in the use of digital devices.

In addition, 38% of the students stated that they were comfortable with distance learning and that they learned as much as they did with face-to-face lessons. 30% said they learned less, but developed other skills (such as technological skills). 28% reported a drop in their learning level and tried to implement personal strategies to adapt to the situation. 5% stated that they did not like distance learning and learned very little.

In general, among the critical elements underlined by the students regarding this emergency teaching method there are the excessive number of daily hours spent in front of the PC to follow lessons (36%), the slow or unreliable connection (23%), the excessive amount of activities to be carried out autonomously assigned by the teachers (13%), the uninvolving didactic offer with lessons not adapted to the new online mode (10%).

Students rate fairly adequate both their level of participation in online classes (70%) and their commitment in daily study (59%).

For 39% of the sample, distance learning could only be useful for special needs in normal conditions, for 31% it could be integrated with classroom lessons in normal conditions, while for 30% it should only be used in emergency conditions.

Concerning the motivation, students expressed a very positive opinion. Considering that negative consensus was calculated summing the answers "total disagreement" and "Disagreement". Positive Consensus was calculated summing the answers "Agreement", "Total Agreement" and "More than agreement". Hence, 88% found the course very motivating and stimulating, highlighting a clear satisfaction with the proposed teaching activity (see Figure 4).

Figure 4. Students' level motivation recorded at the end of the course

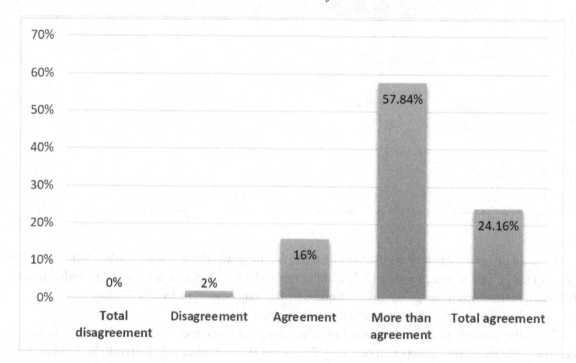

Students' Performances Outcomes

Since the beginning of the lessons, gamification activities have aroused great curiosity and interest in the students. All 120 students enrolled at the course actively participated in the proposed learning units. They stated that they felt motivated and gratified by the innovative approach to the lessons, which helped to develop a better relational climate and to experience the distance learning and individual study with greater awareness and serenity.

As mentioned in the section "LabG@me: the gaming platform", during the gamification activities, students received prizes, and accumulated points, which increased both the personal score and the team score. Thus, a final ranking was created with a prize for the first ones in the ranking. The students that at the end of the course, had the highest score did not carry out a part of the final test.

The reward, i.e. the final prize, prevented a loss of interest as students proceeded with the game activities, encouraging greater engagement in the LabG@me activities, increasing the sense of gratification.

At the end of the course, the assigned marks reflected the level of knowledge and skills acquired by students along the educational path. In particular, it emerged that the overall performances of the course students were of high quality. In fact, 46.67% of the students received an "Excellent" score. 30% of students had a "Good" mark. Only 23.33% of the students got a "Sufficient" mark on the final exam.

CONCLUSION

Today, Education agencies and all stakeholders are facing an unstoppable Copernican revolution that is affecting culture and society globally. In this revolution process, ICT plays a major role as a driving force behind a development that is proceeding at an exponential rate.

Hence, teachers are called upon to implement new actions, strategies and didactic paths to promote in learners creative and innovative skills, competence in the responsible and effective use of media, critical and reflective thinking and all those intangible and soft skills necessary for individual, professional and civic development.

This means that there is a need to go outside the closed approach typical of traditional education and training systems, extending the spaces, times and tools of training, encouraging the interconnection between formal, non-formal and informal environments, and exploring new ways of learning. formal, non-formal and informal spheres, also exploring new ways of learning.

As highlighted in the literature (Deterding et al., 2011; Sassoon, Maestri &Polsinelli, 2019; Zainud-din et al., 2020; XU et al., 2021), the integration of gamification in educational contexts can make a significant contribution to updating those teaching practices that have become obsolete and uninteresting, in which the student is considered as a passive receiver of knowledge.

The experimental work described in this chapter, even though it was carried out in a difficult and emergency period, can be considered positive both as regards the direct feedback received from the students in the satisfaction questionnaire and the indirect feedback represented by the interactions and participation recorded during the gamification activities.

The results confirm that there is an increasing need to implement teaching methods that are more flexible in terms of the ways in which knowledge is transmitted, more interactive and more engaging.

In this way, the activities proposed can be stimulating for the different intelligences and cognitive styles of the students, giving greater emphasis to the social, emotional and experiential dimensions of the learning processes.

The familiarity that the new generations have with technologies and game components makes it even easier to design educational experiences based on games.

The use of network environments such as LabG@me with learning games inside, if well organised and placed in a context that is meaningful for students, is able to act on the personal sphere of self-esteem and motivation, leading to a full integration between playful elements and those of an educational nature.

The challenge, the interactivity, the low cost of failure, the acceptance of error as a method of acquiring new knowledge, are characteristics that make the game highly suitable for education.

Therefore, gamification can represent an appropriate approach to face contemporary society's needs and requirements, since it favours problem solving, risk, creativity, communication, relationship, critical transversal and soft skills.

In addition, the results show that it is not the digital and technological tools that generate knowledge, but it is the way in which they are used and the "how" they are used to foster the construction of new knowledge.

DISCUSSION

Werbach& Hunter (2015) identifies a series of fundamental factors (Constraints, Emotions, Storytelling, Progression and Relationships) that can determine or not the success of gamification. Among these, one of the basic dynamics as well as one of the most important components to take into account during the designing of the gamification are emotions.

Emotions drive the behaviour of the subject, inducing him to abandon or to continue to use the platform. Therefore, it is absolutely necessary to understand how to generate the right emotions in users, taking into account the user's needs: some elements can arouse negative emotions in someone (e.g. frustration and discouragement due to the numerous repetitions), while can produce positive ones in others (e.g. stimulate a sense of competition to achieve the highest possible score).

This latter aspect was particularly important during the pandemic period, when motivation to attend an educational pathway was closely related to the emotions aroused in the subject.

In fact, all the sample actively participated in the educational proposed activities and the high success rate (46.67% excellent score and 30% good score) in the students' performance were of high quality (see Students' performances outcomes section).

The emotions and attitude we assume towards an experience, activity or task deeply affect our perception and therefore our performance and the final result. For this reason, the authors have developed some educational activities that leverages on metacognitive and affective aspects with the aim of making learning more enjoyable, fun and therefore more effective.

Digital environments such as LabG@me are capable to approach the needs and behaviours of the new generations and allow to shift the focus of learning from an individual and solitary dimension to an open dimension oriented towards social interactions, approaching the informality of the relationships that they develop spontaneously online, in social networks and in digital communities. Indeed, 56% of the participants asserted that they would like to use environments similar to LabG@me in the continuation of their studies.

LIMITATIONS AND FUTURE RESEARCH

The presented work is still completely empirical and not based on an experimental plan. However, results and feedback collected at the end of the Basic Computer Science Laboratory course, were relevant from different points of view: how students can be successfully motivated as regards the dimensions of participation, interaction, involvement and the classroom climate among peers and with the teacher.

It represents an important starting point for making improvements and proposing the gamification activity again in the future years. In the next experimentation, researchers planned a pre and post-test in order to enrich the study by using reliability analysis.

For the future, it is planned to experiment LabG@me within courses of years subsequent to the first, involving teachers from other disciplines, taking into account also the idea expressed by students to integrate gamification environments in other curricular topics.

It should be noted that the idea is not to massively introduce gamification in every aspect of specific teachings, but to use it in a well-calibrated way together with more traditional approaches and methodologies, taking into account the characteristics of the knowledge to be transmitted and the interests of teacher and students.

One of the limitations that are expected to improve concern the mechanism of content insertion in the Platform. At the moment, the teaching materials of the Learning Units are inserted manually via the Ftp protocol, and only subsequently are made visible to the students. Following the typical logic of the main Learning Content Management Systems, changes will be made to LabG@me in order to allow the teacher to carry out these operations in a completely automatic way, without having to possess specific advanced skills in the IT field. Further improvements to be made concern the graphics and the possibility of inserting, at the discretion of the teacher, a maximum number of attempts in carrying out quizzes, games and activities by the students.

REFERENCES

Aqda, M. F., Hamidi, F., & Ghorbandordinejad, F. (2011). The impact of constructivist and cognitive distance instructional design on the learner's creativity. *Procedia Computer Science*, *3*, 260–265. doi:10.1016/j.procs.2010.12.044

Azar, A. S., & Tan, N. H. I. (2020). The application of ICT techs (mobile-assisted language learning, gamification, and virtual reality) in teaching English for secondary school students in malaysia during Covid-19 pandemic. *Univers J Educ Res*, *8*(11), 55–63. doi:10.13189/ujer.2020.082307

Bauman, Z., & Lyon, D. (2015). *Sixth power: surveillance in liquid modernity*. Gius. Laterza & Figli Spa.

Bilotta, E., Bertacchini, F., Gabriele, L., Giglio, S., Pantano, P. S., & Romita, T. (2020). Industry 4.0 technologies in tourism education: Nurturing students to think with technology. *Journal of Hospitality, Leisure, Sport and Tourism Education*, 100275.

Biondi, G. (2007). *The school after the new technologies*. Apogeo Editore.

Cárdenas, L. A. V., Tavernise, A., Bertacchini, F., Gabriele, L., Valenti, A., Pantano, P., & Bilotta, E. (2016). An Educational Coding Laboratory for Elementary Pre-service Teachers: A Qualitative Approach. *International Journal of Engineering Pedagogy*, *6*(1), 11–17. doi:10.3991/ijep.v6i1.5364

Chan, E., Nah, F. F. H., Liu, Q., & Lu, Z. (2018, July). Effect of gamification on intrinsic motivation. In *International Conference on HCI in Business, Government, and Organizations* (pp. 445-454). Springer. 10.1007/978-3-319-91716-0_35

de Las Heras, S. C., Gargalo, C. L., Weitze, C. L., Mansouri, S. S., Gernaey, K. V., & Krühne, U. (2021). A framework for the development of Pedagogical Process Simulators (P2Si) using explanatory models and gamification. *Computers & Chemical Engineering*, *151*, 107350. doi:10.1016/j.compchemeng.2021.107350

De Pietro, O., De Rose, M., & Muoio, P. (2010). e-Underline: a tool to support collaborative learning. In *Proceedings of Elearn 2010, World conference on E-learning in Corporate Governement, Healthcare e Higher Education*. Association for the Advancement of Computing in Education (AACE).

Deterding, S., Dixon, D., Khaled, R., & Nacke, L. (2011, September). From game design elements to gamefulness: defining "gamification". In *Proceedings of the 15th international academic MindTrek conference: Envisioning future media environments* (pp. 9-15). 10.1145/2181037.2181040

Edmonds, E. A., Weakley, A., Candy, L., Fell, M., Knott, R., & Pauletto, S. (2005). The studio as laboratory: Combining creative practice and digital technology research. *International Journal of Human-Computer Studies*, *63*(4-5), 452–481. doi:10.1016/j.ijhcs.2005.04.012

Frissen, V., Lammes, S., De Lange, M., De Mul, J., & Raessens, J. (2015). *Homo ludens 2.0: Play, media, and identity*. Academic Press.

Gabriele, L., Bertacchini, F., Tavernise, A., Leticia, V. C., Pantano, P., & Bilotta, E. (2019). Lesson Planning by Computational Thinking Skills in Italian Pre-service Teachers. *Informatics in Education*, *18*(1), 69–104. doi:10.15388/infedu.2019.04

Gabriele, L., Marocco, D., Bertacchini, F., Pantano, P., & Bilotta, E. (2017). An educational robotics lab to investigate cognitive strategies and to foster learning in an arts and humanities course degree. *International Journal of Online Engineering*, *13*(04), 7–19. doi:10.3991/ijoe.v13i04.6962

Goehle, G. (2013). Gamification and web-based homework. *PRIMUS (Terre Haute, Ind.)*, *23*(3), 234–246. doi:10.1080/10511970.2012.736451

Gómez-Carrasco, C. J., Monteagudo-Fernández, J., Moreno-Vera, J. R., & Sainz-Gómez, M. (2019). Effects of a gamification and flipped-classroom program for teachers in training on motivation and learning perception. *Education Sciences*, *9*(4), 299. doi:10.3390/educsci9040299

Hartsell, T. (2017). Digital Storytelling: An Alternative Way of Expressing Oneself. *International Journal of Information and Communication Technology Education*, *13*(1), 72–82. doi:10.4018/IJICTE.2017010107

Legaki, N. Z., Xi, N., Hamari, J., Karpouzis, K., & Assimakopoulos, V. (2020). The effect of challenge-based gamification on learning: An experiment in the context of statistics education. *International Journal of Human-Computer Studies*, *144*, 102496. doi:10.1016/j.ijhcs.2020.102496 PMID:32565668

Lévy, P. (2002). *Collective intelligence. For an anthropology of cyberspace*. Feltrinelli editor.

Lister, M. (2015). Gamification: The effect on student motivation and performance at the post-secondary level. *Issues and Trends in Educational Technology, 3*(2).

Mandujano, G. G., Quist, J., & Hamari, J. (2021). Gamification of backcasting for sustainability: The development of the gamefulbackcasting framework (GAMEBACK). *Journal of Cleaner Production*, *302*, 126609. doi:10.1016/j.jclepro.2021.126609

Muoio, P. (2018). Open Source systems and software in teacher training for a school without excluded. In *Proceedings of EDEN 2018 Annual Conference* (pp. 691-700). European Distance and E-Learning Network.

Nakamura, J., & Csikszentmihalyi, M. (2014). The concept of flow. In *Flow and the foundations of positive psychology* (pp. 239–263). Springer.

Nesti, R. (2017). *Game-based learning: Game and play design in education*. ETS.

Nieto-Escamez, F. A., & Roldán-Tapia, M. D. (2021). Gamification as online teaching strategy during COVID-19: A mini-review. *Frontiers in Psychology*, *12*, 12. doi:10.3389/fpsyg.2021.648552 PMID:34093334

Nordby, A., Øygardslia, K., Sverdrup, U., & Sverdrup, H. (2016). The art of gamification; teaching sustainability and system thinking by pervasive game development. *Electronic Journal of e-Learning, 14*(3), 152-168.

Oe, H., Takemoto, T., & Ridwan, M. (2020). Is gamification a magic tool?: Illusion, remedy, and future opportunities in enhancing learning outcomes during and beyond the COVID-19. *Budapest International Research and Critics in Linguistics and Education Journal, 3*(3), 1401–1414.

Ott, M., & Pozzi, F. (2010). Towards a model to evaluate creativity-oriented learning activities. *Procedia: Social and Behavioral Sciences, 2*(2), 3532–3536. doi:10.1016/j.sbspro.2010.03.547

Papert, S. (1986). *Constructionism: A New Opportunity for Elementary Science Education*. A MIT Proposal to the National Science Foundation.

Papert, S. (1991). Situating Constructionism. In I. Harel & S. Papert (Eds.), *Constructionism*. Ablex Publishing.

Papert, S. A. (2020). *Mindstorms: Children, computers, and powerful ideas*. Basic books.

Pérez-Serrano, M. J., Fernández-Sande, M., & Pallares, M. R. (2020). Entorns d'aprenentatgedigitals en l'àrea d'Empresa Informativa. «Gaming» i incidència en activitats i avaluació. *Anàlisi: quaderns de comunicacióicultura*, (62), 111-130.

Piaget, J. (1967). *The mental development of the child*. Einaudi.

Psomos, P., & Kordaki, M. (2015). A novel educational digital storytelling tool focusing on students misconceptions. *Procedia: Social and Behavioral Sciences, 191*, 82–86. doi:10.1016/j.sbspro.2015.04.476

Raju, P., Ahmed, V., & Anumba, C. (2011). special issue on use of virtual world technology in architecture, engineering and construction. *Journal of Information Technology in Construction, 16*(11), 163–164.

Ryan, R. M., & Deci, E. L. (2000). Intrinsic and extrinsic motivations: Classic definitions and new directions. *Contemporary Educational Psychology, 25*(1), 54–67. doi:10.1006/ceps.1999.1020 PMID:10620381

Ryan, R. M., Rigby, C. S., & Przybylski, A. (2006). The motivational pull of video games: A self-determination theory approach. *Motivation and Emotion, 30*(4), 344–360. doi:10.100711031-006-9051-8

Sassoon, J., Maestri, A., & Polsinelli, P. (2019). *Games to be taken seriously. Gamification, storytelling and game design for innovative projects*. Franco Angeli.

Šimonová, I., & Bílek, M. (2012, April). On Individually Adapted ICT Applications in Computer-supported University Instruction. In DIVAI 2012 (p. 301). Academic Press.

Taladriz, C. C. (2021, April). Flipped mastery and gamification to teach Computer networks in a Cyber-security Engineering Degree during COVID-19. In *2021 IEEE Global Engineering Education Conference (EDUCON)* (pp. 1624-1629). IEEE. 10.1109/EDUCON46332.2021.9453885

Werbach, K., & Hunter, D. (2012). *For the Win. How Game Thinking Can Revolutionize Your Business*. Wharton Digital Press.

Werbach, K., & Hunter, D. (2015). *The gamification toolkit: dynamics, mechanics, and components for the win.* University of Pennsylvania Press.

Xu, J., Lio, A., Dhaliwal, H., Andrei, S., Balakrishnan, S., Nagani, U., & Samadder, S. (2021). Psychological interventions of virtual gamification within academic intrinsic motivation: A systematic review. *Journal of Affective Disorders, 293*, 444–465. doi:10.1016/j.jad.2021.06.070 PMID:34252688

Zain, N. H. M., Othman, Z., Noh, N. M., Teo, N. H. I., Zulkipli, N. H. B. N., & Yasin, A. M. (2020). GAMEBC model: Gamification in health awareness campaigns to drive behaviour change in defeating COVID-19 pandemic. *International Journal of Advanced Trends in Computer Science and Engineering, 9*(4).

Zainuddin, Z., Chu, S. K. W., Shujahat, M., & Perera, C. J. (2020). The impact of gamification on learning and instruction: A systematic review of empirical evidence. *Educational Research Review, 30*, 100326. doi:10.1016/j.edurev.2020.100326

KEY TERMS AND DEFINITIONS

Active Learning Approach: This approach refers to a set of teaching strategies the encourages students to engage higher-order skills and to reflect on what they are doing. The teacher role is as a "coach" who guides students in discovering phenomena, in problem solving, and in building knowledge. Students have an active role in the learning process rather than passively listening the teacher.

Distance Education: Teaching method that allows students and teachers to carry out the training and learning path even if "physically" distant. Online support and its tools play a fundamental role.

Educational Technology: It refers to an area of research aimed to develop and implement innovative educational approaches to learning using a broad set of software and hardware to improve student achievement.

Extrinsic Motivation: Rewards or incentives or reinforcements, both positive and negative external to the individual.

Gamification: It combines the use of mechanisms and dynamics game in the learning context to foster motivation and make learning more exciting and interactive.

Information and Communication Technology: It refers to all communication technologies (internet, smartphone, computers, software, social networking, and other media applications and services enabling users to access, retrieve, store, transmit, and manipulate information digitally.

Intrinsic Motivation: A behaviour driven by an internal rewards rather than by external ones. Hence, individual acts for the fun or for its own satisfaction.

Transmissive Learning Approach: Teaching approach based on the passive transfer of knowledge and notions from the teacher to the student.

APPENDIX 1

Table 3. Questionnaire items

Question	Dimension
Question 1: Which technological device did you mainly use for distance learning? 1 – Notebook 2 – Desktop pc 3 – Smartphone 4 – Tablet	user's relationship with distance learning technologies
Question 2: Do you think that the platform used is suitable for distance learning? 1 – Totally unacceptable 2 – Slightly acceptable 3 – Acceptable 4 – Perfectly Acceptable	user's relationship with distance learning technologies
Question 3: Did the teaching activities proposed meet your expectations? 1 – Totally unacceptable 2 – Slightly acceptable 3 – Acceptable 4 – Perfectly Acceptable	user's relationship with distance learning technologies
Question 4: How do you rate the remote communication with the lecturer? 1 – Not at all satisfied 2 – Slightly satisfied 3 – Moderately satisfied 4 – Very satisfied 5 – Extremely satisfied	user's relationship with distance learning technologies
Question 5: Regarding the level of confidence with technology, how do you rate your lecturer? 1 – Very competent in the use of remote tools 2 – Fairly competent in the use of remote tools 3 – Not very competent in the use of remote tools	user's relationship with distance learning technologies
Question 6: How do you rate your experience with distance learning? 1 - I feel comfortable and am learning as much as in face-to-face classes 2 – I am learning a little less, but I am developing other skills (e.g. technological skills) 3 – I am learning less, but I am trying to adapt to the situation 4 – I don't like it, so I am learning very little	user's relationship with distance learning technologies
Question 7: What are the critical issues experienced in distance learning? 1 - Slow or not sufficiently reliable Internet connection 2 - Technological platforms used not always working 3 - Overload of autonomous tasks assigned by lectures 4 - Excessive number of hours per day at the PC to follow the lessons 5 - Lessons and teaching proposals not very engaging 6 - Lack of willingness to communicate on the part of teachers 7 - No particular criticism	user's relationship with distance learning technologies

Continued on following page

Gamification as an Engaging Approach for University Students in Distance Education

Table 3. Continued

Question	Dimension
Question 8: How do you rate your commitment and participation in the video lessons? 1 – Inappropriate 2 – Slightly inappropriate 3 – Appropriate 4 – Absolutely appropriate	User perception
Question 9- How do you rate your engagement in daily study? 1 – Inappropriate 2 – Slightly inappropriate 3 – Appropriate 4 – Absolutely appropriate	User perception
Question 10: In your opinion Distance Learning 1 - It could be integrated to classroom lessons in normal conditions 2 - It could be useful only for special needs in normal conditions 3 - It should be used only in emergency conditions	User perception
Question 11: Personal overall opinion on distance learning 1 – Not at all satisfied 2 – Slightly satisfied 3 – Moderately satisfied 4 – Very satisfied 5 – Extremely satisfied	User perception
Question 12: Overall rating of the Basic Computer Laboratory Course 1 – Not at all satisfied 2 – Slightly satisfied 3 – Moderately satisfied 4 – Very satisfied 5 – Extremely satisfied	User perception
Question 13: Did you use LabG@me during the course? 1 - Very frequently 2 - Sometimes 3 - Never	Experience with LabG@me
Question 14: The activities proposed within LabG@me were useful for your study? 1 - Yes 2 - More Yes than No 3 - More No than Yes 4 – No	Experience with LabG@me
Question 15: In your opinion, with the use of LabG@me games, the transmission of concepts and the understanding of topics was: 1 - Better than of a traditional course 2 - Similar to a traditional course 3 - Worse than a traditionally course	Experience with LabG@me
Question 16: Which technological device did you mainly use to connect and play on LabG@me? 1 – Notebook 2 – Desktop pc 3 – Smartphone 4 – Tablet	Experience with LabG@me
Question 17: At the end of the course, how do you rate your level of competence on the deepen topics? 1 - Better than the initial level 2 - Same as the initial level 3 - Worse than the initial level	Experience with LabG@me

Continued on following page

Table 3. Continued

Question	Dimension
Question 18: What did you appreciate about LabG@me? 1 - The possibility to learn using games 2 - The possibility of competing with your colleagues 3 - Being able to review topics without having to ask the teacher 4 - The clarity and simplicity of use 5 - The possibility of seeing the points scored and the updated ranking in real time	Experience with LabG@me
Question 19: Please, on a scale from 1 to 5, indicate how motivating and stimulating the course you attended was: 1 – Not at all stimulating 2 – Slightly stimulating 3 – Moderately stimulating 4 – Very stimulating 5 – Extremely stimulating	Experience with LabG@me
Question 20: Would you like to follow courses in the future that use games and environments similar to LabG@me? 1 - Yes, I would like very much 2 - It doesn't matter 3 - No, I prefer a course run in the traditional way	Experience with LabG@me
Question 21: Please, add your suggestions on the the Course and about the LabG@me platform.	Experience with LabG@me

Chapter 6
User–Centered Virtual Reality Environments for Elementary School Children in Times of COVID–19

Héctor Cardona-Reyes
https://orcid.org/0000-0002-9626-6254
Center for Research in Mathematics, Mexico

Miguel Angel Ortiz Esparza
Universidad Autónoma de Aguascalientes, Mexico

ABSTRACT

Derived from the current situation, in which physical contact and closeness between people must be taken care of due to COVID-19, emerging technologies such as virtual reality have taken a fundamental role in continuing with activities in various areas of society. This chapter proposes the use of virtual reality environments as an alternative for the acquisition of learning skills for children in an immersive and interactive way with user-centered content. The design elements of the software, the user-centered aspects, and the involved actors considered for the production of the proposed interactive virtual reality environments are presented. As a result, the evaluation of the user experience resulting from the use of the proposed interactive environments with elementary school children is presented. Virtual reality is a technology that nowadays can be an effective support for the acquisition of learning skills through the execution of various tasks designed by a multidisciplinary group and above all encourages the user to continue acquiring learning skills in a friendly and fun way.

INTRODUCTION

With the constant evolution of information and communication technologies, education has been transformed. This new technological revolution has caused a digital transformation in the school curriculum

DOI: 10.4018/978-1-7998-9732-3.ch006

and in the way of presenting content, being increasingly dynamic, increasing interactivity on the part of students, thus achieving positive benefits and an increase in school performance (Ocete et al., 2003; Yu-Che & Yi-Ru, 2019).

However, the development of these new technologies has generated some drawbacks when incorporating them into the classroom. For example, teachers are not prepared for the use and application of technologies in the classroom. Teachers must be updated and take ownership of the tools and then bring them to the classroom. That the design of new learning environments is according to the learning context and existing technologies (Llorente et al., 2018).

This is mainly due to the variety of learning styles and the generation of content that does not have enough attributes to fit the student's needs, thus not generating a learning experience (Buzio et al., 2017). In this sense, according to (Ferreiro, 2006), it is not about inserting the new into the old or continuing to do the same with current technologies. It is about having personalized attention from teachers.

In the context of the COVID-19 pandemic, the use of technology allows students and teachers to continue with their classes from home or any safe place, even flexible schedules can be established to continue learning. This type of modality also implies that the student must take the role of self-directed and learn simultaneously and asynchronously at any time (Maatuk et al., 2021).

However, other challenges derived from this situation may emerge and special attention should be paid to them, ranging from lack of technological resources, reliability in e-learning, misuse of technology, lack of face-to-face learning experience, among others. Therefore, when incorporating technology in the teaching-learning process, the greatest possible consideration should be taken to ensure its correct adoption (Yuhanna et al., 2020).

In this sense, virtual reality has been an alternative that allows the transmission of knowledge in an immersive and interactive way where it can help to have a positive effect on both teachers and students by creating a motivating effect and fostering a learning environment in which they can safely explore fictional scenarios from anywhere. It also allows students to establish concrete thinking about their experiences within virtual reality (Upayanto & Wuryandani, 2020).

Derived from the current situation, in which physical contact and closeness between people must be taken care of due to COVID-19 (Cabezas, 2021), these technologies have taken a fundamental role to continue activities in various areas of society (Burgess & Sievertsen, 2020; Daniel, 2020).

In the case of elementary education, this is not exempt from these technological changes and global scenarios of today, so the existing learning theories are constantly susceptible to adaptations in order to continue with the teaching processes. It is also important to consider that within the classroom there is a diversity of students with different needs and therefore must be taken into account (Dean, 2002).

As a solution to this current situation, the development of user-centered virtual reality environments will allow offering virtual reality environments that contribute to student learning and that is based on the special needs in their education, through the creation of a development model that allows generating virtual reality components with a gamification approach for learning environments (Alsawaier, 2018; Buzio et al., 2017; Vera et al., 2005). Having these innovation strategies, in addition, can lead educators to design resources based on students' needs and competencies so that they can be a complement to learning (Dalgarno, 2002).

This work presents a model for the production of virtual reality environments as a complement to the teaching-learning process in primary school children through scenarios defined by a multidisciplinary team and a user-centered approach for students to build knowledge using virtual reality environments.

This work is composed of seven sections, then the theoretical foundations related to the proposal are presented, then a section of related works, the existing initiatives to generate virtual reality environments are presented and discussed, the problem section presents the challenges for the production of virtual reality environments according to the context of the user, section five presents a proposed model for the production of virtual reality environments according to the needs, the context of the user and design elements. The discussion section describes the advantages and challenges of the proposal, technological considerations, and adoption within the classroom. Finally, a section of conclusions and future work is presented.

BACKGROUND

Virtual Reality

Virtual reality is a technology that today can be an effective support for the acquisition of learning skills through the execution of various tasks designed by a multidisciplinary group and above all encouraging the user to continue acquiring learning skills in a friendly and fun way.

Virtual reality today is present in various fields of application, such as (Council, 2020):

- Real-time medical education: through proposals that help training and simulation with gamification strategies that allow the student to practice from anywhere and under conditions of surgery, rehabilitation, and various scenarios that represent medical treatments (Council, 2020).
- Handling of hazardous materials: virtual reality allows technicians to perform training where they can use machines to move hazardous materials, radioactive and various pollutants, and follow safety protocols to prevent accidents (Council, 2020).
- Collaborative work: virtual reality allows several people to collaborate remotely in a shared environment where they can establish meetings, brainstorming, among other activities, all in a virtual scenario where avatars can be used to make the experience enjoyable (Council, 2020).
- Virtual exhibitions and entertainment: virtual reality gives the possibility of having 3D scenarios where you can hold exhibitions of artistic works, virtual tours, visits to museums, among others.
- Gamification of fitness: in recent years virtual reality has been oriented to gamify physical activities in a dynamic and fun way, taking advantage of the benefits offered by virtual reality viewers. Applications such as Beat Saber, Box VR allow a person to perform physical activity in an immersive and playful way (Council, 2020).
- Virtual reality in education: virtual reality has spread to schools to offer contents that represent teaching and learning situations. In addition, it has been oriented to the study of various disorders suffered by children during their school age, such as Attention Deficit Hyperactivity Disorder (ADHD), Autism Spectrum Disorder (ASD), learning disabilities, among others (Council, 2020).

Virtual reality allows the user to interact with computer-generated 3D elements and offers an immersive experience to the user where they can experience a sense of realism when interacting with all the elements of the system (Biocca & Delaney, 1995; Mandal, 2013). According to (Bashiri et al., 2017) the benefits of virtual reality consist of providing real-time feedback to the user, offering safety when interacting with the 3D scenarios presented, and incorporation of natural movements such as gestures and movement patterns for the user to interact with the 3D objects. Therefore, virtual reality-based solutions offer (Parsons et al., 2007; Yeh et al., 2012):

- Create virtual environments that adapt to the user's needs.
- Simulate training dynamics that are safe and close to the real experience.
- Provide stability between users and stimuli.
- Allow the user to express him/herself naturally within the virtual environment.
- Have a complete record of patient behaviors and functionalities.
- Save time and costs.
- Provide a more entertaining tool to motivate patients to use this technology.

Virtual Reality Environments in the School Context

In the school context, students in the classroom face several challenges ranging from having adequate content for learning to have access to technological means to carry out their activities. In addition to this, today's global factors such as the health restrictions of the COVID-19 pandemic have caused students to become frustrated and opt for dropping out of school (Pachay-López & Rodríguez-Gámez, 2021).

Nowadays, the transmission of knowledge is not limited only to the theoretical knowledge provided by the teacher; the student must be responsible and co-responsible for constructing knowledge, understanding it, and applying it in real-life situations. To achieve this, they rely on various technologies and new forms of interaction that allow them to develop and realize meaningful learning through the resolution of practical problems (Bellocchio Albornoz, 2009).

Virtual reality, by offering a high degree of immersion to the user and a variety of interaction possibilities when performing a task, can help the student to abstract objects and cognitive processes that are difficult to visualize or imagine and concepts that are difficult to represent or explain verbally (Sanchez et al., 2000). They also offer the advantage of addressing areas where traditional methods have little or no presence (Bell & Fogler, 1995).

Based on the 5 dimensions of (Felder et al., 1988), virtual reality environments can help the student to adapt to different learning styles, among which we can find:

- Sensorial-Intuitive: The sensorial where sensorial ones prefer to be patient with details referring to experimental facts and intuitive ones prefer concepts and theories being faster, but neglecting details.
- Visual-Verbal: Visuals prefer images and graphic elements, verbal's lean more towards texts, discussions, explanations, etc.
- Deductive-Inductive: Deductive ones from observations formulate principles and observations. Inductive learners start from guiding principles and consequently develop applications.
- Active learning by doing and participating. Reflective learning by thinking and reflecting.
- Sequential-Global: Sequential learners learn step-by-step, gaining a partial understanding. Global learners get a representation of the big picture in order to understand the topic.
- Active-Reflective: Active learners learn by doing and participating. Reflective learners think or reflect introspectively.

According to (Jimenez et al., 2000), there are learning situations in which an adaptation of traditional training to training using virtual reality can be established. These situations are presented in Table 1 below.

Table 1. Comparison between different teaching situations, traditional vs. virtual reality

Learning Situation	Traditional	Virtual reality
Fully Synchronous	Typical class session involving a trainer and several students.	The class meets via the Internet in an immersive environment and participants present ideas using audio, text, virtual elements in real-time.
Partially Synchronous	Groups of students meet outside of class time to complete an assignment.	Groups of students, using immersive environments to perform a task.
Asynchronous	Students perform assigned tasks individually, mainly reading and writing assignments that they submit to the teacher.	Students perform assigned tasks individually using immersive environments in which they then have to report their experience to the teacher.

Adapted from (de Antonio Jimenez et al., 2000).

Virtual reality environments can offer the means of interaction and the representation of previous situations as the possibility of building new ones considering their cultural and social environment solving problems with practical sense. In addition, the teaching activity is also supported with the promotion of new ways of learning so that the student can develop their capacity and concretize meaningful learning (Velásquez, 2017).

It is therefore important to identify and consider the cases in which virtual reality can be used within the classroom. Some of these are when (Ball et al., 2021; de Antonio Jimenez et al., 2000; Pantelidis, 1996):

- A simulation can be performed.
- When real-world teaching can represent a risk that is impossible to perform.
- When significant errors can occur in the real world.
- When you want to highlight the knowledge in an interactive, attractive way, offer an experience where the student can develop their manual and physical skills.
- When it is required to create learning experiences that can include people with disabilities that otherwise would not be possible.

RELATED WORK

In the literature, we can find proposals that have tried to integrate ICT into educational processes. In this sense, virtual reality as an emerging technology has taken relevance to be part of the educational processes modifying the learning theories used to develop virtual reality scenarios. The following are some proposals with the potential to create interactive environments in which students can learn representations of various concepts and support learning.

The SIMX platform (SIMX, 2020), through virtual reality users, can experience various training scenarios ranging from military medical assistance, surgeries, COVID-19 patient care protocols, among others. Figure 1 presents a scenario of the SIMX simulation environment.

Figure 1. SIMX Medical Simulation Environment (SIMX, 2020), video available at https://youtu. be/2RYQeSxPWa0

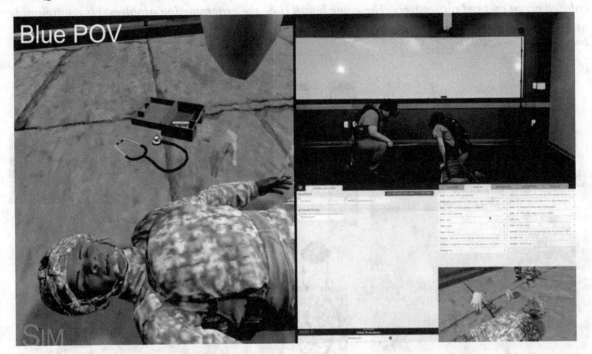

Authors such as (Kim et al., 2019) propose mixed reality programming learning platforms where the user must write a program that creates a path to guide his avatar to a goal. This program is built through instructions or commands given in the platform interface and to execute the code the user is involved by physically moving the avatar following the instructions he created, while the system tracks the movements in real-time generating visual feedback of code errors, helping users to identify them faster and reduce the cognitive load.

Figure 2. Mixed reality programming learning platform. The system tracks the avatar's movement in real-time (with image tracking), to give immediate visual feedback. Correct and incorrect code blocks are colored green and red respectively. The game board (i.e., the programming problems) is configurable, as are all virtual objects
Image by (Kim et al., 2019)

(Seo et al., 2017) presents a virtual reality system called Anatomy Builder VR and is intended to support the teaching of anatomy. The authors take as a basis an alternative constructivist pedagogical model for learning canine anatomy. In Anatomy Builder students identify and assemble bones in live animal orientation, using real thoracic limb bones in a digital limb bone box. The results of their study led them to conclude that participants enjoy interacting with the anatomical content within the virtual reality program.

Figure 3. Example of the use of the Anatomy Builder VR system, under the HTC VIVE platform
Image by (Seo et al., 2017)

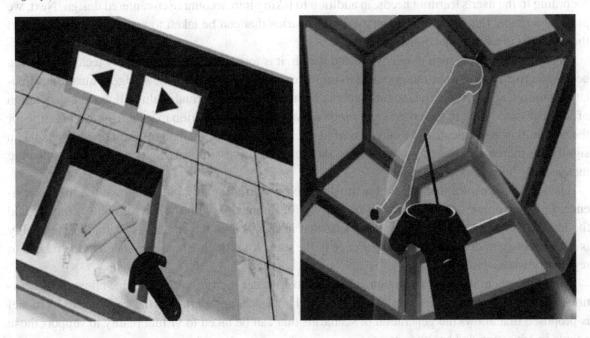

The virtual reality game Job Simulator (Labs, 2019) allows the user to play various roles in different scenarios where work activities must be performed, such as a mechanical workshop, a self-service store, a kitchen, an office, among others. The user through physical controls can interact with the objects around him to accomplish the tasks indicated by intelligent avatars.

Figure 4. Example of an office scenario within the virtual reality game Job Simulator
Image by (Labs, 2019)

These proposals lead us to reflect on the need for design guides that allow the generation of scenarios according to the user's learning needs, in addition to taking into account user-centered design. Next, we propose a model that allows the generation of scenarios that can be taken to virtual reality to support those people in educational contexts.

In application fields such as education and health, it is foreseen that virtual reality technologies can be an effective support to be incorporated to improve processes related to knowledge acquisition, simulated training, task completion, among others. With the ease that virtual reality allows the generation of scenarios according to the criteria and needs of each expert, in addition to establishing a baseline for the creation, improvement, and evaluation of application scenarios. Although virtual reality has had a significant increase in recent years allowing devices to be accessible and low cost to users, allowing increasingly immersive content.

One of the obstacles that persist for the adoption of virtual reality is to improve the user experience, i.e., the complexity of the hardware, the way of interaction with the virtual reality content, and the immersive experience. Another obstacle is that in many cases the content is scarce, or the quality is not necessary to offer a pleasant experience to the user. And finally, there are other aspects related to regulatory issues, risks, etc.

Therefore, there is a need for design guidelines to consider the various factors that allow the generation of scenarios, such as user experience and natural interfaces appropriate to the user's needs. A model is proposed that allows the generation of scenarios that can be taken to virtual reality to support those people in education and health contexts.

PROBLEM OUTLINE

The use of virtual reality solutions is becoming more and more common and the demand is increasing. This opens a door to consider it as an alternative within the educational context, either for its high interactivity, ease of representation of content, its motivating factor to the user, its versatility among other aspects. In this way, we seek to promote its adoption as an alternative and support for classroom teaching and that can be a support for situations such as those experienced today due to the COVID-19 pandemic.

Therefore, it is important to pay attention to the factors that lead to the production of this type of solutions according to the needs of the required context, the needs of the users, the reduction of the number of errors, the reduction of cognitive work, and foster ease of learning (Guzman Mendoza et al., 2019; Stanziola et al., 2014). Some of the challenges in producing user-centered virtual reality environments are (Ortiz-Aguinaga et al., 2020):

- Identify multidisciplinary teams formed by experts, technologists, and users.
- Identify how virtual reality can be adopted in the classroom.
- Raise awareness among teachers, students and look for technological alternatives that may be within their reach, such as mobile devices, cardboard, among others.
- Identify user skills to design user interaction within the virtual reality scenario.
- Determine the design artifacts and virtual reality elements appropriate to the user's needs.
- Define UX evaluation strategies that allow the constant improvement of virtual reality environments.

The following section presents a model for the production of virtual reality environments that takes into account aspects of virtual reality design, the stakeholders involved, the forms of interaction of the system with the user, the context of the application, and feedback strategies such as the evaluation of the user's experience.

PROPOSED MODEL

This section presents a proposed model for the production of user-centered virtual reality environments. It also presents some examples of virtual reality environments produced for elementary school children which are described under the stages of the proposed model.

This model responds to the need for strategies that allow education specialists, teachers, and technologists to produce solutions that can support the learning needs that take place in the classroom.

This model is mainly based on the multidisciplinary work of the various stakeholders involved in the creation of virtual environments and in which the user-centered approach will allow the identification of target users according to their skills and learning needs, and then propose virtual scenarios that can be put into practice by teachers and students as part of their activities. In addition to having elements that allow an evaluation of both the user experience on the content presented, as well as feedback on the virtual environment itself.

Figure 5. User-centered model for the production of virtual reality environments

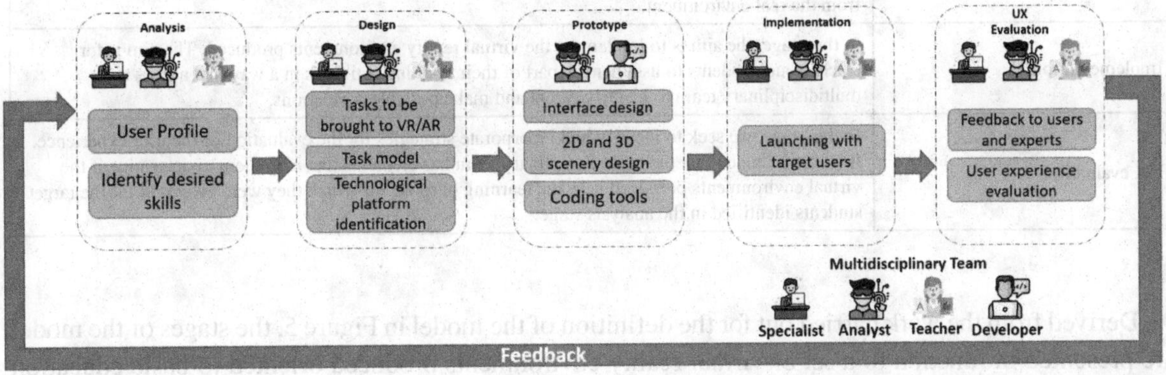

The model shown in Figure 5 is composed of 5 stages and in each of them, various stakeholders participate in its design. The following is a description of the identified stakeholders that make up the model's multidisciplinary team:

- Specialists: is composed of education specialists such as pedagogues, psychologists, and education experts.
- Analyst: software analyst captures the user's needs and abstracts the requirements to generate a design of the interactive environment in a computational context and terms of virtual reality so that it can then be taken to coding by the developer.

- Teacher: Provides the contents and defines the guidelines for the teaching-learning process under which the interactive environment will be based, as well as helping to identify the children's skills and needs to be taken to the virtual environment.
- Developer: is responsible for identifying the appropriate platforms and coding tools according to the requirements identified by the software analyst

Table 2 below presents a description of each of the stages of the model shown in Figure 5.

Table 2. Description of the stages of the model for the production of virtual reality environments

Stage	Description
Analysis	This stage seeks to define the user profile and identify the skills of the target users. For this, the multidisciplinary work in this stage includes education specialists, teachers, and software technologists, in order to know the activities and contents that are carried out in the classroom and determine which can be taken to virtual reality and can be a support to the learning needs.
Design	In this stage, with the identification of the user profile and the contents used by teachers and specialists in the previous stage, it is possible to determine those tasks that can be carried out in virtual reality scenarios. Therefore, for their design, task models can be generated to know the different interactions that the user will have with the system so that the multidisciplinary team can determine if these task designs are adequate for the profiles indicated in the previous stage. Finally, the identification of the technological platforms that may be appropriate and that above all may be accessible to both teachers and students within the learning context is addressed.
Prototype	In this stage, based on the designs obtained in the previous stage. Software developers and analysts determine the user interfaces of the virtual reality environments, the 2D and 3D objects within the virtual scenario, the interactions of these objects with the user, and the dynamics that are represented from the real environment.
Implementation	In this stage, the aim is to implement the virtual reality environments produced. The aim is for teachers and students to use them as part of their learning activities in a way that allows the multidisciplinary team to identify errors and make possible corrections.
UX evaluation	In this stage, we seek to identify and incorporate strategies for the evaluation of the user experience. It is also intended that the multidisciplinary team has elements that help them to determine if the virtual environments produced help the learning purpose for which they were proposed for the target students identified in the analysis stage.

Derived from the work carried out for the definition of the model in Figure 5, the stages of the model are presented in function to a set of virtual reality environments produced oriented to basic education students. These environments met the need for multidisciplinary teams formed to support children with diverse learning needs during the health contingency period due to the COVID-19 pandemic. This situation allowed to take advantage of the developed environments and they could be implemented in basic education institutions in Mexico.

Table 3 presents a description of the virtual reality environments in which the proposed model served as a basis for their development.

Table 3. Virtual reality environments developed the proposed model oriented to elementary education

VR environment	Description	Target
Memorama VR	It is a virtual reality environment oriented to children of basic education in order that they can develop their skills in learning syllables and words in an interactive way through 3D objects and representations of objects.	Elementary education children of the first and second grades. Elementary education children with language problems.
Drone simulator	This virtual reality environment is oriented to develop the student's skills in basic drone piloting. This environment presents tasks that the user must perform according to recreational user training. Another objective is to have a safe and low-cost environment in which the user can fly a drone in a fun way and go through various obstacles.	Elementary education children from 5th grade and up. Secondary school children High school students.
Puzzle VR	This virtual reality environment is oriented to elementary school children with attention problems. The environment consists of solving a puzzle with cards, each card shows an element in 3D and the total of these cards represents the scene to be solved.	Elementary education students of all grades. Elementary education students with attention problems.

For the development of these virtual reality environments, several educational and health institutions in Mexico were involved, which allowed the model to have several multidisciplinary teams.

To carry out the research work in each of the cases, formal requests were made in each of the institutions in order to conduct interviews with specialists and teachers. In the case of the participating children and groups, requests for the consent of both parents and authorities of the institutions were made.

The following is a description of each of the stages that make up the proposed model, presenting artifacts of the virtual reality environments described in Table 3:

Analysis

In this stage, the teaching process carried out in elementary education institutions is identified. The stakeholders involved are identified, such as specialists, teachers, and software analysts. They work together to know the dynamics carried out in class by teachers, the contents used in class, and if the specialists have evaluations for student follow-up. The user profile of the students who will use the proposed virtual reality environment is also identified. With these initial elements, the software analyst can identify those activities that can be taken to a virtual reality context and propose an initial technological platform on which the proposed virtual reality environment will be executed.

Figure 6. Example of contents used by experts and teachers of USAER-19 Aguascalientes, Mexico, in 4th-grade elementary school children

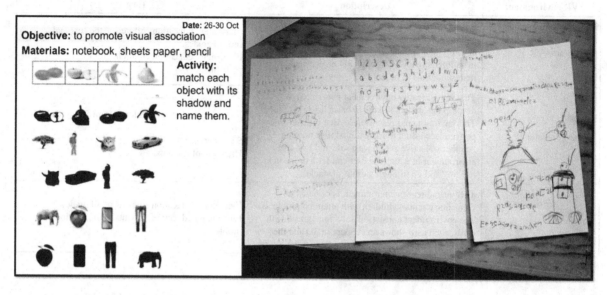

Figure 6 shows some examples of materials used by teachers and experts from the Regular Education Support Services Unit (Unidad de Servicios de Apoyo a la Educación Regular USAER-19) in Mexico with students in 4th grade of elementary education as part of the support provided to mitigate educational backwardness and identify learning problems in the classroom.

It is also important to identify the current conditions of the teaching process in the institutions since with the guidelines established by the health institutions there are sanitary protocols to follow. This is important to consider since the proposed virtual environments and the proposed platforms must comply with the established health protocols for their use. Figure 7 presents the dynamics in a classroom of an elementary education institution under the health protocols established for the COVID-19 contingency. These include having small groups, taking the temperature of each of the students and teachers, keeping a distance, using masks, and applying the antibacterial gel, among other measures.

Figure 7. Dynamics carried out in the classroom in elementary education students

Design

The design stage translates the requirements identified in the analysis stage into a set of software artifacts needed to design the virtual reality environment. In this stage, the specialists and teachers collaborate with the software analyst to:

- Identify the appropriate technology according to the user profile.
- The interaction strategies with which the user will interact within the virtual environment are designed. These can be based on the use of gestures, use of devices such as controls, body movements, etc. It is worth mentioning that the definition of the interaction will depend on the user's skills, so experts and teachers will be an important support for the software analyst to determine the appropriate design.
- Identify the virtual scenarios based on the educational content.
- Establish the modeling of user tasks.

It is also important at this stage to determine the learning strategies (Bueno & Fitzgerald, 2004; H.-M. Huang et al., 2010) under which the virtual reality environment will be governed. These strategies may consist of role-playing, the collaboration between users within the virtual environment, strategies based on problem-solving, among others.

Figure 8. Example of task modeling under the CTT notation for a virtual environment for teaching drone piloting to recreational users

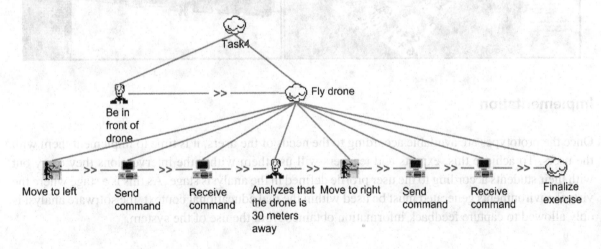

Figure 8 presents an example of task modeling under the Concur Task Tree (CTT) notation (Paternò, 2004) for a virtual environment proposed for teaching drone piloting through virtual reality environments oriented to recreational users such as teenagers and children (Trujillo-Espinoza et al., 2020). The modeling of Figure 8 presents the various interactions identified to carry out a task within the virtual environments. The actions are the responsibility of the user, those that are delegated to the system, and those that depend on specific processing.

Prototype

At this stage, the software analyst and the developer collaborate to carry out the section of the appropriate software components according to the established design to generate the prototype of the virtual reality environment. This phase may even incorporate other roles such as multimedia designers to produce 3D models, sounds, and representations of objects that will be part of the scenario in which the user will perform their tasks.

Figure 9 shows 2 examples of prototype development under the Unity3D platform (Unity3D, n.d.). The image on the left shows the virtual environment "Memorama" based on augmented reality (Videla Rodríguez et al., 2017) oriented to the development of cognitive skills in elementary education children receiving speech therapy (Redondo Romero, 2008). The image on the right shows the design of an avatar of the virtual environment called "Attention-VR", which is oriented to elementary school children who present characteristics associated with Attention deficit hyperactivity disorder (ADHD).

Figure 9. Example of prototype design of virtual reality environments under the Unity3D platform. (left) Virtual environment representing a memorama game in augmented reality. (right) Avatar design and programming

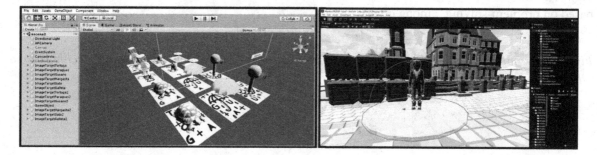

Implementation

Once the prototypes are available according to the needs of the users, it is time to implement them with the users. To achieve this, experts and teachers will use them within the interventions they carry out with their students according to the user profile defined in the analysis stage. As this is a stage where the virtual environments generated must be used within the real educational context, the software analyst is only allowed to capture feedback information obtained from the use of the system.

Figure 10. Example of the implementation stage of virtual reality environments. The student can use the various virtual environments at home as a complement to school learning. Students in class under the guidance of the teacher use virtual environments to support classroom learning

Figure 10 presents 2 examples of implementation of the virtual reality environments produced. One scenario may consist of the child being able to use these environments at home and the parents being the guide for supervision and correct use. A second scenario is for teachers to use these environments as part of the teaching-learning process in the classroom. The selection of these settings will depend on the health conditions established by the COVID-19 pandemic for educational institutions.

Feedback and UX Evaluation

Feedback is an essential part when implementing interactive environments as part of learning, it is expected that these can contribute to the development of knowledge of the students for whom they were designed. In this sense, teachers and specialists as part of the multidisciplinary team must carry out strategies to maintain constant feedback and monitoring of children using virtual reality environments. Figure 11 presents some examples of evaluations made to basic education students as part of their learning process.

Figure 11. Examples of evaluations performed by teachers and specialists on 4th-grade basic education children. On the left is an example of a language acquisition assessment. On the right, an example of an assessment of mathematical thinking acquisition

The evaluation of the user experience allows to increase the overall level of satisfaction that a user has with the virtual reality environments produced, this allows the user to obtain a benefit and integrate these solutions as part of their daily activities. According to (Farrell, 2017) there are several considerations when considering user experience evaluation. Some of these considerations include understanding the user-related processes and the actual generation of virtual reality environments, identifying the necessary resources, testing the virtual environments created with identified potential users, and finally collecting user feedback after participating in testing. Some of the instruments used for user experience evaluation are presented below.

- UEQ(User Experience Questionnaire (Schrepp et al., 2014): the questionnaire scales cover an overall impression of the user experience. Both the classic aspects of usability (effectiveness, insight, reliability) and those of user experience (originality, stimulation) are measured.
- SUS (System Usability Scale) (Lewis, 2018): enables the evaluation of a wide variety of products and services, such as hardware, software, mobile devices, websites, and applications.
- UMUX(Usability Metric for User Experience) (Lewis, 2018): aims to measure perceived usability using fewer items that more closely match the ISO 9241 definition of usability.
- AttrakDif (Hassenzahl et al., 2003): allows determining the emotional impact on the evaluation of a product.

DISCUSSION

This work presents a proposed model for the production of virtual reality environments. The context of this model is that it can serve as a support for the generation of these environments derived from the current health contingency COVID-19.

During this contingency, it was possible to work with several basic education institutions and it was possible to observe the need to offer solutions based on technology that would allow the personnel of these schools to continue under the sanitary restrictive conditions.

It was also possible to identify different types of users who were strongly affected in their knowledge acquisition process by the pandemic. These groups are composed of students who have a disability, learning disability, or disorder and who received personalized attention from school staff.

These findings also helped to orient the model towards a user-centered approach, since this implies mainly considering knowing the end-users, designing products that fit the needs and capabilities of these users, as well as establishing evaluation and feedback strategies.

Although this work addresses the model for the production of virtual reality environments, this is a technology that is little known or unknown in most educational institutions. However, during the interventions carried out, it was possible to carry out awareness-raising and research work with multidisciplinary groups in order to encourage the adoption of this type of technology within the educational context.

It should also be recognized that the technological and adoption aspect is a part that must be constantly worked on because although virtual reality can be attractive for professionals and educators as part of their teaching work, several factors are ranging from lack of budget or spaces for its incorporation to the resistance of the educational staff. Therefore, the benefits and disadvantages of virtual reality must be made aware of its benefits and disadvantages for its correct adoption.

In this sense, the work presented had as a premise the awareness of the multidisciplinary team and for the design and production of the proposed virtual reality environments, the analysis of the available and accessible technology was a key point so that they could be used by students and teachers.

CONCLUSION AND FUTURE WORK

This work presents the proposal of a model for the production of virtual reality environments oriented to the needs of the users, particularly for the production of environments oriented to primary school children as an alternative to strengthen the teaching-learning strategies that have been affected by the health measures imposed by the COVID-19 pandemic.

Under the proposed model, the design elements considered in each of the stages presented are presented and emphasis is placed on the conformation of multidisciplinary teams integrated by experts in education, teachers, and specialists in software design. The presentation of the model during this work is complemented with several examples of design artifacts in each of the stages presented. These examples are the result of the research work and the generation of several virtual reality environments proposed to teachers and institutions from different educational centers in Mexico.

The challenge of this proposal is to continue improving the model by incorporating new design elements, new actors to identify new needs within the teaching-learning process, and strategies so that the virtual environments produced can have a variety of scenarios according to the existing contents in education.

The benefits of the model are that it is a model adaptable to different technologies such as virtual or augmented reality, involves the formation of multidisciplinary teams to better identify the needs of users, and establishes user profiles and evaluation and feedback strategies in a precise manner.

The model during this research served as a starting point to raise awareness and encourage the use of emerging technologies within the educational context. Thus, each of the institutions involved was able to perform an analysis of their capabilities to define a strategy for the adoption of both technology and the personnel involved.

There are also several improvements identified for the model, these include considering specific criteria for different learning styles found in the classroom, as well as strategies to train educational staff in emerging technologies, the incorporation of evaluation instruments used by teachers and specialists to be part of virtual reality environments, among others.

Regarding virtual reality, several studies are still underway to define the feasibility of virtual reality for children and the problems that may arise from its use. Therefore, the model should consider these implications and count on continuous improvements (Freina & Ott, 2015; H. M. Huang et al., 2010; Ocete et al., 2003; Vera et al., 2005; Yamada-Rice et al., 2017).

Although the model is a starting proposal, the future work and challenges are vast, so it is necessary to propose new case studies in which evaluations of the user experience can be carried out in order to know the perception of both teachers and children and to be able to design mechanisms for continuous improvement.

REFERENCES

Alsawaier, R. S. (2018). The effect of gamification on motivation and engagement. *The International Journal of Information and Learning Technology*.

Ball, C., Huang, K.-T., & Francis, J. (2021). Virtual reality adoption during the COVID-19 pandemic: A uses and gratifications perspective. *Telematics and Informatics, 65*, 101728. doi:10.1016/j.tele.2021.101728 PMID:34887619

Bashiri, A., Ghazisaeedi, M., & Shahmoradi, L. (2017). The opportunities of virtual reality in the rehabilitation of children with attention deficit hyperactivity disorder: A literature review. *Korean Journal of Pediatrics, 60*(11), 337. doi:10.3345/kjp.2017.60.11.337 PMID:29234356

Bell, J. T., & Fogler, H. S. (1995). The investigation and application of virtual reality as an educational tool. *Proceedings of the American Society for Engineering Education Annual Conference*, 1718–1728.

Bellocchio Albornoz, M. (2009). Competency-based education and constructivism. An approach and a model for pedagogical training in the 21st century. *Issue F, 378*, B4.

Biocca, F., & Delaney, B. (1995). Immersive virtual reality technology. *Communication in the Age of Virtual Reality, 15*, 32.

Bueno, P. M., & Fitzgerald, V. L. (2004). Problem-based learning. *Theoria: Science, Arts and Humanities, 13*. https://campus.usal.es/~ofeees/NUEVAS_METODOLOGIAS/ABP/13.pdf

Burgess, S., & Sievertsen, H. H. (2020). *Schools, skills, and learning: The impact of COVID-19 on education*. Academic Press.

Buzio, A., Chiesa, M., & Toppan, R. (2017). Virtual reality for special educational needs. *Proceedings of the 2017 ACM Workshop on Intelligent Interfaces for Ubiquitous and Smart Learning*, 7–10. 10.1145/3038535.3038541

Cabezas, C. (2020). COVID-19 pandemic: Storms and challenges. *Rev Peru Med Exp Public Health., 37*(4), 603–604. doi:10.17843/rpmesp.2020.374.6866 PMID:33566897

Council, F. T. (2020). *15 Effective Uses Of Virtual Reality For Businesses And Consumers*. https://www.forbes.com/sites/forbestechcouncil/2020/02/12/15-effective-uses-of-virtual-reality-for-businesses-and-consumers/?sh=469c9d52f2b2

Dalgarno, B. (2002). The potential of 3D virtual learning environments: A constructivist analysis. *Electronic Journal of Instructional Science and Technology, 5*(2), 3–6.

Daniel, J. (2020). Education and the COVID-19 pandemic. *Prospects, 49*(1), 91–96. doi:10.100711125-020-09464-3 PMID:32313309

Dean, A. (2002). Telelearning: Invention, Innovation Implications: Towards a Manifesto. *Australasian Journal of Educational Technology, 5*(2), 1–12.

Farrell, S. (2017). *UX Research Cheat Sheet*. Interaction Design Foundation. https://www.nngroup.com/articles/ux%5C-research%5C-cheat%5C-sheet/

Felder, R. M., Silverman, L. K., & ... (1988). Learning and teaching styles in engineering education. *Engineering Education, 78*(7), 674–681.

Ferreiro, R. F. (2006). The challenge of education in the 21st century: The N-Generation. *Apertura (Guadalajara, Jal.), 5*.

Freina, L., & Ott, M. (2015). A literature review on immersive virtual reality in education: State of the art and perspectives. *Proceedings of ELearning and Software for Education (ELSE), 8*. doi:10.12753/2066-026X-15-020

Guzman Mendoza, J. E., Munoz Arteaga, J., Cardona Reyes, H., & Zapata Gonzalez, A. (2019). Digital Divide Strategy Based-on ICT Services Model. *Proceedings - 2019 International Conference on Inclusive Technologies and Education, CONTIE 2019*. 10.1109/CONTIE49246.2019.00013

Hassenzahl, M., Burmester, M., & Koller, F. (2003). AttrakDiff: A questionnaire to measure perceived hedonic and pragmatic quality. *Mensch & Computer, 57*, 187–196.

Huang, H.-M., Rauch, U., & Liaw, S.-S. (2010). Investigating learners' attitudes toward virtual reality learning environments: Based on a constructivist approach. *Computers & Education, 55*(3), 1171–1182.

Huang, H. M., Rauch, U., & Liaw, S. S. (2010). Investigating learners' attitudes toward virtual reality learning environments: Based on a constructivist approach. *Computers & Education, 55*(3), 1171–1182. doi:10.1016/j.compedu.2010.05.014

Jiménez, A. A., Abarca, M. V., & Ramírez, E. L. (2000). When and how to use Virtual Reality in Teaching. *IE Comunicaciones: Iberoamerican Journal of Educational Informatics, 16*, 4.

Kim, J., Agarwal, S., Marotta, K., Li, S., Leo, J., & Chau, D. H. (2019). Mixed reality for learning programming. *Proceedings of the 18th ACM International Conference on Interaction Design and Children, IDC 2019, 2*, 574–579. 10.1145/3311927.3325335

LabsO. (2019). *JobSimulator*. https://jobsimulatorgame.com/

Lewis, J. R. (2018). Measuring perceived usability: The CSUQ, SUS, and UMUX. *International Journal of Human-Computer Interaction, 34*(12), 1148–1156. doi:10.1080/10447318.2017.1418805

Llorente, J. G. S., Córdoba, Y. A. P., & Mora, B. R. (2018). Causes of difficulties in incorporating ICT in the classroom. *Panorama, 12*(22), 31–41. Available at: https://www.redalyc.org/articulo.oa?id=343968243004

Maatuk, A. M., Elberkawi, E. K., Aljawarneh, S., Rashaideh, H., & Alharbi, H. (2021). The COVID-19 pandemic and E-learning: Challenges and opportunities from the perspective of students and instructors. *Journal of Computing in Higher Education*. Advance online publication. doi:10.100712528-021-09274-2 PMID:33967563

Mandal, S. (2013). Brief introduction of virtual reality & its challenges. *International Journal of Scientific \& Engineering Research, 4*(4), 304–309.

Ocete, G. V., Carrillo, J. A. O., & González, M. Á. B. (2003). Virtual reality and its didactic possibilities. *Etic@ net. Scientific Electronic Journal of Education and Communication in the Knowledge Society,* (2), 12.

Ortiz-Aguinaga, G., Cardona-Reyes, H., Muñoz-Arteaga, J., & Barba-Gonzalez, M. L. (2020). Model for the Generation of Scenarios in Virtual Reality Applied in Health. *2020 3rd International Conference of Inclusive Technology and Education (CONTIE)*, 154–161.

Pachay-López, M., & Rodríguez-Gámez, M. (2021). Dropping out of school: A complex perspective in times of pandemic. *Polo del Conocimiento*, 6(1), 130–155. doi:10.23857/pc.v6i1.2129

Pantelidis, V. S. (1996). Suggestions on when to use and when not to use virtual reality in education. *VR in the Schools*, 2(1), 18.

Parsons, T. D., Bowerly, T., Buckwalter, J. G., & Rizzo, A. A. (2007). A controlled clinical comparison of attention performance in children with ADHD in a virtual reality classroom compared to standard neuropsychological methods. *Child Neuropsychology*, 13(4), 363–381. doi:10.1080/13825580600943473 PMID:17564852

Paternò, F. (2004). ConcurTaskTrees: an engineered notation for task models. The Handbook of Task Analysis for Human-Computer Interaction, 483–503.

Redondo Romero, A. M. (2008). Language disorders. *Pediatria Integral, 12*(9), 859–872. https://cdn.pediatriaintegral.es/wp-content/uploads/2017/xxi01/02/n1-015-022_SergiAguilera.pdf

Sanchez, A., Barreiro, J. M., & Maojo, V. (2000). Design of virtual reality systems for education: A cognitive approach. *Education and Information Technologies*, 5(4), 345–362. doi:10.1023/A:1012061809603

Schrepp, M., Hinderks, A., & Thomaschewski, J. (2014). Applying the user experience questionnaire (UEQ) in different evaluation scenarios. *International Conference of Design, User Experience, and Usability*, 383–392. 10.1007/978-3-319-07668-3_37

Seo, J. H., Smith, B. M., Cook, M., Malone, E., Pine, M., Leal, S., Bai, Z., & Suh, J. (2017). Anatomy builder VR: Applying a constructive learning method in the virtual reality canine skeletal system. *International Conference on Applied Human Factors and Ergonomics*, 245–252. 10.1109/VR.2017.7892345

SIMX. (2020). *Virtual Reality Medical Simulation.* https://www.simxvr.com/

Stanziola, E., Ortiz, J. M., & Simón, M. (2014). UX in healthcare: lessons learned in a complex environment. In *Interaction South America (ISA 14): 6th Lationamerican Conference on Interaction Design.* Interaction Design Association; Asociación de Profesionales en Experiencia de Usuario; Internet Society; Universidad Católica Argentina. Available at: https://repositorio.uca.edu.ar/handle/123456789/7953

Trujillo-Espinoza, C., Cardona-Reyes, H., & Guzmán-Mendoza, J. E. (2020). Model Proposed for the Production of User-Oriented Virtual Reality Scenarios for Training in the Driving of Unmanned Vehicles. *International Conference on Software Process Improvement*, 258–268.

Unity3D. (n.d.). *Unity Real-Time Development Platform | 3D, 3D VR & AR Engine.* Author.

Upayanto, I. D., & Wuryandani, W. (2020). Utilizing virtual reality in learning for elementary schools during COVID 19 pandemic. *ISoLEC Proceedings, 4*(1), 26–30.

Velásquez, C. T. (2017). *Competency-Based Training and the Constructivist Approach to Teaching in Higher Education*. https://enlinea.santotomas.cl/blog-expertos/la-formacion-basada-competencias-enfoque-constructivista-ensenanza-la-educacion-superior/

Vera, L., Herrera, G., & Vived, E. (2005). Virtual reality school for children with learning difficulties. *Proceedings of the 2005 ACM SIGCHI International Conference on Advances in Computer Entertainment Technology*, 338–341. 10.1145/1178477.1178541

Videla Rodríguez, J. J., Sanjuán Pérez, A., Martínez Costa, S., & Seoane Nolasco, A. (2017). Usability and design for augmented reality learning interfaces. *Digital Education Review*, *31*, 61–79. doi:10.1344/der.2017.31.61-79

Yamada-Rice, D., Mushtaq, F., Woodgate, A., Bosmans, D., Douthwaite, A., Douthwaite, I., Harris, W., Holt, R., Kleeman, D., Marsh, J., & others. (2017). *Children and virtual reality: Emerging possibilities and challenges*. Academic Press.

Yeh, S.-C., Tsai, C.-F., Fan, Y.-C., Liu, P.-C., & Rizzo, A. (2012). An innovative ADHD assessment system using virtual reality. *2012 IEEE-EMBS Conference on Biomedical Engineering and Sciences*, 78–83. 10.1109/IECBES.2012.6498026

Yu-Che, H., & Yi-Ru, C. (2019). The Study of Virtual Reality Product Design in Education Learning. *Proceedings of the 2019 The 3rd International Conference on Digital Technology in Education*, 9–11. 10.1145/3369199.3369207

Yuhanna, I., Alexander, A., & Kachik, A. (2020). Advantages and disadvantages of Online Learning. *Journal Educational Verkenning*, *1*(2), 13–19. doi:10.48173/jev.v1i2.54

KEY TERMS AND DEFINITIONS

Immersive Environment: 3D software that through virtual reality devices allows the user to interact with 3D elements isolated from the real world through a simulation.

Interactive Environment: Software system-oriented so that the user with a specific profile interacts with the available technologies and through tasks can be supported to meet their needs for the acquisition of skills or knowledge.

Multidisciplinary Team: Group of people with expertise in different areas who work together to develop a solution.

Task Modeling: Design artifact that allows identifying the various interactions between the user and a computer system.

User-Centered Design: Approach oriented to the creation of products according to the specific needs of end-users.

UX Evaluation: Capturing user perceptions before and after interactions with a product or service.

Virtual Scenario: Set of 3D objects and multimedia elements that represent a context of reality with which users interact under specific rules.

Chapter 7
The Role of Serious Games in Healthcare and Its Contribution to the Healthcare Ecosystem:
Serious Games vs. Wearables

Kartheka Bojan
BrainBerry Ltd., UK

Aikaterini Christogianni
Brainberry Ltd., UK

Elizabeta Mukaetova-Ladinska
Leicester University, UK

ABSTRACT

Serious gaming (SG) is an emerging field that has a unique role in healthcare. With big data and continuous monitoring becoming a new trend in healthcare, SG is evolving faster in the medical field due to its fit into psychology and neuroscience. The SG multi-perspective and multi-functioning framework has the potential to add new dimensions to current treatment pathways and make a significant contribution to healthcare big data. SG data will add more perspective and value to clinical data both from psychological and neurological perspectives, which are still underplayed fields. SG research directed into intensive scientific and clinical pathways is critical for the next level of evolution of health data and health systems. This chapter addresses the importance of psychological data being implemented into health data and SG's role and its future in contributing to new treatment pathways for any disease condition.

INTRODUCTION

With digital health being at forefront of the new post-pandemic world of the 21st century, continuous monitoring of health and generating health data has become prominent. The priority and focus of both

DOI: 10.4018/978-1-7998-9732-3.ch007

the healthcare market and different stakeholders are within improvements of any healthcare system.

Serious Games (SG) are becoming a key instrument in positive digital user experience in the present time. The use of SG in healthcare has received attention in recent years especially in problem-solving and in learning ability skills. SG can make an impact on the unmet psychological needs of any subject by making treatment therapies interesting, entertaining, engaging and motivating (Drummond et al., 2017). There is a plethora of literature to prove the benefits of SG in healthcare and how the implementation of these new digital systems, game platforms and interface devices assist patients' treatment and recovery methods (Wattanasoontorn et al., 2013). SG is an outstanding computer-human interaction protocol that can change, adapt or promote patient's behaviour benefiting both patients and health care systems (Sawesi et al., 2016).

This chapter aims to discuss the importance of health data and the role of SG in big data, and their advantages in the psychological and neurological sectors. These big data from SG can contribute to the evolution of conscious data contributing to human behaviours and society restructuring - a topic of research that has received less attention. It also highlights the quality and the importance of the SG data collected either from clinical or home settings that might also provide insights into diagnosis, treatment, monitoring and prognosis of many diseases (Nøhr & Aarts, 2010; Wattanasoontorn et al., 2013).

BACKGROUND

Digital Health holds greater importance in the 21st century, due to the healthcare systems' evolving technologies, advanced facilities to hold, store and analyse a large amount of data that can provide insight into any demographics. According to researchers at IBM Watson, "the average person is likely to generate more than 1 million gigabytes of health-related data in their lifetime" (University of Illinois Chicago, 2021). Today, we have the right technologies to handle these large data such as advanced server architectures, machine learning, neural network, and other artificial intelligence methodologies to predict, monitor, prognosis or treat any disease condition.

With all these advanced facilities and technologies, the healthcare industry still faces various challenges including regulatory frameworks to handle these large data, the quality of the data generated and methods to understand and distinguish between the necessary and junk data, appropriate use of data analysis to reach goals. Cloud computing platforms are storing these datasets and make them available for clinical applications for the benefit of patients (Zou et al., 2015). The computing platforms create models of biological functions with high predictable rates in diagnosis and disease prognosis (Hasselmo, 2001).

When focusing on the healthcare industry, it is important to understand different types of health data, and how important they are in screening, monitoring, and diagnosing different disease conditions. These big data, when categorised as per their importance, quality, and priority, contribute to both health economics and health informatics.

The healthcare system services aim not only to provide the right treatment plans but also to satisfy the unmet needs worldwide (Pereno & Eriksson, 2020). In this endeavour, they face challenges and emergencies to maintain a good level of care. Nonetheless, the new technologies have played a positive role in maintaining treatment procedures optimal with screening, monitoring, and diagnosing fast enough so that many patients benefit (Pereno & Eriksson, 2020). Healthcare needs to be sustainable, able to respond to population health needs, applying quality and responsibility of healthcare services that are used (Durrani, 2016). Although there are many issues regarding organisation and distribution of the services among individuals, several healthcare departments foster them into organisational designs, to tackle the challenges faced by the healthcare system (Durrani, 2016). The collaboration of such teams is important to establish communication between different stakeholders who use the technology.

Health economics also plays a role in investigating the health behaviour outcomes of different stakeholders and especially those of patients (Phelps, 2017). It investigates the relationship between healthcare systems and health behaviours, aiming to promote healthy lifestyles (Phelps, 2017). Thus, economic evaluations of products are necessary to examine benefits and drawbacks that might cause either positive life outcomes or disparities and cost issues that will impact the stakeholders (Phelps, 2017). Also, this field is of interest to evaluate how easy or difficult it is to promote healthcare resources in the most efficient way (Frank, 2004). Health economics also evaluates all new technological advancements and supports strategies and actions from academia and industry to develop solutions for health (Phelps, 2017).

Another important field of collaboration with healthcare economics is healthcare informatics. Healthcare informatics is the field of science that develops computational systems, such as engineering software, data computing systems; and medical informatics to assist in healthcare information processing (Eysenbach, 2000). This field includes brain databases, such as neuroinformatic, brain mapping, and other motor activity data collections (Ravì et al., 2016). The computing applications used are unique to the recording devices and experts in communicating the medical data to the healthcare (Ravì et al., 2016). The computational methodologies aim to understand biomedical research data sets and model them in a way that would show the individual behaviour via motor and cognitive analysis and interpretation (Eysenbach, 2000). Computer algorithms assist in diagnostic processes through analysis technologies and computational health informatics (Ravì et al., 2016).

1. The health data currently collected in health care systems are mainly categorised into physiological, biological, and psychological data sets.
    a. Physiological measurement systems are generally collected from surface electrodes and non-invasive medical devices. These include heart rate, body temperature, skin conductance, blood pressure, blood volume changes in photoplethysmography, respiration rate, brain waves in electroencephalogram, cardiac input in the electrocardiogram, blood oxygen saturation, body and brain neuroimages in computerized tomography and magnetic resonance imaging etc, (Viceconti et al., 2020; Xu et al., 2020). The physiological data can detect abnormalities through the knowledge already existing about medical conditions (Xu et al., 2020). Therefore, they assist in the medical diagnoses of diseases and syndromes. The physiological databases can provide detailed health reports and suggest medical management tailored to the individual's health issues. In addition, it is possible to measure, monitor and track changes in the physiological data daily, benefitting the overall body's well-being (Xu et al., 2020). Mostly, the common physiological measurements made through wearables target maintaining good health and fitness.
    b. Biological data are series of data from biological materials, such as bodily waste (e.g., sweat, urine, saliva), organ tissue following autopsies, and blood (e.g., DNA, RNA, proteins, plasma, glucose) etc. These are essential to investigate diseases and syndromes in individuals. They are collected in large biobanks or biorepositories for specific research and examination purposes (Zou et al., 2015). The methodologies used to acquire this kind of data sets are invasive most of the time, in comparison to the physiological data. The accumulation of biological data is quite challenging as the specimens do not last over a long period and the procedure to

obtain them can be painful to individuals (Zou et al., 2015). When those data are integrated into organized readable reports with the help of application programming interfaces, they are crucial for disease diagnosis.

c. Psychological data collection is generally categorised into behavioural data, informants' data, self-report data and life data (Mortier et al., 2014). Behavioural data is the most important data which can validate any treatment methods. Most of the current drug-based and treatments are trying to collect behavioural data (Moncrieff, 2018). But the challenge with any collection of psychological data is that they are not independent entities since the social or physical environment can massively impact these datasets (Dalgard et al., 2015; Li et al., 2013). For example, a person behaves differently in a group setting compared to being alone, or a persons' daily mood changes might intervene with the psychological testing measurements. This makes psychological data incomparable at different time intervals leading to relatively small datasets that can be analysed and cross-compared. Most psychological datasets are a form of questionaries developed by different psychiatrists or scientists, which were validated under reliable and repeated experiments. Most of the mental issues around the world are measured or monitored by these standard psychological questionaries for the last few centuries (Shim & Jeong, 2018). Today, the digital world has also made it easy for people to take these tests as often as possible online, to monitor their mental health and contributing to big-data sets.

2. The source of these healthcare data is being measured in 2 different cases, the information created by health and care professionals, and the information created by patients.

a. When information is created by the healthcare providers the electronic health records and the National healthcare databases are holding items like patient data, medical and diagnostic tests, data from tissue samples which can be used to derive genetic information, data from images, (e.g., x-rays, MRI, CT images, data from psychological questionnaires or paper test) etc. to help the patients (Hermon & Williams, 2014). Information created by patients is the information about the monitoring of illnesses and healthy lifestyles such as diet, screening tests, using mobile phone applications (Hermon & Williams, 2014). Wearable devices such as smartwatches for fitness are monitoring and tracking changes relevant to medical conditions (Casola et al., 2016).

b. The information collected from the healthcare providers remains confidential and is only used to help the patients (Casola et al., 2016). However, data collected from the patients themselves which are in their legal possession can be discussed online and distributed (e.g., when using fitness apps). Social media posts or forums aim to understand how many people are discussing certain side effects of a new treatment or the improvement of their disease.

The correct diagnosis of an individual's health status depends on the specifics and the quality of the data collected. However, there are several other challenges involved when choosing the correct physiological measurement device to screen, monitor and diagnose disease. The device selection requires a deep understanding of the individuals' health state and what they need to acquire accurate results. e.g., Electroencephalogram (EEG) or Electro-Cardiogram (ECG) taken when a patient is highly anxious or distressed might result in improper interpretation or sometimes even incorrect diagnosis.

The collection of physiological and biological data sets is encompassing health and medical practices to fight for the good health of individuals. It is important to understand how these data are recorded, collected, and analysed as they play a major role in understanding how treatment plans have an impact on many different patients.

Even though health economics and healthcare informatics are developing effective plans for how the health care systems are distributed among the stakeholders via large individual databases, the focus has remained on physiological and biological functions. Most of the tools and databases already existing in the market do not collect enough data psychological information is missing. Thus, they do not allow psychological and monitoring interventions to manage mental health issues and psychological therapies along with other disease treatments. Computer engineering in healthcare might benefit from improved clinical services that implement the collection of psychological data. Psychological data sets may refine the healthcare treatment plans, and they may customize the therapies according to the knowledge received from the health informatics tools. Various sources of data collection, physiological, biological, and psychological might be necessary, to integrate clinical data stores and repositories to coordinate better the treatment plans. The lack of psychological data in most cases has limited patient's support and investment in the right therapies.

The utility of psychological data is equally important to successfully implement, change or improve any treatment method. Psychological measurements are important to understand the level of discomfort an individual feels during medical assessments in clinical settings, or when using medical devices to record physical health at home (Lazar et al., 2017). In addition, although a patient might not suffer from a mental illness, the level of comfort/discomfort during the medical assessment is essential in order not to get the data biased. There are several factors to consider that might affect how the data interpretation and its cause-and-effect relationships. Besides these, other confounding factors that may affect how the data are being interpreted and generalised to a specific group of patients are not being measured. When this happens these confounding factors are usually psychological, e.g., anxiety or stress, which if not recorded before and after an investigation, lead to biased results (Lazar et al., 2017). In terms of diagnosing a disease or disorder, neuropsychological assessments provide enough psychological data sets to complement neurological reports. The strength of the psychological data is such that they can give precise answers to specific questions related to psychological health in individuals. They explore questions related to real-world views and scenarios and thus, they acquire how people feel, behave and live, in specific life settings. Examples of psychological data collections are, mental health questionnaires (e.g. stress, depression, anxiety) (Chen et al., 2004), mood states and emotions (e.g. happiness, sadness) (Lenton et al., 2013), neuropsychological evaluations (e.g. visuospatial ability, perception) (Howieson & Lezak, 2002).

Considering the progress in data collection in clinics and at home, the psychological data are rarely considered in physiological and biological reports. There is a clear direction on the kind of data that is most preferred to be collected. Healthcare providers have always focused their attention on recording data that are related to physiological and biological measurements. They have been disregarding the presence of any psychological factors that might affect the progress of a disease or disorder. The reason is that it is strongly believed that physiological and biological measurements are very strong indicators of someone's health (Goh et al., 2007). Although psychological data sets are collected in some instances, most of the time the healthcare providers reject these data because they are not as important as in the health patient reports.

BIG-DATA AND ROLE OF SG IN HEALTHCARE

Continuous Monitoring in Healthcare

The national healthcare system of any country is strongly connected with different stakeholders, namely patients, carers and families, doctors, consultants, insurance companies, pharma companies, drug and medical device suppliers, for its successful functioning (Banerjee et al., 2018). The organisation of healthcare services is important to cover the multi-dimensional needs of the stakeholders (Mosadeghrad, 2013). The quality of these services has the goal to satisfy the stakeholder expectations, considering ethical considerations and safe interactions with them (Mosadeghrad, 2013).

In the current digital world, the empowerment and benefit of patients are highly recognisable and important for a stronger healthcare system. Specifically, the patient needs and preferences have been prioritized to meet the clinical expectations, using equipment and methodologies suitable to medical guidelines (Mosadeghrad, 2013). The data collected from such methodologies provide a great opportunity for patients and their families to participate in treatment planning processes and monitor patients' health conditions (Mosadeghrad, 2013). The empowerment of patients can happen today with continuous data monitoring and with advanced modern technologies i.e., wearables, which acquire continuous health data from home-based environments (Ahmed et al., 2017). Accordingly, the procedure of collecting, measuring and analysing data needs to be efficient, safe and secure to improve quality of life and patient health status (Mosadeghrad, 2013).

Wearables and healthcare apps have leapt into the market by generating necessary and continuous health data sets e.g., heart rate, blood pressure, in today's world. The biological data are being gathered usually once before diagnosis and again if the patient's health deteriorates (Ancker et al., 2015). In contrast, psychological data have rarely been continuously recorded and they are usually collected once, upon complaints received from either patients or their families regarding serious mental health issues, or cognitive symptoms. It could be difficult to understand patients' medical history and create optimal health reports due to data collections being biased towards one direction leading to patients' incomplete profiles.

Wearable devices

Wearable devices (wearables) are domineering the industry today and the main purpose of these is to monitor the present health condition and maintain good health. The widespread use of wearable health monitors has amassed vast stores of health information for patients and users from home or work without the need of being in any clinical setting. With racing technology, these wearables are measuring key biological vital signs like heart rate, blood pressure, temperature, pulse etc., but also other physiological signs and symptoms that are important to specific groups of patients i.e., the glucose levels to monitor diabetes. However, all these wearables are limited to their functionalities, they measure only specific biological parameters.

Wearable technologies are mainly recording and monitoring physiological and biological functions (Wu & Luo, 2019). These allow short-term or long-term continuous monitoring of the patients' health status, which represent valuable personalised information about the body physiology (Poongodi et al., 2020; Wu & Luo, 2019). This is particularly beneficial when patients are at home, outside of clinical settings (Hung et al., 2004). For example, blood oxygen saturation and respiration monitors, biosensors such as electrocardiogram electrodes, temperature and blood flow sensors (Poongodi et al., 2020). Wearable technologies can identify information from the location of the sensors that touch the body and share this information with other devices (Banerjee et al., 2018). They may even record while walking, performing high and low-intensity activities and measuring calories (Poongodi et al., 2020; Wu & Luo, 2019). Nonetheless, wearable devices might suffer from privacy risks and limited consent notices about how these data are being processed and distributed (Banerjee et al., 2018; Cilliers, 2020).

Besides, the tracking of physical activities, the wearables may scan brainwaves i.e., with an electroencephalograph, and thus, may have access to feelings, moods, stress levels, sleeping patterns and other neuropsychological parameters (Poongodi et al., 2020). However, even if it may seem possible to understand psychological functions, the research of such data collection is something new and has little documentation. Because of this, many health wearable consumers are using these to track only physiological responses, with the most popular being tracking of weight, diet and healthy daily routines (Wu & Luo, 2019).

Specific groups of patients who are reported to frequently use these wearables during hospital monitoring or at home are people with cardiovascular diseases, asthma and dementia (Banerjee et al., 2018). In these patients, the data collection from the wearables assists in medical interventions, administration of correct prescriptions and therapeutic outcomes (Banerjee et al., 2018).

The collection of these large health data over time will depict the behavioural pattern of both patients and healthcare providers for any demographics which will help different stakeholders within any healthcare system. The wearable devices collect large datasets and store them into big data domains that can be analysed as a group or an individual level (Poongodi et al., 2020; Wu & Luo, 2019). These are a great source of knowledge.

Mobile Health Apps (e-Health Apps)

Mobile health apps have revolutionised the market in the last decade and have provided the opportunity for individuals to get personalised data. The mobile health apps are available to anyone who would like to track a healthy habit with the assistance of wearables, tablets, and other technological advancements.

The health apps can be mainly classified into 5 sectors that include (i) Clinical and diagnostic apps that allow practitioners to gather, evaluate, share data about their patients and provide access to access electronic health records (EHRs) (Detmer et al., 2008); (ii) Remote monitoring apps are generally combined with wearables and can help both the individual and their practitioners to keep track of the patients' healthcare information without frequent clinic visits (Treskes et al., 2016). There are also standard mental-health, general health questionaries available in the app forms which can be the most efficient way of self-monitoring (Chandrashekar, 2018); (iii) Clinical reference apps offer digital access to the ICD-9 and ICD-10 coding (Mansorian & Dorodgar, 2014) for evaluation and management services and other specialized reference materials (Matthew-Maich et al., 2016); (iv) Productivity apps include apps designed for making the management of the healthcare system easy and convenient for all stakeholders involved (Aungst, 2013; Ventola, 2014); and (v) Healthy living apps designed with patients' engagement in mind, healthy living apps to track health metrics such as diet, exercise, heart rate, and sleep (Lee & Cho, 2017).

Clinicians may have access to those datasets to prevent deterioration in a patient's health and quickly implement their treatment plans. The personalization of these data sets may increase the awareness of one's health and reduce the chance of being hospitalized. For example, the Fitbit app collects heart rate, and sleeping data (Balbim et al., 2021); the Strava app, tracks the distance a cyclist covers by using GPS systems (West, 2015). The apps focus on the health status of the individuals with the help of the data obtained. The physicians might benefit from these data sets because they are being recorded remotely, outside of clinical settings and they are resourceful.

Mental health apps exist but their use is not that frequent when it comes to continuous monitoring. For example, WorryTree (Ennis et al., 2014), Chill Panda (Morrison, 2020) and Beat Panic (Haidrani, 2015) are apps being used by the National Health Services (NHS) in the UK to record and control anxiety and changes in mood. These kinds of apps are advantageous for patients and clinicians because they allow patients to self-monitor the progress of their psychological issues. These channels can deliver interventions based on information already stored on cloud technologies about how data are interpreted. Therefore, patients may find it to be a convenient way of regulating their mental health condition without waiting for appointments with clinicians.

Apart from these, there is another category of a health app that includes SG, which is still an emerging field but has gained more focus in both neuroscience and psychology. However, most of the app-based applied games are based on gamification, which is not scientifically tested. Nonetheless, there are very few industry experts that are approaching clinical routes which are highly essential for the future. The games can be categorised into Exergames (Göbel et al., 2010), Virtual Reality Games (Ma & Zheng, 2011), Cognitive Behaviour Therapy (CBT)-Based Serious Games and Gamification (Eichenberg & Schott, 2017), Entertainment Computer Games (Boyle et al., 2012), Biofeedback-Based Games (Travers et al., 2018) and Cognitive Training Games (Imbeault et al., 2011).

The prevalence of SG in healthcare has become prominent with the industry focusing on brain rehabilitation (Bonnechère, 2018), cancer therapy (Loerzel et al., 2020), new treatment pathways in ADHD (Frutos-Pascual et al., 2014), dementia (Imbeault et al., 2011) etc. The SG offer entertainment and engagement during multitasking activities and are claimed to be personalised treatment experiences. The use of such technology is to initiate desired physiological changes in the brain to improve cognitive processes in clinical populations (Akili, 2021).

Gaps in the Continuous Monitoring Data

With the wearable sensor market growing, the real need for monitoring mental health has become both a necessity and a priority in this modern technical world. Though, many health apps are trying to monitor users' psychological parameters through standardised psychological questionaries or battery tests; these are limited in addressing the specifics of any disease condition.

Wearables, though promote monitoring of fitness and health conditions; are limited to measuring certain physiological parameters which might not provide insights into any disease condition in the long term. There are few exceptions to such wearables, like continuous glucose monitoring, where these wearable sensors measure glucose levels and monitor insulin levels which can be a great tool in managing diabetics. However, the global wearable devices market fails to adopt cognitive, emotional, and behavioural status reports. This is a key issue in understanding psychological health and overall wellbeing in patients, especially those who suffer from chronic diseases. The unavailability of such data collection keeps the patient health status reports limited when they use only wearable technology data collection.

The development of wearable devices that monitor mental health is a new domain. There is very little input and inconclusive results to suggest that this method is effective with wearables. It is indeed unknown if the sensors attached to the body would detect and monitor accurately the mental health in patients. For example, EEG-biofeedback devices are claimed to measure cognitive functions; however, the collection of brain wave signal data sets are not able to pinpoint the cognitive functions that challenge the patients (Peake et al., 2018). Even more, when considering the possibility of wearables to measure cognitive function improvement, emotion (i.e. stress) and behaviour (i.e. sleep), physiological responses such as breathing rate and raises in body activity might provide feedback (Blount et al., 2021). Nonetheless, these kinds of methods are not clinically validated, and they do not take into consideration that an individual might exhibit symptoms because of infections/diseases and not mental/psychological burdens. Besides the above fundamental issue, we know from research that when sensors are attached to the skin for a long period, they might create discomfort and changes in behaviour (Wu & Luo, 2019) that may create important issues during investigations and biased psychological outcomes (Stephenson et al., 2017).

The sensors and e-health apps are limited in measuring human psychological and behavioural patterns. In the case of SG, there is emerging evidence that they may be contributing to generating cognitive, emotional, and behavioural patterns of any user with a disease-specific condition. SG has the potential to accelerate both environmental psychology and neuroscience field, contributing to addressing mental-health disorders. People with mental health issues, even individuals who experienced the 21st-century pandemic and acquired psychological issues because of the continuous lockdowns, may find helpful such psychological monitoring.

There are advantages when continuously monitoring psychological data. Thus, immediate feedback about someone's mental health can be recorded. This kind of information might centralise appropriate treatment plans but can also mitigate the risk of evolving serious mental health issues that are untreated. Faster remedies and therapeutic interventions might timely help patients, without unnecessary delays.

Serious Games in Healthcare

Based on the current literature, it is evident that SG behavioural data can impact the quality of care any patient receives. These data will provide an insight into the overall characteristics of any disease condition but will also help in improving the current clinical practices and new treatment pathways or healthcare plans (Sawesi et al., 2016). The data collections may answer fundamental questions about the user performance and the efficacy of the digital software to change patient's behaviour (Loh et al., 2007).

SG has the advantage and uniqueness of addressing any groups of patients, networks of people who share the same diagnosis/symptomatology. These data may impact the collective information of any disease condition and can induce behavioural changes in many patients at the same time (Nardi, 1996; Rusnak, 2008). The navigation structure of such games are usually digital gaming simulations that explore real-world scenarios and patients can work on problem-solving, reasoning, critical thinking, and personal responsibility together (Starks, 2014).

SG may potentially assist in preventing diseases, such as diabetes, mental health issues and even promote healthy habits, such as healthier lifestyles and nutrition, in healthy individuals (Nøhr & Aarts, 2010). For example, an exercise gaming environment aims to engage patients in active lifestyles and prevent obesity (Schuller et al., 2013). Also, for patients with a high risk of self-harming who suffer i.e., from depression, anxiety, drug addiction and suicidal thoughts, behavioural interventions via SG can be radical and preventative (Ong, 2020). SG virtual reality experiments demonstrate that they can prevent deterioration of cognitive functions e.g. in stroke rehabilitation, SG may improve patients' performance and help them develop strategies to answer cognitive tasks, promoting better brain functionalities (Tran et al., 2016).

Also, SG can create a surrounding environment for the patient or any user and can influence their biological, psychological, and clinical health. The advantage of SG data is that they can stimulate and monitor specific behavioural and environmental changes continuously filling the gap which is not achievable via wearables. SG focus on large patient data sets that might assist in enhancing patient care in areas such as neuro-restoration, neurorehabilitation and brain trauma associated with cognitive and motor functions (Mindmaze, 2021). These industry-based SG designs are committed to the idea of both personalisation and group treatment options that benefit patients (McCallum, 2012).

The data collection of these user-SG interactions has entailed cognitive, behavioural, and motor function data in patient studies (Jonsdottir et al., 2018; Samarasinghe et al., 2017). In particular, these data banks include assessments of low to a huge amount of analytic information, such as organised demographic characteristics, users' health history, users' gaming performance, overall physiological, cognitive functioning and well-being, pre-, during and post-playing (Loh et al., 2007). This SG will assist and increase the understanding of how the patients' progress with rehabilitation and manage their disease (Jonsdottir et al., 2018).

For example, the Executive Timed Target Game has been developed to stimulate cognitive functions in people with dementia (Tong et al., 2017). The game may monitor cognitive functions in the patients over time but also act as a clinical cognitive assessment during cognitive screening. The game focuses on target inhibition. The players are required to focus and suppress their attention to the stimuli on the screen. The tack is challenging and requires ignoring specific stimuli and not respond to them. In addition, other SG might assist in personalised health, in dementia patients, for example, the MasterQuiz (McCallum, 2012). In this game the users answer general and personal knowledge questions, part of reminiscence therapy.

SG in Neuroscience

Cognitive behavioural therapy and Cognitive training games are gaining attention in the rehabilitation sector with both industrial and academic research showing interest in this sector. SG challenge cognitive functions and target users' enjoyment whilst playing games (Tong et al., 2017). SG is widely used in healthcare training and rehabilitation. The training-based games are usually education games which can be significant for carers, hospital staff and doctors to train themselves for perfection to treat their patients (Ricciardi & De Paolis, 2014). Examples of such training SG include Code Orange, which is a game based on the Hospital Emergency Incident Command System (HEICS) protocol for training players and staff to treat patients injured by a weapon-of-mass-destruction event (Ricciardi & De Paolis, 2014). Nuclear Event Triage Challenge, Radiation Hazards Assessment Challenge, and Peninsula City are other examples of emergency personnel training (Ricciardi & De Paolis, 2014). Pulse!! is an SG developed for healthcare professionals or medical students, with accurate physiology models and fluid dynamics used to simulate blood flow in the human body, to learn and understand better the anatomy and physiology of the human body in 3D views (Ricciardi & De Paolis, 2014). Another example is Méli-Mélo Glucidique, a quiz form SG, that improves the dietetic knowledge of patients (Ricciardi & De Paolis, 2014).

The rehabilitation-based SG is widespread in different health sectors. Affaire Birman is a game developed for dietary terms, insulin injection and physical activity (Ricciardi & De Paolis, 2014); Timeout is developed for teenagers and adults with type 1 diabetes and pump treatment (Ricciardi & De Paolis, 2014); iSpectrum for social interaction abilities improvement for people affected with Autistic Spectrum Disorders, including Asperger's syndrome (Ricciardi & De Paolis, 2014); Treasure Hunt supports the psychotherapeutic treatment of children (Ricciardi & De Paolis, 2014); Free Dive aims to entertain and distract children who often undergo painful medical procedures (Ricciardi & De Paolis, 2014); some have developed an EEG-based serious game that can be used for pain management (Ricciardi & De Paolis, 2014).

There are several brain training gamification apps on the market focusing on cognition with only a few backed by research studies. Most of them are primarily designed for cognitively healthy older people, while some, designed originally as games for younger adults, were repurposed for older adults, following research studies. Nintendo Wii-Fit console, in an apt example which converted its physical exercise videos like yoga, strength training, aerobics into virtual trainers based games to assist people with dementia in their environment (Sultana et al., 2020; Tripette et al., 2017). Other examples include Big Brain Academy (BBA) (Asad et al., 2019), video games when compared to the Integrated Psychostimulation Program (IPP) in a research study, which showed that this game can help significantly decrease depression in Alzheimer's patients (Fernández-Calvo et al., 2011).

Few industrial pioneers are effectively using SG to improve patients' symptomatology, promote fast rehabilitation and provide entertaining therapy interventions with clinical validation, thus marking the future direction of SG in healthcare. BrainBerry Ltd uses SG for people with mild cognitive impairment and dementia to delay the progression of the disease by improving cognitive and emotional well-being (Brainberry Ltd., 2021). The company is currently focusing on SG specifically designed for people with dementia symptoms to improve their cognitive and emotional well-being. They are building a data ecosystem of their own for the collection of cognitive score data to predict both behavioural changes and progression of dementia, which is one great example of how the big data in SG can evolve and how the market needs are met.

MindMaze is claiming to utilize multidisciplinary sciences, such as neuroscience, biosensing, engineering, mixed reality and artificial intelligence to assist people will neurological diseases to recover and adapt to their illnesses (Mindmaze, 2021). Their innovative technological advancements involve AI digital therapies, cloud computer system resources, data storage and computing systems, and algorithms that aim to change patients' behaviour (Mindmaze, 2021). The company's research focuses on stroke, Parkinson's Disease and dementia (Cervera et al., 2018). They use big data storage for patient-machine interactions and digital assessments to measure motor and cognitive function. They propose that the large patient data sets may assist in transforming patient care with neuro-restoration, neurorehabilitation, neuroplasticity, and brain repair of the cognitive and motor functions (Mindmaze, 2021).

Akili Interactive has created a personalized digital therapeutics engineered to directly improve cognitive impairments (Akili, 2021). The company uses video game research in a technology platform that aims to deliver sensory and motor stimuli in specific cognitive neural systems in the brain. The use of such technology is to initiate desired physiological changes in the brain to improve cognitive processes in clinical populations (Akili, 2021). The company's products focus on paediatric attention deficit hyperactivity disorder (ADHD), and adults with Major Depressive Disorder (Davis et al., 2018): they offer entertainment and engagement during multitasking activities, claimed to be personalised treatment experiences.

There are various challenges or fundamental research stages still to be achieved in the field of SG. One such main challenge is the design method on SG for different disease conditions and different cognitive functions. Moreover, the long-term sight of collecting all this data has been overlooked. The collection of big data only at this stage focuses on the 'motivation' factor with 'Leader board Scores'.

Leader Boards are the one which shows the team performance of all the individuals involved just to motivate any user to do better in the team.

The future direction of research on SG must focus on SG designs for specific accurate cognitive functions e.g., attention, orientation, memory measurements; the designs need to consider the arousal and motivation along with relevant information for a specific use case, such as feedback of normal and actual performances and achieving the specific cognitive skills targeted for an individual. The emotional and psychological improvements should not be underestimated in the SG designs. Also, the collection of these data from SG needs to investigate different scientific parameters that could contribute to scores that achieve precision and accuracy for diagnosis, therapy, and prognosis. And this could be only achieved when the SG undergo scientific and clinical validation to prove the efficiency and efficacy of the measurements made.

SG in psychology

SG designs aim at engaging the target audience in tasks that would inspire specific behavioural, cognitive and psychological outcomes; such as an increase in motivation (Dickey, 2007; Freitas & Liarokapis, 2011), induction of learning (Mayer, 2012), creation of planning strategies (Wittland et al., 2015) and improvement of mood (Fleming et al., 2014, 2017). Games for the ageing populations and people at risk to be diagnosed with dementia were rated as enjoyable and showed engagement in playing cognitive games designed to challenge their cognitive processes (Tong et al., 2017). The cognitive training games relies on the concept that patients with a great cognitive reserve will be able to have a better cognitive outcome while living with their disease (Stern, 2012). To avoid disengagement and cognitive overload (Duplaa & Taiwo, 2013), the cognitive games are designed with animations and colours that may focus on a digital environment which might prepare individuals to train on one's cognitive skills (Bojan et al., 2021).

SG has the potential to rehabilitate, be a therapy; but they may also assist in gaining positive attitudes about health conditions and treatment plans (Nøhr & Aarts, 2010), with well-planned SG designs. This may be especially applicable for patients who require diligent management of their long-term illness issues i.e., cancer, dementia.

The SG methodologies are used to measure behaviour in clinical settings and these have some mentions that are worth considering (Sawesi et al., 2016). For example, positive behavioural changes in adults with chronic illnesses have been studied based on changes in physical activity, medication adherence, and self-management (Thomas et al., 2020). In these methodologies, the data collection sets were assessed before, during and after gamification to quantify the behavioural changes in each disease group (Thomas et al., 2020). These kinds of quality data can assist in developing SG that can be used to implement motivation and adapt new healthy habits and lifestyles (Nøhr & Aarts, 2010).

EVOLUTION OF SG IN EFFECTIVE TREATMENTS FOR FUTURE

SG is the emerging field of science in psychology and is growing parallelly along with environmental, social, and biological psychology. Environmental psychology is an interdisciplinary science that studies the relationship between human psychology and the environment. New studies are emerging in this field, and they picture the importance of psychology in human society. They aim to make people involved in pro-environmental behaviour that can mitigate many environmental challenges e.g. climate change, environmentally sustainable behaviour (Parsons et al., 2017), environmentalism (Dietz et al., 1998) and conservation (Cialdini, 2003). Social neuroscience investigates how social processes and behaviours are implemented by biological systems (Parsons et al., 2017). SG can stimulate "mental processes involved in perceiving, attending to, remembering, thinking about, and making sense of the people in our social world" (Parsons et al., 2017).

Similarly, biological psychology is under-researched in the current era. The field has gained recent attention, since changing patients' emotional and psychological well-being, may positively impact their behaviour and experiences. This positive psychological change in a patient may assist in biological changes that are associated with a reduced risk of chronic illnesses (Steptoe et al., 2012).

Most of the studies in biological psychology focus on cognitive and behavioural activities like thinking, learning, feeling, sensing, and perceiving, the functional activity of the brain and the central nervous system (Breedlove & Watson, 2013). These studies have been exploring the relationship between the psychological bases and the physical factors that directly affect the nervous system (Meissner & Wittmann, 2011). Though the need for and importance of these emerging psychology branches are understood by the scientific community, these fields are still in experimental and pilot study stages. SG can be one such capable tool since it can bring these experiments to the real-time world and could make some serious changes in human behaviour.

SG can stimulate and influence both environmental and social changes. SG can be utilised to be the most powerful tool that can trigger environmental and social psychology (Baldwin & Dandeneau, 2009; Morganti et al., 2017). They are not just measurement tools but can change the brain's perspective and the psychological environment of patients with any condition. Virtual reality games can offer virtual environments, allow the presentation of social stimuli, emotional narratives and environmental awareness that might engender a perspective in users to enhance social responsibilities, personal emotional perspectives in any user (Parsons et al., 2017).

The brain does not distinguish between imagined and physical events that can be judged either as real or unreal (Parsons et al., 2017). The brain emotional responses are similar either triggered by imaginary or physical situations. Various studies have suggested that this is the ability of sensory information of the brain, along with its motor action, to instantiate a stimulation of its sensory outcome. This magical ability of the brain to be undistinguished can make any SG, designed with the right aims to become a powerful tool in making an impact in patients' psychological environment. The positive change in the psyche of a patient might trigger a placebo effect in their treatment pathways, adding additional benefit to full or faster recovery.

The examples above show that SG can play a significant role in mental healthcare by generating positive biological variations. However, one has to consider that SGs haven't evolved themselves at this stage to address the potentials mentioned above. SG are still in an experimental stage with a focus on cognition and learning disabilities with academic and industrial interests pointing only towards the field of neuroscience. It is rather important to turn SG's uniqueness and multi-level benefits into the field of psychology since it could be one of the most important tools in creating or framing a necessary mental and psychological environment for any patient or group of people in shaping a better society. This direction of research could start with simple gamification models designed for answering psychological questionaries instead of paper-based models used in clinics or digital questionnaires in the app form. To measure the biased results between a questionnaire and gamification could open new doors to SG in psychology.

CONCLUSION

Patients benefit from a variety of physical and biological examinations which are essential to diagnose medical diseases and disorders. The heavy burden that patients are facing to get screened, monitored, and diagnosed has been uplifted with the use of non-invasive wearable devices. The methodologies used to help patients are important and accurate; however, they often disregard the importance of psychological factors. Psychological data remain unavailable from health reports, most of the time.

SG promises new innovative treatment methodologies at both home and clinical settings. Therefore, it is essential to focus the attention on these technological advancements and how they can positively impact patients' and healthcare systems. SG has a great capacity to evolve above wearables, not only in assisting the current health status of an individual but to simulate and create a positive psychological environment that will benefit human well-being.

Healthcare stakeholders are in a very advantageous state in which health technological advances have contributed to the improvement of well-being and quality of life in individuals; however, they would be greatly benefitted from the implementation of psychological aspects and data to these health reports to make the screening, monitoring, and diagnosing, trustworthy. In this endeavour, SG is an amazing tool to collect psychological data and can be used in a series of healthcare examinations in clinics, but also at home settings, where continuous monitoring might be both possible and necessary. SG may stand as a solution to the missing puzzles in any healthcare examinations and will be a great source of data collection and continuous monitoring. SG is still in its initial stages of development into the healthcare field, and it is necessary to direct the SG developments in healthcare towards a scientific approach to validate and prove the efficacy and efficiency of SG designs and their framework to work for any specific disease.

REFERENCES

Ahmed, M. N., Toor, A. S., O'Neil, K., & Friedland, D. (2017). Cognitive computing and the future of health care cognitive computing and the future of healthcare: The cognitive power of IBM Watson has the potential to transform global personalized medicine. *IEEE Pulse*, 8(3), 4–9. doi:10.1109/MPUL.2017.2678098 PMID:28534755

Akili. (2021). *Science and Technology*. https://www.akiliinteractive.com/

Ancker, J. S., Witteman, H. O., Hafeez, B., Provencher, T., Van de Graaf, M., & Wei, E. (2015). "You get reminded you're a sick person": Personal data tracking and patients with multiple chronic conditions. *Journal of Medical Internet Research*, 17(8), e202. doi:10.2196/jmir.4209 PMID:26290186

Asad, J., Kousar, S., & Mehmood, N. Q. (2019). Dementia-Related Serious Games: A Comparative Study. *University of Sindh Journal of Information and Communication Technology*, 3(4), 171–177.

Aungst, T. D. (2013). Medical applications for pharmacists using mobile devices. *The Annals of Pharmacotherapy*, 47(7–8), 1088–1095. doi:10.1345/aph.1S035 PMID:23821609

Balbim, G. M., Marques, I. G., Marquez, D. X., Patel, D., Sharp, L. K., Kitsiou, S., & Nyenhuis, S. M. (2021). Using Fitbit as an mHealth intervention tool to promote physical activity: Potential challenges and solutions. *JMIR mHealth and uHealth*, 9(3), e25289. doi:10.2196/25289 PMID:33646135

Baldwin, M. W., & Dandeneau, S. D. (2009). Putting social psychology into serious games. *Social and Personality Psychology Compass, 3*(4), 547–565. doi:10.1111/j.1751-9004.2009.00185.x

Banerjee, S., Hemphill, T., & Longstreet, P. (2018). Wearable devices and healthcare: Data sharing and privacy. *The Information Society, 34*(1), 49–57. doi:10.1080/01972243.2017.1391912

Blount, D. S., McDonough, D. J., & Gao, Z. (2021). Effect of Wearable Technology-Based Physical Activity Interventions on Breast Cancer Survivors' Physiological, Cognitive, and Emotional Outcomes: A Systematic Review. *Journal of Clinical Medicine, 10*(9), 2015. doi:10.3390/jcm10092015 PMID:34066752

Bojan, K., Stavropoulos, T. G., Lazarou, I., Nikolopoulos, S., Kompatsiaris, I., Tsolaki, M., Mukaetova-Ladinska, E., & Christogianni, A. (2021). The effects of playing the COSMA cognitive games in dementia. *International Journal of Serious Games, 8*(1), 45–58. doi:10.17083/ijsg.v8i1.412

Bonnechère, B. (2018). Serious games in physical rehabilitation. In *Serious games in physical rehabilitation. From Theory to practice* (pp. 49–109). Springer.

Boyle, E. A., Connolly, T. M., Hainey, T., & Boyle, J. M. (2012). Engagement in digital entertainment games: A systematic review. *Computers in Human Behavior, 28*(3), 771–780. doi:10.1016/j.chb.2011.11.020

Brainberry Ltd. (2021). *Healthcare Ecosystem for the Evolution of Mental Health.* https://brainberry.co.uk/

Breedlove, S. M., & Watson, N. V. (2013). *Biological psychology: An introduction to behavioral, cognitive, and clinical neuroscience.* Sinauer Associates.

Casola, V., Castiglione, A., Choo, K.-K. R., & Esposito, C. (2016). Healthcare-related data in the cloud: Challenges and opportunities. *IEEE Cloud Computing, 3*(6), 10–14. doi:10.1109/MCC.2016.139

Cervera, M. A., Soekadar, S. R., Ushiba, J., Millán, J. del R., Liu, M., Birbaumer, N., & Garipelli, G. (2018). Brain-computer interfaces for post-stroke motor rehabilitation: A meta-analysis. *Annals of Clinical and Translational Neurology, 5*(5), 651–663. doi:10.1002/acn3.544 PMID:29761128

Chandrashekar, P. (2018). Do mental health mobile apps work: Evidence and recommendations for designing high-efficacy mental health mobile apps. *mHealth, 4*, 4. doi:10.21037/mhealth.2018.03.02 PMID:29682510

Chen, T.-H., Chang, S.-P., Tsai, C.-F., & Juang, K.-D. (2004). Prevalence of depressive and anxiety disorders in an assisted reproductive technique clinic. *Human Reproduction (Oxford, England), 19*(10), 2313–2318. doi:10.1093/humrep/deh414 PMID:15242992

Cialdini, R. B. (2003). Crafting normative messages to protect the environment. *Current Directions in Psychological Science, 12*(4), 105–109. doi:10.1111/1467-8721.01242

Cilliers, L. (2020). Wearable devices in healthcare: Privacy and information security issues. *The HIM Journal, 49*(2–3), 150–156. doi:10.1177/1833358319851684 PMID:31146589

Dalgard, F. J., Gieler, U., Tomas-Aragones, L., Lien, L., Poot, F., Jemec, G. B. E., Misery, L., Szabo, C., Linder, D., Sampogna, F., Evers, A. W. M., Halvorsen, J. A., Balieva, F., Szepietowski, J., Romanov, D., Marron, S. E., Altunay, I. K., Finlay, A. Y., Salek, S. S., & Kupfer, J. (2015). The psychological burden of skin diseases: A cross-sectional multicenter study among dermatological out-patients in 13 European countries. *The Journal of Investigative Dermatology*, *135*(4), 984–991. doi:10.1038/jid.2014.530 PMID:25521458

Davis, N. O., Bower, J., & Kollins, S. H. (2018). Proof-of-concept study of an at-home, engaging, digital intervention for pediatric ADHD. *PLoS One*, *13*(1), e0189749. doi:10.1371/journal.pone.0189749 PMID:29324745

De Freitas, S., & Liarokapis, F. (2011). Serious Games: A New Paradigm for Education? In J. L. In M. Ma & A. Oikonomou (Eds.), *Serious Games and Edutainment Applications* (pp. 9–23). Springer. doi:10.1007/978-1-4471-2161-9_2

Detmer, D., Bloomrosen, M., Raymond, B., & Tang, P. (2008). Integrated personal health records: Transformative tools for consumer-centric care. *BMC Medical Informatics and Decision Making*, *8*(1), 1–14. doi:10.1186/1472-6947-8-45 PMID:18837999

Dickey, M. D. (2007). Game design and learning: A conjectural analysis of how massively multiple online role-playing games (MMORPGs) foster intrinsic motivation. *Educational Technology Research and Development*, *55*(3), 253–273. doi:10.100711423-006-9004-7

Dietz, T., Stern, P. C., & Guagnano, G. A. (1998). Social structural and social psychological bases of environmental concern. *Environment and Behavior*, *30*(4), 450–471. doi:10.1177/001391659803000402

Drummond, D., Hadchouel, A., & Tesnière, A. (2017). Serious games for health: Three steps forwards. *Advances in Simulation (London, England)*, *2*(1), 1–8. doi:10.118641077-017-0036-3 PMID:29450004

Duplaa, E., & Taiwo, E. (2013). Cognition and theory of flow for elders: can digital games help. *Proceedings of World Congress on Social Sciences*.

Durrani, H. (2016). Healthcare and healthcare systems: Inspiring progress and future prospects. *mHealth*, *2*. PMID:28293581

Eichenberg, C., & Schott, M. (2017). Serious games for psychotherapy: A systematic review. *Games for Health Journal*, *6*(3), 127–135. doi:10.1089/g4h.2016.0068 PMID:28628385

Ennis, L., Robotham, D., Denis, M., Pandit, N., Newton, D., Rose, D., & Wykes, T. (2014). Collaborative development of an electronic Personal Health Record for people with severe and enduring mental health problems. *BMC Psychiatry*, *14*(1), 1–7. doi:10.118612888-014-0305-9 PMID:25403285

Eysenbach, G. (2000). Consumer health informatics. *BMJ (Clinical Research Ed.)*, *320*(7251), 1713–1716. doi:10.1136/bmj.320.7251.1713 PMID:10864552

Fernández-Calvo, B., Rodríguez-Pérez, R., Contador, I., Rubio-Santorum, A., & Ramos, F. (2011). Efficacy of cognitive training programs based on new software technologies in patients with Alzheimer-type dementia. *Psicothema*, *23*(1), 44–50. PMID:21266141

Fleming, T. M., Bavin, L., Stasiak, K., Hermansson-Webb, E., Merry, S. N., Cheek, C., Lucassen, M., Lau, H. M., Pollmuller, B., & Hetrick, S. (2017). Serious games and gamification for mental health: Current status and promising directions. *Frontiers in Psychiatry, 7*(JAN). Advance online publication. doi:10.3389/fpsyt.2016.00215 PMID:28119636

Fleming, T. M., Cheek, C., Merry, S. N., Thabrew, H., Bridgman, H., Stasiak, K., Shepherd, M., Perry, Y., & Hetrick, S. (2014). Serious games for the treatment or prevention of depression: A systematic review. *Revista de Psicopatología y Psicología Clínica, 19*(3), 227–242. doi:10.5944/rppc.vol.19.num.3.2014.13904

Frank, R. G. (2004). *Behavioral economics and health economics*. National Bureau of Economic Research. doi:10.3386/w10881

De Freitas, S., & Liarokapis, F. (2011). Serious Games: A New Paradigm for Education? In J. L. In M. Ma & A. Oikonomou (Eds.), *Serious Games and Edutainment Applications* (pp. 9–23). Springer., doi:10.1007/978-1-4471-2161-9

Frutos-Pascual, M., Zapirain, B. G., & Buldian, K. C. (2014). Adaptive cognitive rehabilitation interventions based on serious games for children with ADHD using biofeedback techniques: assessment and evaluation. *Proceedings of the 8th International Conference on Pervasive Computing Technologies for Healthcare*, 321–324. 10.4108/icst.pervasivehealth.2014.255249

Göbel, S., Hardy, S., Wendel, V., Mehm, F., & Steinmetz, R. (2010). Serious games for health - Personalized exergames. *MM'10 - Proceedings of the ACM Multimedia 2010 International Conference*, 1663–1666. 10.1145/1873951.1874316

Goh, K.-I., Cusick, M. E., Valle, D., Childs, B., Vidal, M., & Barabási, A.-L. (2007). The human disease network. *Proceedings of the National Academy of Sciences of the United States of America, 104*(21), 8685–8690. doi:10.1073/pnas.0701361104 PMID:17502601

Haidrani, L. (2015). Beat Panic app. Nursing Standard (Royal College of Nursing (Great Britain): 1987), 30(15), 29.

Hasselmo, M. E. (2001). Neural Systems: Models of Behavioral Functions. In International Encyclopedia of the Social & Behavioral Sciences (pp. 10575–10578). Elsevier.

Hermon, R., & Williams, P. A. H. (2014). Big data in healthcare: What is it used for? *Australian EHealth Informatics and Security Conference.*

Howieson, D. B., & Lezak, M. D. (2002). The neuropsychological evaluation. In S. C. Yudofsky & R. E. Hales (Eds.), *The American Psychiatric Publishing textbook of neuropsychiatry and clinical neurosciences* (pp. 217–244). American Psychiatric Publishing, Inc.

Hung, K., Zhang, Y.-T., & Tai, B. (2004). Wearable medical devices for tele-home healthcare. *The 26th Annual International Conference of the IEEE Engineering in Medicine and Biology Society, 2*, 5384–5387.

Imbeault, F. F., Bouchard, B., & Bouzouane, A. (2011). Serious games in cognitive training for Alzheimer's patients. *2011 IEEE 1st International Conference on Serious Games and Applications for Health (SeGAH)*. 10.1109/SeGAH.2011.6165447

Jonsdottir, J., Bertoni, R., Lawo, M., Montesano, A., Bowman, T., & Gabrielli, S. (2018). Serious games for arm rehabilitation of persons with multiple sclerosis. A randomized controlled pilot study. *Multiple Sclerosis and Related Disorders*, *19*, 25–29. doi:10.1016/j.msard.2017.10.010 PMID:29112939

Lazar, J., Feng, J. H., & Hochheiser, H. (2017). *Research methods in human-computer interaction*. Morgan Kaufmann.

Lee, H. E., & Cho, J. (2017). What motivates users to continue using diet and fitness apps? Application of the uses and gratifications approach. *Health Communication*, *32*(12), 1445–1453. doi:10.1080/1041 0236.2016.1167998 PMID:27356103

Lenton, A. P., Slabu, L., Sedikides, C., & Power, K. (2013). I feel good, therefore I am real: Testing the causal influence of mood on state authenticity. *Cognition and Emotion*, *27*(7), 1202–1224. doi:10.108 0/02699931.2013.778818 PMID:23574266

Li, H. C. W., Lopez, V., Chung, O. K. J., Ho, K. Y., & Chiu, S. Y. (2013). The impact of cancer on the physical, psychological and social well-being of childhood cancer survivors. *European Journal of Oncology Nursing*, *17*(2), 214–219. doi:10.1016/j.ejon.2012.07.010 PMID:22898653

Loerzel, V. W., Clochesy, J. M., & Geddie, P. I. (2020). Using Serious Games to Increase Prevention and Self-Management of Chemotherapy-Induced Nausea and Vomiting in Older Adults With Cancer. *Oncology Nursing Forum*, *47*(5), 567–576. doi:10.1188/20.ONF.567-576 PMID:32830802

Loh, C. S., Anantachai, A., Byun, J., & Lenox, J. (2007). Assessing what players learned in serious games: in situ data collection, information trails, and quantitative analysis. *10th International Conference on Computer Games: AI, Animation, Mobile, Educational & Serious Games (CGAMES 2007)*, 25–28.

Ma, M., & Zheng, H. (2011). Virtual reality and serious games in healthcare. In *Advanced computational intelligence paradigms in healthcare 6. Virtual reality in psychotherapy, rehabilitation, and assessment* (pp. 169–192). Springer. doi:10.1007/978-3-642-17824-5_9

Mansorian, A., & Dorodgar, K. (2014). Designing a software for systematic registration of oral and maxillofacial diseases based on the latest update of the World Health Organization ICD-10 classification system in 2010. *The Journal of Dental Medicine*, *27*(1), 51–60.

Matthew-Maich, N., Harris, L., Ploeg, J., Markle-Reid, M., Valaitis, R., Ibrahim, S., Gafni, A., & Isaacs, S. (2016). Designing, implementing, and evaluating mobile health technologies for managing chronic conditions in older adults: A scoping review. *JMIR mHealth and uHealth*, *4*(2), e5127. doi:10.2196/mhealth.5127 PMID:27282195

Mayer, I. (2012). Towards a Comprehensive Methodology for the Research and Evaluation of Serious Games. *Procedia Computer Science*, *15*, 233–247. doi:10.1016/j.procs.2012.10.075

McCallum, S. (2012). Gamification and serious games for personalized health. *PHealth*, *177*(February), 85–96. doi:10.3233/978-1-61499-069-7-85 PMID:22942036

Meissner, K., & Wittmann, M. (2011). Body signals, cardiac awareness, and the perception of time. *Biological Psychology*, *86*(3), 289–297. doi:10.1016/j.biopsycho.2011.01.001 PMID:21262314

Mindmaze. (2021). *Mindmaze: Healthcare*. https://www.mindmaze.com/

Moncrieff, J. (2018). Research on a 'drug-centred' approach to psychiatric drug treatment: Assessing the impact of mental and behavioural alterations produced by psychiatric drugs. *Epidemiology and Psychiatric Sciences*, 27(2), 133–140. doi:10.1017/S2045796017000555 PMID:29022518

Morganti, L., Pallavicini, F., Cadel, E., Candelieri, A., Archetti, F., & Mantovani, F. (2017). Gaming for Earth: Serious games and gamification to engage consumers in pro-environmental behaviours for energy efficiency. *Energy Research & Social Science*, 29, 95–102. doi:10.1016/j.erss.2017.05.001

Morrison, C. (2020). *Review of Current Use of Digital Solutions for Mental Health*. University of Strathclyde.

MortierR.HaddadiH.HendersonT.McAuleyD.CrowcroftJ. (2014). Human-data interaction: The human face of the data-driven society. *Available at* SSRN 2508051. doi:10.2139/ssrn.2508051

Mosadeghrad, A. M. (2013). Healthcare service quality: Towards a broad definition. *International Journal of Health Care Quality Assurance*, 26(3), 203–219. doi:10.1108/09526861311311409 PMID:23729125

Nardi, B. A. (1996). Studying context: A comparison of activity theory, situated action models, and distributed cognition. *Context and Consciousness: Activity Theory and Human-Computer Interaction, 69102*.

Nøhr, C., & Aarts, J. (2010). Use of "serious health games" in health care: a review. *Information Technology in Health Care: Socio-Technical Approaches*, 160.

Ong, E. (2020). Can digital games serve as potential intervention or suicide risk? *International Journal of Serious Games*, 7(1), 127–132. doi:10.17083/ijsg.v7i1.303

Parsons, T. D., Gaggioli, A., & Riva, G. (2017). Virtual reality for research in social neuroscience. *Brain Sciences*, 7(4), 42. doi:10.3390/brainsci7040042 PMID:28420150

Peake, J. M., Kerr, G., & Sullivan, J. P. (2018). A critical review of consumer wearables, mobile applications, and equipment for providing biofeedback, monitoring stress, and sleep in physically active populations. *Frontiers in Physiology*, 9, 743. doi:10.3389/fphys.2018.00743 PMID:30002629

Pereno, A., & Eriksson, D. (2020). A multi-stakeholder perspective on sustainable healthcare: From 2030 onwards. *Futures*, 122, 102605. doi:10.1016/j.futures.2020.102605 PMID:32834076

Phelps, C. E. (2017). *Health economics* (6th ed.). Routledge. doi:10.4324/9781315460499

Poongodi, T., Krishnamurthi, R., Indrakumari, R., Suresh, P., & Balusamy, B. (2020). Wearable devices and IoT. In *A handbook of Internet of Things in biomedical and cyber physical system* (pp. 245–273). Springer. doi:10.1007/978-3-030-23983-1_10

Ravì, D., Wong, C., Deligianni, F., Berthelot, M., Andreu-Perez, J., Lo, B., & Yang, G.-Z. (2016). Deep learning for health informatics. *IEEE Journal of Biomedical and Health Informatics*, 21(1), 4–21. doi:10.1109/JBHI.2016.2636665 PMID:28055930

Ricciardi, F., & De Paolis, L. T. (2014). A comprehensive review of serious games in health professions. *International Journal of Computer Games Technology*, 2014, 2014. doi:10.1155/2014/787968

Rusnak, P. J. (2008). *The Science of Gaming Consciousness: A Lesson for Teachers and Parents*. Canadian Society for the Study of Education.

Samarasinghe, H. A. S. M., Weerasooriya, W. A. M. S., Weerasinghe, G. H. E., Ekanayaka, Y., Rajapakse, R., & Wijesinghe, D. P. D. (2017). Serious games design considerations for people with Alzheimer's disease in developing nations. *2017 IEEE 5th International Conference on Serious Games and Applications for Health, SeGAH 2017*. 10.1109/SeGAH.2017.7939301

Sawesi, S., Rashrash, M., Phalakornkule, K., Carpenter, J. S., & Jones, J. F. (2016). The impact of information technology on patient engagement and health behavior change: A systematic review of the literature. *JMIR Medical Informatics, 4*(1), e4514. doi:10.2196/medinform.4514 PMID:26795082

Schuller, B. W., Dunwell, I., Weninger, F., & Paletta, L. (2013). Serious gaming for behavior change: The state of play. *IEEE Pervasive Computing, 12*(3), 48–55. doi:10.1109/MPRV.2013.54

Shim, G., & Jeong, B. (2018). Predicting suicidal ideation in college students with mental health screening questionnaires. *Psychiatry Investigation, 15*(11), 1037–1045. doi:10.30773/pi.2018.08.21.3 PMID:30380820

Starks, K. (2014). Cognitive behavioral game design: A unified model for designing serious games. *Frontiers in Psychology, 5*, 28. doi:10.3389/fpsyg.2014.00028 PMID:24550858

Stephenson, A., McDonough, S. M., Murphy, M. H., Nugent, C. D., & Mair, J. L. (2017). Using computer, mobile and wearable technology enhanced interventions to reduce sedentary behaviour: A systematic review and meta-analysis. *The International Journal of Behavioral Nutrition and Physical Activity, 14*(1), 1–17. doi:10.118612966-017-0561-4 PMID:28800736

Steptoe, A., Demakakos, P., de Oliveira, C., & Wardle, J. (2012). Distinctive biological correlates of positive psychological well-being in older men and women. *Psychosomatic Medicine, 74*(5), 501–508. doi:10.1097/PSY.0b013e31824f82c8 PMID:22511728

Stern, Y. (2012). Cognitive reserve in ageing and Alzheimer's disease. *Lancet Neurology, 11*(11), 1006–1012. doi:10.1016/S1474-4422(12)70191-6 PMID:23079557

Sultana, M., Bryant, D., Orange, J. B., Beedie, T., & Montero-Odasso, M. (2020). Effect of Wii Fit© exercise on balance of older adults with neurocognitive disorders: A meta-analysis. *Journal of Alzheimer's Disease, 75*(3), 817–826. doi:10.3233/JAD-191301 PMID:32310168

Thomas, T. H., Sivakumar, V., Babichenko, D., Grieve, V. L. B., & Klem, M. (2020). Mapping Behavioral Health Serious Game Interventions for Adults With Chronic Illness: Scoping Review. *JMIR Serious Games, 8*(3), e18687. doi:10.2196/18687 PMID:32729836

Tong, T., Chan, J. H., & Chignell, M. (2017). Serious games for dementia. *Proceedings of the 26th International Conference on World Wide Web Companion*, 1111–1115. 10.1145/3041021.3054930

Tran, M. K. P., Robert, P., & Bremond, F. (2016). A Virtual Agent for enhancing performance and engagement of older people with dementia in Serious Games. *Workshop Artificial Compagnon-Affect-Interaction 2016*.

Travers, B. G., Mason, A. H., Mrotek, L. A., Ellertson, A., Dean, D. C. III, Engel, C., Gomez, A., Dadalko, O. I., & McLaughlin, K. (2018). Biofeedback-based, videogame balance training in autism. *Journal of Autism and Developmental Disorders, 48*(1), 163–175. doi:10.100710803-017-3310-2 PMID:28921103

Treskes, R. W., van der Velde, E. T., Barendse, R., & Bruining, N. (2016). Mobile health in cardiology: A review of currently available medical apps and equipment for remote monitoring. *Expert Review of Medical Devices*, *13*(9), 823–830. doi:10.1080/17434440.2016.1218277 PMID:27477584

Tripette, J., Murakami, H., Ryan, K. R., Ohta, Y., & Miyachi, M. (2017). The contribution of Nintendo Wii Fit series in the field of health: A systematic review and meta-analysis. *PeerJ*, *5*, e3600. doi:10.7717/peerj.3600 PMID:28890847

University of Illinois Chicago. (2021). *Big Data and Wearable Health Monitors: Harnessing the Benefits and Overcoming Challenges*. https://healthinformatics.uic.edu/blog/big-data-and-wearable-health-monitors-harnessing-the-benefits-and-overcoming-challenges

Ventola, C. L. (2014). Mobile devices and apps for health care professionals: Uses and benefits. *P&T*, *39*(5), 356. PMID:24883008

Viceconti, M., Zannoni, C., Baruffaldi, F., Pierotti, L., Toni, A., & Cappello, A. (2020). CT-scan data acquisition to generate biomechanical models of bone structures. *Computer Methods in Biomechanics and Biomedical Engineering*, *2*, 279–287.

Wattanasoontorn, V., Boada, I., García, R., & Sbert, M. (2013). Serious games for health. *Entertainment Computing*, *4*(4), 231–247. doi:10.1016/j.entcom.2013.09.002

West, L. R. (2015). Strava: Challenge yourself to greater heights in physical activity/cycling and running. *British Journal of Sports Medicine*, *49*(15), 1024. doi:10.1136/bjsports-2015-094899 PMID:25964665

Wittland, J., Brauner, P., & Ziefle, M. (2015). Serious Games for Cognitive Training in Ambient Assisted Living Environments – A Technology Acceptance Perspective. In *Human-Computer Interaction – INTERACT 2015* (pp. 453–471). Springer International Publishing. doi:10.1007/978-3-319-22701-6_34

Wu, M., & Luo, J. (2019). Wearable technology applications in healthcare: A literature review. *On-Line Journal of Nursing Informatics*, *23*(3).

Xu, Z., Yu, B., & Wang, F. (2020). Artificial intelligence/machine learning solutions for mobile and wearable devices. *Digital Health: Mobile and Wearable Devices for Participatory Health Applications*, 55.

Zou, D., Ma, L., Yu, J., & Zhang, Z. (2015). Biological databases for human research. *Genomics, Proteomics & Bioinformatics*, *13*(1), 55–63. doi:10.1016/j.gpb.2015.01.006 PMID:25712261

ADDITIONAL READING

Ahmad, S., Mehmood, F., Khan, F., & Whangbo, T. K. (2022). Architecting Intelligent Smart Serious Games for Healthcare Applications: A Technical Perspective. *Sensors (Basel)*, *22*(3), 810. doi:10.339022030810 PMID:35161556

De Croon, R., Wildemeersch, D., Wille, J., Verbert, K., & Vanden Abeele, V. (2018). Gamification and serious games in a healthcare informatics context. *2018 IEEE International Conference on Healthcare Informatics (ICHI)*, 53–63. 10.1109/ICHI.2018.00014

Dietlein, C., Eichberg, S., Fleiner, T., & Zijlstra, W. (2018). Feasibility and effects of serious games for people with dementia: A systematic review and recommendations for future research. *Gerontechnology (Valkenswaard)*, *17*(1), 1–17. doi:10.4017/gt.2018.17.1.001.00

Graafland, M., & Schijven, M. (2018). How serious games will improve healthcare. In *Digital Health* (pp. 139–157). Springer. doi:10.1007/978-3-319-61446-5_10

Lu, A. S. (2013). *Serious Games for healthcare: applications and implications*. Mary Ann Liebert, Inc.

Maheu-Cadotte, M.-A., Cossette, S., Dubé, V., Fontaine, G., Lavallée, A., Lavoie, P., Mailhot, T., & Deschênes, M.-F. (2021). Efficacy of serious games in healthcare professions education: A systematic review and meta-analysis. *Simulation in Healthcare*, *16*(3), 199–212. PMID:33196609

Spil, T. A. M., Romijnders, V., Sundaram, D., Wickramasinghe, N., & Kijl, B. (2021). Are serious games too serious? Diffusion of wearable technologies and the creation of a diffusion of serious games model. *International Journal of Information Management*, *58*, 102202. doi:10.1016/j.ijinfomgt.2020.102202 PMID:32836650

KEY TERMS AND DEFINITIONS

Digital Health: Is health information technology that supports clinical decisions in healthcare systems to improve diagnosis, treatment outcomes and delivery of health in patients.

E-Health Apps: Are electronic health record software applications which are collecting health data from patients, and they communicate them to healthcare teams and professionals with the aim to exchange important clinical information about patients.

Health Economics: Is an economical application to the field of health care and aims to maximize the goods and services from the health resources to effectively deliver quality of health in patients.

Healthcare Data: Are data related to the health of a patient or population and include demographic characteristics, medical history, and any recorded information about a patient.

Healthcare Informatics: Refers to health information systems that are based on informative technological advances to promote benefits in healthcare systems.

Serious Games: Are games designed especially for clinical populations, and they promote comprehensive and professional therapeutic models as game therapies.

Wearables: Are technologically advanced devices that can be worn by an individual and record important physiological data.

Chapter 8
Money Management:
Serious Games for the Elderly

Ana Maria Gonzaga
Hospital Magalhães Lemos, Portugal

Maria Céu Lamas
Escola Superior Saúde, Instituto Politécnico do Porto, Portugal

ABSTRACT

With the increase in average life expectancy and the demographic ageing of the worldwide population, several challenges have emerged at the social, economic, and health are levels. To improve this process, the WHO advocates active ageing, where cognitive stimulation is one of the important aspects to consider for the adoption of a healthy lifestyle and the care of one's mental health. In this framework, serious games can bring more benefits to older people and caregivers. In order to assess the contribution of serious games, a bibliographic research was carried out in the Web of Science database, using the terms "serious game" and "elderly." It is found that the use of serious games has benefits in several domains. Within the scope of cognitive stimulation, there are several games, although they do not value the difficulties that individuals have in their IADLs. In this context, it is important to stimulate skills related to money management. This intervention will help to maintain daily living skills and optimize responses to functional losses, resulting in active aging.

INTRODUCTION

People live in communities in constant change, subject to various and rapid technological innovations with applicability in various domains. The improvement in quality of life and health care has contributed to the longevity of people around the world and, consequently, the ageing of populations.

The phenomenon of ageing is characterized by structural and functional changes in various body systems, with implications for functionality and quality of life, which may limit independence and performance in carrying out activities of daily living and social participation (Fontaine, 2000; López-Otín et al, 2013; Divo et al, 2014). However, the changes associated with ageing are not expressed at the

DOI: 10.4018/978-1-7998-9732-3.ch008

same time in life in all individuals. On a singular level, several factors – physical, psychological, and cognitive problems associated with external, environmental, social, professional, and economic factors – may influence it (Firmino et al, 2014). As ageing is a biological stage in which it is important to live with quality and dignity, cognitive stimulation is one of the activities that is often implicit in healthy and pathological ageing, with a focus on dementia. This reflects that lack of cognitive activity leads to cognitive loss (Woods et al, 2012). Cognitive deficits will limit the elderly in their decisions, and consequently, lower their self-esteem. On the other hand, the loss of autonomy, associated with these deficits and loss of mobility, also contribute to the decrease in self-esteem of the elderly (Firmino et al, 2014). In this context, it is understood that one of the great challenges is focused on screening and early diagnosis of cognitive decline.

To promote the maintenance of the elderly for as long as possible in their respective communities, it is a priority to provide conditions and provision of multimodal care by formal and informal caregivers, whether the latter is a family member or not. Elderly people and their caregivers are often advised to do mental exercises to help delay the decline in memory and reasoning common at this stage of the life cycle. Nevertheless, this type of cognitive stimulation aimed at stimulating reasoning and memory can involve a panoply of activities such as word games, puzzles, music, and practical everyday activities such as cooking and gardening (Woods et al, 2012).

With the increasing technological influence in everyday life, today's societies are becoming digital societies, in which attention is increasingly directed towards new technologies (Barbosa et al, 2017). However, if people live in a society that is constantly evolving technologically, how can cognitive stimulation tools possibly keep up with this evolution? Could these methodologies not be more active, and transformed into games/digital applications, associated with the use of information and communication technologies?

In this sense, the objective of this chapter was to characterize demographic ageing, particularly in Portugal, as well as the main challenges associated with this worldwide phenomenon, with a focus on cognitive decline. In this context, the authors highlight the importance of basic and instrumental activities of daily living, which allow the assessment of independence or degree of dependence in different areas of daily life. By reviewing the bibliography, the authors searched for what serious games existed, sought to understand the impact of their use in this segment of the population, and to find out in which domains they are developed. Finally, some recommendations are made about the possibility of working with the elderly in the field of money management, aiming to contribute to the maintenance of functionality in their daily lives. This is an area related to other aspects of a person's life, such as shopping and taking public transport. By remaining independent in these activities, functioning in these areas, and being integrated in their environment, the older person will surely have an active and healthy ageing throughout life.

BACKGROUND

Ageing Population

The ageing of the population is a worldwide phenomenon, resulting from the improvement of living conditions and the evolution of medicine and health care (WHO, 2015).

In Portugal, as in other countries of the European community, the trend of demographic ageing has been maintained for several decades, due to the reduction of the youth population at working-age and to the increase in the number of elderly people because of low birth rates, increased longevity, and negative migration balances until 2016, leading to an increase in the median age of the resident population. Consequently, in 2019, the ageing rate was 163.2 people per 100 young people, with this rate increasing in all regions, the Alentejo being the region with the oldest population (206.1). Although they occur at different rhythms, these changes in the population's age pyramid (Figure 1) influence the degree of dependency of populations (INE, 2019).

Figure 1. Age pyramids according to estimates (2019) and projections (2080) of the population residing in Portugal
Source: Adapted from INE (2019)

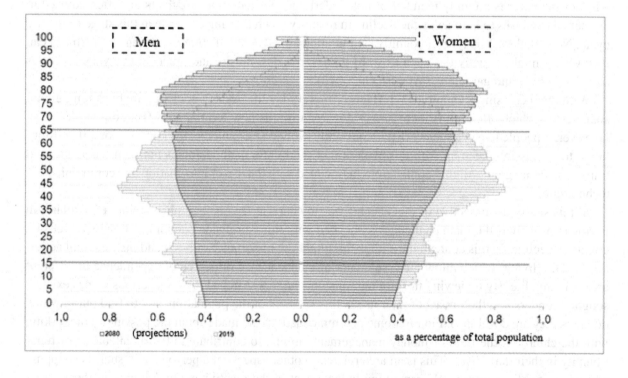

The dependency index measures the weight of the elderly in the working-age population. It is estimated that the rate of dependence of the elderly, between 2019 and 2080, may increase from 34.5 to 72.4 elderly per 100 potentially active people - Figure 2 (INE, 2019).

Figure 2. Age pyramids according to estimates (2019) and projections (2080) of the population residing in Portugal
Source: Adapted from INE (2019)

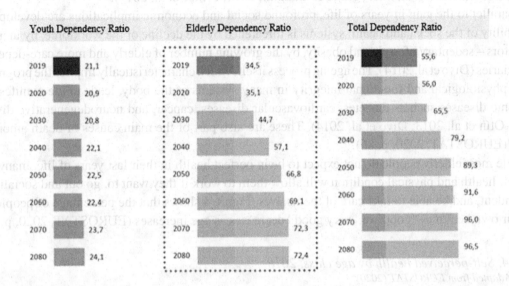

In 2018, Portugal had a proportion of young people lower than that of the EU-28 and one of the lowest among the other countries, while the proportion of elderly people was higher than that of the EU-28, Portugal being the 4th country with the highest percentage of elderly people - Figure 3 (INE, 2019).

Figure 3. Percentage of elderly people in the EU-28, 2018
Source: Adapted from EUROSTAT (2020)

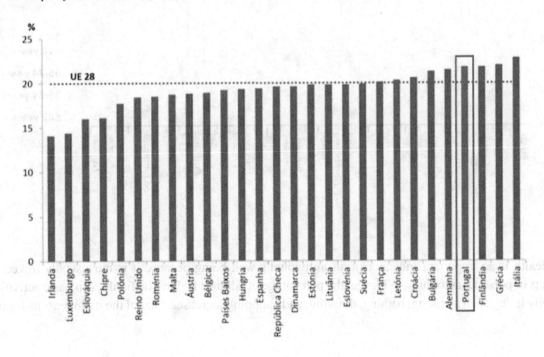

This reveals that Portugal faces problematic societal issues (EC, 2015; OECD, 2017; SNS, 2017), namely the increased prevalence of neurocognitive disorders, usually referred to as mild cognitive decline and dementia (Prince et al, 2013; Hugo & Ganguli, 2014; Prince et al, 2015).

In parallel to the gain in years of life, profound social and economic implications are developed, as the viability of the social and health systems is threatened by the decline of the workforce, by increased risk factors – sedentary lifestyle and obesity, by the growing number of elderly and more care-dependent beneficiaries (Divo et al, 2014). The ageing process itself, which characteristically implies the progressive loss of physiological and functional integrity in many systems of the body, leads to the manifestation of chronic diseases such as diabetes, cardiovascular diseases, cancer, and neurodegenerative diseases (López-Otín et al, 2013; Divo et al, 2014). These are also part of the main causes of death among the elderly (EUROSTAT, 2020, p. 86).

While most elderly people do not expect to be in perfect health in their last years of life, many hope that their health and physical condition will allow them to work if they want to, go out and socialize, be independent, and be able to take care of themselves. Figure 4 shows that the percentage of people who see their own health as "good" or "very good" decreases as age increases (EUROSTAT, 2020, p. 53).

Figure 4. Self-perceived health by age class, 2018
Source: Adapted from EUROSTAT (2020)

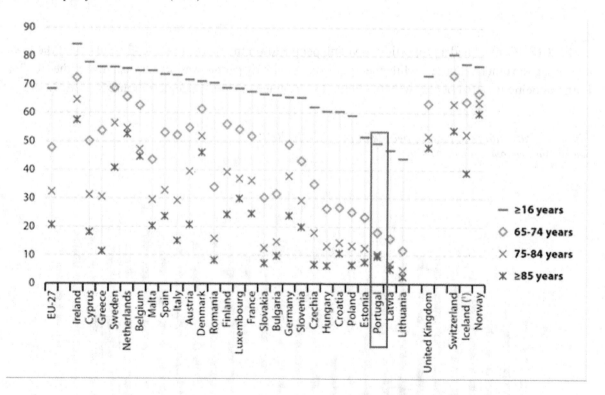

Health is an important indicator of an individual's well-being because it is intrinsically linked to aspects of personal autonomy. With age, the percentage of adults who have difficulties in basic activities of daily living such as eating, bathing, dressing, and shopping increases. One of the main reasons for the use of this standardized model is the relatively high proportion of old people suffering from physical and sensory functional limitations, with an impact on their vision, hearing, mobility, communication, or ability to remember. Most elderly people suffer from diseases or organ dysfunctions. However, if they can carry out their activities alone, independently, and autonomously, they are considered healthy, as they are not limited in their activities or restricted from social participation (Moraes, 2009; Connolly at al, 2017; Feger et al, 2020).

Realizing that the increase in longevity is not directly related to active, healthy, and independent ageing most of the time (Oxley, 2009), in 2015, the World Health Organization (WHO, 2005) proposed "Active Ageing" as a strategy to promote healthy ageing. The notion of active ageing allows people to be the protagonists in this process and to be responsible for their physical, social, and mental well-being throughout the course of life. It considers that active participation in regular and moderate physical and cognitive activities can delay functional declines and is of great importance for a healthy lifestyle (WHO, 2005; Santos et al, 2019). For ageing to be a positive experience, a longer life must be accompanied by continuous opportunities for health, social participation, and safety.

The normal ageing process implies a physical, mental, and functional deficit in all individuals, although to varying degrees of intensity. And the intensity of this deficit determines the degree of dependence that will affect the elderly in the various areas of their individual and social life. According to Demir et al (2014), with age, cognitive impairment worsens. Patients in their study had a rate of cognitive impairment of 56.8%.

The goal of global geriatric assessment is to better understand the condition of the elderly and their problems, allowing for a more complete, coordinated, and integrated response from professionals. Consequently, it facilitates the maintenance of functional capacity, decreases the risk of hospitalization, and provides a better quality of life for the elderly (Sousa, 2019). The Figure 5 expresses some of the self-reported difficulties that people aged 75 and over experience in their daily lives.

Figure 5. Self-reported difficulties for household and personal care activities among people aged ≥ 75 years by sex, UE-27, 2014
Source: Adapted from EUROSTAT (2020)

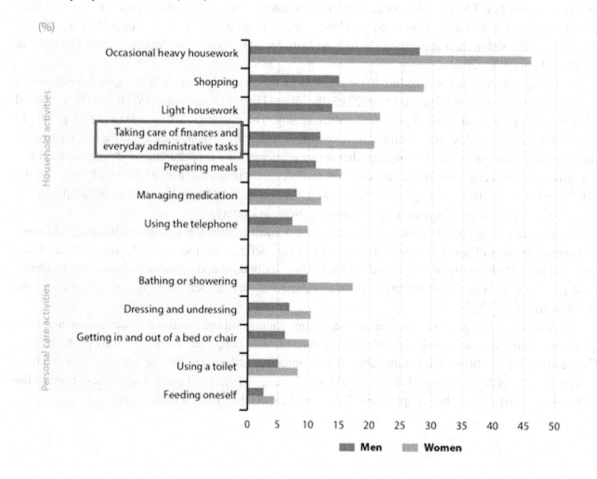

In 2014, 39.2% of the elderly people in the EU-27 had serious difficulties in occasionally performing heavy housework, mainly women (45.9%) compared to men (27.9%), as well as for each of the domestic and personal care activities. On the other hand, more than one tenth of all persons (both genders) in the EU-27 aged 75 years or older had serious difficulties in medication management (10.4%), in the preparation of meals (13.8%), in the bath and shower (14.3%), in the care of finances and daily administrative tasks (17.1%), or in light housework - washing dishes, ironing, making beds and caring for children - (18.6%), and more than one fifth in shopping (23.2%) (EUROSTAT, 2020, p. 72).

Ageing and Cognitive Functions

The ageing process is associated with a set of brain alterations that induce changes in cognitive functions, namely in attention, memory, in the spatial perspective and adaptive capacity, in executive functions and processing speed (Fontaine, 2000; Parents, 2008), which may result in difficulty in adapting to new roles and changes, in lack of motivation, self-esteem, autonomy and difficulty in planning the future (Fontaine, 2000). However, cognitive decline is not a uniform process in all individuals, therefore several authors report that it is associated with health factors and previous lifestyles (Drag & Bieliauskas, 2010). Through psychological theory, it seeks to explain the ageing process, describing the different ways of ageing related to intelligence, memory, personality, motivation, and skills. Thus, when exercised, it contributes to the preservation of the functional capacity and well-being of the elderly (Fonseca, 2006). The educational level itself – which the higher it is – is considered a reliable indicator of cognitive reserve (Drag & Bieliauskas, 2010).

On the other hand, the individual perspective of the ageing process as a pathological event and the beginning of the countdown of life, lessens the will to remain active and participative in the social environment in which the person is involved. This passive, inactive and progressively less reflective role may represent damage to physical and mental health, even constituting a risk factor for cognitive decline (Souza & Chaves, 2005).

According to Baltes and Smith (2003), adults and the elderly have a set of favourable conditions to develop their cognitive abilities at their disposal, considering that the increase in cognitive reserves is related to different cultural variables such as: better health, favourable material conditions, literacy instruments available and lifelong educational systems. Thus, cognitive abilities when properly stimulated and exercised tend to suffer a later and less pronounced decline. The same authors, through the BASE study, showed that the elderly have a high plasticity, and an important ability to accept and process the losses that occur. However, with advancing age, neuroplasticity decreases, and it is necessary to stimulate it through activities that favour intellectual, emotional, relational, and physical capacities, in an integral way (Fontaine, 2000; Paúl, 2006). Thus, the more the brain is exercised with intellectual activities, the longer it will take to lose its connections and, consequently, present symptomatic losses (Nordon et al, 2009).

Currently, dementia is one of the main pathologies associated with ageing, in which age remains the most important risk factor. In Portugal, it is estimated that there are 153,000 people with dementia, of which 90,000 have Alzheimer's disease, which corresponds to approximately 1% of the national population. In Europe, the data amount to 7.3 million people with dementia, with an increasing incidence expected in the coming decades (Luz & Miguel, 2015).

The definition of the clinical diagnosis of dementia is related to the understanding of a syndrome that encompasses multiple cognitive deficits. Although cognitive decline is heterogeneous among the elderly population, the different studies (Demir et al, 2014; Feber et al, 2020; Romero-Ayuso et al, 2021) are consensual in the evidence that dementia tends to accentuate deficits in cognitive functions, which in turn, interfere in various domains – social, occupational, and instrumental activities of daily living. In short, it is a pathology that strongly limits the quality of life of the elderly, because it interferes with the occupational and social functioning of individuals (Luz & Miguel, 2015).

Dementia in the elderly is also a common condition of vulnerability, for which pharmacological intervention is not always effective. In this context, several proposals for non-pharmacological interventions have emerged with the aim of reducing the negative impacts associated with the progression of the disease. Thus, considering the cognitive state of each individual, strategies aimed at the prevention of functional losses and maintenance of the basic and instrumental capacities of daily life are established (Luz & Miguel, 2015).

This last aspect is of paramount importance, since older adults may reveal some difficulty in performing daily life activities, which compromises their functional performance. These activities can be divided into:

1)   Basic Activities of Daily Living (BADLs), which include various self-care activities. They are bathing, going to the bathroom, getting in and out of bed, eating, getting dressed and bowel/bladder movements.

2)   Instrumental Activities of Daily Living (IADLs), involved in the integration of the person in his/her environment, and these are:

   a.   tasks that involve physical health: taking care of the house, washing clothes, preparing meals and shopping.

   b.   tasks that require cognitive resources: using means of transport, using the telephone, taking responsibility for financial matters and responsibility for their own medication.

In the study developed by Demir et al. (2014), no difference was found between the two groups of patients who were classified as normal or with impaired cognitive function in terms of activities such as watching television or resting, which required less functional capacity. They noted that patients with no cognitive impairment had better social participation and interaction, including more leisure, exercise, and shopping, as well as a better mood. The assessment of elderly people's daily activities could provide valuable health information. In this sequence, to evaluate functionality, the Lawton & Brody Scale can be used, because it allows the evaluation of the autonomy of the person to perform the activities necessary to live independently in the community, called IADL. The information can be obtained through a questionnaire directly answered by the person, family members or caregivers. For each IADL the person is classified as: Independent (1 point) or Dependent (2, 3, 4 or 5 points).

It is common throughout life for people to worry about whether they will have enough money when they retire, but they rarely worry about their ability to manage it. This indifference is probably associated with the fact that many financial activities are routine and rely on "crystallized" intelligence, which consists of knowledge that accumulates over time. However, normal cognitive ageing can lead to financial errors because people lose much of their "fluid" intelligence when they reach their 70s or 80s. Even in situations of normal cognitive ageing, changes may occur that limit their ability to handle their financial affairs, such as the death or incapacity of the spouse responsible for these activities. For older people with cognitive decline, the challenges will be greater. In its milder forms, such a decline affects their judgment but not their ability to make financial decisions, which puts older people at risk of potentially serious mistakes and fraud. The ability of retirees to handle their own financial affairs is completely eroded by more serious forms of cognitive impairment, making it more likely that someone more capable will take over their finances. However, because of their reliance, dementia patients are at risk of financial exploitation by their caregivers (Belbase & Sanzenbacher, 2017).

Financial capability is the ability to manage one's finances in one's own best interest and involves a variety of tasks ranging from the simplest procedures, such as paying bills, to the most critical exercises, such as evaluating the potential return on an investment relative to its risk (Caboral-Stevens & Medetsky, 2014; Schaie et al, 2016), as expressed in Table 1.

Table 1. Types of Abilities Measured by Tests of Financial Capacity

Type of ability	Example of tasks
Basic money skills	Identify and understand the value of banknotes and coins.
Cash transactions	Analyse the price of a product and comprehend the sales receipt.
Checkbook Management	Recognize when and how to use a check.
Bill payment	Understand how to read bills, pay them, and dispute them.
Bank statement management	Find deposits, withdrawals, and balances in a bank statement.
Asset and estate management	Identify assets and incomes.
Knowledge of financial concepts	Understand concepts like debt, insurance, and asset returns.
Financial decision	Determine the value of an asset, as well as fraud and other threats.

Source: Adapted from Marson et al. (2009)

Normal cognitive ageing does not have enough of an impact on financial capacity to warrant intervention. Unlike the normal cognitive changes associated with ageing, cognitive impairment, which is becoming more common among people in their 80s, can quickly diminish financial ability. This condition can manifest itself in a variety of ways, ranging from mild cognitive impairment (MCI) to severe dementia. These issues may be temporary or indicate the onset of dementia (Belbase & Sanzenbacher, 2017). Thus, in the "Money Management" function, it is necessary to perceive if the person has some difficulties: i) When going shopping, only notes of a certain value are used; ii) Forgets to receive change; iii) Does not check the change received; and iv) Loses the money taken.

There are many instruments used to assess these capacities. Their use stems from options dictated by various reasons: objectives; costs; technical availability; simplicity; reliability. For the objectives aimed at in the Global Geriatric Assessment and because they are the most used for this purpose, those that are presented in this chapter are recommended, because they are simple, reliable, easy to perform, little time-consuming and well accepted by the elderly. However, the innovative mechanism based on games that mix the real world with the virtual, through the simulation of practical situations of daily life, enable more frequent, accessible, and pleasant interventions, capable of involving and motivating the elderly (Santos et al, 2019) and empowering them to stay more functional and ensure their autonomy for longer.

In ageing populations, neurodegenerative diseases, such as Alzheimer's, are a major challenge for the health system, so it is important to continue to develop instruments to better assess the severity and progression of the disease, improve treatment, stimulation, and rehabilitation of these people (Robert et al, 2014; Ben-Sadoun et al, 2018).

Cognitive Stimulation

Intervention in cognition consists of a process of cooperation between the individual with cognitive deficit and health professionals, family members and other members of the community, such as caregivers, to balance or mitigate cognitive deficits resulting from neurological damage (Pais, 2008). Initially, the different intervention techniques aim at clinical restoration and later the compensation of functions, with the objective of minimizing the disorders of executive functions, attention and memory, language, visual processing, reasoning, and problem solving (Pais, 2008; Apostle et al, 2014; Apostle & Cardoso, 2014). To maximize the effectiveness of the various intervention techniques, these should express specific outlined objectives and should be carried out over several sessions in a sequential and continuous manner (Pais, 2008; Apostle et al, 2014; Apostle & Cardoso, 2014).

In the context of neurocognitive disorders, cognitive stimulation is particularly relevant due to the growing clinical, social, and economic impact of these clinical conditions (Woods et al, 2012; Apostle et al, 2014; Apostle & Cardoso, 2014). There is some evidence that supports the efficacy of cognitive stimulation, resulting in gains in health, particularly in cognition, mood, well-being, functional activity, quality of life and communication skills (Woods et al, 2006; Yuill & Hollis, 2011; Woods et al, 2012; Aguirre et al, 2014; Apostle et al, 2014; Apostle & Cardoso, 2014) and in the reduction of the burden of the caregiver and the consumption of human and economic resources (Woods et al, 2006; Woods et al, 2012; Apostle et al, 2014; Apostle & Cardoso, 2014).

In this field, the provision of care must contribute to increase the potential of self-care through the promotion of autonomy and self-esteem, adaptation to deficits and by the involvement and training of the family and respective support and care network (Woods et al, 2012). This will be a way of delaying institutionalisation, while enhancing dependency.

With the development of new technologies, the use of digital resources for the prevention and rehabilitation of cognitive alterations has been the subject of several studies and research in this area, which support the possibility that leisure activities associated with computing devices – computers, tablets, smartphones, or serious games – can be a protective factor for the development of cognitive deficits and dementia. The cognitive stimulation through these digital tools tends to be more flexible and personalised than the traditional methods, due to providing results or comments on the performance in real time, with the possibility of being adjusted to the skill level of the user and therefore, allowing for a motivating or even fun activity (Xavier et al, 2014).

Serious games

Notwithstanding the various definitions for serious games, all share the existence of having an explicit educational purpose as a priority, rather than simply serving as entertainment and fun. Which does not mean they cannot accumulate those characteristics (Michael & Chen, 2006).

The use of Serious Games in Health is expanding, particularly in Mental Health. The recent closeness between technologies and rehabilitation led to the evolution of the traditional system being practically supported in the connection between therapist and patient, for systems where technology takes on a supporting role to therapy (Luz & Miguel, 2015; Lau & Agius, 2021). The use of technology in this field reveals itself as being demanding and challenging (Barbosa et al, 2017), mainly when it involves individuals with dementia. In this field, it is necessary to contemplate many factors, namely: the needs of these people, the human-computer interaction, emotions, and comfort, among others. Although it causes game development to be more complicated, a well-planned and friendlier graphic interface helps people to concentrate more on the game (Foti et al, 2014). The application of information and communication technologies to serious games, can contribute to improve the ludic aspect of the computerised cognitive training and provide motivating solutions for elderly patients (Robert et al, 2020). On the other hand, Serious Games can provide interesting and useful data and statistics for monitoring an individual's condition, which can then be analysed more objectively by health professionals or other specialists.

When it is considered that many older adults are not familiar with digital games, it is necessary to pose the question, can this lack of experience cause stress and consequently limit or hinder the motivations of the users to use them? In the study developed by Khalili et al (2020), it was concluded that the experience in playing digital games was not stressful for the elderly participants, although they advised the need to include an element of fun in the games.

In any case, the main underlying premise to the development of Serious Games (Robert et al, 2014), will be the involvement of multidisciplinary teams (health professionals, computer experts, project managers), patients and respective caregivers (Ben-Sadoun et al, 2018). Nonetheless, increasingly, the recourse to digital devices is an effective potential option for cognitive rehabilitation (Bonavitta et al, 2015; Taylor & Griffin, 2015), even having a positive impact in various motor and cognitive functions (Maillot et al, 2012), so incapacitating chronic illnesses can benefit greatly from digital therapy (Abbadessa et al, 2021; Lau & Agius, 2021).

This category of games has the advantage of combining knowledge with fun and involvement from the players to be able to attain specific objectives, which can relate to social problems, health (Machado et al, 2011; Lopez-Basterretxea et al, 2014; Pessini et al, 2015), money management assessment and stimulation of the skills needed for the carrying out of everyday activities. In this perspective, and in the domain of "Money Management" there are implicit circumstantial and functional evaluations.

As the population ages, so does the number of people diagnosed with dementia, making early detection of cognitive decline critical. As a result of the increased use of mobile technology by older adults, assessments for early detection of cognitive impairment are becoming more convenient and cost-effective (Koo et al, 2019). According to Thompson-Bradley et al. (2012), smartphone-based puzzle games can be used to accurately assess and monitor cognitive function in the elderly. Instead of instrumenting existing games, Tong and colleagues (2016) developed a serious game to assess cognition in the emergency department and increase engagement while performance is tested. They found that the majority of patients (96.6%) completed the game successfully, and that performance was significantly correlated with Montreal Cognitive Assessment (MoCA), Mini-Mental State Examination (MMSE), and Confusion Assessment Method scores (CAM).

The use of money in the different areas of daily life needs specific skills: payment of household bills (electricity, gas, water, among others), purchasing of personal articles (clothes, shoes, items of personal hygiene), personal care (hairdresser, manicure, pedicure, massage), household shopping (food, medication, hygiene products for the house, utensils for the house, among others) purchase of personal interest items (books, magazines, CDs, among others).

Some studies (Manera et al, 2015; Hina et al, 2016) have shown the acceptance of serious games, mentioning an improvement in autonomy and health in general. Therefore, the authors believe that the development of serious games in this domain, directed at cognitive stimulation, having as a basis the use of money, can be a contribution which will allow older people to maintain or develop skills in this area and remain integrated into their family or social context.

As an intervention focused on improving specific aspects of cognition, computerized cognitive training (CCT) has been shown to improve memory, self-control, reasoning, attention deviation, and processing speed. This is why it has been successfully applied in clinical research to combat mental illness and cognitive deficits in disorders such as dementia and other neurodegenerative diseases (Birk & Mandryk, 2019). Although mental illness is on the rise, therapies have not kept pace. Computerized interventions delivered at scale have the potential to reduce clinical demand and make interventions available to those who do not qualify for or cannot afford traditional therapies. Their findings suggest that increasing in-the-moment engagement via interface customization and personalization can boost training effectiveness.

METHODOLOGY

A literature review was conducted through a literature search between the years 2010 and 2021, through the scientific databases Web of Science, restricted to the Portuguese and English language. For this, the descriptors "serious games" and "elderly" and "money" were used, in both English and Portuguese. The inclusion criteria for this review were scientific articles that addressed the referred topic as well as articles that had the topic in question and were referenced in the articles. It was previously defined that the search terms would be present in the abstract and title. Articles that, upon review, did not fit the concept of this chapter were removed, while the remaining articles were read and included in this review.

The research was specifically targeted to answer the questions initially posed by the authors: Is it possible to improve care for older people with cognitive decline? What are possible ways to improve money management through serious games while also improving the autonomy of older people? What games already exist and what can we learn from them?

RESULTS

By analysing the obtained results, the authors realised that the therapy which involved serious games has been a hotspot regarding the care of individuals with dementia and therefore, highlighted a cognitive decline. Valladares-Rodriguez and contributors (2017) highlighted that the use of non-invasive methods, such as serious games, can detect the beginning of MCI or Alzheimer's disease. Also, the study by Chen and colleagues (2021), through two serious PC based games, evaluated the reaction times and the accuracy rates related to cognitive skills between normal individuals, individuals with a minor cognitive deficit and individuals with dementia. The performance result of each elderly person was compared by neuropsychological tests of cognitive functioning based on the Mini Mental State, and weaker results were confirmed in individuals who had signs of cognitive decline.

Initially, the games were more directed towards computerising more traditional games, such as board games, like for example Jigsaws (Dartigues et al, 2013). With technological development there appeared videogames confirming a good performance in dementia treatment, games such as Angry Birds and Kart Rider (Bing, 2014). At this time, the issue emerged relating to the fact that none of them had been specifically designed for the particular treatment of this pathology. In line with this, emerges a window of opportunity for the development of more personalised games directed to dementia. In this context, some games were developed to treat cognitive deficiencies: Minwii, Big Brian Academy, Kitchen and Cooking (Benveniste et al, 2010; Manera et al, 2015; Dinis et al, 2019), while games as Wiifit, Wii Sports are created to work with movement alterations (Padala et al, 2012).

As a result, from technological development and knowledge, various well-planned serious games have appeared with applicability to assess cognitive skills (McCallum, 2013; Allain et al, 2014; Valladares-Rodríguez, 2017; Fontana et al, 2017; Chi et al, 2017). This aspect was approached in the study of Tong & Chignell (2016) which assessed the potential of serious games as a screening tool for delirium, due to the fact the literature highlighted the cognitive deficits, such as dementia and delirium, which many times are not detected in the elderly in the context of urgency. In this way, an automated cognitive test, to detect the onset of delirium can be a helpful complement in the cognitive assessment to support its prevention and treatment. Various cognitive rehabilitation games have been proposed to complement or to substitute the traditional approach to rehabilitation, with the intention to contribute to a better engagement (Lau &

Agius, 2021). In this perspective, the authors consider that although there is a variety of serious games frameworks and proposals for serious rehabilitation games, there is a clear lack of ones that care for the specific and distinct characteristics of individuals who suffer with a mild cognitive deficit. Therefore, in the attempt to optimise the inherent advantages of serious games, the MCI-GaTE (MCI-Game Therapy Experience) was proposed – a structure which can be used to develop serious games as effective tools for cognitive and physical rehabilitation. This came about because it results from the combination of the analysis of the institutionalised residents' profiles, structured interviews with occupational therapists who work daily with this kind of individuals and bibliographical research.

With the aim of highlighting the gains associated with virtual reality, directed to cognitive stimulation in the elderly and this one possibly being linked to serious games, a controlled case study was conducted where an experimental group was subjected to cognitive stimulation based in virtual reality and a controlled group was subjected to cognitive stimulation with paper and pencil. The results highlighted positive effects in the dimensions of general cognition, executive functioning, attention, and visual memory in the first group (Gamito et al, 2020). With the aim of improving concentration and minimizing the effects of cognitive decline in attention for the elderly, Fontana and contributors (2017) developed the game TrainBrain which can be also extended to children with attention deficit hyperactivity disorder. However, more studies must be developed to consolidate if such effects can be broadened to functionality and well-being of the elderly with cognitive decline (Gamito et al, 2020). Many of the investigations contemplated the evaluation through questionnaires, as for example the MMSE or MoCA (Kurlowicz & Wallace, 1999; Smith et al, 2007), while other investigators used physiological signs resorting to electroencephalogram (EEG) and electrodermal activity (EDA) to explore the effects of the games on the people (Qi et al, 2004; Wen et al, 2018). Nonetheless, a model of evaluation of cognitive stimulation efficacy, should be multimodal, combining the tests results by questionnaires, the games results, the physiological signs, and the re-evaluations from the professional team.

In the scope of evaluation of memory and flexibility/mental attention in patients with neurocognitive disorders, the effectiveness of the MeMo (Memory Motivation) web application was studied, which can be used in a computer or tablet. The randomised controlled study compared the cognition and behavioural progress among patients who do not use MeMo (control group) and patients who use MeMo (MeMo Group) for 12 weeks (4 sessions/week). After 12 weeks, improvement was observed in attention and motivation, simply by the regular use of the application (Robert et al, 2020).

Generally, the digital interventions are centred in the cognitive deficits, disregarding the difficulties the patients experience in the IADL. In this domain, various virtual environments were developed aimed at the movement within the community (Foreman et al, 2005; Gamito et al, 2017), meal preparation (Klinger et al, 2009; Manera et al, 2015) and cleaning and maintenance of the home (Man et al, 2012; Oliveira et al, 2018; Gamito et al, 2019; Cabinio et al, 2020).

Given that cognitive decline cannot be reversed, all efforts and interventions should be focused on improving the quality of life of these people as much as possible and promoting an autonomous and normalized lifestyle. Based on the findings of Lopez et al. (2014), the authors also believe that intervention tools that focus on maintaining and training skills through technological devices and leisure could help this population live more independently. However, more research is needed. As a result, the authors define additional research lines as follows:

- Create Serious Games to improve other skills and abilities.
- Include as many currencies and grades as possible in the games.

- Conceptualize and develop activities based on real-life scenarios, such as shopping at the supermarket.

The sensation of being effectively "present" in the virtual world, acting and experiencing sensations as if they were inserted in real context, can allow for the transference to a reality of capacities and behaviours meanwhile practiced (Tieri et al, 2018). Triggered by the COVID-19 pandemic, the authors felt the prolific importance of digital interventions in the provision of health services. In this sense, it investigated the viability and potential of rehabilitation through interactive virtual environments incredibly realistic for the neurorehabilitation of patients with mild cognitive decline. Images of a medium size supermarket were taken to create a neurorehabilitation platform - NeuroVRehab.PT, due to being the sort of shop more visited for buying food and products for the home. The platform is made of three independent game modes: supermarket, recipes, and shopping lists. The adopted design, associated with the analysis of IADL patients' previous experiences, is a promising methodology to develop effective digital interventions to promote functioning in the real world (Ferreira-Brito et al, 2020).

SOLUTIONS AND RECOMMENDATIONS

In the present investigation, there was found to be a gap in the serious games segment which dealt with the use of money. Only one study was found dealing with the context of the daily life of older people which can be one of the first signs of cognitive decline interfering with the person's functionality and for which the caregiver must be attentive to. However, it is possible to include Lopez-Basterretxea and collaborators' (2014) study, which was based on serious games and addressed money management skills in people with intellectual disabilities.

Serious games have an important place in the care of people with cognitive decline, assuming itself as an interface between computer science, calculation and biomedical sciences but demanding strict communication among the different investigators and the creators of the games to ensure specific objectives of effective application. This next connection is essential to be able to characterise the game in levels in accordance with mild or moderate cognitive decline – for being more effective in the initial and intermediary phase – and domains of activity. Following this logic, Ning and contributors (2020) proposed the creation of a Serious Game Hospital to provide care to people with dementia and in this way offer a systematic professional treatment aimed at the individual. Nonetheless, there is still the need for more investigation into the evaluation of therapeutic efficacy and respective evaluation models. For the authors, the question, and the interest in applying serious games to the specific context of the use of money in the everyday life of older people, are the main assumed challenges. The authors believe that these types of applications, which address money management habits, are essential for an independent and autonomous life, as Lopez-Basterretxea et al. (2014) found in their study. This is because being able to manage money means being able to live a more normal life: i) shopping, getting a cup of coffee, and so on; and ii) continuing to engage in other types of activities.

CONCLUSION

The ageing population demands contributory interventions to improve the quality of life of the elderly and assure their integrated permanence in society and family. For such, it is necessary that in line with the medium life expectancy the authors also associate the quality of the years lived. It is one of the WHO objectives, through the promotion of intervention policies with the intention of obtaining health gains.

In the present panorama of older populations, the mild cognitive decline and dementia, where Alzheimer disease can be emphasised, are a global health problem. Thus, early detection of cognitive decline enables us to distinguish it from physiological ageing in contrast to pathological conditions such as dementia. Not excluding the transitional situations which can be subtle. According to Woods and contributors (2012) there is consistent evidence coming from several clinical trials that cognitive stimulation programmes favour the cognition in people with light to moderate dementia, than any medicinal effect. In this field, medicinal therapy has very little success. Nonetheless, the use of serious games has been emerging as an alternative for the evaluation of cognition and treatment of dementia, with better effects regarding cognitive skills. The serious games applied to health without an entertainment purpose, are generally used in different devices for training, simulation, and education, allowing the people to experience real life situations to improve their skills and their performance in various tasks.

The literature suggests that using serious games has benefits in various domains. As it is possible to see throughout the chapter, although there are several studies related to the topic, there is still a need for more consistent results on the framework and games aimed at individuals with these characteristics. Usually, the digital interventions focus on the cognitive deficit, not valuing the difficulties the patients present in their instrumental daily activities. As with other investigators (Ferreira-Brito et al, 2020; Gamito et al, 2020), the authors also consider that these tools must focus on activities/tasks of daily life which, because they are like reality can benefit from the transfer of the gains of the exercises to the person's daily life.

With the objective of stimulating the skills related with responsibility for financial matters needed to manage money, the focus of a serious game must centre on the first two items: i) Takes care of financial matters on his/her own; and ii) Makes daily purchases but needs help with large purchases and at the bank. Also, must have as its main objective the identification of the money and the respective connection necessary for daily life purchases. Through this type of intervention, the authors think that a programme of digital cognitive stimulation in this field will allow for the maintenance of daily life skills and the optimisation of the answers in the domain of functional losses and therefore, to be a contributor in active ageing.

REFERENCES

Abbadessa, G., Brigo, F., Clerico, M., De Mercanti, S., Trojsi, F., Tedeschi, G., Bonavita, S., & Lavorgna, L. (2021). Digital therapeutics in neurology. *Journal of Neurology*, 1–16. doi:10.100700415-021-10608-4 PMID:34018047

Aguirre, E., Hoare, Z., Spector, A., Woods, R. T., & Orrell, M. (2014). The Effects of a Cognitive Stimulation Therapy [CST] Programme for People with Dementia on Family Caregivers' Health. *BMC Geriatrics*, *14*(31), 1–16. doi:10.1186/1471-2318-14-31 PMID:24628705

Allain, P., Foloppe, D., Besnard, J., Yamaguchi, T., Etcharry-Bouyx, F., Le Gall, D., Nolin, P., & Richard, P. (2014). Detecting Everyday Action Deficits in Alzheimer's Disease Using a Nonimmersive Virtual Reality Kitchen. *Journal of the International Neuropsychological Society*, 20(5), 468–477. doi:10.1017/S1355617714000344 PMID:24785240

Apóstolo, J., & Cardoso, D. (2014). Estimulação Cognitiva em Idosos - Síntese da evidência e intervenção: programa de manutenção [Cognitive Stimulation in the Elderly - Synthesis of the evidence and intervention: maintenance program]. In Envelhecimento, Saúde e Cidadania [Aging, Health and Citizenship]. Coimbra: Unidade de Investigação em Ciências da Saúde: Enfermagem.

Apóstolo, J., Cardoso, D., Rosa, A. I., & Paúl, C. (2014). The Effect of Cognitive Stimulation on Nursing Home Elders: A Randomized Controlled Trial. *Journal of Nursing Scholarship*, 46(3), 157–166. doi:10.1111/jnu.12072 PMID:24597922

Barbosa, H., Vieira, A. C., & Carrapatoso, E. (2017). Exercises and Serious Games Applied to the TEG 2020 - Special Session on Technology, Elderly Games 288 Rehabilitation for Older Adults. *Proceedings of the Portuguese Association for Information Systems Conference*. 10.18803/capsi.v17.354-361

Belbase, A., & Sanzenbacher, G. T. (2017). Cognitive Aging and the Capacity to Manage Money. *Issues in Brief (Alan Guttmacher Institute)*, 17(1).

Ben-Sadoun, G., Manera, V., Alvarez, J., Sacco, G., & Robert, P. (2018). Recommendations for the Design of Serious Games in Neurodegenerative Diseases. *Frontiers in Aging Neuroscience*, 10(13), 13. Advance online publication. doi:10.3389/fnagi.2018.00013 PMID:29456501

Benveniste, S., Jouvelot, P., & Péquignot, R. (2010). The MINWii project: Renarcissization of patients suffering from Alzheimer's disease through video game-based music therapy. In *International Conference on Entertainment Computing*. Springer. 10.1007/978-3-642-15399-0_8

Bing, S. (2014). The research of digital game interactive technology on the prevention and rehabilitation of diseases in the elderly. *Art panorama*, 6, 102.

Birk, M. V., & Mandryk, R. L. (2019). Improving the Efficacy of Cognitive Training for Digital Mental Health Interventions Through Avatar Customization: Crowdsourced Quasi-Experimental Study. *Journal of Medical Internet Research*, 21(1), e10133. Advance online publication. doi:10.2196/10133 PMID:30622095

Bonavita, S., Sacco, R., Della Corte, M., Esposito, S., Sparaco, M., d'Ambrosio, A., Docimo, R., Bisecco, A., Lavorgna, L., Corbo, D., Cirillo, S., Gallo, A., Esposito, F., & Tedeschi, G. (2015). Computer-aided cognitive rehabilitation improves cognitive performances and induces brain functional connectivity changes in relapsing remitting multiple sclerosis patients: An exploratory study. *Journal of Neurology*, 262(1), 91–100. doi:10.100700415-014-7528-z PMID:25308631

Boulay, M., Benveniste, S., Boespflug, S., Jouvelot, P., & Rigaud, A. S. (2011). A pilot usability study of MINWii, a music therapy game for demented patients. *Technology and Health Care: Official Journal of the European Society for Engineering and Medicine*, 19(4), 233–246. doi:10.3233/THC-2011-0628

Cabinio, M., Rossetto, F., Isernia, S., Saibene, F. L., Di Cesare, M., Borgnis, F., Pazzi, S., Migliazza, T., Alberoni, M., Blasi, V., & Baglio, F. (2020). The Use of a Virtual Reality Platform for the Assessment of the Memory Decline and the Hippocampal Neural Injury in Subjects with Mild Cognitive Impairment: The Validity of Smart Aging Serious Game (SASG). *Journal of Clinical Medicine*, *9*(5), 1355. Advance online publication. doi:10.3390/jcm9051355 PMID:32384591

Caboral-Stevens, M., & Medetsky, M. (2014). The Construct of Financial Capacity in Older Adults. *Journal of Gerontological Nursing*, *40*(8), 30–37. doi:10.3928/00989134-20140325-02 PMID:24694046

Chen, Y. T., Hou, C. J., Derek, N., Huang, S. B., Huang, M. W., & Wang, Y. Y. (2021). Evaluation of the reaction time and accuracy rate in normal subjects, MCI, and dementia using serious games. *Applied Sciences (Basel, Switzerland)*, *11*(2), 1–14. doi:10.3390/app11020628

Chi, H., Agama, E., & Prodanoff, Z. G. (2017). Developing serious games to promote cognitive abilities for the elderly. *Proceedings of the 2017 IEEE 5th International Conference on Serious Games and Applications for Health (SeGAH)*.

Connolly, D., Garvey, J., & McKee, G. (2017). Factors associated with ADL/IADL disability in community dwelling older adults in the Irish longitudinal study on ageing (TILDA). *Disability and Rehabilitation*, *39*(8), 809–816. doi:10.3109/09638288.2016.1161848 PMID:27045728

Dartigues, J. F., Foubert-Samier, A., Le Goff, M., Viltard, M., Amieva, H., Orgogozo, J. M., Barberger-Gateau, P., & Helmer, C. (2013). Playing board games, cognitive decline and dementia: A French population-based cohort study. *BMJ Open*, *3*(8), e002998. doi:10.1136/bmjopen-2013-002998 PMID:23988362

Demir Akça, A. S., Saraçli, Ö., Emre, U., Atasoy, N., Güdül, S., Özen Barut, B., Şenormanci, Ö., Büyükuysal, M. Ç., Atik, L., & Atasoy, H. T. (2014). Relationship of Cognitive Functions with Daily Living Activities, Depression, Anxiety and Clinical Variables in Hospitalized Elderly Patients. *Nöro Psikiyatri Arşivi*, *51*(3), 267–274. doi:10.4274/npa.y7053 PMID:28360637

Dinis, A. C., Silvano, A., Casado, D., Espadinha, C., & Noriega, P. (2019). Usability and UX of Nintendo Wii big brain academy game in the elderly as a resource of psychomotor intervention. *Proceedings of the International Conference Healthcare Ergonomics and Patient Safety*. 10.1007/978-3-030-24067-7_31

Divo, M. J., Martinez, C. H., & Mannino, D. M. (2014). Ageing and the epidemiology of multimorbidity. *The European Respiratory Journal*, *44*(4), 1055–1068. doi:10.1183/09031936.00059814 PMID:25142482

Drag, L. L., & Bieliauskas, L. A. (2010). Contemporary Review 2009: Cognitive Aging. *Journal of Geriatric Psychiatry and Neurology*, *23*(2), 75–93. doi:10.1177/0891988709358590 PMID:20101069

European Commission. (2015). *Demography report*. Publications Office of the European Union.

EUROSTAT. (2020). *Ageing Europe. Looking at the lives of older people in the EU*. Publications Office of the European Union., doi:10.2785/628105

Feger, D. M., Willis, S. L., Thomas, K. R., Marsiske, M., Rebok, G. W., Felix, C., & Gross, A. L. (2020). Incident Instrumental Activities of Daily Living Difficulty in Older Adults: Which Comes First? Findings From the Advanced Cognitive Training for Independent and Vital Elderly Study. *Frontiers in Neurology*, *11*, 550577. Advance online publication. doi:10.3389/fneur.2020.550577 PMID:33192982

Ferreira-Brito, F., Alves, S., Santos, O., Guerreiro, T., Caneiras, C., Carriço, L., & Verdelho, A. (2020). Photo-Realistic Interactive Virtual Environments for Neurorehabilitation in Mild Cognitive Impairment (NeuroVRehab.PT): A Participatory Design and Proof-of-Concept Study. *Journal of Clinical Medicine*, *9*(12), 3821. Advance online publication. doi:10.3390/jcm9123821 PMID:33255869

Firmino, H., Nogueira, V., Neves, S., & Lagarto, L. (2014). Psicopatologia das pessoas mais velhas [Psychopathology of Older People]. In Geriatria Fundamental. Saber e Praticar [Fundamental Geriatrics. Knowing and Practicing]. Lidel Edições Técnicas.

Fonseca, A. (2006). O Envelhecimento. Uma abordagem psicológica (2ª edição) [Aging. A Psychological Approach (2nd Edition)]. Lisbon: Universidade Católica Portuguesa.

Fontaine, R. (2000). *Piscologia de envelhecimento* [Psychology of Aging]. Climepsi Editores.

Fontana, E., Gregorio, R., Lucia, E., & Carolina, A. (2017). TrainBrain: A Serious Game for Attention Training. *International Journal of Computers and Applications*, *160*(4), 1–6. doi:10.5120/ijca2017913027

Foreman, N., Stanton-Fraser, D., Wilson, P. N., Duffy, H., & Parnell, R. (2005). Transfer of Spatial Knowledge to a Two-Level Shopping Mall in Older People, Following Virtual Exploration. *Environment and Behavior*, *37*(2), 275–292. doi:10.1177/0013916504269649

Fotis, L., Kurt, D., Athanasios, V., Panagiotis, P., & Alina, E. (2014). Comparing interaction techniques for serious games through braincomputer interfaces: A user perception evaluation study. *Entertainment Computing*, *5*(4), 391–399. doi:10.1016/j.entcom.2014.10.004

Gamito, P., Oliveira, J., Alghazzawi, D., Fardoun, H., Rosa, P., Sousa, T., Maia, I., Morais, D., Lopes, P., & Brito, R. (2017). The Art Gallery Test: A Preliminary Comparison between Traditional Neuropsychological and Ecological VR-Based Tests. *Frontiers in Psychology*, *8*, 1–8. doi:10.3389/fpsyg.2017.01911 PMID:29204128

Gamito, P., Oliveira, J., Alves, C., Santos, N., Coelho, C., & Brito, R. (2020). Virtual Reality-Based Cognitive Stimulation to Improve Cognitive Functioning in Community Elderly: A Controlled Study. *Cyberpsychology, Behavior, and Social Networking*, *23*(3), 150–156. doi:10.1089/cyber.2019.0271 PMID:32031888

Gamito, P., Oliveira, J., Morais, D., Coelho, C., Santos, N., Alves, C., Galamba, A., Soeiro, M., Yerra, M., French, H., Talmers, L., Gomes, T., & Brito, R. (2019). Cognitive Stimulation of Elderly Individuals with Instrumental Virtual Reality-Based Activities of Daily Life: Pre-Post Treatment Study. *Cyberpsychology, Behavior, and Social Networking*, *22*(1), 69–75. doi:10.1089/cyber.2017.0679 PMID:30040477

Hina, M. D., & Dourlens, A. R. S. (2016). Serious Gaming: Autonomy and Better Health for the Elderly. *Proceedings of the 17th International Conference on Computer Systems and Technologies*. 10.1145/2983468.2983519

Hugo, J., & Ganguli, M. (2014). Dementia and Cognitive Impairment: Epidemiology, Diagnosis and Traetment. *Clinics in Geriatric Medicine*, *30*(3), 421–442. doi:10.1016/j.cger.2014.04.001 PMID:25037289

Instituto Nacional de Estatística [National Institute of Statistics]. (2019). *Estatísticas Demográficas* [Demographic Statistics]. https://www.ine.pt/ngt_server/attachfileu.jsp?look_parentBoui=463528670&att_display=n&att_download=y

Khalili-Mahani, N., Assadi, A., Li, K., Mirgholami, M., Rivard, M. E., Benali, H., Sawchuk, K., & De Schutter, B. (2020). Reflective and Reflexive Stress Responses of Older Adults to Three Gaming Experiences In Relation to Their Cognitive Abilities: Mixed Methods Crossover Study. *JMIR Mental Health*, *7*(3), e12388. Advance online publication. doi:10.2196/12388 PMID:32213474

Klinger, E., Cao, X., Douguet, A. S., & Fuchs, P. (2009). Designing an ecological and adaptable virtual task in the context of executive functions. *Studies in Health Technology and Informatics*, *144*, 248–252. PMID:19592774

Koo, B. M., & Vizer, L. V. (2019). Mobile Technology for Cognitive Assessment of Older Adults: A Scoping Review. *Innovation in Aging*, *3*(1). Advance online publication. doi:10.1093/geroni/igy038 PMID:30619948

Kurlowicz, L., & Wallace, M. (1999). The mini-mental state examination (MMSE). *Journal of Gerontological Nursing*, *25*(5), 8–9. doi:10.3928/0098-9134-19990501-08 PMID:10578759

Lau, S. Y. J., & Agius, H. (2021). A framework and immersive serious game for mild cognitive impairment. *Multimedia Tools and Applications*, *80*(20), 31183–31237. Advance online publication. doi:10.100711042-021-11042-4

Lawton, M. P., & Brody, E. M. (1969). Assessment of older people: Self-maintaining and instrumental activities of daily living. *The Gerontologist*, *9*(3), 179–186. doi:10.1093/geront/9.3_Part_1.179 PMID:5349366

Lopez-Basterretxea, A., Mendez-Zorrilla, A., & Garcia-Zapirain, B. (2014). A Telemonitoring Tool based on Serious Games Addressing Money Management Skills for People with Intellectual Disability. *International Journal of Environmental Research and Public Health*, *11*(3), 2361–2380. doi:10.3390/ijerph110302361 PMID:24573223

López-Otín, C., Blasco, M. A., Partridge, L., Serrano, M., & Kroemer, G. (2013). The hallmarks of aging. *Cell*, *153*(6), 1194–1217. doi:10.1016/j.cell.2013.05.039 PMID:23746838

Machado, L. S., Moraes, R. M., Nunes, F. L. S., & Costa, R. M. E. M. (2011). Serious Games baseados em realidade virtual para educação médica [Virtual reality-based Serious Games for medical education]. *Revista Brasileira de Educação Médica*, *35*(2), 254–262. doi:10.1590/S0100-55022011000200015

Maillot, P., Perrot, A., & Hartley, A. (2012). Effects of interactive physical-activity video-game training on physical and cognitive function in older adults. *Psychology and Aging*, *27*(3), 589–600. doi:10.1037/a0026268 PMID:22122605

Man, D. W., Chung, J. C., & Lee, G. Y. (2012). Evaluation of a virtual reality-based memory training programme for Hong Kong Chinese older adults with questionable dementia: A pilot study. *International Journal of Geriatric Psychiatry*, *27*(5), 513–520. doi:10.1002/gps.2746 PMID:21681818

Manera, V., Petit, P. D., Derreumaux, A., Orvieto, I., Romagnoli, M., Lyttle, G., David, R., & Robert, P. H. (2015). "Kitchen and cooking", a serious game for mild cognitive impairment and Alzheimer's disease: A pilot study. *Frontiers in Aging Neuroscience*, 7(24). Advance online publication. doi:10.3389/fnagi.2015.00024 PMID:25852542

Marson, D. C., Martin, R. C., Wadley, V., Griffith, H. R., Snyder, S., Goode, P. S., Kinney, F. C., Nicholas, A. P., Steele, T., Anderson, B., Zamrini, E., Raman, R., Bartolucci, A., & Harrell, L. E. (2009). Clinical interview assessment of financial capacity in older adults with mild cognitive impairment and Alzheimer's disease. *Journal of the American Geriatrics Society*, 57(5), 806–814. doi:10.1111/j.1532-5415.2009.02202.x PMID:19453308

McCallum, S., & Boletsis, C. (2013). Dementia Games: A Literature Review of Dementia-Related Serious Games. In *Proceedings of the 4th International Conference on Serious Games Development and Applications*. 10.1007/978-3-642-40790-1_2

Michael, D., & Chen, S. (2006). *Serious games: Games that educate, train, and inform*. Thomson Course Technology PTR.

Miguel, I., & Amaro da Luz, M. H. (2015). New technologies towards cognitive stimulation in elderly with dementia: Effects and potential. *Proceedings of the 2015 10th Iberian Conference on Information Systems and Technologies*. http://hdl.handle.net/11328/1487

Neto, J. M., & Costa, J. N. (2016). *Dissertation for obtaining the Master's Degree in Computer Engineering, Specialization Area: Computer Systems*. ISEP.

Ning, H., Li, R., Ye, X., Zhang, Y., & Liu, L. (2020). A Review on Serious Games for Dementia Care in Ageing Societies. *IEEE Journal of Translational Engineering in Health and Medicine*, 8, 1–11. Advance online publication. doi:10.1109/JTEHM.2020.2998055 PMID:32537264

Nordon, D. G., Guimarães, R. R., Kozonoe, D. Y., Mancilha, V. S., & Neto, V. S. D. (2009). Perda cognitiva em idosos [Cognitive Loss in the Elderly]. *Revista da Faculdade de Ciências Médicas de Sorocaba*, 11(3), 5–8.

Observatory on Health Systems and Policies (OECD). (2017). Portugal: Country health profile 2017. State of Health in the EU, OECD Publishing, Paris/European Observatory on Health Systems and Policies, Brussels.

Oliveira, J., Gamito, P., Alghazzawi, D. M., Fardoun, H. M., Rosa, P. J., Sousa, T., Picareli, L. F., Morais, D., & Lopes, P. (2018). Performance on naturalistic virtual reality tasks depends on global cognitive functioning as assessed via traditional neurocognitive tests. *Applied Neuropsychology. Adult*, 25(6), 555–561. doi:10.1080/23279095.2017.1349661 PMID:28805447

Oxley, H. (2009). Policies for Healthy Ageing: An Overview. *OECD Health Working Papers*, 42, 6–30.

Padala, K. P., Padala, P. R., Malloy, T. R., Geske, J. A., Dubbert, P. M., Dennis, R. A., Garner, K. K., Bopp, M. M., Burke, W. J., & Sullivan, D. H. (2012). Wii-fit for improving gait and balance in an assisted living facility: A pilot study. *Journal of Aging Research*, 2012, 1–6. Advance online publication. doi:10.1155/2012/597573 PMID:22745909

Pais, J. (2008). As Dificuldades de Memória no Idoso [Memory Difficulties in the Elderly]. In *Memória, Funcionamente, Perturbações e Treino* [Memory, Functioning, Disorders and Training]. Lidel Edições Técnicas.

Paúl, C. (2006). Psicossomática do Envelhecimento [Psychosomatics of Aging]. In *Psicogeriatria* [Psychogeriatrics]. Psiquiatria Clínica.

Pessini, A., Kemczinski, A., & Hounsell, M. (2015). *Uma Ferramenta de Autoria para o desenvolvimento de Jogos Sérios do Gênero RPG* [An Authoring Tool for Developing Serious RPG Games]. Computer on the Beach. doi:10.14210/cotb.v0n0.p071-080

Prince, M., Bryce, R., Albanese, E., Wimo, A., Ribeiro, W., & Ferri, C. P. (2013). The global prevalence of dementia: A systematic review and metaanalysis. *Alzheimer's & Dementia*, 9(1), 63–75. doi:10.1016/j.jalz.2012.11.007 PMID:23305823

Prince, M., Wimo, A., Guerchet, M., Ali, G., Wu, Y., & Prina, M. (2015). World Alzheimer Report: The Global Impact of Dementia. London: Alzheimer's Disease International (ADI).

Qi, H., Wan, B., & Zhao, L. (2004). Mutual information entropy research on dementia EEG signals. *The Fourth International Conference on Computer and Information Technology*.

Robert, P., Manera, V., Derreumaux, A., Ferrandez, Y., Montesino, M., Leone, E., Fabre, R., & Bourgeois, J. (2020). Efficacy of a Web App for Cognitive Training (MeMo) Regarding Cognitive and Behavioral Performance in People With Neurocognitive Disorders: Randomized Controlled Trial. *Journal of Medical Internet Research*, 22(3), e17167. Advance online publication. doi:10.2196/17167 PMID:32159519

Robert, P. H., König, A., Amieva, H., Andrieu, S., Bremond, F., Bullock, R., Ceccaldi, M., Dubois, B., Gauthier, S., Kenigsberg, P. A., Nave, S., Orgogozo, J. M., Piano, J., Benoit, M., Touchon, J., Vellas, B., Yesavage, J., & Manera, V. (2014). Recommendations for the use of Serious Games in people with Alzheimer's Disease, related disorders and frailty. *Frontiers in Aging Neuroscience*, 6(54). Advance online publication. doi:10.3389/fnagi.2014.00054 PMID:24715864

Romero-Ayuso, D., Cuerda, C., Morales, C., Tesoriero, R., Triviño-Juárez, J. M., Segura-Fragoso, A., & Gallud, J. A. (2021). Activities of Daily Living and Categorization Skills of Elderly with Cognitive Deficit: A Preliminary Study. *Brain Sciences*, 11(2), 213. Advance online publication. doi:10.3390/brainsci11020213 PMID:33578677

Santos, L. H., Okamoto, K., Hiragi, S., Yamamoto, G., Sugiyama, O., Aoyama, T., & Kuroda, T. (2019). Pervasive game design to evaluate social interaction effects on levels of physical activity among older adults. *Journal of Rehabilitation and Assistive Technologies Engineering*, 6. Advance online publication. doi:10.1177/2055668319844443 PMID:31285836

Schaie, K., & Willis, S. (2016). *Handbook of the Psychology of Aging* (8th ed.). Academic Press.

Smith, T., Gildeh, N., & Holmes, C. (2007). The Montreal cognitive assessment: Validity and utility in a memory clinic setting. *Canadian Journal of Psychiatry*, 52(5), 329–332. doi:10.1177/070674370705200508 PMID:17542384

Sousa, L., Oliveira, A. I., Marques, A. R., Morais, J., Mendes, M., Cardoso, R., Costa, S., & Capela, C. (2019). Global Geriatric Assessment at Internal Medicine: A More Appropriate Model in The Evaluation of Hospitalized Elderly Patients. *Revista da Sociedade Portuguesa de Medicina Interna, 26*(1), 40–46. doi:10.24950/rspmi/original/214/1/2019

Souza, J., & Chaves, E. (2005). O efeito do exercício de estimulação da memória em idosos saudáveis [The effect of memory stimulation exercise in healthy elderly]. *Revista da Escola de S. Paulo, 39*(1), 13–19.

Taylor, M. J., & Griffin, M. (2015). The use of gaming technology for rehabilitation in people with multiple sclerosis. *Multiple sclerosis (Houndmills, Basingstoke, England), 21*(4), 355–371. doi:10.1177/1352458514563593 PMID:25533296

Thompson-Bradley, O., Barrett, S., Patterson, C., & Craig, D. (2012). Examining the Neurocognitive Validity of Commercially Available, Smartphone-Based Puzzle Games. *Psychology (Irvine, Calif.), 3*(07), 525–526. doi:10.4236/psych.2012.37076

Tieri, G., Morone, G., Paolucci, S., & Iosa, M. (2018). Virtual reality in cognitive and motor rehabilitation: Facts, fiction and fallacies. *Expert Review of Medical Devices, 15*(2), 107–117. doi:10.1080/1743 4440.2018.1425613 PMID:29313388

Tong, T., Chignell, M., Tierney, M. C., & Lee, J. S. (2016). Test-Retest Reliability of a Serious Game for Delirium Screening in the Emergency Department. *Frontiers in Aging Neuroscience, 8*, 258. doi:10.3389/fnagi.2016.00258 PMID:27872590

Valladares-Rodríguez, S., Perez-Rodriguez, R., Facal, D., Fernández-Iglesias, M. J., Anido-Rifon, L., & Mouriño-Garcia, M. (2017). Design process and preliminary psychometric study of a video game to detect cognitive impairment in senior adults. *PeerJ, 5*, 5. doi:10.7717/peerj.3508 PMID:28674661

Wen, D., Lan, X., Zhou, Y., Li, G., Hsu, S. H., & Jung, T. P. (2018). The study of evaluation and rehabilitation of patients with different cognitive impairment phases based on virtual reality and EEG. *Frontiers in Aging Neuroscience, 10*, 88. Advance online publication. doi:10.3389/fnagi.2018.00088 PMID:29666577

WHO - World Health Organization. (2005). *Envelhecimento ativo: uma política de saúde* [Active aging: a health policy]. Author.

WHO - World Health Organization. (2015). *Relatório mundial de envelhecimento e saúde* [World Aging and Health Report]. https://sbgg.org.br//wp-content/uploads/2015/10/OMS-ENVELHECIMENTO-2015-port.pdf

Woods, B., Aguirre, E., Spector, A. E., & Orrell, M. (2012). Cognitive stimulation to improve cognitive functioning in people with dementia. *Cochrane Database of Systematic Reviews, 2*. Advance online publication. doi:10.1002/14651858.CD005562.pub2 PMID:22336813

Woods, B., Thorgrimsen, L., Spector, A., Royan, L., & Orrell, M. (2006). Improved quality of life and cognitive stimulation therapy in dementia. *Aging & Mental Health, 10*(3), 219–226. doi:10.1080/13607860500431652 PMID:16777649

Xavier, A. J., d'Orsi, E., de Oliveira, C. M., Orrell, M., Demakakos, P., Biddulph, J. P., & Marmot, M. G. (2014). English longitudinal study of aging: Can Internet/E-mail use reduce cognitive decline? *The Journals of Gerontology. Series A, Biological Sciences and Medical Sciences*, *69*(9), 1117–1121. doi:10.1093/gerona/glu105 PMID:25116923

Yuill, N., & Hollis, V. (2011). A systematic review of cognitive stimulation therapy for older adults with mild to moderate dementia: An occupational therapy perspective. *Occupational Therapy International*, *18*(4), 163–186. doi:10.1002/oti.315 PMID:21425381

KEY TERMS AND DEFINITIONS

Cognition: Is a complex set of mental functions that include attention, perception, comprehension, learning, memory, problem-solving, and reasoning, among others, that allow the individual to understand and relate to the surrounding world.

Cognitive Stimulation: Is an intervention for people with cognitive decline that uses a panoply of specific activities that stimulate reasoning, concentration, calculation, and memory, usually in a sociable environment, such as small groups, guided by health professionals or caregivers.

Money Management: Managing money in various activities of daily life.

Serious Games: Serious games created for the purpose of non-entertainment, although they may be included.

Chapter 9
Improving Emergency Management Training Within Organizations:
TiER–Tool – A Serious Game

Patricia Quiroz-Palma

ⓘ https://orcid.org/0000-0002-2300-6101

Universitat Politècnica de València, Spain & University "Eloy Alfaro" of Manabi, Ecuador

M. Carmen Penadés

Universitat Politècnica de València, Spain

Ana Gabriela Núñez

University of Cuenca, Ecuador & Universitat Politècnica de València, Spain

ABSTRACT

As serious games are nowadays more frequently used for learning purposes in different domains, the success of the tasks in the organization depends on the stakeholders' training and capabilities, and in the emergency management domain, this is no exception. Accordingly, stakeholders in emergency management need adequate training to respond effectively to an incident. Their perception of safety is a goal for organizations, and proper training could ensure their adequate participation in the activities of emergency plan management. This chapter presents a serious game for training stakeholders to respond to emergency incidents designed to optimize the costs involved. For this purpose, a tool was developed that allowed the learning process to be evaluated through an experiment with a group of workers in an organization. The results obtained were found to be valuable assessments of the learning objectives and showed that serious games contributed to improving continuous training in organizations.

DOI: 10.4018/978-1-7998-9732-3.ch009

INTRODUCTION

The use of serious games, simulations, and gamification techniques (Gaitán, 2013) is now widely used in emergency management training, as it allows the continuous improvement of the knowledge obtained in the training and learning processes, providing improved coordination and unstressful conditions for all those involved. Although there are various tools available for training in emergencies, such as Save Yourself (Alsura, 2021), Stop Disasters (ISDR, 2021), and Emergency and Evacuation Simulator (Galicia, 2021), among others, there is no available tool to evaluate learning in order to validate feedback and enhance the learning process and the continuous improvement of emergency management training.

Proper training of all potential stakeholders in an emergency is of vital importance for obtaining an effective and opportune response. Customized training in the emergency management domain is critical for organizations. Training for the emergency plan must be customized for each stakeholder in each phase of emergency management. Investment in training benefits both the person who receives it and the organization that instructs them. The support of Information Technology (IT) tools in training are also essential (and decreases costs) for the continuous improvement of disaster prevention, emergencies, and reconstruction.

We present a training tool based on serious games and gamification techniques to optimize the response to an emergency, known as a *tool for training in emergency response* (TiER) (Quiroz-Palma et al., 2019). This tool promotes the development of skills in emergencies, establishing users' knowledge aspects, and achieving specific learning goals. First, we identified the emergency domains and dimensions of the training plan content. The training content must include theoretical information, experience, and practice (Xing and Hu, 2010). As good training not only includes a set of activities to be carried out periodically but also contains learning objectives, the concept of the capability or training plan was introduced, which incorporates both aspects.

The TiER Tool allows an organization to carry out the training of participants through gaming and provides feedback after each interaction to improve the learning process. It can be used by organizations, communities, and educational institutions because it does not require further resources for its implementation and correct functioning. Its portability means that it can be applied to remote sites with no access to network connections. *TiER* has been presented in its first version (*TiER Tool* v1.0) as a tool for training people to evacuate in a fire scenario. It has been evaluated in small and medium organizations but has not yet been evaluated in large organizations; the evaluations were carried out with different stakeholders in the performance of three missions in the case of fire. Currently, we have the second version (*TiER Tool* v2.0), with some improvements carried out after evaluation. This new version of the tool allows for a pre-game assessment and collects information to determine the relationship between learning and other variables such as age and prior knowledge in case of fire.

This chapter is organized as follows: Section 2 describes the key concepts of e-learning, serious games, gamification, and training for emergency management. Sections 3 and 4 describe the proposed *TiER tool* and its versions. Section 5 reports on an experiment carried out to test the proposal, the results of which are given in Section 6, and Section 7 contains our conclusions and outlines future work.

BACKGROUND

The tools for training in emergency management are important for the adequate preparation of those involved since the effectiveness of the execution of each of the phases (planning, response, and analysis) of emergency management depends on it. The support of IT tools in training is also important (and reduces costs) for the continuous improvement of disaster prevention, emergencies, and reconstruction (Prasanna et al., 2011). Tools that incorporate serious games in training, and in this case in emergency management, have been increasing, and there are now e-learning tools that integrate these practices into their digital platforms.

Training in Emergency Management

Organizations need to form teams to work together toward shared goals and require individuals or teams to cooperate. Social relationships within teams can drive a player's desire to perform well (Peng et al., 2012), and cooperation between team members can provide a positive social environment. Unlike interactivity, cooperation can provide a shared goal that can promote people's psychological needs satisfaction (Sailer et al., 2017). Although competition has been the most studied multiuser gamification, it is also useful to explore cooperation (Liu et al., 2017). In this context, appropriate training of all potential participants involved in an emergency is of vital importance to achieving effective knowledge and timely response.

Training in emergency management allows stakeholders to obtain skills and knowledge to face emergency situations. A training plan should contain activities that improve stakeholders' capabilities; training should be periodic to avoid knowledge obsolescence. (Quiroz-Palma et al., 2019).

Ferradas et al. (2006) define techniques for training processes such as interviews, participant observation, life histories, surveys, focus groups, participatory diagnosis, and role identification. Additionally, expert trainers identify six techniques, including on-the-job training, lectures, role-plays, audiovisuals, programmed learning, and simulations.

- The on-the-job training technique consists of assigning new employees to experienced workers or supervisors who are in charge of the actual training.
- The lecture technique is practical and easy to implement and is a quick and easy way to provide knowledge to large groups.
- The role-playing technique is used to teach sales techniques interviewing techniques, address groups, resolve conflicts and achieve negotiations, occupy positions of greater responsibility, and consist of professionals playing roles according to the position or tasks they perform.
- Audiovisual techniques are related to the presentation of information to employees through audiovisual techniques such as films, closed-circuit television, audio, or video tapes.
- The programmed learning technique consists of presenting a set of questions or facts for the learner to answer, then reviewing and comparing the answers, and repeating the questions with wrong answers until all have been answered correctly. This technique is effective because it provides employees with immediate feedback on the accuracy of their answers and on the learning, they are achieving.
- Simulation is a technique in which employees learn on real or simulated equipment for the execution of their tasks, for example, simulated operation of machines, vehicles, or airplanes. This

training corrects errors without putting learners in dangerous situations and is almost a necessity in positions where it is too expensive or dangerous to train employees directly (Adibi, 2000).

E-learning offers many opportunities for business organizations and employees as learners (Singh et al., 2015). Technology offers opportunities for the effective use of IT, delivery of up-to-date knowledge and technologies anytime, anywhere, and to anyone, cost cutting of training, and just-in-time philosophy. Other tools such as serious games, as explained in two case studies, the first case is a simulated evacuation of a burning ship and the second case the simulator provides train crash response training (Heldal, 2016).

The aim of training in emergency management is to develop local capabilities to respond to unexpected events and/or to prevent disasters. Therefore, it is essential to start from the knowledge of the causes of disasters and their consequences to determine the different factors that constitute hazards and vulnerability for stakeholders.

Figure 1. Emergency Management dimensions
(Quiroz-Palma et al., 2019)

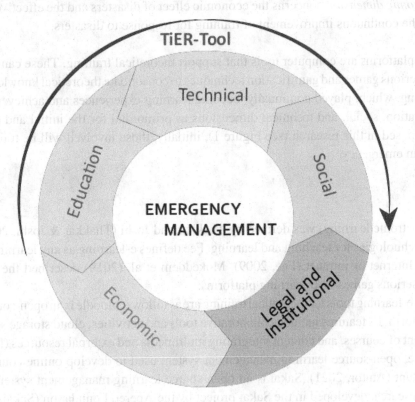

The expertise required to perform tasks or activities in an organization is usually developed through training. In the emergency management field, the purpose of training is to build capacities to respond to unforeseen events and/or to prevent disasters. To avoid knowledge becoming obsolete, periodic emergency training must be performed. Ferradas et al. (2006) identified the training dimensions in *education*, *social*, *technical*, *legal*, *institutional*, and *economic* areas.

- The *education dimension* refers to risk management theory and planning for development, disasters, livelihoods, rehabilitation, and reconstruction from the perspective of development and minimum standards for humanitarian aid.
- The *social dimension* is related to the organization and leadership, ethics and values, memory and history of disasters, perceptions of risk, prevention and adaptation strategies, prevention culture, information needs, communication media, informal communication, information networks, and information campaigns.
- The *technique dimension* refers to risk assessment, preparation of risk maps, use of databases for geo-referencing and geographic information systems, preparedness and emergency response plans, technologies for disaster prevention and emergency response, early warning systems, damage and needs assessment, psychosocial rehabilitation, operational emergency management, and the implementation of temporary shelters.
- The *legal and institutional dimensions* are related to the current legislation applicable to disaster prevention and response, law and regulation of civil defense, local laws and state policies in emergencies, priorities, support systems, and supply of aid.
- The *economic dimension* concerns the economic effect of disasters and the effectiveness of investment in the continuous improvement of training for response to disasters.

E-learning platforms are computer tools that support theoretical training. These can be added tools that integrate serious games and gamification techniques to consolidate theoretical knowledge simulating practical training, which, played continually, become learning experiences and achievements. Considering the education, social, and technical dimensions as primordial for the initial and actual versions of the tool proposed in this research (see Figure 1), initially, those involved will be trained to respond effectively in an emergency.

E-Learning

E-learning (electronic learning) was defined by Thakkar and Joshi (Thakkar & Joshi, 2016) as the use of electronic technologies for teaching and learning. Fee defines e-learning as any learning that involves the use of the Internet or intranet (Fee, 2009). Mokeddem et al. (2019) described the importance of incorporating serious games on e-learning platforms.

Some of the e-learning tools for theoretical training are as follows: Moodle is an open-source web-based e-learning platform. Its features include collaborative tools and activities, cloud storage services, design and management of courses, and content integrating multimedia and external resources (Moodle, 2021). ATutor is a free, open-source learning management system used to develop online courses and create e-learning content (Atutor, 2021). Sakai is an open-source learning management system for teaching, learning, and research, developed in the Sakai project by the Apereo Foundation (Sakai, 2021). Learning.com provides tools to seamlessly organize access and share digital content (Learning, 2021). Udemy is an online learning platform for adult professionals, but there are people who do not like the massive open online course (MOOC) (Mooc, 2021), because academic programs are created like traditional courses. Udemy uses content from online creators to sell for profit (Udemy, 2021). Coursera is a virtual education platform developed by academics at Stanford University in October 2011 to bring mass education offerings to the population (Coursera, 2021). EvolMind is a learning management system (LMS) that facilitates the creation, delivery, evaluation, and analysis of online training. It makes life easier for students and teachers with amazing features and powerful tools (Evolmind, 2021).

E-learning is one of the most popular forms of training, but it has limitations in some areas that require practical training, as in the case of emergency management. As they have been designed, they are too general and do not integrate interactive games to simulate practical scenarios in the domain of emergency management.

Serious Games and Gamification

Serious games (Capuano & King, 2015) were created with a purpose other than entertainment. Simulations are designed for education, often in the form of a serious game (Adam & Andonoff, 2019). The use of simulations and serious games are increasing in training in different fields of education. Serious games are now widely accepted for their learning potential and the achievement of non-technical skills (Turcotte *et al.*, 2019).

Gamification is defined as the use of game design components in contexts without games (Deterding, 2011). Previous research has found that, in line with the theory of self-determination, autonomy, competence, and interrelationships determine the motivations of the players in the games (Ryan, 2006). Zhang developed a set of design principles for motivational interface design based on self-determination (Zhang, 2008). Zhang proposed ten principles based on five motivational sources: autonomy and being, competence and achievement, social and psychological relationships, leadership and support, and affect and emotion. The latter requires that the game induce emotions during initial exposure and intensive interaction. The context of a game is expected to promote affective and emotional responses (Irfan & Kanat, 2013).

A game model operates because it motivates users, develops greater commitment to people, and encourages improvement. Gamification techniques are manual (*points, levels, prizes, gifts, classifications, challenges, and missions*) and dynamic (*reward, status, achievement, competition*) (Gaitán, 2013). Gamification provides advantages as it motivates and reinforces skills and knowledge, encourages competition and offers a status, stimulates social connections, and gradually increases the degree of difficulty.

Research conducted (Almeida, 2014) established that building occupants do not have adequate training and do not apply the best exit choice strategies; it then becomes a chaotic process that depends on many variables, among which the predefined exit route is blocked due to an unpredictable situation, such as smoke, fire, or partial collapse due to an earthquake. Evacuation procedures and decision-making processes must be rehearsed and evaluated (Kolen, 2011) in the context of constantly evolving social and institutional actors and physical infrastructure. When entities lack first-hand experience in orchestrating large-scale evacuations, simulations can be used to prepare governmental and institutional stakeholders and decision-makers. The use of simulations and serious games are growing in emergency management training (Heldal, 2016).

Serious games (Capuano & King, 2015) are applied and designed with a purpose other than entertainment; the difference lies in the fact that the video game is used as a training modality that promotes the development of skills in the face of emergencies, establishing cognitive aspects in the users, and reaching certain learning achievements. Serious games become a virtual evacuation training tool, which serves to address this problem and can produce useful information; it has the advantage that employees do not move away from their workplaces (Ribeiro, 2012). The use of simulations and serious games have been growing in emergency management training. The most common forms of emergency management training are in classroom situations or live training. The technology in simulations and serious games allows for the continuous evaluation and improvement of the knowledge acquired in the training process.

Some proposals for serious games and evacuation simulators are described below. Some tools partially support training in emergency management, such as *Save yourself,* which is a web-based game created by the company *"Seguros de Riesgos Laborales Suramericana SA,"* in which the user can choose between a house, a building, or a company as the site of the emergency, which may be for example a fire or seismic movement (Alsura S.A., 2021). *Stop disasters* are web-based games in which several scenarios are proposed, and the goal is to select actions that save the greatest number of lives. ISDR is the acronym of the UN's International Strategy for Disaster Reduction. This strategy links numerous organizations, universities, and institutions with a common purpose: to reduce the number of deaths and injuries caused by disasters and natural hazards (ISDR, 2021). *An emergency and evacuation simulator* is a web-based game, which is an interactive simulator that allows the members of the emergency team and the workers of a company to carry out emergency drills in a series of situations such as a fire, flood, explosion, or a work accident (Galicia, 2021). This platform allows the integration of scenarios with a synthetic environment that merges the game with people, both individually and in groups (CONAF, 2021). *Hazmat Hotzone* illustrates the learning potential of such training well; although this was only one of several options and scenarios, the intent was clear that, after repeated training, fire personnel could potentially become as safe as handling hazardous materials and terrorist incidents as conventional fire incidents (Gamasutra, 2021). The tools described support several features for emergency training, as shown in the next section (Table 2), but are limited to training, because they do not allow learning evaluation for the improvement of training. We are convinced of the need for knowledge to be evaluated and reinforced to consolidate evaluation and feedback, which are important features of the tool proposed here.

TIER: A PROPOSAL FOR CONTINUOUS IMPROVEMENT OF TRAINING

Our proposal is based on the theoretical concept of the continuous improvement of training presented in the quality of emergency plan management framework (Núñez *et al.*, 2015). QuEP assesses the planning process and analyzes the capabilities of the participants. All the activities carried out in the emergency plan management life cycle, and the issues involved in each of these practices at the different maturity levels. Five types of stakeholders are involved in QuEP: organization, planner, worker, citizen, and responder.

Figure 2. Maturity Levels
(Núñez et al., 2015)

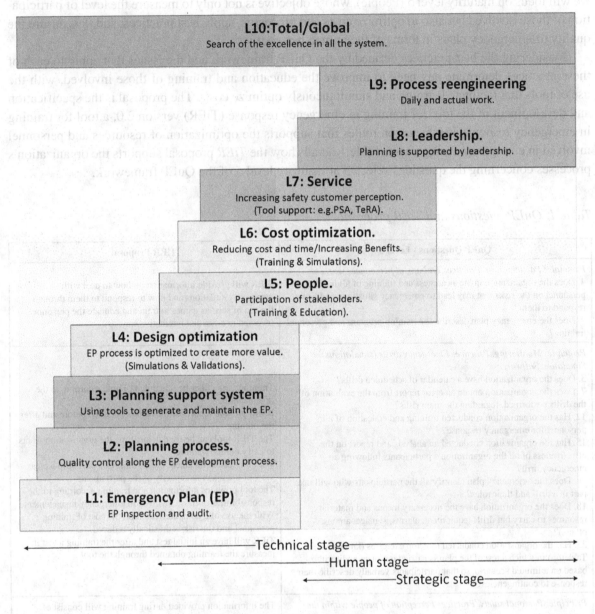

The QuEP framework defines ten maturity levels, numbered from 1 to 10, as shown in Figure 2. "A maturity level is a well-defined evolutionary phase to achieve total quality in emergency plan management" (Núñez et al., 2015). Levels 1 to 4 refer to the technical stage, which is oriented to increase the quality of the emergency plan. Levels 5 to 7 refer to the human stage, oriented toward human participation in the planning process. Levels 8 and 9 represent the strategic stage; the main idea is the quality of the emergency plans as a strategic decision within organizations. Finally, Level 10 seeks excellence in the emergency plan management process.

Once the maturity levels determined by the QuEP framework have been analyzed, for this research, we will focus on maturity level 5 (People), whose objective is not only to measure the level of participation of those involved but also to optimize costs and processes, apply best practices, and thus ensure the quality of emergency plans in terms of the human perspective.

Considering the best practices defined by the QuEP framework and the issues that apply to each of these practices determine any need to improve the education and training of those involved, with the use of tools that facilitate learning and simultaneously optimize costs. The proposal is the specification and development of the tool for training in emergency response (TiER) version 2.0, a tool for training in emergency response in evacuation routes that supports the optimization of resources and personnel involved in emergency management. Table 1 details how the *TiER* proposal supports the organization's processes concerning the questions selected at maturity level 5 of the QuEP framework.

Table 1. QuEP questions and TiER proposal

QuEP Questions - Level 5	TiER Proposal
Principle: Participation. Practice: Training of personnel / workers. 4. Does the organization invite awareness and training of all building personnel on the risks that may lead to emergency situations and how to respond to them? 7. Does the emergency plan describe the training program and personnel training?	TiER will provide information on how to deal with emergency situations and how to respond to them through the use of serious games to train and educate the personnel involved in a fun and interactive way.
Principle: Monitoring. Practice: Emergency drills (simulations) Simulation Software. 3. Does the organization have a calendar of scheduled drills? 7. Does the organization obtain an error report from the evaluation of the drills performed, regarding the main risks? 12. Has the organization conducted training and education of all personnel for emergency response? 15. Has the organization conducted an analysis and report on the effectiveness of all the organization's participants following an emergency drill? 16. Does the emergency plan identify all the participants who will take part in a drill and their roles? 18. Does the organization have the necessary means and material resources to carry out drills (equipment, alarms, signage, among others)? 23. Has the organization conducted tabletop exercises (known as Tabletop) in which a test of the plan is carried out in an auditorium based on a limited scenario, so that participants verbally describe their response to contingencies?	Trainings can either be scheduled or not, according to the organization. It will provide reports of the results obtained before and after the training. The TiER tool can be used at any time the organization wants to carry out the training. With the results obtained, the organization will have a clear view of the reaction capacity of the participants. The tool provides information and training according to the responsibilities of those involved in emergency management. With the use of a computerized tool, the cost of training personnel and the risk is drastically reduced. TiER will have an initial test and after the training a test to measure the learning obtained through the tool.
Principle: Personal safety. Practice: Perception of people within the organization. 1. Does the organization and all its personnel know the operation of alarms and evacuation signals (audible and/or visual)? 3. Has the organization provided access to technological tools to face an emergency (for example: mobile applications, social networks, among others)? 4. Does the organization's personnel have adequate theoretical and practical training to consider all the aspects that will allow them to face an emergency situation? 5. In the organization, after a drill, do the personnel feel fully prepared to act in the event of an emergency in the future? 6. Is emergency information provided through tools to staff and citizens in general easily accessible and usable in the organization?	The information provided during training will consist of training in evacuation signals. TiER will be the answer to this question, as it will be available to all personnel. The tool includes theoretical and practical information: before, during and after the game, to face an emergency situation. Through the post-training test, the user and the organization will know their level of preparedness for emergency situations, the users can repeat the training as many times as required to consolidate their knowledge. TiER will be available to staff and citizens in an accessible way and will be easy to use considering that it uses the techniques of serious games.

TiER integrates the training dimensions through its implemented features; that is, situational awareness is created through education in risk and disaster identification, social awareness of the scenarios posed, technical knowledge in emergency response (such as, for example, about the types of fire extinguishers and their correct use), legal issues, and internal regulations of the organization regarding safety standards in evacuation (for example, evacuation signage and the non-use of elevators in case of fire), and with respect to the economic issue, it presents a low-cost alternative for training those involved in emergency management.

Although others support emergency training, the *TiER* proposal differs from the others because it allows continuous evaluation and coaching for training improvement, as shown in Table 2.

Table 2. General table comparing characteristics of serious games and TiER

Features	Save Yourself	Stop disasters	Disaster decision making	Virtual Emergency and Evacuation Simulator	Hazmat: Hotzone	TiER
Response Training			•		•	•
Citizen Training	•	•	•			•
Evacuation route training		•	•		•	•
Natural disaster training		•	•		•	•
Fire training	•	•				•
Use Avatar		•		•	•	
Various scenarios	•	•	•		•	•
Information on signage and fire extinguishers	•	•		•		•
Evaluates learning						•
Reference	(Alsura S.A., 2021)	(ISDR, 2021)	(CONAF, 2021)	(Galicia, 2021)	(Gamasutra, 2021)	(Quiroz-Palma et al.,2019)

TIER TOOL

TiER (Quiroz-Palma et al., 2019) is a tool for emergency response training that optimizes resources and training of the personnel involved. According to Table 2, the most important characteristics that should be considered for inclusion in a capacitation tool based on serious games are response training, citizen training, and evacuation routes.

The need to improve the training of all those involved in emergency plan management can be achieved using tools that facilitate learning. For this, the objective is not only to measure the stakeholder's participation but also to optimize costs and processes, applying the best practices to ensure the quality of emergency plans in human terms. The proposed *TiER* was designed according to the following requirements (RQ) specifications:

RQ1: To provide the necessary information to be able to face an emergency (natural or man-made disaster) and know how to act, using serious games to train the personnel involved (workers, citizens, and responders) in a fun and interactive way.

RQ2: To use an avatar

RQ3: To provide various emergency scenarios.

RQ4: To be able to be used at any time.

RQ5: To report the results obtained before and after training.

RQ6: To have a clear idea of the stakeholders' reaction capacity.

RQ7: To provide information and training according to the different responsibilities of stakeholders in emergency management (stakeholders identified by QuEP).

RQ8: Offering a pre- and post-training test to measure the level of learning obtained.

RQ9: To make the training available to all stakeholders The tool includes theoretical-practical information before, during, and after the game.

RQ10: To be easily accessible and user-friendly.

RQ11: To give the organization an idea of the level of preparedness for emergencies and allow stakeholders to repeat the training as many times as they want.

The *TiER* domain model provides a global view of the tool, identifying the characteristics, and how different stakeholders can interact. Figure 3 shows the *TiER* concept as a serious game that concentrates theoretical and practical training using gamification techniques to make the activity dynamic. *The* advantage of TiER is that it can evaluate learning to provide valuable feedback. The content of the training can be customized for each of the 5 types of stakeholders.

Figure 3. TiER Domain model
(Quiroz-Palma et al.,2019)

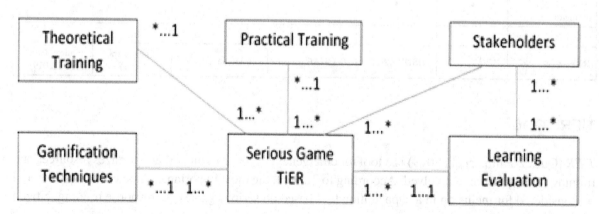

TiER is aimed at those involved in the emergency management of organizations and educational centers. Table 3 gives the disaster types and their most common scenarios, the missions or activities in each of them, and the stakeholders involved.

Table 3. TiER Missions

Disaster Type	Scenario	Missions	Stakehoders*
Hazards	Fire	1. Identify the signage	O, P, W, C, R
		2. Sound alarm	R, W, C
		3. Identify fire extinguishers	O, P, W, C, R
		4. Turn off fire level 1	R, W, C
		5. Evacuate	O, P, W, C, R
		6. Ask for help	O, P, W, C, R
		7. Exit	O, P, W, C, R
		8. Search for a safe place	O, P, W, C, R
		9. Rescue	R
		10. Help others	O, P, W, C, R
	Bomb threat	1. Evacuate	O, P, W, C, R
		2. Search for a safe place	O, P, W, C, R
		3. Deactivate Bomb	R
	Terrorist attack	1. Evacuate	O, P, W, C, R
		2. Search Safe place	O, P, W, C, R
		3. Rescue	R
Natural disasters	Earthquake Tsunami Floods Hurricanes Wind Avalanches Volcanic eruption …	1. Evacuate	O, P, W, C, R
		2. Search for a safe place	O, P, W, C, R
		3. Rescue	R
		4. Ask for help	O, P, W, C, R
		5. Help others	O, P, W, C, R

***O**rganization, **P**lanner, **W**orker, **C**itizen, **R**esponder

TiER was developed following the Scrum methodology (Scrum, 2021). Some references as (Mountain-Software, 2021) indicate, "Scrum is an agile way to manage a project, usually software development. Agile software development with Scrum is often perceived as a methodology, but rather than viewing Scrum as methodology, think of it as a framework for managing a process." Figure 4 shows three iterations of the Scrum process that allow valid versions to be obtained in each sprint. The team defined the requirements that will be met in each sprint. Each iteration lasts three weeks, with daily meetings in which the Scrum Master and the development team review the results obtained so far. The TiER was validated at the end of the first iteration. According to this method, the following iterations generate later versions. TiER v1.0 includes an evacuation mission. Evacuation is common to all scenarios and involves getting away from danger to safety in the three types of hazards described. Evacuating a building involves a similar procedure, but in a large-scale natural disaster, it depends on the topography of the place and the type of disaster (for example, in a tsunami or flood evacuation, this means going to higher areas such as hills or mountains).

Figure 4. SCRUM process for the development of TiER
(Quiroz-Palma et al.,2019)

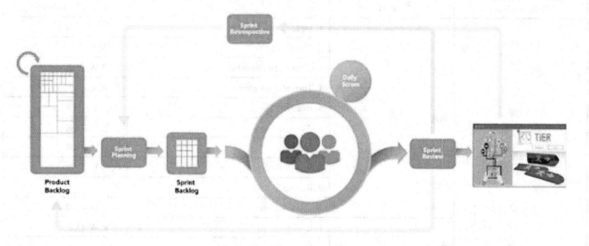

We used Azure DevOps (Microsoft, 2021) to carry out the development monitoring and identified *TiER*'s main characteristics, including the configuration of scenarios (C1) and user roles (C2), theoretical training (C3) and practice (C4), gamification techniques (C5), evaluation of learning (C6), and results (C7), as shown in Figure 5.

Figure 5. General Specifications TiER in Azure DevOps
(Quiroz-Palma et al.,2019)

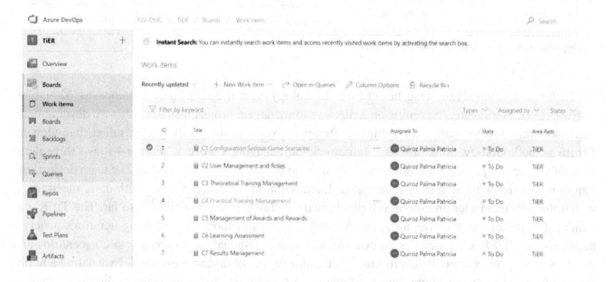

TiER Versions

TiER v1.0 was obtained from three sprints. The aim of the sprints is to achieve the tool's strong point: the evaluation of the actors' learning in the training process. Initially, information is displayed on what to do before and after a fire, and is part of the training that the tool provides to the user. Similarly, when the action "Learning fire signage" or "Learning evacuation routes" Learning evacuation routes' is selected, the corresponding information is displayed. Selecting "Learning fire extinguishers" action shows users information about fire extinguishers, and selecting "Learning extinguisher types" action displays information on the types of extinguishers according to the fire to be extinguished; when the missions are completed, it allows the user to measure the learning obtained in the interaction with *TiER*. In the next section, we present the interfaces (Figures 8 and 10).

TiER v2.0 was obtained in one sprint; this version enhancement consisted of the addition of an initial pre-game assessment to evaluate the level of prior knowledge, as well as a final stakeholder data collection interface to analyze variables such as name, e-mail, age, feedback, and game skill, as well as sending the results via the stakeholder's registered email address. In the next section, we present the interfaces (Figures 13, 14, and 15).

The technology used in both versions was Microsoft Visual Basic (Visual Studio, 2021), which was chosen to obtain a visual, interactive, portable final product that did not require any additional software.

TiER Interface

TiER trains stakeholders through a game consisting of three challenges in which they have to assess the knowledge acquired in each interaction. Pressing the start button shows possible scenarios. In this first version, the fire scenario was active, as shown in Figure 6.

Figure 6. TiER Scenarios

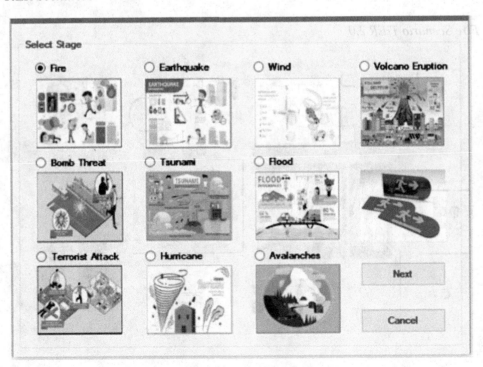

In selecting the fire scenario, the missions that must be carried out in each scenario are shown in the order that they have to be performed, as shown in Figure 7. The player is represented by an avatar on the map of the building, with a specific signage for fires and evacuation routes. The exit is on the opposite side of the player, as shown in Figure 8. The maps are configured by an administrator; in later versions, this option will be included in the tool for the end-user to make.

Figure 7. TiER Fire missions

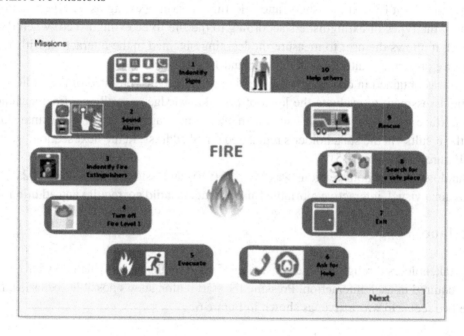

Figure 8. Fire Scenario TiER 2.0

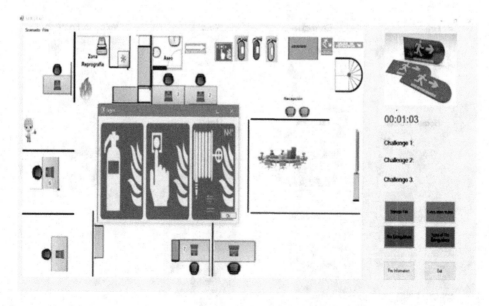

In the fire scenario interface (Figure 8), the player must perform each of the missions assigned to him, for which he has information buttons on the right that allow him to review fire procedures, fire signals, evacuation, and types of extinguishers. While the game is in progress, the time elapsed from the start of the mission until the emergency exit is reached. After completing the missions, the knowledge acquired through the game was evaluated. This process can be repeated to evaluate learning evolution.

TIER EVALUATION

An experiment was carried out to evaluate the prototypes *TiER* v1.0 and *TiER* v2.0 in which we followed Dana Chisnell's definition (Chisnell, 2009): an experiment is a "practical test or tests carried out to prove the effectiveness of a thing or examine its properties".

TiER V1.0 Evaluation

The case study involved stakeholders of an organization in the worker's role. The organization selected was the UPV's Building 1F. The following steps were performed:

Step 1: Preparation of the executable application was compatible with desktops without any additional software.

Step 2: An introduction was given on serious games with gamification

Step 3: *TiER* was described to the participants.

Step 4: The stakeholders downloaded the application

Step 5: They started playing in the Worker Role

Step 6: Scenario: Fire (see Figure 8)

Step 7: Three challenges were involved:

Challenge1: Evacuate the offices (Mission 5) using the signs (Mission 1) shown on the plan, avoiding elevators and fire area, and finally exit (Mission 7).

Challenge 2: Put out the fire (Mission 4) with a suitable extinguisher (Mission 3), evacuate the offices (Mission 5), and exit (Mission 7).

Challenge 3: Alarm (Mission 2), put out the fire (Mission 4) with the correct extinguisher (Mission 3), evacuate the offices (Mission 5), and exit (Mission 7).

Step 8: The time elapsed for each challenge is shown in Figure 9. The same application evaluated learning through questionnaires (see Figure 10).

Step 9: Challenges were repeated to measure results

Step 10: The data was recorded to send the results by email

Step 11: The learning evolution through results was calculated.

Figure 9. TiER v1.0 Fire scenario: challenges completed

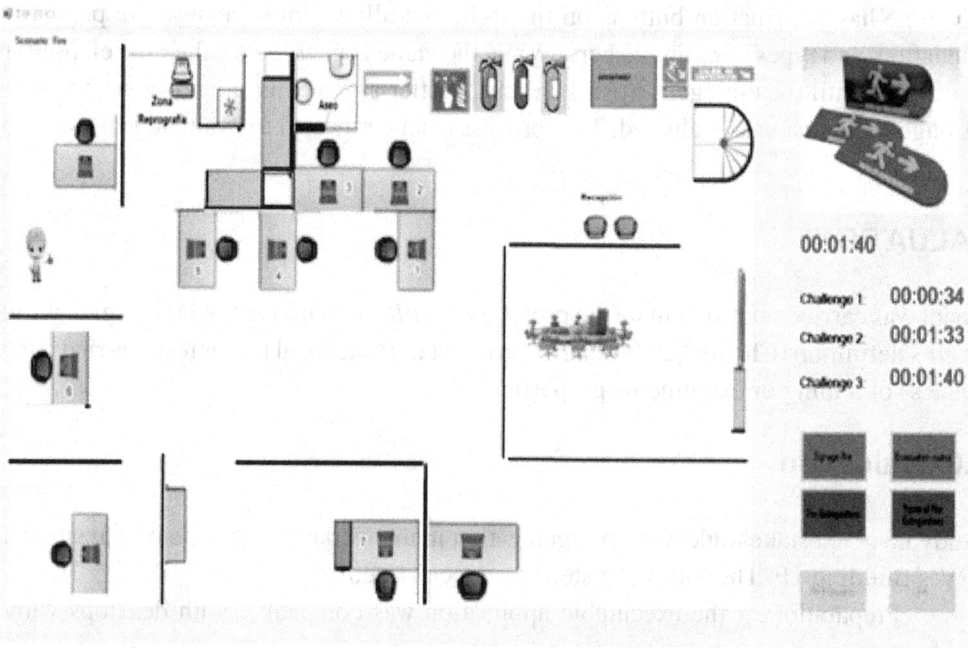

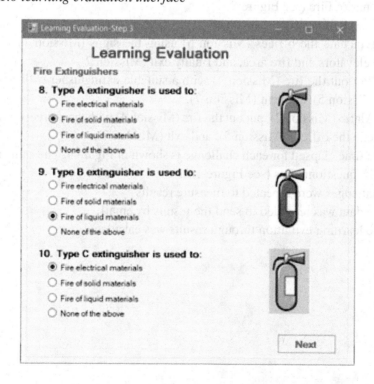

Figure 10. TiER v1.0 learning evaluation interface

Figure 11. TiER v1.0 learning evaluation

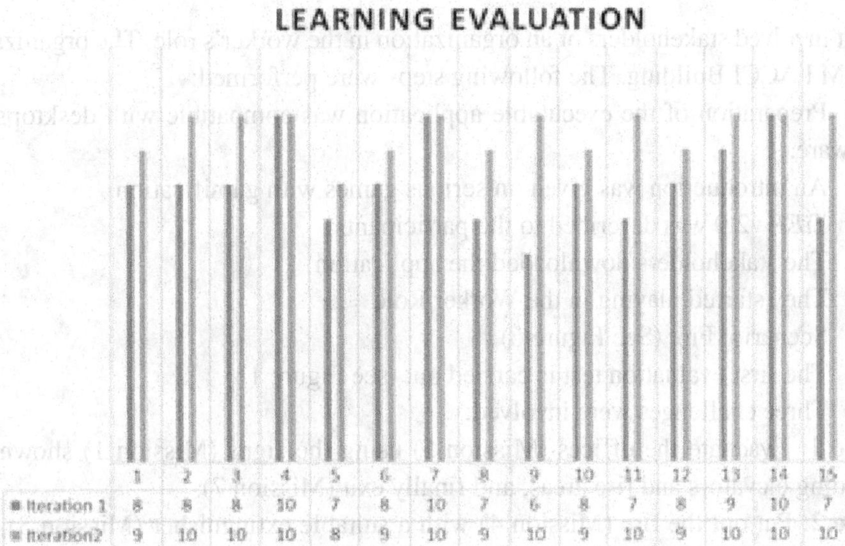

LEARNING EVALUATION
1 2 3 4 5 6 7 8 9 10 11 12 13 14 15
Iteration 1 8 8 8 10 7 8 10 7 6 8 7 8 9 10 7
Iteration2 9 10 10 10 8 9 10 9 10 9 10 9 10 10 10

The *TiER* v1.0 validation allowed us to evaluate the learning variables and the time required for each stakeholder to achieve the set challenges. The repetition provided the data to determine the knowledge learned with respect to the first iteration.

The results obtained in the test were grouped by iteration and compared to determine the learning effect. 93% of the stakeholders improved their times in Challenges 1 and 2. 87% improved their times in Challenge 3, while 13% did not show any improvement.

In Figure 11, it can be seen that 80% improved their score, while the other 20% had the maximum score (10). The increased scores in the second iteration are shown in Figure 12. Although the sample size was small, the average improvement in learning was 14.67%, and the standard deviation was 11.87%.

Figure 12. Training improvement

PERCENTAGE OF INCREASE
10% 20% 20% 0% 10% 10% 0% 20% 40% 10% 30% 10% 10% 0% 30%
1 2 3 4 5 6 7 8 9 10 11 12 13 14 15
LEARNERS

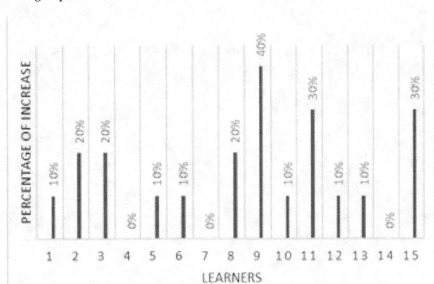

TiER V2.0 Evaluation

The experiment involved stakeholders of an organization in the worker's role. The organization selected was the ULEAM FACCI Building. The following steps were performed:

Step 1: Preparation of the executable application was compatible with desktops without any additional software.

Step 2: An introduction was given on serious games with gamification

Step 3: *TiER* v2.0 was described to the participants.

Step 4: The stakeholders downloaded the application

Step 5: They started playing in the Worker Role

Step 6: Scenario: Fire (See Figure 6)

Step 7: The first evaluation test is carried out (see Figure 13).

Step 8: Three challenges were involved:

Challenge 1: Evacuate the offices (Mission 5) using the signs (Mission 1) shown on the plan, avoiding elevators and fire areas, and finally exit (Mission 7).

Challenge 2: Put out the fire (Mission 4) with a suitable extinguisher (Mission 3), evacuate the offices (Mission 5), and exit (Mission 7).

Challenge 3: Alarm (Mission 2), put out the fire (Mission 4) with the correct extinguisher (Mission 3), evacuate the offices (Mission 5), and exit (Mission 7).

Step 9: The time required for each challenge is shown in Figure 8.

Step 10: *TiER* evaluated learning through second test questionnaires.

Step 11: Challenges (Step 8) were repeated to measure results

Step 12: *TiER* evaluated learning through the third test.

Step 13: The data were recollected and recorded (see Figure 14) to send the results by email (email address registered by the stakeholder) (see Figure 15).

Step 14: The learning evolution through results was calculated.

The *TiER* v2.0 validation evaluated the learning variables and the time required for each stakeholder to achieve the set challenges. An initial test and another after each iteration made it possible to determine the stakeholders' progress in each iteration.

Figure 13. Initial evaluation

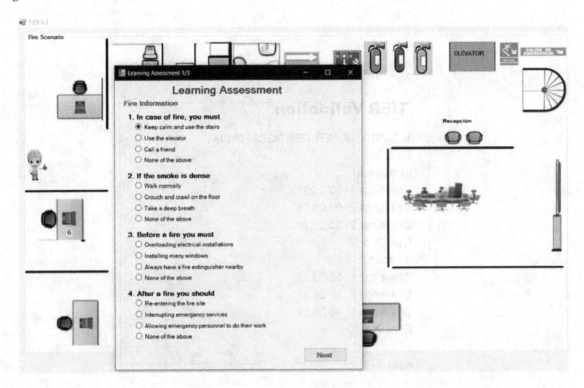

Figure 14. Player data

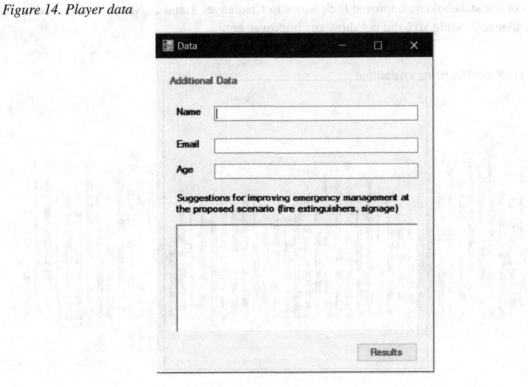

Figure 15. Results sent to player's email

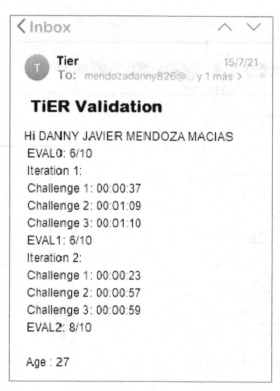

The results obtained in the test were grouped by iteration and compared to determine the learning effect. 97% of the stakeholders improved their times in Challenges 1 and 2. Ninety% improved their times in Challenge 3, while 10% did not show any improvement.

Figure 16. TiER v2.0 learning evaluation

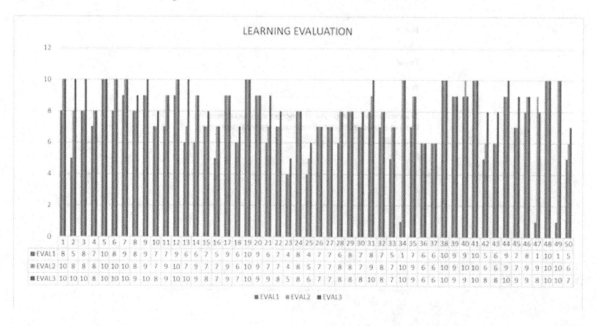

In Figure 16, it can be seen that 70% improved their score, while the other 30% had the maximum score (10). The increased scores in the second iteration are shown in Figure 17. The average improvement in learning was 16.67%, and the standard deviation was 20.56%.

Figure 17. TiER v2.0 training improvement

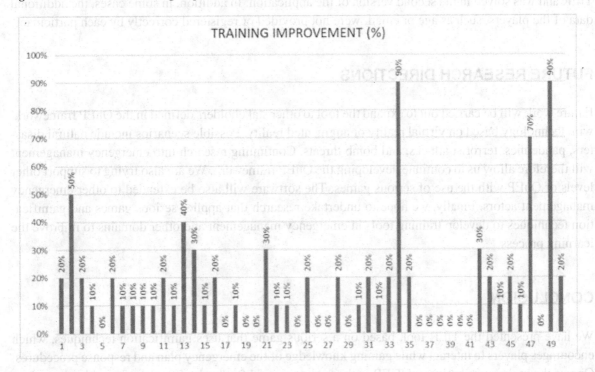

DISCUSSION

TiER v1.0 and *TiER* v2.0 managed to train stakeholders to be ready for emergencies and capture their attention in emergency training, as reflected by the scores of the learning assessment. Regarding the learning process, some stakeholders already knew that an elevator could not be used in fires but learned new information regarding signage and types of extinguishers. Overall, learning scores increased, and in cases where the times of the second iteration did not improve, the evaluation of learning scores did increase, suggesting that during the second iteration, time was spent on learning the information on fires, signage, and extinguishers available in the tool. On the other hand, certain standard behaviours were detected, such as myths or erroneous beliefs (using the elevator during a fire, correct signage, location, and importance of meeting points). In addition, it was also shown that in most cases, the correct path to the exit was followed on the evacuation route. However, some stakeholders tried to go over the desks to get to the exit faster. Curiously, it was found that these stakeholders had already lived through an emergency (earthquake) in their own countries.

TiER v2.0 provided us with more information to validate indicators such as age and pre-game knowledge. The *TiER* v2.0 experiment was more agile even though it was conducted virtually because of the exceptional circumstances experienced due to the pandemic, unlike the first version, which was face-to-face. Another aspect to highlight was that the game was learned faster, and this can be attributed to the fact that the average age of the students in the second experiment was around 21 years old, the age at which they generally practice entertainment games.

The problems that occurred in the experiment were that the participants did not follow the order of the instructions, and therefore, the mission was not concluded. This error was detected in the first version of TiER and was solved in the second version of the application. In addition, in some cases, the additional data of the players, such as age or email, were not provided or registered correctly by each participant.

FUTURE RESEARCH DIRECTIONS

Future work will be carried out to expand the tool to other stakeholders defined in the QuEP framework, with technology based on virtual reality or augmented reality. Possible scenarios include natural disasters, pandemics, terrorist attacks, and bomb threats. Continuing research into emergency management will therefore allow us to continue developing the QuEP framework. We are also trying to support other levels of QuEP with the use of serious games. The software will also be extended to other emergency management actors. Finally, we hope to undertake research that applies serious games and gamification techniques to develop training tools in emergency management and other domains to improve the learning process.

CONCLUSION

We have presented the TiER tool, based on a serious game that uses gamification techniques, which encourages players to interact while gaining knowledge of the emergency plan and response procedures. One of the main contributions of TiER is the evaluation and feedback of the learning objectives. As a result, TiER manages to capture the user's attention during emergency training, which is reflected in the learning assessment score. Due to its ease of use, TiER can be implemented in organizations such as schools and small, medium, and large businesses. On the other hand, TiER can be used to analyze human behavior in an emergency and obtain contributions through the scenarios presented in the game.

ACKNOWLEDGMENT

This research was supported by the Spain's Ministerio de Ciencia e Innovación [grant MIGRATE (PID2019-105414RB-C31)]; the Ecuadorian University "Eloy Alfaro" of Manabi supported partially the work of P. Quiroz-Palma, and "Universidad de Cuenca" of Ecuador supported partially the work of A.G. Núñez.

REFERENCES

Adam, C., & Andonoff, E. (2019, May). VigiFlood: a serious game for understanding the challenges of risk communication. ISCRAM.

Adibi, M. M. (2000). Bulk Power System Restoration Training Techniques. In Power System Restoration: Methodologies & Implementation Strategies. IEEE. pp. doi:10.1109/9780470545607.ch39

Almeida, P. N. (2014). Serious games for the Elicitation of way-finding behaviours. In *Conferencia Ibérica de Sistemas de Información y Tecnologías*. IEEE Xplore.

Alsura, S. A. (2021). *Save yourself who knows*. https://www.arlsura.com/salvesequiensepa/

Atutor. (2021). *Expert Tutoring Advice*. https://www.atutor.ca

Capuano, N., & King, R. (2015). Adaptive Serious Games for Emergency Evacuation Training. *Proceedings - 2015 International Conference on Intelligent Networking and Collaborative Systems*, 308–313. 10.1109/INCoS.2015.32

Chisnell, D. (2009). *Usability Testing Demystified*. http://alistapart.com/article/usability-testing-demystified

CONAF. (2021). *Ceinina: Center for Research and Applied Research*. http://www.ceinina.cl/?q=node/213

Coursera. (2021). *Cursos en línea*. https://es.coursera.org/

Deterding, S. L. (2011). Gamification. using game-design elements in non-gaming contexts. *Proceedings of the 2011 annual conference extended abstracts*, 24–25. 10.1145/1979742.1979575

Evolmind. (2021). *La plataforma e-learning que simplifica la formación en línea*. https://www.evolmind.com/

Fee, K. (2009). *Delivering E-learning - A complete strategy for design, application and assessment*. Kogan Page. https://www.emerald.com/insight/publication/issn/1477-7282

Ferradas, P., Vargas, A., & Santillán, G. (2006). *Metodologías y herramientas para la capacitación en gestión de riesgo de Desastres*. Codex.

Gaitán, V. (2013). *Gamification: fun learning*. https://www.educativa.com/blog-articulos/gamificacion-el-aprendizaje-divertido/

Galicia, C. de E. (2021). *Virtual Emergency and Evacuation Simulator*. http://www.prevencion.ceg.es/modulos/senalizacion/index.html

Gamasutra. (2021). *Hazmat*. http://www.gamasutra.com

Heldal, I. (2016). Simulation and Serious Games in Emergency Management, *Proceedings of the 2016 International Conference on Virtual Systems and Multimedia*, 201–209.

Irfan, S. S., & Kanat, E. (2013). Gamification of Emergency Response Training. In *ISI 2013* (pp. 134–136). IEEE.

ISDR. (2021). *Stop Disasters Retrieved*. https://www.stopdisastersgame.org/home.html

Kolen, T. Z. (2011). Evacuation a serious game for preparation. In *IEEE International Conference on Networking, Sensing and Control*. IEEE Xplore.

Learning. (2021). *Suite of Digital Literacy Curriculum*. https://www.learning.com/

Liu, D., Santhanam, R., & Webster, J. (2017). Toward meaningful engagement: A framework for design and research of gamified information systems. *Management Information Systems Quarterly, 41*(4), 1011–1034. doi:10.25300/MISQ/2017/41.4.01

Microsoft. (2021). *Azure DevOps*. https://azure.microsoft.com/en-us/services/devops/?nav=min

Mokeddem, A., Plaisent, M., & Prosper, B. (2019). Learning with the Games: A Competitive Environment based on Knowledge. *The Journal of Learning in Higher Education, 2019*, 1–6. doi:10.5171/2019.133016

Moodle. (2021). *Proyecto Moodle*. https://www.moodle.org

Mountain-Software. (2021). *Agile Projects*. https://www.mountaingoatsoftware.com/agile/scrum

Núñez, A.-G., Penadés, M. C., & Canos, J.H. (2015). Towards a total quality framework for the evaluation and improvement of emergency plans management. *ISCRAM 2015 Conference Proceedings - 12th International Conference on Information Systems for Crisis Response and Management.*

Peng, W., Lin, J. H., Pfeiffer, K. A., & Winn, B. (2012). Need satisfaction supportive game features as motivational determinants: An experimental study of a self-determination theory guided exergame. *Media Psychology, 15*(2), 175–196. doi:10.1080/15213269.2012.673850

Prassana, R., Yang, L., & King, M. (2011). Evaluation of a Software Prototype for Supporting Fire Emergency Response. *ISCRAM 2011 Conference Proceedings - International Conference on Information Systems for Crisis Response and Management 2011.*

Quiroz-Palma, P., Penadés, M. C., & Núñez, A. G. (2019). TiER: A Serious Games for Training in Emergency Scenarios. International Business Information Management Association (IBIMA 2019).

Ribeiro, A. R. (2012). Using serious games to train evacuation behavior. In *Iberian Conference on Information Systems and Technologies*. IEEE Xplore.

Ryan, R. M., Rigby, C. S., & Przybylski, A. (2006). The motivational pull of video games: A self-determination theory approach. *Motivation and Emotion, 30*(4), 344–360. doi:10.100711031-006-9051-8

Sailer, M., Hense, J. U., Mayr, S. K., & Mandl, H. (2017). How gamification motivates: An experimental study of the effects of specific game design elements on psychological need satisfaction. *Computers in Human Behavior, 69*, 371–380. doi:10.1016/j.chb.2016.12.033

Sakai, A. F. (2021). *Learning Management System*. https://www.sakaiproject.org

Scrum. (2021). *Scrum*. https://www.scrum.org/

Singh, H., & Singh, B. P. (2015). E-Training: An assessment tool to measure business effectiveness in a business organization. *2015 2nd International Conference on Computing for Sustainable Global Development (INDIACom)*, 1229-1231.

Thakkar, S. R., & Joshi, H. D. (2016). E-Learning Systems: A Review. *Proceedings - IEEE 7th International Conference on Technology for Education*, 37–40. 10.1109/T4E.2015.6

Turcotte, I. (2019). Serious gaming for training non-technical skills in crisis management and emergency response. *Proceedings of the 16th International Conference on Information Systems for Crisis Response & Management (ISCRAM).*

Udemy. (2021). *Online courses.* https://www.udemy.com/

Visual Studio. (2021). *Microsoft Visual Studio.* https://visualstudio.microsoft.com/

Xing, Y., & Hu, S. (2010). Following Construction Study of One Village One College Student Training Plan in Heilongjiang Province. *International Conference on e-Education, e-Business, e-Management and e-Learning,* 436–439. 10.1109/IC4E.2010.46

Zhang, P. (2008). Motivational affordances: Reasons for ICT design and use. *Communications of the ACM, 51*(11), 145–147. doi:10.1145/1400214.1400244

ADDITIONAL READING

Babu, S. K., Mclain, M. L., Bijlani, K., Jayakhrishnan, R., & Bhavani, R. R. (2016). Collaborative Game Based Learning of Post-Disaster Management. *IEEE 8th Int. Conf. Technol. Educ. Collab.,* 80–87.

Ilmi, N., & Hendradjaya, B. (2018, November). Serious Game Design for Simulation of Emergency Evacuation by Using Virtual Reality. In *2018 5th International Conference on Data and Software Engineering (ICoDSE)* (pp. 1-6). IEEE. 10.1109/ICODSE.2018.8705860

Jain, S., & McLean, C. R. (2005). Integrated simulation and gaming architecture for incident management training. In *Proceeding Winter Simul. Conf.,* 2005, pp. 904–913. 10.1109/WSC.2005.1574338

Kimura, Y., & Kawamoto, P. N. (2018). Gamifying the Element of Forgetting in E-learning Systems. *Proceeding IEEE International Conference on Teaching, Assessment, and Learning for Engineering (TALE),* 751–754. 10.1109/TALE.2018.8615352

Menestrina, Z., De Angeli, A., & Busetta, P. (2014) APE: End User Development for Emergency Management Training. *Proceeding 6th International Conference on Games and Virtual Worlds for Serious Applications (VS-GAMES),* 1–4. 10.1109/VS-Games.2014.7012030

Oulhaci, M. A., Tranvouez, E., Espinasse, B., & Fournier, S. (2013). Intelligent Tutoring Systems and Serious Game for Crisis Management: A Multi-agents Integration Architecture. *2013 Workshops on Enabling Technologies. Infrastructure for Collaborative Enterprises, 2013,* 253–258.

Rocha, R. V., Campos, M. R., Boukerche, A., & Araujo, R. B. (2012). From Behavior Modeling to Communication, 3D Presentation and Interaction: An M&S Life Cycle for Serious Games for Training. *2012 IEEE/ACM 16th International Symposium on Distributed Simulation and Real Time Applications,* 132–139.

Silva, J. F., Almeida, J. E., Rossetti, R. J. F., & Coelho, A. L. (2013). A serious game for Evacuation training. *2013 IEEE 2nd International Conference on Serious Games and Applications for Health (SeGAH),* 1–6.

Stroe, I. P., Ciupe, A., Meza, S. N., & Orza, B. (2019). FireScape: a Gamified Coordinative Approach to Multiplayer Fire-Safety Training. *2019 IEEE Global Engineering Education Conference (EDUCON),* 1316-1323. 10.1109/EDUCON.2019.8725148

Vargas, M. R. R., Díaz, P., Zarraonandia, T., & Aedo, I. (2012). Safety villages: A computer game for raising children's awareness of risks. *Proceeding ISCRAM 2012 Conference - 9th Int. Conf. Inf. Syst. Cris. Response Manag.,* 1–5.

KEY TERMS AND DEFINITIONS

E-Learning: E-learning is teaching and learning we receive online, i.e. through the Internet and technology.

Emergency Management: The organization and management of resources and responsibilities for addressing all aspects of emergencies, in particular preparedness, response, and initial recovery steps.

Gamification: Gamification is a learning technique that transfers the full potential of games to the educational environment to improve results.

Hazard: A dangerous phenomenon, substance, human activity or condition that may cause loss of life, injury or other health impacts, property damage, loss of livelihoods and services, social and economic disruption, or environmental damage.

QuEP Maturity-Level: A maturity level is a well-defined evolutionary phase toward achieving total quality in emergency plan management.

Risk: The combination of the probability of an event and its negative consequences.

Serious Games: Serious games are games designed with an educational purpose rather than for entertainment purposes.

Simulations: Simulations are experimentation with a model that mimics certain aspects of reality.

Chapter 10
Serious Games Integrated With Rehabilitation Structures and Assist–as–Need Techniques

Lucas Antonio Oliveira Rodrigues
Federal University of Uberlândia, Brazil

Leonardo Assis Gaspar
Federal University of Uberlândia, Brazil

Rogério Sales Gonçalves
Federal University of Uberlândia, Brazil

ABSTRACT

The video game market has been experiencing constant growth throughout the last decade, especially after 2008 with the rise of mobile gaming and after 2016 with virtual and augmented reality technologies. As a result of the ever-growing applications of games, the rehabilitation process of disabilities caused by stroke, cerebral palsy, and other neurological diseases has incorporated games designed to assist recovery. Based on these facts, this chapter deals with the development of two serious games designed to be integrated with two structures: ReGear, a new design for interlimb rehabilitation mechanisms, and HOPE-G, a novel gait rehabilitation structure capable of balance training. Both systems apply assist-as-needed control techniques to improve the outcomes of the treatment. The first clinical trials in one of the structures were conducted on a group of healthy volunteers and another with post-stroke patients, showing encouraging results regarding the serious game and the mechanical design.

INTRODUCTION

Videogames became a permanent part of modern society, consolidating one of the current largest entertainment markets. A 159 billion dollars projection is estimated for this market only in 2020, where almost 48% of the revenues come from games developed specifically for mobile applications (Hall, 2020).

DOI: 10.4018/978-1-7998-9732-3.ch010

The stability of the games market has opened space for important innovations and experiments that brought contributions beyond entertainment. Studies have shown positive impacts of electronic games for educational purposes (Gee, 2003; Tokarieva et al., 2019) and in the visual-motor skill (Cornejo et al., 2021; Green & Bavelier, 2003).

Recently, it became popular to include game characteristics in educational programs, process control, and activity management. This inclusion process is known as "gamification," and some studies already demonstrate that it promotes cognitive, motivational, and educational gain in the learning process (Kim, Song, Lockee, & Burton, 2018; Sailer & Homner, 2020).

Following this same principle and expanding the appliances and benefits of video games, a specific group of games is developed with therapeutical purposes, called "serious games" (Rego, Moreira, & Reis, 2010). The use of electronic games combined with the human rehabilitation process and assisted by robotic structures is becoming a reality throughout recent years, where most of the systems developed for this purpose already include serious game to be played during the training sessions (Hesse et al., 2003; T. G. Susko, 2015; Veneman et al., 2007).

Within the "serious games" concept, there are well-defined concepts that guide the development process of the games and contribute effectively to improve the treatment results of the patients. Some of these concepts are the field of applications, interaction technology, game interface, number of players, game genre, adaptability, and active assistance (Buchinger & da Silva Hounsell, 2018; Rego et al., 2010).

Robotic structures applied in human body rehabilitation are considered an important tool to assist the treatment of patients with several neurological impairments like stroke and cerebral palsy (PC) (Bateni & Maki, 2005; Hu et al., 2017; Molteni, Gasperini, Cannaviello, & Guanziroli, 2018). Although many positive results have been proven in recent literature, there is still a need for further innovation, especially regarding structures designed for human gait and interlimb interaction between upper and lower limbs (Rogério S. Gonçalves & Rodrigues, 2021; Rogério Sales Gonçalves, Hamilton, Daher, Hirai, & Hermano, 2017; Rogério Sales Gonçalves & Rodrigues, 2019).

A common point in both the development of serious games and rehabilitation structures is the need to adapt to the behavior of the player/patient. Adaptability and customization are features with a high impact in the consolidation of the positive outcomes of serious games (Streicher & Smeddinck, 2016). Likewise, studies demonstrate that structures able to adapt their control actions based on the behavior of the patients have a positive impact on the treatment (Alves, Chaves D'Carvalho, & Gonçalves, 2019; Asl, Narikiyo, & Kawanishi, 2019; Lauretti, Cordella, Guglielmelli, & Zollo, 2017).

Therefore, this chapter presents the development of two serious games designed to integrate distinct rehabilitation structures: ReGear, and HOPE-G (Rogério S. Gonçalves & Rodrigues, 2021; Rogério Sales Gonçalves & Rodrigues, 2019). The first section presents a review of the background in serious games integrated with robotic rehabilitation structures.

Next, the basics of both rehabilitation structures to be integrated with the games are presented, including their main goals, mechanical principles, and control design.

The third section details the design of the serious games developed for these robotic structures, explaining the project concepts, the definition of the visual elements, game mechanics, score systems, and the communication with the controller of the robotic systems.

Finally, the results of the first clinical trials performed with groups of healthy and post-stroke volunteers are presented, including a discussion of the data obtained so far.

STATE OF THE ART OF REHABILITATION STRUCTURES AND SERIOUS GAMES

As mentioned in the Introduction, serious games are widely present among robotic devices applied in human rehabilitation, contributing to better results and experience during the training sessions of the patients. In this section, a review of the state of the art of serious games integrated with robotic structures is presented.

In Health Care, the major efficiency of serious games is linked to cognitive/affective responses of the patients, being some of them: sensorial pleasure, emotion, and sensation of control. With this, the rehabilitation process is no longer a group of repetitive movements and exercises, and becomes a joyful experience of an individual's routine, resulting in better outcomes from the treatment (Lourenço, 2018).

An example of a patient using a rehabilitation structure integrated with serious games is presented in Figure 1.

Figure 1. Photo of a patient using MIT Skywalker, a rehabilitation robotic structure integrated with serious games
(*T. Susko, Swaminathan, & Krebs, 2016*)

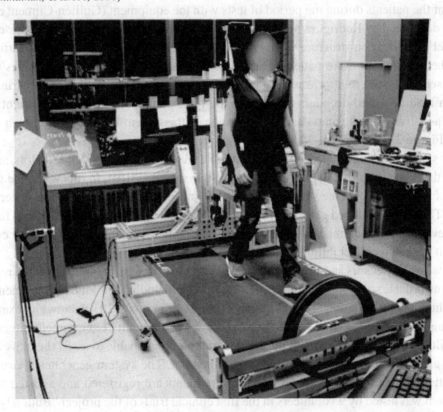

To improve the organization of these sections, the review of the rehabilitation structures and their respective serious games are divided into two groups: upper limb rehabilitation, and lower limb rehabilitation.

Upper Limb Rehabilitation

The rehabilitation process of the human upper limb assisted by robotic structures is highly consolidated with several approaches found in the literature. It is possible to find examples of structures developed applying serial chains directly coupled with the paretic limb of the patient, parallel systems using mobile platforms, cable-driven systems, and technologies that apply remote and/or wearable sensors integrated with the serious games.

The robotic system MERLIN is an example of serial rehabilitation structure integrate with serious games (Guillén-Climent et al., 2021). This structure is based on the Arm Assist system (TECNALIA, 2021), developed by TECNALIA®, and the telemedicine platform Antari (GMV, 2021), which allows the remote monitoring of the rehabilitation activities of a patient by a health professional. The system is integrated with 7 different types of games, where the patient moves its paretic limb with the assistance of the serial structure to accomplish the objectives of the game. The games available in this device include word formation, solitaire, card games to find pairs, and puzzles (Guillén-Climent et al., 2021). The first clinical studies have been performed in a group with 9 post-stroke patients with different levels of impairments. Preliminary results show promising results, where almost 100% of the participants described the system as useful, safe, and encouraging, and also promoting moderate motor improvements to the paretic limb of the patients during the period of tests with the equipment (Guillén-Climent et al., 2021).

The work developed by Rodrigues and Gonçalves (Rodrigues & Gonçalves, 2014) presents a cable-driven parallel rehabilitation structure with 4 degrees of freedom, applying a mobile platform directly attached to the upper limb of the patient. The structure is integrated with serious games using a Wii Remote as a sensor central to interface the game and the structure. The cables of the structure are associated with load cells and encoders to monitor the forces and trajectory of the patient upper limb and perform assistive actions when needed. An image of the system being operated by a volunteer is presented in Figure 2.

A similar system was developed utilizing a mobile platform with similar actuators and operated indirectly by the patients, with 2 degrees of freedom (Alves et al., 2019). In this work, the games had a higher level of integration with the structure, without the need of an intermediate sensor central like the Wii Remote. Thus, the developed games were designed to monitor and respond to the need for assistance at the same level of the structure. The games applied comprehensive situations with easy controls, like moving a fruit basket to collect falling fruits or drive a motorcycle on a track.

Recently, wearable sensors and immersive technologies like virtual and/or augmented reality are becoming more affordable solutions. Therefore, new research is including this kind of equipment in projects designed for human rehabilitation. The "Butterfly" project (Elor et al., 2019) shows an example of this concept. In this work, a serious game was developed in a virtual reality environment integrated with a smart suit built, named "CRUX", with neoprene and micromotor capable to assist the movements of the paretic limb, and synchronized with a virtual reality headset. The system generates a virtual scenario where the patient must protect a butterfly and all movements are registered and assisted by the smart suit. The system was tested by 9 volunteers in the first clinical trials of the project "Butterfly", reporting major positive results regarding the assistance of the suit, ease of use, and comfort.

The development of the serious games integrated with the rehabilitation structures is the focus of this chapter, the characteristics of the games observed in these structures were the main reference, especially the utilization of adaptative methodologies like the assist-as-needed system in Alves et al. (Alves et al., 2019).

Figure 2. Photo of a volunteer operating the rehabilitation structure integrated with serious games using a Wii Remote
(Rodrigues & Gonçalves, 2014)

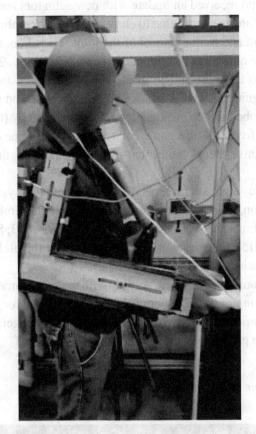

Lower Limb Rehabilitation

Robotic systems dedicated to the rehabilitation of the human lower limb face a different level of challenge from the therapeutic perspective since the objective of the structure can be focused on specific joint training, performing exercises separately, or dedicated to a functional goal of the paretic limb in human gait training.

An example of a structure dedicated to a single joint of the lower limb is presented in Khoshdel et al. (Khoshdel, Akbarzadeh, Naghavi, Sharifnezhad, & Souzanchi-Kashani, 2018). Here, a study was conducted to obtain surface electromyography signals (sEMG) of the active muscles that control the knee flexion of the lower limb and apply this data to train a neural network associated with fuzzy logic to control the mechanical impedance of a robotic structure with one degree-of-freedom directly connected to the paretic knee of the patient.

This approach based on biometric data and adaptive systems obtained satisfactory results and eliminated the need for complete dynamic modeling of the mechanical structure to perform the proper impedance control of the structure. A similar approach is applied in ReGear to assist the movement of the entire paretic side of the patients, combining the movement of both limbs.

Another single spot structure for the lower limb is Rutgers CP (Cioi et al., 2011), developed for ankle rehabilitation. This structure was originally proposed as a parallel platform dedicated to the ankle movements (Girone et al., 2000), and received an update with new actuators and new serious games (Cioi et al., 2011), Figure 5. The structure was submitted to clinical tests with cerebral palsy patients, with results pointing to significant strength and motor control of the joint. Therefore, these outcomes also affected the control and stability of the human gait of the participants (Cioi et al., 2011).

Single Spot structures also takes advantage of the use of Serious Games. The work developed by Banh et al. (2021) describes guidelines for game development focused on post-stroke patients with age 65+. They built a prototype robot able to evaluate the force produced by the paretic ankle of the player and generate real-time visual feedback on a game environment. The game currently integrated with the prototype is a colorful interactive thermometer that measures the strength of the patient's movements and compare with a goal.

In addition to the structures dedicated to specific joints, there are systems developed to cover the entire human gait rehabilitation, working with the healthy and paretic limb simultaneously. One of the main references of this kind of structure is LOKOMAT (Hesse et al., 2003; Swinnen, Baeyens, Knaepen, Michielsen, Clijsen, et al., 2015), an exoskeleton capable to assist the global movement of both lower limbs in treadmill training sessions.

LOKOMAT is still being constantly updated. A study with the same game type developed in this work, "endless runner" based on the inputs of the structure, has been proposed for LOKOMAT (Michaud et al., 2017). The objective of the game is to improve disabled children's engagement with their rehabilitating treatment. A screenshot of the game developed is shown in Figure 3.

Figure 3. Endless Runner game developed for LOKOMAT
(Michaud et al., 2017)

Another successful structure in the literature is known as LOPES (Veneman et al., 2007). Games applied in this device are based on the detection of the active participation level of the patient while executing the human gait movements. Whenever the patient can maintain a regular gait by himself/herself, a signal is sent to the game, resulting in higher scores.

Although some of the most known names of lower limb rehabilitation has been proposed in the last decade, there are still innovative solutions being proposed. One alternative design is cable-driven structures such as the one proposed by Tang and Shi (2021). Their solution is based on a treadmill combined with four pairs of active cables connected to two cuffs working as end-effectors. The cuffs are mounted on the thigh shank of the paretic limb of the patient, arranged as a parallelogram. The structure is still under development, with simulation results demonstrating that the design is suitable for human gait rehabilitation.

An illustration of the cable-driven design is shown in Figure 4.

Figure 4. Cable-Driven design proposed for gait rehabilitation
(Tang & Shi, 2021)

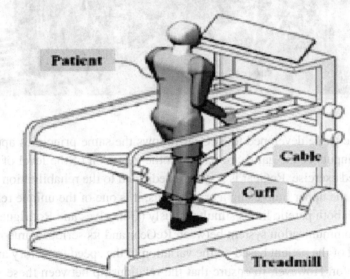

Some structures work with the indirect action in the human gait, promoting movements as similar to the natural ones as possible. One of the main references in this kind of gait rehabilitation system is the MIT-Skywalker (Rogério S Gonçalves, Hamilton, Daher, Hirai, & Hermano, 2017; Rogério Sales Gonçalves et al., 2017; T. Susko et al., 2016). This equipment induces the gait movements on patients' lower limbs indirectly using a pair of basculation treadmills associated with linear cams, which allows the system to use the gravitational force to reproduce the gait mechanism. The structure also includes a rotation system to simulate irregular grounds and train the patient balance. This structure is represented in Figure 1.

Figure 5. Photo of the Rutgers rehabilitation structure
(Cioi et al., 2011; Girone et al., 2000)

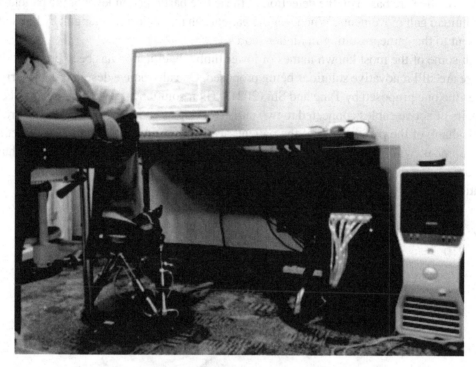

In this chapter, the game developed to ReGear follows the same principles applied in the LOPES structure, where the inputs of the game are based on the detection of the level of participation of the patient in the specified exercise. ReGear is a system dedicated to the rehabilitation of the knee flexion, while also exercising the upper limb using a crank. Thus, it is one of the unique rehabilitation systems designed to work with both paretic limbs simultaneously (Gonçalves and Rodrigues, 2021).

The control and communication system between ReGear and its serious game is designed to detect the participation level of the patient based on the variation of the speed trajectory and electrical current variations in its actuator. However, to ensure that the relationship between these parameters with the muscular activity, the tests performed with this system also applied sEMG sensors to measure the activity of the main muscles trained in the sessions, and the data collected were compared with the scores of each participant.

The second game described in this work deals with the HOPE-G structure and is mainly based on the MIT-Skywalker case (Rogerio S Gonçalves et al., 2017; Rogerio Sales Gonçalves et al., 2017; T. Susko et al., 2016), but using active bodyweight support to perform the balance training.

This game receives and sends more commands from the robotic structure. Here, the position of the patient is estimated in the structure and sent to the game, which uses this data to update the main character's position. The environment of the game also generates active outputs to the structure to simulate the displacement effect and assist the patient's movements whenever needed.

Therefore, the game and robotic device described in this work aim to assist the rehabilitation process of post-stroke patients, especially with the topics listed:

- Muscular control and strength of the paretic limbs.
- Functional independence of the patients.
- Motor coordination between the paretic limbs.
- Gait and balance control.

This work deals with the development of two serious games, specially designed to work with two rehabilitation structures: ReGear and HOPE-G. Both games are based on control adaptive techniques to adjust the events following the patients' needs throughout the training sessions. In this section, a brief description of these structures is presented.

REGEAR: AN INTERLIMB REHABILITATION STRUCTURE

ReGear was originally proposed as a collection of passive rehabilitation structures, dedicated to specific movements of the joints of the human lower limb. Previously, the movement assistance was provided by the patient himself/herself using a crank-rocker mechanism associated with a passive chain-belt system and a reduction system (Rogério S. Gonçalves & Rodrigues, 2021; Rodrigues, 2017).

Robotic Structure Development

The knee prototype was updated to be suitable for the rehabilitation training of post-stroke patients. The update included a 12 V DC motor with a gearbox and a rotary encoder linked to the mechanism to provide assistive actions when needed. With this new configuration, the structure is now able to assist the movements of both paretic limbs during a training session. This new version of the structure, now named ReGear, is presented in Figure 6.

Figure 6. (a) Prototype of the ReGear rehabilitation structure, (b) detail of the new actuator of the system

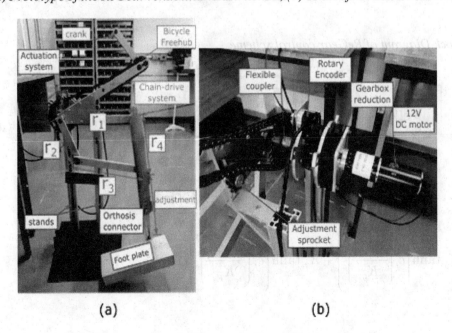

(a)   (b)

The new design of ReGear allows it to set up for each of the lower limb joints, where this prototype is dedicated to the knee. The workspace of the structure is designed specifically to the complete flexion/ extension amplitude and is reproduced in the patient's leg using a 4-bar linkage, configured as a crank-rocker mechanism, Figure 6(a). Thus, bars r_1 to r_4 are designed to allow r_1 to perform a complete rotation, and r_4 oscillates with the amplitude of the knee movement (Rogério S. Gonçalves & Rodrigues, 2021).

The actual version of the structure connects the actuator to the main gear using an elastic coupler, Figure 6(b). The transmission system of the main crank is connected with a manipulator for the patient to allow the motion input from the upper limb. The system also includes a tension adjustment sprocket in the chain-drive system and a freehub to allow patients to perform active movements only in one direction. This element was necessary to assist patients with less mobility in one of the paretic limbs and to avoid the need for a mirror setup of the structure for patients with different paretic sides.

The structure is controlled by a microcontroller Arduino Uno R3 with a current driver shield for 12V DC motors VNH2SP30. The microcontroller receives velocity data of the structure using a 2000 pulses rotary encoder and generates PWM outputs for the actuator based on the control logic implemented.

The entire control of the structure is oriented by the rotational speed of the main gear, where the rotary encoder and the crank are connected. Thus, to apply the assist-as-need methodology, a specific function was implemented directly in the digital controller of the microcontroller.

The assist-as-needed function was created based on the work of Asl et al. (Asl et al., 2019), and described in Figure 7. In this function, the error between the input from the rotary encoder and the reference from the desired speed trajectory is calculated and, in case it is close to zero, a proportional suppression is applied, creating a "dead zone." Thus, the actuator action is suppressed when the patient can perform the specified movement on its own and increases smoothly in case any assistance is needed to maintain the speed trajectory.

To create this dead zone, a function based on the hyperbolic tangent of the signals is applied after the controller calculation, as described in Equation (1). The final output of the controlled is yet added by a fraction of the reference signal in a "feed-forward" branch to avoid subtle stops in the equipment.

Figure 7. Block Diagram of ReGear control scheme

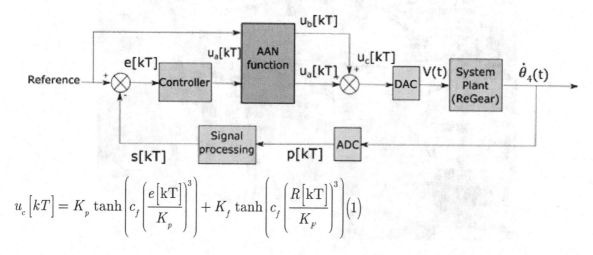

$$u_c\left[kT\right] = K_p \tanh\left(c_f \left(\frac{e\left[\text{kT}\right]}{K_p}\right)^3\right) + K_f \tanh\left(c_f \left(\frac{R\left[\text{kT}\right]}{K_F}\right)^3\right) \quad (1)$$

Therefore, the control system of ReGear can be resumed as described ahead: the output of the system is represented by the angular velocity of the bar r_4, described as $\dot{\theta}_4$. This angular speed is monitored by the rotary encoder, sending the raw signal $p[kT]$ to the microcontroller, which will then be converted into an angular speed $s[kT]$. This signal is compared with the reference $R[kT]$ to obtain the error $e[kT]$. Thus, a PID controller process this error, and the output is modulated by Equation (1) and summed up with a fraction of $R[kT]$ to create the output $u_c[kT]$, which is converted to a PWM $V(t)$ and sent back to the actuator.

In addition to the control logic described above, the microcontroller is also responsible to maintain direct communication with the serious game using a USB port to send and receive commands. The microcontroller sends periodically information regarding the participation level of the patient based on the output of the AAN function. It also receives important commands from the game like start and stop the seed trajectory calculation, which is the calibration process of the structure, and start or stop the training session.

JUMPING JACK: SERIOUS GAME FOR REGEAR

The serious game for ReGear was named "Jumping Jack." This game is based on the classic 2D adventure and platform games, remarkably present in vintage videogames and mobile devices. This game genre was chosen to compose with ReGear simple operation. A screenshot of the game is presented in Figure 8.

Figure 8. Screenshot of Jumping Jack

The game was developed with the Unity 2D engine, applying built-in resources and custom C# scripts. The main goal of the game is to control Jack, a fox humanoid referred to like the main character, throughout an infinite track with it collects fruits along the way. During the sessions, the character may follow the path of running or walking, depending on the level of participation in the exercises in ReGear structure.

During the training session, Jack will find collectible fruits with different associated scores. There is also a level system connected to the level of participation of the patient. Depending on the total time that the patient performed the active movement in the rehabilitation structure, a special impulse appears on the screen and, if he/she manages to make the main character pass through it running, it will trigger a super jump and give access to a new level with new fruits that worth more points.

Game-Structure Interaction

The game starts with an initial screen, where the health professional that will monitor the training session specifies the desired duration in minutes. Before moving to the next screen, he/she must ensure that the setup of the equipment with the lower limb of the patient is correct.

In the next screen, there is a button to perform a calibration of the speed trajectory of the micro-controller. Since the required gains are different for each patient, this is an important step that allows the system to apply the assist-as-needed control strategy correctly. During the calibration, the patient is oriented to let the actuator of ReGear perform a complete cycle without any muscular action. Therefore, the microcontroller will build the reference based on the passive weight of the patient's lower limb.

Once the calibration is complete, the health professional may start the game on the next screen. As the game starts, the structure will start a continuous movement in one direction, and the patient must try to maintain this movement without the assistance of the actuator. Since the system is connected to both upper and lower paretic limbs, the patient may combine or alternate the movements of both limbs to keep the participation in the game.

The serious game also shows up the current score and the remaining time in the session, as shown in Figure 8. Once the time for the session expires, the main character and the structure stop moving, and the final score is displayed on the screen.

Main Character Control Design

The main character of the game, Jack, has only one degree of freedom controlled by the participation level of the patient: walk, when the main movement action is performed by the actuator of ReGear; and run, when the patient is performing the active movement. When Jack is running, he moves 70% faster than walking. The animation sprites of the main character are presented in Figure 9.

Figure 9. Animation sprites of Jack, the main character of the first serious game. (a) Jumping, (b) walking, (c) running

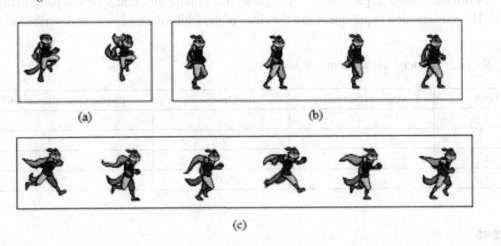

The control system implemented for the main character is based on the serial communication between the microcontroller and the serious game. ReGear sends a periodical signal every 500ms containing a character that indicates whether the patient is performing the active movement or not. When the game receives a signal of a state different than the actual one 3 times in a row, the main character changes its behavior. For example, if Jack is currently walking and the game receives 3 consecutive messages indicating that the patient is performing the active movement, it will start running.

Score Fruits

Fruits are the score source of the game. The main objective of the game is to collect them as they appear. There are two types of fruits in the game: the common type appears at the ground level and can be easily collected, and the rare ones appear some meters above the ground, requiring a jump and an impulse to be collected. Jack will only jump to collect the rare fruits if he passes through the impulse running. Thus, the patient must maintain a high level of participation to collect the most valuable fruits. The fruits applied in the game are displayed in Figure 10.

Figure 10. Fruits applied in the scoring system of Jumping Jack

The score of each fruit depends if it is a common or rare fruit, and on the current level that Jack is. There are 4 different levels implemented in the game, that require different levels of participation to be accessed. The participation requirement and the value of the fruits of each level are described in Table 1.

Table 1. Score detail per level in Jumping Jack

Level	Common fruit score	Rare fruit score	Required participation level (%)
1	1	5	-
2	2	10	50%
3	5	20	70%
4	10	50	85%

Impulses

One of the elements that enrich the interactions of the game is the jump impulses, represented as chevrons as shown in Figure 11. They appear in specific moments of the game and allow the main character to jump if it is running, and consequently if the patient is participating in the exercises.

Figure 11. Chevrons applied to represent the jump impulses. (a) Simple jump Chevron, (b) level up Chevron

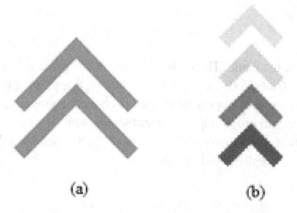

(a)   (b)

The simple chevrons always appear closely before a rare fruit. That way, Jack must be running as it passes through the chevron, trigger a jump and collects the fruit. The level-up chevrons will appear only if the patient matches the requirement of level up, based on the amount of time he spent with active participation in the movement on the structure.

The overall participation of the patient in the movement is evaluated in the game every 1 minute, and if it is enough to move to the next level, the level up chevron will spawn. However, Jack will only jump to the next level if it is running, so the patient must time well the movements to access the level. The level-up requirements of each level are presented in Table 1.

In case the required activity level drops below the requirement of a certain level after 1 minute, the platform of that level will end, and Jack will fall to the previous level.

HOPE-G: A NOVEL STRUCTURE FOR HUMAN GAIT REHABILITATION

The second structure in this chapter is named HOPE-G, and is subdivided into 3 modules:

- **Active Bodyweight Support (BWS) module:** This module consists of a parallel robotic structure with 5 degrees of freedom: 3 translations, and 2 rotations. The main goal of this module is to promote assist-as-needed actions to the pelvic joint, especially regarding the gait balance, while suppressing part of the bodyweight of the patient. Therefore, the structure is designed to provide efficient training and balance function (Lefeber, Swinnen, & Kerckhofs, 2017).
- **Dual Treadmill Module:** This module is composed of two dropping treadmills, positioned below the feet of the patient, associated with pneumatic pistons to perform the basculation. Thus, this module is responsible to induce human gait movements indirectly. The design of this module is based on MIT-Skywalker (T. Susko et al., 2016) improving the original project regarding the mechanical structure and control system.
- **Markerless Control & Monitoring Module:** The human gait is monitored by a markerless system, which applies "Microsoft Kinect 2.0", a camera system designed for games, to identify and quantify the movements of the lower limbs. This module will be responsible to control the movements of the dual treadmill module and is already developed and validated in clinical trials (Salim, 2018).

The concept model of HOPE-G and the detail of its modules is presented in Figure 12.

Figure 12. The main concept of the HOPE-G rehabilitation system

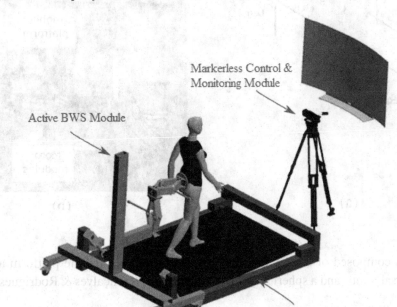

The main innovation of HOPE-G is related to the active BWS module, developed based on a closed kinematic chain little explored in rehabilitation systems. Robotic structures that promote BWS treadmill training sessions for gait rehabilitation affect the pelvic joint movements and the gait balance (Gonçalves et al., 2017a, 2017b; Swinnen, Baeyens, Hens, et al., 2015; Swinnen, Baeyens, Knaepen, Michielsen, Hens, et al., 2015)

Therefore, the active BWS module of HOPE-G may contribute to the balance training of the patients with the dual treadmill module, a simple treadmill, or directly overground.

The HOPE-G system is already fully designed and modeled, with a built prototype for the Active BWS module in Robotics and Automation Laboratory of the Federal University of Uberlândia (R.S. Gonçalves & Rodrigues, 2019).

Therefore, the serious game for this structure will be designed for the Active BWS Module and its control system. This structure has its workspace based on the meaningful movements for the pelvic joint (Roberts, 2004), and is designed as a "multiperson" mechanism (C. Gosselin, Laliberté, & Veillette, 2015; C. M. Gosselin et al., 2007). Thus, this structure is a closed kinematic chain system with low coupling between the actuators and almost singularity-free, while allowing an even load distribution over the structure (R.S. Gonçalves & Rodrigues, 2019). The configuration of the Active BWS module is presented in Figure 7.

Figure 13. (a) schematics of the Active BWS module of HOPE-G, (b) prototype built in Laboratory of Automation and Robotics (LAR) of the Federal University of Uberlândia

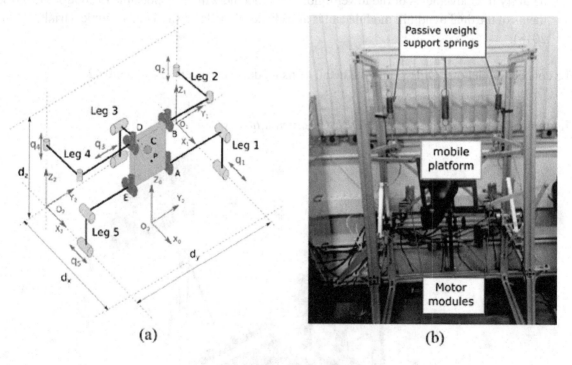

The structure is composed of 5 legs, Figure 9(b), connected to a mobile platform applying rotational joints, universal joints, and a spherical joint (only on leg 3) (Gonçalves & Rodrigues, 2019b). The structures provide to the patient bodyweight suppression through a monocycle seat and a safety vest. The passive weight of the patient is suppressed by 3 springs, one positioned directly above the mobile platform, and others above each vertical actuator, q_2 and q_4, as shown in Figure 9(b).

The actuators of the structure, q_1 to q_5, are originally designed as linear devices. To allow the appliance of DC motors, specific modules for the structure were developed. These modules are composed of a crank-rod mechanism, designed to convert angular movement into linear using a motor bracket with a rotary encoder and linear rails. The schema developed for the motor modules is presented in Figure 14.

All modules were designed to allow the patient to move passively, while also monitoring its movements and efforts to apply assist-as-needed actions.

The structure is controlled by a microcontroller Arduino MEGA 2560 with 3 current driver shields VNH2SP30, adjusted to operate with DC motors in 16V, rotary encoders, and endpoint sensors installed at the extremities of the linear rails.

The control of the structure is based on the position read on the rotary encoders, assisted by the endpoint sensors. For each motor module, a PID controller was implemented, and the parameters were tuned applying a differential evolution algorithm with an iterative process over several step responses of each module. Each module was tested based on 50 initial conditions over 200 iterations to obtain the optimum control parameters (Gonçalves et al., 2016; Lobato et al., 2007).

A similar assist-as-needed function, Eq. (1), is also applied in the controller output of each motor module, without the feedforward branch. Thus, as long as the error between the position of the coordinates q_n and the reference is low, the structure does not perform corrections in the position of the patient. In addition, whenever the error starts rising, the dead zone function smoothly allows the control actions of the PID controllers to take place and induce corrections.

Figure 14. CAD model of the motor module, (b) schematic drawing of the mechanism

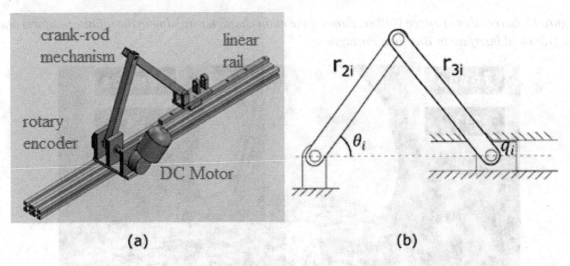

(a) (b)

During the operation, the BWS module starts by adjusting its translations in $OXYZ_0$ to the patient's neutral position. After this, the structure starts monitoring the movements of the patients in the training sessions. Eventually, the structure performs slight rotations on the coronal or transversal plane of the patient, that is, around axes X_0 and Z_0. These rotations are designed to train the balance of the patient during the gait in a controlled environment.

Like ReGear, the microcontroller of the Active BWS module of HOPE-G is also responsible to communicate with the serious game using a USB connection. In this case, the microcontroller receives commands from the game to calibrate the neutral position of the patient, start/stop the training sessions, assist actively the patient to reach a specific position, and perform the controlled rotations in the mobile platform.

The microcontroller also sends periodical information to the serious game, which is applied as the input commands to the main character. This information is based on the position of the patient measured by the encoder of q_3 along axis Y_0. In case the patient struggles to maintain the requested positions in the game, assistive actions are performed by q_3 to complete the movement.

SPACE WALKER: SERIOUS GAME FOR HOPE-G

The second game presented in this chapter is named "Space Walker", developed to integrate the Active BWS module of the HOPE-G rehabilitation system. Therefore, this game is designed to match the required characteristics to react to the movements in the training sessions with HOPE-G.

Since this rehabilitation structure deals with tridimensional movements, the game was designed using Unity 3D engine, adopting the "Endless Runner" genre, which follows similar principles applied in Jumping Jack. In Space Walker, the main character of the game is a humanoid robot that walks on an infinite platform with 3 main lanes, one to the left, one in the middle, and one to the right. During the walk, the player must avoid collisions with obstacles and collect bonus items. A screenshot of the final game is presented in Figure 15.

Figure 15. Screenshot of Space Walker, showing the main character walking in the infinite platform and the graphical interface in Brazilian Portuguese

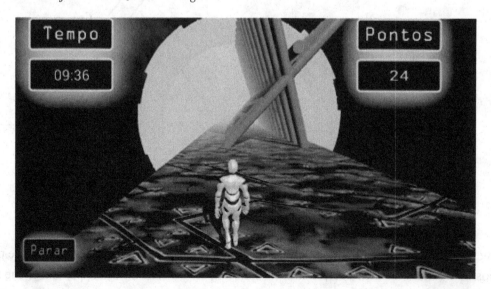

Game-Structure Interaction

The interaction of Space Walker with HOPE-G has common points with the one designed for Jumping Jack and ReGear. It also starts with an initial screen where the health professional enters the desired duration for the training session, but in this case, the structure adjusts the translation of the mobile platform to the neutral position of the patient as soon as the game is opened.

After the position is adjusted, the treadmill is turned on and the game starts. HOPE-G will send periodical data containing information of the patient position that controls which lane the main character should walk in. The structure will also receive commands to perform the rotations on the platform depending on the events of the game.

The periodical signals of the microcontroller are sent through the USB connection every 500 milliseconds, with the position of the patient along Y_0 measured in the rotary encoder of q_3. Each encoder of the structure has 500 pulses per cycle, resulting in a workspace of around 200 pulses for the motor modules.

Therefore, 3 zones are defined to represent the lanes of the game based on the encoder readings: up to 60 pulses, the microcontroller sends a message indicating the left lane; from 61 to 120, it indicates the central lane, and above 120 pulses, the right lane.

If the player finds difficulties avoiding collisions with the obstacles, the game will send a command to activate the active assistance in q_3 to assist the patient to move the character to the correct lane of the current tile. To do this, a script counts the collisions per minute of the player, and if the value is greater or equal to 4, this command is sent to the structure. Once the collisions per minute are reduced, the assistance is turned off.

Once the session runs out of time, the final screen with the obtained score of the session is displayed and both treadmill and Active BWS module are turned off.

Scenario and Obstacles

In Space Walker, a C# script running in the game controls the generation of the infinite platform where the main character walks. To allow the platform to be generated indefinity, it is subdivided into pre-created tiles, so that only a controlled and pre-determined quantity of tiles exists in the scene.

As the main character advances, the tiles of the track already walked and invisible to the game camera are destroyed, and new tiles are created behind a portal that maintains a constant distance from the player. Thus, the new spawning tiles are not visible by the player and will only be revealed once it crosses the portal.

The pre-created tiles of the platform already contain the obstacles that the player must avoid while walking on it. Therefore, the script that manages the tile creation shuffles their order, and generates new ones randomly, making each training session unique. More than 20 different models of tiles with obstacles were created for this game. An example of a pre-created tile is shown in Figure 16.

Figure 16. Example of pre-created tile of the platform

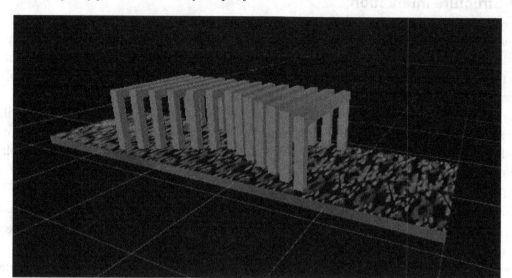

Score System

The score in Space Walker is directly proportional to the time of the session, where the player continuously earns points as long as the training session is active. The game also has an extra points system that can be obtained by collecting bonus cubes or multiplying the base score when the mobile platform of the active BWS is rotated.

The main source of extra scores in the game comes from the multipliers. Every time the game sends a rotation command to the rehabilitation structure, the scenario of the game is also rotated, and a multiplying factor is applied to the score. This factor stays active as long as the player does not collide with any obstacle and is removed if any collision is detected. The multiplying factors are stackable up to 4 times the base score rate if the player manages to avoid collisions until the next rotation of the platform.

Another scoring element in the game is the bonus cubes, small floating green objects that spawn eventually with the tiles, as shown in Figure 17. These cubes appear in one of the lanes of the platform, but they are not always easily reachable. Therefore, a challenging situation is created, where the patient must always evaluate the tradeoff of trying to get a bonus cube and risking getting a collision and lose active multipliers if there are any.

Figure 17. Bonus Cube in the scene

Main Character and Camera

The main character of Space Walker is a humanoid blue robot, capable to walk in a straight line and change lanes. Its position is hardwired to the encoder readings of q_3 in the active BWS module of HOPE-G. Thus, the main character should follow the same position as the patient, creating an immersive sensation with the serious game.

The game implements a third-person vision system, where a game camera constantly follows the main character, with a fixed perspective, and maintaining a constant distance. In addition, a special playability element was added to the camera to improve the experience: the camera is affected by the same rotations induced in the mobile platform of the active BWS of HOPE-G.

The rotations of the game are controlled by a script and are randomly activated in an arbitrary interval between 60 and 100 seconds. The same command sent to the rehabilitation structure is sent to the camera, creating a sensation that the same action happening in the virtual environment is being replicated in the reality.

During the platform rotations, an animated icon also pops up in the game interface, indicating visually what kind of rotation is active at the moment.

User Interface

During the sessions, an interface is kept active displaying information of the current session. Most of the time, the interface will the remaining time in the session on the upper left corner with a countdown clock, and the current score at the upper right corner.

When the rotations occur, the animated icon that indicates the rotation shows up in the upper-middle level. This icon is displayed only when a rotation is active.

Another element in the interface is the multiplying factor. It appears on the left side of the current score and indicates the actual score scaling rate. This indicator remains on the screen until the player collides with an obstacle and is updated every time a new rotation is activated.

There is also a button to stop the session before the session time runs out, in case it is necessary. All these elements are described in Figure 18.

Figure 18. Interface diagram

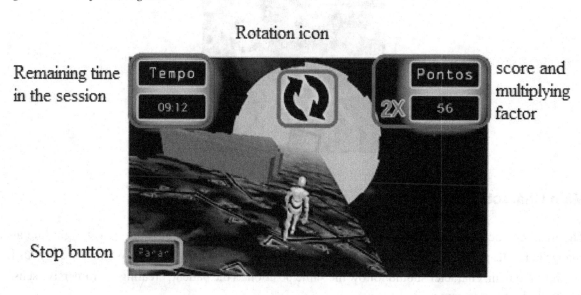

EXPERIMENTAL TESTS

To validate the design applied in the rehabilitation structures and the serious games, experimental tests were proposed featuring two groups of volunteers, one composed of healthy people and the other with post-stroke patients. At the current state of the research, the first clinical trials with ReGear and Jumping Jack are already concluded, and the trials with Space Walker and HOPE-G are scheduled. Both research projects are authorized by the Ethical Committee of Human Research under the research projects number 34857520.6.0000.5152 and 01305318.2.0000.5152.

The tests were conducted in the Laboratory of Automation and Robotics and the Physiotherapy Clinic of the Federal University of Uberlândia. An image of one of the volunteers testing ReGear during a training session with Jumping Jack is presented in Figure 19.

Figure 19. Healthy volunteer testing ReGear

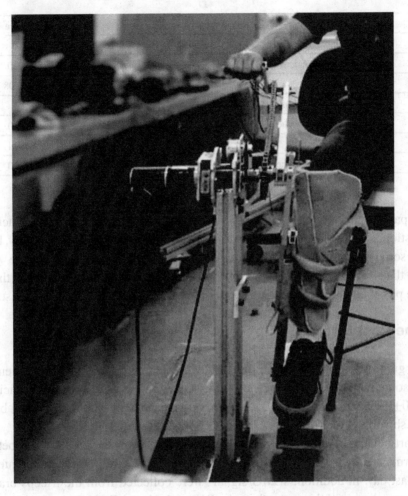

Tests with the Healthy Group

The first testing group was composed of 10 people of both genders and ages above 18 years. Before the beginning of the tests, all participants received a document with all the terms, conditions, and all the necessary instructions about the research. After signing up the term, the setup of ReGear with the lower limb is performed, and a single training session with a duration of 10 minutes is conducted. First, the calibration of the equipment is performed to obtain the speed trajectory, and then the session with the game is started.

At the end of the session, the score obtained by each volunteer was registered, and a questionnaire regarding the main characteristics of the game was applied. The results of the healthy group are consolidated in Table 2.

Table 2. Test results of the healthy group

Metric	Value
Number of sessions	10
Average score	4020
Average score per minute	402.08
Standard deviation	474
Minimum value	3250
Median	3994
Maximum value	4700

After participation in the training sessions, most participants gave positive feedback regarding the game in the questionnaire. In this group, all participants reported that the game was easy, but two of them reported that at some moments, they were required attention and coordination. Some volunteers were able to maintain the character running using only one of the limbs, but it was observed that to obtain the maximum score possible, they needed to use both upper and lower limbs in the exercise.

Tests with the Post-Stroke Group

The second test group was composed of 5 individuals, 4 men, and 1 woman, all of them chronic post-stroke patients, some with the left paretic side, and some with the right side. All participants had ages 65 ± 5 years, 1.60 ± 0.12 m height, 70 ± 11 kg weight, and muscular spasticity evaluated between 1+ and 2 in Modified Ashworth Scale (MAS).

The group participated in training sessions over one week, with session durations between 5 and 10 minutes. The terms and instructions were presented on the first day, and the game questionnaire was applied on the last day. In addition, sEMG signals were collected from the triceps brachii long head (TBLH) of the upper limb and the rectus femoris (RF) of the lower limb. These signals were applied to measure the muscular activity of each limb during the training sessions.

The results obtained by the post-stroke group are consolidated in Table 3.

Table 3. Test results of the post-stroke group

Metric	Value
Number of sessions	13
Average score	1633.26
Average score per minute	163.33
Standard Deviation	1240.90
Minimum value	240
Median value	1093
Maximum Value	3917

Some participants of the post-stroke group were not able to finish all the scheduled training sessions due to health complications unrelated to the clinical trials. However, the group managed to perform 13 complete training sessions. It was noticed during the tests the game is more challenging to the post-stroke group compared with the healthy group, requiring more attention to the game mechanics and the movements executed by both limbs.

The assist-as-needed behavior of ReGear was evident during the tests, as participants with lower mobility were able to perform complete movements with the assistance of the actuator, activated whenever they had more difficulties. At the same time, the game was constantly encouraging them to move the structure by themselves.

The differences in the mobility of the participants were highly reflected in the score obtained by them, where participants with better mobility obtained scores close to the obtained by the healthy group, while the ones with more spasticity needed more assistance from the motor during the session.

Participants with the right paretic side had a better performance with the structure compared with the ones with the left paretic side due to the current design of ReGear. They were able to perform full rotations on the crank with the upper limb, while the participants with the left paretic side had to use the freehub to perform oscillating movements.

However, some left paretic side participants learned to time the active movements of each limb to maximize the participation level detected by ReGear and prioritize the movements near chevrons to get a higher score. Therefore, they worked with better motor coordination between the upper and lower limb and obtained competitive scores compared with the other participants.

The post-stroke group gave positive overall feedback regarding the structure and the game. Most of the participants described the game as interesting, challenging, and fun. One of the participants also reported he felt his joints lighter and easier to move after the end of the training sessions.

With the sEMG data collected in the training sessions, moderate and correlations were found between the muscular activity of the participants and the obtained scores in each session, divided by the session duration to compensate for the different time durations. Results are presented in Table 4.

Table 4. Correlation between the observed characteristic in the data collected from sEMG signals and the score per minute of the post-stroke group

Feature	Correlation
Average of clusters RMS	0,64
RMS of TBLH cluster	0,60
RMS of RF cluster	0,36
Std. of RF cluster	0,30

The clinical tests of the HOPE-G structure with Space Walker serious game are scheduled. At the moment, its basic functionalities and conditions of use are already tested. A similar test protocol adopted with ReGear is planned for HOPE-G, focusing the analysis on the comparison of the results between healthy and post-stroke groups regarding the performance in the game and the effectiveness of the assist-as-needed function in the training sessions.

CONCLUSION

This chapter presented the current state of development of two serious games integrated with distinct rehabilitation robotic structures that applies assist-as-needed systems: ReGear and HOPE-G.

The current state of the art in rehabilitation structure integrated with serious games was presented, highlighting the alignment of these structures with trends observed in the literature.

A brief description of the structures to be integrated with the serious games is presented, detailing its mechanics and clinical objectives, and demonstrating the positive contribution to the literature with the interlimb rehabilitation perspective of ReGear, and the novel design applied in the Active BWS of HOPE-G.

The development process of both serious games is presented, highlighting the main characteristics for each case, and how the design is aligned with the clinical objectives of each structure. In addition, the first clinical trials of ReGear with Jumping Jack are presented.

Results demonstrate that the assist-as-needed principle explored in structure and the serious game has been successfully implemented. The system was able to provide active assistance to the participants only when necessary, and the serious game was able to use the participation level obtained from the structure as the input for the main character's behavior.

The first clinical trials with ReGear provide encouraging results for the next tests to be performed with HOPE-G and Space Walker, which are already scheduled.

Based on the obtained results, future works with ReGear should focus on improvements of the mechanical design to provide better support for left paretic side patients and expand the clinical trials for larger groups of volunteers and for a longer period to observe possible gains related to the training sessions with the structure and the serious game.

For HOPE-G, the next steps consist in evaluate the design of the interactions between the structure and the game considering the behavior of healthy and post-stroke volunteers and the effects of the balance training and adaptative assistance. All evaluations should also consider the feedback from the participants to perform adjustments in the game and the structure.

ACKNOWLEDGMENT

The authors thank the Federal University of Uberlândia, FAPEMIG, CNPq, and CAPES [grant number 0001] for the partial funding for this work.

REFERENCES

Alves, T., Chaves D'Carvalho, M., & Gonçalves, R. S. (2019). Assist-as-needed control in a cable-actuated robot for human joints rehabilitation. *Journal of Mechanical Engineering and Biomechanics*, *3*(5), 57–62. doi:10.24243/JMEB/3.5.214

Asl, H. J., Narikiyo, T., & Kawanishi, M. (2019). An assist-as-needed control scheme for robot-assisted rehabilitation. *Proceedings of the American Control Conference*, 198–203. 10.23919/ACC.2017.7962953

Banh, S., Zheng, E., Kubota, A., & Riek, L. D. (2021, March 8). A Robot-based Gait Training System for Post-Stroke Rehabilitation. *Companion of the 2021 ACM/IEEE International Conference on Human-Robot Interaction*. 10.1145/3434074.3447212

Bateni, H., & Maki, B. E. (2005). Assistive devices for balance and mobility: Benefits, demands, and adverse consequences. In Archives of Physical Medicine and Rehabilitation (Vol. 86, Issue 1, pp. 134–145). doi:10.1016/j.apmr.2004.04.023

Buchinger, D., & da Silva Hounsell, M. (2018). Guidelines for designing and using collaborative-competitive serious games. *Computers & Education*, *118*, 133–149. Advance online publication. doi:10.1016/j.compedu.2017.11.007

Cioi, D., Kale, A., Burdea, G., Engsberg, J., Janes, W., & Ross, S. (2011). Ankle control and strength training for children with cerebral palsy using the Rutgers Ankle CP. *2011 IEEE International Conference on Rehabilitation Robotics*, 1–6. 10.1109/ICORR.2011.5975432

Cornejo, R., Martínez, F., Álvarez, V. C., Barraza, C., Cibrian, F. L., Martínez-García, A. I., & Tentori, M. (2021). Serious games for basic learning mechanisms: Reinforcing Mexican children's gross motor skills and attention. *Personal and Ubiquitous Computing*, *25*(2), 375–390. Advance online publication. doi:10.100700779-021-01529-0

Elor, A., Lessard, S., Teodorescu, M., & Kurniawan, S. (2019). Project Butterfly: Synergizing Immersive Virtual Reality with Actuated Soft Exosuit for Upper-Extremity Rehabilitation. *2019 IEEE Conference on Virtual Reality and 3D User Interfaces (VR)*, 1448–1456. 10.1109/VR.2019.8798014

Gee, J. P. (2003). What video games have to teach us about learning and literacy. *Computers in Entertainment*, *1*(1), 20–20. doi:10.1145/950566.950595

Girone, M., Burdea, G., Bouzit, M., Popescu, V., & Deutsch, J. E. (2000). Orthopedic rehabilitation using the "Rutgers ankle" interface. *Studies in Health Technology and Informatics*, *70*, 89–95. PMID:10977590

GMV. (2021). *Antari by GMV*. https://www.gmv.com/en/Products/antari_ehealth_epidemiology_solutions/antari_tele_rehab/

Gonçalves, R. S., Carvalho, J. C. M., & Lobato, F. S. (2016). Design of a robotic device actuated by cables for human lower limb rehabilitation using self-adaptive differential evolution and robust optimization. *Bioscience Journal*, 1689–1702. doi:10.14393/BJ-v32n1a2016-32436

Gonçalves, R. S., Hamilton, T., Daher, A. R., Hirai, H., & Hermano, I. (2017a). MIT-Skywalker: Considerations on the Design of a Body Weight Support System. *Journal of Neuroengineering and Rehabilitation*, *14*(1), 1–12. doi:10.118612984-017-0302-6 PMID:28877750

Gonçalves, R. S., Hamilton, T., Daher, A. R., Hirai, H., & Hermano, I. (2017b). MIT-Skywalker : Evaluating Comfort of Bicycle / Saddle Seat. *2017 International Conference on Rehabilitation Robotics (ICORR)*, 516–520. 10.1109/ICORR.2017.8009300

Gonçalves, R. S., & Rodrigues, L. A. O. (2019a). Development of a Novel Parallel Structure for Gait Rehabilitation. In Handbook of Research on Advanced Mechatronic Systems and Intelligent Robotics (pp. 42–81). doi:10.4018/978-1-7998-0137-5.ch003

Gonçalves, R. S., & Rodrigues, L. A. O. (2019b). Development of a novel parallel structure for gait rehabilitation. In Handbook of Research on Advanced Mechatronic Systems and Intelligent Robotics. doi:10.4018/978-1-7998-0137-5.ch003

Gonçalves, R. S., & Rodrigues, L. A. O. (2021). Development of nonmotorized mechanisms for lower limb rehabilitation. *Robotica*, 1–18. doi:10.1017/S0263574721000412

Gosselin, C., Laliberté, T., & Veillette, A. (2015). Singularity-Free Kinematically Redundant Planar Parallel Mechanisms With Unlimited Rotational Capability. *IEEE Transactions on Robotics*, *31*(2), 457–467. doi:10.1109/TRO.2015.2409433

Gosselin, C. M., Masouleh, M. T., Duchaine, V., Richard, P.-L., Foucault, S., & Kong, X. (2007). Parallel Mechanisms of the Multipteron Family: Kinematic Architectures and Benchmarking. *Proceedings 2007 IEEE International Conference on Robotics and Automation*, 555–560. 10.1109/ROBOT.2007.363045

Green, C. S., & Bavelier, D. (2003). Action video game modifies visual selective attention. *Nature*, *423*(6939), 534–537. doi:10.1038/nature01647 PMID:12774121

Guillén-Climent, S., Garzo, A., Muñoz-Alcaraz, M. N., Casado-Adam, P., Arcas-Ruiz-Ruano, J., Mejías-Ruiz, M., & Mayordomo-Riera, F. J. (2021). A usability study in patients with stroke using MERLIN, a robotic system based on serious games for upper limb rehabilitation in the home setting. *Journal of Neuroengineering and Rehabilitation*, *18*(1), 41. doi:10.118612984-021-00837-z PMID:33622344

Hall, S. (2020). *How COVID-19 is taking gaming and esports to the next level*. World Economic Forum. https://www.weforum.org/agenda/2020/05/covid-19-taking-gaming-and-esports-next-level/

Hesse, S., Schmidt, H., Werner, C., & Bardeleben, A. (2003). Upper and lower extremity robotic devices for rehabilitation and for studying motor control. In Current Opinion in Neurology (Vol. 16, Issue 6, pp. 705–710). Lippincott Williams & Wilkins. doi:10.1097/00019052-200312000-00010

Hu, W., Li, G., Sun, Y., Jiang, G., Kong, J., Ju, Z., & Jiang, D. (2017). A Review of Upper and Lower Limb Rehabilitation Training Robot. In Y. Huang, H. Wu, H. Liu, & Z. Yin (Eds.), *Intelligent Robotics and Applications* (pp. 570–580). Springer International Publishing. doi:10.1007/978-3-319-65289-4_54

Khoshdel, V., Akbarzadeh, A., Naghavi, N., Sharifnezhad, A., & Souzanchi-Kashani, M. (2018). sEMG-based impedance control for lower-limb rehabilitation robot. *Intelligent Service Robotics*, *11*(1), 97–108. doi:10.100711370-017-0239-4

Kim, S., Song, K., Lockee, B., & Burton, J. (2018). What is Gamification in Learning and Education? In *Gamification in Learning and Education* (pp. 25–38). Springer International Publishing., doi:10.1007/978-3-319-47283-6_4

Lauretti, C., Cordella, F., Guglielmelli, E., & Zollo, L. (2017). Learning by Demonstration for Planning Activities of Daily Living in Rehabilitation and Assistive Robotics. *IEEE Robotics and Automation Letters*, *2*(3), 1375–1382. doi:10.1109/LRA.2017.2669369

Lefeber, N., Swinnen, E., & Kerckhofs, E. (2017). The immediate effects of robot-assistance on energy consumption and cardiorespiratory load during walking compared to walking without robot-assistance: a systematic review. In Disability and Rehabilitation: Assistive Technology (Vol. 12, Issue 7, pp. 657–671). doi:10.1080/17483107.2016.1235620

Lobato, F. S., Steffen, V., Jr., & Oliveira-Lopes, L. C. (2007). An evolutionary approach based on search chaotic pattern associated to differential evolution algorithm. *17° Symposium of the Mechanical Engineering Post-Graduation Program*, 9.

Lourenço, J. M. B. (2018). *Serious Games for Motor Rehabilitation Applying Virtual Reality*. Academic Press.

Michaud, B., Cherni, Y., Begon, M., Girardin-Vignola, G., & Roussel, P. (2017, June). A serious game for gait rehabilitation with the Lokomat. *2017 International Conference on Virtual Rehabilitation (ICVR)*. 10.1109/ICVR.2017.8007482

Molteni, F., Gasperini, G., Cannaviello, G., & Guanziroli, E. (2018). Exoskeleton and End-Effector Robots for Upper and Lower Limbs Rehabilitation: Narrative Review. *PM & R*, *10*(9), S174–S188. doi:10.1016/j.pmrj.2018.06.005 PMID:30269804

Rego, P., Moreira, P. M., & Reis, L. P. (2010). Serious Games for Rehabilitation: A survey and a classification towards a taxonomy. *Proceedings of the 5th Iberian Conference on Information Systems and Technologies, CISTI 2010*.

Roberts, M. (2004). *A robot for gait rehabilitation*. Academic Press.

Rodrigues, L. A. O. (2017). *Development of nonmotorized mechanisms for human lower limb rehabilitation*. Federal University of Uberlândia.

Rodrigues, L. A. O., & Gonçalves, R. S. (2014). Development of games Applied to Human Upper limb Rehabilitation. *XXIV Brazilian Conference of Biomedic – CBEB*, 396–399.

Sailer, M., & Homner, L. (2020). The Gamification of Learning: A Meta-analysis. *Educational Psychology Review*, *32*(1), 77–112. doi:10.100710648-019-09498-w

Salim, V. V. (2018). Development of a markerless control system for a human gait rehabilitation robot. Federal University of Uberlândia.

Streicher, A., & Smeddinck, J. D. (2016). *Personalized and Adaptive Serious Games*. doi:10.1007/978-3-319-46152-6_14

Susko, T., Swaminathan, K., & Krebs, H. I. (2016). MIT-Skywalker: A Novel Gait Neurorehabilitation Robot for Stroke and Cerebral Palsy. *IEEE Transactions on Neural Systems and Rehabilitation Engineering*, *24*(10), 1089–1099. doi:10.1109/TNSRE.2016.2533492 PMID:26929056

Susko, T. G. (2015). *MIT Skywalker: A novel robot for gait rehabilitation of stroke and cerebral palsy patients*. Academic Press.

Swinnen, E., Baeyens, J. P., Hens, G., Knaepen, K., Beckwe, D., Michielsen, M., Clijsen, R., & Kerckhofs, E. (2015). Body weight support during robot-assisted walking: Influence on the trunk and pelvis kinematics. *NeuroRehabilitation, 36*(1), 81–91. Advance online publication. doi:10.3233/NRE-141195 PMID:25547772

Swinnen, E., Baeyens, J. P., Knaepen, K., Michielsen, M., Clijsen, R., Beckwée, D., & Kerckhofs, E. (2015). Robot-assisted walking with the Lokomat: The influence of different levels of guidance force on thorax and pelvis kinematics. *Clinical Biomechanics (Bristol, Avon), 30*(3), 254–259. doi:10.1016/j.clinbiomech.2015.01.006 PMID:25662678

Swinnen, E., Baeyens, J.-P., Knaepen, K., Michielsen, M., Hens, G., Clijsen, R., Goossens, M., Buyl, R., Meeusen, R., & Kerckhofs, E. (2015). Walking with robot assistance: The influence of body weight support on the trunk and pelvis kinematics. *Disability and Rehabilitation. Assistive Technology, 10*(3), 252–257. doi:10.3109/17483107.2014.888487 PMID:24512196

Tang, L., & Shi, P. (2021). Design and analysis of a gait rehabilitation cable robot with pairwise cable arrangement. *Journal of Mechanical Science and Technology, 35*(7), 3161–3170. Advance online publication. doi:10.100712206-021-0637-6

TECNALIA. (2021). *Arm Assist*. http://armassist.eu/

Tokarieva, A. v., Volkova, N. P., Harkusha, I. v., & Soloviev, V. N. (2019). *Educational digital games: models and implementation*. Освітній Вимір. doi:10.31812/educdim.v53i1.3872

Veneman, J. F., Kruidhof, R., Hekman, E. E. G., Ekkelenkamp, R., Van Asseldonk, E. H. F., & Van Der Kooij, H. (2007). Design and evaluation of the LOPES exoskeleton robot for interactive gait rehabilitation. *IEEE Transactions on Neural Systems and Rehabilitation Engineering, 15*(1), 379–386. doi:10.1109/TNSRE.2007.903919 PMID:17894270

Chapter 11
Immersive Learning in Neonatal Resuscitation Education:
An Overview of the RETAIN Project

Maria Cutumisu
University of Alberta, Canada

Simran K. Ghoman
University of Alberta, Canada

Georg M. Schmölzer
University of Alberta, Canada

ABSTRACT

Resuscitation Training for healthcare professionals (RETAIN) is an immersive simulation-based platform that aims to improve access for neonatal resuscitation providers. This review of the research that measures the educational outcomes of training with RETAIN identified nine original research papers, two review papers, and one case study. Findings show that RETAIN is clinically relevant, engaging, improves short-and long-term knowledge and transfer of the key steps of neonatal resuscitation, and may be used as a formative or summative assessment. Further, performance on the RETAIN digital simulator was moderated by healthcare professional (HCP) attitudes, including growth mindset, and was compared across clusters obtained based on HCPs' attitudes towards technology. This simulator presents an attractive and accessible immersive learning approach towards training and assessing neonatal resuscitation competence. By improving the knowledge and skills of neonatal resuscitation providers, immersive media such as RETAIN may ultimately improve health outcomes for our smallest patients.

INTRODUCTION

You are working the night shift in the neonatal intensive care unit and have just been called to the labor and delivery ward, as a baby is about to be born. You enter the room right in time to see the mother

DOI: 10.4018/978-1-7998-9732-3.ch011

deliver her first child—a baby boy. Surrounding her at the bedside are the baby's father, grandparents, aunts, and uncles—who for the past nine months have expectantly waited for the day they would finally meet their newest family member. You look over to the obstetrician, who encourages the mom to give one final push. Everyone in the room anxiously holds their breath, anticipating the baby's first cry... But the room remains silent. All at once, the delivery room breaks out in a flood of sound and activity. The doctor clamps the umbilical cord, and a team of healthcare professionals (HCPs) quickly rush the baby away from his family and into the adjacent room. The family is left with nothing to do but wait, while the healthcare team tries to get their newborn baby to take his first breaths.

Each year, approximately 10% of newborn babies will need help to breathe at birth (Wyckoff et al., 2015). Sadly, one million of these babies will never make it back to their family's expectant arms (Lawn et al., 2007). Helping babies breathe is the cornerstone of neonatal resuscitation (American Heart Association, 2016). During neonatal resuscitation, HCPs must work together to provide complex and coordinated care under intense pressures of time and stress. HCPs must synthesize information simultaneously from the baby's case history, visual appearance, and cardiorespiratory status to appropriately provide care (e.g., ventilation, intubation, chest compressions, and intravenous medication; American Heart Association, 2016). Neonatal resuscitation is a cognitively and physically demanding medical emergency, and therefore errors by HCPs are common (Joint Commission, 2004; LeBlanc et al., 2005). The delivery room is one of the highest risk areas in a hospital where errors can have devastating consequences for infant morbidity and mortality (Joint Commission, 2004; Lipman et al., 2011).

To address this gap, the International Liaison Committee on Resuscitation has developed the Neonatal Resuscitation Program (NRP), a standardized training course and education program to teach neonatal resuscitation providers the guidelines of evidence-based care (American Heart Association, 2016). The NRP is rooted in simulation-based education, prioritizing immersive and interactive learning experiences over a pedagogical approach (American Heart Association, 2016; Lipman et al., 2011).

Neonatal Resuscitation Program (NRP)

The NRP consists of two parts. First, an at-home portion enables learners to read the neonatal resuscitation textbook and complete an online multiple-choice exam. Second, an in-class portion offers learners an opportunity to attend hands-on individual-skills stations and group simulation scenarios (American Heart Association, 2016). The NRP course has set a global standard for immersive learning through simulation in critical care medicine. However, neonatal resuscitation providers are only required to complete the course once every two years (American Heart Association, 2016), which may be insufficient to maintain long-term competence (Matterson et al., 2018). While more frequent simulation sessions are needed, traditional simulation can be resource-consuming, requiring a manikin, access to a simulation lab, and supervision by a trained instructor (Binotti et al., 2019; Mileder et al., 2014). Moreover, as neonatal resuscitation is a high-acuity, low-occurrence (HALO) event, HCPs have limited opportunities to learn by attending actual clinical cases (Cutumisu et al., 2019).

Barriers towards frequent immersive learning experiences prohibit neonatal resuscitation providers from adequately maintaining their knowledge and skills, leaving them dangerously underprepared to act quickly and correctly during a clinical emergency (Joint Commission, 2004). An alternative approach to simulation training is needed—one that is effective, engaging, and efficient (Ghoman et al., 2020). Immersive media like tabletop, digital, and virtual reality simulators offer promising solutions to augment traditional neonatal resuscitation education and teach relevant knowledge or skills within an engaging learning environment (Ghoman et al., 2020; Bellotti et al., 2010).

Resuscitation Training (RETAIN)

The RETAIN (REsuscitation TrAINing) platform for healthcare professionals represents one such solution. RETAIN is a tabletop simulator and a digital simulator, with previous iterations including a video game (Ghoman & Schmölzer, 2020; RETAIN Labs Medical Inc., 2018).

In RETAIN, learners select a simulation scenario from over 200 resuscitation cases of varying difficulty. Using the appropriate equipment pieces, monitors, and actions, learners practice safely stabilizing the simulated newborn baby in distress. Feedback (i.e., the baby's clinical status) guides decision-making, where correct adherence to NRP guidelines results in the baby's health eventually stabilizing and inappropriate or incorrectly-ordered tasks cause the baby's health to decline (RETAIN Labs Medical Inc., 2018).

Thus, the goal of this book chapter is to synthesize the results of the empirical studies conducted using the RETAIN training platform, discuss a framework for development, summarize the reported results, and detail the landscape of similar educational tools. By doing so, this review aims to deepen the investigation of immersive media for neonatal resuscitation education.

DEVELOPMENT AND THEORETICAL FRAMEWORK

The RETAIN platform was developed in collaboration with neonatologists, neonatal clinical researchers, computer scientists, educational psychologists, and graphic and industrial designers. Since its inception as a computer role-playing game (Figure 1C; Bulitko et al., 2015; Cutumisu et al., 2018; Cutumisu et al., 2020), RETAIN has been developed into a tabletop simulator (Figure 1A; Cutumisu et al., 2019; Ghoman, Cutumisu, & Schmölzer, 2020b), and then into a more streamlined digital simulator (Figure 1B; Lu et al., 2020). At each stage of development, RETAIN underwent hypothesis-driven research in a population of neonatal resuscitation providers from a tertiary level perinatal center. The process and outcomes were documented in open-access scientific literature, to provide useful information for other serious game developers in health (Bulitko et al., 2015; Cutumisu et al., 2019; Ghoman & Schmölzer, 2020; Cutumisu et al., 2018; Ghoman, Cutumisu, & Schmölzer, 2020a; Ghoman et al., 2020; Ghoman, Cutumisu, & Schmölzer, 2020b; Lu et al., 2020).

RETAIN adheres to a recent framework proposed to inform the development of evidence-based serious games for health. This framework guides developers, designers, researchers, and health care professionals in serious game development and it comprises five stages (Verschueren, Buffel, & Vander Stichele, 2019).

Stage 1 (scientific foundations) is designed to provide a theoretical evidence-based approach to serious games development in health (Verschueren et al., 2019). It includes considerations regarding the target audience, learning outcomes, theoretical foundations for the outcomes, and trial evaluation (Verschueren et al., 2019). RETAIN was designed to meet the re-training needs of HCPs who do not have many opportunities to refresh their neonatal resuscitation skills outside of infrequent NRP requirements. The learning outcomes include the steps in the NRP algorithm (e.g., ventilation corrective steps acronymized MR. SOPA). RETAIN draws on principles of game-based learning, such as incorporating challenging but precise goals, well-order tasks in increasing order of difficulty, immediate feedback following each action, and assuming different meaningful identities (Gee, 2005).

Stage 2 (design foundations) outlines the design elements informed by Stage 1. It includes the game mechanics mapped to the learning outcomes, the design requirements, and the trial design (Verschueren et al., 2019). RETAIN was designed as a simulation to mimic the conditions of a real delivery room. Players assume the identity of an HCP who is tasked with saving a newborn under time constraints that simulate the stress and urgency of an actual delivery room. To enhance verisimilitude of the scenarios, delivery room footage was reviewed to determine the average time taken to complete clinical tasks (e.g., attach pulse oximeter) during neonatal resuscitation. This information was used to help recreate realistic timing after players initiate a task in the game. Learning outcomes are mapped to the objectives of increasing-difficulty scenarios.

Stage 3 (development) includes the choice of genre, rules, content, and visuals (Verschueren et al., 2019). RETAIN has progressed from a video game (Figure 1C; Bulitko et al., 2015; Cutumisu et al., 2018) designed using a commercial computer role-playing game (BioWare Corp., 2021) to a tabletop simulator (Figure 1A; Cutumisu et al., 2019; Ghoman, Cutumisu, & Schmölzer, 2020b), followed by a digital simulator (Figure 1B; Lu et al., 2020). In each case, the rules and content were dictated by the game genre, but they were based on the NRP protocol. The visuals were inspired by the delivery room environment, but they were kept at an abstract level, as too much realism may detract from learning in some cases.

Stage 4 (validation) includes the clinical validation studies (Verschueren et al., 2019). All versions of RETAIN have undergone several testing cycles with HCPs (Bulitko et al., 2015; Cutumisu et al., 2018; Cutumisu et al., 2019; Cutumisu et al., 2020; Ghoman, Cutumisu, & Schmölzer, 2020a; Ghoman, Cutumisu, & Schmölzer, 2020b; Lu et al., 2020; Lu et al., 2021).

Finally, Stage 5 (implementation) includes the game dissemination, rollout, and follow up (Verschueren et al., 2019). The rollout of the first RETAIN version (i.e., the video game) led to the development of the tabletop simulator that, in turn, led to the development of the digital simulator (Ghoman & Schmölzer, 2020). Thus, the lessons learned from each version informed the subsequent version.

RELATED WORK: OTHER IMMERSIVE NEONATAL RESUSCITATION MEDIA

RETAIN belongs to a broader landscape of alternative approaches to neonatal resuscitation training and teaching neonatology (Ghoman et al., 2020). For instance, the NRP has developed a digital simulation, called the eSim, in partnership with Laerdal Medical (Stavanger, Norway). The eSim contains 4 neonatal resuscitation training scenarios. HCPs may complete these scenarios in preparation to attending the in-class portion of the NRP certification course (American Heart Association, 2016; Ghoman et al., 2020; Zaichkin, Mccarney, & Weiner, 2016). Neogames (Hu et al., 2021) is a computer game designed to improve the long-term retention of neonatal resuscitation knowledge of medical students. Similar to the results of the RETAIN studies, an experimental study using Neogames sampled 81 undergraduate medical students and found evidence of long-term improvement in neonatal resuscitation knowledge. However, another experiment sampling 162 HCPs found no digital game effects in neonatal resuscitation knowledge retention after six months (Yeo et al., 2020). In contrast, the RETAIN studies also examined long-term learning transfer from one environment (digital game) to another (analog tabletop game) using the games themselves as assessment instruments. The e-Baby (Fonseca et al., 2014) serious game is a digital game that evaluates the respiratory process in pre-term infants and also integrates a Moodle-based course, *Clinical Evaluation of the Preterm Baby*. An empirical study examined 14 Portuguese nursing students' perceptions on learning with e-Baby as part of an extracurricular course (Fonseca et al., 2015). The study found that students' self-reports were largely favorable (e.g., regarding ease of use, motivational aspects, perceptions of learning), but no actual performance measures were collected to corroborate with the students' perceptions. A randomized controlled trial found learning gains of 572 neonatal care clinicians as a result of adaptive and standard feedback provided by an Android game app, with a small effect of adaptive feedback, after controlling for learner differences (Tuti et al., 2020).

Moreover, there are tabletop games, which have been described in the literature, designed to train learners in neonatology and neonatal resuscitation. These include the Neonatology Game (University of Glasgow, Glasgow, UK), the Neonatal Emergency Trivia Game (Neonatal Education Specialties, Greensboro, North Carolina, USA), and the Neonopoly game (South Africa; Ghoman et al., 2020). However, these tabletop games use strategy-based gameplay to teach users information about neonatal resuscitation along with many other topics in neonatal medicine. Meanwhile, the RETAIN tabletop simulator uses simulation-based conventions to train neonatal resuscitation specifically.

Further, alternative digital and virtual reality media have been developed for neonatal resuscitation, including the Scottish Neonatal Resuscitation Game (National Health Service Education for Scotland, Edinburgh, UK), the Singaporean Neonatal Resuscitation Game (Singapore General Hospital, Bukit Merah, Singapore), eHelping Babies Breathe (eHBB, University of Washington, Seattle, Washington, USA, and Oxford University, Oxford, UK), Life-Saving Instructions for Emergencies (LIFE, Nuffield Department of Medicine, Oxford University, Oxford, UK), and the Compromised Neonate Program (University of Newcastle, Callaghan, Australia; Ghoman et al., 2020). These media are diverse in terms of the location, culture, and resource background of the intended user, however only some have been investigated for measurable educational improvement after training. Although RETAIN was developed primarily for HCPs in a tertiary perinatal center in North America, it is being developed for use across a wider range of locations, languages, cultures, and resource backgrounds (Ghoman & Schmölzer, 2020; RETAIN Labs Medical Inc., 2018).

METHODS

To identify studies examining the RETAIN simulation platform, the PubMed, EMBASE, Web of Science, CINAHL, Cochrane Central Register of Controlled Trials, and Google Scholar were searched from database inception to July 31, 2021. The RETAIN platform encompasses several immersive media including a tabletop simulator, digital simulator, and video game. Therefore, search terms included "RETAIN", "computer game", "board game", "video game", "digital simulat*" (to retrieve both digital simulators and digital simulations), "tabletop simulat*", "virtual reality", and "neonatal resuscitation". No language restrictions were applied and all publications describing RETAIN (e.g., regarding the video game, tabletop simulation, and digital simulation) were included. Additionally, the reference lists of retrieved articles were manually screened and publications were selected based on their title and abstract if they described RETAIN.

RESULTS

Learning Outcomes

Nine original research studies, two review papers, and one case study were identified describing the RETAIN simulator (Table 1).

Table 1. Summary of studies describing the RETAIN training simulator

Reference	Simulator	Objectives	Outcomes
Original Research			
Bulitko et al., 2015	Video Game	Development of the video game and pilot testing for usability and relevance	Users reported the game as stressful, engaging, clinically relevant, and useful for basic neonatal resuscitation training
Cutumisu et al., 2018	Video Game	Moderation effect of fixed vs. growth mindset on video game performance	Mindset moderated the relationship between 50 HCP performance and time since their NRP training
Cutumisu et al., 2019	Tabletop	Assessment of short-term knowledge retention after tabletop simulation training	30 HCPs significantly improved their performance after training, with most gains in temperature management
Cutumisu et al., 2020	Video Game	Use of the video game simulator to explore the relationship between perceptions of the simulator and their performance	Mindset moderated the relation between 50 HCP perceived terminology used in RETAIN and their video game performance; HCP reported enjoying the game
Ghoman, Cutumisu, & Schmölzer, 2020b	Tabletop	Use of the tabletop simulator as a summative assessment tool	20 HCP performed better on the tabletop summative assessment, if they had more years of board game experience
Ghoman, Cutumisu, & Schmölzer, 2020c	Digital, Tabletop	Use of the digital simulator as a learning and assessment tool; use of the tabletop simulator as an assessment of knowledge transfer	The digital simulator improved, maintained (after 2 months), and helped transfer (after 5 months) 50 HCP neonatal resuscitation knowledge
Ghoman, Cutumisu, & Schmölzer, 2020d	Tabletop	Use of the tabletop simulator as a summative assessment of neonatal resuscitation knowledge	Years of board game experience of 20 HCP moderated the relation between their written pre-test and tabletop game performance
Lu et al., 2020	Digital	Use of machine learning to examine attitudes and longitudinal digital simulation performance	Three attitudinal clusters were identified, each exhibiting a different learning path. All clusters showed knowledge improvement after training
Lu et al., 2021	Digital, Tabletop	Facilitation of neonatal resuscitation knowledge gain, retention, and transfer; moderation effect of growth mindset on longitudinal performance in neonatal resuscitation	50 HCP improved their neonatal resuscitation knowledge after the digital simulator training, retained their knowledge on the 2-month delayed posttest, and transferred their knowledge to the tabletop simulator after 5 months; growth mindset moderated the relationship between pretest and long-term knowledge retention

Continued on following page

Table 1. Continued

Reference	Simulator	Objectives	Outcomes
Original Research			
Review			
Ghoman et al., 2020	Video Game, Tabletop, Digital	Review of the landscape of technology-enhanced and game-based neonatal education	The RETAIN digital and tabletop simulators are two of the nine identified alternative tools for neonatal resuscitation/neonatology education
Ghoman & Schmölzer, 2020	Video Game, Tabletop, Digital	Review of the existing literature describing the educational outcomes of RETAIN simulators	Three original papers and one conference proceeding were identified and summarized
Case Study			
Ghoman, Cutumisu, & Schmölzer, 2020a	Tabletop	Description of the methodology and study design of the tabletop simulation clinical studies	Information summarized about how training and assessment studies were conducted, including decision-making and troubleshooting

Notes: HCP - Healthcare Professional; NRP - Neonatal Resuscitation Program

All studies were conducted with neonatal resuscitation providers from the Royal Alexandra Hospital (Edmonton, Canada) Neonatal Intensive Care Unit, which specializes in the care of very premature infants. This site has a total catchment area equivalent to one third of Canada's land mass, admitting more than 350 babies weighing less than 1,500 grams each year. In the RETAIN video game, learners take on the role of an HCP and must correctly navigate the neonatal resuscitation algorithm, while making no more than 4 mistakes throughout a scenario. In the RETAIN tabletop simulator, learners take turns, working through each step of neonatal resuscitation as a team, and debrief afterwards by answering questions about their performance (Figure 1A). In the RETAIN digital simulator, learners' time-stamped actions are used to provide individualized feedback to identify areas of proficiency and improvement (Figure 1B).

Figure 1. The RETAIN immersive media training platform including the a) tabletop simulator, b) digital simulator, and c) video game simulator. Permission for reprint obtained from RETAIN Labs Medical Inc

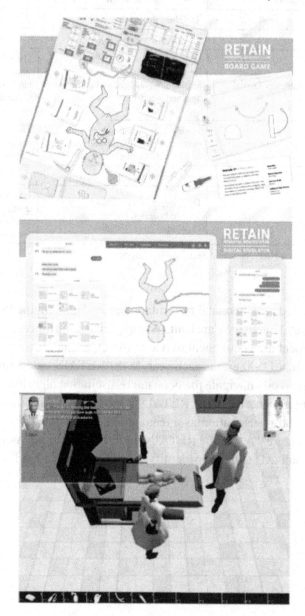

Video game simulator

Bulitko et al. (2015) described the development and preliminary evaluation of the RETAIN computer role-playing game (Figure 1C) by computer scientists and clinical neonatologists, respectively. Authors reported that participants perceived the video game as stressful, engaging, and useful for basic neonatal resuscitation training.

Next, Cutumisu et al. (2018) investigated the video game with 50 HCPs to understand if performance was moderated by participants' growth mindset. Individuals endorsing a growth mindset believe that effort and deliberate practice can improve one's abilities and performance, whereas individuals endorsing a fixed mindset believe that one's abilities cannot be changed (Mangels, Butterfield, Lamb, Good, & Dweck, 2006; Martin, 2015). Participants' growth mindset was assessed using a pre-survey and participants' performance was measured by the number of attempts required to successfully complete three resuscitation scenarios (Cutumisu et al., 2018). Findings showed that growth mindset moderated the relationship between time since participants' last NRP certification course and their performance in the video game (Cutumisu et al., 2018). Further, participants also made fewer mistakes if they endorsed a higher growth mindset (Cutumisu et al., 2018). A recent review of mindset theory in health professions education found mixed results for the association between mindset and other measures in the 27 studies examined (e.g., self-reported medical errors, stress, anxiety, well-being, and communication; Wolcott et al., 2021). Therefore, more studies that include mindset measures concomitantly with performance and affective measures are needed to explore their role in the uptake of serious games. The review also calls for mindset teaching and interventions to support learners in the medical domain.

More recently, Cutumisu et al. (2020) conducted a study to uncover the predictors of performance in computer-based simulation environments for neonatal resuscitation. They used the RETAIN video game simulator based on the Neverwinter Nights game and developed using its Aurora Toolset (BioWare Corp., 2021). The study explored the relationship between 50 HCPs' perceptions of the video game simulator via a post-game survey and their performance in the simulator. Specifically, they investigated the moderating role of mindset on the association between the perceived understanding of the terminology used in the video game and their game performance on three rounds of increasingly difficult tasks. Their results revealed that mindset moderated the relation between the HCPs' perceived terminology used in the RETAIN video game simulator and their performance on the video game. Additionally, HCP reported enjoying the game. Findings showed that participants who perceived the terminology as being useful also performed better on the game tasks but only when they adopted a growth mindset. Conversely, they also performed worse when they adopted a fixed mindset. Regarding the terminology used in the tutorial specifically, results showed that the more the HCPs reported that the tutorial terminology was accessible and in the game was accessible, the better they performed on the video game, but only when adopting a higher level of a growth mindset.

Tabletop simulator

Cutumisu et al. (2019) evaluated if training with the RETAIN tabletop simulator improved HCPs' knowledge of neonatal resuscitation guidelines (Cutumisu et al., 2019). Thirty experienced neonatal HCPs were recruited to complete a pre-test (open-answer neonatal resuscitation knowledge instrument), three scenarios using RETAIN, and a post-test (i.e., repeated pre-test). The pre-test and post-test were scored using the 7th edition NRP guidelines (American Heart Association, 2016) with a maximum score of 16 points and compared to measure short-term knowledge improvement after training with RETAIN (Ghoman, Cutumisu, & Schmölzer, 2020a). Participants improved their knowledge of the neonatal resuscitation guidelines by 12% (49-61% from pre- to post-test). Actions related to temperature management experienced the most improvement after training (Cutumisu et al., 2019), such as placement of a hat (10-43%), plastic wrap (27-67%), and temperature probe (7-30%).

Ghoman et al. (2020) investigated whether the tabletop simulator could also function as an assessment method (Ghoman, Cutumisu, & Schmölzer, 2020a; Ghoman, Cutumisu, & Schmölzer, 2020b). To investigate, 20 HCPs individually underwent both a traditional open-answer neonatal resuscitation assessment, as well as a RETAIN scenario (Ghoman, Cutumisu, & Schmölzer, 2020b). Participants' performance on both instruments were recorded, scored using 7th edition NRP guidelines (American Heart Association, 2016), and compared (Ghoman, Cutumisu, & Schmölzer, 2020b). Authors reported that HCP scores between the two assessment methods were moderately correlated and that participants with lower scores on the traditional assessment performed better on RETAIN if they reported more years of game board experience (Ghoman, Cutumisu, & Schmölzer, 2020b).

Importantly, the tabletop simulator was employed as an assessment of transfer of 50 HCPs' neonatal resuscitation knowledge that they had originally acquired via the digital simulator (Ghoman, Cutumisu, & Schmölzer, 2020c). Here, transfer denotes the process whereby knowledge that was mastered in one situation can be applied successfully to another context (e.g., a different learning simulation environment). Thus, they measured HCPs' neonatal resuscitation knowledge after 5 months using a different medium (i.e., the tabletop simulator, which is not a digital instrument) than that used in the learning stage (i.e., the digital simulator). They found that the tabletop simulator was able to elicit HCPs' neonatal resuscitation knowledge that may have been missed by more traditional ways of assessment. This shows the importance of a versatile set of assessments that may uncover different areas of knowledge that may be neglected by others.

Ghoman, Cutumisu, and Schmölzer (2020d) conducted a study in which the tabletop simulator was used as a summative assessment of neonatal resuscitation knowledge. They found that the years of board game experience of 20 HCP moderated the relation between their written pre-test and tabletop game performance.

Lu, Ghoman, Cutumisu, and Schmölzer (2021) sampled 50 HCP to explore the facilitation of neonatal resuscitation knowledge gain, retention, and transfer using a combination of tabletop and digital simulators, as well as a possible moderation effect of growth mindset on longitudinal performance in neonatal resuscitation. Results show that the HCP improved their neonatal resuscitation knowledge after the digital simulator training, retained their knowledge on the 2-month delayed posttest, and transferred their knowledge to the tabletop simulator after 5 months. Concomitantly, growth mindset moderated the relationship between pretest and long-term knowledge retention.

Digital simulator

Lu et al. (2020) explored whether HCP attitudes towards technology and their self-endorsed mindset affected their performance on the RETAIN digital simulator (Lu et al., 2020). Fifty participants completed a pre-test, two training scenarios with the RETAIN digital simulator, and a post-test. Information about participants' clinical position, attitudes towards technology, and self-endorsed mindset was collected using a post-session questionnaire. A hierarchical clustering algorithm was used to identify three attitudinal clusters based on participants' survey answers. While all clusters demonstrated improved neonatal resuscitation knowledge overall after training with RETAIN, each cluster exhibited a different learning path leading to the learning outcomes (Lu et al., 2020).

Ghoman, Cutumisu, and Schmölzer (2020c) employed the RETAIN digital simulator as a learning and assessment tool for 50 HCPs, as well as in combination with the RETAIN tabletop simulator employed to assess participants' knowledge transfer. They found that the digital simulator improved and maintained (after 2 months) HCPs' neonatal resuscitation knowledge.

Motivation and Engagement

Data from 150 HCPs were collected to understand motivational processes while playing RETAIN (Ghoman & Schmölzer, 2020; Ghoman, Cutumisu, & Schmölzer, 2020a; Ghoman, Cutumisu, & Schmölzer, 2020c). Overall, HCPs received RETAIN well and reported the length of time and pacing during the game was appropriate to retain information of the basic resuscitation steps, the terminology used in the game was appropriate, and the game facilitated quick decision making. On a five-point Likert scale, HCPs evaluated RETAIN as realistic (mean = 3.88, SD = 0.8), simulated the stressful nature of neonatal resuscitation (mean = 3.63, SD = 0.75), and enjoyable to play (mean = 3.8, SD = 0.8). HCPs evaluated the RETAIN video game and digital simulation as more stressful and less enjoyable to play, compared to the tabletop simulator. HCPs also reported that RETAIN could be beneficial for NRP training (mean = 4.14, SD = 0.64), and that they liked this way of learning (mean = 3.7, SD = 0.8; Ghoman & Schmölzer, 2020; Ghoman, Cutumisu, & Schmölzer, 2020a). Caserman et al. (2020) proposed several criteria for high-quality serious games, including keeping players in a state of flow (Czikszentmihalyi, 1990). The motivational and engaging aspects of the RETAIN games are important ingredients in the design of serious games to ensure that players keep on practicing their knowledge or skills. They are also necessary criteria for achieving a state of flow. Another important criterion of high-quality serious games is fidelity or realism of the simulation (Caserman et al., 2020). This is an important aspect in creating immersive games and in supporting learning transfer, for instance, from the simulation to the real-world delivery room (Kuipers et al., 2017). Therefore, these aspects will be further probed in future research studies based on the RETAIN games, with a focus on their relationship with performance.

DISCUSSION

The literature search presented a robust body of research describing the various RETAIN simulators and examining their related outcomes. In regards to educational outcomes as a result of training, the reviewed studies showed that the digital and tabletop simulators improved HCP short-term (Cutumisu et al., 2019) and longer-term (Lu et al., 2020) knowledge retention of neonatal resuscitation guidelines. These results indicate that training with RETAIN may improve neonatal HCPs awareness to prevent negative outcomes like hypothermia, late-onset sepsis, and mortality (Laptook & Watkinson, 2008; Lunze, Bloom, Jamison, & Hamer, 2013). While training can have important consequences to improve patient outcomes, no studies identified in this review measured changes in actual clinical care after training. Further, the different media (i.e., tabletop vs. digital) appeared to elicit different outcomes based on learners' experience with and attitudes towards either technology, board games, and other variables (Ghoman, Cutumisu, & Schmölzer, 2020b; Lu et al., 2020). Future studies focusing on RETAIN will expand both the repetition of the games and the length of the follow-up assessments to 1 year and 2 years, respectively, to improve the long-term effectiveness of the simulation and to align with the recommendations of a recent scoping review (Sharifzadeh et al., 2020).

Several studies investigated the interaction between learners' mindset and their performance on the RETAIN simulator. Across the studies reviewed, mindset was found to moderate the relationships between HCP perceptions of the different simulators and their performance on the simulators used. Within the video game, there was a significant interaction between time since participants' last NRP course and growth mindset in predicting the number of attempts taken to complete the scenario, suggesting that practical training opportunities such as RETAIN may be most effective for HCPs who would be most likely to seek out and find training to be most valuable (Cutumisu et al., 2018). Moreover, when learners' mindset was considered using a machine learning algorithm, different training pathways were uncovered based on their performance outcomes in the digital and tabletop simulators (Lu et al., 2020). The RETAIN project is the first to study growth mindset together with neonatal resuscitation training (Cutumisu et al., 2018) and, therefore, it warrants continued investigation to further understand the relationship. One implication of this work is allotting more attention to meta-cognitive aspects of learning (e.g., mindsets) in supporting HCPs learning and transfer of complex neonatal resuscitation knowledge in game-based learning environments. These results may also help guide effective implementation of RETAIN as an educational intervention. A systematic review on the role of transfer in designing games and simulations for health examined 15 studies of game-like interventions aimed at transfer (Kuipers at al., 2017). The review found a paucity of game-like interventions for health that focus on transfer. Thus, one of the contributions of the RETAIN studies is the provision of design choices in each of the game media as well as design principles that researchers and practitioners could employ in future work (e.g., how transfer is embedded in the design of learning interventions across the game media).

In contrast to implementing RETAIN for training, some of the reviewed studies identified in this review examined the tabletop simulator for the purpose of assessment. RETAIN was demonstrated to successfully assess participant neonatal resuscitation knowledge when compared to more traditional assessment instruments (Ghoman, Cutumisu, & Schmölzer, 2020b). These results suggest that RETAIN may be used as an attractive, enjoyable, and resource-conservative method for simulation-based assessment of HCPs' neonatal resuscitation competence (Ghoman, Cutumisu, & Schmölzer, 2020b). More likely, RETAIN offers an intermediate solution between low-resource/low-immersive written paper tests and high-resource/high-immersive in-person simulation. Additional investigation is needed to compare assessment outcomes using the tabletop simulator to traditional simulation.

Importantly, HCPs received the various simulators well, and reported enjoyment and motivation (Ryan & Deci, 2000) when using these immersive media (Bulitko et al., 2015; Cutumisu et al., 2019; Cutumisu et al., 2018; Ghoman, Cutumisu, & Schmölzer, 2020b; Lu et al., 2020). However, all of the observational studies were conducted in a relatively homogenous population of experienced neonatal resuscitation providers from a tertiary perinatal center. Therefore, outcomes reported from this research have potentially limited application across geographical locations, resource backgrounds, and educational/clinical experience levels. Furthermore, randomized controlled studies comparing RETAIN to traditional and alternative educational media would also benefit the project.

Finally, RETAIN is a low-cost alternative to traditional simulation, it is easy to use anytime and for sessions of varying durations, which fits the time frame of HCPs, and it can be played individually as well as collaboratively. Future plans include the development of a virtual reality version of RETAIN. The present review highlights the data-driven contributions of RETAIN to acquisition of knowledge across short, medium, and long term as well as multiple types of assessment and media, concomitantly offering a way to measure players' mindset and perceptions of technology, the game, and their own learning. This enables the examination of cognitive and meta-cognitive skills within the same environment and of learning transfer across game media (from digital to analog and vice versa). The games were designed as dynamic assessments (Vygotsky, 1997), as the feedback and the game mechanics provides multiple opportunities to learn during the assessment. As such, it is possible that the core mechanics for learning in RETAIN might be employed beyond the particular context of neonatal resuscitation. Researchers, clinicians, and instructors may select a suitable combination of the RETAIN games for research, training, and teaching purposes that could further inform teaching and learning.

CONCLUSION

The RETAIN training platform leverages immersive simulation-based learning to train neonatal resuscitation providers. RETAIN may provide an accessible solution for HCPs looking for additional training to their NRP certification. Future steps include extending RETAIN into virtual reality and augmented reality to enhance the immersive nature of the neonatal resuscitation simulation. More research is also needed to elucidate whether training with RETAIN improves HCPs' adherence to neonatal resuscitation guidelines in the delivery room and, consequently, improves health outcomes for newborn babies under their care.

ACKNOWLEDGMENT

We would like to thank the public for donating money to our funding agencies: SKG is a recipient of the CIHR Frederick Banting and Charles Best Canada Graduate Scholarship, Maternal and Child Health (MatCH) Scholarship (supported by the University of Alberta, Stollery Children's Hospital Foundation, Women and Children's Health Research Institute, and the Lois Hole Hospital for Women), Canadian Federation of University Women Edmonton (CFUW), University of Alberta Department of Pediatrics Graduate Recruitment Scholarship, and the Faculty of Medicine & Dentistry/Alberta Health Services Graduate Student Recruitment Studentship. MC is a recipient of the SSHRC, NSERC DG, and Killam Trust Grants. GMS is a recipient of the Heart and Stroke Foundation/University of Alberta Professorship of Neonatal Resuscitation, a National New Investigator of the Heart and Stroke Foundation Canada and an Alberta New Investigator of the Heart and Stroke Foundation Alberta.

REFERENCES

American Heart Association. (2016). Textbook of neonatal resuscitation (NRP) (7th ed.). American Academy of Pediatrics.

Bellotti, F., Berta, R., & De Gloria, A. (2010). Designing effective serious games: Opportunities and challenges for research. *International Journal of Emerging Technologies in Learning*, 5(3), 22–35. doi:10.3991/ijet.v5s3.1500

Binotti, M., Genoni, G., Rizzollo, S., De Luca, M., Carenzo, L., Monzani, A., & Ingrassia, P. L. (2019). Simulation-based medical training for paediatric residents in Italy: A nationwide survey. *BMC Medical Education*, 19(161), 1–7. doi:10.118612909-019-1581-3 PMID:31113417

BioWare Corp. (2021). *BioWare*™. Retrieved from https://www.bioware.com

Bulitko, V., Hong, J., Kumaran, K., Swedberg, I., Thoang, W., Von Hauff, P., & Schmölzer, G. M. (2015). *RETAIN: A neonatal resuscitation trainer built in an undergraduate video-game class.* https://www. researchgate.net/publication/279808492_RETAIN_a_Neonatal_Resuscitation_Trainer_Built_in_an_Undergraduate_Video-Game_Class

Caserman, P., Hoffmann, K., Müller, P., Schaub, M., Straßburg, K., Wiemeyer, J., Bruder, R., & Göbel, S. (2020). Quality criteria for serious games: Serious part, game part, and balance. *JMIR Serious Games, 8*(3), e19037. doi:10.2196/19037 PMID:32706669

Cutumisu, M., Brown, M. R. G., Fray, C., & Schmölzer, G. M. (2018). Growth mindset moderates the effect of the neonatal resuscitation program on performance in a computer-based game training simulation. *Frontiers in Pediatrics, 6. Article, 195*, 1–10. doi:10.3389/fped.2018.00195 PMID:30023355

Cutumisu, M., Ghoman, S. K., Lu, C., Patel, S. D., Garcia-Hidalgo, C., Fray, C., Brown, M. R. G., Greiner, R., & Schmölzer, G. M. (2020). Health care providers' performance, mindset, and attitudes toward a neonatal resuscitation computer-based simulator: Empirical study. *Journal of Medical Internet Research (JMIR) Serious Games, 8*(4), e21855. doi:10.2196/21855 PMID:33346741

Cutumisu, M., Patel, S. D., Brown, M. R. G., Fray, C., von Hauff, P., Jeffery, T., & Schmölzer, G. M. (2019). RETAIN: A board game that improves neonatal resuscitation knowledge retention. *Frontiers in Pediatrics, 7*(13), 13. Advance online publication. doi:10.3389/fped.2019.00013 PMID:30766862

Czikszentmihalyi, M. (1990). *Flow: The psychology of Optimal Experience.* Harper & Row.

Fonseca, L. M. M., Dias, D. M. V., Góes, F. D. S. N., Seixas, C. A., Scochi, C. G. S., Martins, J. C. A., & Rodrigues, M. A. (2014). Development of the e-Baby serious game with regard to the evaluation of oxygenation in preterm babies: Contributions of the emotional design. *CIN: Computers, Informatics. Nursing, 32*(9), 428–436. PMID:25010051

Fonseca, L. M. M., Aredes, N. D. A., Dias, D. M. V., Scochi, C. G. S., Martins, J. C. A., & Rodrigues, M. A. (2015). Serious game e-Baby: Nursing students' perception on learning about preterm newborn clinical assessment. *Revista Brasileira de Enfermagem, 68*, 13–19. doi:10.1590/0034-7167.2015680102p PMID:25946489

Gee, J. P. (2005). Learning by design: Good video games as learning machines. *E-Learning and Digital Media, 2*(1), 5–16. doi:10.2304/elea.2005.2.1.5

Ghoman, S. K., Cutumisu, M., Schmölzer, G. M. (2020a). Using the RETAIN neonatal resuscitation game to train and assess health care professionals' competence in an observational study design. *SAGE Research Methods Cases: Medicine and Health.* doi:10.4135/9781529734461

Ghoman, S. K., Cutumisu, M., & Schmölzer, G. M. (2020b). Simulation-based summative assessment of neonatal resuscitation providers using the RETAIN serious board game - A pilot study. *Frontiers in Pediatrics, 8*, 1–14. doi:10.3389/fped.2020.00014 PMID:32083041

Ghoman, S. K., Cutumisu, M., & Schmölzer, G. M. (2020c). Digital simulation improves, maintains, and helps transfer healthcare providers' neonatal resuscitation knowledge. *Frontiers in Pediatrics: Neonatology, 8*, 599638. Advance online publication. doi:10.3389/fped.2020.599638 PMID:33537263

Ghoman, S. K., Cutumisu, M., & Schmölzer, G. M. (2020d). Using the RETAIN tabletop simulator as a summative assessment tool for neonatal resuscitation healthcare professionals: A pilot study. *Frontiers in Pediatrics: Neonatology, 8,* 569776. doi:10.3389/fped.2020.569776 PMID:33224907

Ghoman, S. K., Patel, S. D., Cutumisu, M., von Hauff, P., Jeffery, T., Brown, M. R. G., & Schmölzer, G. M. (2020). Serious games, a game changer in teaching neonatal resuscitation? A review. *Archives of Disease in Childhood. Fetal and Neonatal Edition, 105*(1), 98–107. doi:10.1136/archdischild-2019-317011 PMID:31256010

Ghoman, S. K., & Schmölzer, G. M. (2020). The RETAIN simulation-based serious game— A review of the literature. *Healthcare (Basel), 8*(1), 3–3. doi:10.3390/healthcare8010003 PMID:31877882

Hu, L., Zhang, L., Yin, R., Li, Z., Shen, J., Tan, H., Wu, J., & Zhou, W. (2021). NEOGAMES: A serious computer game that improves long-term knowledge retention of neonatal resuscitation in undergraduate medical students. *Frontiers in Pediatrics, 9,* 645776. doi:10.3389/fped.2021.645776 PMID:33968850

Joint Commission. (2004). Sentinel event alert: Preventing infant death and injury during delivery. The Joint Commission, 4(4), 180-181. doi:10.1016/j.adnc.2004.08.005

Kuipers, D. A., Terlouw, G., Wartena, B. O., van't Veer, J. T., Prins, J. T., & Pierie, J. P. E. (2017). The role of transfer in designing games and simulations for health: Systematic review. *JMIR Serious Games, 5*(4), e7880. doi:10.2196/games.7880 PMID:29175812

Laptook, A. R., & Watkinson, M. (2008). Temperature management in the delivery room. *Seminars in Fetal & Neonatal Medicine, 13*(6), 383–391. doi:10.1016/j.siny.2008.04.003 PMID:18501693

Lawn, J. E., Manandhar, A., Haws, R. A., & Darmstadt, G. L. (2007). Reducing one million child deaths from birth asphyxia - A survey of health systems gaps and priorities. *Health Research Policy and Systems, 5*(4), 1–10. doi:10.1186/1478-4505-5-4 PMID:17506872

LeBlanc, V. R., MacDonald, R. D., McArthur, B., King, K., & Lepine, T. (2005). Paramedic performance in calculating drug dosages following stressful scenarios in a human patient simulator. *Prehospital Emergency Care, 9*(4), 439–444. doi:10.1080/10903120500255255 PMID:16263679

Lipman, S. S., Daniels, K. I., Arafeh, J., & Halamek, L. P. (2011, April). The case for OBLS: A simulation-based obstetric life support program. *Seminars in Perinatology, 35*(2), 74–79. doi:10.1053/j.semperi.2011.01.006 PMID:21440814

Lu, C., Ghoman, S. K., Cutumisu, M., & Schmölzer, G. M. (2020). Unsupervised machine learning algorithms examine healthcare providers' perceptions and longitudinal performance in a digital neonatal resuscitation simulator. *Frontiers in Pediatrics, 8. Article, 544,* 1–11. doi:10.3389/fped.2020.00544s

Lu, C., Ghoman, S. K., Cutumisu, M., & Schmölzer, G. M. (2021). Mindset moderates healthcare providers' longitudinal performance in a digital neonatal resuscitation simulator. *Frontiers in Pediatrics: Neonatology, 8,* 594690. Advance online publication. doi:10.3389/fped.2020.594690 PMID:33665174

Lunze, K., Bloom, D., Jamison, D., & Hamer, D. (2013). The global burden of neonatal hypothermia: Systematic review of a major challenge for newborn survival. *BMC Medicine, 11*(24), 24. Advance online publication. doi:10.1186/1741-7015-11-24 PMID:23369256

Matterson, H. H., Szyld, D., Green, B. R., Howell, H. B., Pusic, M. V., Mally, P. V., & Bailey, S. M. (2018). Neonatal resuscitation experience curves: Simulation based mastery learning booster sessions and skill decay patterns among pediatric residents. *Journal of Perinatal Medicine*, *46*(8), 934–941. doi:10.1515/jpm-2017-0330 PMID:29451862

Mangels, J., Butterfield, B., Lamb, J., Good, C., & Dweck, C. (2006). Why do beliefs about intelligence influence learning success? A social cognitive neuroscience model. *Social Cognitive and Affective Neuroscience*, *1*(2), 75–86. doi:10.1093can/nsl013 PMID:17392928

Martin, A. (2015). Implicit theories about intelligence and growth (personal best) goals: Exploring reciprocal relationships. *The British Journal of Educational Psychology*, *85*(2), 207–223. doi:10.1111/bjep.12038 PMID:24904989

Mileder, L. P., Urlesberger, B., Schwindt, J., Simma, B., & Schmölzer, G. M. (2014). Compliance with guidelines recommending the use of simulation for neonatal and infant resuscitation training in Austria. *Klinische Padiatrie*, *226*(1), 24–28. doi:10.1055-0033-1361106 PMID:24435789

RETAIN Labs Medical Inc. (2018). *RETAIN Neonatal Resuscitation.* Retrieved from: https://www.playretain.com

Ryan, R. M., & Deci, E. L. (2000). Self-determination theory and the facilitation of intrinsic motivation, social development, and well-being. *The American Psychologist*, *55*(1), 68–78. doi:10.1037/0003-066X.55.1.68 PMID:11392867

Sharifzadeh, N., Kharrazi, H., Nazari, E., Tabesh, H., Khodabandeh, M. E., Heidari, S., & Tara, M. (2020). Health education serious games targeting health care providers, patients, and public health users: Scoping review. *JMIR Serious Games*, *8*(1), e13459. doi:10.2196/13459 PMID:32134391

Tuti, T., Winters, N., Edgcombe, H., Muinga, N., Wanyama, C., English, M., & Paton, C. (2020). Evaluation of adaptive feedback in a smartphone-based game on health care providers' learning gain: Randomized controlled trial. *Journal of Medical Internet Research*, *22*(7), e17100. doi:10.2196/17100 PMID:32628115

Verschueren, S., Buffel, C., & Vander Stichele, G. (2019). Developing theory-driven, evidence-based serious games for health: Framework based on research community insights. *JMIR Serious Games*, *7*(2), e11565. doi:10.2196/11565 PMID:31045496

Vygotsky, L. S. (1997). *The collected works of L.S. Vygotsky: Problems of the theory and history of psychology.* Springer US, Science & Business Media. doi:10.1007/978-1-4615-5893-4

Wolcott, M. D., McLaughlin, J. E., Hann, A., Miklavec, A., Beck Dallaghan, G. L., Rhoney, D. H., & Zomorodi, M. (2021). A review to characterise and map the growth mindset theory in health professions education. *Medical Education*, *55*(4), 430–440. doi:10.1111/medu.14381 PMID:32955728

Wyckoff, M. H., Aziz, K., Escobedo, M. B., Kapadia, V. S., Kattwinkel, J., Perlman, J. M., Simon, W. M., Weiner, G. M., & Zaichkin, J. G. (2015). Part 13: Neonatal resuscitation. 2015 American Heart Association guidelines update for cardiopulmonary resuscitation and emergency cardiovascular care. *Circulation*, *132*(18, suppl 2), S543–S560. doi:10.1161/CIR.0000000000000267 PMID:26473001

Yeo, C. L., Ho, S. K. Y., Tagamolila, V. C., Arunachalam, S., Bharadwaj, S. S., Poon, W. B., Tan, M. G., Edison, P. E., Yip, W. Y., Haium, A. A. A., Jayagobi, P. A., Vora, S. J., Khurana, S. K., Allen, J. C., & Lustestica, E. I. (2020). Use of web-based game in neonatal resuscitation-is it effective? *BMC Medical Education, 20*(1), 1–11. doi:10.118612909-020-02078-5 PMID:32456704

Zaichkin, J., Mccarney, L., & Weiner, G. (2016). NRP 7th Edition: Are You Prepared? Neonatal Network, 35(4), 184-191. doi:10.1891/0730-0832.35.4.184

KEY TERMS AND DEFINITIONS

Game-Based Learning: Subcategory of serious games with the main purpose of learning and education, rather than just of entertainment.

Healthcare Professional (HCP): An individual who may provide health care treatment and advice based on formal training and experience.

Infant: A human being within the first year after birth.

Neonatal Resuscitation: The set of interventions at the time of birth to re-establish and support infants' breathing and circulation.

Neonatal Resuscitation Program (NRP): A program designed to help build neonatal resuscitation knowledge, skills, and confidence to prepare trainees to resuscitate a newborn infant (neonate).

Newborn: A human being within the first 28 days after birth.

Retain: Resuscitation Training for healthcare professionals constitutes a collection of computer games, video games, and tabletop games for neonatal resuscitation.

Simulation: Training, practice, and learning technique that aims to replicate essential aspects of real experiences or situations.

Chapter 12
Immersive Games for Neurodiversity and Mental Health in Children and Young Adults

Richard Chen Li

The Hong Kong Polytechnic University, Hong Kong

Meike Belter

HIT Lab NZ, University of Canterbury, New Zealand

Zoë Platt-Young

🆔 https://orcid.org/0000-0001-7966-6291

HIT Lab NZ, University of Canterbury, New Zealand

Heide Karen Lukosch

🆔 https://orcid.org/0000-0002-9585-0723

HIT Lab NZ, University of Canterbury, New Zealand

ABSTRACT

Mental health and neurodevelopmental disorders are common among children and young adults. They can negatively affect children's social behaviour, development, and performance in school. This chapter discusses three common mental health and neurodevelopmental disorders and how serious immersive games could support this group. Serious immersive games are games that are designed with a certain purpose in mind and make use of immersive technologies like virtual or augmented reality. As games are a vital element of youth culture, the authors claim that immersive game elements could be utilized to engage a larger group with the health system and offer safe and motivating environments. This chapter shows that work exists to explore the use of games or immersive technologies in mental health support. However, the authors also show that there are shortcomings in the current research and propose research directions to address those.

DOI: 10.4018/978-1-7998-9732-3.ch012

INTRODUCTION

In this chapter, we discuss the state of the art of immersive games for children and young adults with mental health disorders and neurodevelopmental diversities. The World Health Organisation states that mental health problems are a challenging public health issue worldwide, with approximately one in five children and young adults suffering from psychiatric disorders (World Health Organization, 2001). Social anxiety disorder (SAD) is one of the mental health disorders that has an early age of onset, and can be triggered by situations where public performance or social interactions, such as public speaking, are required (Elizabeth et al., 2006). Autism Spectrum Disorder (ASD) and Attention-Deficit Hyperactivity Disorder (known as ADHD) are the most common neurodevelopmental diversities in children. They can have a huge impact on the lives of the children affected, and their families. Children with these disorders may find it more difficult to engage with others, to follow formal education, and to manage daily life (Elizabeth et al., 2006). ASD and ADHD share a number of underlying conditions, symptoms, and co-morbidities, or symptoms that often occur together (Hansen et al., 2018).

For many children and young adults, games are a ubiquitous element of culture. Children and young adults are familiar with games, they use them for distraction, socialising, and having fun. Immersive games are a promising approach to help children and young adults to overcome challenges related to mental health disorders, but they are still an underexplored field. In our work, we approach immersive games as a sub-group of serious games that make use of immersive technologies such as virtual or augmented reality. We discuss immersive games as a support tool for the group of children and young adults who are affected by anxiety disorders and neurodevelopmental diversities, such as ASD, ADHD and SAD.

Our chapter discusses typical challenges children and young adults with SAD, ADHD, and ASD face. We discuss what kind of common measures are taken for the distinct conditions, and the role of serious and immersive games amongst these. We then summarize the findings, highlighting the contribution of immersive games and promising game elements for mental health. We conclude with opportunities and limitations of immersive games for mental health, and how future work could be progressed.

SERIOUS AND IMMERSIVE GAMES FOR MENTAL HEALTH AND NEURODIVERSITY

Games, especially video games or digital games, are ubiquitous in the life of children and young adults. They can also be used for 'serious' purposes such as learning or support of mental health. Called serious games, these games are defined as games that do not have entertainment, enjoyment or fun as their primary purpose (Michael & Chen, 2005). A central goal of serious games is that the learning in the game generalizes to improve real life outcomes (Whyte, Smyth, & Scherf, 2015).

Serious games in the health sector include games to actively involve young people in the treatment of cancer, in the field of psychotherapy, or to treat conditions such as eating disorders (Lau et al., 2017). Serious games which address mental health may make use of evidence-based mental health therapy, such as CBT or exposure therapy (Fleming et al., 2017). Fleming et al. (2017) define three processes linked to serious games and their impact on mental health. First, serious games can represent an addition to online health programs, and reach those who otherwise might not engage with these programs. Secondly, the motivational factor of games can be used to keep users engaged. And thirdly, combined with therapeutic processes, game elements can lead to change. When well designed, games can enhance concentration, improve retention of learning content, facilitate deep learning, and lead to behavioural change. While serious games promise to show positive effects on psychological and behavioural change or symptom relief, as initial studies show the field of serious games for mental health is still in its infancy – with sometimes poorly described interventions. For example, the studies examined by Fleming et al. (2017) treat diverse approaches as homogenous.

Serious immersive games are games that have a purpose such as learning, training, or mental health support, and make use of immersive technologies such as virtual reality (VR) or augmented reality (AR). Serious immersive games offer a promising approach to overcome the weaknesses of traditional learning media, that are often not intrinsically motivating or able to retain attention, and to make learning more engaging, satisfying, and probably more effective (Kickmeyer-Rust et al., 2007). The term serious immersive game includes more than the technology-use alone. Immersive games, especially when Head Mounted Displays (HMDs) are used, enable users to engage in stimulating interactive experiences, feeling a sense of presence, or 'as if being there', in a virtual world (Biocca, 1997; Sanchez-Vives & Slater, 2005; Garrett et al., 2018; Tao et al., 2021). Serious or applied games adopt immersive technologies to create realistic and engaging environments for learning and support. Recent technological advancements have made Virtual Reality (VR) games accessible to the broad consumer market and therefore, also feasible for implementation in formal education (Virvou & Katsionis, 2008). They offer a safe and realistic environment to try out actions and decisions, and provide immediate feedback to a player which often includes audio-visual and other sensory stimuli. In a literature review by Freina and Ott (2015), it was concluded that VR is often used for scenarios or environments which cannot be experienced in reality or for experiencing physically inaccessible objects such as the solar system. In addition, game characteristics such as challenge, fantasy, and curiosity make games appealing and strong tools for learning (Malone, 1981). In general, studies have shown that games can have a positive effect on cognitive skills, and that they can lead to persistent motivation (Granic et al., 2014). The same study discussed the effects of games on emotional states of players, but also reports that more research is needed here.

Immersive games show potential to address challenges children and young adults may experience in relation to mental health and neurodevelopmental disorders because of their appealing power, evidenced by the huge popularity of games played by children and young adults. These characteristics may help to reach a group that do not (yet) receive treatment (Fleming et al., 2017). Dynamics of games that make them enjoyable and offer a challenge would likely increase the engagement of users, and support the learning process by offering a safe space in which a state of 'flow' can be achieved (Nakamura & Csikszentmihalyi, 2009; Fleming et al., 2017). Flow describes the experience of complete absorption in the present moment, or 'optimal experience', when people enjoy what they are doing. It is also described as intense and focused concentration, a sense that one can control one's actions, and the experience of the activity as intrinsically rewarding (Csikszentmihalyi 1997; Nakamura & Csikszentmihalyi, 2009). Flow is experienced as a product of one's own actions, whereas feelings of presence within a virtual environment result from experiences that are influenced by the objects of the external environment (Scoresby & Shelton, 2011). A state of flow can have a positive effect on someone's experience, and can be more easily reached when someone can engage with a task without disruptions. Engaging in this way is an advantage of immersive games that exclude the 'real' world and allow a player to be fully immersed in the virtual environment. While on paper these aspects seem to be very promising, there have been few studies that have looked into the use of immersive games in the fields that we focus on. As Fleming et al. (2017) show, there are less than 10 studies which report on the results of such games, with the majority only including a small number of participants.

In comparison to serious games in the sense of 2D or 3D digital games, displayed on a computer or mobile device screen, immersive games represent interactive spaces in which the participant becomes a co-creator of the experience (Garrett et al., 2018). First-person immersive environments may be used in therapy, e. g. in the treatment of phobia, or as stress relief applications that offer a calming, meditative environment (Tao et al., 2021). However, these environments do not necessarily make use of game elements. Game elements are already used in immersive environments for rehabilitation or pain management (Regenbrecht et al., 2012). For example, the game elements of incremental difficulty and visual feedback may help a patient to feel motivated to 'level up' their physical skills during their path to recovery from injury.

This brief overview of the use of serious and immersive serious games in the health sector shows that games are already in use to help individuals with mental health disorders. However, it also shows that more research on distinct game elements and their effects in relation to specific mental health issues is needed, especially in relation to immersive technologies and games. In our chapter, we differentiate between three disorders, and show how serious immersive games could be used to support children and young adults diagnosed with ASD, ADHD, and SAD.

MENTAL HEALTH DISORDERS AND NEURODIVERSITY IN CHILDREN AND YOUNG ADULTS

A large number of children and young adults face challenges relating to mental health disorders or neurodevelopmental diversities. Amongst these are depression, anxiety, autism, and ADHD. Neurodiversity refers to the variability of neurological impairment and neurological diversity (Krcek, 2013). It is obvious that these disorders and diversities put a lot of pressure on the young individuals, their families, and the educational and health system. These conditions can lead to situations where children behave differently than others, leading to stigma and exclusion from activities and groups. Mental health discussions occur more openly now than in the past, but impairments such as SAD, ASD and ADHD still present a silent epidemic in our society. Neurodiverse individuals are at greater risk for suicidal ideation and behaviour (Horowitz et al., 2018). Children with ADHD, for example, may struggle with remembering instructions from a teacher, and young adults with ASD or SAD may miss out on a lot of experiences that are common activities for their peers, such as sport activities, after-school-clubs, or parties. Moreover, some disorders and their symptoms are present together – called comorbidity. For example, comorbidity with ADHD in youth includes oppositional, conduct, mood, and anxiety disorders, with a co-occurrence of ADHD and mood disorders found in 15% to 75% of children and young adults (Spencer, 2006). When looking at the National Comorbidity Survey of the US, it shows that half of all serious adult psychiatric illnesses — including major depression, anxiety disorders, and substance abuse — start around 14 years of age, and three fourths of them are present by 25 years of age (Kessler et al., 2005). For children and young adults with ASD or ADHD, it can be challenging to cope with day-to-day situations such as formal learning or social interactions. Both impairments often co-occur (Ashwood et al., 2015), and can lead to language production deficits, attention difficulties, and poor working memory.

Social anxiety disorder (SAD) is described as an intense 'fear of failure' in a given social situation, for example when having to deliver a speech in front of a number of people, and as the third most common mental health disorder (Leigh & Clark, 2018). Many people experience fear before events such as a public talk, or meeting new people. However, individuals with social anxiety experience such situations more persistently, which can lead to complete avoidance of social situations, compromising their quality of life (Khalid-Khan et al., 2007).

Similar to children and young adults with SAD, ASD and ADHD can exclude them from their peers, and make it difficult to perform in school. As such, support tools are needed. As we have shown, comorbidities between the disorders exist, and some symptoms are similar to all three disorders we are focusing on. Yet, SAD, ASD and ADHD show different characteristics and causes. In the next three sections, we go into more detail regarding the specific characteristics of ASD, ADHD, and SAD. We then present what immersive game applications (if any) already exist to support children and young adults in this space, what is missing, and what future research directions may look like in the field of immersive games to increase the health and quality of life for these individuals.

IMMERSIVE GAMES FOR CHILDREN AND YOUNG ADULTS WITH ASD

Autism Spectrum Disorder (ASD) is a neurodevelopmental disorder. It is characterised by one's persistent deficits in social communication and interaction across multiple contexts as well as restricted and repetitive patterns of behaviour. These may cause significant impairments in social and occupational functioning (American Psychiatric Association, 2013). Individuals with ASD can show weak central coherence, executive function, and the lack of a Theory of Mind (ToM). Weak central coherence refers to the individuals' preference for local detail over global processing (Frith, 1989). A person with weak central coherence would for example see every single tree instead of the forest as a whole. There is evidence showing that due to weak central coherence, learners with ASD can understand the immediate or literal meaning of their teachers' verbal instructions but may persistently be pre-occupied with only one part of the instructions and persevere with smaller details, hindering them from extracting and digesting knowledge from the details (Happé & Frith, 2006; de Jager & Condy, J, 2020). ToM is a socio-cognitive ability to think about one's own or someone else's mental state. A lack of ToM makes it more difficult to understand other people, their intentions, and follow their lines of thought (Baron-Cohen, 1997). Weak central coherence and a lack of ToM are considered to be interacting facets of the disorder. Both can explain why behaviour among individuals may be implausible because they do not belong to a coherent system of thought (Pellicano et al., 2006; Delli et al., 2017). Executive function is a set of mental skills that include working memory, flexible thinking, and self-control; these skills are vital to handle everyday situations, in learning, working, or generally managing daily life (Pennington & Ozonoff, 1996; Hill, 2004; Demetriou et al., 2018). Trouble with executive function can make it hard to focus, follow directions, and handle emotions. One can imagine that all these impairments, which affect individuals on the Spectrum of Autism Disorders more or less severely, present difficult challenges when engaging in social life.

Currently, there is no clinical evidence that fully supports a particular treatment for ASD. However, a great number of evidence-based interventions have been developed and delivered to help children with ASD at young ages. The most widely delivered evidence-based interventions include Applied Behaviour Analysis (ABA) (Foxx, 2008), Picture Exchange Communication System (PECS) (Bondy & Frost, 1994), Treatment and Education of Autistic and Related Communication Handicapped Children (TEACCH) (Mesibov et al., 2005), and Social-Communication, Emotional Regulation and Transactional Support (SCERTS) (Rubin et al., 2013). These interventions may potentially reduce ASD-related symptoms and improve the children's daily living skills, thus enhancing their ability of functioning and participating in the communities (Dawson et al., 2012; Weitlauf et al., 2014; Tachibana et al., 2017). However, these interventions always require to be administered by trained professionals, causing a bottleneck for accessing the much-needed intervention services.

A number of low-tech games exist that teach children with ASD to cope with situations in school (*What would you do at school if…*®), how to (better) remember faces (*I never forget a face*®), recognize emotions (*Feelings in a Flash*®), or trigger sensory stimuli such as *Kinetic Sand*®. However, whilst many of these games may have a positive effect on some players, many have not been designed as a therapeutic tool on the basis of psychological insights, and even fewer with young individuals in mind. The above examples are mainly entertainment games or toys, that have been shown to be useful to address some issues children and young adults with ASD face, and therefore are mentioned on websites that offer support for teachers and care-givers of children with ASD.

Technology-based ASD intervention could be a possible solution to address gaps in the support system (Grynszpan et al., 2014). Among the various types of technologies, immersive technology, such as virtual reality and augmented reality, has been empirically studied since the late 1990s (Strickland, 1997). Both the hardware and software technologies are getting more mature. Regarding the hardware, the enabling technology, such as virtual reality HMDs, has matured out of research laboratories and become off-the-shelf commercial products. However, the ASD population's acceptance of virtual reality headsets still needs to be further studied. Besides headsets, projection-based virtual environments, such as the Cave Automatic Virtual Environment (CAVE), have become more accessible and are used for delivering ASD interventions (e.g. Maskey et al., 2014; Ip et al., 2018; Maskey et al., 2019). The development of software technologies enables complex physical environments and dynamic social interactions being simulated in virtual environments. By adding gamification elements, such simulations can be highly interactive and engaging, making immersive games a promising tool for delivering interventions to children and young adults with ASD. Simulations of real-life scenarios in VR games can help children and young adults generalize what they have learned through gameplay, and relate it back to real-life situations (Parsons & Mitchell, 2002). Next to the promising technological advancement, there are still, there are three major concerns in academic research and practice on using immersive games for ASD intervention.

- **Effectiveness** - there is still a lack of evidence regarding the effectiveness of immersive games on ASD intervention due to small sample sizes, erratic game designs, and flawed experiment designs (Karami et al., 2021). Also, very few longitudinal studies have been carried out to investigate the retention of the interventional effects.
- **Design Theories and Models** - although a few educational and psychiatric theories and models have been applied to guide the immersive game design, most of the existing immersive games for ASD intervention are designed based on experiences rather than well-established educational and psychiatric theories.
- **Contributing Factors** - among those studies that showed immersive games' effects on ASD intervention, few have investigated the factors that contributed to the results.

Effectiveness In recent years, there are a few high-quality publications on empirical studies of using immersive games, or immersive technologies in general, for ASD intervention among children and young adults (see for an overview e.g. Parsons & Mitchell, 2002). In these publications, scholars have reported studies on investigating the effectiveness with sizable samples and rigorous experiment designs, such as randomised controlled trials (RCT). For example, Ip et al. studied the use of virtual reality for enhancing social and emotional skills among children with ASD (Ip et al., 2018). The study employed the RCT design involving 94 children between the ages of 6 to 12 with a clinical diagnosis of ASD. A total number of six virtual scenarios were developed and used across 28 interventional sessions. These scenarios simulated various school scenes in which social interactions took place in the corresponding contexts. The children were asked to complete tasks by navigating in virtual scenarios, getting involved in social interactions, and following certain social rules (e.g., being quiet in the school library). Although the authors did not label the scenarios as games, the use of task lists and rewarding the children virtually after completing the tasks can be considered as the gameplay elements, which, according to the authors, motivated the children during the sessions. The results are very encouraging; statistical analysis showed that comparing the assessments between the control group and the intervention group, there were significant improvements in the children's emotion expression and regulation and social-emotional reciprocity. Such research studies provided valuable and solid evidence in the effectiveness of using games, or immersive technologies in general, for children and young adults with ASD. However, at the same time, we should also notice that many studies in this area of research suffer from flaws in experiment designs in terms of *"selection of participants, type and duration of intervention, and choice of a measurement tool"* (Karami et al., 2021, p. 21).

Design Theories and Models Some conventional educational and psychiatric theories and models have been applied to guide immersive game designs. For example, Kolb's experiential learning model (ELM) (Kolb, 1984) seems to be applicable for designing immersive games for ASD intervention (Li et al., 2021). Originated in conventional classroom teaching and learning, ELM requires an interactive learning environment and related facilitation. In such environment, learners can understand the problem through interaction and observation, come up with strategies based on previous experiences and knowledge, apply the strategies to tackle the problem, and reflect if the strategies do or do not work (Kolb, 1984). The iterative process is generally a trial-and-error process. Immersive games are the perfect environment in which ELM can be applied. Games are highly interactive and should be engaging enough to encourage the iterative process of learning with various rewarding mechanisms. Facilitation can be pre-designed and gradually provided as the gameplay goes. The facilitation of immersive games by a trusted person such as a teacher or caregiver could be beneficial for children with ASD (Li et al., 2021). Another example is the adoption of Cognitive Behavioural Therapy (CBT) in immersive games. Conventionally, CBT is a talk therapy, during which the therapists will help the patients with certain challenges by changing how the patients think and behave. The adoption of CBT in game design seems to be quite effective in addressing anxiety and stress among children and young adults with ASD (Maskey et al., 2014; Maskey et al., 2019). Unlike conventional talk therapy, immersive games can provide concrete and vivid visual tactics when the therapists are trying to address a specific anxiety among the patients, which could be quite crucial to the success of CBT (Moree & Davis, 2010). Since many evidence-based approaches nowadays also rely on concrete visual tactics, it is more or less straightforward to use immersive games or generally interactive media to deliver such approaches. However, how to maximise the power of immersive games, such as how to make good use of the gameplay elements for educational or psychoeducational purposes, still remains largely unexplored. Game elements that could leverage the motivation of players, and enable personalisation of learning, are seen as beneficial for children and adolenscents with ASD (Whyte, Smyth, & Scherf, 2015).

Contributing Factors A small number of studies hypothetically attributed the effects of immersive games on ASD to the strength in visual thinking among the ASD population (Ip et al., 2018). Yet, we think this needs to be more carefully investigated. Although based on eye tracking data, the gaze patterns of the ASD population are found to be different, especially in social contexts (Papagiannopoulou et al., 2014; Chita-Tegmark, 2016), how they receive, process, and respond to visual stimulations, is still largely unexplored (Anger et al., 2019). Thus, identifying the contributing factors to the effects of immersive games on ASD intervention requires more in-depth investigations.

In summary, a number of studies on immersive technologies to support children and young adults with ASD exist. Some of them make use of game elements. On the other hand, the specific needs of this population seem to correspondent with the characteristics of immersive games, such as providing a safe, controllable space. More research is needed on the effectiveness, the underlying design principles, and the contributing factors of immersive games for this group. The next section will further explore the situation of immersive games to support individuals with ADHD.

IMMERSIVE GAMES FOR CHILDREN AND YOUNG ADULTS WITH ADHD

Similar to children and young adults with ASD, weak executive function can be a symptom of individuals with ADHD, who may also show signs of impulsiveness or inattention. These traits demonstrate challenges and make it difficult for children and young adults to 'perform' in school, 'function' in social situations, and develop skills needed in our modern society. Symptoms of ADHD vary widely, but are commonly grouped into two clusters of symptoms (Roberts, Milich, & Barkley, 2015):

- **Hyperactivity/Impulsivity** - characterised by an inability to control impulses, acting without thinking, and poor executive function.;
- **Inattention** - characterised by difficulty controlling attention, becoming distracted easily, and impaired working memory.

ADHD has been included in the Global Burden of Disease Study for the first time in 2010 (Erskine et al., 2013). Its symptoms can have a significant negative impact on ones' academic and social engagements (American Psychiatric Association, 2013; Booster, DuPaul, Eiraldi, & Power, 2012). When looking at gender, young males seem to be more often affected by this neurodevelopmental condition compared to young females. Expressions of inattention are found to be the dominant ADHD symptoms for girls (Teichner, 2016). Resulting social and behavioural problems appear to impact children diagnosed with ADHD regardless of gender identity (Hinshaw et al., 2012). The developmental complications of ADHD may include poor academic achievements, problems with peer relationships, or substance abusive behaviour (Teichner, 2016). Children with ADHD can be distracted by daydreaming, may engage in creating sounds, and may have severe difficulties in following and remembering instructions. It is obvious that a child who simply cannot remember the instructions for a certain task will not be able to produce the same result as a neurotypical child, regardless their intellectual skills. There are medications to help children deal with the symptoms of ADHD, such as Ritalin. However, not all children react to the medication in the same way, and not all caregivers want their children to take a medication on a long-term basis. Moreover, a combination of pharmacological and non-pharmacological treatment appears to be most effective (Brown et al., 2018). Researchers and practitioners alike are looking for alternative ways to support young adults and children with ADHD cope with the challenges that come with their neurodiversity. However, the majority of studies in relation to games and ADHD that can be found in literature report on the use of these tools for assessment rather than support or intervention (Rizzo et al., 2001; Nolin, Stipanicic, Henry, Lachapelle, Lussier-Desrochers & Allain, 2016; Parsons, Duffield, & Asbee, 2019).

Games that aim to support children with ADHD often focus on building concentration and attention, such as Memory games, or Escape room games. EndeavorRx® is the first digital game-based device that is aimed at children with ADHD, and offers an engaging method to develop skills in a way that addresses the specific challenges of children with ADHD (Canady, 2020). Wegrzyn, Hearrington, Martin & Randolph (2012) investigated the use of brain games as a non-pharmaceutical alternative for children with ADHD. They found that daily use of these games helped the children to improve their ability to focus and improved the executive function in adolescents. Pandian, Jain, Raza, & Sahu (2021) found in their literature review that digital games can have a positive effect on some of the symptoms of ADHD, but that long-term studies are still lacking. The usefulness of games in their view is based on the insight that improvements of cognitive functions can be achieved by digital means, including games. The same study also summarizes findings on how video games can alter brain structure and function, which can also lead to improved brain functioning in children with ADHD. Beyond games, VR environments are used to support children with ADHD, too. In their review of the use of VR for the rehabilitation of ADHD, Bashiri, Ghazisaeedi and Shahmoradi (2017) list 20 studies, of which seven make use of a continuous performance test (CPT). 13 of the studies in the review were VR classroom simulations, designed to either measure inattention, or to train and improve children's ability to focus and engage in a physical classroom. One of these studies (Cho et al., 2002) developed a virtual classroom with simple tasks designed to improve subjects' attention over the course of two weeks. Participants undertook a CPT test before and after training to measure their improvement. While not tested on children diagnosed with ADHD, the study found that VR can be an effective tool to train attention in children and adolescents. In a study by Rohani et al. (2014), a novel brain-computer interface (BCI) based system was used to support ADHD rehabilitation through feedback games, aiming at increasing attention in affected children. This was combined with an immersive VR room simulating distractions. The researchers report promising findings which underlines the potential for immersive technologies in ADHD support.

Immersive VR gaming can offer unique features that can particularly be helpful to children with ADHD. Children with ADHD often struggle with internalization of speech. This makes it hard for them to translate heard information into concrete action (Kray et al., 2009). A VR game environment is customizable to the unique need for more frequent and verbal cues, fostering internalization of speech. This individualized approach can usually not be taken in a traditional classroom scenario. Similarly, VR gaming can accommodate for an increased support in working memory. Difficulties in working memory are often present in children with ADHD, especially showing through difficulties in holding and processing information (Klingberg et al., 2005). VR environments can be customized by displaying limited information at a time to avoid cognitive overload. Also, practice time can be customized to their needs, and game challenges and goals can be created to match the learner's ability and needs (Kalyuga et al., 2009). VR generates simulations of one's own body in the world, through the developed scenario. It allows exploring and manipulating that environment, improving self-regulation and learning through the representation from the prediction of the internal (of the body itself) and external (environmental) sensory stimuli (Romero-Ayuso et al., 2021).

Despite the promising outlook for VR games in education, it is still difficult to integrate them into traditional learning routines. Limiting factors include availability of time and space (Egenfeldt-Nielsen, 2006). Additionally, games often fail to address the required learning goals of individual curricula, because they are developed with broader application areas in mind (Kirriemuir & McFarlane, 2004). However, immersive games could include virtual representations of social situations like a school playground, or a park, or basic activities of daily living (Romero-Ayuso et al., 2021).

Using games in classroom education can still prove difficult due to a lack of technical knowledge and scepticism regarding learning effectiveness (Egenfeldt-Nielsen, 2006), but this might be a question of time, and overall higher adoption of immersive technologies in educational environments. Future studies should include the long-term effects of such interventions. Only one application for ADHD so far, EndeavorRx®, has been accredited in parts of the world. While VR games could offer an engaging and accessible way for children with ADHD to cope with their specific challenges, a great deal of research remains to be done in this field. The next section of this chapter looks into the situation in a related field, the case of immersive games for SAD.

IMMERSIVE GAMES FOR CHILDREN AND YOUNG ADULTS WITH SAD

Social Anxiety Disorder (SAD) is a condition in which individuals have an extreme fear of being evaluated and judged by others, to the point where it becomes debilitating, and prevents them from being able to participate and engage in healthy social activities and relationships. According to clinical guidelines, SAD may involve avoiding situations where one may be "the centre of attention", and those with SAD "may be concerned that others might notice the anxiety and be critical" (Andrews et al., 2018, p. 2). SAD is the most common anxiety disorder (Weinstock, 1999; Stein & Stein, 2008) with an age of onset by 11 years old in 50 per cent of individuals with SAD (Stein & Stein, 2008). Compared to ASD and ADHD, SAD is not a neurodevelopmental disorder, but can be caused by a specific event, the (family) environment, modelling of behaviours by family, long-term stress, and genetics. Having a parent with anxiety increases the chances of having the condition (Festa & Ginsburg, 2011). As with people who experience ASD and ADHD, SAD can make it difficult for children and young adults to develop a positive self-image, engage in social interactions, and may lead to poor performance in learning environments, e.g. when group work or presentation skills are expected. Such challenges can impact life chances, and without intervention can lead to the development of other conditions such as depression (Stein, Fuetsch, Müller, Höfler, Lieb, & Wittchen, 2001), suicidal ideation (Buckner et al, 2018), and comorbid substance abuse issues (Leichsenring & Leweke, 2017).

Cognitive Behavioural Therapy (CBT) is often used to address SAD in traditional therapeutic practice. As Coyle et al. (2011) describe, CBT involves focusing on thoughts, feelings and behaviours, and how these are interrelated. CBT focuses on "breaking the cycle" (Coyle et al. 2011) by providing skills to identify recurring thought patterns and challenge negative 'core beliefs' – those beliefs we may have about ourselves, our image, and what we are capable of. Clinical professional bodies recommend CBT for treatment of youth social anxiety over alternatives like medication given the age of clients (Andrews et al., 2018). Despite the efficacy of CBT for anxiety disorders, access to effective treatments can be challenging. Barriers include cost, stigma, geographic factors, waitlists and availability of therapists (Cardwell, 2021).

Further, identification and disclosure of the condition can be difficult given the nature of SAD as an internalising condition – one which presents limited external signals. For example, compared to other disorders there may be few obvious or behavioural hints that communicate its existence. Given these barriers, aspects of CBT have been implemented into computer cognitive behavioural therapy – CCBTs. However, CCBTs that are solely online can present engagement problems and dropouts from therapy.

Other work has explored translating features of CBT into games, as in the example of Quest Te Whitianga, a game which describes being based on principles of CBT, adapted for its game context and utilising New Zealand's cultural elements (Christie et al, 2019).

Next to these therapeutic and non-game applications, a growing number of entertainment games are also addressing anxiety and depression in a range of forms, such as Sea of Solitude®, Celeste®, or Sym®. Sea of Solitude® is a video game that illustrates depression, anxiety, and loneliness utilising specific aesthetics. In this game, the player takes over the role of the main character, Kay, who experiences great loneliness. The player has agency over the action unfolding in the game that plays with light and colour to represent mental health. The adventure game illustrates how depression and mental health issues can impact ones' life and the lives of loved ones. In Celeste®, the main character Madeline is confronted with a dark reflection of herself, and has to climb a dark-looking, dangerous mountain. Developed as a speed-running game, Celeste® can also be seen as a game about overcoming challenges and fighting one's fears. These two games are examples of entertainment games that deal loosely with mental health themes such as loneliness and depression, though do not address social anxiety specifically. By contrast, Sym® is a puzzle adventure exploring shyness and social anxiety directly. The main character, Josh, has to deal with two worlds in the game – the light side of the 'real' world, and the dark side of his personal, inner world. He faces his fears in the 'real' world, but also has a place to hide in his inner world. These games have all been highly praised, and Celeste® has reached a large group of players worldwide. However, of these games, only Sym© has been developed specifically as an intervention for people with social anxiety. All three games described above can foster empathy for what it means to suffer from depression and anxiety, but are not created to help someone who experiences a mental health disorder themselves. Though targeting SAD, Sym© has not been designed on the basis of clinical insights with the intention of being utilized as clinical intervention. When looking into the scientific literature, a number of studies can be found on the relation of social anxiety and gaming behaviour (Lo, Wang, & Fabg, 2005; Park et al., 2016; Wang, Sheng, & Wang, 2019; Karaca et al., 2020) but not how games could be used specifically as an intervention for children and young adults with social anxiety.

Recent work into serious games for social anxiety presents examples of games that have been designed for those with SAD. This has been done in varying ways, with different aspects of therapy included such as psychoeducation and cognitive restructuring. The work of Baldy et al. (2021) describes a serious game designed to improve awareness of CBT strategies, by presenting various scenarios such as attending a party, reflecting on events through cognitive restructuring, and falling in a public space as a form of exposure therapy (Baldy, Hansen and Bjorner, 2021). Results indicate that though this appears a viable form of education regarding skills for SAD, recall may have been improved if high arousal elements for CBT knowledge retention were included, with the authors stating this may help people remember (Baldy et al., 2021). Another interesting comment made is that participants who preferred action genre games rated engagement lower than those who preferred RPGs (Baldy et al., 2021), which is a challenge for designers considering how to balance the needs and preferences of multiple people and player types. How to make games, and immersive games particularly both useful for a wide range of people experiencing a particular condition, while also being personally contextually relevant is a complex research and design challenge.

Virtual reality is another technology medium that offers potential for those with social anxiety. Virtual reality exposure therapy, known as VRET, is a promising tool for social anxiety disorder. As exposure therapy can be difficult and time-intensive to conduct "in vivo", having the ability to enter an immersive environment to role play various social scenarios presents a promising augmentation or alternative to traditional treatment. When clinicians working in mental health were surveyed, VRET was described as being most beneficial for targeting anxiety disorders (Linder et al., 2019). Despite this, however, VR has not become commonplace in clinical practice, which presents a challenge to researchers and designers, to probe how effective and usable VRETs can be designed so they address clinician concerns, whilst also being engaging for young clients. In recommendations regarding how to improve VRET systems, Lindner et al. (2019) describe how gamified scenarios may increase the likelihood of continuing to confront adverse stimuli, suggesting that game elements may help with motivation in the face of challenging tasks. They however caution that game elements should not distract from the goals of the exposure therapy (Lindner et al., 2017). In their work comparing treatment of SAD by use of virtual environments and serious games, Biedel et al. (2021) found both treatment modalities to have similar efficacy in terms of reducing SAD symptoms.

It therefore seems worthwhile to investigate in more depth how game elements may complement virtual reality systems targeting youth anxiety, and how VR systems can be made more usable for clinicians and clients alike, as well as those who support them. Investigation of specific game mechanics that may help motivate young clients whilst also maintaining treatment efficacy of such systems is an important research direction, as is how to offer some degree of exploration and personalisation. As Emmelkamp et al. (2020) discuss, VRETs also need to allow for 'unpredictable social interaction' and incorporate flexibility in dialogue systems. Further, including game features explicitly in descriptions of systems would help other researchers and designers. There are open questions regarding which particular elements of games can be meshed with virtual reality as well as treatment paradigms for strong engagement and efficacy. One step towards addressing this could be to collaboratively engage with those who have lived experience of the target anxiety disorders themselves, clinicians, families and support people, to provide nuanced understanding not only of the manifestations of the condition, but also to understand usability concerns, and age and cultural considerations.

SUMMARY

Mental health and neurodevelopmental disorders in children and young adults is a topic that is increasingly discussed both in public and in academia. Whether more people talk about it, or more people actually experience it is not clear yet. One can imagine that the use of social media and confrontation with serious global events at a young age can have an impact on mental health. Public discussion will hopefully lead to more acceptance, and better solutions for individuals experiencing mental health problems, neurodiversity and developmental disorders such as ASD, ADHD, and SAD. While children and young adults diagnosed with one of these conditions may share similar symptoms of insecurity, depression, and anxiety, the underlying reasons for these symptoms differ, and require distinct support and intervention.

Immersive games appear to be a promising approach for the groups discussed in this chapter, and some examples already exist. Games may be included as an engaging, and easy-to-access addition to online health programs, reaching those who might otherwise not engage with health programs, or who are on a long waiting list. Game examples from other areas in health care show that they can be used for behavioural change. Immersive games have the ability to create engaging, realistic, and safe environments that enable players to experience and 'train' for certain scenarios. These scenarios can represent social situations, such as a busy classroom, a test setting, or a moment before a public speech. Immersive games can also be designed as clean and calming environments, making use of colour schemes and sounds that can uplift or calm users. Immersive games can offer rewards and positive feedback, further motivating players to progress with treatment. They make use of motivating story lines, and provide a meaningful learning context (Whyte et al., 2015). Following the theory of flow Csikszentmihalyi (1997), immersive games could evaluate and adapt to a specific skill level of the learner, increasing difficulty according to a learner's skill level. These elements underpin the possible usability of games to help children and young adults with ASD, ADHD, and SAD.

However, only one game could be found that is accredited as a health intervention already, EndevaourXR®, a game made for children diagnosed with ADHD. The majority of games in this space illustrate topics such as depression and loneliness, but are not developed following medical guidelines, or based on therapeutic insights. A new relationship between these and game design principles could be a promising approach towards evidence-based development and usage of immersive games in the field. Games are a vital part of youth and adolescent culture, and could therefore reach a large group of users facing mental health and neurodevelopmental disorders. However, research could not be found that explored long-term effects in a large test group at present. Generally, research demonstrates that young people appreciate the use of immersive technologies, especially in learning, but most studies only include a small number of participants, and the research field is fragmented (Checa & Bustillo, 2019). There is no evidence yet for which game elements would work best in particular contexts, and how games should be implemented – as part of a therapy, as preparation for face-to-face meetings, as an online tool. How to make games, and immersive games particularly both useful for a wide range of people experiencing a particular condition, while also being personally contextually relevant is a complex research and design challenge.

These and more questions are still unanswered and need to be incorporated in future research on games as a means for children and young adults who experience neurodiversity and mental health problems. Little is currently known about specific game elements and which effects those elements produce in the domains discussed. Future research should explore which elements are most effective in particular scenarios. None of the approaches, expect for EndevaourXR®, is an accredited tool yet. We could not find any evidence-based approaches in the literature. Furthermore, in research, the health and safety of participating children have to be addressed. Children with mental health and neurodevelopmental disorders represent an especially vulnerable group. Specific risks of the use of immersive game technology, such as being too realistic and overwhelming for some children, have to be addressed in research set-ups. However, there are a number of research directions that can be identified, which are listed below.

FUTURE RESEARCH DIRECTIONS

Future research on the design and use of immersive games for mental health and neurodiversity, especially in children and young adults, should focus on following aspects, based on our findings discussed above:

1. **Focus on the Target Group**: Immersive games for children and young adults with mental health and neurodevelopmental disorders should be designed for this specific group in mind. The youth in general is very familiar with games, and has certain expectations towards any game developed for 'serious' purposes. However, children with ASD, ADHD, and SAD have special needs when it comes to immersive environments and games. For example, children with ADHD would benefit from clean, calming game environments without time pressure. Children with ASD could learn from

immersive games that help them to learn social scripts in familiar environments. And immersive games for young adults with SAD could provide realistic situations that prepare them for real-life and enable players to develop strategies to cope with their anxiety.

2. **Design Based on Clinical and Psychological Insights**: We have seen that many games and toys to support children and young adults with ASD, ADHD, and SAD are not explicitly developed based on clinical and psychological insights. While some of these games might still be useful in e.g. training one's attention span, or representing social situations, insights from these fields should be used to develop immersive games tailored to the specific needs of this group. In addition, insights from human-interface design, user experience, and game design should drive the actual development. Therefore, interdisciplinary research teams should be formed.

3. **Mixed-Methods Evaluation Strategies**: There is still little evidence of the effects of immersive games on the above discussed impairments. A lack of long-term studies with a larger population is the main reason for this. On the other hand, studies often focus on the effects of full-fledged games and environments, making it difficult to identify which element of an immersive game or environment would lead to a certain outcome. Evaluation of the games designed for this target group should be designed as long-term, mixed methods approaches, to find out how these games are experienced, and what kind of effect they show, related to which of their elements.

To conclude our chapter, we formulate below questions based on our insights, that may help to advance the scientific knowledge in this field with mixed-research method studies. These will support future ways to explore the effect of applied immersive games on children and young adults with special needs.

1. How can the unique traits of immersive technology, such as the ability to induce a sense of presence and embodiment, contribute to the learning and/or psychoeducational effects?

2. How can gameplay design, such as rules and rewards of a game, contribute to the learning and/or psychoeducational effects for children and young adults with mental health and neurodevelopmental diversities?

CONCLUSION

Immersive games may be a promising approach to help children and young adults with ASD, ADHD, and SAD, among others. They provide safe, experiential environments with engaging elements and immediate feedback, and may help to address issues of access to treatment. Immersive games can be used to represent challenging situations, and train vital skills for these specific user groups. However, their design and application would benefit from interdisciplinary, mixed methods research both into their distinct elements as well as their effects. Further research into the design and use of immersive games for children and young adults with mental health and neurodevelopmental disorders is necessary to explore the effectiveness of digital interventions and their use and acceptability in clinical practice. Several promising elements of immersive games in this field are outlined below, and should be addressed in future research:

*   **Engaging Game Design** - Game-based therapeutic approaches have an increased appeal for children, thus making treatment an enjoyable experience;

- **User-Friendly Design** – Design that is focused on the target group leads to increased understanding and identification of relevant scenarios, and can improve treatment adherence;
- **Accessible Technology** – Immersive games can be used at home without any medical supervision. Accessible technology like mobiles and wearable technologies can give increased access to patients as it is easy to carry around and can be accessed at any time by the patient if needed;
- **Improved Inclusion** – Immersive games can negate the undesirable side effects and stigmatization caused by medications, as well as help to remove some of the barriers to treatment.

ACKNOWLEDGMENT

This research is supported by the Tertiary Education Commission New Zealand and the University of Canterbury, Christchurch, NZ, as part of the Applied Immersive Gaming Initiative (AIGI). All authors contributed evenly to this chapter.

REFERENCES

American Psychiatric Association. (2013). *Diagnostic and statistical manual of mental disorders (DSM-5®)*. American Psychiatric Association.

Andrews, G., Bell, C., Boyce, P., Gale, C., Lampe, L., Marwat, O., Rapee, R., & Wilkins, G. (2018). Royal Australian and New Zealand College of Psychiatrists clinical practice guidelines for the treatment of panic disorder, social anxiety disorder and generalised anxiety disorder. *The Australian and New Zealand Journal of Psychiatry*, 52(12), 1109–1172. doi:10.1177/0004867418799453

Anger, M., Wantzen, P., Le Vaillant, J., Malvy, J., Bon, L., Guénolé, F., Moussaoui, E., Barthelemy, C., Bonnet-Brilhault, F., Eustache, F., Baleyte, J.-M., & Guillery-Girard, B. (2019). Positive effect of visual cuing in episodic memory and episodic future thinking in adolescents with autism spectrum disorder. *Frontiers in Psychology*, 10, 1513. doi:10.3389/fpsyg.2019.01513 PMID:31354565

Ashwood, K. L., Tye, C., Azadi, B., Cartwright, S., Asherson, P., & Bolton, P. (2015). Brief report: Adaptive functioning in children with ASD, ADHD and ASD+ ADHD. *Journal of Autism and Developmental Disorders*, 45(7), 2235–2242. doi:10.100710803-014-2352-y PMID:25614019

Baron-Cohen, S. (1997). *Mindblindness: An essay on autism and theory of mind*. MIT press.

Bashiri, A., Ghazisaeedi, M., & Shahmoradi, L. (2017). The opportunities of virtual reality in the rehabilitation of children with attention deficit hyperactivity disorder: A literature review. *Korean Journal of Pediatrics*, 60(11), 337–343. doi:10.3345/kjp.2017.60.11.337 PMID:29234356

Beidel, D. C., Tuerk, P. W., Spitalnick, J., Bowers, C. A., & Morrison, K. (2021). Treating childhood social anxiety disorder with virtual environments and serious games: A randomized trial. *Behavior Therapy*, 52(6), 1351–1363. doi:10.1016/j.beth.2021.03.003 PMID:34656191

Biocca, F. (1997). The cyborg's dilemma: Progressive embodiment in virtual environments. *Journal of Computer-Mediated Communication, 14*(1), 27–50. doi:10.1111/j.1083-6101.1997.tb00070.x

Bondy, A. S., & Frost, L. A. (1994). The picture exchange communication system. *Focus on Autistic Behavior, 9*(3), 1–19. doi:10.1177/108835769400900301

Booster, G. D., DuPaul, G. J., Eiraldi, R., & Power, T. J. (2012). Functional impairments in children with ADHD: Unique effects of age and comorbid status. *Journal of Attention Disorders, 16*(3), 179–189. doi:10.1177/1087054710383239 PMID:20876886

Brown, K. A., Samuel, S., & Patel, D. R. (2018). Pharmacologic management of attention deficit hyperactivity disorder in children and adolescents: A review for practitioners. *Translational Pediatrics, 7*(1), 36–47. doi:10.21037/tp.2017.08.02 PMID:29441281

Buckner, J. D., Lemke, A. W., Jeffries, E. R., & Shah, S. M. (2017). Social anxiety and suicidal ideation: Test of the utility of the interpersonal-psychological theory of suicide. *Journal of Anxiety Disorders, 45*, 60–63. doi:10.1016/j.janxdis.2016.11.010 PMID:27940416

Canady, V. A. (2020). FDA approves first video game Rx treatment for children with ADHD. *Mental Health Weekly, 30*(26), 1–7. doi:10.1002/mhw.32423

Cardwell, H. (2021). *Shortage of psychologists leaving patients on waitlist for 9 to 12 months. Radio New Zealand.* https://www.rnz.co.nz/news/political/451062/shortage-of-psychologists-leaving-patients-on-waitlist-for-9-to-12-months

Checa, D., & Bustillo, A. (2019). A review of immersive virtual reality serious games to enhance learning and training. *Multimedia Tools and Applications, 79*(9-10), 5501–5527. doi:10.100711042-019-08348-9

Christie, G. I., Shepherd, M., Merry, S. N., Hopkins, S., Knightly, S., & Stasiak, K. (2019). Gamifying CBT to deliver emotional health treatment to young people on smartphones. *Internet Interventions: the Application of Information Technology in Mental and Behavioural Health, 18*, 100286–100286. doi:10.1016/j.invent.2019.100286 PMID:31890633

Csikszentmihalyi, M. (1997). *Finding flow.* Basic Books.

Chita-Tegmark, M. (2016). Social attention in ASD: A review and meta-analysis of eye-tracking studies. *Research in Developmental Disabilities, 48*, 79–93. doi:10.1016/j.ridd.2015.10.011 PMID:26547134

Cho, B.-H., Ku, J., Jang, D. P., Kim, S., Lee, Y. H., Kim, I. Y., Lee, J. H., & Kim, S. I. (2002, April). The Effect of Virtual Reality Cognitive Training for Attention Enhancement. *Cyberpsychology & Behavior, 5*(2), 129–137. doi:10.1089/109493102753770516 PMID:12025879

Coyle, D., McGlade, N., Doherty, G., & O'Reilly, G. (2011). Exploratory evaluations of a computer game supporting cognitive behavioural therapy for adolescents. *Proceedings of the SIGCHI Conference on Human Factors in Computing Systems*, 2937-2946. 10.1145/1978942.1979378

Dawson, G., Jones, E. J., Merkle, K., Venema, K., Lowy, R., Faja, S., Kamara, D., Murias, M., Greenson, J., Winter, J., Smith, M., Rogers, S. J., & Webb, S. J. (2012). Early behavioral intervention is associated with normalized brain activity in young children with autism. *Journal of the American Academy of Child and Adolescent Psychiatry, 51*(11), 1150–1159. doi:10.1016/j.jaac.2012.08.018 PMID:23101741 de Jager, P. S., & Condy, J. (2020). Weak central coherence is a syndrome of autism spectrum disorder during teacher-learner task instructions. *South African Journal of Childhood Education*, *10*(1), 1–11. doi:10.4102ajce.v10i1.785

Delli, C. K. S., Varveris, A., & Geronta, A. (2017). Application of the Theory of Mind, Theory of Executive Functions and Weak Central Coherence Theory to Individuals with ASD. *Journal of Educational and Developmental Psychology*, *7*(1), 102–102. doi:10.5539/jedp.v7n1p102

Demetriou, E. A., Lampit, A., Quintana, D. S., Naismith, S. L., Song, Y. J. C., Pye, J. E., Hickie, I., & Guastella, A. J. (2018). Autism spectrum disorders: A meta-analysis of executive function. *Molecular Psychiatry*, *23*(5), 1198–1204. doi:10.1038/mp.2017.75 PMID:28439105

Egenfeldt-Nielsen, S. (2006). Overview of research on the educational use of video games. *Nordic Journal of Digital Literacy*, *1*(03), 184–214. doi:10.18261/ISSN1891-943X-2006-03-03

Elizabeth, J., King, N., Ollendick, T. H., Gullone, E., Tonge, B., Watson, S., & Macdermott, S. (2006). Social anxiety disorder in children and youth: A research update on aetiological factors. *Counselling Psychology Quarterly*, *19*(2), 151–163. doi:10.1080/09515070600811790

Emmelkamp, P., Meyerbröker, K., & Morina, N. (2020). Virtual Reality Therapy in Social Anxiety Disorder. *Current Psychiatry Reports*, *22*(7), 32. doi:10.100711920-020-01156-1 PMID:32405657

Erskine, H. E., Ferrari, A. J., Nelson, P., Polanczyk, G. V., Flaxman, A. D., Vos, T., Whiteford, H. A., & Scott, J. G. (2013). Research Review: Epidemiological modelling of attention-deficit/hyperactivity disorder and conduct disorder for the Global Burden of Disease Study 2010. *Journal of Child Psychology and Psychiatry, and Allied Disciplines*, *54*(12), 1263–1274. doi:10.1111/jcpp.12144 PMID:24117530

Festa, C. C., & Ginsburg, G. S. (2011). Parental and peer predictors of social anxiety in youth. *Child Psychiatry and Human Development*, *42*(3), 291–306. doi:10.100710578-011-0215-8 PMID:21274620

Foxx, R. M. (2008). Applied behavior analysis treatment of autism: The state of the art. *Child and Adolescent Psychiatric Clinics of North America*, *17*(4), 821–834. doi:10.1016/j.chc.2008.06.007 PMID:18775372

Freina, L., & Ott, M. (2015). A literature review on immersive virtual reality in education: state of the art and perspectives. *The International Scientific Conference eLearning and Software for Education*, *1*(133), 10-1007.

Frith, U. (1989). *Autism: Explaining the enigma*. Blackwell Publishing.

Garrett, B., Taverner, T., Gromala, D., Tao, G., Cordingley, E., & Sun, C. (2018). Virtual reality clinical research: Promises and challenges. *JMIR Serious Games*, *6*(4), e10839. doi:10.2196/10839 PMID:30333096

Granic, I., Lobel, A., & Engels, R. C. (2014). The benefits of playing video games. *The American Psychologist*, *69*(1), 66–78. doi:10.1037/a0034857 PMID:24295515

Grynszpan, O., Weiss, P. L., Perez-Diaz, F., & Gal, E. (2014). Innovative technology-based interventions for autism spectrum disorders: A meta-analysis. *Autism*, *18*(4), 346–361. doi:10.1177/1362361313476767 PMID:24092843

Hansen, B. H., Oerbeck, B., Skirbekk, B., Petrovski, B. É., & Kristensen, H. (2018). Neurodevelopmental disorders: Prevalence and comorbidity in children referred to mental health services. *Nordic Journal of Psychiatry*, *72*(4), 285–291.

Happé, F., & Frith, U. (2006). The weak coherence account: Detail-focused cognitive style in autism spectrum disorders. *Journal of Autism and Developmental Disorders*, *36*(1), 5–25.

Hill, E. L. (2004). Evaluating the theory of executive dysfunction in autism. *Developmental Review*, *24*(2), 189–233.

Hinshaw, S. P., Owens, E. B., Zalecki, C., Huggins, S. P., Montenegro-Nevado, A. J., Schrodek, E., & Swanson, E. N. (2012). Prospective follow-up of girls with attention-deficit/hyperactivity disorder into early adulthood: Continuing impairment includes elevated risk for suicide attempts and self-injury. *Journal of Consulting and Clinical Psychology*, *80*(6), 1041.

Horowitz, L. M., Thurm, A., & Farmer, C. (2018). Autism and Developmental Disorders Inpatient Research Collaborative. Talking about death or suicide: Prevalence and clinical correlates in youth with autism spectrum disorder in the psychiatric inpatient setting. *Journal of Autism and Developmental Disorders*, *48*(11), 3702–3710.

Ip, H. H., Wong, S. W., Chan, D. F., Byrne, J., Li, C., Yuan, V. S., ... Wong, J. Y. (2018). Enhance emotional and social adaptation skills for children with autism spectrum disorder: A virtual reality enabled approach. *Computers & Education*, *117*, 1–15.

Kalyuga, S., & Plass, J. L. (2009). Evaluating and managing cognitive load in games. In *Handbook of research on effective electronic gaming in education* (pp. 719–737). IGI Global.

Karaca, S., Karakoc, A., Gurkan, O. C., Onan, N., & Barlas, G. U. (2020). Investigation of the online game addiction level, sociodemographic characteristics and social anxiety as risk factors for online game addiction in middle school students. *Community Mental Health Journal*, *56*(5), 830–838.

Karami, B., Koushki, R., Arabgol, F., Rahmani, M., & Vahabie, A. H. (2021). Effectiveness of Virtual/Augmented Reality-based therapeutic interventions on individuals with autism spectrum disorder: A comprehensive meta-analysis. *Frontiers in Psychiatry*, *12*, 887.

Kessler, R. C., Berglund, P., Demler, O., Jin, R., Merikangas, K. R., & Walters, E. E. (2005). Lifetime prevalence and age-of-onset distributions of DSM-IV disorders in the National Comorbidity Survey Replication. *Archives of General Psychiatry*, *62*, 593–602.

Kirriemuir, J.K. & McFarlane, A. (2004). *Literature Review in games and learning*. University of Bristol: FutureLab Series 8.

Klingberg, T., Fernell, E., Olesen, P. J., Johnson, M., Gustafsson, P., Dahlström, K., ... Westerberg, H. (2005). Computerized training of working memory in children with ADHD-a randomized, controlled trial. *Journal of the American Academy of Child and Adolescent Psychiatry*, *44*(2), 177–186.

Kolb, D. A. (1984). *Experiential learning: Experience as the source of learning and development*. Prentice-Hall.

Kray, J., Kipp, K. H., & Karbach, J. (2009). The development of selective inhibitory control: The influence of verbal labeling. *Acta Psychologica, 130*(1), 48–57.

Krcek, T. E. (2013). Deconstructing Disability and Neurodiversity: Controversial Issues for Autism and Implications for Social Work. *Journal of Progressive Human Services, 24*, 1, 4–22.

Leichsenring, F., & Leweke, F. (2017). Social anxiety disorder. *The New England Journal of Medicine, 376*(23), 2255–2264.

Leigh, E., & Clark, D. M. (2018). Understanding Social Anxiety Disorder in Adolescents and Improving Treatment Outcomes: Applying the Cognitive Model of Clark and Wells (1995). *Clinical Child and Family Psychology Review, 21*(3), 388–414.

Li, C., Ip, H. H. S., & Ma, P. K. (2021). Experiential learning for children with autism spectrum disorder using virtual reality headsets: A preliminary report. *International Journal of Innovation and Learning, 30*(3), 317–333.

Lindner, P., Miloff, A., Zetterlund, E., Reuterskiöld, L., Andersson, G., & Carlbring, P. (2019). Attitudes toward and familiarity with virtual reality therapy among practicing cognitive behavior therapists: A cross-sectional survey study in the era of consumer VR platforms. *Frontiers in Psychology, 10*, 176–176.

Lindner, P., Miloff, A., Hamilton, W., Reuterskiöld, L., Andersson, G., Powers, M. B., & Carlbring, P. (2017). Creating state of the art, next-generation virtual reality exposure therapies for anxiety disorders using consumer hardware platforms: Design considerations and future directions. *Cognitive Behaviour Therapy, 46*(5), 404–420.

Lo, S. K., Wang, C. C., & Fang, W. (2005). Physical interpersonal relationships and social anxiety among online game players. *Cyberpsychology & Behavior, 8*(1), 15–20.

Malone, T. W. (1981). *Toward a theory of intrinsically motivating instruction. Cognitive Science, 4*, 333–369.

Maskey, M., Lowry, J., Rodgers, J., McConachie, H., & Parr, J. R. (2014). Reducing specific phobia/fear in young people with autism spectrum disorders (ASDs) through a virtual reality environment intervention. *PLoS One, 9*(7), e100374.

Maskey, M., Rodgers, J., Grahame, V., Glod, M., Honey, E., Kinnear, J., ... Parr, J. R. (2019). A randomised controlled feasibility trial of immersive virtual reality treatment with cognitive behaviour therapy for specific phobias in young people with autism spectrum disorder. *Journal of Autism and Developmental Disorders, 49*(5), 1912–1927.

Mesibov, G. B., Shea, V., & Schopler, E. (2005). *The TEACCH approach to autism spectrum disorders.* Springer Science & Business Media.

Michael, D. R., & Chen, S. L. (2005). Serious Games: Games That Educate, Train, and Inform. *Education,* 1–95.

Moree, B. N., & Davis, T. E. III. (2010). Cognitive-behavioral therapy for anxiety in children diagnosed with autism spectrum disorders: Modification trends. *Research in Autism Spectrum Disorders, 4*(3), 346–354.

Nakamura, J., & Csikszentmihalyi, M. (2009). In S. J. Lopez & C. R. Snyder (Eds.), *Flow theory and research. Handbook of positive psychology* (pp. 195–206). University Press.

Nolin, P., Stipanicic, A., Henry, M., Lachapelle, Y., Lussier-Desrochers, D., & Allain, P. (2016). ClinicaVR: Classroom-CPT: A virtual reality tool for assessing attention and inhibition in children and adolescents. *Computers in Human Behavior, 59*, 327–333.

Papagiannopoulou, E. A., Chitty, K. M., Hermens, D. F., Hickie, I. B., & Lagopoulos, J. (2014). A systematic review and meta-analysis of eye-tracking studies in children with autism spectrum disorders. *Social Neuroscience, 9*(6), 610–632.

Park, J. H., Han, D. H., Kim, B. N., Cheong, J. H., & Lee, Y. S. (2016). Correlations among social anxiety, self-esteem, impulsivity, and game genre in patients with problematic online game playing. *Psychiatry Investigation, 13*(3), 297.

Parsons, S., & Mitchell, P. (2002). The potential of virtual reality in social skills training for people with autistic spectrum disorders. *Journal of Intellectual Disability Research, 46*(5), 430–443.

Parsons, T. D., Duffield, T., & Asbee, J. (2019). A Comparison of Virtual Reality Classroom Continuous Performance Tests to Traditional Continuous Performance Tests in Delineating ADHD: A Meta-Analysis. *Neuropsychology Review*, 1–19.

Pellicano, E., Maybery, M., Durkin, K., & Maley, A. (2006). Multiple cognitive capabilities/deficits in children with an autism spectrum disorder: "Weak" central coherence and its relationship to theory of mind and executive control. *Development and Psychopathology, 18*(1), 77–98.

Pennington, B. F., & Ozonoff, S. (1996). Executive functions and developmental psychopathology. *Journal of Child Psychology and Psychiatry, and Allied Disciplines, 37*(1), 51–87.

Regenbrecht, H., Hoermann, S., McGregor, G., Dixon, B., Franz, E., Ott, C., Hale, L., Schubert, T., & Hoermann, J. (2012). Visual manipulations for motor rehabilitation. *Computers & Graphics, 36*(7), 819–834.

Rizzo, A. A., Bowerly, T., Buckwalter, J. G., Humphrey, L., Neumann, U., Kim, L., ... Chua, C. (2001). A Virtual Reality Environment for the Assessment of ADHD. *The ADHD Report, 9*(2), 9–13.

Roberts, W., Milich, R., & Barkley, R. A. (n.d.). Primary symptoms, diagnostic criteria, subtyping, and prevalence of ADHD. In Attention-Deficit Hyperactivity Disorder: A Handbook for Diagnosis and Treatment (4th ed., pp. 51–80). New York: The Guilford Press.

Rohani, D. A., Sørensen, H. B. D., & Puthusserypady, S. (2014). Brain-computer interface using P300 and virtual reality: A gaming approach for treating ADHD. In *2014 36th Annual International Conference of the IEEE Engineering in Medicine and Biology Society* (pp. 3606–3609). IEEE.

Romero-Ayuso, D., Toledano-González, A., Rodríguez-Martínez, M. del C., Arroyo-Castillo, P., Triviño-Juárez, J. M., González, P., & Ariza-Vega, P., Del Pino González, A., & Segura-Fragoso, A. (2021). Effectiveness of Virtual Reality-Based Interventions for Children and Adolescents with ADHD: A Systematic Review and Meta-Analysis. *Children (Basel, Switzerland), 8*(2), 70.

Rubin, E., Prizant, B. M., Laurent, A. C., & Wetherby, A. M. (2013). Social communication, emotional regulation, and transactional support (SCERTS). In *Interventions for Autism Spectrum Disorders* (pp. 107–127). Springer.

Scoresby, J., & Shelton, B. E. (2011). Visual perspectives within educational computer games: Effects on presence and flow within virtual immersive learning environments. *Instructional Science, 39*(3), 227–254.

Sanchez-Vives, M. V., & Slater, M. (2005). From presence to consciousness through virtual reality. *Nature Reviews. Neuroscience, 6*(4), 332–339.

Spencer, T. J. (2006). ADHD and comorbidity in childhood. *The Journal of Clinical Psychiatry, 67*, 27.

Sripada, C. S., Angstadt, M., Banks, S., Nathan, P. J., Liberzon, I., & Phan, K. L. (2009). Functional neuroimaging of mentalizing during the trust game in social anxiety disorder. *Neuroreport, 20*(11), 984–989.

Stein, M. B., Fuetsch, M., Müller, N., Höfler, M., Lieb, R., & Wittchen, H.-U. (2001). Social Anxiety Disorder and the Risk of Depression: A Prospective Community Study of Adolescents and Young Adults. *Archives of General Psychiatry, 58*(3), 251–256.

Stein, M. B., & Stein, D. J. (2008). Social anxiety disorder. *Lancet, 371*(9618), 1115–1125.

Strickland, D. (1997). Virtual reality for the treatment of autism. *Virtual Reality in Neuro-Psycho-Physiology, 44*, 81–86.

Tachibana, Y., Miyazaki, C., Ota, E., Mori, R., Hwang, Y., Kobayashi, E., ... Kamio, Y. (2017). A systematic review and meta-analysis of comprehensive interventions for pre-school children with autism spectrum disorder (ASD). *PLoS One, 12*(12), e0186502.

Tao, G., Garrett, B., Taverner, T., Cordingley, E., & Sun, C. (2021). Immersive virtual reality health games: A narrative review of game design. *Journal of Neuroengineering and Rehabilitation, 18*(1), 1–21.

Teichner, G. (2016). *Attention-deficit/hyperactivity disorder in children and adolescents: A dsm-5 handbook for medical and mental health professionals.* Retrieved from https://ebookcentral.proquest.com

Virvou, M., & Katsionis, G. (2008). On the usability and likeability of virtual reality games for education: The case of VR-ENGAGE. *Computers & Education, 50*(1), 154–178.

Wang, J. L., Sheng, J. R., & Wang, H. Z. (2019). The association between mobile game addiction and depression, social anxiety, and loneliness. *Frontiers in Public Health, 7*, 247.

Wegrzyn, S. C., Hearrington, D., Martin, T., & Randolph, A. B. (2012). Brain games as a potential nonpharmaceutical alternative for the treatment of ADHD. *Journal of Research on Technology in Education, 45*(2), 107–130.

Weinstock, L. S. (1999). Gender differences in the presentation and management of social anxiety disorder. *The Journal of Clinical Psychiatry, 60*(9), 9–13.

Weitlauf, A. S., McPheeters, M. L., Peters, B., Sathe, N., Travis, R., Aiello, R., . . . Warren, Z. (2014). Therapies for children with autism spectrum disorder: Behavioral interventions update. Comparative Effectiveness Review, 137.

Whyte, E. M., Smyth, J. M., & Scherf, K. S. (2015). Designing Serious Game Interventions for Individuals with Autism. *Journal of Autism and Developmental Disorders, 45*(12), 3820–3831.

World Health Organization. (2001). *The World Health Report 2001: Mental health: new understanding, new hope.* World Health Organisation.

Chapter 13
Gamifying Interventions:
Sweetening Mental Health Interventions for Children

Nicholas Kun Lie Goh

https://orcid.org/0000-0001-9347-1204

Institute of Mental Health, Singapore

Tze Jui Goh

Institute of Mental Health, Singapore

Choon Guan Lim

Institute of Mental Health, Singapore

Daniel Shuen Sheng Fung

https://orcid.org/0000-0003-0718-9363

Institute of Mental Health, Singapore

ABSTRACT

A key ingredient in successful psychological therapies is found in patients' motivation and willingness to engage in and follow through with the therapy program. Engaging children is challenging for various reasons, such as their role in their presentation for treatment and differences in parent and child motivations. This chapter explores the utility of serious games as a potential option that offers an engaging and effective approach to psychiatric treatment for children and adolescents with mental health difficulties. The authors review research projects utilizing the serious games methodology at the Child Guidance Clinic, an outpatient psychiatric clinic for children and adolescents in Singapore, in the management of various mental health concerns. The utility and feasibility of gamified interventions for autism spectrum disorders, attention-deficit hyperactive disorder, anxiety disorders, and anger management issues are discussed, along with practical implications for the application of serious games in mental healthcare.

DOI: 10.4018/978-1-7998-9732-3.ch013

INTRODUCTION

Singapore is a small island city-state in Southeast Asia, about 728 km^2 in size (Singapore Land Authority, 2021), with about 5.7 million residents (Department of Statistics, Singapore, 2021). The nation places emphasis on innovation and research to remain competitive (World Trade Organisation, 2012).

Singapore has also done well in providing quality and affordable healthcare (World Bank, 2019, 2021). In recent years, there has been an increasing awareness and focus on mental illness and its associated disease burden on the population. Mental Disorders are the second leading contributor of Years Lived with Disability (YLDs) in Singapore. It also accounts for the majority of YLDs in youths aged between 10 and 34 years old (Ministry of Health Singapore, Epidemiology & Disease Control Division & Institute for Health Metrics and Evaluation, 2019). Mental disorders place a significant financial burden on society, with an estimated average annual excess cost of US$2897.83 per person in Singapore (Abdin et al., 2021). These costs arise from both direct medical costs of seeking professional help and lost productivity due to absenteeism. Unsurprisingly, mental illnesses have greater adverse effects on vulnerable and at-risk groups of people with lower socioeconomic status, who have relatively poorer access to resources such as disposable income, health literacy, and social support systems, as compared to the general population (Lund et al., 2011; Murali & Oyebode, 2004). It is therefore imperative to design new and innovative ways to treat and manage mental illness more cost-effectively.

Mental illness refers to a wide range of conditions that affect a person's mood, cognition, and behavior (American Psychiatric Association, 2013). A significant proportion of mental health disorders has onset in childhood and adolescence. Hence, early intervention is critical for a better prognosis (Goodman et al., 2011). Successful mental health intervention in childhood can initiate important positive cascading effects into adulthood. In Singapore, public healthcare services incorporate technology to improve productivity and enhance access to healthcare (Smart Nation and Digital Government Office, 2021). There has been an increased national focus on utilizing technology to reduce barriers to mental health services (Ministry of Health, Singapore, 2020; Ong, 2017). Hence, serious games can be a potential tool to better engage children and adolescents in enhancing mental health and well-being.

This chapter provides an overview of the current challenges faced by mental health professionals in providing mental health services to children in Singapore, and discusses the utilization of serious games as a potential solution to these challenges. Specifically, this chapter explores the utility of serious games as a means to increase access to treatment and improve treatment engagement amongst children and adolescents presenting with mental health difficulties. The authors describe projects on serious games conducted at an outpatient psychiatric setting and share important findings as well as practical implications for clinicians and researchers looking to adopt serious games in treating the pediatric psychiatry population.

BACKGROUND

Child Mental Health in Singapore

Global estimates indicate that 10-20% of youths aged between 10 to 19 years old have experience of a mental health condition (Kessler et al., 2007). Recent statistics from a nationwide survey on the prevalence of mental illness in Singapore indicate that young adults between 18 to 34 years old are at a high risk of mood and alcohol use disorders (Subramaniam et al., 2019). Large-enough epidemiological studies for children aged 18 and below have not been completed locally. However, smaller community studies offer a glimpse into the prevalence of mental illness in Singaporean children. For instance, the prevalence of depression was estimated to be between 2% and 2.5% for depression in children below the age of 18 (Woo et al., 2004). Additionally, an estimated 9.6% of Singaporean children between 6 to 12 years old hit screening cut-offs for clinically significant anxiety (Woo et al., 2007).

Apart from depression and anxiety, neurodevelopmental disorders such as Autism Spectrum Disorder (ASD) and Attention-Deficit Hyperactive Disorder (ADHD) make up a significant portion of children seeking mental health services. Global studies have estimated that about 1 in 6 children have a neurodevelopmental disability (Dietrich et al., 2005). In 2016, developmental disabilities (including ASD and ADHD) accounted for 13% of the 29.3 million YLDs in young children globally (Olusanya et al., 2018). The symptoms associated with neurodevelopmental disorders are typically pervasive and longstanding. The conditions are compounded by impairment in various domains such as school, emotional, and psychosocial functioning with a high risk of co-occurring problems such as other mental health diagnoses or social-emotional repercussions such as law-breaking. Children with ADHD have been reported to have worse psychosocial, financial, and occupational outcomes, including anxiety problems, poor self-esteem, persistent peer rejection, and a higher risk of tobacco use and delinquency, when compared to children without ADHD (Harpin et al., 2016; Mrug et al., 2012; Pelham III et al., 2020; Shaw et al., 2012). Undiagnosed ADHD is also linked to greater depressive and emotional issues, and conduct problems such as aggression, deceitfulness, insubordination, and destructive behavior (Okumura et al., 2018).

The co-occurrence of conditions can also significantly impair daily functioning and overall quality of life for children with mental health concerns and/or neurodevelopmental disorders. Notably, about 83% of children with ASD present with co-occurring symptoms and conditions on top of symptoms directly attributed to the ASD diagnosis (Levy et al., 2010; Tsai, 2014; van Steensel et al., 2011; Vannucchi et al., 2014; Williams et al., 2014; Zaboski & Storch, 2018). These co-occurring issues may constitute a secondary diagnosis, such as Intellectual Disability and ADHD, or may simply be an associated feature such as elevated anxiety or depressive levels (Jong et al., 2012; Seligman & Ollendick, 1998; Simonoff et al., 2008)

In Singapore, the Institute of Mental Health (IMH) is the only tertiary hospital dedicated to psychiatric care in the public healthcare system. The Child Guidance Clinic (CGC), a pediatric outpatient psychiatric service run by IMH, receives approximately 2000 new referrals per year for various mental health concerns, neurodevelopmental disabilities, and other psychosocial problems. The service consists of several multi-disciplinary teams comprising psychiatrists, clinical psychologists, social workers, and occupational therapists, and includes an inpatient service for acute psychiatric treatment.

Existing Gaps in Mental Health Services

Patient motivation and engagement play an important role in the success and efficacy of psychosocial interventions. Like the keys to a car, patient motivation and engagement have to be "plugged in" and consistent throughout patients' recovery journeys for them to "go the distance" (Thompson et al., 2007). However, establishing patient motivation to engage in therapy is one of the most challenging tasks for mental health professionals, and much research has been done on the topic (e.g., Dean et al., 2016; Holdsworth et al., 2014; Oshotse et al., 2020). There could be various factors impacting engagement and adherence in therapy. Practical barriers to access services such as the financial cost of therapy, physical distance and lack of transportation options, long wait times, and clashes in schedule between therapy and other commitments can impede treatment adherence, and even therapy alliance. At times, parents and children may have different motivations. Parents may engage with therapists in therapeutic tasks, such as identifying problems and the solutions to these problems. However, children may lack the understanding or desire to do so and might actively resist participation in therapy (Hutchby & O'Reilly, 2010).

Additionally, behavioral activation exercises such as exposure and generalization of skills for some conditions such as phobia can be challenging to simulate within a traditional clinical setting. For example, a therapist may bring in a live spider to address arachnophobia, but it may be impractical to simulate situations for a phobia of flying. Younger children or children with developmental delays may also experience barriers in communication and expression. While they may benefit from more hands-on, experiential learning, the opportunity to process complex events, emotions, and thoughts or even the management of behaviors may be hard to come by in the therapy room.

Another critical factor that can significantly impact treatment engagement would be stigma against mental illness (Pang et al., 2017). Stigma refers to prejudice and discrimination against people with mental illness due to reasons such as misinformation and ignorance (Link & Phelan, 2001). People with mental illness often have poorer self-esteem as a result of stigmatizing attitudes and actions against them (Link et al., 2001), making them reluctant to seek help (Corrigan, 2004; Kessler et al., 2001). These individuals may benefit from less formal means of help, such as self-help applications and serious games, which might offer a more discreet manner of administration.

In summary, while the healthcare system in Singapore is relatively well-established, barriers to the administration of effective, affordable, and accessible treatments in mental healthcare remain. A large part of these barriers lies with patients' motivation to engage in therapy. In pediatric settings, treatment options need to appeal to children to engage in therapeutic learning and opportunities to practice new skills and behaviors. This must be done in affordable, convenient, and scalable ways to maximize reach and parent buy-in.

SERIOUS GAMES: A POTENTIAL SOLUTION?

Given that advances in computer and internet-based therapies such as internet Cognitive Behavior Therapy (iCBT) are widely available and have shown promise in offering similar efficacy rates as traditional modes of therapy (Newman et al., 2011), one would gravitate towards the use of technology as a means to increase access to treatment in a cost-effective, scalable manner. Technology-based methods have the potential to increase reach without drastically increasing costs and so can be theoretically done cost-effectively. Additionally, using technology would reduce the reliance on human therapists, potentially improving the availability of treatment after-hours.

Computer and Internet-based adaptations to traditional modes of therapy are more relevant in countries with adequate infrastructure and internet penetration rates. People need to be able to access such services without worries of disruption due to power or internet outages. Additionally, people who use these services need to be able to accept and navigate service platforms (e.g., computers, online booking, video-calling software) comfortably enough to ensure a smooth user experience that facilitates continual and consistent use of services. With 98% of households with internet access and 89% of individuals with access to a computer at home (Infocomm Media Development Authority, 2020), Singapore is in a prime position to use technology to scale up mental health services and provide accessible and affordable care.

Efforts to computerize services can range in complexity, from digital questionnaires that automatically score and save data to Artificial Intelligence (AI) programs that assist with diagnosis and treatment (e.g., WYSA; Inkster et al., 2018). These can occur in various stages of the therapy process, including triaging, assessment and diagnosis, intervention, and tracking progress. Internet-based Cognitive Behavioral Therapy (iCBT) is a successful example of psychotherapy administered digitally. It has been found to be effective for various mental health conditions, with comparable outcomes to traditional CBT (Andersson & Cuijpers, 2009; Andrews et al., 2010; Cuijpers et al., 2011; Williams & Andrews, 2013).

Advances in smartphone technology also help make digital interventions more feasible and accessible today. Mobile applications for mental health concerns are readily available and allow for quick and easy access to mental health support. The mobile penetration rate in Singapore is one of the highest globally, at around 150% (Infocomm Media Development Authority, 2019), putting the country in an ideal place to adopt mobile interventions. Applications range from autonomous chatbots offering coping strategies and resources, to journaling and mood-tracking applications, many of which are free for download. The ubiquity of mobile phones and mental health applications means that immediate support is readily available in one's pocket in times of emotional distress.

While computerized interventions significantly boost the scalability and accessibility of psychological therapy, the delivery of therapeutic content such as coping strategies and psychological concepts still tends to model the style of delivery in traditional therapy. For example, patients may be encouraged to peruse psychoeducational material, journal negative thoughts on digital worksheets, or practice coping strategies. This didactic style of delivery might not appeal to children and adolescents who may not be orientated to therapeutic learning and growth.

Serious games are the next logical step in the adoption of technology in psychological therapies. Generally, children and adolescents play games on the computer or their mobile phones (Gentile & Walsh, 2002; Granic et al., 2014). Hence, they would be savvy with such platforms to use them to access therapeutic material. The gamification of therapeutic interventions leverages on adolescents' captivation with computer games to promote engagement and motivate them to commit to therapy by breaking down walls between the therapist (or, in this case, the game) and themselves. Emerging work on serious games may offer the solution to improve engagement in therapy and other digitalized interventions. By borrowing principles from educational psychology (Cheek et al., 2015; Dickey, 2005), serious games facilitate learning skills that might be difficult or unappealing for children. For example, children might not be willing to engage in exposure therapy to address a phobia but might be receptive towards a serious game approach to overcoming the fear. A common goal that serious games can share with traditional therapy is to ensure the generalization of skills learned in-game to real-life situations outside of the game. This is also the main difference between serious games and entertainment games; the latter is not meant for skills training.

Serious games integrate principles of learning pedagogy and game design to create immersive environments. This co-op aims to combine evidence-based learning theories and common motivational tools in game design to increase players' intrinsic motivation to engage in skills training. Additionally, the serious game aims to emulate real-life situations in its game environment to increase the generalizability of lessons taught in the program. While there are many considerations relevant to successful game design, this chapter outlines design elements that enhance motivation to play and engage in serious games, which is the main draw of serious games in bridging the existing gaps in treatment for youth with mental health concerns.

Immersive Storylines/Narratives

Creating a narrative is one of the most effective ways to increase players' motivation to engage in games. Good, integrated storylines help put target skills and goals into context, increasing enjoyment, player motivation, and immersion in the game. Character development of playable and non-playable characters can also provide a potential avenue for learning social skills and empathy. For example, players may identify with characters' backstories and actions or take on roles that help facilitate learning during gameplay (Marchiori et al., 2012). When learning opportunities are directly woven into the game narrative, players may experience intrinsic motivation to engage in learning (Baranowski et al., 2008; Lu et al., 2012). In turn, the players may apply these learned skills in real life, increasing the generalizability of in-game learning to real-life settings.

Goals Directed at Target Skills

As with all games, serious games utilize goals to facilitate players' learning and application of target skills, albeit for therapeutic purposes. Goals tend to fall into one of two classifications – primary end-goals and intermediate, or incremental, goals. Primary end-goals refer to goals required for game completion. In contrast, intermediate goals keep users engaged by providing consistent challenges and feedback on progress (Garris et al., 2002). Completing intermediate goals provides a sense of achievement when players successfully learn and apply skills needed to complete bigger tasks relevant to longer-term goals (Baranowski et al., 2008; Habgood & Ainsworth, 2011). This ensures consistent encouragement and validation of players' effort and maintains intrinsic motivation of players to continue playing the game, even when game difficulty is gradually increased. When paired with an immersive game narrative, goals become less mundane, increasing opportunities for learning and practicing skills. Consequently, this may help to increase the likelihood of actual change.

Feedback and Reward Systems

Consistent feedback and rewards are essential for learning and behavioral change. When integrating feedback and reward systems into serious games, developers must consider their effects on both intrinsic and extrinsic motivation (Habgood & Ainsworth, 2011). For example, visual and auditory cues that signal progress or good performance (e.g., sparkle and ring when characters level up), cumulative point summaries, or leaderboards make up some of the rewards frequently employed in commercial games. While this effectively reinforces player motivation in typical gaming contexts, learning theories suggest that they may not promote sustained and self-directed behavior change (Gagné & Deci, 2005). Often, the feedback on progress alone can act as a tremendous intrinsic reward for players. Such feedback can offer players a deep sense of achievement that extends beyond the game's context and boost players' intrinsic motivation to learn and apply taught skills in real life (Kapp, 2012). As such, a good mix of intrinsic and extrinsic rewards will help to ensure optimal play whereby players are sufficiently motivated to engage in the game and generalize skills out of the game.

Gradual Increments in Difficulty

To provide a platform for skills training for individuals who would benefit from but struggle with applying relevant skills in daily life situations, the focus of serious games should be on maximizing the learning of target skills via optimal engagement (Mishra & Gazzaley, 2014). In particular, negative feedback in response to failure can backfire and reduce player motivations to continue playing (Lepper & Chabay, 1985). This would diminish the utility of serious games in providing learning opportunities for youth with mental health concerns. As such, feedback and reward systems are often tied with game difficulty when considering game design elements for optimal player engagement. To facilitate learning, serious games must walk a tightrope between being too challenging and too easy. Serious games aim to achieve this balance by providing adequate challenges that players can reasonably expect to overcome, but with sufficient and incremental difficulty such that players continuously feel compelled to engage optimally with the game (Przybylski et al., 2010). This aligns with various theories in psychology, such as Vygotsky's Zone of Proximal Development (Vygotsky, 1978, 1980), and Csikszentmihalyi's state of "Flow" (Csikszentmihalyi et al., 2014; Nakamura & Csikszentmihalyi, 2014). Specifically, these theories suggest that learning and engagement in tasks are optimized when the learning is performed under sufficiently, but not excessively, difficult conditions. "Flow" theory suggests that concentration, interest, and enjoyment in tasks peak when people perceive a match between the difficulty of the task and their skill level (Shernoff et al., 2014). On the other hand, the Zone of Proximal Development suggests that optimal growth and learning occurs when children are placed in situations just slightly above their skill level but are supported with scaffolds to enable them to develop and grow their skills (Shabani et al., 2010). Following these, children can either be supported in-game by adult models or via game-play assistance (e.g., tutorial levels, temporary power-ups, or multiple lives). Serious games can structure and scaffold new behavior by gradually increasing game difficulty to match players' abilities.

While there are many other ways to increase the attractiveness of a game, such as the use of bright colors and multi-sensory experiences (e.g., tactile output on controllers in addition to visual and audio output), this chapter focuses on elements potentially useful in the context of mental health intervention. Game design elements aim to enhance patient motivation to engage in therapeutic learning and boost opportunities for learning in patients during play. These learning opportunities are contextualized to aid understanding, and structured to provide a clear step-by-step path for completion. Rewards and feedback can motivate patients to engage in-game activities and apply real-life lessons, while game difficulty is adjusted to match each patient's skill level and ensure optimal levels of stimulation and learning.

SERIOUS GAMES FOR MENTAL HEALTH IN SINGAPORE

In Singapore, the study of serious games as a potential therapeutic tool in child mental health is a growing field. At CGC, researchers hypothesized that serious games would help children and adolescents better engage with therapeutic content. The authors and colleagues have developed and tested serious games on various game platforms for usability and treatment efficacy across different mental health conditions.

Brain-Computer Interface: Cogo™Land

The earliest projects on serious games at CGC focused on using Brain-Computer Interfaces (BCIs) to help children with ADHD improve attention. A progressive series of games were developed to be played on an electroencephalogram (EEG) based BCI. In these games, electrical signals from the frontal and parietal regions of the brain are recorded via EEG leads placed on the child's head. These signals were filtered and separated into various frequency bands, such as theta, alpha, and beta waves. A machine learning model analyzed the EEG input as quantifiable markers of attention, which generated attention scores used to control players' game responses. Models unique to each player are generated by collecting EEG data while players perform attention and relaxation tasks during an initial calibration stage before playing the game. This constitutes a neuro-feedforward mechanism whereby players' attention levels are used to control the game directly.

The initial pilot study of the BCI project involved children with ADHD undergoing the BCI game sessions at the clinic twice weekly over ten weeks (Lim et al., 2010). Therapists were trained to position the EEG leads correctly and administer the game following a manualized protocol. The game's speed was programmed to be proportional to the child's attention level. Children were presented with a series of games in increasing difficulty as they progressed through each session. Therapists can adjust the difficulty of game tasks to ensure children stay optimally engaged during each 30-minute game session. After every second session, children complete two worksheets consisting of Mathematics and English questions tailored to their school grade to help children generalize learned attention-regulation skills to their learning. While the pilot study did not find statistically significant differences between the experimental and control groups in terms of change scores, there was still an improvement in the attention of children who completed 20 game sessions compared to the control group.

A subsequent version of the BCI game was developed following the completion of the initial pilot study (Lim et al., 2012). A wireless headband with mounted dry EEG electrodes that sent signals to the BCI via Bluetooth-enabled protocol replaced the original tethered EEG cap. Figure 1 illustrates the use of the wireless EEG headband.

Figure 1. A view of the BCI Cogo™Land game set-up
(Lim et al., 2012)

A similar neuro-feedforward mechanism was used in the updated BCI interface, with refinements to reduce signal noise from eye movement and increase the specificity of recorded EEG frequency bands. Twenty children with ADHD aged between 6 to 12 years old were recruited for this study. EEG head-bands worn around players' foreheads measured EEG signals from frontal regions of the brain. After completing calibration tasks, children played Cogo™Land, a computerized 3-dimensional graphic game developed for the study. Players controlled their avatars using the detected EEG signals. EEG signals were measured and fed into the BCI platform to compute a score measuring ADHD severity. This score was displayed on the player's screen, providing a reference to how much "concentration" players were putting in. Players must "concentrate" to move their avatar, and a higher concentration score would increase the speed of their avatar. The game's main goal was for players to navigate their avatar around a pre-set course in the fastest time possible. As players advanced through the BCI program, additional goals were added to increase the game's difficulty level. For example, at the intermediate difficulty level, players had to collect as many fruits as they could within the time limit, by pressing a key on the computer to make their avatars jump. At the highest difficulty level, players had to collect fruits in a pre-specified order presented on the game screen. Figure 2 illustrates the game interface and game-play.

Figure 2. Game interface of the Cogo™Land game
(Lim et al., 2012)

Players attended 30-minute sessions thrice-weekly over eight weeks. At the end of the main program, children were asked to return for booster sessions once a month for three months. Like the 2010 BCI Pilot, players were also asked to complete English and Mathematics worksheets after every alternate session to evaluate the generalizability of their learning to educational settings. This study found statistically significant reductions in parent-reported inattention, hyperactive-impulsive, and combined (inattention and hyperactivity-impulsivity symptoms) symptoms on the ADHD Rating Scale. These results support the potential use of BCI-based serious games as an attention-training intervention program for children with ADHD.

The positive results of the Cogo™Land trial encouraged researchers to pursue further studies on the use of Cogo™Land in children with co-occurring ASD and ADHD. The trial aimed to examine the efficacy of Cogo™Land in reducing inattention symptoms and improving social responsiveness in children with both ASD and ADHD. In this trial, a similar protocol to the previous Cogo™Land trial was adopted. Preparation to report findings in a journal article is underway, but results are promising. Following these encouraging findings, natural next steps in using the use of the Cogo™Land and the BCI-EEG platform would be in a take-home attention training format, specifically for children with

ADHD or attentional difficulties. Ongoing trials are being conducted on the feasibility and efficacy of a home-based Cogo™Land program.

Virtual Reality Games

The use of Virtual Reality (VR) technology in mental health has also been mooted as a way to augment traditional therapies (Boeldt et al., 2019). VR allows for the construction of a fully immersive, three-dimensional environment that allows people to engage and interact with virtual stimuli realistically. This can potentially enhance therapeutic engagement and learning via physiologically and emotionally evocative experiences that might be difficult to achieve in person (Jerdan et al., 2018). VR Exposure Therapy is an example of mental health treatment that utilizes VR technology to expose patients to feared stimuli or situations safely and acceptably (Hembree et al., 2003). In the field of serious games, the addition of VR technology can help to enhance the immersiveness of the game, increasing player engagement and motivation to continue playing. Additionally, VR environments modeled to mimic real-life settings potentially allow for better generalization of learned skills from game to real-life situations.

At CGC, VR games have been developed to teach youths Mindfulness strategies to cope with anxiety. The VR-Mindfulness project at CGC was conceptualized as a serious game that could potentially function as an intervention program for adolescents struggling with anxiety issues. Mindfulness-based interventions tend to be more experiential and consist of formal mindfulness practices such as body scan and breathing meditations. These exercises might be challenging for adolescents with clinically significant anxiety, as sustained practice is needed before benefits can be observed (Bergomi et al., 2015). Hence, adolescents will need to be highly motivated and disciplined to practice these skills to reap the benefits of mindfulness. The gamification of mindfulness practice in the VR-Mindfulness program helps adolescents engage in and stay motivated to continue their mindfulness practice.

The VR-Mindfulness program consists of 2 parts – a didactic mindfulness program to teach concepts and strategies used in Mindfulness-based anxiety regulation and a VR game involving players' reactions to 'avoid' oncoming rocks. Adolescents put on a portable EEG headband around their forehead, as well as a VR headset display. Each session consists of a 20-minute lesson on mindfulness concepts, followed by 10 minutes of game-play. During game-play, players are asked to respond to an oncoming rock by clicking a button corresponding to the direction of an arrow shown (i.e., left or right) for about 1 minute before being taken to a calming scene for 4-minutes. The game is programmed to track the player's performance via EEG measurements, reaction time, and accuracy. The speed of the oncoming rock is tied to players' performance in the game. Players are given feedback on their performance via a score on the screen. EEG measurements of arousal are taken, like in Cogo™Land, and determine whether players are taken from the game to the calming scene and vice versa. For example, if arousal levels are too high for a set duration (e.g., 30 seconds), the game will take players to the calming scene to calm down. Once arousal levels fall below a set level for a specific duration, players are taken back to the game to resume game-play. During the calming scene, adolescents are instructed to apply the mindfulness techniques taught in the lessons to regulate their arousal levels back to baseline. After undergoing a calibration run on the first session, adolescents are asked to attend a total of eight 30-minute sessions over four weeks. A trial of the VR-Mindfulness game is still underway.

Mobile Games

Given the ubiquity of mobile devices such as tablet computers and smartphones in Singapore (Infocomm Media Development Authority, 2019), mobile applications are a viable platform to host serious games for mental health. Mobile games are portable and convenient to use, making it extremely easy for children to engage in therapeutic learning from anywhere. At CGC, two serious games – RegnaTales and Autism Cognitive Rehabilitation program for Executive functioning skills (ACRES), were developed for use on mobile devices.

RegnaTales

RegnaTales (Ong et al., 2019), consisting of 6 mobile applications, was developed to help children learn anger management skills using a Cognitive-Behavioral framework. Specifically, RegnaTales was adapted from the Social Problem-Solving Skills Training (SPSST) for anger management (Ooi et al., 2007), a manualized intervention initially administered in-person via a workbook. SPSST was subsequently adapted into an internet-based game, Socialdrome (Coyle et al., 2011). Following positive feedback of playability in an early prototype (Tan et al., 2011), RegnaTales was developed in collaboration with a professional game development company.

RegnaTales was developed as a Role-Playing Game (RPG) set in a fantasy world caught between "light" and "dark" forces, where relatable situations help children apply skills learned in-game. Players navigate the RPG environment and are required to complete missions to complete the game. Missions involve acquiring and using skills such as identifying one's emotions, perspective-taking, and problem-solving. Games are designed to test and reinforce target anger management skills while remaining integrated within the in-game narrative to deliver an enjoyable and immersive experience. The first four installments of the RegnaTales series aim to teach various strategies for anger management such as emotional literacy, relaxation techniques, perspective-taking, reframing, and restructuring thoughts, as well as interpersonal effectiveness skills (e.g., assertiveness). The last two installments focus on generalizing learning outside of the game. These installments involve exercises for children to practice in real life, such as reminders to use anger management strategies and a log to monitor progress (Ong et al., 2019).

Players navigate their character through a storyline in which the main antagonist has kidnapped the main character's parents in his quest for world domination. The player must navigate through challenges to save his parents and complete the game. Non-playable characters are also included in the game to guide the player and encourage players to use learned skills and make "good" decisions despite temptations to act maladaptively. Rewards are also given to players via a "village elder" to encourage skill use. To keep players motivated, hints are available if players need help completing challenging missions. Players also get feedback on their performance via a "health" bar that is topped up when players do well and deducted from when players behave in an inappropriate, aggressive, or unhelpful manner. When players' health becomes too low, their character's movement is slowed down, and players must practice positive skills to recover. Players can also exchange health points for in-game currency to buy or upgrade their character's items. Figures 3 and 4 illustrate different tasks taught during game-play in RegnaTales.

Figure 3. An example of a deep breathing task being taught during game-play
(Ong et al., 2019)

Figure 4. An example of perspective-taking skills taught during game-play
(Ong et al., 2019)

Each of the six RegnaTales applications was developed and tested sequentially. For each app, children with a disruptive behavior disorder, such as ADHD, Conduct Disorder (CD), or Oppositional Defiance Disorder (ODD), were recruited to test the application. Typically developing children were also invited to test the app. Children were asked to play their assigned RegnaTales installment on a tablet computer for 50 minutes. Following their game session, they were administered questionnaires on user experience and questionnaires measuring aggression. In general, most children found the games enjoyable and playable, and were keen to continue using RegnaTales and apply learned skills outside of the game. Preliminary analyses also found a significant decrease in reactive and overall aggression immediately after children completed the game. These results offer some evidence on the efficacy of RegnaTales in helping children manage their anger and reduce anger-related aggression. A randomized controlled trial on the efficacy of RegnaTales for children referred for anger-management issues is in progress.

ACRES

ACRES was developed to function as a computerized cognitive rehabilitation program to help children with ASD improve their executive functioning skills. Executive function refers to a suite of higher-order cognitive processes that aid in goal-directed behavior, such as studying for an exam or traveling to a specified destination. Executive functioning skills include planning, impulse control, working memory, and flexible thinking. These skills are essential in helping individuals perform everyday tasks and live independently.

The behavioral problems that children with ASD face daily, such as the need for sameness, difficulties switching attention between tasks, have been hypothesized to be a result of deficits in executive function (Dawson et al., 2002). Additionally, children with ASD frequently report difficulties with everyday demands that involve time management, planning and organization, and coordinating multiple tasks and activities. These difficulties lead to overall impairment across separate contexts of home, school, and work. Notably, research has found that children with ASD have difficulties in 3 areas of executive function – Planning, Mental Flexibility, and Inhibitory Control (Hill, 2004).

Cognitive rehabilitation aims to help affected people cope with impairments in cognitive function, including executive function difficulties, by guiding them to learn and use compensatory strategies and skills (Morris, 2007). This helps to bolster overall functioning levels in various settings (Ylvisaker et al., 2003). Computerized cognitive rehabilitation programs have been developed and implemented in multiple populations facing a wide array of cognitive difficulties due to conditions like brain injury (Laatsch et al., 2007), brain cancer (Kesler et al., 2011) as well as neurodevelopmental disorders like ADHD (Tajik-Parvinchi et al., 2014; van der Oord et al., 2014). Studies have mostly found promising results, although there is little evidence that skills learned in these programs are generalized outside of the program

ACRES was developed by approaching a computerized cognitive rehabilitation program for ASD with a serious game design perspective. Tasks that would traditionally be repetitive and menial were transformed into a set of mini-games that emulate everyday tasks. For example, one collection of mini-games required players to pack their bags based on a pre-determined school schedule to train organization skills. In addition, to help players practice mental flexibility, certain levels would involve changes or additions to the calendar. These changes were introduced via "post-it" notes that players were prompted to check and adjust for during bag-packing. Figures 5 and 6 illustrate the gameplay in the Home mini-game.

Figure 5. Game interface during the Home Minigame. Players click on the day of the week corresponding to the day given at the top-most bar to activate a packing list. Relevant items are dragged from different "rooms" in the house into players' bags on the sidebar before players submit their answers

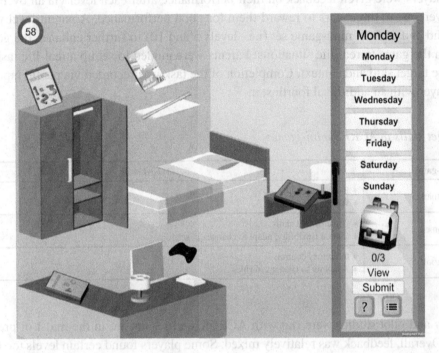

Figure 6. An example of a reward that players get for good task performance

Each set of mini-games emulated a different real-life setting and target skill. Table 1 describes the various mini-games and respective target skills. Difficulty levels were increased as players moved up each level. Players were given feedback on their performance after each level via an overall score and were also given one to three stars to reward them for good performance. A parent level was set up at the middle and end of each mini-game set (i.e., levels 5 and 10) to further enhance the generalization of skills from the game to real-life situations. Parents were guided to set up a real-life task for players relevant to the target skill and context. Completion of the task was recorded via parent input and would award the player with an additional fourth star.

Table 1. Target skills in ACRES mini-games

Mini-game	Target skill
Supermarket	• Planning • Working Memory
Home	• Organization skills • Mental flexibility; adapt to changes in schedule
School	• Inhibitory control • Adapting to changes in rules

Feasibility and pilot studies were run with ACRES, and results are in the midst of preparation for publication. Overall, feedback was relatively mixed. Some players found certain levels too tricky, while others found levels too easy and boring. Parents generally did not feel the parent component was enjoyable for them. This was evident when game usage data showed that parents rarely engaged in the game with their children.

RECOMMENDATIONS AND FUTURE WORK

In their experience with serious game research in mental health, the authors faced several difficulties in running research programs for serious game-based interventions for mental health. The lessons learned from the authors' struggles and reflections are summarized here to help future researchers design serious games and plan intervention programs for children.

Parent Buy-In is as Important as Child Buy-In

In pediatric mental health, the family and immediate support system around the child are typically involved in treatment to achieve best results. This means that serious games in child mental health need to appeal to and increase treatment engagement in both parents and children. In the authors' experience, most parents were keen to let their children try non-pharmacological treatment options. Children and adolescents were equally enthusiastic when presented with the option of "playing games" that would potentially help them. As expected in randomized controlled trials, parents tended to prefer being assigned to the experimental group instead of a waitlist control group. However, the administration of such trials to establish the efficacy of the game-based programs are not without challenges. For the

BCI-based programs, participants are required to make multiple visits to the clinic per week, so it was not surprising that scheduling issues and inconvenience were commonly–cited as reasons for premature dropping-out of the trials. On the other hand, in contrast to the rationale of convenience, some parents were less receptive to having the serious game programs be administered at home. While the authors hypothesize that this is related to the requirement of supervision and management of devices, further exploration of these consumer preferences would be necessary.

Serious game-based interventions that actively involve parents either as a moderator of a child's in-game responses, or as a co-player in the game also need to appeal to and engage parents. Like any other player, parent players need to be motivated to continuously engage in the game for parent interventions to work. The authors see the importance of parent motivation (or lack thereof) in one of their studies, where most enrolled parents did not complete the parent levels with their children, and parents who did engage in the parent levels did so only inconsistently. Feedback on parent levels was that they were boring and not engaging for parents. A significant percentage of parents reported expectations of independence and immediate generalization from the child as a consequence of game-play. Hence, as with entertainment games, serious games must be enjoyable for all involved players for maximum engagement.

Acceptance towards games as a platform for therapeutic change aside from "educational" games is considerably lukewarm. In particular, Singaporean parents may have a hyper-focus on academic performance; i.e., some parents may be hesitant to commit their children to game-play despite it being a means of treatment due to fears that their children's academic performance would be negatively impacted. However, researchers must also be careful when labeling games as educational or medical. While pitching the games as a medium of learning might help get some parents on board, the same can backfire when used with children and undermine the child's motivation to engage in the game (Shen et al., 2009). Hence, for serious games to be effective, developers have to consider both parent and child motivations and find a balance between the two to achieve better overall buy-in. Specifically, impressions of the game need to fit parent expectations of being helpful, productive, and useful while also serving child expectations of being enjoyable and engaging.

As researchers and developers explore the feasibility and receptivity of home protocols, the impact of cost on consumer receptivity towards serious game programs would require further consideration. Additionally, non-adherence to sessions or problems with treatment fidelity when the programs are administered at home may also limit the efficacy of the treatment. Hence, adjustments to treatment protocol would be important for optimal home use. These are pertinent issues in mobile health research (Eysenbach, 2005). Researchers can expect that serious game research using mobile games would face similar problems.

Maintaining Motivation to Play Requires Constant Work

The authors noted a low adherence to the prescribed duration and frequency for take-home serious game programs such as the ACRES. For example, instead of adhering to the recommended daily duration of play over one month, ACRES participants typically "binge-played" (i.e., completed the whole game at home in one sitting). Some other participants played only intermittently and "binge-played" the game towards the end of the program. Similarly, parents were rarely interested in being involved in the therapeutic games and supervision. The BCI and VR-Mindfulness programs were appointment-based, and researchers experienced difficulties with missed appointments and non-adherence to prescribed schedules of gameplay. It was often difficult to schedule and reschedule clinic visits to ensure that children played the games at the specified frequency.

Approaching this problem from a serious game design perspective, games must hence be appealing enough to encourage consistent play and have built-in safeguards against protocol deviations. Maintenance and adherence are secondary objectives that feed into the achievement of primary game objectives and hence can also be gamified. For example, notifications and reminders can be built into games to remind patients to play the game consistently. Rewards, such as premium in-game currency (e.g., diamonds and gold), can also be given out for achieving maintenance goals to encourage consistent play. In order to prevent "binge-playing" of serious games and promote a steady pattern of play adhering to prescribed intervention protocols, game-play can be limited via a daily "energy" limit. Players expend "energy" for each level they play and cannot continue after exhausting their energy, until their character has rested sufficiently (i.e., until the next day).

Actual motivation to play the games was also impeded by boredom, especially when tasks are repetitive and laborious. For skills training programs that involve repetition and are less stimulating, increasing the number of game levels and rewards would allow developers to incorporate novel obstacles. This would help to increase difficulty levels and stimulation for players. Additionally, there needs to be an adequate number of game levels so that increments in difficulty can be noticeable but not overwhelming to players. For complex tasks, games can offer more support to players in the form of hints or power-ups. These can be provided when players have difficulties completing game tasks, or can be bought with in-game currency earned from previous levels and consistent play.

Who Should Pay for Serious Games?

Game development is resource-intensive and it is often taxing for development teams to build entire games from scratch. Additionally, constant updates are needed to troubleshoot bugs and add new game content so that players remain motivated to play the game. This requires entire development teams to continually monitor application performance, troubleshoot problems, and conceptualize and develop new game content. The sustainability of this process needs to be considered. While the cost to patients needs to be kept as low as possible, game developers also need to be able to fund their operations profitably.

Game equipment, such as VR headsets and EEG headbands, can also be expensive in a business-to-consumer model. A potential solution to pay game developers while minimizing costs to patients would be via a business-to-business model. Healthcare providers could buy serious games and equipment directly from developers and loan them to patients as a prescribed healthcare intervention. This is similar to how some medical technologies are used today, such as 24-hour Holter monitors in cardiology clinics. Patients pay for cardiologists to assess potential heart rhythm problems, and cardiologists use medical tools to achieve that goal. As a prescriptive tool, healthcare subsidies or national insurance programs may cover the cost of serious games. However, national regulatory bodies lack information that would prompt decisive action. Current research findings are limited by the small number of studies on the topic (David et al., 2020). Most studies focus on user experience and feedback rather than actual changes experienced in the patient. The results from these usability studies do not give clinicians and national regulatory bodies adequate information about the utility and cost-effectiveness of serious games in mental healthcare. Future studies on the utility of serious games need to examine the therapeutic efficacy and cost-effectiveness of these games to better inform clinicians in making decisions that balance effectiveness and cost concerns.

CONCLUSION

Serious games offer huge potential in changing how mental health professionals approach skills training and behavioral change in therapy. Incorporating game design elements meant to increase player motivation in therapy processes, such as skills acquisition, skills practice, and progress monitoring, help to improve treatment engagement in children and adolescents. Specifically, the use of immersive storylines to engage players and frame skill-specific goals, in-game feedback and reward systems, and gradual increments in difficulty all play a role in keeping players engaged and invested in game-play. These are invaluable to the design of mental health interventions, especially those for children and adolescents, to increase patient motivation to engage in therapy. The potential for convenient, affordable, and effective treatment is also boosted by the portability of current game technologies, such as mobile games and web-based applications. This could bridge the gap in existing mental healthcare for children and adolescents, where patients tend to feel unmotivated to engage in repetitive and difficult tasks in therapy. Additionally, the portability of serious games would help to increase overall access to treatment to children and adolescents.

In about a decade's worth of work with serious games at CGC, researchers have explored serious games on various platforms and experienced different results from each. While this chapter has only covered serious games hosted on computerized platforms (i.e., computers and mobile devices), the authors believe that serious games for mental health treatment do not have to be high-tech. High-tech games have their own set of considerations as opposed to low-tech games such as board games. For example, technological limitations such as game-device compatibility (e.g., Apple iOS systems versus Android operating systems) and data security concerns would likely be more relevant to high-tech games than low-tech games. These concerns would constitute another topic of discussion on their own. Most importantly, serious games must not be treated as simple adaptations of treatment delivery, but rather as games rooted in treatment goals. This means that serious games must be entertaining and engaging to best motivate players to play consistently and as specified by treatment protocol. This is the main advantage games have over traditional skills training programs for mental health, and will likely be the active ingredient in enhancing the success of skills training in mental health.

While serious games may serve as an innovative approach in mental health treatment, it may still be premature in terms of what serious games currently can offer (David et al., 2020). The skills and strategies incorporated in serious games may be able to help people change the way they cope with stressors in their lives in a more light-hearted manner. However, mental health treatment has never been a one-size-fits-all solution. The involvement of a human therapist and the therapeutic alliance inherent in traditional therapy can be hard to recreate in serious games. It would be helpful to consider having serious games as a complement to conventional therapy, whereby the therapist may incorporate the serious games program in the individualized treatment. At the same time, the therapist can also act as a facilitator to check in on the utilization and adherence in the use of the serious game component.

It might also be worth exploring the use of serious games as an educational tool to improve mental health literacy and reduce stigma more engagingly. This approach focuses on upstream processes of awareness, literacy, and stigma, and would potentially lead to positive cascades in the overall mental health of the population. Serious games have demonstrated their value as a tool to teach skills and knowledge that would otherwise be difficult to engage people in, and could likely support preventative efforts in public mental health campaigns. The authors look forward to more work in these areas in the future.

ACKNOWLEDGMENT

This research studies presented in this chapter was supported by the Lee Foundation [study reference numbers 2018/00693; 2019/00085; 2015/00841]; the National Medical Research Council [grant numbers CIRG11nov087; NIG11may025; 477-2015]; the Rehabilitation Research Institute of Singapore [grant number RRG1/16002]; and the National Research Foundation, Singapore [grant number NRF2010NRF-POC002-017].

REFERENCES

Abdin, E., Chong, S. A., Ragu, V., Vaingankar, J. A., Shafie, S., Verma, S., Ganesan, G., Tan, K. B., Heng, D., & Subramaniam, M. (2021). The economic burden of mental disorders among adults in Singapore: Evidence from the 2016 Singapore Mental Health Study. *Journal of Mental Health (Abingdon, England)*, *0*(0), 1–8. doi:10.1080/09638237.2021.1952958 PMID:34338569

American Psychiatric Association. (2013). *Diagnostic and Statistical Manual of Mental Disorders (DSM-5®)*. American Psychiatric Pub.

Andersson, G., & Cuijpers, P. (2009). Internet-Based and Other Computerized Psychological Treatments for Adult Depression: A Meta-Analysis. *Cognitive Behaviour Therapy*, *38*(4), 196–205. doi:10.1080/16506070903318960 PMID:20183695

Andrews, G., Cuijpers, P., Craske, M. G., McEvoy, P., & Titov, N. (2010). Computer Therapy for the Anxiety and Depressive Disorders Is Effective, Acceptable and Practical Health Care: A Meta-Analysis. *PLoS One*, *5*(10), e13196. doi:10.1371/journal.pone.0013196 PMID:20967242

Baranowski, T., Buday, R., Thompson, D. I., & Baranowski, J. (2008). Playing for Real: Video Games and Stories for Health-Related Behavior Change. *American Journal of Preventive Medicine*, *34*(1), 74–82.e10. doi:10.1016/j.amepre.2007.09.027 PMID:18083454

Bergomi, C., Tschacher, W., & Kupper, Z. (2015). Meditation Practice and Self-Reported Mindfulness: A Cross-Sectional Investigation of Meditators and Non-Meditators Using the Comprehensive Inventory of Mindfulness Experiences (CHIME). *Mindfulness*, *6*(6), 1411–1421. doi:10.100712671-015-0415-6

Boeldt, D., McMahon, E., McFaul, M., & Greenleaf, W. (2019). Using Virtual Reality Exposure Therapy to Enhance Treatment of Anxiety Disorders: Identifying Areas of Clinical Adoption and Potential Obstacles. *Frontiers in Psychiatry*, *10*, 773. doi:10.3389/fpsyt.2019.00773 PMID:31708821

Cheek, C., Fleming, T., Lucassen, M. F., Bridgman, H., Stasiak, K., Shepherd, M., & Orpin, P. (2015). Integrating Health Behavior Theory and Design Elements in Serious Games. *JMIR Mental Health*, *2*(2), e11. doi:10.2196/mental.4133 PMID:26543916

Corrigan, P. (2004). How stigma interferes with mental health care. *The American Psychologist*, *59*(7), 614–625. doi:10.1037/0003-066X.59.7.614 PMID:15491256

Coyle, D., McGlade, N., Doherty, G., & O'Reilly, G. (2011). *Exploratory evaluations of a computer game supporting cognitive behavioural therapy for adolescents*. Academic Press.

Csikszentmihalyi, M., Abuhamdeh, S., & Nakamura, J. (2014). Flow. In M. Csikszentmihalyi (Ed.), *Flow and the Foundations of Positive Psychology: The Collected Works of Mihaly Csikszentmihalyi* (pp. 227–238). Springer Netherlands. doi:10.1007/978-94-017-9088-8_15

Cuijpers, P., Donker, T., Johansson, R., Mohr, D. C., van Straten, A., & Andersson, G. (2011). Self-Guided Psychological Treatment for Depressive Symptoms: A Meta-Analysis. *PLoS One, 6*(6), e21274. doi:10.1371/journal.pone.0021274 PMID:21712998

David, O. A., Costescu, C., Cardos, R., & Mogoaşe, C. (2020). How Effective are Serious Games for Promoting Mental Health and Health Behavioral Change in Children and Adolescents? A Systematic Review and Meta-analysis. *Child and Youth Care Forum, 49*(6), 817–838. doi:10.100710566-020-09566-1

Dawson, G., Webb, S., Schellenberg, G. D., Dager, S., Friedman, S., Aylward, E., & Richards, T. (2002). Defining the broader phenotype of autism: Genetic, brain, and behavioral perspectives. *Development and Psychopathology, 14*(3), 581–611. doi:10.1017/S0954579402003103 PMID:12349875

de Jong, P. J., Sportel, B. E., de Hullu, E., & Nauta, M. H. (2012). Co-occurrence of social anxiety and depression symptoms in adolescence: Differential links with implicit and explicit self-esteem? *Psychological Medicine, 42*(3), 475–484. doi:10.1017/S0033291711001358 PMID:21798114

Dean, S., Britt, E., Bell, E., Stanley, J., & Collings, S. (2016). Motivational interviewing to enhance adolescent mental health treatment engagement: A randomized clinical trial. *Psychological Medicine, 46*(9), 1961–1969. doi:10.1017/S0033291716000568 PMID:27045520

Department of Statistics. Singapore. (2021, July 7). *Singapore Population*. Department of Statistics, Singapore. https://www.singstat.gov.sg/modules/infographics/population

Dickey, M. D. (2005). Engaging by design: How engagement strategies in popular computer and video games can inform instructional design. *Educational Technology Research and Development, 53*(2), 67–83. doi:10.1007/BF02504866

Dietrich, K. N., Eskenazi, B., Schantz, S., Yolton, K., Rauh, V. A., Johnson, C. B., Alkon, A., Canfield, R. L., Pessah, I. N., & Berman, R. F. (2005). Principles and Practices of Neurodevelopmental Assessment in Children: Lessons Learned from the Centers for ' 'Children's Environmental Health and Disease Prevention Research. *Environmental Health Perspectives, 113*(10), 1437–1446. doi:10.1289/ehp.7672 PMID:16203260

Eysenbach, G. (2005). The Law of Attrition. *Journal of Medical Internet Research, 7*(1), e11. doi:10.2196/jmir.7.1.e11 PMID:15829473

Gagné, M., & Deci, E. L. (2005). Self-determination theory and work motivation. *Journal of Organizational Behavior, 26*(4), 331–362. doi:10.1002/job.322

Garris, R., Ahlers, R., & Driskell, J. E. (2002). Games, Motivation, and Learning: A Research and Practice Model. *Simulation & Gaming, 33*(4), 441–467. doi:10.1177/1046878102238607

Gentile, D. A., & Walsh, D. A. (2002). A normative study of family media habits. *Journal of Applied Developmental Psychology, 23*(2), 157–178. doi:10.1016/S0193-3973(02)00102-8

Goodman, A., Joyce, R., & Smith, J. P. (2011). The long shadow cast by childhood physical and mental problems on adult life. *Proceedings of the National Academy of Sciences of the United States of America, 108*(15), 6032–6037. doi:10.1073/pnas.1016970108 PMID:21444801

Granic, I., Lobel, A., & Engels, R. C. M. E. (2014). The benefits of playing video games. *The American Psychologist, 69*(1), 66–78. doi:10.1037/a0034857 PMID:24295515

Habgood, M. P. J., & Ainsworth, S. E. (2011). Motivating Children to Learn Effectively: Exploring the Value of Intrinsic Integration in Educational Games. *Journal of the Learning Sciences, 20*(2), 169–206. doi:10.1080/10508406.2010.508029

Harpin, V., Mazzone, L., Raynaud, J. P., Kahle, J., & Hodgkins, P. (2016). Long-Term Outcomes of ADHD: A Systematic Review of Self-Esteem and Social Function. *Journal of Attention Disorders, 20*(4), 295–305. doi:10.1177/1087054713486516 PMID:23698916

Hembree, E. A., Rauch, S. A. M., & Foa, E. B. (2003). Beyond the manual: The ' 'insider's guide to Prolonged Exposure therapy for PTSD. *Cognitive and Behavioral Practice, 10*(1), 22–30. doi:10.1016/S1077-7229(03)80005-6

Hill, E. L. (2004). Executive dysfunction in autism. *Trends in Cognitive Sciences, 8*(1), 26–32. doi:10.1016/j.tics.2003.11.003 PMID:14697400

Holdsworth, E., Bowen, E., Brown, S., & Howat, D. (2014). Client engagement in psychotherapeutic treatment and associations with client characteristics, therapist characteristics, and treatment factors. *Clinical Psychology Review, 34*(5), 428–450. doi:10.1016/j.cpr.2014.06.004 PMID:25000204

Hutchby, I., & O'Reilly, M. (2010). ' 'Children's participation and the familial moral order in family therapy. *Discourse Studies, 12*(1), 49–64. doi:10.1177/1461445609357406

Infocomm Media Development Authority. (2019, August 8). *Mobile Penetration Rate*. Data.Gov.Sg. https://data.gov.sg/dataset/mobile-penetration-rate

Infocomm Media Development Authority. (2020, March 11). *Infocomm Usage-Households and Individuals*. Infocomm Media Development Authority. https://www.imda.gov.sg/infocomm-media-landscape/research-and-statistics/infocomm-usage-households-and-individuals

Inkster, B., Sarda, S., & Subramanian, V. (2018). An Empathy-Driven, Conversational Artificial Intelligence Agent (Wysa) for Digital Mental Well-Being: Real-World Data Evaluation Mixed-Methods Study. *JMIR mHealth and uHealth, 6*(11), e12106. doi:10.2196/12106 PMID:30470676

Jerdan, S. W., Grindle, M., van Woerden, H. C., & Kamel Boulos, M. N. (2018). Head-Mounted Virtual Reality and Mental Health: Critical Review of Current Research. *JMIR Serious Games, 6*(3), e14. doi:10.2196/games.9226 PMID:29980500

Kapp, K. M. (2012). *The Gamification of Learning and Instruction: Game-based Methods and Strategies for Training and Education*. John Wiley & Sons.

Kesler, S. R., Lacayo, N. J., & Jo, B. (2011). A pilot study of an online cognitive rehabilitation program for executive function skills in children with cancer-related brain injury. *Brain Injury: [BI], 25*(1), 101–112. doi:10.3109/02699052.2010.536194 PMID:21142826

Kessler, R. C., Angermeyer, M., Anthony, J. C., De Graaf, R., Demyttenaere, K., Gasquet, I., De Gi-rolamo, G., Gluzman, S., Gureje, O., Haro, J. M., Kawakami, N., Karam, A., Levinson, D., Medina Mora, M. E., Oakley Browne, M. A., Posada-Villa, J., Stein, D. J., Adley Tsang, C. H., Aguilar-Gaxiola, S., ... Üstün, T. B. (2007). Lifetime prevalence and age-of-onset distributions of mental disorders in the World Health ' 'Organization's World Mental Health Survey Initiative. *World Psychiatry; Official Journal of the World Psychiatric Association (WPA)*, *6*(3), 168–176. PMID:18188442

Kessler, R. C., Berglund, P. A., Bruce, M. L., Koch, J. R., Laska, E. M., Leaf, P. J., Manderscheid, R. W., Rosenheck, R. A., Walters, E. E., & Wang, P. S. (2001). The prevalence and correlates of untreated serious mental illness. *Health Services Research*, *36*(6 Pt 1), 987–1007. PMID:11775672

Laatsch, L., Harrington, D., Hotz, G., Marcantuono, J., Mozzoni, M. P., Walsh, V., & Hersey, K. P. (2007). An Evidence-based Review of Cognitive and Behavioral Rehabilitation Treatment Studies in Children With Acquired Brain Injury. *The Journal of Head Trauma Rehabilitation*, *22*(4), 248–256. doi:10.1097/01.HTR.0000281841.92720.0a PMID:17667068

Lepper, M. R., & Chabay, R. W. (1985). Intrinsic Motivation and instruction: Conflicting Views on the Role of Motivational Processes in Computer-Based Education. *Educational Psychologist*, *20*(4), 217–230. doi:10.120715326985ep2004_6

Levy, S. E., Giarelli, E., Lee, L.-C., Schieve, L. A., Kirby, R. S., Cunniff, C., Nicholas, J., Reaven, J., & Rice, C. E. (2010). Autism Spectrum Disorder and Co-occurring Developmental, Psychiatric, and Medical Conditions Among Children in Multiple Populations of the United States. *Journal of Developmental and Behavioral Pediatrics*, *31*(4), 267–275. doi:10.1097/DBP.0b013e3181d5d03b PMID:20431403

Lim, C. G., Lee, T. S., Guan, C., Fung, D. S. S., Cheung, Y. B., Teng, S. S. W., Zhang, H., & Krishnan, K. R. (2010). Effectiveness of a brain-computer interface based programme for the treatment of ADHD: A pilot study. *Psychopharmacology Bulletin*, *43*(1), 73–82. PMID:20581801

Lim, C. G., Lee, T. S., Guan, C., Fung, D. S. S., Zhao, Y., Teng, S. S. W., Zhang, H., & Krishnan, K. R. R. (2012). A brain-computer interface based attention training program for treating attention deficit hyperactivity disorder. *PLoS One*, *7*(10), e46692. doi:10.1371/journal.pone.0046692 PMID:23115630

Link, B. G., & Phelan, J. C. (2001). Conceptualizing Stigma. *Annual Review of Sociology*, *27*(1), 363–385. doi:10.1146/annurev.soc.27.1.363

Link, B. G., Struening, E. L., Neese-Todd, S., Asmussen, S., & Phelan, J. C. (2001). Stigma as a Barrier to Recovery: The Consequences of Stigma for the Self-Esteem of People With Mental Illnesses. *Psychiatric Services (Washington, D.C.)*, *52*(12), 1621–1626. doi:10.1176/appi.ps.52.12.1621 PMID:11726753

Lu, A. S., Thompson, D., Baranowski, J., Buday, R., & Baranowski, T. (2012). Story Immersion in a Health Videogame for Childhood Obesity Prevention. *Games for Health Journal*, *1*(1), 37–44. doi:10.1089/g4h.2011.0011 PMID:24066276

Lund, C., De Silva, M., Plagerson, S., Cooper, S., Chisholm, D., Das, J., Knapp, M., & Patel, V. (2011). Poverty and mental disorders: Breaking the cycle in low-income and middle-income countries. *Lancet*, *378*(9801), 1502–1514. doi:10.1016/S0140-6736(11)60754-X PMID:22008425

Marchiori, E. J., Torrente, J., del Blanco, Á., Moreno-Ger, P., Sancho, P., & Fernández-Manjón, B. (2012). A narrative metaphor to facilitate educational game authoring. *Computers & Education, 58*(1), 590–599. doi:10.1016/j.compedu.2011.09.017

Ministry of Health Singapore. (2020). *Healthier Together: Partnering Singaporeans for Better Health*. Ministry of Health, Singapore. https://www.moh.gov.sg/docs/librariesprovider5/cos2020/cos-booklet-2020.pdf

Ministry of Health Singapore, Epidemiology & Disease Control Division & Institute for Health Metrics and Evaluation. (2019). *The burden of disease in Singapore, 1990-2017 report: An overview of the global burden of disease study 2017 results*. IMHE.

Mishra, J., & Gazzaley, A. (2014). Harnessing the neuroplastic potential of the human brain & the future of cognitive rehabilitation. *Frontiers in Human Neuroscience, 0*. Advance online publication. doi:10.3389/fnhum.2014.00218 PMID:24782745

Morris, J. (2007). Cognitive Rehabilitation: Where We Are and What is on the Horizon. *Physical Medicine and Rehabilitation Clinics of North America, 18*(1), 27–42. doi:10.1016/j.pmr.2006.11.003 PMID:17292811

Mrug, S., Molina, B. S. G., Hoza, B., Gerdes, A. C., Hinshaw, S. P., Hechtman, L., & Arnold, L. E. (2012). Peer Rejection and Friendships in Children with Attention-Deficit/Hyperactivity Disorder: Contributions to Long-Term Outcomes. *Journal of Abnormal Child Psychology, 40*(6), 1013–1026. doi:10.100710802-012-9610-2 PMID:22331455

Murali, V., & Oyebode, F. (2004). Poverty, social inequality and mental health. *Advances in Psychiatric Treatment, 10*(3), 216–224. doi:10.1192/apt.10.3.216

Nakamura, J., & Csikszentmihalyi, M. (2014). The Concept of Flow. In M. Csikszentmihalyi (Ed.), *Flow and the Foundations of Positive Psychology: The Collected Works of Mihaly Csikszentmihalyi* (pp. 239–263). Springer Netherlands. doi:10.1007/978-94-017-9088-8_16

Newman, M. G., Szkodny, L. E., Llera, S. J., & Przeworski, A. (2011). A review of technology-assisted self-help and minimal contact therapies for anxiety and depression: Is human contact necessary for therapeutic efficacy? *Clinical Psychology Review, 31*(1), 89–103. doi:10.1016/j.cpr.2010.09.008 PMID:21130939

Okumura, Y., Sugiyama, N., & Noda, T. (2018). Timely follow-up visits after psychiatric hospitalization and readmission in schizophrenia and bipolar disorder in Japan. *Psychiatry Research, 270*, 490–495. doi:10.1016/j.psychres.2018.10.020 PMID:30326432

Olusanya, B. O., Davis, A. C., Wertlieb, D., Boo, N.-Y., Nair, M. K. C., Halpern, R., Kuper, H., Breinbauer, C., de Vries, P. J., Gladstone, M., Halfon, N., Kancherla, V., Mulaudzi, M. C., Kakooza-Mwesige, A., Ogbo, F. A., Olusanya, J. O., Williams, A. N., Wright, S. M., Manguerra, H., ... Kassebaum, N. J. (2018). Developmental disabilities among children younger than 5 years in 195 countries and territories, 1990–2016: A systematic analysis for the Global Burden of Disease Study 2016. *The Lancet. Global Health, 6*(10), e1100–e1121. doi:10.1016/S2214-109X(18)30309-7 PMID:30172774

Ong, B. (2017). Inaugural Chee Kuan Tsee Lecture: Mental Health Care for the 21st Century. *Annals of the Academy of Medicine, Singapore, 46*(6), 5. PMID:28733694

Ong, J. G., Lim-Ashworth, N. S., Ooi, Y. P., Boon, J. S., Ang, R. P., Goh, D. H., Ong, S. H., & Fung, D. S. (2019). An Interactive Mobile App Game to Address Aggression (RegnaTales): Pilot Quantitative Study. *JMIR Serious Games*, *7*(2), e13242. doi:10.2196/13242 PMID:31066682

Ooi, Y. P., Ang, R., Fung, D. S. S., Wong, G., & Cai, Y. (2007). Effects of CBT on children with disruptive behaviour disorders: Findings from a Singapore study. *ASEAN Journal of Psychiatry*, *8*(2), 71–81.

Oshotse, C. O., Bosworth, H. B., & Zullig, L. L. (2020). Treatment Engagement and Adherence. In A. Hadler, S. Sutton, & L. Osterberg (Eds.), The Wiley Handbook of Healthcare Treatment Engagement (pp. 15–32). John Wiley & Sons, Ltd. doi:10.1002/9781119129530.ch1

Pang, S., Liu, J., Mahesh, M., Chua, B. Y., Shahwan, S., Lee, S. P., Vaingankar, J. A., Abdin, E., Fung, D. S. S., Chong, S. A., & Subramaniam, M. (2017). Stigma among Singaporean youth: A cross-sectional study on adolescent attitudes towards serious mental illness and social tolerance in a multiethnic population. *BMJ Open*, *7*(10), e016432. doi:10.1136/bmjopen-2017-016432 PMID:29042379

Pelham, W. E. III, Page, T. F., Altszuler, A. R., Gnagy, E. M., Molina, B. S. G., & Pelham, W. E. Jr. (2020). The long-term financial outcome of children diagnosed with ADHD. *Journal of Consulting and Clinical Psychology*, *88*(2), 160–171. doi:10.1037/ccp0000461 PMID:31789549

Przybylski, A. K., Rigby, C. S., & Ryan, R. M. (2010). A Motivational Model of Video Game Engagement. *Review of General Psychology*, *14*(2), 154–166. doi:10.1037/a0019440

Seligman, L. D., & Ollendick, T. H. (1998). Comorbidity of Anxiety and Depression in Children and Adolescents: An Integrative Review. *Clinical Child and Family Psychology Review*, *1*(2), 125–144. doi:10.1023/A:1021887712873 PMID:11324302

Shabani, K., Khatib, M., & Ebadi, S. (2010). Vygotsky's Zone of Proximal Development: Instructional Implications and Teachers' Professional Development. *English Language Teaching*, *3*(4), 237. doi:10.5539/elt.v3n4p237

Shaw, M., Hodgkins, P., Caci, H., Young, S., Kahle, J., Woods, A. G., & Arnold, L. E. (2012). A systematic review and analysis of long-term outcomes in attention deficit hyperactivity disorder: Effects of treatment and non-treatment. *BMC Medicine*, *10*(1), 99. doi:10.1186/1741-7015-10-99 PMID:22947230

Shen, C., Wang, H., & Ritterfeld, U. (2009). Serious Games and Seriously Fun Games: Can They Be One and the Same? In U. Ritterfeld, M. Cody, & P. Vorderer (Eds.), *Serious Games: Mechanisms and Effects* (1st ed., pp. 48–62). Routledge.

Shernoff, D. J., Csikszentmihalyi, M., Schneider, B., & Shernoff, E. S. (2014). Student Engagement in High School Classrooms from the Perspective of Flow Theory. In M. Csikszentmihalyi (Ed.), *Applications of Flow in Human Development and Education: The Collected Works of Mihaly Csikszentmihalyi* (pp. 475–494). Springer Netherlands. doi:10.1007/978-94-017-9094-9_24

Simonoff, E., Pickles, A., Charman, T., Chandler, S., Loucas, T., & Baird, G. (2008). Psychiatric disorders in children with autism spectrum disorders: Prevalence, comorbidity, and associated factors in a population-derived sample. *Journal of the American Academy of Child and Adolescent Psychiatry*, *47*(8), 921–929. doi:10.1097/CHI.0b013e318179964f PMID:18645422

Singapore Land Authority. (2021, June 23). *Total Land Area of Singapore*. Data.Gov.Sg. https://data.gov.sg/dataset/total-land-area-of-singapore

Smart Nation and Digital Government Office. (2021, May 11). *Initiatives: Health*. Smart Nation Singapore. https://www.smartnation.gov.sg/what-is-smart-nation/initiatives

Subramaniam, M., Abdin, E., Vaingankar, J. A., Shafie, S., Chua, B. Y., Sambasivam, R., Zhang, Y. J., Shahwan, S., Chang, S., Chua, H. C., Verma, S., James, L., Kwok, K. W., Heng, D., & Chong, S. A. (2019). Tracking the mental health of a nation: Prevalence and correlates of mental disorders in the second Singapore mental health study. *Epidemiology and Psychiatric Sciences, 29*, e29. doi:10.1017/S2045796019000179 PMID:30947763

Tajik-Parvinchi, D., Wright, L., & Schachar, R. (2014). Cognitive Rehabilitation for Attention Deficit/Hyperactivity Disorder (ADHD): Promises and Problems. *Journal of the Canadian Academy of Child and Adolescent Psychiatry, 23*(3), 207–217. PMID:25320614

Tan, J. L., Goh, D. H.-L., Ang, R. P., & Huan, V. S. (2011). Child-centered interaction in the design of a game for social skills intervention. *Computers in Entertainment, 9*(1), 2:1-2:17. doi:10.1145/1953005.1953007

Thompson, S. J., Bender, K., Lantry, J., & Flynn, P. M. (2007). Treatment Engagement: Building Therapeutic Alliance in Home-Based Treatment with Adolescents and their Families. *Contemporary Family Therapy, 29*(1–2), 39–55. doi:10.100710591-007-9030-6 PMID:20556209

Tsai, L. Y. (2014). Prevalence of Comorbid Psychiatric Disorders in Children and Adolescents with Autism Spectrum Disorder. *Journal of Experimental and Clinical Medicine (Taiwan), 6*(6), 179–186. doi:10.1016/j.jecm.2014.10.005

van der Oord, S., Ponsioen, A. J. G. B., Geurts, H. M., Brink, E. L. T., & Prins, P. J. M. (2014). A Pilot Study of the Efficacy of a Computerized Executive Functioning Remediation Training With Game Elements for Children With ADHD in an Outpatient Setting: Outcome on Parent- and Teacher-Rated Executive Functioning and ADHD Behavior. *Journal of Attention Disorders, 18*(8), 699–712. doi:10.1177/1087054712453167 PMID:22879577

van Steensel, F. J. A., Bögels, S. M., & Perrin, S. (2011). Anxiety Disorders in Children and Adolescents with Autistic Spectrum Disorders: A Meta-Analysis. *Clinical Child and Family Psychology Review, 14*(3), 302–317. doi:10.100710567-011-0097-0 PMID:21735077

Vannucchi, G., Masi, G., Toni, C., Dell'Osso, L., Erfurth, A., & Perugi, G. (2014). Bipolar disorder in adults with ' 'Asperger's Syndrome: A systematic review. *Journal of Affective Disorders, 168*, 151–160. doi:10.1016/j.jad.2014.06.042 PMID:25046741

Vygotsky, L. (1978). Interaction between learning and development. *Readings on the Development of Children, 23*(3), 34–41.

Vygotsky, L. (1980). *Mind in Society: The Development of Higher Psychological Processes*. Harvard University Press. doi:10.2307/j.ctvjf9vz4

Williams, A. D., & Andrews, G. (2013). The Effectiveness of Internet Cognitive Behavioural Therapy (iCBT) for Depression in Primary Care: A Quality Assurance Study. *PLoS One*, *8*(2), e57447. doi:10.1371/journal.pone.0057447 PMID:23451231

Williams, L. W., Matson, J. L., Beighley, J. S., Rieske, R. D., & Adams, H. L. (2014). Comorbid symptoms in toddlers diagnosed with autism spectrum disorder with the DSM-IV-TR and the DSM-5 criteria. *Research in Autism Spectrum Disorders*, *8*(3), 186–192. doi:10.1016/j.rasd.2013.11.007

Woo, B. S. C., Chang, W. C., Fung, D. S. S., Koh, J. B. K., Leong, J. S. F., Kee, C. H. Y., & Seah, C. K. F. (2004). Development and validation of a depression scale for Asian adolescents. *Journal of Adolescence*, *27*(6), 677–689. doi:10.1016/j.adolescence.2003.12.004 PMID:15561310

Woo, B. S. C., Ng, T. P., Fung, D. S. S., Chan, Y. H., Lee, Y. P., Koh, J. B. K., & Cai, Y. (2007). Emotional and behavioural problems in Singaporean children based on parent, teacher and child reports. *Singapore Medical Journal*, *48*(12), 1100–1106. PMID:18043836

World Bank. (2019, April 9). *Singapore Overview* [Text/HTML]. World Bank. https://www.worldbank.org/en/country/singapore/overview

World Bank. (2021). *World Development Indicators*. The World Bank | Country Profile. https://databank.worldbank.org/views/reports/reportwidget.aspx?Report_Name=CountryProfile&Id=b450fd57&tbar=y&dd=y&inf=n&zm=n&country=SGP

World Trade Organisation. (2012). *Trade policy review—Singapore* (WT/TPR/S/267). World Trade Organisation. https://www.wto.org/english/tratop_e/tpr_e/tp367_e.htm

Ylvisaker, M., Robin, H., & Doug, J.-G. (2003). Rehabilitation of Children and Adults With Cognitive-Communication Disorders After Brain Injury (No. TR2003-00146). American Speech-Language-Hearing Association. doi:10.1044/policy.TR2003-00146

Zaboski, B. A., & Storch, E. A. (2018). Comorbid autism spectrum disorder and anxiety disorders: A brief review. *Future Neurology*, *13*(1), 31–37. doi:10.2217/fnl-2017-0030 PMID:29379397

ADDITIONAL READING

Bryant, J., & Fondren, W. (2009). Psychological and Communicological Theories of Learning and Emotion Underlying Serious Games. In U. Ritterfeld, M. Cody, & P. Vorderer (Eds.), *Serious Games* (pp. 125–138). Routledge.

Dickey, M. D. (2005). Engaging by design: How engagement strategies in popular computer and video games can inform instructional design. *Educational Technology Research and Development*, *53*(2), 67–83. doi:10.1007/BF02504866

Dickey, M. D. (2006). Game Design Narrative for Learning: Appropriating Adventure Game Design Narrative Devices and Techniques for the Design of Interactive Learning Environments. *Educational Technology Research and Development*, *54*(3), 245–263. doi:10.100711423-006-8806-y

Galli, L., & Fraternali, P. (2014). Achievement Systems Explained. In Y. Baek, R. Ko, & T. Marsh (Eds.), *Trends and Applications of Serious Gaming and Social Media* (pp. 25–50). Springer. doi:10.1007/978-981-4560-26-9_3

Gee, J. P. (2009). Deep Learning Properties of Good Digital Games: How Far Can They Go? In U. Ritterfeld, M. Cody, & P. Vorderer (Eds.), *Serious Games*. Routledge.

Hagger, M. S., & Protogerou, C. (2020). Self-determination Theory and Autonomy Support to Change Healthcare Behavior. In A. Hadler, S. Sutton, & L. Osterberg (Eds.), The Wiley Handbook of Healthcare Treatment Engagement (pp. 141–158). John Wiley & Sons, Ltd. doi:10.1002/9781119129530.ch7

Oshotse, C. O., Bosworth, H. B., & Zullig, L. L. (2020). Treatment Engagement and Adherence. In A. Hadler, S. Sutton, & L. Osterberg (Eds.), The Wiley Handbook of Healthcare Treatment Engagement (pp. 15–32). John Wiley & Sons, Ltd. doi:10.1002/9781119129530.ch1

Rapoff, M. A., & Calkins-Smith, A. (2020). Enhancing Treatment Adherence in Young People with Chronic Diseases. In A. Hadler, S. Sutton, & L. Osterberg (Eds.), The Wiley Handbook of Healthcare Treatment Engagement (pp. 354–364). John Wiley & Sons, Ltd. doi:10.1002/9781119129530.ch19

Shen, C., Wang, H., & Ritterfeld, U. (2009). Serious Games and Seriously Fun Games: Can They Be One and the Same? In U. Ritterfeld, M. Cody, & P. Vorderer (Eds.), *Serious Games: Mechanisms and Effects* (1st ed., pp. 48–62). Routledge.

Subrahmanyam, K., & Greenfield, P. (2009). Designing Serious Games for Children and Adolescents: What Developmental Psychology Can Teach Us. In U. Ritterfeld, M. Cody, & P. Vorderer (Eds.), *Serious Games*. Routledge.

Whyte, E. M., Smyth, J. M., & Scherf, K. S. (2015). Designing Serious Game Interventions for Individuals with Autism. *Journal of Autism and Developmental Disorders*, *45*(12), 3820–3831. doi:10.100710803-014-2333-1 PMID:25488121

KEY TERMS AND DEFINITIONS

Cognitive Behavioral Therapy: A form of psychological therapy that targets and attempts to change unhelpful patterns of thinking and behavior to relieve psychological problems.

Disease Burden: The total, cumulative consequences of a defined disease or range of diseases with respect to disabilities in a population.

Feasibility: The degree to which a proposed product is a practical solution for all involved stakeholders.

Feedforward: A control mechanism in which information is collected and used to generate a control signal to counteract measured disturbance in the system. In Cogo™ Land, in-game EEG signals are used to counteract attentional disturbances measured during the calibration phase.

Playability: The degree to which a game is enjoyable and usable.

Social Communication: The way people use verbal and nonverbal language, gestures, and cues in social situations to express themselves and interpret others' intentions. This includes following unspoken rules of conversation such as turn-taking, adjusting tone of voice when addressing different people, and speaking at an appropriate volume depending on the context.

Treatment Effectiveness: The likelihood that a specific treatment protocol will benefit patients in a specific clinical population when administered in clinical practice.

Treatment Efficacy: The extent to which a specific treatment protocol will bring about desired clinical outcomes in patients under controlled conditions.

Treatment Engagement: The degree of commitment to the therapeutic process and active participation in one's collaboration with a therapist to work towards recovery. This includes adhering to treatment plans, coming to appointments, and being honest about one's condition.

Usability: A measure of how well a user in a specific context can effectively use a product to achieve a defined goal.

Chapter 14
A Rationale for Leveraging Serious Game Design Through Sociocultural Theory

Ilias Karasavvidis
University of Thessaly, Greece

ABSTRACT

The present work focuses on the issue of serious game design (SGD) through the lens of sociocultural theory. First, the main challenges that the field of SGD faces are briefly outlined. Second, Vygotsky's sociocultural theory is introduced and explored as a means to address these challenges. Third, a rationale for SGD that is informed by Vygotsky's ideas is introduced. This rationale is based on (1) viewing concepts as psychological tools and (2) conceptualizing two types of resources for SGD: exploration and application. According to this rationale, SGD needs to include a problem, exploration resources, and application resources. The chapter concludes with a discussion of the major implications of the proposed rationale for SGD.

INTRODUCTION

Over the course of the past four decades, video games have become an established medium for entertainment. In recent years, digital games are increasingly being considered as a very promising medium for learning. This new trend comes in many forms such as Game-Based Learning (GBL) or more commonly Serious Games (SG). SGs are explicitly designed to serve purposes other than entertainment, without necessarily excluding it (de Freitas & Liarokapis, 2011; Mitgutsch, 2011).

The transition from entertainment games to SG is not exactly smooth as many new parameters need to be factored in. Undoubtedly, the entertainment industry has developed very elaborate and refined ways to make games fun. However, the "serious" component of SG, namely the one that pertains to learning, is practically terra incognita. Hence, developing a SG is an entirely different affair compared to the development of a game whose sole aim is to entertain players. Creating SG is a very complicated process and a sophisticated enterprise.

DOI: 10.4018/978-1-7998-9732-3.ch014

Generally, SGD might swing back and forth from fun to learning, the two polar extremes along which the design space can be defined. In the first case, the design might drift more toward fun, potentially undermining learning. The experience will be pleasant but the learning outcome might be questionable. In the second case, the design might drift more toward learning, diminishing the fun. In this case learning might be insured, though the overall game experience might not be entertaining enough, spoiling the fun. Based on this design space, we can chart two main game design routes.

Prioritizing Fun

At the one end of the spectrum, the first route entails that fun takes precedence over learning. This route involves using the good-old fashioned, generic Analyse, Design, Develop, Implement, and Evaluate (AD-DIE) model (e.g. Bethke, 2003). This represents a more traditional game design approach as this model has a long and successful history of application in several fields. The main idea behind this route is to utilize the knowledge and expertise that the game industry has accumulated over the past four decades in the context of game design. This is a successful, and well-established route in which fun dominates because it is the ultimate goal. In this route, the learning component – the one that corresponds to the serious dimension of SG – is practically an add-on to an existing, well-established process. While this route may seem to be the default option – judging by the sheer numbers related to gaming – it falls short in some important respects.

First, striking a balance between fun and learning. The seamless integration of game play and learning has been one of the main challenges in SG design. As prioritizing learning might not preserve the fun, finding the right balance between gaming and learning is the single most important challenge for educators and game designers (Charsky, 2010; Sanchez, 2011; Kiili, 2005; Kelle, Klemke & Specht, 2011). In the context of SGD, there is a pressing need to combine fun and learning (Plass, Homer, Mayer & Kinzer, 2020).

Second, bridging the game design - educational design gap. Due to the disconnect between established game development models and the design of learning, the integration of game design and educational design principles is a major challenge (Arnab et al, 2014; Bellotti, Berta, De Gloria, D'ursi & Fiore, 2012; Van Staalduinen & de Freitas, 2011).

Third, integrating academic content into games. Figuring out how to integrate academic content in a game is difficult for one cannot simply inject academic content into a game, at least not without denaturing it. As the sugar-coating of educational content with game elements is sub-optimal, educational content should not be a mere add-on to a game (Boyan & Sherry, 2011).

Fourth, SGD is a collaborative process requiring multiple forms of expertise. In addition to the experts that were initially involved in creating a digital game, even more professionals are called for in the creation of a serious game: content experts, educators, and learning scientists. The communication between all those experts is not easy for a number of reasons: lack of a a common vocabulary, different demands and perspectives. Cross-communication among all the areas of expertise that are involved is the key. As De Troyer, Van Broeckhoven and Vlieghe (2017) noted, developing a common language that would facilitate the communication of the many experts involved in SGD is a major challenge.

Finally, basing game design on learning theory and research. As Mayer (2011a; 2016; 2020) argued, the foundations of game design should be empirically established design principles that are based both on the science of instruction and on the science of learning. On the one hand, there is no clear mapping between game design and Instructional Design (ID): game designers need principled ID guidelines.

On the other hand, because the application of empirically proven learning principles to game design is not straightforward, the need to support designers is compelling (Mayer, 2011a; Clark & Mayer, 2008; Mayer, 2011b; 2020; Clark, Yates, Early & Moulton, 2010; O'Neil & Perez, 2008)

Prioritizing Learning

At the other end of the spectrum, the second route takes a completely different approach to the design problem, prioritizing learning over fun. In this case, the design is not geared around the streamlined game design process that characterizes entertainment games. Rather, the design revolves primarily around learning, which after all is the ultimate goal of SG. This second route foregrounds learning and involves basing SGD in the learning sciences, capitalizing advances in theory and research for designing SG. We call this route principled SGD.

There have been many calls for principled SGD. In particular, it has been repeatedly stressed that game design needs to be based on principles of learning (Mayer, 2016; 2020; Karasavvidis, 2018; Westera, 2019; Watt & Smith, 2021). This emphasis has been manifested in the literature in various forms: evidence-based design, psychological design, learning design, instructional design, pedagogical design, and - more broadly - educational design. On the one hand scholars have stressed the need to design SG based on learning theory and research. Mayer (2016; 2020) has argued that psychology can offer many solutions when it comes to improving the instructional effectiveness of digital games. Similarly, Westera (2019) emphasized the need for SGD to draw on the empirical findings of research on teaching and learning. On the other hand, reviews of SGD models also reveal the need to focus more on learning frameworks. For instance, Watt and Smith (2021) pointed out that few SGD models are based on psychological or educational models of cognitive development. Karasavvidis (2018) also concluded that the majority of SGD models are limited in how they conceptualize learning and employ learning science principles.

Principled SGD might be obtained by drawing on advances from both learning theory and empirical learning research.

Regarding research, recent scholarship is gradually beginning to consider empirical research findings in a systematic manner. For instance, Mayer (2020) proposed that Multimedia Learning Theory (MLT) can be used for the design of GBL (see also Plass, Homer, Mayer & Kinzer, 2020). Mayer (2020) examined how extraneous processing and generative processing might influence learning during game play. According to his proposal, we need to design SG so as to strike a balance between (a) instructional features, which minimize extraneous processing and support essential processing and (b) game features, which promote generative processing. Undoubtedly, SGD has a lot to gain from such evidence-based approaches because many features that are taken for granted by the entertainment industry turn out to be suboptimal learning-wise (e.g. immersion in the form of virtual reality).

Regarding theory, SGD models have often turned to both psychology (for learning theories) and education (for teaching methods). While several SGD models have been put forward in recent years, there is a noticeable lack of emphasis on the science of learning. Karasavvidis (2018) concluded that the degree to which SGD models are based on the learning sciences varies considerably. Similarly, Ávila-Pesántez, Rivera and Alban (2017) report that about 2 in 3 SGD models appear to utilize learning theories (e.g. Behaviorist, Cognitivist, Constructivist and Sociocultural theories) while 1 in 3 SGD papers that presented SGD models addressed issues related to teaching methods.

For instance, some of the SGD models that have been proposed lack a solid grounding in the learning sciences e.g. DICE - (Djaouti, 2020), SGDA (Mitgutsch & Alvarado, 2012) (see also the SGD models proposed by Andreoli et al., 2017 and Valenza, Gasparini & Hounsell, 2019). At the other end of the extreme, other SGD models are based on a learning framework but only loosely such as the ATTAC-L design tool (De Troyer, Van Broeckhoven & Vlieghe, 2017) that is based on Social Cognitive Theory or the extension to AT SGD model to include game analytics (Callaghan, McShane, Eguíluz & Savin-Baden, 2018).

Recent reviews of the theoretical underpinnings of GBL, such as the one by Homer, Raffaele and Henderson (2020), focus more on the classical psychological frameworks put forward by J. Piaget and L.S. Vygotsky. The present work draws on Vygotsky's sociocultural theory as a framework for principled SGD. With a few exceptions (Theodosiou & Karasavvidis, 2015a; 2015b), Vygotsky's sociocultural framework is used more as a general learning theory backdrop for SGD rather as an explicit framework to inform SGD.

Most contemporary theoretical thinking about games, such as the work of Gee (2003), use gaming as their starting point. Gee attempted to draw parallels between the principles from learning theory and research and the ways in which they are implemented in games. He convincingly illustrated how the learning sciences theory and research is actualized in video games. Gee's (2003) account may be very comprehensive, but it is purely descriptive in nature: it is neither psychological nor is it based on learning theory. Thus, in his conceptualization the links from games to the broader context of psychological, sociological, and educational dimensions are either implicit or missing altogether.

Vygotsky's cultural-historical psychology constitutes one of the most comprehensive accounts of learning that have been given to date. What makes Vygotsky's approach particularly interesting is that it is the only learning theory in which play is a principal component. In fact, to the best of our knowledge, no other learning theory explicitly accounts for the role of play in cognitive development or learning in general. In Vygotskian theory, play is inherently integrated into learning and cognitive development. Interestingly enough, neither his ideas on play and how it impacts learning and cognitive development nor his learning theory have been systematically explored for game design purposes in the field of SGD.

This work aims to provide a brief outline of what I consider to be some core ideas of Vygotsky's framework. Then I will propose a rationale for SGD that is derived from these core ideas.

SOCIOCULTURAL THEORY

Firstly, I need to stress that Vygotsky's theory on cognitive development is both complex and multi-faceted (van der Veer & Valsiner, 1991). The actual reasons are beyond the scope of this work (for a comprehensive historical account see Dafermos, 2018). I will present a brief and selective account of his ideas, one that is exclusively tailored to the goals of this chapter.

Based on Dialogical Materialism, Vygotsky's primary focus was to describe the structure and function of consciousness in terms of Marx's theory. In the given sociohistorical context he lived and worked, his main goal was to establish a Marxist Psychology (Dafermos, 2018). Given the focus of the present chapter, I have selected five main constructs from his theory: social interaction, mediation, concept formation, learning potential, and play.

Social Interaction

Vygotsky considered social interaction as the primary and driving source of cognitive development. Vygotsky (1978) proposed the general genetic law of cultural development, according to which every cognitive function appears first on a social level (i.e. between people) and then on an individual level (i.e. within the person). As Vygotsky argued, all higher psychological functions emerge as social relations, being primarily manifested between people before they are manifested at an individual level. To emphasize the distinctively social dimension of human thinking, Vygotsky (1960/1981b) pointed out that even solitary thinking is of an inherent social nature:

even when we turn to mental processes, their nature remains quasi-social. In their own private sphere, human beings retain the functions of social interaction (p. 164)

In the Vygotskian framework, human psychological functioning consists in internalizing social relations, interactions, and practices.

Mediation

Human activity is both goal-oriented and tool-based (Wertsch, 1991; 1998). On the one hand, humans act to pursue a specific goal, which is meant to satisfy a certain need. On the other hand, this action is mediated by tools: people use various physical and mental tools in carrying out an activity. Vygotsky considered mediation to be the most defining feature of his approach because it is the building block for the development of consciousness. In particular, Vygotsky examined how humans develop and use tools to mediate and ultimately control their behavior. His approach consisted in examining how mediating tools shape consciousness. Drawing on the ideas of Marx and Engels, Vygotsky argued that material tools are similar to cultural tools (van der Veer & Valsiner, 1991)

the sign acts as an instrument of psychological activity in a manner analogous to the role of a tool in labor (Vygotsky, 1978, p. 52).

Vygotsky focused on a particular class of cultural tools, which he called psychological tools. Psychological tools include all the auxiliary means that humans construct in order to mediate mental functions:

language; various systems for counting; mnemonic techniques; algebraic symbol systems; works of art; writing; schemes, diagrams, maps and mechanical drawings; all sorts of conventional signs (Vygotsky, 1960/1981a, p. 137).

However, unlike material tools whose energy is directed at an external object (e.g. a hammer on a nail), psychological tools are inward-directed: they are meant to control oneself (e.g. take a note as a reminder to do something) (Vygotsky, 1978).

Vygotsky distinguished between *biological* psychological processes, such as direct perception, involuntary attention, and natural memory, and *cultural* psychological processes, such as verbalized perception, voluntary attention, mediated memory, thinking, and speech. For instance, while in the case of natural (i.e. biological) memory remembering amounts to retrieving information from memory, in the case of cultural (i.e. artificial) memory remembering amounts to reading information off a paper or screen. Writing information down using symbols for the purposes of remembering has transformed the process from recalling information to reading information (i.e. decoding symbols). Although in both cases the outcome is the same, namely remembering, the processes of retrieving information are markedly different.

The use of signs has an enormous impact on psychological functions because it transforms them, expands their scope, and elevates them to a new, higher level. Symbolic tools transform a biological function (low-level one) into a cultural one (higher-level), elevating it into a new level, changing its course and function. Due to this, Vygotsky referred to biological psychological functions as lower psychological functions and to the culturally mediated ones as higher psychological functions. Consequently, all higher mental functions are sign-based.

Concept Formation: Everyday and Scientific Concepts

Vygotsky (1987) was interested primarily in how signs influence consciousness and studied the transition from lower to higher mental functions. He focused on a particular class of signs, words, and explored the relationship between thinking and speech. His approach involved using word meaning as an analytic unit. He examined how various forms of speech (egocentric speech, inner speech) are related to cognitive development. As he argued

the word plays a decisive role in the formation of the true concept. It is through the word that the child voluntarily directs his attention on a single feature, synthesizes these isolated features, symbolizes the abstract concept, and operates with it as the most advanced form of the sign created by human thinking (p. 159, emphasis added).

In the process of exploring how word meanings are related to concept formation, Vygotsky concluded that there are two very different categories of concepts: everyday and scientific ones.

Everyday concepts develop spontaneously in the context of social interactions with others. They are empirically saturated and their developmental path consists in moving from the concrete to the abstract, namely from an experience to a generalization. The defining property of everyday concepts is the way in which they are related to the object they designate: their relationship to the object is unmediated – it does not involve other concepts (Vygotsky, 1987). In this sense, everyday concepts are non-systemic: a concept is self-standing, involving no direct reference to other concepts.

On the other hand, scientific concepts do not enter a child's consciousness in the same way everyday concepts do, that is in a natural and non-systematic manner. On the contrary, scientific concepts emerge as a result of ad hoc instruction. As opposed to the rich empirical dimension that characterizes everyday concepts, the formation of scientific concepts does not initiate from direct experience. A scientific concept enters a child's consciousness through a word followed by a verbal definition. Consequently, their developmental path involves moving from the abstract to the concrete. Another distinctive feature of scientific concepts is their systemic nature: defining any scientific concept necessitates a reference to a network of other scientific concepts. Due to their inherently systemic nature, their relationship to the object they designate is mediated, namely it is realized only through other concepts (Vygotsky, 1987).

Learning Potential: Independent versus Assisted Performance

Vygotsky explored the differences between static and dynamic conceptualizations of cognitive potential. His research led him distinguish two types of cognitive potential: (a) the actual cognitive potential, which involves the independent solution to a given problem by a learner, and (b) the developmental potential, which designates a solution given to a problem by a learner who is assisted by more capable social others. In this context, Vygotsky (1978) advanced the concept of the zone of proximal development (ZPD). The ZPD is defined as

the distance between the actual developmental level as determined by independent problem solving and the level of potential development as determined through problem solving under adult guidance or in collaboration with more capable peers. (p. 86).

The importance of the ZPD lies in that it expanded the standard psychological unit of analysis: the individual. The concept of ZPD broadens the focus of attention beyond the single individual, taking into consideration a dyad (e.g. more capable social other-child / student) or an even larger social group.

The ZPD offers an alternative approach to learning. In other psychological and educational approaches, learning follows development (maturation) much like the shadow follows an object. In the context of cultural-historical psychology, however, learning precedes development in the sense that it activates the cognitive potential and paves the way for subsequent development. As Vygotsky (1978) put it, learning

...awakens a variety of internal developmental processes (p. 90).

Essentially, the ZPD constitutes the link between everyday and scientific concepts as the latter restructure the former, forming a zone of proximal development that elevates spontaneous concepts to a higher level.

Play and Cognitive Development

As opposed to the way other learning theorists approached play, Vygotsky's (1978) contribution is unique in the sense that play is an integral part of his theory, exerting a huge influence on cognitive development.

Vygotsky proposed that the first major contribution of play concerns the development of imagination. As he argued, imagination is a new psychological process for the child that develops when the child transitions from the real world to an imaginary world. Imagination develops as a means of liberating from the constraints of reality: when a specific need or drive is not satisfied in the real world, the child mentally constructs an alternative imaginary world in which the need is met. On the part of the child, this mental construction is an important psychological process that requires a concerted and conscious effort.

The second major contribution of play pertains to the relation of perception and thought. Initially, the child is constrained by the situation she finds herself in: it is the objects themselves that suggest to her what she could do with them. However, through play the child achieves independence from visual perception: she sees a thing but does not act according to what the thing suggests. As Vygotsky argued, before play, separating the field of meaning from the visual field is practically impossible for the young child. However, play allows children to be liberated from the constraints of the visual field, enabling them to detach themselves from their concrete reality. It is through play that children can transition from the field of things to another field, that of ideas and meanings.

The final contribution of play concerns how it changes children's relation to reality. Vygotsky pointed out that initially human perception could be described in terms of an object / meaning ratio: it is the object that dominates and determines the meaning. Through play, however, the inverse ratio could be used to describe perception: meaning / object. Rather than the object and its properties it is the child's intention that is dominant and determines the meaning. Vygotsky observed that the same pattern occurs in the case of action. Initially, action dominates meaning (i.e. the ratio is action / meaning) but through play the ratio is eventually inverted: meaning gets to determine the action. In the context of play, an action can represent another action much like an object can stand for another object. Play facilitates the transition from the perceptual field to a field of meaning to which objects and actions are subservient.

Overall, Vygotsky argued that play constitutes a major source of development because it *"creates a zone of proximal development of the child. In play a child always behaves beyond his average age, above his daily behavior"* (p. 102). Play helps children reach a higher level of consciousness, thereby paving the way for abstract thought.

CONCEPTUALIZING A NOVEL RATIONALE FOR PRINCIPLED SGD

In this section I will outline how Vygotsky's framework can provide a rationale for principled SGD. First, I discuss how human knowledge consists of concepts and how these could be seen as functional solutions to problems. Then I argue that science concepts can be seen as psychological tools and examine the main implications of this position. Next, I focus on problems and I consider how they are at the core of game design. Finally, I explore the two main resource types that could be used for configuring problems in SGD and relate each resource to everyday and scientific concepts.

Disciplinary Concepts as Psychological Tools

Human knowledge is typically organized in scientific disciplines (and other non-scientific fields). Concepts are the building blocks of this knowledge. All knowledge in each scientific field can be represented as a hierarchically structured network of concepts.

It is important to consider the nature of concepts in detail. In functional terms, **concepts constitute solutions to problems** that emerged in a given socio-historical context. In particular, in the course of history a certain group of individuals in a given cultural context attempted to achieve a specific goal. This group were part of a collective practice that was facing a problem. Through contributions from various individuals in a continuous process of successive approximations, this group eventually manages to solve the problem. It should be noted that - depending on the specific problem that is being tackled - this solution process might span years, decades or even longer time frames. Once the problem is solved, this solution is crystallized as an artifact, material or conceptual, that is further stored in various forms so that it becomes available to future generations. From this viewpoint, concepts are representations of solutions to problems; they constitute tools that are meant to solve problems.

It is important to note that the starting point behind concept development is a problem: concepts emerge as responses to this problem. Hence, **problems are fundamental for understanding concepts** in functional terms. It is also important to observe the origins of problems, namely the fact that problems are not self-standing. Rather, problems indicate human agency, reflecting a drive to achieve a goal. It is in this process of attempting to meet a specific need that concepts are constructed. Interestingly, the history of science supports this view, as science concepts are abstract and de-contextualized, devoid of any visible agency (Gooding, 1990).

Drawing on Kozulin's (1998) seminal work, I put forward a conceptualization of learning that treats disciplinary concepts as psychological tools. More specifically, I propose viewing concepts from all scientific fields as cultural artifacts and in particular as psychological tools. From a Vygotskian perspective, concepts from all disciplines constitute scientific concepts. Seen as psychological tools, concepts constitute both meaning carriers and codified forms of social behaviors and practices.

In traditional education concepts are typically approached in terms of curricular subjects rather than from a psychological perspective, namely in terms of cognitive development. Treating concepts from all science fields as scientific concepts entails that learning any concept from any curricular subject can be seen as a **special class** or **subset** of learning and cognitive development in general. Consequently, the development of any science concept could be approached in the same terms as the development any psychological process.

The main implication of this conceptualization is that the curricular concepts no longer need to be considered in terms of content: a host of other psychological concepts and methods can be brought to bear on their study. In this sense, learning e.g. the concept of inertia in Physics has a dual focus. First, it involves understanding the development of the physical concept itself in terms of semiotic content (e.g. the concept definition, relations to other concepts). Second, it involves examining the concept in psychological terms, namely consider the psychological processes involved in appropriating the concept itself.

Two Types of Resources for SGD

As described above, mediation is a fundamental idea for sociocultural theory. Human action is goal-directed and tool-mediated: a person does not interact with an object directly but through a tool, i.e. indirectly. In this sense, signs mediate the achievement of a goal, being instrumental for its attainment. This relation is depicted in figure 1.

Figure 1. Subject-Tool-Object relationship

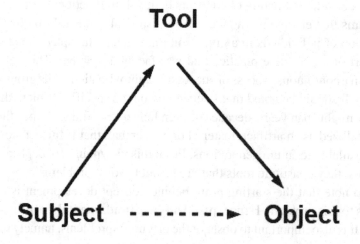

This fundamental concept of mediation can be directly applied to SGD. More specifically, the player (learner) assumes the identity of the hero who uses the resources provided to overcome the obstacle which stands in the way of achieving a goal. This relationship is depicted in figure 2.

Figure 2. Hero-Resources-Obstacles relationship

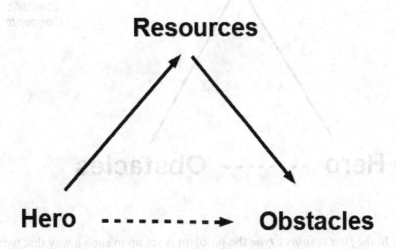

Essentially, in the context of a game the player needs to overcome a series of obstacles of increasing difficulty to achieve the ultimate goal. These obstacles constitute problems that the player needs to solve, using the resources that are provided within the game. The main implication of this is that SGD consists in establishing worlds in which problems are situated and for which solutions are required. It should be noted that for the purposes of SGD, the solutions to these problems need to correspond to the concepts that students need to learn, namely the academic content of the game.

The core idea of the rationale that is presented in this work is that game playing amounts to problem solving. Consequently, **game design is problem design**. The implication is that problem design should be the starting point for SGD. Next, **problems could be resolved by using the resources** that the game furnishes. **Two major resource types** can be distinguished, **exploration** and **application**. Figure 3 features the enriched relations. While both resource types revolve around a problem, the way these resources are set up is very different.

Figure 3. The two main resource types

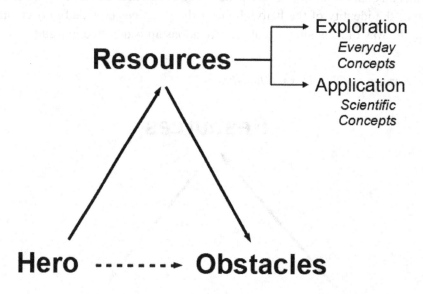

Exploration. In the *first resource type* the problem is set up in such a way that working on it inductively enables players to form the **connections** between their actions in the game and the subsequent game responses. Based on the outcomes obtained and through successive generalizations, the players are gradually led to develop the concept. This is what Salen and Zimerman (2004) refer to as 'meaningful play' in their revolutionary work. As they argued, the purpose of game design is to create meaningful play. They defined meaningful play as the relationship that a player forms by observing an action she makes in the game and the outcome of this action. According to their reasoning, players find meaning during gameplay when they associate a move they make with the response of the game system to their move.

Games naturally afford a type of learning that is empirical, which allows for exploration, discovery, experimentation, and hypothesis testing. The players explore the game world, make hypotheses, and test them in successive trials, eventually arriving at the requisite conclusions, i.e. generalizations. This process involves going from the concrete to the abstract: take an action, observe the outcomes, and draw a conclusion on how the two are related in the specific situation.

This type of learning based on exploration is a hallmark of digital games. For instance, in his seminal work Gee (2003) identified principles that are indicative of this type of learning – chief among which are probing and discovery. With respect to the probing principle Gee argued:

learning is a cycle of probing the world (doing something); reflecting in and on this action and, on this basis, forming a hypothesis; reprobing the world to test this hypothesis; and then accepting or rethinking the hypothesis (p. 107).

Concerning the discovery principle, Gee observed that in digital games

overt telling is kept to a well-thought-out minimum, allowing ample opportunity for the learner to experiment and make discoveries. (p. 138).

It is clear that both principles above reflect the empirical type of learning that digital games afford.

It should be noted that this property of games fully corresponds to everyday concepts and how these are formed. As mentioned above, Vygotsky (1987) pointed out their developmental path, which originates from the concrete, lived experience and is then turned into abstractions. Consequently, learning from a digital game is somewhat natural and resembles how everyday concepts are developed: it takes place in a natural context, through trial and error, exploration, and generalization. While conventional entertainment games might not formally teach anything directly, Gee (2003) has noted that they are carefully designed so as to allow for progressive exploration and experimentation, which eventually lead to generalizations and learning.

Let us take a look at a SG to elaborate on the concept of exploration. We will examine the Stop Disasters game UNDDR (2018) that has been developed by the United Nations Office for Disaster Risk Reduction (UNDRR). Stop Disasters is a single player game that can be played online through a web browser. The objective of the game is stop disasters and save lives. The players accomplish this by learning the risks posed by natural hazards. The game focuses on disasters like tsunamis, floods, hurricanes, wildfires, and earthquakes. Depending on the scenario, the idea is to build various defenses (e.g. schools, hospitals, houses, hotels etc.) to help the local populations survive all sorts of natural disasters. The game UI is presented in figure 4.

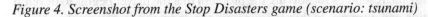

Figure 4. Screenshot from the Stop Disasters game (scenario: tsunami)

The game provides the player with some background information on each scenario and then the player is free to explore deploying various defenses to either prevent disasters or minimize the casualties. In each disaster scenario the player has a fixed budget that he/she can spend to prevent the respective disaster. The players are given a specific budget which they can spend however they want in building defenses. For instance, in the case of the tsunami scenario, the player can select among the following defenses: breakwater structures, buildings (huts, houses, hotels, schools, hospitals), trees, and sand dunes. The player can try different configurations of these resources, varying their location, arrangement and quantity. Once the players are confident that they have deployed all necessary resources and used up the budget, they can run the tsunami simulation and see the outcomes of their choices. Depending on the death toll, the players can try again using different configurations in order to further minimize the risks. After some experimentation, the players come to a viable resolution, saving all lives in the local community.

I consider this game to be very typical of exploration because the player is only given some background information about the context and overall game objective. The player is free to experiment with different configurations of defenses in order to reach the ultimate goal, i.e. minimize casualties. The whole game environment is developed around exploration: players are encouraged to try out different combinations of resources. This requires a trial and error approach that can be materialized using many different strategies. With the exception of the necessary background information, the players are not given anything else, such as instruction or other resources that could potentially encapsulate solutions. Hence, no direct instruction, tutorials, demonstrations or other informational resources are provided whatsoever. The players need to figure out how to combine the resources given in order to achieve the game goal and this involves systematic exploration.

Application. In the *second resource type* the player is also facing a problem but in this case the focus is not on inference-based generalizations. The problem-resource configuration is set up very differently: a **set of resources are provided** (tools, concepts, procedures, artifacts etc.) and the player is required to figure out how to best use them to resolve the task. Depending on the design and context, these resources could embed or embody full or partial solutions to the problem.

It is in this process of applying the resources for solving the problem that the player begins to develop an understanding of their function and purpose. In this case, learning is deductive in nature: the players are given a resource that comprises a solution and are expected to apply it to a problem. Thus, instead of going from the concrete to the abstract, as is the case with the exploration resources described above, in this case the leaner is required to go in the opposite direction, from the abstract to the concrete. The key difference with the first resource type (exploration) is that – given a problem – the learner is furnished with an artifact (conceptual or material in the game context) that can be applied to solve the task.

Meaning-making emerges from applying the tool to similar tasks first and then to novel tasks. The use of the tool for resolving the problem paves the way for meaning-making as it creates opportunities for the player to develop intuitions of how things work in a concrete and contextualized way. This type of work on the problem enables the player to gain direct experience of the problem-solution link. Essentially, the artifacts that are given to the player constitute solutions which the player is then required to apply to a problem or series of problems.

In terms of Vygotskian theory, the learner is given a solution in the form of an artifact (concept, tool, algorithm – any type of cultural artifact) and is required to use it on a problem in order to understand how it is related to the problem and how it can be used to resolve it. Much like concept formation, which begins with a word and a verbal definition, in this case the player is provided with a resource that represents a solution to a problem. Hence, meaning will emerge not through exploration and inference but through application, comparison, analysis, and reflection.

This resource type fits squarely into scientific concepts and the way Vygotsky (1987) described their developmental course. Scientific concepts are introduced to learners through a word, which is followed by a formal definition and then examples and use cases. As Vygotsky noted, initially, words are empty vessels which do have any meaning for the learners because they are abstract, de-contextualized generalizations that are introduced verbally. These empty vessels are gradually filled with meaning, as the learner gains direct experience from applying the concept on various problems. The same holds with games as the resources that are provided for resolving the problem initially make little sense to the player: he/she is given an artifact that is pretty much meaningless in the given context. It is in the process of applying this resource to resolving a problem in order to accomplish a goal that the player begins to understand how it is linked with the problem, what strategies it embodies, and how it codifies knowledge or action. Observing the application of this artifact to the solution of the problem paves the way for appreciating its potential for resolving the problem. This application involves cycles of comparison, analysis, and reflection which ultimately help the player grasp how the particular artifact responds to the challenge that the problem poses. Thus, in this case learning emerges in the process of moving from an abstraction to its usage in concrete, situated problems.

To illustrate the meaning of application in the context of SG, let us take a closer look at a game that embodies such resources. Specifically, we will examine Materials Hunter (Materials for a Sustainable Future, 2015), a game that was developed in the context of an EU funded project. This is a puzzle game that runs on multiple devices and operating systems. The focus of the game is on advanced materials and how these help shape societies today and tomorrow. The objective of the game is to craft new technologies by combining different materials. The player accomplishes this by learning about materials through interacting with the game. Materials Hunter covers materials in many different historical periods, ranging from ancient times to present day nanotechnologies. Once finished crafting a technology, the players need to sell it to a community member. When the community members no longer have requests for technologies, the specific historical age is considered complete and the player is taken to a more recent age. The main game UI is presented in figure 05.

Figure 5. Screenshot from the Materials Hunter game (period: ancient age)

What sets this game apart compared to Stop Disasters is the different paradigm that is adopted for its design. More specifically, two NPC characters, Max and Lily, help the player in many different ways: introduce the context of each task, provide specific information, give instructions, and provide guidelines.

The gameplay is very streamlined: the players need to follow a specific route, which progressively familiarizes them with simple technologies before moving on to more complex ones. For instance, to get the player started, Max and Lily provide explicit guidance and demonstrations. Tutorials are also available, especially in the beginning of the game. A screenshot from one of the guided tutorials is given in figure 6.

Figure 6. Game screenshot illustrating Max tutoring the player

Throughout the game information can be provided upon request. For example, the player can inquire information about a specific material. Figure 7 presents an example of a piece of information that the player had retrieved for a a specific material.

Figure 7. Screenshot of an information card returned in response to a player probe on a material

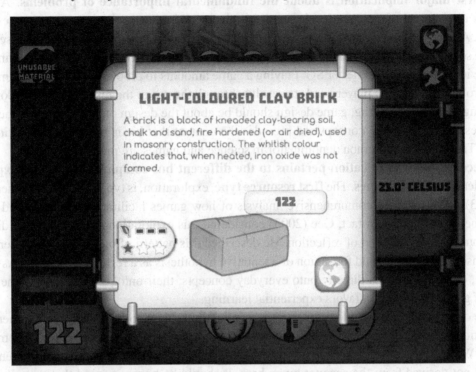

The material recipes used in the game involve a mix of explicit and implicit information (in the form of clues), which the players will need to decode.

I consider this game to be typical of application because many types of either direct or indirect assistance are masterfully embedded in the game. Unlike the Stop Disasters game, in which exploration is the main approach and there is hardly any information or help provided, the Materials Hunter game includes many different layers of help, both indirect (e.g. clues) and direct (e.g. explicit information about materials). Overall, there is a layer of guided instruction in the form of provision of information embedded in the game. The player is both guided and instructed in many different ways in the various game contexts. The element of help is highly conspicuous in Materials Hunter. In terms of sociocultural theory, this approach parallels the development of scientific concepts: conceptual resources are provided and the player needs to apply them to practice, crafting different technologies by combining various materials.

Needless to say that Materials Hunter also includes exploration: the player is encouraged to explore different material combinations to craft specific technologies. However, exploration is neither the main nor the only mediational resource provided, as was the case with the Stop Disasters game. In Materials Hunter application takes center stage and exploration is secondary.

IMPLICATIONS FOR SGD

Based on concepts as psychological tools and the problems-resources configurations outlined above, three major implications for SGD can be derived.

The first major implication is about the fundamental importance of problems. As argued, **problems** are integral to concept development in science and concepts emerge as responses to these problems. As it was pointed out, concepts are functionally related to the problems in the sense that they constitute solutions. The same pattern can be said to apply for SGD: **problems** are also fundamental for games, be it entertainment games or SG. Playing a game amounts to problem solving: the game assigns various problems which the player needs to resolve through the use of the resources given. Considering that gaming is problem solving, game design should be about the design of problems. It is the problem that creates the need for the concept and provides the context that binds the artifact (solution) to the problem. Therefore, the common denominator in science and games are problems.

The **second major implication pertains to the different but complimentary roles exploration and application play in games**. The **first resource type**, exploration, is typical of entertainment games. Gee (2003) has provided a comprehensive analysis of how games facilitate exploration and how this leads to meaning-making. In fact, Gee (2003) considered this exploration to be not only indicative of spontaneous learning but also of reflection. He described this pattern of player action - observation of the response by the game – and formation of a tentative hypothesis as a reflective practice. As I pointed out above, exploration maps directly onto everyday concepts, their ontology and development. In the context of games, exploration favors experiential learning.

On the other hand, the **second resource type**, application, is less common for entertainment games. The adoption of resource types related to application is minimal – at least based on the aforementioned rationale. While in some games certain resources (artifacts) are provided, the particular implementation method is not derived from the account given here. It should be borne in mind that that all academic subjects include concepts and procedures for which SG are perfect exploration environments. With the proper contextualization and an assortment of tasks, the students could be given ample opportunities for exploring relations between factors, identifying cause and effect, determining rates of change, isolate the effect of hidden variables etc. Although the players could be furnished with such opportunities, it is completely unrealistic to expect them to simply "discover" the constructs that are the product of the collective work of humans since the dawn of time. Thus, while some concepts could be 'discovered', exploration is not possible with the majority of concepts. In all such cases, the students need to be given the solutions. Based on this reasoning, **SGD also necessitates the second type of resources**, where artifacts are provided and the players learn from their application. As discussed in the previous section, application maps perfectly onto scientific concepts.

It should be noted that, while exploration is a distinctive feature of entertainment games, it does mean that SG cannot take advantage of it. On the contrary, exploration can very well be integrated in SG, though the configuration of problem-resource set needs to be structured differently. Much like learners gradually "fill" an abstract concept with meaning in the process of applying it in various contexts, players also make sense of a resource in the process of utilizing it in the tasks the game system provides.

Ideally, SGD should seek to strike a balance between exploration and application. On the one hand, certain facts and relations between concepts could be inferred by the players in a discovery fashion. On the other hand, once certain artifacts have been provided to the players who are then expected to apply them to practice, exploration is perfectly possible. It should be noted, however, that this type of exploration is not based on inference.

The final major implication centers around the properties of generalization. In the case of exploration, the player is expected to proceed from a concrete experience to an abstraction. This movement corresponds fully to Vygotsky's account of everyday concepts that are spontaneously developed in an empirically rich context. In the case of application, the player is expected to start off an abstraction and populate it with meaning. This movement corresponds fully to Vygotsky's idea of scientific concepts which are not 'developed' empirically, rather they are given in a finished, fully articulated form. While in the case of exploration the player is expected to **construct** a generalization, in the case of application the player is expected to move in the opposite direction, namely to **deconstruct** a generalization. Both processes, construction and de-construction are essential for SGD.

Figure 8. Overview of the SG design rationale

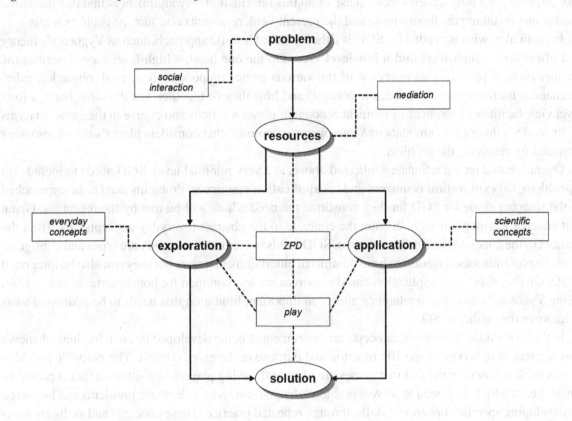

A complete overview of the rationale for SGD that is advanced in this work is given in figure 8. This figure illustrates the interrelations between the main game elements (problem-solution) and the influence of constructs from Sociocultural theory (social interaction, mediation, ZPD and play). As can be seen in the figure, the problem is the starting point and its solution is the ultimate goal. However, players do not tackle the problem unassisted. Rather, they reach a solution by making use of two classes of mediating artifacts, exploration and application. The former corresponds to everyday concepts and involves going from the concrete to the abstract. The latter involves going from the abstract to the concrete and maps to scientific concepts. The ZPD represents the bridge between everyday and scientific concepts, linking both resources types. Finally, the whole context involves social interaction and play facilitates meaning making through both concept construction (i.e. everyday concepts) and the concept deconstruction (i.e. scientific concepts).

CONCLUSION

Contemporary scholarship on SGD is increasingly taking into account advances in research. For instance, Mayer (2020) has recommended considering several principles from MLT for SGD. While research-based advances are very a promising route for SGD, it should be noted that due to its origin (information processing theory), MLT is mostly preoccupied with presenting factual and conceptual information to learners – the well-known principles of multimedia learning are highly indicative of this orientation. However, we need to go beyond the presentation of information and focus more on the broader meaning-making process, exploring how students make sense of all this information. My argument is that this particular need is met by taking the theory route and the present work represents one such possible example.

In particular, what is needed for SGD is a theory-based holistic approach, such as Vygotsky's theory that offers both a **high-level and a low-level view.** On the one hand, a high-level view describes the broader picture, providing an overview of the various game components (e.g. goal, obstacles, rules, mechanics, narrative context, academic content) and how they fit together. On the other hand, a low-level view facilitates a moment-to-moment account of player's actions and course in the game. In terms of Vygotsky's theory, this amounts to a microgenetic approach that considers player's use of resources provided for resolving the problem.

Overall, based on the rationale explicated above, at a very minimal level, SGD needs to include (a) a **problem,** (b) **exploration resources** and (c) **application resources.** Problems need to be approached as the stepping stone for SGD for they constitute the need which will be met by the resources. Given that concept learning moves both from the concrete to the abstract (everyday concepts) and from the abstract to the concrete (scientific concepts), SGD needs to facilitate both resource types and configurations. Exploration-based resources have dominated entertainment games but they can also be integrated in SG. On the other hand, application-based resources are less common for both entertainment and SG. Using Vygotsky's theory as a reference, this is an important limitation that needs to be addressed so as to improve the quality of SG.

In the Vygotskian framework, concepts are instrumental, being developed by an individual whenever they are required, serving a specific function and purpose in the given context. The rationale provided in this work is based on the fact that games are ideal at throwing players in a situation that is problem-based, i.e. in which they need to solve a problem of some sort. As a rule, these problems can be solved by developing specific concepts or skills, through repeated practice. These concepts and skills are inextricably tied to the problem and are instrumental in its solution.

To conclude, as opposed to starting off the design process from the perspective of game design (traditional entertainment industry approach) or the perspective of academic content (conventional educational approach), the rationale advanced in this work fundamentally re-frames the design problem in terms of learning. Essentially, it draws on Vygotsky's ideas treating concepts as mediational artifacts and finds parallels in how the game resources provided could be utilized to solve problems.

Sociocultural Theory provides a comprehensive and holistic framework for describing learning by taking into consideration the academic content to be learned, the specific context in which learning takes place, the practices that are actualized in this context, the social interaction that is involved, and the mediational artifacts that are utilized. I have used this framework for developing a comprehensive rationale for SGD that covers both types of concept formation. Readers are advised to approach this work as a first, tentative proposal of a principled theoretical formulation, which can be greatly improved in the future.

REFERENCES

Andreoli, R., Corolla, A., Faggiano, A., Malandrino, D., Pirozzi, D., Ranaldi, M., Santangelo, G., & Scarano, V. (2017). A framework to design, develop, and evaluate immersive and collaborative serious games in cultural heritage. *Journal on Computing and Cultural Heritage, 11*(1), 1–22. doi:10.1145/3064644

Arnab, S., Lim, T., Carvalho, M. B., Bellotti, F., de Freitas, S., Louchart, S., Suttie, N., Berta, R., & De Gloria, A. (2014). Mapping learning and game mechanics for serious games analysis. *British Journal of Educational Technology.* Advance online publication. doi:10.1111/bjet.12113

Ávila-Pesántez, D., Rivera, L. A., & Alban, M. S. (2017). Approaches for serious game design: A systematic literature review. *Computers in Education Journal, 8*(3).

Bellotti, F., Berta, R., De Gloria, A., D'ursi, A., & Fiore, V. (2012). A serious game model for cultural heritage. *Journal on Computing and Cultural Heritage, 5*(4), 17. doi:10.1145/2399180.2399185

Bethke, E. (2003). *Game development and production.* Wordware Publishing.

Boyan, A., & Sherry, J. L. (2011). The challenge in creating games for education: Aligning mental models with game models. *Child Development Perspectives, 5*(2), 82–87. doi:10.1111/j.1750-8606.2011.00160.x

Callaghan, M., McShane, N., Eguíluz, A., & Savin-Baden, M. (2018). Extending the activity theory based model for serious games design in engineering to integrate analytics. *International Journal of Engineering Pedagogy, 8*(1), 109–126. doi:10.3991/ijep.v8i1.8087

Charsky, D. (2010). From edutainment to serious games: A change in the use of game characteristics. *Games and Culture, 5*(2), 177–198. doi:10.1177/1555412009354727

Clark, R. C., & Mayer, R. E. (2008). Learning by viewing versus learning by doing: Evidence-based guidelines for principled learning environments. *Performance Improvement, 47*(9), 5–13. doi:10.1002/pfi.20028

Clark, R. E., Yates, K., Early, S., & Moulton, K. (2010). An analysis of the failure of electronic media and discovery-based learning: Evidence for the performance benefits of guided training methods. In K. H. Silber & W. R. Foshay (Eds.), *Handbook of improving performance in the workplace* (pp. 263–297). Pfeiffer. doi:10.1002/9780470592663.ch8

Czauderna, A., and Guardiola., E., (2019). The Gameplay Loop Methodology as a Tool for Educational Game Design. *The Electronic Journal of e-Learning, 17*(3), 207-221.

Dafermos, M. (2018). *Rethinking cultural-historical theory: A dialectical perspective to Vygotsky.* Springer. doi:10.1007/978-981-13-0191-9

de Freitas, S., & Liarokapis, F. (2011). Serious Games: a new paradigm for education? In M. Ma, A. Oikonomou, & L. C. Jain (Eds.), *Serious games and edutainment applications* (pp. 9–23). Springer. doi:10.1007/978-1-4471-2161-9_2

De Troyer, O., Van Broeckhoven, F., & Vlieghe, J. (2017). Linking serious game narratives with pedagogical theories and pedagogical design strategies. *Journal of Computing in Higher Education, 29*(3), 549–573. doi:10.100712528-017-9142-4

Djaouti, D. (2020). DICE: A Generic Model for the Design Process of Serious Games. *International Journal of Game-Based Learning, 10*(2), 39–53. doi:10.4018/IJGBL.2020040103

Gee, J. P. (2003). *What video games have to teach us about language and literacy.* Palgrave Macmillan.

Gooding, D. (1990). *Experiment and the making of meaning. Human agency in scientific observation and experiment.* Kluwer Academic Publishers. doi:10.1007/978-94-009-0707-2

Homer, B. D., Raffaele, C., & Henderson, H. (2020). Games as Playful Learning: Implications of Developmental Theory for Game-Based Learning. In J. L. Plass, R. E. Mayer, & B. D. Homer (Eds.), *Handbook of Game-Based Learning* (pp. 25–52). MIT Press.

Karasavvidis, I. (2018). Educational Serious Games Design: An Overview. In M. Khosrow-Pour (Ed.), *Encyclopedia of Information Science and Technology* (4th ed., pp. 3287–3295). IGI Global.

Kelle, S., Klemke, R., & Specht, M. (2011). Design patterns for learning games. *International Journal of Technology Enhanced Learning, 3*(6), 555–569. doi:10.1504/IJTEL.2011.045452

Kiili, K. (2005). Digital game-based learning: Towards an experiential gaming model. *The Internet and Higher Education, 8*(1), 13–24. doi:10.1016/j.iheduc.2004.12.001

Kozulin, A. (1998). *Psychological Tools. A Socio-Cultural Approach to Education.* Cambridge University Press.

Materials for a Sustainable Future. (2015). *Materials Hunter* [Online game]. STIMULATE. http://www.materialsfuture.eu/en/game/

Mayer, R. E. (2011a). Multimedia learning and games. In S. Tobias & J. D. Fletcher (Eds.), *Computer Games and Instruction* (pp. 281–305). Information Age Publishing.

Mayer, R. E. (2011b). Instruction based on visualizations. In R. E. Mayer & P. A. Alexander (Eds.), *Handbook of Research on Learning and Instruction* (pp. 427–445). Routledge.

Mayer, R. E. (2016). What should be the role of computer games in education? *Policy Insights from the Behavioral and Brain Sciences, 3*(1), 20–26. doi:10.1177/2372732215621311

Mayer, R. E. (2014). Mutlimedia instruction. In J. M. Spector, M. D. Merrill, J. Elen, & M. J. Bishop (Eds.), *Handbook of Research on Educational Communications and Technology* (4th ed., pp. 385–399). Springer. doi:10.1007/978-1-4614-3185-5_31

Mayer, R. E. (2020). Cognitive Foundations of Game-Based Learning. In J. L. Plass, R. E. Mayer, & B. D. Homer (Eds.), *Handbook of Game-Based Learning* (pp. 83–110). MIT Press.

Mitgutsch, K. (2011). Serious Learning in Serious Games. In Serious Games and Edutainment Applications (pp. 45-58). Springer. doi:10.1007/978-1-4471-2161-9_4

Mitgutsch, K., & Alvarado, N. (2012). Purposeful by design? A serious game design assessment framework. In *Proceedings of the International Conference on the Foundations of Digital Games - FDG '12* (p. 121). Raleigh, NC: ACM Press. 10.1145/2282338.2282364

O'Neil, H. F., & Perez, R. S. (Eds.). (2008). *Computer games and team and individual learning.* Elsevier.

Oubahssi, L., Piau-Toffolon, C., Loup, G., & Sanchez, E. (2020). From Design to Management of Digital Epistemic Games. *International Journal of Serious Games*, 7(1), 23–46. doi:10.17083/ijsg.v7i1.336

Plass, J. L., Homer, B. D., Mayer, R. E., & Kinzer, C. K. (2020). Theoretical Foundations of Game-Based and Playful Learning. In J. L. Plass, R. E. Mayer, & B. D. Homer (Eds.), *Handbook of Game-Based Learning* (pp. 3–24). MIT Press.

Salen, K., & Zimmerman, E. (2004). *Rules of play: Game design fundamentals*. MIT press.

Sanchez, E. (2011). Key criteria for Game Design. A Framework. MEET Project. European Commission.

Silva, F. G. (2020). Practical methodology for the design of educational serious games. *Information (Basel)*, *11*(1), 14. doi:10.3390/info11010014

Siriaraya, P., Visch, V., Vermeeren, A., & Bas, M. (2018). A cookbook method for Persuasive Game Design. *International Journal of Serious Games*, 5(1), 37–71. doi:10.17083/ijsg.v5i1.159

Theodosiou, S. & Karasavvidis, I. (2015b). Serious games design: a mapping of the problems novice game designers experience in designing games. *Journal of e-Learning and Knowledge Society*, *11*(3), 133-148.

Theodosiou, S., & Karasavvidis, I. (2015a). An Exploration of the Role of Feedback on Optimizing Teachers' Game Designs. *Bulletin of the IEEE Technical Committee on Learning Technology*, *17*(4), 2.

UNDDR. (2018). *Stop Disasters* [Online game]. UN Office for Disaster Risk Reduction. https://www.stopdisastersgame.org

Valenza, M. V., Gasparini, I., & Hounsell, M. da S. (2019). Serious Game Design for Children: A Set of Guidelines and their Validation. *Journal of Educational Technology & Society*, 22(3), 19–31.

Van der Veer, R., & Valsiner, J. (1991). *Understanding Vygotsky: A Quest for Synthesis*. Blackwell.

Van Staalduinen, J. P., & de Freitas, S. (2011). A Game-Based Learning Framework: Linking Game Design and Learning. In M. S. Khine (Ed.), *Learning to play: Exploring the future of education with video games* (pp. 29–53). Peter Lang.

Vygotsky, L. S. (1981a). The Instrumental Method in Psychology. In *The concept of activity in Soviet psychology* (J. V. Wertsch, Ed. & Trans.; pp. 134–143). M.E. Sharpe. Inc. (Original work published 1960)

Vygotsky, L. S. (1981b). The Genesis of Higher Mental Functions (J.V. Wertsch, Ed. & Trans.). In The Concept of Activity in Soviet Psychology (pp. 144-188). M.E. Sharpe. (Originally published 1960)

Vygotsky, L. S. (1978). *Mind in Society: The Development of Higher Psychological Processes* (M. Cole, V. John-Steiner, S. Scribner, & E. Souberman, Eds. & Trans.). Harvard University Press.

Vygotsky, L. S. (1987). The Collected Works of L.S. Vygotsky. Vol. 1. Problems of General Psychology (Rieber, R.S. & Carton, A.S. Eds., N. Minick Trans.). Plenum Press.

Watt, K., & Smith, T. (2021). Based Game Design for Serious Games. *Simulation & Gaming*.

Wertsch, J. V. (1991). *Voices of the Mind. A Socio-Cultural Approach to Mediated Action*. Harverster-Wheatsheaf.

Wertsch, J. V. (1998). *Mind as Action*. Oxford University Press.

Westera, W. (2019). Why and How Serious Games can Become Far More Effective: Accommodating Productive Learning Experiences, Learner Motivation and the Monitoring of Learning Gains. *Journal of Educational Technology & Society*, 22(1), 59–69.

KEY TERMS AND DEFINITIONS

Application: In this work, application is defined as the second mediational resource type that players utilize in solving game problems. It involves deduction, namely going from the abstract to the concrete and corresponds to scientific concepts.

Concept Formation: In the context of sociocultural theory, concepts are generalizations that are represented through signs (words). Vygotsky distinguished between naturally occurring concepts (everyday ones) and formally introduced concepts (scientific ones). Concepts constitute collectively constructed and shared artifacts that either embody or represent solutions to problems.

Exploration: In this work, exploration is defined as the first mediational resource type that players utilize in overcoming game obstacles. It involves induction, that is moving from the concrete to the abstract and corresponds to everyday concepts.

Mediation: The term denotes any material or conceptual artifacts that humans utilize in accomplishing cognitive tasks. In Vygotskian theory mediation is one of the two main pillars as it shapes consciousness.

Serious Games: Serious Games are games whose primary objective is not related to entertainment. Typically, such games aim to foster the learning of concepts, skills, and attitudes in various disciplines. While Serious Games are not mainly focused on entertainment, they certainly do not exclude it.

Serious Games Design: The processes involved in creating games whose principal target is the learning of concepts, skills, and attitudes. It is an interdisciplinary endeavor, involving experts from the different disciplines such as graphic, audio, product, and interaction design, programming, animation, writing, content experts, educators, and learning scientists.

Social Interaction: Social interaction is one of two main foundational pillars of the Vygotskian framework. It constitutes the primary and driving source of cognitive development as all higher psychological functions emerge as social relations.

Sociocultural Theory: Coined by contemporary scholars, the term refers to a set of theoretical frameworks that originated in the Soviet Union in the beginning of the 20th century by Lev Vygotsky and his colleagues, Alexander Luria, and Alexei Leont'ev. These frameworks included Vygotsky's Cultural-Historical Psychology and Leont'ev's Activity Theory.

Chapter 15
Serious Games Applications for Cultural Heritage:
Benefits and Main Design Issues

Paola Falcone

Sapienza University of Rome, Italy

ABSTRACT

The chapter aims to explore how serious games can provide cultural organizations with opportunities to attract audiences. In the first part, main terms (games, serious games, gamification, meaningful gamification) are defined, along with some features of players as well as game-related aspects, like dynamics and mechanics, that are identified and described. The chapter presents the main features of an effective design of serious games for cultural heritage. This part is supported by the application of gamification literature concepts and models to cultural heritage and by evidence from applications in the field. In the last part, some controversial aspects connected to the use of gamification for cultural heritage are presented. Some problems in implementing, mostly connected to the lack of resources, and some possible solutions are outlined.

INTRODUCTION

The mission of cultural institutions has two main dimensions: to take care and preserve cultural heritage, and to promote its knowledge and enjoyment, engaging audiences (see among others Black, 2012; Falk, 2016). This is clear in the ICOM definition of what a museum is and does to be *"in the service of society and its development"*: in addition to acquisition, preservation and research activities, a museum *"communicates and exhibits the tangible and intangible heritage of humanity and its environment for the purposes of education, study and enjoyment"* (Museum Definition, n.d.). Cultural organizations, within their domain and according to available resources, put effort into promoting and diffusing culture, connecting and engaging audiences.

As pointed out by several scholars (see among others Black, 2012), museums and other cultural institutions are on one side eroding their traditional audiences, and on the other side appear not able to turn

DOI: 10.4018/978-1-7998-9732-3.ch015

out to be attractive enough for new audiences. A particular concern regards young generations, which often appear to be a hard target to reach. Children attend museums, when carried there by their teachers in school field trips or by their parents, somehow conscious, on rainy Sundays. As reported by Falk (2016) from a survey on several US museums, families -meant as groups with at least one adult and one or more children- are the most frequent type of museums visitors. The survey pointed out that on average most represented people are adults aged 25-44 and children aged 5-12 years old; some distinctions occur considering the type of museum, as the average audience age is older for art and history museums and younger for science museums (Falk, 2016). But will these non-voluntary children visits generate free-choice young visitors? The distance with certain audiences is a problem of promotion, as well as contents and used languages. So it appears to be strictly related to communication. Cultural organizations need to find fitting means and codes to reach and engage their publics (Black, 2012). Serious games applications to cultural heritage (Anderson et al., 2009) can be an effective tool, especially for young people, who are used to these and enjoy playing videogames (Apostolellis et al., 2018; Yanev, 2019).

Games attractive potential and people inclination to a frequent play got the attention of both managers and researchers, and found interesting applications in many different for profit and not-for-profit environments in recent years (Djaouti et al., 2011) for different goals (Kuo, 2015a).

Game-based applications make game elements enter the cultural context (Anderson et al., 2009; Apostolellis et al., 2018), to reach educational goals. These applications also have has a promotional aim, as cultural organizations need to develop their audiences, improve their brand image, increase their visibility and revenues.

In this perspective, the purpose of the chapter is to explore how serious games can provide cultural organizations opportunities to engage audiences. Both academic and technical literature are examined. In the background main concepts are defined and some features of players, as well as game-related aspects (mechanics, dynamics, and aesthetics) are identified and described. Then the chapter presents main features of an effective design of serious games for cultural heritage, providing evidences from some international applications. The third part identifies and describes some controversial aspects, main related problems and some possible solutions.

BACKGROUND

Games and Gamification: Terms and Definitions

The first term appeared in this relatively recent field of research is gamification. It can be defined as "*the use of game design elements in non-game contexts*" (Deterding et al., 2011, p. 10). Players are rewarded for some specific completed tasks. As new applications and classification needs emerged, this gamification has been often qualified as "BLAP gamification", where BLAP is for typical mechanics later described, such as badges, levels and leaderboards, achievements, and points (see among others Kapp & Boller, 2017; Schell, 2019).

In order to distinguish such games from typical entertainment games, the term "serious games" emerged in literature to identify those games designed with a wider scope than the sole entertainment for the players (Abt, 1987; Dörner et al., 2016). Djaouti et al. (2011, p. 2) describe this process: "*serious game designers use people's interest in video games to capture their attention for a variety of purposes that go beyond pure entertainment*". Serious games have their focus in the goal, that's why for some authors this term should not be considered as a synonymous of gamification (King, 2021). This does not mean that fun and entertainment are out of serious games; simply these are not their main purpose (Abt, 1987; Bruckman, 1999). The term "*serious games*" was not considered fully satisfying for all scholars, as it attains to the context, and does not specify much more about (Nicholson, 2012). Schell (2012) goes beyond this concept, introducing the concept of transformative games, and emphasizing the "*impact the game has from the perspective of the player*" (Nicholson, 2012, p.4). Schell's work is rooted in Mezirow's research (1991) on transformative learning, which is able to make learners change their previous assumptions and meanings of the world. This change regards attitudes, as well as expectations and behaviors.

In line with Schell, Nicholson (2012; 2015) proposes to qualify this gamification process as "meaningful". Specifically, "*meaningful gamification is the use of game elements to help someone find meaning in a non-game context, and is therefore a tool to help people learn through changing their perspectives on life*" (Nicholson, 2012, p.2).

Games, Learning, and Culture

A heartfelt matter for cultural organizations' managers and officers is audience development. Related strategies aim at reaching and engaging new audiences, and fidelize current audiences (Black, 2012). An engaged audience appreciates the value of arts and culture and increases its cultural consumptions; so the entire cultural sector can take advantage from effective actions carried on by single institutions.

Cultural heritage can benefit from serious games. Some museums are not new to use games as a tool to diffuse knowledge and visitors engagement. Children's museums and science museums, have been long used to favor visitors participation and active involvement; on such experiences more recently also some art museum launched their own projects (Hunter, 2009). These actions support the creation of a "participatory museum" (Nicholson, 2012), which is a place where visitors can play and engage during the visit. In such game-based experiences a "*visitor is assimilating and mastering skills through practice and problem-solving*" (Grenier, 2010, p. 79).

Within a digital, interactive and emotionally involving context audiences like young people are more likely to spend their time and engage (Prensky, 2001). Through their interface, graphics, and storylines video games offer immersive experiences where it's possible to approach arts, history, culture, and related sites in an engaging way.

Gamification Applications Design Elements

Why do some games become so popular and are so appreciated? Asking this question to the fans of a game, probably collected answers will mostly regard the game process aspects and its aesthetics, both influencing the player experience. Such aspects are at the basis of the MDA model (Hunicke et al., 2004), that identifies three main games design elements: mechanics, dynamics, and aesthetics.

Mechanics are game rules and process aspects, driving players' actions and their engagement. Some examples are: calls to action, assigned tasks (combats or more complex 'boss fights'), challenges and missions with different and progressive levels of difficulty, cooperation and competition mechanisms, playing turns, feedbacks to players, transactions, rewards and so on (Werbach & Hunter, 2012). Limitations and constraints are also to be included, in order to set some difficulties on the path.

The game sets some achievements - like bonuses, discount, badges, gadgets, or content unlocking - for gamers who successfully complete the given tasks. So, mechanics are made of components, which are their specific installation in the game (Werbach & Hunter, 2012); they provide a feedback to gamers, support their motivation to play, and engage them. Most popular components are points, badges, and leaderboards. Points to collect are necessary for tracking and feedback. They are mostly skill points related to the gamer's ability. Games design can provide also redeemable points, experience points, karma points -connected to positive behaviors-, online reputation points (Werbach and Hunter, 2012), and social points, depending on others' behavior. Badges are another popular game component. They are rewarding systems attesting goals achievement (Gopaladesikan, 2013; Werbach & Hunter, 2012). Antin and Churchill (2011) identify several main badges motivational features: badges are goals to achieve, and also reputational markers within the group of players. Leaderboards make scores and progresses visible to the game community, help compare performances, create ranking, and so stimulate competition (Werbach & Hunter, 2012). Performance graphs support progress tracking (Sailer et al., 2017), also regarding specific actions.

Game design can also include other components, as quests, virtual goods, currency, gifting/sharing, levels (see Werbach & Hunter, 2012; Wood & Reiners, 2015).

Game dynamics are the second element of the MDA model. Kapp and Boller (2017) list and describe some dynamics, easy to find also in both games and video-games, like race to the finish, territory acquisition, exploration, collecting items, rescue or escape, items alignment or matching, construct, and finding solution (to problems, quizzes, and so on). Dynamics are strictly connected to motivational aspects and gamers preferences. In the Octalysis model, Chou (2014) identifies eight core drives, useful to design game dynamics. These core drives act as rational or emotional stimuli and are (Chou, 2014): epic meaning and calling, development and accomplishment, empowerment of creativity and feedback, ownership and possession, social influence and relatedness, scarcity and impatience, unpredictability and curiosity, loss and avoidance. These drives are later described, in their cultural application. Dynamics aspire to positively engage players in the so called "*blissful productivity*" (McGonigal, 2010; Rekhi, 2017). When the game is engaging, gamers experience goes with the "flow" and players stay focused and feel happy; Csikszentmihalyi connects this state with optimal experiences, and describes it as "*the state in which people are so involved in an activity that nothing else seems to matter*" (1990, p.3). The flow results in balanced games able to keep players away from both frustration/anxiety (when over-challenged) and boredom (when under-challenged), balancing challenges and skills (Csikszentmihalyi, 1990).

The MDA model also focuses its attention on aesthetics. The game environment is important for players' emotional engagement, as it generates curiosity, surprise, and fun, for a satisfactory experience. Technological progresses favor immersive experiences thanks to virtual environments and 3d reconstructions (Liarokapis et al., 2017).

Types of Gamers

Gamers show different attitudes towards the game and different behaviors. Bartle identifies four types of players according to their being more oriented towards themselves and own actions, or rather towards the environment and the interaction with other players (Bartle, 1996; Rekhi, 2017):

- *achievers*, wanting to succeed by getting rewards, points, levels. They engage in challenges to win. Challenges, feedbacks, and rewards drive their motivation to play; if they can't win, they can lose their interest in the game;

- *explorers*, who enjoy discovering the game environment. They view, rate, review, and most of all appreciate the quality of the virtual environment;
- *socializers*, enjoying social interaction; for them the game "*is a backdrop for meaningful long-term social interactions. It's the context and catalyst, not the end in itself*" (Zichermann & Cunnigham, 2011, p. 22). They support, share, comment, like, post: they are motivated by the social dimension of a game;
- *killers*, who want to win other players and play harassing behaviors: they are motivated by competition. Unlike achievers they want to win beating other competitors (Zichermann & Cunningham, 2011).

So, different gamers have different motivations and enjoy different game features. In this view achievers' primarily search for challenge, explorers appreciate discovery, socializers search for interactions, and killers search for a hard competition (Bartle, 1996; Schell, 2019). So, game designers have to take into account these preferences, offering different types of gamers the features they appreciate.

SERIOUS GAMES FOR CULTURAL HERITAGE: BENEFITS AND MOTIVATIONAL ASPECTS

Benefits and Goals

The strength of serious games is clear: "*games are fun and engaging*" (Ge & Ifenthaler, 2018, p. 2). So, meaningful gamification can be an effective tool (Kuo, 2015a) for audience development strategies, in order to attract and possibly engage new target groups. This is particularly true for young audiences (Apostolellis et al., 2018).

In particular, serious games applications to cultural heritage can help organizations to achieve multiple goals:

- *informative goals*. Games offer visibility to cultural sites, their collections, and their opportunities. In some cases people do not even know about the existence of a given site. Games can be the fly-wheel for a visit;
- *educational/learning goals*. Games are ways to provide cultural educational contents to gamers (Ge & Ifenthaler, 2018). Such content useful to get audiences familiar to cultural properties and to support them in decoding cultural content. Studies show that people visiting a museum or any other cultural site with a prior basic information earn a deeper and better learning experience from the visit, than those who do not (Falk, 2016). As Falk remarks: "*both prior interest and prior knowledge are important and vital predictors of what and how much someone learns from a museum experience*" (2016, p. 27) Audiences become active players, rather than passive information receivers. This improves learning effectiveness (Prensky, 2001), in line with experiential learning theories (Kolb & Kolb, 2010);
- *engaging goals*. Games are able to engage audiences (Black, 2012), as players find spaces for being active and simulate real actions. In his pioneering book Abt writes: "*In dreams begin responsibilities' said the poet, and in games begin realities. Games offer expanded possibilities for*

action in mode that, while chiefly mental, includes the felt freedom, intuitive speed, and reactive responses of physical movements" (1970, p. 5);

- *attitude changing goals.* Games are enjoyable and so they can support a positive attitude towards cultural experiences, which can be other than tedious, but fun. This change of perspective is rational, but supported by enjoyment and positive emotions (Mezirow, 1991). For example the conviction that culture is boring can be broken by the perception of beauty in a picture, the surprise in a story, the fun in an activity, and so on. In this process also sharing the learning experience with other players and getting new points of view is important (Kolb & Kolb, 2010);
- *behavioral goals.* Games can promote behaviors, as planning a visit to a cultural site, searching for information about an artist or an artistic style, buying books, and so on;
- *digital marketing goals.* Games can be also useful in lead generation, lead qualification and nurturing (see among others Baker, 2021).

The organization proposing the game directly benefits from an effective game project as above described. But the benefits of a change of attitude towards arts and culture, or the promotion of cultural consumptions are for the entire cultural sector.

Motivational Issues

Serious games for cultural heritage are forms of meaningful gamification (Nicholson, 2012; 2015). Not all games are transformative, according to the provided Schell's definition (2012); e.g., pastimes are not. On the contrary, those games aiming at getting new audiences closer to cultural heritage are potentially transformative. This is particularly visible for young people, who can start appreciating new things, improve school performances and even find new inspirations for their education and future career.

The key factor is motivation, which moves people to act, and can be intrinsic or extrinsic (Djaouti et al., 2011; Rekhi, 2017). People completing tasks for pure enjoyment from the task itself are intrinsically motivated (Malone, 1981): so arts lovers attend exhibitions and participate in cultural events in town; when they travel they plan visits to local archeological sites and museums and so on. On the contrary, people doing things and completing tasks to get rewards and incentives - e.g. attending a cultural event for social reasons - are driven by an extrinsic motivation. Serious games design has to balance the two types of motivation drivers and make players draw motivation and stimuli from the experience. A successful project is able to make players play and go further, beyond the game, in terms of learning, attitudes, behaviors, as described. This is a crucial aspect to take into account, which makes the design of serious games more complicated than pure games one.

DESIGN ISSUES

The Ludic Learning Space

A ludic learning space is a *"free and safe space that provides the opportunity for individuals to play with their potentials and ultimately commit themselves to learn, develop, and grow"* (Kolb & Kolb, 2010, p.27). The term "ludic" deals with the game experience. As Abt (1987) remarks, serious games are not incompatible with fun. Zichermann & Cunningham note that *"everything has the potential to be fun"*

(2011 p.2) and so analyze the need to introduce a *"fun quotient"* in game design. This is true also for cultural heritage and the ludic learning space has to couple entertainment and education (Bruckman, 1999).

An effective design of such space has to start from a careful target audience analysis, in order to tailor the ludic learning space design to it. Is the game mainly tailored to adolescents, young adults or to families? Different target audiences require different game features. Besides main target audience, other two basic elements are to be defined: a clear purpose and the design of the players journey. Once made these basic choices, operational game features like the choice of the type of game, its storytelling and the dyad mechanics-dynamics, can be defined. These aspects are described in the next paragraphs.

A Clear Purpose

As Schell (2019) suggests, a good start for serious game design is a problem statement. So, towards the solution of which problem is the game called to contribute? problem is the game called to try to solve for the cultural organization?
Some good examples of clear purposes for game development are presented here:

- *Virtual Songline* is a project made of interactive cultural heritage survival games, supported by virtual reality and augmented reality technologies. The project is aiming at *"simulating, representing and promoting the cultural heritage of First Nations across Australia"* (Virtual Songlines, n.d.);
- *Race against Time* is a game created for the Tate Gallery. Its purpose is *"to informally inspire and educate users simply by playing through the beautiful artscapes"* (Nelson, in Tate Gallery, 2012);
- *Find the future* is the game launched in 2011 for the 100 years anniversary of the New York Public Library. Creators present it so: *"the game is designed to empower young people to find their own futures by bringing them face-to-face with the writings and objects of people who made an extraordinary difference"* (McGonigal, in The New York Public Library, n.d.);
- *The World of Lexica*, is an awarded 3D action videogame (The World of Lexica, n.d.) whose purpose is to *"inspire kids to pursue reading on their own and simultaneously to get them familiar with characters from classical literature"* (Schell, in Toppo, 2013). In order to encourage reading, players can interact with some literary popular characters, like the Cheshire cat from Alice's Adventures in Wonderland. And most of all, players are encouraged to read the stories, also with the support of an e-reader allowing them to access the texts.

As it is possible to argue from the examples, a clear purpose helps keep the project focused on the goal, evaluating each possible dynamic, mechanic, component, and add-on, according to their potential contribution (or distraction) from the goal itself. Besides, a clear purpose also sets the specific and measurable objectives which inform control and evaluation.

Designing the journey(s)

The quality and memorability of the user/player experience is crucial for any game (King, 2021; Schell, 2019). A positive, engaging experience supports the decision to spend time in playing, so, the journey for the players has to be carefully designed. Each game has a starting point and in most cases a final objective. Between the two a player makes a progression from being novice, to expert, up to master

(Zichermann & Cunningham, 2011), and each step has to be characterized by specific objectives, and is facilitated by narrative and engagement loops (King, 2021).

In serious games this journey has to support a main journey, to achieve main goals of the game project. Making players enjoy playing the game and become masters, in fact, is not enough in serious games. Main journey in serious games applications for cultural heritage is related to audience development. Each of the two journeys has to be carefully designed in all its stages, contents and dynamics according to specific objectives. Process maps (Kim et al., 2013) are useful to visualize the steps of each journey and the interplay between the journeys.

It's important to define a proper level of challenge for each step (Malone, 1981), so to avoid players feeling frustrated (in case of too difficult tasks) or bored (in case of too easy ones).

Novice players need to be encouraged to join the game through a welcome message, clear goals and instructions, as well as accessible initial tasks. Learning has to be supported through information and knowledge, which can be step by step provided. Designers have to think about possible prior knowledge requirements. In most cases, e.g., "Race against Time", required no prior art knowledge (Nelson, in Tate Gallery, 2012). This favors players' inclusion. Otherwise some scaffolding systems are necessary. Young audiences draw motivation from visible progress tracking and rewards through immediate feedbacks, points or badges (e.g., to get after a correct answer to a quiz regarding an art work or a painter's life), challenges from missions and goals, as well as social recognition from interactions. This generates engagement and positive reinforcement (Mak, 2016); besides, it also provides useful data for game monitoring.

As players keep going with the game, they start "*to learn how the system works*" (Zichermann & Cunningham, 2011, p.30) and become experts. At this stage they need new contents, as well as status and gratifications (e.g., from badges); in fact pride, surprise, and share with friends are positive motivational drivers in this stage. Designers have to decide at which level players become experts, as well as which information and knowledge are to be provided for their learning. At the same time designers have to define how to support main journey and identify expected progresses in players' intrinsic interest and positive attitude towards cultural heritage at this level. Specific cultural consumption behaviors to promote are to be identified, e.g., online cultural contents to explore, or a visit to plan. A good engagement loop can be in quizzes asking questions whose answer can be found searching for content online, or visiting a cultural site (Kim et al., 2013; King, 2021) This way the game is supporting main journey, on an extrinsic motivation base, as these actions are rewarded. But this is acceptable at low levels of cultural awareness.

Players at the last step of their journey become masters. Here too designers have to decide at which level players become masters, as well as which information and knowledge are to be provided for their learning, identifying specific behaviors to promote. Players at this level need to see their mayorship confirmed. Pride and competition can push them to play, in order to get special benefits, like exclusive unlocks and accesses. But most of all at this stage designers have to support specifically main journey. What kind of players' cultural consumption behaviors do designers want to promote? Performed behaviors mean that players are progressing in the main journey.

As seen, intrinsic and extrinsic motivation are involved in the interplay between the two journeys. Extrinsic motivation can support the journey in the first stages. A successful serious game for cultural heritage is able to stimulate audiences' interest and engagement towards it. This means to have audiences who are intrinsically motivated to discover cultural heritage. In fact, the goal is not to have systems where progresses in main journey only serve the function of getting points to progress in the game. This is the paradox of having main journey supporting the game journey.

Previous considerations show the need to carefully choose game dynamics and mechanics, as later described.

Choosing the Game

Several different types of game applications for cultural heritage can be identified. Most of them are outcome oriented games, pushing participants to complete specific tasks and achieve specific goals. Others are process-oriented games, that do not really have an end-game final objective (like Second Life), but support participants' objectives like exploration, decision making improvement, and training purposes through simulations (King, 2021). Some games are easier to design and play than others, which are definitely more complex, also for the adopted technology. The following is a list of main types of games designed for field applications.

1. Action/adventure games

As a cited study has shown (Yanev, 2019), players prefer action games. These, supported by an effective narrative related to the cultural site (e.g., being it an archeological site or a modern art museum), can provide engaging dynamics.

A possible classic game of this type, to play online or on-site, is the scavenger or treasure hunt. An example is "Find the Future", the game of the New York Public Library, involving gamers in a search for hidden objects through the corridors of the secret library basement.

The Smithsonian American Art Museum launched in 2008 'Ghosts of a chance', the first alternate reality game (ARG) for a museum (Goodlander, 2009) . Players were engaged in a three months play, including interconnected online and on-site activities. The museum was the set for a ghost story, where participants had to solve a mystery.

2. Role playing and simulation games

Role playing and simulation games are also an interesting solution for a meaningful gamification. Players analyze, directly experience, solve problems, and make decisions, in a real experiential learning process (Kolb & Kolb, 2010).

A good and simple example is the game proposed by National Museums Scotland, "Build a Pyramid" (Explore our Collections - Games, n.d.): players go back to Ancient Egypt and must build a pyramid for the Pharaoh. They have to make decisions about aspects like the terrain to build upon, the materials for the construction, the dimension of the pyramid, as well as the number of employees to hire. For each choice the player has three choices and receives from the Prime Minister information about different solutions. At the end of the game the player receives a feedback, including the evaluation of the appropriateness of the choices and the results of the construction in terms of stability, expected durability, and prestige. The game is very simple, and well designed. It encourages thinking, problem solving, information evaluation, use of pieces of advice, and decision making. National Museums Scotland proposes other similar games (Explore our Collections - Games, n.d.), to learn history and approach world cultures, e.g., learning how an Egyptian, or a Roman soldier got dressed.

An interesting simulation game is provided by the Canada Aviation and Space Museum's. Ace Academy is a flight simulation app released in 2014, bringing players back to World War I and experience an aviation training to learn how to fly a biplane (Kuo, 2015c). App designers reconstructed online vintage aircraft models and described real historical facts in the storyline, so they are able to support students' studying history.

3. Shooter games

Shooter games are easy to design, as it only takes to define a conflict and the involved parts. But they provide a limited learning experience, easily fall into triteness, and so are less suitable for a meaningful gamification. Besides, with their narrative, shooter games are the typical controversial type of video game (see later). For this reason, they are not suitable for applications for cultural heritage.

4. Specific knowledge and skill games

In some cases the game is a test and a training at specific skills. For example, the game "Latin Translators required" of National Museums Scotland (currently no more available) encouraged students -and not only- to use their own latin knowledge in order to translate some latin inscriptions.

5. "Tell me about me" games

Some games combine learning with some sort of self-exploration. They are not psychological tests, of course, but ask profiling questions. An example is the game of National Museums Scotland "Which primate are you?" (Explore our Collections - Games, n.d.). Players are asked a series of questions about their behavior in some given situations (e.g. "What are you like when hanging out in a crowd?"). Multiple choice provided answers describe typical reactions and behaviors of specific primates. Curious players discover something about themselves and learn at the same time some primates habits. In such cases self-exploration acts as an extrinsic motivational factor.

6. Casual games formats

Game formats like digital quizzes, puzzles, hidden objects to find in a picture, crosswords and so on (Partarakis et al., 2017) are typical formats for casual games. They are seemingly superficial for a meaningful gamification. On the contrary, organizations can decide to propose sets of several little games like these, connected to form a learning path. They are cheap to be implemented and besides they are familiar to people playing, so don't require to provide long rules explanations to players.

7. Can you do it the same? Look-alike

In some cases cultural organizations can use existing popular games with their platforms, or apps, in a creative way, according to own goals. A popular videogame, Minecraft, offers a good example of such opportunity. Both the British Museum (Marshall, n.d.) and the Smithsonian Museum (Smith, 2017) successfully launched open calls for volunteers to make online reproductions of their sites through Minecraft. Another Minecraft project regards the online reconstruction of the Ancient Rome (Kuo, 2012) to educate young people about history.

Main Elements in Serious Games Design

Serious games applications for cultural heritage provide cultural content within a game context. In order to transmit the content it is necessary to create a motivating environment to learn and engage (King, 2021), and this can be done through: a. an effective storytelling, b. engaging dynamics and effective mechanics, plus c. a nice aesthetics.

1. Storytelling

An effective storytelling for cultural heritage (Falcone, 2020) is able to engage audiences on both rational and emotional basis. The game storyline has to be interesting, connected to the context and the learning goals of the game. Gamers enter the story and become leading players; so they become story-holders of the museum stories and story-doers at the same time.

For example in "Father and Son", the videogame launched by the National Archeological Museum in Naples (Father and Son - the game, n.d.), the main character in the videogame is the young Michel, who receives a letter from his father and starts his adventure in the Museum and around. Gamers so can virtually visit museum roots and areas, with multiple turning points.

Museums and other cultural sites have many stories to tell. How to choose the ones to situate in the game storytelling? This is done through a cross evaluation considering the potential appeal of the story, its cultural value, and the importance of sharing it with audiences. It's important to identify possible gateways for the players. Gateways are open accesses for players to cross. A gateway can be a known artwork in the collection (e.g., the Mona Lisa for the Louvre), or a story able to attract audiences' curiosity, with an overlap between the story and the audience's world, in terms of culture, interests and so on. A good gateway can be a starting point for a game design or even its entire topic. For example, the Metropolitan Museum of Art designed a whole game on one of its most representative artworks: Virginie Gautreau -Madame X- painted by John Singer Sargent. In "Murder at the Museum" (Murder at the Museum, n.d.), a mobile detective game set back in 1899, visitors are called to identify the killer of Madame X, the lady portrayed in the homonymous picture. During the game, visitors explore the museum and interview different characters. Through interviews cultural contents are conveyed.

The game narrative is set in a specific time and space (set of action). There are several possible choices:

- a real cultural location -such as a museum- at the present time;
- a real cultural location, but back in time, such as going back to Ancient Rome, for a travel in both time and space;
- a fantasy world, in the past, present, or future time.

The first two options are frequently used, as they are able to promote the specific cultural property proposing the game. In other cases the game set of action proposes mixed forms of the above mentioned solutions. In the mentioned game "Father and Son" (Father and Son - the game, n.d.) past and present alternate in the player's travel, with multiple historical locations, related to the museum collection, such as life before the Vesuvius volcanic eruption which destroyed the city of Pompeii in 79, life in the ancient Egypt or ancient Rome, and so on.

2. Aesthetics

Video games are immersive experiences, so the aesthetics of a game matters to gamers and contributes to attract players. Technological advances allowed an exponential development of graphic interface, sound quality, and the general game environment design during last years. Games aesthetics is always more realistic, engaging, sophisticated, also thanks to virtual 3D reconstructions of the environments. First game applications like Pacman or Tetris can be hardly compared with modern settings in games like Assassin's Creed, so perfect to be considered as a possible useful documentary source in the reconstruction process of the Notre Dame Cathedral immediately after the fire in 2019. Experts rejected this possibility for a matter of both lack of exact interiors proportions and some details in the reconstruction, but the accurate virtual reconstruction of the Cathedral which took one year work by its designers (Rea, 2019) is anyway valuable. It is interesting that a virtual setting in a videogame was so accurate to be considered eligible for becoming a documentary source. Any form of mapping and digitalization of cultural heritage is a way to document and preserve it (Santos et al, 2017; Verbiest et al., 2017) and this is also true for digital reconstructions in commercial and serious games. Immersive and reliable reproductions (Liarokapis et al., 2017) support an advanced storytelling (Maietti et al., 2017) and players engaging explorations. This is possible thanks to the increasing use of multimodal games technologies, like augmented or virtual reality, in both artistic and archeological reconstructions (Liarokapis et al, 2017). An interesting example is "Rome reborn", an international project offering an accurate and trustworthy 3d high resolution reconstruction of the Ancient Rome with its streets and main monuments, which can be virtually visited thanks to the accurate work of a team made of international arts scholars and technology experts (Anderson et al., 2009).

CHOOSING DYNAMICS AND MECHANICS

Dynamics and connected mechanics can drive engagement (Hunicke et al., 2004). The Octalysis model (Chou, 2014) above mentioned can be applied to cultural heritage applications. The identified eight basic key motivators are operative tools able to leverage intrinsic or extrinsic motivation and support both players' journeys.

1. *Epic Meaning and Calling.* An epic meaning is a higher meaning making the game more engaging for its players. Serious games have relevant (and somehow really epic) meanings, but a creative (and fantasy) epic one is always effective. In "Race against time" (Tate Gallery, 2012) the main character is a chameleon, whose epic meaning is to save the world from Dr. Greyscale's plan is to eliminate colors from the world. In doing so, players are engaged in a travel from 1890 until today, exploring modern art. Level by level they discover main pictures and art movements.
2. *Development and Accomplishment.* Dynamics connected to development and accomplishment typically leverage people's desire to improve own skills and make progresses. These dynamics can be connected to the main goal of the serious game, through a cultural knowledge progressively provided, suggestions to learn more, and privileges connected to the goal (e.g., an invitation for the exhibition opening or any other event at the cultural site).
3. *Empowerment of Creativity and Feedback.* Games can favor creative expression of the players. For example in "Ghosts of a chance" players were asked to create artifacts (Goodlander, 2009). Another

way to favor creativity is to provide players digital elements to be combined together in modular original compositions. These elements can regard the background and the general environment, as well as some features of the adventure (missions or paths). Players can personalize some cues and colors of the interface, the dashboard, their profile, or their character/avatar. In "The World of Lexica" (The World of Lexica, n.d.), players can personalize the appearance of their fantastic character. Alternative forms of animals, plus some add-ons, as parts of other animals or pieces of clothes are provided. Each option for creativity expression in the game connects players to their fantasy. Social feedbacks can be asked and provide gratification.

4. *Ownership and Possession.* The sense of ownership can regard concrete rewards, e.g., gadgets to be picked at the cultural site, or items to collect completing a set. But sense of ownership is also stimulated by the availability of a personal area or an account on the game app, or the personalization features mentioned at point C. of this list. When players feel some sense of ownership, they will be more likely playing and interacting with the institution;

5. *Social influence and Relatedness.* In order to accomplish social needs, it's important for meaningful gamification projects to promote social visibility, sharing, collaborative learning, and social feedbacks. Players can be encouraged to see others' profiles, to produce user generated contents like pictures or selfies, to face team challenges, to express their opinions with likes, rates, and comments, to earn some social points or other rewards for doing actions like inviting friends to play and so on. Social influence is also related to status, which is *"the relative position of an individual in relation to others, especially in a social group"* (Zichermann & Cunningham, 2011, p.10). Transmedia content diffusion can include videos, text, pictures, conveyed also through social media, as for "Ghosts of a chance" (Goodlander, 2009). Players' posts about the game can provide the cultural organization earned media content;

6. *Scarcity and Impatience.* Scarcity pushes action. All games offer scarce benefits, like rewards, which are only for the best players, limited edition gadgets, seats to an exclusive event, or exclusive memberships. Also time in time-based competition on certain tasks is scarce, so designers can fix deadlines to complete tasks or to get benefits.

7. *Unpredictability and Curiosity.* Well designed games surprise players. Surprise favors exploration, questions and curiosity. This can be done through storytelling, anecdotes, revelations about works or artist's life. Easter eggs and unexpected rewards are helpful. Unpredictable events can occur during the play, and they can be either positive or negative;

8. *Loss and Avoidance.* At the basis of dynamics like time-based rewards, there is also the aversion to the risk of losing. The fear to miss an opportunity can solicit an action by players.

Above listed main key motivators regard each type of game. Most of them leverage extrinsic motivation. Meaningful gamification needs to balance intrinsic and extrinsic motivation, so it can leverage the BLAP components to engage players (Gopaladesikan, 2013) towards the goal of the application. Among the listed key motivators, as players go on with the game, becoming experts and masters, Development and Accomplishment can be used as key motivator for intrinsic motivation to get closer to arts and culture. Players' interest and autonomy can be fostered; they can grow in knowledge and competence about cultural heritage, as well as the understanding of their meaning. Players can be encouraged to explore, learn, and discover, going beyond the game and searching for information on their own. In order to activate this motivation driver, Unpredictability and Curiosity can be useful, with proper attractive gateways like a story, a detail, some funny or surprising cultural content.

Dynamics and mechanics designers also have to take into account the described different basic features of gamers (Bartle, 1996). Achievers' interest in getting rewards, reaching a goal, and improving their status is different than explorers' interest, who are more interested in the quality of the experience and want to be surprised at special effects in their dynamic immersive exploration of this virtual environment. As Zichermann and Cunningham (2011) note, even though the majority of designers are achievers, the majority of players are socializers; followed by explorers and achievers, with a minority of killer gamers. For this reason, respectively: rewards, visual aspects, social aspects, and competition can be good extrinsic motivators for each type of gamers, to keep in consideration (Rekhi, 2017). Achievers and killers prefer action; on the contrary socializers and explorers prefer inter-action with the environment and with other players. The latter together are the most copious part of players; they prefer inter-action with the environment and with other players. For this reason, some organizations are starting opting for multiplayers' games solutions, also thanks to technologically advanced interactive game platforms making possible communication, interaction and competition for distant players. Examples are "Mystery at the Museum" (Klopfer et al., 2005), which was meant for groups of parents and children, or "Ghosts of a chance" (Goodlander, 2009) which favors multiplayer collaboration, and leverages collective intelligence. Also events and meetings in presence, like in "Ghosts of a chance" (Goodlander, 2009) meet social needs.

CONTROVERSIES

There are some general concerns about (meaningful or not) gamification applications.

General concerns regard the potential abuse of video games, with three main charges (see Schell, 2019): violence (the conflict in video games narrative often offers simulations of violent actions), risk of addiction (videogames engaging loops are designed in order to make people play and re-play), and negative effects on physical and mental health (Barlett et al., 2009).

Researchers' remarks recall that relevant goals of serious games should not lead to under-evaluate the problems connected to the use of the means.

Serious games applications to cultural heritage present some specific controversial aspects. First of all in some historical locations and museums their use is not appropriated (Akhtar, 2016; Kuo, 2015b). Some curators are skeptical about any application of serious games to cultural heritage, and concerned about the possibility of trivialization induced by the game component. One issue is how to avoid the risk to "*compromise the museum's credibility by supporting the fiction of the game*" (Goodlander, 2009). A second issue is how can games solve big problems like spreading culture or get new generations interested in cultural heritage. A game is a game, and for some authors mixing and matching education and entertainment is not functional. In this view, these applications could render approaching cultural heritage just a sort of "side effect" of playing a game. The result is the risk of visitors walking through museum corridors "*passing Picasso in search of Pikachu*", as Vonn deplores (2016) referring to Pokémon Go, the popular location-based game whose gamers go through city locations using their smartphone with a GPS locator in search of Pokémons, shown by augmented reality on their smartphone screen. Games can be useful to attract new audiences, but developing and engaging an audience is something more complex (Black, 2012).

Some concerns about mixing culture and games also regard the ludic dimension. Bruckman (1999) for example remarks that an educational game loses most of its fun, and so is not a game anymore, but an exercise. Granic et al. (2014) define educational games similar to "*chocolate-covered broccoli*". Children love chocolate and hate broccoli. Can their mix be enough to encourage children to appreciate eating broccoli - the educational goal of the game - and start eating broccoli? Or is the result an unpalatable mix? As Schell remarks: "*if you make a game that is really good for people, but no one likes it (the game version of a broccoli smoothie), you haven't helped anyone* (2019, p. 456).

The problem is the asymmetric relation between means and ends. Cultural sites managers supporting designers in serious games applications are aware of educational goals, and that a ludic engaging experience is just a mean. On the contrary, gamers approaching the application can consider the educational dimension just a mean - it's in the game characterization, with its storyline and its setting - and having fun is their real goal. This is strictly connected to the problem of players' motivation. Main strength of games is their ability to attract audiences and most of all young people. But the point is that it "*replaces an intrinsic reward with an extrinsic one. In other words, it shifts a participant's motivation from doing something because it is inherently rewarding to doing it for some other reason that isn't as meaningful. This (...) is ultimately less motivating*" (Sierra, cited in Finley, 2012, p.1). After all, in case of lack of irrecoverable motivation, serious games are not enough to move people to a specific behavior, like visiting a museum. Besides, organizations run the risk of actions devaluation, considering them to be necessarily sustained by the game in order to be done (Deterding et al., 2011). Players can't remain for the whole journey in a reward loop. Zichermann and Cunningham recognize that "*Gamification works better if and when we can align intrinsic motivations and extrinsic rewards, and we should strive to achieve that wherever possible*" (2011, p.28). But the authors go on assuming that: "*our new belief is that we should accept players and their motivational states as they are, and try to help them get to where they would like to go, as well as where we'd like them to be*" (2011, p.28).

Other concerns regard the risk of decontextualization: when a game -like a treasure or scavenger hunt, but also a quiz- focuses on a single artifact, a single moment of an artist's life, it "*encourages students to see the museum as a bunch of disconnected, decontextualized artifacts*" (Klopfer et al., 2005, p.2). This could be an obstacle to develop a systemic view.

PROBLEMS TO CONSIDER

When managers approach serious games projects for cultural heritage, they face above all problems related to financial resources (Black, 2012) and skills. An investigation showed that cultural organizations managers recognize the lack of both mentioned resources as the real obstacle to technological or digital innovations implementation (Dosdoce, 2013).

A professional meaningful gamification project requires consistent investments in the architectural and interface design, involving many different professionals in the project. Contrary to a business project, which has to produce direct revenues, serious games for cultural heritage are not meant to be profitable and often are free applications. Maybe they can generate more sold tickets, but outcomes of such programs are long-term and intangible, regarding awareness, knowledge acquisition, and so on. Temporary exhibitions maybe do not offer time and returns adequate to recoup what organizations might spent to create a serious game. On the contrary, this seems to better fit a cultural site or a museum's permanent collection. Financial resources for such projects can be from own museum funds, result from public funds for Arts and Culture, from crowdfunding, fundraising campaigns, or from a sponsorship program.

A second problem regards skills. Serious games design is a team work requiring:

- digital design skills (by professionals like programmers, UX design experts, motion graphic designers, storytellers, and so on);
- specific cultural knowledge, by internal staff or external consultants, providing cultural contents;
- project management competencies;
- marketing and communication skills.

Most of the above listed skills are not available within cultural organizations. They are to be acquired on a regular base, also considering necessary adjustments to the games, to make them still playable on all web browsers after some time from their design.

SOLUTIONS AND RECOMMENDATIONS

Serious Games are not a Fix-All Tool

Games, even serious ones, are not appropriate to any heritage site, as said. Besides, they clearly cannot fill educational and cultural gaps, nor change audiences' attitude towards cultural heritage. Motivational theories above described clearly show that a serious game is not enough to ensure attitude and behavioral changes, nor most of all audience development by itself. But serious games can be a good tool to attract and reach audiences, especially young generations, who maybe would never plan a visit to a heritage site. It's essential to provide not just a nice and fun online game experience, but to encourage new audiences -and most of all young generations- to on-site engaging experiences. In other terms, a serious game can be a first step, a sort of lead magnet (Baker, 2021) to attract new audiences, but it's not sufficient to retain and develop them. In order to reach this goal, the whole heritage site, along with its cultural proposal and related communication, needs to be transformed within a project of audience development. A serious game has to be part of a structured audience development plan, made of innovation in the cultural activities as well as in their communication, also with the support of ICTs. The Tate Gallery strategy is a good example of such approach. The institution structured and adopted in 2013 its digital strategy plan. Its strategy *"is audience centred and responds to their needs"*; it *"has multichannel and multimedia mindset"* and *"considers online and offline experiences as one"* (Tate Gallery, 2013). An effective interplay between online and on-site experiences is crucial for the audience journey, in the game (e.g. rewarded missions to be accomplished by a visit to the cultural site) and beyond. Curiosity and competition drive exploration and discovery. So, the live game experience proposed by "Find the future" (New York Public Library) in 2011, combined *"real-world missions with virtual clues and online collaboration — all inspired by 100 works from the amazing collections of The New York Public Library"* (Werbach & Hunter, 2012).

Different tools can be used to reach different target audiences, taking into account their habits and preferences and serious games are one of them. As Birchall, manager at the Wellcome Collection, clearly explains, games:

are part of a larger strategy of using many different things to engage the public. You use video games to reach those who play games, like you create documentaries for those who watch television. We're not trying to convert museum people into games players (Birchall, in Marshall, n.d.).

A serious game project has to fix clear priorities, and never misunderstand means (the game) for goals (cultural heritage promotion, audience development). Mixing education and fun requires a specific ability (Bruckman, 1999), which is the ability to structure the path of the two interconnected above described journeys. As Birchall states: "*Our motto is 'no chocolate-covered broccoli here'. We're not making unpalatable things tasty by wrapping game magic around them*" (Birchall in Marshall, n.d.).

It's not easy to find a balance between online and on-site experiences, between intrinsic and extrinsic motivation, as well as to make progresses in the game journey support progresses also in the main journey. But this balance is necessary for the success of a serious game project.

Facing the Lack of Resources

The lack of both skills and financial resources is common among cultural organizations (Dosdoce, 2013). This can be an obstacle for them to an own game implementation, but they can lean on other games, in the wake of big video games productions. An example of this option is the mentioned popular game Pokémon Go, a mobile game based on a geolocalized augmented reality. The goal of the game is to search for Pokémons dispersed among locations. PokéStops are points of interest in the game, where gamers can find Pokémons (Vonn, 2016). They can be both public or private locations; most of them are chosen by the game developer, but other cultural organizations can ask to be included in the list and become one of the game points of interest, getting visibility and traffic. Some experts are concerned about this traffic made of extrinsically motivated, unaware museums visitors from the game (Vonn, 2016). Some organizations tried to leverage the opportunity of these visits, offering specific art Tours; an art-tour guide at the Metropolitan Museum of Art explains: "*We were seeing people playing PokémonGO in the museum (...) and it's awesome the game is getting people in the door — but we figured we could combine the game with our tours and give people the best of both worlds*" (Downey, in Mercado, 2016).

The above mentioned use of Minecraft is another example of using existing video games: many young people know how this game works, so an open call or a contest to reconstruct heritage sites through this game can be welcomed. In the words of a curator "*it's an innovative way to get the public interested in collections, especially audiences that wouldn't normally engage with them*" (Wisdom, in Marshall, n.d.).

A second possible solution to the lack of resources is to search for partnerships with digital game design schools and universities. This is what National Museums Scotland did with Robots, a game designed and created by university students (Explore our Collections - Games, n.d.). This is interesting for both players. In fact, on one hand students can make an interesting learning experience; on the other cultural organizations can get good products at reasonable, or even almost zero, costs.

FUTURE RESEARCH DIRECTIONS

Several topics can be explored through future research in the field.

First in the list are serious games for cultural heritage case studies, describing best practices in design. It's important to focus on assessing their both short and medium-term outcomes, in order to evaluate the effectiveness towards different audiences also through a cost-benefit analysis (Dörner et al., 2016). Did games support -in gamers' view- any change in their attitude towards cultural heritage in general? And what about the specific cultural heritage site and institution signing the game? Did the experience support any behavioral change in their general cultural consumptions (beyond the specific cultural property site), such as visiting cultural sites, attending exhibitions, making virtual visits to heritage places, and so on?

It's important also to investigate the role of social components on this effectiveness. Studies could compare results from individual gaming, and those from class involvement at school.

Another specific aspect to understand some more is the player experience (Dörner et al., 2016) and the evidence regarding how extrinsic motivation cues contribute to feed intrinsic motivation, in the interplay between the two described journeys. It will also be important to explore how serious games interact with intrinsically motivated audiences (Bowser et al., 2013). What about cultural content provided in games? Is it just a must-go-through in order to pass to the next level, or do gamers real find interest in it? And which types of communication styles are more effective to learn from cultural contents provided in games?

CONCLUSION

Serious games applications can be an effective tool within an audience development plan, especially to attract young audiences. Cultural organizations need to know their target audiences, their needs and preferences, and target game dynamics and mechanics. They have to define goals and share them with game designers, in order to identify which behaviors are to be encouraged by the game. It's also important to invest in the graphic interface and in the storyline, as well as in the cultural content provided through the game, also through a transmedia narrative. Extrinsic and intrinsic motivation can interplay, the first related to the means, the second to the goals. They can be combined in the two gamers journeys, which are to be carefully designed in their main aspects, including cultural content to provide and goals to achieve in different stages, providing interconnections between online and on-site visitor experience.

Serious games are to be inserted in wider audience development plans, providing the modernization of proposed cultural activities and their communication to audiences, in terms of content, language, and channels. In this view, serious games can be modern and interesting tools for cultural organizations.

ACKNOWLEDGMENT

The author is thankful to the Editors and to the anonymous reviewers for their reviews.

REFERENCES

Abt, C. C. (1987). *Serious Games*. University Press of America.

Akhtar, A. (2016, July 12). Holocaust Museum, Auschwitz want Pokémon Go hunts out. *USA Today*. https://eu.usatoday.com/story/tech/news/2016/07/12/holocaust-museum-auschwitz-want-pokmon-go-hunts-stop-pokmon/86991810/

Anderson, E. F., McLoughlin, L., Liarokapis, F., Peters, C., Petridis, P., & de Freitas, S. (2009). Serious Games in Cultural Heritage. In *Proceedings of the 10th VAST International Symposium on Virtual Reality, Archaeology and Cultural Heritage—STARs Session* (pp. 29-48). Eurographics.

Antin, J., & Churchill, E. F. (2011). Badges in Social Media: A Social Psychological Perspective. In *Proceedings of the SIGCHI Conference on Human Factors in Computing Systems*. ACM.

Apostolellis, P., Bowman, D. A., & Chmiel, M. (2018). Supporting Social Engagement for Young Audiences with Serious Games and Virtual Environments in Museums. In AMuseum Experience Design. Springer Series on Cultural Computing. doi:10.1007/978-3-319-58550-5_2

Baker, R. (2021). *Marketing Funnel*. Barnes & Noble Press.

Barlett, C., Anderson, C., & Swing, E. (2009). Video Game Effects - Confirmed, Suspected, and Speculative: A Review of the Evidence. *Simulation & Gaming*, *40*(3), 377–403. doi:10.1177/1046878108327539

Bartle, R. (1996). *Hearts, clubs, diamonds, spades: players who suit MUDs*. http://mud.co.uk/richard/hcds.htm#1

Black, G. (2012). *Transforming Museums in the Twenty-First Century*. Routledge. doi:10.4324/9780203150061

Bowser, A., Hansen, D., & Preece, J. (2013). Gamifying Citizen Science: Lessons and Future Directions. *Proceedings of CHI 2013: Workshop Designing Gamification: Creating Gameful and Playful Experiences*. http://gamification-research.org/wp-content/uploads/2013/03/Bowser_Hansen_Preece.pdf

Bruckman, A. (1999, March 17). *Can Educational Be Fun?* [Paper presentation]. Game Developer's Conference, San Jose, CA. https://www.cc.gatech.edu/~asb/papers/conference/bruckman-gdc99.pdf

Chou, Y. (2015). *Actionable Gamification: Beyond Points, Badges and Leaderboards*. Octalysis Media.

Csikszentmihalyi, M. (1990). *Flow: The Psychology of Optimal Experience*. Harper & Row.

Deterding, S., Dixon, D., Khaled, R., & Nacke, L. (2011). From Game Design Elements to Gamefulness: Defining "Gamification". In *Proceedings of the 15th International Academic MindTrek Conference: Envisioning Future Media Environments*. (pp. 9–15). ACM. 10.1145/2181037.2181040

Djaouti, D., Alvarez, J., & Jessel, J. P. (2011). Classifying serious games: The G/P/S model. In P. Felicia (Ed.), *Handbook of research on improving learning and motivation through educational games: Multidisciplinary approaches* (pp. 118–136). IGI Global. doi:10.4018/978-1-60960-495-0.ch006

Dörner, R., Göbel, S., Effelsberg, W., & Wiemeyer, J. (2016). *Serious games: foundations, concepts and practice*. Springer. doi:10.1007/978-3-319-40612-1

Dosdoce. (2013). *Museums in the digital age* [Paper presentation]. Museum Next. http://www.dosdoce.com/upload/ficheros/noticias/201305/museums_in_the_digital_age__a_dosdoce_survey.pdf

Explore our Collections – Games. (n.d.). *National Museums Scotland*. https://www.nms.ac.uk/explore-our-collections/?type=13119

Falcone, P. (2020). Heritage storytelling. In A. dos Santos Queirós (Ed.), *Examining a New Paradigm of Heritage with Philosophy, Economy, and Education* (pp. 142–156). IGI Global. doi:10.4018/978-1-7998-3636-0.ch010

Falk, J. H. (2016). *Identity and the Museum Visitor Experience*. Routledge. doi:10.4324/9781315427058

Father and Son - the game. (n.d.). *MANN Naples*. https://mannapoli.it/father-and-son-the-game/

Finley, K. (2012, November 14). How 'Gamification' Can Make Your Customer Service Worse. *Wired*. https://www.wired.com/2012/11/gamification-customer-service/

Ge, X., & Ifenthaler, D. (2018). Designing Engaging Educational Games and Assessing Engagement in Game-Based Learning. In Gamification in Education: Breakthroughs in Research and Practice (pp. 1-19). IGI Global. doi:10.4018/978-1-5225-5198-0.ch001

Goodlander, G. (2009). Fictional Press Releases and Fake Artifacts: How the Smithsonian American Art Museum is Letting Game Players Redefine the Rules. In J. Trant & D. Bearman (Eds.), *Museums and the Web 2009: Proceedings*. Archives & Museum Informatics. https://www.archimuse.com/mw2009/papers/goodlander/goodlander.html

Gopaladesikan, S. (2013, January 8). How to Use Badges for Positive Growth. *Gamification.co*. https://www.gamification.co/2013/01/08/how-to-use-badges-for-positive-growth/

Granic, I., Lobel, A., & Engels, R. C. M. E. (2014). The Benefits of Playing Video Games. *The American Psychologist*, *69*(1), 66–78. doi:10.1037/a0034857 PMID:24295515

Grenier, R. (2010). All work and no play makes for a dull museum visitor. *New Directions for Adult and Continuing Education*, *127*(127), 77–85. doi:10.1002/ace.383

Hunicke, R., Leblanc, M., & Zubek, R. (2004). MDA: A Formal Approach to Game Design and Game Research. In *Proceedings of 19th National Conference on Artificial Intelligence - AAAI Workshop on Challenges in Game AI*. AAAI Press.

Kapp, K. M., & Boller, S. (2017, September 5). Core Dynamics: A Key Element in Instructional Game Design. *Atd Blog*. https://www.td.org/insights/core-dynamics-a-key-element-in-instructional-game-design

Kim, H., Hong, J., & Kim, S. H. (2013, October 13). Seoul Museum Week 2013: Collaboration Using Gamification. In N. Proctor & R. Cherry (Eds.), *Museums and the Web*. https://mwa2013.museumsandtheweb.com/paper/seoul-museum-week-2013-collaboration-using-gamification/

King, N. (2021, February 1). Serious Games Guide: Everything You Need To Know In 2021. *Chaostheorygames*. https://www.chaostheorygames.com/blog/serious-games-guide-everything-you-need-to-know-in-2021

Klopfer, E., Perry, J., Squire, K., Jan, M. F., & Steinkuehler, C. (2005). Mystery at the museum: A collaborative game for museum education. In *Proceedings of the 2005 conference on Computer support for collaborative learning: learning 2005: the next 10 years!* (pp. 316-320). International Society of the Learning Sciences. 10.3115/1149293.1149334

Kolb, A. Y., & Kolb, D. A. (2010). Learning to Play, Playing to Learn: A Case Study of a *Ludic* Learning Space. *Journal of Organizational Change Management*, *23*(1), 26–50. doi:10.1108/09534811011017199

Kuo, I. (2012, June 14). *Exploring Ancient Rome through Minecraft*. https://www.gamification.co/2012/06/14/exploring-ancient-rome-through-minecraft/

Kuo, I. (2015a, July 7). Does Gamification Work? Recent Empirical Study Shows Positive Results. *Gamification.co*. https://www.gamification.co/2015/07/07/does-gamification-work-recent-empirical-study-shows-positive-results/

Kuo, I. (2015b, July 15). Educational Games: Approaching Controversial Topics with Care. *Gamification.co*. https://www.gamification.co/2015/07/15/educational-games-approaching-controversial-topics-with-care/

Kuo, I. (2015c, July 21). Reliving WWI Flight History with Mobile Gamification App: Ace Academy. *Gamification.co*. https://www.gamification.co/2015/07/21/reliving-wwi-flight-history-with-mobile-gamification-app-ace-academy/

Liarokapis, F., Petridis, P., Andrews, D., & de Freitas, S. (2017). Multimodal Serious Games Technologies for Cultural Heritage. In M. Ioannides, N. Magnenat-Thalmann, & G. Papagiannakis (Eds.), *Mixed Reality and Gamification for Cultural Heritage* (pp. 371–392). Springer. doi:10.1007/978-3-319-49607-8_15

Mak, H. W. (2016, January 20). Three beneficial Impact of Games in Education for Students. *Gamification.co*. https://www.gamification.co/2016/01/20/3-beneficial-impact-games-education-students/

Malone, T. W. (1981). Toward a theory of intrinsically motivating instruction. *Cognitive Science*, *5*(4), 333–369. doi:10.120715516709cog0504_2

Marshall, S. (n.d.). *Video games in museums: fine art or just fun?* https://stonemarshall.com/news/minecraft-news/video-games-museums-fine-art-just-fun/

McGonigal, J. (2010, October 17). Ideas for modern living: blissful productivity. *The Guardian*. https://www.theguardian.com/lifeandstyle/2010/oct/17/ideas-modern-living-productivity-video-computer-games

Mercado, A. (2016, July 22). Take a PokÃ©mon GO Tour Through the Met Museum This Weekend. *This is New York*. https://www.dnainfo.com/new-york/20160722/upper-east-side/take-pokmon-go-tour-through-met-museum-this-weekend/

Mezirow, J. (1991). *Transformative Dimensions of Adult Learning*. Jossey- Bass.

Murder at the Museum. (n.d.). *Metropolitan Museum of Art*. https://metmystery.oncell.com/pages/

Museum Definition. (n.d.). *ICOM*. https://icom.museum/en/resources/standards-guidelines/museum-definition/

Nicholson, S. (2012). *Strategies for meaningful gamification: Concepts behind transformative play and participatory museums* [Paper presentation]. Meaningful Play 2012, Lansing, MI. https://scottnicholson.com/pubs/meaningfulstrategies.pdf

Nicholson, S. (2015). A RECIPE for Meaningful Gamification. In T. Reiners & L. Wood (Eds.), Gamification in Education and Business (pp. 1-20). Springer. doi:10.1007/978-3-319-10208-5_1

Partarakis, N., Grammenos, D., Margetis, G., Zidianakis, E., Drossis, G., Leonidis, A., Metaxakis, G., Antona, M., & Stephanidis, C. (2017). Digital Cultural Heritage Experience in Ambient Intelligence. In M. Ioannides, N. Magnenat-Thalmann, & G. Papagiannakis (Eds.), *Mixed Reality and Gamification for Cultural Heritage* (pp. 473–505). Springer. doi:10.1007/978-3-319-49607-8_19

Prensky, M. (2001). *Digital Game-based Learning*. McGraw-Hill.

Rea, N. (2019, April 18). Can 'Assassin's Creed' Help Rebuild Notre Dame? How Restoring the Cathedral Will Rely on Both New Tech and Ancient Knowhow. *Artnet*. https://news.artnet.com/market/how-technologies-old-and-new-will-be-needed-to-rebuild-notre-dame-1520689

Rekhi, S. (2017, January 3). Understanding User Psychology: Thinking like a Game Designer. *Medium*. https://medium.com/@sachinrekhi/understanding-user-psychology-thinking-like-a-game-designer-3aafde81ae2d

Sailer, M., Hense, J., Mayr, S. K., & Mandl, H. (2017). How Gamification motivates: An experimental study of the effects of specific game design elements on psychological need satisfaction. *Computers in Human Behavior*, *69*, 371–380. doi:10.1016/j.chb.2016.12.033

Santos, P., Ritz, M., Fuhrmann, C., Monroy, R., Schmedt, H., Tausch, R., Domajnko, M., Knuth, M., & Fellner, D. (2017). Acceleration of 3D Mass Digitization Process: Recent Advances and Challenges. In M. Ioannides, N. Magnenat-Thalmann, & G. Papagiannakis (Eds.), *Mixed Reality and Gamification for Cultural Heritage* (pp. 99–128). Springer. doi:10.1007/978-3-319-49607-8_4

Schell, J. (2012). What Games are Good At [Paper presentation]. 9th Annual Games for Change Festival, New York, NY.

Schell, J. (2019). *The Art of Game Design: A Book of Lenses* (3rd ed.). Taylor & Francis Ltd.

Smith, R. P. (2017, September 15). Fans of Minecraft Are Sure to Dig this Nationwide Museum Fest. *Smithsonianmag*. https://www.smithsonianmag.com/smithsonian-institution/minecraft-fans-dig-museum-fest-180964888/

Tate Gallery. (2012, January 4). *Tate's new art game for mobiles - Race Against Time. Press Release*. https://www.tate.org.uk/press/press-releases/tates-new-art-game-mobiles-race-against-time

Tate Gallery. (2013). *Digital transformation. July 2013 - February 2015*. https://www.tate.org.uk/about-us/projects/digital-transformation

The New York Public Library. (n.d.). *Find the Future: The Game*. http://exhibitions.nypl.org/100/digital_fun/play_the_game

The World of Lexica. (n.d.). *Schell Games*. https://www.schellgames.com/games/the-world-of-lexica

Toppo, G. (2013, June 18). Can a video game encourage kids to read the classics? *USA Today*. https://eu.usatoday.com/story/tech/gaming/2013/06/18/lexica-game-classic-books/2431337/

Verbiest, F., Proesmans, M., & Van Goal, L. (2017). Autonomous Mapping of the Priscilla Catacombs. In M. Ioannides, N. Magnenat-Thalmann, & G. Papagiannakis (Eds.), *Mixed Reality and Gamification for Cultural Heritage* (pp. 75–98). Springer. doi:10.1007/978-3-319-49607-8_3

Virtual Songlines. (n.d.). www.virtualsonglines.org

Vonn, C. (2016, July 12). Pokémon Go Users Flock to Museums, Passing Picasso in Search of Pikachu. *Hyperallergic*. https://hyperallergic.com/310589/pokemon-go-users-flock-to-museums-passing-picasso-in-search-of-pikachu/

Werbach, K., & Hunter, D. (2012). *For the Win: How Game Thinking can Revolutionize your Business.* Wharton Digital Press.

Wood, L. C., & Reiners, T. (2015). Gamification. In M. Khosrow-Pour (Ed.), *Encyclopedia of Information Science and Technology* (3rd ed., pp. 3039–3047). IGI Global. doi:10.4018/978-1-4666-5888-2.ch297

Yanev, V. (2019, May 2). Video Game Demographics - Who Plays. *Games, 2020.* https://techjury.net/stats-about/video-game-demographics/#gref

Zichermann, G., & Cunningham, C. (2011). *Gamification by Design: Implementing Game Mechanics in Web and Mobile Apps.* O'Reilly Media.

ADDITIONAL READING

Alcorn, S., & Turner, W. (2015). *42 Rules for Engaging Members through Gamification: Unlock the Secrets of Motivation, Community and Fun.* Super Star Press.

Dickey, M. D. (2011). Murder on Grimm Isle: The impact of game narrative design in an educational game-based learning environment. *British Journal of Educational Technology, 42*(3), 456–469. doi:10.1111/j.1467-8535.2009.01032.x

Dymek, M., & Zackariasson, P. (2018). *The Business of Gamification: A Critical Analysis.* Taylor and Frances Ltd.

Larsen, I., & Daisy, S. (2014). *Gamification: A Motivational Tool for Achieving Serious Tasks.* Globeedit.

Salen, K. (Ed.). (2008). *The Ecology of Games: Connecting Youth, Games, and Learning.* MIT Press.

Wilkinson, P. (n.d.). *A Brief History of Serious Games.* http://eprints.bournemouth.ac.uk/30697/1/A%20Brief%20History%20of%20Serious%20Games.pdf

Wouters, P., Van Nimwegen, C., Van Oostendorp, H., & Van Der Spek, E. D. (2013). A meta-analysis of the cognitive and motivational effects of serious games. *Journal of Education & Psychology, 105*(2), 249–266. doi:10.1037/a0031311

KEY TERMS AND DEFINITIONS

Audience Engagement: The effort of a cultural organization in reaching an audience and engaging it in its cultural activities.

Badge: A recognition unit for gamers, on achieving a given goal.

Lead Magnet: Any attractive content for an audience (e.g., an e-book or a special discount) able to attract visitors of a website and convert them into leads.

Leaderboard: Visible ranking of gamers according to their performances.

Leads: Potential organization customers who showed some interest in the product and left own contacts.

Points: Value units that gamers collect on progressing in their play.

Chapter 16
A Serious Game for Cultural Heritage?

Maureen Thomas
Inland Norway University of Applied Sciences, Lillehammer, Norway

Bendik Stang
Snowcastle Games, Norway

ABSTRACT

Queens Game explores the potential of creating a serious game for cultural heritage through collaborative intersectorial research and production. Popular neo-medieval entertainment-games lack correct historical content and the appeal of modern character-based screen period drama, which often focuses on female protagonists: princesses attract large followings. Female player-characters in games usually act and dress like males – though studies show that female gamers prefer atmospheric exploration, interactive drama, and gathering and crafting to defeating enemies. The Queens Game incorporates well-researched history and features exploration and gathering, utilizing period-drama and musical approaches to characterization and staging. The player-character, based on a real medieval princess, lives in a virtual, populated, explorable version of her real castle, now built over. Medieval visual, musical, and storytelling modes in a historically accurate setting immerse visitors in the Middle Ages, potentially attracting players who don't normally enjoy games as well as those who do.

INTRODUCTION

The *Queens game* project (2018 -2021) brings together film and interactive media storytelling research at the Norwegian Film School with commercial 3D interactive games-development for entertainment at Snowcastle Games, Oslo, in an innovative approach to serious game, defined as "a game created with the intention to entertain and to achieve at least one additional characterizing goal" (Dörner, Göbel et al., 2016, p.3) - in this case, immersing players in the medieval world. *Queens game* draws on the expertise of the Norwegian Armed Forces Museum and Visitor Centre, Akershus Fortress and Castle [AFCM] to model the 14th-century home (Tschudi-Madsen & Moberg, 1999) of its child queen player-character,

DOI: 10.4018/978-1-7998-9732-3.ch016

Margrete I (1353-1412) of Norway, Denmark and Sweden. This through-designed *HiStoryGame* - not a gamification - addresses dramatic storytelling on the borders of film, animated musical, television period drama and interactive game, including inclusive and exclusive gender appeal. The chapter presents the pilot prototype in relation to neomedieval games for entertainment, and historicity and authenticity for tangible and intangible cultural heritage and virtual tourism. Granström's classification of desirable components for an interactive cultural-heritage serious game, divided into five categories and 17 elements derived from a review of virtual cultural heritage research and applied to existing games for entertainment (Granström, 2013, pp.12-19), provides an analytical framework for *Queens game*. The chapter also summarises some challenges and mutual benefits of intersectorial research and content development designed to maximise social and economic impact.

BACKGROUND: THE APPEAL OF CULTURAL HERITAGE

Cultural Heritage plays a significant part in economic and social life (Katsoni, Upadhya & Stratigea, 2016). "Heritage tourism is one of the fastest-growing segments in the industry and equates to a $171 billion annual spend. (…) Heritage tourists travel (…) in search of authentic experiences and want to learn something new" (Payne, 2018). The United Nations World Tourism Organization suggests that they seek the "distinctive material, intellectual, spiritual and emotional features of a society (…); arts and architecture, historical and cultural heritage, culinary heritage, literature, music, (…) lifestyles, value systems, beliefs and traditions" (UNTWO, 2017). The US National Trust for Historic Preservation defines cultural heritage tourism as "travelling to experience the places, artifacts and activities that authentically represent the stories and people of the past" (NTHP, 2015).

The global covid 19 pandemic of 2020-2022 drastically restricted travel and increased online virtual exploration, where "viewers can experience activities, locations, and destinations from the comfort of their own homes (…); see and experience a destination without traveling to it" (Fredericks, 2021). But in digital cultural heritage the focus is on photogrammetry – the realistic recording of sites to create navigable 360-degree computer models – for virtual tours, gamified with quizzes (Georgopoulos et al., 2017): not on bringing to life the emotional, cultural and personal. Tourism employs gamification to enhance experience, create brand loyalty and increase consumer spending (Xu & Buhalis, 2021). Can video games devised for entertainment help give access to the stories and people of the past and their cultures?

The global market for serious games rose from USD $2,731 million in 2016 to an expected USD $9,167 million by 2023 (Sonawane, 2017). The global entertainment games market estimate for 2021 is USD $175 billion, with 2.9 billion gamers (Wijman, 2021). In 2021, Netflix included video games in subscription packages at no extra cost. Accessing television, social media and games on computers and mobile devices and accessing the internet on smart televisions is now common: Netflix saw the potential of channeling everything to their subscribers. The possibility of crossover audiences opens the way to new demands and opportunities for content.

Historicity and Gaming

Detailed neohistorical video games are popular. Granström (2013) argues that *Elder scrolls v: skyrim* (2011), set in a neomedieval world, offers all the features desirable for a cultural heritage serious game - except cultural and historical correctness (Granström, 2013, p.19). She suggests it might offer a template for serious heritage games, though she deems the development and marketing costs - approximately $85 million USD (Statistic Brain, 2012) - prohibitive (Granström, 2013, p.21; pp. 34-35). The game *Medieval dynasty* (2020), a first-person life-sim with realistic environment and characters, also fulfils Granström's criteria - except for historical and cultural correctness. *Assassin's Creed II* (2009) and *The witcher 3: wild hunt* (2015) are both set in neomedieval worlds and contain history-like detail: but these, like *Skyrim* or *Medieval dynasty,* are not primarily devised to communicate real history (Bontchev, 2015) and also lack cultural and historical correctness. It has been argued that such simulation games legitimately "provide alternate schemas for apprehending the historically real (our perception of what actually happened in the past) that privileges story, genre, and details over critical analysis or the production of new historical knowledge," employing, like television and film period drama "selective authenticity" which "challenge traditional historic discourse" (Salvati and Bullinger, 2013, pp.152-153).

Television costume historical dramatizations like *The white queen* (Kent & Teague, 2013), portraying the lives of real medieval characters and historical documentary, such as *The real white queen and her rivals* (Gregory, 2013), *The Normans* (Bartlett, 2010) or *The Plantagenets* (Bartlett, 2014), which attract a wide audience (St Andrews, 2014), are meticulously researched and incorporate intangible as well as material cultural heritage. The dramatized television documentary, *Historien om Danmark* [History of Denmark] (DRTV, 2017), blends scholarly analysis and commentary with staged scenes based on historical evidence, to tell the stories of people of the past. All these incorporate material, intellectual, spiritual and emotional aspects, encompassing arts, architecture, historical and cultural heritage, culinary heritage, music, lifestyles, value systems, beliefs and traditions. Helen Castor (2019), historian, broadcaster and author of *She-wolves: the women who ruled England before Elizabeth* (2010), adapted for television as *She-wolves: England's early queens* (2012) and of made-for-television miniseries *Medieval lives: birth, marriage, death* (2013), claims that "historical drama can offer the illusion of three-dimensional immersion in the past with unrivalled immediacy". *Queens game* explores some approaches from period drama to enhance immersion in a HiStoryGame without actively distorting the past.

The issue of authenticity in games is perennially debated (Lorber & Zimmerman, 2020, pp. 7-17; Kapell & Elliott, 2013, pp.151-212). What is "the past" and how does it relate to "true myth", perhaps a game-form of "authentic history" (Kapell & Elliott, 2013 pp. 357-369)? Brandenburg argues that in *The Witcher 3: wild hunt* (2015) history and fantasy collide, eliding medievalism and neomedievalism, to portray a kind of "Dark Age" (Brandenburg, 2020, pp. 203-205). This world is broadly similar to that of the popular *Witcher* games (2007-2021) first developed in Sapowski's cult fantasy novels, *The witcher saga* (1994-1999) and adapted for the internationally successful Netflix television series, *The witcher* (2019 -2021) (Wanat, 2020). The game-action takes place after the final book in the *Saga* series and the games are not connected with the television franchise; but the worlds of the novels, television series and games conflate into a Dark-Age universe much like that of *Game of thrones* (Benioff & Weiss, 2013-2019), another successful example of transmedia neomedieval production.

Grand ages: medieval (2015), a life-sim game, on the other hand, contains careful period detail in buildings and the wares available to trade from the cities players build. However, since the goal - to develop the richest city and rule the largest empire - is set, the story develops according to player choice as an experimental simulation. The characterization is role-based, not personality-based, and costume is neomedieval. What differentiates this from other such games is that you build your empire not primarily through military conquest, but trade. The survival and building RPG life-sim game, *Medieval dynasty* (2020), also inhabits a hybrid neomedieval world. It initially takes the perspective not of warriors or war-leaders, but of ordinary people whose lives are devastated by war: the first-person player-character works his way up from nothing to building a house; enlisting workers to develop a village; acquiring a wife and begetting a son to succeed him as the leader of his dynasty.

Gender Appeal and Inclusion

The women in *Medieval dynasty* do the same work as the men, but can aspire only to becoming wife and mother, not founding dynasties themselves or bringing up daughters to continue their lines. This sparked heat on the game's early-release: female players enjoyed the gameworld but felt excluded by having to play a first-person male - including flirting with potential wives (Steamcommunity, 2020). In *Grand ages: medieval* (2015) a female player-character can become Empress of the World, but she turns out to act exactly like the male default PC and the game's dialogue texts refer to her as "him".

History games explicitly directed towards girls rarely offer proactive female protagonists. *Little big planet 3: women in history costume pack* (2016) suggests that on Women's Day girls try "dressing Sack-girl® up as 4 of the most famous and influential women from the pages of history": Cleopatra, Elizabeth I of England, Joan of Arc and China's Wu Zetian. *A princess tale* (Introduction, 2016) offers "the most irresponsible bubblehead … life's good when you're the Princess; no responsibilities, nobody telling you what to do or where to go, just running around, having fun and flitting your life away".

Even in the classic, highly-popular Nintendo game-series *The Legend of Zelda* (1986 -), set in neomedieval fantasy-land Hyrule, Princess Zelda, a goddess of wisdom reincarnated in various times and guises, is usually lost or captive and has to be rescued by Link, the real (male) hero. Although there are two piratical *Zelda* episodes - *wind waker* (2002/2013) and *Phantom hourglass* (2007/2013) - where Zelda is somewhat proactive, this is in male attire, as Tetra the female pirate: a girl playing a boy. It seems that if they don't play girls in boys' clothing, behaving like boys, fighting with bow or sword, girls are expected to play dress-up with period fashion or play ditzy princesses.

The player-character in *Queens game,* based on Danish Princess Margrete Valdemarsdatter, who married and became Queen of Norway at the age of 10, is no bubblehead; nor does she dress as a boy or fight with a sword. History says that she grew up to be a powerful ruler who achieved success through intelligent strategy and diplomacy, dressed in the clothes of a royal woman: and that she made every effort to ensure that swords were drawn as rarely as possible (Etting, 2004).

Overtly historical video-games, since the early days of 'edutainment' in the 1990's, are overwhelmingly driven by war, combat and strategy, featuring male protagonists: for example, *The great war: 1914-1918* (1992); *Historion* (Klett, 2002*)*; *Napoleon: total war* (2010); *Ways of history* (2017). Some historically-oriented games do address medieval social history: for example *Medieval defenders* (2016), *The plague* (2015), *The black death* (2016) and *A plague tale: innocence* (2019) - all set, like *Queens game*, in the European Middle Ages. Unusually, *Innocence* has a female protagonist – though dressed as a boy and acting like one - who battles plague-rats in a photorealistic, devastated medieval European landscape.

Award-winning, war-based, open-world, action-adventure role-playing game *Kingdom come: deliverance* (2018) is scrupulous on 15th-century Bohemian period detail, winning 4-star ratings (Hood, 2018) and rapidly selling two million copies (Jones, 2019). Its impressive, authentic medieval environments, costume and battle-techniques offer historical verisimilitude: but its story is fictitious. Its DownLoadable Content [DLC] addition, *A woman's lot* (2019), as well as a female NPC visionary, Johanka, protected by hero Henry, does offer a female player-character, Teresa - there are virtually no women in the original game, with the exception of Lady Stephanie, a hostage in need of rescue.

The stereotyped portrayal of women and girls in video-games, where even the most apparently proactive and dynamic often wilt rapidly into damsels in distress is well attested (Sarkeesian, 2013). Although Teresa the milkmaid does not dress as a boy, she quickly becomes a fighter, using the combat and stealth skills of original player-character, Henry. This is neomedieval fantasy: though history records some medieval women leading soldiers, they are not normally portrayed with warrior skills themselves (McLaughlin 1990; Eads, 2012). In most core computer games, the default animation for the player-character - as in *Medieval dynasty* - is male. Heroism is intimately linked with combat: so a woman hero player-character tends to be the male default character revamped as a female, in trousers - easily adapted from the original male animation - complete with his programmed behaviours: typically, defeating enemies.

However, statistics suggest that female players are more attracted to activity-based *casual games,* played by a single player against their own highest score, often with objects rather than human characters (Soha, 2021). More complex *core games* that take much longer to learn to play, but contain deeper content and narratives, appear to attract more male gamers. In 2021, around half of all gamers were women (Brune, 2021), slightly up from 2017, when females accounted for 46% (Bosman, 2019). Among players of casual games, by the 21st century there was gender symmetry; while male core-game players outnumbered female by 70% to 30% (Clement, 2021) which may be partially accounted for by a difference between male and female responses to incentive stimuli (Warthen et al., 2020). Gameplay analysis suggests that the top three activities in games played mainly by males are *attack and defend* (combat), *maneuver and steer* and *tactics and planning,* while the top three activities for female players, who "want to make creative choices", are *puzzle solving, gathering, build and design* (Brune, 2021), *atmospheric exploration* and *interactive drama* (Campbell, 2017).

Investing time in mastering the interface to games with complex rules seems to be a barrier for players with feminine "gender culture" (Campa et al., 2011) - a set of behaviours which operates from childhood: "girls playing house promotes personal relationships, and playing house does not necessarily have fixed rules or objectives. Boys (…) tend to play more competitive team sports with different goals and strategies", including complex rulesets (Cochise College, 2016). Core games reward specific behaviour according to defined rules, thus activating dopamine in masculine gender-cultured reward-centres (Brandt, 2008).

The 21st century has seen a rise in numbers of female gamers - still predominantly casual - but in 2021 the gender balance in game development and company management still lagged behind (Yokoi, 2021). Brie Code, previously an AI programmer at game-developers Ubisoft and Relic Entertainment, set up TRULUV Studios, Canada in 2016, because, an avid gamer herself, she wanted to make games for her female friends "who don't like video games", which "lack depth"; who think they "don't learn anything" from games or "change as a person"; or were "just flat out repulsed by video games. Few women, for example, are going to play a video game with terrible portrayals of women". "They don't find their own cultural references or interests in video games" and are irritated by "failing at things [they] didn't care about in the first place" (Code, 2016). *Queens game*, whose core creative team is predominantly female, is fully cognizant of these issues.

The convention in neomedieval games whereby female protagonists adopt male behaviours - particularly fighting - and eschew skirts is also found in twenty-first century action-adventure films. For example, hero Princess Diana in *Wonderwoman* (Jenkins, 2017), who finally decides to use her immortal fighting skills to try to stop mortal men warring and making women weep, is an Amazon, trained as a warrior, who scorns the apparel of 20th-century femininity in favour of fantasy buskins. Still, more work has been done in examining the role and perception of female protagonists in film with a view to transforming them (Jacey, 2010; Murdock,1990) than in game - although *Feminist frequency* (n.d.) continues to analyze and critique game role-stereotyping.

Some fantasy neomedieval films are more medieval than others. *The Lord of the Rings* (Jackson, 2001-2003) and *The Chronicles of Narnia* (Adamson, 2005-2010), both adapted from fiction written by Oxford University medievalists shaping medieval material for modern readers (Duriez, 2015), have contributed greatly to the popular sense of the cultural heritage of the Middle Ages. Expertise and effort go into researching historical sources to generate visuals, costumes and aesthetics that create detailed, convincing onscreen worlds (Lafortune, 2020), into which viewers are beguiled by storytelling and performance, leaving a vivid picture in the minds of audiences. The internationally popular fantasy television series, *Game of Thrones* (Benioff & Weiss, 2013-2019), with strong characters and a compelling story that wake echoes of real history, draw on these worlds, feeding the appetite for the neomedieval past (Thomas, 2021). The sense of identification with real people of long ago in their own setting doing real things has, however, so far been little-explored in the interactive games environment, despite the well-researched engagement offered by interactivity (Ryan, 2016).

The highly-influential world of Disney musical-animation films signposts possibilities for change in a male-dominated landscape. *Frozen* (Buck & Lee, 2013) was the highest grossing film of the year (O'Neill, 2021) and *Frozen II* (Buck & Lee, 2019) was the 10th most successful film of all time (Stoll, 2021). The stories were co-written and directed by a woman, Jennifer Lee, and the lyrics were also written by a woman, Kristen Anderson-Lopez. They brought a new type of character to Disney's cast of princesses: "innovative leaders" rather than the "passive dreamers, lost dreamers, active leaders and sacrificing dreamers" featured in earlier films (Muir, 2020). The dramatic portrayal of *Frozen*'s Elsa and Anna and their expression of their feelings in song have been credited, from a psychodynamic perspective, with helping girls to understand themselves through identification with the onscreen characters (Kowalski & Bhalla, 2018), partially accounting for their extreme popularity.

Queens game enables the player-character to recognize her own potential through interaction with the effective, credible medieval women she meets. The lyricist is female, as is the composer and performer, who sings for the characters in the game. In fact the core research and creative team, led by a woman, consisted of four women and two men – a gender-balance unusual in game development (Clement, 2021, March 3), enabled by the Norwegian creative practice research environment.

QUEENS GAME

Immersion in History as Characterizing Goal in a Serious Game

Queens game starts from the principle that interactive engagement comes fundamentally through satisfying game experience (GX) - "having fun, being challenged, being immersed and involved in the game, feeling emotions, and being absorbed" (Dörner, Göbel et al., 2016, p. 3). The project constitutes the investigative and experimental phase of developing a potential commercial offering, exploring immersive virtual cultural heritage as the additional characterizing goal, personalising social, cultural and political history through identification with the player character. It also aims to provide players who don't like fighting and frustration and/or want to play a female character conceived from the outset as female with a compelling way to experience the Middle Ages.

Queens game invites players to move between two realms: MARGRETE'S WORLD, the grey stronghold home of 10-year old Margrete, just married to 23-year old King Håkon of Norway; and LUNETE'S WORLD, the bright, legendary realm of King Arthur and Queen Gunvor (Guinevere in medieval Scandinavian); the contrasting castles in each are shown in Figure 1.

Figure 1. Margrete's castle in "real" medieval Norway and Lunete's Arthurian castle
(© 2021, Queens game. Used with permission.)

Queen's game and its methodology are described below, using Granström's classifications of successful neomedieval games for entertainment which would qualify as serious games did they not lack "correct" culture and history (Granström, 2013, p.19; see also Introduction to this chapter). The text below, using Granström's five main categories - *Interactivity, Meaning, Player Character, Other Characters, Accuracy and Realism* - and their sub-categories, shows how *Queens game* fulfils the qualities of the entertainment games she analyses, and how it fills the lacks she finds in them in cultural meaning and historical correctness.

Interactivity: Ability to Affect, Use or Communicate

Exploration: Openly Navigable Environment

MARGRETE'S WORLD: The fully explorable setting for player-character 10-year-old Princess Margrete's story is, in the pilot prototype, the North Wing and Inner Ward of the virtual historical stronghold of medieval Akersborg, Oslo. Set in the surrounding terrain as it was in the fourteenth century, the whole forensic architectural model was transposed into Unreal Engine 4.26 (2021), as shown in Figure 2.

Figure 2. Fully explorable medieval Akersborg castle
(© 2021, Queens game. Used with permission.)

LUNETE'S WORLD: Lunete's contrasting white-turreted castle (which has the same footprint as Margrete's grey Akersborg), inspired by a medieval manuscript-illustration and set in the fully navigable legendary world of King Arthur and Queen Gunvor, is shown in Figure 3.

Figure 3. Lunete's castle in the legendary world of King Arthur and Queen Gunvor
(© 2021, Queens game. Used with permission.)

Tasks: Assignments, Errands, Missions, Quests, Challenges

MARGRETE'S WORLD: In her new home - the castle of medieval Akersborg - 10-year old Margrete has to find her runaway cat and the chess piece it has stolen. She gets to know Ingegerd, her new Head of Household's daughter - in real life a close lifelong friend. Margrete has to discover what her new subjects in Norway think about her, her family and their own situations. Finding her cat, Margrete discovers a hidden chess-room, shown in Figure 4.

Figure 4. Margrete finds the hidden chess-room (ingame) and places her dragon chess-pawn on the board (concept art)
(© 2021, Queens game. Used with permission.)

Her chess-piece enables Margrete to travel through the wall-hanging depicting the land of King Arthur and Queen Gunvor into the legendary story-realm itself, shown in Figure 5.

Figure 5. Margrete passes through the wall-hanging (here concept art) and becomes player.character Lunete (ingame)
(© 2021, Queens game. Used with permission.)

Here, the player-character is Lunete; whatever she discovers or learns, Margrete brings back to her own world.

LUNETE'S WORLD: Lunete has to find her own path in life, acquiring skills and knowledge which Margrete can use. Lunete starts by learning to play the harp and sing to earn her bread, before finally becoming Queen Gunvor's minstrel: shown in Figure 6.

Figure 6. Lunete learns to play and sing and becomes Queen Gunvor's minstrel (concept art)
(© 2021, Queens game. Used with permission.)

As she explores the land, Lunete collects a chess-set, piece by piece, each representing a character in the gameworld and giving access to original songs. As Lunete interacts with each new character, they appear on Queen Gunvor's tapestry.

Dialogue: Communication/Conversation Between Player and Non-Player Character

MARGRETE'S WORLD: The player-character Margrete talks with Ingegerd, the friend she makes at Akersborg. Players can also choose to play Ingegerd, who has slightly different adventures in Lunete's World – though in this pilot game, her adventures are not yet implemented. In Margrete's World, player-character Margrete overhears the NPC castle folk discussing her, their own lives and the kings who determine their fate. Figure 7 shows the great hall and bakehouse at Akersborg.

Figure 7. Margrete overhears conversations in the great hall and the bakehouse
(© 2021, Queens game. Used with permission.)

LUNETE'S WORLD: NPC statues and a fantasy bird-creature - derived from a 14th-century manuscript - give clues and help with tasks. Lunete converses with the characters she meets - the alewife, tapster and drinkers at an alehouse; travelling musicians; an abbess and nuns singing over a dead Black-Death victim; a spinner and weaver and others. Dialogue is randomized to avoid repetition in a session - experimentation enabled by the research context. In the pilot, all dialogue is audio, as in film and television, not text. Both Lunete and the characters she encounters sing original songs, which, as in a musical or Disney animated-feature, express character and emotion while telling the story.

Quiz: Test with Questions

There is no quiz in the pilot prototype, but the structure of the game could facilitate a quiz element. For example, in MARGRETE'S WORLD, in the Chancellery at Akersborg, where documents and books are kept and written, players might choose to discover, as part of a crafting system, how medieval manuscript books are made. A quiz could be added if desired. In LUNETE'S WORLD, the player can gain the skills of playing the harp, spinning and weaving, brewing ale and gathering the herbs the Middle Ages believed cured various ailments. These skills could potentially be tested in Margrete's World through an active quizlike format.

Meaning: Elements Specifically Adding Deeper Meaning

Culture and History: Intangible Heritage, Cultural Expressions, Rituals, Traditions, Customs, Skills, Beliefs, Values. Historical Events and Developments

In MARGRETE'S WORLD, historical events and developments are seen through the eyes of 10-year old Margrete. For example, Ingegerd learns from Margrete that Queen Blanka, who travelled to Copenhagen to attend Margrete's wedding to her son Håkon, died there shortly afterwards.

News also comes through Ingegerd's mother (who teaches and cares for both girls) from Ingegerd's grandmother, Birgitta - later Saint Birgitta of Sweden. In 1363, when the HiStoryGame is set, Birgitta is in Rome, seeking official status for the religious order she founded in the great house at Vadstena donated by Margrete's mother-in-law, Queen Blanka of Sweden, whose Head of Household Birgitta had been. Birgitta remained in Rome as an advisor to the Pope; she had decided views on politics, expressed in her letters, which survive (Nyberg, 2003, pp. 29-44).

Margrete, freshly arrived from Denmark, learns more about the state of affairs in Norway through interacting with the pirate cabin-boy Eskil, who comes up secretly to the castle with much-needed, smuggled food-supplies. The harbour is blockaded by German Hansa League merchant-ships, in support of their sea-trade monopoly. Margrete learns that Eskil lost his father in one of the many violent clashes between the Hansa-merchants and Margrete's father, the King of Denmark. Eskil thought being a pirate would be better than struggling to scrape a living on land after the terrible shortages following the Black Death; but Margrete and Ingegerd discover that now he is not so sure – too much beating and hard work. Ingegerd and Eskil learn that in the sea-battle at Elsinore Castle, where Eskil's father died, Margrete's only surviving brother was fatally wounded, precipitating her marriage. Her two other brothers and a sister died in infancy; Margrete's only living sibling went to be married to the Duke of Mecklenburg when she was 11 and Margrete six, and first betrothed to Håkon of Norway. Historically, as Queen, Margrete succeeded in bringing about a peaceful settlement with the Hansa League; she also used piratical privateers to bolster Norway's economy. In the game, her encounters with Eskil lay the foundation for these policies.

In LUNETE'S WORLD, intangible medieval cultural heritage is played out through Lunete's interactions with the various characters. In historical drama, "Costume plays an essential role (…) because clothing is intrinsically linked to time, place, culture and identity" (Lafortune, 2020, p.1). The costume of the Alewife, who refuses Lunete food until she plays for her customers, shows how manuscript illustration underpins the game in Figure 8.

Figure 8. The Alewife
(© 2021, Queens game. Used with permission.)

Story: Plot, Narrative

MARGRETE'S WORLD: On a winter's afternoon just before Christmas, 1363, 10-year old Queen Margrete of Norway, formerly Princess of Denmark, arrives at Akersborg by ship from Copenhagen, where she was married in April to 23-year old King Håkon VI of Norway. Her cat jumps ashore and Margrete gives chase, meeting a beggar girl shown in Figure 9

Figure 9. Margrete arrives by ship at Akersborg, Oslo, and, chasing her cat, which jumps ashore, meets a beggar-girl (ingame)
(© 2021, Queens game. Used with permission.)

She has been in mourning for her mother-in-law, Queen Blanka of Sweden, who died shortly after the wedding. Margrete's new husband is away fighting, along with her father and father-in law.

At the dockside, Margrete's cat jumps ashore, stealing the dragon pawn from Margrete's chess-set: Margrete runs after her. The cat leads Margrete through the snow to a smugglers' tunnel below Akersborg castle, where Ingegerd - the same age as Margrete - is signalling a pirate-ship with a lantern. The two girls discover each other's identity and cautiously begin to make friends. As the cat runs into the tunnel and the girls follow, Ingegerd introduces Margrete to Eskil, the pirate cabin-boy bringing smuggled food to Akersborg.

The three children sneak through the kitchens, collecting apples, freshly-baked bread and small beer. They try to get fish to tempt the cat. Margrete explores her new home incognito: her official reception is planned for the following day, for which Ingegerd should be rehearsing a welcoming song. Margrete and Ingegerd follow the cat into a cosy bookroom, concealing the entrance to a hidden chamber where Margrete passes through the wall-hanging depicting Lunete's Tale into the tale itself.

LUNETE'S WORLD: Through the wall-hanging, on her twelfth birthday, to avoid marrying the husband her father has chosen, Lunete runs away into the bright landscape shown in Figure 10.

Figure 10. Lunete's World (ingame)
(© 2021, Queens game. Used with permission.)

The overall narrative structure of the HiStoryGame is episodic, echoing medieval storytelling, which derives from oral forms and is spatially-organised rather than linear, both in drama (Axton, 1974) and prose - for example Malory's *Le Morte D'Arthur* (Cooper (Ed.), 2008). Lunete can explore the locations in any order, in a landscape filled with music and song, as she learns the skills and develops the courage to find her own way.

Player Character

Roleplay: the Player Assuming the Role of the Player Character

The player-character is initially 10-year old Queen Margrete of Norway. When she passes through the wall-hanging in the secret chess-room at Akersborg castle, the player-character becomes Lunete, in the world of King Arthur and Queen Gunvor.

Avatar: Visual Representation of the Player Character

Players play in the third person. In Margrete's world, in a future development, they can hopefully opt to play Margrete, funloving but responsible - destined for queenship, brought up to royal life; or Ingegerd, curious and sprightly - destined to become abbess of her grandmother's powerful religious order of sisters and brothers. Derived from 14th-century manuscripts, their 3D model avatars, along with Arthurian player-character, Lunete, are shown in Figure 11.

Figure 11. Reference paintings from medieval manuscripts & 3D model avatars of player-characters Ingegerd, Margrete and Lunete
(© 2021, Queens game. Used with permission.)

Personalised Avatar: Possibility to Alter the Appearance of the Player Character

The player-characters in *Queens game* have fixed appearances. In Lunete's World, Lunete, who chooses to rebel against her destiny, bears a physical resemblance to both Margrete and Ingegerd: she is a kind of freer alter-ego, through whom the player can discover more of the medieval world than might be accessible to a child queen.

Other Characters: Real or Virtual Characters/Actors

Like the player-characters, NPC's are not motion-captured, but expressively animated. Their occupations and behaviours, like their looks, are based on medieval and scholarly sources and interaction contributes to the player-character's skill-tree of acquired capabilities.

Multiplayer: Ability to Play with Other Players in the Same Environment

Queens game pilot-prototype is a single-player RPG. Using the same assets, a multiplayer version may be developed, as a medieval life-sim based on skill progression, a format not unlike *Medieval Dynasty* (2020), but devised from a female perspective.

Accuracy and Realism: Elements Improving Sense of Authenticity

Cultural and Historical: Cultural and Historical Correctness

The events of Scandinavian history which resulted in the 10-year old Danish princess Margrete being married to 23-year old Norwegian King Håkon form the background to the story of Margrete and Ingegerd's historically-attested friendship, which lasted all their lives (Etting, 2004, pp. 6-7).

Margrete's home, today mostly-invisible, was mapped from the meticulous historical notes and plans prepared during the early 20th-century restoration of Akershus Castle (Sinding-Larsen 1924; Tshudi-Madsen & Moberg, 1999), as in Figure 12.

Figure 12. Generating the forensic architectural 3D computer-model of medieval Akershus Castle
(© 2021, Queens game. Used with permission.)

The forensic architectural model was finalised with AFCM historianTom Andersen, before being transposed into Unreal Engine and furnished, following medieval sources. The bookroom, through which Margrete enters the realm of Queen Gunvor, is conceived in the game as belonging to Queen Eufemia, Margrete's husband Håkon's great, great, grandmother, probably the first queen to live at Akersborg. She had stories of the knights of the Round Table translated into old Scandinavian for her daughter Ingeborg when, aged 11, Ingeborg married 30-year old Erik Magnusson (1282 – 1318), second son of King Magnus III of Sweden (Layher, 2015, pp. 128-31). The bookroom floor, modelled on surviving medieval tiles, is shown in Figure 13.

Figure 13. Akersborg castle: bookroom flooring modelled on medieval tiles
(© 2021, Queens game. Used with permission.)

Like the castle interior, the player-characters and NPC's in both Margrete's World and Lunete's World were developed using medieval depictions and descriptions in literature, archaeology and scholarship, expressively animated to create a lively, varied cast. Props in the game are also modelled after surviving medieval artifacts and visual representations from the period: a royal gold *hanaper* - a large covered vessel - and an *aquamanile* - a bronze water-jug used at table to wash the hands - are shown in Figure 14.

Figure 14. Royal gold hanaper and bronze aquamanile modelled for Queens Game after surviving medieval regal tableware
(© 2021, Queens game. Used with permission.)

A great source of inspiration was Dover Castle, Kent, England, remodelled by King Henry II in the 1180's, around the time the original castle at Akershus was built. It has been sensitively restored and furnished, based on meticulous research; the medieval love of colour and luxury are reflected in the guest-bed, painted in bright red, green and blue, the basis for the *Queen's Game* model in Figure 15.

Figure 15. Top right and left: 3D-modelled beds based on re-creation guest-bed below, from Dover Castle, photographed by Queens Game art team
(© 2021, Queens game. Used with permission.)

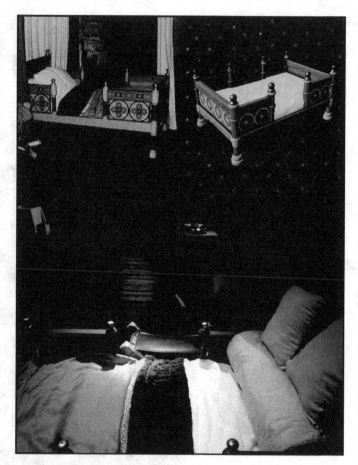

The NPC's at Akersborg Castle and King Arthur and Queen Gunvor's castle where the halls are festively decked, prepare the Christmas meal, to the accompaniment of original music arranged, played, sung and produced for the game. Each individual the player meets, whether in Margrete's World or Lunete's, is based on contemporary literature, historical documentation, manuscript illustrations and archaeology, dramatized using dialogue and expressive animation, as they engage in medieval activities, customs and crafts.

Visual and Behavioral: 3D Models, Textures, Shaders. Animation, Artificial Intelligence, Crowd Simulation, Physics

Snowcastle implemented a pre-production Unreal-Engine version of part of the architectural model of Akersborg Castle in its natural environment, the topography for which (Hoydedata, n.d.) was converted into a height-map applied to a landscape-module in the Unreal Engine. Differences between the 14th and 21st-century landscapes were sculpted, retracting the shoreline along the coast of Bjørvika before the castle geometry was imported into the game-engine in its historical position.

In playtesting, the initial landscape proved too big for the pilot, requiring too much processing power. Travelling on foot is tedious in prototype quality and players would soon lose interest in exploring. In a commercial iteration, more design effort will make travelling a fun gameplay activity, but this was beyond the scope of the research production, which therefore scaled the map down to 60% of its original size: making game-distances practical, while the scenery remains true to the geographical area. The pilot environment in Unreal focused on incorporating historical detail into the buildings, furnishings, terrain and NPC models, iteratively developing story architecture, gameplay, concept art, dramaturgy, characters and character-models. The forensic architectural model of Akersborg North Wing and Inner Ward was finally transferred to Unreal, textured, lit and populated, as shown in Figure 16.

Figure 16. Exterior of Akersborg medieval castle forensic architectural 3D model North Wing and Inner Ward transposed into Unreal Engine 4.26 and populated with NPC's
(© 2021, Queens game. Used with permission.)

On top of Unreal Engine 4.26 (2021) from Epic Games, the first iteration of *Queens game* was tested using the Superior RPG Kit (2019), containing code modules for *Save and load games*, *Character creation*, *Character skills*, *Character stats*, *Player inventory*, *Store inventory & pricing*, *NPC behaviour*, *NPC dialogue* and *Quest* systems, until a skilled Unreal programmer could join the team.

Environmental: Weather, Day and Night Cycle, Wildlife, Vegetation

With the *Sky & Atmosphere* module (Building worlds, n.d.) included in Unreal Engine 4.26, *Queens game* will be able to simulate a full night and day cycle. Snowcastle Games has developed an ecological simulator, a dynamic climate system and a weather-storm system, as well as an animal behaviour AI, all of which can be adapted for a commercial version of *Queens game*. The HistoryGame will then be able to offer convincing night and day cycle, change of seasons, semi-realistic animal-behaviour and vegetation-growth to set the stage for immersion in the medieval experience.

Auditory: Sound

Sound is very important in *Queens game*. The music is all original: composed, performed and produced using Logic X Pro with Best Service Audio's Medieval Library of acoustic instruments. The songs express the personality, preoccupations and dramatic role of the character who sings them, as well as telling parts of the story. Some songs, like the ballad of King Valdemar - player-character Margrete's father - sung by the blacksmith and his lad as they work making and mending armour at Akersborg castle, recount historical events. This ballad - created for the game - gives an ironic account of Valdemar's notorious victory, in 1361, over farmers armed only with farm implements, mercilessly cut down outside the gates of Visby town on the island of Gotland, from which the Hansa League merchants traded.

The player-character Lunete composes and sings a new song-verse about each adventure she has, until finally she wins her place as Queen Gunvor's minstrel, by singing her whole ballad - bringing out each character from her adventures on the great tapestry in Gunvor's Hall. Some of the songs and all the game-music are reconfigurable, never playing exactly the same way twice, no matter how many repeated visits. The in-game music works dramatically, like film-music, creating the atmosphere for each scene.

As the player collects a chess-piece from each scene they play in Lunete's World, a giant stone chess-set forms in the heart of the forest, which the player can reach through an enchanted stone circle to activate individual pieces and hear the songs associated with them - as often as desired.

CHALLENGES AND SOLUTIONS

Modelling Cultural Heritage

The project, running for 22 months over three years (somewhat disrupted by the Covid 19 pandemic), comprised progressive interlinked iterative experiments developing historical research, story-architecture, gameplay, set and character design. In consultation with AFCM, the project created as correct as possible a 3D computer-model of Margrete's medieval home, which the core research and production team, supported by Snowcastle Games, transposed into Unreal Engine to make a playable pilot. Expressively-animated 3D characters and original music and song provide emotional depth as the explorable, spatially-organised HiStoryGame unfolds interactively in real time, promoting an engaging, immersive relationship between player, characters and story.

In the game, the ever-popular legendary world of King Arthur provides a contrast to Margrete's actual Norway, recovering in the 14th century from the effects of the Black Death, which killed more than a third of its population. Buildings, props and characters as true as possible to authentic medieval sources bring the fantasy-realm of Gunvor and Arthur to life, offering 21st-century players an engaging way-in to real medieval history, as shown in Figure 17.

Figure 17. The Unreal Round Table, based on medieval illustration
(© 2021, Queens game. Used with permission.)

The legendary realm evokes the intangible cultural heritage, events and developments of Margrete's time without dramatizing incidents in her life for which there is no historical evidence. Records of a royal girl's childhood in the Middle Ages are rare - for many, the date of their birth, and often their death, is unknown, only being reconstructed, if they married, from the date of their wedding.

In Margrete's case, the fourteenth-century *Sjællandske Krønike* [Zealand's Chronicle] (Olsen,1981), which recorded in Latin events concerning her father, King Valdemar IV of Denmark, mentions her birth in 1353 (Olsen, 1981, p. 38), her betrothal, aged 6, to Håkon VI of Norway in 1359 (Olsen, 1981, p. 57) and her marriage to him in Copenhagen in 1363 (Olsen, 1981, p. 65). "A chronicle from Vadstena convent records that Merete Ulvsdatter brought up Margrete with her own daughter Ingegerd, and they were 'often whipped with the same rod'" (Etting, 2004, pp. 6-7). Little else is known about Margrete's childhood and education, but *Queens game* draws on modern scholarship for the practices of the time (Orme, 2003; Power, 1975; Svensson, 1962). Margrete and Ingegerd would have learnt not only to read, write and figure, but also the courtly accomplishments of manners, dancing, music and fine sewing; as well as how to run every aspect of a large medieval castle, which activities are incorporated into the storygame. They could be expanded in detail so that players could progressively increase crafting skills and gain experience points.

The acclaimed Danish television documentary series, *Historien om Danmark* [*History of Denmark*] (DRTV, 2017), which manages a fine balance between a visual dramatization of historical events with voice-over commentary and interviews with historians and archaeologists, covers Margrete's childhood in two scenes: her birth and her marriage to Håkon VI, which is represented by a short, silent sequence of the 11-year old girl sitting meekly at table opposite her 24-year old husband, in a gloomy stone castle. The scrupulous documentary approach, where scenes are shot on the locations where they happened, does not recreate or reconstruct the culture of the time in a detailed studio set - as does the BBC *White Queen* television series (Kent & Teague, 2013) - but leaves the impression that off the battlefield, high-status people in the Middle Ages lived in drafty, bare-walled, unfurnished castles (Thomas, 2021 130-131). There are no servants waiting on Margrete and Håkon and they have no companions; dressed sombrely in shades of brown, they dine alone from brown earthenware vessels at a brown-clothed table for two, in a whitewashed stone castle corner - as though colour and royal ceremony were unknown to them. There is no sign of Merete or Ingegerd. Håkon seems bored and slightly churlish; Margrete is meek and awkward.

Creating the explorable virtual Akersborg castle for *Queens game* enables the evocation of as accurate a version as possible of the setting for Margrete's childhood, built from archaeological, pictorial and documentary evidence, offering players an immersive experience of what her life might have felt like. Margrete was brought up from infancy to queenship. She was well-educated and in later life courteous, confident and respected; even aged ten, she would have been trained in poise and polite court manners. Her subsequent life suggests an enterprising and decisive character and a determination to bring about and maintain peace (Etting, 2004, pp. 96-108; p. 139).

The legendary world of King Arthur and Queen Guinevere has, from its early literary manifestations in the works of Chrétien de Troyes (c.1180), been a locus for depicting idealized behaviours (Archibald & Johnson, 2020), but also for challenging the values, conventions and norms of society (Archibald, 2009). Staging Lunete's adventures in this longstanding and well-known "true myth"-world (Kapell & Elliott, 2013, pp. 357-369), permits *Queens game* to bring together many aspects of medieval culture in a coherent, explorable HiStoryGameworld, where medieval artistic modes of presentation echo Arthurian storytelling of the Middle Ages.

Margrete, in *Queens game*, escapes into this world just as her distant cousin Ingeborg, who lived at Akersborg before her, doubtless also did, through the translated Arthurian tales her mother - Margrete's husband's great, great grandmother, Queen Eufemia - commissioned (Kalinke, 2015, p.17).

Snowcastle Games believes that developers can deliver most kinds of content, so long as players have fun and can find out how to proceed. The amount of characterizing additional immersive cultural heritage and historical information enriching a game may range from minimum to maximum, but fun factor and market potential - how wide the reach of the game is - are pre-eminent considerations.

Inclusivity

As well as gamers, *Queens game* aims to appeal to and include both those who want to discover the stories of people of the past and players who traditionally do not play video games - one subset of whom Brie Code (2016) identifies as female. She realizes that when her cousin who doesn't like video games

gets home from a long day, she doesn't want to battle it out in a game or get frustrated in a game. She wants to experiment with who she is in a social context of characters whom she cares about and who care about her. Because we as an industry fail at the first two, my friends don't get to experience that gaming is perhaps the most powerful medium for learning and for growing and changing as a person. (Code, 2016)

Queens game recognizes, with Brie Code, the full power of this medium.

Code concludes that women gamers "want not to be repulsed, to recognize their own tastes, and to find depth." She also notes that her cousin, "is the first woman in her family to earn a university degree and build a big career," and that "she is tiny and so even though she is also very smart and very strong, people often don't take her seriously." Perhaps most importantly, "she has no obvious role models. She is figuring everything out herself" (Code, 2016). The historical Margrete was also small of stature, very smart and strong, and has to figure everything out herself. It is hoped that players will be able to identify with her, as audiences do with Elsa in *Frozen* (Kowalski & Bhalla, 2018), and enjoy discovering, with Margrete and her best friend, Ingegerd, how to acquire and celebrate their skills and strengths.

Margrete makes a good role-model. In the realm of Gunvor, the player-character, Lunete runs away to explore the world and become the Queen's minstrel or *jougleresse* – one of the few careers open to medieval women (Amt, 1993, p. 168; Coldwell, 1986, pp. 39-56). As she finds her own way and grows in skill and confidence, players meet a range of challenges in a social context and learn to celebrate the qualities needed by a young medieval queen - still needed by many girls today.

CHALLENGES AND SOLUTIONS

Testing many possibilities using the Superior RPG Kit (2019), which would be risky for a game developer, was realistic and useful in this collaboration. The incorporation into the team of the advanced students and early-career artistic researchers who used the kit brought a high level of talent, energy and commitment, but also involved mentoring and guidance to develop experience and competence. Members claim to have benefitted from working in a small, close team, expanding their skillsets by taking on whatever challenges emerged and contributing to the whole creative process, as opposed to focusing only on one role on a commercial production. Since time is money, trial and error and mentoring are luxuries game-developers can ill afford: the company gained less from the incorporation of BA student interns in the early stages of the project than the students and the research-team, who benefitted from the opportunity to try out ideas under guidance. Although trials involved placeholders, they enabled playtesting, adjusting story-architecture, rethinking aspects of the storyworld and iteratively rewriting dialogue, without compromising a commercial production pipeline.

At the pre-production stage of *Queens game*, BA-level interns under Snowcastle's mentorship prototyped game-design from the draft story-architecture, characterization and setting, to create an examinable BA project - for which they achieved good marks - while acquiring industry experience. After graduation, one returned to Snowcastle as an apprentice and another joined the *Queens game* team after completing a postgraduate diploma course in game design. The *Queens game* practice-led research team experimented in the pre-production environment, developing the spatially-organized narrative, trying out characters and dialogue and refining NPC models. The later phases of the project, where experienced game designers from Snowcastle supported and contributed directly to the work of the core team based at the Norwegian Film School, were mutually beneficial: while the artist research-assistants improved their skills, Snowcastle creatives discovered different aspects of narrativity, characterization and music for immersive dramatic effect. It is hoped that this new hybrid skillset will inform developing the game from prototype to commercial product.

The production successfully, though not without some heated discussions, harmonized working processes from stage, film and television - where a project typically begins with dramatic story architecture, characters and an action-and-dialogue script, which evolve through mise-en scene and editing - with the practice in games development, which typically starts from a 3D gameworld, mechanics and gameplay, then develops the story, characterisation, action and dialogue. In order to manage the many states the gamestory goes through, the project tested the software tools CeltX (2021), originally designed for screenwriting and drama, which incorporates an interactive option; and 'Logic Driver Pro (2021), an Unreal c ++ plug-in which starts from a flowchart approach to game design. Both were useful in planning and developing the project. CeltX, conceived for audiovisual scripting including action and dramatic dialogue, has a useful storyboarding which relates these in the interactive option directly to gameplay flowcharts. 'Logic Driver Pro' works well with the Unreal Game Engine to speed up prototyping the story and gameplay directly in the game environment. The project found that utilizing both these programs from the pre-production stage could optimize and streamline the development flow; but becoming fluent involves a significant learning curve. The project's principal investigator, a dramatist and interactive story architect familiar with screenwriting software, and the commercial game designer/director familiar with game design software, found them the most helpful, especially as a way of working together.

Queens game integrated dramatic script and characters with 3D-world building and gameplay, developing and testing everything iteratively and avoiding pre-made animated cut-scenes to communicate the story as far as possible, instead leaving the player in control of the player-character to discover the drama in real time. The project incorporated from the beginning medieval aesthetics and storytelling modes - spatially organised narrative, a (reconfigurable) storyteller's voice and songs - as well as locations, props and visuals inspired by medieval sources. Whereas, typically, game and often film and television makers involve composers only towards the end of the production process, losing significant opportunities for mutual enrichment, the *Queens game* team worked on dramatic, expressive music in tandem with characters and action - as when developing original musicals or opera.

The *Queens game* team share the view (Dörner et al., 2016, p. 3-4) that there is no necessary binary distinction between a video game and a serious game. Commercial video gameworlds include meticulously detailed geography and place, containing complex lore: culture - customs, beliefs, crafts, music, visual arts, poems, characters, stories - and physical entities: food, clothing, plants and animals (Wolf,

2019). The additional characterizing feature in a cultural-heritage history-based serious game is immersion and insight into specific historical events and characters. The *Queens game* project demonstrates that cultural and historical correctness can be incorporated into the normal parameters of a video game without abandoning the principle of fun, absorbing strygameplay.

Immersive History

In games, 'character' is most commonly expressed as *level-based progression* or *skill-based progression*. Players take their character through *level-based progression* to gain Experience Points (XP) for activities such as completing quests or killing monsters. Once the XP bar is full, your character 'levels up' or qualifies to enter the next level of play, where players can choose to spend skill points on any skill they prefer. As in *Final Fantasy* (1997-), type of activity and skill increase are not interdependent: XP gained from fighting monsters can be used to increase any skill. By contrast, *Ultima Online* (1987-) uses *skill-based progression*, requiring the character to use a specific skill to reach a given end; skill level increases with increased practice.

In *Queens game*, skill progression intensifies historical immersion, as the player becomes familiar with each new medieval activity. When Margrete explores the castle scriptorium/chancellery, players will be able, as, under the guidance of an NPC scribe, Margrete discovers each process involved in making a medieval book, to adopt the role of an apprentice training under a master. Players do not need to choose a character-class (such as Bard, or Scribe) at the beginning, as in the conventional Role Playing Game (RPG); instead, over time, through their choice of activities, they can become a specialized Bard or Scribe. This enables players to try out various trades and skills, learning something about each before settling on those they enjoy most and most want to explore fully. Historical immersion is inseparable from game immersion as Skill Points (SP) instantiate knowledge acquisition and testing, without recourse to non-diagetic measures like questionnaires: players can roleplay characters in the HiStoryGameworld and progress as they might in its time-period. The relationship of constituents is shown as a diagram in Figure 18.

Figure 18. Diagram showing how HiStoryGame imparts cultural heritage understanding and knowledge through historical immersion and skill-based craft progression
(© 2021, Queens game. Used with permission.)

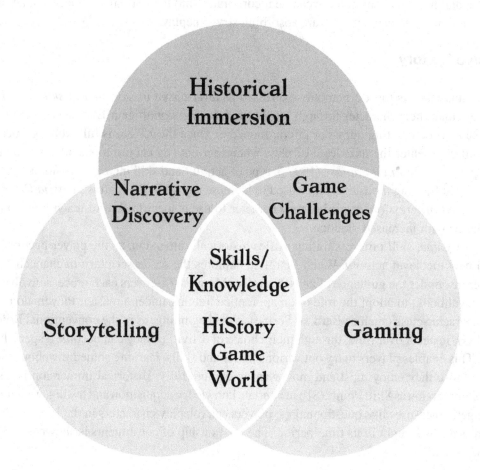

FUTURE DIRECTIONS

For exhibition in 2022 at AFCM, alongside an interactive standalone excerpt from *Queens Game* enabling visitors to fly, as an owl, around medieval Akersborg castle and environs and, as a cat, to explore the furnished and populated interior of the North Wing, the forensic architectural computer-model was 3D-printed and lit with projection-mapped textures and digital signage.

There is no business model for developing HiStoryGames using the collaborative intersectorial approach tested in the *Queens game* pilot project, a first step. Further research and production could potentially be financed through local Cultural Heritage, EEA Protecting Cultural Heritage and/or EU Creative Europe funding. The existence of a pilot prototype increases the chances of commercial uptake and setting up internet access; also of applying the approach to other cultural heritage sites.

Research could continue into historical immersion for intangible cultural heritage, where gaining craft skills and experience imparts understanding and knowledge of a period, its people and the way they lived. Further scholarly analysis of everyday life in the medieval castles of the North (Svensson, 1962, pp.

21-28) could be incorporated into the HiStoryGameworld. Already both stories and storytelling-modes offer "correct" history and narrative of the time, including visual and musical forms, an approach building on Maureen Thomas's earlier interactive work bringing intangible cultural heritage to life (Prager, Thomas & Selsjord, 2015).

The complete plan for the *Queens Game* storyworld, for which the project described in this chapter is a pilot prototype, incorporates the tale, inspired by original medieval poems by Chrétien de Troyes and Geoffrey Chaucer, of 13-year-old Galven, whose quest it is to become a Knight of the Round Table. Galven and Lunete share some adventures; Lunete can choose for herself how she relates to Galven. The original scripts, developed with support from the Norwegian Film Institute, also include the story of Princess Philippa of England (1394-1430), to whom Margrete married her heir, Erik of Pomerania. Philippa sailed to Elsinore in 1406 at the age of 12 to marry 24 year-old King Erik, and in the original *Queens game* concept, Philippa explores Akershus Castle, where she discovers the story of Margrete as well as the tales of Lunete and Galven.

The *Queens game* project explored, with the Danish Company Interaktive Oplivelser (https://make-mefeel.dk/), the potential for an on-site Augmented Reality (AR) experience at modern-day Akershus Castle, incorporating research and some assets from the HiStoryGame. Through an "ic3D" stereoscopic viewer, recorded ingame footage provides instant time-travel on site: hands-free, headset-free immersion in the colourful, 3D animated world of *Queens game*'s furnished and populated virtual castle, as it was in the fourteenth century – shown in Figure 19.

Figure 19. ic3D viewer on site gives access to game footage. (© 2021, Queens game. Used with permission)

Queens game's collaborative research production-budget of 5 million Norwegian kroner (including in-kind contributions), or c. $600,000 US dollars, to reach playable pilot prototype stage, was very small compared with $36 million spent on *Kingdom come: deliverance* (Hood, 2018) or $85 million on *Skyrim V: the elder scrolls* (Statistic Brain, 2012): successful entertainment games that Granström found satisfied all the criteria for an absorbing and chellenging serious cultural heritage game, save "cultural and historical correctness". Snowcastle estimates that to develop the *Queens game* pilot prototype, with its careful, vivid historical and cultural detail and medieval skills-progression gameplay, into a commercial offering, would take its 30 developers three years, requiring a modest budget of about 50 million Norwegian kroner - less than $6 million US dollars.

Start-up funding for a commercial offering could come from a number of sources. Since the game's setting is Norwegian history, the Norwegian Film Institute's interactive fund would be able to part-fund it, to a likely ceiling of 10 million Norwegian kroner, based on Snowcastle's past experience. 18% tax credits are available for game-development R&D; so a team of 30 developers would attract tax credit amounting to roughly 2 million Norwegian kroner per year over three years, totaling 6 million kroner. Innovation Norway could support such a project with a risk-loan of up to 5 million kroner. Creative Europe can grant up to €150 000 per project. It would thus be reasonable to anticipate a total of 22.5 million Norwegian kroner in funding support and loans. The rest, 27.5 million Norwegian kroner, could come from a variety of sources: a forward-looking independent production company operating like Netflix and/or such potential stakeholders as virtual cultural heritage tourism and education. Created, like all Snowcastle's games, with the intention to entertain, but achieving the additional characterizing goal of historical immersion in a convincing, well-researched medieval environment rich in dramatic storytelling, *Queens game* fits well into Snowcastle's overall development slate, to support which it leverages venture capital - for example, from Egmont's Nordisk Game arm.

Research suggests that "Playing commercial video games has been found to improve (…) desirable skills and competencies (…) in students" (Toh & Lim, 2022), and the growing market for entertainment games in relation to education could include HiStoryGames.

The emerging convergence of television and interactive gaming on subscriber channels portends new possibilities for marketing. In *Queens game*, collaborative intersectorial research and production have developed a promising, playable pilot, which it is hoped will provide the foundation for a marketable, primarily fun, serious HiStoryGame, demonstrating an innovative format with strong artistic and commercial potential.

CONCLUSION

Queens game is a emerged as a pilot prototype which amalgamates serious medieval cultural heritage and history with gameplay for entertainment, enriched with the innovative use of reconfigurable music, dramatic dialogue and narration. It trials a female-centred format that both gamers and people who don't like video games will hopefully find beguiling, entertaining, absorbing and rewarding as a locus for growing and learning. It offers emotional depth in the player-characters: Margrete - destined to become a powerful queen, a leader in a world organized by men; Ingegerd - destined to become Abbess of a powerful religious house, the medieval equivalent of a college; and Lunete, the rebel who finds her own creative way in the world. In these roles modern girls can hopefully recognize their own tastes and interests, and finding encouragement and growth.

As a result of collaborative intersectorial research and production, *Queens game*'s serious game innovative format offers the joy of entertaining gaming with the additional characterizing goal of immersing players, using medieval aesthetic and storytelling modes, in "correct" fourteenth-century history and culture, personalized through characters inspired by real people and places. Social and economic impact could be increased by developing existing assets from this RPG into a multiplayer life-sim and/or extending the gamestory world and interactive crafting skill-progression to include any number of medieval activities.

Rather than a photogrammetrically-produced virtual tour, converting a forensic historical architectural model into the Unreal Game Engine makes a fully navigable and explorable, furnished and populated medieval castle, now only partially visible at the actual site, potentially accessible to those who want to see and experience the destination and discover the stories of people of the past without travelling. The game can, however, also enhance visitor experience to the location itself; the format could be transferred to different historical sites and personages.

The HiStoryGame, based on characters, place, atmospheric exploration, interactive drama, gathering and creativity, rather than frustrating combats and violence, uses music and techniques from stage and screen to enrich emotional identification and dramatic effect. The main player-character is a real historical princess, who found her own way to innovative leadership. To those chiefly female-cultured, potential buyers who don't find their experiences reflected in existing offerings, or feel excluded by gaming's male-culture-centred ethos- who represent a virtually untapped market - these factors should prove attractive, increasing both social and economic impact.

Team

Iðunn Ágústsdóttir (sound design).

Tom Andersen (chief curator and historian, Norwegian Armed Forces Museum and Visitor Centre, Akershus Fortress and Castle [AFCM]).

Ann Iren Bratt (higher executive officer, finance, Norwegian Film Scool).

Kariina Gretere (music composition, production and performance).

Rafal Hanzl (3D art, modelling and creative technology).

Wenche Hellekås (concept art, character design, 3D modelling and animation).

Nikola Kuresevic (game-design and intern mentor, Snowcastle Games).

Sindre Lie (3D environment and props design and modelling).

Sindre Majgren Uthaug (NPC character design and modelling).

Amir Soltani (forensic architectural modelling, metrowave).

Bendik Stang (game direction, Snowcastle Games).

Maureen Thomas (research, story architecture, dramatization, directing, producing).

Emil Walseth (Unreal Game Engine programming).

ACKNOWLEDGMENTS

This research was supported by "Norwegian Artistic Research Programme" (Project Grant 29, 2018); "Norwegian Film School, Inland Norway University of Applied Sciences"; "Snowcastle Games Oslo" and the "Norwegian Armed Forces Museum and Visitor Centre, Akershus Fortress and Castle". Development of the original script for *Queens game* was supported by "Norwegian Film Institute".

REFERENCES

A Plague Tale: Innocence. (2019). [Video Game]. Asobo Studios SARL/ Focus Home Interactive SAS.

A Princess Tale: Introduction (2016). [Video Game]. Warfare Studios/Adorlea https://www.youtube.com/watch?v=yn9tSs9v0WE

A Woman's Lot: [Kingdom Come: Deliverance]. (2019). [Video Game]. DownLoadable Content (DLC). Warhorse Studios s.r.o.

Adamson, A. & Apted. M. (Directors). (2005-2010). *The Chronicles of Narnia* [Feature film series]. Walt Disney Pictures, Walden Media, Ozumi Films & Fox 2000 Pictures.

Amt, E. (1993). *Women's lives in medieval Europe.* Routledge.

Andrews, S. (2014). Documenting the Middle Ages on television. *REF 2014 Impact Case Studies.* https://impact.ref.ac.uk/casestudies/CaseStudy.aspx?Id=35308

Archibald, E. (2009). Questioning Arthurian ideals. In E. Archibald & A. Putter (Eds.), *The Cambridge companion to the Arthurian legend* (pp. 39–153). Cambridge University Press., doi:10.1017/CCOL9780521860598.009

Archibald, E., & Johnson, D. F. (2020). Arthurian Literature XXXV. *Arthurian Literature,* 35.

Assassin's Creed II. (2009). [Video Game]. Ubisoft Montreal.

Axton, R. (1974). *European Drama of the Early Middle Ages.* Hutchinson.

Bartlett, R. *(Researcher, Presenter).* (2010). *The Normans* [Television documentary miniseries]. BBC TV.

Bartlett, R. *(Researcher, Presenter).* (2014). *The Plantagenets* [Television documentary miniseries]. BBC TV.

Benioff, D. & Weiss, D.B. (Creators). (2013-2019). *Game of Thrones* [Television series]. HBO, Television 360 & Groki Studio.

Bontchev, B. (2015). Serious games for and as cultural heritage. *Researchgate.* https://www.researchgate.net/publication/301285825_Serious_Games_for_and_as_Cultural_Heritage

Bosman, S. (2019, May 3). Male and female gamers: how their similarities and differences shape the games market. *Newzoo.* https://newzoo.com/insights/articles/male-and-female-gamers-how-their-similarities-and-differences-shape-the-games-market/

Brain, S. (2017, September 12). Skyrim: The Elder Scrolls V statistics. *Statistic Brain Research Institute.* https://www.statisticbrain.com/skyrim-the-elder-scrolls-v-statistics/

Brandenburg, A. (2020). If it's a fantasy world, why bother making it realistic? – Constructing and Debating the Middle Ages of *The Witcher 3: The Wild Hunt*. In M. Lorber & F. Zimmermann (Eds.), *History in games: contingencies of an authentic past* (pp. 201–220). Transcript Verlag. doi:10.1515/9783839454206-011

Brandt, M. (2008). *Video games activate reward regions of brain in men more than women, Stanford study finds*. Stanford Medecine News Center. https://med.stanford.edu/news/all-news/2008/02/video-games-activate-reward-regions-of-brain-in-men-more-than-women-stanford-study-finds.html

Brune, M. (2021, March 31). Zooming in on female gamers with consumer insights data. *Newzoo*. https://newzoo.com/insights/articles/zooming-in-on-female-gamers-with-consumer-insights-data/

Buck, C., & Lee, J. *(Directors).* (2013). *Frozen* [Animated feature film]. Walt Disney Pictures, Walt Disney Animation Studios.

Buck, C., & Lee, J. *(Directors).* (2019). *Frozen II* [Animated feature film]. Walt Disney Pictures, Walt Disney Animation Studios.

Building Worlds. (n.d.) FogEffects_SkyAtmposphere. *Unreal engine documentation 4.6.* https://docs.unrealengine.com/4.26/en-US/BuildingWorlds/FogEffects/SkyAtmosphere/

Campa, P., Casarico, A., & Profeta, P. (2011). Gender culture and gender gap in employment. *CESifo Economic Studies*, *57*(1), 156–182. doi:10.1093/cesifo/ifq018

Campbell, C. (2017, January). Which games are women and girls playing? *Polygon.* https://www.polygon.com/2017/1/20/14337282/games-for-women-and-girls

Castor, H. (2010). *She-wolves: the women who ruled England before Elizabeth*. Faber.

Castor, H. *(Researcher, Presenter).* (2012). *She-wolves: England's early queens* [Television documentary miniseries]. BBC TV.

Castor, H. *(Researcher, Presenter).* (2013). *Medieval Lives: Birth, Marriage, Death* [Television documentary miniseries]. BBC TV.

Castor, H. (2019, February). Good television depends on the care, commitment, resources and skill of those creating it. In How good is television as a medium for history? *History Today*, *69*(2). https://www.historytoday.com/history-today-issues/volume-69-issue-2-february-2019

CeltX 8.82.1. (2020). [Software - audiovisual story and interactive scripting]. CeltX Inc. https://www.celtx.com/

Clement, J. (2021, March 3). Game-developer gender distribution worldwide. *Statista.* https://www.statista.com/statistics/453634/game-developer-gender-distribution-worldwide/

Clement, J. (2021, May 5). Gender split of US computer video gamers. *Statista.* https://www.statista.com/statistics/232383/gender-split-of-us-computer-and-video-gamers/

Cochise College. (2016, May 26). Gender differences in social interaction. *Sociology.* https://courses.lumenlearning.com/cochise-sociology-os/chapter/gender-differences-in-social-interaction/

Code, B. (2016, December 07). Video games are boring. *GameIndustryBiz*. https://www.gamesindustry.biz/articles/2016-11-07-video-games-are-boring

Coldwell, M. (1986). Jougleresses and trobairitz: secular musicians in medieval France. In Women making music: The western art tradition (pp. 39 – 61). University of Illinois Press. doi:10.1007/978-1-349-09367-0_3

Cooper, H. (Ed.). (2008). *Sir Thomas Malory: Le Morte D'Arthur*. Oxford University Press.

Dörner, R., Göbel, S., Effelsberg, W., & Wiemeyer, J. (Eds.). (2016). *Serious games: Foundations, concepts and practice*. Springer. doi:10.1007/978-3-319-40612-1

DRTV. (2017). *Historien om Danmark* [The history of Denmark]. Danish Broadcasting Co. [Television dramatized documentary miniseries]

Duriez, C. (2015). *The Oxford Inklings*. Lion Hudson.

Eads, V. (2012). Means, motive, opportunity: medieval women and the recourse to arms. *De Re Militari*. https://deremilitari.org/2012/09/eads-means-motive-opportunity/

Elder Scrolls V: Skyrim. (2011). [Video Game]. Bethesda Game Studios.

Etting, V. (2004). *Queen Margrete I (1353-1412) and the founding of the Nordic Union*. Brill. doi:10.1163/9789047404798

Feminist Frequency. (n.d.). *Conversations with pop culture*. https://feministfrequency.com/

Final Fantasy. (1987-). [Video Game]. Square Enix.

Fredericks, L. (2021, February 16). The complete guide to virtual tourism in 2021. *Cvent*. https://www.cvent.com/en/blog/hospitality/virtual-tourism

Georgopoulos, A., Kontogianni, G., Koutsaftis, C., & Skamantzari, M. (2017). Serious games at the service of cultural heritage and tourism. In V. Katsoni, A. Upadhya, & A. Stratigea (Eds.), *Tourism, Culture and Heritage in a Smart Economy* (pp. 3–18). Springer., doi:10.1007/978-3-319-47732-9_1

Grand Ages: Medieval. (2015). [Video Game]. Kalypso Media Digital.

Granström, H. (2013). *Elements in games for virtual heritage applications* [Master Degree Project in Informatics Dissertation]. University of Skövde. http://www.diva-portal.org/smash/get/diva2:627227/FULLTEXT01.pdf

Gregory, P. *(Researcher, Presenter)*. (2013). *The Real White Queen and her Rivals* [Television documentary]. BBC TV.

Hissrich, L. (Showrunner, Writer, Executive Producer). (2019-2021). *The Witcher* [Television miniseries]. Netflix.

Historion (2002). [Video Game]. Klett Softwareverlag GmbH.

Hood, V. (2018, March 5). Kingdom Come: Deliverance cost over $36 million to make. *PC Games*. https://www.pcgamesn.com/kingdom-come-deliverance/kingdom-come-deliverance-cost-budget

Hoydedata. (n.d.). https://hoydedata.no

Jacey, H. (2010). *The woman in the story*. Michael Wiese Productions.

Jackson, P. (2001-2003). (Director). *The Lord of the Rings* [Feature film series]. New Line Cinema, WingNut Films, The Saul Zaentz Company.

Jenkins, P. *(Director)*. (2021). *Wonderwoman* [Feature film]. Warner Bros, Atlas Entertainment & Cruel and Unusual Films.

Jones, A. (2019, February 13). Kingdom Come: Deliverance has sold two million copies. *PC Games*. https://www.pcgamesn.com/kingdom-come-deliverance/kingdom-come-deliverance-sales-numbers

Kalinke, M. (2015). The introduction of the Arthurian legend in Scandinavia. In M. Kalinke (Ed.), *The Arthur of the North* (pp. 5–21). University of Wales Press.

Kapell, M., & Elliott, A. (2013). *Playing with the past: digital games and the simulation of history*. Bloomsbury.

Katsoni, V., Upadhya, A., & Stratigea, A. (2016). *Tourism, culture and heritage in a smart economy*. Springer.

Kent, J., Payne, J. & Teague, C. (Directors). (2013). *The White Queen* [Television historical drama miniseries]. BBC TV.

Kingdom Come: Deliverance. (2018). [Video Game]. Warhorse Studios s.r.o.

Kowalski, C., & Bhalla, R. (2018). Viewing the Disney movie *Frozen* through a psychodynamic lens. *The Journal of Medical Humanities*, *39*(2), 145–150. doi:10.100710912-015-9363-3 PMID:26467918

Lafortune, A. (2020). *Clothed in history: costume and medievalism in fantasy film and television* [Master of Arts Thesis, Western University] (Publication number 7198). Electronic Thesis and Dissertation Repository. https://ir.lib.uwo.ca/etd/7198

Layher, W. (2015). The Old Swedish Hærre Ivan leons riddare. In M. Kalinke (Ed.), *The Arthur of the North* (pp. 123–144). University of Wales Press.

Legend of Zelda: Phantom Hourglass. (2007/Wii U 2013). [Video Game]. Nintendo DS.

Legend of Zelda: Wind Waker. (2002/Wii U 2013). [Video Game]. Nintendo GameCube.

Little Big Planet 3: Women In History Costume Pack. (2016). [Video Game]. Sony Interactive Entertainment Europe.

Logic Driver Pro 2.5. (2021). [Software - game development]. Recursive. https://recursoft.com/projects/LogicDriver

Lorber, M., & Zimmerman, F. (Eds.). (2020). *History in games: Contingencies of an authentic past*. Transcript Verlag.

McLaughlin, M. (2010). The woman warrior: Gender, warfare and society in medieval Europe. *Women's Studies*, *17*(3-4), 193–209. doi:10.1080/00497878.1990.9978805

Medieval Defenders. (2016). [Video Game]. Creobit/8floor.

Medieval Dynasty. (2020). [Video Game]. Toplitz Productions.

Muir, R. (2020). *And they all lived happily ever after? A critical analysis of the Disney princess phenomenon* [PhD thesis]. University of Nottingham.

Murdock, M. (1990). *The heroine's journey.* Shambala.

Napoleon: Total War. (2010). [Video Game]. Creative Assembly.

NTHP. (2015). *Preservation glossary.* https://savingplaces.org/stories/preservation-glossary-todays-word-heritage-tourism#.YQfhxY4za44

Nyberg, T. (2003). Birgitta politikern [Birgitta the politician]. In Birgitta av Vadstena [Birgitta of Vadstena] (pp. 29-44). Natur och Kultur.

O'Neill, A. (2021, June 4). Highest grossing film annually: historical. *Statista.* https://www.statista.com/statistics/1072778/highest-grossing-film-annually-historical/

Olsen, R. A. (1981). *Sjællandske krønike* [The Chronicle of Zealand]. Wormianum.

Orme, N. (2003). *Medieval children.* Yale University Press.

Payne, J. (2018, December 30). Heritage tourism: facts and figures. *The Insider.* https://www.buses.org/news/article/insider-exclusive-heritage-toursim-facts-figures

Power, E. (1975). *Medieval women.* Cambridge University Press.

Prager, P., Thomas, M., & Selsjord, M. (2015). Transposing, transforming and transcending tradition in creative digital media. In D. Harrison (Ed.), *Handbook of research on digital media and creative technologies* (pp. 141–199). IGI Global. doi:10.4018/978-1-4666-8205-4.ch008

Ryan, M. (2016). *Narrative as Virtual Reality 2: Revisiting immersion and interactivity in literature and electronic media.* Johns Hopkins University Press.

Sapkowski, A. (2020). *The Witcher Saga.* Gollancz.

Sarkeesian, A. (2013). *Tropes vs women in video games.* https://feministfrequency.com/video-series/

Sinding-Larsen, H. (1924). *Akershus: bidrag til Akershus' slots bygningshistorie i de første 350 aar 1300 – 1650. Paa grundlag av den bygningsarkaeologiske undersøkelse 1905 – 1924* [Akershus: contribution to the history of the building of Akershus castle in the first 350 years 1300-1650. On the basis of the archaeological examination 1905-1924]. Eberh. B. Oppi Kunstforlag.

SOHA. (2021, July 26). Female gamers are on the rise. *Zestvine.* https://www.zestvine.com/female-gamers-are-on-the-rise-trends-stats/

Sonawane, K. (2017, November). Serious games market outlook: 2023. *Allied Market Research.* https://www.alliedmarketresearch.com/serious-games-market

Steamcommunity. (2020, September 19). Playable female character. *Discussions: Medieval Dynasty.* https://steamcommunity.com/app/1129580/discussions/0/2942496178841957805/

Stoll, J. (2021, Jan 13). Box-office revenue of the most successful films of all time. *Statista*. https://www.statista.com/statistics/262926/box-office-revenue-of-the-most-successful-films-of-all-time /

Superior RPG Kit. (2019). *T-games*. https://www.unrealengine.com/marketplace/en-US/product/superior-rpg-kit

Svensson, E. (1962). *The medieval household: daily life in castles and farmsteads. Scandinavian examples in their European context*. Brepols.

The Black Death. (2016). [Video Game]. Small Impact Games & Syrin Studios/Green Man Loaded.

The Great War: 1914-1918 (1992). [Video Game]. Blue Byte Studio GmbH.

The Legend of Zelda. (1986). [Video Game] Nintendo.

The Plague. (2015). [Video Game]. Serious Games Interactive.

The Witcher. (2007-2020). [Video Game Series]. CD Projekt.

The Witcher 3: The Wild Hunt. (2020) [Video Game]. CD Projekt.

Thomas, M. (2021). Cinematic forms and cultural heritage. In M. Breeze (Ed.), *Forms of the cinematic* (pp. 122–142). Bloomsbury. doi:10.5040/9781501361456.0015

Toh, W. & Lim, F. (2022). Learning in digital play: a dual case study of video gamers' independent play. *Research and practice in technology based learning,* 17(article number 6), (introduction). DOI:. doi:10.1186/s41039-022-00182-2

Tolkien, J.R.R. (1954-55). *The Lord of the rings*. Allen and Unwin.

Toplitz (2020). Introduction. *Medieval dynasty*. https://www.toplitz-productions.com/medieval-dynasty.html

Tschudi-Madsen, S., & Moberg, H. (1999). *Akershus: vårt riksklenodium 700 år* [Akershus: gem of our realm 700th anniversary]. Aschehaug.

Ultima Online. (1997). [Video Game]. Origin Systems. https://uo.com/

Unreal Engine 4.26. (2021). [Software - game engine]. Epic Games. https://www.unrealengine.com/

UNWTO. (2017). Tourism and culture. *UNWTO General Assembly*. https://www.unwto.org/ethics-culture-and-social-responsibility

Wanat, G. (2020, June 19). Popularity of Netflix production *The Witcher* by region. *Statista*. https://www.statista.com/statistics/1085978/popularity-of-netflix-production-the-witcher-by-region/

Warthen, K., Boyce-Peacor, A., Jones, K., Love, T., & Mickey, B. (2020). Sex differences in the human reward system: Convergent behavioral, autonomic and neural evidence. *Social Cognitive and Affective Neuroscience, 15*(7), 789–801. doi:10.1093can/nsaa104 PMID:32734300

Ways of History. (2017). [Video Game]. Glyph Worlds.

Wijman, T. (2021, May 6). *Newzoo*. https://newzoo.com/insights/articles/global-games-market-to-generate-175-8-billion-in-2021-despite-a-slight-decline-the-market-is-on-track-to-surpass-200-billion-in-2023/

Wolf, M. J. P. (2019). *The Routledge companion to imaginary worlds*. Routledge.

Wu, Y. (2020). The analysis of Elsa's growth from the perspective of ecofeminism. *Open Journal of Social Sciences*, *8*(6), 30–36. Advance online publication. doi:10.4236/jss.2020.86003

Xu, F., & Buhalis, D. (2021). *Gamification for tourism*. Channel View Publications.

Yokoi, T. (2021, March 3). Female gamers are on the rise – can the gaming industry keep up? *Forbes*. https://www.forbes.com/sites/tomokoyokoi/2021/03/04/female-gamers-are-on-the-rise-can-the-gaming-industry-catch-up/

KEY TERMS AND DEFINITIONS

Attack and Defend Combat: gameplay to defeat one's enemies or be defeated.

Crafting: mechanics allowing combination of items into new items.

Empire building: game objective to conquer opponent's territory.

Gathering: harvesting and collection of resources.

Life-sim: genre where player develops relationships with NPCs.

Maneuver and Steer: controlling avatar with precision to progress.

RPG: Role Playing Game, where avatar has skills and stats that can be developed.

Skill-tree: gated avatar skill progression.

Survival game: player must eat and drink to survive, typically combined with gathering, crafting, and combat.

Tactics and Planning: gameplay choices that have consequences later.

Chapter 17
Serious Games for Recruitment in the New Humanism

Tetiana Luhova

 https://orcid.org/0000-0002-3573-9978

Odessa National Polytechnic University, Ukraine

ABSTRACT

Serious games are analyzed through the principles of New Humanism, the humanization of computer games for training. The chapter defined the types of serious games for Western and Japanese management. Based on this, the characteristics and criteria that serious next-generation games must meet are described. In particular, hard-skills serious games are focused on Western management; emphasize gameplay on formalization, logic, clear rules, and work functionality; and have the aesthetics of a challenge aimed at academic training and practice of skills. The core of soft-skills serious games are creativity, innovation, research, personal qualities, and implicit knowledge aimed at solving cognitive and social problems, so they best embody the principles of the Japanese approach to management. The threats and shortcomings of such games have been clarified. The trends in the development of serious games in automated recruiting systems are revealed. It is emphasized that in the "education-recruitment-spirituality" system, serious games play a connecting and integrating role.

INTRODUCTION

The information age has led to the emergence of new competitive models of the labor market. The competencies of adaptability, mobility and high professionalism gain weight for both recruiters and job applicants. It is a readiness for lifelong learning, continuous professional development, and retraining. Compliance of the education content with modern labor market requirements is an important criterion for the quality of higher education (Recommendations, 2020). All this causes close cooperation of higher education institutions with stakeholders, employers, and graduates. But, in such a partnership model, a stage of recruitment mediation is leveled. In fact, the process of employment of a young specialist is the most exciting topic for graduates. So, recruitment systems play the role of litmus tests on the current needs of the labor market.

DOI: 10.4018/978-1-7998-9732-3.ch017

The rapid development of recruitment information systems and career-oriented social networks is transforming recruitment into a dynamic human resources industry, and video games into platforms for professional training and recruitment. Serious games are teaching people to perform real-life tasks in the virtual world, simulating the work of a real process system in time. Serious games can be the bridge that combines academic education and direct employment of a young specialist, his adaptation to the fleeting demands of the labor market. Therefore, it is time to study the essence of serious games for training and recruitment, develop criteria for them, and understand the place and role of such forms of techno communication between all education subjects and employment in the New Humanism ideology (Pechchei, 1977). In particular, "no techniques will be effective unless they are based on positive personality traits" (Covey, 2020). This formulation of the question provides an opportunity to take a fresh look at the human qualities as objects of upbringing, education, career growth, gamification, and cultural values through serious games.

BACKGROUND

The discovery of great opportunities for video games in a wide range of social life (business, education, entertainment, management, public administration, etc.) has aroused considerable scientists' interest in various aspects of serious games and gamification. As of July 1, 2021, the scientific platform Google Scholar has about 103,000 scientific papers on the use of serious games in recruitment. The theory of serious games is studied (Dörner, Göbel, Effelsberg, & Wiemeyer, 2016), their frameworks are developed (Loh, Sheng, & Ifenthaler, 2015), the classification is given(Ratan & Ritterfeld, 2009), their possibilities (Stapleton, 2004) and evaluation methods (Emmerich & Bockholt, 2016) are described.

In recruitment, serious games were considered from the perspective of defining the role of gamification and game thinking in human resource management (Armstrong, Landers, & Collmus, 2016),(Fetzer, McNamara, & Geimer, 2017), analyzed the advantages and disadvantages of this approach (Stănescu, Ioniță, & Ioniță, 2020). The dependence of the recruiters' characteristics on their use of selection technology has been established (Oostrom, Van Der Linden, Born, & Van Der Molen, 2013); new technologies for evaluating and selecting candidates as part of the company's strategy. In particular, the impact of intelligence on employment policy, personality tests, analysis of social interaction in the interview process, the impact of social networks on applicants' perceptions, competency modeling (Nikolaou & Oostrom, 2015). The effects of the game evaluation of the job candidate were presented as a method for increasing the objectivity of the selection process, reducing anxiety, and better evaluation of job candidates (Stănescu, Ioniță, & Ioniță, 2020). This has led to a certain shift in the research of serious games for recruitment towards the formalization of competencies (hard- and soft-skills), motivating factors, and so on. This trend of research is justified by both economic pragmatism and technical proposals of the information society, the progress of global data accounting networks.

However, as N. Wiener writes: "We can no longer judge a person by the work he does. We must evaluate it as a human being" (Wiener, 1964, p. 323), otherwise, a "routine human being" can be replaced by a machine. The ideologue of the New Humanism A. Pechchei notes: "The most important thing on which the fate of humanity depends are human qualities" (Pechchei, 1977, p. 73). And further: "People are seen as biological organisms, economic beings or - in a more general form - as consumers. And the primary attention, therefore, is almost only focused on the material needs of their existence. Other most important needs, desires, and aspirations related to the social, cultural and spiritual nature of man are considered not primary, secondary" (Pechchei, 1977, p. 76). So, it seems important to define the ways of embedding the concept of New Humanism in the outline of serious games to form a person's worldview. "The New humanism <...> must be creative and convincing to radically renew, if not completely replace, the principles and norms that now seem inviolable; to promote the emergence of new values and motivations that meet the requirements of our time - spiritual, philosophical, ethical, social, aesthetic and artistic" (Pechchei, 1977, p. 212). All this should be embodied in new pedagogical concepts, methods, and developments that offer a holistic view of the world, deep responsibility, systematic, and high spirituality.

The theme of New Humanism has rich and long-standing historiography. The phenomenon of New Humanism was analyzed (Sarton, 1924),(Brooks, 2011). It was considered as a significant stage in the history of religions (Eliade, 1961), as the spirituality and culture meaning restoration through archetypal myths and symbols (Eliade, 1961), (Cave, 1993), as "a new critical humanist pedagogy, an approach to reading the world that puts the struggle against capitalism and the imperialism", "the pedagogical project, that is powered by the oxygen of socialism's universal quest for human freedom and social justice" (McLaren & Jaramillo, 2007). In the education system, the issues of the peculiarities of teaching new humanism (Belle-Isle, 1986), its role in pedagogy (Biesta, 1998) and media literacy (Tornero & Tapio, 2010), education for global citizenship (Ikeda, 2010) have been investigated. New humanism as a worldview concept has been described as a reference model of education (Stallman, 2003) (Halimi, 2014), associated with the deep thinking, spirituality formation (Bostad, 2012), and stable development(d'Orville, 2016). "The new humanism therefore advocates the social inclusion of every human being at all levels of society and underlines the transformative power of education, sciences, culture and communications"(d'Orville, 2016).

Training and organizational management of personnel, including recruitment, are interrelated elements of a single social system. The connection between these elements is manifested in the concepts of dual education, student-centered learning, fitness for purpose (NAQA, 2020), and professional-oriented video games. All of this forms a broad field of research: game-based learning (Gee, 2003), transmedia learning (Raybourn, 2014); the use of serious games in the corporate sector (Donovan, 2012). We also initiated a discussion on the implementation of the game design principles in the methodological work of higher education institutions, bringing the content of education closer to the real needs of the labor market (Luhova T. A., 2021); development of professionally-oriented video games for the managers training of various profiles (Luhova, Chursyn, Blazhko, & Rostoka, 2019), (Luhova T. A., 2020), games with open data sets for public administration (Blazhko, Luhova, Melnik, & Ruvinska, 2017). But, to this day, the topic of the humanization of computer games for training and recruitment, which has gained tangible social significance, remains unsolved.

RESEARCH METHODOLOGY OR APPROACH

The study aims to identify ways to transform serious recruitment games through the principles of New Humanism.

The study objectives are:

- to analyze well-known professionally-oriented games in terms of the principles of the New Humanism;

- to define the serious games types according to Western and Japanese management. On this basis, to describe the characteristics and criteria that must meet the new generation serious games;
- to reveal trends in the development of serious games in automated recruitment systems.

The methodological basis of the study was a comparative analysis of serious games based on their classifications (Ratan & Ritterfeld, 2009), (Djaouti, Alvarez, Jessel, Methel, & Molinier, 2008); generalizations to supplement the "basic map of the serious games" (Ratan & Ritterfeld, 2009). And also a humanitarian examination of serious games based on principles of the New Humanism (Pechchei, 1977).

MAIN FOCUS OF THE CHAPTER

Serious Games in the Light of the New Humanism

The designer of serious games not only determines the game situations (settings, rules, levels, etc.), but also determines the selective attitude to certain abilities, competencies and human qualities that are put forward to the player. Therefore, the game designer is the architect of digital human competencies, but also a harbinger of social change. This was written in particular (Michael & Chen, 2006). Therefore, it is expedient to determine the basic requirements of the New Humanism to human qualities, to find out the features of their implementation in different serious games for recruitment, using the known classifications of video games (Ratan & Ritterfeld, 2009), (Djaouti, Alvarez, Jessel, Methel, & Molinier, 2008), (Kirizleev, 2014).

A. Pechchei points to the features of the New Humanism: a sense of global responsibility and the ability to evaluate the results of their actions, a clear and unambiguous understanding of how to live in harmony with an ever-changing world, love of justice and intolerance of violence (Pechchei, 1977, pp. 84, 211, 214). Scientists note that the results of serious games are always useful for players, facilitate the learning process, and have no negative or harmful effects (Ratan & Ritterfeld, 2009, p. 11). The metaphorical system of such a game should not contradict human values (Blazhko, Luhova, Melnik, & Ruvinska, 2017). «Games that would elide aggression or addiction would not qualify as serious games. On the contrary, serious games should always work as intended, contributing to a self-guided, enjoyable, and therefore deeply sustained learning experience" (Ratan & Ritterfeld, 2009, p. 11). E.g., the children's game "Job Simulator" (Job Simulator, 2016) could be useful for career guidance, imitating the details of the work of a restaurant chef, office worker, shop assistant and other professions. But it does not belong to serious games, because some of its elements of game aesthetics (fun) are unacceptable for ethics: game started by "Run the boss with a stapler!"; besides useful actions, the game provides the ability to break physical objects, "eat questionable food from the trash" (Job Simulator, 2016).

In game design, the means of "fun" is used to attract players, and hence the economic success of the game project. But in serious games, the "fun" should not be identified with permissiveness, violate taboo boundaries, contain elements of aggression. This is an important requirement for the mechanics (rules) of serious games. E.g. the well-known ROBLOX gaming platform has introduced players to block a gaming account for various periods of time for swearing, harassment, fraud, begging and sexual harassment. The player must feel the limits of what is allowed, be aware of responsibility for their actions. The most prominent characteristic of "responsibility" is revealed in the game "Stop Disaster" (Stop Disaster, 2018), which according to the results of game actions and strategies of the player shows the statistics of rescued and killed during a natural disaster. Similarly, the game "Not For Broadcast" (Not For Broadcast, 2020) shows an assessment of the player's actions, his mistakes and likely influences on the social processes of the game world.

In modern digital game theories, the "fun" is a certain emotional state of the gamer without pragmatic goals. It can be not only fun, but also communication, boasting, leadership, ownership, sadness, horror, and so on. There are different classifications of fun types: emotional, cognitive and social (Kim, Jung, & Kim, 2015); easy (curiosity, curiosity, chances, quick bonuses, free unexpected gifts); difficult (challenge, challenge, overcome obstacles, perform a significant task); social (friendship, communication, receiving "likes", "messages", "reposts", being in a team, performing common tasks, uniting by interests); serious (importance, helping others, creating something useful, answering forums, advising, tidying up work folders, etc.) (Lokteva, 2017). Accordingly, there are types of players: destroyers (will try to break everything), consumers (will use while there is something to take), creators (will offer improvements) (Lokteva, 2017)

For serious games of the New Humanism, transforming the player-destroyer and the player-consumer into the creator is important. The correct ethical metaphorization of the game is important for this. Thus, the "destroy" action encourages the player to destroy, collect or catch objects of the game for their further purposeful collection and accumulation. The "Shoot" action is also not considered in the literal sense, but invites the player to touch an object at a distance, or somehow affect it (Djaouti, Alvarez, Jessel, Methel, & Molinier, 2008). Therefore, negative connotations of breath actions appear only in a certain context when they are aimed at people, order, beauty, and so on. A. Pechchei argues that the New Humanism can ensure the human transformation, to raise his qualities and opportunities to a new increased responsibility at the world level (Pechchei, 1977, p. 211). These guidelines are essential for developers of serious games.

The global feeling is associated with another important quality - holism (Come On!, 2018); (Pechchei, 1977, p. 214), and hence with holistic pedagogy. "Instead of well-educated citizens and productive economic workers, which are the goal of traditional educational systems, holistic education emphasizes the importance of cultivating spirituality, respect for the environment and a sense of social justice" (Zabolotna, 2012, pp. 225-226), (Mercogliano, 2005, p. 153). The principles of holistic pedagogy include: understanding the unity and integrity of all living things, deep, comprehensive development of personality, especially its creativity, imagination, compassion, spirituality, self-knowledge, social skills and emotional intelligence; giving preference to synthesis and integration over analysis and separation (Mercogliano, 2005), (Zabolotna, 2012), (Lemkow, 1990).

This vision is confirmed in the New Humanism ideology, the requirement to establish a new balance between knowledge of details and the ability to synthesize, giving it a clear focus on important goals (Pechchei, 1977, p. 111). Such characteristics correspond to games with a deep history, guided by the player's choice (based on his moral guidelines, creativity, responsibility, ability to strategic think), with many alternatives to the finale. Thus, in the game (1979 Revolution: Black Friday, 2016) the protagonist - a novice photojournalist decides on life and death on the streets of Iran in the late 1970s. This game teaches novice journalists the basics of hotspot behavior and can recruit reporters into various media. It also helps to establish the level of the player's humanity, his ability to partner, mercy, and decisive action.

The special attention of holistic pedagogy and the New Humanism to the problems of ecology, ecosystems and community conservation is noticeable (Pechchei, 1977), (Come On!, 2018) (Zabolotna, 2012, p. 229). This is consistent with the game "Stop Disaster", created under the auspices of UNDRR (Stop Disaster, 2018). The primary goal of the game is to raise public awareness about disaster risk reduction. The developers of the game proceed from the idea that "Children are the future architects, mayors, doctors, and parents of the world of tomorrow. If they know what to do to reduce the impact of disasters, they will create a safer world" (Stop Disaster, 2018). In different locations around the world, the player must take anti-crisis actions against various natural disasters: earthquakes, floods, tsunamis, storms, fires. The player's actions must be strategic, systematic, based on laws and logic.

Serious games simulate the various ways of solving the problems outlined by the Club of Rome (Pechchei, 1977, p. 120). Thus, the Game for change website presents serious games in the following categories: civil law, conflict, business, education, compassion, ecology, finance, gender and social equality, globalism, health care, history, International Women's Day, politics, safety, science, technology, transportation.

Another important human quality that the New Humanism needs is respect for complex systems in which the interests of man and nature are intertwined. A. Pechchei points to a new role of man in the informatized world - it is "the role of an arbiter who regulates life on the planet, including his own life" (Pechchei, 1977, pp. 70-71). Therefore, serious games should instill in the player an understanding of the connectivity of the world, contextuality: "each problem is related to all others, and any seemingly obvious solution of one of them may complicate or somehow influence the decisions of others" (Pechchei, 1977, p. 120). Preference should be given to games with a non-linear plot, because "no problem or combination of them can be solved by applying the methods of the past based on a linear approach" (Pechchei, 1977, p. 120). Examples of such games are (Stop Disaster, 2018) and (Branches of Power, 2010). The latter game allows the player to feel like an "arbiter", taking part in the legislative process in terms of all three branches of government.

Thus, based on the principles of New Humanism (Pechchei, 1977) and Holistic pedagogy (Zabolotna, 2012), we can identify the main vectors and points of application of game designers in developing serious games for training and recruitment (Table 1).

Table 1. Vectors for serious games through New Humanism and Holistic pedagogy

Key principles	Interconnectedness	Wholeness	Human qualities	Game
Key concepts	Globality, interdependence, interconnectedness, mutual involvement, nonlinearity	Integrity of systems, multilevel perception, multilevel	Humanity, creativity, development, self-sufficiency, responsibility	Mechanics, dynamics, aesthetics
The key values	Compassion, community, ecosystems	Diversity in unity (pluralism), sustainable development, cultural identity	Spirituality, love, goodness, charity, responsibility, insight, empathy, wisdom, conscience, honor, dignity	Social significance
Social problems	Cultural identity, globalization, loneliness	Inclusion, ecosystems	Equality, ethics, change	Adaptation, socialization, communication, self-fulfillment
Curriculum	Inter- (trans-, cross-, inter-) discipline, interaction	Integration	Curiosity, identity, choice	Game design
Learning process	Dialogue, partnership, co-creation, cooperation, collaboration	Integral personality, integral community, integral life, system thinking, meta-cognition	Reflexivity, experimentation, curiosity, attentiveness, imagination, inspiration, joy of knowledge, self-management	Gamification, motivation, self-directed learning

Continued on following page

Table 1. Continued

Key principles	Interconnectedness	Wholeness	Human qualities	Game
Learning outcome	Significance, positive relationships, friendliness, trust, academic mindset	Health, integrity, happiness, care, empathy, confidence, independence	Self-expression, curiosity, flexibility, competence, purposefulness, indifference, critical thinking and problem solving	Hard-skills, soft-skills, involvement
Serious games	Systematic, contextual	Balance	The role of the arbitrator, creativity, independence, choice, responsibility, courage, sensitivity, awareness of the value of life, a sense of boundaries, systematic thinking	Social adaptation, social employment, content mastery

Types of Serious Games According to Management Schools

Serious games for recruitment should focus on personnel strategies within certain business models. It is worth considering two opposite schools of management (Western and Japanese), and determine which serious games correspond to each of the areas. I. Nonaka described the Japanese approach to managing the company, contrasting it with the Western tradition of management from F. Taylor(Taylor, 1919) to H. Simon (Simon, 2013).

Western management is characterized by "limited rationality" (Simon, 1990), hierarchy, behavioral approach, administrative behavior (Simon, 2013), design thinking (Serrat, 2017) as a rational problem-solving activity (Kimbell, 2009), (Simon HA, 1969), decision-making models (Simon, 1979).

If a company in Western management is associated with a machine, then in Japanese management it is understood as a living organism, an individual with a collective sense, identity, and fundamental purpose. This is an approach to the creation of knowledge that belongs at the center of the company's human resources strategy (Nonaka, 2007, p. 163).

I. Nonaka argues that the new knowledge creation is not limited to the mechanical processing of objective information. It depends on "unspoken and often very subjective ideas, intuition and premonitions of individual employees and providing these ideas for testing and use by the company. The key to this process is personal commitment, a sense of identity of employees with the company, and its mission. Mobilizing this commitment and translating implicit knowledge into real technologies and products requires managers who are versed in images and symbols, slogans, metaphors, as hard numbers, market share measurements, productivity or return on investment as well" (Nonaka, 2007, p. 163). A. Pechchei emphasized the perspective resourcefulness of implicit knowledge as objects of management and human existence: "This (materialistic - TL) approach leaves aside the main property of a person - his own unrealized, undiscovered, or incorrectly used possibilities. It is in their development that not only the solution of all problems is concluded but also the basis of general self-improvement and self-expression of humans" (Pechchei, 1977, p. 214).

From the cybernetics point of view, the metaphor of Western management is the "management situation": a clear algorithm of actions to achieve certain goals. This is the situation of optimizing the choice (Chursin, 2010, p. 76). Japanese management is associated with a "development situation". It is modeled not by an algorithm but by a "calculus" (Chursin, 2010, pp. 39, 76). Here, the calculus is understood as "a way to sets by specifying the original elements (axioms) and derivation rules, each of which describes how to build new elements from the original and already built" (Maslov, 1979).

From the pedagogical point of view, Western management is characterized by a competency-based approach that meets the needs of the manufacturing sector. And Japanese - a value-based approach that meets innovation. Thus, both control models are different cognitive situations: freedom or non-freedom of the player, the determinism or stochastic behavior, the nature of game actions based on "calculus" or "algorithm" (Chursin, 2010, p. 40). D. Gray points to two types of business games (Gray, Brown, & Macanufo, 2010) with a specific purpose (optimization of business processes, re-engineering, improving productivity and sales, management decisions, etc.); and with an uncertain purpose in case of the need to develop innovative ideas, develop innovative projects, etc. Based on the above, recruiting serious games can be divided into two groups: Hard-skills-serious games (HSSG) for Western business models and Soft-skills-serious games (SSSG) for Japanese business models. The differences between the basic principles in these games are summarized in Table 2.

Table 2. Serious games through Western and Japanese approaches to management

Serious games for Western management	Serious games for Japanese management
Hard-skills-SG	**Soft-skills-SG**
Management situation	Development situation
Algorithm	Compute
Dots	Vector
Limit choices to optimize actions	Many choices
Competence approach	Value approach
Practice skills	Exploration and cognitive problem solving
To achieve the goal	The creative process
Focus on analysis	Focus on synthesis
Positive feedback loops	Negative feedback loops
Game	Play
The game finish is one, has tangible criteria for achieving the goal, standard solutions.	There are many alternatives to the finale. The criteria for achieving the goal are implicit. There are no standard solutions.

Hard-skills Serious Games (Hard-skills-SG, HSSG)

Serious games, emphasizing practical skills, a clear list of competencies, and professional knowledge, are rooted in the traditions of Western management, promoting the view of the organization as a machine for "information processing". According to this view, the only useful knowledge is formal and systematic-hard (read: quantifiable) data, codified procedures, universal principles. And key indicators for measuring the value of new knowledge are just as complex and quantifiable — increasing efficiency, lower costs, improved return on investment (Nonaka, 2007, p. 163).

The "Western" approach to game development is showed by D. Gray, who notes that "business, like many other human activities, came about through goals. Only the target presence makes you move from point A to point B; from where we are, to where we want to go. There is a voltage between the current state A - the initial condition - and the desired future state B - the target. What is between, we call the problem space. It is what needs to be overcome to achieve the goal" (Gray, Brown, & Macanufo, 2010). All this brings together business, any game, project activities, and, in fact, the business game. The game plot in this structure is embodied in a sequence of steps to overcome the space of the problem, which creates a causal chain that leads to the desired result - the finish of the game and the goal achievement for the business. This type includes logic games with deterministic, transitive rules. These games have been classified as based on the «primary learning principle of practicing skills», they "induce players to practice and solidify basic or advanced skills", and often "focus on a narrow scope of information and activity" (Ratan & Ritterfeld, 2009, p. 16).

HSSGs focus on professional skills practice. E.g. attributions of art objects (ARTigo), programming of office processes (Human Resource Machine, 2015), ability to work with streaming videos and determine censorship in the media (Not For Broadcast, 2020), to tool a set of actions against natural disasters (Stop Disaster, 2018). These are games that mimic business or production processes, which can be an important stage of competitive testing to hire specialists. The main purpose of such games is to acquaint the candidate with the future work functionality and to form an understanding of the work process in the company, identify realistic expectations with future work: lawyer-simulator (Objection!, 1992), ice cream makers (Stone City-Cold Stone Creamery, Inc, 2003). So, the HSSG reveals the close links between game content and academic education content (Ratan & Ritterfeld, 2009, p. 13). In such games, the player acts as a "learning machine", he must not just play by strict rules, with a constant strategy, but periodically or continuously must review the results to determine whether to change in favor of certain parameters, certain values in the strategy" (Wiener, 1964, p. 322). This is the basis that allows involving experts in professional issues.

HSSGs use a game balancing mechanism "positive feedback loops". This term comes from the biology and describes flexible biological modules of cells that provide background bistability in genetic networks, allows cells to remember past events and make discrete decisions in response to graduated signals" (Ingolia & Murray, 2007). For game design, the "positive feedback loop" (Yunyongying, 2014) refers to game mechanics to motivate and stimulate the player based on a direct interdependence: the one who is faster, stronger, smarter, smarter, first, richer, etc. A "positive feedback loop" is an indicator of a player's progress. Such games are the most favorable for the use of gamification tools: ratings, bonuses, competitions, because the better the player plays, the better his results. E.g. professional sports, races, chess, competitions, quizzes, testing, etc. Therefore, recruiting statistics are determined at the end of the game. Based on the structural model of the business game (Gray, Brown, & Macanufo, 2010), presented the place of game statistics for recruitment in Hard-skills-SG (Fig. 1)

Figure 1. Game statistics for recruitment in Hard-skills-SG

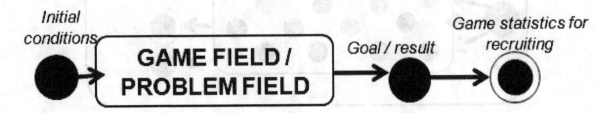

Game situations that mimic actual business processes can be an important stage of competitive testing to hire professionals.

Soft-Skills Serious Games (Soft-skills-SG, SSSG)

Serious games based on the Japanese approach should focus on a range of soft skills: sociability, teamwork, involvement, leadership, persuasive talent, public qualities, management skills, creativity, thinking paradigms and non-standard solutions, critical thinking, time management, emotional intelligence, intuition, self-management, etc. SSSG attracts universal non-specialized and supra-professional competencies and personal qualities that lead to successful participation in the work process and high productivity. Such games are not related to a specific profession but form or test the ability to solve life's problems and work with other people. SSSGs reproduce the experience of being in certain situations according to the industry (social, medical, military, business, etc.). SSSG includes games based on research, solving cognitive and social problems, creative tasks (Ratan & Ritterfeld, 2009, p. 16). These are puzzles, complex hypothetical situations, games with a deep history with elements of social fun, non-transitive rules, non-linear plots, and an open world. Contrary to practicing skills games, these games focus on a broad scope of information with a small amount of competition (Ratan & Ritterfeld, 2009, p. 17). Thus, they meet New Humanism regarding the balance between analysis and synthesis, the value-vector direction of analytical activity. This, of course, does not mean that it is necessary to stop any analytical activity, it just needs a clear orientation, submission to broader general goals, the ability to live in harmony with themselves and the world in conditions of high uncertainty and change (Pechchei, 1977, p. 111).

I. Nonaka points the essence of innovation is to re-create the world according to a particular vision or ideal. Such human qualities will be useful in the "Knowledge-creating company", inventing new knowledge is not a specialized activity (of the R&D department, marketing, or strategic planning), but "a nonstop process of personal and organizational self-renewal" (Nonaka, 2007, p. 164). SSSG focuses not on the result, but the process. So its statistics for recruitment forms not by the results of the game finish, but at checkpoints throughout the game (Fig. 2). This creates a collision of SSSG: an increased level of gameplay freedom gans increases the control of game statistics for recruitment.

Figure 2. Game statistics for recruitment in SSSG

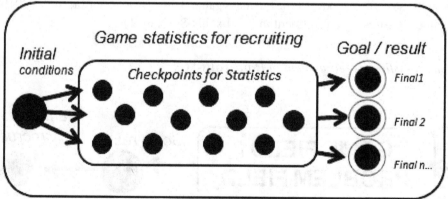

SSSGs use "negative feedback loops" as an element of game mechanics. This is a situation where the player receives more (bonuses, gifts, levels, hidden artifacts, etc.) if he is in a losing situation. This mechanism allows you to better adapt to new conditions, without rushing to reflect, explore, experiment. This is not only a certain system of psychological support for the player (beginner, non-professional, weak, or slow person), giving him the opportunity to stay in the game. But it is also a kind of game behavior focused on innovation. It is this mechanism that shifts the emphasis from performance to productivity.

SSSGs can be divided into those that explicitly form and test soft skills for employers; and those who do so implicitly. The first group includes games in which players interact with colleagues and managers, learn workplace ethics and company policy, learn management skills and work functionality. E.g. the Marriott Hotel Facebook game is a recruitment tool for Marriott Hotel employees. Gamers can create their own restaurant, where they will buy equipment and ingredients for budget money, hire and train staff, and serve guests (My Marriott Hotel). The major result is gaining experience in managing the hotel and restaurant business. The integration principle of "learning and employment" and the economic benefits of serious games have been declared in this game. The possibility of deploying the same game for recruitment and general training justifies the cost of developing Marriott (Donovan, 2012, pp. 25-26).

Games with implicit influence form or test a player's soft skills in deep game histories, solving complex social, civic, political, and environmental problems. In particular, the fight against world poverty, refugee problems (Darfur is Dying, 2006), environmental protection (Alba: A Wildlife Adventure, 2020), social unrest, and the journalist's hotspots behavior (1979 Revolution: Black Friday, 2016). Such games focus on the player's free choice, his civic activity. E.g., collecting signatures on a petition to protect the reserve, compiling a catalog of local animals (Alba: A Wildlife Adventure, 2020), the player's communication and leadership skills(Activate, 2010).

Such games show the influence of each person on various processes (social or natural) through bottom-up initiatives, volunteering, alternative worlds, personal moral choice, communication with other players, taking responsibility as a team member (Ratan & Ritterfeld, 2009, p. 17). New Humanism's demand for responsibility, a sense of globalism, and coherence is most clear in such serious games. Unlike HSSG, a sense of responsibility is not created by game statistics, but by game dynamics. Notable in this perspective is games with alternative stories when the player changes events in the past to solve certain problems of the present.

SSSG also includes creative games or research games, such as "Minecraft" - a computer indie game in the genre of the sandbox. This game has a significant potential for both the education and career guidance of children, their entry into vocational schools and higher, and for future recruitment. Because besides entertainment, the game forms/tests different soft skills. E.g. in architecture (modeling cities), physics (to study probability theory), chemistry (to experiment with chemical elements), biology (to model the human body structure), ecology (to study the deforestation and soil change), programming (program Minecraft inside Minecraft, learning the basics of network security), agriculture, etc. It is noteworthy that SSSG uses the capabilities of multiplayer gameplay, which encourages the communication skills of collaboration, co-creation, and thus promotes innovation creation(Patricio, Moreira, Zurlo, & Melazzini, 2020).

It is believed that soft skills are a certain type of skill (agree, change, analyze, etc.), the ability to act independently and effectively within their powers. And are not identified with human qualities (kind, intelligent, calm). But, the SSSG reveals the characteristics of the player's personality through his moral choice in the game situation. E.g. in his attitude to confidential information, protection of personal data, the ability to create a useful information product (Data Dealer, 2013), (Datak, 2016).

We can see, SSSG is most in line with the New Humanism ideology: the development of human social, cultural, and spiritual nature; its creative potential; a sense of global responsibility; and the ability to evaluate the results of their actions; an unambiguous understanding of how to live in harmony with an ever-changing world; love of justice and intolerance of violence; integrity, the balance between knowledge of details and ability to synthesis (Pechchei, 1977, pp. 84, 211, 214). However, in the fascination with SSSG, we see the threat of transforming such games into the genre of "Submission" (Djaouti, Alvarez, Jessel, Methel, & Molinier, 2008), which is defined as a "life simulator", "pastime" without the limitations. Here, a serious game can lose its meaningful purpose and meaning, leading to chaos, aggression, and gambling addiction. In this case, the confrontation is not based on the poles "authoritarianism - liberalism", but on the poles "order - chaos". The existence of the rules of the game and their strict observance, on the one hand, and the complete chaos when the rules of the game are not established. When the rules of the game are not established, aggression increases" (Terno, 2018).

So, we believe serious games should combine the HSSG and SSSG approaches, using Spinoza's formula "Freedom is a conscious necessity" (Kisner, 2011). Namely: to balance the creativity processes (new ideas, perceptions, new context and vision, discoveries and research) and formalization (rules, substantiation of ideas), positive and negative feedback, explicit and implicit educational influence, focus not only on goals (effectiveness) but also on values (productivity). Only under such conditions can serious games for training and recruitment be able to embody the principles of New Humanism. A holistic view of the relationship between two opposing types of serious games, their features, and the corresponding types of game aesthetics (Djaouti, Alvarez, Jessel, Methel, & Molinier, 2008) is presented (Figure 3).

Figure 3. The holistic view of serious games for recruitment

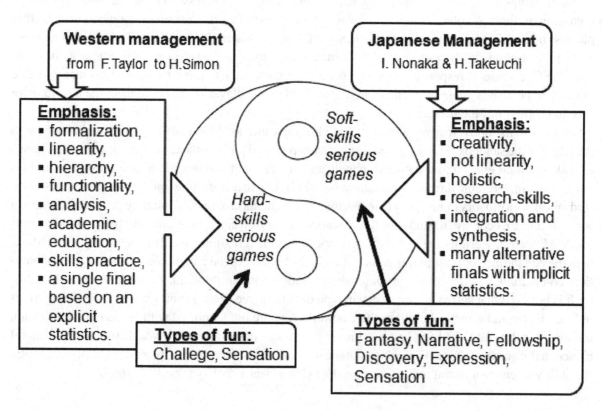

Integration of Serious Games with Automated Recruitment Systems

It is possible to predict the peculiarities of serious games development in automated recruitment systems based on globalization and integration trends in information and document scope (Luhova & Akimov, 2013), (Luhova, Raieva, Bezuhla, & Hrebeniuk, 2019). They include:

- Social networks and software integration in a single global database of vacancies and resumes. Integration of serious games in social networks commissioned by companies. E.g. (My Marriott Hotel). This dictates the need for data interoperability.
- Integration TQM and Knowledge management into the recruitment information network. It will expand the field of criteria for personnel selection, including informal knowledge: experience, professional skills, talents, emotional intelligence, connections, and contacts, etc.
- Applying the visualization and mapping tools of employment trajectories, maps of competencies, and achievements as elements of game-level design (Luhova & Melnyk, 2014).
- Creating transparency of work achievements of all people as potential job seekers. This is shown, in particular, by such systems as Unified State Database on Education, electronic employment records, electronic portals of the Pension Fund, Unified Register of Insurers, electronic queue to the center employment, etc. All this must be regulated under the current legislation in the fields of information, documentation, work, protection in automated systems, etc.
- Designing virtual environments, aiming not only at entertainment, professional, and soft skills training but also hiring of personnel.
- Introduction the Data-and Web-mining into the system of game statistics to predict the behavior of the player/specialist, predict his future interests, requirements, and recruitment headhunting. It will promote developing the global integrated decision support systems for recruitment based on serious games (Fig. 4).

Figure 4. Development trends of recruitment decision support systems based on serious games

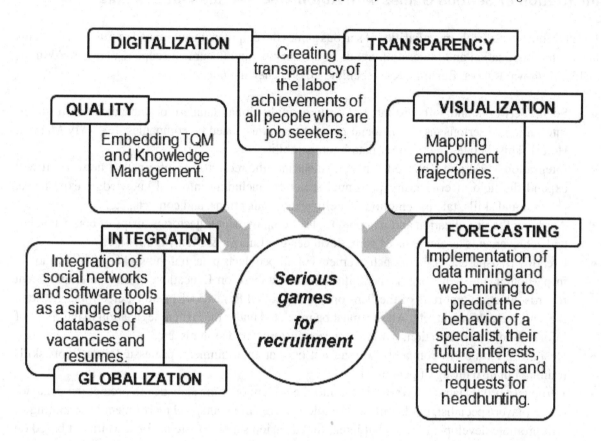

FUTURE RESEARCH DIRECTIONS

The presented research is in line with the broader issues of humanization of computer games, their pedagogical examination to educating spirituality. Serious games are an effective tool for converging theoretical and practical parts of education, bringing the content of education to the real and current requirements of specific employers, increasing student satisfaction with educational outcomes. So research to design and use the serious games on the examples of higher education disciplines as a response to the specific employer's requirements seems promising. Studies of the classifications of serious games deserve special attention. In the long run, serious games, applying the principles of the New Humanism and Holistic pedagogy, embedded in global information-educational-recruitment systems, will promote the evolution of "Homo economicus" through Homo Ludens (Huizinga, 1997), Homo Digital (Klekovkin, 2019) to Homo Moral.

An important area of research is also seen to detail and deepen the analysis of serious games under different management models: American, English, German, Japanese, Slavic. This will make it possible to clarify the professional profiles for recruiting and therefore will give new methods and ideologies in the train of future specialists.

CONCLUSION

The study made it possible to formulate the following conclusions:

1. Analysis of well-known professionally-oriented games in terms of implementing the principles of the New Humanism showed it is serious games form in gamers a sense of global responsibility and the ability to evaluate the results of their actions; holistic mindset; understanding how to live in harmony in conditions of uncertainty and constant change, love of justice and intolerance of violence; awareness of the value of knowledge and responsibility for it. Knowledge management ideologues write: "In an economy where the only certainty is uncertainty, the only reliable source of long-term competitive advantage is knowledge. As markets change, technology spreads, competitors multiply, and products become obsolete in almost one night, successful companies are those that create new knowledge, disseminate it throughout the organization, and translate it into new technologies and products. This activity defines a company that "creates knowledge", the only activity of which is continuous innovation" (Nonaka, 2007, p. 162). Knowledge is a value category that combines education, business as a customer of new professionals, and recruitment. But, it is worth emphasizing the historical tendency to objectify knowledge that the separation from the subject (man as a carrier of information). This led to the shift of the axiological center from man to his knowledge, the mechanized view of man as a generator and disseminator of knowledge. This devaluation of the man himself and his qualities. Today the moral aspect of the use of knowledge, knowledge in human qualities, and human choice is actualized. Serious games of the New Humanism should be aimed at the formation, definition, and search for human qualities in which knowledge gains sociocultural, moral, and ethical connotations.

2. According to Western and Japanese management, it is proposed to supplement the known classifications of serious games with the types Hard-skills-SG and Soft-skills-SG. Their features are described: HSSGs are focused on Western management, emphasize gameplay on formalization, logic, clear rules, work functionality, have the aesthetics of the challenge, aimed at academic training and practice of skills. The core of SSSG is creativity, innovation, research, personal qualities, implicit knowledge aimed at solving cognitive and social problems, so they best embody the principles of the Japanese approach to management. The threats and shortcomings of such games have been clarified: the routinization and "mechanization" of man in the HSSG and the collision of the SSSG - the lack of rules, increased control of game statistics, and because of aggression. Therefore, the key criterion that must meet the serious games of the new generation is the balance and harmony of the HSSG and SSSG.

3. Identified and described the following trends in the development of the serious game within automated recruitment systems are integration, globalization, quality, transparency, digitization, visualization, and forecasting. On this basis, the emergence of global integrated decision support systems for recruitment based on serious games is predicted.

REFERENCES

Activate. (2010). *iCivics*. Retrieved 07 17, 2021, from Game for change: https://www.gamesforchange.org/game/game-3/

Alba: A Wildlife Adventure [Digital game]. (2020). *Ustwo Games*. Retrieved 07 17, 2021, from STEAM: https://store.steampowered.com/app/1337010/Alba_A_Wildlife_Adventure/

Armstrong, M. B., Landers, R. N., & Collmus, A. B. (2016). Gamifying recruitment, selection, training, and performance management: Game-thinking in human resource management. In *Emerging research and trends in gamification* (pp. 140–165). IGI Global.

ARTigo [Digital game]. (n.d.). *IT-Group Humanities*. Retrieved from https://www.artigo.org/

Belle-Isle, R. (1986). Learning for a new humanism. *The International Schools Journal*, 27.

Biesta, G. J. (1998). Pedagogy without humanism: Foucault and the subject of education. *Interchange*, *29*(1), 1–16.

Blazhko, O., Luhova, T., Melnik, S., & Ruvinska, V. (2017). Communication Model of Open Government Data Gamification Based on Ukrainian Websites. In *International conference on Intelligent Data Acquisition and Advanced Computing Systems: Technology and Applications (IDAACS): 4th Experiment International Conference (exp.at'17)* (pp. 181-186). Faro, Portugal: University of Algarve.

Bostad, I. (2012). Existential Education and the Quest for a New Humanism: How to Create Disturbances and Deeper Thinking in Schools and Universities? *Enlightenment. Creative Education*, 45–59.

Branches of Power [Digital game]. (2010). *Filament Games*. Retrieved 07 11, 2021, from Game for change: https://www.gamesforchange.org/game/branches-of-power/

Brooks, D. (2011, March 7). The new humanism. *New York Times*.

Cave, D. (1993). *Mircea Eliade's vision for a new humanism*. Oxford University Press.

Chursin, N. N. (2010). The conception of thesaurus in the information view of the world. Luhansk: Noulydzh.

Covey, S. R. (2020). *The 7 habits of highly effective people*. Simon & Schuster.

d'Orville, H. (2016). New humanism and sustainable development. *Cadmus, 2*(5).

Darfur is Dying [Digital game]. (2006). *interFUEL, LLC*. Retrieved 07 19, 2021, from Game for change: https://www.gamesforchange.org/game/darfur-is-dying/

Data Dealer [Digital game]. (2013). *Cuteacute Media OG*. Retrieved from Game for change: https://www.gamesforchange.org/game/data-dealer/

Datak. (2016). *RTS*. Retrieved 07 19, 2021, from Game for change [Digital game]: https://www.gamesforchange.org/game/datak/

Djaouti, D., Alvarez, J., Jessel, J. P., Methel, G., & Molinier, P. (2008). A gameplay definition through videogame classification. *International Journal of Computer Games Technology*, 1–6.

Donovan, L. (2012). *The use of serious games in the corporate sector. A State of the Art Report*. Learnovate Centre.

Dörner, R., Göbel, S., Effelsberg, W., & Wiemeyer, J. (2016). *Serious games*. Springer International Publishing.

Eliade, M. (1961). History of religions and a new humanism. *History of Religions*, *1*(1), 1–8.

Emmerich, K., & Bockholt, M. (2016). Serious games evaluation: processes, models, and concepts. In *Entertainment Computing and Serious Games* (pp. 265–283). Springer.

Fetzer, M., McNamara, J., & Geimer, J. L. (2017). Gamification, serious games and personnel selection. In J. P. Pulakos & C. Semedo (Eds.), *The Wiley Blackwell handbook of the psychology of recruitment, selection and employee retention* (pp. 293–309). Wiley Online Library.

Fitness for purpose. Glossary. Methodical recommendations for experts of the National Agency on the application of the Criteria for evaluating the quality of the educational program [Hlosarii. Metodychni rekomendatsii dlia ekspertiv Natsionalnoho ahentst]. (2020). Retrieved 2021, from NAQA: https://naqa. gov.ua/wp-content/uploads/2020/01/%D0%93%D0%BB%D0%BE%D1%81%D0%B0%D1%80%D1%96 %D0%B9.pdf

Gee, J. P. (2003). What video games have to teach us about learning and literacy. Palgrave Macmillan.

Gray, D., Brown, S., & Macanufo, J. (2010). *Gamestorming: A Playbook for Innovators, Rulebreakers, and Changemaker*. O'Reilly Media, Inc.

Halimi, S. (2014). A new humanism? Heritage and future prospects. *International Review of Education*, *60*(3), 311–325.

Huizinga, J. (1997). Homo Ludens. A person who plays. Articles on the history of culture. Moscow: Progress-Tradition.

Human Resource Machine [Digital game]. (2015). *Tomorrow Corporation*. Retrieved from STEAM: https://store.steampowered.com/app/375820/Human_Resource_Machine/

Ikeda, D. (2010). *A new humanism: The university addresses of Daisaku Ikeda*. Bloomsbury Publishing.

Ingolia, N. T., & Murray, A. W. (2007). Positive-feedback loops as a flexible biological module. *Current Biology*, *17*(8), 668–677.

Job Simulator [Digital game]. (2016). Retrieved 07 10, 2021, from ag.ru: https://ag.ru/games/job-simulator

Kim, J., Jung, J., & Kim, S. (2015). The relationship of game elements, fun and flow. *Journal of Science and Technology*, (8), 405–411.

Kimbell, L. (2009). Design practices in design thinking. *European Academy of Management*, *5*, 1–24.

Kirizleev, A. (2014). *Classification of computer games genres*. Retrieved 07 10, 2021, from GamesIsArt: https://gamesisart.ru/janr.html

Kisner, M. J. (2011). *Spinoza on human freedom: Reason, autonomy and the good life*. University Press.

Klekovkin, O. (2019). Homo Digital: Formula of Consumption. *Art culture. Current issues, 15*(1), 69-77.

Lemkow, A. (1990). *The Wholeness Principle: Dynamics of Unity Within Science, Religion and Society.* Quest Books.

Loh, C. S., Sheng, Y., & Ifenthaler, D. (2015). Serious games analytics: Theoretical framework. In *Serious games analytics* (pp. 3–29). Springer.

Lokteva, E. (2017). *Fan in Learning: Refusal Cannot Be Provided.* Retrieved 07 21, 2021, from etutorium.ru: https://www.youtube.com/watch?v=gQ2thBXfxTY

Luhova, T., & Akimov, O. Y. (2013). Evolution of enterprises electronic document management systems. *Bibliotekoznavstvo. Dokumentoznavstvo. Informolohiia,* (1), 16-20.

Luhova, T., Chursyn, M., Blazhko, O., & Rostoka, M. (2019). Stages of developing narrative material for educational video games for the formation of managerial competencies in decision making. *Online Journal for Research and Education Resource,* (17), 213–221.

Luhova, T., Raieva, V., Bezuhla, S., & Hrebeniuk, V. (2019). Promising areas of research on information and document data consolidation. *ΛΟΓΟΣ. The Art of Scientific Thought,* (7), 63-68.

Luhova, T. A. (2020). Narrative and storytelling in the knowledge structure of educational and business video games as factors of synergy of information technologies and spiritually-oriented pedagogy. *Open Educational E-Environment of Modern University,* (8), 42-59.

Luhova, T. A. (2021). Game-design-oriented approach to development of educational disciplins of higher educational institutions. *Information Technologies and Learning Tools, 81*(1), 235–254.

Luhova, T. A., & Melnyk, S. P. (2014). Knowledge mapping as a tool for studying the intellectual potential of employees of secondary schools and universities. *Nasha shkola,* (1), 29-35.

Maslov, S. I. (1979). Inference search theory and questions of the psychology of creativity. *Semiotics and Informatics,* (13), 17-46.

McLaren, P., & Jaramillo, N. (2007). Pedagogy and praxis in the age of empire: Towards a new humanism. *Review Symposium,* 206.

Mercogliano, C. (2005). Philosophical Sources of Holistic Education. *Turkish Journal of Values Education, 3*(10), 150–161.

Michael, D., & Chen, S. (2006). *Serious games. Games that educate, train, and inform.* Thomson.

My Marriott Hotel Social Media Game Trailer [Video]. (n.d.). Retrieved from https://www.youtube.com/watch?v=ULOwlkiRM18

Nikolaou, I., & Oostrom, J. K. (Eds.). (2015). Employee recruitment, selection, and assessment: Contemporary issues for theory and practice (1st ed. ed.). London: Psychology Press.

Nonaka, I. (2007, July–August). The Knowledge-Creating Company. *Harvard Business Review,* 162–171.

Not For Broadcast [Digital game]. (2020). *NotGames.* Retrieved 17 07, 2021, from STEAM: https://store.steampowered.com/app/1147550/Not_For_Broadcast/

Objection! [Digital game]. (1992). *TransMedia Productions*. Retrieved from Old-Games.RU: https://www.old-games.ru/game/4107.html

Oostrom, J. K., Van Der Linden, D., Born, M. P., & Van Der Molen, H. T. (2013). New technology in personnel selection: How recruiter characteristics affect the adoption of new selection technology. *Computers in Human Behavior*, 29(6), 2404–2415.

Patricio, R., Moreira, A., Zurlo, F., & Melazzini, M. (2020). Co-creation of new solutions through gamification: A collaborative innovation practice. *Creativity and Innovation Management*, (29), 146–160.

Pechchei, A. (1977). Chelovecheskie kachestva [The Human Quality] 312 (O. V. Zaharova, Trans.). Moscow: Progress.

Ratan, R. A., & Ritterfeld, U. (2009). Classifying serious games. In *Serious games* (pp. 32–46). Routledge.

Raybourn, E. M. (2014). A new paradigm for serious games: Transmedia learning for more effective training and education. *Journal of Computational Science*, (5(3)), 471–481.

Recommendations for applying criteria for evaluating the quality of an educational program. (2020, November 17). *Approved by the National Agency for quality assurance of Higher Education*, 66. Kyiv: LLC "Ukrainian educational publishing center "Orion"".

Revolution: Black Friday [Digital game]. (2016). *iNK Stories*. Retrieved 07 11, 2021, from Games for change: https://www.gamesforchange.org/game/1979-revolution-black-friday/

Sarton, G. (1924). The new humanism. *Isis*, 9–42.

Serrat, O. (2017). Design thinking. *Knowledge Solutions*, 129-134.

Simon, H. A. (1979). Rational decision making in business organizations. *The American Economic Review*, 69(4), 493–513.

Simon, H. A. (1990). Bounded rationality. *Utility and Probability*, 15-18.

Simon, H. A. (2013). *Administrative behavior* (4th ed.). Simon and Schuster.

Stallman, J. (2003). John Dewey's new humanism and liberal education for the 21st century. *Education and Culture*, 19(2), 18–22.

Stănescu, D. F., Ioniță, C., & Ioniță, A. M. (2020). Game-thinking in Personnel Recruitment and Selection: Advantages and Disadvantages. *Postmodern Openings/Deschideri Postmoderne, 11*(2), 267-276.

Stapleton, A. J. (2004). *Serious games: Serious opportunities. Australian Game Developers" Conference*. Academic Summit.

Stone City-Cold Stone Creamery, Inc. [Digital game]. (2003). Retrieved 17 07, 2021, from Persuasive games: https://persuasivegames.com/game/coldstone

Stop Disaster. (2018). *UNDRR, Producer, & playerthree*. Retrieved 2021, from Play and learn to STOP DISASTERS!: https://www.stopdisastersgame.org/

Taylor, F. W. (1919). *Scientific management*. Harper & Brothers Publishers.

Terno, S. (2018). *Educational institution as a social institution: chaos or order?* Retrieved 07 20, 2021, from Prometheus: https://courses.prometheus.org.ua/assets/courseware/v1/228bd74b5c310bb220998b 4fc174746b/asset-v1:Prometheus+CTFT102+2018_T3+type@asset+block/Лекція_3.2.pdf

Tornero, J. P., & Tapio, V. (2010). *Media literacy and new humanism.* UNESCO Institute for Information Technologies in Education.

Weizsäcker, E., & Wijkman, A. (2018). *Come On! Capitalism, Short-termism, Population and the Destruction of the Planet A Report to the Club of Rome, prepared for the Club of Rome's 50th Anniversary in 2018.* Springer Science+Business Media LLC.

Wiener, N. (1964, February 24). Machines Smarter than Men? Interview with Dr. Norbert Wiener, Noted Scientist. *U.S. News & World Report,* 84–86.

Yunyongying, P. (2014). Gamification: Implications for curricular design. *Journal of Graduate Medical Education, 6*(3), 410–412.

Zabolotna, O. (2012). Holistic pedagogy as a theoretical source of alternative school education. *Psychological and Pedagogical Problems of Rural Schools,* (41), 224-230.

Chapter 18
CircuSChain Game:
A Serious Game to Explore Circular Supply Chains

Asiye Kurt
G-SCOP, University of Grenoble Alpes, France & LIG, Université Grenoble Alpes, France

Mario Cortes-Cornax
LIG, Université Grenoble Alpes, France

Van-Dat Cung
G-SCOP, Université Grenoble Alpes, France

Fabien Mangione
G-SCOP, Université Grenoble Alpes, France

Soufiane Kaddouri
G-SCOP, Université Grenoble Alpes, France

ABSTRACT

The circular economy has gained attention in recent years as a sustainable alternative to the current linear economic model. Supply chains have an essential role in the transition towards a circular economy. However, the transition towards circular supply chains is challenging for companies due to the lack of knowledge and awareness among the supply chain members. In order to overcome this barrier, the CircuSChain Game was developed based on the well-known Beer Distribution Game. The CircuSChain Game is a multi-player board game supported by a calculation sheet. The game considers reuse, refurbishing, remanufacturing, and recycling activities within closed-and open-loops, as well as CO_2 emissions and material scarcity concepts. An experiment was conducted with industrial engineering students in order to test the CircuSChain Game and assess its educational value, game pace, entertainment value, and simplicity.

DOI: 10.4018/978-1-7998-9732-3.ch018

INTRODUCTION

Our economy has been following the "take-make-dispose" model since the industrial revolution (Ellen MacArthur Foundation, 2013). In such a model, also called linear economy, products are being produced using raw materials; they are then used and thrown away when they are considered obsolete. Due to overall economic development and population growth, the production activities and the demand for raw materials are also increasing, while the natural resources remain limited. This fact may have significant consequences: natural resource depletion and environmental pollution (Yuan et al., 2006). In addition to the environmental pressure, this situation raises resource prices, price volatility, and material scarcity, which are challenging for organizations (Ellen MacArthur Foundation, 2013). This situation is not long-term sustainable. A new economic model needs to be designed to ensure our future and solve these problems.

The Circular Economy concept has gained attention as a sustainable substitute to the linear economic model (Lahane et al., 2020). Supply chains play an essential role in the transition towards Circular Economy (Aminoff & Kettunen, 2016; Bianchini et al., 2019; Ellen MacArthur Foundation, 2014; Howard et al., 2019).

However, the transition from linear supply chains to Circular Supply Chains is challenging for companies due to barriers such as the inadequacy of knowledge and awareness among supply chain members (Mangla et al., 2018) and customers (Vermunt et al., 2019), as well as lack of appropriate training and development programs about Circular Economy for supply chain members (Mangla et al., 2018).

Besides, serious games have been used in training in business and management areas since the 1950s and 1960s (Qualters et al., 2008). The serious games that combine gaming and learning (Neck & Greene, 2011) help participants learn decision-making in complex systems (Qualters et al., 2008). Scholars stated as well the advantages of serious games for attracting students' attention and helping them retain the acquired knowledge (Madani et al., 2017). Moreover, serious games could be a way to increase environmental awareness (Ponce et al., 2020; Wikipedia, 2021).

Therefore, in order to overcome the lack of knowledge and awareness about Circular Supply Chains that are complex systems as the backbone of Circular Economy, the researchers developed a serious game named CircuSChain Game, based on the well-known Beer Distribution Game (Sterman, 1989). This chapter presents the background of the work, the conception of the serious game within the used methodology, the game flows, and the experiment, as well as its analysis and future research directions.

BACKGROUND

In this section, the context of this work is described. First, the Circular Economy and the Circular Supply Chains are introduced, including its activities and loops, which will be present in the CircuSChain Game. Second, the serious games in the literature about Circular Supply Chains or their related domains are presented.

Circular Economy and Circular Supply Chains

The Circular Economy has gained attention worldwide in recent years as a potential solution to the problems related to the linear economy, it is defined as follows:

CE aims to keep products, components, and materials at their highest utility and value at all times. The value is maintained or extracted through the extension of product lifetimes by reuse, refurbishment, and remanufacturing as well as closing of resource cycles—through recycling and related strategies (Bocken et al., 2017).

Supply chains play a vital role in the transition towards Circular Economy since they support strategies also called Circular Economy activities outlined in the definition above. These activities have been already mentioned in the literature in Green Supply Chain, Sustainable Supply Chain and Closed-Loop Supply Chain domains. Besides these themes, the Circular Supply Chain concept has emerged in the literature recently. A Circular Supply Chain is described as a combination of closed- and open-loops (Batista et al., 2018; De Angelis et al., 2017) of circular activities in addition to linear supply chains. The CircuSChain Game is based on the Extended Model of Circular Supply Chains (Kurt et al., 2019).

As seen in Figure 1, a linear supply chain consists of material extraction, part manufacturing, module manufacturing, distribution and use activities. These closed- and open-loops concern reverse logistics flows. The closed-loops consist of collecting used products and integrating them into the original supply chain through circular activities such as direct reuse, reuse with remanufacturing, recycling, etc. The open-loops relates integrating collected products into a different supply chain through Circular Economy activities such as direct repurposing, repurposing with remanufacturing, etc. Repurposing activities allows using collected products in other applications different from their original function, for example, repurposing electric vehicle li-ion batteries in stationary applications (Alamerew & Brissaud, 2020; Canals Casals et al., 2017; Richa et al., 2017). In CircuSChain Game, repurposing activities are called open-loop Circular Economy activities, while reuse activities are called closed-loop Circular Economy activities. For instance, open-loop remanufacturing (repurposing with remanufacturing), closed-loop refurbishing (reuse with refurbishing), etc.

Figure 1. The extended model of circular supply chains (Kurt et al., 2019)

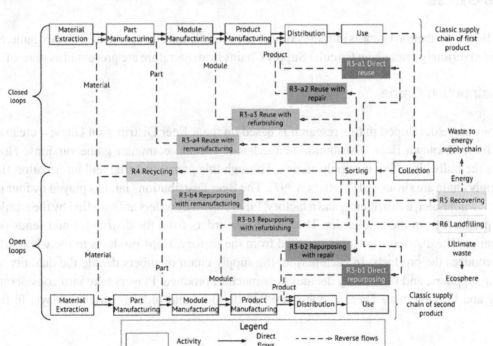

The Circular Economy activities require a different amount of modification in the used product. For example, while reuse activity allows reselling products with minor changes, recycling requires the destruction of the used product's added value to transform it into the material and use it in the production activities. The inertia principle, which relates to replacing or treating the smallest possible part of the used product in order to keep existing value, helps to hierarchize the Circular Economy activities. This principle is reformulated as the power of inner circle, promoting shorter loops, by (Ellen MacArthur Foundation, 2014). Parallel to the inertia principle, this principle highlights savings in material, energy, labor and pollution through shorter loops. The inertia principle is described below:

Do not repair what is not broken, do not remanufacture something that can be repaired, do not recycle a product that can be remanufactured. (Stahel, 1982, 2010)

As stated above, the power of inner circle and the inertia principles concern choosing the most circular activity, according to the used product's state. The hierarchy of Circular Economy activities considering the inertia and the power of inner circle principles is represented by a green gradient in Figure 1. According to this hierarchy, direct reuse or direct repurposing place at the top of the hierarchy since that requires minor modifications. Landfilling (R6 in Figure 1), which is the destruction of used products, is at the bottom of the hierarchy.

Moreover, (Kurt et al., 2021) proposed another approach based on the power of inner circle principle. This approach promotes multiple Circular Economy activities. Having multiple Circular Economy activities in a supply chain allows handling collected products by the most circular activity according to their state, to keep more value and gain more savings. For instance, through a supply chain that has only repair and recycling activities, the returned products, which cannot be repaired but can be remanufactured, will be recycled. However, a supply chain that has these three activities (repair, remanufacturing, and recycling) would allow remanufacturing of the products that are not repairable but still in a good state.

Serious Games

First, the Beer Distribution Game is introduced since the CircuSChain Game is based on this game. Second, some related serious games about Circular Supply Chains from literature are presented as state-of-the-art.

Beer Distribution Game

The serious game developed in this research is based on the « Beer Distribution Game » created in the 1960s. The well-known Beer Distribution Game has board and computer game versions. This game illustrates the bullwhip effect in supply chains. Through this game, material and information flow in a linear supply chain are simulated (Metters, 1997). The Beer Distribution Game is played by four players: a retailer, a wholesaler, a distributor, and a factory. Final customer orders are satisfied by the retailer, who receives products from the wholesaler. The wholesaler orders from the distributor and sends products to the retailer. The distributor, who is supplied from the factory, ships products to the wholesaler. The factory produces the products. In each period, the supply chain members decide the quantity to order from their suppliers, and the factory decides how much to produce. Players take into consideration the inventory and backlog cost. There is one period of shipping and order receiving delays. In the Beer

Distribution Game, materials flow from upstream to downstream actors, and information moves in the reverse direction via material flows, like real supply chains.

Serious Games related to the Circular Supply Chains

Since the Circular Supply Chain concept is new in the literature, in this section, some serious games from related concepts, such as Closed-Loop Supply Chains or Sustainable Supply Chains, are also included. Table 1 presents selected serious games and their contents.

Table 1. Serious games about the Circular Economy

Serious Game Name and Reference	Contents	Serious Game type
Chain of Command (Cuesta & Nakano, 2017) Looper (Aguiar et al., 2018)	• Environment: Closed-loop Supply Chain, recycle remanufacturing, CO_2 emissions, government environmental regulations, and investment in green technologies. • Economic: Supply chain optimization through lead times and production efficiency • Social: Ethics between firms • Risk management: Supply risk mitigation	Board Game
In The Loop (Whalen et al., 2018)	• Material criticality • Circular Economy concepts (Product as service, maintenance, repair, reuse, remanufacturing, refurbishing) • Other potential solutions (Diversify supply chain or increase supply chain transparency, material substitution, invest in new technologies etc.) • Economic: Profit	Board Game
Shortfall (Sivak et al., 2007)	• Environment: Waste disposal, recovery, and recycling • Economic: Profit	Board and Digital Game
CircuSChain Game	• Circular Economy concepts: CSCs, CO_2 emissions, reuse, refurbishing, remanufacturing, recycling, repurposing, waste disposal • Material scarcity • Economic: Profit	Board Game

As seen in Table 1, repurposing activities or open-loops are not considered by these games. However, repurposing activities and their related open-loops constitute a new potential for Circular Supply Chains. Moreover, these works complement this work since they consider other approaches, such as social, risk (Aguiar et al., 2018; Cuesta & Nakano, 2017), new technologies, and material substitution (Whalen et al., 2018), etc.

CIRCUSCHAIN GAME

In this section, the CircuSChain Game is presented. First, the methodology adopted to develop the game is introduced. Second, the game is described within its key characteristic. Finally, the game flow is explained.

Methodology

As suggested by (Carrión-Toro et al., 2020), the development of serious games requires a specific design methodology. In this article, the authors mentioned several serious game design methodologies, such as (Avila-Pesantez et al., 2019; Jimenez-Hernandez et al., 2016; Marfisi-Schottman et al., 2010). Since the CircuSChain Game is a board game, the seven steps methodology proposed by (Marfisi-Schottman et al., 2010) that is designed for both digital and board games has been chosen. The other methodologies mainly target video/digital games. Besides, this methodology suits CircuSChain Game better because it contains a pedagogical quality control step for board games that allows determining the game parameters and testing the game during the design phase.

Furthermore, to develop the CircuSChain Game, the researchers relied on the well-known Beer Distribution Game to simulate the material and information flows. The elements of the Beer Distribution Game is maintained in some steps. The seven steps of the adopted methodology can be stated as follows:

Step 1: concerns the determination of the pedagogical objectives, which is defined as one of the first steps of other serious game design methodologies (Avila-Pesantez et al., 2019; Carrión-Toro et al., 2020; Jimenez-Hernandez et al., 2016). Note that the objectives of the CircuSChain Game are different from those of the Beer Distribution Game (bullwhip effect, inventory management, order and transport lead-times, etc.). Through the CircuSChain Game, the researchers want to raise knowledge and awareness of: (1) circularity and the importance of circular activities in Circular Supply Chains, (2) natural resource depletion, and (3) CO^2 footprints.

Step 2: is about choosing a predefined model for serious games such as board games, investigation games, puzzles, etc. In the same line, identification of video game genre type is indicated in many serious game design methodologies (Avila-Pesantez et al., 2019; Carrión-Toro et al., 2020; Jimenez-Hernandez et al., 2016). The researchers chose a board game (Figure 2) supported by a shared calculation spreadsheet as in the Beer Distribution Game. Moreover, the Beer Distribution Game has also a digital version.

Step 3: gives the general description of the scenario and the virtual environment. This step, which is also stated in other works (Avila-Pesantez et al., 2019; Carrión-Toro et al., 2020), determines the elements such as characters, storyline, etc. In Beer Distribution Game, a linear supply chain is simulated with retailor, distributor, wholesaler, and manufacturer. Compared with the Beer Distribution Game, the researchers changed the storyline by modifying characters slightly (part manufacturer, module manufacturer, product manufacturer, and distributor), adding circular scenarios (*i.e.,* closed-loop and open-loop reuse, refurbishing, remanufacturing and recycling) and a new character who manages reverse logistics related to circular scenarios.

Step 4: is about searching for reusable software components. For the moment, the only software component of this game is a shared calculation spreadsheet inspired by (Aguiar et al., 2018) that manage the players' decisions and compute indicators. However, for the development of the digital version of the game, this step would be further considered to increase automation.

Step 5: consists in describing the details of the scenario. Here, the flows and the players' interactions with the game are described. For instance, linear material flows and information flows are simulated as in the Beer Distribution Game. Furthermore, the way and the tools to simulate the uncertain quantity and quality of collected products that are not considered in the Beer Distribution Game are defined.

Step 6: addresses pedagogical quality control, which aims at minimizing the testing processes. In this step, different scenarios are simulated using the calculation spreadsheets in order to define the initial state of the game as well as to define the different thresholds concerning parameters of the game, players' decisions and adequacy to the pedagogical objectives.

Step 7: is to precise game specifications for subcontractors of the game development process such as graphic designer, sound manager, etc. The researchers are currently developing a tool prototype to study the possibility of providing more flexibility to the supply chain configuration and the game rounds. Since the game is still a prototype, the researchers still do not have subcontractors. This step will be completed when a digital version of the game is established.

Figure 2. Board of the CircuSChain Game with all possible Circular Economy activities

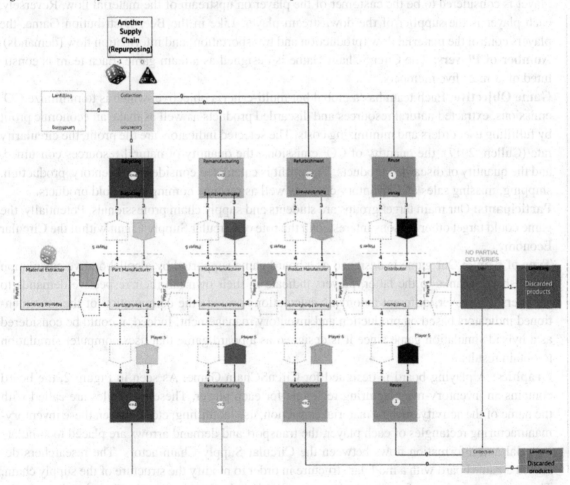

Game Description

In order to present the CircuSChain Game, the researchers relied on the characterization proposed by Madani et al., (2017), diving it into different vital points such as the theme, the player's role or the number of players. Below, the different characteristics of the CircuSChain Game are presented:

- **Theme:** The theme of the CircuSChain Game is Circular Supply Chains. The game is based on a modular product Circular Supply Chain, such as electric and electronic equipment. Therefore, this supply chain is composed of activities such as material extraction, part manufacturing, module manufacturing, product manufacturing, distribution, use, collection, and the different closed or open-loop Circular Economy activities (reuse, refurbishing, remanufacturing, and recycling). The Circular Supply Chain structure is based on the Circular Supply Chain model (Kurt et al., 2019).
- **Player's Role:** The players' roles vary slightly from the Beer Distribution Game. They represent supply chain actors: the material extractor, the part manufacturer, the module manufacturer, the product manufacturer, the user. Note that the actors map with the aforementioned activities, each player is considered to be the customer of the player on upstream of the material flow. Reversely, each player is the supplier of the downstream player. Like in the Beer Distribution Game, the players control the material flow (production and transportation) and information flow (demands).
- **Number of Players:** The CircuSChain Game is designed as a team game. Each team is constituted of at most five members.
- **Game Objective:** Each team has a global but multi-criteria objective, which is to minimize CO_2 emissions, extracted natural resources and discarded products as well as make an economic profit by fulfilling user orders and minimizing costs. The selected indicators are the profit, the circularity rate (Cullen, 2017), the quantity of CO_2 emissions, the quantity of natural resources consumed, and the quantity of discarded products. The profit is calculated considering inventory, production, shipping, missing sales and inventory costs, as well as revenue coming from sold products.
- **Participants:** Our main target groups are students and supply chain professionals. Potentially, the game could target other persons interested in the role of Circular Supply Chain within the Circular Economy.
- **Type of Game:** Our game is designed as a board game supported by a collaborative calculation spreadsheet. Thanks to the latter, players indicate in their own tab their respective demands to suppliers. Moreover, different automatic calculations provide the computation of the aforementioned indicators based on production and inventory management. Indeed, it could be considered as a hybrid simulation game since it is designed as a board game that uses computer simulation to obtain results.
- **Graphics:** A playing board is designed for CircuSChain Game. As seen in Figure 2, the board contains an inventory-manufacturing rectangle for each player. These rectangles are called with the name of the activity, such as material extraction, use landfilling, etc. Between these inventory-manufacturing rectangles of each player, the transport and demand arrows are placed to simulate material and information flows between the Circular Supply Chain actors. The researchers designed a game board with a modular structure in order to modify the structure of the supply chain. This structure eases transforming the linear supply chain in Circular Supply Chain by plugging the collection and the selected Circular Economy activities into the linear supply chain.

Game Flows

As Beer Distribution Game, there is one period of delay in material and information flows. In the CircuSChain Game, in order to simulate the products, tokens are used. The total raw materials available for the extraction are limited for the whole game. Additionally, the available quantity of raw materials is considered limited and uncertain for each round. It is simulated by a 6-sided dice. The demands are represented by cards filled by players (and noted in their respective calculation spreadsheet's tab). Final customer order quantities represented by order cards are drawn at random and unknown to the players at the beginning of each round, represented by order cards.

The first version of the CircuSChain Game is played in three years. Each year has six rounds that represent a period of two months. This division is justified thanks to previous simulations and tests in order to fit in a three hours session. During each year, the players manage the material and information flows (demands). The game flows in each year are explained below.

First Year Simulation: Linear Supply Chain

In the first year, the players manage a linear supply chain as in the Beer Distribution Game. The game board of this year is represented in Figure 3. This year is designed in order to learn the game flows and raise awareness of natural resource depletion and CO_2 emissions.

The steps to follow in each round are explained in round flow cards (Figure 4). In order to facilitate the game, the steps described in these cards are also represented by numbers on the board (Figure 3).

At each round, each player takes the delivery of the products that are waiting in the transport arrow (colorful arrows) by shifting the tokens towards their procurement-manufacturing rectangle (Step 1). Then, each player checks her/his customer's demand card (Step 2) that is located in the demand arrow (white arrows) and send the products towards the transport arrow between the player and her/his customer (Step 3). Afterwards, each player fills the demand card and puts it to the demand arrow (Step 4) as a demand order for her/his supplier. The member (Player 1) who plays the material extractor role has an additional step, which is to determine the raw material availability of the round by rolling the dice (Step 0). Player 5, who plays the user role, has only one step this year, which consists in receiving materials from the supplier (Step 1).

Figure 3. The game board for the first year of CircuSChain Game

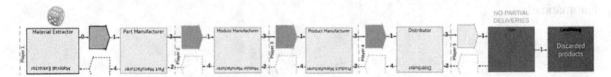

Partial deliveries are possible between players 1, 2, 3 and 4. When a supplier sends less product than the actual demand to their customer, there are no penalties. The missing orders are not expected to be satisfied in the next round, there are no demand backlogs; they are ignored for simplicity reasons. However, the final customer order should be satisfied entirely; no partial deliveries are allowed. In other words, if the distributor's (Player 4) inventory is lesser than the demand, they cannot ship the final customer order and keep the products in their stock. In that case, a penalty is applied according to the missed order quantity and missed orders are not expected to send in the next round, they are considered as lost.

Figure 4. Round flow cards

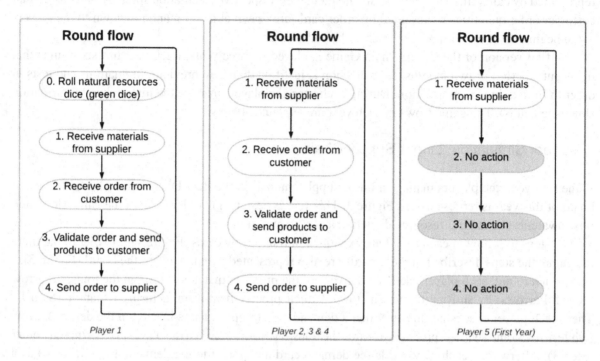

The players fill collaboratively a record sheet that contains different tabs for each player at the end of each round (Figure 5). In order to simplify the game, some cases, such as the order received from the customer, is filled automatically according to the cases in the other tabs. Moreover, the quantity sent to the customer is filled automatically, since the players send either the quantity ordered by the customer (if they have enough products in stock) or all products in the stock (if they have less products than the ordered quantity). In addition, at the end of each year, indicators of the game objective are calculated automatically.

Figure 5. Record Sheet (Tab for Player 1)

	Round	Raw material availability (green dice)	Quantity received from extractor	Quantity received from reverse logistics provider	Order received from customer	Quantity sent to customer	Order sent to extractor	Order sent to reverse logistics provider	Quantity in stock at the end of the round
	0	4	4		4	4	4		0
Year 1	1		4		4	4			0
	2								
	3								
	4								
	5								
	6								
Year 2	7			0					
	8								
	9								
	10								
	11								
	12								
Year 3	13								
	14								
	15								
	16								
	17								
	18								

Initialization boxes (do not touch)
Boxes filled automatically
Boxes to fill
Boxes not taken into account for the year

Second Year Simulation: Closed-Loop Supply Chain

Before starting the second year, all team members decide together to invest in a closed-loop Circular Economy activity to invest during a debriefing session. This decision leads players to discuss the Circular Economy activities, which is one of the game's objectives. The Circular Economy activities to invest in are presented to players by the so-called strategy cards (Figure 6). These cards show information about the corresponding Circular Economy activities, such as the investment cost, potential CO^2 reduction, and the returned product availability.

Figure 6. Strategy cards

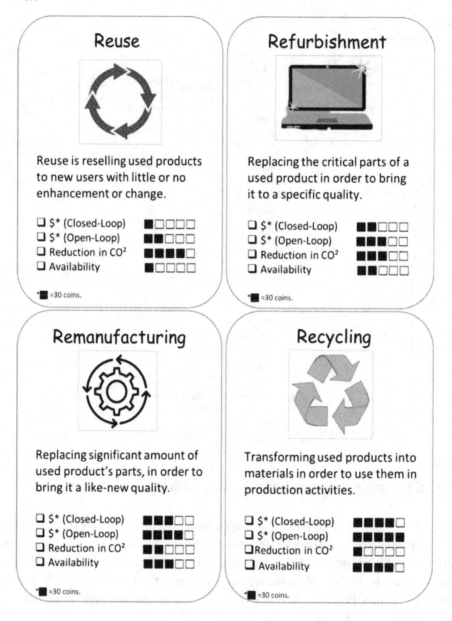

The **investment cost** ($ symbol on the cards) is supposed to be the highest for recycling activity, which requires specific technologies to transform used products into materials and the lowest for reuse, which is reselling used products with minor changes. The investment cost for open-loop activities is considered slightly higher than closed-loop ones since open-loop activities prepare the used product for a different function.

The Circular Economy activities allow a **reduction in CO_2** by skipping some linear activities. For instance, when a used product is recycled, the extraction activity is skipped; while a used product is reused, even more activities are skipped. Therefore, reuse activity has the most potential of reduction in CO_2. Indeed, the shorter the loop, the more savings are in emissions (Ellen MacArthur Foundation, 2014).

The **availability** of products is related to the used products state. The researchers supposed that the returned products are not all eligible for all Circular Economy activities. For instance, reuse activity requires a good product state, while recycling does not have any requirement. Therefore, all collected products are supposed to be recyclable. In other words, it is considered that all products, even the most damaged ones, could be recycled. Therefore, the availability is the highest for recycling and the lowest for reuse.

Through the modular structure of the board, the collection activity and the selected Circular Economy activity are added to the board. In the second year, the member who plays the user role (Player 5) also under-takes the reverse logistics provider role and manages the added collection and Circular Economy activities.

In order to simulate the uncertainties of the quantity and the quality state of the returned products, which are the biggest challenges in reverse logistics (Werning & Spinler, 2020), a 6-sided and a 4-sided dice are used, respectively. For instance, reuse requires a good product state (represented by 1 on the 4-sided dice), while the others have less stringent requirements, such as refurbishing (≤ 2 on the 4-sided dice), remanufacturing (≤ 3 on the 4-sided dice), and recycling (≤ 4 on the 4-sided dice). In order to remind the quality state requirements of each Circular Economy activity, numbers from 1 to 4 are indicated on each Circular Economy activity rectangle on the game board.

Collection and sorting of the used products are simulated by Player 5 (reverse logistics provider). The round flow card for Player 5 designed for the second and third years is represented by Figure 7. Player 5 rolls the 6-sided dice in order to determine the quantity of the collected product (Step -1) and then the 4-sided dice to determine the state of the returned products (Step 0). If the products' state is eligible for the selected Circular Economy activity, s/he moves the products through the corresponding Circular Economy activity's rectangle (Step 0). In the other cases, products are moved to landfill rectangle. Then, s/he checks the customer's order (Step 2) and send products to their customer (Step 3). The customer of Player 5 is one of the other players who manage the linear supply chain.

Figure 7. Round flow card of Player 5 for the second and third years

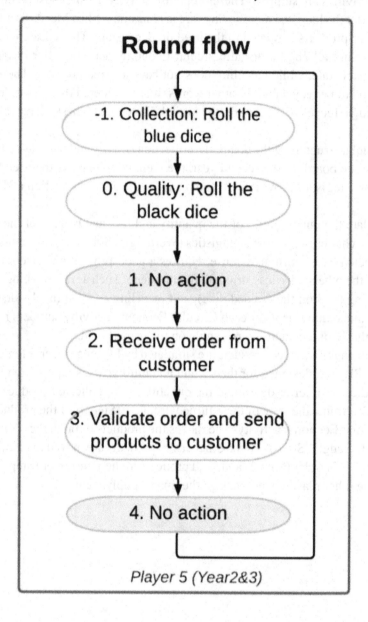

Furthermore, according to the selected Circular Economy activity, a player among players 1, 2, 3 and 4 gets another supplier from a Circular Economy activity in addition to their supplier in the first year. This player sends demand to their two suppliers and receives products from each of them. For example, Figure 8 represents the scenario where reuse activity is selected. In that case, Player 4, with the distributor role, needs to receive products from her/his two suppliers (products at the orange arrow and black arrow) and send an order to her/his two suppliers.

Figure 8. The scenario where reuse activity is selected

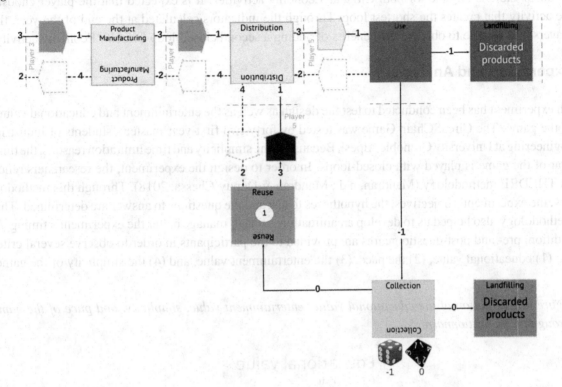

At the end of each round, players fill the calculation sheet collaboratively. In this year, Player 5 and the player who gets a second supplier have an additional case to fill, which is "Order sent to reverse logistics provider" (Figure 5). At the end of this second year, through the calculation sheet, the indicators are calculated again. The players are invited to discuss the evolution of indicators and the benefits of adding a Circular Economy activity.

Third Year Simulation: Multiple-Loops Supply Chain

After playing the second year, the players are asked to invest in an additional Circular Economy activity. The selected activity is added to the board through the board's modular structure. For the third year, two versions of the game are proposed. As in the second year, Player 5 and another player (related to chosen Circular Economy activity) have more steps to execute and more cases to fill in the calculation sheet.

Open-loop Version: Players invest in another Circular Economy activity, which will be open-loop for this version. Another collection activity and selected open-loop Circular Economy activity will be added to the board. Reverse Logistics Provider (Player 5) will manage these activities as in the second year. Through the indicators calculated at the end of the third year, the players will be able to observe the benefits of adding an open-loop Circular Economy activity to the supply chain built in the second year simulation with only one closed-loop Circular Economy activity.

Closed-loop Version: Players of the team invest in another closed-loop Circular Economy activity. In this version, the reverse logistics provider should decide the Circular Economy activity when the returned products' state is eligible for both Circular Economy activities. It is expected that the player chooses the activity that creates the shortest loop. Through the indicators calculated at the end of the year, the players will be able to observe the benefits of adding a second closed-loop Circular Economy activity.

Experiment and Analysis

An experiment has been conducted to test the design as well as the entertainment and educational values of the game. The CircuSChain Game was tested by forty-two first-year master's students of industrial engineering at University Grenoble Alpes[1]. Because of the simplicity and time limitation reasons, the third year of the game is played with closed-loops. In order to design the experiment, the researchers relied on THEDRE methodology (Mandran, n.d.; Mandran & Dupuy-Chessa, 2018). Through this methodology, the experiment's objectives, the hypotheses to test and the questions to answer are determined. This methodology also helped us to develop an animation guide to manage better the experiment's timing. In addition, pre- and post-questionnaires are provided to the participants in order to observe several criteria: (1) educational value, (2) the pace, (3) the entertainment value, and (4) the simplicity of the game.

Figure 9. Evaluation of the educational value, entertainment value, simplicity, and pace of the game through post-questionnaire

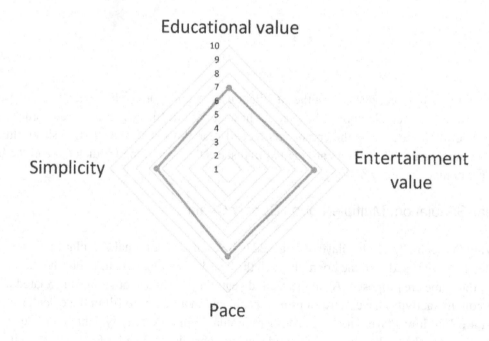

The game was tested with forty-two students, and the 3 hours were allocated for the experiment. The experiment is carried out over three stages, one stage per year. Each stage contains the presentation of the concepts, playing one year of the game and discussions on the indicators. During the first stage, the considered linear supply chain and the game rules for the first year are explained through a slide presentation. After playing the first year, the participants are invited to discuss on their obtained results. The second stage of the experiment starts with the presentation of the Circular Supply Chain (with only closed-loops), followed by the distribution of strategy cards. Each team discuss the proposed Circular Economy activities and decide to invest in one of them. After playing the second year of the game, the results are discussed. During the third stage of the experiment, the closed-loop version of the game is played. First, the players discuss the Circular Economy activities, and they are asked to choose a second Circular economy activity and invest in it. Then, players play the third year of the game. The third stage of the experiment also ends with a discussion.

Moreover, pre- and post-questionnaires are provided to assess the educational value, the pace, the entertainment value, and the simplicity of the game. The participants were asked to evaluate the game on a scale from 1 to 10, according to the aforementioned criteria in the post questionnaire. The results are shown in Figure 9. According to the results, participants have enjoyed their experience with the CircuSChain Game (average: 7.40) and found the pace suitable (average: 7.35). However, more work is needed to make the game simpler (average: 6.92). However, this result has to be nuanced by the fact that the students have already played the Beer Distribution Game. Besides, the average educational value given is 6.93.

In addition, in order to further analyze the educational value, the participants were asked to answer questions about the Circular Supply Chain and the Circular Economy activities in the pre and post-questionnaires to assess their knowledge after playing the game. The researchers graded then their answers.

Finally, the results of both questionnaires are compared in order to check and validate the knowledge acquisition. Note that the students did not answer all the questions since they were informed that their answers would not be marked.

The participants were asked to define the Circular Economy and Circular Supply Chains. The answers are expected to include cyclic structure or return flows, waste management, pollution (CO_2), end-of-life and revaluation notions. Approximately 15% of the participants gained knowledge about these concepts; they mentioned them in the post-questionnaires, while they did not mention them in the pre-questionnaire.

The participants were also asked to define Circular Economy activities (reuse, refurbishing, remanufacturing and recycling). The answers were expected to include two notions: revaluation of used products and level of modification or product state. The results in each concept are represented in Figure 10, with the percentage of the participants that acquired knowledge, the participants that acquired any knowledge and the participants that have already knowledge. The participants who did not indicate these notions correctly both in pre- and in post-questionnaires are considered as "Participants acquired any knowledge" (grey columns). "Participants acquired knowledge" are the participants who could not answer correctly in the pre-questionnaire but provided a correct answer in post-questionnaire. The participants who provided a correct answer in pre-questionnaires are considered as "Participants already have knowledge".

Figure 10. Knowledge acquisition about circular economy activities

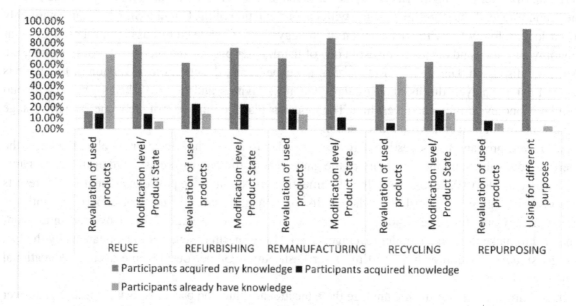

Concerning revaluation of used products, most of the participants have already aware of reuse (69%) and recycling (50%) activities. They mentioned the revaluation of used products notion in the post-questionnaires. However, approximately 14% of participants had knowledge about refurbishing and remanufacturing activities. After playing the game, respectively, 23% and 19% of participants gained knowledge about refurbishing and remanufacturing.

Concerning the level of modification or product state, percentage of knowledge before the game (average 7% for all activities except repurposing), and 20% of participants gained knowledge through the game.

The gained knowledge is the lowest for repurposing as it is expected since, in this experiment, it is not included. The repurposing activity is only presented at the end of the game. Moreover, the percentage of participants that have indicated changing used products' function through repurposing is low (11%), which shows the lack of knowledge about this activity.

Moreover, through this game, the researchers aimed to show participants the inertia and the power of inner circle principles. Therefore, two multiple-choice questions with supply chain figures are included in the questionnaires to evaluate the knowledge about the benefits of having shorter and multiple loops (Figure 11). The results related to these two questions are represented in Figure 12.

Figure 11. Questions about having multiple and shorter loops

1. Which supply chain do you think is the most circular?

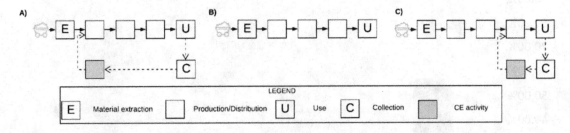

2. Which supply chain do you think is the most circular?

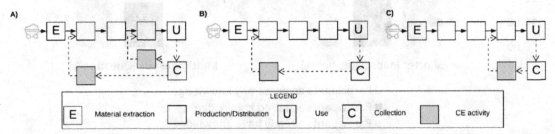

For the first question the participants were supposed to choose the supply chain with the shortest loop as the most circular one (option C). However, 45% of the participants marked the supply chain with recycling (option A) as the most circular. Since when they invested in only reuse activity (option C), the team made less profit due to the low availability of reusable products (25% of availability with 4-sided dice).

For the second question, the participants were supposed to choose option A since it has more loops than the other options. 81% of participants answered this question in the pre-questionnaires correctly before playing the game. The rest of the participants gained knowledge through the game and answered the question correctly in the post-questionnaires. Therefore, concerning the shorter loops, 19% of the participants gained knowledge.

Figure 12. Knowledge acquisition about shorter and multiple loops

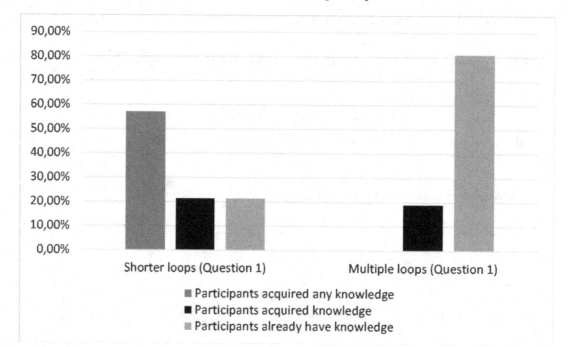

■ Participants acquired any knowledge
■ Participants acquired knowledge
■ Participants already have knowledge

SOLUTIONS AND RECOMMENDATIONS

The CircuSChain Game is designed in order to contribute to raise awareness and knowledge about Circular Supply Chains. The game has been tested with forty-two industrial engineering students. The results of this first experiment are promising about the simplicity, the pace, as well as the educational and the entertainment value of the game, although more experiments are needed.

Furthermore, in order to highlight the learning outcomes of the CircuSChain Game, the researchers relied on learning principles and orientations presented by (Madani et al., 2017). Our game adopts constructivism as a learning orientation and situated cognition principle. Constructivism concerns learning by constructing meaning from experience. Our game works well for constructivism since it represents reality by a simulation (Madani et al., 2017).

Moreover, situated cognition is experiencing scenarios in a contextualized environment. According to this principle, players receive feedback related to their actions. For example, CircuSChain Game provides a supply chain environment, where players experience a supply chain management process. The players have feedback such as indicators calculated at the end of each year that correspond to their strategic decisions (selection of Circular Economy activities). Through this feedback, the players are expected to gain knowledge about increasing CO_2 emissions and natural resource depletion, as well as the benefits of setting up Circular Economy activities and managing Circular Supply Chains to reduce them.

FUTURE RESEARCH DIRECTIONS

Since the CircuSChain Game is designed as a board game, the simulation of the supply chain operations is conducted by players. Therefore, in order to make the game simple for players, some aspects are not taken into consideration. For example, no modular tokens are chosen to represent products, despite the modular nature of the considered products. In a future version of the CircuSChain Game, modular tokens (using Lego blocks, for instance) could be considered to have a more realistic simulation of the manufacturing processes. In that case, an indicator that considers the recirculated product quantity, such as the product level circularity metric (Linder et al., 2017), could be used. Each team member's contribution to circularity could be calculated through this indicator. Thus, each player could have a local objective additionally to a global objective for the whole team.

Moreover, while designing the experiment, the researchers included a closed-loop activity instead of an open-loop activity in the third year for time limitation and simplicity reasons. However, repurposing activities and their related open-loops constitute a new potential for Circular Supply Chains. In addition, this concept is new among scholars and industrials. Therefore, future validation experiments, including the open-loops, are needed.

Furthermore, according to the experiment's analysis, the game is not efficient enough to help players gain knowledge about shorter and multiple loops. Therefore, the game parameters need to be better tuned, and the questions about these concepts are needed to be detailed in the questionnaires.

Moreover, as seen in Figures 10 and 12, the participants could not answer most of the questions correctly, neither in pre nor post-questionnaires. Most of these questions were left blank. An online questionnaire with mandatory answers could increase the number of answers to be analyzed. In order to include the aforementioned concepts in the CircuSChain Game and keep it simple to manage and play at the same time, the researchers are working on a digital version of the game. This could permit: (1) a physically decentralized but collaborative game through a web interface, (2) more flexible management of the time horizon as well as the computation of indicators, and (3) the automation of the material and information flow control.

Finally, the experiment was conducted solely with forty-two first-year master's students of industrial engineering. More experiments are needed with more participants and different audiences, such as supply chain professionals, final clients, Circular Economy experts and public authorities. A future experiment with the partners of the Cross Disciplinary Program CIRCULAR is planned.

CONCLUSION

The Circular Supply Chains play a critical role in the transition towards Circular Economy, which is proposed as a sustainable solution for pollution and resource depletion problems. The lack of knowledge and awareness about Circular Supply Chains constraint the adoption of Circular Supply Chains. In order to overcome this barrier, the CircuSChain Game is introduced. This game is developed based on the well-known Beer Distribution Game to simulate the material and information flows. Concepts related to Circular Supply Chains, such as reuse, refurbishing, remanufacturing, and recycling activities within closed- and open-loops, as well as CO_2 emissions and material scarcity, are considered in this game. The CircuSChain Game proposes a complementary approach to existing serious games with related concepts in Circular Supply Chains, considering repurposing and open-loops concepts as first-class citizens.

The game was tested by an experiment with forty-two industrial engineering students. Participants were asked to fill pre- and post-questionnaires in order to assess the game and observe the knowledge acquired through the game. The results showed that the CircuSChain Game would be an efficient tool to raise awareness and knowledge about Circular Supply Chains. Moreover, this game could be useful in overcoming resistance to change when transitioning to a Circular Supply Chain.

The game does not represent all the aspects of the complex Circular Supply Chains because of simplicity and time constraints due to the board structure of the game. However, a computer version of the game could be a solution to overcome these constraints. Moreover, more testing experiments are needed to further investigate the educational value of the game.

ACKNOWLEDGMENT

This research is supported by the French National Research Agency under the "Investissements d'avenir" program [grant number ANR-15-IDEX-02] through the Cross Disciplinary Program CIRCULAR.

REFERENCES

Aguiar, V. A. C., Rosly, M. M., & Nakano, M. (2018). A Single Player Serious Game for Sustainable Supply Chain Management. *Studies in Simulation and Gaming*, 28(1), 60–72.

Alamerew, Y. A., & Brissaud, D. (2020). Modelling reverse supply chain through system dynamics for realizing the transition towards the circular economy: A case study on electric vehicle batteries. *Journal of Cleaner Production*, 254, 120025. doi:10.1016/j.jclepro.2020.120025

Aminoff, A., & Kettunen, O. (2016). Sustainable supply chain management in a circular economy—towards supply circles. *International Conference on Sustainable Design and Manufacturing*, 52, 61–72. 10.1007/978-3-319-32098-4_6

Avila-Pesantez, D., Delgadillo, R., & Rivera, L. A. (2019). Proposal of a Conceptual Model for Serious Games Design: A Case Study in Children with Learning Disabilities. *IEEE Access: Practical Innovations, Open Solutions*, 7, 161017–161033. doi:10.1109/ACCESS.2019.2951380

Batista, L., Bourlakis, M., Liu, Y., Smart, P., & Sohal, A. (2018). Supply chain operations for a circular economy. *Production Planning and Control*, 29(6), 419–424. doi:10.1080/09537287.2018.1449267

Bianchini, A., Rossi, J., & Pellegrini, M. (2019). Overcoming the main barriers of circular economy implementation through a new visualization tool for circular business models. *Sustainability (Switzerland)*, 11(23), 6614. doi:10.3390u11236614

Bocken, N. M. P., Olivetti, E. A., Cullen, J. M., Potting, J., & Lifset, R. (2017). Taking the Circularity to the Next Level: A Special Issue on the Circular Economy. *Journal of Industrial Ecology*, 21(3), 476–482. doi:10.1111/jiec.12606

Canals Casals, L., Amante García, B., & Cremades, L. V. (2017). Electric vehicle battery reuse: Preparing for a second life. *Journal of Industrial Engineering and Management, 10*(2), 266–285. doi:10.3926/jiem.2009

Carrión-Toro, M., Santorum, M., Acosta-Vargas, P., Aguilar, J., & Pérez, M. (2020). iPlus a user-centered methodology for serious games design. *Applied Sciences (Switzerland), 10*(24), 1–33. doi:10.3390/app10249007

Cuesta, V., & Nakano, M. (2017). Chain of command: A sustainable supply chain management serious game. *International Journal of Automotive Technology, 11*(4), 552–562. doi:10.20965/ijat.2017.p0552

Cullen, J. M. (2017). Circular Economy: Theoretical Benchmark or Perpetual Motion Machine? *Journal of Industrial Ecology, 21*(3), 483–486. doi:10.1111/jiec.12599

De Angelis, R., Howard, M., & Miemczyk, J. (2017). Supply Chain Management and the Circular Economy : Towards the Circular Supply Chain. *Production Planning and Control, 29*(6), 425–437. doi:10.1080/09537287.2018.1449244

Ellen MacArthur Foundation. (2013). *Towards the Circular Economy* (Vol. 1). Author.

Ellen MacArthur Foundation. (2014). *Towards the Circular Economy Vol.3: Accelerating the scale-up across global supply chains*. Author.

Howard, M., Hopkinson, P., & Miemczyk, J. (2019). The regenerative supply chain: A framework for developing circular economy indicators. *International Journal of Production Research, 57*(23), 7300–7318. doi:10.1080/00207543.2018.1524166

Jimenez-Hernandez, E. M., Oktaba, H., Piattini, M., Arceo, F. D. B., Revillagigedo-Tulais, A. M., & Flores-Zarco, S. V. (2016). Methodology to construct educational video games in software engineering. *Proceedings - 2016 4th International Conference in Software Engineering Research and Innovation, CONISOFT 2016*, 110–114. 10.1109/CONISOFT.2016.25

Kurt, A., Cortes-Cornax, M., Cung, V.-D., Front, A., & Mangione, F. (2021). A Classification Tool for Circular Supply Chain Indicators. *Advances in Production Management Systems*, 644–653.

Kurt, A., Cung, V.-D., Mangione, F., Cortes-Cornax, M., & Front, A. (2019). An Extended Circular Supply Chain Model Including Repurposing Activities. *International Conference on Control, Automation and Diagnosis*, 1–6. 10.1109/ICCAD46983.2019.9037929

Lahane, S., Kant, R., & Shankar, R. (2020). Circular supply chain management: A state-of-art review and future opportunities. *Journal of Cleaner Production, 258*, 120859. doi:10.1016/j.jclepro.2020.120859

Linder, M., Sarasini, S., & van Loon, P. (2017). A Metric for Quantifying Product-Level Circularity. *Journal of Industrial Ecology, 21*(3), 545–558. doi:10.1111/jiec.12552

Madani, K., Pierce, T. W., & Mirchi, A. (2017). Serious games on environmental management. *Sustainable Cities and Society, 29*, 1–11. doi:10.1016/j.scs.2016.11.007

Mandran, N. (n.d.). *Experiment Guides*. Retrieved July 30, 2021, from http://thedre.imag.fr/?page_id=606

Mandran, N., & Dupuy-Chessa, S. (2018). Supporting experimental methods in information system research. *Proceedings - International Conference on Research Challenges in Information Science,* 1–12. 10.1109/RCIS.2018.8406654

Mangla, S. K., Luthra, S., Mishra, N., Singh, A., Rana, N. P., Dora, M., & Dwivedi, Y. (2018). Barriers to effective circular supply chain management in a developing country context. *Production Planning and Control, 29*(6), 551–569. doi:10.1080/09537287.2018.1449265

Marfisi-Schottman, I., George, S., & Frank, T.-B. (2010). Tools and Methods fo Efficiently Designing Serious Games. *4th Europeen Conference on Games Based Learning ECGBL2010, October,* 226–234.

Metters, R. (1997). Quantifying the bullwhip effect in supply chains. *Journal of Operations Management, 15*(2), 89–100. doi:10.1016/S0272-6963(96)00098-8

Neck, H. M., & Greene, P. G. (2011). Entrepreneurship Education: Known Worlds and New Frontiers. *Journal of Small Business Management, 49*(1), 55–70. doi:10.1111/j.1540-627X.2010.00314.x

Ponce, P., Meier, A., Méndez, J. I., Peffer, T., Molina, A., & Mata, O. (2020). Tailored gamification and serious game framework based on fuzzy logic for saving energy in connected thermostats. *Journal of Cleaner Production, 262,* 121167. doi:10.1016/j.jclepro.2020.121167

Qualters, D. M., Isaacs, J., Cullinane, T., Laird, J., & McDonald, A. (2008). A Game Approach to Teach Environmentally Benign Manufacturing in the Supply Chain. *International Journal for the Scholarship of Teaching and Learning, 2*(2). Advance online publication. doi:10.20429/ijsotl.2008.020214

Richa, K., Babbitt, C. W., & Gaustad, G. (2017). Eco-Efficiency Analysis of a Lithium-Ion Battery Waste Hierarchy Inspired by Circular Economy. *Journal of Industrial Ecology, 21*(3), 715–730. doi:10.1111/jiec.12607

Sivak, S., Sivak, M., Isaacs, J., Laird, J., & McDonald, A. (2007). Managing the tradeoffs in the digital transformation of an educational board game to a computer-based simulation. *Proceedings of the 2007 ACM SIGGRAPH Symposium on Video Games,* 97–102. 10.1145/1274940.1274961

Stahel, W. R. (1982). The Product-Life Factor. In S. G. Orr (Ed.), *An Inquiry Into the Nature of Sustainable Societies: The Role of the Private Sector.* NARC.

Stahel, W. R. (2010). The Preformance Economy (2nd ed.). Springer.

Sterman, J. D. (1989). Modeling Managerial Behavior: Misperceptions of Feedback in a Dynamic Decision Making Experiment. *Management Science, 35*(3), 321–339. doi:10.1287/mnsc.35.3.321

Vermunt, D. A., Negro, S. O., Verweij, P. A., Kuppens, D. V., & Hekkert, M. P. (2019). Exploring barriers to implementing different circular business models. *Journal of Cleaner Production, 222,* 891–902. doi:10.1016/j.jclepro.2019.03.052

Werning, J. P., & Spinler, S. (2020). Transition to circular economy on firm level: Barrier identification and prioritization along the value chain. *Journal of Cleaner Production, 245,* 118609. doi:10.1016/j.jclepro.2019.118609

Whalen, K. A., Berlin, C., Ekberg, J., Barletta, I., & Hammersberg, P. (2018). 'All they do is win': Lessons learned from use of a serious game for Circular Economy education. *Resources, Conservation and Recycling, 135*(May), 335–345.

Wikipedia. (2021). *The climate Fresk*. https://en.wikipedia.org/wiki/The_Climate_Fresk

Yuan, Z., Bi, J., & Moriguichi, Y. (2006). The circular economy: A new development strategy in China. *Journal of Industrial Ecology, 10*(1–2), 4–8. doi:10.1162/108819806775545321

KEY TERMS AND DEFINITIONS

Circular Economy Activity: Reprocessing activity allows maintaining used products value by integrating them into linear supply chains through closed- or open-loops.

Circular Supply Chain: Management process of material and information flows, starting with raw material extraction activity, encompasses production, distribution, use, collection, and Circular Economy activities, and ends with landfilling. Circular Supply Chains consist of a combination of closed- and open-loops.

Closed-Loop: Material flow, starting with collection activity, encompassing Circular Economy activities, and integrating into the linear Supply Chain of the original product.

Closed-Loop Activity: Circular Economy activities allow revaluating used products for the same purpose, integrating them into the linear Supply Chain of the original product. For example, closed-loop reuse, closed-loop refurbishing, etc.

Linear Supply Chain: Management process of material and information flows, starting with raw material extraction activity, encompasses production, distribution and use activities, and ends with landfilling.

Open-Loop: Material flow, starting with collection activity, encompassing Circular Economy activities, and integrating into a different linear supply chain of another product different from the original one.

Open-Loop Activity: Circular Economy activities, also called repurposing activities, allow revaluating used products for a different purpose from the original one, integrating them into the linear Supply Chain of another product. For example, open-loop reuse, open-loop refurbishing, etc.

Recycling: Transforming used products into materials in order to use them in production activities.

Refurbishment: Replacing the critical parts of a used product in order to bring it to a specific quality.

Remanufacturing: Replacing a significant amount of used product's parts, in order to bring it a like-new quality.

Repurposing: Reprocessing used product in order to give it another function through reuse, refurbishing, remanufacturing or recycling activities. These activities constitute open-loops.

Reuse: Reselling used products with minor modifications.

Reverse Logistics: Management process of return flows (closed or open-loops) in a Circular Supply Chain.

Chapter 19
Promoting Agroforestry Using Geo–Spatially Enabled Serious Gaming

Nadeem Ahmed Khan

Dr. B. R. Ambedkar National Institute of Technology, Jalandhar, India

Arun Khosla

(iD) https://orcid.org/0000-0001-8571-7614

Dr. B. R. Ambedkar National Institute of Technology, Jalandhar, India

Girish S. Pujar

National Remote Sensing Centre, Hyderabad, India

Parampreet Singh

Dr. B. R. Ambedkar National Institute of Technology, Jalandhar, India

ABSTRACT

Agroforestry is a type of land management in which trees or shrubs are planted around or amid crops or pastureland. It integrates agriculture and forestry technology to create land-use systems. This approach aids farmers in raising production, managing nutrient cycling, and enhancing their socio-economic standing. However, well-managed systems have several advantages over monocultures, although this approach is not widely used in the country. Agroforestry is hampered by a lack of competent management, a lack of technological help, a rigorous regulation of tree harvesting, and an irregular, unorganized market. As a result of these factors, farmers are hesitant to plant trees on their land, leading to the notion of agroforestry not being widely used in the world. Through this chapter, the authors attempt to understand the reasons for the lack of knowledge about agroforestry and help in designing solutions using serious gaming to alter farmers' behavior and propose a method in the form of a serious game to promote agroforestry practices among the farmers.

DOI: 10.4018/978-1-7998-9732-3.ch019

INTRODUCTION

India is an agriculturally intensive country with a traditional cropping pattern that has contributed to the country's food security. Owing to depletion of native nutrient stores and development of their inadequacies, lowering of the under-ground water, and return of insects and illnesses due to overexploitation, the productivity of this system has plateaued, if not decreased in certain places. The necessity for diversification from this system has been emphasized as a result of this. Agroforestry has emerged as one of the most effective options for crop rotation diversification. Different tree species are historically cultivated in the country's various agroclimatic zones.

For better profits, appropriate tree species, high-quality planting material, and profitable crop combinations must be chosen. Adopting the right cultural and managerial techniques may help boost agroforestry systems' productivity and economic benefits.

According to the National Forest Policy (1988), at least one-third of the nation must be covered in forests in order to preserve ecological balance and fulfill wood-based requirements. It also says that forest cover should cover at least 60% of the land in hills and 20% of the area in plains. The demand for wood and other tree-based goods is steadily rising. The only viable option for meeting such a demand would be to implement agroforestry practices, since this is the only system that can supply both wood and food while also conserving and rehabilitating the environment. But due to lack of awareness and shortage of technical support, farmers are not adopting agroforestry at large scale in the country.

For increasing the engagement in agroforestry practices serious games can play a crucial role. The geo spatial data in serious games provide a more realistic environment for researchers and stakeholders. Environment system has complicated and inter-disciplinary features that not only challenging to manage, but also difficult to train students and stakeholders in this area.

This chapter provides an overview of environmental management and agriculture games that can help researchers and students in finding a tool appropriate to their purpose. In this chapter, a method is proposed in the form of geo-information based serious game for increasing the engagement of farmers in agroforestry systems that incorporates gaming techniques to add a competitive aspect.

BACKGROUND

Agroforestry

Agroforestry is a land use management method that benefits in the conservation and protection of natural resources, and its advantages contribute to a significant increase in agricultural economic and resource sustainability. Agroforestry, which is founded on ecological principles, is essential in regions where agricultural production is very insecure owing to erratic and severe weather. Forestry and agriculture work together to sustain the agricultural system by providing stability and reliable revenue. Agroforestry has the potential to reduce the effect and consequences of these environmental constraints. Agroforestry has been practiced since the dawn of time, but it has been the subject of focused scientific research in the past 43 years only after the creation of the World Agroforestry Centre (International Centre for Research in Agroforestry, ICRAF) in 1978. Fruit tree cultivation on arable or grazing areas developed through time in various European countries, including England, France, and Germany, and was formerly known as pre-verger or Streuobst in its home country. In the Mediterranean zone of Spain and Portugal, the Dehesa and Montado (4500-year-old) systems are discovered. Another particular technique that developed in north-western Germany is Hauberg of the Siegerland. The Greek Chania System is also present (Dagar and Tewari, 2009).

The Hununoo of the Philippines developed a complicated and sophisticated form of shifting agriculture in southeast Asia. Agroforestry techniques such as Pekarangan and Kebentalun in Indonesia, Satoyama in Japan, and KGF in Sri Lanka are also well-known.

Traditional methods include the Quezungal system in western Honduras, the Riberno system in the Peruvian Amazon (forest clearance followed by multi-species home gardens), the silvipastoral system in Brazil, and 'Sweden fallow agroforestry and Amazonian home gardens.Multipurpose trees are used in the parks system of West African dryland. Tanzania's Kihamba and Ngitili Agroforestry Systems are also significant.

More than 40% of the world's agricultural fields have a tree cover of at least 10%. In terms of potential, there are now 1023 million hectares under agroforestry throughout the globe. Agroforestry and silvopastoral systems are projected to cover 823 million hectares worldwide. In India, the area under agroforestry is projected to be 25.31 million hectares, or 8.2 percent of the country's total reported geographical area, with the potential to grow further (Dhyani et al., 2009). In India, 13.5 million hectares of agroforestry are used to decrease rural unemployment, with wood production on farms providing 450 employment days per ha per year. In 2014, India became the first nation to enact the National Agroforestry Policy. The Ministry of Agriculture, Government of India, also has a national sub-mission on agroforestry.

Besides producing tangible products, agroforestry systems also provide intangible services such as territory to wildlife, bees habitats for fertilization for crop plants, carbon capture in soil and biomass, enhancement of surrounding environment, regulation of micro-climates, nitrogen obsession, soil erosion control, soil formation, social values, among others. Agroforestry system can control water runoff and soil erosion, thus reducing losses of water, soil minerals, organic matter and nutrients. Solar energy can be more effectively used in an Agroforestry system in the comparison of monoculture systems. The fertility of soil can be increased by roots and biomass of agroforestry system.

Benefits of agroforestry

The agriculture industry played an important role in the country's total income. The monoculture system of farming has been expanded due to increasing the demand of agriculture based goods. The agricultural land is limited, so the natural forests are converted into agricultural land. Globally, conversion has severe environmental consequences such as forest destruction, habitat fragmentation, and climate change. Because the activities are environmentally harmful, they are deemed unsustainable because the systems reduce the value of the natural environment over time. Many researchers are researched on agroforestry systems to better understand this phenomenon. Agroforestry systems are land use methods that maximize agricultural land use to produce diverse outputs while protecting natural resources. Systems are considered sustainable farming practices as they contribute to the healthy growth of the agricultural industry with respect to environmental, social, and economic factors.

Air quality

Furthermore, the advantages of agroforestry on air quality are heavily reliant on the proper selection of components, as well as their integration and arrangements. Windbreaks and shelterbelts are created by planting trees in straight lines to protect agricultural crops and animals. Furthermore, including plant materials into agricultural land may help to minimize soil erosion and reduce odors produced by wind from animal feces and urine. As a result, agroforestry systems that integrate agricultural products, plant materials, and animal species improve the air quality of the surrounding area.

Quality of water

Monoculture systems have an 80 percent lower water saving value than agroforestry systems. In agroforestry systems, better interaction of belowground plant materials aids the farm's water quality. Furthermore, agriculture regulations in the United States actively promote and support the use of plant materials as riparian buffers owing to their benefits in enhancing water quality. Riparian buffers, which are planted or developed beside water bodies, have the potential to reduce the amount of fertilizer or nutrient carried by surface runoff from agricultural land. As a result, the quantity of nutrients transported by runoff to ground and surface water may be decreased, reducing nonpoint source water pollution. According to literature, riparian buffers along first-order streams have the highest potential for enhancing water quality when compared to bigger streams. They claimed that slowing water flow, trapping contaminants, boosting infiltration, enhancing nutrient absorption and storage, increasing perspiration and promoting denitrification in the shallower subsoil all enhanced water quality.

Enhancement of soil

Agroforestry offers important environmental services in land management, such as soil improvement. According to Nair (1993), soil improvement through agro-forestry systems may be determined in the light of three conditions:

1. Increased nitrogen gas (N_2) by fixation of the plants and the ground;
2. Increased nutrient available by breakdown and biomass production of vegetation materials; and
3. Nutrient use of deeply rooted plant materials.

Preservation of biodiversity

Agroforestry systems that mix and interact with different kinds of flora and animals provide biodiversity with a home. Agroforestry systems, provide environmental services in the agricultural sector via their advantages in biodiversity conservation. Through the promotion and intensification of agricultural techniques, it was discovered that an agroforestry system may assist to maintain a greater degree of biodiversity as well as offer sustainable landscape connectivity. It can withstand a certain amount of disturbance if sustainable and profitable agricultural methods are used instead of monoculture systems. This is due to the fact that the systems require the clearing of natural forests, which disrupts the habitat of a variety of flora and fauna species. The reason for the agroforestry system's good response to biodiversity is based on three elements:

1. Agroforestry system accumulation protects areas from corruption;
2. Agroforestry system extension increases land area for biodiversity habitation in connection to landscape objectives; and

3. Agroforestry system diversification diversifies plant materials species in agricultural systems.

Climate Change Mitigation and Carbon Sequestration

Natural growth resources such as light, nutrients, and water may be captured and used by agroforestry systems that include different kinds of plant materials. The systems have a greater chance of sequestering carbon (C) than single-species crop farming because the integration of trees and crops may act as carbon sinks and offer temporary carbon storage. Carbon stocks are obtained from the compartments and tree usage or form systems, according to Somarriba, Cerda, Orozco, Cifuentes, Davila, Espin, Mavisoy, Avila, Alvarado, Poveda, Astorga, Say, and Deheuvels. Aboveground, root, soil, litter, and dead wood all play a role in compartment systems. Meanwhile, agricultural crops, wood species, fruit tree species, palms, ornamentals, and other components interact in tree use or form systems. Furthermore, the variety and richness of plant materials species on agricultural land influences greater soil organic carbon (C) content.

Important Aspects That Encourage Agroforestry Adoption

*   Guaranteed returns – this is particularly important in rain-fed agriculture, where farmers rely on tree components during times of shortage.
*   Increased demand for forest goods - as our population grows, so does the need for wood and wood-based products.
*   Better economic returns – compared to conventional farming systems – as shown by the use of a popular-based agroforestry model in riverbed regions of Punjab with a stable pH and reliable irrigation.
*   Harvesting time – can be changed according to market demands.
*   When compared to producing only agricultural crops, the system uses fewer natural resources.
*   Long-term system – because it improves soil, sequesters carbon, and aids in nutrient cycle, among other things.

Serious Games

Games have an essential role in the development of the human brain. The game's reward offer a chemical reaction that is related to brain areas involved in decision-making and behavior organization (Schultz, 2004). While simple analog games emerge naturally during a person's development, any multimedia information is quickly incorporated into the cognitive flow of a person (Andrews, Hull, & Donahue, 2009). Videogames combines human interaction with a user interface to provide visual feedback on a video device like a television or a computer monitor, were part of the multimedia revolution that swept the world in the twentieth century (Wikipedia, 2004). In today's society, videogames are a popular topic. Since the first titles were developed, many years and generations have passed, improving the design and range of the options available today. Since 1996, several authors and the media have used the term "game culture" to describe the habits and trends of videogame consumers (Shaw et al., 2010). Adventures, first-person shooters, and casual games are among the numerous genres of digital games that may be categorized based on their mechanics and design. The names are often used in entertainment games, which are games designed only for enjoyment (which is the most common objective of a game). What if a game had a secondary purpose in addition to entertainment? The game is then classified as a Serious

Game. Serious games, whether analog or digital, are those that serve a purpose other than entertainment (Backlund, Engstrom, Johannesson, &Lebram, 2010; Romero, Usart, & Ott, 2014). The serious goal of a serious game can be anything from educational to athletic to just attractive (Devine, 2015). There are subcategories and naming standards depending on the goal, such as educational games, exergames, art games, advergames, and so on, due to the wide range of purposes. By experimenting with serious games, companies and scholars may discover more about how multimedia content connects with people and how that content might be modified to improve its serious outcome. Adams et al. (2012), for example, looked at Crystal Island and Cache 17, two narrative 3D adventure learning games. They tried with concepts including Discovery, Narrative, and Distraction. Learning via the discovery of a realistic environment, according to the Discovery hypothesis, leads to better cognitive function. According to the Story hypothesis, a game's narration and narrative enhance the user's motivation to play and complete the game, resulting in more learning. Finally, according to the Distraction hypothesis, game content and activities that are unrelated to the instructional objective may distract a learner's attention away from the session's most essential instructional information. They find that narration and story are not sufficiently proven to improve the learning outcomes of both games when compared to a conventional slideshow presentation. Andrews, Hull, and Donahue (2009), on the other hand, conducted a classification of military instructional games that improved player immersion and reflection, resulting in a better understanding of what they were being taught and, as a result, a more effective retention of the knowledge due to the emotional engagement. Games, as previously mentioned, may serve other purposes than teaching, such as providing physical exercise. Exergames (Väätänen&Leikas, 2009; Yang, 2010) are video games that focus on generating several kinds of exercises, such as strength, balance, and flexibility activities. Unlike other serious games, exergames may make use of a wider variety of technologies. In their prototype, Väätänen and Leikas (2009) utilized GPS position tracking to have players roam around different parts of a city.

GIS / GEO-SPATIAL DATA

The use of geographic information systems (GIS), which is a set of computer hardware and software to analyze and display geographically referenced data, can facilitate the planning process. A Geographic Information System (GIS) is a data management system used to capture, store, extract, manipulate, analyzeand display spatial data for search and decision-makingpurposes.A database is linked to the mapping features of a GIS, and the data values are geo-referenced, allowing resource managers to space-based representation of information such as soil types and plant communities.A database is linked to map features in a GIS, and data values are geo-referenced, allowing resource managers to space-based representation of information such as soil types and plant communities. Because farm use and a variety of related subjects (such as agricultural production, forest management, exurban planning, and preservation) all deal with the geographical features of terrains, GIS has become widely used in land management and natural-resource planning, that provide a spatial way to assist in decision-making.

GIS is frequently associated with other technologies, like global positioning systems (GPS) as well as remote sensing. GPS is a method of entering spatial information into a GIS using real-world location, it's become a crucial tool for engineers to locating and recording data in the field. Remote sensing is the process of analyzing and interpreting spatial information from picture and satellite pictures that used software applications. GIS may be defined as "a software method for gathering, verifying, combining, and analyzing data associated to the earth's surface." As it stands, the need for large-scale modelling and map modeling processes for a wide range of classically manual processes is becoming increasingly apparent. Foresters also see GIS (a computer-based application) as a useful management solution for their day-to-day operations.

Datasets, yield and yield component models, nature conservation models, agro forestry knowledge-based systems, financial models, geographical information systems (GIS), and visualization tools are among the software applications available to support forest management decision making. Each application typically will have its own interface and information format, so managers need to be able each functionality and manual process convert data from one setup to another in order to use multiple tools. Given the breadth of topics that might need to be discussed in a typical ecology management issue, and the need to run several to many applications as a result, mechanical orchestration of the entire analytical process can quickly become a major roadblock. The Learning Management System (LMS) solves this problem by directing information flow through pre-programmed pathways in its core component. To project changes on forested landscapes over time, LMS combines landform location data, stand-level inventory records, and length independent tree height models.

Suitability evaluations may be developed using geographic information layers such as type of soil, slope, and land cover to determine ideal sites for agroforestry techniques to address landowner and public concerns. This evaluation method may be used to design agroforestry operations at any scale by choosing data with the proper spatial resolution. The ability to integrate various evaluations to identify places where numerous goals may be met is the most important advantage of utilizing GIS-guided suitability.

Crop yield estimates and monitoring are crucial for the country's timely knowledge of crop yields, as well as the formulation of food import and export policies and pricing. It is a major priority for the United Nations Food and Agriculture Organization (FAO) and most nations. Crop yield estimates has two major aspects: one is estimating the crop planting area, and the other is determining the yield model using the yield model and long-distance remote sensing monitoring. This job may be completed quickly and accurately using GIS. In production, remote sensing pictures of crop development are acquired, RS image information is processed, different spatial data information is evaluated in GIS, crop kinds are recognized, and planting area is estimated using statistics. Then, in order to estimate the yield and growth of large-area crops, use the model function of the GIS system to construct a crop growth model and various estimation models under various conditions, and the above factors are introduced into the model to estimate the yield and growth of large-area crops. To undertake a case study of Haiphong Province in northern Vietnam, Thanh Van Hoang and Tien Yin Chou combined a GIS tool with a SALUS (Land Use Sustainability System Approach) model. To begin, research demonstrates the effect of climate change on agriculture in northern Vietnam, using Haiphong Province as a case study. Second, the SALUS model is incorporated into the GIS in order to forecast rice production in case studies as well as other environmental variables. This comparison shows a confidence level of more than 80% when using the root mean square error to correctly represent the model. Rice yield has been effectively simulated under climate change using this model.

RELATED WORK

Serious Games for Environment Management

Serious environmental management games are assisting individuals get a better understanding of real-world environmental sustainability problems by enabling them to participate in first-hand experiences that would otherwise be too costly, difficult, or dangerous to duplicate in real life.

The value of interdisciplinary collaboration and a systems approach in environmental management has long been recognized (Hoekstra, 2012; Rusca et al., 2012), providing a solid foundation for game-based learning (GBL). Games may be utilized in educational contexts to promote environmental and sustainability consciousness among individuals who are more exposed to information-age products. Learners may role-play in environments that would be difficult to reproduce without the use of computer graphics and realistic simulations (Kirriemuir & McFarlane, 2004). This capability is critical for environmental management education because it is required to make important decisions about "wicked" environmental planning and management problems (e.g., climate change and extreme weather events, ocean acidification, desertification, and biodiversity loss, among others), rather than well-defined, end-in-view "tame problems" (Rittel& Webber, 1973). The first generation to grow up with digital technology such as the internet, computers, video games, MP3 players, and smartphones is known as the Net-generation, sometimes known as the Digital-generation or digital natives (Prensky, 2001). Prensky (2001) argues that digital natives perceive and process information differently than previous generations due to the pervasiveness of technology exposure, which is a significant characteristic of today's youth who use their time differently than previous generations. In 2009, American teenagers aged 8 to 18 were expected to spend 10:45 hours per day watching television, up from 8:33 hours in 2004 and 7:29 hours in 1999. (Rideout et al., 2010). People spend 73 minutes per day on average playing video games in 2009, up from 49 minutes in 2004 and 26 minutes in 1999(Rideout et al., 2010).

In contrast to the real world, video games provide a practical method of personal and social fulfillment, as gamers enjoy the challenge of beating the game and other players in an exciting, unbiased "level playing field" (Sherry et al., 2006). Video games are not just played by young children and teenage men. Gamers are on average 30 years old, with 47 percent of females and 53 percent of males participating in games (Entertainment Software Association, 2012). In the past decade, as technological advances have made electronic media more accessible and digital games more widely available, "serious games" (SG) designed for instructional purposes have gotten greater attention (Young et al., 2012). SGs are seen to have a particularly high potential for addressing the limitations of traditional lecture-driven classrooms in science, technology, engineering, and math (STEM) courses (Levine, 2011; Mayo, 2007). Students leave STEM programs for a variety of reasons, including a lack of interest in the topic, a loss of academic self-confidence as a result of a competitive environment (Seymour & Hewitt, 1997), or incompatible personal learning styles (Bernold et al., 2007). The prevalence of lecture-style classrooms (Blickenstaff, 2005), which account for over 95% of engineering courses, may be related to a drop in interest in engineering degrees (Deshpande &Huang, 2011). Mayo (2007) lists five reasons why SGs may increase STEM majors' interest and retention: wide reach, effective learning paradigms, better brain chemistry, more time on task, and improved learning outcomes. Games in K-12 may help expose youngsters to STEM professions in a fun and engaging manner, perhaps boosting college-bound students' interest in STEM degrees and retention. With so much interest in technology, especially gaming, the educational potential of games is receiving more attention outside of academia. The NMC Horizon Report: Higher

Education (2013) was developed to offer information about new and emerging technology and its potential impact on teaching, learning, and research to education leaders, policymakers, and academics (Johnson et al., 2013). A significant trend noted in the research is the evolution of higher education teaching to incorporate more informal learning, such as online learning, hybrid learning, and collaborative models. The popularity of the US government-sponsored National STEM Video Game Challenge is on the rise. President Barack Obama launched the Video Game Challenge in 2010 to encourage middle and high school students to develop STEM-related games to promote learner independence (Robertson & Howells, 2008), systems thinking, and higher-order skills, all of which are critical to STEM learning (Resnick, 2012). The E-TECH Caucus in the US Congress was formed to educate lawmakers and the public about the educational and economic benefits that the gaming industry can offer (Levine, 2011). In addition, in 2012, the first national policy effort on the role of digital gaming in education, health, civic engagement, and other areas was established (Toppo, 2012).

The potential of GBL and serious environmental management games to improve cognitive development, professional skills, and learning experience in the area of environmental management is investigated in this research. GBL has been proven to improve soft skills such as critical thinking, problem-solving creativity, and cooperation, as well as learning retention, cognitive development, and socialization (Johnson et al., 2013; Gee, 2004). It adjusts to different learning styles and works as a supplement to traditional methods to suit a broader variety of learning styles (Squire, 2008; Kirriemuir & McFarlane, 2004; Levine & Vaala, 2013; Van Eck, 2006). The present state of SGs in environmental management is discussed, as well as their variations in terms of subject, aim, intended participants, game style, and availability, among other things.

SERIOUS GAMING FOR AGRICULTURE

Agriculture has often been utilized as a source of amusement. Many serious games have been made about it, as well as thecurrent craze for board games.In casual games, there are a few instances. In games like FarmMania, VitualFarm, and The Farmer Game, the players' main tasks are to plant, fertilize, and irrigate fields in order to produce crops. Farmville, one of the most popular Facebook games, is based on the same concepts and thousands of individuals have participated in the game.

SimAgri, for example, has a persistent online environment. SimAgri is comparable to the simulation gamesJohn Deere American Farmer andSimFarm in terms of game principles, however it is practiced on a different timeframe and includes thousands of participants.

While farming is a common subject in video games, the bulk of them were not designed with seriousness in mind. However, there are certain exceptions. NASA's BioBlast is best example, has been utilized in educational institutions to assist students comprehend the mechanisms involved in plant development. The player's objective is to generate enough oxygen and food (biomass) to keep a six-person crew alive in space for three years. Participants manage a greenhouse in which they grow a variety of vegetables. To observe how the plants respond, they may experiment with temperature, CO_2 levels, and light exposure. Bet the Farm is another example, in which players establish agricultural policy before witnessing the long-term effects of their choices. The choices are many; for example, the player may choose to use precision farming, provide antibiotics to animals, or plant genetically engineered seeds, and after each choice, the player is given advise or a warning. The goal is to have the most money at the end of the year. The game promotes re-playability, allowing the user to experiment with different tactics. Another example is 3rd World Farmer16, a game in which players control a little virtual farm in a developing third-world country and go through the hardships and tribulations of a poor family. In addition to agricultural problems, this game addresses political, social, and health issues. For example, the player may be urged to invest in the local development of the hamlet and send children to school. Design-A- Even though it is not an agricultural game, Plant is noteworthy because it explores the use of animated teaching agents to enhance knowledge-based learning in game-like settings. In Design-A-Plant, students learn about botanical anatomy and physiology by graphically creating customized plants that thrive in certain environments. The goal for the players is to figure out what makes a plant grow stronger in each scenario. With the possible exception of certain warnings in Bet the Farm, none of the above games discuss the impact of agriculture on the environment. Environmental issues, on the other hand, should not be ignored since they may be significant, as we will see in the next section. On the other side, there are a plethora of games concerning environmental issues (some of which may be found on the Games For Change website), but none of them are about agriculture. For the reasons mentioned above, we view the development of a game that analyzes environmental problems related to agriculture as an important potential and viable route. We believe that, given the popularity of agricultural games, the topic of agriculture might be a great approach to introduce environmental issues in general.

GAME FRAMEWORK

Agroforestry Suitability

In our serious game first we evaluate the agroforestry suitability of the land. So in this research our first aim is find land suitability for agroforestry in India by using temperature, soil, water data and other geo-spatial data. GIS is used to evaluate the suitability of Agroforestry from geo-spatial data. India is an agriculturally intensive country where the traditional farming method has helped the country's food security. Due to depletion of native nutrient stores and the emergence of their deficiencies, lowering of the under-ground water table, and recurrence of insects and diseases due to overexploitation, the productivity of this system has plateaued, if not declined in certain regions. The need for diversification from this system has been emphasized as a result of this. Agroforestry has emerged as one of the feasible alternatives to traditional rice-wheat rotation diversification. Varied tree species traditionally grow in the country's various agroclimatic zones. For increased profits, appropriate tree species, high-quality planting material, and profitable crop combinations must be chosen. Adopting the appropriate cultural and managerial techniques can also boost the productivity and economic returns from agroforestry systems.

According to the National Forest Policy (1988), at least one-third of the country must be covered in forests in order to maintain ecological balance and supply wood-based needs. It also stipulates that forest cover should cover at least 60% of the land in the hills and 20% of the area in plains. The demand for wood and other tree-based products is steadily expanding. Adoption of agroforestry practices is the only viable option for meeting such a need, as it is the only system that can offer both wood and food while also conserving and rehabilitating the ecosystem.

Nutrient Availability and Capacity for Retention

The nutrients of soil are important for the agroforestry. The data about nutrition in soil and nutrition holding capacity are used to determine that a piece of land is suitable for agroforestry or not. Soil nutrient parameter was also used for determining the suitability of agroforestry. Data for nutrient availability were derived from soil structure, organic C, humas and water content and particle size. The data for capacity of nutrient retention were derived from organic C of soil, soil structure and ion exchange capabilities of clay and soil. The map for nutrition availability and capacity of retention for India is derived by combining both of the factors in the GIS domain and giving them equal weightage.

Availability of Oxygen in the Root Zone

Plant development is influenced by oxygen availability in soils, which is mainly controlled by drainage features of earth. If there is no sufficient oxygen in layer of soil, roots are not capable of nutrient absorption. The roots use available oxygen to send the nutrient to other parts of tree. By using these nutrient leaves make food.FAO established methods for determining soil drainage grades. Different soil categories, soil structure, rise and fall of terrain are considered in these processes.

Rooting circumstances

The roots provide physiologic tasks such as water and nutrient absorption, which are critical for plant development. Because root of trees is growing too deep in the soil and offer sufficient knowledge of optimal plant crop selection depending on soil properties. The rooting conditions are essential elements for agroforestry suitability. Gravel and stoniness may influence rooting conditions, limit the actual depth of rootedness and reducing the actual volume that can be accessed for root penetration into the soil, lowering agricultural output. The root conditioning data of our countrydemonstrates an important relationship between soil conditions in the rooting area and crop development.

Figure 1. India map for Rooting circumstances (Ahmad et al, 2019)

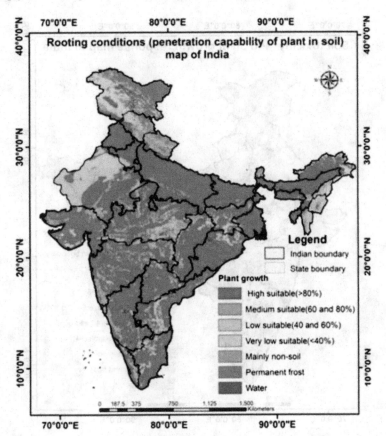

Toxicity

Low pH results in toxicity associated with acidity, which are reason for phosphorus and molybdenum shortages, both of which are necessary for plant development. Micronutrient shortages like iron, manganese, and zinc, as well as molybdenum toxicity, are common in calcareous soils. Gypsum significantly reduces the amount of moisture accessible in the soil. As a result, this soil toxicity solely includes calcium carbonate and gypsum-related issues. The availability of calcium carbonate and gypsum, has a negative impact on plant development.

Figure 2. Plant growth response and soil toxicities map of India (Ahmad et al, 2019)

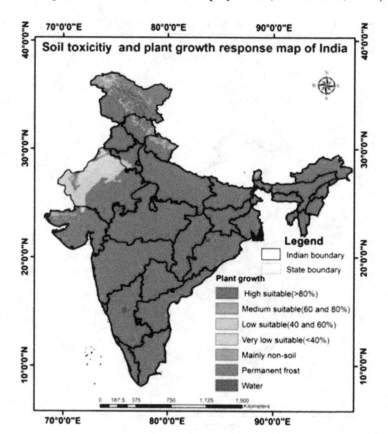

Vegetation map—NDVI

Normalized Difference Vegetation Index (NDVI) is the popular vegetation index that is a measure of trees' greenery and photosynthetic process. In this research, an NDVI map produced by MODIS can utilized. The connection between NDVI values and plant density has been shown to be substantial. In figure the greater NDVI score shows higher greenness and lower soil erosion.

Generation of Slope Maps from Digital Elevation Model

Variability in topography has an impact on the plants' growth and productivity. The QGIS software can handle large datasets for a variety of applications. One of them is the Spatial Analyst module. The Space Analyst module's surface sub-module mayuseto analyze the GTOPO30 DEM and create a slope map. Slope gradient is a major topographic element that influences soil erosion severity and, as a result, plant development. When slope rises, infiltration capacity of the soil diminishes, resulting in substantial increases in runoff quantities, which leads to soil erosion.

Temperature and Precipitation Map

Plant species' growth is influenced by the climate. Monthly temperature and precipitation data will used to create annual average temperature map and annual average precipitationmaps, where the GIS modeling was used exclusively. FAO (1976) suggested that the temperature and rainfall map are main parameter for evaluating the agroforestry suitability.

TREE GROWTH MODEL

In yield estimate, stand description, and damage assessments, the connection between tree height and diameter is important (Parresol, 1992). For different tree species, several height and diameter equations have been established (Wykoff et al., 1982; Huang et al., 1992). Sigmoidal or non-linear growth functions are frequently utilized in creating tree height and diameter equations among the many mathematical equations available. Foresters often employ height-diameter models to estimate tree or stand volume and site quality by predicting total tree height based on observed diameter at breast height (DBH). As a result, precise height-diameter functions are critical in estimating tree or stand volume and site quality. Because of the impact of both internal and external variables on height development, there is no standard height/age connection for trees, although the fundamental pattern is sigmoidal. Forest researchers and managers may benefit from growth models in a variety of ways. Foresters, for example, may want to know the long-term impact of a specific silvicultural choice, such as altering harvesting cutting restrictions, on both the forest and future harvests. They may evaluate the probable consequences, both with the planned and alternative cutting limits, using a growth model, and make an objective choice. The process of creating a growth model may also provide fresh and fascinating insights about forestry. Growth models can potentially play a larger role in forest management and policy development. The same may be utilized to generate predictions, develop prescriptions, and direct forest management choices into stand dynamics when combined with other resource and environmental data.

Table 1. Tree growth model of some tree species. (Devaranavadgi et al., 2013)

S. No.	Tree species	Height- Age Equation
1.	Acacia auriculiformis	H=7.005*exp (-6.034*exp (-0.523*T))
2.	Acacia catechu	H=5.966*exp (-3.0001/ TX+0.3501))
3.	Acacia nilotica	H=7.9211*exp (-2.9119exp (-0.2918*T)
4.	Leucaena leucocephala	H=11.465*(1-exp (-0.0161*T^1.993))
5.	Albizzia lebbeck	H=7.1478*(1-exp (-0.3316*T)) ^2.9981)
6.	Azadirachta indica	H=5.2672*(1-exp (-0.3253*T)) ^3.3731
7.	Bahunia purpurea	H=5.6821*exp (-3.265*exp (-0.4934*T
8.	Butea monosperma	H=2.836*exp (-4.932*exp (-0.4029*T)
9.	Casuarina equsitefolia	H=5.0717*exp (-2.3623*exp (-0.2219*T)
10.	Cassia siamea	H=6.721*exp (-2.918*exp (-0.2002*T))
11.	Dalbergia sissoo	H=5.5179*(1-exp (-0.0675*T^-1.4036))
12.	Emblicaofficianalis	H=11.975*exp (-5.674/(T+1.684)
13.	Eucalyptus citriodara	H=12.539*(1-exp (-0.0625*T^-1.2829)
14.	Eucalyptus hybrid	H=15.879*exp (-11.356/(T+2.573)
15	Hardwickiabinata	H=10.403*(1-exp (-0.0253*T^-1.495))
16.	Inga dulce	H=6.6737*exp (-2.7339*exp (-0.236)
17.	Peltoferrumferrugeneum	H=9.334*(1-exp (-0.0139*T^1.78)

Where H- Height & T-Age of tree (in years)

BIOMASS OF TREE

Biomass is a weight-based measurement of biological stuff. The biomass of a forest is a vast subject that encompasses all creatures, trees, fungus, insects, and so on, and is beyond the scope of this book. Tree biomass is the subject of this chapter. The biomass of a single tree or the biomass of all trees in a certain region is called biomass. Because trees have a high moisture content, weights may be green or oven dry. The decision in agroforestry system is devoted to oven-dry biomass and the relationship between biomass and usage in individual trees.

Tree biomass is often split into above- and below-ground components, with sub-divisions within each. Foliage, branches, stems, and bark, for example, make up above-ground biomass. Components may be defined in a variety of ways by various scholars. Many commercial tree species found in the Pacific Northwest have formulae for calculating oven-dry biomass components (Gholz et al., 1979).

Table 2 depicts an example of biomass distribution derived from the equations for a 16-inch (40.64-cm) dbh Douglas-fir tree. This tree has an above-ground biomass of 83 percent and a below-ground biomass of 17 percent. The stem, including the bark, accounts for about 72% of total biomass. When analyzing biomass statistics, caution is required. The stem (with bark) of a 16-inch Douglas-fir accounts for 87 percent of its above-ground biomass, according to some studies.

Table 2. A 16-inch dbh Douglas-fir tree's biomass distribution

Crown	Oven-dry weight (In Kg)	Percent (%)
foliage	32	2.8
barky live branches	62	6.0
barky dead branches	19	1.7
Total	120	10.5
Stem or Bole wood	719	62.8
bark	109	9.5
Total Above Ground	948	82.8
Below Ground roots and stump	197	17.2
TOTAL TREE	1145	100.00

BIOLOGICAL NITROGEN FIXING

Through biological nitrogen fixation, organic matter addition, and nutrient recycling, agroforestry plants, especially leguminous trees, improve soil. Some trees, such as Leucaena, Acacia, and Alnus, have been reported to fix up to 400-500 kg, 270 kg, and 100-300 kg nitrogen per hectare per year. Fixed nitrogen may provide a symbiotic advantage to the crops that grow alongside it, as well as aid in soil fertility development. The quantity of nitrogen taken up by the first crop from legumes or tree species trimming is very low, with a significant part remaining in the soil organic matter, suggesting a long-term nitrogen benefit rather than an instant benefit. Various decomposition rates exist for different tree components, including as leaves, twigs, fruit, and wood, which serves to spread nutrient release throughout time. Table 3 lists some of the most significant nitrogen-fixing plants. Symbiotic and non-symbiotic nitrogen fixation is used in biological nitrogen fixation. Plant roots collaborate with nitrogen-fixing microbes to achieve symbiotic fixation. Many legumes have Rhizobium symbionts, whereas a few non-leguminous plants have Frankia symbionts. Free-living soil organisms are responsible for non-symbiotic nitrogen fixation, which may be a major component in natural ecosystems with low nitrogen needs from external sources (Nair, 1993).

Table 3. Important nitrogen fixing plants species (Nair, 1993)

Family	Botanical Name	Plants	N_2fixed (kg N/ha/yr)
Mimosoideae	*Acaciamearnsii*	Blackwattle	200
Casuarinaceae	*Casurinaequisetifolia*	Beefwood,Saru	60-110
Pipilonaceae	*Erythrinapoeppigiana*	Erythrina	60
Fabaceae	*Gliricidiasepium*	Applering, Areca	13
Mimosoideae	*Ingajincicuil*	Inga	34-50
Mimosoideae	*Leucaenaleucocephala*	Subabul	100-500
Betulaceae	*Alnusnepalensis*	Indianalder	-
Fabaceae	*Viciafaba*	Horsebean	68-88

NUTRIENT PUMPING

Tree root systems have a role in a variety of beneficial soil impacts, including carbon enrichment via root turnover, nutrient interception, and the physical enhancement of compact soil layers. Tree roots are deep and spread out, allowing them to absorb nutrients and water from deeper soil strata where herbaceous crop roots are unable to reach. Trees are known for 'nutrient pumping,' which involves their absorbing nutrients from deeper in the soil profile and depositing them on the top layers through litter-fall and other processes. The features of tree species, as well as other soil, climatic, and topographic variables, play a major role in this process. In contrast to trees grown in high moisture soils, trees grown in low moisture soils have deep root systems that aid in nutrient and water pumping (Makumba et al., 2009; Schroth and Sinclair, 2003; Schroth, 1999).

NUTRIENT IN SOIL

Land degradation has direct consequences such as decreased soil productivity and a shortage of food and cash crops. There are 175 million hectares of degraded land in India. It has a number of issues with soil erosion and land degradation. These are significant contributors to land degradation and soil nutrient loss. We take an example of nutrient stored by different system.

Table 4. Amount of nitrogen stored in above-ground plants under various conditions (Bargli, 1995; Tokey et al., 1989; Sharma et al. 1988)

S. No.	Different systems	Nutrient (Kg/ha)		
		N	P	K
1	*Agrisilvi- horticultural system*	532	40	461
2	*Eucalyptus tereticornis*	246	21	276
3	*Delbergia sissoo*	1063	68	434

Table 5. Some fast-growing tree species employed in agroforestry produce dry matter and have high nutritional content (Misra, 2011)

S. No.	Trees	Nutrient release (Kg/ha/yr)			DM (Ton/ha/yr)
		P	N	K	
1	*Eucalyptus globules*	5	58	48	8.5
2	*Delbergia sissoo*	3	67	16	4.2
3	*Eucalyptus hybrid*	9	22	7	4.6

Table 6. Under a prosopis-based agroforestry system, available nitrogen, and phosphorus as organic matter (Misra, 2011)

S. No.	Tree Name	P (%)	N (%)	Organic matter (%)
1	*Prosopis juliflora*	0.28	0.033	0.38
2	*Prosopis cineraria*	0.42	0.042	0.57
3	*Barefield*	0.28	0.020	0.37

Table 7. Nutrientvariationin open field system and agroforestry (Misra, 2011)

S. No.	TreeName	N (%)	P (%)	Organic matter (%)
1	*Prosopis juliflora*	10.3	409	250
2	*Open field*	7.7	370	203
3	*Prosopis cineraria*	22.9	633	250

Table 8. Soil nutrients in various silvipastoral systems (Misra, 2011)

S. No.	Treetypes	Nitrogen (%)	Phosphorus (%)	Organic matter (%)
1	*Acacianilotica*	216	15.6	0.71
2	*Albizia lebbeck*	208	15.0	0.68
3	*Albizia Procera*	197	14.2	0.62
4	*Luceana leucocephala*	273	16.3	0.98
5	*Open field*	178	13.0	0.28

Tree roots, litterfall, and root exudates in the rhizosphere all provide organic matter to the soil system in different ways. These additions serve as the primary food source for a diverse variety of species engaged in soil biological activity and interactions, and they have significant implications for soil nutrients and fertility. Trees contribute to carbon buildup in soils as a result of their participation in these complicated processes, a subject that is becoming more prominent in debates about greenhouse gas reduction in the context of global warming and climate change. Although carbon (C) makes up nearly half of the dry weight of branches and a third of the dry weight of foliage, the majority of C sequestration (roughly 2/3) takes place belowground, involving living biomass such as roots and other belowground plant parts, soil organisms, and C stored in various soil horizons (Nair, 1993).

DESIGNING OF SERIOUS GAME

This serious game is designed in the Unity software that is a well known game engine. In this game first player evaluate the agroforestry suitability in the region with help of GIS data. After the evolution of agroforestry suitability player will select the tree that is best for that region with the help of database. Growth models of tree will give basic idea for the growth of trees with respect to time.

Figure 3. Flow of game designing

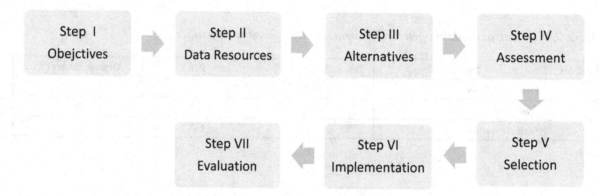

SCORING PROCESS OF AGROFORESTRY GAME

Methods to assess land suitability have been authorized by the Food and Agricultural Organization (FAO). Today's geospatial technology, along with the availability of many free datasets, makes it simple to study the land in order to accomplish a particular objective depending on their use. GIS modeling software allows you to group various thematic levels according to their significance. Appropriate data-sets, highly experienced GIS specialists familiar with modeling concepts, and sufficient lab equipment are all required for this kind of research.

For scoring of serious game, when the data of different variable are suitable for agroforestry then the game system adds high reward in the players' score. If the conditions are not suitable for agroforestry practicing the game mechanism does not add any rewards in players' score. The game mechanism shows a warning on system for non-suitability of agroforestry. In short the game score reflects the suitability for agroforestry that it is highly, medium, low or not suitable.

Table 9. Weightage in score for different land characteristics

Region Properties	Factors	Weightage in Score (%)
Energy sufficiency	Average yearly temperature (⁰C)	16.66
Water sufficiency	Precipitation(mm)	16.66
Nutrients sufficiency	Nutrition availability and retention capacity	16.66
Oxygen sufficiency and roots' conditions	Available oxygen in the roots	8.34
	Capacity of root penetration in soil	8.33
Toxicity	Toxicity	16.67
Level of erosion/ease of water management	Vegetation score/NDVI	8.34
	Angle of slope	8.34
Ease of cultivation	Rocks/ dams/Iceandsnow	–

Table 10. Game rewards conditions

Land characteristics	Categories for Game Rewards			
Average yearly temperature (⁰C)	<16	16–20	20–24	>24
Precipitation(mm)	–	<900	1300-900	>1300
Available nutritionand retentioncapacity	–	Low	Medium	High
Available oxygen in the roots	–	Low	Medium	High
Capacity of root penetration in soil	–	Low	Medium	High
Toxicities	–	High	Medium	Low
Vegetation score / NDVI	–	Low	Medium	High
Slope (in degree)	>35	15–35	1–15	0–1
Boulders/ rocks/ dams/ ice and snow	–	–	–	–
	No Reward	Low Reward	Medium Reward	High Reward

DISCUSSION

Any essential thematic layers such as oxygen available for the root zone, soil nutrient and retention capacity, rooting conditions, soil toxicity, yearly average temperature, vegetation (NDVI), yearly precipitation, and slope of soil were pooled as per their weight percentage factors based on relative significance to create score agroforestry land suitability serious game. The agroforestry suitability is classified into four types according to game score - High score (Highly suitable), Medium score (Moderately suitable), Low score (Marginally suitable), No score (Not suitable).

Table 11. Agroforestry decision making

Score	Class	Details
High	Highly suitable (S1)	Land with no major restrictions on how it may be used, or just small restrictions that won't decrease production or benefits and won't increase inputs beyond an appropriate standard.
Medium	Moderately suitable (S2)	Land with fairly severe restrictions for continuous implementation of a particular use will decrease production or profits and boost needed inputs to the degree that the total benefit to be obtained from the use is reduced.
Low	Marginally suitable (S3)	Land with significant restrictions for continuous implementation of a particular use, which will reduce production and profits, or boost needed inputs, to the point where this investment will only be partially justified.
No score	Not suitable (NS)	Land with significant constraints for continuous implementation of a particular use, which will decrease production and profits or raise needed inputs to the point where this investment will only be partially justified

- **High Score (High Suitability Areas)**

High score shows the high suitability of agroforestry in given region. These are regions where the average annual temperature (°C) is higher than 24, the average rainfall is higher than 1300 mm, and the soil water content is quite high. Plants have a high availability of nutrients and nutrient retention in the soil, as well as sufficient oxygen in the plant roots. The soil toxicity is minimal, with appropriate root's penetration capacity, primarily on plains (slope lower than one percent), with high NDVI index (lower erosion degree) giving enough helpful circumstances for tree development.

- **Medium Score (Moderate Suitability)**

In these regions, average rainfall is ranging from 1300 to 900 mm and average yearly temperature is ranging from 20 to 24°C range. The availability and retention capacity of soil nutrients, as well as the amount of oxygen availability in roots of plants, are modest. Soil poisoning and root's penetration capacity are moderate, mainly in the rolling region (slope range is 1 – 15 percent) with moderate NDVI index (moderate erosion degree), giving moderately helpful plant development conditions.

- **Low Score (Marginal Suitability)**

These are regions with yearly rainfall is lower than 900 mm and average yearly temperature is ranging from 16 to 20°C range. The availability and retention capacity of soil nutrients, as well as the amount of oxygen availability in the roots of plants, are lowest. Low soil toxicities and root penetration capacity, mainly in the undulating region (slope range from 15 to 35%), with lower NDVI index (low erosion degree), provide less helpful conditions for tree development.

- **No Score (Not Suitable Areas)**

Because of the very low temperatures and constant frost, as well as the presence of a snow area, dams, river, rock, and steep slopes (higher than 35 percent), these locations are extremely unsuitable for agroforestry.

In extreme weather events (floods and droughts, climate change), the quality of soils degrades quickly, and alternative environmentally dangerous scenarios, an agroforestry system is a feasible practice that can be socially, economically and ecologically sustainable. Farmers' annual income can be expanded by multiple folds without detriment to our existing ecosystem if they use land resources wisely and take appropriate soil and water conservation measures. All agroecological zones have been studied for their appropriateness and productive potential under specific applications by the FAO. It is necessary to encompass a diverse range of tree species that are compatible with current environmental circumstances and farmers' requirements. Table 11 illustrates the agro - ecological map of the area of India, which was generally categorized in five states of the ecosystem and subsequently assessed with categories of agroforestry suitability (S1, S2, S3, and NS). In just the farmland area/utilized agricultural area, the research illustrates the agroforestry appropriateness in different agroecological zones.

Agroforestry suitability (S3) is poor in dry and semiarid environment, that are described by harsh climatic conditions like low rain, high sun radiation, higher wind velocity, and enhanced evapotranspiration. Because of juvenile, extremely rough and unstructured soil texture with limited water retention ability and poor nutritional condition, the land's production potential is generally low.

In this area, agroforestry techniques like cultivation under the trees are also a long tradition. Soil and water conservation, as well as rainwater harvesting, must be adopted aggressively in order to store seasonal rainwater, keep the soil moist for longer and prevent it from eroding. Cultivatedland may be used for Silvipastoral, Agrisilvipastoral and Horti-pastoral. Prosopis cineraria, Acacia nilotica, Azadirachta indica, Acacia tortilis, and Albizia lebbeck are examples of tree species that may be cultivated alongside agricultural crops. Shelterbelt plantations around agricultural fields will be very beneficial in protecting the land from strong winds and conserving soil moisture in hot conditions.

The subhumid and humid–paranoid ecosystems, both are ideal ecosystem for agroforestry implementation because they have good meteorological conditions such as enough rainfall, rich soil, plentiful soil nutrients, and sufficient soil moisture retention capacity. Home gardens, multilayer tree gardens, plantation crop combinations, alley cropping, and remaining inter-cropping systems may all be done in the humid and subhumid lowlands. Small check dams, ponds will all helpful in these areas. In situ humidity preservation techniques including mulching, ridge, and furrow systems, zero tillage and strip cropping will be beneficial. These methods will save rainwater while also providing moisture to the crop for the next season. This technique will improve soil moisture, decrease soil erosion and nutritional loss, and may be used effectively in an agrisilvihorticulture system. Mangifera indica, Artocarpus heterophyllus, Syzygiumcumini, banana, papaya, and other fruit plants may be cultivated. The silvipastoral system may be used in the highlands with rouged ground.

CONCLUSION

This study utilized the GIS modeling concept by integrating serious gaming together. Game-based decision support system from various datasets and its logical evaluation in GIS domain greatly helps in decision-making. The government of India has adopted agroforestry policy realizing its potentiality. It is the first nation in the world to do so. Agroforestry has tremendous capacity to achieve sustainability in agriculture and allied sector while optimizing the land productivity to help poor and marginalized farmers suffering from climate change impact. Agroforestry is seen as a viable solution which can fulfill the demand of food, nutrition, energy, and employment and can protect our threatened environment. Our research for agroforestry decision support system using serious gaming will be of great help to the agro-forestry policy makers of India for extending the projects to new areas. This research shows the ability of geospatial technology as well as pooling of various themes of land, soil, climate, and topographic data, which can be brought within GIS domain. GIS modeling software has enormous scope to evaluate land potentiality in terms of its productivity for certain specific uses if integrated logically. There is a need to evaluate the land capacity for India at various levels (village, district, and state) utilizing the significant themes/layers/parameters which will greatly help in the growth of agroforestry crops.

This research on game-based approach for decision support in agroforestry will help farmers to experience the long-term advantages of agroforestry without actually doing it and just by playing a game that replicates visualization, intuitive management and analysis of geospatial, hydrologic and economic data in agroforestry systems. The serious game will provide virtual environment for decision making in agroforestry system. Use of geospatial data in this serious game provides such a complex information in such an easy and understandable manner that it may motivate people in the agroforestry practices. Serious games have promoted new and creative communication techniques to inform and engage participants with logical research. This research analyses that the productivity and engagement in agroforestry practices will increase through decision-making process using serious game.

FUTURE WORK

This research of geo spatially enabled agroforestry game shows that combination of geospatial data and agroforestry practice through serious gaming can provide good platform for the decision making in agroforestry systems. Based on recent literature and serious games for agroforestry we recommend that virtual reality serious gaming can provide more effective decision support for agroforestry systems in future as it is even more engaging and can have a deep impact on the users' mind.

REFERENCES

Adams, D. M., Mayer, R. E., MacNamara, A., Koenig, A., & Wainess, R. (2012). Narrative games for learning: Testing the discovery and narrative hypotheses. *Journal of Educational Psychology*, *104*(1), 235–249. doi:10.1037/a0025595

Ahmad, F., Uddin, M. M., & Goparaju, L. (2019). Agroforestry suitability mapping of India: A geospatial approach based on FAO guidelines. *Agroforestry Systems*, *93*(4), 1319–1336. doi:10.100710457-018-0233-7

Andrews, D. H., Hull, T. D., & Donahue, J. A. (2009). Storytelling as an Instructional Method: Definitions and Research Questions. *The Interdisciplinary Journal of Problem-Based Learning*, *3*(2), 10–26. doi:10.7771/1541-5015.1063

Backlund, P., Engstrom, H., Johannesson, M., & Lebram, M. (2010). Games for traffic education: An experimental study of a game-based driving simulator. *Simulation & Gaming*, *41*(2), 145–169. doi:10.1177/1046878107311455

Bernold, L. E., Spurlin, J. E., & Anson, C. M. (2007). Understanding our students: A longitudinal-study of success and failure in engineering with implications for increased retention. *Journal of Engineering Education*, *96*(3), 263–274. doi:10.1002/j.2168-9830.2007.tb00935.x

Blickenstaff, J. C. (2005). Women and science careers: Leaky pipeline or gender filter? *Gender and Education*, *17*(4), 369–386. doi:10.1080/09540250500145072

Dagar, J. C., & Tewari, V. P. (2017). Evoluation of agroforestry as modern science. In Agroforestry: Anecdotal to Modern Science. Springer Nature Singapore Pvt. Ltd.

Deshpande, A. A., & Huang, S. H. (2011). Simulation games in engineering education: A state-of-the-art review. *Computer Applications in Engineering Education*, *19*(3), 399–410. doi:10.1002/cae.20323

Devaranavadgi, S. B., Bassappa, S., Jolli, R.B, Wali, S.Y., & Bagali, A.N. (2013). Height-Age Growth Curve Modelling for Different Tree Species in Drylands of North Karnataka. *Global Journal of Science Frontier Research Agriculture and Veterinary Sciences*.

Devine, T. C. (2015). *Integrating Games into the Artworld: A Methodology and Case Study Exploring the Work of Jason Rohrer*. Games and Culture.

Dhyani, S. K., Newaj, R., & Sharma, A. R. (2009). Agroforestry: Its relation with agronomy, Challenges and opportunities. *Indian Journal of Agronomy*, *54*(3), 249–266.

Eck, R. (2006). Digital game-based learning: It's not just the digital natives that are restless. *EDUCAUSE Review*, *41*(2), 1–16.

Gee, J. P. (2004). *What video games have to teach us about learning and literacy*. Palgrave Macmillan.

Hoekstra, A. Y. (2012). Computer-supported games and role plays in teaching water management. *Hydrology and Earth Systems Sciences*, 2885-2994.

Johnson, W. L., & Wu, S. (2008). Assessing aptitude for learning with a serious game for foreign language and culture. *Proceedings of the ninth international conference on intelligent tutoring systems*. 10.1007/978-3-540-69132-7_55

Katsaliaki, K., &Mustafee, N. (2012). A survey of serious games on sustainable development. In *Proceedings of the 2012 Winter* (pp. 1-13). IEEE.

Levine, M. H. (2011, March 11). *Congress launches caucus for competitiveness in entertainment technology*. Retrieved from www.joanganzcooneycenter.org/cooney-center-blog-127.html

Levine, M. H., & Vaala, S. E. (2013). Games for learning: Vast wasteland or a digital promise? In F. C. Blumberg (Ed.), *New Directions for Child and Adolescent Development, no. 139* (pp. 71–82). doi:10.1002/cad.20033

Makumba, W., Akinnifesi, F. K., & Janssen, B. H. (2009). Spatial rooting patterns of gliricidia, pigeon pea and maize intercrops and effect on profile soil N and P distribution in southern Malawi. *African Journal of Agricultural Research*, *4*(4), 278–288.

Mayo, M. J. (2007). Games for science and engineering education. *Communications of the ACM*, *50*(7), 30–35. doi:10.1145/1272516.1272536

Misra, P. K. (2011). Soil Fertility Management in Agroforestry System. *International Journal of Biotechnology and Biochemistry, 7*(5), 637-644.

Nair, P. K. R. (1993). *An introduction to agroforestry*. Kluwer Academic Publishers. doi:10.1007/978-94-011-1608-4

Prensky, M. (2001). Digital natives, digital immigrants part 1. *On the Horizon, 9*(5), 1–6. doi:10.1108/10748120110424816

Resnick, M. (2012). Mother's Day, Warrior Cats, and Digital Fluency: Stories from the Scratch Online Community. *Proceedings of the Constructionism 2012 Conference.*

Rideout, V. J., Foehr, U. G., & Roberts, D. F. (2010). *Generation M^2: Media in the lives of 8 to 18 year olds. Henry J. Kaiser Family Foundation*. Henry J. Kaiser Family Foundation.

Rittel, H. W., & Webber, M. M. (1973). Dilemmas in a general theory of planning. *Policy Sciences, 4*(2), 155–169. doi:10.1007/BF01405730

Robertson, J., & Howells, C. (2008). Computer game design: Opportunities for successful learning. *Computers & Education, 50*(2), 559–578. doi:10.1016/j.compedu.2007.09.020

Romero, M., Usart, M., & Ott, M. (2014). Can Serious Games Contribute to Developing and Sustaining 21st Century Skills? *Games and Culture, 10*(2), 148–177. doi:10.1177/1555412014548919

Rusca, M., Huen, J., & Schwartz, K. (2012). Water management simulation games and the construction of knowledge. *Hydrology and Earth System Sciences, 16*(8), 2749–2757. doi:10.5194/hess-16-2749-2012

Schroth, G. (1999). A review of belowground interactions in agroforestry, focussing on mechanisms and management options. *Agroforestry Systems, 43*(1/3), 5–34. doi:10.1023/A:1026443018920

Schroth, G., & Sinclair, F. L. (2003). *Trees, crops and soil fertility concepts and research methods*. CABI Publishing.

Schultz, W. (2004). Neural coding of basic reward terms of animal learning theory, game theory, microeconomics and behavioural ecology. *Current Opinion in Neurobiology, 14*(2), 139–147. doi:10.1016/j.conb.2004.03.017 PMID:15082317

Seymour, E., & Hewitt, N. M. (1997). *Talking about leaving: Why undergraduates leave the sciences*. Westview Press.

Shaw, A. (2010). What Is Video Game Culture? Cultural Studies and Game Studies. *Games and Culture, 5*(4), 403–424. doi:10.1177/1555412009360414

Sherry, J. L., Lucas, K., Greenberg, B. S., & Lachlan, K. (2006). Video game uses and gratifications as predictors of use and game preference. In P. Vorderer & J. Bryant (Eds.), *Playing computer games: Motives, responses, and consequences* (pp. 213–224). Erlbaum.

Toppo, G. (2012). White House office studies benefits of video games. *USA Today.*

Väätänen, A., & Leikas, J. (2009). Human-Centered Design and Exercise Games: Users' Experiences of a Fitness Adventure Prototype. *Design and Use of Serious Games, 37*, 33–47. Available at: http://en.scientificcommons.org/41680703

Watson, W. R., Mong, C. J., & Harris, C. A. (2011). A case study of the in-class use of a video game for teaching high school history. *Computers & Education, 56*(2), 466–474. doi:10.1016/j.compedu.2010.09.007

Wikipedia. (n.d.). *Video game*. Available at: https://en.wikipedia.org/wiki/Video_game

Yang, S. (2010). Defining Exergames & Exergaming. *Proceedings of Meaningful Play*, 1–17. Available at: https://meaningfulplay.msu.edu/proceedings2010/mp2010_paper_63.pdf

Young, M. F., Slota, S., Cutter, A. B., Jalette, G., Mullin, G., Lai, B., & Yukhymenko, M. (2012). Our princess is in another castle: A review of trends in serious gaming for education. *Review of Educational Research, 82*(1), 61–89. doi:10.3102/0034654312436980

Chapter 20
A Framework for a Location–Specific Self–Adaptive Serious Game for Watershed Management

Sonali Beri
Dr. B. R. Ambedkar National Institute of Technology, Jalandhar, India

Arun Khosla
🆔 https://orcid.org/0000-0001-8571-7614
Dr. B. R. Ambedkar National Institute of Technology, Jalandhar, India

Girish S. Pujar
National Remote Sensing Centre, India

Parampreet Singh
Dr. B. R. Ambedkar National Institute of Technology, Jalandhar, India

ABSTRACT

Serious games are potential providers of education and are in trend nowadays as they are a combination of education and fun. There are various applications for it, and one of those is in the context of natural resource management. Water scarcity is an issue that is being witnessed nowadays all over the world. Annual water consumption is much more than that of groundwater recharge. To overcome such issues, a watershed can be an efficient approach leading towards groundwater replenishment and improving the quality of water, along with other benefits like preventing soil erosion, floods, etc. A GIS-based serious game for watershed management will be a good way to increase stakeholder participation in water resource conservation and management. Adding an extra element to this project can be beneficial. It is to make the game GIS or geospatially adaptive (i.e., a framework to be implemented to replicate the game to different locations without human intervention).

DOI: 10.4018/978-1-7998-9732-3.ch020

INTRODUCTION

Games are nowadays in trend as an alternating method of training and educating in a better way as compared to the older techniques. There are several applications which include the use of such games for education purposes like in as an illustrative game in medical fields, military, urban development planning, policy making, natural resource management, heritage learning, and the list remains countless. The games with such a goal are said to be serious games. These games have the capabilities to identify the vulnerabilities, better knowledge about a specific serious issue, helps in decision making, how to respond to a disaster, etc.

One such usage of serious games can be for the watershed management. Through the game the participants can learn how to manage a proper watershed just by playing the game. This will add on to their interest in management of the watershed and will make them know about the pros and cons of the decision they will take during the game.

Serious games are the games designed for purposes like education and not for entertainment as a primary goal. Like the games it has features like a gameplay story, rewards, punishments, etc. but also it includes knowledge providing element for a particular cause for which the game is being designed. These games provide a virtual environment for the players to learn about a specific activity without practising in the real-world scenario. The serious game will include watershed management as a purpose to be served. There is another added on element to the serious game for watershed management. That added on element is the ability of the serious game to alter itself according to the location chosen. This alteration and location selection both are the backend processes. The benefit of this framework would be for the designing part itself that the game can be altered quickly according to the location.

SERIOUS GAME

In our surroundings we have aspects with which we are not familiar to, most of the times. At times this unfamiliarity becomes an issue to cope up with the aspects and their upcoming results. Location based or geo based serious games can help in addressing such issues by providing a measure to explore new places with the serious gaming as a medium to it. This will make the players aware of what to do next. For an instance, we can look on an example by a game point of view, hide and seek. Imagine you are visiting an acquaintance's home and playing this game there. You start thinking about where to hide as soon as the countdown begins, hide under a bed, behind a sofa or a curtain. Can you just notice the fact that under a situation of this game play you are thinking of to hide behind a curtain but in normal situation would you do so? No, right, so this is just all in the influence of the game that you are eager to do so and your way of interacting with the surroundings around you changed. It is not strange to do so in context to the game. This is a way of the game to combine the rules, storyline and mechanics to just encourage the player to get involved in the game with keen potential to win it. Relating to this hide and seek game it provides imaginative skills to reach a new place or to just escape from one to another without getting caught. This forms a framework for the game and similarly, such frameworks can be applied to the games to make it include both the fun as well as an informative source for the player. This fun plus information element in a game forms the bases of a serious game. Serious games with several different motives can be designed which may provide an exposure to a place or a situation, giving a virtual first-hand experience which would not be possible otherwise. This first-hand experience to the players about the tasks being performed in the game can be of real help to them. Serious games need a key ingredient and an initial point to start with to enhance the participation of the players. Serious games for environmental management can enhances the understanding regarding the environmental issues by providing the opportunity to have first -hand experiences which otherwise in reality will be of much cost, difficult to re-correct it or even dangerous at times. Serious games-based learning increases the soft skills like thinking ability for critical situations, problem solving approach, creative solutions, better cognitive development, etc., these all skills are essential in efficient environment management. The serious games are getting in trend and are being progressively used for the governance of natural resources and environment. These games are getting in use for data collection, teaching and training the stakeholders.

New ways to look over a certain situation are provided by the serious games. There are certain issues pertaining in our society that needs proper attention and to make the public look over those very issues we need to opt for certain good examples. In this virtual era serious gaming can do a part to make people learn about the things and enjoying the game.

Serious Games for Disaster Management

The growth in the technology has made it possible for us to better foresee the risks related to the disasters and emerging technologies have enabled us to take preventive measures before-hand regarding an upcoming disaster. However, it has been seen in developing countries that the efficient scientific methods of disaster management do not always go in coordination with its implementation, as after several warnings and alerts people tend to stay in the exposed areas itself. For an example the super typhoon Haiyan (2005) in Philippines, because of lack of communicating the early alarms about the disaster made it the deadliest disaster in the records. According to the research the scale of danger could had been reduced if there was a proper communication with the locals and if they had been evacuated to safer places on time then there would have been lesser loss of lives taken place. So, even after knowing about the coming disaster, despite of early actions there has been losses due to various hazards like droughts, floods, tsunamis, etc. This scenario talks about a gap between the science based beforehand knowledge about the disaster and the practices and implementations to avoid the risks (Dekanter & Nick, 2005). The strategy making and decision taking by the government departments regarding the hazards is a traditional approach which is being followed. This top-down approach involving the authorities and not the locals is not an effective way to cope the hazards. To have an effective risk control communication and actions to be taken should include participation of local community as well as the authorities in proper coordination to fight back the hazard. To achieve this coordinated participation the people, need to be educated about the disaster risk management. The concept of serious games may help in serving this purpose by providing an interactive virtual environment and enhancing the participation for various issues like disaster management, management of watershed conservation, climatic control, etc. (Medema et al., 2019).

There will be artificially constructed scenarios governed by some rules and storyline resulting in quantified outcomes. The game play utilises the person's thinking ability in the most natural and creative manner to learn facilely. The players must take decisions, see the outcomes, and learn from them. There may be immediate feedbacks given to the players making them fully involved in the game. It is a human tendency to learn more by the experiences and exposures and serious games making it practically possible to do so. Learning with participation and involvement is potentially more powerful in retention process as compared to the traditional learning methods. Also, in studies it can be seen that practical learning results in better retention (say about 75%) whereas the traditional methods of learning conclude 5-7% information holding. In the traditional methods the learning is all about memorizing and the serious games will focus on deep understanding and proper involvement in the domain (Medema et al., 2019). The existence of serious games can be in any of the forms like a mobile application, a web-based game, mashup of social software, or a computer game, having a purpose of creating a virtual interactive environment.

The games with specific role play allow the player to perform the roles of disaster manager or a planner or a decision maker. There is a game known as Disaster Imagination Game where the players are appointed persons of the virtually created commanding post for relief activities. The several recorded details on the map help in identifying the vulnerable spaces and the ways to have the relief activities. In another game known as Evacuation Challenge Game the player performs as a member of evacuation team and locals affected by the disaster and needs to be evacuated. In the game the participants must go through the information, help the needy with mobility services or health or other related services. The main objective of such games consisting of a role play is to enhance their knowledge about the topic and letting them to explore various elements which they would not think of it the other ways.

These location-based or geo games are an enhancing parameter in the serious games. Again, if we look the hide and seek game and you are playing this at your friend's place and your task be either hiding or seeking the other people you will have to rethink about the landscape of the place. A sofa is no longer a thing to sit on for you as in your mind you will be thinking if somebody is hiding behind or not. Thus, it makes you look at things differently with new lenses on and not just a standard view. Every location comes with a different landscape and provides a different view and if we can have this self-adapting of the location's landscape, we choose in the serious gaming background then it will be of real help. Games in such a context along with the game play, story line and mechanics will enhance the players participation more.

Serious Game for Watershed Management

Serious games as an application for natural resource management can be used for a watershed management. Watershed management focus on issues like water conservation, replenishment of ground water, reduce soil erosion, better vegetation and with many other benefits to society. There are factors over which the watershed depends on, and it is classified in the sections ahead. The game based on watershed has a DEM of a place at which the game is being designed. Like, starting with a game with a DEM of a particular location which is a backend work which includes higher and lower elevation, having a view to a waterbody, settlements around it and so on.

Then in the story line we can have a budget, a timeline, a success bar, and finally in results we can see the consequences of what we did. There is game based on this known as Stop Disaster Game. In this game is divided in various scenarios like different disasters and terrains are there for which the game is designed. For instance, for southeast Asia the game is designed on tsunami and the terrain is coastal village, in another variation for eastern Mediterranean the terrain is lowland hills, and the disaster is the earthquake. The game is divided among three difficulty levels i.e., easy, medium, and hard. The game starts with an introduction to the mission and providing a challenge say to provide accommodation to N number of people before the tsunami hits the coastal area. It provides various housing and other related equipment that could be brought up in use to fix the issue. In the game a specific budget is being provided and the tasks are to be performed in specific given time and taking in consideration the risk factor. This is how a serious game with a storyline will help the government officials and even the locals to look for the alternative and helpful ways to cope up with such disasters.

In similar ways a serious game for watershed management can be designed. The design parameters be like the terrain (keeping in mind the ridge to valley concept), the budget, the various methods for watershed like planting a small pond, a check dam, etc. There is another important constraint related to it is time, as serious games are real based games and time is an important factor.

Then comes a possibility to design a game from already designed game for a particular DEM. In this process the backend work would reduce as the designer will already know that how the game is to be adjusted. Those adjustments could be made just by analyses of various watersheds and the factors affecting the watershed. There should be some mechanism to alter these changes by itself when the game designer just changes the DEM in the backend of the game. This backend process will reduce the time span for the development of the serious game on watershed management for different locations. Further we will be looking for the steps that are involved to be worked on to make the game self-adaptive to the location. Such a designed game can make it more realistic and learnable to have achieve the goals accordingly. In this chapter we are going to look over this self-adapting serious game according to the location. This could be done with the help of Artificial Intelligence. Other parameters involving in such type of game are the factors that change with the change in location for the watershed. The GIS components are further fed to some machine learning algorithms to train it to specify the location. Then this specified location will be shown with the help of the gaming end.

Benefits of Serious Game for Watershed Management

The watershed management needs proper planning before its implementation. The game will be beneficial for the government officials and even for the stakeholders. This will help the stakeholders to have an experience in virtual formed world. The watershed management consumes a lot of time and money. So, one step wrong and it becomes difficult to alter the damage. To avoid any such condition serious games can play a part by providing a virtual environment for the stakeholders and make them conveniently familiar to the watershed management. It will add one step closer to the realisation of an efficient watershed and its management. Also, it will educate the locals about the watershed and its benefits. Such a game will help in narrowing the participation gap for the watershed management of both the stakeholders as well as the locals. Though the local community participation may only hold a small amount of potential when it comes to decision making but these steps need to involve the locals as the benefits would be coming to them and it will create more employment possibilities.

GIS-Based Serious Game

The approach that combines the game design with the GIS engine so that the serious game can adjust itself according to the GIS data (Cheng et al., 2011) GIS being a professional thing to cope with the spatial data that is related to a particular location and its combination with the gaming engine will help in reducing the problems and difficulties that arrive while developing the geospatial game. The serious game engine model and its connection with GIS engine can be seen in the Figure 1.

In the combination of gaming engine with the GIS, the GIS engine gives the spatial data to the game engine through the GIS game interface module which acts as an interface between both engines. The gaming engine can work directly with the terrain data and may not require the map data. To have a smooth working of the interface and hardware there is a need of game graphic engine. The GIS engine will only be the provider for the map data, but the game engine will process it and upload it. The artificial intelligence added in the game will make the game more interactive. The sound effect engine will influence in the generation of the interest of the players.

Figure 1. GIS and serious game

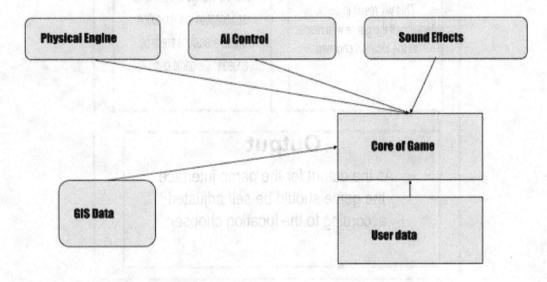

FRAMEWORK FOR THE SERIOUS GAME TO ALTER THE GAME OBJECTS AUTOMATICALLY

A layered model is required as the framework for such a game. While the already available games are based on a specific GIS model. The existing models relating to such games are wholly based on a specific code. For this model implementation we need to look for alternating methods that can be brought up in practise that will ensure in easy game design and quick changes can be brought up in the game just by changing the DEM. The GIS data is an essential requirement for the game.

Say if a game is already designed for a specific GIS but we want to design it for another GIS location. Though we can design the game all over again from the very start. But how if we can conclude a framework to redesign the game to a new location in certain steps itself. For a GIS game we will be having a DEM as the base. For a self-changing game, we need proper set of data related to a DEM say how much ground water recharge is available here, hydrology of the location, topography, terrain, elevation, etc. For instance, to finalize what kind of structure is required for a catchment area all such details are required. Say if the area is with more slope, then the structure to be used will be a check dam and areas for lesser slopes can have farm ponds as the structures. This all is to be done by the artificial intelligence and having the output as a self-adjusted game.

Figure 2. Framework of concept

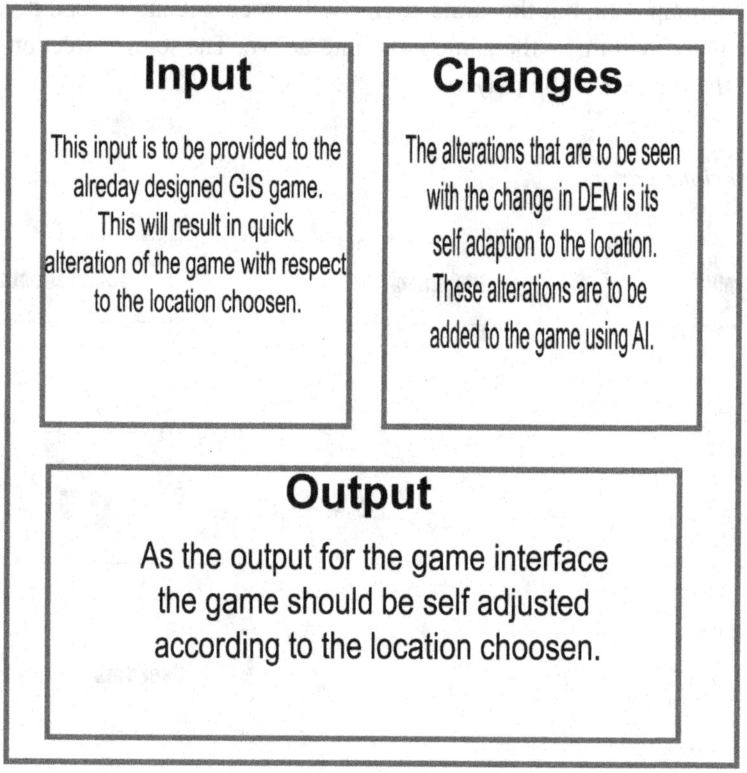

Input

This input is to be provided to the alreday designed GIS game. This will result in quick alteration of the game with respect to the location choosen.

Changes

The alterations that are to be seen with the change in DEM is its self adaption to the location. These alterations are to be added to the game using AI.

Output

As the output for the game interface the game should be self adjusted according to the location choosen.

In the Figure 3 the framework can be modelled as:

- The input to the AI model is the DEM, Hydrology, Flow direction, classified images, different watershed structures and where to use those structures, data about the junctions, outlets, etc.
- Once the AI model is trained, it will process this data when provided with a test DEM and as an output it will provide features related to the DEM that will be helpful in designing a game scene.
- For instance, by looking over the test DEM it can be resulted out that what kind of watershed structure and where to be placed will be beneficial for that respective DEM.
- This knowledge regarding the DEM for which the game will be designed will be helpful and make the game self-adaptive by just changing those features in the game scene.
- So, this concludes that the output of AI model will become the input to the gaming software (UNITY) and will help in realising a location specific self-adaptive serious game for watershed management.

Figure 3. Model for game to be self-adaptive

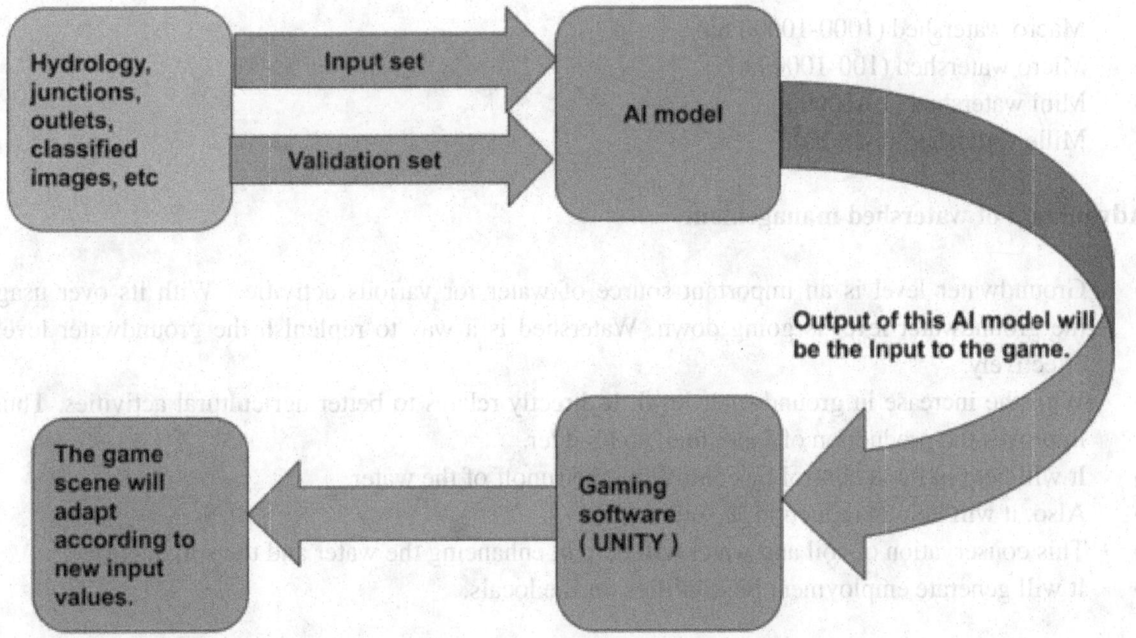

For instance, to finalize what kind of structure is required for a catchment area all such details are required. Say if the area is with more slope, then the structure to be used will be a check dam and areas for lesser slopes can have farm ponds as the structures. This all is to be done by the artificial intelligence and having the output as a self-adjusted game.

WATERSHED

Watershed is an area where all the streams and precipitation are drained to a common outlet, for instance a reservoir, a bay, or any point along a stream channel. The size of a watershed can be anything from as small as a footprint or large enough to hold all the water.

At times, 'watershed' as a word is interchanged with a catchment or a drainage basin. The separation of two watersheds by the ridges and hills is known as a drainage divide. The watershed comprises of water from surface (lakes, streams, rivers), wetlands, and the groundwater. The large size watersheds consist of many small watersheds into them. Watersheds are of great importance as stream flow and water's quality and quantity of a river is being affected at much higher extent by humans ("Watersheds and Drainage Basin," 2019). Watershed is a precipitation collector that collects all the precipitation that falls within the drainage area.

Watershed Classification

The watershed can be classified according to the size, shape, drainage patterns and land use patterns.

Watershed classification based on the size:

- Macro watershed (1000-10000 ha)
- Micro watershed (100-1000 ha)
- Mini watershed (10-100 ha)
- Mille watershed (1-10 ha)

Advantages of watershed management:

- Groundwater level is an important source of water for various activities. With its over usage the groundwater level is going down. Watershed is a way to replenish the groundwater levels effectively.
- With the increase in groundwater level, it directly relates to better agricultural activities. Thus, improves the production of food, fuel, and fodder.
- It will help in flood control by controlling the runoff of the water.
- Also, it will help in reduction of soil erosion.
- This conservation of soil and water will help in enhancing the water and the soil quality.
- It will generate employment possibilities for the locals.

Factors which Affect the Watershed Management

- **Watershed characters:**
  - Size and shape of the watershed: the shape of the watershed effects the speed of runoff of water with which it reaches the outlet for an example the long thin catchment takes longer time to drain s compared to the circular shaped catchment. Though basin shape is not directly included in the hydrology design method. There is an infinite number of shapes that a watershed can have and is just a way to look on the runoff towards the outlet point. For instance, an elliptical shaped watershed with the outlet at one end of the major axis compared to a circular watershed with the same size in area would result in spread out runoff over time and thereby, concluding a smaller flood peak in comparison to the circular watershed. Size contributes to the amount of water reaching the outlet, the greater potential for flooding is related to the larger size of the catchment.
  - Topography: it contributes to determining the speed related to the runoff with which it will reach the outlet. For instance, in steep mountainous areas the rain will reach the primary waterbody in the watershed faster as compared to the lightly sloped or flat areas.
  - Slope: the slope of watershed is seen effecting the momentum of the runoff, also, the channel and the watershed slope are both are matter of concern. The rate of change of elevation in contract to the distance with the flow path is shown by the watershed slope. Usually, it is calculated as the elevation difference between the endpoints of the main flowing path which is divided by the length.
- **Climatic characteristics:**
  - Precipitation: The precipitation that flows in the watershed may be either as rain or snow is an important factor playing role in controlling the stream flow. But most likely not all the

water falling the watershed flow out, and as result of it the stream will continue to flow with no direct contact with the recent precipitation.

○ Amount and intensity of rainfall: the amount of rainfall contributes to the flow of waterbodies in the watershed and directly relates to the water stored as groundwater. This amount of rainfall is different for different geographic locations.

• **Water resources and their capabilities:** The hydrology of a place is an essential factor for the watershed. The hydrology of a place consists of various orders of waterbodies. The hydrology is also divided in the categories depending over the age of the waterbody i.e., young, mature, or old. Also, the rivers are categorised as a perennial river or a seasonal river. This categorisation of the waterbodies results in differences in their capabilities.

• **Land use pattern:** Watershed contributes to betterment of various elements like the forests, wetlands, coastal resources, agriculture, and localities.

○ Vegetation cover: In any watershed the vegetation cover is an essential landscape. There can be diversity in the vegetation species across a watershed.

○ Density: Density can be calculated by the total length of all waterbodies in a drainage basin which is to be divided by the total drainage basin area. It reflects that how well/ badly the watershed is drained by the channels. The river' shape is affected by the drainage density during a rainstorm. A high drainage density will usually have a flashy hydrography with steep limb (Olais, 2014).

Figure 4. Factors affecting watershed management

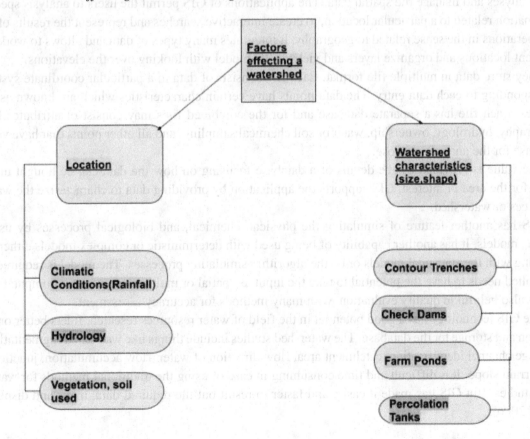

These factors vary from location to location. This variability in such factors for different geo spatial locations are going to make the whole difference for the serious game to be self-adapting to the location chosen.

Say for an example the hydrology is different for different locations and over this the watershed depends directly. Also, the cropping system is different. Also, the benefits achieved by a particular arrangement for watershed management will vary according to the location.

There is another concept which is important for the watershed management and is to be included in the game i.e., Ridge to Valley concept. The ridge to valley concept for watershed is one of the most worthwhile options to ensure optimized benefits and outcomes from the watershed. It is a scientific approach to cope with the degraded area under watershed. Watershed development is to be taken in regard from topmost point from where the precipitation begins to flow in downward direction. The topmost point is called the ridge and from that ridge point it starts flowing down towards the valley. This makes the consumption of each drop falling to its worth.

Further, going to look on the GIS components for the watershed management.

GIS FOR WATERSHED MANAGEMENT

Geographic Information Systems refers to the databases that relate to a spatial component for storing and processing the data. They are potential enough for storage and creation of map products. Also, multiple analyses could be performed using these systems. GIS is a system designed to store, capture, manipulate, analyses and manage the spatial data. The applications of GIS permit the users to analysis special information related to a particular location, to create interactive searches and represent the results of all the operations in the sense related to geography. It integrates many types of data and allows to work on different locations and organize layers and view its 3D model with looking over the elevations.

They store data in multiple file format. Each file consists of data in a particular coordinate system corresponding to each data entry. The data points have certain characteristics which are known as attributes. Each file has a separate database and for the combined files may consist of attributes like topography, hydrology, ownership, water or soil chemical sampling, and all other points that have valid response for the analysis purpose.

The value is provided by the details of a database focusing on how the data can be bought up in usage for the area of interest. GIS supports the application by providing data to characterize the water resources or watershed.

GIS has another feature of simulating the physical, chemical, and biological processes by using various models. It has another capability of being used with deterministic or complex models either by applying with the statistical models or by the algorithm simulating processes. The model is required to be applied needs to have the potential to take the input as spatial or multiple file data for computation. GIS is also helpful in quality evaluation, with many methods for accuracy assessment.

The GIS technology has a good potential in the field of water resources research. It lets better organization and storage for the database. The watershed studies include things like watershed segmentation, drainage channel identification, catchment area, flow direction of water, flow accumulation, junctions, and terrain slope. It is difficult and time consuming in case of using the traditional methods for watershed studies. But GIS has made it easier and faster to result out the required data, maps and displays (Gale, 2006).

DEM

The main purpose in this section is to process a Digital Elevated Model (DEM) and have rapid and automated evaluated results about the properties of a watershed. The input here will be a DEM over which the whole work would be done. The test DEM taken for the processing purpose is of around location having latitude and longitude coordinates as 30.975254, 76.527328. The DEM is taken from Bhuvan. The location chosen is so that it can support the ridge valley concept which is important for an efficient watershed. The processing of the DEM is done on the software QGIS. It is a free and an open-source software that provides the platform for viewing, editing, analysis of the geo spatial data.

Figure 5. DEM of test area

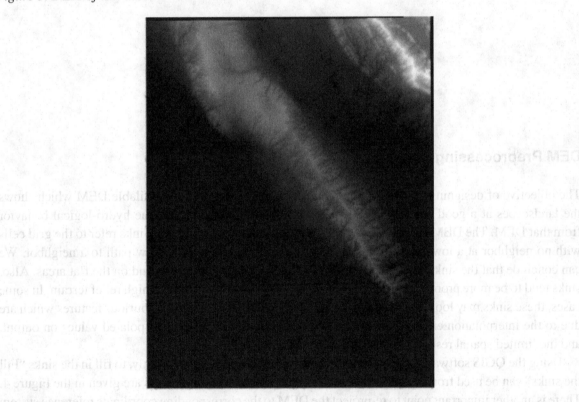

Figure 6. 3D view of DEM

DEM Preprocessing

The objective of designing of a DEM is to emphasize the analysis of the available DEM which shows the landscapes at a good resolution to provide the opportunity to extract the hydro-logical behavior from that DEM. The DEMs usually have problems of sinks present in them. Sinks refer to the grid cells with no neighbor at a lower elevation and resulting with no down-slope flow path to a neighbor. We can conclude that the sinks can be present over both the closed depressions and on the flat areas. Also, sinks tend to be more prominent in the low relief areas as compared to that in high relief terrain. In some cases, these sinks may look like real landscape but in majority cases it is the spurious features which are due to the interpolation errors while generation of DEM, truncation of interpolated values on output, and the limited spatial resolution of the DEM grid.

Using the QGIS software for the whole processing of GIS being done. Firstly, to fill in the sinks "Fill the sinks" can be used from the processing toolbox. The results of the process are given in the Figure 4. There is another important point to re-project the DEM to the corresponding coordinate reference system (CRS) to have proper function. There is a 3D view of the test area DEM in the Figure 5.

Drainage Network

Using the "Strahler Order" the stream/ drainage pattern can be produced. The streams can be of different orders as specified in the Figure 6. The different orders represent that how big the water body is, like the order 1 stream is smaller in size as compared to order 2 which is formed by the combination of the two or more 1 order stream, and this goes on. In the Figure 8 the darker blue lines represent the higher order stream, and the lighter blue colour represents the smaller order water body.

Figure 7. Different order waterbodies

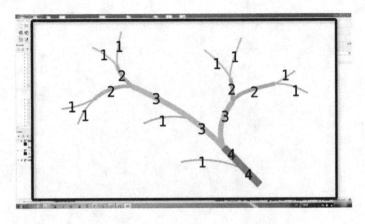

Figure 8. Delineation

Figure 9. Different order channels

This further can be seen on the base map as well. Also, in the attribute table (Figure 9) related to the channel network the order and the length of the water body is specified. This whole process of highlighting the hydrology in the test DEM is known as 'Delineation' as in Figure 7. This process of delineating the channel network of a DEM is important for a proper watershed management.

Figure 10. Attribute table for channels

Channels — Features Total: 4667, Filtered: 4667, Selected: 0

	SEGMENT_ID	NODE_A	NODE_B	BASIN	ORDER	ORDER_CELL	LENGTH
610	610	636	631	23	1	5	214.1993024100
611	611	633	642	23	2	6	115.5614418800
612	612	639	567	23	2	6	1392.0463738000
613	613	637	657	33	1	5	1536.4981761000
614	614	640	621	23	4	8	285.9999771800
615	615	638	693	23	1	5	752.3520940800
616	616	643	667	33	1	5	1758.5579083000
617	617	644	640	23	1	5	69.7475000660
618	618	641	645	23	2	6	28.8903604690
619	619	646	635	23	1	5	192.3189188600
620	620	647	730	23	1	5	1082.1128384000
621	621	642	700	23	3	7	791.1560589800
622	622	645	659	23	2	6	353.6943025400
623	623	648	639	23	1	5	336.7707212000
624	624	650	630	23	5	9	702.4318028700
625	625	649	642	23	2	6	512.1660587200
626	626	651	657	33	1	5	110.6046396600
627	627	653	604	23	1	5	865.8603612600
628	628	652	708	33	3	7	723.4617336100
629	629	655	639	23	1	5	238.1328606700
630	630	656	649	23	1	5	69.7475000660
631	631	658	667	33	1	5	122.5714187900
632	632	654	668	26	2	6	827.9068491700
633	633	662	650	23	5	9	151.4617792600
634	634	666	664	23	3	7	168.3853606000

Figure 11. Junctions

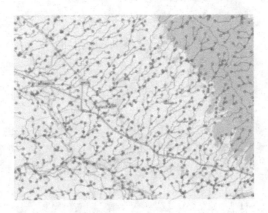

Figure 12. Attribute table for junctions

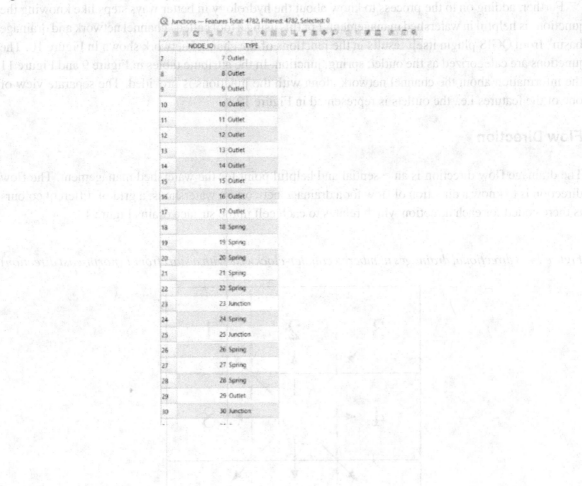

Figure 13. Outlets in the DEM

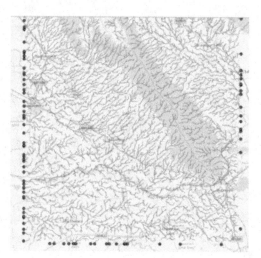

Further, adding on to the process to know about the hydrology in better ways steps like knowing the junctions is helpful in watershed management. For this using a tool called "channel network and drainage basin" from QGIS plugin itself results in the junctions of the channel network shown in Figure 10. The junctions are categorized as the outlet, spring, junction. In the attribute tables in Figure 9 and Figure 11 the information about the channel network along with the junctions is provided. The separate view of one of the features i.e., the outlets is represented in Figure 12.

Flow Direction

The drainage flow direction is an essential and helpful point for the watershed management. The flow direction is to know a direction of flow for a drainage network or watersheds, a grid of different colours is there coded for each direction which relates to each cell in the surface drains Figure 13.

Figure 14. 8 directional drainages numbered counter-clockwise with a start from 1 (north-east direction)

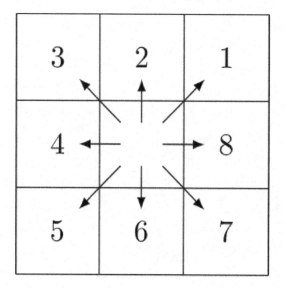

The direction in degrees could be achieved by multiplication of the positive values by 45 which will correspond to the surface run off that will travel from the cell. The 0 (zero) value relates to the depression area of the cell which is defined by the depression input map. The depression is basically the map of sinkholes in the landscape which are large enough to slow down and store the surface runoff from a storm event. The surface runoff which is leaving the boundaries of the current geographic region is indicated by the negative value the direction flow for these negative cells in indicated by the absolute values of the respective negative cell.

For the test DEM, the flow direction is being concluded by different colours corresponding to the different bands. The band range for the test DEM is from to (Figure 14). the corresponding colours for the different bands could be seen in the fig14. For the test DEM the zoomed in image could be seen in fig 15.

Figure 15. Different colour for different bands

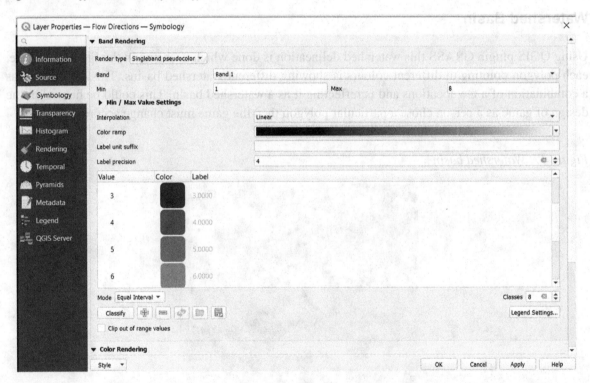

Figure 16. Zoomed in view for flow direction

Watershed Basin

Using QGIS plugin GRASS this watershed delineation is done which is shown in the Figure 16. Here, each polygon pointing to different colours is showing different watershed basins. This can be said as a combination of a few locations and is reflecting it as a watershed basin. This could be helpful in the design of game as a person chose a particular polygon then the game must change accordingly.

Figure 17. Watershed basin

Image Classification

This particular step is important in terms of identifying various classes in a particular image, i.e., the classification of the settlement areas, vegetation area, waterbody, etc. This is shown in the Figure 17 (but the image is not of the same location already used in the examples above). There have been three different classes for the exampled image. Using a machine learning algorithm called as decision tree the results were acquired. Result of image classification by decision tree came out with an accuracy of 88.5%.

In similar conditions by taking a satellite image of different locations can be used to make the training and the validation sets according to the different classes that we can visualise in the image. Further, image classification can be done using different machine learning algorithms. This can be done by using a QGIS plugin known as Orfeo Toolbox (OTB).

Figure 18. Classified image

CRITICAL PERSPECTIVE IN DESIGNING SUCH A GAME

The serious game for watershed management with adaptability to different locations has a critical point in its design which is to collect a good amount of data to have this design. This game is to be developed and deployed with the goal of educating the stakeholders for their awareness, inquiry, and their engagement in the watershed management. Also, a specific GIS location-based game is different from automatically location adaptive games. These games are to change according to the DEM in a faster way and not involving the whole designing again from the start. Say, if we change the DEM in the backend then the game changes accordingly, having alterations in the elevations, waterbodies or say hydrology, the consequences of the watershed arrangements would change, the structures to be used will change, and so on. For such a game it is essential to take in consideration the impact of the game on the participants of the game. This is an important factor the designers and players as well who will be involved in the game with different places and cultures as outsiders. It will be providing a thorough knowledge in context to the watershed. Such a game would not only be focusing on the locals but anybody who plays it would get to know that how the watershed management requires changes according to the change in the location and signifies that it can't be same for all the places.

Few critical steps that can be involved in the designing of the game includes:

- Keeping in mind the factors related to multiplication of places.

- Considering a proper reflective design and play of game that could be related to the places being chosen.
- Keeping in mind that this serious game will be helping the stakeholders to increase their active and efficient participation. For that the introduction to the game should be provided accordingly.
- Activation of various learning can be added on to the watershed management by showing how it can be beneficial in other activities.

SOFTWARE TO RELATE THE GIS DATA AND THE GAME ENGINE

- ArcGIS: City Engine by ArcGIS is a modelling software with advanced properties to convert a DEM directly into a game scene for Unity. Using this 3D models can be designed by using the satellite images and 3D terrain. There is a plugin in ArcGIS called as ArcGIS Maps SDK which enables direct access of the ArcGIS data to the gaming engine. City Engine allows users to create a very realistic model of the terrain based on real map data like DEM, OSM map, satellite map etc. It also allows the user to modify the 3d models in City Engine only so that the output product is finished to be used directly in unity without any modifications. The only demerit of City Engine by ArcGIS is that it is not an open-source software.
- Google SketchUp: Another modelling software through which we can easily design a 3D model for games is google SketchUp. Here also we can upload the DEM and get a game scene. As SketchUp is designed for 3d modelling, we can use the DEM and modify it in any way, add any kinds of buildings, trees roads etc. to give it a very realistic look. Unlike City Engine, SketchUp cannot understand itself from other map data like satellite data or OSM data. All the modelling must be done by the user itself.
- UNITY plugin Gaia: It is plugin in UNITY which is powerful enough to generate terrain and scene in few minutes. An example of a game scene generated by using Gaia from a DEM is shown in the Figure 19. A DEM is used as a base for this scene created and Gaia itself converts into a game scene by placing different objects randomly. The upper portion in the figure is showing Game design view and the lower portion represents the game view as is visible to the gamer. The DEM is imported in Unity by converting it into .raw format in photoshop. We cannot import .hgt file directly in Unity. Before converting to RAW file, QGIS can be used to carry out minor modifications in the DEM like cropping it.

Figure 19. Game scene using Gaia: A UNITY plugin

- Blender: We can do similar work using blender also with its plugin known as blender GIS which merges different kinds of map data and produces the result as a game scene. Its other functions include managing a scene's georeferencing information, creating a terrain mesh using Delaunay triangulation, placing items on a terrain mesh, doing terrain analysis using shader nodes, creating new cameras from geotagged pictures, and rendering a new georeferenced raster with Blender. We can add maps from google, OSM map data, satellite data and SRTM height map data and use them for modelling of a scene.

CONCLUSION AND FUTURE WORK

There arises another question that motivation for the idea may be good but how can the idea growth be facilitated? Though the idea of combining this self-adaption method with a designed GIS specific serious game for watershed seems to be effective once deployed. But how to gain that effectiveness, what path is to be led to gain traction? A game which will be adapting easily according to the DEM chosen will be advantageous in increasing the stakeholder participation. Also, it can help in proper implementation of a watershed and resulting it to be a success story.

When a watershed is being constructed various factors are to be focused on and that too on priority bases as any alternation in the work done will cost too much and at times it even becomes difficult to alter the defaults. Thereby, such a serious game would prove to be an effective experience provider to the people involved in the watershed management. The locally focused design of the game would even help in enhancing the local participation as their interest would increase to know better about their own location.

The growth in this idea can be broadly divided into three area i.e., platforms, frameworks, and community. In the first very area of platforms, more platforms are needed that can make the nonprogrammers even to build a design of such a media. As generally the game designing platforms like UNITY require C sharp for scripting the game. At least a few of such platforms should be designed which are free of such content. Also, the platform for GIS is also needed to be understood that how to bring it in use. Framework is needed to be worked upon to model a game with the required results. The whole idea of making a game with self-adapting nature depends on the framework that how convenient it is to be brought in actual practice. There exists a challenge of how to use the framework to design a quality game with proper functioning for such an application. For the game to be of diverse nature there is a need to bring in the community perspective in this research field. For the future work a good amount of data is required to train the model so that this whole concept can be brought in practise.

REFERENCES

Cheng, Z., Hao, F., Jianyou, Z., & Yun, S. (2011, January). *Research on Design of Serious Game based on GIS*. doi:10.1109/CAIDCD.2010.5681365

Dkanter, N. (2005). Gaming Redefines Interactivity for Learning. In ERIC (pp. 26-33). doi:10.1007/BF02763644

Gale, I. N. (2006). *Managed Aquifer Recharge: Lessons Learned from The Agrar Study*. Academic Press.

Jaiswal, D. (n.d.). *Watershed Management: Meaning, Types, Steps and Programmes*. https://www.yourarticlelibrary.com/watershed-management/watershed-management-meaning-types-steps-and-programmes/77309

Medema, W., Mayor, I., Adamowaski, J., & Wals, C. (2019). *The Potential of Serious Games to Solve Water Problems: Editorial to the Special Issue on Game-Based Approaches to Sustainable Water Governance*. https://www.hindawi.com/journals/ijcgt/2014/358152/

Olais, R. (2014, March 6). *Factors Affecting Watershed Management and Amount of Water*. https://prezi.com/ad_lxddphop-/factors-affecting-watershed-management-and-amount-of-water/

Sen, J., & Vaghasia, D. (n.d.). *Ridge to valley Approach in Watershed Experience of Teliamba Village of AKRSP, Netrang*. http://www.dscindia.org/dwnld.php?path=dXBsb2FkL3BkZi9wdWJsaWNhdGlvbnMv&filename=Ridgetovalleywatershed.pdf

SketchUp. (2021, January 16). In *Wikipedia*. https://en.wikipedia.org/wiki/SketchUp

Susi, T., Johannesson, M., & Backlund, P. (2007). *Serious games: An Overview*. Academic Press.

Watersheds and Drainage Basin. (2019, June 8). *Water Science School*. https://www.usgs.gov/special-topics/water-science-school/science/watersheds-and-drainage-basins

Chapter 21
Multiplayer Game–Based Language Learning

Sam Redfern
Newby Chinese Ltd., Ireland

Richard McCurry
Newby Chinese Ltd., Ireland

ABSTRACT

In this chapter, the authors discuss the Newby Chinese game-based learning (GBL) platform for group-based teaching of beginners Mandarin Chinese as a second language. Details are provided on the design of games within the platform, the pedagogical theories which they support, and the ways that theories of fun and teaching intersect to produce an effective learning experience which students actually enjoy. While aspects of the games within the platform have been designed to specifically support modern Chinese-learning pedagogy, the approaches taken and lessons learned should be useful for a range of GBL content. Newby Chinese has been used by thousands of students over the last three years, and its continued development has been informed by this practical experience.

INTRODUCTION

This chapter provides a practice-based and theory-based exploration of co-located multiplayer Game Based Learning (GBL) as a way of supporting the nuanced requirements of learning Chinese as a second language (CSL). It explores and develops modern pedagogies for teaching Mandarin Chinese. It discusses the various games within the Newby Chinese platform, including an exposition of how they support effective language learning and practice of the various skills required by language learners. Throughout the chapter, there is a particular focus on the strengths of co-located and collaborative multiplayer as a gaming paradigm for GBL, and on how games can be effectively designed to make use of it.

Chinese is well known to be a very difficult language for non-native speakers (and indeed, Chinese writing is difficult even for native Chinese children). The difficulty emanates not from its simple grammar, but the pictorial or logo syllabic system of writing, which has thousands of complex characters.

DOI: 10.4018/978-1-7998-9732-3.ch021

Because "it is still early days in the field of CSL" (Orton & Scrimgeour, 2019, p.12), and "although the visual complexity of the Chinese writing system has been widely recognized in the literature, little is known about the units of character perception or how insight into the architecture of Chinese characters develops in children" (Anderson at al., 2013, p.41). Thus the core architecture and many of the games in Newby Chinese are specifically designed to study and support this emerging field of Chinese-learning pedagogy, drawing on recent approaches by Orton, Shu, Anderson, and others (e.g. Anderson at al., 2013; Orton 2016a, 2016b; Orton & Scrimgeour, 2019). However, its approach and games could be successfully applied to other languages as it focuses on vocabulary, sentence construction, listening and speaking. From a GBL perspective, Newby Chinese focuses very much on the motivational strengths inherent in social (multiplayer) learning environments - including direct competition, visual (avatar) rewards, and the social pressure to perform well for the sake of success of one's team.

BACKGROUND

Gamification

Gamification is the use of game elements and design techniques in non-game contexts; it seeks to promote both intrinsic and extrinsic motivation in the task at hand, through concepts such as scores, leaderboards, and badges (Werbach & Hunter, 2012). Intrinsic motivation refers to internal motivation: the desire to improve on your own previous attempts; extrinsic motivation refers to external motivation: the desire to out-perform other people and to have your achievements visible to them (Werbach & Hunter, 2012). While the term "gamification" was coined in 2002, its use in education first started to appear in the literature in 2011 (Caponetto at al., 2014). It has been well established that the gamification of education is gaining support among educators who recognize that effectively designed games can stimulate large gains in productivity and creativity among learners (Johnson at al., 2014).

While gamification focuses explicitly on rewards and goals, it does not focus specifically on other sources of fun. While it may provide the internal and the extrinsic motivation discussed above (which suits some personality types – e.g. Bartle *achievers* or *killers*; Bartle, 1996), it does little to leverage the power of social pressure and cooperation (which much better suits Bartle *socialisers*). A wider definition of GBL requires that play and learning activities are intimately linked; that games are designed to incorporate learning activities *within* them – as opposed to using game techniques in *non-game* contexts.

GAME BASED LEARNING

Game Based Learning (GBL) is the use of games for learning, in which explicit pedagogical goals as well as explicit entertainment and engagement goals have been considered in the game design – it is a learning strategy focused on achieving the particular objectives of given educational content through game play (Kim et al., 2009). GBL progresses far beyond the simple reward mechanisms of gamification, and can provide a range of learning outcomes in a variety of paradigms including behaviourist through to constructivist (Whitten, 2011). Behaviourist learning focuses on drill-and-response practice, while in Constructivist learning students construct their own knowledge via direct experience in problem solving and collaborative work (Behlol & Dad, 2010).

One of the most well established and enduring theories of engagement is that of *flow* (Nakamura & Csikszentmihalyi, 2014). Flow refers to a state of deep engagement in an activity which is intrinsically enjoyable, and people in a state of flow report their actions to be successful and pleasurable, and the activity at hand to be worth doing for its own sake, regardless of higher goals. Flow is achieved by providing a challenge which matches well to the player's skill level – thereby avoiding boredom (where the player is under-challenged) or frustration (where the player is over-challenged). Thus, flow runs deep in many aspects of modern game design – be it analogue or digital; purely entertainment focused or GBL focused; singleplayer or multiplayer. It is flow that allows the goals of pedagogy, engagement and entertainment to be integrated successfully in a GBL experience.

For many years, studies have indicated that GBL offers a variety of benefits to second language (L2) learners – including possibilities for collaboration and meaningful interaction, vocabulary acquisition, reduced anxiety and a willingness to communicate (Poole & Clarke-Midura, 2020).

Researchers have also focused on task-based language learning (TBLL) – the central argument being that functional tasks are fundamental to L2 learners, despite traditional classroom teaching which focuses on the practice of discrete linguistic or grammatical components (York & deHaan, 2018). TBLL requires that learners undertake meaningful communication rather than mere rote-learning and repetition; it provides higher-level goals which may be achieved through meaningful communication in the target language rather than the use of discrete linguistic elements (Ellis, 2003).

COLLABORATIVE GAME BASED LEARNING

Collaborative learning is a social interaction that involves a community of learners and teachers who acquire knowledge while sharing a common experience. The central features of collaborative learning are positive interdependence, individual accountability, face-to-face and verbal interaction, social skills, and team reflection. As a result, students develop individual responsibility for group results (Sumtsova et al., 2018; Zhu, 2012). At their best, collaborative game based learning (CGBL) can support collaborative learning through game tasks whose solutions require collaboration, discussion, alternative solutions and viewpoints (Oksanen & Hämäläinen, 2013).

In CGBL, tasks may include cooperation, competition between individuals, and competition between teams – the latter includes aspects of both cooperation and competition. Games which require students to cooperate with their teammates while competing with other teams appear to provide both a heightened sense of community within the team, and also a higher motivation for winning than would be provided by competition between individuals (Denholm at al. 2013; Romero, 2011). Carefully designed tasks even have the potential to enhance learning by providing opportunities for intra-group cooperation and positive interdependence (Romero at al., 2012). In a cooperative situation, CGBL converts knowledge into social capital, since peer acknowledgement is shown to be a powerful motivator (Herz, 2002).

While clear definitions and guidelines for effective CGBL are not yet well defined, a recent review by Wang & Huang provides a useful systematic review of empirical research articles on the use of serious games for collaborative learning (Wang & Huang, 2021). Furthermore, the influential game design book by Schell (2008) provides a taxonomy of game mechanics, together with design rationales for their use. Schell's game mechanics include a number which are applicable to the design of CGBL experiences:

- Mechanics of space – which foster feelings of shared activities, and promote cooperation and help seeking;
- Mechanics of objects, attributes and states – which support tradeable resources, division of information, and indirect action, thereby promoting communication, sharing and individual accountability;
- Mechanics of actions – including the majority of 'traditional' skill-based/arcade game mechanics as well as multi-user communication, enabling both communication and competition;
- Mechanics of rules and goals – which include teams and group membership, leadership, partial goals, common goals and rewards, thereby promoting teamwork, team spirit and individual value and accountability, while reducing the possibility for one person to dominate proceedings.

LEARNING MANDARIN CHINESE AS A SECOND LANGUAGE

The Chinese language suffers from a number of unsolved problems which prevent it from being scaled to a truly global 2nd language. This is seen internationally whereby Chinese language programs consistently experience a drop-out rate of 95% from early on (Orton, 2016a). Despite noble aspirations,

Engagement with the reality of Chinese learning is often a cold shower. In international publications and conference papers, evidence constantly shows that what most school age and under-graduate learners from Europe, North America and Australia find to be 'hitherto unthinkable' in their encounter with Chinese language are the overwhelming challenges they meet when trying to learn it. Far from being led along an empowering path, many end up despondent about success. (Orton & Scrimgeour, 2019, p. 5)

Aside from stark differences in socio-cultural educational paradigms, the principal hurdle for foreign learners as previously mentioned, is the system of writing with its nonalphabetic orthography, which represents the spoken language in a largely irregular and unsystematic manner (Everson, 1998). There are competing methods for committing to memory the thousands of Chinese characters required for fluency. The first is to view each as a unique piece of art, to be memorized in its entirety (Everson, 1997). This *en masse* memorization technique has been correlated with poor reading levels and poor comprehension.

A second approach, analysing the graphic units or 'units of perception' that make up an individual character - whether done subconsciously or systematically, has been shown to provide a marked advantage (Anderson at al., 2013). This approach - analysing the graphic units - may be further broken into two main schools of thought. The far more established approach studies the graphic units inside a character which offer semantic or phonetic (meaning or pronunciation) clues for the overall character – treating the other constituent graphic units as an assembled 'piece of art'. This approach has its weaknesses. Studies of the 2,500 characters typically learned in primary classrooms in China, have shown that 58% of the characters contain a graphic unit giving a somewhat useful hint to the meaning, while only 39% contain a graphic unit offering a useful hint to pronunciation (Shu at al., 2003). Also, a discrete graphic unit which offers a useful semantic or phonetic clue in one character, often flips roles in another character, or is relegated to 'a piece of art' in a third, leaving it impossible to routinely predict whether a graphic unit will have a significant role outside of its visual presence. In the words of Orton and Scrimgeour, this system is of no use to the young learner with limited vocabulary, since:

for these novice learners, information related to the function of the semantic radical and the phonetic side is rendered next to meaningless, not only because transfer of sound and meaning information is unreliable, but, more importantly, because learners simply have not encountered sufficient related characters for such transfers or reliabilities to become evident (Orton & Scrimgeour 2019, p. 61).

The second, and newly emerging school of thought, is to treat the graphic units in a purely visual-orthographic way, which means analysing the graphic units of the Chinese written system independently from phonological, morphological and semantic information (Anderson at al. 2013). This is akin to allowing learners to "spell out" all of the discrete graphic units of a character "as a way to remember the totality of the graphic information" (Orton & Scrimgeour 2019, p.64). Again this approach has its weaknesses, as no consensus exists on how many graphic units there are. Nor do all graphic units actually have a name, which leaves discussing them rather difficult; "The piece on the left/bottom/top-right/inside of/outside of ... xCharacter" is how these nameless visual-orthographic graphic units are currently referred to in Chinese. Without a large body of orthographic knowledge and vocabulary to draw from, a new learner currently has no way of even referencing these graphic units.

The incomplete nature of each of these systems results in a hybrid approach: when the more practiced semantic-phonological-morphological system routinely fails, the "memorizing unique pieces of art" approach steps in, and if a diligent student spends long enough, consciously or subconsciously they begin to assemble their own visual-orthographic system (Anderson at al.. 2013) – most likely unaware they are headed into territory where the work is incomplete. Without a single comprehensive standardized system, it is left to individual teachers and students to invent their own. It is here that multiple parallel and contradictory, historically inaccurate folk-etymologies have emerged as memory aids, where contradictory rules bring about despondency in otherwise enthusiastic learners, and where "that's just the way it is" is the common answer.

The dearth of research into how a standardized approach might be developed to tackle the Chinese written system has left Chinese language suffering from an underdeveloped pedagogy and resources (Orton, 2016b). In this light, it is easy to understand the feeling amongst learners that Chinese is inaccessible and impossible to learn (Zhang & Li, 2010). Thus the aim of the Newby Chinese platform is to build a comprehensive visual-orthographic solution, based on how learners best perceive the graphic units, or "units of perception" of Chinese characters. This is further discussed below in the sections entitled *Chinese for English Speakers* and *Pedagogy in Newby Chinese*.

NEWBY CHINESE

Technology and Classroom Setup

The Newby Chinese platform has been created to be lightweight and rapidly deployable, in order to allow the teacher to arrive on-site and start teaching with a minimum of fuss. It is essentially a cloud-based system, written using HTML5 and JavaScript. The teacher connects to the platform's server through a web browser, and projects their screen at the front of the class. The students connect via web browsers on their personal devices – typically phones or tablets. Thus, there is no software installation required.

The platform provides teacher-directed multimedia learning via a collection of rich media, interactive media, and multiplayer games. Students interact using their own devices, with the interface presented to them changing to suit the task at hand. The concept of 'smart private screens' for players in a game is one with huge potential, not only because it allows a variety of input interfaces, but also because game designs can take advantage of the information presented privately to individual players. This approach has been very successfully employed, for example, by Jackbox Games and on the Nintendo Wii U console.

The Newby Chinese server is written using Node.js and performs a minimum of processing – as much as possible, student and teacher (client) devices do the 'heavy lifting' of game processing and network packet parsing. This makes the system highly scalable. Websockets are used for bi-directional communication between the server and clients. Many of the multimedia elements of the platform are developed using Adobe Animate, which exports to HTML5/JavaScript with a reliance on the Easel.js graphics library. Thus, Easel.js is also the library that has been chosen to support graphical and audio aspects of the system which do not use media developed in Adobe Animate (e.g. the multiplayer games).

From a practical point of view, the authors have learned that a high-performance router is valuable to bring to a teaching session, allowing the system to be served via LAN from the teacher's laptop, should this be necessary due to Internet (or local router) performance issues.

CO-LOCATED GROUP LEARNING

Effective learning occurs not only when the student constructs their own knowledge via pedagogical scaffolds but also benefits greatly from the social support of a community of learners. Language learning, of course, particularly benefits from taking place within a social group, since language is a communication tool which by definition requires multiple actors.

While online (distributed) multiplayer games are hugely popular, they are less effective than co-located multiplayer when it comes to infusing the play with a sense of shared purpose and good-natured fun. Co-location also makes it trivial to monitor the engagement of students and to make sure that none of them have disappeared.

The Newby Chinese platform uses a variety of games to take advantage of different aspects of game-based learning and gamification. Some games for example focus on competition, points scoring or racing – while others focus on team-based cooperation and communication. The individual games within the platform are discussed later.

ORCHESTRATING THE CLASS DYNAMIC

Effective learning benefits greatly from the real-time input of a facilitator, who can monitor in real-time the engagement and focus of the class and can orchestrate the sequence of activities in order to maintain effective learning. The authors' experience over the past 3 years and delivering the Newby Chinese platform to thousands of students has allowed them to develop a nuanced and responsive approach, delivering a sequence of activities which directs the focus and energy of the class: at times chaotic, at times reflective and calm; at times competitive, at times cooperative; at times individual, at times group-based. Thus, *flow* can be maintained in the classroom. Newby Chinese provides a range of different activities and games from which the facilitator can select in real time, in order to manage the flow.

The social psychology concepts of shame and guilt have recently been discussed as they apply to L2 learners, in order to introduce more subtlety to our understanding of negative emotions during second language acquisition (Teimouri, 2018). With Newby Chinese, the authors have observed the value of time-critical, chaotic team-based games in displacing such negative emotions with more positive feelings of camaraderie, and the effect that this has, as laughter and deep engagement in the activity removes the time to dwell on negatives.

Since language learning requires a variety of skills to be mastered (reading, writing, listening, speaking, vocabulary acquisition), a variety of GBL approaches are appropriate. In some cases, activities are by their nature personal and unexciting (e.g. handwriting practice of Chinese characters) – and in these cases, the use of "reward" games has been found to have a huge impact on engagement. By providing fun-first (as opposed to learning-first) games as a reward to those students who perform best in the more boring activity, a huge improvement in overall engagement with those difficult activities has been observed. Of course, fun-first games can also be an opportunity for some lesser focus on learning too.

In many cases, individual games are preceded by a short, focused knowledge-gathering activity. In anticipation of the impending game, students are typically hyper-focused for a short period of time – in order to gather the necessary information, they know they will need in the game. This is a fantastic opportunity for learning. For example, one of the fun-first games on the platform is *Battle Fall*. In this game, players run and jump around a 'platformer' game arena, while throwing bombs at each other. Points may only be scored by hitting opponents with the correct Chinese number over their head. The teacher's device calls out various numbers as the game progresses. Before each *Battle Fall* session, the teacher's screen presents and calls out the Chinese numbers which the teacher has chosen for the session (individual digits, or more complex numbers involving multiple digits). Students pay absolute attention to this pre-game knowledge-gathering activity. Figure 1 shows a game of *Battle Fall* in progress.

Figure 1. The Battle Fall game

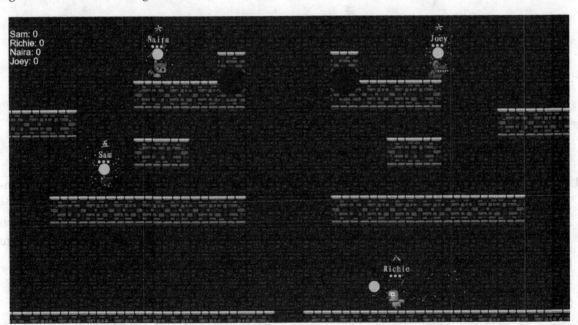

CHINESE FOR ENGLISH SPEAKERS

In order to understand the particular set of challenges that the Chinese written system presents to the minds and eye muscles of new learners, some issues are highlighted below. Here the authors will imagine Chinese graphic units as being somewhat analogous to English letters, and Chinese characters as being analogous to English words.

1.   Unlike English words, read as a string of uni-directional letters (left-to-right), Chinese has no set order for the visual reading of the 'letters' (graphic units) of a character. Imagine encountering the word 'Teacher', but instead of scanning the word left-to-right, you scan the entire word without order as you memorize the collection of letters. Perhaps the order in which your eyes move from one letter to another is **H-a-r-e-c-e-t**.

2.   The order is not important, as the combination of letters do not actually create the pronunciation of the word. Rather, with the experience and orthographic insight gained by already having memorized 2,500 words (characters), then 39% of the time, one of the letters above provides a useful clue to the pronunciation of the overall word. And 58% of the time, one of the letters provides a useful clue to the meaning of the word (Shu at al., 2003)

3.   Unlike English words read as a linear string, Chinese characters are a 2-D composition of letters (graphic units), with vertical, horizontal, diagonal, and even internal - external relationships. The word 'Teacher' now requires your eye to move in two dimensions as it scans the assembled letters, while your mind memorizes the spatial relationships – as shown in figure 2.

Figure 2. Chinese characters are a composition of graphic units aligned in various directions

4.   The letters (graphic units) also stretch, warp, shrink, and grow, to assume different spatial relationships, while maintaining a fairly square symmetry to the overall structure of the character. This means some are hard to see (note the c in figure 3) as search performance for letters has been shown to decrease for smaller targets (Clayden at al., 2020). Some units also warp and twist (note the 'mild' warping of the T in figure 3). Others change shape dramatically.

Figure 3. The graphic units within characters are frequently distorted

5. If the English alphabet included a number of symbols without name or Unicode number, the words containing them would be impossible to spell. Not all Chinese graphic units have names, or Unicode numbers - as represented by the three unpronounceable 'letters' in figure 4. At this stage our 'Teacher' example becomes un-spellable, even for native speakers. Instead, these un-named graphic units must be referenced by their location within other characters already known by all parties to a discussion.

Figure 4. Some graphic units have no name and are thus unpronounceable

6. Identical graphic units - because of etymological differences - may not be classed as being the same graphic unit. In the example in figure 4, if perhaps the 'e' served a stand-in role for a 'y' at some stage in the past, it is not here regarded as an 'e'. This is further explained in a section below.

7. Imagine the sense of unease that would arise in foreign learners if the English alphabet had a disputed number of letters – this is the case with the discrete graphic units in the Chinese written system, with some academics claiming around 400.

Overcoming the particular challenges of the Chinese written system outlined above will require scaffolding a learning framework very different to that of other languages. One reason is that with no set order to the reading of graphic units, and with un-named graphic units, learners can neither consciously nor subconsciously use rhythm to remember and replicate the structure of characters. Rhythm plays an organizational role in the prosody and phonology of language, and a lack of rhythm is a predictor of poor reading and spelling (Lundetrae & Thomson, 2018). A learner must also physically train their eye muscles and minds to an entirely new skillset to scan these 2-D compositions. Orton & Scrimgeour have suggested pattern perception training exercises (Orton & Scrimgeour, 2019) from which the authors have developed the sequence shown in figure 5.

Figure 5. Pattern perception training exercises

According to Orton & Scrimgeour, the current state of teaching Chinese is thus:

The resources do not start where the students are, on the starting line, nor do they even consider what it is that the learners on the starting line need to master in order to reach the perfect texts on the finishing line. As a result, exercises and activities often do not form a scaffolded path between starting line and finishing line. In fact, the learning path has been far less regarded or studied, so much of the necessary information about it is simply not available. Instead the finishing line is presented with an underlying assumption that the learners will already have available what is needed to attain the goal and all that needs to be added is determination and diligence. … To develop the most basic capacities in Chinese – to hear and utter, to read and write – requires these foreign learners as a starting point to extend fundamental motor skills and to change long ingrained habits in perception and production of spoken and written language (Orton & Scrimgeour, 2019, p.6).

PEDAGOGY IN NEWBY CHINESE

Central to Newby Chinese is the creation of an original and comprehensive glossary of the graphic units of the Chinese written system (a complete visual-orthographic system), while scaffolding a framework of sequential presentation and testing by which a learner can rapidly access the written and spoken Chinese language. With a comprehensive glossary made accessible, instead of viewing each logo-syllabic character as a unique piece of art to be memorized in its entirety, a new learner could instead routinely 'spell out' the entire collection of graphic units inside an individual character, something that is currently impossible to do. With a ready glossary, a learner could then leverage rhythm to memorize the 2-D spatial relationships of graphic units within a character.

Many of these graphic units also function as fundamental characters in their own right, and can be immediately applied to meaningful sentence construction, for speech, writing and reading. The Newby Chinese pedagogy attempts to 'start where the learner is', by presenting the discrete graphic units of the written system as a learner most effectively perceives them, but also presenting them in a sequence which gives a learner the most rapid access to meaningful language. To this end the Newby Chinese pedagogy is constantly informed and refined through real world feedback from thousands of learners throughout the development process.

Creating a fictional representation of graphic units allows the sidestepping of a mostly unknowable and heavily disputed ancient etymological origin of the language. It also avoids, for the learner's sake, gaping inconsistencies in phonological, morphological, and semantic approaches to the study of graphic units as is evidenced in a study (Shu et al., 2003). Furthermore it allows the blending of identical graphic units under one entry, thus reducing the overall corpus of graphic units to remember. It also allows for names to be given to previously 'un-named' graphic units.

Core to the presentation of this glossary of graphic units are animated audio-visual anthropomorphised characters - which introduce the graphic units through short animated stories in which the graphic units are decorated so as to appear as a human or animal engaged in a memorable (often funny) activity. For example, the graphic unit 不 ('bu'), which also happens to be a standalone character meaning 'no' or 'not' in Chinese, is introduced through a mnemonic animation involving a character bungee-jumping on screen while yelling "Boo! No, it's not!" - in response to a question posed by the narrator. The association of a spoken English word, repeated often, with the target Chinese graphic unit which it sounds like, is a strong memory support. The animation and its 'story' further support this. Another example, illustrated in figure 6, is of 人 ('ren') – an important graphic unit as well as standalone character meaning 'person'. The sound of this character is associated with that of a motor scooter as it revs up (RREEENNNN RRREEENNN). The animation here involves a person excitedly revving their scooter and then crashing it, before standing up again in the shape of the target Chinese character.

Figure 6. The Chinese word for Person – "Ren"

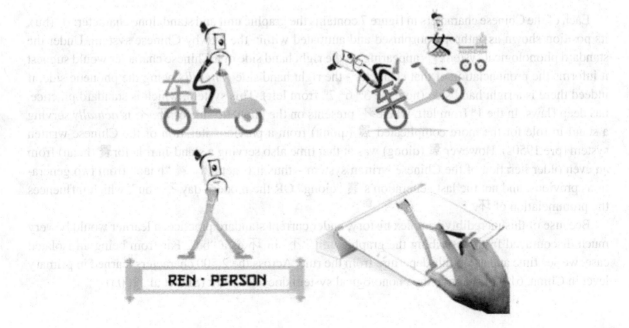

Apart from the laughter and sense of fun they generally evoke – displacing any previously ingrained sense of language learning shame (Teimouri, 2018), these anthropomorphised graphic units allow for immediate reading, enunciation (speaking) and even 'phrasal chunking'. These anthropomorphised characters appear throughout the games in Newby Chinese; some of its more basic games, for example, involve timed exercises in which players score points by rapidly and accurately identifying target graphic units, entire characters, or 'phrasal chunks' in screensful of Chinese words. The payoff, apart from scoring points and running faster, is to see these dynamic and humorous graphic units, unique to the Newby Chinese system, come to life.

Once an anthropomorphised graphic unit is mastered by a learning group, the following step is to present a learning framework where learners begin to discriminate between, and remember, different spatial arrangements of graphic units within 2-D compound characters. To this end Newby Chinese has developed a set of exercises which are explained below. However, to more clearly explain the rationale behind this learning platform, several of the problems with the existing phonological and morphological system will be highlighted, in figure 7.

Figure 7. The 'Stall Guys' preparation page – where characters which share one or more identical graphic units are contrasted and discussed

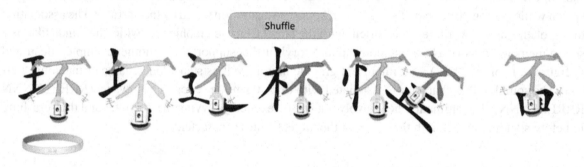

Each of the Chinese characters in figure 7 contains the graphic unit and standalone character: 不 (bu), its position shown as anthropomorphised and animated within the Newby Chinese system. Under the standard phonological system, 不 appearing on the right hand side of a Chinese character would suggest it informs the pronunciation of that character - the right hand side *generally* being the phonetic side, if indeed there is a right hand side (note the 3rd 6th 7th from left). This system, which is standard practice, has deep flaws. In the 1st from left, where 不 presents on the phonetic side of 环, 不 is *actually* serving a stand-in role for the more complicated 瞏 (qiong) from a previous iteration of the Chinese written system (pre 1950s). However 瞏 (qiong) was at that time also serving a stand-in role for 瞏 (huan) from an even older iteration of the Chinese written system – thus it is actually 瞏 "huan" from two generations previous, and not the last generation's 瞏 "qiong" OR the modern day 不 "bu", which influences the pronunciation of 环.

Because of this incredibly complex history, under current standard practice, a learner would be very much discouraged from describing the graphic unit: '不' in 环 as a "bu". Far from being an isolated case, we see time and again this departure from the rule. Across the 2,500 characters learned in primary level in China, 61% of the time the phonological system does not work (Shu et al., 2003)

In the line-up of characters in figure 7, 不 fails to provide a close hint to the pronunciation of a single target character - despite being the 'phonetic side' in all but one. Thus most teachers, without a comprehensive knowledge of the deep and archaic orthography themselves, shy away from students' questions regarding visual structure, instead insisting they should be memorized like 'pieces of art'. Their attitude should not be mocked, as even researching this headache-inducing morphology of the language – as a nearly fluent Chinese language speaker, creates a confusing and foggy trail of broken associations. Nor are the dictionaries and resources always in agreement. Complex phonology, semantics and morphology, twinned with the hesitancy any rookie L2 learner feels, creates a very unempowering path to effective learning.

Thus once introduced in the Newby Chinese system, a 不 *is always called* a "bu", with the rationale that this visual-orthographic approach allows a learner to immediately enunciate and commit to memory 50% of the graphic unit content in the above seven characters, as well as an unspecified percentage of other Chinese characters containing the graphic unit 不. The fact that this learning outcome can be achieved after the introduction of a single fifteen second anthropomorphic animation provides a powerful mechanism for accelerated Chinese learning. This is proving far more effective than the 'drill and repetition' approach of traditional Chinese learning (as shown by Andersen at al., 2013). During Newby Chinese sessions, it is common to hear utterances such as: "I've learned more Chinese in a few hours than French in three years!" (15 year old girl, Dublin, Ireland) or "Somebody please tell my English teacher I'm finally good at something!" (16 year old girl, Dublin, Ireland).

Encouraging learners to engage with sets of characters which have one or more graphic units in common, but differing spatial arrangements, helps them rapidly increase their 'reading' vocabulary, but also to learn to differentiate by scanning in different planes: diagonally, vertically, and horizontally. As previously described, this is an entirely new perceptive skill for the eye muscles and brains of English speakers whose prior reading experience is to scan uni-directional strings of alphabetic letters.

One of the games on the Newby Chinese platform that follows from this scaffolded 2-D perceptive learning, is *Stall Guys*. This game stress tests this graphic unit scanning activity - by putting the whole class together in an arena where they must pick the correct character (called out by the teacher's computer) from among a candidate set of visually similar characters. An incoming wall of spikes puts time pressure on the students, and in addition a level of chaotic fun is injected by allowing the students to push each other's avatars around as they compete to run through the narrow entrance of the arena's exit tunnel.

GAMES FOR READING AND WRITING

A number of games within Newby Chinese focus on the core skills of reading, writing (including handwriting), vocabulary, and sentence construction. The games include a variety of tasks involving translation between Chinese, English, and Pinyin, as well as basic word 'spotting' – i.e. identifying Chinese words correctly. There is a particular focus on the use of virtual keyboards on modern phones and browsers – which allow the user to write Chinese via Pinyin input and even via speech recognition. Pinyin is a system of Romanization of the Chinese written language, allowing characters to be spelled out using the Roman alphabet. Once spelled out, the correct character can be chosen from a list, as shown in figure 8.

Figure 8. The result from typing "b...u..." in Pinyin, on a standard keyboard with Pinyin activated

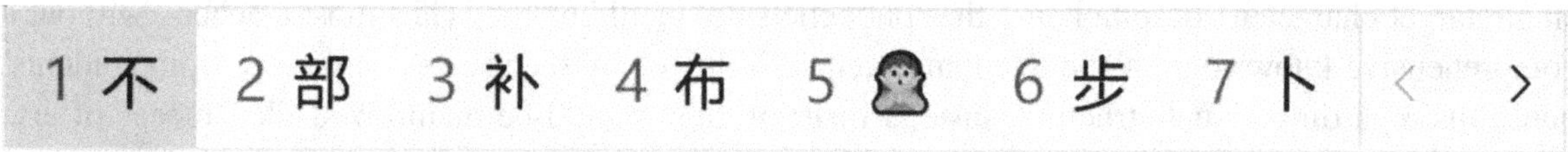

| 1 不 | 2 部 | 3 补 | 4 布 | 5 🧟 | 6 步 | 7 卜 | ‹ › |

The more basic games in Newby Chinese – in which students practice core skills – are displayed on their own devices, rather than in a multiplayer arena on the teacher's screen. Thus, these are essentially singleplayer experiences. These games are supported by displaying user avatars in a running race on the teacher's screen, whereby avatars run faster if their owners score well in the games. This is, of course, simply an engaging alternative to a scoreboard, which is a basic gamification technique. A running race in progress is shown in figure 9.

Figure 9. A running race

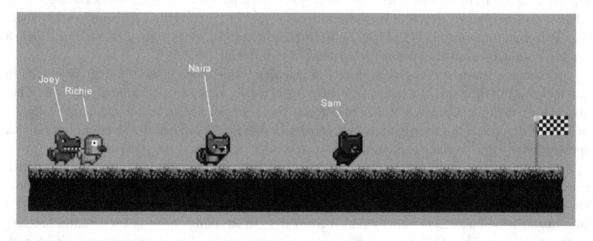

In the games *Word Grid*, *Sentence Grid*, and *Invaders*, students perform word and sentence spotting tasks in a time-critical situation – whereby completing tasks rapidly and without error scores higher points.

In *Maze Hunters* students compete by running around a maze filled with Chinese words. Students use virtual joysticks presented on their personal devices to move around the maze, seeking out target words which are called out by the teacher's computer. The game itself displays on the teacher's screen, and thus is a 'proper' multiplayer game. See figure 10. Since there are not as many target words as avatars in the maze, *Maze Hunters* progresses in a fashion similar to the child's game 'musical chairs': students are knocked out in successive rounds of play until one finally wins. *Maze Hunters* is one of the platform's more chaotic games, where students jump around and shout out Chinese words at each other, hurriedly explaining what a word looks like to each other, and so on. This leads to incredible engagement and powerful learning outcomes. This video shows a class of 15 year old students playing Maze Hunters: https://www.youtube.com/watch?v=9D9nrsf_dwA

Figure 10. The Maze Hunters game

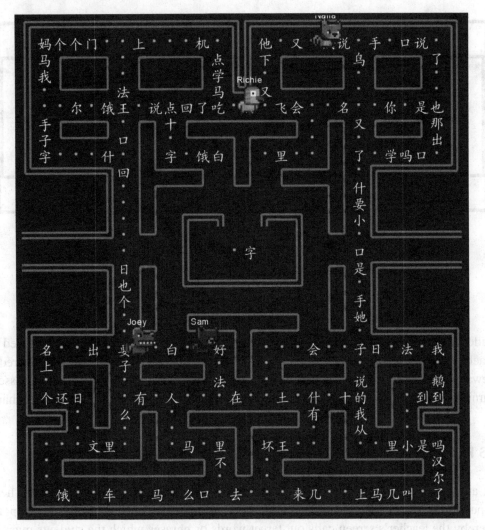

Aspects of the Newby Chinese reading and writing games take a 'training wheels' approach, whereby novice learners are given assistance, and this assistance is gradually taken away. For example, handwriting starts by tracing characters/graphic units which are shown onscreen. The outline being traced gradually gets fainter, and eventually disappears leading to unassisted freeform writing. Because visual-motor symbol production has been shown to facilitate letter recognition in young children (Zemlock at al., 2018) this step is perceived by the authors to be particularly important for a learner experiencing the nuances of the Chinese written system.

An intermediate game, *Sentence Builder*, involves the construction of sentences by scrolling through candidate Chinese words in sequence, before they are to be traced. This is shown in figure 11.

Figure 11. The Sentence Builder game

As students submit their work in the various writing games, all submitted work is displayed together on the teacher's screen where it can be discussed. The best and fastest submissions are scored and are further rewarded by inviting those students into a game of *Battle Fall* - which is further discussed below in the Gamification section, since reward games are best considered to be gamification mechanisms.

GAMES FOR LISTENING AND SPEAKING

Speaking and listening is critical in language learning, and all-too-frequently learners are hesitant to speak in public for fear of sounding stupid. A number of the games in Newby Chinese support listening – whereby the teacher's screen calls out target words or phrases which the students must identify. However, the game *Chase Team* is uniquely effective at encouraging practice of spoken Chinese.

In *Chase Team*, a team of players are running away from an evil robot: see figure 12. One of the players will see a phrase in Chinese on their device and they must quickly call it out across the classroom so that their team-mates can select that phrase (from a set of candidate phrases) on their own devices. Rapid, correct responses lead to their avatars running faster and eventually escaping, while failure means that the robot runs faster and eventually catches the avatars. *Chase Team* effectively puts social pressure on players to perform well for the sake of the team - and in the excitement and time-pressure of gameplay, anxiety about speaking a foreign language disappears.

Figure 12. The Chase Team game

Various other games on the platform also encourage learners to speak into their devices - which use voice recognition to convert this to Chinese. It is time pressure in the competitive game environment which encourages students to speak rather than type, since speaking is faster than Pinyin input. Efficiently inputting into the student's device becomes more important to them than any social anxiety they might have in speaking.

Another of the multiplayer games on the platform is *Boss Battle*, in which teams of players face an evil robot in an arena. In order to defeat the robot, players must cooperate in their use of shields to defend each other and in their earning and shooting of bullets. Shields and bullets are earned by completing short sentence or word tasks on their individual devices. Again, learners are motivated to engage with the tasks by their desire to support their team. Social pressure and a reluctance to let down one's teammates are powerful motivators.

GAMIFICATION

Battle Fall is a chaotic battle game in which students run and jump around a platformer arena while throwing bombs at each other. This is a reward game which is used as a way to encourage students to perform well in handwriting and other unexciting tasks: only the most accurate and rapid submissions in these tasks lead to an invitation to join the game of *Battle Fall*. Encouraging rapid submission has been observed to help overcome reluctance to engage with the platform due to either social hierarchy or embarrassment. It has also greatly reduced behavioural issues and increased learning outcomes by focusing attention within the time envelope of the class. Despite being a 'fun-first' (reward) game, *Battle Fall* is also an opportunity to study numbers in Chinese: players can only attack other players who have the correct Chinese number above their head.

In addition to the games described above, Newby Chinese also makes use of traditional gamification approaches - leaderboards, timing, scoring, prize avatars and clothing/hats - which although blunt, are still useful mechanisms to promote engagement. These are forms of gamification and thus are longstanding GBL techniques; they will not therefore be discussed in depth. Figure 13 shows the winners' podium, which is displayed after various games – rewarding top performing students with animation, a cheering crowd, and the subsequent satisfaction of having their avatars displayed in this way in front of the whole class.

Figure 13. The winners' podium

DISCUSSION

A co-located approach to group learning infuses Newby Chinese, and is central to the design of all of its games. The social supports afforded by face-to-face co-operation and instruction, as well as the good natured atmosphere which face-to-face competition encourages are important, and would be much harder to achieve in a fully distributed (online) learning platform.

Newby Chinese has been in active use in classrooms for more than 3 years. Its games have been modified and re-balanced to support pedagogical goals over this time, and thus the following key lessons learned may be valuable to other developers and researchers:

1. The presentation of short multimedia mnemonics is a powerful way of assisting language learners to recall the sound, shape and meaning of Chinese characters - through the use of a brief narrative occurrence and the repetition of the Chinese pronunciation in a way that fits the narrative while also sounding like an English word.
2. Some teaching and learning goals are by their nature unexciting and repetitive. In these cases the authors have found that simple gamification techniques (scoring and leaderboards) are not sufficient to motivate some students. The addition of 'fun first' reward games (offered to those scoring well in the repetitive tasks) can have an enormous impact on this - much greater levels of engagement have been observed in the repetitive tasks when performing these well leads to a coveted spot in a limited-membership team game which is played out in front of the whole class.

3. The interleaving of reflective activities, chaotic fun activities, and short intense activities focused on knowledge acquisition can be very effective when well-orchestrated by the teacher. In particular, students are observed to be hyper-focused on short knowledge acquisition tasks when the knowledge being gathered will have a direct bearing on a group game which follows immediately afterwards.

4. Through use of time-critical games, students competing in tasks will naturally want to use the most efficient data-input approach available to them: this motivation quickly outweighs the shyness to speak a foreign language, for example, as students choose to use speech recognition on their devices purely for efficiency of input.

5. In addition to using time-critical tasks as a way of overcoming a reluctance to speak, team-based games are also a powerful addition which can encourage students to speak, listen and converse in the target language. In team-based games, students desire to do well for the sake of their team-mates as well as themselves, and again this rapidly overcomes their reluctance to speak or to engage in other tasks.

FUTURE RESEARCH DIRECTIONS

There are numerous future directions in which further investigation would be fruitful. These generally emanate from this chapter's investigation of (i) the use of co-located multiplayer GBL for language learning, and (ii) the pedagogy of teaching Chinese as a second language.

Multiplayer systems – particularly co-located multiplayer – are highly appropriate for GBL as they are much more effective and engaging than singleplayer – this is especially relevant for language learning where the core skills relate to communication and thus require other people. However clear definitions and guidelines for effective Collaborative GBL are not yet well defined, and this would be a very useful direction for further formal research.

It is still early days in the field of CSL (Orton & Scrimgeour, 2019, page 12) and so little is known about the units of character perception or how insight into the architecture of Chinese characters develops in children (Anderson at al., 2013). Thus further studies into how learners *actually* perceive the 'units of perception' of Chinese language would, in the opinions of the authors, be of prime importance to advance the field of CSL. It is within the Newby Chinese ethos to adapt to how best a learner actually learns, thus further research will undoubtedly inform the development process. An AI (machine learning) system of feedback analyzing a users' interactions with the Newby Chinese platform – to systematically and independently test and refine our best 'guesses' as to the optimal presentation of graphic units and sequence leading to meaningful language construction, is currently in the design phase.

Extending the existing Newby Chinese glossary of animated anthropomorphized graphic units to become fully comprehensive of the entire Chinese written system is an ongoing process which will take some time. The current Newby Chinese glossary of 50 animated graphic units allows for the complete graphical 'reading' by the learner of roughly 200 high frequency Chinese characters, challenging the learner with games involving 350 target Chinese characters. This also allows for the partial graphical 'reading' of roughly 2,500 high frequency Chinese characters. With increased resources it would be feasible to roll out a fully comprehensive glossary of all Chinese graphic units contained in high frequency characters within 18 months. This would have immediate applications for both native and non-native novice and expert speakers of the language.

Despite its effectiveness at beginner tasks and vocabulary acquisition, Newby Chinese still has some way to go to fully embrace task-based language learning and other constructivist approaches in support of intermediate and advanced learners. Ongoing developments focus on tasks which require meaningful communication, rather than games which mostly practice discrete linguistic elements. Prototype concepts are in development for:

- Text-based adventure games, in which the entire class discusses a narrative which is displayed (in Chinese) on the teacher's screen, and together decides what actions to take in order to explore and solve puzzles. In the game's current form, player actions are chosen from a list of options. Later, the authors plan to incorporate a text parser so that freeform Chinese input (of simple sentences) can be accepted, in the style of the classic text adventure games of the 1970s and 80s.
- A variation of the text-based adventure games will allow students to co-exist in a shared, networked multi-user domain (MUD) and to explore and solve puzzles as individuals or in ad-hoc groups. The collaborative game mechanics laid out by Schell (2008) will be of particular importance to this variation – as discussed briefly above, in the section titled "Collaborative Game Based Learning".

The work described in this chapter is primarily applied and commercial rather than academic. Thus, although the concepts and games of Newby Chinese have certainly been informed through observation of what works well in practice, there have not been formal experiments undertaken to measure the efficacy of learning. Such experiments would be an important addition to the body of work described here.

CONCLUSION

China is an economic behemoth, and the economic and social implications of the growth of Chinese language are very real. However, despite having far more native speakers than any other global language, large scale competency in the language outside of China has proved rather elusive, with second language learners feeling it is inaccessible and impossible to learn (Zhang & Li, 2010). This has ramifications for individuals, societies, and even the national security of countries, as relying on someone else to gather information or represent your interests and views, whether economic, social or political, is risky.

The importance of engaging with Chinese as a second language has never been more important, yet approaches to doing so are hampered by arcane and inappropriate approaches. Even native Chinese children struggle to read and write the language. Recent work by leading scholars has begun to define the various natures of the problem, and suggest better ways to approach it. The Newby Chinese system embraces these modern pedagogies for teaching Chinese as a second language, while also illuminating the use of co-located multiplayer GBL technologies to improve the experience and learning outcomes in a more general way.

Newby Chinese is showing one effective way of integrating various gaming and GBL concepts into a coherent whole – including class dynamic and multiplayer game flow, mitigation of negative emotions during L2 learning, and the careful use of gamification into aspects of a broader GBL system.

This chapter concludes with some comments from secondary school teachers and GBL academics who have used the system:

I was shocked at the students' response - so used to the 'non reactive/difficult to impress teenager', when I saw total engagement it was surprising. That was the best thing we have done so far! They absolutely loved it and asked could they do it every week. I explained budget restrictions and they said they would pay for it themselves (E. Dempsey, Teaching coordinator at St. Mels. College, Longford, Ireland).

Never mind just Chinese, this is the best language-learning platform I've ever seen! (E. Bertozzi, Associate Professor of Game Design & Development, Quinnipiac University, USA).

Awesome, one of the most enjoyable and engaging classroom tools you'll ever use. I can't believe the progress the students have made after just 6 hours ... Newby Chinese was voted favourite activity of the year by my students, and this in a year jam packed with surfing, skiing and crime scene investigation. It's amazing. (R. Conboy, teaching coordinator at St Joseph's College, Galway, Ireland).

I haven't seen these students so excited about anything before - they loved it! (M. Corboy, Teaching coordinator, Sacred Heart, Drogheda, Ireland).

ACKNOWLEDGMENT

We acknowledge the support of Enterprise Ireland. Newby Chinese is a Pre HPSU client in receipt of Competitive Start Fund funding.

REFERENCES

Anderson, R. C., Ku, Y. M., Li, W., Chen, X., Wu, X., & Shu, H. (2013). Learning to see the patterns in Chinese characters. *Scientific Studies of Reading*, *17*(1), 41–56. doi:10.1080/10888438.2012.689789

Bartle, R. (1996). Hearts, clubs, diamonds, spades: Players who suit MUDs. *Journal of MUD Research*, *1*(1), 19.

Behlol, M. G., & Dad, H. (2010). Concept of learning. *International Journal of Psychological Studies*, *2*(2), 231. doi:10.5539/ijps.v2n2p231

Bricker, L. J., Tanimoto, S. L., Rothenberg, A. I., Hutama, D. C., & Wong, T. H. (1995). Multiplayer Activities That Develop Mathematical Coordination. *Proceedings of CSCL 1995*.

Caponetto, I., Earp, J., & Ott, M. (2014). Gamification and education: A literature review. In *European Conference on Games Based Learning* (Vol. *1*, p. 50). Academic Conferences International Limited.

Clayden, A. C., Fisher, R. B., & Nuthmann, A. (2020). On the relative (un) importance of foveal vision during letter search in naturalistic scenes. *Vision Research*, *177*, 41–55. doi:10.1016/j.visres.2020.07.005 PMID:32957035

Csikszentmihalhi, M. (2020). Finding flow: The psychology of engagement with everyday life. Hachette UK.

Denholm, J. A., Protopsaltis, A., & de Freitas, S. (2013). The value of team-based mixed-reality (TBMR) games in higher education. *International Journal of Game-Based Learning, 3*(1), 18–33. doi:10.4018/ijgbl.2013010102

Ellis, R. (2003). *Task-based language learning and teaching*. Oxford University Press.

Everson, M. (1997). An inquiry into the reading the reading strategies of intermediate and advanced learners of Chinese as a foreign language. *Journal of the Chinese Language Teacher Association, 32*, 1–20.

Everson, M. (1998). Word recognition among learners of Chinese as a foreign language: Investigating the relationship between naming and knowing. *Modern Language Journal, 82*(2), 194–204. doi:10.1111/j.1540-4781.1998.tb01192.x

Herz, J. C. (2002). Gaming the System. In What Higher Education Can Learn from Multiplayer Online Worlds. In R. LM Devlin, Internet and the University: 2001 Forum (pp. 169-191). Academic Press.

Johnson, L., Becker, S. A., Estrada, V., Freeman, A., Kampylis, P., Vuorikari, R., & Punie, Y. (2014). *NMC Horizon Report Europe: 2014 schools edition*. The New Media Consortium.

Kim, B., Park, H., & Baek, Y. (2009). Not just fun, but serious strategies: Using meta-cognitive strategies in game-based learning. *Computers & Education, 52*(4), 800–810. doi:10.1016/j.compedu.2008.12.004

Lundetræ, K., & Thomson, J. M. (2018). Rhythm production at school entry as a predictor of poor reading and spelling at the end of first grade. *Reading and Writing, 31*(1), 215–237. doi:10.100711145-017-9782-9 PMID:29367807

Nakamura, J., & Csikszentmihalyi, M. (2014). The concept of flow. In *Flow and the foundations of positive psychology* (pp. 239–263). Springer.

Oksanen, K., & Hämäläinen, R. (2013). Perceived sociability and social presence in a collaborative serious game. *International Journal of Game-Based Learning, 3*(1), 34–50. doi:10.4018/ijgbl.2013010103

Orton, J. (2016a). Issues in Chinese language teaching in Australian schools. *Chinese Education & Society, 49*(6), 369–375. doi:10.1080/10611932.2016.1283929

Orton, J. (2016b). *Building Chinese language capacity in Australia*. The Australia-China Relations Institute.

Orton, J., & Scrimgeour, A. (2019). *Teaching Chinese as a second language: The way of the learner*. Routledge. doi:10.4324/9781351206877

Poole, F. J., & Clarke-Midura, J. (2020). A systematic review of digital games in second language learning studies. *International Journal of Game-Based Learning, 10*(3), 1–15. doi:10.4018/IJGBL.2020070101

Romero, M. (2011). Supporting collaborative game based learning knowledge construction through the use of knowledge group awareness. NoE games and learning alliance. *Lecture at the GaLa 1st Alignment School, 20*.

Romero, M., Usart, M., Ott, M., Earp, J., de Freitas, S., & Arnab, S. (2012). Learning through playing: for or against each other? Promoting collaborative learning in digital game based learning. *European Conference on Information Systems*.

Schell, J. (2008). *The Art of Game Design: A book of lenses*. CRC press. doi:10.1201/9780080919171

Shu, H., Chen, X., Anderson, R. C., Wu, N., & Xuan, Y. (2003). Properties of school Chinese: Implications for learning to read. *Child Development, 74*(1), 27–47. doi:10.1111/1467-8624.00519 PMID:12625434

Sumtsova, O., Aikina, T., Bolsunovskaya, L., Phillips, C., Zubkova, O., & Mitchell, P. (2018). Collaborative learning at engineering universities: Benefits and challenges. *International Journal of Emerging Technologies in Learning, 13*(1), 160–177. doi:10.3991/ijet.v13i01.7811

Teimouri, Y. (2018). Differential roles of shame and guilt in L2 learning: How bad is bad? *Modern Language Journal, 102*(4), 632–652. doi:10.1111/modl.12511

Wang, C., & Huang, L. (2021). A Systematic Review of Serious Games for Collaborative Learning: Theoretical Framework, Game Mechanic and Efficiency Assessment. *International Journal of Emerging Technologies in Learning, 16*(6), 88. doi:10.3991/ijet.v16i06.18495

Werbach, K., & Hunter, D. (2012). For the win: how game thinking can revolutionize your business. Wharton Digital Press.

Whitton, N. (2011). Encouraging engagement in game-based learning. *International Journal of Game-Based Learning, 1*(1), 75–84. doi:10.4018/ijgbl.2011010106

York, J., & deHaan, J. W. (2018). A constructivist approach to game-based language learning: Student perceptions in a beginner-level EFL context. *International Journal of Game-Based Learning, 8*(1), 19–40. doi:10.4018/IJGBL.2018010102

Zemlock, D., Vinci-Booher, S., & James, K. H. (2018). Visual–motor symbol production facilitates letter recognition in young children. *Reading and Writing, 31*(6), 1255–1271. doi:10.100711145-018-9831-z

Zhang, G. X., & Li, L. M. (2010). Chinese language teaching in the UK: Present and future. *Language Learning Journal, 38*(1), 87–97. doi:10.1080/09571731003620689

Zhu, C. (2012). Student satisfaction, performance, and knowledge construction in online collaborative learning. *Journal of Educational Technology & Society, 15*(1), 127–136.

ADDITIONAL READING

Admiraal, W., Huizenga, J., Akkerman, S., & Ten Dam, G. (2011). The concept of flow in collaborative game-based learning. *Computers in Human Behavior, 27*(3), 1185–1194. doi:10.1016/j.chb.2010.12.013

Csikszentmihalyi, M. (1990). *Flow: The psychology of optimal experience*. Harper & Row.

Long, M. (2014). *Second language acquisition and task-based language teaching*. John Wiley & Sons.

Pine, N., Ping'an, H., & Ren Song, H. (2003). Decoding strategies used by Chinese primary school children. *Journal of Literacy Research, 35*(2), 777–812. doi:10.120715548430jlr3502_5

Redfern, S., & McCurry, R. (2018). A Gamified System for Learning Mandarin Chinese as a Second Language. In *2018 IEEE Games, Entertainment, Media Conference* (pp. 1-9). IEEE.

Werbach, K., & Hunter, D. (2012). *For the win: How game thinking can revolutionize your business.* Wharton Digital Press.

Xu, Y., Chang, L. Y., & Perfetti, C. A. (2014). The effect of radical-based grouping in character learning in Chinese as a foreign language. *Modern Language Journal, 98*(3), 773–793. doi:10.1111/modl.12122

KEY TERMS AND DEFINITIONS

Co-Located Group Learning: A socially integrated learning experience where participants are physically located together and may therefore interact directly, see each other's expressions and gestures, and communicate more effectively (Bricker et al., 1995).

Collaborative Game-Based Learning (CFBL): A method of Game Based Learning (GBL) where learners and teachers share a socially integrated learning experience.

Collaborative Learning: A social interaction that involves a community of learners and teachers who acquire knowledge while sharing a common experience (Sumtsova et al., 2018).

CSL: (Learning) Chinese as a second language.

Flow: A theory of engagement which describes a state of deep concentration while the participant(s) in an activity are in a creative and rewarding state of mind.

Game-Based Learning (GBL): A learning strategy focused on achieving the particular objectives of given educational content through game play (Kim et al., 2009).

Gamification: The use of game elements and design techniques in non-game contexts.

Pinyin: A system of Romanization of the Chinese written language, allowing characters to be spelled out phonetically using the Roman alphabet.

Chapter 22
Game–Based Practices for Radical Urban Visions

Roger Paez

ELISAVA Barcelona School of Design and Engineering, University of Vic, Central University of Catalonia, Spain & ETSALS, University Ramon Llull, Spain

ABSTRACT

The chapter explores disruptive uses of serious games to achieve radical urban visions through the presentation and critical discussion of three recent case studies developed in graduate and postgraduate university courses. The chapter addresses the underpinnings of game-based design practices and discusses their untapped potential to spark imagination and bring about new urban visions. The focus is on subverting the expectations of the aims, methods, and results of spatial design projects in the context of higher educational institutions. Most importantly, games and play are used to radically address pressing technical, societal, and environmental topics in a disruptive way, generating new urban visions that push the limits of what is considered probable, desirable, and even imaginable.

INTRODUCTION

The book chapter explores disruptive uses of serious games to achieve radical urban visions through the presentation and critical discussion of recent case studies developed in postgraduate or postdoctoral educational environments associated with programmes in architecture, design and urbanism. Based on the author's practical experience in graduate and postgraduate university courses at ELISAVA (Universitat de Vic-Universitat Central de Catalunya) and ETSALS (Universitat Ramon Llull)

The chapter addresses the underpinnings of disruptive game-based design practices and discusses three case studies that illustrate their potential to generate and communicate radical urban visions. The author's personal research and his involvement in all of the case studies presented allows for an in-depth discussion of the opportunities and the shortcomings of these explorative practices.

The main objective of the chapter is to present and discuss the ability of playful environments and game-based practices to articulate radically explorative approaches to urban futures. Often used in merely instrumental ways to address problem-solving, participation or simulation, urban-oriented serious games

DOI: 10.4018/978-1-7998-9732-3.ch022

Figure 1. Dalia Al-Akki, Jana Antoun, Juan Arizti, Marta Borreguero, Elena Caubet, Ines Fernández, Tanvi Gupta, Stephanie Ibrahim, Tracy Jabbour, Yunling Jin, Jad Karam, Selen Kurt, Alexa Nader, Joelle Nader, Assil Naji, Mokshuda Narula, Tiago Rosado, Eirini Sampani, Montserrat Sevilla, Brentsen Solomon, Kuan Yi Wu [faculty: Roger Paez, Toni Montes, Bhavleen Kaur and Atrey Chhaya], 2020. Community Plugins

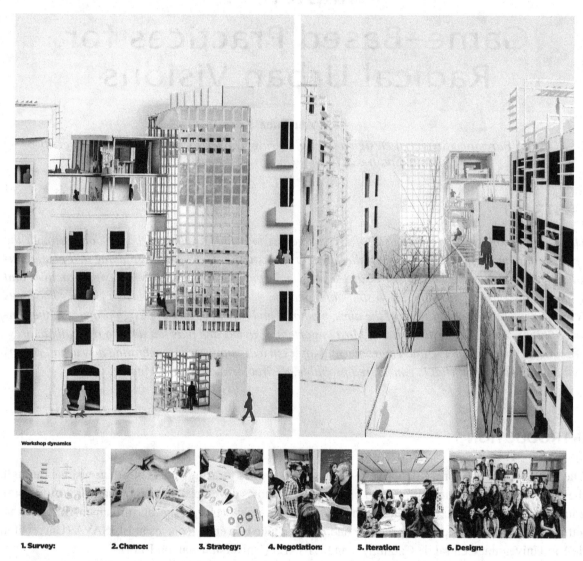

Workshop dynamics

1. Survey: 2. Chance: 3. Strategy: 4. Negotiation: 5. Iteration: 6. Design:

Figure 2. Xenia Armengol, Dorian Bella, Victoria Caballero, Agustina Cainzo, Albert Chavarria, Alex Font, Ronald Grebe, Marco Mosca, Alaa Osman, Charisa Paredes, Laura Prudence, Carlota Puigrefagut, Aurora Santallusia [faculty: Roger Paez and Jordi Mansilla], 2018. El Núvol [The Cloud]

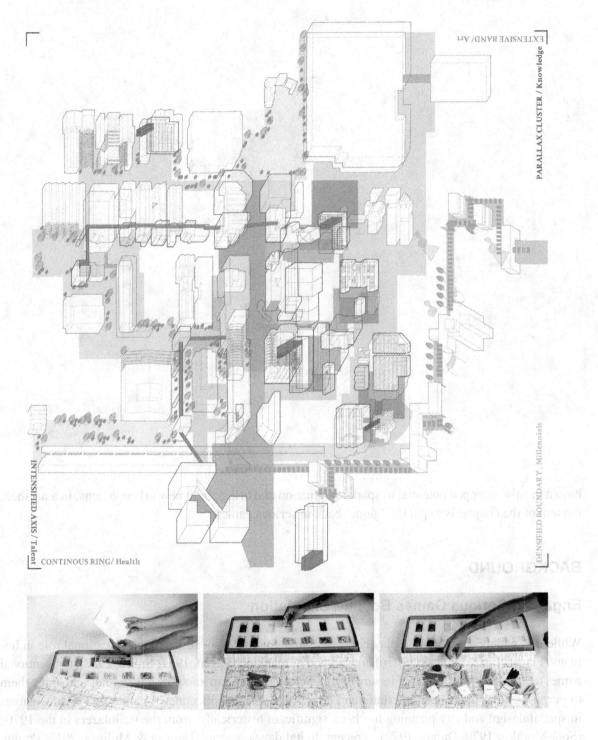

Figure 3. Roger Paez [faculty: Enric Miralles, Carme Ribas, Ton Salvadó], 1998. EisTenPolin [Towards the City]

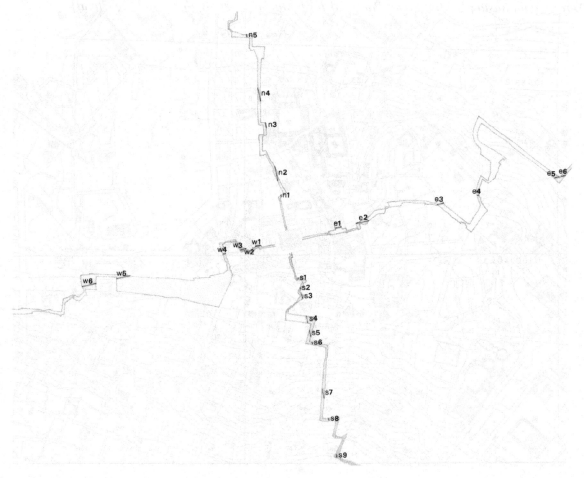

have a mostly untapped potential to spark imagination and bring about new urban visions. In a nutshell, the aim of the chapter is to put the 'game' back in serious games.

BACKGROUND

Engaging Serious Games Beyond Simulation

While it is widely accepted that play has a profound cognitive, socialising and educational role in humans (Piaget, 1962; Vygotsky, 2016) and beyond humankind (Fagen, 1981; Smith, 1982), conventional games tend to stress the aspect of leisure or fun. Serious games tap into play's potentials and apply them to purposes other than sheer entertainment (Abt, 1970). The application of games and serious games in spatial design and city planning has been significant historically, from the trailblazers in the 1970s (Solà-Morales, 1970; Dupuy, 1972) to recent digital developments (Henriot & Molines, 2019; Poplin, 2011). However, there are two questions that potentially restrict the enormous capabilities of serious games as applied to architecture, design and urbanism. First, most serious games attempt to simulate real-world behaviours (however simplified) in order to train specific skills: such as in flight, medical or urban simulators. Second, serious games often formalise play through a rigid (albeit complex) set of protocols that sometimes curtail the open nature of play, whereas play's strength lies in the unresolved tension between closure (limits, rules) and openness (chance). Some authors (Graeber, 2015; Walther, 2003) establish a distinction between the open-endedness of play and the bounded qualities of games that is relevant in this discussion. Graeber, particularly, is very explicit about the political implications of exploring play as free creativity versus engaging in games as predictable, regulated action. Indeed, the current tendency to overregulate every aspect of life "ultimately derives from a tacit cosmology in which the play principle (and by extension, creativity) is itself seen as frightening, while game-like behaviour is celebrated as transparent and predictable" (Graber, 2015, p. 196). We claim that in engaging serious games in design both principles should be critically combined to ensure performance (through the regulated, territorialising aspect of games) while expanding imagination (through the creative, deterritorialising aspect of play).

Play's Contribution to Design Practices

Play addresses three basic questions: limits, self and chance. Play can challenge the relevance and test the operativity of a set of accepted rules (whether temporal, spatial or behavioural). It can push the boundaries of conventional authorship by enacting fluid roles (often unrelated to the player's actual worldview or set of beliefs). And it can let players actively explore the agency of chance—ultimately working in an open environment unrestrained by solution-provider logics, embracing serendipity and exploring indeterminacy as a positive design value. Elsewhere, the author has discussed how an expanded notion of play holds a huge potential for design, identifying play's contribution in three concepts that mirror the triad of play's pursuits: facilitating an explorative use of factual or self-imposed constraints, prompting new types of engagement and authorship through dialogism and creatively embracing chance (Paez, in press; Elvira & Paez, 2019).

Radical Exploration through Game-Based Formats

In recent practice, serious games have been used extensively in collaborative or participatory urbanism to articulate consensual conflict-mediation approaches (Arenas et al., 2020). These approaches harness the potential of non-competitive games to negotiate and address collaborative problem-solving (Tan, 2020). However, there is a radically explorative aspect of play that is left untapped by consensual approaches. This chapter will focus on that radicality. Playful environments and serious games have the potential to generate an environment that is predisposed to a radical exploration of the aims, methodologies and results of city-making processes, leading to radical urban visions. By radical urban visions, we refer to a design approach that focuses on providing visionary and often disruptive scenarios with the potential to thoroughly rearrange current preconceptions of what cities are, could, or should be. Beyond urban gamification and the playable city paradigm (Watershed, 2014), a responsible yet bold approach to speculative urban futures offers a perspective that is sorely needed in today's world, characterised above all by uncertainty and a lack of cohesive shared horizons. Exploring playful environments and game-based practices in educational and research centres can contribute to that general aim. Serious game methodologies can be used in urban design to explore different interests and respond to different ethical horizons. While collaborative urbanism focuses on the conflict-resolution capabilities of serious games, speculative radical practices focus on exploration, using serious game's abilities to incorporate chance and creatively deal with indeterminacy. For all the value of consensual approaches, if the inevitable conflict in our societies is to be addressed as a positive city-making force (Mouffe, 2013) antagonism must also be taken into account, understood as a proactive attitude driving a critical reckoning with hegemonic truths, voluntarily instrumentalising conflict, but also critique, imagination and desire (Paez and Valtchanova, 2021).

Indeterminacy as a Positive Urban Factor

Expanding the means at our disposal to understand today's cities and project future urban scenarios through game-based practices responds to a holistic approach to the city. The author understands the city as a complex medium beyond the binaries of top-down/bottom-up, planned/self-organised, infrastructure/event, and so on. The city is made up of an interconnected web of environmental, spatial, socio-cultural, economic and political systems (BCNEcologia, 2019), and both formal and informal processes, strategies and tactics (Certeau, 1984) and designed and improvisational practices (Dell, 2019) have agency in tapping into these different urban dimensions. It is important to clarify that this holistic approach by no means seeks out or presupposes a 'final' or 'ideal' state of the complex system (the city) but assumes a radical indeterminacy and embraces it as a source of urban imagination.

CASE STUDIES FROM BARCELONA RADICAL LANDSCAPES

Overview

Although the case studies presented in this chapter are diverse in terms of both topic and tone, they are three iterations of the same basic design studio methodology, called Barcelona Radical Landscapes. It uses playful environments and game formats to address radical urban visions at multiple scales, from territorial strategies to situated practices. The focus is on subverting the expectations of the aims, methods and results of spatial design projects in the context of higher educational institutions, as well as obstructing conventional teacher-student roles. Most importantly, game and play are used to radically address all-too-real, highly relevant and pressing technical, societal and environmental topics in a disruptive way, generating new urban visions that push the limits of what is considered probable, desirable, and even imaginable. Thus, serious game formats are not used to address problem-solving through simulation but are purposefully used as heuristic devices shedding light on improbable yet potential urban horizons and, especially, as open frameworks to explore radical urban visions using speculative design approaches (Dunne & Raby, 2013).

In the discussion that follows, the author will offer a brief description of the context and methodology for each case study and then focus on presenting the specific results of each iteration. The boldness of the design statements, the variety of topics addressed, the richness of the specific solutions proposed, and the diversity of tones used to convey the messages are proof of the ability of open-ended game-based practices to inform design. It is important to clarify that the open-endedness of this design approach precludes a rigid application of a clear-cut, step-by-step methodology. Consequently, the evaluation of the case studies' results must be qualitative rather than quantitative.

The main focus of this section lies in presenting the results attained for the purpose of identifying relevant topics and matters of concern raised and addressed by the radical urban visions developed through game-based formats and playful environments. The accompanying figures, generated by the students and edited by the author, are not mere illustrations of the text but the medium through which the radical urban visions were explored and the design intent was communicated.

Context

Barcelona Radical Landscapes is a five-year programme within the BCN Unit design studio, led by the author and Pedro García at the School of Architecture of La Salle (ETSALS) – Ramon Llull University. It is a semester-long design studio for advanced undergraduate architecture students (4th and 5th year), both local and international. The name highlights the explorative ethos of the course. 'Radical', meaning "from the root" (from Latin *radix* "root", from Proto Indo-European *wrād- "branch, root"), indicates our desire to use design to explore core potentialities of urban life in an epoch of global crises, expanding the apparently immutable horizon of expectation of today's world through the exploration and visualisation of new spaces of experience (both concepts taken form Koselleck, 2004, pp. 255-275). 'Landscapes' suggests a more open approach to city making, beyond the disciplinary schism between architecture, urbanism and design. Last but not least, 'Barcelona' entails using Barcelona as a lab to investigate, explore and test contemporary architectural and urbanistic approaches applicable worldwide. While the issues addressed are of global interest, their architectural materialisation is local, establishing a feedback loop between generic questions and specific conditions in order to achieve a high level of both ambition and precision in design research.

Methodology

Barcelona Radical Landscapes proposes a game-based design studio methodology to uncover latent urban sites and opportunities in the apparently built-up city of Barcelona and propose radical visions that challenge expectations on the future of urban habitats.

The methodology activates serious game logics on two distinct levels: formal and informal. Formally, it uses game-based formats such as rule-sets, formal constraints, time management, combinatory logics, aleatorics (Motte, 1986), and the purposeful incorporation of chance dynamics. Informally, it fosters a playful atmosphere through a lively and carefree approach to pressing current global emergencies to supersede 'designer's block' when facing wicked problems, a somewhat mischievous disavowal of conventional expectations regarding what can design do in this context, and a curated subversion of the authority roles in a university setting.

The basic methodology of the course includes five steps: localisation and references, programme and vision, formalisation, development, and final presentation. First, students identify 16 potential sites using game tools, such as the randomised selection of an area (Chora & Bunschoten, 2001) and experiential derives (Paez, 2014). Simultaneously, students collect architectural and urban references related to the course's specific topic approach (in this case, waterfronts). All this work is compiled into a shared, pre-defined card-like graphic format, so that each site and each reference is represented by a single card. Through a game-like process including role play and chance, four site-cards are chosen. Second, students discuss the reference-cards and distil some of the urban topics addressed in them—topics that are relevant to the course's general direction and the team's specific interests. Loosely based on these topics, they propose one programme for each of the four chosen sites. Programmes are briefly presented through a single programme-card following the same graphic format as the site and reference cards. Combining a site-card with one or more reference-cards and a programme-card, each of the four programme-sites is quickly tested by using a single graphic document (collage, sketch, model) to generate a radical urban vision. Third, all the students together discuss each team's four urban visions in a situation room format. This helps to clarify the interests and galvanise the design ethos of the whole class, while at the same time facilitating the cross-pollination between the different teams. In the following phase, each team begins formalising their design proposal, concentrating most of their efforts on a single 'wow' document that captures the crucial research questions addressed and the team's core design intentions. Fourth, each team develops their proposal following the logics intrinsic to their specific design claim and urban vision. Finally, each student individually develops a specific aspect of the team's proposal, with the intention of proliferating the proposal to explore various paths and test different implications of the common design. All phases except for the last one are done in teams to prompt dialogic and playful practices that subvert conventional approaches to individual authorship. A few transversal practices, such as strict game-like time management (e.g., turns and rounds) and the introduction of wild cards (e.g., lectures unrelated to the studio's topic, unscheduled out-of-class activities, unexpected visits from external faculty/alumni), further reinforce the course's playful atmosphere and build an environment open to experimentation and discovery.

The presentations of the case studies begin with a description of the radical urban vision resulting from the exercise. This is followed by a description of the unique game-related methods organically developed by each team to enrich the general methodology. Finally, there is an identification of the complex topics raised and addressed by the design proposal. Three case studies with very different focuses (environmental, cultural and social) have been selected in order to showcase the richness of this design approach.

Environmental Focus: Sea Wall

Urban vision

A massive wall, triangular in plan, protects the historical city centre from the rising sea levels.

Figure 4 shows an aerial view of the centre of Barcelona identifying the area protected by the sea wall, as well as the flooded low-lying areas of Poblesec to the southwest and Poblenou to the northeast. The historical port and the beaches of Barceloneta and Icària have become an interior sea, maintaining the coastline of the early 21st century. The schematic plans at the bottom of the image show the progressive construction of the sea wall, responding to the changes in the coastline as a result of continuing sea level rise. The worst forecasts have come to pass and due to man-made environmental changes, the levels of all bodies of water have risen drastically, including contained seas like the Mediterranean.

Figure 5 shows how the construction of the sea wall separates the protected coastline from the rising sea beyond. Like most port cities, a large part of Barcelona is dramatically affected by this change. Given the scale of the problem, there is no way to save all the waterfront districts. A decision is made to pour all efforts into safeguarding the historical core of Barcelona, where the city was founded more than 2,000 years ago. This is due to the symbolic relevance of the foundational kernel of the city, which is singled out as the low-lying area that needs to be protected.

The section through the city centre in Figure 6 shows the basic configuration of the sea wall as a protective infrastructure as well as a support for urbanity. The open sea, to the left of the image, is prevented

Figure 4. Carles Gesa, Carlos González, Martin Nicholls [faculty: Roger Paez , Pedro Garcia, Albert Chavarria TA], 2021. Sea Wall

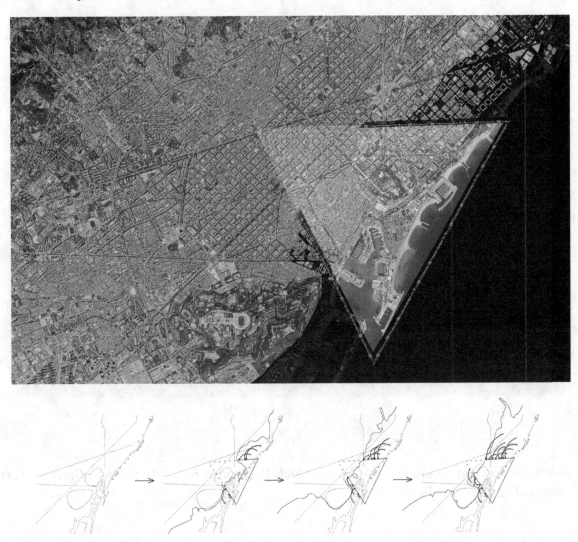

from flooding the historical core of Barcelona while it is used as a source of renewable energy. The sea wall itself, in the centre of the image, becomes the foundation for a new linear city, a vibrant community between waters. To the right of the picture, the old coastline and some of Barcelona's beaches are preserved. The unfolded plan at the bottom of Figure 6 shows the sea wall as the hard boundary between the old (below) and the new (above) sea levels. Some districts, like the industrial and logistic port of Zona Franca, will move upland, while other areas, like the Poblenou-22@ neighbourhood, will suffer a major transformation, allowing lower floors to be progressively flooded and becoming a modern-day Venice. In 1848, the old medieval walls were demolished due to public pressure. Ironically, barely 200 years later, an equally widespread social sentiment supports the construction of a new wall. Updating bygone logics of protection, the Sea Wall encloses the city on three sides, creating a new hard boundary

Figure 5. Carles Gesa, Carlos González, Martin Nicholls [faculty: Roger Paez , Pedro Garcia, Albert Chavarria TA], 2021. Sea Wall

Figure 6. Carles Gesa, Carlos González, Martin Nicholls [faculty: Roger Paez , Pedro Garcia, Albert Chavarria TA], 2021. Sea Wall

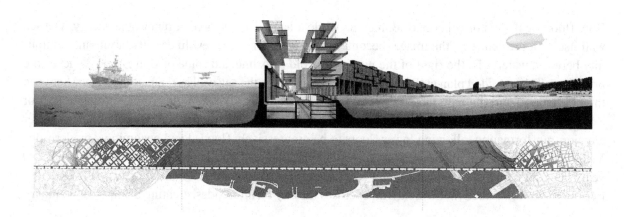

Figure 7. Carles Gesa, Carlos González, Martin Nicholls [faculty: Roger Paez , Pedro Garcia, Albert Chavarria TA], 2021. Sea Wall

between city and territory. Only this time around, the city does not stop at the wall, but sprawls upland as far as the eye can see.

Figure 7 captures a view from a high apartment on the sea wall, looking inland toward the city centre. The sea wall penetrating the urban fabric can be seen at a distance. As long as the sea levels keep rising, the wall will keep extending inland. The Sea Wall is not a mere dyke but a veritable foundation for a linear urbanity. A city-generator. The infrastructure designed to retain the rising sea and harness its vast energy potential, also serves, quite literally, as the new ground where the displaced population from the flooded areas can rebuild a home and hearth. Fifty meters wide, the wall houses an astonishing variety of spaces and all imaginable functions: from dwellings to theatres, from offices to parks, from shops to universities. Compelled by the need to be higher than the ever-rising waters, the new datum defines a problematic ground floor that enters into strange and often conflicting relations with the existing city. Below it, transportation, logistics and services occupy the dark, humid spaces. Above it, there is a proliferation of sun-drenched spaces for living and relating. Every thousand meters there is a gate, a site of connection between inside and outside, with all the trappings such places of exchange tend to have. Between two gates, an agora marks the core of public life of a kilometre-long neighbourhood. Between these main points, urban life unfolds in its complex and unforeseeable ways.

Figure 8 features diagrammatic plans showing the organisational sequence of a generic part of the sea wall. On both edges of the image, the gates control access to the protected city centre; in the centre, an agora concentrates neighbourhood life. Further spatial subdivisions define ever more specific levels of community. The actual spatial layout can be freely developed within the basic infrastructural constraints.

Figure 8. Carles Gesa, Carlos González, Martin Nicholls [faculty: Roger Paez , Pedro Garcia, Albert Chavarria TA], 2021. Sea Wall

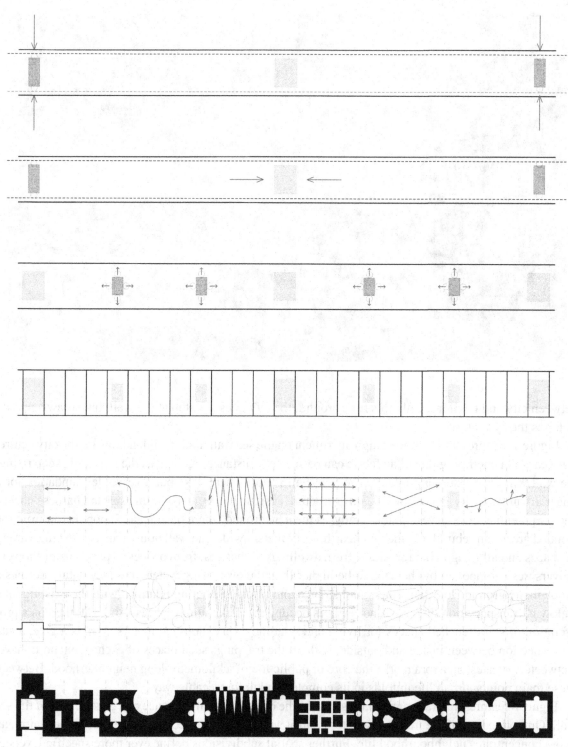

Figure 9. Carles Gesa, Carlos González, Martin Nicholls [faculty: Roger Paez , Pedro Garcia, Albert Chavarria TA], 2021. Sea Wall

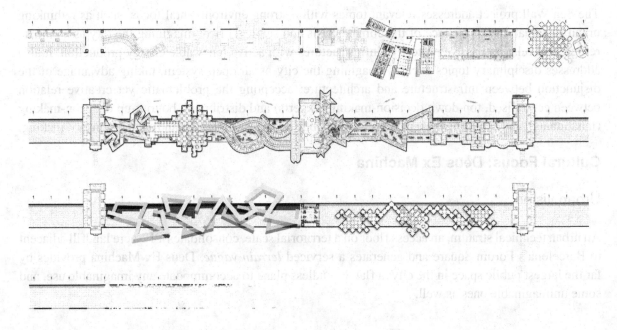

Method

The Sea Wall team enriched the course's general serious game methodology in two ways. First, they purposefully introduced role playing techniques resulting in multiple outcomes, stressing the open-endedness of the design proposal. Together, the team members defined three iterations of the project and developed them individually in the final stage of the course, thus enacting and communicating the proposal's multiple outcomes and the tension between common design strategies and individual tactical interpretations thereof. Second, they chose to use a self-imposed formal constraint and graphically present their work in a continuous line This made it easier to follow the proposal's narrative while at the same time reinforcing the linearity of the design.

Figure 9 shows the plan, rearranged here to fit the page, originally developed and presented in a five-metre-long continuous line. The section above shows the basic sea wall configuration and a number of modern and contemporary architectural references to scale. These serve as the starting point to propose three distinct playful sea wall layout proposals. The first one, in the second row, addresses the district scale between two gates and is generated through an articulated combination and rearrangement of multiple references, seeking out spatial continuities and the generation of a cohesive public space. The second one, to the left of the third row, addresses the block scale and is generated through the morphing of two specific references, using formal operations such as extend, multiply, slice, or rotate to spawn a hybrid architecture. The third one, to the right of the third row, addresses the building scale and is generated through the modular proliferation of a single reference in both plan and section. The fourth row is purposefully left open to indicate the potentiality of the sea wall to accommodate any type of architecture.

Topics

The Sea Wall project addresses relevant topics with a strong environmental focus, such as rethinking urban sustainability in the face of the climate crisis and sea-level rise; imagining the city as a climate refuge; and relating passive protective infrastructures with active renewable energy production. It also addresses disciplinary topics such as imagining the city as an open system, taking advantage of the disjunction between infrastructure and architecture; accepting the problematic yet creative relation between centralised, top-down decision-making (experts) and distributed, bottom-up decision-making (inhabitants); and exploring the tension between public and private interests and agencies in city-making.

Cultural Focus: Deus Ex Machina

Urban vision

An urban technical stratum, an access floor on a territorial scale, consolidates a 12-acre landfill adjacent to Barcelona's Forum Square and generates a serviced *terrain vague*. Deus Ex Machina provides by far the largest public space in the city: a flat, boundless plane to accommodate any imaginable use, and some unimaginable ones as well.

Figure 10. Pau Garrofé, Guillem Hernández [faculty: Roger Paez , Pedro Garcia, Albert Chavarria TA], 2021. Deus Ex Machina

Figure 11. Pau Garrofé, Guillem Hernández [faculty: Roger Paez , Pedro Garcia, Albert Chavarria TA], 2021. Deus Ex Machina

Figure 10 boldly captures the essence of the proposal, based on the radical disjunction between the servicing space below and the serviced surface above. This new *terrain vague*, purposefully built as an area of opportunity with no specific function, harnesses temporality to accommodate different levels of urban activation, from major festivals for 50,000 people to solitary experiences.

Figure 11 shows three different intensities of use for the top surface based on programme and season: the top of the image depicts a concert in spring, the centre a nudist solarium in summer, and the bottom an empty landscape in winter. While the top surface is featureless and extensive, it is lavishly served by

Figure 12. Pau Garrofé, Guillem Hernández [faculty: Roger Paez , Pedro Garcia, Albert Chavarria TA], 2021. Deus Ex Machina

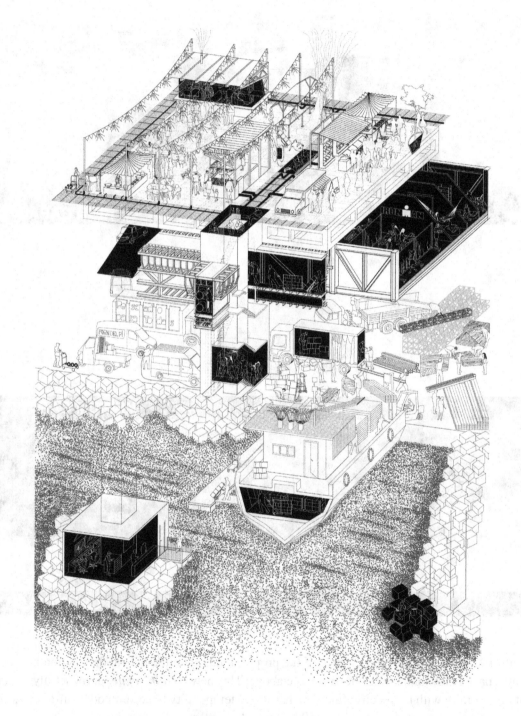

Figure 13. Pau Garrofé, Guillem Hernández [faculty: Roger Paez , Pedro Garcia, Albert Chavarria TA], 2021. Deus Ex Machina

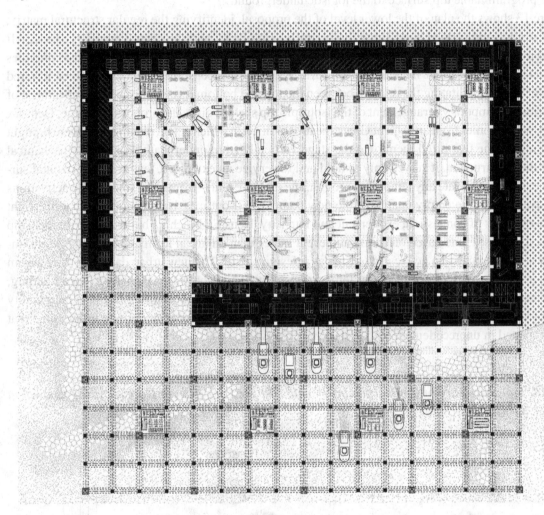

a vast underground world, on both land and sea, that houses all the technical facilities, infrastructural services, and auxiliary space to support any temporary uses of the top surface.

Figure 12 is a detailed axonometric drawing showing the configuration of the top surface resulting from the complex spaces below. The top of the image depicts one of the myriad possibilities for temporarily activating the top surface, while service elements such as accessibility, water, drainage and electricity can be seen coming from below. The load-bearing structure that holds the top surface in place is also used to condition indoor spaces that require higher environmental control. The bottom part of the image shown the man-made landfill and the sea as ancillary logistic spaces, essential to irrigate the smooth *terrain vague* above. The load-bearing structure is simple yet monumental, due to its sheer scale. A forest of pillars holds a brand-new urban datum on the waterfront that connects directly to the city level, erasing the physical boundary of the city's perimetral highway, now under the new datum and thus hidden from view. The regular load-bearing structure facilitates the construction of an isotropic public space above, regulated by large-scale square units. A regular matrix of vertical circulation cores provides accessibility from the programmable top surface to the logistic underground.

Figure 13 shows the plan of the lower level of the proposal, identifying the regular structural matrix, the hard storage and service band along the perimeter (in black), and the central auxiliary space, left open and available to support any activity programmed above. The sea below the top surface provides direct boat access. To further increase the top surface's performance, some of the units can be lowered to the level below, facilitating the relation between the top and bottom levels. The sudden appearance of any imaginable temporary arrangement of the isotropic top surface gives the proposal its name, Deus Ex Machina, which comes from an ancient Greek theatre tradition in which actors playing gods were brought on using a machine that lifted them onto the stage vertically from underneath. For all the mechanical might of the construction, it serves only to hold and to service an extensive, featureless horizontal surface that can accommodate any temporary programme, use or event—from calm small-scale activations taking advantage of the empty quality of the new datum to all-out massive celebrations that highlight the urban qualities of congestion, excitement and intensity. Deus Ex Machina builds a new relationship between city and sea, one based on action and event rather than on urban form and iconicity. More importantly still, it suggests an active use of time as a design vector. The new urban datum, serviced from below, is a smooth space of opportunities temporarily activated in any way imaginable. Not a building, not a square, not a park, Deus Ex Machina fulfils the promise of freedom resulting from the marginality offered by a *terrain vague*: urban interstices, ambiguous spaces without a predefined programme that can be activated in unprecedented, unexpected and creative.

Figure 14. Pau Garrofé, Guillem Hernández [faculty: Roger Paez , Pedro Garcia, Albert Chavarria TA], 2021. Deus Ex Machina

The eight variations shown in Figure 14 are a token of the manifold possibilities of use afforded, whether planned or improvised: a popup nudist beach, an illegal street party, a funfair, urban agriculture, sports, farmer's markets, private celebrations, or a drive-in cinema. Deus Ex Machina is a place to test the imagination, to enact citizen empowerment, and to radically explore what it means to live in cities.

Method

The Deus Ex Machina team enriched the course's serious game methodology by designing a board game as part of their proposal. The eponymous board game, consisting of a physical board, a rule booklet and a set of tokens, uses playful logics explore the design proposal's potential configurations. It is a cross between a strategy game and a role-playing game, activating both negotiation between players and chance.

Figure 15. Pau Garrofé, Guillem Hernández [faculty: Roger Paez , Pedro Garcia, Albert Chavarria TA], 2021. Deus Ex Machina

Figure 15 shows the physical gameboard and the tokens at different stages of the game. The game was used to expand the proposal's possibilities well beyond the expected configurations of the Deus Ex Machina multipurpose urban platform.

Topics

The Deus Ex Machina project addresses relevant topics with a strong cultural focus, such as defining urban spaces through use rather than form, exploring a performative approach to urban design; using temporality as a design tool; proposing a politically charged yet playful activation of fringe urban spaces; purposefully building a *terrain vague*, an unprogrammed yet enabling space activated through specific appropriations by citizens; and exploring a new form of commons. It also addresses disciplinary topics such as articulating an active relation between hard physical infrastructure and soft civic superstructure.

Social Focus: Travellers' Platform

Urban vision

An iconic oil platform is transported in front of Barcelona and repurposed as a hub for travellers.

Figure 16. Martina Blázquez, Diego Lahoz [faculty: Roger Paez , Pedro Garcia, Albert Chavarria TA], 2021. Travellers' Platform

The montage in Figure 16 is a bold graphic statement showing the interaction of the main elements of the design: the repurposed oil platform in the centre of the image, the tourist cruise boats to the left, and the rescue vessels to the right. In the distance, the iconic skyline of the city of Barcelona is a reminder of the extraterritorial quality of the proposal. Due to insufficient oil reserves, the Casablanca platform, in use since 1981 and situated 44 km off the coast of southern Catalonia, recently shut down operations. Leaving this large man-made structure in the middle of the sea supposes a serious environmental risk, but dismantling it has a significant cost and offers no returns—or does it? By transforming an obsolete extractive infrastructure into an innovative productive hub focusing on servicing the myriad people travelling to Barcelona by sea, the cost of dismantling and transporting the oil platform is sidestepped.

Figure 17. Martina Blázquez, Diego Lahoz [faculty: Roger Paez , Pedro Garcia, Albert Chavarria TA], 2021. Travellers' Platform

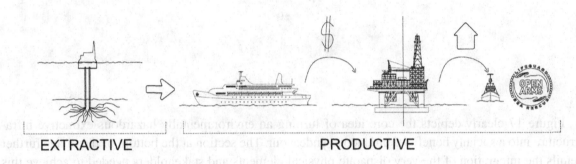

EXTRACTIVE   PRODUCTIVE

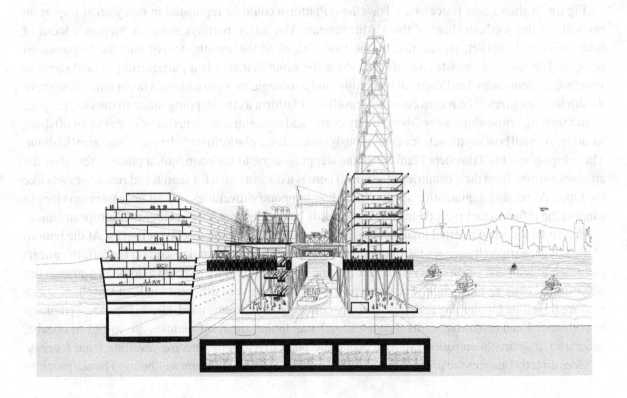

Figure 18. Martina Blázquez, Diego Lahoz [faculty: Roger Paez, Pedro Garcia, Albert Chavarria TA], 2021. Travellers' Platform

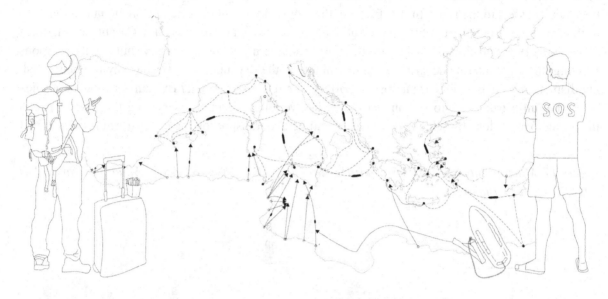

Figure 17 clearly depicts the core idea of turning an environmentally hazardous extractive infrastructure into a socially beneficial productive endeavour. The section at the bottom of the image further details the integration of the very disparate physical elements and stakeholders needed to achieve this transformation. The Travellers' Platform caters to travellers of all sorts, both sightseeing tourists and refugees seeking a better life.

Figure 18 shows how Barcelona's Travellers' Platform could be replicated in many other important ports along the northern shore of the Mediterranean. The image portrays *mare nostrum* as a locus of both desire and conflict, represented by the twin images of the wealthy tourist and the dispossessed refugee. The fact that tourists and refugees share the same structure is a purposeful political move to visualise contemporary landscapes of inequality, and a strategic move to address a fairer redistribution of wealth and resources. The tourists use the Travellers' Platform as the stepping-stone to the city, keeping contaminating cruise ships away from the city centre and concentrating touristic services in an offshore location. A small boat shuttle service continuously connects the platform with the city's historical harbour. The refugees use the Travellers Platform as the stepping-stone to the continent, a place to rest after the arduous journey from their countries of origin. There is a docking area for search and rescue vessels like the Open Arms, and a quarantine section including temporary dwellings and all necessary services to support the refugees and meet their immediate needs before they are able to enter the European Union.

Figure 19 shows an internal image of the temporary housing for the rescued refugees. At the bottom of the image, a triptych narrates the dramatic experience of migration and rescue on the left; the uncertain stage of temporary hospitality in the centre; and the hopeful future to make a home in a strange but welcoming country on the right. The close proximity between very different kinds of travellers, those who are travelling for pleasure and those who are compelled by extreme need, allows for some symbiosis in both social and economic terms. From a social standpoint, different realities are forced to coexist, generating a desirable empathy. From an economic point of view, the income resulting from tourists' services directly finances the immediate needs of the refugees and their future wellbeing. The sea provides

Figure 19. Martina Blázquez, Diego Lahoz [faculty: Roger Paez , Pedro Garcia, Albert Chavarria TA], 2021. Travellers' Platform

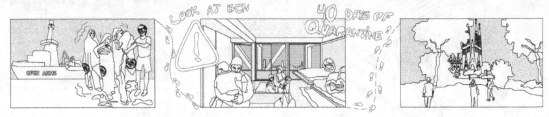

a continuous supply of renewable energy to sustain the whole operation, while non-recyclable trash is used as fuel, taking advantage of the oil platform's incinerating systems. The extra-territoriality of the offshore platform, afforded by its location 12 nautical miles off the coast, implies a special legal status that grants both types of travellers certain advantages: duty free shopping for tourists and legal protection for refugees. The Travellers' Platform is a step towards the realisation of the dream of equality, using an obsolete industrial infrastructure for social purposes—a welfare state re-enactment of Ellis Island using the iconic image of a transformed oil platform as a beacon of justice and civic sustainability.

Method

The Travellers' Platform team enriched the course's general serious game methodology in two ways. First, they incorporated more players into the design process, inviting people initially unrelated to the design team to participate in the roles of the most relevant stakeholders: i.e., the tourist and the refugee.

Figure 20. Martina Blázquez, Diego Lahoz [faculty: Roger Paez , Pedro Garcia, Albert Chavarria TA], 2021. Travellers' Platform

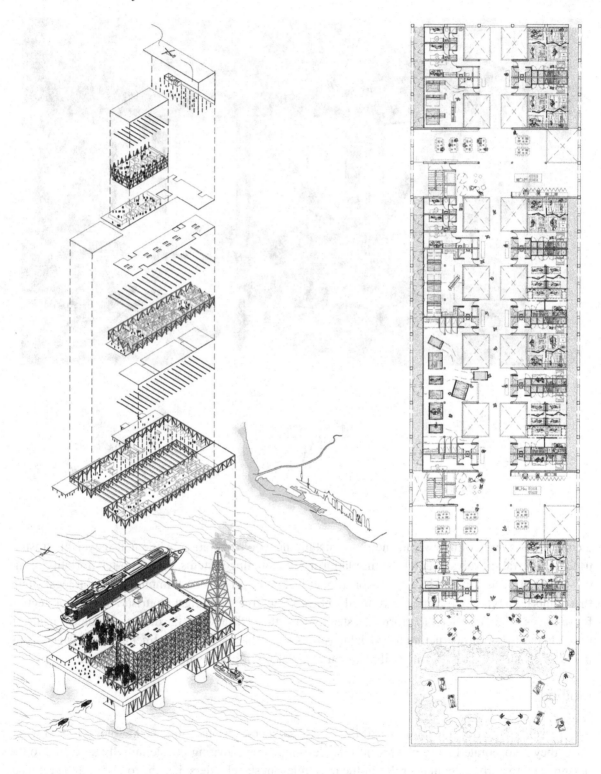

That move forced them to relate to external voices, not invested in the design proposal on a personal level. Second, they consciously introduced game logics such as taking turns and playing rounds to explore and communicate the design's proliferating qualities. In the final phase of the project, each student took turns making individual decisions that were reacted to by the next student and so on, thus erasing the boundary of conventional authorial design and generating a design proposal as a direct result of the interaction between players

The left side of Figure 20 shows an exploded axonometric drawing of the common spatial organisation, while the right side of the image shows a partial result of the different layouts of the adaptable temporary housing units generated separately by the members of the design team and subsequently pasted together on either side of the central corridor.

Topics

The Travellers' Platform project addresses relevant topics with a strong social focus, such as treating migration as a beneficial social resource; using tourism to finance social economies; transitioning from an extractive to a productive economy; enacting ethics of care and social co-responsibility; counteracting urban segregation caused by tourist-generated gentrification; and rethinking the social and environmental impacts of large-scale cruise tourism on coastal cities. It also addresses disciplinary topics such as the adaptive reuse of obsolete infrastructures.

FUTURE RESEARCH DIRECTIONS

An initial direction for future research might involve a shift in the specific dimension of the city that is addressed in the design approach. The city is a complex phenomenon, simultaneously *urbs*, *civitas* and *polis*. *Urbs* refers to the physical space, the morphological framework of the city, made up of buildings and infrastructure. *Civitas* refers to the social reality construed by citizens inhabiting the city and exercising citizenship rights. Finally, *polis* refers to the political community articulated around the city and city-life (Jennings, 2001, 89; Capel, 2003). While dealing simultaneously with all three dimensions, the case studies focus mainly on the physical component of cities (*urbs*) through the methodological approach based on the choice of site/reference/programme. Slight variations in this game-based methodology could shift the focus onto the relational (*civitas*) or the political (*polis*) components of the city and would likely yield very different, yet complementary results. This iteration would be relevant to exploring a larger array of design approaches and generating more varied urban visions. For instance, the game-based design process could take social relations (e.g., intergenerational relations) or policies (e.g., migratory policy) as its starting point, rather than physical sites (e.g., waterfronts).

A second future research direction could involve implementing the game-based practices at a different stage of the design process. The case studies use a serious games approach in the conceptualisation and design development phases, but they fail to do so in the problematisation or performance monitoring phases. For instance, game-based practices could be used to explore a disruptive approach to an initial problematisation phase, using scenario-writing and what-if questions, or a proposal resulting from a conventional design methodology could be stress-tested in the final performance monitoring phase through role-play practices.

A third future research direction might deal with an in-depth exploration of game-based digital environments and their ability to proliferate radical urban visions, for instance through parametric design techniques or AR/VR environments.

CONCLUSION

Rethinking Authorship in Design

Recent societal challenges, technological developments and cultural shifts have pushed traditional hard authorship in design away from centre stage (Elvira, 2005; Waldheim, 2006; Ortega, 2017, p. 47ff). More complex and supple decision-making processes are being tested to respond to changing perceptions of the role of design and of how designers should proceed in an agonistic society. An exploratory approach to game-based design formats has a massive transformative potential, and rethinking authorship in design is one of its most salient outcomes. As the case studies have shown, the relationship between design intent, game-based formats, and playful practices is a very rich one. The author posits play itself as a way to critically design cities, using play's capacities to expand conventional design approaches and reinvent contemporary authorship. Game-based design practices offer a stupendous arsenal to expand on traditional modes of authorship leading to the concept of the augmented designer, "a figure that expands on the designer's conventional authorship through an enhancement of his or her performative capacities based on the incorporation of new conceptual, methodological, and technological devices" (Paez, 2019, p. 312). As developed by the author elsewhere, "understanding design as playground is based on facilitating an explorative use of factual or self-imposed constraints, prompting new types of engagement and authorship through dialogism and creatively embracing chance" (Paez, in press).

The case studies presented here show how "through a specific definition of constraints, designers can creatively organise and relate a sub-set of reality and turn it into a laboratory to explore specific questions, explicitly addressing the setup of the game as a crucial design question." As far as dialogism goes, they show that designers use role-play to "rewire intrasubjective responses and challenge dominant forms of subjectivation" and use negotiation to "explore new modes of intersubjectivity, which problematize post-Romantic authorship centred on an autarkic subject." Finally, "through the incorporation of chance, designers articulate a different relationship between design intent and effect, dismantling hard control and top-down design approaches and inviting non-human, asubjective agency" (Paez, in press).

Although the case studies draw on all three of these aspects (constraints, dialogism and chance), they place a special focus on an explorative use of factual and self-imposed constraints. One of the most relevant roles game-based practices play in design is the articulation of subjective decision-making processes with objective rule-based formats. As is the case with literary constraint-based creation systems, such as classical poetic metres (e.g., dactylic hexameter, alexandrine, skaldic poetry, sonnet) or modernist combinatory literature (e.g., Raymond Roussel, OuLiPo, David Foster Wallace, Erasure poetry), the purposeful acceptance of self-imposed constraints is a source of disciplinary invention in design. As the case studies show, based on—yet moving beyond—design informed by constraints (Eames, 1969), game formats can successfully articulate the creative tension between an objective, pre-given rule-set (either chosen or imposed) and a subjective, expressive desire (Bogost, 2016, 146-153). They may also offer new insights on co-creation, co-responsibility, participation (LaCol, 2018) and design for the unforeseen (Fannon et al., in press).

The Need for Radical Imagination and Active Speculation

As the world we inhabit witnesses the unfolding of emergencies of all kinds that should remind us of the precariousness of the material and symbolic armature that holds our dominant worldview in place, we seem intent in ignoring this call, plunging ourselves into business-as-usual approaches. This generalised attitude "reduces futures to matters of anticipation, calculation, management and pre-emption of risks and uncertainties in the present" (Savransky et al., 2017, p. 1), effectively generating a suspension of time as an open horizon of invention, exploration and experimentation. The author claims this is a highly toxic tendency that cements the understanding of an apparently immutable present, blocking any possibility of imagining the occurrence of something radically different. Specifically, the case of urban futures is particularly relevant; given the tendencies of population growth and increased urbanisation, cities remain one of the world's most crucial fronts in social, political, cultural, economic and environmental terms. From both an epistemological and an ethical point of view, the author claims it is necessary to break with this suspension of time and mobilise radicality to speculate on futures that go beyond the mere management of our continuous present (Mitrović & Šuran, 2016).

The case studies presented in this chapter use regulated game-based formats as a methodological scaffolding that allows designers to go beyond what they consider proper or adequate and surpass their own expectations of what is acceptable as a design result, using the game's cohesive internal logic as a protective magic circle (Huizinga, 1948), within which the possibilities of the real are augmented. But above and beyond 'hard' game-based logics, such as rule-sets, role-play and turn-taking, the case studies show the enormous power of playfulness, understood as a 'soft' atmosphere pervading the entire design experience, a collectively generated frame of mind that facilitates the playful (yet not frivolous) contestation of acquired truths and the joyful exploration of expanded realities.

The Disruptive Role of Playful Environments and Game-Based Practices

Notwithstanding serious games' instrumental uses, the author wishes to focus the attention on their radically disruptive potential. While some authors highlight the problem-solving potential of serious games applied to the city (Tan, 2020), others stress their ability to structure complex processes of participatory urbanism (Arenas et al., 2020) and still others focus on their heuristic value as a testing ground for urban theories (Solà-Morales, 1970). In this chapter, the author claims there is a crucial value in playful environments and game-based practices that is usually left untapped: namely, their ability to explore and loosely articulate radically disruptive approaches to urban futures, going well beyond 'correct' and 'desirable' solutions and embracing, if need be, antagonism (Paez and Valtchanova, 2021), playful deviance (Redmon, 2003) or established madness (Blavier, 1972 – *la folie avéré*). Risk is an essential quality of play (Caillois, 2001) and one that should be embraced in all its breadth if we are to tap into games' disruptive potential.

This is a crucial question: serious games can harness affordances and constraints to foster radical, speculative and disruptive design. This disruptive potential of playful environments and game-based practices in urban design is based simultaneously on discovery and imagination. Two sides of the same coin, games have both hermeneutic and projective potential, and one cannot be understood without the other. Discovery means revealing opportunities that exist in a given context that are not yet activated, either because they are not visualised or because they are not conceptualised. A game-based approach can help designers to reveal opportunities and become 'worldful': "like design, creativity reveals itself to have far less to do with our own desires and visions and imaginations, and more to do with the world outside us, and how seriously are we willing to take it. How worldful we will allow our lives to become" (Bogost, 2016, 152). Imagination, on the other hand, uses the expanded interpretation of the world to think outside the box, inventing and communicating new realities. Imagination does not sprout from a blank slate but grows from the fertile soil of exploring reality without submitting to it (Paez, 2019, 313). Playful environments and game-based practices provide us with a rich methodological and relational framework to radically explore both the hermeneutic and projective dimensions of design and the city.

To finalise, it is important to clarify that the main value of the explorations presented in the case studies is not to be found in their desirability, their feasibility, their applicability, or their forecasting potential, but rather in the way they mobilise game-based practices to open up new urban horizons beyond the utopian-dystopian dichotomy, overturning cemented conventions and expectations of what the city is and what constitutes a desirable future. Paradoxically, taking serious games a little less seriously and a lot more playfully is a powerful way to explore current matters of concern without being held back by unsolvable wicked problems, and it lets us imagine disruptive futures that force us to confront both our desires and our limitations, in a fulfilment of design's political responsibility.

REFERENCES

Abt, C. (1970). *Serious Games*. Viking Press.

Arenas-Laorga, E., Basabe-Montalvo, L., Muñoz-Torija, S., & Palacios-Labrador, L. (2020). 'Game Boards'. Soportes urbanos para procesos sociales ['Game Boards'. Urban supports for social processes]. In *EDUMEET International Conference on Transfers for Innovation and Pedagogical Change*. Universidad Politécnica de Madrid / Javeriana de Bogotá. 10.20868/UPM.book.66588

BCNEcologia. (2019). *Charter for the Ecosystemic Planning of Cities and Metropolises*. http://www.cartaurbanismoecosistemico.com/index2eng.html

Blavier, A. (1982). *Les Fous littéraires* [Literary Madmen]. Éditions Henri Veyrier.

Bogost, I. (2016). *Play Anything: The Pleasure of Limits, the Uses of Boredom, and the Secret of Games*. Basic Book.

Caillois, R. (2001). *Man, Play, and Games*. University of Illinois Press.

Capel, H. (2003). *Los Problemas de las Ciudades: Urbs, Civitas y Polis* [The Problems of Cities: Urbs, Civitas and Polis]. Ciudades, Arquitectura y Espacio Urbano.

Chora, & Bunschoten, R. (2001). *Urban Flotsam*. 010 Publishers.

de Certeau, M. (1984). *The Practice of Everyday Life*. The University of California Press.

Dell, C. (2019). *The Improvisation of Space*. Jovis.

Dunne, A., & Raby, F. (2013). *Speculative Everything: Design, Fiction, and Social Dreaming*. The MIT Press.

Dupuy, G. (1972). Les jeux urbains [Urban Games]. *L'Actualite Economique, 48*(1), 85. Advance online publication. doi:10.7202/1003681ar

Eames, C. (1969). *Qu'est ce qu'est le design?* [What is Design?]. Musée des Arts Décoratifs.

Elvira, J. (2005). Control Remot / Remote Control. *Quaderns d'arquitectura i urbanisme, 247*, 84-95.

Elvira, J., & Paez, R. (2019). Design Through Play: The Archispiel Experience. In VII Jornadas sobre Innovación Docente en Arquitectura. UPC IDP, GILDA.

Fagen, R. M. (1981). *Animal Play Behavior*. Oxford University Press.

Fannon, D., Laboy, M., & Wiederspahn, P. (in press). *The Architecture of Persistence: Designing for Future Use*. Routledge.

Gerber, A., & Götz, U. (2020). *Architectonics of Game Spaces*. Transcript Verlag., doi:10.14361/9783839448021

Graeber, D. (2015). *The Utopia of Rules: On Technology, Stupidity, and the Secret Joys of Bureaucracy*. Melville House.

Henriot, C., & Molines, N. (2019). Urban serious games and digital technology. *NETCOM call for papers*. https://journals.openedition.org/netcom/3667?lang=en#actualite-3667

Huizinga, J. (1948). *Homo Ludens: A Study of the Play-Element in Culture*. Routledge & Kegan Paul.

Jennings, B. (2001). From the Urban to the Civic: The Moral Possibilities of the City. *Journal of Urban Health, 78*(1), 88–103. doi:10.1093/jurban/78.1.88 PMID:11368207

Koselleck, R. (2004). *Futures Past: On the Semantics of Historical Time*. Columbia University Press.

LaCol. (2018). *Building Collectively: Participation in Architecture and Urban Planning*. Pollen Editors.

Mitrović, I., & Šuran, O. (Eds.). (2016). Speculative – Post-Design Practice or New Utopia? Ministry of Culture of the Republic of Croatia & Croatian Designers Association.

Motte, W. F. Jr. (1986). *Oulipo: A Primer of Potential Literature*. Dalkey Archive Press.

Mouffe, C. (2013). *Agonistics: Thinking the World Politically*. Verso.

Paez, R. (2014). Derivas Urbanas: la Ciudad Extrañada [Urban Dérives: The Estranged City]. *R.I.T.A. Revista indexada de textos académicos, 1*, 120-129.

Paez, R. (2019). Operative Mapping: Maps as Design Tools. Actar Publishers.

Paez, R., & Valtchanova, M. (2021). Harnessing Conflict: Antagonism and Spatiotemporal Design Practices. *Temes de Disseny, 37 Invisible Conflicts: The New Terrain of Bodies, Infrastructures and Communication*, 183-216. doi:10.46467/TdD37.2021.182-213

Paez, R. (in press). Design as Playground: Exploring Design Through Game-based Formats. *Space and Culture*.

Piaget, J. (1962). *Play, Dreams and Imitation in Childhood*. Norton.

Poplin, A. (2011). Games and Serious Games in Urban Planning: Study Cases. In *Computational Science and Its Applications - ICCSA 2011 - International Conference - Proceedings, Part II*. Springer. 10.1007/978-3-642-21887-3_1

Redmon, D. (2003). Playful Deviance as an Urban Leisure Activity: Secret Selves, Self-validation, and Entertaining Performances. *Deviant Behavior: An Interdisciplinary Journal*, 24(1), 27–51. doi:10.1080/10639620390117174

Savransky, M., Wilkie, A., & Rosengarten, M. (2017). The Lure of Possible Futures. In A. Wilkie, M. Savransky, & M. Rosengarten (Eds.), *Speculative Research* (pp. 1–17). Routledge. doi:10.4324/9781315541860-1

Smith, P. K. (1982). Does play matter? Functional and evolutionary aspects of animal and human play. *Behavioral and Brain Sciences*, 5(1), 139155. doi:10.1017/S0140525X0001092X

Tan, E. (2020). Play the City. In A. Gerber & U. Götz (Eds.), *Architectonics of Game Spaces* (pp. 265–276). Transcript Verlag., doi:10.14361/9783839448021-018

Vygotsky, L. S. (2016). Play and Its Role in the Mental Development of the Child. *International Research in Early Childhood Education, 7*(2).

Waldheim, C. (2006). Strategies of Indeterminacy in Recent Landscape Practice. *Public 33: Errata*, 80-86.

Walther, B.K. (2003). Playing and Gaming: Reflections and Classifications. Game Studies, volume 3, issue 1.

Watershed. (2014). *Playable City*. https://www.playablecity.com/

ADDITIONAL READING

Allen, S. (2000). Mapping the Unmappable: On Notation. In S. Allen (Ed.), *Practice: Architecture, Technique and Representation* (pp. 31–45). Routledge.

Baur, R., & Baur, V. Civic City & Attac. (2017). Our World to Change. Lars Müller Publishers.

Borden, I. (2007). Tactics for a Playful City. In Eds. F. Von Borries, S. P. Walz & M. Boettger (Eds.), Space Time Play: computer games, architecture and urbanism: the next level. Birkhauser.

Flanagan, M. (2009). *Critical Play: Radical Game Design*. The MIT Press. doi:10.7551/mitpress/7678.001.0001

Gill, T. (2007). *No Fear: Growing up in a risk averse society*. Calouste Gulbenkian Foundation.

Stevens, Q. (2007). *The Ludic City: Exploring the potential of public spaces*. Routledge. doi:10.4324/9780203961803

Walz, S. P., & Deterding, S. (Eds.). (2015). *The gameful world: approaches, issues, applications*. The MIT Press. doi:10.7551/mitpress/9788.001.0001

Wilkie, A., Savransky, M., & Rosengarten, M. (Eds.). (2017). *Speculative Research*. Routledge. doi:10.4324/9781315541860

KEY TERMS AND DEFINITIONS

Constraints: Self-imposed or consciously accepted limits within a given spatiotemporal setup.

Disruptive Design: Innovative and ground-breaking design beyond the desirable/undesirable dichotomy.

Game-Based Format: Formal organisational setup following the features of games, such as agreed-upon rules or the introduction of chance, applied to a context of design or research.

Playful Environment: Informal ambiance conducive to ludic interactions between participants.

Radical: Affecting the fundamental nature of something.

Speculative Design: The space between foresight and fantasy, driven by imagination and with the purpose of proliferating reality.

Urban Vision: Sudden and bold visualisation of potential urban futures to collectively redefine our relationship to (existing) reality.

Chapter 23
Unveiling the Potential of Learning Analytics in Game–Based Learning:
Case Studies With a Geometry Game

Jose A. Ruipérez Valiente
(iD) https://orcid.org/0000-0002-2304-6365
University of Murcia, Spain

ABSTRACT

Due to technological advancement, the authors see a huge change in the way of teaching and learning. Game-based learning (GBL) is applied in order to motivate students, improve their knowledge, and make the process of education more enjoyable. This chapter will focus on explaining the process of learning analytics (LA) in the context of GBL, which can play a meaningful role in transforming learning pathways in games into interpretable information for teachers. Respectively, the overarching aim of this work is to verify the potential of GBL and LA applied to the educational process through four case studies, each of which presents an important metric in the geometry game Shadowspect, developed in order to train geometry and spatial reasoning skills by solving a series of geometry puzzles. The case studies will be focused on data-driven game design, learner modelling and adaptive learning, game-based assessment (GBA) of 21st-century skills, and teacher-oriented visualization dashboards.

BACKGROUND

Technology is gradually being applied into our everyday life affecting many fundamental processes, including education. Accordingly, in recent years, we see a considerable change in the way of teaching and learning (Dabbagh et al., 2016). In this sense, a key transformative approach is gamification, which has been broadly defined as "the use of game design elements in non-game contexts" (Deterding, Dixon, Khaled, & Nacke, 2011), and is frequently implemented with these new technologies. There are multiple elements that are being implemented in this context, such as points, badges, levels, leader boards, virtual

DOI: 10.4018/978-1-7998-9732-3.ch023

goods, avatars, or even whole games (Hamari, Koivisto, & Sarsa, 2014). We focus on this last item, since nowadays it is common to involve game-based learning (GBL) in order to motivate students, improve their knowledge and increase the enjoyment of such an essential process as education (Plass, Homer, & Kinzer, 2015). However, while there are obvious benefits, current educational systems are still suffering from numerous issues that require transformative changes. GBL holds the potential to improve many of the problems that are currently present within the educational process (De Freitas, 2006). One issue is that even though many teachers report a positive attitude towards games being used in K12 classrooms and believe that they can improve learning and curriculum, the actual number of teachers who are implementing digital games in their curriculum is contrarily low. There are several factors affecting the possibility of implementing games into as formative assessment, including the doubts on how to effectively implement games in the classroom, how to support evidence-based decisions based on game data, or how to assess students using the games (Watson & Yang, 2016).

Within the context of these challenges, we argue that learning analytics (LA) could be a vital novelty being able to address the problems as mentioned earlier. LA was defined in 2011 in the first Learning Analytics and Knowledge (LAK) conference as the "*the measurement, collection, analysis and reporting of data about learners and their contexts, for purposes of understanding and optimising learning and the environments in which it occurs*" (Society for Learning Analytics Research (SoLAR), 2021). While the work presented in this article focuses on the process for implementing LA, there are numerous other cross-cutting factors to consider during this process that are highly important for success. In the first place, it should be noted that the rise of research in LA has been given by the introduction of technology in education and that as it continues to be introduced more in the educational fabric (US Department of Education, 2016), we could expect a greater demand for implementing it. In turn, it could lead to greater ease in certain parts of introducing this process into education. Secondly, there is a need to highlight the need to anchor LA projects in real educational applications that can improve learning. However, there is a risk of implementing technology and analytics that are totally disconnected from the best pedagogical practices and educational theories developed in recent decades (Gašević, Dawson, & Siemens, 2015). Third, nowadays, people are more concerned about their privacy, and it is especially crucial to guarantee the privacy of students and teachers for the ethical development of this technology, which is a problem that has already been tackled by numerous policies (H. Drachsler & Kalz, 2016). On the other hand, it is a critical question whether educational systems want to move in the same direction as the large Internet companies, which continuously monitor their users (Slade & Prinsloo, 2013).

Accordingly, we must take into account the fact that students or their representatives must consent to their data being used for these purposes and have the freedom to choose which data can be used or if they wish to withdraw that consent at any point in the process; all of this requires major orchestration among the actors in this process, not only students but also teachers, designers and system administrators (Pardo & Siemens, 2014). This can lead to several difficulties in the implementation process, including one of the most crucial concerns - time which can be highly affected due to bureaucratic issues. Finally, we highlight the need for the proper implementation and systematization of LA in education. It is essential to achieve the involvement of educational institutions and the generation of national educational policies, which could generate problems that may not initially be obvious (Macarini et al., 2019).

Despite all the challenges that could arise while introducing games into the educational process and using LA techniques accordingly, there are very important benefits, including, first of all, a better experience for students and teachers (Freire et al., 2016). This includes the academic achievement, enjoyment of the process from both sides, concentration, and classroom dynamics in general. Moreover, we would be able to address the individual needs of every student, which is performed in the context of adaptive learning (Liu, McKelroy, Corliss, & Carrigan, 2017). Additionally, it can help to understand and improve the effectiveness of teaching practices and respectively inform institutional decisions and strategies. Respectively, the overarching aim of this work is to verify the potential of GBA and LA applied to the educational process through four case studies, each of which presents an important metric. In this study, we will explore four case studies of LA applied in a geometry game Shadowspect. The game was developed in order to train geometry and spatial reasoning skills by solving a series of geometry puzzles. The case studies will be focused on data-driven game design, learner modelling & adaptive learning, game-based assessment (GBA) of a the 21st-century skill persistence, and teacher-oriented visualization dashboards.

The organization of the chapter is as follows: in Section 2, we will describe the LA process in GBL. In Section 3, we will introduce a geometry puzzle game Shadowspect. Section 4 will focus on a series of metrics that can provide comprehensive information about the learning process and the students. We will perform the puzzle difficulty, the competency of students by the use of the Elo rating system, and the persistence metric. Next, we will describe the implementation of a real-time dashboard of the metrics as mentioned earlier. Finally, in Section 5, we will discuss the obtained results and draw our conclusions.

THE LEARNING ANALYTICS PROCESS AND GAME-BASED LEARNING

In this section, we review the LA process in GBL and studies that fall within each one of these stages (Ruipérez-Valiente, 2020). We will delve into the following steps in the process:

1. Game-based learning environments. What is the context, and who are the students?
2. Raw data collection. Which data needs to be generated, and how to store it?
3. Data manipulation and feature engineering. What features are needed and how to obtain them?
4. Analytics and modelling. Which analysis and models should be implemented?
5. Educational application. What is the objective application and the final user?

In addition, there are other issues that must be taken into account in a transversal way, such as the technologies to be applied, the theories and learning sciences to be used, the privacy of users, as well as educational institutions and policies. Finally, it is important to mention that depending on the project, it is not necessary to go through all the steps that we will describe. Most researchers and experts in the field of LA focus only on steps 3 and 4. We now delve into each of these stages.

Figure 1. The Learning Analytics implementation process

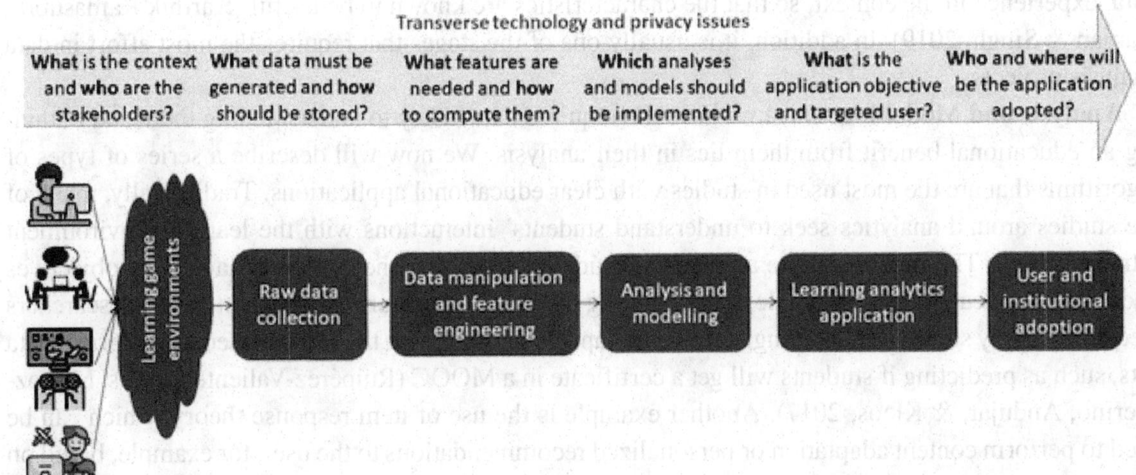

Learning Environments: In Figure 1, we illustrate the LA implementation process. The first step of the process takes place in the learning game environment and the users who interact with it. Traditionally, in distance or digital education, we find digital environments such as Learning Management Systems (LMSs), including Moodle, Sakai, dotLRN, among many others (Romero, Ventura, & García, 2008). Then, with the advent of Massive Open Online Courses (MOOCs), there was an explosion in terms of being able to collect large amounts of data from students around the world (Breslow, et al., 2013) which favoured the emergence of numerous studies in the area. LA projects have also been carried out in less common settings, such as smart tutors (Jaques, Conati, Harley, & Azevedo, 2014) or educational games (Freire et al., 2016). Each of these environments has its specificities that make the implementation of their analytics hard to implement.

Raw Data Collection: On the other hand, in this context, the ability to easily collect data was strengthened with the advent of education through digital environments. The most common way that most virtual learning environments have followed is to save the traces of all the clicks that users make in the environment as events, in the format that is usually known in the literature, as clickstream data. This approach is not only followed in educational settings, but it is universal in a multitude of digital domains to model human behaviour (Bollen et al., 2009). Besides, in recent years, the use of sensors in education has also become increasingly common, both to capture audiovisual signals and biometric signals from students such as the heartbeat or electrodermal activity, which is especially promising for the evaluation of complex tasks (Blikstein & Worsley, 2016). From the Shadowspect side, it generates a vast amount of clickstream data that we save and can generate the analytics out of it.

Data Manipulation and Feature Engineering: Once the data has been collected, the manipulation process begins. Because these low-level events represent isolated actions of the students, they are not very informative in the raw format, and therefore it is necessary to go through a process known as feature engineering (Veeramachaneni, Reilly, & Taylor, 2014). During this process, data is transformed into actionable and valuable educational information (Muñoz-Merino, Ruipérez Valiente, & Kloos, 2013). For example, these virtual environments will save the actions of each student, but this information will not be handy until we algorithmically calculate the total time that the user has spent actively interacting with the learning platform. This process requires a high technical knowledge level to manipulate the data, experience in the context, so that the characteristics are known to be useful (Karthik Ramasubramanian & Singh, 2019). In addition, it is usually one of the stages that requires the most effort in data analysis projects.

Analysis and Modelling: Once we have the required data, a key to understanding them and obtaining an educational benefit from them lies in their analysis. We now will describe a series of types of algorithms that are the most used in studies with clear educational applications. Traditionally, many of the studies around analytics seek to understand students' interactions with the learning environment retrospectively. The methods to be applied are evident and direct when projects have clear objectives and future applications. For example, for generating predictions of future learning outcomes, researchers frequently apply supervised learning algorithms capable of modelling the future based on historical data sets, such as predicting if students will get a certificate in a MOOC (Ruipérez-Valiente, Cobos, Muñoz-Merino, Andujar, & Kloos, 2017). Another example is the use of item response theory, which can be used to perform content adaptation or personalized recommendations to the user, for example, based on the user's current difficulty and skill level (Chen, Lee, & Chen, 2005). These are a few examples of the most common modelling and analysis methods that are widespread in the LA area, but others can be applied as well. Finally, it should be noted that the data manipulation and feature engineering process, in conjunction with the analysis and modelling phase, is an iterative process that can be repeated until the desired results are achieved (Ruipérez-Valiente, 2020).

Learning Analytics Application: The analysis of the previous phase usually has an educational application associated with them. However, the reality is that on many occasions, this application is not usually put into practice and the research usually ends in the analysis and modelling phase. This means that most of the research is not transferred to practice, and therefore, it cannot be evaluated if it really has a positive educational impact or not (Clow, 2012).

In other cases, the most typical applications seen in LA projects include visualization interfaces, which are normally used by instructors to monitor how their students are progressing but can also be accessed by students to reflect on their own learning process (Park & Jo, 2015; Ruiperez-Valiente, Gomez, Martinez, & Kim, 2021) and applications that introduce fully adaptive modules or systems (Brusilovsky, Wade, & Conlan, 2007). Moreover, another application is a recommendation system that sends personalized recommendations to the student about what might interest them (Dwivedi & Bharadwaj, 2015). Finally, it is also expected that the final application of the analysis generates a high-level report on an educational context of an institution, course or subject, to better understand the context and adapt educational policies (Reich & Ruipérez-Valiente, 2019). These applications or final analyses should generate feedback in the educational contexts where the data was generated that allows improving the learning process, and with this, the cycle of the implementation of LA would be closed (Clow, 2012). Furthermore, the effect of these changes should be evaluated, which could be done using again a LA methodology (Ruipérez-Valiente, Muñoz-Merino, Pijeira Díaz, Ruiz, & Kloos, 2017). This evaluation is essential to be able to measure the impact of the changes introduced in the educational context.

User and Institutional Adoption: In the coming years, the LA field and educational institutions in general, face the challenge of the prospect of implementing the above-mentioned methods on a large scale and in a systematic way to finally be able to reach the high potential that all researchers converge on. To do so, there are numerous barriers that the entire community of actors involved in education must contribute to breaking down (Tsai & Gasevic, 2017). Policies should be developed to allow a correct implementation with educational impact, without losing sight of the importance of ethics and security in using these data, preserving the privacy to which students are entitled. These projects must be focused on users, empowering them and putting them at the centre of development in order to implement applications that can be used sustainably over time (Chatti et al., 2020). For this, it is recommended that institutions in the coming years focus on implementing LA applications such as visualization interfaces or content evaluation through analytics in a proper way. In a more distant future, other challenges await the area at the research level, such as transferring machine learning models when contexts and even platforms change or facilitating the interpretability of all the analytics to be more accessible to the users who have limited competencies in data analysis (Bonikowska, Aneta; Sanmartin, Claudia; Frenette, 2019; Raffaghelli, 2019). The area also goes through a critical period to start developing more open educational science (Zee & Reich, 2018), in which hypotheses are pre-registered, data and analysis are open, and articles published are free for any researcher and educator.

SHADOWSPECT: A GEOMETRY PUZZLE SOLVING GAME

As part of this research proposal, we will use a geometry puzzle-solving game Shadowspect (https://shadowspect.org/). The objective of the game is to solve a series of puzzles by selecting, placing, and rotating 3D geometric primitives such as cubes, cylinders, spheres, cones, or pyramids based on the three orthogonal views of a figure. Figure 2 shows a puzzle example in Shadowspect, with some zones delimited by red parallelograms and a letter to facilitate the following description. When users start a puzzle, they see its overall description (A), and they receive a set of silhouettes (B) from different views that represent the figure they need to build. Users can create (C) cubes, pyramids, ramps, cylinders, cones and spheres. Additionally, several puzzles set up constraints, such as using a maximum number of objects or a maximum number of shapes of each type. Learners can use various tools (D) to achieve in-game goals by moving, rotating, and scaling shapes around the stage to match the silhouettes provided.

Additionally, users can delete and select multiple shapes at the same time. Students can change the camera view (E) to see the figure they are building from different angles and then use the Snapshot functionality (G) in order to generate the silhouette from the current view. Snapshots can help them know if their shapes match any of the solution silhouettes. Finally, users must submit (G) their current shapes, and the system will evaluate if the solution is correct and provide them with feedback. Any interaction that users perform with Shadowspect is stored as clickstream data that will allow us to reconstruct the learning process that students undergo to solve each puzzle.

The data used for this work were collected as a part of assessment machinery development that later will be implemented in Shadowspect. The team recruited seven teachers to use the game for two hours in their 7th grade to 10th grade math and geometry classes. All students' interactions with the game were collected without any identifiable or personal data except for a nickname provided by each student.

Figure 2. A puzzle example in a geometry game Shadowspect

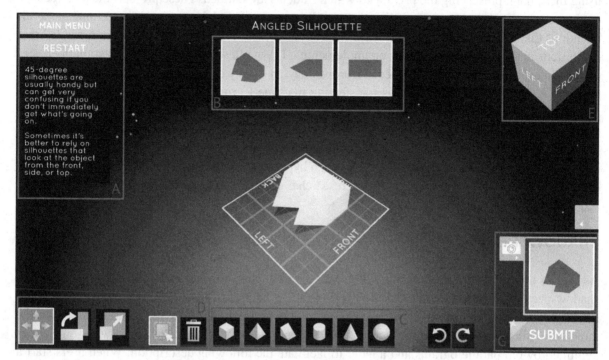

LEARNING ANALYTICS CASE STUDIES IN SHADOWSPECT

In this section we present the four case studies that will exemplify the potential of LA in GBL.

Data-Driven Game Design

In game development, data from users have excellent potential to be used for accomplishing the learning and assessment goals. Analysis of these data results in deriving insightful metrics which can explain both players' overall enjoyment and efficiency of learning and qualities of assessment. The difficulty is one of the most common core game elements that game developers compute and apply data-driven methods on (Kim & Ruipérez-Valiente, 2020). Game designers state that the difficulty should balance boredom and frustration so that the players can experience a "well-shaped difficulty curve" (Aponte, Levieux, & Natkin, 2009). Several authors (Gee, 2005; Hamari et al., 2016) proved that the challenging and therefore motivating game atmosphere positively affects learning. In this case study, the authors explore the potential of LA within the explanation of how the metrics of difficulty were created and applied to the Shadowspect geometry game.

The primary objective is to estimate the relative difficulty of each puzzle in Shadowspect. Additionally, we aimed to determine the sequence of puzzles where the game has a well-shaped difficulty curve. Moreover, we questioned the time that players of varying abilities would take to complete a number of puzzles. For fulfilling the goals as mentioned earlier, we performed a data-driven approach. Accordingly, we identified that difficulty consists of two measures: firstly, the level of effort required by learners to solve the puzzle and secondly, the relative complexity of the puzzle (i.e., fewer players can solve it). For example, difficulty value is affected if a user needs to make more actions or needs more time to complete the puzzle or if a vast majority of users are not capable of finishing the task. Based on these estimations, we computed the following four metrics per each puzzle level which directly influence the difficulty:

1. Average time per puzzle completed - total time spent in puzzles divided by the number of puzzles completed correctly.
2. An average number of actions per puzzle completed - a total number of actions performed divided by the number of puzzles completed correctly.
3. Percentage incorrect - the number of wrong submissions divided by the total number of submissions.
4. Percentage abandoned - number of different puzzles that were started and not completed correctly divided by the number of puzzles started.

For the reason that the metrics stated above are represented in different units such as percentage and time, we generated a composite difficulty measure. On these grounds, we first compute the z-scores of each metric and then normalize the sum of the four z-scores over the maximum. Accordingly, the final range of the composite puzzle difficulty of the geometry game Shadowspect varies from 0 (the easiest puzzle) to 1 (the hardest puzzle). In Figure 3, we illustrate the results of all four metrics per puzzle and the normalized composition of them called general difficulty measure. The puzzles are ordered in the way they appear in the game, so the game developers considered that the puzzle named "1. One Box" is the easiest, and the puzzle "Zzz" is the hardest. However, we can see that there are several puzzles that have a maximum difficulty, and at the same time, they appear in the middle of the game.

Figure 3. General difficulty measure and four metrics that compose it

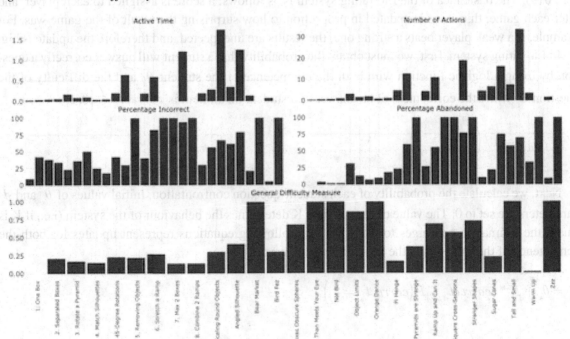

This allowed us to revaluate the distribution and allocation of puzzles into basic, intermediate, and advanced groups of puzzles. Based on this difficulty representation, we had to review the overall difficulty curve of the entire game and fine-tuned the sequence of the puzzles. For estimating the amount of time that players of varying skills would take to complete a number of puzzles, we calculated the amount of puzzles completed per unit of time. We concluded that during a one-hour session, a student with standard abilities would be able to finish on average 12 ± 1 puzzles. In contrast, in a two-hour session, the amount of puzzles would increase to 15 ± 1 puzzles. By computing these empirical and realistic estimations, we were able to provide them to teachers who want to use the Shadowspect geometry game in their classrooms. We proved that difficulty could be operationalized based on the varying notions in the literature (Kim & Ruipérez-Valiente, 2020).

Learner Modelling and Adaptive Learning

There is an extensive variety of methods that aim to measure the existing knowledge and forecast the future performance of users. They often fall within the context of a sequence of knowledge inference problems whose main goal consists of predicting or modelling the students' knowledge (or its absence) over questions as they interact with a learning platform at a specific time. In this case study, we will exemplify how we can use multivariate Elo learner modelling to predict if students are going to solve the next puzzle correctly and consequently adapt the sequence of puzzles.

Elo rating is a system for relative skill calculation of players (Pelánek, 2016) that has been predominantly used to rank players, for example, in competitive games such as chess tournaments. It was primarily developed for measuring how strong the players are, but it was also adapted into the context of educational research and was used for measuring both learner ability and task difficulty (Pankiewicz, et al., 2019). The basic idea of the Elo rating system is as follows: a score is assigned to each player, and after each game, this score is updated in proportion to how surprising the result of the game was. For example, if a weak player beats a strong one, the results are unexpected, and therefore the update is big.

In Elo rating system, first, we must obtain the probability that a student will answer correctly a question by using a logistic function with both the competence of the student θ_s and the difficulty of the question d_i while the correctness of an answer of a student on an item is $correct_{si} \in \{0,1\}$:

$$P_{correct_{si} \epsilon \{0,1\}} = 1 / \left(1 + e^{-(\theta_s - d_i)}\right)$$

Next, we calculate the probability of each student-question confrontation. Initial values of θ_s and d_i parameters are set to 0. The value of the constant K determines the behaviour of the system (i.e., if K is small, the estimation converges too slowly). The following equations represent updates for both the competence of the student and the difficulty of the puzzle:

$$\theta_s = \theta_s + K * \left(correct_{si} - P\left(correct_{si} = 1\right)\right)$$

$$d_i = d_i + K * \left(\left(P\left(correct_{si} = 1\right)\right) - correct_{si}\right)$$

In the current case study, we were mainly interested in the competency of the student since we already calculated the puzzles' difficulty during the first case study. Therefore, in Figure 4, we represent the result obtained by using the equations stated above.

Figure 4. Students' competency by KC according to the Elo rating system

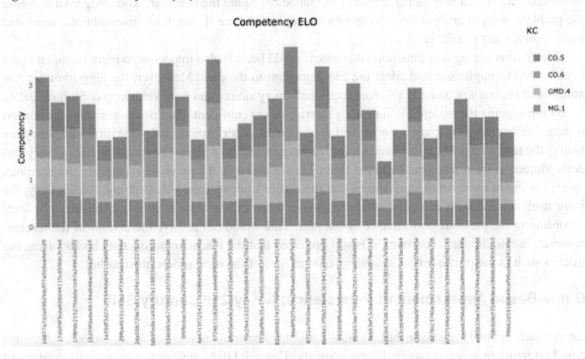

We illustrated the competency of each student for each Knowledge Component (KC) which are the skills needed to complete a puzzle successfully. In the visualization, each KC is differentiated by colours, normalized to 1; therefore, the maximum score of a student can be four since we work with four competencies. Across Shadowspect, experts defined four main KCs:

1. MG.1: Use geometric shapes, their measurements and their properties to describe objects.
2. GMD.4: Identify the shapes of the two-dimensional cross sections of the three-dimensional objects, and identify the three-dimensional objects generated by the rotations of the two-dimensional objects.
3. CO.5: Given a geometrical figure and a rotation, reflection or translation, draw the transformed figure using, for example, graph paper, tracing paper or geometry software. Specify a sequence of transformations that will take one given figure to another.
4. CO.6: Use geometric descriptions of rigid movements to transform figures and predict the effect of a given rigid movement on a given figure; in the case of two figures, use the definition of congruence in terms of rigid movements to decide if they are congruent.

As can be observed in Figure 4, the teacher, at a glance, could obtain the students' score for evaluation and can also identify where each student fails or if they have any mastered skills. Several interesting cases appear to be analysed in the class visualization. First, we see that the user "86e8f92f3a09a2f-64ae0c8eedfbf7e53" stands out above the rest with the best competence; in addition he draws attention that it has a high value for all the KCs, so we can consider that he has solved the puzzles and acquired the expected knowledge. In contrast, we can see the case of "a283b675d67d1d68be3638180a7e5be3" where the scores of the components are all weak. In this situation, the teacher can quickly see that the student has not shown interest in the task or has failed to acquire the necessary knowledge. To diagnose the problem, we can analyse the activity of such students to see if they have invested time, generated events, solved any puzzle, etc.

Finally, after seeing how beneficial this metric could be, it is also important to mention that it is not complicated to implement and adapt the Elo algorithm to the data. Moreover, the algorithm has few adjustment parameters, and it is also computationally very simple and fast (Veldkamp & Sluijter, 2019).

By introducing the students' competency metric, we are confident that this can serve for the context of adaptive learning. By knowing how well each student is performing and what difficulties they are facing, the teacher would be able to adapt the learning process to address the special needs of every student. Moreover, the teacher can build the future classes based on the previous experience, for example, by explaining in more detail some topics that the earlier students found challenging. Additionally, the game itself automatically can be adapted to each user by providing hints or choosing the difficulty level according to the previous performance of the user. This would not involve the actions of the teacher; however, in a traditional classroom, it is still preferred that the teacher controls the class by using the metrics such as the puzzle difficulty and the competency of the user as described earlier.

Game-Based Assessment of Persistence: A Key 21st Century Skill

LA is widely applied to estimate the continually updated learners' knowledge, skills, and other attributes based on multiple observations in diverse contexts. Through GBA, we can behave in a diagnostic and formative way – to analyse how the student's way of thinking becomes "visible", thereby informing both learners and teachers about their train of thought, beyond right or wrong answers. Additionally, most children and teenagers play games on an almost everyday basis and consider them as an activity that makes life way more enjoyable. At the same time, game developers benefited from this situation and created a lot of games that are capable not only to entertain but also to educate even those users who are typically not very interested in learning. In this way, stealth assessment methods in GBA provide the opportunity of evaluating users without interrupting the gaming flow. Previous research has proved that learners are only able to show their actual skills and perform well if they are appropriately motivated and under no stress situations, and accordingly, GBA can help with this. As we mentioned earlier, gamification in learning is a perfect solution for maximising both enjoyment and engagement through capturing the interest of users and inspiring them to continue the learning process. In this case study, we will exemplify the potential of GBA in LA by measuring persistence in the Shadowspect geometry game. Persistence is a facet of conscientiousness that reflects a dispositional need to complete complex tasks and the desire to exhibit high-performance standards in the face of frustration (Ventura, Shute, & Zhao, 2013).

While exploring other works that have calculated the persistence metric, we found one example (Shute et al., 2015) where time spent on unresolved trials is a critical factor. Time in resolved practices is also important; however, it is more linked to the previous knowledge. The authors of (Shute et al., 2015) made an experiment consisting of exposing students to six problems, three easy and three impossible (the complete solution was not possible). In this way, we could see the time that each student invested to the tasks that were impossible, so it is a critical factor of the persistence that it presented. In (Israel-Fishelson & Hershkovitz, 2020), we saw how another measure of persistence is used. In this case, the indicator is the number of attempts to achieve solutions to different types of difficulty. The authors collected the number of attempts for each of the difficulties and the average.

Although there are few indicators on how to calculate persistence, it can be observed that time, both for completed and uncompleted activities, and the number of attempts are essential characteristics for persistence. Following some related works, it can be seen that the rest of the parameters are more linked to the specifications of each scenario where it has been implemented.

For the Shadowspect case study, in order to see if the student has been persistent or not in a puzzle, we face it as a problem of measuring a student's constancy in the face of adversity by considering several metrics, including a number of basic persistence parameters and others that help contextualise, give flavours and see the evolution over time. First of all, the more complex the puzzle is, the more persistent it should be since it is more challenging. Secondly, we will build the persistence metric on a time/attempts basis, with multipliers for the difficulty. Accordingly, we will consider percentiles of each of the parameters considered (time, attempts), supposing that the student was persistent if the respective value exceeds the value of 75%. Lastly, for each student, we will identify the puzzles in which he has been persistent. Then, we will calculate if the student globally has been persistent or not according to the number of puzzles in which he has been persistent. For example, to compute persistence at a puzzle attempt level, for each puzzle attempt, we point out the ratio with the features related to the persistence. To calculate persistence at a student level, we point out the ratio with all puzzle attempts for each student.

Based on the assumptions and examples listed above, in Figure 5, we illustrate the persistence levels of a particular class where the beach figure means low persistence, desert stands for medium persistence, and mountain signifies high persistence. We can observe the fact that most of the students demonstrate a medium persistence level which is a common situation because initially, this metric was evaluated by the example of real students, and on average, they had medium persistence. Surprisingly, there are many more students who have low persistence in comparison with a few who have a high level of persistence. This could be explained by the fact that there was low interest or motivation in this particular class.

Figure 5. The persistence levels of a particular class

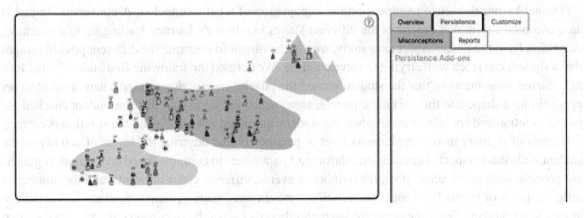

Moreover, teachers may build their own filters or create alerts for specific features they are interested in. In the case of persistence, an alert can be established when a student is experiencing difficulties in solving the puzzles and therefore appears as less persistent. This would allow teachers to take some actions in order to motivate the student and point them to the right solution. It brings flexibility for teachers and a more unique learning process for students.

Teacher-Oriented Visualization Dashboards

While games proved to have a positive effect on the learning process, they are not so frequently used as part of classroom activities. One of the main reasons for that is related to the competencies of teachers. Moreover, most of them do not totally understand how the students interact with the game and how beneficial it is to implement and utilize it in their classrooms (Ruipérez-Valiente & Kim, 2020). On the other hand, there are more routine-related and logistic issues connected to the limited time available in the classroom and the impossibility of introducing games in the context of the regular classroom.

Educational games were brought into regular classrooms to transform the sceptical mindset of all the people involved in the learning process. In order to help teachers better navigate and monitor the interactions of students, there were introduced various tools, including providing LA dashboards that present low-level interactions in visualizations easy to understand. While their power and strengths are apparent, it is not a trivial task to create an intuitive and easy to use dashboard. Therefore, the design of a dashboard for games for classroom use should be user-centred and take into account the usability and the needs of the teachers. In this case study, we will explore the potential of implementing a LA dashboard to support teachers that are using games in the classroom.

The working group for creating the dashboard was composed of two learning designers, one educator, one assessment scientist, and one LA expert. Each member of the team proposed straightforward ideas of measures that would be interesting to consider for the dashboard using data from Shadowspect. After the initial ideas were formulated, we conducted the session where each proposed metric was discussed and voted for. All the metrics could not be included because the scope of the project was limited. Therefore, we decided that the dashboard should include only those metrics that can directly help teachers to improve the learning process at the same time, considering how difficult it would be to technically implement these metrics (Ruiperez-Valiente et al., 2021). The final dashboard consists of various metrics. Next, we will explain the most important ones that were not described before.

Funnel by puzzle metric requires first the explanation of what a funnel is. A conversion funnel is an e-commerce term that describes the different stages in a buyer's journey leading up to a purchase. Accordingly, in the Shadowspect case study, we use the funnel to illustrate the different possible stages that a student can reach while trying to solve a puzzle. We defined the following four stages for the funnel: *started stage* meaning that the student started the puzzle, *create_shape stage* when the student set up a primitive shape into this particular puzzle, *submitted stage* signifying that the student checked the puzzle solution and *completed stage* when the student submitted the puzzle and the solution is correct.

Levels of Activity metric implements a set of parameters that describe the levels of activity of the student with Shadowspect. These are straightforward parameters to compute based on a feature engineering process, such as the active time, the number of events, different types of events, and the number of different types of events like snapshots, rotations, movements, scaling, shape creations and deletions, among several others. For our case study, we highlight only two of the parameters as mentioned earlier, namely, active time and the number of events; since these are the most important to look at when analyzing students' interaction with the game, however, we would like to denote that all of them are available for the teacher.

Finally, sequence within puzzles metric obtains a sequence of actions of every student in each puzzle. By doing that, we can know every single action a student performed while solving a puzzle. We only keep the main events that are related to the puzzle-solving process, which are starting a puzzle, manipulation events on a shape, puzzle submitting, snapshots and perspective change. To reduce the number of rows in the data, we collapse identical consecutive events, adding a field that indicates the number of times that an event has been performed in a row.

Next, in Figure 6 and Figure 7, we represented two examples of a real-time dashboard that we generated. Through them, teachers can see the metrics of the entire class or filter by a particular student. These dashboards can be used in a regular classroom for dynamically visualizing the different metrics to support the sessions and provide personalized feedback. For example, by analysing the sequence within puzzles metric represented in Figure 6, the teacher can see the sequence of actions, denoting that the student performed a large number of actions in order to solve the puzzle. As the student made a significant amount of actions between submits, we know that the student was mindfully trying to solve the puzzle, instead of making random actions.

Figure 6. A real-time teacher-oriented visualisations dashboard (sequence within puzzles metric)

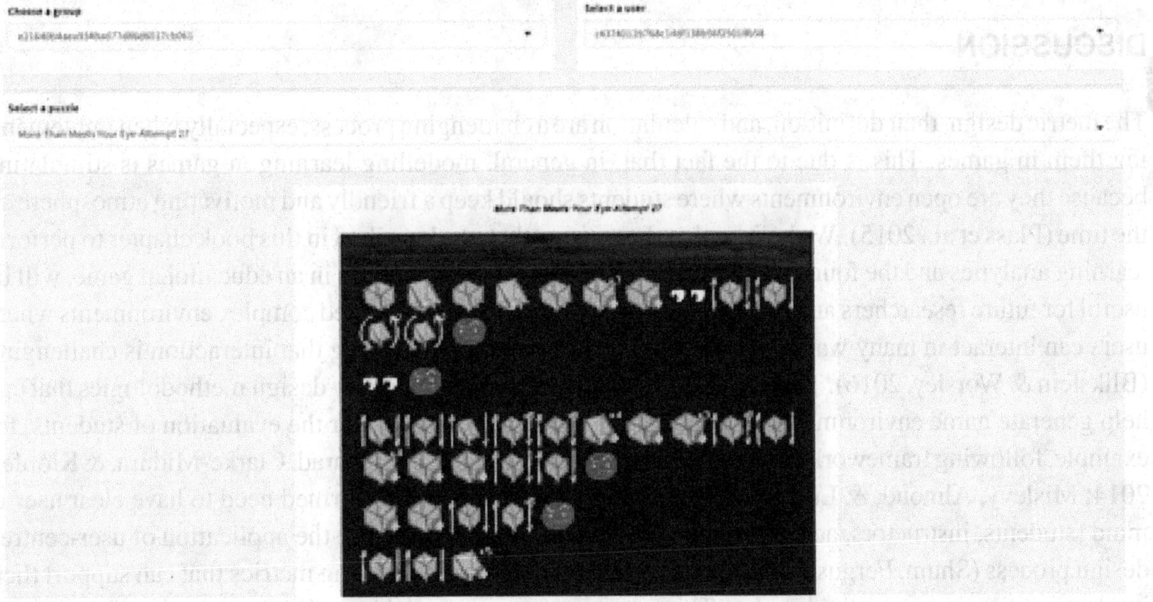

Figure 7. A real-time teacher-oriented visualisations dashboard (levels of activity metric)

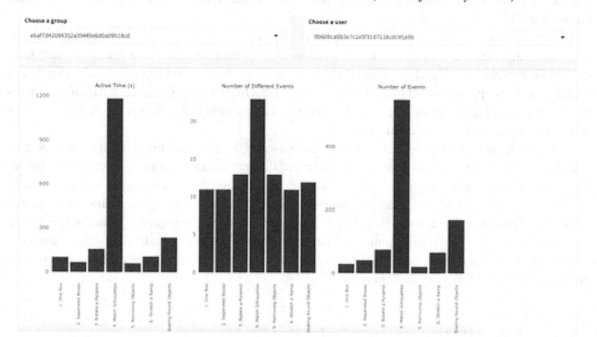

DISCUSSION

The metric design, their definition, and calculation are a challenging process, especially when implementing them in games. This is due to the fact that, in general, modelling learning in games is stimulating because they are open environments where students should keep a friendly and motivating atmosphere all the time (Plass et al., 2015). We believe that the process that we described in this book chapter to perform learning analytics and the four use cases of real learning analytics studies in an educational game, will be useful for future researchers and practitioners. Since games are open-ended complex environments where users can interact in many ways with the virtual environment, modelling that interaction is challenging (Blikstein & Worsley, 2016). Therefore, we recommend authors to follow design methodologies that can help generate game environments that collect the necessary evidence for the evaluation of students, for example, following frameworks like evidence-centred design (ECD) (Conrad, Clarke-Midura, & Klopfer, 2014; Mislevy, Almond, & Lukas, 2003). Moreover, the analytics performed need to have clear user in mind (students, instructors, administrators, etc), therefore, we encourage the application of user-centred design process (Shum, Ferguson, & Martinez-Maldonado, 2019) targeting metrics that can support their implementation in our particular case. This process often requires the work of a multidisciplinary team that can bring diverse perspectives to the LA design process, including analytics, technology, learning sciences, game design and assessment (Ruiperez-Valiente et al., 2021). Finally, we also recommend to align the developments with the concept of translucent LA (Martinez-Maldonado et al., 2020) in order to make learning visible, improve awareness and accountability. If all these design guidelines are followed, this can help the production of learning-oriented video games that can even target different user profiles and diverse goals.

However, in order to accomplish such goals, there are also some barriers and key points that need to be addressed. One is related to the development of privacy-preserving LA solutions (Pardo & Siemens, 2014). Otherwise, students or teachers might develop negative feelings about these applications. One key aspect is that the involved stakeholders should always have the opportunity to opt-out or opt-in, and the learning analytics applications should be able to handle these decisions without problems (Hendrik Drachsler & Greller, 2016). By developing these user-centred applications, the acceptance and adoption will improve (Tsai & Gasevic, 2017). In turn, this can provide potential benefits to students, in order to become more self-aware of their game activity, to receive personalize recommendations about their next game actions, or to have adaptive learning experiences in games based on their preferences and previous actions. In the case of teachers, these learning analytics can be especially useful to better understand what their students are doing in the game and to be able to assess students with detailed information, and complex metrics driven by analytics and artificial intelligence, completely developed for the purpose evaluating students using game data.

Finally, we would like to also share some words about the potential of educational games during remote learning, and the key role that LA can have to support students and teachers based on the previously shared applications. COVID-19 pandemic highlighted the need to rethink how to perform effective remote learning, and the use of games and simulations have been depicted as one of the most promising mediums to support it (Colao et al., 2020). While this pandemic was an isolated event, we can expect in the future more emergency situations due to other pandemics or events derived from climate change, that will force society to undergo additional periods or a more frequent remote teaching. Therefore, the use of games and LA can greatly support the future of education.

CONCLUSION

The objective of this research was diverse: first, to explain how beneficial it is to introduce GBA and LA into the educational process but also what challenges it brings. The following goal consisted of describing the LA process. We described the context of the environment, the raw data collection and its storage in the scope of the paper. Next, we delved into the steps of data manipulation, feature engineering and data analytics. In the last step, we characterised the educational application of this process.

After describing the LA process and motivating the research in this area, we introduced Shadowspect - a geometry puzzle game created for the development of geometry and spatial reasoning skills. In its context, we aimed to propose a series of metrics that can provide comprehensive information regarding the learning means of students while solving the puzzles in the game. We computed the puzzle difficulty, then we calculated the competency of students by the use of the Elo rating system, and lastly, we presented the persistence metric. Finally, we described the implementation of a real-time dashboard with simple but detailed visualisations of the metrics as mentioned above that can allow teachers to track the students within their class. Accordingly, the teachers will be able to evaluate or detect problems quickly and effectively, addressing the unique needs of each student and giving them personalised attention.

We believe that our work presented a significant advancement for the implementation of GBA and LA into the educational process in the classroom. By performing the case studies as mentioned earlier, we have proved that GBA has a vast potential to be easily adapted in the class. The dashboard that we presented depicts an excellent opportunity for educators to perform a live monitoring of their students directly during the class. Data-driven game design, particularly for educational games, could help designers and researchers to ensure that a game is not only playable and enjoyable but satisfies other educational purposes such as learning and assessment. This can serve for supporting formative assessment and moreover developing more LA dashboards in GBA and other environments that we characterised during our work.

REFERENCES

Aponte, M., Levieux, G., & Natkin, S. (2009). Scaling the Level of Difficulty in Single Player Video Games Entertainment Computing – ICEC 2009. *International Conference on Entertainment Computing*, 25–35.

Blikstein, P., & Worsley, M. (2016). Multimodal learning analytics and education data mining : Using computational technologies to measure complex learning tasks. *Journal of Learning Analytics*, *3*(2), 220–238. doi:10.18608/jla.2016.32.11

Bollen, J., van de Sompel, H., Hagberg, A., Bettencourt, L., Chute, R., Rodriguez, M. A., & Balakireva, L. (2009). Clickstream data yields high-resolution Maps of science. *PLoS One*, *4*(3), e4803. Advance online publication. doi:10.1371/journal.pone.0004803 PMID:19277205

Bonikowska, A., Sanmartin, C., & Frenette, M. (2019). Data Literacy: What It Is and How to Measure It in the Public Service. Analytical Studies Branch, Statistics Canada, (11).

Breslow, L., Pritchard, D. E., DeBoer, J., Stump, G. S., Ho, A. D., & Seaton, D. T. (2013). Studying Learning in the Worldwide Classroom: Research into edX's First MOOC. *Research and Practice in Assessment*, *8*, 13–25.

Brusilovsky, P., Wade, V., & Conlan, O. (2007). From Learning Objects to Adaptive Content Services for E- Learning. In *Architecture Solutions for E-Learning Systems* (pp. 243–261). Academic Press.

Chatti, M. A., Muslim, A., Guesmi, M., Richtscheid, F., Nasimi, D., Shahin, A., & Damera, R. (2020). How to Design Effective Learning Analytics Indicators? A Human-Centered Design Approach. In *European Conference on Technology Enhanced Learning* (pp. 303–317). 10.1007/978-3-030-57717-9_22

Chen, C. M., Lee, H. M., & Chen, Y. H. (2005). Personalized e-learning system using Item Response Theory. *Computers & Education*, *44*(3), 237–255. doi:10.1016/j.compedu.2004.01.006

Clow, D. (2012). The learning analytics cycle: closing the loop effectively. In *Proceedings of the 2nd International Conference on Learning Analytics and Knowledge* (pp. 134–138). 10.1145/2330601.2330636

Colao, A., Piscitelli, P., Pulimeno, M., Colazzo, S., Miani, A., & Giannini, S. (2020). Rethinking the role of the school after COVID-19. *The Lancet. Public Health*, *5*(7), e370. doi:10.1016/S2468-2667(20)30124-9 PMID:32464100

Conrad, S., Clarke-Midura, J., & Klopfer, E. (2014). A Framework for Structuring Learning Assessment in a Massively Multiplayer Online Educational Game. *International Journal of Game-Based Learning*, *4*(1), 37–59. doi:10.4018/IJGBL.2014010103

Dabbagh, N., Benson, A. D., Denham, A., Joseph, R., Al-Freih, M., Zgheib, G., ... Guo, Z. (2016). *Learning Technologies and Globalization*. Springer International Publishing. doi:10.1007/978-3-319-22963-8

De Freitas, S. (2006). Learning in Immersive worlds A review of game-based learning. *JISC ELearning Innovation, 3.3*(October), 73. doi:10.1111/j.1467-8535.2009.01024.x

Deterding, S., Dixon, D., Khaled, R., & Nacke, L. E. (2011). Gamification : Toward a Definition. In *ACM CHI Conference on Human Factors in Computing Systems* (pp. 12–15). ACM.

Drachsler, H., & Kalz, M. (2016). The MOOC and learning analytics innovation cycle (MOLAC): A reflective summary of ongoing research and its challenges. *Journal of Computer Assisted Learning, 32*(3), 281–290. doi:10.1111/jcal.12135

Drachsler, H., & Greller, W. (2016). Privacy and analytics - it's a DELICATE issue a checklist for trusted learning analytics. In *Proceedings of the sixth international conference on learning analytics \& knowledge* (pp. 89–98). ACM. doi:10.1145/2883851.2883893

Dwivedi, P., & Bharadwaj, K. K. (2015). E-Learning recommender system for a group of learners based on the unified learner profile approach. *Expert Systems: International Journal of Knowledge Engineering and Neural Networks, 32*(2), 264–276. doi:10.1111/exsy.12061

Freire, M., Serrano-laguna, Á., Iglesias, B. M., Martínez-ortiz, I., Moreno-ger, P., & Fernández-manjón, B. (2016). Game Learning Analytics: Learning Analytics for Serious Games. In Learning, Design, and Technology: An International Compendium of Theory, Research, Practice, and Policy (pp. 1–29). Springer. doi:10.1007/978-3-319-17727-4

Gašević, D., Dawson, S., & Siemens, G. (2015). Let's not forget: Learning analytics are about learning. *TechTrends, 59*(1), 64–71. doi:10.100711528-014-0822-x

Gee, J. P. (2005). Learning by Design: Good Video Games as Learning Machines. *E-Learning and Digital Media, 2*(1), 5–16. doi:10.2304/elea.2005.2.1.5

Hamari, J., Koivisto, J., & Sarsa, H. (2014). Does Gamification Work? -- A Literature Review of Empirical Studies on Gamification. In *2014 47th Hawaii International Conference on System Sciences* (pp. 3025–3034). IEEE. 10.1109/HICSS.2014.377

Hamari, J., Shernoff, D. J., Rowe, E., Coller, B., Asbell-Clarke, J., & Edwards, T. (2016). Challenging games help students learn: An empirical study on engagement, flow and immersion in game-based learning. *Computers in Human Behavior, 54*, 170–179. doi:10.1016/j.chb.2015.07.045

Israel-Fishelson, R., & Hershkovitz, A. (2020). Persistence in a Game-Based Learning Environment: The Case of Elementary School Students Learning Computational Thinking. *Journal of Educational Computing Research, 58*(5), 891–918. doi:10.1177/0735633119887187

Jaques, N., Conati, C., Harley, J., & Azevedo, R. (2014). Predicting Affect from Gaze Data during Interaction with an Intelligent Tutoring System. In *Proceedings 12th International Conference, Intelligent Tutoring Systems 2014, Honolulu, HI, USA.* (pp. 29–38). Springer International Publishing. 10.1007/978-3-319-07221-0_4

Karthik, R., & Singh, A. (2019). *Machine Learning Using R. Frontiers in Artificial Intelligence and Applications* (Vol. 321). doi:10.3233/FAIA200024

Kim, Y. J., & Ruipérez-Valiente, J. A. (2020). Data-driven game design: The case of difficulty in educational games. Lecture Notes in Computer Science, 12315, 449–454. doi:10.1007/978-3-030-57717-9_43

Liu, M., McKelroy, E., Corliss, S. B., & Carrigan, J. (2017). Investigating the effect of an adaptive learning intervention on students' learning. *Educational Technology Research and Development, 65*(6), 1605–1625. doi:10.100711423-017-9542-1

Macarini, L. A., Ochoa, X., Cechinel, C., Rodés, V., Dos Santos, H. L., Alonso, G. E., ... Díaz, P. (2019). Challenges on implementing learning analytics over countrywide K-12 data. *ACM International Conference Proceeding Series*, 441–445. 10.1145/3303772.3303819

Martinez-Maldonado, R., Elliott, D., Axisa, C., Power, T., Echeverria, V., & Buckingham Shum, S. (2020). Designing translucent learning analytics with teachers: An elicitation process. *Interactive Learning Environments, 0*(0), 1–15. doi:10.1080/10494820.2019.1710541

Mislevy, R. J., Almond, R. G., & Lukas, J. F. (2003). A Brief Introduction to Evidence-Centered Design. *ETS Research Report Series*, (1), i–29. doi:10.1002/j.2333-8504.2003.tb01908.x

Muñoz-Merino, P. J., Ruipérez Valiente, J. A., & Kloos, C. D. (2013). Inferring higher level learning information from low level data for the Khan Academy platform. In *Proceedings of the Third International Conference on Learning Analytics and Knowledge - LAK '13* (pp. 112–116). ACM Press. 10.1145/2460296.2460318

Pankiewicz, M., & Bator, M. (2019). Elo Rating Algorithm for the Purpose of Measuring Task Difficulty in Online Learning Environments. *E-Mentor, 82*(5), 43–51. doi:10.15219/em82.1444

Pardo, A., & Siemens, G. (2014). Ethical and privacy principles for learning analytics. *British Journal of Educational Technology, 45*(3), 438–450. doi:10.1111/bjet.12152

Park, Y., & Jo, I. (2015). Development of the Learning Analytics Dashboard to Support Students ' Learning Performance Learning Analytics Dashboards (LADs). *Journal of Universal Computer Science, 21*(1), 110–133.

Pelánek, R. (2016). Applications of the Elo rating system in adaptive educational systems. *Computers & Education, 98*, 169–179. doi:10.1016/j.compedu.2016.03.017

Plass, J. L., Homer, B. D., & Kinzer, C. K. (2015). Foundations of Game-Based Learning. *Educational Psychologist, 50*(4), 258–283. doi:10.1080/00461520.2015.1122533

Raffaghelli, J. E. (2019). Developing a Framework for Educators' Data Literacy in the European Context: Proposal, Implications and Debate. *EDULEARN19 Proceedings, 1*(July), 10520–10530. 10.21125/edulearn.2019.2655

Reich, J., & Ruipérez-Valiente, J. A. (2019). The MOOC pivot. *Science, 363*(6423), 130–131. doi:10.1126cience.aav7958 PMID:30630920

Romero, C., Ventura, S., & García, E. (2008). Data mining in course management systems: Moodle case study and tutorial. *Computers & Education*, *51*(1), 368–384. doi:10.1016/j.compedu.2007.05.016

Ruiperez-Valiente, J. A., Gomez, M. J., Martinez, P. A., & Kim, Y. J. (2021). Ideating and Developing a Visualization Dashboard to Support Teachers Using Educational Games in the Classroom. *IEEE Access: Practical Innovations, Open Solutions*, *9*, 83467–83481. doi:10.1109/ACCESS.2021.3086703

Ruipérez-Valiente, J. A., Cobos, R., Muñoz-Merino, P. J., Andujar, Á., & Kloos, C. D. (2017). Early prediction and variable importance of certificate accomplishment in a MOOC. Lecture Notes in Computer Science, 10254. doi:10.1007/978-3-319-59044-8_31

Ruipérez-Valiente, J. A., Muñoz-Merino, P. J., Pijeira Díaz, H. J., Ruiz, J. S., & Kloos, C. D. (2017). Evaluation of a learning analytics application for open edX platform. *Computer Science and Information Systems*, *14*(1), 51–73. Advance online publication. doi:10.2298/CSIS160331043R

Ruipérez-Valiente, J. A., & Kim, Y. J. (2020). Effects of solo vs. collaborative play in a digital learning game on geometry: Results from a K12 experiment. *Computers & Education*, *159*(September), 104008. Advance online publication. doi:10.1016/j.compedu.2020.104008

Ruipérez-Valiente, J. A. (2020). El Proceso de Implementación de Analiticas de Aprendizaje. *RIED. Revista Iberoamericana de Educación a Distancia*, *23*(2), 85–101. doi:10.5944/ried.23.2.26283

Shum, S. B., Ferguson, R., & Martinez-Maldonado, R. (2019). Human-centred learning analytics. *Journal of Learning Analytics*, *6*(2), 1–9. doi:10.18608/jla.2019.62.1

Shute, V. J., D'Mello, S., Baker, R., Cho, K., Bosch, N., Ocumpaugh, J., Ventura, M., & Almeda, V. (2015). Modeling how incoming knowledge, persistence, affective states, and in-game progress influence student learning from an educational game. *Computers & Education*, *86*, 224–235. doi:10.1016/j.compedu.2015.08.001

Slade, S., & Prinsloo, P. (2013). Learning Analytics: Ethical Issues and Dilemmas. *The American Behavioral Scientist*, *57*(10), 1510–1529. doi:10.1177/0002764213479366

Society for Learning Analytics Research (SoLAR). (2021). *What is Learning Analytics?* Retrieved from https://www.solaresearch.org/about/what-is-learning-analytics/

Tsai, Y. S., & Gasevic, D. (2017). Learning analytics in higher education - Challenges and policies: A review of eight learning analytics policies. In Seventh international learning analytics & knowledge conference (pp. 233–242). doi:10.1145/3027385.3027400

US Department of Education. (2016). Future ready learning. *2016 National Education Technology Plan*, 1–106.

Veeramachaneni, K., Reilly, U. O., & Taylor, C. (2014). *Towards feature engineering at scale for data from massive open online courses.* ArXiv Preprint ArXiv:1407.5238.

Veldkamp, B. P., & Sluijter, C. (2019). *Theoretical and practical Advances in Computer-based Educational Measurement.* Academic Press.

Ventura, M., Shute, V., & Zhao, W. (2013). The relationship between video game use and a performance-based measure of persistence. *Computers & Education, 60*(1), 52–58. doi:10.1016/j.compedu.2012.07.003

Watson, W., & Yang, S. (2016). Games in schools: Teachers' perceptions of barriers to game-based learning. *Journal of Interactive Learning Research, 27*(2), 153–170.

van der Zee, T., & Reich, J. (2018). Open Education Science. *AERA Open, 4*(3). doi:10.1177/2332858418787466

ADDITIONAL READING

Abdi, S., Khosravi, H., Sadiq, S., & Gasevic, D. (2019). A multivariate Elo-based learner model for adaptive educational systems. *EDM 2019 - Proceedings of the 12th International Conference on Educational Data Mining, 1*, 228–233.

Dicerbo, K. E. (2014). International Forum of Educational Technology & Society Game-Based Assessment of Persistence. *Journal of Educational Technology & Society, 17*(1), 17–28.

Gomez, M. J., Ruipérez-Valiente, J. A., Martínez, P. A., & Kim, Y. J. (2021). Applying learning analytics to detect sequences of actions and common errors in a geometry game. *Sensors (Switzerland), 21*(4), 1–16. doi:10.339021041025 PMID:33546167

Lu, O. H. T., Huang, J. C. H., Huang, A. Y. Q., & Yang, S. J. H. (2017). Applying learning analytics for improving students engagement and learning outcomes in an MOOCs enabled collaborative programming course. *Interactive Learning Environments, 25*(2), 220–234. doi:10.1080/10494820.2016.1278391

Montgomery, A. L., Li, S., Srinivasan, K., & Liechty, J. C. (2004). Modeling online browsing and path analysis using clickstream data. *Marketing Science, 23*(4), 579–595. doi:10.1287/mksc.1040.0073

Scruggs, R., Baker, R. S., & McLaren, B. M. (2020). Extending deep knowledge tracing: Inferring interpretable knowledge and predicting post-system performance. *ICCE 2020 - 28th International Conference on Computers in Education. Proceedings, 1*, 195–204.

KEY TERMS AND DEFINITIONS

Clickstream Data: The traces of all clicks that users make, normally, in the game context.

Game-Based Assessment: A field which goal is to use games in order to educate and learn.

Item Response Theory: A group of mathematical models whose goal is to find a relationship between latent traits.

Knowledge Component: The skills needed to complete a task correctly.

Learning Analytics: A collection of students-related data and their analysis in the educational context.

Learning Management System: A software application for various tasks including administration, documentation, tracking, automation and reporting of educational courses or learning processes.

Massive Open Online Course: An online course whose main goal is to educate and normally provide an option of free and open registration and a publicly shared curriculum.

Chapter 24
Improving Immigrant Inclusion Through the Design of a Digital Language Learning Game

Heidi T. Katz
 https://orcid.org/0000-0003-4763-1953
Åbo Akademi University, Finland

Emmanuel O. Acquah
Åbo Akademi University, Finland

Anette Bengs
 https://orcid.org/0000-0003-4489-0087

Åbo Akademi University, Finland

Fredrik Sten
Åbo Akademi University, Finland

Mattias Wingren
 https://orcid.org/0000-0003-4269-5093
Åbo Akademi University, Finland

ABSTRACT

Technology has garnered attention as a successful tool for second language learning that could help improve immigrant integration and inclusion. More specifically, digital learning games have been identified as an effective tool for enhancing a variety of outcomes related to second language learning, including language acquisition, motivation, and confidence. Digital learning games differentiate instruction, provide immediate feedback, situate the learning, and offer a safe and engaging environment to practice the target language. However, it is important that digital learning games are designed with the end-users in mind. For that reason, this study outlines how researchers and game developers can utilize user-centered design to develop a context-specific digital language learning game for immigrants. As an example, the authors present the four-phase process of an ongoing game design project in Finland, including general findings from interviews with teachers.

DOI: 10.4018/978-1-7998-9732-3.ch024

INTRODUCTION

As immigration increases around the world, countries must work to support social inclusion and integration by providing newly arrived immigrants with effective second language (L2) education. While some view immigrant education as an additional burden on society and the economy, underserving the immigrant community is of no benefit. People with an immigrant background contribute greatly to society through entrepreneurship, filling labor shortages, being highly skilled in their professions, having foreign language abilities, and creating more openness in society (Huddleston et al., 2013). Huddleston et al. (2013) believe, "if policymakers want to reduce unemployment in their country, create a knowledge-based society, and encourage active citizens, then immigrants are a major target group," (Huddleston et al., 2013, p. 48). More importantly, immigrant children and adolescents have a right to a comprehensive education that meets their needs and enables them to achieve their personal goals.

Supporting the needs of learners who are both linguistically and culturally diverse is no easy feat. In most OECD countries, PISA data consistently shows a performance gap between immigrant student populations and their native-born peers (OECD, 2019a). The underperformance of students with an immigrant background is not due to a lack of ambition; rather, it can be attributed to the segregation of immigrants into low-income neighborhoods and disadvantaged schools, students' limited proficiency in the language of instruction, lack of teachers trained to support diverse learners, inadequate assessments of student needs, and integration of language and content learning (European Commission, 2019; Huddleston et al., 2013; OECD, 2019a). Though some of these challenges must be addressed through country-specific social policies, digital tools have also been suggested as a useful means for supporting the integration and inclusion of people with an immigrant background (Ahad & Benton, 2018). Ahad and Benton (2018) note that digital tools can aid teachers in creating personalized learning experiences, collecting data (to make more informed assessments), and supporting students in overcoming barriers, including those related to language.

We specifically advocate for the development of digital language learning games (DLLG) for improving immigrant integration and inclusion. To be effective and practical for use in school and as an individual player, DLLGs must meet the needs of various stakeholders (immigrant students, teachers, schools, adult immigrants, etc.) within a given region. In the development of DLLGs, we suggest researchers and game designers follow user-centered design (UCD), a four-phase iterative process that combines rigorous background research, active involvement of targeted end-users, and multi-disciplinary design team (ISO, 2010; Ritter et al., 2014). UCD is particularly beneficial for developing a DLLG for immigrants because the process ensures the game is pedagogically, culturally, and geographically grounded, and as a result, the final product is designed to support the real-life application of newly acquired language skills.

In this chapter, we demonstrate how UCD can be used to develop a DLLG for immigrants by presenting our ongoing project in Finland. The targeted population are both first and second-generation immigrants who do not already have proficient language skills in the official language(s) of Finland. The chapter begins with an overview of approaches and challenges related to immigrant L2 education worldwide for school age and adult immigrants. We then connect research on digital learning games (DLGs) and DLLGS with theories of learning, before outlining the UCD approach to developing a DLLG. Next, we tie all the research together by demonstrating the ongoing design process of a DLLG for immigrants in Finland. We conclude by presenting societal implications as well as recommendations for those interested in applying a similar approach to developing a DLLG within other contexts. We believe being transparent about the game design process will benefit future designers of DLGs as well as educators who wish to understand the pedagogical considerations that make DLLGs effective tools.

APPROACHES TO IMMIGRANT L2 EDUCATION

Integration is a two-way process involving the host country and immigrant populations, meaning there must be policies and programs in place that support immigrant success by targeting both the native-born and immigrant populations (Council of the EU, 2004; Heugh & Mohamed, 2020). Effective integration policies and programs can lead to immigrants experiencing a greater sense of social inclusion, belonging, and the ability to contribute to one's new country. Conversely, a lack of effective integration support can result in higher rates of school dropout, lower academic outcomes, challenges entering the labor market, and a lower sense of well-being (Ahad & Benton, 2018; European Commission, 2019; OECD, 2015, 2019b). This chapter will focus on supports that target the immigrant population, but it is equally as important to establish policies and programs for the native-born population to promote social cohesion, and reduce intolerance, prejudice, and any sense of economic or social threat (OECD, 2019b).

It is indisputable that for immigrant populations, acquiring the host country language can help alleviate issues related to integration (Huddleston et al., 2013; Magos & Politi, 2008; Salant & Benton, 2017). However, policies for L2 immigrant education are often unclear or not grounded in evidence, and there lacks consensus over which L2 education model should be taken in compulsory school settings (European Commission, 2019; Heugh & Mohamed, 2020). The common approaches schools and countries take tend to fall under one of the following three categories:

- **Direct integration:** Students are directly integrated into mainstream classrooms, but typically are provided L2 support either through additional classes, individualized or small-group instruction, or teaching assistants/specialists in the general education classroom (European Commission, 2017; Sugarman, 2018).
- **Preparatory (or introductory, transition, reception) classes:** Schools provide intensive training in the language of instruction, which is generally organized in one of three ways: 1) students take some lessons in separate groups; 2) students take most lessons in separate groups; or 3) students take all lessons in separate groups (European Commission, 2019). In Europe, these classes last on average one to two years, but can last up to six years (European Commission, 2019).
- **Dual language education (or mother tongue-based programs):** The goal is to provide students support in developing both L1 and L2 proficiency, thus it is commonly referred to as an additive model (Heugh & Mohamed, 2020; Sugarman, 2018).

While preparatory classes provide more time for language instruction, they also may hinder integration by separating immigrant and native-born students (Ahad & Benton, 2018; Benton & Glennie, 2016; European Commission, 2019). Preparatory classes also can impede educational progress if other curricular learning is halted (Ahad and Benton, 2018; European Commission, 2019). A study conducted in one U.S. school found that under the school's preparatory model, very few students were able to successfully exit within one year, and those who were unable to exit fell increasingly behind in other core content (Sugarman, 2017). To avoid this, the European Commission (2015) and OECD (2015, 2018) recommend having target language coursework offered in addition to the regular class because immediate integration is associated with better outcomes both academically and socially (Huddleston et al., 2013). However, direct integration can pose a challenge when students are unable to understand the language of instruction (European Commission, 2019).

Other researchers advocate for dual language/mother tongue-based approaches as they enable learners to build L1 skills (their language of identity), maintain a connection to their home country, feel a greater sense of empowerment, and - at a broader level - promote more intercultural understanding (Heugh & Mohamed, 2020; OECD, 2019b; Sugarman, 2018). Unfortunately, this model can be difficult to arrange due to the resources and initial investments that are required (Heugh & Mohamed, 2020). Given the challenges surrounding each approach, there must be flexibility, open communication, and cooperation within education systems and among various stakeholders (European Commission, 2017; Magos and Politi, 2008).

Although the focus of L2 immigrant education is often placed on children and adolescents enrolled in formal education, it is imperative that countries also provide L2 support for adult immigrants as it facilitates both economic and social integration (Ahad & Benton, 2018; OECD, 2019b, 2021). L2 learning for adults can be particularly challenging and intimidating; thus, host countries must remove barriers and provide positive incentives to motivate adults to participate (OECD, 2021). One of the most significant barriers to L2 education for immigrants is cost (OECD, 2021). Although some countries offer (co-) financed L2 education for adult immigrants, this often depends on the reason for migration (OECD, 2021). Therefore, the OECD (2021) claim that countries should provide all newly arrived adult immigrants' access to affordable or free L2 courses. These courses should be offered in a flexible format to remove additional barriers related to busy schedules or family responsibilities. To further motivate participation, the learning should be meaningful and applied to everyday situations (OECD, 2021).

Regardless of the age of students or the educational model used, many teachers feel ill prepared to teach in classrooms that are ethnically, culturally, and linguistically diverse (European Commission, 2019; Heugh & Mohamed, 2020; OECD, 2015, 2019b). Though many countries recommend that teachers have additional qualifications to provide L2 instruction for immigrant students, it is rarely required (European Commission, 2017, 2019). This is unfortunate because all staff working with immigrant students should have diversity awareness and effective strategies to support students with different backgrounds (Salant & Benton, 2017; Villegas & Lucas, 2007). These strategies include differentiated and scaffolded instruction (Lucas & Villegas, 2013), though this can be challenging even for highly trained teachers (Ahad and Benton, 2018).

To address this, researchers suggest teachers adopt digital resources as a means to systematically collect data in order to better understand the students' needs and provide objective feedback (Ahad & Benton, 2018; OECD, 2021). Digital tools can be particularly useful for adult learners whose age, language competencies, and level of education will vary greatly (OECD, 2021). For job seekers, working immigrants, or immigrants with children, digital tools provide flexibility in learning schedules. Digital apps or games may also be more affordable than attending in-person learning courses. However, the OECD (2021) suggests that digital tools not replace in-person courses; instead, it is optimal for them to be used in a blended fashion, where teachers integrate the tools into the classroom experience. These tools enable teachers to differentiate instruction, reduce preparation time, create more variation in learning formats, and establish a more efficient use of class time (OECD, 2021).

DIGITAL LEARNING GAMES AND LANGUAGE ACQUISITION

Numerous systematic literature reviews demonstrate that DLGs have a positive effect on a variety of L2-related outcomes, such as language acquisition, retention, and motivation (Acquah & Katz, 2020; Hung et al., 2018; Young et al., 2012; Yudintseva, 2015). DLLGs have also been found to reduce speaking anxiety and to enhance confidence, making them an ideal environment for learning a new language (Reitz et al., 2016; Wu & Huang, 2017; Young & Wang, 2014). The success of DLLGs can partly be attributed to the simple fact that they increase engagement and exposure to the target language (Klimova & Kacet, 2017; Yudintseva, 2015). However, researchers have also discussed the natural relationship between gaming and what is known about effective learning and second language acquisition. In the words of James Paul Gee (2008), renowned scholar of linguistics, education, and video games, "Game design is applied learning theory," (p. 24).

Gee (2008) believes experiences are key to learning, given they meet the following conditions: 1) they are structured by specific goals; 2) we interpret them during and after the experience based on how our goals relate to our choices; 3) we receive immediate feedback in order to assess and explain our errors; 4) we engage in practice by applying the previous experiences to new situations; 5) and we debrief and reflect with others. When people have a meaningful experience, the experience is stored in their long-term memory, which can later be used to help problem-solve in new situations (Gee, 2008). From these experiences, people construct various simulations in their minds to consider how they might act in the future to improve outcomes (Gee, 2008). The aforementioned criteria for meaningful learning experiences occur in games, where players must consider diverse options to meet their goals, test those options, engage with other players, receive feedback for their choices, and later reflect on what could have been done better. Over time, players learn from their mistakes and improve in the process.

The real-time feedback and learner-centered approach found in DLGs aligns with the sociocultural perspective on learning because users can learn within their zone of proximal development (ZPD; Peterson, 2010): the point at which learners are challenged within their own skill range, but able to succeed with the proper support (Vygotsky, 1978). From the sociocultural perspective, teachers and learners are active in a collaborative process (Gibbons, 2015), with the goal of enabling students to stay within their ZPD (Peterson, 2010). Oftentimes schools struggle to differentiate instruction based on students' unique skills and needs. DLLGs can be used to support differentiation because of their ability to collect data and personalize the learning experience for students to learn at their own rate. For example, designers and developers of DLLGs can integrate a spaced-repetition algorithm, which uses machine learning techniques to capture the students' achievement during a lesson, and then calculate the interval of time that should pass between sessions to produce optimal learning outcomes (Schimanke et al., 2014; Settles & Meeder, 2016). The idea of spaced repetition comes from Ebbinghaus's (1885) discovery of the "spacing effect," which highlights the positive effect repetitive content exposure can have on learning retention, as opposed to learning through intense short-term cramming (Schimanke et al., 2014; Settles & Meeder, 2016). Relatedly, the "lag effect" (Melton, 1970) demonstrates how the interval of time between practices should increase as the learning improves (Schimanke et al., 2014; Settles & Meeder, 2016). These effects have been found to be particularly effective for language learning (Settles & Meeder, 2016).

The effectiveness of DLLGs can also be attributed to the role of play and relevance of context in learning. Vygotsky advocated for rule-based play, meaning children learn through structured play (within their ZPD) with the necessary guidance and support from teachers or peers (Piker, 2013). This aligns with the aforementioned ideas from Gee (2008) regarding experiences, where explicit goals and social debriefing are important for learning. DLLGs are a form of rule-based play that situates the learner in meaningful, interactive, goal-driven experiences. Rather than expose learners to content out of context, as is often done in traditional language classrooms and textbooks, DLLGs provide "'situated meanings' for words," (Gee, 2008, p. 36). Namely, learning occurs in the appropriate context where students learn about the points of view of the system and develop identities within that system (Gee, 2008; Squire, 2008). The situated nature of DLGs allows for new knowledge and skills to be transferred and applied to other contexts, especially when the game context mirrors that of real life (Plass et al., 2015).

Situated learning that occurs within one's ZPD is important for learner engagement and intrinsic motivation (Plass et al., 2015). When students are faced with activities that are challenging and cognitively complex, they are likely to experience a heightened level of enjoyment and deepened concentration (Hamari et al., 2016). Many DLGs integrate challenging work and play, which can result in users entering a state of mind called flow. Flow, as defined by psychologists, is a positive experiential state where one is fully immersed in a task to the point at which the person and task become one, and all outside distractions or thoughts about past and present disappear (Csikszentmihalyi & Asakawa, 2016). Experiencing flow during gameplay signifies the highest level of engagement, which can lead to positive learning outcomes and increased motivation to continue to improve one's skills (Hamari et al., 2016).

In sum, DLLGs consist of numerous features that are important for L2 learning, including experiences (situated and meaningful), real-time interaction and feedback, learner-centered approach, appropriate levels of challenge and complexity (ZPD), and rule-based play. L2 learning can feel intimidating at first; thus, DLLGs can help motivate learners, both young and old, to experiment and practice their new skills within an interactive and safe learning environment. However, to achieve all of this requires a careful and intentional approach to game design that centers the target end-users.

Designing a Digital Language Learning Game

The effectiveness of DLLGs on L2 acquisition depends on whether they were designed to be both engaging and educative (Egenfeldt-Nielsen, 2011; Harteveld et al., 2010). To accomplish this, we suggest user-centered design (UCD), a valuable approach that may be applied to the design and development of any kind of artefact, process, or experience, including educational ones (Lyon & Koerner, 2016). UCD requires the involvement of various stakeholders who can provide feedback and insight throughout the entire process, as well as a multi-disciplinary design team (Braad et al., 2016). Including different experts in the design process enables the team to address elements and mechanics relevant to game design, as well as didactical design. Furthermore, the benefits resulting from the involvement of stakeholders extends beyond the game design: research shows that when parents are involved in decision-making processes for education (and language education), they become more invested in their child's education (Heugh & Mohamed, 2020).

The application of UCD for designing a DLLG makes it possible to bridge the different roles of the end-users – in this case, language learner, game player, and user of an interactive interface - in the context of researching, designing and development (Braad et al., 2016; Pagulayan et al., 2008). This is because targeted end-users are actively involved throughout the design and development process (Braad et al., 2016; Rankin et al., 2008). The information gathered from end-users ensures the design of a DLLG is based on, and in line with, the end-users' values, needs, preferences, abilities and constraints in a specific context. This is crucial for developing successful digital solutions that are meaningful and enjoyable for the end-users (Hassenzahl, 2010). The general structure offered in UCD aligns with the learner-centered approach to education, thus it is well suited for designing DLLGs. Schimanke et al. (2014) explain, "Interactivity and a user-centered design [applied to learning games] enable students to make a 'learning by doing' experience which is far more immersive than just reading about a certain topic," (p. 202).

The UCD process is typically broken down into four iterative phases in the development cycle: (1) identifying, understanding and empathizing with the intended end-users, the context of use, and tasks involved; (2) identifying and defining user requirements and design goals; (3) iteratively designing and developing an intervention, product, system or service; and (4) implementing and evaluating whether the solution meets end-user needs, requirements and abilities that were identified and defined in previous phases (ISO, 2010; Keinonen, 2009; Ritter et al., 2014). In the next section, we will present the application of the UCD phases to our ongoing project for designing a DLLG for immigrants in Finland.

ONGOING GAME DESIGN FOR IMMIGRANT L2 LEARNING IN FINLAND

Finland was under Swedish rule from the 14th to 19th century, and as a result, Finland has two official languages: Finnish and Finland Swedish. Of the 5.5 million people living in Finland, 86.9% speak Finnish, 5.2% speak Swedish, and 7.8% speak another language, the most common being Russian, Estonian, Arabic and English (Official Statistics Finland [OSF], 2020). The pronunciation of Finland Swedish is different from the Swedish spoken in Sweden, and there are also differences in vocabulary. The majority of people with Finland Swedish as their mother tongue are located at the western and southern coasts of Finland (OSF, 2020). In most cases, the bilingual regions in Finland have separate schools for students to learn in their preferred language. When immigrants arrive and settle in bilingual municipalities, they can choose whether to attend Finland Swedish language integration training or Finnish language integration training. In fact, in 2014 it was reported that 15% of first-generation immigrants claim to speak Swedish better than Finnish (Finnish Institute for Health and Welfare [THL], 2021)

Finland has seen an increase in immigration since the 1990s, with around 6% of students in Finland having an immigrant background in 2018, an increase of 3.2% from 2009 (OECD, 2019a). The largest populations of people with an immigrant background are from Russia, Estonia, Iraq, and Somalia (OSF, 2021). Despite the international recognition Finland often receives for its equitable, high-quality education, it has failed to ensure equity to the influx of immigrant students. Newly arrived immigrant children and adolescents are typically placed in preparatory classes, resulting in some of the highest rates of immigrant segregation within OECD countries (European Commission, 2019; OECD, 2019a). According to Sinkkonen and Kyttälä (2014), when students in Finland leave preparatory classes, they barely reach the level necessary for academic learning and it is not mandatory to provide additional support. Moreover, it is often difficult for teachers to distinguish between actual learning difficulties and challenges related to cultural or linguistic differences (Sinkkonen & Kyttälä, 2014). This means a disproportionate number of immigrants are placed in special education, which could be attributed to the lack of quality assessment methods (European Commission, 2015; Sinkkonen & Kyttälä, 2014). Those wrongly placed in special education risk remaining less educated, instead of reaching their potential (EUMC, 2004; Sinkkonen & Kyttälä, 2014). In recent years, immigrant (first and second generation) students in Finland were twice as likely than their native peers to fail to achieve baseline levels of academic proficiency on PISA (OECD, 2018a, 2019a). In fact, the difference in 2018 reading scores between native and immigrant students was 74 points, one of the biggest gaps found in OECD countries (OECD, 2019a). As a result, only 7.9% of immigrant students are deemed academically resilient (i.e., scored in top quarter of reading performance amongst students in Finland; OECD, 2019a).

Variation in levels of immigrant success tend to depend on the country of departure, reason for migration, age of migration, and time spent in Finland (THL, 2021). For instance, of those arriving at age 20 or younger, almost all have completed their primary education, though just a little over half have also completed their secondary education (THL, 2021). Due to feelings of exclusion and lack of knowledge in the language of instruction, many immigrant youth wish to start working and therefore do not continue into secondary education (THL, 2021). The Finnish Institute for Health and Welfare (THL, 2021) argue that grasping the official language(s) is essential for both children and adults in Finland, as it helps immigrants use services, obtain employment, access more study possibilities, and adapt to society. Many jobs in the public sector require a good command of at least one - and sometimes both - of the official languages, which significantly reduces the number of jobs one can pursue without proficient Finnish or Finland Swedish skills (OECD, 2018b). A lack of knowledge in the Finnish education system, language(s) and culture can also create barriers for parents who wish to be more involved in their children's schooling (Ismail, 2019). In some cases, adult immigrants in Finland have access to publicly organized, subsidized language training, but integration services are not available to all immigrant groups (OECD, 2021). Those who are ineligible for these services (e.g., some labor immigrants and their families, longer-term residents) may struggle to find affordable and/or convenient L2 learning opportunities, and as a result, they may never fully grasp the language(s).

According to the 2021 InterNations' rankings of 59 best countries for expats, Finland ranks 50th for ease of settling in, and 46th for career prospects and satisfaction. More specifically, 50% of foreigners living in Finland perceive local career options negatively, and 71% struggle to learn the local language (InterNations, 2021). Similarly, a survey on work and well-being among people of foreign origin (UTH-survey) found that nearly one in five immigrants feel the language education is insufficient, and thus THL (2021) recommends exploring new solutions for improving L2 skills. One option is through digital tools, given that Finland ranks number one for digital life on the InterNations (2021) report, and according to the Finnish Ministry of Education and Culture (2017), "It is of utmost importance that Finland remains at the forefront of utilizing language technology" (p. 26). A digital L2 tool could supplement existing integration services, and it could offer an affordable and convenient solution for immigrants who fall through the cracks.

Game Design Process

In the ongoing project, targeted end-users are people with an immigrant background living in Finland who wish to learn Finnish and/or Swedish. Although the focus is on designing a DLLG for the inclusion of immigrants, the game could also be used by Finnish speakers who wish to learn Swedish, and vice versa. We seek to address the needs of learners of all ages, and we consider how the game can be applicable both within formal learning environments and at home. This means we must also consider how the game could be used as an effective tool for educators. To do so, we involve various stakeholders, such as teachers of adult L2 learners, teachers in preparatory classrooms, teachers in mainstream classrooms, parents of children with an immigrant background, school leaders, etc.

Figure 1. Four UCD phases applied to designing a digital L2 learning game for immigrants in Finland

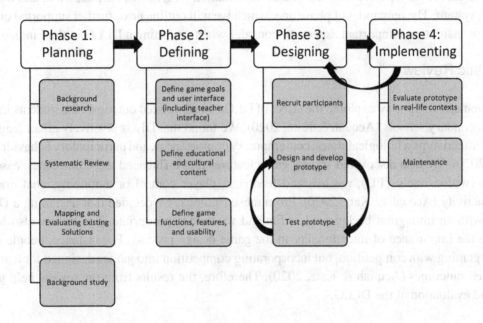

We also recognize the importance of diversity within the design team (see Braad et al., 2016). Thus, our team includes experts in user experience, game design, and game development; current and former educators; and researchers in psychology and education (multicultural education, culturally and linguistically responsive teaching, educational equity, inclusion, etc.). The members of our team are also linguistically, culturally, and ethnically diverse, with both native Finns and immigrants to Finland.

The project follows the four phases of UCD, and we are currently at phase two of the development cycle. Rather than present a completed DLLG, we emphasize the iterative design process that centers the end-users because it is the process that can inform the design of DLLGs in other contexts, not the final product. Therefore, we will outline the approach to research and development within each of the four phases (see Figure 1), and we will also present results from the first phase. Given that our team members work within Swedish-speaking institutions in Finland, the initial game design is focused on Finland Swedish, but in later iterations we will develop the Finnish language version.

Phase 1

The goals of this phase were to evaluate whether the project was worth pursuing, to understand the current state of Finnish L2 education for immigrant students, and to assess the needs of educators and immigrant students in Finland. To accomplish these goals, we conducted background research, a systematic review, a review of existing solutions, and a background study. We have already summarized the background research under the previous sections on immigrant education, the benefits of digital learning games, and the Finnish context. As part of the background research, we also reviewed the current Finnish curriculum for preparatory education in Finland. The background research provided evidence that L2 education for immigrant students in Finland is lacking, and that digital tools could be used to enhance L2 learning and inclusion for immigrants of all ages. Throughout the duration of the project, we will continuously review literature to ensure we have the most up-to-date information on DLLGs, L2 education, and the Finnish education system. The remainder of phase one, which we will outline next, further supported our vision, and gave us insight into important aspects to consider when designing a DLLG in the Finnish context.

Systematic Review

In the systematic review, we explored the effect of DLGs on L2-related outcomes for students in primary through secondary schools (Acquah & Katz, 2020). We found that DLGs positively affect language acquisition, affective/psychological states, contemporary competences, and participatory behavior (Acquah & Katz, 2020). We also discovered six key game features that influenced these outcomes: ease-of-use, challenge (within one's ZPD), rewards and feedback, player control or autonomy, goal orientation, and interactivity (Acquah & Katz, 2020). From these findings, we decided that designing a DLLG for students with an immigrant background in Finland would be appropriate. The review also helped us recognize the importance of intentionality in the game design process. For instance, people naturally associate gaming with competition, but incorporating competition into games designed for learning can have mixed outcomes (Acquah & Katz, 2020). Therefore, the results from the review help guide the design and evaluation of the DLLG.

Mapping and Evaluating Existing Solutions

Prior to developing a new product, it is necessary to investigate whether a similar solution already exists. Thus, we sought to explore what digital tools currently exist for learning Finnish or (Finland) Swedish. We discovered a range of existing digital tools, including websites and applications providing basic L2 lessons, a game for early literacy, and a mobile application for watching news programs with Finnish or Swedish subtitles. We also looked into popularized language learning applications, such as Duolingo.

Used in combination, we could see the potential benefits of these solutions, but as individual tools they each had numerous limitations. For instance, some of the solutions only offered preliminary language training or were only appropriate for a specific age group. Others lacked engaging features as well as a structured learning program. Moreover, the majority did not offer Finland Swedish, nor did they align with the preparatory curriculum for immigrants in Finland. Although we believe there is much to be learned from the existing tools, we concluded that our proposed solution could help fill the gaps and provide a much-needed tool for both immigrants and educators.

Background Study

The aim of the background study was to inform the design of a DLLG at the front end of the design process. The background study focused on teachers' experiences and needs related to teaching Finland Swedish and/or Finnish to immigrant students. Although we initially had hoped to involve more students during this phase of the project, Covid-19 made it challenging to collect data in schools. Rather than stall the process, we decided to move forward without initial student interviews (excluding one interview we conducted early on), but we aim to include students with an immigrant background throughout the remainder of the project. With that said, from the data collection we learned that the students in the teachers' classrooms were diverse in terms of literacy skills, previous education, reasons for immigrating to Finland, and country of origin, which included Syria, Nigeria, Iraq, Thailand, Peru, Ukraine, USA, and more.

Data for the background study was collected through semi-structured interviews with twelve teachers in Ostrobothnia, Western Finland. We identified educational institutions offering preparatory education for immigrants (both children/adolescents and adults), then contacted and recruited teachers in the schools by either e-mail or phone. Two of the team's researchers conducted the interviews, with one focusing on the schools in the South Ostrobothnia region and the other on schools in the Ostrobothnia region. To ensure similar data collection procedures by the two researchers, a data collection protocol and checklist was created. The interview questions were aimed at understanding the current state, needs and preferences related to L2 teaching and learning for immigrant students, with a particular focus on the availability and use of digital tools. The interviews were anonymized and transcribed verbatim, but minute details like pauses and word stress were not usually included, except when they were deemed too important to ignore. The transcripts were then translated to English by one of the researchers who conducted the interviews.

The translated interview transcripts were imported into NVivo qualitative analysis software where they were analyzed using thematic analysis (Braun & Clarke, 2006), resulting in three key themes: (1) importance of a differentiated, flexible approach; (2) need for context-specific integration education; and (3) positive perspective on digital tools and games for L2 acquisition. Many of the teachers admitted they were generally unprepared when they began teaching students with an immigrant background, but through trial-and-error and experience, they learned the necessity of being flexible in daily activities and incorporating a variety of tools and teaching methods. Due to the linguistic, cultural, educational, and sometimes age diversity among their students, they felt it was crucial to differentiate instruction in order to meet students' individual needs:

There isn't a schema that's applicable to everybody. We've had teenage boys which have come to secondary school...who are illiterate, who haven't gone to any school. They're also supposed to attend school. So, you have to evaluate everything from case to case.

Being able to adapt their teaching and come up with creative solutions was key to reaching each student. Given they did not share a common language with their students, they had to find other means to effectively communicate, such as through visuals.

The teachers emphasized that education for immigrants was not merely about language acquisition, but also about providing social support and information specific to Finnish life. As one teacher pointed out, "It's called an integration education — not language education. So, that means you don't only work on language. You also learn about, for example, Finnish society, working in Finland." The challenge to accomplishing this was the lack of Finland Swedish material available:

The problem is that our material comes from Sweden. You notice it in every detail...The currency is always kronor and the date is written in the Swedish way, with the month before if it's written with numbers — like year, month, day... Well, the holidays are the same, of course. So, stuff like that we bring up with a Finnish view of course...We listen to the texts as well. We listen to those which are recorded with the materials own recording, and then I also read it to get a Finland Swedish pronunciation.

Another teacher discussed the lack of digital Finland Swedish content: "there exists apps and digital material, but it's with standard Swedish pronunciation. There's a vast amount of YouTube films, but they have Swedish pronunciation everywhere." Finland's unique language situation makes it difficult for teachers to have Swedish material that is relevant within the Finnish context. Many of the teachers found themselves adapting the material from Sweden, or creating their own. Thus, they expressed a need for more context-specific material, including in the digital form.

Most of the teachers appeared very comfortable using digital tools, often incorporating them into their lessons. The teachers used digital tools to break up lectures, adding a fun, visual element to the learning. Overall, the teachers perceived digital tools and games positively. When asked about whether a DLLG developed specifically for Finland would be beneficial, one teacher responded,

...it would be very good to have things like games and stuff like that, when you don't know the language yet and can't communicate. But you could do it through pictures, and stuff like that...there is very little material for the preparatory students in Finland Swedish...Saying something to [immigrant students] doesn't do anything. You need to show pictures and your hands and stuff like that. So, if there's one place you could make an enormous difference if you made games and stuff like that, it's there.

Another teacher put it simply, "I really think games in learning is the way of the future. It's something we definitely will use more and more."

The background study confirmed that there is a need for more innovative L2 education solutions for immigrants in Finland. A DLLG could be used to help teachers differentiate instruction, and it would provide an alternative approach to learning through a visual, engaging platform (OECD, 2021). Importantly, the teachers in this study perceived digital tools and DLLGs positively, but they simply lacked relevant, engaging, easy-to-use resources. A DLLG could help fill this gap and introduce more culturally relevant learning content.

Phase 2

Upon consideration of the combined findings from phase one (systematic review, background research, evaluating existing solutions, and background study) we safely concluded that a DLLG would be beneficial for immigrants' L2 learning and social inclusion in Finland, and it would be a well-received tool among educators of immigrants in Finland. Thus, we moved on to the second phase where we defined design goals and made design choices based on the findings from phase one, and guided by the curriculum for preparatory education in Finland. During the second phase, our team's game designers and educational experts collaborated to make decisions regarding the game goals, player interface, educational content, cultural content, game functions and features, teacher interface, and usability.

Game Goal and User Interface

The goals of the game are to help players improve their Finnish and/or Finland Swedish, and to provide a general understanding of Finnish culture and everyday life. This requires the design of a game that is both engaging and educative, resulting in frequent play and enjoyment. To achieve these goals, we chose to create mini games that are played in venues based on locations one can find in most Finnish cities or towns. The players begin by selecting their age and creating their own avatar, which can move around a city map and enter venues to play mini games. The mini games expose players to age-appropriate content that is relevant and applicable within that given context. The content becomes increasingly more advanced as the player progresses through the game and they can unlock more challenging levels, including bonus games.

Educational and Cultural Content

The educational content stems from the Finnish National Curriculum, feedback from educators and immigrants in Finland, and research on L2 learning and challenges to integration. The age adaptability function means the content will be relevant based on the different spaces children, youth, and adults will most likely occupy, consequently supporting age differences in integration needs. For children, the school will be an important venue early on, but they may also choose to enter and learn within other locations, such as a store, a park, a library, "their" home, etc. Within the school venue, the player will be exposed to words related to the classroom environment (e.g., pencil, colors, book), the people within school (e.g., teachers, students, friends), an average school day (e.g., lunch time, recess, art class) as well as basic language to communicate (e.g., help, please, thank you, I am..., my name is..., etc.). Enabling children to understand academic content and effectively communicate with school staff and native-born peers is essential for supporting their integration (Sinkkonen & Kyttälä, 2014; THL, 2021)

Given the challenges adult immigrants in Finland have with settling in and finding work (InterNations, 2021), they must be introduced to everyday vocabulary, as well as language skills that will improve integration. For this reason, the workplace will be an important venue for adults, and even when entering the same venue, the content will be adjusted to be age appropriate. For instance, at the home venue, both children and adults will be exposed to vocabulary about furniture, cooking, and family, but adults will also learn about paying the rent in Finland and getting home insurance. It is imperative that adults learn language around practical matters, such as paying taxes, accessing healthcare, applying for a job, and how the education system works.

Language education extends beyond the mere acquisition of language; it is about understanding the relationship between culture, identity, and language (Heugh & Mohamed, 2020). In other words, it involves providing learners with the cultural capital required to be successful and obtain opportunities within the host country (Ismail, 2019). Therefore, we also use each location to share culture-specific knowledge, practices, and traditions. The cultural content may be presented either through mini games, or through stories that are shared at different points in the game. An example of an important cultural practice within the adult Finnish context is the coffee break, which is a time during the workday where colleagues briefly meet to share a cup of coffee and conversation. Integrating cultural content into the games creates situated meanings for language; consequently, newly arrived immigrants may feel more comfortable and confident applying their new skills at work, school, or in social situations (see Gee, 2008). This also addresses the need raised by teachers where they lack Swedish language material that is relevant in the Finnish context.

Functions and features

We have also planned to include a variety of functions and features that help the player establish an in-game identity, guide the player through the game, motivate the player to continue to practice, prompt the player to review and refresh their learning, and inform the player of their learning progress. Each function and feature must be carefully designed for optimal efficacy. One such feature is the reward system, where positive reinforcement is provided to users through the dispersion of some virtual symbol or object (i.e., digital badges; Yang et al., 2016), whether it be coins, stars, points, hearts, etc. Although simple in theory, in practice the optimization of a reward system requires careful consideration of a variety of factors to ensure the reward is meaningful, and to avoid distracting the player from the learning content (Schimanke et al., 2014). One must consider the value of the reward, how often and how much it should be dispersed, and whether it can be used for some further purpose (e.g., to make virtual purchases, to re-do a task, to open new levels). If rewards are dispersed too easily, then players will not feel a sense of challenge; in contrast, if they are dispersed infrequently, then the challenge of acquiring them may be too great and the player may simply ignore them. Other forms of feedback must be dispersed in a similar manner to provide the adequate level of support needed for players to learn within their ZPD, and feel motivated to continue playing (Acquah & Katz, 2020; Plass et al., 2015). Through the integration of a spaced-repetition algorithm, we hope to optimize language acquisition, retention, and player behavior (Schimanke et al., 2014). The inclusion of features that create the right level of balance between challenge and support have the potential of inducing the state of flow, which offers a myriad of benefits to the users (Hamari et al., 2016; Plass et al., 2015).

Teacher interface

Another important consideration is how the game could easily be adopted in schools to help inform educators' instruction. This entails the safe collection of user data that teachers can use to track progress and provide differentiated support within students' ZPD (Ahad & Benton, 2018; OECD, 2021; Peterson, 2010). To enable this feature, we decided to also develop a teacher interface, where teachers can connect to each of their students' profiles. The teacher then will have access to individual student progress, including game level, frequency of play, proficiency in certain learning goals, errors, and overall language proficiency. The tracking of student proficiency and errors must occur over time to exclude one-time mistakes or lucky guesses. It also should not merely present vocabulary recognition and understanding of grammar rules, but it should also provide information regarding students' L2 skills (reading, writing, listening, etc.; see European Commission, 2017). This ensures proper identification of learning challenges, and will hopefully reduce the number of immigrants wrongly placed in special education classes (Sinkkonen & Kyttälä, 2014). For example, a teacher can see whether patterned errors are a result of the student not understanding a grammar rule, or whether they are struggling to understand the spoken language. Although we have a preliminary idea of what student information could be provided to teachers, further discussions with teachers in Finland will help determine the data they deem useful.

Usability

Finally, we must highlight the importance of usability through an intuitive game design because, as discussed by the teachers, visuals are key for communication when there is no common language. Scaffolding not only applies to supporting a learner to acquire knowledge within their ZPD, but it also refers to providing proper support early on to make certain users understand how to play the game (Plass et al., 2015). Given the cultural, linguistic, and age diversity within the target users, the DLLG must be made to avoid player frustration and ensure ease-of-use (Acquah & Katz, 2020). This means we must carefully select visual and auditory cues to guide the player through the game in a way that does not require the understanding of Finnish or Swedish. The selection of visual or auditory cues requires an exploration into the various meanings associated with certain colors or symbols across cultures. At the same time, to ensure the game is culturally relevant in Finland, we seek to include symbols that are commonly used throughout the country. An example of this is the check mark (✓), which in some contexts represents right or good, but in Finnish schools is used to mark something wrong. There is a fine balance between making the game both culturally relevant and easy to understand; thus, testing the game with a diverse group of potential end-users will help us improve aspects of the game (including cultural aspects) that are unclear.

Phase 3

The benefit of using UCD is that we do not expect to get everything right on the first try. There may be some features we have planned for that distract from gameplay and others that are completely ignored by the players. There may be aspects of the interface the players find confusing, or mini games that are too difficult. However, during the third phase we will be able to assess the game design and usability, and engage in an iterative process of design, development, and testing until we have reached the optimal product for L2 learning. At this phase, the game will be developed starting from early prototypes based on the phase two design decisions, and exceeding to more mature ones once we begin user-testing and are able to evaluate what does or does not work.

In addition to our design team, we will involve teachers, students, a graphic designer, a programmer, and other outside experts in the design and evaluation of the evolving prototypes. At this stage, it is necessary to recruit a group of participants who represent the diversity within potential end-users, and as a result can give insight into the range of needs and preferences of the target group (Aykin, 2005; Bengs et al., 2018). This includes diversity in ethnicity, age, language, gender, gaming experience, years in Finland, etc. Although earlier prototypes will be designed to fit the needs of school-age users, we will eventually expand upon those to make the game relevant for adults with an immigrant background.

A mixed-methods approach will be applied in order to gain insights into usability, playability, and L2-related outcomes. A mixed-methods approach enables validation and triangulation of findings (Wiklund-Engblom & Högväg, 2014). It also allows for the identification of inconsistencies in responses and evaluations, which might be due to lack of familiarity with the types of scales employed, social desirability bias in the face-to-face interview, or cultural background (Bengs et al., 2018). The application of multiple methods further enables evaluation and validation of users' actions, reactions, and experiences, not only retrospectively, but also during the actual experience of playing the game. The following is a list of potential methods that could be used to inform the design process for a DLLG during this phase of the development cycle:

- **Interviews:** used to gather information about demographics and technographics of the participants before the test (Rubin & Chasnell, 2008). Post-test, semi-structured interviews can also be used to gain insights into why certain tasks, functions or features were experienced as problematic or especially helpful. The post-test interviews should target participants' perceptions of usability (including pedagogical usability), user experience, motivation, and learning related to playing the game.
- **Concurrent think aloud:** enables participants to verbalize their thought process and motivations for actions as they are playing the game and completing the tasks (Wiklund-Engblom & Högväg, 2014). The sound is recorded with a microphone integrated into eye tracking equipment.

- **Questionnaires:** can measure students' perspectives, emotions, and experiences related to the game. More specifically, there are existing validated questionnaires that measure affective/ psychological states, mental effort, challenge, and cognitive load.
- **Task success:** used to calculate participants' general success rate (Rubin & Chasnell, 2008). It provides information about task-level usability problems and enables a validation of improvements made in later prototypes by comparing task success rates with earlier prototypes.
- **Eye tracking:** eye-tracking devices can be used to measure eye movements, capture patterns of fixations (or ignored functions/content), and to give insight into users' general interaction with the game (Duchowski, 2017; Guestrin & Eizenman, 2006). Long fixations on stimuli indicate interest and focus or that something is difficult to understand and requires mental effort (Duchowski, 2017; Holmqvist & Andersson, 2017).
- **Observations:** provide insight into participants' behavior, screen behavior, and learning process during the test (Rankin et al., 2008; Rubin & Chasnell, 2008). Recording behavior can also be used as a validity check for the eye tracking data in cases where, for instance, a participant is looking away from the screen.

In Table 1, we organize each method by the stage of testing where they would be most valuable, as well as the type of data they would provide. However, this is meant merely as a guide; a vital part of UCD is being flexible, thus the method(s) can be adapted and used at different stages when the need arises.

Table 1. Potential user research methods according to test stage and type of data collected

Test stage	Type of data			
	Subjective **Formative Summative**		**Objective** **Formative Summative**	
Before	Interview	Questionnaire	-	-
During	Think aloud	-	Eye tracking Behavior observation Screen behavior observation	Task success rate Eye tracking
After	Interview	Questionnaire	-	-

Phase 4

In the fourth phase, the game will be implemented and evaluated in real life contexts, and a continuous process of maintenance will begin. This entails assessing gameplay over an extended period to observe L2 retention within participants, as well as player behavior. Evidence shows that a spaced-repetition algorithm supports both retention as well as user behavior (Schimanke et al., 2014), but if we find user retention and behavior stagnates or declines, then the algorithm and possibly other features of the game will have to be adjusted.

The ultimate aim of the game is to promote social inclusion of immigrants living in Finland by enhancing their Finnish or Finland Swedish skills. If players are not motivated to continue playing, and they stop before reaching the point where they can use the language in everyday life, then the game will not be viewed as a success. Assessing this may require further data collection with the participants as it is important to know whether the game has had an impact on their ability to effectively integrate within society. In addition, we will assess the use of the game in school contexts, including how well the teacher interface serves the teachers' needs. With school-age users, the hope is that the game promotes quicker integration into mainstream classrooms, resulting in social inclusion among Finnish peers.

Societal Impact

For immigrants living in Finland, grasping Finnish and/or Finland Swedish opens the doors to numerous opportunities (social, economic, educational, and occupational) that enable active participation in society, and can generally ease challenges to settling in (InterNations, 2021). This has implications for immigrants' overall sense of well-being and ability to form relationships (InterNations, 2021). With that said, the design of a DLLG for immigrants in Finland not only has implications for the immigrant population, but also the Finnish population, education sector, and work force (see Figure 2; OECD, 2017, 2018b). A DLLG would benefit Finnish society because it could improve cross-cultural communication, understanding, awareness, and connection. Moreover, Finland has an ageing population making it crucial to introduce more highly trained workers with diverse skill sets into the labor market. This means young immigrant students must have access to the same level of education as their Finnish peers, and parents must be provided with relevant cultural knowledge to support their children's educational needs (Ismail, 2019). A DLLG could also support Finnish teachers of immigrants who may not share a common language with their students making it difficult to differentiate instruction and objectively assess learning (Ahad & Benton, 2018). As a result of improved L2 education, immigrants of all ages may be able to integrate more quickly and successfully into mainstream schools, the labor market, and society at large.

Figure 2. Potential impact of a digital L2 learning game for immigrants in Finland

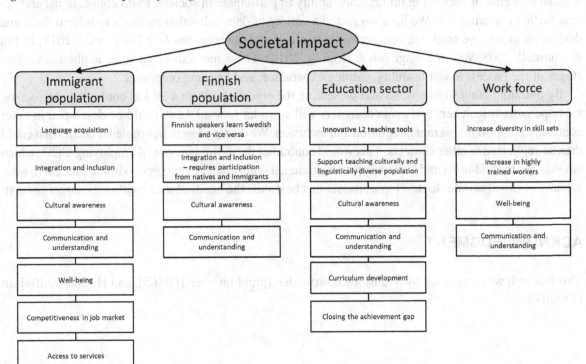

DISCUSSION AND CONCLUSION

In this chapter, we presented our ongoing project aimed at supporting immigrant integration and inclusion in Finland through the design of a DLLG. We have highlighted benefits of DLLGs for immigrant L2 acquisition, modeled the four-phase UCD process, and presented challenges that may occur during the design process. The choice to design a DLLG for immigrants arose from extensive evidence demonstrating the need to improve immigrant L2 education and integration in Finland (InterNations, 2021; OECD, 2019a; Sinkkonen & Kyttälä, 2014; THL, 2021), and research showing the benefits of DLLGs on L2 outcomes (Acquah & Katz, 2020). DLLGS are especially effective due to their ability to differentiate, motivate, enhance L2 speaking confidence, and improve language acquisition (Peterson, 2010; Squire, 2008). They also provide the possibility of incorporating other content into the game so that language is not the sole focus, but immigrant students can continue to progress in other content areas.

However, the efficacy of the DLLG largely depends on the game design decisions, which is why we suggest researchers and game designers use UCD. UCD involves a multi-disciplinary design team, as well as active involvement of targeted end-users and various stakeholders (ISO, 2010; Ritter et al., 2014). The iterative design process can lead to the development of a game that is appropriate for the selected context, enabling it to address the linguistic and cultural needs of end-users. As a result of incorporating a combination of linguistic and cultural content into the game, immigrants should be better prepared to apply their new skills within the appropriate contexts. This outcome is not possible without equipping the game with functions and features that not only support language education, but also motivate users to engage in frequent gameplay (Acquah & Katz, 2020; Schimanke et al., 2014). The inclusion of rewards, feedback, and spaced repetition can ensure the game is engaging and users are supported within their ZPD (Plass et al., 2015; Schimanke et al., 2014; Yang et al., 2016). Moreover, providing teachers with data on student progress can support them in differentiating instruction and identifying problem areas (Lucas & Villegas, 2013; OECD, 2021). Each game design decision arises from thorough user research, with an end-goal of improving immigrants' ability to participate in society, build connections, and access further opportunities. We have suggested a variety of data collection methods to inform the game design, including eye-tracking, concurrent think-aloud and observations (see Duchowski, 2017; Rubin & Chasnell, 2008; Wiklund-Engblom & Högväg, 2014). These methods can also be applied at various stages of the process to test usability, gaming experience, and learning outcomes.

By outlining our design process and presenting the potential impact a DLLG could have on society, we hope more researchers and game designers will consider how a DLLG could be developed in other contexts to support immigrant integration and inclusion. We do not present a completed DLLG that could then be replicated in other contexts. This would contradict the entire purpose of employing UCD, which emphasizes the end-users and iterative process. Rather, it is necessary to undergo a similar process to what we have outlined in order to develop a product that best suits the needs of users within the target context.

ACKNOWLEDGMENT

This research was supported by Svenska Kulturfonden [grant number 160465], and Högskolestiftelsen i Österbotten.

REFERENCES

Acquah, E. O., & Katz, H. T. (2020). Digital game-based L2 learning outcomes for primary through high-school students: A systematic literature review. *Computers & Education, 143*, 143. doi:10.1016/j. compedu.2019.103667

Ahad, A., & Benton, M. (2018). *Mainstreaming 2.0: How Europe's education systems can boost migrant inclusion*. Academic Press.

Bengs, A., Hägglund, S., Wiklund-Engblom, A., Majors, J., & Ashfaq, A. (2018). Designing for social inclusion of immigrant women: The case of TeaTime. *Innovation (Abingdon), 31*(2), 106–124. doi:10. 1080/13511610.2017.1348931

Benton, M., & Glennie, A. (2016). *Digital humanitarianism: How tech entrepreneurs are supporting refugee integration*. Migration Policy Institute.

Braad, E., Žavcer, G., & Sandovar, A. (2016). Processes and models for serious game design and development. In R. Dörner, S. Göbel, M. Kickmeier-Rust, M. Masuch, & K. Zweog (Eds.), *Entertainment computing & serious games* (pp. 92–118). Springer. doi:10.1007/978-3-319-46152-6_5

Braun, V., & Clarke, V. (2006). Using thematic analysis in psychology. *Qualitative Research in Psychology, 3*(2), 77–101. doi:10.1191/1478088706qp063oa

Csikszentmihalyi, M., & Asakawa, K. (2016). Universal and cultural dimensions of optimal experiences. *The Japanese Psychological Research, 58*(1), 4–13. doi:10.1111/jpr.12104

Duchowski, A. (2017). *Eye tracking methodology: Theory and practice* (3rd ed.). Springer. doi:10.1007/978-3-319-57883-5

Ebbinghaus, H. (1885). *Memory: A contribution to experimental psychology*. Dover.

Egenfeldt-Nielsen, S. (2011). What makes a good learning game? Going beyond edutainment. *ELearn Magazine, 2*.

EUMC. (2004). *Migrants, minorities and education: Documenting discrimination and integration in 15 member states of the European Union*. EUMC.

European Commission/EACEA/Eurydice. (2017). *Key data on teaching languages at school in Europe - 2017 edition* (Eurydice Report). Publications Office of the European Union. https://op.europa.eu/en/publication-detail/-/publication/73ac5ebd-473e-11e7-aea8-01aa75ed71a1/language-en/format-PDF

European Commission/EACEA/Eurydice. (2019). *Integrating students from migrant backgrounds into schools in Europe: National Policies and Measures (Eurydice Report)*. Publications Office of the European Union.

European Commission. (2015). *Language teaching and learning in multilingual classrooms*. Publications Office of the European Union.

Finnish Institute for Health and Welfare (THL). (2021). *Koulutus ja kielitaito*. https://thl.fi/fi/web/maahanmuutto-ja-kulttuurinen-%0Amoninaisuus/kotoutuminen-ja-osallisuus/koulutus-ja-kielitaito%0A

Gee, J. P. (2008). Learning and Games. In *The ecology of games: Connecting youth, games, and learning* (pp. 21–40). The MIT Press. doi:10.1162/dmal.9780262693646.021

Gibbons, P. (2015). *Scaffolding language, scaffolding learning: Teaching English language learners in the mainstream classroom*. Heinemann.

Guestrin, E. D., & Eizenman, M. (2006). General theory of remote gaze estimation using the pupil centre and conreal reflections. *IEEE Transactions on Biomedical Engineering, 53*(6), 1124–1133. doi:10.1109/TBME.2005.863952 PMID:16761839

Hamari, J., Shernoff, D. J., Rowe, E., Coller, B., Asbell-Clarke, J., & Edwards, T. (2016). Challenging games help students learn: An empirical study on engagement, flow and immersion in game-based learning. *Computers in Human Behavior, 54*, 170–179. doi:10.1016/j.chb.2015.07.045

Harteveld, C., Guimarães, R., Mayer, I. S., & Bidarra, R. (2010). Balancing play, meaning and reality: The design philosophy of levee patroller. *Simulation & Gaming, 41*(3), 316–340. doi:10.1177/1046878108331237

Hassenzahl, M. (2010). *Technology for all the right reasons*. Morgan and Claypool.

Heugh, K., & Mohamed, N. (2020). Approaches to language in education for migrants and refugees in the Asia-Pacific region. In *UNESCO Bangkok*. UNESCO-UNICEF.

Holmqvist, K., & Andersson, R. (2017). *Eye tracking: A comprehensive guide to methods, paradigms and measures* (2nd ed.). Lund Eye-Tracking Institute.

Huddleston, T., Niessen, J., & Tjaden, J. T. (2013). Using EU indicators of immigrant integration: Final Report for Directorate-General for Home Affairs. Home Affairs, European Commission.

Hung, H., Yang, J. C., Hwang, G., Chu, H., & Wang, C. (2018). A scoping review of research on digital game-based language learning. *Computers & Education, 126*, 89–104. doi:10.1016/j.compedu.2018.07.001

InterNations. (2021). *Expat Insider 2021: The year of uncertainty*. InterNations.

Ismail, A. A. (2019). Immigrant children, educational performance and public policy: A capability approach. *Journal of International Migration and Integration, 20*(3), 717–734. doi:10.100712134-018-0630-9

ISO. (2010). *Ergonomics of human system interaction - Part 210: Human-centred design for interactive systems*. https://www.iso.org/obp/ui/#iso:std:iso:9241:-210:ed-1:v1:en

Keinonen, T. (2009). Design contribution square. *Advanced Engineering Informatics, 23*(2), 142–148. doi:10.1016/j.aei.2008.10.002

Klimova, B., & Kacet, J. (2017). Efficacy of computer games on language learning. *The Turkish Online Journal of Educational Technology, 16*(4).

Lucas, T., & Villegas, A. M. (2013). Preparing linguistically responsive teachers: Laying the foundation in preservice teacher education. *Theory into Practice, 52*(2), 98–109. doi:10.1080/00405841.2013.770327

Lyon, A. R., & Koerner, K. (2016). User-centred design for psychosocial intervention development and implementation. *Clinical Psychology: Science and Practice, 23*(2), 180–200. doi:10.1111/cpsp.12154 PMID:29456295

Magos, K., & Politi, F. (2008). The creative second language lesson: The contribution of the role-play technique to the teaching of a second language in immigrant classes. *RELC Journal, 39*(1), 96–112. doi:10.1177/0033688208091142

Melton, A. W. (1970). The situation with respect to the spacing of repetitions and memory. *Journal of Verbal Learning and Verbal Behavior, 9*(5), 596–606. doi:10.1016/S0022-5371(70)80107-4

Ministry of Education and Culture - Finland. (2017). *Multilingualism as a strength: Procedural recommendations for developing Finland's national language reserve.* https://minedu.fi/docu-ments/1410845/4150027/Multilingualism+as+a+strength.pdf/766f921a-%0A1456-4146-89ed-899452cb5af8/Multilingualism+as+a+strength.pdf.%0A

OECD. (2015). *Helping immigrant students to succeed at school-and beyond.* OECD Publishing. https://www.oecd.org/education/Helping-immigrant-students-to-succeed-at-school-and-beyond.pdf

OECD. (2017). *Finding the way: A discussion of the Finnish migrant integration system.* OECD Publishing. https://www.oecd.org/els/mig/Finding_the_Way_Finland.pdf

OECD. (2018a). *The resilience of students with an immigrant background: Factors that shape well-being.* OECD Publishing. doi:10.1787/9789264292093-

OECD. (2018b). *Working together: Skills and labour market integration of immigrants and their children in Finland.* OECD Publishing. doi:10.1787/9789264305250-

OECD. (2019a). *PISA 2018 results: Where all students can succeed: Vol. II.* OECD Publishing.

OECD. (2019b). The road to integration: Education and migration. In *OECD Reviews of Migrant Education.* OECD Publishing. doi:10.1787/d8ceec5d-

OECD. (2021). Language training for adult migrants. In *Making Integration Work.* OECD Publishing. doi:10.1787/02199d7f-

Pagulayan, R. J., Keeker, K., Wixon, D., Romero, R., & Fuller, T. (2008). User-centered design in games. In J. Jacko & A. Sears (Eds.), *Handbook of Human-Computer Interaction in Interactive Systems.* Lawrence Erlbaum Associates, Inc.

Peterson, M. (2010). Massively multiplayer online role-playing games (MMORPGs) as arenas for language learning. *Computer Assisted Language Learning, 23*(5), 429–439. doi:10.1080/09588221.2010.520673

Piker, R. A. (2013). Understanding influences of play on second language learning: A microethnographic view in one Head Start preschool classroom. *Journal of Early Childhood Research, 11*(2), 184–200. doi:10.1177/1476718X12466219

Plass, J. L., Homer, B. D., & Kinzer, C. K. (2015). Foundations of game-based learning. *Educational Psychologist, 50*(4), 258–283. doi:10.1080/00461520.2015.1122533

Rankin, Y. A., McNeal, M., Shute, M. W., & Gooch, B. (2008). User centered game design: Evaluating massive multiplayer online role playing games for second language acquisition. *Sandbox Symposium,* 43–50. 10.1145/1401843.1401851

Reitz, L., Sohny, A., & Lochmann, G. (2016). VR-based gamification of communication training and oral examination in a second language. *International Journal of Game-Based Learning, 16*(4), 391–404. doi:10.4018/IJGBL.2016040104

Ritter, F. E., Baxter, G. D., & Churchill, E. F. (2014). *Foundations for designing user-centered systems.* Springer-Verlag. doi:10.1007/978-1-4471-5134-0

Rubin, J., & Chasnell, D. (2008). *Handbook of usability testing: How to plan, design, and conduct effective tests* (2nd ed.). Wiley Publishing, Inc.

Salant, B., & Benton, M. (2017). *Strengthening local education systems for newly arrived adults and children: Empowering cities through better use of EU instruments.* Migration Policy Institute Europe. https://ec.europa.eu/futurium/sites/futurium/files/mpieurope_urbanagenda_education.pdf

Schimanke, F., Mertens, R., & Vornberger, O. (2014). Spaced repetition learning games on mobile devices: Foundations and perspectives. *Interactive Technology and Smart Education, 11*(3), 201–222. doi:10.1108/ITSE-07-2014-0017

Settles, B., & Meeder, B. (2016). A trainable spaced repetition model for language learning. *54th Annual Meeting of the Association for Computational Linguistics*, 1848–1858. https://www.duolingo.com

Sinkkonen, H. M., & Kyttälä, M. (2014). Experiences of Finnish teachers working with immigrant students. *European Journal of Special Needs Education, 29*(2), 167–183. doi:10.1080/08856257.2014.891719

Squire, K. D. (2008). Video games and education: Designing learning systems for an interactive age. *Educational Technology, 48*(2), 17–26.

Sugarman, J. (2017). *Beyond teaching English: Supporting high school completion by immigrant and refugee students.* Migration Policy Institute.

Sugarman, J. (2018). A matter of design: English learner program models in K-12 education (Issue 2). Migration Policy Institute.

Villegas, A. M., & Lucas, T. (2007, March). The culturally responsive teacher. *Educational Leadership.* https://www.ascd.org/el/articles/the-culturally-responsive-teacher

Vygotsky, L. S. (1978). *Mind in society: The development of higher psychological processes.* Harvard University Press.

Wiklund-Engblom, A., & Högväg, J. (2014). The quest for integrating data in mixed research: User experience research revisited. In M. Horsely, M. Elliot, B. A. Knight, & R. Reilly (Eds.), *Current trends in eye tracking research* (pp. 161–175). Springer. doi:10.1007/978-3-319-02868-2_12

Wu, T., & Huang, Y. (2017). A mobile game-based English vocabulary practice system based on portfolio analysis. *Journal of Educational Technology & Society, 20*(2), 265–277.

Yang, J. C., Quadir, B., & Chen, N. S. (2016). Effects of the badge mechanism on self-efficacy and learning performance in a game-based english learning environment. *Journal of Educational Computing Research, 54*(3), 371–394. doi:10.1177/0735633115620433

Young, M. F., Slota, S., Cutter, A. B., Jalette, G., Mullin, G., Lai, B., Simeoni, Z., Tran, M., & Yukjymenko, M. (2012). Our princess is in another castle: A review of trends in serious gaming for education. *Review of Educational Research*, *82*(1), 61–89. doi:10.3102/0034654312436980

Young, S.-S.-C., & Wang, Y.-H. (2014). The game embedded call system to facilitate english vocabulary acquisition and pronunciation. *Journal of Educational Technology & Society*, *17*(3), 239–251.

Yudintseva, A. (2015). Synthesis of research on video games for the four second language skills and vocabulary practice. *Open Journal of Social Sciences*, *3*(11), 81–89. doi:10.4236/jss.2015.311011

ADDITIONAL READING

Bengs, A., Wiklund-Engblom, A., Majors, J., Teirilä, M., & Oraviita, T. (2016). Cross-cultural digital design: Lessons learned from the case of ImageTestLab. In C. M. Schmidt (Ed.), *Crossmedia-Kommunikation in kulturbedingten Handlungsräumen: Mediengerechte Anwendung und zielgruppenspezifische Ausrichtung*. Springer VS. doi:10.1007/978-3-658-11076-5_15

Bradley, L., Berbyuk Lindström, N., & Sofkova Hashemi, S. (2017). Integration and language learning of newly arrived migrants using mobile technology. *Journal of Interactive Media in Education*, *1*(3), 1–9. doi:10.5334/jime.434

Hodent, C. (2018). *The gamer's brain: How neuroscience and ux can impact video game design*. Taylor & Francis.

Jones, A., Kukulska-Hulme, A., Norris, L., Gaved, M., Scanlon, E., Jones, J., & Brasher, A. (2017). Supporting immigrant language learning on smartphones: A field trial. *Studies in the Education of Adults*, *49*(2), 228–252. doi:10.1080/02660830.2018.1463655

Lankoski, P., & Björk, S. (Eds.). (2015). *Game Research Methods: An Overview*. Lulu.com.

Lantolf, J. P., & Thorne, S. L. (2006). Sociocultural theory and second language learning. In B. VanPatten & J. Williams (Eds.), *Theories in second language acquisition: An introduction* (1st ed., pp. 197–221).

Takeuchi, L., & Vaala, S. (2014). *Level up learning: A national survey on teaching with digital games*. The Joan Ganz Cooney Center at Sesame Workshop.

Wastiau, P., Kearney, C., & Van den Berghe, W. (2009). *How are digital games used in schools?* (Final Report). European Schoolnet.

KEY TERMS AND DEFINITIONS

Differentiated Instruction: Adjusting the educational approach and content to meet students' individual needs and to build off their background knowledge.

Digital Language Learning Game: A game designed specifically for learning a language using an electronic device.

Digital Learning Game: A game designed for any form of learning using an electronic device.

Digital Tool: An electronic resource that can be used to support a wide range of objectives and purposes.

Flow State: Experiencing an optimal level of concentration, enjoyment, and immersion while engaged in an activity or task.

Host Country: The place to which an immigrant has relocated.

Immigrant: A person who has moved (by choice or force) to another country with the aim of establishing residence (short or long-term).

Preparatory Education: Formal learning environments where newly arrived immigrants are provided host country language instruction and other relevant skills to prepare them for integration into mainstream classrooms and/or society.

Situated Learning: Presenting content in the relevant context and enabling learners to be actively involved in the meaning-making process.

User-Centered Design: An iterative design process in which intended end users are involved in each phase through a variety of design and research methods.

Compilation of References

Revolution: Black Friday [Digital game]. (2016). *iNK Stories*. Retrieved 07 11, 2021, from Games for change: https://www.gamesforchange.org/game/1979-revolution-black-friday/

A Plague Tale: Innocence. (2019). [Video Game]. Asobo Studios SARL/ Focus Home Interactive SAS.

A Princess Tale: Introduction (2016). [Video Game]. Warfare Studios/Adorlea https://www.youtube.com/watch?v=yn9tSs9v0WE

A Woman's Lot: [Kingdom Come: Deliverance]. (2019). [Video Game]. DownLoadable Content (DLC). Warhorse Studios s.r.o.

Abbadessa, G., Brigo, F., Clerico, M., De Mercanti, S., Trojsi, F., Tedeschi, G., Bonavita, S., & Lavorgna, L. (2021). Digital therapeutics in neurology. *Journal of Neurology*, 1–16. doi:10.100700415-021-10608-4 PMID:34018047

Abdin, E., Chong, S. A., Ragu, V., Vaingankar, J. A., Shafie, S., Verma, S., Ganesan, G., Tan, K. B., Heng, D., & Subramaniam, M. (2021). The economic burden of mental disorders among adults in Singapore: Evidence from the 2016 Singapore Mental Health Study. *Journal of Mental Health (Abingdon, England)*, *0*(0), 1–8. doi:10.1080/09638237.2021.1952958 PMID:34338569

Abidin, H. Z., & Zaman, F. K. (2017, November). Students' perceptions on game-based classroom response system in a computer programming course. In *2017 IEEE 9th International Conference on Engineering Education (ICEED)* (pp. 254-259). IEEE.

Abt, C. C. (1987). *Serious Games*. University Press of America.

Acquah, E. O., & Katz, H. T. (2020). Digital game-based L2 learning outcomes for primary through high-school students: A systematic literature review. *Computers & Education*, *143*, 143. doi:10.1016/j.compedu.2019.103667

Activate. (2010). *iCivics*. Retrieved 07 17, 2021, from Game for change: https://www.gamesforchange.org/game/game-3/

Adam, C., & Andonoff, E. (2019, May). VigiFlood: a serious game for understanding the challenges of risk communication. ISCRAM.

Adams, D. M., Mayer, R. E., MacNamara, A., Koenig, A., & Wainess, R. (2012). Narrative games for learning: Testing the discovery and narrative hypotheses. *Journal of Educational Psychology*, *104*(1), 235–249. doi:10.1037/a0025595

Adamson, A. & Apted. M. (Directors). (2005-2010). *The Chronicles of Narnia* [Feature film series]. Walt Disney Pictures, Walden Media, Ozumi Films & Fox 2000 Pictures.

Adibi, M. M. (2000). Bulk Power System Restoration Training Techniques. In Power System Restoration: Methodologies & Implementation Strategies. IEEE. pp. doi:10.1109/9780470545607.ch39

Aguiar, V. A. C., Rosly, M. M., & Nakano, M. (2018). A Single Player Serious Game for Sustainable Supply Chain Management. *Studies in Simulation and Gaming*, *28*(1), 60–72.

Aguirre, E., Hoare, Z., Spector, A., Woods, R. T., & Orrell, M. (2014). The Effects of a Cognitive Stimulation Therapy [CST] Programme for People with Dementia on Family Caregivers' Health. *BMC Geriatrics*, *14*(31), 1–16. doi:10.1186/1471-2318-14-31 PMID:24628705

Ahad, A., & Benton, M. (2018). *Mainstreaming 2.0: How Europe's education systems can boost migrant inclusion.* Academic Press.

Ahmad, A., Zeeshan, F., Marriam, R., Samreen, A., & Ahmed, S. (2020b). Does one size fit all? Investigating the effect of group size and gamification on learners' behaviors in higher education. *Journal of Computing in Higher Education*, 1–32.

Ahmad, A., Zeshan, F., Khan, M. S., Marriam, R., Ali, A., & Samreen, A. (2020a). The impact of gamification on learning outcomes of computer science majors. *ACM Transactions on Computing Education*, *20*(2), 1–25. doi:10.1145/3383456

Ahmad, F., Uddin, M. M., & Goparaju, L. (2019). Agroforestry suitability mapping of India: A geospatial approach based on FAO guidelines. *Agroforestry Systems*, *93*(4), 1319–1336. doi:10.100710457-018-0233-7

Ahmed, M. N., Toor, A. S., O'Neil, K., & Friedland, D. (2017). Cognitive computing and the future of health care cognitive computing and the future of healthcare: The cognitive power of IBM Watson has the potential to transform global personalized medicine. *IEEE Pulse*, *8*(3), 4–9. doi:10.1109/MPUL.2017.2678098 PMID:28534755

Akhtar, A. (2016, July 12). Holocaust Museum, Auschwitz want Pokémon Go hunts out. *USA Today*. https://eu.usatoday.com/story/tech/news/2016/07/12/holocaust-museum-auschwitz-want-pokmon-go-hunts-stop-pokmon/86991810/

Akili. (2021). *Science and Technology*. https://www.akiliinteractive.com/

Alamerew, Y. A., & Brissaud, D. (2020). Modelling reverse supply chain through system dynamics for realizing the transition towards the circular economy: A case study on electric vehicle batteries. *Journal of Cleaner Production*, *254*, 120025. doi:10.1016/j.jclepro.2020.120025

Alami, D., & Dalpiaz, F. (2017, September). A gamified tutorial for learning about security requirements engineering. In *2017 IEEE 25th International Requirements Engineering Conference (RE)* (pp. 418-423). IEEE. 10.1109/RE.2017.67

Alba: A Wildlife Adventure [Digital game]. (2020). *Ustwo Games*. Retrieved 07 17, 2021, from STEAM: https://store.steampowered.com/app/1337010/Alba_A_Wildlife_Adventure/

Alexander, A. L., Brunyé, T., Sidman, J., & Weil, S. A. (2005). *From Gaming to Training: A Review of Studies on Fidelity, Immersion, Presence, and Buy-in and Their Effects on Transfer in PC-Based Simulations and Games.* DARWARS Training Impact Group.

AlJarrah, A., Thomas, M. K., & Shehab, M. (2018). Investigating temporal access in a flipped classroom: Procrastination persists. *International Journal of Educational Technology in Higher Education*, *15*(1), 1–18. doi:10.118641239-017-0083-9

Allain, P., Foloppe, D., Besnard, J., Yamaguchi, T., Etcharry-Bouyx, F., Le Gall, D., Nolin, P., & Richard, P. (2014). Detecting Everyday Action Deficits in Alzheimer's Disease Using a Nonimmersive Virtual Reality Kitchen. *Journal of the International Neuropsychological Society*, *20*(5), 468–477. doi:10.1017/S1355617714000344 PMID:24785240

Almeida, P. N. (2014). Serious games for the Elicitation of way-finding behaviours. In *Conferencia Ibérica de Sistemas de Información y Tecnologías*. IEEE Xplore.

Alonso-Fernandez, C., Calvo, A., Freire, M., Martinez-Ortiz, I., & Fernandez-Manjon, B. (2017). Systematizing game learning analytics for serious games. *IEEE Global Engineering Education Conference, EDUCON*, (April), 1111–1118. 10.1109/EDUCON.2017.7942988

Alsawaier, R. S. (2018). The effect of gamification on motivation and engagement. *The International Journal of Information and Learning Technology*.

Alsura, S. A. (2021). *Save yourself who knows*. https://www.arlsura.com/salvesequiensepa/

Alves, T., Chaves D'Carvalho, M., & Gonçalves, R. S. (2019). Assist-as-needed control in a cable-actuated robot for human joints rehabilitation. *Journal of Mechanical Engineering and Biomechanics*, *3*(5), 57–62. doi:10.24243/JMEB/3.5.214

American Heart Association. (2016). Textbook of neonatal resuscitation (NRP) (7th ed.). American Academy of Pediatrics.

American Psychiatric Association. (2013). *Diagnostic and statistical manual of mental disorders (DSM-5®)*. American Psychiatric Association.

American Psychiatric Association. (2013). *Diagnostic and Statistical Manual of Mental Disorders (DSM-5®)*. American Psychiatric Pub.

Aminoff, A., & Kettunen, O. (2016). Sustainable supply chain management in a circular economy—towards supply circles. *International Conference on Sustainable Design and Manufacturing*, *52*, 61–72. 10.1007/978-3-319-32098-4_6

Amt, E. (1993). *Women's lives in medieval Europe*. Routledge.

Ancker, J. S., Witteman, H. O., Hafeez, B., Provencher, T., Van de Graaf, M., & Wei, E. (2015). "You get reminded you're a sick person": Personal data tracking and patients with multiple chronic conditions. *Journal of Medical Internet Research*, *17*(8), e202. doi:10.2196/jmir.4209 PMID:26290186

Anderson, E. F., McLoughlin, L., Liarokapis, F., Peters, C., Petridis, P., & de Freitas, S. (2009). Serious Games in Cultural Heritage. In *Proceedings of the 10th VAST International Symposium on Virtual Reality, Archaeology and Cultural Heritage—STARs Session* (pp. 29-48). Eurographics.

Anderson, J. R., Boyle, C. F., & Reiser, B. J. (1985). Intelligent tutoring systems. *Science*, *228*(4698), 456–462. doi:10.1126cience.228.4698.456 PMID:17746875

Anderson, R. C., Ku, Y. M., Li, W., Chen, X., Wu, X., & Shu, H. (2013). Learning to see the patterns in Chinese characters. *Scientific Studies of Reading*, *17*(1), 41–56. doi:10.1080/10888438.2012.689789

Andersson, G., & Cuijpers, P. (2009). Internet-Based and Other Computerized Psychological Treatments for Adult Depression: A Meta-Analysis. *Cognitive Behaviour Therapy*, *38*(4), 196–205. doi:10.1080/16506070903318960 PMID:20183695

Andrade, F. R., Mizoguchi, R., & Isotani, S. (2016, June). The bright and dark sides of gamification. In *International conference on intelligent tutoring systems* (pp. 176-186). Springer. 10.1007/978-3-319-39583-8_17

Andreoli, R., Corolla, A., Faggiano, A., Malandrino, D., Pirozzi, D., Ranaldi, M., Santangelo, G., & Scarano, V. (2017). A framework to design, develop, and evaluate immersive and collaborative serious games in cultural heritage. *Journal on Computing and Cultural Heritage*, *11*(1), 1–22. doi:10.1145/3064644

Andrews, S. (2014). Documenting the Middle Ages on television. *REF 2014 Impact Case Studies*. https://impact.ref.ac.uk/casestudies/CaseStudy.aspx?Id=35308

Andrews, D. H., Hull, T. D., & Donahue, J. A. (2009). Storytelling as an Instructional Method: Definitions and Research Questions. *The Interdisciplinary Journal of Problem-Based Learning*, *3*(2), 10–26. doi:10.7771/1541-5015.1063

Andrews, G., Bell, C., Boyce, P., Gale, C., Lampe, L., Marwat, O., Rapee, R., & Wilkins, G. (2018). Royal Australian and New Zealand College of Psychiatrists clinical practice guidelines for the treatment of panic disorder, social anxiety disorder and generalised anxiety disorder. *The Australian and New Zealand Journal of Psychiatry, 52*(12), 1109–1172. doi:10.1177/0004867418799453

Andrews, G., Cuijpers, P., Craske, M. G., McEvoy, P., & Titov, N. (2010). Computer Therapy for the Anxiety and Depressive Disorders Is Effective, Acceptable and Practical Health Care: A Meta-Analysis. *PLoS One, 5*(10), e13196. doi:10.1371/journal.pone.0013196 PMID:20967242

Anger, M., Wantzen, P., Le Vaillant, J., Malvy, J., Bon, L., Guénolé, F., Moussaoui, E., Barthelemy, C., Bonnet-Brilhault, F., Eustache, F., Baleyte, J.-M., & Guillery-Girard, B. (2019). Positive effect of visual cuing in episodic memory and episodic future thinking in adolescents with autism spectrum disorder. *Frontiers in Psychology, 10*, 1513. doi:10.3389/fpsyg.2019.01513 PMID:31354565

Antin, J., & Churchill, E. F. (2011). Badges in Social Media: A Social Psychological Perspective. In *Proceedings of the SIGCHI Conference on Human Factors in Computing Systems*. ACM.

Aponte, M., Levieux, G., & Natkin, S. (2009). Scaling the Level of Difficulty in Single Player Video Games Entertainment Computing – ICEC 2009. *International Conference on Entertainment Computing*, 25–35.

Apostolellis, P., Bowman, D. A., & Chmiel, M. (2018). Supporting Social Engagement for Young Audiences with Serious Games and Virtual Environments in Museums. In AMuseum Experience Design. Springer Series on Cultural Computing. doi:10.1007/978-3-319-58550-5_2

Apóstolo, J., & Cardoso, D. (2014). Estimulação Cognitiva em Idosos - Síntese da evidência e intervenção: programa de manutenção [Cognitive Stimulation in the Elderly - Synthesis of the evidence and intervention: maintenance program]. In Envelhecimento, Saúde e Cidadania [Aging, Health and Citizenship]. Coimbra: Unidade de Investigação em Ciências da Saúde: Enfermagem.

Apóstolo, J., Cardoso, D., Rosa, A. I., & Paúl, C. (2014). The Effect of Cognitive Stimulation on Nursing Home Elders: A Randomized Controlled Trial. *Journal of Nursing Scholarship, 46*(3), 157–166. doi:10.1111/jnu.12072 PMID:24597922

Aqda, M. F., Hamidi, F., & Ghorbandordinejad, F. (2011). The impact of constructivist and cognitive distance instructional design on the learner's creativity. *Procedia Computer Science, 3*, 260–265. doi:10.1016/j.procs.2010.12.044

Archibald, E. (2009). Questioning Arthurian ideals. In E. Archibald & A. Putter (Eds.), *The Cambridge companion to the Arthurian legend* (pp. 39–153). Cambridge University Press., doi:10.1017/CCOL9780521860598.009

Archibald, E., & Johnson, D. F. (2020). Arthurian Literature XXXV. *Arthurian Literature*, 35.

Arenas-Laorga, E., Basabe-Montalvo, L., Muñoz-Torija, S., & Palacios-Labrador, L. (2020). 'Game Boards'. Soportes urbanos para procesos sociales ['Game Boards'. Urban supports for social processes]. In *EDUMEET International Conference on Transfers for Innovation and Pedagogical Change*. Universidad Politécnica de Madrid / Javeriana de Bogotá. 10.20868/UPM.book.66588

Armstrong, M. B., Landers, R. N., & Collmus, A. B. (2016). Gamifying recruitment, selection, training, and performance management: Game-thinking in human resource management. In *Emerging research and trends in gamification* (pp. 140–165). IGI Global.

Arnab, S., Lim, T., Carvalho, M. B., Bellotti, F., de Freitas, S., Louchart, S., Suttie, N., Berta, R., & De Gloria, A. (2014). Mapping learning and game mechanics for serious games analysis. *British Journal of Educational Technology*. Advance online publication. doi:10.1111/bjet.12113

ARTigo [Digital game]. (n.d.). *IT-Group Humanities*. Retrieved from https://www.artigo.org/

Asad, J., Kousar, S., & Mehmood, N. Q. (2019). Dementia-Related Serious Games: A Comparative Study. *University of Sindh Journal of Information and Communication Technology*, 3(4), 171–177.

Ashwood, K. L., Tye, C., Azadi, B., Cartwright, S., Asherson, P., & Bolton, P. (2015). Brief report: Adaptive functioning in children with ASD, ADHD and ASD+ ADHD. *Journal of Autism and Developmental Disorders*, 45(7), 2235–2242. doi:10.100710803-014-2352-y PMID:25614019

Asikainen, H. (2014). *Successful learning and studying in Biosciences: Exploring how students conceptions of learning, approaches to learning, motivation and their experiences of the teaching-learning environment are related to study success* [Unpublished doctoral dissertation] University of Helsinki.

Asl, H. J., Narikiyo, T., & Kawanishi, M. (2019). An assist-as-needed control scheme for robot-assisted rehabilitation. *Proceedings of the American Control Conference*, 198–203. 10.23919/ACC.2017.7962953

Assassin's Creed II . (2009). [Video Game]. Ubisoft Montreal.

Atutor. (2021). *Expert Tutoring Advice*. https://www.atutor.ca

Aungst, T. D. (2013). Medical applications for pharmacists using mobile devices. *The Annals of Pharmacotherapy*, 47(7–8), 1088–1095. doi:10.1345/aph.1S035 PMID:23821609

Avila-Pesantez, D., Delgadillo, R., & Rivera, L. A. (2019). Proposal of a Conceptual Model for Serious Games Design: A Case Study in Children with Learning Disabilities. *IEEE Access: Practical Innovations, Open Solutions*, 7, 161017–161033. doi:10.1109/ACCESS.2019.2951380

Ávila-Pesántez, D., Rivera, L. A., & Alban, M. S. (2017). Approaches for serious game design: A systematic literature review. *Computers in Education Journal*, 8(3).

Axton, R. (1974). *European Drama of the Early Middle Ages*. Hutchinson.

Azar, A. S., & Tan, N. H. I. (2020). The application of ICT techs (mobile-assisted language learning, gamification, and virtual reality) in teaching English for secondary school students in malaysia during Covid-19 pandemic. *Univers J Educ Res*, 8(11), 55–63. doi:10.13189/ujer.2020.082307

Backlund, P., Engstrom, H., Johannesson, M., & Lebram, M. (2010). Games for traffic education: An experimental study of a game-based driving simulator. *Simulation & Gaming*, 41(2), 145–169. doi:10.1177/1046878107311455

Baker, R. (2021). *Marketing Funnel*. Barnes & Noble Press.

Balbim, G. M., Marques, I. G., Marquez, D. X., Patel, D., Sharp, L. K., Kitsiou, S., & Nyenhuis, S. M. (2021). Using Fitbit as an mHealth intervention tool to promote physical activity: Potential challenges and solutions. *JMIR mHealth and uHealth*, 9(3), e25289. doi:10.2196/25289 PMID:33646135

Baldwin, M. W., & Dandeneau, S. D. (2009). Putting social psychology into serious games. *Social and Personality Psychology Compass*, 3(4), 547–565. doi:10.1111/j.1751-9004.2009.00185.x

Ball, C., Huang, K.-T., & Francis, J. (2021). Virtual reality adoption during the COVID-19 pandemic: A uses and gratifications perspective. *Telematics and Informatics*, 65, 101728. doi:10.1016/j.tele.2021.101728 PMID:34887619

Banerjee, S., Hemphill, T., & Longstreet, P. (2018). Wearable devices and healthcare: Data sharing and privacy. *The Information Society*, 34(1), 49–57. doi:10.1080/01972243.2017.1391912

Banh, S., Zheng, E., Kubota, A., & Riek, L. D. (2021, March 8). A Robot-based Gait Training System for Post-Stroke Rehabilitation. *Companion of the 2021 ACM/IEEE International Conference on Human-Robot Interaction.* 10.1145/3434074.3447212

Baranowski, T., Blumberg, F., Buday, R., DeSmet, A., Fiellin, L. E., Green, C. S., Kato, P. M., Lu, A. S., Maloney, A. E., Mellecker, R., Morrill, B. A., Peng, W., Shegog, R., Simons, M., Staiano, A. E., Thompson, D., & Young, K. (2016). Games for Health for Children-Current Status and Needed Research. *Games for Health Journal, 5*(1), 1–12. doi:10.1089/g4h.2015.0026 PMID:26262772

Baranowski, T., Buday, R., Thompson, D. I., & Baranowski, J. (2008). Playing for Real: Video Games and Stories for Health-Related Behavior Change. *American Journal of Preventive Medicine, 34*(1), 74–82.e10. doi:10.1016/j.amepre.2007.09.027 PMID:18083454

Barata, G., Gama, S., Fonseca, M. J., & Gonçalves, D. (2013, October). Improving student creativity with gamification and virtual worlds. In *Proceedings of the First International Conference on Gameful Design, Research, and Applications* (pp. 95-98). 10.1145/2583008.2583023

Barbosa, H., Vieira, A. C., & Carrapatoso, E. (2017). Exercises and Serious Games Applied to the TEG 2020 - Special Session on Technology, Elderly Games 288 Rehabilitation for Older Adults. *Proceedings of the Portuguese Association for Information Systems Conference.* 10.18803/capsi.v17.354-361

Barlett, C., Anderson, C., & Swing, E. (2009). Video Game Effects - Confirmed, Suspected, and Speculative: A Review of the Evidence. *Simulation & Gaming, 40*(3), 377–403. doi:10.1177/1046878108327539

Baron-Cohen, S. (1997). *Mindblindness: An essay on autism and theory of mind.* MIT press.

Bartle, R. (1996). *Hearts, clubs, diamonds, spades: players who suit MUDs.* http://mud.co.uk/richard/hcds.htm#1

Bartle, R. (1996). Hearts, clubs, diamonds, spades: Players who suit MUDs. *Journal of MUD Research, 1*(1), 19.

Bartlett, R. *(Researcher, Presenter).* (2010). *The Normans* [Television documentary miniseries]. BBC TV.

Barton, K., & Maharg, P. (2007). E-Simulations in the wild: interdisciplinary research, design, and implementation. In D. Gibson, C. Aldrich, & M. Prensky (Eds.), Games and simulations in online learning: Research and development frameworks. Academic Press.

Bashiri, A., Ghazisaeedi, M., & Shahmoradi, L. (2017). The opportunities of virtual reality in the rehabilitation of children with attention deficit hyperactivity disorder: A literature review. *Korean Journal of Pediatrics, 60*(11), 337. doi:10.3345/kjp.2017.60.11.337 PMID:29234356

Bateni, H., & Maki, B. E. (2005). Assistive devices for balance and mobility: Benefits, demands, and adverse consequences. In Archives of Physical Medicine and Rehabilitation (Vol. 86, Issue 1, pp. 134–145). doi:10.1016/j.apmr.2004.04.023

Batista, L., Bourlakis, M., Liu, Y., Smart, P., & Sohal, A. (2018). Supply chain operations for a circular economy. *Production Planning and Control, 29*(6), 419–424. doi:10.1080/09537287.2018.1449267

Baum, D. R., Riedel, S., & Hays, R. T. (1982). *Training Effectiveness as a Function of Training Device Fidelity.* Alexandria, VA: U.S. Army Research Institute: ARI Technical Report 593.

Bauman, Z., & Lyon, D. (2015). *Sixth power: surveillance in liquid modernity.* Gius. Laterza & Figli Spa.

BCNEcologia. (2019). *Charter for the Ecosystemic Planning of Cities and Metropolises.* http://www.cartaurbanismo-ecosistemico.com/index2eng.html

Becker, K., & Parker, J. (2012). *The Guide to Computer Simulations and Games.* Wiley.

Beed, P. L., Hawkins, E. M., & Roller, C. M. (1991). Moving learners toward independence: the power of scaffolded instruction. *The Reading Teacher, 44*, 648-655. doi:10.2307/20200767

Behlol, M. G., & Dad, H. (2010). Concept of learning. *International Journal of Psychological Studies, 2*(2), 231. doi:10.5539/ijps.v2n2p231

Beidel, D. C., Tuerk, P. W., Spitalnick, J., Bowers, C. A., & Morrison, K. (2021). Treating childhood social anxiety disorder with virtual environments and serious games: A randomized trial. *Behavior Therapy, 52*(6), 1351–1363. doi:10.1016/j.beth.2021.03.003 PMID:34656191

Belbase, A., & Sanzenbacher, G. T. (2017). Cognitive Aging and the Capacity to Manage Money. *Issues in Brief (Alan Guttmacher Institute), 17*(1).

Belle-Isle, R. (1986). Learning for a new humanism. *The International Schools Journal, 27*.

Bell, J. T., & Fogler, H. S. (1995). The investigation and application of virtual reality as an educational tool. *Proceedings of the American Society for Engineering Education Annual Conference*, 1718–1728.

Bellocchio Albornoz, M. (2009). Competency-based education and constructivism. An approach and a model for pedagogical training in the 21st century. *Issue F, 378*, B4.

Belloti, F., Berta, R., & De Gloria, A. (2010). Designing Effective Serious Games: Opportunities and Challenges for Research. *International Journal of Emerging Technologies in Learning (iJET), 5*(SI 3), 22-35.

Bellotti, F., Berta, R., De Gloria, A., Lavagnino, E., Antonaci, A., Dagnino, F. M., & Ott, M. (2013, July). A gamified short course for promoting entrepreneurship among ICT engineering students. In *2013 IEEE 13th International Conference on Advanced Learning Technologies* (pp. 31-32). IEEE. 10.1109/ICALT.2013.14

Bellotti, F., Berta, R., & De Gloria, A. (2010). Designing effective serious games: Opportunities and challenges for research. *International Journal of Emerging Technologies in Learning, 5*(3), 22–35. doi:10.3991/ijet.v5s3.1500

Bellotti, F., Berta, R., De Gloria, A., D'ursi, A., & Fiore, V. (2012). A serious game model for cultural heritage. *Journal on Computing and Cultural Heritage, 5*(4), 17. doi:10.1145/2399180.2399185

Bengs, A., Hägglund, S., Wiklund-Engblom, A., Majors, J., & Ashfaq, A. (2018). Designing for social inclusion of immigrant women: The case of TeaTime. *Innovation (Abingdon), 31*(2), 106–124. doi:10.1080/13511610.2017.1348931

Benioff, D. & Weiss, D.B. (Creators). (2013-2019). *Game of Thrones* [Television series]. HBO, Television 360 & Groki Studio.

Ben-Sadoun, G., Manera, V., Alvarez, J., Sacco, G., & Robert, P. (2018). Recommendations for the Design of Serious Games in Neurodegenerative Diseases. *Frontiers in Aging Neuroscience, 10*(13), 13. Advance online publication. doi:10.3389/fnagi.2018.00013 PMID:29456501

Benton, M., & Glennie, A. (2016). *Digital humanitarianism: How tech entrepreneurs are supporting refugee integration*. Migration Policy Institute.

Benveniste, S., Jouvelot, P., & Péquignot, R. (2010). The MINWii project: Renarcissization of patients suffering from Alzheimer's disease through video game-based music therapy. In *International Conference on Entertainment Computing*. Springer. 10.1007/978-3-642-15399-0_8

Bergeron, B. (2006). *Developing Serious Games (Game Development Series)*. Charles River Media.

Bergomi, C., Tschacher, W., & Kupper, Z. (2015). Meditation Practice and Self-Reported Mindfulness: A Cross-Sectional Investigation of Meditators and Non-Meditators Using the Comprehensive Inventory of Mindfulness Experiences (CHIME). *Mindfulness*, *6*(6), 1411–1421. doi:10.100712671-015-0415-6

Bernold, L. E., Spurlin, J. E., & Anson, C. M. (2007). Understanding our students: A longitudinal-study of success and failure in engineering with implications for increased retention. *Journal of Engineering Education*, *96*(3), 263–274. doi:10.1002/j.2168-9830.2007.tb00935.x

Bethke, E. (2003). *Game development and production*. Wordware Publishing.

Bianchini, A., Rossi, J., & Pellegrini, M. (2019). Overcoming the main barriers of circular economy implementation through a new visualization tool for circular business models. *Sustainability (Switzerland)*, *11*(23), 6614. doi:10.3390u11236614

Biesta, G. J. (1998). Pedagogy without humanism: Foucault and the subject of education. *Interchange*, *29*(1), 1–16.

Bilotta, E., Bertacchini, F., Gabriele, L., Giglio, S., Pantano, P. S., & Romita, T. (2020). Industry 4.0 technologies in tourism education: Nurturing students to think with technology. *Journal of Hospitality, Leisure, Sport and Tourism Education*, 100275.

Bing, S. (2014). The research of digital game interactive technology on the prevention and rehabilitation of diseases in the elderly. *Art panorama*, *6*, 102.

Binotti, M., Genoni, G., Rizzollo, S., De Luca, M., Carenzo, L., Monzani, A., & Ingrassia, P. L. (2019). Simulation-based medical training for paediatric residents in Italy: A nationwide survey. *BMC Medical Education*, *19*(161), 1–7. doi:10.118612909-019-1581-3 PMID:31113417

Biocca, F. (1997). The cyborg's dilemma: Progressive embodiment in virtual environments. *Journal of Computer-Mediated Communication*, *14*(1), 27–50. doi:10.1111/j.1083-6101.1997.tb00070.x

Biocca, F., & Delaney, B. (1995). Immersive virtual reality technology. *Communication in the Age of Virtual Reality*, *15*, 32.

Biondi, G. (2007). *The school after the new technologies*. Apogeo Editore.

BioWare Corp. (2021). *BioWare™*. Retrieved from https://www.bioware.com

Birk, M. V., & Mandryk, R. L. (2019). Improving the Efficacy of Cognitive Training for Digital Mental Health Interventions Through Avatar Customization: Crowdsourced Quasi-Experimental Study. *Journal of Medical Internet Research*, *21*(1), e10133. Advance online publication. doi:10.2196/10133 PMID:30622095

Bizzocchi, J., Lin, M. B., & Tanenbaum, J. (2011). Game, narrative, and the design of interface. *International Journal of Art and Technology*, *4*(4), 460–479. doi:10.1504/IJART.2011.043445

Blackburn, N. N. (2021). *OGrES Welcome! Toward a Systematic Theory for Serious Game Design. In CHI PLAY '21*. ACM.

Black, G. (2012). *Transforming Museums in the Twenty-First Century*. Routledge. doi:10.4324/9780203150061

Blavier, A. (1982). *Les Fous littéraires* [Literary Madmen]. Éditions Henri Veyrier.

Blazhko, O., Luhova, T., Melnik, S., & Ruvinska, V. (2017). Communication Model of Open Government Data Gamification Based on Ukrainian Websites. In *International conference on Intelligent Data Acquisition and Advanced Computing Systems: Technology and Applications (IDAACS): 4th Experiment International Conference (exp.at'17)* (pp. 181-186). Faro, Portugal: University of Algarve.

Blickenstaff, J. C. (2005). Women and science careers: Leaky pipeline or gender filter? *Gender and Education*, *17*(4), 369–386. doi:10.1080/09540250500145072

Blikstein, P., & Worsley, M. (2016). Multimodal learning analytics and education data mining : Using computational technologies to measure complex learning tasks. *Journal of Learning Analytics, 3*(2), 220–238. doi:10.18608/jla.2016.32.11

Blount, D. S., McDonough, D. J., & Gao, Z. (2021). Effect of Wearable Technology-Based Physical Activity Interventions on Breast Cancer Survivors' Physiological, Cognitive, and Emotional Outcomes: A Systematic Review. *Journal of Clinical Medicine, 10*(9), 2015. doi:10.3390/jcm10092015 PMID:34066752

Blumberg, F. C., Almonte, D. E., Anthony, J. S., & Hashimoto, N. (2012). Serious Games: What Are They? What Do They Do? Why Should We Play Them? In K. E. Dill (Ed.), *The Oxford Handbook of Media Psychology.* Oxford University Press. doi:10.1093/oxfordhb/9780195398809.013.0019

Blumler, J. G., & Katz, E. (1974). The Uses of Mass Communications: Current Perspectives on Gratifications Research. Sage Annual Reviews of Communication Research, 3.

Bocken, N. M. P., Olivetti, E. A., Cullen, J. M., Potting, J., & Lifset, R. (2017). Taking the Circularity to the Next Level: A Special Issue on the Circular Economy. *Journal of Industrial Ecology, 21*(3), 476–482. doi:10.1111/jiec.12606

Boeldt, D., McMahon, E., McFaul, M., & Greenleaf, W. (2019). Using Virtual Reality Exposure Therapy to Enhance Treatment of Anxiety Disorders: Identifying Areas of Clinical Adoption and Potential Obstacles. *Frontiers in Psychiatry, 10*, 773. doi:10.3389/fpsyt.2019.00773 PMID:31708821

Bogost, I. (2016). *Play Anything: The Pleasure of Limits, the Uses of Boredom, and the Secret of Games.* Basic Book.

Bojan, K., Stavropoulos, T. G., Lazarou, I., Nikolopoulos, S., Kompatsiaris, I., Tsolaki, M., Mukaetova-Ladinska, E., & Christogianni, A. (2021). The effects of playing the COSMA cognitive games in dementia. *International Journal of Serious Games, 8*(1), 45–58. doi:10.17083/ijsg.v8i1.412

Bollen, J., van de Sompel, H., Hagberg, A., Bettencourt, L., Chute, R., Rodriguez, M. A., & Balakireva, L. (2009). Clickstream data yields high-resolution Maps of science. *PLoS One, 4*(3), e4803. Advance online publication. doi:10.1371/journal.pone.0004803 PMID:19277205

Bonavita, S., Sacco, R., Della Corte, M., Esposito, S., Sparaco, M., d'Ambrosio, A., Docimo, R., Bisecco, A., Lavorgna, L., Corbo, D., Cirillo, S., Gallo, A., Esposito, F., & Tedeschi, G. (2015). Computer-aided cognitive rehabilitation improves cognitive performances and induces brain functional connectivity changes in relapsing remitting multiple sclerosis patients: An exploratory study. *Journal of Neurology, 262*(1), 91–100. doi:10.100700415-014-7528-z PMID:25308631

Bondy, A. S., & Frost, L. A. (1994). The picture exchange communication system. *Focus on Autistic Behavior, 9*(3), 1–19. doi:10.1177/108835769400900301

Bonikowska, A., Sanmartin, C., & Frenette, M. (2019). Data Literacy: What It Is and How to Measure It in the Public Service. Analytical Studies Branch, Statistics Canada, (11).

Bonnechère, B. (2018). Serious games in physical rehabilitation. In *Serious games in physical rehabilitation. From Theory to practice* (pp. 49–109). Springer.

Bontchev, B. (2015). Serious games for and as cultural heritage. *Researchgate.* https://www.researchgate.net/publication/301285825_Serious_Games_for_and_as_Cultural_Heritage

Booster, G. D., DuPaul, G. J., Eiraldi, R., & Power, T. J. (2012). Functional impairments in children with ADHD: Unique effects of age and comorbid status. *Journal of Attention Disorders, 16*(3), 179–189. doi:10.1177/1087054710383239 PMID:20876886

Bosman, S. (2019, May 3). Male and female gamers: how their similarities and differences shape the games market. *Newzoo.* https://newzoo.com/insights/articles/male-and-female-gamers-how-their-similarities-and-differences-shape-the-games-market/

Bostad, I. (2012). Existential Education and the Quest for a New Humanism: How to Create Disturbances and Deeper Thinking in Schools and Universities? *Enlightenment. Creative Education,* 45–59.

Botra, A., Rerselman, M., & Ford, M. (2014, May). Gamification beyond badges. In *2014 IST-Africa Conference Proceedings* (pp. 1-10). IEEE. 10.1109/ISTAFRICA.2014.6880651

Boulay, M., Benveniste, S., Boespflug, S., Jouvelot, P., & Rigaud, A. S. (2011). A pilot usability study of MINWii, a music therapy game for demented patients. *Technology and Health Care: Official Journal of the European Society for Engineering and Medicine,* *19*(4), 233–246. doi:10.3233/THC-2011-0628

Bowser, A., Hansen, D., & Preece, J. (2013). Gamifying Citizen Science: Lessons and Future Directions. *Proceedings of CHI 2013: Workshop Designing Gamification: Creating Gameful and Playful Experiences.* http://gamification-research. org/wp-content/uploads/2013/03/Bowser_Hansen_Preece.pdf

Boyan, A., & Sherry, J. L. (2011). The challenge in creating games for education: Aligning mental models with game models. *Child Development Perspectives,* *5*(2), 82–87. doi:10.1111/j.1750-8606.2011.00160.x

Boyle, E. A., Connolly, T. M., Hainey, T., & Boyle, J. M. (2012). Engagement in digital entertainment games: A systematic review. *Computers in Human Behavior,* *28*(3), 771–780. doi:10.1016/j.chb.2011.11.020

Boyle, E. A., Hainey, T., Connolly, T. M., Gray, G., Earp, J., Ott, M., Lim, T., Ninaus, M., Ribeiro, C., & Pereira, J. (2016). An update to the systematic literature review of empirical evidence of the impacts and outcomes of computer games and serious games. *Computers & Education,* *94,* 178–192. doi:10.1016/j.compedu.2015.11.003

Braad, E., Žavcer, G., & Sandovar, A. (2016). Processes and models for serious game design and development. In R. Dörner, S. Göbel, M. Kickmeier-Rust, M. Masuch, & K. Zweog (Eds.), *Entertainment computing & serious games* (pp. 92–118). Springer. doi:10.1007/978-3-319-46152-6_5

Brain, S. (2017, September 12). Skyrim: The Elder Scrolls V statistics. *Statistic Brain Research Institute.* https://www.statisticbrain.com/skyrim-the-elder-scrolls-v-statistics/

Brainberry Ltd. (2021). *Healthcare Ecosystem for the Evolution of Mental Health.* https://brainberry.co.uk/

Branches of Power [Digital game]. (2010). *Filament Games.* Retrieved 07 11, 2021, from Game for change: https://www.gamesforchange.org/game/branches-of-power/

Brandenburg, A. (2020). If it's a fantasy world, why bother making it realistic? – Constructing and Debating the Middle Ages of *The Witcher 3: The Wild Hunt.* In M. Lorber & F. Zimmermann (Eds.), *History in games: contingencies of an authentic past* (pp. 201–220). Transcript Verlag. doi:10.1515/9783839454206-011

Brandt, M. (2008). *Video games activate reward regions of brain in men more than women, Stanford study finds.* Stanford Medecine News Center. https://med.stanford.edu/news/all-news/2008/02/video-games-activate-reward-regions-of-brain-in-men-more-than-women-stanford-study-finds.html

Braun, V., & Clarke, V. (2006). Using thematic analysis in psychology. *Qualitative Research in Psychology,* *3*(2), 77–101. doi:10.1191/1478088706qp063oa

Breedlove, S. M., & Watson, N. V. (2013). *Biological psychology: An introduction to behavioral, cognitive, and clinical neuroscience.* Sinauer Associates.

Breslow, L., Pritchard, D. E., DeBoer, J., Stump, G. S., Ho, A. D., & Seaton, D. T. (2013). Studying Learning in the Worldwide Classroom: Research into edX's First MOOC. *Research and Practice in Assessment, 8*, 13–25.

Breuer, J., & Bente, G. (2010). Why so serious? On the Relation of Serious Games and Learning. *Eludamos (Göttingen), 4*(1), 7–24.

Bricker, L. J., Tanimoto, S. L., Rothenberg, A. I., Hutama, D. C., & Wong, T. H. (1995). Multiplayer Activities That Develop Mathematical Coordination. *Proceedings of CSCL 1995*.

Brooks, D. (2011, March 7). The new humanism. *New York Times*.

Brown, K. A., Samuel, S., & Patel, D. R. (2018). Pharmacologic management of attention deficit hyperactivity disorder in children and adolescents: A review for practitioners. *Translational Pediatrics, 7*(1), 36–47. doi:10.21037/tp.2017.08.02 PMID:29441281

Bruckman, A. (1999, March 17). *Can Educational Be Fun?* [Paper presentation]. Game Developer's Conference, San Jose, CA. https://www.cc.gatech.edu/~asb/papers/conference/bruckman-gdc99.pdf

Brune, M. (2021, March 31). Zooming in on female gamers with consumer insights data. *Newzoo*. https://newzoo.com/insights/articles/zooming-in-on-female-gamers-with-consumer-insights-data/

Brusilovsky, P., Wade, V., & Conlan, O. (2007). From Learning Objects to Adaptive Content Services for E- Learning. In *Architecture Solutions for E-Learning Systems* (pp. 243–261). Academic Press.

Brydges, R., Carnahan, H., Rose, D., Rose, L., & Dubrowski, A. (2010). Coordinating Progressive Levels of Simulation Fidelity to Maximize Educational Benefit. *Academic Medicine, 85*(5), 806–812. doi:10.1097/ACM.0b013e3181d7aabd PMID:20520031

Buchinger, D., & da Silva Hounsell, M. (2018). Guidelines for designing and using collaborative-competitive serious games. *Computers & Education, 118*, 133–149. Advance online publication. doi:10.1016/j.compedu.2017.11.007

Buck, C., & Lee, J. *(Directors)*. (2013). *Frozen* [Animated feature film]. Walt Disney Pictures, Walt Disney Animation Studios.

Buckner, J. D., Lemke, A. W., Jeffries, E. R., & Shah, S. M. (2017). Social anxiety and suicidal ideation: Test of the utility of the interpersonal-psychological theory of suicide. *Journal of Anxiety Disorders, 45*, 60–63. doi:10.1016/j.janxdis.2016.11.010 PMID:27940416

Bueno, P. M., & Fitzgerald, V. L. (2004). Problem-based learning. *Theoria: Science, Arts and Humanities, 13*. https://campus.usal.es/~ofeees/NUEVAS_METODOLOGIAS/ABP/13.pdf

Building Worlds. (n.d.) FogEffects_SkyAtmposphere. *Unreal engine documentation 4.6*. https://docs.unrealengine.com/4.26/en-US/BuildingWorlds/FogEffects/SkyAtmosphere/

Bulitko, V., Hong, J., Kumaran, K., Swedberg, I., Thoang, W., Von Hauff, P., & Schmölzer, G. M. (2015). *RETAIN: A neonatal resuscitation trainer built in an undergraduate video-game class*. https://www.researchgate.net/publication/279808492_RETAIN_a_Neonatal_Resuscitation_Trainer_Built_in_an_Undergraduate_Video-Game_Class

Burgess, S., & Sievertsen, H. H. (2020). *Schools, skills, and learning: The impact of COVID-19 on education*. Academic Press.

Butgereit, L. (2016, May). Gamifying mobile micro-learning for continuing education in a corporate IT environment. In *2016 IST-Africa Week Conference* (pp. 1-7). IEEE.

Butt, A., Naaranoja, M., & Savolainen, J. (2016). Project change stakeholder communication. *International Journal of Project Management, 34*(8), 1579–1595. doi:10.1016/j.ijproman.2016.08.010

Buzio, A., Chiesa, M., & Toppan, R. (2017). Virtual reality for special educational needs. *Proceedings of the 2017 ACM Workshop on Intelligent Interfaces for Ubiquitous and Smart Learning*, 7–10. 10.1145/3038535.3038541

Cabezas, C. (2020). COVID-19 pandemic: Storms and challenges. *Rev Peru Med Exp Public Health., 37*(4), 603–604. doi:10.17843/rpmesp.2020.374.6866 PMID:33566897

Cabinio, M., Rossetto, F., Isernia, S., Saibene, F. L., Di Cesare, M., Borgnis, F., Pazzi, S., Migliazza, T., Alberoni, M., Blasi, V., & Baglio, F. (2020). The Use of a Virtual Reality Platform for the Assessment of the Memory Decline and the Hippocampal Neural Injury in Subjects with Mild Cognitive Impairment: The Validity of Smart Aging Serious Game (SASG). *Journal of Clinical Medicine, 9*(5), 1355. Advance online publication. doi:10.3390/jcm9051355 PMID:32384591

Caboral-Stevens, M., & Medetsky, M. (2014). The Construct of Financial Capacity in Older Adults. *Journal of Gerontological Nursing, 40*(8), 30–37. doi:10.3928/00989134-20140325-02 PMID:24694046

Caillois, R. (2001). *Man, Play, and Games*. University of Illinois Press.

Cain, R., & Lee, V. R. (2016). Measuring Electrodermal Activity to Capture Engagement in an Afterschool Maker Program. *Proceedings of the 6th Annual Conference on Creativity and Fabrication in Education - FabLearn '16, 1*(718), 78–81. 10.1145/3003397.3003409

Callaghan, M. J., McShane, N., & Eguiluz, A. G. (2014). Using game analytics to measure student engagement/retention for engineering education. *Proceedings of 2014 11th International Conference on Remote Engineering and Virtual Instrumentation, REV 2014*, (February), 297–302. 10.1109/REV.2014.6784174

Callaghan, M., McShane, N., Eguíluz, A., & Savin-Baden, M. (2018). Extending the activity theory based model for serious games design in engineering to integrate analytics. *International Journal of Engineering Pedagogy, 8*(1), 109–126. doi:10.3991/ijep.v8i1.8087

Campa, P., Casarico, A., & Profeta, P. (2011). Gender culture and gender gap in employment. *CESifo Economic Studies, 57*(1), 156–182. doi:10.1093/cesifo/ifq018

Campbell, C. (2017, January). Which games are women and girls playing? *Polygon.* https://www.polygon.com/2017/1/20/14337282/games-for-women-and-girls

Canady, V. A. (2020). FDA approves first video game Rx treatment for children with ADHD. *Mental Health Weekly, 30*(26), 1–7. doi:10.1002/mhw.32423

Canals Casals, L., Amante García, B., & Cremades, L. V. (2017). Electric vehicle battery reuse: Preparing for a second life. *Journal of Industrial Engineering and Management, 10*(2), 266–285. doi:10.3926/jiem.2009

Capel, H. (2003). *Los Problemas de las Ciudades: Urbs, Civitas y Polis* [The Problems of Cities: Urbs, Civitas and Polis]. Ciudades, Arquitectura y Espacio Urbano.

Caponetto, I., Earp, J., & Ott, M. (2014). Gamification and education: A literature review. In *European Conference on Games Based Learning* (*Vol. 1*, p. 50). Academic Conferences International Limited.

Capuano, N., & King, R. (2015). Adaptive Serious Games for Emergency Evacuation Training. *Proceedings - 2015 International Conference on Intelligent Networking and Collaborative Systems*, 308–313. 10.1109/INCoS.2015.32

Cárdenas, L. A. V., Tavernise, A., Bertacchini, F., Gabriele, L., Valenti, A., Pantano, P., & Bilotta, E. (2016). An Educational Coding Laboratory for Elementary Pre-service Teachers: A Qualitative Approach. *International Journal of Engineering Pedagogy*, *6*(1), 11–17. doi:10.3991/ijep.v6i1.5364

Cardwell, H. (2021). *Shortage of psychologists leaving patients on waitlist for 9 to 12 months. Radio New Zealand.* https://www.rnz.co.nz/news/political/451062/shortage-of-psychologists-leaving-patients-on-waitlist-for-9-to-12-months

Carrión-Toro, M., Santorum, M., Acosta-Vargas, P., Aguilar, J., & Pérez, M. (2020). iPlus a user-centered methodology for serious games design. *Applied Sciences (Switzerland)*, *10*(24), 1–33. doi:10.3390/app10249007

Caserman, P., Hoffmann, K., Müller, P., Schaub, M., Straßburg, K., Wiemeyer, J., Bruder, R., & Göbel, S. (2020). Quality criteria for serious games: Serious part, game part, and balance. *JMIR Serious Games*, *8*(3), e19037. doi:10.2196/19037 PMID:32706669

Casola, V., Castiglione, A., Choo, K.-K. R., & Esposito, C. (2016). Healthcare-related data in the cloud: Challenges and opportunities. *IEEE Cloud Computing*, *3*(6), 10–14. doi:10.1109/MCC.2016.139

Castor, H. (2010). *She-wolves: the women who ruled England before Elizabeth*. Faber.

Castor, H. (2019, February). Good television depends on the care, commitment, resources and skill of those creating it. In How good is television as a medium for history? *History Today*, *69*(2). https://www.historytoday.com/history-today-issues/volume-69-issue-2-february-2019

Cave, D. (1993). *Mircea Eliade's vision for a new humanism*. Oxford University Press.

CeltX 8.82.1. (2020). [Software - audiovisual story and interactive scripting]. CeltX Inc. https://www.celtx.com/

Cervera, M. A., Soekadar, S. R., Ushiba, J., Millán, J. del R., Liu, M., Birbaumer, N., & Garipelli, G. (2018). Brain-computer interfaces for post-stroke motor rehabilitation: A meta-analysis. *Annals of Clinical and Translational Neurology*, *5*(5), 651–663. doi:10.1002/acn3.544 PMID:29761128

Chalmers, A., & Debattista, K. (2009). Level of Realism for Serious Games. In 2009 Conference in Games and Virtual Worlds for Serious Applications (pp. 225-232). Coventry.

Chalmers, A., Debattista, K., & Ramic-Brkic, B. (2009). Towards high-fidelity multi-sensory virtual environments. *The Visual Computer*, *25*(12), 1101–1108. doi:10.100700371-009-0389-2

Chandrashekar, P. (2018). Do mental health mobile apps work: Evidence and recommendations for designing high-efficacy mental health mobile apps. *mHealth*, *4*, 4. doi:10.21037/mhealth.2018.03.02 PMID:29682510

Chan, E., Nah, F. F. H., Liu, Q., & Lu, Z. (2018, July). Effect of gamification on intrinsic motivation. In *International Conference on HCI in Business, Government, and Organizations* (pp. 445-454). Springer. 10.1007/978-3-319-91716-0_35

Charleer, S., Santos, J. L., Klerkx, J., & Duval, E. (2014). Improving teacher awareness through activity, badge and content visualizations. In New Horizons in Web Based Learning (pp. 143–152). doi:10.1007/978-3-319-13296-9_16

Charlier, N. (2011). Game-based assessment of first aid and resuscitation skills. *Resuscitation*, *82*(4), 442–446. doi:10.1016/j.resuscitation.2010.12.003 PMID:21277070

Charsky, D. (2010). From Edutainment to Serious Games: A Change in the Use of Game Characteristics. *Games and Culture*, *5*(2), 177–198. doi:10.1177/1555412009354727

Chatti, M. A., Muslim, A., Guesmi, M., Richtscheid, F., Nasimi, D., Shahin, A., & Damera, R. (2020). How to Design Effective Learning Analytics Indicators? A Human-Centered Design Approach. In *European Conference on Technology Enhanced Learning* (pp. 303–317). 10.1007/978-3-030-57717-9_22

Checa, D., & Bustillo, A. (2019). A review of immersive virtual reality serious games to enhance learning and training. *Multimedia Tools and Applications*, 79(9-10), 5501–5527. doi:10.100711042-019-08348-9

Cheek, C., Fleming, T., Lucassen, M. F., Bridgman, H., Stasiak, K., Shepherd, M., & Orpin, P. (2015). Integrating Health Behavior Theory and Design Elements in Serious Games. *JMIR Mental Health*, 2(2), e11. doi:10.2196/mental.4133 PMID:26543916

Chen, C. M., Lee, H. M., & Chen, Y. H. (2005). Personalized e-learning system using Item Response Theory. *Computers & Education*, 44(3), 237–255. doi:10.1016/j.compedu.2004.01.006

Cheng, Z., Hao, F., Jianyou, Z., & Yun, S. (2011, January). *Research on Design of Serious Game based on GIS*. doi:10.1109/CAIDCD.2010.5681365

Chen, T.-H., Chang, S.-P., Tsai, C.-F., & Juang, K.-D. (2004). Prevalence of depressive and anxiety disorders in an assisted reproductive technique clinic. *Human Reproduction (Oxford, England)*, 19(10), 2313–2318. doi:10.1093/humrep/deh414 PMID:15242992

Chen, Y. T., Hou, C. J., Derek, N., Huang, S. B., Huang, M. W., & Wang, Y. Y. (2021). Evaluation of the reaction time and accuracy rate in normal subjects, MCI, and dementia using serious games. *Applied Sciences (Basel, Switzerland)*, 11(2), 1–14. doi:10.3390/app11020628

Chi, H., Agama, E., & Prodanoff, Z. G. (2017). Developing serious games to promote cognitive abilities for the elderly. *Proceedings of the 2017 IEEE 5th International Conference on Serious Games and Applications for Health (SeGAH)*.

Chisnell, D. (2009). *Usability Testing Demystified*. http://alistapart.com/article/usability-testing-demystified

Chita-Tegmark, M. (2016). Social attention in ASD: A review and meta-analysis of eye-tracking studies. *Research in Developmental Disabilities*, 48, 79–93. doi:10.1016/j.ridd.2015.10.011 PMID:26547134

Cho, B.-H., Ku, J., Jang, D. P., Kim, S., Lee, Y. H., Kim, I. Y., Lee, J. H., & Kim, S. I. (2002, April). The Effect of Virtual Reality Cognitive Training for Attention Enhancement. *Cyberpsychology & Behavior*, 5(2), 129–137. doi:10.1089/109493102753770516 PMID:12025879

Chora, & Bunschoten, R. (2001). *Urban Flotsam*. 010 Publishers.

Chou, Y. (2015). *Actionable Gamification: Beyond Points, Badges and Leaderboards*. Octalysis Media.

Christie, G. I., Shepherd, M., Merry, S. N., Hopkins, S., Knightly, S., & Stasiak, K. (2019). Gamifying CBT to deliver emotional health treatment to young people on smartphones. *Internet Interventions: the Application of Information Technology in Mental and Behavioural Health*, 18, 100286–100286. doi:10.1016/j.invent.2019.100286 PMID:31890633

Christy, K. R., & Fox, J. (2014). Leaderboards in academic contexts: A test of stereotype threat and social comparison explanations for women's math performance. *Computers & Education, 78*, 66-77. . doi:10.106/j.compedu.2014.05.005

Chursin, N. N. (2010). The conception of thesaurus in the information view of the world. Luhansk: Noulydzh.

Cialdini, R. B. (2003). Crafting normative messages to protect the environment. *Current Directions in Psychological Science*, 12(4), 105–109. doi:10.1111/1467-8721.01242

Cilliers, L. (2020). Wearable devices in healthcare: Privacy and information security issues. *The HIM Journal*, 49(2–3), 150–156. doi:10.1177/1833358319851684 PMID:31146589

Cioi, D., Kale, A., Burdea, G., Engsberg, J., Janes, W., & Ross, S. (2011). Ankle control and strength training for children with cerebral palsy using the Rutgers Ankle CP. *2011 IEEE International Conference on Rehabilitation Robotics*, 1–6. 10.1109/ICORR.2011.5975432

Clark, R. C., & Mayer, R. E. (2008). Learning by viewing versus learning by doing: Evidence-based guidelines for principled learning environments. *Performance Improvement*, *47*(9), 5–13. doi:10.1002/pfi.20028

Clark, R. E., Yates, K., Early, S., & Moulton, K. (2010). An analysis of the failure of electronic media and discovery-based learning: Evidence for the performance benefits of guided training methods. In K. H. Silber & W. R. Foshay (Eds.), *Handbook of improving performance in the workplace* (pp. 263–297). Pfeiffer. doi:10.1002/9780470592663.ch8

Classcraft. (2021). Available at https://www.classcraft.com/

Clayden, A. C., Fisher, R. B., & Nuthmann, A. (2020). On the relative (un) importance of foveal vision during letter search in naturalistic scenes. *Vision Research*, *177*, 41–55. doi:10.1016/j.visres.2020.07.005 PMID:32957035

Clement, J. (2021, March 3). Game-developer gender distribution worldwide. *Statista*. https://www.statista.com/statistics/453634/game-developer-gender-distribution-worldwide/

Clement, J. (2021, May 5). Gender split of US computer video gamers. *Statista*. https://www.statista.com/statistics/232383/gender-split-of-us-computer-and-video-gamers/

Clow, D. (2012). The learning analytics cycle: closing the loop effectively. In *Proceedings of the 2nd International Conference on Learning Analytics and Knowledge* (pp. 134–138). 10.1145/2330601.2330636

Cochise College. (2016, May 26). Gender differences in social interaction. *Sociology*. https://courses.lumenlearning.com/cochise-sociology-os/chapter/gender-differences-in-social-interaction/

Code, B. (2016, December 07). Video games are boring. *GameIndustryBiz*. https://www.gamesindustry.biz/articles/2016-11-07-video-games-are-boring

Colao, A., Piscitelli, P., Pulimeno, M., Colazzo, S., Miani, A., & Giannini, S. (2020). Rethinking the role of the school after COVID-19. *The Lancet. Public Health*, *5*(7), e370. doi:10.1016/S2468-2667(20)30124-9 PMID:32464100

Coldwell, M. (1986). Jougleresses and trobairitz: secular musicians in medieval France. In Women making music: The western art tradition (pp. 39 – 61). University of Illinois Press. doi:10.1007/978-1-349-09367-0_3

CONAF. (2021). *Ceinina: Center for Research and Applied Research*. http://www.ceinina.cl/?q=node/213

Connolly, D., Garvey, J., & McKee, G. (2017). Factors associated with ADL/IADL disability in community dwelling older adults in the Irish longitudinal study on ageing (TILDA). *Disability and Rehabilitation*, *39*(8), 809–816. doi:10.3109/09638288.2016.1161848 PMID:27045728

Connolly, T. M., Boyle, E. A., MacArthur, E., Hainey, T., & Boyle, J. M. (2012). A systematic literature review of empirical evidence on computer games and serious games. *Computers & Education*, *59*(2), 661–686. doi:10.1016/j.compedu.2012.03.004

Conrad, S., Clarke-Midura, J., & Klopfer, E. (2014). A Framework for Structuring Learning Assessment in a Massively Multiplayer Online Educational Game. *International Journal of Game-Based Learning*, *4*(1), 37–59. doi:10.4018/IJGBL.2014010103

Cooper, H. (Ed.). (2008). *Sir Thomas Malory: Le Morte D'Arthur*. Oxford University Press.

Corbett, A., Kauffman, L., Maclaren, B., Wagner, A., & Jones, E. (2010). A Cognitive Tutor for Genetics Problem Solving: Learning Gains and Student Modeling. *Journal of Educational Computing Research*, *42*(2), 219–239. doi:10.2190/EC.42.2.e

Cornejo, R., Martínez, F., Álvarez, V. C., Barraza, C., Cibrian, F. L., Martínez-García, A. I., & Tentori, M. (2021). Serious games for basic learning mechanisms: Reinforcing Mexican children's gross motor skills and attention. *Personal and Ubiquitous Computing*, *25*(2), 375–390. Advance online publication. doi:10.100700779-021-01529-0

Cornel, C. J., Rowe, D. C., & Cornel, C. M. (2017, September). Starships and cybersecurity: Teaching security concepts through immersive gaming experiences. In *Proceedings of the 18th Annual Conference on Information Technology Education* (pp. 27-32). 10.1145/3125659.3125696

Corrigan, P. (2004). How stigma interferes with mental health care. *The American Psychologist*, *59*(7), 614–625. doi:10.1037/0003-066X.59.7.614 PMID:15491256

Council, F. T. (2020). *15 Effective Uses Of Virtual Reality For Businesses And Consumers*. https://www.forbes.com/sites/forbestechcouncil/2020/02/12/15-effective-uses-of-virtual-reality-for-businesses-and-consumers/?sh=469c9d52f2b2

Coursera. (2021). *Cursos en línea*. https://es.coursera.org/

Covey, S. R. (2020). *The 7 habits of highly effective people*. Simon & Schuster.

Cowls, J., & Schroeder, R. (2015). Causation, Correlation, and Big Data in Social Science Research. *Policy and Internet*, *7*(4), 447–472. doi:10.1002/poi3.100

Coyle, D., McGlade, N., Doherty, G., & O'Reilly, G. (2011). *Exploratory evaluations of a computer game supporting cognitive behavioural therapy for adolescents*. Academic Press.

Coyle, D., McGlade, N., Doherty, G., & O'Reilly, G. (2011). Exploratory evaluations of a computer game supporting cognitive behavioural therapy for adolescents. *Proceedings of the SIGCHI Conference on Human Factors in Computing Systems*, 2937-2946. 10.1145/1978942.1979378

Csikszentmihalhi, M. (2020). Finding flow: The psychology of engagement with everyday life. Hachette UK.

Csikszentmihalyi, M. (1990). *Flow: the psychology of optimal experience*. Harper & Row.

Csikszentmihalyi, M. (1990). *Flow: The Psychology of Optimal Experience*. Harper & Row.

Csikszentmihalyi, M. (1997). *Finding flow*. Basic Books.

Csikszentmihalyi, M., Abuhamdeh, S., & Nakamura, J. (2014). Flow. In M. Csikszentmihalyi (Ed.), *Flow and the Foundations of Positive Psychology: The Collected Works of Mihaly Csikszentmihalyi* (pp. 227–238). Springer Netherlands. doi:10.1007/978-94-017-9088-8_15

Csikszentmihalyi, M., & Asakawa, K. (2016). Universal and cultural dimensions of optimal experiences. *The Japanese Psychological Research*, *58*(1), 4–13. doi:10.1111/jpr.12104

Cuesta, V., & Nakano, M. (2017). Chain of command: A sustainable supply chain management serious game. *International Journal of Automotive Technology*, *11*(4), 552–562. doi:10.20965/ijat.2017.p0552

Cuijpers, P., Donker, T., Johansson, R., Mohr, D. C., van Straten, A., & Andersson, G. (2011). Self-Guided Psychological Treatment for Depressive Symptoms: A Meta-Analysis. *PLoS One*, *6*(6), e21274. doi:10.1371/journal.pone.0021274 PMID:21712998

Cullen, J. M. (2017). Circular Economy: Theoretical Benchmark or Perpetual Motion Machine? *Journal of Industrial Ecology*, *21*(3), 483–486. doi:10.1111/jiec.12599

Cutumisu, M., Brown, M. R. G., Fray, C., & Schmölzer, G. M. (2018). Growth mindset moderates the effect of the neonatal resuscitation program on performance in a computer-based game training simulation. *Frontiers in Pediatrics, 6. Article, 195*, 1–10. doi:10.3389/fped.2018.00195 PMID:30023355

Cutumisu, M., Ghoman, S. K., Lu, C., Patel, S. D., Garcia-Hidalgo, C., Fray, C., Brown, M. R. G., Greiner, R., & Schmölzer, G. M. (2020). Health care providers' performance, mindset, and attitudes toward a neonatal resuscitation computer-based simulator: Empirical study. *Journal of Medical Internet Research (JMIR) Serious Games, 8*(4), e21855. doi:10.2196/21855 PMID:33346741

Cutumisu, M., Patel, S. D., Brown, M. R. G., Fray, C., von Hauff, P., Jeffery, T., & Schmölzer, G. M. (2019). RETAIN: A board game that improves neonatal resuscitation knowledge retention. *Frontiers in Pediatrics, 7*(13), 13. Advance online publication. doi:10.3389/fped.2019.00013 PMID:30766862

Czauderna, A., and Guardiola., E., (2019). The Gameplay Loop Methodology as a Tool for Educational Game Design. *The Electronic Journal of e-Learning, 17*(3), 207-221.

Czikszentmihalyi, M. (1990). *Flow: The psychology of Optimal Experience*. Harper & Row.

d'Orville, H. (2016). New humanism and sustainable development. *Cadmus, 2*(5).

Dabbagh, N., Benson, A. D., Denham, A., Joseph, R., Al-Freih, M., Zgheib, G., ... Guo, Z. (2016). *Learning Technologies and Globalization*. Springer International Publishing., doi:10.1007/978-3-319-22963-8

Dafermos, M. (2018). *Rethinking cultural-historical theory: A dialectical perspective to Vygotsky*. Springer. doi:10.1007/978-981-13-0191-9

Dagar, J. C., & Tewari, V. P. (2017). Evoluation of agroforestry as modern science. In Agroforestry: Anecdotal to Modern Science. Springer Nature Singapore Pvt. Ltd.

Dalgard, F. J., Gieler, U., Tomas-Aragones, L., Lien, L., Poot, F., Jemec, G. B. E., Misery, L., Szabo, C., Linder, D., Sampogna, F., Evers, A. W. M., Halvorsen, J. A., Balieva, F., Szepietowski, J., Romanov, D., Marron, S. E., Altunay, I. K., Finlay, A. Y., Salek, S. S., & Kupfer, J. (2015). The psychological burden of skin diseases: A cross-sectional multicenter study among dermatological out-patients in 13 European countries. *The Journal of Investigative Dermatology, 135*(4), 984–991. doi:10.1038/jid.2014.530 PMID:25521458

Dalgarno, B. (2002). The potential of 3D virtual learning environments: A constructivist analysis. *Electronic Journal of Instructional Science and Technology, 5*(2), 3–6.

Dameff, C. J., Selzer, J. A., Fisher, J., Killeen, J. P., & Tully, J. L. (2019). Clinical Cybersecurity Training Through Novel High-Fidelity Simulations. *The Journal of Emergency Medicine, 56*(2), 233–238. doi:10.1016/j.jemermed.2018.10.029 PMID:30553562

Daniel, J. (2020). Education and the COVID-19 pandemic. *Prospects, 49*(1), 91–96. doi:10.100711125-020-09464-3 PMID:32313309

Daniel, M., & Garry, C. (2018). *Video Games As Culture*. Routledge. doi:10.4324/9781315622743

Dankbaar, M. E., Alsma, J., Jansen, E. E., van Merrienboer, J. J., van Sasse, J. L., & Schuit, S. C. (2016). An experimental study on the effects of a simulation game on students' clinical cognitive skills and motivation. *Advances in Health Sciences Education: Theory and Practice, 21*(3), 505–521. doi:10.100710459-015-9641-x PMID:26433730

Danowska-Florczyk, E., & Mostowski, P. (2012). *Gamification as a new direction in teaching Polish as a foreign language*. ICT for Language Learning.

Darfur is Dying [Digital game]. (2006). *interFUEL, LLC*. Retrieved 07 19, 2021, from Game for change: https://www.gamesforchange.org/game/darfur-is-dying/

Dartigues, J. F., Foubert-Samier, A., Le Goff, M., Viltard, M., Amieva, H., Orgogozo, J. M., Barberger-Gateau, P., & Helmer, C. (2013). Playing board games, cognitive decline and dementia: A French population-based cohort study. *BMJ Open*, *3*(8), e002998. doi:10.1136/bmjopen-2013-002998 PMID:23988362

Data Dealer [Digital game]. (2013). *Cuteacute Media OG*. Retrieved from Game for change: https://www.gamesforchange.org/game/data-dealer/

Datak. (2016). *RTS*. Retrieved 07 19, 2021, from Game for change [Digital game]: https://www.gamesforchange.org/game/datak/

David, O. A., Costescu, C., Cardos, R., & Mogoaşe, C. (2020). How Effective are Serious Games for Promoting Mental Health and Health Behavioral Change in Children and Adolescents? A Systematic Review and Meta-analysis. *Child and Youth Care Forum*, *49*(6), 817–838. doi:10.100710566-020-09566-1

Davis, N. O., Bower, J., & Kollins, S. H. (2018). Proof-of-concept study of an at-home, engaging, digital intervention for pediatric ADHD. *PLoS One*, *13*(1), e0189749. doi:10.1371/journal.pone.0189749 PMID:29324745

Dawson, G., Jones, E. J., Merkle, K., Venema, K., Lowy, R., Faja, S., Kamara, D., Murias, M., Greenson, J., Winter, J., Smith, M., Rogers, S. J., & Webb, S. J. (2012). Early behavioral intervention is associated with normalized brain activity in young children with autism. *Journal of the American Academy of Child and Adolescent Psychiatry*, *51*(11), 1150–1159. doi:10.1016/j.jaac.2012.08.018 PMID:23101741

Dawson, G., Webb, S., Schellenberg, G. D., Dager, S., Friedman, S., Aylward, E., & Richards, T. (2002). Defining the broader phenotype of autism: Genetic, brain, and behavioral perspectives. *Development and Psychopathology*, *14*(3), 581–611. doi:10.1017/S0954579402003103 PMID:12349875

De Angelis, R., Howard, M., & Miemczyk, J. (2017). Supply Chain Management and the Circular Economy : Towards the Circular Supply Chain. *Production Planning and Control*, *29*(6), 425–437. doi:10.1080/09537287.2018.1449244

de Certeau, M. (1984). *The Practice of Everyday Life*. The University of California Press.

De Freitas, S. (2006). Learning in Immersive worlds A review of game-based learning. *JISC ELearning Innovation*, *3*(October), 73. doi:10.1111/j.1467-8535.2009.01024.x

De Freitas, S., & Liarokapis, F. (2011). Serious Games: A New Paradigm for Education? In J. L. In M. Ma & A. Oikonomou (Eds.), *Serious Games and Edutainment Applications* (pp. 9–23). Springer. doi:10.1007/978-1-4471-2161-9_2

de Jager, P. S., & Condy, J. (2020). Weak central coherence is a syndrome of autism spectrum disorder during teacher-learner task instructions. *South African Journal of Childhood Education*, *10*(1), 1–11. doi:10.4102ajce.v10i1.785

de Jong, P. J., Sportel, B. E., de Hullu, E., & Nauta, M. H. (2012). Co-occurrence of social anxiety and depression symptoms in adolescence: Differential links with implicit and explicit self-esteem? *Psychological Medicine*, *42*(3), 475–484. doi:10.1017/S0033291711001358 PMID:21798114

de Las Heras, S. C., Gargalo, C. L., Weitze, C. L., Mansouri, S. S., Gernaey, K. V., & Krühne, U. (2021). A framework for the development of Pedagogical Process Simulators (P2Si) using explanatory models and gamification. *Computers & Chemical Engineering*, *151*, 107350. doi:10.1016/j.compchemeng.2021.107350

De Pietro, O., De Rose, M., & Muoio, P. (2010). e-Underline: a tool to support collaborative learning. In *Proceedings of Elearn 2010, World conference on E-learning in Corporate Governement, Healthcare e Higher Education*. Association for the Advancement of Computing in Education (AACE).

De Troyer, O., Van Broeckhoven, F., & Vlieghe, J. (2017). Linking serious game narratives with pedagogical theories and pedagogical design strategies. *Journal of Computing in Higher Education, 29*(3), 549–573. doi:10.100712528-017-9142-4

Dean, A. (2002). Telelearning: Invention, Innovation Implications: Towards a Manifesto. *Australasian Journal of Educational Technology, 5*(2), 1–12.

Dean, S., Britt, E., Bell, E., Stanley, J., & Collings, S. (2016). Motivational interviewing to enhance adolescent mental health treatment engagement: A randomized clinical trial. *Psychological Medicine, 46*(9), 1961–1969. doi:10.1017/S0033291716000568 PMID:27045520

Delen, D. (2010). A comparative analysis of machine learning techniques for student retention management. *Decision Support Systems, 49*(4), 498–506. doi:10.1016/j.dss.2010.06.003

Dell, C. (2019). *The Improvisation of Space*. Jovis.

Delli, C. K. S., Varveris, A., & Geronta, A. (2017). Application of the Theory of Mind, Theory of Executive Functions and Weak Central Coherence Theory to Individuals with ASD. *Journal of Educational and Developmental Psychology, 7*(1), 102–102. doi:10.5539/jedp.v7n1p102

Demetriou, E. A., Lampit, A., Quintana, D. S., Naismith, S. L., Song, Y. J. C., Pye, J. E., Hickie, I., & Guastella, A. J. (2018). Autism spectrum disorders: A meta-analysis of executive function. *Molecular Psychiatry, 23*(5), 1198–1204. doi:10.1038/mp.2017.75 PMID:28439105

Demir Akça, A. S., Saraçli, Ö., Emre, U., Atasoy, N., Güdül, S., Özen Barut, B., Şenormanci, Ö., Büyükuysal, M. Ç., Atik, L., & Atasoy, H. T. (2014). Relationship of Cognitive Functions with Daily Living Activities, Depression, Anxiety and Clinical Variables in Hospitalized Elderly Patients. *Nöro Psikiyatri Arşivi, 51*(3), 267–274. doi:10.4274/npa.y7053 PMID:28360637

Denholm, J. A., Protopsaltis, A., & de Freitas, S. (2013). The value of team-based mixed-reality (TBMR) games in higher education. *International Journal of Game-Based Learning, 3*(1), 18–33. doi:10.4018/ijgbl.2013010102

Denny, P. (2013, April). The effect of virtual achievements on student engagement. In *Proceedings of the SIGCHI conference on human factors in computing systems* (pp. 763-772). 10.1145/2470654.2470763

Department of Statistics. Singapore. (2021, July 7). *Singapore Population*. Department of Statistics, Singapore. https://www.singstat.gov.sg/modules/infographics/population

Deshpande, A. A., & Huang, S. H. (2011). Simulation games in engineering education: A state-of-the-art review. *Computer Applications in Engineering Education, 19*(3), 399–410. doi:10.1002/cae.20323

Deterding, S. (2012). Gamification: Designing for motivation. *Interactions, 19*(4), 14-17.

Deterding, S. L. (2011). Gamification. using game-design elements in non-gaming contexts. *Proceedings of the 2011 annual conference extended abstracts*, 24–25. 10.1145/1979742.1979575

Deterding, S., Dixon, D., Khaled, R., & Nacke, L. (2011, September). From game design elements to gamefulness: defining "gamification". In *Proceedings of the 15th international academic MindTrek conference: Envisioning future media environments* (pp. 9-15). 10.1145/2181037.2181040

Deterding, S., Dixon, D., Khaled, R., & Nacke, L. E. (2011). Gamification : Toward a Definition. In *ACM CHI Conference on Human Factors in Computing Systems* (pp. 12–15). ACM.

Detmer, D., Bloomrosen, M., Raymond, B., & Tang, P. (2008). Integrated personal health records: Transformative tools for consumer-centric care. *BMC Medical Informatics and Decision Making*, 8(1), 1–14. doi:10.1186/1472-6947-8-45 PMID:18837999

Devaranavadgi, S. B., Bassappa, S., Jolli, R.B, Wali, S.Y., & Bagali, A.N. (2013). Height-Age Growth Curve Modelling for Different Tree Species in Drylands of North Karnataka. *Global Journal of Science Frontier Research Agriculture and Veterinary Sciences*.

Devine, T. C. (2015). *Integrating Games into the Artworld: A Methodology and Case Study Exploring the Work of Jason Rohrer*. Games and Culture.

Dhyani, S. K., Newaj, R., & Sharma, A. R. (2009). Agroforestry: Its relation with agronomy, Challenges and opportunities. *Indian Journal of Agronomy*, 54(3), 249–266.

Dickey, M. D. (2005). Engaging by design: How engagement strategies in popular computer and video games can inform instructional design. *Educational Technology Research and Development*, 53(2), 67–83. doi:10.1007/BF02504866

Dickey, M. D. (2007). Game design and learning: A conjectural analysis of how massively multiple online role-playing games (MMORPGs) foster intrinsic motivation. *Educational Technology Research and Development*, 55(3), 253–273. doi:10.100711423-006-9004-7

Dietrich, K. N., Eskenazi, B., Schantz, S., Yolton, K., Rauh, V. A., Johnson, C. B., Alkon, A., Canfield, R. L., Pessah, I. N., & Berman, R. F. (2005). Principles and Practices of Neurodevelopmental Assessment in Children: Lessons Learned from the Centers for ' 'Children's Environmental Health and Disease Prevention Research. *Environmental Health Perspectives*, 113(10), 1437–1446. doi:10.1289/ehp.7672 PMID:16203260

Dietz, T., Stern, P. C., & Guagnano, G. A. (1998). Social structural and social psychological bases of environmental concern. *Environment and Behavior*, 30(4), 450–471. doi:10.1177/001391659803000402

Dinis, A. C., Silvano, A., Casado, D., Espadinha, C., & Noriega, P. (2019). Usability and UX of Nintendo Wii big brain academy game in the elderly as a resource of psychomotor intervention. *Proceedings of the International Conference Healthcare Ergonomics and Patient Safety*. 10.1007/978-3-030-24067-7_31

Divjak, B., & Tomić, D. (2011). The impact of Game-based learning on the achievement of learning goals and motivation for learning mathematics - literature review. *Journal of Information and Organizational Sciences*, 35(1). jios.foi.hr/index.php/jios/article/view/182

Divo, M. J., Martinez, C. H., & Mannino, D. M. (2014). Ageing and the epidemiology of multimorbidity. *The European Respiratory Journal*, 44(4), 1055–1068. doi:10.1183/09031936.00059814 PMID:25142482

Djaouti, D. (2020). DICE: A Generic Model for the Design Process of Serious Games. *International Journal of Game-Based Learning*, 10(2), 39–53. doi:10.4018/IJGBL.2020040103

Djaouti, D., Alvarez, J., & Jessel, J. P. (2011). Classifying serious games: The G/P/S model. In P. Felicia (Ed.), *Handbook of research on improving learning and motivation through educational games: Multidisciplinary approaches* (pp. 118–136). IGI Global. doi:10.4018/978-1-60960-495-0.ch006

Djaouti, D., Alvarez, J., Jessel, J. P., Methel, G., & Molinier, P. (2008). A gameplay definition through videogame classification. *International Journal of Computer Games Technology*, 1–6.

Dkanter, N. (2005). Gaming Redefines Interactivity for Learning. In ERIC (pp. 26–33). doi:10.1007/BF02763644

Domínguez, A., Saenz-de-Navarrete, J., De-Marcos, L., Fernández-Sanz, L., Pagés, C., & Martínez-Herráiz, J. J. (2013). Gamifying learning experiences: Practical implications and outcomes. *Computers & Education*, *63*, 380–392. doi:10.1016/j.compedu.2012.12.020

Donovan, L. (2012). *The use of serious games in the corporate sector. A State of the Art Report*. Learnovate Centre.

Dörner, R., Göbel, S., Effelsberg, W., & Wiemeyer, J. (2016). *Serious games*. Springer International Publishing.

Dörner, R., Göbel, S., Effelsberg, W., & Wiemeyer, J. (2016). *Serious Games: Foundations, Concepts and Practice*. Springer International. doi:10.1007/978-3-319-40612-1

Dosdoce. (2013). *Museums in the digital age* [Paper presentation]. Museum Next. http://www.dosdoce.com/upload/ficheros/noticias/201305/museums_in_the_digital_age__a_dosdoce_survey.pdf

Drachsler, H., & Greller, W. (2016). Privacy and analytics - it's a DELICATE issue a checklist for trusted learning analytics. In *Proceedings of the sixth international conference on learning analytics \& knowledge* (pp. 89–98). ACM. doi:10.1145/2883851.2883893

Drachsler, H., & Kalz, M. (2016). The MOOC and learning analytics innovation cycle (MOLAC): A reflective summary of ongoing research and its challenges. *Journal of Computer Assisted Learning*, *32*(3), 281–290. doi:10.1111/jcal.12135

Drag, L. L., & Bieliauskas, L. A. (2010). Contemporary Review 2009: Cognitive Aging. *Journal of Geriatric Psychiatry and Neurology*, *23*(2), 75–93. doi:10.1177/0891988709358590 PMID:20101069

DRTV. (2017). *Historien om Danmark* [The history of Denmark]. Danish Broadcasting Co. [Television dramatized documentary miniseries]

Drummond, D., Hadchouel, A., & Tesnière, A. (2017). Serious games for health: Three steps forwards. *Advances in Simulation (London, England)*, *2*(1), 1–8. doi:10.118641077-017-0036-3 PMID:29450004

Duchowski, A. (2017). *Eye tracking methodology: Theory and practice* (3rd ed.). Springer. doi:10.1007/978-3-319-57883-5

Dunne, A., & Raby, F. (2013). *Speculative Everything: Design, Fiction, and Social Dreaming*. The MIT Press.

Duplaa, E., & Taiwo, E. (2013). Cognition and theory of flow for elders: can digital games help. *Proceedings of World Congress on Social Sciences*.

Dupuy, G. (1972). Les jeux urbains [Urban Games]. *L'Actualite Economique*, *48*(1), 85. Advance online publication. doi:10.7202/1003681ar

Duriez, C. (2015). *The Oxford Inklings*. Lion Hudson.

Durrani, H. (2016). Healthcare and healthcare systems: Inspiring progress and future prospects. *mHealth*, *2*. PMID:28293581

Dwivedi, P., & Bharadwaj, K. K. (2015). E-Learning recommender system for a group of learners based on the unified learner profile approach. *Expert Systems: International Journal of Knowledge Engineering and Neural Networks*, *32*(2), 264–276. doi:10.1111/exsy.12061

Eads, V. (2012). Means, motive, opportunity: medieval women and the recourse to arms. *De Re Militari*. https://deremilitari.org/2012/09/eads-means-motive-opportunity/

Eames, C. (1969). *Qu'est ce qu'est le design?* [What is Design?]. Musée des Arts Décoratifs.

Easley, D., & Ghosh, A. (2016). Incentives, Gamification, and Game Theory: An Economic Approach to Badge Design. *ACM Transactions on Economics and Computation (TEAC)*, *4*(3).

Ebbinghaus, H. (1885). *Memory: A contribution to experimental psychology*. Dover.

Eck, R. (2006). Digital game-based learning: It's not just the digital natives that are restless. *EDUCAUSE Review, 41*(2), 1–16.

Edmonds, E. A., Weakley, A., Candy, L., Fell, M., Knott, R., & Pauletto, S. (2005). The studio as laboratory: Combining creative practice and digital technology research. *International Journal of Human-Computer Studies, 63*(4-5), 452–481. doi:10.1016/j.ijhcs.2005.04.012

Egenfeldt-Nielsen, S. (2011). What makes a good learning game? Going beyond edutainment. *ELearn Magazine, 2*.

Egenfeldt-Nielsen, S. (2006). Overview of research on the educational use of video games. *Nordic Journal of Digital Literacy, 1*(03), 184–214. doi:10.18261/ISSN1891-943X-2006-03-03

Eichenberg, C., & Schott, M. (2017). Serious games for psychotherapy: A systematic review. *Games for Health Journal, 6*(3), 127–135. doi:10.1089/g4h.2016.0068 PMID:28628385

Eichler, M. L., Perry, G. T., Lucchesi, I. L., & Melendez, T. T. (2018). Mobile game-based learning in STEM subjects. In *Encyclopedia of Information Science and Technology* (4th ed., pp. 6376–6387). IGI Global.

Eichner, S. (2014). *Agency and Media Reception: Experiencing Video Games, Film, and Television*. Springer VS. doi:10.1007/978-3-658-04673-6

El-Deghaidy, H., & Mansour, N. (2015). Science Teachers' Perceptions of STEM Education: Possibilities and Challenges. *International Journal of Learning, 1*(1), 51–54. doi:10.18178/ijlt.1.1.51-54

Elder Scrolls V: Skyrim. (2011). [Video Game]. Bethesda Game Studios.

Eliade, M. (1961). History of religions and a new humanism. *History of Religions, 1*(1), 1–8.

Elizabeth, J., King, N., Ollendick, T. H., Gullone, E., Tonge, B., Watson, S., & Macdermott, S. (2006). Social anxiety disorder in children and youth: A research update on aetiological factors. *Counselling Psychology Quarterly, 19*(2), 151–163. doi:10.1080/09515070600811790

Ellen MacArthur Foundation. (2013). *Towards the Circular Economy* (Vol. 1). Author.

Ellen MacArthur Foundation. (2014). *Towards the Circular Economy Vol.3: Accelerating the scale-up across global supply chains*. Author.

Ellis, R. (2003). *Task-based language learning and teaching*. Oxford University Press.

Elor, A., Lessard, S., Teodorescu, M., & Kurniawan, S. (2019). Project Butterfly: Synergizing Immersive Virtual Reality with Actuated Soft Exosuit for Upper-Extremity Rehabilitation. *2019 IEEE Conference on Virtual Reality and 3D User Interfaces (VR)*, 1448–1456. 10.1109/VR.2019.8798014

Elorriaga, M., Antúnez, M. E., & Nicolino, M. S. (2016, October). The game as a way to destructuration: Learning to reason through game. In *2016 International Conference on Interactive Mobile Communication, Technologies and Learning (IMCL)* (pp. 43-45). IEEE. 10.1109/IMCTL.2016.7753768

Elvira, J. (2005). Control Remot / Remote Control. *Quaderns d'arquitectura i urbanisme, 247*, 84-95.

Elvira, J., & Paez, R. (2019). Design Through Play: The Archispiel Experience. In VII Jornadas sobre Innovación Docente en Arquitectura. UPC IDP, GILDA.

Emmelkamp, P., Meyerbröker, K., & Morina, N. (2020). Virtual Reality Therapy in Social Anxiety Disorder. *Current Psychiatry Reports, 22*(7), 32. doi:10.100711920-020-01156-1 PMID:32405657

Emmerich, K., & Bockholt, M. (2016). Serious games evaluation: processes, models, and concepts. In *Entertainment Computing and Serious Games* (pp. 265–283). Springer.

Ennis, L., Robotham, D., Denis, M., Pandit, N., Newton, D., Rose, D., & Wykes, T. (2014). Collaborative development of an electronic Personal Health Record for people with severe and enduring mental health problems. *BMC Psychiatry*, *14*(1), 1–7. doi:10.118612888-014-0305-9 PMID:25403285

Erskine, H. E., Ferrari, A. J., Nelson, P., Polanczyk, G. V., Flaxman, A. D., Vos, T., Whiteford, H. A., & Scott, J. G. (2013). Research Review: Epidemiological modelling of attention-deficit/hyperactivity disorder and conduct disorder for the Global Burden of Disease Study 2010. *Journal of Child Psychology and Psychiatry, and Allied Disciplines*, *54*(12), 1263–1274. doi:10.1111/jcpp.12144 PMID:24117530

ESA. (2019). *2019 Essential Facts About the Computer and Video Game Industry*. Retrieved from https://www.theesa.com/resource/essential-facts-about-the-computer-and-video-game-industry-2019/

Etting, V. (2004). *Queen Margrete I (1353-1412) and the founding of the Nordic Union*. Brill. doi:10.1163/9789047404798

EUMC. (2004). *Migrants, minorities and education: Documenting discrimination and integration in 15 member states of the European Union*. EUMC.

European Commission. (2015). *Demography report*. Publications Office of the European Union.

European Commission. (2015). *Language teaching and learning in multilingual classrooms*. Publications Office of the European Union.

European Commission/EACEA/Eurydice. (2017). *Key data on teaching languages at school in Europe - 2017 edition* (Eurydice Report). Publications Office of the European Union. https://op.europa.eu/en/publication-detail/-/publication/73ac5ebd-473e-11e7-aea8-01aa75ed71a1/language-en/format-PDF

European Commission/EACEA/Eurydice. (2019). *Integrating students from migrant backgrounds into schools in Europe: National Policies and Measures (Eurydice Report)*. Publications Office of the European Union.

EUROSTAT. (2020). *Ageing Europe. Looking at the lives of older people in the EU*. Publications Office of the European Union., doi:10.2785/628105

Everson, M. (1997). An inquiry into the reading the reading strategies of intermediate and advanced learners of Chinese as a foreign language. *Journal of the Chinese Language Teacher Association*, *32*, 1–20.

Everson, M. (1998). Word recognition among learners of Chinese as a foreign language: Investigating the relationship between naming and knowing. *Modern Language Journal*, *82*(2), 194–204. doi:10.1111/j.1540-4781.1998.tb01192.x

Evolmind. (2021). *La plataforma e-learning que simplifica la formación en línea*. https://www.evolmind.com/

Explore our Collections – Games. (n.d.). *National Museums Scotland*. https://www.nms.ac.uk/explore-our-collections/?type=13119

Eysenbach, G. (2000). Consumer health informatics. *BMJ (Clinical Research Ed.)*, *320*(7251), 1713–1716. doi:10.1136/bmj.320.7251.1713 PMID:10864552

Eysenbach, G. (2005). The Law of Attrition. *Journal of Medical Internet Research*, *7*(1), e11. doi:10.2196/jmir.7.1.e11 PMID:15829473

Fagen, R. M. (1981). *Animal Play Behavior*. Oxford University Press.

Falcone, P. (2020). Heritage storytelling. In A. dos Santos Queirós (Ed.), *Examining a New Paradigm of Heritage with Philosophy, Economy, and Education* (pp. 142–156). IGI Global. doi:10.4018/978-1-7998-3636-0.ch010

Falk, J. H. (2016). *Identity and the Museum Visitor Experience*. Routledge. doi:10.4324/9781315427058

Fang, X., Chan, S., Brzezinski, J., & Nair, C. (2010). Development of an instrument to measure enjoyment of computer game play. *International Journal of Human-Computer Interaction, 26*(9), 868–886. doi:10.1080/10447318.2010.496337

Fannon, D., Laboy, M., & Wiederspahn, P. (in press). *The Architecture of Persistence: Designing for Future Use*. Routledge.

Farrell, S. (2017). *UX Research Cheat Sheet*. Interaction Design Foundation. https://www.nngroup.com/articles/ux%5C-research%5C-cheat%5C-sheet/

Father and Son - the game. (n.d.). *MANN Naples*. https://mannapoli.it/father-and-son-the-game/

Fee, K. (2009). *Delivering E-learning - A complete strategy for design, application and assessment*. Kogan Page. https://www.emerald.com/insight/publication/issn/1477-7282

Feger, D. M., Willis, S. L., Thomas, K. R., Marsiske, M., Rebok, G. W., Felix, C., & Gross, A. L. (2020). Incident Instrumental Activities of Daily Living Difficulty in Older Adults: Which Comes First? Findings From the Advanced Cognitive Training for Independent and Vital Elderly Study. *Frontiers in Neurology, 11*, 550577. Advance online publication. doi:10.3389/fneur.2020.550577 PMID:33192982

Feinstein, A. H., & Cannon, H. M. (2002). Constructs of simulation evaluation. *Simulation & Gaming, 33*(4), 425–440. doi:10.1177/1046878102238606

Felder, R. M., Silverman, L. K., & ... (1988). Learning and teaching styles in engineering education. *Engineering Education, 78*(7), 674–681.

Feminist Frequency. (n.d.). *Conversations with pop culture*. https://feministfrequency.com/

Fernández-Calvo, B., Rodríguez-Pérez, R., Contador, I., Rubio-Santorum, A., & Ramos, F. (2011). Efficacy of cognitive training programs based on new software technologies in patients with Alzheimer-type dementia. *Psicothema, 23*(1), 44–50. PMID:21266141

Ferradas, P., Vargas, A., & Santillán, G. (2006). *Metodologías y herramientas para la capacitación en gestión de riesgo de Desastres*. Codex.

Ferreira-Brito, F., Alves, S., Santos, O., Guerreiro, T., Caneiras, C., Carriço, L., & Verdelho, A. (2020). Photo-Realistic Interactive Virtual Environments for Neurorehabilitation in Mild Cognitive Impairment (NeuroVRehab.PT): A Participatory Design and Proof-of-Concept Study. *Journal of Clinical Medicine, 9*(12), 3821. Advance online publication. doi:10.3390/jcm9123821 PMID:33255869

Ferreiro, R. F. (2006). The challenge of education in the 21st century: The N-Generation. *Apertura (Guadalajara, Jal.), 5*.

Festa, C. C., & Ginsburg, G. S. (2011). Parental and peer predictors of social anxiety in youth. *Child Psychiatry and Human Development, 42*(3), 291–306. doi:10.100710578-011-0215-8 PMID:21274620

Fetzer, M., McNamara, J., & Geimer, J. L. (2017). Gamification, serious games and personnel selection. In J. P. Pulakos & C. Semedo (Eds.), *The Wiley Blackwell handbook of the psychology of recruitment, selection and employee retention* (pp. 293–309). Wiley Online Library.

Final Fantasy. (1987-). [Video Game]. Square Enix.

Finley, K. (2012, November 14). How 'Gamification' Can Make Your Customer Service Worse. *Wired.* https://www.wired.com/2012/11/gamification-customer-service/

Finnish Institute for Health and Welfare (THL). (2021). *Koulutus ja kielitaito.* https://thl.fi/fi/web/maahanmuutto-ja-kulttuurinen-%0Aoninaisuus/kotoutuminen-ja-osallisuus/koulutus-ja-kielitaito%0A

Firmino, H., Nogueira, V., Neves, S., & Lagarto, L. (2014). Psicopatologia das pessoas mais velhas [Psychopathology of Older People]. In Geriatria Fundamental. Saber e Praticar [Fundamental Geriatrics. Knowing and Practicing]. Lidel Edições Técnicas.

Fitness for purpose. Glossary. Methodical recommendations for experts of the National Agency on the application of the Criteria for evaluating the quality of the educational program [Hlosarii. Metodychni rekomendatsii dlia ekspertiv Natsionalnoho ahentst]. (2020). Retrieved 2021, from NAQA: https://naqa.gov.ua/wp-content/uploads/2020/01/%D0%93%D0%BB%D0%BE%D1%81%D0%B0%D1%80%D1%96%D0%B9.pdf

Fleming, T. M., Bavin, L., Stasiak, K., Hermansson-Webb, E., Merry, S. N., Cheek, C., Lucassen, M., Lau, H. M., Pollmuller, B., & Hetrick, S. (2017). Serious games and gamification for mental health: Current status and promising directions. *Frontiers in Psychiatry, 7*(JAN). Advance online publication. doi:10.3389/fpsyt.2016.00215 PMID:28119636

Fleming, T. M., Cheek, C., Merry, S. N., Thabrew, H., Bridgman, H., Stasiak, K., Shepherd, M., Perry, Y., & Hetrick, S. (2014). Serious games for the treatment or prevention of depression: A systematic review. *Revista de Psicopatología y Psicología Clínica, 19*(3), 227–242. doi:10.5944/rppc.vol.19.num.3.2014.13904

Fleury, A., Nakano, D., & Cordeiro, J. H. (2014). *Mapeamento da Indústria Brasileira e Global de Jogos Digitais.* BNDES.

Fonseca, A. (2006). O Envelhecimento. Uma abordagem psicológica (2ª edição) [Aging. A Psychological Approach (2nd Edition)]. Lisbon: Universidade Católica Portuguesa.

Fonseca, L. M. M., Aredes, N. D. A., Dias, D. M. V., Scochi, C. G. S., Martins, J. C. A., & Rodrigues, M. A. (2015). Serious game e-Baby: Nursing students' perception on learning about preterm newborn clinical assessment. *Revista Brasileira de Enfermagem, 68*, 13–19. doi:10.1590/0034-7167.2015680102p PMID:25946489

Fonseca, L. M. M., Dias, D. M. V., Góes, F. D. S. N., Seixas, C. A., Scochi, C. G. S., Martins, J. C. A., & Rodrigues, M. A. (2014). Development of the e-Baby serious game with regard to the evaluation of oxygenation in preterm babies: Contributions of the emotional design. *CIN: Computers, Informatics. Nursing, 32*(9), 428–436. PMID:25010051

Fontaine, R. (2000). *Piscologia de envelhecimento* [Psychology of Aging]. Climepsi Editores.

Fontana, E., Gregorio, R., Lucia, E., & Carolina, A. (2017). TrainBrain: A Serious Game for Attention Training. *International Journal of Computers and Applications, 160*(4), 1–6. doi:10.5120/ijca2017913027

Foreman, N., Stanton-Fraser, D., Wilson, P. N., Duffy, H., & Parnell, R. (2005). Transfer of Spatial Knowledge to a Two-Level Shopping Mall in Older People, Following Virtual Exploration. *Environment and Behavior, 37*(2), 275–292. doi:10.1177/0013916504269649

Fotis, L., Kurt, D., Athanasios, V., Panagiotis, P., & Alina, E. (2014). Comparing interaction techniques for serious games through braincomputer interfaces: A user perception evaluation study. *Entertainment Computing, 5*(4), 391–399. doi:10.1016/j.entcom.2014.10.004

Foxx, R. M. (2008). Applied behavior analysis treatment of autism: The state of the art. *Child and Adolescent Psychiatric Clinics of North America, 17*(4), 821–834. doi:10.1016/j.chc.2008.06.007 PMID:18775372

Frank, R. G. (2004). *Behavioral economics and health economics.* National Bureau of Economic Research. doi:10.3386/w10881

Franzwa, C., Tang, Y., Johnson, A., & Bielefeldt, T. (2014). Balancing Fun and Learning in a Serious Game Design. *International Journal of Game-Based Learning*, *4*(4), 37–57. doi:10.4018/ijgbl.2014100103

Fredericks, L. (2021, February 16). The complete guide to virtual tourism in 2021. *Cvent.* https://www.cvent.com/en/blog/hospitality/virtual-tourism

Freina, L., & Ott, M. (2015). A literature review on immersive virtual reality in education: State of the art and perspectives. *Proceedings of ELearning and Software for Education (ELSE)*, 8. doi:10.12753/2066-026X-15-020

Freina, L., & Ott, M. (2015). A literature review on immersive virtual reality in education: state of the art and perspectives. *The International Scientific Conference eLearning and Software for Education*, *1*(133), 10-1007.

Freire, M., Serrano-laguna, Á., Iglesias, B. M., Martínez-ortiz, I., Moreno-ger, P., & Fernández-manjón, B. (2016). Game Learning Analytics: Learning Analytics for Serious Games. In Learning, Design, and Technology: An International Compendium of Theory, Research, Practice, and Policy (pp. 1–29). Springer. doi:10.1007/978-3-319-17727-4

Freitas, S. (2006). Using games and simulations for supporting learning. *Learning, Media and Technology*, *31*(4), 343–358. doi:10.1080/17439880601021967

Freitas, S. d. (2018). Are Games Effective Learning Tools? A Review of Educational Games. *Journal of Educational Technology & Society*, *21*(2), 74–84.

Frissen, V., Lammes, S., De Lange, M., De Mul, J., & Raessens, J. (2015). *Homo ludens 2.0: Play, media, and identity.* Academic Press.

Frith, U. (1989). *Autism: Explaining the enigma.* Blackwell Publishing.

Frutos-Pascual, M., Zapirain, B. G., & Buldian, K. C. (2014). Adaptive cognitive rehabilitation interventions based on serious games for children with ADHD using biofeedback techniques: assessment and evaluation. *Proceedings of the 8th International Conference on Pervasive Computing Technologies for Healthcare*, 321–324. 10.4108/icst.pervasivehealth.2014.255249

Fu, F. L., Su, R. C., & Yu, S. C. (2009). EGameFlow: A scale to measure learners' enjoyment of e-learning games. *Computers & Education*, *52*(1), 101–112. doi:10.1016/j.compedu.2008.07.004

Gabarron, E., Schopf, T., Serrano, J. A., Fernandez-Luque, L., & Dorronzoro, E. (2012). Gamification Strategy on Prevention of STDs for Youth. *Studies in Health Technology and Informatics*, *192*, 1066–1066. PMID:23920840

Gabriele, L., Bertacchini, F., Tavernise, A., Leticia, V. C., Pantano, P., & Bilotta, E. (2019). Lesson Planning by Computational Thinking Skills in Italian Pre-service Teachers. *Informatics in Education*, *18*(1), 69–104. doi:10.15388/infedu.2019.04

Gabriele, L., Marocco, D., Bertacchini, F., Pantano, P., & Bilotta, E. (2017). An educational robotics lab to investigate cognitive strategies and to foster learning in an arts and humanities course degree. *International Journal of Online Engineering*, *13*(04), 7–19. doi:10.3991/ijoe.v13i04.6962

Gagné, M., & Deci, E. L. (2005). Self-determination theory and work motivation. *Journal of Organizational Behavior*, *26*(4), 331–362. doi:10.1002/job.322

Gaitán, V. (2013). *Gamification: fun learning.* https://www.educativa.com/blog-articulos/gamificacion-el-aprendizaje-divertido/

Gale, I. N. (2006). *Managed Aquifer Recharge: Lessons Learned from The Agrar Study.* Academic Press.

Galicia, C. de E. (2021). *Virtual Emergency and Evacuation Simulator*. http://www.prevencion.ceg.es/modulos/senalizacion/index.html

Gamasutra. (2021). *Hazmat*. http://www.gamasutra.com

Gamito, P., Oliveira, J., Alghazzawi, D., Fardoun, H., Rosa, P., Sousa, T., Maia, I., Morais, D., Lopes, P., & Brito, R. (2017). The Art Gallery Test: A Preliminary Comparison between Traditional Neuropsychological and Ecological VR-Based Tests. *Frontiers in Psychology*, 8, 1–8. doi:10.3389/fpsyg.2017.01911 PMID:29204128

Gamito, P., Oliveira, J., Alves, C., Santos, N., Coelho, C., & Brito, R. (2020). Virtual Reality-Based Cognitive Stimulation to Improve Cognitive Functioning in Community Elderly: A Controlled Study. *Cyberpsychology, Behavior, and Social Networking*, 23(3), 150–156. doi:10.1089/cyber.2019.0271 PMID:32031888

Gamito, P., Oliveira, J., Morais, D., Coelho, C., Santos, N., Alves, C., Galamba, A., Soeiro, M., Yerra, M., French, H., Talmers, L., Gomes, T., & Brito, R. (2019). Cognitive Stimulation of Elderly Individuals with Instrumental Virtual Reality-Based Activities of Daily Life: Pre-Post Treatment Study. *Cyberpsychology, Behavior, and Social Networking*, 22(1), 69–75. doi:10.1089/cyber.2017.0679 PMID:30040477

Gao, F., Li, L., & Sun, Y. (2020). A systematic review of mobile game-based learning in STEM education. *Educational Technology Research and Development*, 68(4), 1791–1827. doi:10.100711423-020-09787-0

Garrett, B., Taverner, T., Gromala, D., Tao, G., Cordingley, E., & Sun, C. (2018). Virtual reality clinical research: Promises and challenges. *JMIR Serious Games*, 6(4), e10839. doi:10.2196/10839 PMID:30333096

Garris, R., Ahlers, R., & Driskell, J. E. (2002). Games, motivation, and learning: A research and practice model. *Simulation & Gaming*, 33(4), 441–467. doi:10.1177/1046878102238607

Gašević, D., Dawson, S., & Siemens, G. (2015). Let's not forget: Learning analytics are about learning. *TechTrends*, 59(1), 64–71. doi:10.100711528-014-0822-x

Ge, X., & Ifenthaler, D. (2018). Designing Engaging Educational Games and Assessing Engagement in Game-Based Learning. In Gamification in Education: Breakthroughs in Research and Practice (pp. 1-19). IGI Global. doi:10.4018/978-1-5225-5198-0.ch001

Gee, J. P. (2003). What video games have to teach us about learning and literacy. Palgrave Macmillan.

Gee, J. P. (2008). Learning and games. *The Ecology of Games: Connecting Youth, Games, and Learning*, 21–40. doi:10.1162/dmal.9780262693646.021

Gee, J. P. (2003). *What video games have to teach us about language and literacy*. Palgrave Macmillan.

Gee, J. P. (2003). What video games have to teach us about learning and literacy. *Computers in Entertainment*, 1(1), 20. doi:10.1145/950566.950595

Gee, J. P. (2004). *What video games have to teach us about learning and literacy*. Palgrave Macmillan.

Gee, J. P. (2005). Learning by design: Good video games as learning machines. *E-Learning and Digital Media*, 2(1), 5–16. doi:10.2304/elea.2005.2.1.5

Geithner, S., & Menzel, D. (2016). Effectiveness of Learning Through Experience and Reflection in a Project Management Simulation. *Simulation & Gaming*, 47(2), 228–256. doi:10.1177/1046878115624312

Gentile, D. A., & Walsh, D. A. (2002). A normative study of family media habits. *Journal of Applied Developmental Psychology*, 23(2), 157–178. doi:10.1016/S0193-3973(02)00102-8

Georgopoulos, A., Kontogianni, G., Koutsaftis, C., & Skamantzari, M. (2017). Serious games at the service of cultural heritage and tourism. In V. Katsoni, A. Upadhya, & A. Stratigea (Eds.), *Tourism, Culture and Heritage in a Smart Economy* (pp. 3–18). Springer., doi:10.1007/978-3-319-47732-9_1

Gerber, A., & Götz, U. (2020). *Architectonics of Game Spaces*. Transcript Verlag., doi:10.14361/9783839448021

Ghoman, S. K., Cutumisu, M., Schmölzer, G. M. (2020a). Using the RETAIN neonatal resuscitation game to train and assess health care professionals' competence in an observational study design. *SAGE Research Methods Cases: Medicine and Health.* doi:10.4135/9781529734461

Ghoman, S. K., Cutumisu, M., & Schmölzer, G. M. (2020b). Simulation-based summative assessment of neonatal resuscitation providers using the RETAIN serious board game - A pilot study. *Frontiers in Pediatrics, 8,* 1–14. doi:10.3389/fped.2020.00014 PMID:32083041

Ghoman, S. K., Cutumisu, M., & Schmölzer, G. M. (2020c). Digital simulation improves, maintains, and helps transfer healthcare providers' neonatal resuscitation knowledge. *Frontiers in Pediatrics: Neonatology, 8,* 599638. Advance online publication. doi:10.3389/fped.2020.599638 PMID:33537263

Ghoman, S. K., Cutumisu, M., & Schmölzer, G. M. (2020d). Using the RETAIN tabletop simulator as a summative assessment tool for neonatal resuscitation healthcare professionals: A pilot study. *Frontiers in Pediatrics: Neonatology, 8,* 569776. doi:10.3389/fped.2020.569776 PMID:33224907

Ghoman, S. K., Patel, S. D., Cutumisu, M., von Hauff, P., Jeffery, T., Brown, M. R. G., & Schmölzer, G. M. (2020). Serious games, a game changer in teaching neonatal resuscitation? A review. *Archives of Disease in Childhood. Fetal and Neonatal Edition, 105*(1), 98–107. doi:10.1136/archdischild-2019-317011 PMID:31256010

Ghoman, S. K., & Schmölzer, G. M. (2020). The RETAIN simulation-based serious game— A review of the literature. *Healthcare (Basel), 8*(1), 3–3. doi:10.3390/healthcare8010003 PMID:31877882

Gibbons, P. (2015). *Scaffolding language, scaffolding learning: Teaching English language learners in the mainstream classroom.* Heinemann.

Giessen, H. (2015). Serious games effects: An Overview. *Procedia: Social and Behavioral Sciences, 17,* 2240–2244. doi:10.1016/j.sbspro.2015.01.881

Gillard, S. (2009). Soft Skills and Technical Expertise of Effective Project Managers. *Proceedings of the 2009 InSITE Conference.* 10.28945/3378

Girone, M., Burdea, G., Bouzit, M., Popescu, V., & Deutsch, J. E. (2000). Orthopedic rehabilitation using the "Rutgers ankle" interface. *Studies in Health Technology and Informatics, 70,* 89–95. PMID:10977590

Gloria, A., Belloti, F., Berta, R., & Lavagnino, E. (2014, January). Serious Games for education and training. *International Journal of Serious Games, 1*(1). Advance online publication. doi:10.17083/ijsg.v1i1.11

GMV. (2021). *Antari by GMV.* https://www.gmv.com/en/Products/antari_ehealth_epidemiology_solutions/antari_tele_rehab/

Göbel, S., Hardy, S., Wendel, V., Mehm, F., & Steinmetz, R. (2010). Serious games for health - Personalized exergames. *MM'10 - Proceedings of the ACM Multimedia 2010 International Conference,* 1663–1666. 10.1145/1873951.1874316

Goehle, G. (2013). Gamification and Web-based Homework. *PRIMUS (Terre Haute, Ind.), 23*(3), 234–246. doi:10.1080/10511970.2012.736451

Goh, K.-I., Cusick, M. E., Valle, D., Childs, B., Vidal, M., & Barabási, A.-L. (2007). The human disease network. *Proceedings of the National Academy of Sciences of the United States of America, 104*(21), 8685–8690. doi:10.1073/pnas.0701361104 PMID:17502601

Gómez-Carrasco, C. J., Monteagudo-Fernández, J., Moreno-Vera, J. R., & Sainz-Gómez, M. (2019). Effects of a gamification and flipped-classroom program for teachers in training on motivation and learning perception. *Education Sciences, 9*(4), 299. doi:10.3390/educsci9040299

Gomez, M. J., Ruipérez-Valiente, J. A., Martínez, P. A., & Kim, Y. J. (2021). Applying Learning Analytics to Detect Sequences of Actions and Common Errors in a Geometry Game. *Sensors (Basel), 21*(4), 1025. doi:10.339021041025 PMID:33546167

Gonçalves, R. S., & Rodrigues, L. A. O. (2019a). Development of a Novel Parallel Structure for Gait Rehabilitation. In Handbook of Research on Advanced Mechatronic Systems and Intelligent Robotics (pp. 42–81). doi:10.4018/978-1-7998-0137-5.ch003

Gonçalves, R. S., Carvalho, J. C. M., & Lobato, F. S. (2016). Design of a robotic device actuated by cables for human lower limb rehabilitation using self-adaptive differential evolution and robust optimization. *Bioscience Journal*, 1689–1702. doi:10.14393/BJ-v32n1a2016-32436

Gonçalves, R. S., Hamilton, T., Daher, A. R., Hirai, H., & Hermano, I. (2017a). MIT-Skywalker: Considerations on the Design of a Body Weight Support System. *Journal of Neuroengineering and Rehabilitation, 14*(1), 1–12. doi:10.118612984-017-0302-6 PMID:28877750

Gonçalves, R. S., Hamilton, T., Daher, A. R., Hirai, H., & Hermano, I. (2017b). MIT-Skywalker : Evaluating Comfort of Bicycle / Saddle Seat. *2017 International Conference on Rehabilitation Robotics (ICORR)*, 516–520. 10.1109/ICORR.2017.8009300

Gonçalves, R. S., & Rodrigues, L. A. O. (2021). Development of nonmotorized mechanisms for lower limb rehabilitation. *Robotica*, 1–18. doi:10.1017/S0263574721000412

Gooding, D. (1990). *Experiment and the making of meaning. Human agency in scientific observation and experiment.* Kluwer Academic Publishers. doi:10.1007/978-94-009-0707-2

Goodlander, G. (2009). Fictional Press Releases and Fake Artifacts: How the Smithsonian American Art Museum is Letting Game Players Redefine the Rules. In J. Trant & D. Bearman (Eds.), *Museums and the Web 2009: Proceedings*. Archives & Museum Informatics. https://www.archimuse.com/mw2009/papers/goodlander/goodlander.html

Goodman, A., Joyce, R., & Smith, J. P. (2011). The long shadow cast by childhood physical and mental problems on adult life. *Proceedings of the National Academy of Sciences of the United States of America, 108*(15), 6032–6037. doi:10.1073/pnas.1016970108 PMID:21444801

Gopaladesikan, S. (2013, January 8). How to Use Badges for Positive Growth. *Gamification.co*. https://www.gamification.co/2013/01/08/how-to-use-badges-for-positive-growth/

Gordillo, A., Gallego, D., Barra, E., & Quemada, J. (2013). The city as a learning gamified platform. In *Frontiers in Education Conference* (pp. 372-378). IEEE. 10.1109/FIE.2013.6684850

Gosselin, C. M., Masouleh, M. T., Duchaine, V., Richard, P.-L., Foucault, S., & Kong, X. (2007). Parallel Mechanisms of the Multipteron Family: Kinematic Architectures and Benchmarking. *Proceedings 2007 IEEE International Conference on Robotics and Automation*, 555–560. 10.1109/ROBOT.2007.363045

Gosselin, C., Laliberté, T., & Veillette, A. (2015). Singularity-Free Kinematically Redundant Planar Parallel Mechanisms With Unlimited Rotational Capability. *IEEE Transactions on Robotics, 31*(2), 457–467. doi:10.1109/TRO.2015.2409433

Graafland, M., & Schijven, M. (2018). How Serious Games Will Improve Healthcare. In H. Rivas & K. Wac (Eds.), Digital health: scaling healthcare to the world (pp. 137-157). Springer International Publishing. doi:10.1007/978-3-319-61446-5_10

Graafland, M., Bemelman, W. A., & Schijven, M. P. (2015). Appraisal of Face and Content Validity of a Serious Game Improving Situational Awareness in Surgical Training. *Journal of Laparoendoscopic & Advanced Surgical Techniques. Part A., 25*(1), 1–7. doi:10.1089/lap.2014.0043 PMID:25607899

Graafland, M., Schraagen, J., & Schijven, M. (2012). Systematic review of serious games for medical education and surgical skills training. *British Journal of Surgery, 99*(10), 1322–1330. doi:10.1002/bjs.8819 PMID:22961509

Graeber, D. (2015). *The Utopia of Rules: On Technology, Stupidity, and the Secret Joys of Bureaucracy.* Melville House.

Grand Ages: Medieval . (2015). [Video Game]. Kalypso Media Digital.

Granic, I., Lobel, A., & Engels, R. C. (2014). The benefits of playing video games. *The American Psychologist, 69*(1), 66–78. doi:10.1037/a0034857 PMID:24295515

Granström, H. (2013). *Elements in games for virtual heritage applications* [Master Degree Project in Informatics Dissertation]. University of Skövde. http://www.diva-portal.org/smash/get/diva2:627227/FULLTEXT01.pdf

Grant, E. S., Shankararaman, V., & Loong, J. L. K. (2014, December). Experimenting with Gamification in the Classroom. In *2014 IEEE 6th Conference on Engineering Education (ICEED)* (pp. 79-83). IEEE. 10.1109/ICEED.2014.7194692

Gray, D., Brown, S., & Macanufo, J. (2010). *Gamestorming: A Playbook for Innovators, Rulebreakers, and Changemaker.* O'Reilly Media, Inc.

Green, C. S., & Bavelier, D. (2003). Action video game modifies visual selective attention. *Nature, 423*(6939), 534–537. doi:10.1038/nature01647 PMID:12774121

Grenier, R. (2010). All work and no play makes for a dull museum visitor. *New Directions for Adult and Continuing Education, 127*(127), 77–85. doi:10.1002/ace.383

Grubic, N., Badovinac, S., & Johri, A. (2020). Student mental health in the midst of the COVID-19 pandemic: A call for further research and immediate solutions. *The International Journal of Social Psychiatry, 66*(5), 517–518. doi:10.1177/0020764020925108 PMID:32364039

Grynszpan, O., Weiss, P. L., Perez-Diaz, F., & Gal, E. (2014). Innovative technology-based interventions for autism spectrum disorders: A meta-analysis. *Autism, 18*(4), 346–361. doi:10.1177/1362361313476767 PMID:24092843

Guestrin, E. D., & Eizenman, M. (2006). General theory of remote gaze estimation using the pupil centre and conreal reflections. *IEEE Transactions on Biomedical Engineering, 53*(6), 1124–1133. doi:10.1109/TBME.2005.863952 PMID:16761839

Guillén-Climent, S., Garzo, A., Muñoz-Alcaraz, M. N., Casado-Adam, P., Arcas-Ruiz-Ruano, J., Mejías-Ruiz, M., & Mayordomo-Riera, F. J. (2021). A usability study in patients with stroke using MERLIN, a robotic system based on serious games for upper limb rehabilitation in the home setting. *Journal of Neuroengineering and Rehabilitation, 18*(1), 41. doi:10.118612984-021-00837-z PMID:33622344

Guzman Mendoza, J. E., Munoz Arteaga, J., Cardona Reyes, H., & Zapata Gonzalez, A. (2019). Digital Divide Strategy Based-on ICT Services Model. *Proceedings - 2019 International Conference on Inclusive Technologies and Education, CONTIE 2019.* 10.1109/CONTIE49246.2019.00013

Habgood, M. P. J., & Ainsworth, S. E. (2011). Motivating Children to Learn Effectively: Exploring the Value of Intrinsic Integration in Educational Games. *Journal of the Learning Sciences, 20*(2), 169–206. doi:10.1080/10508406.2010.508029

Haidrani, L. (2015). Beat Panic app. Nursing Standard (Royal College of Nursing (Great Britain): 1987), 30(15), 29.

Halimi, S. (2014). A new humanism? Heritage and future prospects. *International Review of Education, 60*(3), 311–325.

Hall, S. (2020). *How COVID-19 is taking gaming and esports to the next level.* World Economic Forum. https://www.weforum.org/agenda/2020/05/covid-19-taking-gaming-and-esports-next-level/

Hamari, J., Koivisto, J., & Sarsa, H. (2014). Does Gamification Work? -- A Literature Review of Empirical Studies on Gamification. In *2014 47th Hawaii International Conference on System Sciences* (pp. 3025–3034). IEEE. 10.1109/HICSS.2014.377

Hamari, J., Koivisto, J., & Sarsa, H. (2014, January). Does gamification work? A literature review of empirical studies on gamification. In *2014 47th Hawaii international conference on system sciences* (pp. 3025-3034). IEEE.

Hamari, J. (2013). Transforming homo economicus into homo ludens: A field experiment on gamification in a utilitarian peer-to-peer trading service. *Electronic Commerce Research and Applications, 12*(4), 236–245. doi:10.1016/j.elerap.2013.01.004

Hamari, J., Shernoff, D. J., Rowe, E., Coller, B., Asbell-Clarke, J., & Edwards, T. (2016). Challenging games help students learn: An empirical study on engagement, flow and immersion in game-based learning. *Computers in Human Behavior, 54*, 170–179. doi:10.1016/j.chb.2015.07.045

Hamstra, S. J., Brydges, R., Hatala, R., Zendejas, B., & Cook, D. A. (2014). Reconsidering Fidelity in Simulation-Based Training. *Academic Medicine, 89*(3), 387–392. doi:10.1097/ACM.0000000000000130 PMID:24448038

Hansen, B. H., Oerbeck, B., Skirbekk, B., Petrovski, B. É., & Kristensen, H. (2018). Neurodevelopmental disorders: Prevalence and comorbidity in children referred to mental health services. *Nordic Journal of Psychiatry, 72*(4), 285–291.

Hanus, M. D., & Fox, J. (2015). Assessing the effects of gamification in the classroom: A longitudinal study on intrinsic motivation, social comparison, satisfaction, effort, and academic performance. *Computers & Education, 80*, 152–161. doi:10.1016/j.compedu.2014.08.019

Happé, F., & Frith, U. (2006). The weak coherence account: Detail-focused cognitive style in autism spectrum disorders. *Journal of Autism and Developmental Disorders, 36*(1), 5–25.

Haring, P., Chakinska, D., & Ritterfeld, U. (2011). Understanding serious gaming. A psychological perspective. In P. Felicia (Ed.), *Handbook of Research on Improving Learning and Motivation through Educational Games: Multidisciplinary Approaches* (pp. 29–50). IGI Global. doi:10.4018/978-1-60960-495-0.ch020

Harpin, V., Mazzone, L., Raynaud, J. P., Kahle, J., & Hodgkins, P. (2016). Long-Term Outcomes of ADHD: A Systematic Review of Self-Esteem and Social Function. *Journal of Attention Disorders, 20*(4), 295–305. doi:10.1177/1087054713486516 PMID:23698916

Harteveld, C. (2011). Triadic Game Design: Balancing Reality, Meaning, and Play. Springer. doi:10.1007/978-1-84996-157-8

Harteveld, C., Guimarães, R., Mayer, I. S., & Bidarra, R. (2010). Balancing play, meaning and reality: The design philosophy of levee patroller. *Simulation & Gaming, 41*(3), 316–340. doi:10.1177/1046878108331237

Hartsell, T. (2017). Digital Storytelling: An Alternative Way of Expressing Oneself. *International Journal of Information and Communication Technology Education, 13*(1), 72–82. doi:10.4018/IJICTE.2017010107

Hasselmo, M. E. (2001). Neural Systems: Models of Behavioral Functions. In International Encyclopedia of the Social & Behavioral Sciences (pp. 10575–10578). Elsevier.

Hassenzahl, M., Burmester, M., & Koller, F. (2003). AttrakDiff: A questionnaire to measure perceived hedonic and pragmatic quality. *Mensch & Computer, 57*, 187–196.

Hassenzahl, M. (2010). *Technology for all the right reasons*. Morgan and Claypool.

Hays, R. T., & Singer, M. J. (1989). Simulation fidelity in training system design: Bridging the gap between reality and training. Springer-Verlag. doi:10.1007/978-1-4612-3564-4

Heldal, I. (2016). Simulation and Serious Games in Emergency Management, *Proceedings of the 2016 International Conference on Virtual Systems and Multimedia*, 201–209.

Hembree, E. A., Rauch, S. A. M., & Foa, E. B. (2003). Beyond the manual: The ' 'insider's guide to Prolonged Exposure therapy for PTSD. *Cognitive and Behavioral Practice, 10*(1), 22–30. doi:10.1016/S1077-7229(03)80005-6

Henriot, C., & Molines, N. (2019). Urban serious games and digital technology. *NETCOM call for papers*. https://journals.openedition.org/netcom/3667?lang=en#actualite-3667

Hermon, R., & Williams, P. A. H. (2014). Big data in healthcare: What is it used for? *Australian EHealth Informatics and Security Conference*.

Herz, J. C. (2002). Gaming the System. In What Higher Education Can Learn from Multiplayer Online Worlds. In R. LM Devlin, Internet and the University: 2001 Forum (pp. 169-191). Academic Press.

Hesse, S., Schmidt, H., Werner, C., & Bardeleben, A. (2003). Upper and lower extremity robotic devices for rehabilitation and for studying motor control. In Current Opinion in Neurology (Vol. 16, Issue 6, pp. 705–710). Lippincott Williams & Wilkins. doi:10.1097/00019052-200312000-00010

Heugh, K., & Mohamed, N. (2020). Approaches to language in education for migrants and refugees in the Asia-Pacific region. In *UNESCO Bangkok*. UNESCO-UNICEF.

Heutte, J., Fenouillet, F., Kaplan, J., Martin-Krumm, C., & Bachelet, R. (2016). The EduFlow Model: A Contribution Toward the Study of Optimal Learning Environments. In L. Harmat, F. Ø. Andersen, F. Ullén, J. Wright, & G. Sadlo (Eds.), *Flow Experience: Empirical Research and Applications* (pp. 127–143). doi:10.1007/978-3-319-28634-1_9

Hill, E. L. (2004). Evaluating the theory of executive dysfunction in autism. *Developmental Review, 24*(2), 189–233.

Hill, E. L. (2004). Executive dysfunction in autism. *Trends in Cognitive Sciences, 8*(1), 26–32. doi:10.1016/j.tics.2003.11.003 PMID:14697400

Hina, M. D., & Dourlens, A. R. S. (2016). Serious Gaming: Autonomy and Better Health for the Elderly. *Proceedings of the 17th International Conference on Computer Systems and Technologies*. 10.1145/2983468.2983519

Hinshaw, S. P., Owens, E. B., Zalecki, C., Huggins, S. P., Montenegro-Nevado, A. J., Schrodek, E., & Swanson, E. N. (2012). Prospective follow-up of girls with attention-deficit/hyperactivity disorder into early adulthood: Continuing impairment includes elevated risk for suicide attempts and self-injury. *Journal of Consulting and Clinical Psychology, 80*(6), 1041.

Hissrich, L. (Showrunner, Writer, Executive Producer). (2019-2021). *The Witcher* [Television miniseries]. Netflix.

Historion (2002). [Video Game]. Klett Softwareverlag GmbH.

Hoekstra, A. Y. (2012). Computer-supported games and role plays in teaching water management. *Hydrology and Earth Systems Sciences,* 2885-2994.

Holdsworth, E., Bowen, E., Brown, S., & Howat, D. (2014). Client engagement in psychotherapeutic treatment and associations with client characteristics, therapist characteristics, and treatment factors. *Clinical Psychology Review, 34*(5), 428–450. doi:10.1016/j.cpr.2014.06.004 PMID:25000204

Holliday, E. L. (2021). *Breaking the Magic Circle: Using a Persuasive Game to Build Empathy For Nursing Staff and Increase Citizen Responsibility During a Pandemic. In CHI PLAY '21.* ACM. doi:10.1145/3450337.3483511

Holman, C., Aguilar, S., & Fishman, B. (2013, April). GradeCraft: What can we learn from a game-inspired learning management system? In *Proceedings of the third international conference on learning analytics and knowledge* (pp. 260-264). 10.1145/2460296.2460350

Holmqvist, K., & Andersson, R. (2017). *Eye tracking: A comprehensive guide to methods, paradigms and measures* (2nd ed.). Lund Eye-Tracking Institute.

Holstein, K., McLaren, B. M., & Aleven, V. (2017). Intelligent tutors as teachers' aides: Exploring teacher needs for real-time analytics in blended classrooms. *ACM International Conference Proceeding Series,* 257–266. 10.1145/3027385.3027451

Homer, B. D., Raffaele, C., & Henderson, H. (2020). Games as Playful Learning: Implications of Developmental Theory for Game-Based Learning. In J. L. Plass, R. E. Mayer, & B. D. Homer (Eds.), *Handbook of Game-Based Learning* (pp. 25–52). MIT Press.

Hood, V. (2018, March 5). Kingdom Come: Deliverance cost over $36 million to make. *PC Games.* https://www.pcgamesn.com/kingdom-come-deliverance/kingdom-come-deliverance-cost-budget

Horowitz, L. M., Thurm, A., & Farmer, C. (2018). Autism and Developmental Disorders Inpatient Research Collaborative. Talking about death or suicide: Prevalence and clinical correlates in youth with autism spectrum disorder in the psychiatric inpatient setting. *Journal of Autism and Developmental Disorders, 48*(11), 3702–3710.

Howard, M., Hopkinson, P., & Miemczyk, J. (2019). The regenerative supply chain: A framework for developing circular economy indicators. *International Journal of Production Research, 57*(23), 7300–7318. doi:10.1080/00207543.2018.1524166

Howieson, D. B., & Lezak, M. D. (2002). The neuropsychological evaluation. In S. C. Yudofsky & R. E. Hales (Eds.), *The American Psychiatric Publishing textbook of neuropsychiatry and clinical neurosciences* (pp. 217–244). American Psychiatric Publishing, Inc.

Hoydedata. (n.d.). https://hoydedata.no

Huang, H.-M., Rauch, U., & Liaw, S.-S. (2010). Investigating learners' attitudes toward virtual reality learning environments: Based on a constructivist approach. *Computers & Education, 55*(3), 1171–1182.

Huang, H. M., Rauch, U., & Liaw, S. S. (2010). Investigating learners' attitudes toward virtual reality learning environments: Based on a constructivist approach. *Computers & Education, 55*(3), 1171–1182. doi:10.1016/j.compedu.2010.05.014

Huddleston, T., Niessen, J., & Tjaden, J. T. (2013). Using EU indicators of immigrant integration: Final Report for Directorate-General for Home Affairs. Home Affairs, European Commission.

Hugo, J., & Ganguli, M. (2014). Dementia and Cognitive Impairment: Epidemiology, Diagnosis and Traetment. *Clinics in Geriatric Medicine, 30*(3), 421–442. doi:10.1016/j.cger.2014.04.001 PMID:25037289

Huizinga, J. (1997). Homo Ludens. A person who plays. Articles on the history of culture. Moscow: Progress-Tradition.

Huizinga, J. (1948). *Homo Ludens: A Study of the Play-Element in Culture*. Routledge & Kegan Paul.

Huizinga, J. (2008). *Homo Ludens: O Jogo como Elemento na Cultura*. Perspectiva.

Hu, L., Zhang, L., Yin, R., Li, Z., Shen, J., Tan, H., Wu, J., & Zhou, W. (2021). NEOGAMES: A serious computer game that improves long-term knowledge retention of neonatal resuscitation in undergraduate medical students. *Frontiers in Pediatrics*, *9*, 645776. doi:10.3389/fped.2021.645776 PMID:33968850

Human Resource Machine [Digital game]. (2015). *Tomorrow Corporation*. Retrieved from STEAM: https://store.steampowered.com/app/375820/Human_Resource_Machine/

Hung, K., Zhang, Y.-T., & Tai, B. (2004). Wearable medical devices for tele-home healthcare. *The 26th Annual International Conference of the IEEE Engineering in Medicine and Biology Society, 2*, 5384–5387.

Hung, H., Yang, J. C., Hwang, G., Chu, H., & Wang, C. (2018). A scoping review of research on digital game-based language learning. *Computers & Education*, *126*, 89–104. doi:10.1016/j.compedu.2018.07.001

Hunicke, R., Leblanc, M., & Zubek, R. (2004). MDA: A Formal Approach to Game Design and Game Research. In *Proceedings of 19th National Conference on Artificial Intelligence - AAAI Workshop on Challenges in Game AI*. AAAI Press.

Hutchby, I., & O'Reilly, M. (2010). ' 'Children's participation and the familial moral order in family therapy. *Discourse Studies*, *12*(1), 49–64. doi:10.1177/1461445609357406

Hu, W., Li, G., Sun, Y., Jiang, G., Kong, J., Ju, Z., & Jiang, D. (2017). A Review of Upper and Lower Limb Rehabilitation Training Robot. In Y. Huang, H. Wu, H. Liu, & Z. Yin (Eds.), *Intelligent Robotics and Applications* (pp. 570–580). Springer International Publishing. doi:10.1007/978-3-319-65289-4_54

Ikeda, D. (2010). *A new humanism: The university addresses of Daisaku Ikeda*. Bloomsbury Publishing.

Imbeault, F. F., Bouchard, B., & Bouzouane, A. (2011). Serious games in cognitive training for Alzheimer's patients. *2011 IEEE 1st International Conference on Serious Games and Applications for Health (SeGAH)*. 10.1109/SeGAH.2011.6165447

Imlig-Iten, N., & Petko, D. (2018). Comparing Serious Games and Educational Simulations: Effects on Enjoyment, Deep Thinking, Interest and Cognitive Learning Gains. *Simulation & Gaming*, *49*(4), 401–422. doi:10.1177/1046878118779088

Infocomm Media Development Authority. (2019, August 8). *Mobile Penetration Rate*. Data.Gov.Sg. https://data.gov.sg/dataset/mobile-penetration-rate

Infocomm Media Development Authority. (2020, March 11). *Infocomm Usage-Households and Individuals*. Infocomm Media Development Authority. https://www.imda.gov.sg/infocomm-media-landscape/research-and-statistics/infocomm-usage-households-and-individuals

Ingolia, N. T., & Murray, A. W. (2007). Positive-feedback loops as a flexible biological module. *Current Biology*, *17*(8), 668–677.

Inkster, B., Sarda, S., & Subramanian, V. (2018). An Empathy-Driven, Conversational Artificial Intelligence Agent (Wysa) for Digital Mental Well-Being: Real-World Data Evaluation Mixed-Methods Study. *JMIR mHealth and uHealth*, *6*(11), e12106. doi:10.2196/12106 PMID:30470676

Instituto Nacional de Estatística [National Institute of Statistics]. (2019). *Estatísticas Demográficas* [Demographic Statistics]. https://www.ine.pt/ngt_server/attachfileu.jsp?look_parentBoui=463528670&att_display=n&att_download=y

InterNations. (2021). *Expat Insider 2021: The year of uncertainty*. InterNations.

Ip, H. H., Wong, S. W., Chan, D. F., Byrne, J., Li, C., Yuan, V. S., ... Wong, J. Y. (2018). Enhance emotional and social adaptation skills for children with autism spectrum disorder: A virtual reality enabled approach. *Computers & Education*, *117*, 1–15.

Irfan, S. S., & Kanat, E. (2013). Gamification of Emergency Response Training. In *ISI 2013* (pp. 134–136). IEEE.

Irshad, S., & Perkis, A. (2020). *Serious Storytelling in Virtual Reality: The Role of Digital Narrative to Trigger Mediated Presence and Behavioral Responses. In CHI PLAY '20 EA.* ACM. doi:10.1145/3383668.3419908

Isaac, J., & Babu, S. V. (2016, March). Supporting computational thinking through gamification. In *2016 IEEE Symposium on 3D User Interfaces (3DUI)* (pp. 245-246). IEEE. 10.1109/3DUI.2016.7460062

ISDR. (2021). *Stop Disasters Retrieved.* https://www.stopdisastersgame.org/home.html

Ismail, A. A. (2019). Immigrant children, educational performance and public policy: A capability approach. *Journal of International Migration and Integration*, *20*(3), 717–734. doi:10.100712134-018-0630-9

ISO. (2010). *Ergonomics of human system interaction - Part 210: Human-centred design for interactive systems.* https://www.iso.org/obp/ui/#iso:std:iso:9241:-210:ed-1:v1:en

Israel-Fishelson, R., & Hershkovitz, A. (2020). Persistence in a Game-Based Learning Environment: The Case of Elementary School Students Learning Computational Thinking. *Journal of Educational Computing Research*, *58*(5), 891–918. doi:10.1177/0735633119887187

Jacey, H. (2010). *The woman in the story.* Michael Wiese Productions.

Jackson, P. (2001-2003). (Director). *The Lord of the Rings* [Feature film series]. New Line Cinema, WingNut Films, The Saul Zaentz Company.

Jaiswal, D. (n.d.). *Watershed Management: Meaning, Types, Steps and Programmes.* https://www.yourarticlelibrary.com/watershed-management/watershed-management-meaning-types-steps-and-programmes/77309

Japiassú, P., & Marcondes, D. (2001). Dicionário Básico de Filosofia (3rd ed.). Rio de Janeiro: Zahar.

Jaques, N., Conati, C., Harley, J., & Azevedo, R. (2014). Predicting Affect from Gaze Data during Interaction with an Intelligent Tutoring System. In *Proceedings 12th International Conference, Intelligent Tutoring Systems 2014, Honolulu, HI, USA.* (pp. 29–38). Springer International Publishing. 10.1007/978-3-319-07221-0_4

Jenkins, P. *(Director).* (2021). *Wonderwoman* [Feature film]. Warner Bros, Atlas Entertainment & Cruel and Unusual Films.

Jennings, B. (2001). From the Urban to the Civic: The Moral Possibilities of the City. *Journal of Urban Health*, *78*(1), 88–103. doi:10.1093/jurban/78.1.88 PMID:11368207

Jeong, E. J., & Lee, H. R. (2015). Addictive use due to personality: Focused on big five personality traits and game addiction. *International Journal of Psychology and Behavioral Sciences*, *9*(6), 2032–2036.

Jeong, K. Y., & Bozkurt, I. (2014). Evaluating a Project Management Simulation Training Exercise. *Simulation & Gaming*, *45*(2), 183–203. doi:10.1177/1046878113518481

Jerdan, S. W., Grindle, M., van Woerden, H. C., & Kamel Boulos, M. N. (2018). Head-Mounted Virtual Reality and Mental Health: Critical Review of Current Research. *JMIR Serious Games*, *6*(3), e14. doi:10.2196/games.9226 PMID:29980500

Jiménez, A. A., Abarca, M. V., & Ramírez, E. L. (2000). When and how to use Virtual Reality in Teaching. *IE Comunicaciones: Iberoamerican Journal of Educational Informatics*, *16*, 4.

Jimenez-Hernandez, E. M., Oktaba, H., Piattini, M., Arceo, F. D. B., Revillagigedo-Tulais, A. M., & Flores-Zarco, S. V. (2016). Methodology to construct educational video games in software engineering. *Proceedings - 2016 4th International Conference in Software Engineering Research and Innovation, CONISOFT 2016*, 110–114. 10.1109/CONISOFT.2016.25

Job Simulator [Digital game]. (2016). Retrieved 07 10, 2021, from ag.ru: https://ag.ru/games/job-simulator

Johnson, L., Becker, S. A., Estrada, V., Freeman, A., Kampylis, P., Vuorikari, R., & Punie, Y. (2014). *NMC Horizon Report Europe: 2014 schools edition*. The New Media Consortium.

Johnson, W. L., & Wu, S. (2008). Assessing aptitude for learning with a serious game for foreign language and culture. *Proceedings of the ninth international conference on intelligent tutoring systems*. 10.1007/978-3-540-69132-7_55

Joint Commission. (2004). Sentinel event alert: Preventing infant death and injury during delivery. The Joint Commission, 4(4), 180-181. doi:10.1016/j.adnc.2004.08.005

Jones, A. (2019, February 13). Kingdom Come: Deliverance has sold two million copies. *PC Games*. https://www.pcgamesn.com/kingdom-come-deliverance/kingdom-come-deliverance-sales-numbers

Jonsdottir, J., Bertoni, R., Lawo, M., Montesano, A., Bowman, T., & Gabrielli, S. (2018). Serious games for arm rehabilitation of persons with multiple sclerosis. A randomized controlled pilot study. *Multiple Sclerosis and Related Disorders*, 19, 25–29. doi:10.1016/j.msard.2017.10.010 PMID:29112939

Kahoot. (2021). Available at https://kahoot.com/

Kalinke, M. (2015). The introduction of the Arthurian legend in Scandinavia. In M. Kalinke (Ed.), *The Arthur of the North* (pp. 5–21). University of Wales Press.

Kalyuga, S., & Plass, J. L. (2009). Evaluating and managing cognitive load in games. In *Handbook of research on effective electronic gaming in education* (pp. 719–737). IGI Global.

Kapell, M., & Elliott, A. (2013). *Playing with the past: digital games and the simulation of history*. Bloomsbury.

Kapp, K. M., & Boller, S. (2017, September 5). Core Dynamics: A Key Element in Instructional Game Design. *Atd Blog*. https://www.td.org/insights/core-dynamics-a-key-element-in-instructional-game-design

Kapp, K. M. (2012). *The Gamification of Learning and Instruction: Game-based Methods and Strategies for Training and Education*. John Wiley & Sons.

Kapp, K. M. (2012). *The gamification of learning and instruction: Game-based methods and strategies for training and education*. Pfieffer.

Karaca, S., Karakoc, A., Gurkan, O. C., Onan, N., & Barlas, G. U. (2020). Investigation of the online game addiction level, sociodemographic characteristics and social anxiety as risk factors for online game addiction in middle school students. *Community Mental Health Journal*, 56(5), 830–838.

Karami, B., Koushki, R., Arabgol, F., Rahmani, M., & Vahabie, A. H. (2021). Effectiveness of Virtual/Augmented Reality-based therapeutic interventions on individuals with autism spectrum disorder: A comprehensive meta-analysis. *Frontiers in Psychiatry*, 12, 887.

Karasavvidis, I. (2018). Educational Serious Games Design: An Overview. In M. Khosrow-Pour (Ed.), *Encyclopedia of Information Science and Technology* (4th ed., pp. 3287–3295). IGI Global.

Karthik, R., & Singh, A. (2019). *Machine Learning Using R. Frontiers in Artificial Intelligence and Applications* (Vol. 321). doi:10.3233/FAIA200024

Katirci, N. (2017). *The Influence of DragonBox on Student Attitudes and Understanding in 7th Grade Mathematics Classroom*. University at Albany, State University of New York. Retrieved from https://search.proquest.com/openview /967700b0c633db144a461e8fff33347d/1?pq-origsite=gscholar&cbl=18750&diss=y

Katsaliaki, K., &Mustafee, N. (2012). A survey of serious games on sustainable development. In *Proceedings of the 2012 Winter* (pp. 1-13). IEEE.

Katsoni, V., Upadhya, A., & Stratigea, A. (2016). *Tourism, culture and heritage in a smart economy*. Springer.

Ke, F., & Hsu, Y.-C. (2015). Mobile augmented-reality artifact creation as a component of mobile computer-supported collaborative learning. *The Internet and Higher Education, 26*, 33–41. doi:10.1016/j.iheduc.2015.04.003

Keinonen, T. (2009). Design contribution square. *Advanced Engineering Informatics, 23*(2), 142–148. doi:10.1016/j.aei.2008.10.002

Kekuluthotuwage, P., & Fernando, P. (2017, September). HomeSchool: An interactive educational tool for child education. In *2017 National Information Technology Conference (NITC)* (pp. 34-39). IEEE. 10.1109/NITC.2017.8285652

Kelle, S., Klemke, R., & Specht, M. (2011). Design patterns for learning games. *International Journal of Technology Enhanced Learning, 3*(6), 555–569. doi:10.1504/IJTEL.2011.045452

Kent, J., Payne, J. & Teague, C. (Directors). (2013). *The White Queen* [Television historical drama miniseries]. BBC TV.

Ker, J., & Bradley, P. (2010). Simulation in medical education. Understanding Medical Education: Evidence, Theory, and Practice, 164-180.

Kesler, S. R., Lacayo, N. J., & Jo, B. (2011). A pilot study of an online cognitive rehabilitation program for executive function skills in children with cancer-related brain injury. *Brain Injury: [BI], 25*(1), 101–112. doi:10.3109/02699052.2010.536194 PMID:21142826

Kessler, R. C., Angermeyer, M., Anthony, J. C., De Graaf, R., Demyttenaere, K., Gasquet, I., De Girolamo, G., Gluzman, S., Gureje, O., Haro, J. M., Kawakami, N., Karam, A., Levinson, D., Medina Mora, M. E., Oakley Browne, M. A., Posada-Villa, J., Stein, D. J., Adley Tsang, C. H., Aguilar-Gaxiola, S., ... Üstün, T. B. (2007). Lifetime prevalence and age-of-onset distributions of mental disorders in the World Health ' 'Organization's World Mental Health Survey Initiative. *World Psychiatry; Official Journal of the World Psychiatric Association (WPA), 6*(3), 168–176. PMID:18188442

Kessler, R. C., Berglund, P. A., Bruce, M. L., Koch, J. R., Laska, E. M., Leaf, P. J., Manderscheid, R. W., Rosenheck, R. A., Walters, E. E., & Wang, P. S. (2001). The prevalence and correlates of untreated serious mental illness. *Health Services Research, 36*(6 Pt 1), 987–1007. PMID:11775672

Kessler, R. C., Berglund, P., Demler, O., Jin, R., Merikangas, K. R., & Walters, E. E. (2005). Lifetime prevalence and age-of-onset distributions of DSM-IV disorders in the National Comorbidity Survey Replication. *Archives of General Psychiatry, 62*, 593–602.

Khalili-Mahani, N., Assadi, A., Li, K., Mirgholami, M., Rivard, M. E., Benali, H., Sawchuk, K., & De Schutter, B. (2020). Reflective and Reflexive Stress Responses of Older Adults to Three Gaming Experiences In Relation to Their Cognitive Abilities: Mixed Methods Crossover Study. *JMIR Mental Health, 7*(3), e12388. Advance online publication. doi:10.2196/12388 PMID:32213474

Khoshdel, V., Akbarzadeh, A., Naghavi, N., Sharifnezhad, A., & Souzanchi-Kashani, M. (2018). sEMG-based impedance control for lower-limb rehabilitation robot. *Intelligent Service Robotics, 11*(1), 97–108. doi:10.100711370-017-0239-4

Kiili, K. (2005). Digital game-based learning: Towards an experiential gaming model. *The Internet and Higher Education, 8*(1), 13–24. doi:10.1016/j.iheduc.2004.12.001

Kim, Y. J., & Ruipérez-Valiente, J. A. (2020). Data-driven game design: The case of difficulty in educational games. *Lecture Notes in Computer Science, 12315*, 449–454. doi:10.1007/978-3-030-57717-9_43

Kim, B., Park, H., & Baek, Y. (2009). Not just fun, but serious strategies: Using meta-cognitive strategies in game-based learning. *Computers & Education, 52*(4), 800–810. doi:10.1016/j.compedu.2008.12.004

Kimbell, L. (2009). Design practices in design thinking. *European Academy of Management, 5*, 1–24.

Kim, H., Hong, J., & Kim, S. H. (2013, October 13). Seoul Museum Week 2013: Collaboration Using Gamification. In N. Proctor & R. Cherry (Eds.), *Museums and the Web*. https://mwa2013.museumsandtheweb.com/paper/seoul-museum-week-2013-collaboration-using-gamification/

Kim, J., Agarwal, S., Marotta, K., Li, S., Leo, J., & Chau, D. H. (2019). Mixed reality for learning programming. *Proceedings of the 18th ACM International Conference on Interaction Design and Children, IDC 2019, 2*, 574–579. 10.1145/3311927.3325335

Kim, J., Jung, J., & Kim, S. (2015). The relationship of game elements, fun and flow. *Journal of Science and Technology*, (8), 405–411.

Kim, S., Song, K., Lockee, B., & Burton, J. (2018). What is Gamification in Learning and Education? In *Gamification in Learning and Education* (pp. 25–38). Springer International Publishing., doi:10.1007/978-3-319-47283-6_4

Kim, Y. J. (2015). Opportunities and Challenges in Assessing and Supporting Creativity in Video Games. *Video Games and Creativity*.

Kim, Y. J., Almond, R. G., & Shute, V. J. (2016). Applying Evidence-Centered Design for the Development of Game-Based Assessments in Physics Playground. *International Journal of Testing, 16*(2), 142–163. doi:10.1080/15305058.2015.1108322

Kim, Y. J., & Shute, V. J. (2015). The interplay of game elements with psychometric qualities, learning, and enjoyment in game-based assessment. *Computers & Education, 87*, 340–356. doi:10.1016/j.compedu.2015.07.009

King, N. (2021, February 1). Serious Games Guide: Everything You Need To Know In 2021. *Chaostheorygames*. https://www.chaostheorygames.com/blog/serious-games-guide-everything-you-need-to-know-in-2021

Kingdom Come: Deliverance . (2018). [Video Game]. Warhorse Studios s.r.o.

Kirizleev, A. (2014). *Classification of computer games genres*. Retrieved 07 10, 2021, from GamesIsArt: https://gamesisart.ru/janr.html

Kirriemuir, J.K. & McFarlane, A. (2004). *Literature Review in games and learning*. University of Bristol: FutureLab Series 8.

Kirriemuir, J., & Mcfarlane, A. (2004). *Literature Review in Games and Learning*. Futurelab.

Kisekka, V., Han, W., & Sharman, R. (2014). Utilizing the Uses and Gratification Theory to Understand Patients Use of Online Support Groups. *AMCIS 2014 Proceedings*. Available at: https://aisel.aisnet.org/amcis2014/Posters/HealthIS/11

Kisner, M. J. (2011). *Spinoza on human freedom: Reason, autonomy and the good life*. University Press.

Klekovkin, O. (2019). Homo Digital: Formula of Consumption. *Art culture. Current issues, 15*(1), 69-77.

Klimova, B., & Kacet, J. (2017). Efficacy of computer games on language learning. *The Turkish Online Journal of Educational Technology, 16*(4).

Klingberg, T., Fernell, E., Olesen, P. J., Johnson, M., Gustafsson, P., Dahlström, K., ... Westerberg, H. (2005). Computerized training of working memory in children with ADHD-a randomized, controlled trial. *Journal of the American Academy of Child and Adolescent Psychiatry, 44*(2), 177–186.

Klinger, E., Cao, X., Douguet, A. S., & Fuchs, P. (2009). Designing an ecological and adaptable virtual task in the context of executive functions. *Studies in Health Technology and Informatics, 144*, 248–252. PMID:19592774

Klopfer, E., Perry, J., Squire, K., Jan, M. F., & Steinkuehler, C. (2005). Mystery at the museum: A collaborative game for museum education. In *Proceedings of the 2005 conference on Computer support for collaborative learning: learning 2005: the next 10 years!* (pp. 316-320). International Society of the Learning Sciences. 10.3115/1149293.1149334

Kluge, A., & Dolonen, J. (2015). Using Mobile Games in the Classroom. In H. Crompton & J. Traxler (Eds.), *Mobile Learning and Mathematics: Foundations, Design, and Case Studies* (pp. 106–121). Taylor & Francis.

Kochmar, E., Do Vu, D., Belfer, R., Gupta, V., Serban, I. V., & Pineau, J. (2020). Automated Personalized Feedback Improves Learning Gains in An Intelligent Tutoring System. In I. I. Bittencourt, M. Cukurova, K. Muldner, R. Luckin, & E. Millán (Eds.), *Artificial Intelligence in Education* (pp. 140–146). Springer International Publishing. doi:10.1007/978-3-030-52240-7_26

Koivisto, J., & Hamari, J. (2014). Demographic differences in perceived benefits from gamification. *Computers in Human Behavior, 35*, 179–188. doi:10.1016/j.chb.2014.03.007

Kolb, A. Y., & Kolb, D. A. (2010). Learning to Play, Playing to Learn: A Case Study of a *Ludic* Learning Space. *Journal of Organizational Change Management, 23*(1), 26–50. doi:10.1108/09534811011017199

Kolb, D. A. (2006). *Experiential learning: Experience as the source of learning and development*. Prentice Hall, Inc.

Kolen, T. Z. (2011). Evacuation a serious game for preparation. In *IEEE International Conference on Networking, Sensing and Control*. IEEE Xplore.

Koo, B. M., & Vizer, L. V. (2019). Mobile Technology for Cognitive Assessment of Older Adults: A Scoping Review. *Innovation in Aging, 3*(1). Advance online publication. doi:10.1093/geroni/igy038 PMID:30619948

Koselleck, R. (2004). *Futures Past: On the Semantics of Historical Time*. Columbia University Press.

Kowalski, C., & Bhalla, R. (2018). Viewing the Disney movie *Frozen* through a psychodynamic lens. *The Journal of Medical Humanities, 39*(2), 145–150. doi:10.100710912-015-9363-3 PMID:26467918

Kozulin, A. (1998). *Psychological Tools. A Socio-Cultural Approach to Education*. Cambridge University Press.

Kray, J., Kipp, K. H., & Karbach, J. (2009). The development of selective inhibitory control: The influence of verbal labeling. *Acta Psychologica, 130*(1), 48–57.

Krcek, T. E. (2013). Deconstructing Disability and Neurodiversity: Controversial Issues for Autism and Implications for Social Work. *Journal of Progressive Human Services, 24*, 1, 4–22.

Kuipers, D. A., Terlow, G., Wartena, B. O., Veer, J. T., Prins, J. T., & Pierie, J. P. (2017). The Role of Transfer in Designing Games and Simulations for Health: Systematic Review. *JMIR Serious Games, 5*(4), 1–9. doi:10.2196/games.7880 PMID:29175812

Kuo, I. (2012, June 14). *Exploring Ancient Rome through Minecraft*. https://www.gamification.co/2012/06/14/exploring-ancient-rome-through-minecraft/

Kuo, I. (2015a, July 7). Does Gamification Work? Recent Empirical Study Shows Positive Results. *Gamification.co*. https://www.gamification.co/2015/07/07/does-gamification-work-recent-empirical-study-shows-positive-results/

Kuo, I. (2015b, July 15). Educational Games: Approaching Controversial Topics with Care. *Gamification.co*. https://www.gamification.co/2015/07/15/educational-games-approaching-controversial-topics-with-care/

Kuo, I. (2015c, July 21). Reliving WWI Flight History with Mobile Gamification App: Ace Academy. *Gamification.co*. https://www.gamification.co/2015/07/21/reliving-wwi-flight-history-with-mobile-gamification-app-ace-academy/

Kurlowicz, L., & Wallace, M. (1999). The mini-mental state examination (MMSE). *Journal of Gerontological Nursing*, *25*(5), 8–9. doi:10.3928/0098-9134-19990501-08 PMID:10578759

Kurt, A., Cortes-Cornax, M., Cung, V.-D., Front, A., & Mangione, F. (2021). A Classification Tool for Circular Supply Chain Indicators. *Advances in Production Management Systems*, 644–653.

Kurt, A., Cung, V.-D., Mangione, F., Cortes-Cornax, M., & Front, A. (2019). An Extended Circular Supply Chain Model Including Repurposing Activities. *International Conference on Control, Automation and Diagnosis*, 1–6. 10.1109/IC-CAD46983.2019.9037929

Laamarti, F., Eid, M., & Saddik, A. E. (2014). An Overview of Serious Games. *International Journal of Computer Games Technology*, *2014*, 1–15. doi:10.1155/2014/358152

Laatsch, L., Harrington, D., Hotz, G., Marcantuono, J., Mozzoni, M. P., Walsh, V., & Hersey, K. P. (2007). An Evidence-based Review of Cognitive and Behavioral Rehabilitation Treatment Studies in Children With Acquired Brain Injury. *The Journal of Head Trauma Rehabilitation*, *22*(4), 248–256. doi:10.1097/01.HTR.0000281841.92720.0a PMID:17667068

LabsO. (2019). *JobSimulator*. https://jobsimulatorgame.com/

LaCol. (2018). *Building Collectively: Participation in Architecture and Urban Planning*. Pollen Editors.

Lafortune, A. (2020). *Clothed in history: costume and medievalism in fantasy film and television* [Master of Arts Thesis, Western University] (Publication number 7198). Electronic Thesis and Dissertation Repository. https://ir.lib.uwo.ca/etd/7198

Lahane, S., Kant, R., & Shankar, R. (2020). Circular supply chain management: A state-of-art review and future opportunities. *Journal of Cleaner Production*, *258*, 120859. doi:10.1016/j.jclepro.2020.120859

Lambruschini, B. B., & Pizarro, W. G. (2015, July). Tech—Gamification in university engineering education: Captivating students, generating knowledge. In *2015 10th International Conference on Computer Science & Education (ICCSE)* (pp. 295-299). IEEE.

Laptook, A. R., & Watkinson, M. (2008). Temperature management in the delivery room. *Seminars in Fetal & Neonatal Medicine*, *13*(6), 383–391. doi:10.1016/j.siny.2008.04.003 PMID:18501693

Lauretti, C., Cordella, F., Guglielmelli, E., & Zollo, L. (2017). Learning by Demonstration for Planning Activities of Daily Living in Rehabilitation and Assistive Robotics. *IEEE Robotics and Automation Letters*, *2*(3), 1375–1382. doi:10.1109/LRA.2017.2669369

Lau, S. Y. J., & Agius, H. (2021). A framework and immersive serious game for mild cognitive impairment. *Multimedia Tools and Applications*, *80*(20), 31183–31237. Advance online publication. doi:10.100711042-021-11042-4

Lawn, J. E., Manandhar, A., Haws, R. A., & Darmstadt, G. L. (2007). Reducing one million child deaths from birth asphyxia - A survey of health systems gaps and priorities. *Health Research Policy and Systems*, *5*(4), 1–10. doi:10.1186/1478-4505-5-4 PMID:17506872

Lawton, M. P., & Brody, E. M. (1969). Assessment of older people: Self-maintaining and instrumental activities of daily living. *The Gerontologist*, *9*(3), 179–186. doi:10.1093/geront/9.3_Part_1.179 PMID:5349366

Layher, W. (2015). The Old Swedish Hærre Ivan leons riddare. In M. Kalinke (Ed.), *The Arthur of the North* (pp. 123–144). University of Wales Press.

Lazar, J., Feng, J. H., & Hochheiser, H. (2017). *Research methods in human-computer interaction*. Morgan Kaufmann.

Learning. (2021). *Suite of Digital Literacy Curriculum*. https://www.learning.com/

LeBlanc, V. R., MacDonald, R. D., McArthur, B., King, K., & Lepine, T. (2005). Paramedic performance in calculating drug dosages following stressful scenarios in a human patient simulator. *Prehospital Emergency Care*, *9*(4), 439–444. doi:10.1080/10903120500255255 PMID:16263679

Lee, S., & Lim, S. (2014, December). Considerations on gamification of e-learning application: Case study with phrase building training application. In *2014 6th International Conference on Multimedia, Computer Graphics and Broadcasting* (pp. 55-58). IEEE.

Lee, H. E., & Cho, J. (2017). What motivates users to continue using diet and fitness apps? Application of the uses and gratifications approach. *Health Communication*, *32*(12), 1445–1453. doi:10.1080/10410236.2016.1167998 PMID:27356103

Lee, J. J., & Hammer, J. (2011). Gamification in education: What, how, why bother? *Academic Exchange Quarterly*, *15*(2), 146.

Leese, M. (2010). Bridging the gap: Supporting student transitions into higher education. *Journal of Further and Higher Education*, *34*(2), 239–251. doi:10.1080/03098771003695494

Lefeber, N., Swinnen, E., & Kerckhofs, E. (2017). The immediate effects of robot-assistance on energy consumption and cardiorespiratory load during walking compared to walking without robot-assistance: a systematic review. In Disability and Rehabilitation: Assistive Technology (Vol. 12, Issue 7, pp. 657–671). doi:10.1080/17483107.2016.1235620

Legaki, N. Z., Xi, N., Hamari, J., Karpouzis, K., & Assimakopoulos, V. (2020). The effect of challenge-based gamification on learning: An experiment in the context of statistics education. *International Journal of Human-Computer Studies*, *144*, 102496. doi:10.1016/j.ijhcs.2020.102496 PMID:32565668

Legend of Zelda: Phantom Hourglass . (2007/Wii U 2013). [Video Game]. Nintendo DS.

Legend of Zelda: Wind Waker . (2002/Wii U 2013). [Video Game]. Nintendo GameCube.

Leichsenring, F., & Leweke, F. (2017). Social anxiety disorder. *The New England Journal of Medicine*, *376*(23), 2255–2264.

Leigh, E., & Clark, D. M. (2018). Understanding Social Anxiety Disorder in Adolescents and Improving Treatment Outcomes: Applying the Cognitive Model of Clark and Wells (1995). *Clinical Child and Family Psychology Review*, *21*(3), 388–414.

Lemkow, A. (1990). *The Wholeness Principle: Dynamics of Unity Within Science, Religion and Society*. Quest Books.

Lenton, A. P., Slabu, L., Sedikides, C., & Power, K. (2013). I feel good, therefore I am real: Testing the causal influence of mood on state authenticity. *Cognition and Emotion*, *27*(7), 1202–1224. doi:10.1080/02699931.2013.778818 PMID:23574266

Lepper, M. R., & Chabay, R. W. (1985). Intrinsic Motivation and instruction: Conflicting Views on the Role of Motivational Processes in Computer-Based Education. *Educational Psychologist*, *20*(4), 217–230. doi:10.120715326985ep2004_6

Levine, M. H. (2011, March 11). *Congress launches caucus for competitiveness in entertainment technology*. Retrieved from www.joanganzcooneycenter.org/cooney-center-blog-127.html

Levine, M. H., & Vaala, S. E. (2013). Games for learning: Vast wasteland or a digital promise? In F. C. Blumberg (Ed.), *New Directions for Child and Adolescent Development, no. 139* (pp. 71–82). doi:10.1002/cad.20033

Lévy, P. (2002). *Collective intelligence. For an anthropology of cyberspace.* Feltrinelli editor.

Levy, S. E., Giarelli, E., Lee, L.-C., Schieve, L. A., Kirby, R. S., Cunniff, C., Nicholas, J., Reaven, J., & Rice, C. E. (2010). Autism Spectrum Disorder and Co-occurring Developmental, Psychiatric, and Medical Conditions Among Children in Multiple Populations of the United States. *Journal of Developmental and Behavioral Pediatrics, 31*(4), 267–275. doi:10.1097/DBP.0b013e3181d5d03b PMID:20431403

Lewis, J. R. (2018). Measuring perceived usability: The CSUQ, SUS, and UMUX. *International Journal of Human-Computer Interaction, 34*(12), 1148–1156. doi:10.1080/10447318.2017.1418805

Liarokapis, F., Petridis, P., Andrews, D., & de Freitas, S. (2017). Multimodal Serious Games Technologies for Cultural Heritage. In M. Ioannides, N. Magnenat-Thalmann, & G. Papagiannakis (Eds.), *Mixed Reality and Gamification for Cultural Heritage* (pp. 371–392). Springer. doi:10.1007/978-3-319-49607-8_15

Li, C., Dong, Z., Untch, R. H., & Chasteen, M. (2013). Engaging Computer Science Collaborative Learning Environment. *International Journal of Information and Education Technology (IJIET), 3*(1), 72–77. doi:10.7763/IJIET.2013.V3.237

Li, C., Ip, H. H. S., & Ma, P. K. (2021). Experiential learning for children with autism spectrum disorder using virtual reality headsets: A preliminary report. *International Journal of Innovation and Learning, 30*(3), 317–333.

Li, H. C. W., Lopez, V., Chung, O. K. J., Ho, K. Y., & Chiu, S. Y. (2013). The impact of cancer on the physical, psychological and social well-being of childhood cancer survivors. *European Journal of Oncology Nursing, 17*(2), 214–219. doi:10.1016/j.ejon.2012.07.010 PMID:22898653

Lim, C. G., Lee, T. S., Guan, C., Fung, D. S. S., Cheung, Y. B., Teng, S. S. W., Zhang, H., & Krishnan, K. R. (2010). Effectiveness of a brain-computer interface based programme for the treatment of ADHD: A pilot study. *Psychopharmacology Bulletin, 43*(1), 73–82. PMID:20581801

Lim, C. G., Lee, T. S., Guan, C., Fung, D. S. S., Zhao, Y., Teng, S. S. W., Zhang, H., & Krishnan, K. R. R. (2012). A brain-computer interface based attention training program for treating attention deficit hyperactivity disorder. *PLoS One, 7*(10), e46692. doi:10.1371/journal.pone.0046692 PMID:23115630

Linder, M., Sarasini, S., & van Loon, P. (2017). A Metric for Quantifying Product-Level Circularity. *Journal of Industrial Ecology, 21*(3), 545–558. doi:10.1111/jiec.12552

Lindner, P., Miloff, A., Hamilton, W., Reuterskiöld, L., Andersson, G., Powers, M. B., & Carlbring, P. (2017). Creating state of the art, next-generation virtual reality exposure therapies for anxiety disorders using consumer hardware platforms: Design considerations and future directions. *Cognitive Behaviour Therapy, 46*(5), 404–420.

Lindner, P., Miloff, A., Zetterlund, E., Reuterskiöld, L., Andersson, G., & Carlbring, P. (2019). Attitudes toward and familiarity with virtual reality therapy among practicing cognitive behavior therapists: A cross-sectional survey study in the era of consumer VR platforms. *Frontiers in Psychology, 10*, 176–176.

Link, B. G., & Phelan, J. C. (2001). Conceptualizing Stigma. *Annual Review of Sociology, 27*(1), 363–385. doi:10.1146/annurev.soc.27.1.363

Link, B. G., Struening, E. L., Neese-Todd, S., Asmussen, S., & Phelan, J. C. (2001). Stigma as a Barrier to Recovery: The Consequences of Stigma for the Self-Esteem of People With Mental Illnesses. *Psychiatric Services (Washington, D.C.), 52*(12), 1621–1626. doi:10.1176/appi.ps.52.12.1621 PMID:11726753

Lipman, S. S., Daniels, K. I., Arafeh, J., & Halamek, L. P. (2011, April). The case for OBLS: A simulation-based obstetric life support program. *Seminars in Perinatology, 35*(2), 74–79. doi:10.1053/j.semperi.2011.01.006 PMID:21440814

Lister, M. (2015). Gamification: The effect on student motivation and performance at the post-secondary level. *Issues and Trends in Educational Technology, 3*(2).

Little Big Planet 3: Women In History Costume Pack . (2016). [Video Game]. Sony Interactive Entertainment Europe.

Liu, D., Santhanam, R., & Webster, J. (2017). Toward meaningful engagement: A framework for design and research of gamified information systems. *Management Information Systems Quarterly, 41*(4), 1011–1034. doi:10.25300/MISQ/2017/41.4.01

Liu, M., McKelroy, E., Corliss, S. B., & Carrigan, J. (2017). Investigating the effect of an adaptive learning intervention on students' learning. *Educational Technology Research and Development, 65*(6), 1605–1625. doi:10.100711423-017-9542-1

Llorente, J. G. S., Córdoba, Y. A. P., & Mora, B. R. (2018). Causes of difficulties in incorporating ICT in the classroom. *Panorama, 12*(22), 31-41. Available at: https://www.redalyc.org/articulo.oa?id=343968243004

Lobato, F. S., Steffen, V., Jr., & Oliveira-Lopes, L. C. (2007). An evolutionary approach based on search chaotic pattern associated to differential evolution algorithm. *17° Symposium of the Mechanical Engineering Post-Graduation Program*, 9.

Loerzel, V. W., Clochesy, J. M., & Geddie, P. I. (2020). Using Serious Games to Increase Prevention and Self-Management of Chemotherapy-Induced Nausea and Vomiting in Older Adults With Cancer. *Oncology Nursing Forum, 47*(5), 567–576. doi:10.1188/20.ONF.567-576 PMID:32830802

Logic Driver Pro 2.5. (2021). [Software - game development]. Recursive. https://recursoft.com/projects/LogicDriver

Loh, C. S., Anantachai, A., Byun, J., & Lenox, J. (2007). Assessing what players learned in serious games: in situ data collection, information trails, and quantitative analysis. *10th International Conference on Computer Games: AI, Animation, Mobile, Educational & Serious Games (CGAMES 2007)*, 25–28.

Loh, C. S., Sheng, Y., & Ifenthaler, D. (2015). Serious games analytics: Theoretical framework. In *Serious games analytics* (pp. 3–29). Springer.

Lokteva, E. (2017). *Fan in Learning: Refusal Cannot Be Provided*. Retrieved 07 21, 2021, from etutorium.ru: https://www.youtube.com/watch?v=gQ2thBXfxTY

Long, Y., & Aleven, V. (2014). Gamification of Joint Student/System Control Over Problem Selection in a Linear Equation Tutor. In *International conference on intelligent tutoring systems* (Vol. 8474 LNCS, pp. 378–387). doi:10.1007/978-3-319-07221-0

Lopez-Basterretxea, A., Mendez-Zorrilla, A., & Garcia-Zapirain, B. (2014). A Telemonitoring Tool based on Serious Games Addressing Money Management Skills for People with Intellectual Disability. *International Journal of Environmental Research and Public Health, 11*(3), 2361–2380. doi:10.3390/ijerph110302361 PMID:24573223

López-Otín, C., Blasco, M. A., Partridge, L., Serrano, M., & Kroemer, G. (2013). The hallmarks of aging. *Cell, 153*(6), 1194–1217. doi:10.1016/j.cell.2013.05.039 PMID:23746838

Lorber, M., & Zimmerman, F. (Eds.). (2020). *History in games: Contingencies of an authentic past*. Transcript Verlag.

Lo, S. K., Wang, C. C., & Fang, W. (2005). Physical interpersonal relationships and social anxiety among online game players. *Cyberpsychology & Behavior, 8*(1), 15–20.

Lourenço, J. M. B. (2018). *Serious Games for Motor Rehabilitation Applying Virtual Reality*. Academic Press.

Lu, A. S., Thompson, D., Baranowski, J., Buday, R., & Baranowski, T. (2012). Story Immersion in a Health Videogame for Childhood Obesity Prevention. *Games for Health Journal, 1*(1), 37–44. doi:10.1089/g4h.2011.0011 PMID:24066276

Lu, C., Ghoman, S. K., Cutumisu, M., & Schmölzer, G. M. (2020). Unsupervised machine learning algorithms examine healthcare providers' perceptions and longitudinal performance in a digital neonatal resuscitation simulator. *Frontiers in Pediatrics, 8. Article, 544*, 1–11. doi:10.3389/fped.2020.00544s

Lu, C., Ghoman, S. K., Cutumisu, M., & Schmölzer, G. M. (2021). Mindset moderates healthcare providers' longitudinal performance in a digital neonatal resuscitation simulator. *Frontiers in Pediatrics: Neonatology, 8*, 594690. Advance online publication. doi:10.3389/fped.2020.594690 PMID:33665174

Lucas, T., & Villegas, A. M. (2013). Preparing linguistically responsive teachers: Laying the foundation in preservice teacher education. *Theory into Practice, 52*(2), 98–109. doi:10.1080/00405841.2013.770327

Luhova, T. A. (2020). Narrative and storytelling in the knowledge structure of educational and business video games as factors of synergy of information technologies and spiritually-oriented pedagogy. *Open Educational E-Environment of Modern University, (8)*, 42-59.

Luhova, T. A., & Melnyk, S. P. (2014). Knowledge mapping as a tool for studying the intellectual potential of employees of secondary schools and universities. *Nasha shkola, (1)*, 29-35.

Luhova, T., & Akimov, O. Y. (2013). Evolution of enterprises electronic document management systems. *Bibliotekoznavstvo. Dokumentoznavstvo. Informolohiia, (1)*, 16-20.

Luhova, T., Raieva, V., Bezuhla, S., & Hrebeniuk, V. (2019). Promising areas of research on information and document data consolidation. *ΛΟΓΟΣ. The Art of Scientific Thought, (7)*, 63-68.

Luhova, T. A. (2021). Game-design-oriented approach to development of educational disciplins of higher educational institutions. *Information Technologies and Learning Tools, 81*(1), 235–254.

Luhova, T., Chursyn, M., Blazhko, O., & Rostoka, M. (2019). Stages of developing narrative material for educational video games for the formation of managerial competencies in decision making. *Online Journal for Research and Education Resource, (17)*, 213–221.

Lukosch, H., Lukosch, S., Hoermann, S., & Lindeman, R. W. (2019). Conceptualizing Fidelity for HCI in Applied Gaming. In *HCI in Games - 1st International Conference, HCI-Games 2019, Held as part of the 21st HCI International Conference, HCII 2019, Proceedings* (pp. 165-179). Springer.

Lund, C., De Silva, M., Plagerson, S., Cooper, S., Chisholm, D., Das, J., Knapp, M., & Patel, V. (2011). Poverty and mental disorders: Breaking the cycle in low-income and middle-income countries. *Lancet, 378*(9801), 1502–1514. doi:10.1016/S0140-6736(11)60754-X PMID:22008425

Lundetræ, K., & Thomson, J. M. (2018). Rhythm production at school entry as a predictor of poor reading and spelling at the end of first grade. *Reading and Writing, 31*(1), 215–237. doi:10.100711145-017-9782-9 PMID:29367807

Lunze, K., Bloom, D., Jamison, D., & Hamer, D. (2013). The global burden of neonatal hypothermia: Systematic review of a major challenge for newborn survival. *BMC Medicine, 11*(24), 24. Advance online publication. doi:10.1186/1741-7015-11-24 PMID:23369256

Lyon, A. R., & Koerner, K. (2016). User-centred design for psychosocial intervention development and implementation. *Clinical Psychology: Science and Practice, 23*(2), 180–200. doi:10.1111/cpsp.12154 PMID:29456295

Maatuk, A. M., Elberkawi, E. K., Aljawarneh, S., Rashaideh, H., & Alharbi, H. (2021). The COVID-19 pandemic and E-learning: Challenges and opportunities from the perspective of students and instructors. *Journal of Computing in Higher Education*. Advance online publication. doi:10.100712528-021-09274-2 PMID:33967563

Macarini, L. A., Ochoa, X., Cechinel, C., Rodés, V., Dos Santos, H. L., Alonso, G. E., ... Díaz, P. (2019). Challenges on implementing learning analytics over countrywide K-12 data. *ACM International Conference Proceeding Series*, 441–445. 10.1145/3303772.3303819

Machado, L. d., Moraes, R. M., & Nunes, F. L. (2009). Serious Games para Saúde e Treinamento Imersivo. In Abordagens Práticas de Realidade Virtual e Aumentada (Vol. 1, pp. 31-60). Porto Alegre.

Machado, L. S., Moraes, R. M., Nunes, F. L. S., & Costa, R. M. E. M. (2011). Serious Games baseados em realidade virtual para educação médica [Virtual reality-based Serious Games for medical education]. *Revista Brasileira de Educação Médica*, 35(2), 254–262. doi:10.1590/S0100-55022011000200015

Madani, K., Pierce, T. W., & Mirchi, A. (2017). Serious games on environmental management. *Sustainable Cities and Society*, 29, 1–11. doi:10.1016/j.scs.2016.11.007

Madhushree, Revathi, & Aithal. (2019). A Review on Impact of Information Communication & Computation Technology (ICCT) on Selected Primary, Secondary, and Tertiary Industrial Sectors. *Saudi Journal of Business and Management Studies*, 4(1), 106–127. Retrieved from https://econpapers.repec.org/RePEc:pra:mprapa:95150

Magnisalis, I., Demetriadis, S., & Karakostas, A. (2011). Adaptive and intelligent systems for collaborative learning support: A review of the field. *IEEE Transactions on Learning Technologies*, 4(1), 5–20. doi:10.1109/TLT.2011.2

Magos, K., & Politi, F. (2008). The creative second language lesson: The contribution of the role-play technique to the teaching of a second language in immigrant classes. *RELC Journal*, 39(1), 96–112. doi:10.1177/0033688208091142

Maheu-Cadotte, M.-A., Cossette, S., Dubé, V., Fontaine, G., Mailhot, T., Lavoie, P., Cournoyer, A., Balli, F., & Mathieu-Dupuis, G. (2018, March). Effectiveness of serious games and impact of design elements on engagement and educational outcomes in healthcare professionals and students: A systematic review and meta-analysis protocol. *BMJ Open*, 8(3), 1–7. doi:10.1136/bmjopen-2017-019871 PMID:29549206

Maia, R. F., & Graeml, F. R. (2015, October). Playing and learning with gamification: An in-class concurrent and distributed programming activity. In *2015 IEEE Frontiers in Education Conference (FIE)* (pp. 1-6). IEEE.

Maillot, P., Perrot, A., & Hartley, A. (2012). Effects of interactive physical-activity video-game training on physical and cognitive function in older adults. *Psychology and Aging*, 27(3), 589–600. doi:10.1037/a0026268 PMID:22122605

Mak, H. W. (2016, January 20). Three beneficial Impact of Games in Education for Students. *Gamification.co*. https://www.gamification.co/2016/01/20/3-beneficial-impact-games-education-students/

Makumba, W., Akinnifesi, F. K., & Janssen, B. H. (2009). Spatial rooting patterns of gliricidia, pigeon pea and maize intercrops and effect on profile soil N and P distribution in southern Malawi. *African Journal of Agricultural Research*, 4(4), 278–288.

Malone, T. W. (1981). *Toward a theory of intrinsically motivating instruction. Cognitive Science*, 4, 333–369.

Malone, T. W. (1981). Toward a theory of intrinsically motivating instruction. *Cognitive Science*, 5(4), 333–369. doi:10.120715516709cog0504_2

Ma, M., & Zheng, H. (2011). Virtual reality and serious games in healthcare. In *Advanced computational intelligence paradigms in healthcare 6. Virtual reality in psychotherapy, rehabilitation, and assessment* (pp. 169–192). Springer. doi:10.1007/978-3-642-17824-5_9

Man, D. W., Chung, J. C., & Lee, G. Y. (2012). Evaluation of a virtual reality-based memory training programme for Hong Kong Chinese older adults with questionable dementia: A pilot study. *International Journal of Geriatric Psychiatry*, *27*(5), 513–520. doi:10.1002/gps.2746 PMID:21681818

Mandal, S. (2013). Brief introduction of virtual reality & its challenges. *International Journal of Scientific \& Engineering Research, 4*(4), 304–309.

Mandran, N. (n.d.). *Experiment Guides*. Retrieved July 30, 2021, from http://thedre.imag.fr/?page_id=606

Mandran, N., & Dupuy-Chessa, S. (2018). Supporting experimental methods in information system research. *Proceedings - International Conference on Research Challenges in Information Science,* 1–12. 10.1109/RCIS.2018.8406654

Mandujano, G. G., Quist, J., & Hamari, J. (2021). Gamification of backcasting for sustainability: The development of the gamefulbackcasting framework (GAMEBACK). *Journal of Cleaner Production, 302,* 126609. doi:10.1016/j.jclepro.2021.126609

Manera, V., Petit, P. D., Derreumaux, A., Orvieto, I., Romagnoli, M., Lyttle, G., David, R., & Robert, P. H. (2015). "Kitchen and cooking", a serious game for mild cognitive impairment and Alzheimer's disease: A pilot study. *Frontiers in Aging Neuroscience, 7*(24). Advance online publication. doi:10.3389/fnagi.2015.00024 PMID:25852542

Mangels, J., Butterfield, B., Lamb, J., Good, C., & Dweck, C. (2006). Why do beliefs about intelligence influence learning success? A social cognitive neuroscience model. *Social Cognitive and Affective Neuroscience, 1*(2), 75–86. doi:10.1093can/nsl013 PMID:17392928

Mangla, S. K., Luthra, S., Mishra, N., Singh, A., Rana, N. P., Dora, M., & Dwivedi, Y. (2018). Barriers to effective circular supply chain management in a developing country context. *Production Planning and Control, 29*(6), 551–569. doi:10.1080/09537287.2018.1449265

Mansorian, A., & Dorodgar, K. (2014). Designing a software for systematic registration of oral and maxillofacial diseases based on the latest update of the World Health Organization ICD-10 classification system in 2010. *The Journal of Dental Medicine, 27*(1), 51–60.

Maran, J. N., & Glavin, R. J. (2003). Low- to high-fidelity simulation - a continuum of medical education? *Medical Education, 37*(1), 22–28. doi:10.1046/j.1365-2923.37.s1.9.x PMID:14641635

Marchiori, E. J., Torrente, J., del Blanco, Á., Moreno-Ger, P., Sancho, P., & Fernández-Manjón, B. (2012). A narrative metaphor to facilitate educational game authoring. *Computers & Education, 58*(1), 590–599. doi:10.1016/j.compedu.2011.09.017

March, S. T., & Smith, G. F. (1995). Design and natural science research on information technology. *Decision Support Systems, 15*(4), 251–266. doi:10.1016/0167-9236(94)00041-2

Marfisi-Schottman, I., George, S., & Frank, T.-B. (2010). Tools and Methods fo Efficiently Designing Serious Games. *4th Europeen Conference on Games Based Learning ECGBL2010, October,* 226–234.

Marshall, S. (n.d.). *Video games in museums: fine art or just fun?* https://stonemarshall.com/news/minecraft-news/video-games-museums-fine-art-just-fun/

Marson, D. C., Martin, R. C., Wadley, V., Griffith, H. R., Snyder, S., Goode, P. S., Kinney, F. C., Nicholas, A. P., Steele, T., Anderson, B., Zamrini, E., Raman, R., Bartolucci, A., & Harrell, L. E. (2009). Clinical interview assessment of financial capacity in older adults with mild cognitive impairment and Alzheimer's disease. *Journal of the American Geriatrics Society, 57*(5), 806–814. doi:10.1111/j.1532-5415.2009.02202.x PMID:19453308

Martin, A. (2015). Implicit theories about intelligence and growth (personal best) goals: Exploring reciprocal relationships. *The British Journal of Educational Psychology*, *85*(2), 207–223. doi:10.1111/bjep.12038 PMID:24904989

Martínez-López, F. J., Anaya-Sánchez, R., & Aguilar-Illescas, R. (2016). *Online brand communities: Using the social web for branding and marketing*. Springer. doi:10.1007/978-3-319-24826-4

Martinez-Maldonado, R., Elliott, D., Axisa, C., Power, T., Echeverria, V., & Buckingham Shum, S. (2020). Designing translucent learning analytics with teachers: An elicitation process. *Interactive Learning Environments*, *0*(0), 1–15. do i:10.1080/10494820.2019.1710541

Maskey, M., Lowry, J., Rodgers, J., McConachie, H., & Parr, J. R. (2014). Reducing specific phobia/fear in young people with autism spectrum disorders (ASDs) through a virtual reality environment intervention. *PLoS One*, *9*(7), e100374.

Maskey, M., Rodgers, J., Grahame, V., Glod, M., Honey, E., Kinnear, J., ... Parr, J. R. (2019). A randomised controlled feasibility trial of immersive virtual reality treatment with cognitive behaviour therapy for specific phobias in young people with autism spectrum disorder. *Journal of Autism and Developmental Disorders*, *49*(5), 1912–1927.

Maslov, S. I. (1979). Inference search theory and questions of the psychology of creativity. *Semiotics and Informatics*, (13), 17-46.

Materials for a Sustainable Future. (2015). *Materials Hunter* [Online game]. STIMULATE. http://www.materialsfuture.eu/en/game/

Matterson, H. H., Szyld, D., Green, B. R., Howell, H. B., Pusic, M. V., Mally, P. V., & Bailey, S. M. (2018). Neonatal resuscitation experience curves: Simulation based mastery learning booster sessions and skill decay patterns among pediatric residents. *Journal of Perinatal Medicine*, *46*(8), 934–941. doi:10.1515/jpm-2017-0330 PMID:29451862

Matthew-Maich, N., Harris, L., Ploeg, J., Markle-Reid, M., Valaitis, R., Ibrahim, S., Gafni, A., & Isaacs, S. (2016). Designing, implementing, and evaluating mobile health technologies for managing chronic conditions in older adults: A scoping review. *JMIR mHealth and uHealth*, *4*(2), e5127. doi:10.2196/mhealth.5127 PMID:27282195

Mayer, I. (2012). Towards a Comprehensive Methodology for the Research and Evaluation of Serious Games. *Procedia Computer Science*, *15*, 233–247. doi:10.1016/j.procs.2012.10.075

Mayer, R. E. (2011a). Multimedia learning and games. In S. Tobias & J. D. Fletcher (Eds.), *Computer Games and Instruction* (pp. 281–305). Information Age Publishing.

Mayer, R. E. (2011b). Instruction based on visualizations. In R. E. Mayer & P. A. Alexander (Eds.), *Handbook of Research on Learning and Instruction* (pp. 427–445). Routledge.

Mayer, R. E. (2014). Mutlimedia instruction. In J. M. Spector, M. D. Merrill, J. Elen, & M. J. Bishop (Eds.), *Handbook of Research on Educational Communications and Technology* (4th ed., pp. 385–399). Springer. doi:10.1007/978-1-4614-3185-5_31

Mayer, R. E. (2016). What should be the role of computer games in education? *Policy Insights from the Behavioral and Brain Sciences*, *3*(1), 20–26. doi:10.1177/2372732215621311

Mayer, R. E. (2020). Cognitive Foundations of Game-Based Learning. In J. L. Plass, R. E. Mayer, & B. D. Homer (Eds.), *Handbook of Game-Based Learning* (pp. 83–110). MIT Press.

Mayo, M. J. (2007). Games for science and engineering education. *Communications of the ACM*, *50*(7), 30–35. doi:10.1145/1272516.1272536

McCallum, S. (2012). Gamification and serious games for personalized health. *PHealth*, *177*(February), 85–96. doi:10.3233/978-1-61499-069-7-85 PMID:22942036

McCallum, S., & Boletsis, C. (2013). Dementia Games: A Literature Review of Dementia-Related Serious Games. In *Proceedings of the 4th International Conference on Serious Games Development and Applications*. 10.1007/978-3-642-40790-1_2

McGonigal, J. (2010, October 17). Ideas for modern living: blissful productivity. *The Guardian*. https://www.theguardian.com/lifeandstyle/2010/oct/17/ideas-modern-living-productivity-video-computer-games

McGonigal, J. (2011). *Reality is broken: Why games make us better and how they can change the world*. Penguin.

McLaren, P., & Jaramillo, N. (2007). Pedagogy and praxis in the age of empire: Towards a new humanism. *Review Symposium*, 206.

McLaughlin, M. (2010). The woman warrior: Gender, warfare and society in medieval Europe. *Women's Studies*, *17*(3-4), 193–209. doi:10.1080/00497878.1990.9978805

Medema, W., Mayor, I., Adamowaski, J., & Wals, C. (2019). *The Potential of Serious Games to Solve Water Problems: Editorial to the Special Issue on Game-Based Approaches to Sustainable Water Governance*. https://www.hindawi.com/journals/ijcgt/2014/358152/

Medieval Defenders . (2016). [Video Game]. Creobit/8floor.

Medieval Dynasty . (2020). [Video Game]. Toplitz Productions.

Meissner, K., & Wittmann, M. (2011). Body signals, cardiac awareness, and the perception of time. *Biological Psychology*, *86*(3), 289–297. doi:10.1016/j.biopsycho.2011.01.001 PMID:21262314

Melton, A. W. (1970). The situation with respect to the spacing of repetitions and memory. *Journal of Verbal Learning and Verbal Behavior*, *9*(5), 596–606. doi:10.1016/S0022-5371(70)80107-4

Mendonça, F. M. (2015). *Ontoforinfoscience: metodologia para construção de ontologias pelos cientistas da informação - Uma aplicação prática no desenvolvimento da ontologia sobre componentes do sangue humano (HEMONTO)*. Tese de Doutorado.

Mendonça, F. M., & Almeida, M. B. (2012). *Modelos e Teorias para Representação: Uma Teoria Ontológica Sobre o Sangue Humano*. Anais do XIII Encontro Nacional de Pesquisa em Ciência da Informação - XIII ENANCIB.

Mercado, A. (2016, July 22). Take a PokÃ©mon GO Tour Through the Met Museum This Weekend. *This is New York*. https://www.dnainfo.com/new-york/20160722/upper-east-side/take-pokmon-go-tour-through-met-museum-this-weekend/

Mercogliano, C. (2005). Philosophical Sources of Holistic Education. *Turkish Journal of Values Education*, *3*(10), 150–161.

Mesibov, G. B., Shea, V., & Schopler, E. (2005). *The TEACCH approach to autism spectrum disorders*. Springer Science & Business Media.

Metters, R. (1997). Quantifying the bullwhip effect in supply chains. *Journal of Operations Management*, *15*(2), 89–100. doi:10.1016/S0272-6963(96)00098-8

Mezirow, J. (1991). *Transformative Dimensions of Adult Learning*. Jossey- Bass.

Michael, D. R., & Chen, S. L. (2005). Serious Games: Games That Educate, Train, and Inform. *Education*, 1–95.

Michael, D., & Chen, S. (2006). *Serious games. Games that educate, train, and inform*. Thomson.

Michael, D., & Chen, S. (2006). *Serious games: Games that educate, train, and inform*. Thomson Course Technology PTR.

Michaud, B., Cherni, Y., Begon, M., Girardin-Vignola, G., & Roussel, P. (2017, June). A serious game for gait rehabilitation with the Lokomat. *2017 International Conference on Virtual Rehabilitation (ICVR)*. 10.1109/ICVR.2017.8007482

Microsoft. (2021). *Azure DevOps*. https://azure.microsoft.com/en-us/services/devops/?nav=min

Miguel, I., & Amaro da Luz, M. H. (2015). New technologies towards cognitive stimulation in elderly with dementia: Effects and potential. *Proceedings of the 2015 10th Iberian Conference on Information Systems and Technologies*. http://hdl.handle.net/11328/1487

Mileder, L. P., Urlesberger, B., Schwindt, J., Simma, B., & Schmölzer, G. M. (2014). Compliance with guidelines recommending the use of simulation for neonatal and infant resuscitation training in Austria. *Klinische Padiatrie, 226*(1), 24–28. doi:10.1055-0033-1361106 PMID:24435789

Mindmaze. (2021). *Mindmaze: Healthcare*. https://www.mindmaze.com/

Ministry of Education and Culture - Finland. (2017). *Multilingualism as a strength: Procedural recommendations for developing Finland's national language reserve*. https://minedu.fi/documents/1410845/4150027/Multilingualism+as+a+strength.pdf/766f921a-%0A1456-4146-89ed-899452cb5af8/Multilingualism+as+a+strength.pdf.%0A

Ministry of Health Singapore, Epidemiology & Disease Control Division & Institute for Health Metrics and Evaluation. (2019). *The burden of disease in Singapore, 1990-2017 report: An overview of the global burden of disease study 2017 results*. IMHE.

Ministry of Health Singapore. (2020). *Healthier Together: Partnering Singaporeans for Better Health*. Ministry of Health, Singapore. https://www.moh.gov.sg/docs/librariesprovider5/cos2020/cos-booklet-2020.pdf

Mishra, J., & Gazzaley, A. (2014). Harnessing the neuroplastic potential of the human brain & the future of cognitive rehabilitation. *Frontiers in Human Neuroscience, 0*. Advance online publication. doi:10.3389/fnhum.2014.00218 PMID:24782745

Mislevy, R. J., Almond, R. G., & Lukas, J. F. (2003). A Brief Introduction to Evidence-Centered Design. *ETS Research Report Series*, (1), i–29. doi:10.1002/j.2333-8504.2003.tb01908.x

Misra, P. K. (2011). Soil Fertility Management in Agroforestry System. *International Journal of Biotechnology and Biochemistry, 7*(5), 637-644.

Mitgutsch, K. (2011). Serious Learning in Serious Games. In Serious Games and Edutainment Applications (pp. 45-58). Springer. doi:10.1007/978-1-4471-2161-9_4

Mitgutsch, K., & Alvarado, N. (2012). Purposeful by design? A serious game design assessment framework. In *Proceedings of the International Conference on the Foundations of Digital Games - FDG '12* (p. 121). Raleigh, NC: ACM Press. 10.1145/2282338.2282364

Mitrović, I., & Šuran, O. (Eds.). (2016). Speculative – Post-Design Practice or New Utopia? Ministry of Culture of the Republic of Croatia & Croatian Designers Association.

Moccozet, L., Tardy, C., Opprecht, W., & Léonard, M. (2013). Interactive collaborative learning (ICL). In *2013 International Conference on. Interactive Collaborative Learning (ICL), 2013 International Conference on* (pp. 171-179). 10.1109/ICL.2013.6644565

Mokeddem, A., Plaisent, M., & Prosper, B. (2019). Learning with the Games: A Competitive Environment based on Knowledge. *The Journal of Learning in Higher Education, 2019*, 1–6. doi:10.5171/2019.133016

Molteni, F., Gasperini, G., Cannaviello, G., & Guanziroli, E. (2018). Exoskeleton and End-Effector Robots for Upper and Lower Limbs Rehabilitation: Narrative Review. *PM & R*, *10*(9), S174–S188. doi:10.1016/j.pmrj.2018.06.005 PMID:30269804

Moncrieff, J. (2018). Research on a 'drug-centred' approach to psychiatric drug treatment: Assessing the impact of mental and behavioural alterations produced by psychiatric drugs. *Epidemiology and Psychiatric Sciences*, *27*(2), 133–140. doi:10.1017/S2045796017000555 PMID:29022518

Moodle. (2021). *Proyecto Moodle*. https://www.moodle.org

Moree, B. N., & Davis, T. E. III. (2010). Cognitive-behavioral therapy for anxiety in children diagnosed with autism spectrum disorders: Modification trends. *Research in Autism Spectrum Disorders*, *4*(3), 346–354.

Morganti, L., Pallavicini, F., Cadel, E., Candelieri, A., Archetti, F., & Mantovani, F. (2017). Gaming for Earth: Serious games and gamification to engage consumers in pro-environmental behaviours for energy efficiency. *Energy Research & Social Science*, *29*, 95–102. doi:10.1016/j.erss.2017.05.001

Morris, J. (2007). Cognitive Rehabilitation: Where We Are and What is on the Horizon. *Physical Medicine and Rehabilitation Clinics of North America*, *18*(1), 27–42. doi:10.1016/j.pmr.2006.11.003 PMID:17292811

Morrison, C. (2020). *Review of Current Use of Digital Solutions for Mental Health*. University of Strathclyde.

Morris, P., Pinto, J., & Söderlund, J. (2011). *The Oxford Handbook of Project Management*. Oxford University Press. doi:10.1093/oxfordhb/9780199563142.001.0001

MortierR.HaddadiH.HendersonT.McAuleyD.CrowcroftJ. (2014). Human-data interaction: The human face of the data-driven society. *Available at* SSRN 2508051. doi:10.2139/ssrn.2508051

Mosadeghrad, A. M. (2013). Healthcare service quality: Towards a broad definition. *International Journal of Health Care Quality Assurance*, *26*(3), 203–219. doi:10.1108/09526861311311409 PMID:23729125

Motte, W. F. Jr. (1986). *Oulipo: A Primer of Potential Literature*. Dalkey Archive Press.

Mouffe, C. (2013). *Agonistics: Thinking the World Politically*. Verso.

Mountain-Software. (2021). *Agile Projects*. https://www.mountaingoatsoftware.com/agile/scrum

Mrug, S., Molina, B. S. G., Hoza, B., Gerdes, A. C., Hinshaw, S. P., Hechtman, L., & Arnold, L. E. (2012). Peer Rejection and Friendships in Children with Attention-Deficit/Hyperactivity Disorder: Contributions to Long-Term Outcomes. *Journal of Abnormal Child Psychology*, *40*(6), 1013–1026. doi:10.100710802-012-9610-2 PMID:22331455

Muchinsky, P. M. (2006). Psychology Applied to Work: An Introduction to Industrial and Organizational Psychology (8th ed.). Belmont, CA: Thomson Wadsworth.

Muir, R. (2020). *And they all lived happily ever after? A critical analysis of the Disney princess phenomenon* [PhD thesis]. University of Nottingham.

Müller, R., & Turner, J. (2005). The impact of principal–agent relationship and contract type on communication between project owner and manager. *International Journal of Project Management*, *23*(5), 398–403. doi:10.1016/j.ijproman.2005.03.001

Muñoz Merino, P. J., Delgado Kloos, C., Seepold, R., & Crespo García, R. M. (2006). Rating the importance of different LMS functionalities. In *Proceedings - Frontiers in Education Conference, FIE* (pp. 13–18). 10.1109/FIE.2006.322715

Muñoz-Merino, P. J., Ruipérez Valiente, J. A., & Kloos, C. D. (2013). Inferring higher level learning information from low level data for the Khan Academy platform. In *Proceedings of the Third International Conference on Learning Analytics and Knowledge - LAK '13* (pp. 112–116). ACM Press. 10.1145/2460296.2460318

Muoio, P. (2018). Open Source systems and software in teacher training for a school without excluded. In *Proceedings of EDEN 2018 Annual Conference* (pp. 691-700). European Distance and E-Learning Network.

Murali, V., & Oyebode, F. (2004). Poverty, social inequality and mental health. *Advances in Psychiatric Treatment*, *10*(3), 216–224. doi:10.1192/apt.10.3.216

Murder at the Museum. (n.d.). *Metropolitan Museum of Art*. https://metmystery.oncell.com/pages/

Murdock, M. (1990). *The heroine's journey*. Shambala.

Muriel, D., & Crawford, G. (2020). Video Games and Agency in Contemporary Society. *Games and Culture*, *15*(2), 138–157. doi:10.1177/1555412017750448

Museum Definition. (n.d.). *ICOM*. https://icom.museum/en/resources/standards-guidelines/museum-definition/

My Marriott Hotel Social Media Game Trailer [Video]. (n.d.). Retrieved from https://www.youtube.com/watch?v=ULOwlkiRM18

Myers, M. D., Nichols, J. D., & White, J. (2003). Teacher and Student Incremental and Entity Views of Intelligence: The Effect of Self-Regulation and Persistence Activities. *International Journal of Educational Reform*, *12*(2), 97–116. doi:10.1177/105678790301200202

Mylopoulos, J. (1992). Conceptual modeling and telos. In P. Loucopoulos & R. Zicari (Eds.), Conceptual modeling, databases and case: An integrated view of information systems development. John Wiley and Sons.

Nah, F. F. H., Telaprolu, V. R., Rallapalli, S., & Venkata, P. R. (2013, July). Gamification of education using computer games. In *International Conference on Human Interface and the Management of Information* (pp. 99-107). Springer.

Nair, P. K. R. (1993). *An introduction to agroforestry*. Kluwer Academic Publishers. doi:10.1007/978-94-011-1608-4

Nakamura, J., & Csikszentmihalyi, M. (2009). In S. J. Lopez & C. R. Snyder (Eds.), *Flow theory and research. Handbook of positive psychology* (pp. 195–206). University Press.

Nakamura, J., & Csikszentmihalyi, M. (2014). The Concept of Flow. In M. Csikszentmihalyi (Ed.), *Flow and the Foundations of Positive Psychology: The Collected Works of Mihaly Csikszentmihalyi* (pp. 239–263). Springer Netherlands. doi:10.1007/978-94-017-9088-8_16

Nakamura, J., & Csikszentmihalyi, M. (2014). The concept of flow. In *Flow and the foundations of positive psychology* (pp. 239–263). Springer.

Napoleon: Total War . (2010). [Video Game]. Creative Assembly.

Nardi, B. A. (1996). Studying context: A comparison of activity theory, situated action models, and distributed cognition. *Context and Consciousness: Activity Theory and Human-Computer Interaction*, *69102*.

Neck, H. M., & Greene, P. G. (2011). Entrepreneurship Education: Known Worlds and New Frontiers. *Journal of Small Business Management*, *49*(1), 55–70. doi:10.1111/j.1540-627X.2010.00314.x

Nelson, M. J. (2012, October). Soviet and American precursors to the gamification of work. In *Proceeding of the 16th international academic MindTrek conference* (pp. 23-26). 10.1145/2393132.2393138

Nesti, R. (2017). *Game-based learning: Game and play design in education*. ETS.

Neto, J. M., & Costa, J. N. (2016). *Dissertation for obtaining the Master's Degree in Computer Engineering, Specialization Area: Computer Systems.* ISEP.

Newman, M. G., Szkodny, L. E., Llera, S. J., & Przeworski, A. (2011). A review of technology-assisted self-help and minimal contact therapies for anxiety and depression: Is human contact necessary for therapeutic efficacy? *Clinical Psychology Review, 31*(1), 89–103. doi:10.1016/j.cpr.2010.09.008 PMID:21130939

Nicholson, S. (2012). *A user-Centered theoretical framework for meaningful gamification.* Paper presented at the Games+ Learning+ Society 8.0, Madison, WI.

Nicholson, S. (2012). *Strategies for meaningful gamification: Concepts behind transformative play and participatory museums* [Paper presentation]. Meaningful Play 2012, Lansing, MI. https://scottnicholson.com/pubs/meaningfulstrategies.pdf

Nicholson, S. (2015). A RECIPE for Meaningful Gamification. In T. Reiners & L. Wood (Eds.), Gamification in Education and Business (pp. 1-20). Springer. doi:10.1007/978-3-319-10208-5_1

Nicholson, S. (2015). A recipe for meaningful gamification. In *Gamification in education and business* (pp. 1–20). Springer.

Nieto-Escamez, F. A., & Roldán-Tapia, M. D. (2021). Gamification as online teaching strategy during COVID-19: A mini-review. *Frontiers in Psychology, 12*, 12. doi:10.3389/fpsyg.2021.648552 PMID:34093334

Nikolaou, I., & Oostrom, J. K. (Eds.). (2015). Employee recruitment, selection, and assessment: Contemporary issues for theory and practice (1st ed. ed.). London: Psychology Press.

Ning, H., Li, R., Ye, X., Zhang, Y., & Liu, L. (2020). A Review on Serious Games for Dementia Care in Ageing Societies. *IEEE Journal of Translational Engineering in Health and Medicine, 8*, 1–11. Advance online publication. doi:10.1109/JTEHM.2020.2998055 PMID:32537264

Nøhr, C., & Aarts, J. (2010). Use of "serious health games" in health care: a review. *Information Technology in Health Care: Socio-Technical Approaches*, 160.

Nolin, P., Stipanicic, A., Henry, M., Lachapelle, Y., Lussier-Desrochers, D., & Allain, P. (2016). ClinicaVR: Classroom-CPT: A virtual reality tool for assessing attention and inhibition in children and adolescents. *Computers in Human Behavior, 59*, 327–333.

Nonaka, I. (2007, July–August). The Knowledge-Creating Company. *Harvard Business Review*, 162–171.

Nordby, A., Øygardslia, K., Sverdrup, U., & Sverdrup, H. (2016). The art of gamification; teaching sustainability and system thinking by pervasive game development. *Electronic Journal of e-Learning, 14*(3), 152-168.

Nordon, D. G., Guimarães, R. R., Kozonoe, D. Y., Mancilha, V. S., & Neto, V. S. D. (2009). Perda cognitiva em idosos [Cognitive Loss in the Elderly]. *Revista da Faculdade de Ciências Médicas de Sorocaba, 11*(3), 5–8.

Not For Broadcast [Digital game]. (2020). *NotGames.* Retrieved 17 07, 2021, from STEAM: https://store.steampowered.com/app/1147550/Not_For_Broadcast/

NTHP. (2015). *Preservation glossary.* https://savingplaces.org/stories/preservation-glossary-todays-word-heritage-tourism#.YQfhxY4za44

Núñez, A.-G., Penadés, M. C., & Canos, J.H. (2015). Towards a total quality framework for the evaluation and improvement of emergency plans management. *ISCRAM 2015 Conference Proceedings - 12th International Conference on Information Systems for Crisis Response and Management.*

Nyberg, T. (2003). Birgitta politikern [Birgitta the politician]. In Birgitta av Vadstena [Birgitta of Vadstena] (pp. 29-44). Natur och Kultur.

O'Connor, C., Mullane, K., & Luethge, D. (2021). The Management and Coordination of Virtual Teams in Large Classes: Facilitating Experiential Learning. *Journal of Management Education, 5*(4), 739–759. doi:10.1177/1052562921995550

O'Neil, H. F., & Perez, R. S. (Eds.). (2008). *Computer games and team and individual learning*. Elsevier.

O'Neill, A. (2021, June 4). Highest grossing film annually: historical. *Statista*. https://www.statista.com/statistics/1072778/highest-grossing-film-annually-historical/

Objection! [Digital game]. (1992). *TransMedia Productions*. Retrieved from Old-Games.RU: https://www.old-games.ru/game/4107.html

Observatory on Health Systems and Policies (OECD). (2017). Portugal: Country health profile 2017. State of Health in the EU, OECD Publishing, Paris/European Observatory on Health Systems and Policies, Brussels.

Ocete, G. V., Carrillo, J. A. O., & González, M. Á. B. (2003). Virtual reality and its didactic possibilities. Etic@ net. *Scientific Electronic Journal of Education and Communication in the Knowledge Society*, (2), 12.

OECD. (2015). *Helping immigrant students to succeed at school-and beyond*. OECD Publishing. https://www.oecd.org/education/Helping-immigrant-students-to-succeed-at-school-and-beyond.pdf

OECD. (2017). *Finding the way: A discussion of the Finnish migrant integration system*. OECD Publishing. https://www.oecd.org/els/mig/Finding_the_Way_Finland.pdf

OECD. (2018a). *The resilience of students with an immigrant background: Factors that shape well-being*. OECD Publishing. doi:10.1787/9789264292093-

OECD. (2018b). *Working together: Skills and labour market integration of immigrants and their children in Finland*. OECD Publishing. doi:10.1787/9789264305250-

OECD. (2019a). *PISA 2018 results: Where all students can succeed: Vol. II*. OECD Publishing.

OECD. (2019b). The road to integration: Education and migration. In *OECD Reviews of Migrant Education*. OECD Publishing. doi:10.1787/d8ceec5d-

OECD. (2021). Language training for adult migrants. In *Making Integration Work*. OECD Publishing. doi:10.1787/02199d7f-

Oe, H., Takemoto, T., & Ridwan, M. (2020). Is gamification a magic tool?: Illusion, remedy, and future opportunities in enhancing learning outcomes during and beyond the COVID-19. *Budapest International Research and Critics in Linguistics and Education Journal, 3*(3), 1401–1414.

Oksanen, K., & Hämäläinen, R. (2013). Perceived sociability and social presence in a collaborative serious game. *International Journal of Game-Based Learning, 3*(1), 34–50. doi:10.4018/ijgbl.2013010103

Okumura, Y., Sugiyama, N., & Noda, T. (2018). Timely follow-up visits after psychiatric hospitalization and readmission in schizophrenia and bipolar disorder in Japan. *Psychiatry Research, 270*, 490–495. doi:10.1016/j.psychres.2018.10.020 PMID:30326432

Olais, R. (2014, March 6). *Factors Affecting Watershed Management and Amount of Water*. https://prezi.com/ad_lxd-dphop-/factors-affecting-watershed-management-and-amount-of-water/

Oliveira, J., Gamito, P., Alghazzawi, D. M., Fardoun, H. M., Rosa, P. J., Sousa, T., Picareli, L. F., Morais, D., & Lopes, P. (2018). Performance on naturalistic virtual reality tasks depends on global cognitive functioning as assessed via traditional neurocognitive tests. *Applied Neuropsychology. Adult, 25*(6), 555–561. doi:10.1080/23279095.2017.1349661 PMID:28805447

Olsen, R. A. (1981). *Sjællandske krønike* [The Chronicle of Zealand]. Wormianum.

Olusanya, B. O., Davis, A. C., Wertlieb, D., Boo, N.-Y., Nair, M. K. C., Halpern, R., Kuper, H., Breinbauer, C., de Vries, P. J., Gladstone, M., Halfon, N., Kancherla, V., Mulaudzi, M. C., Kakooza-Mwesige, A., Ogbo, F. A., Olusanya, J. O., Williams, A. N., Wright, S. M., Manguerra, H., ... Kassebaum, N. J. (2018). Developmental disabilities among children younger than 5 years in 195 countries and territories, 1990–2016: A systematic analysis for the Global Burden of Disease Study 2016. *The Lancet. Global Health*, *6*(10), e1100–e1121. doi:10.1016/S2214-109X(18)30309-7 PMID:30172774

Ong, B. (2017). Inaugural Chee Kuan Tsee Lecture: Mental Health Care for the 21st Century. *Annals of the Academy of Medicine, Singapore*, *46*(6), 5. PMID:28733694

Ong, E. (2020). Can digital games serve as potential intervention or suicide risk? *International Journal of Serious Games*, *7*(1), 127–132. doi:10.17083/ijsg.v7i1.303

Ong, J. G., Lim-Ashworth, N. S., Ooi, Y. P., Boon, J. S., Ang, R. P., Goh, D. H., Ong, S. H., & Fung, D. S. (2019). An Interactive Mobile App Game to Address Aggression (RegnaTales): Pilot Quantitative Study. *JMIR Serious Games*, *7*(2), e13242. doi:10.2196/13242 PMID:31066682

Ooi, Y. P., Ang, R., Fung, D. S. S., Wong, G., & Cai, Y. (2007). Effects of CBT on children with disruptive behaviour disorders: Findings from a Singapore study. *ASEAN Journal of Psychiatry*, *8*(2), 71–81.

Oostrom, J. K., Van Der Linden, D., Born, M. P., & Van Der Molen, H. T. (2013). New technology in personnel selection: How recruiter characteristics affect the adoption of new selection technology. *Computers in Human Behavior*, *29*(6), 2404–2415.

Orme, N. (2003). *Medieval children.* Yale University Press.

Ortiz-Aguinaga, G., Cardona-Reyes, H., Muñoz-Arteaga, J., & Barba-Gonzalez, M. L. (2020). Model for the Generation of Scenarios in Virtual Reality Applied in Health. *2020 3rd International Conference of Inclusive Technology and Education (CONTIE)*, 154–161.

Orton, J. (2016a). Issues in Chinese language teaching in Australian schools. *Chinese Education & Society*, *49*(6), 369–375. doi:10.1080/10611932.2016.1283929

Orton, J. (2016b). *Building Chinese language capacity in Australia.* The Australia-China Relations Institute.

Orton, J., & Scrimgeour, A. (2019). *Teaching Chinese as a second language: The way of the learner.* Routledge. doi:10.4324/9781351206877

Oshotse, C. O., Bosworth, H. B., & Zullig, L. L. (2020). Treatment Engagement and Adherence. In A. Hadler, S. Sutton, & L. Osterberg (Eds.), The Wiley Handbook of Healthcare Treatment Engagement (pp. 15–32). John Wiley & Sons, Ltd. doi:10.1002/9781119129530.ch1

Ott, M., & Pozzi, F. (2010). Towards a model to evaluate creativity-oriented learning activities. *Procedia: Social and Behavioral Sciences*, *2*(2), 3532–3536. doi:10.1016/j.sbspro.2010.03.547

Oubahssi, L., Piau-Toffolon, C., Loup, G., & Sanchez, E. (2020). From Design to Management of Digital Epistemic Games. *International Journal of Serious Games*, *7*(1), 23–46. doi:10.17083/ijsg.v7i1.336

Oxley, H. (2009). Policies for Healthy Ageing: An Overview. *OECD Health Working Papers*, *42*, 6–30.

Pachay-López, M., & Rodríguez-Gámez, M. (2021). Dropping out of school: A complex perspective in times of pandemic. *Polo del Conocimiento*, *6*(1), 130–155. doi:10.23857/pc.v6i1.2129

Padala, K. P., Padala, P. R., Malloy, T. R., Geske, J. A., Dubbert, P. M., Dennis, R. A., Garner, K. K., Bopp, M. M., Burke, W. J., & Sullivan, D. H. (2012). Wii-fit for improving gait and balance in an assisted living facility: A pilot study. *Journal of Aging Research, 2012*, 1–6. Advance online publication. doi:10.1155/2012/597573 PMID:22745909

Paez, R. (2014). Derivas Urbanas: la Ciudad Extrañada [Urban Dérives: The Estranged City]. *R.I.T.A. Revista indexada de textos académicos, 1*, 120-129.

Paez, R. (2019). Operative Mapping: Maps as Design Tools. Actar Publishers.

Paez, R., & Valtchanova, M. (2021). Harnessing Conflict: Antagonism and Spatiotemporal Design Practices. *Temes de Disseny, 37 Invisible Conflicts: The New Terrain of Bodies, Infrastructures and Communication*, 183-216. doi:10.46467/TdD37.2021.182-213

Paez, R. (in press). Design as Playground: Exploring Design Through Game-based Formats. *Space and Culture*.

Pagulayan, R. J., Keeker, K., Wixon, D., Romero, R., & Fuller, T. (2008). User-centered design in games. In J. Jacko & A. Sears (Eds.), *Handbook of Human-Computer Interaction in Interactive Systems*. Lawrence Erlbaum Associates, Inc.

Pais, J. (2008). As Dificuldades de Memória no Idoso [Memory Difficulties in the Elderly]. In *Memória, Funcionamente, Perturbações e Treino* [Memory, Functioning, Disorders and Training]. Lidel Edições Técnicas.

Pang, S., Liu, J., Mahesh, M., Chua, B. Y., Shahwan, S., Lee, S. P., Vaingankar, J. A., Abdin, E., Fung, D. S. S., Chong, S. A., & Subramaniam, M. (2017). Stigma among Singaporean youth: A cross-sectional study on adolescent attitudes towards serious mental illness and social tolerance in a multiethnic population. *BMJ Open, 7*(10), e016432. doi:10.1136/bmjopen-2017-016432 PMID:29042379

Pankiewicz, M., & Bator, M. (2019). Elo Rating Algorithm for the Purpose of Measuring Task Difficulty in Online Learning Environments. *E-Mentor, 82*(5), 43–51. doi:10.15219/em82.1444

Pantelidis, V. S. (1996). Suggestions on when to use and when not to use virtual reality in education. *VR in the Schools, 2*(1), 18.

Pan, Z., Cheok, A. D., Yang, H., Zhu, J., & Shi, J. (2006). Virtual reality and mixed reality for virtual learning environments. *Computers & Graphics, 30*(1), 20–28. doi:10.1016/j.cag.2005.10.004

Papagiannopoulou, E. A., Chitty, K. M., Hermens, D. F., Hickie, I. B., & Lagopoulos, J. (2014). A systematic review and meta-analysis of eye-tracking studies in children with autism spectrum disorders. *Social Neuroscience, 9*(6), 610–632.

Papert, S. (1986). *Constructionism: A New Opportunity for Elementary Science Education*. A MIT Proposal to the National Science Foundation.

Papert, S. (1991). Situating Constructionism. In I. Harel & S. Papert (Eds.), *Constructionism*. Ablex Publishing.

Papert, S. A. (2020). *Mindstorms: Children, computers, and powerful ideas*. Basic books.

Pardo, A., & Siemens, G. (2014). Ethical and privacy principles for learning analytics. *British Journal of Educational Technology, 45*(3), 438–450. doi:10.1111/bjet.12152

Park, J. H., Han, D. H., Kim, B. N., Cheong, J. H., & Lee, Y. S. (2016). Correlations among social anxiety, self-esteem, impulsivity, and game genre in patients with problematic online game playing. *Psychiatry Investigation, 13*(3), 297.

Park, Y., & Jo, I. (2015). Development of the Learning Analytics Dashboard to Support Students' Learning Performance Learning Analytics Dashboards (LADs). *Journal of Universal Computer Science, 21*(1), 110–133.

Parsons, S., & Mitchell, P. (2002). The potential of virtual reality in social skills training for people with autistic spectrum disorders. *Journal of Intellectual Disability Research*, *46*(5), 430–443.

Parsons, T. D., Bowerly, T., Buckwalter, J. G., & Rizzo, A. A. (2007). A controlled clinical comparison of attention performance in children with ADHD in a virtual reality classroom compared to standard neuropsychological methods. *Child Neuropsychology*, *13*(4), 363–381. doi:10.1080/13825580600943473 PMID:17564852

Parsons, T. D., Duffield, T., & Asbee, J. (2019). A Comparison of Virtual Reality Classroom Continuous Performance Tests to Traditional Continuous Performance Tests in Delineating ADHD: A Meta-Analysis. *Neuropsychology Review*, 1–19.

Parsons, T. D., Gaggioli, A., & Riva, G. (2017). Virtual reality for research in social neuroscience. *Brain Sciences*, *7*(4), 42. doi:10.3390/brainsci7040042 PMID:28420150

Partarakis, N., Grammenos, D., Margetis, G., Zidianakis, E., Drossis, G., Leonidis, A., Metaxakis, G., Antona, M., & Stephanidis, C. (2017). Digital Cultural Heritage Experience in Ambient Intelligence. In M. Ioannides, N. Magnenat-Thalmann, & G. Papagiannakis (Eds.), *Mixed Reality and Gamification for Cultural Heritage* (pp. 473–505). Springer. doi:10.1007/978-3-319-49607-8_19

Paternò, F. (2004). ConcurTaskTrees: an engineered notation for task models. The Handbook of Task Analysis for Human-Computer Interaction, 483–503.

Patricio, R., Moreira, A., Zurlo, F., & Melazzini, M. (2020). Co-creation of new solutions through gamification: A collaborative innovation practice. *Creativity and Innovation Management*, (29), 146–160.

Paúl, C. (2006). Psicossomática do Envelhecimento [Psychosomatics of Aging]. In *Psicogeriatria* [Psychogeriatrics]. Psiquiatria Clínica.

Payne, J. (2018, December 30). Heritage tourism: facts and figures. *The Insider.* https://www.buses.org/news/article/insider-exclusive-heritage-toursim-facts-figures

Peake, J. M., Kerr, G., & Sullivan, J. P. (2018). A critical review of consumer wearables, mobile applications, and equipment for providing biofeedback, monitoring stress, and sleep in physically active populations. *Frontiers in Physiology*, *9*, 743. doi:10.3389/fphys.2018.00743 PMID:30002629

Pechchei, A. (1977). Chelovecheskie kachestva [The Human Quality] 312 (O. V. Zaharova, Trans.). Moscow: Progress.

Peirce, N., Conlan, O., & Wade, V. (2008). Adaptive educational games: Providing non-invasive personalised learning experiences. In *Proceedings - 2nd IEEE International Conference on Digital Game and Intelligent Toy Enhanced Learning, DIGITEL 2008* (pp. 28–35). 10.1109/DIGITEL.2008.30

Pelánek, R. (2016). Applications of the Elo rating system in adaptive educational systems. *Computers & Education*, *98*, 169–179. doi:10.1016/j.compedu.2016.03.017

Pelham, W. E. III, Page, T. F., Altszuler, A. R., Gnagy, E. M., Molina, B. S. G., & Pelham, W. E. Jr. (2020). The long-term financial outcome of children diagnosed with ADHD. *Journal of Consulting and Clinical Psychology*, *88*(2), 160–171. doi:10.1037/ccp0000461 PMID:31789549

Pellicano, E., Maybery, M., Durkin, K., & Maley, A. (2006). Multiple cognitive capabilities/deficits in children with an autism spectrum disorder: "Weak" central coherence and its relationship to theory of mind and executive control. *Development and Psychopathology*, *18*(1), 77–98.

Peng, W., Lin, J. H., Pfeiffer, K. A., & Winn, B. (2012). Need satisfaction supportive game features as motivational determinants: An experimental study of a self-determination theory guided exergame. *Media Psychology*, *15*(2), 175–196. doi:10.1080/15213269.2012.673850

Pennington, B. F., & Ozonoff, S. (1996). Executive functions and developmental psychopathology. *Journal of Child Psychology and Psychiatry, and Allied Disciplines, 37*(1), 51–87.

Pereno, A., & Eriksson, D. (2020). A multi-stakeholder perspective on sustainable healthcare: From 2030 onwards. *Futures, 122*, 102605. doi:10.1016/j.futures.2020.102605 PMID:32834076

Pérez-Serrano, M. J., Fernández-Sande, M., & Pallares, M. R. (2020). Entorns d'aprenentatgedigitals en l'àrea d'Empresa Informativa. «Gaming» i incidència en activitats i avaluació. *Anàlisi: quaderns de comunicaciói cultura,* (62), 111-130.

Pessini, A., Kemczinski, A., & Hounsell, M. (2015). *Uma Ferramenta de Autoria para o desenvolvimento de Jogos Sérios do Gênero RPG* [An Authoring Tool for Developing Serious RPG Games]. Computer on the Beach. doi:10.14210/cotb.v0n0.p071-080

Peterson, M. (2010). Massively multiplayer online role-playing games (MMORPGs) as arenas for language learning. *Computer Assisted Language Learning, 23*(5), 429–439. doi:10.1080/09588221.2010.520673

Phelps, C. E. (2017). *Health economics* (6th ed.). Routledge. doi:10.4324/9781315460499

Piaget, J. (1962). *Play, Dreams and Imitation in Childhood.* Norton.

Piaget, J. (1967). *The mental development of the child.* Einaudi.

Piker, R. A. (2013). Understanding influences of play on second language learning: A microethnographic view in one Head Start preschool classroom. *Journal of Early Childhood Research, 11*(2), 184–200. doi:10.1177/1476718X12466219

Plass, J. L., Homer, B. D., & Kinzer, C. K. (2015). Foundations of Game-Based Learning. *Educational Psychologist, 50*(4), 258–283. doi:10.1080/00461520.2015.1122533

Plass, J. L., Homer, B. D., Mayer, R. E., & Kinzer, C. K. (2020). Theoretical Foundations of Game-Based and Playful Learning. In J. L. Plass, R. E. Mayer, & B. D. Homer (Eds.), *Handbook of Game-Based Learning* (pp. 3–24). MIT Press.

Plecher, D. A., Herber, F., Eichhorn, C., Pongratz, A., Tanson, G., & Klinker, G. (2020, December 4). HieroQuest - A Serious Game for Learning Egyptian Hieroglyphs. *Journal on Computing and Cultural Heritage,* 1-20.

Ponce, P., Meier, A., Méndez, J. I., Peffer, T., Molina, A., & Mata, O. (2020). Tailored gamification and serious game framework based on fuzzy logic for saving energy in connected thermostats. *Journal of Cleaner Production, 262*, 121167. doi:10.1016/j.jclepro.2020.121167

Poole, F. J., & Clarke-Midura, J. (2020). A systematic review of digital games in second language learning studies. *International Journal of Game-Based Learning, 10*(3), 1–15. doi:10.4018/IJGBL.2020070101

Poongodi, T., Krishnamurthi, R., Indrakumari, R., Suresh, P., & Balusamy, B. (2020). Wearable devices and IoT. In *A handbook of Internet of Things in biomedical and cyber physical system* (pp. 245–273). Springer. doi:10.1007/978-3-030-23983-1_10

Poplin, A. (2011). Games and Serious Games in Urban Planning: Study Cases. In *Computational Science and Its Applications - ICCSA 2011 - International Conference - Proceedings, Part II.* Springer. 10.1007/978-3-642-21887-3_1

Power, E. (1975). *Medieval women.* Cambridge University Press.

Prager, P., Thomas, M., & Selsjord, M. (2015). Transposing, transforming and transcending tradition in creative digital media. In D. Harrison (Ed.), *Handbook of research on digital media and creative technologies* (pp. 141–199). IGI Global. doi:10.4018/978-1-4666-8205-4.ch008

Prassana, R., Yang, L., & King, M. (2011). Evaluation of a Software Prototype for Supporting Fire Emergency Response. *ISCRAM 2011 Conference Proceedings - International Conference on Information Systems for Crisis Response and Management 2011*.

Prensky, M. (2001). Fun, Play and Games: What Makes Games Engaging. In Digital Game-Based Learning (pp. 1-31). McGraw-Hill.

Prensky, M. (2006). Don't bother me, Mom, I'm learning! How computer and video games are preparing your kids for 21st century success and how you can help! Paragon House.

Prensky, M. (2001). *Digital Game-based Learning*. McGraw-Hill.

Prensky, M. (2001). Digital natives, digital immigrants part 1. *On the Horizon, 9*(5), 1–6. doi:10.1108/10748120110424816

Prieto, L. P., Rodríguez-Triana, M. J., Kusmin, M., & Laanpere, M. (2017). Smart school multimodal dataset and challenges. *CEUR Workshop Proceedings, 1828*, 53–59. doi:10.1145/1235

Prince, M., Wimo, A., Guerchet, M., Ali, G., Wu, Y., & Prina, M. (2015). World Alzheimer Report: The Global Impact of Dementia. London: Alzheimer's Disease International (ADI).

Prince, M., Bryce, R., Albanese, E., Wimo, A., Ribeiro, W., & Ferri, C. P. (2013). The global prevalence of dementia: A systematic review and metaanalysis. *Alzheimer's & Dementia, 9*(1), 63–75. doi:10.1016/j.jalz.2012.11.007 PMID:23305823

Przybylski, A. K., Rigby, C. S., & Ryan, R. M. (2010). A Motivational Model of Video Game Engagement. *Review of General Psychology, 14*(2), 154–166. doi:10.1037/a0019440

Psomos, P., & Kordaki, M. (2015). A novel educational digital storytelling tool focusing on students misconceptions. *Procedia: Social and Behavioral Sciences, 191*, 82–86. doi:10.1016/j.sbspro.2015.04.476

Qian, M., & Clark, K. R. (2016). Game-based Learning and 21st century skills: A review of recent research. *Computers in Human Behavior, 63*, 50–58. doi:10.1016/j.chb.2016.05.023

Qi, H., Wan, B., & Zhao, L. (2004). Mutual information entropy research on dementia EEG signals. *The Fourth International Conference on Computer and Information Technology*.

Qualters, D. M., Isaacs, J., Cullinane, T., Laird, J., & McDonald, A. (2008). A Game Approach to Teach Environmentally Benign Manufacturing in the Supply Chain. *International Journal for the Scholarship of Teaching and Learning, 2*(2). Advance online publication. doi:10.20429/ijsotl.2008.020214

Quiroz-Palma, P., Penadés, M. C., & Núñez, A. G. (2019). TiER: A Serious Games for Training in Emergency Scenarios. International Business Information Management Association (IBIMA 2019).

Raffaghelli, J. E. (2019). Developing a Framework for Educators' Data Literacy in the European Context: Proposal, Implications and Debate. *EDULEARN19 Proceedings, 1*(July), 10520–10530. 10.21125/edulearn.2019.2655

Raju, P., Ahmed, V., & Anumba, C. (2011). special issue on use of virtual world technology in architecture, engineering and construction. *Journal of Information Technology in Construction, 16*(11), 163–164.

Ranieri, M., Raffaghelli, J., & Bruni, I. (2018). Game-based student response system: Revisiting its potentials and criticalities in large-size classes. *Active Learning in Higher Education, 22*(2), 95–96.

Rankin, Y. A., McNeal, M., Shute, M. W., & Gooch, B. (2008). User centered game design: Evaluating massive multiplayer online role playing games for second language acquisition. *Sandbox Symposium*, 43–50. 10.1145/1401843.1401851

Ratan, R. A., & Ritterfeld, U. (2009). Classifying serious games. In *Serious games* (pp. 32–46). Routledge.

Ravì, D., Wong, C., Deligianni, F., Berthelot, M., Andreu-Perez, J., Lo, B., & Yang, G.-Z. (2016). Deep learning for health informatics. *IEEE Journal of Biomedical and Health Informatics*, *21*(1), 4–21. doi:10.1109/JBHI.2016.2636665 PMID:28055930

Ravyse, W. S., Blignaut, A. S., Leendertz, V., & Woolner, A. (2017). Success factors for serious games to enhance learning: A systematic review. *Virtual Reality (Waltham Cross)*, *21*(1), 31–58. doi:10.100710055-016-0298-4

Raybourn, E. M. (2014). A new paradigm for serious games: Transmedia learning for more effective training and education. *Journal of Computational Science*, (5(3)), 471–481.

Rea, N. (2019, April 18). Can 'Assassin's Creed' Help Rebuild Notre Dame? How Restoring the Cathedral Will Rely on Both New Tech and Ancient Knowhow. *Artnet*. https://news.artnet.com/market/how-technologies-old-and-new-will-be-needed-to-rebuild-notre-dame-1520689

Recommendations for applying criteria for evaluating the quality of an educational program. (2020, November 17). *Approved by the National Agency for quality assurance of Higher Education*, 66. Kyiv: LLC "Ukrainian educational publishing center "Orion"".

Redmon, D. (2003). Playful Deviance as an Urban Leisure Activity: Secret Selves, Self-validation, and Entertaining Performances. *Deviant Behavior: An Interdisciplinary Journal*, *24*(1), 27–51. doi:10.1080/10639620390117174

Redondo Romero, A. M. (2008). Language disorders. *Pediatria Integral*, *12*(9), 859–872. https://cdn.pediatriaintegral.es/wp-content/uploads/2017/xxi01/02/n1-015-022_SergiAguilera.pdf

Regenbrecht, H., Hoermann, S., McGregor, G., Dixon, B., Franz, E., Ott, C., Hale, L., Schubert, T., & Hoermann, J. (2012). Visual manipulations for motor rehabilitation. *Computers & Graphics*, *36*(7), 819–834.

Rego, P., Moreira, P. M., & Reis, L. P. (2010). Serious Games for Rehabilitation: A survey and a classification towards a taxonomy. *Proceedings of the 5th Iberian Conference on Information Systems and Technologies, CISTI 2010.*

Reich, J., & Ruipérez-Valiente, J. A. (2019). The MOOC pivot. *Science*, *363*(6423), 130–131. doi:10.1126cience.aav7958 PMID:30630920

Reiners, T., Wood, L. C., Chang, V., Gütl, C. H., Teräs, H., & Gregory, S. (2012). Operationalising gamification in an educational authentic environment. In IADIS Internet Technologies and Society (pp. 93-100). Academic Press.

Reitz, L., Sohny, A., & Lochmann, G. (2016). VR-based gamification of communication training and oral examination in a second language. *International Journal of Game-Based Learning*, *16*(4), 391–404. doi:10.4018/IJGBL.2016040104

Rekhi, S. (2017, January 3). Understanding User Psychology: Thinking like a Game Designer. *Medium*. https://medium.com/@sachinrekhi/understanding-user-psychology-thinking-like-a-game-designer-3aafde81ae2d

Renkl, A., & Atkinson, R. K. (2007). Interactive Learning Environments: Contemporary Issues and Trends. An Introduction to the Special Issue. *Educational Psychology Review*, *19*(3), 235–238. doi:10.100710648-007-9052-5

Resnick, M. (2012). Mother's Day, Warrior Cats, and Digital Fluency: Stories from the Scratch Online Community. *Proceedings of the Constructionism 2012 Conference.*

RETAIN Labs Medical Inc. (2018). *RETAIN Neonatal Resuscitation*. Retrieved from: https://www.playretain.com

Rezzly. (2021). Available at https://www.rezzly.com/

Ribaupierre, S. d., Kapralos, B., Haji, F., & Stroulia, E. Dubrowski, & Eagleson, R. (2014). Healthcare training enhancement through virtual reality and serious games. In C. Lakhmi, L. Jain, & P. Anderson (Eds.), Virtual, augmented reality and serious games for healthcare (pp. 9-27). Berlin: Springer.

Ribeiro, A. R. (2012). Using serious games to train evacuation behavior. In *Iberian Conference on Information Systems and Technologies*. IEEE Xplore.

Ricciardi, F., & Paolis, L. T. (2014). A Comprehensive Review of Serious Games in Health Professions. *International Journal of Computer Games Technology, 2014*, 1–11. doi:10.1155/2014/787968

Richa, K., Babbitt, C. W., & Gaustad, G. (2017). Eco-Efficiency Analysis of a Lithium-Ion Battery Waste Hierarchy Inspired by Circular Economy. *Journal of Industrial Ecology, 21*(3), 715–730. doi:10.1111/jiec.12607

Rideout, V. J., Foehr, U. G., & Roberts, D. F. (2010). *Generation M^2: Media in the lives of 8 to 18 year olds. Henry J. Kaiser Family Foundation.* Henry J. Kaiser Family Foundation.

Rieber, L. P. (1996). Seriously considering play: Designing interactive learning environments based on the blending of microworlds, simulations, and games. *Educational Technology Research and Development, 44*(2), 43–58. doi:10.1007/BF02300540

Rinnert, G. C., Martens, M., Mooney, A., Talbott, J. A., & Rinnert, B. (2017, June). Energetic alpha, playful handwriting practice for children. In *Proceedings of the 2017 Conference on Interaction Design and Children* (pp. 687-691). 10.1145/3078072.3091981

Ristov, S., Ackovska, N., & Kirandziska, V. (2015, March). Positive experience of the project gamification in the microprocessors and microcontrollers course. In *2015 IEEE Global Engineering Education Conference (EDUCON)* (pp. 511-517). IEEE. 10.1109/EDUCON.2015.7096018

Rittel, H. W., & Webber, M. M. (1973). Dilemmas in a general theory of planning. *Policy Sciences, 4*(2), 155–169. doi:10.1007/BF01405730

Ritter, F. E., Baxter, G. D., & Churchill, E. F. (2014). *Foundations for designing user-centered systems.* Springer-Verlag. doi:10.1007/978-1-4471-5134-0

Rizzo, A. A., Bowerly, T., Buckwalter, J. G., Humphrey, L., Neumann, U., Kim, L., ... Chua, C. (2001). A Virtual Reality Environment for the Assessment of ADHD. *The ADHD Report, 9*(2), 9–13.

Robert, P. H., König, A., Amieva, H., Andrieu, S., Bremond, F., Bullock, R., Ceccaldi, M., Dubois, B., Gauthier, S., Kenigsberg, P. A., Nave, S., Orgogozo, J. M., Piano, J., Benoit, M., Touchon, J., Vellas, B., Yesavage, J., & Manera, V. (2014). Recommendations for the use of Serious Games in people with Alzheimer's Disease, related disorders and frailty. *Frontiers in Aging Neuroscience, 6*(54). Advance online publication. doi:10.3389/fnagi.2014.00054 PMID:24715864

Robert, P., Manera, V., Derreumaux, A., Ferrandez, Y., Montesino, M., Leone, E., Fabre, R., & Bourgeois, J. (2020). Efficacy of a Web App for Cognitive Training (MeMo) Regarding Cognitive and Behavioral Performance in People With Neurocognitive Disorders: Randomized Controlled Trial. *Journal of Medical Internet Research, 22*(3), e17167. Advance online publication. doi:10.2196/17167 PMID:32159519

Roberts, M. (2004). *A robot for gait rehabilitation.* Academic Press.

Roberts, W., Milich, R., & Barkley, R. A. (n.d.). Primary symptoms, diagnostic criteria, subtyping, and prevalence of ADHD. In Attention-Deficit Hyperactivity Disorder: A Handbook for Diagnosis and Treatment (4th ed., pp. 51–80). New York: The Guilford Press.

Robertson, J., & Howells, C. (2008). Computer game design: Opportunities for successful learning. *Computers & Education, 50*(2), 559–578. doi:10.1016/j.compedu.2007.09.020

Robichaud, C. (2020). *Leadership Simulation: Patient Zero.* Harvard Business Publishing Education. https://hbsp.harvard.edu/product/7215-HTM-ENG?Ntt=Leadership

Robson, K., Plangger, K., Kietzmann, J., McCarthy, I., & Pitt, L. (2015). Is it all a game? Understanding the principles of gamification. *Business Horizons*, 58(4), 411–420. doi:10.1016/j.bushor.2015.03.006

Rodrigues, L. A. O. (2017). *Development of nonmotorized mechanisms for human lower limb rehabilitation*. Federal University of Uberlândia.

Rodrigues, L. A. O., & Gonçalves, R. S. (2014). Development of games Applied to Human Upper limb Rehabilitation. *XXIV Brazilian Conference of Biomedic – CBEB*, 396–399.

Rohani, D. A., Sørensen, H. B. D., & Puthusserypady, S. (2014). Brain-computer interface using P300 and virtual reality: A gaming approach for treating ADHD. In *2014 36th Annual International Conference of the IEEE Engineering in Medicine and Biology Society* (pp. 3606–3609). IEEE.

Romero, M. (2011). Supporting collaborative game based learning knowledge construction through the use of knowledge group awareness. NoE games and learning alliance. *Lecture at the GaLa 1st Alignment School, 20.*

Romero, M., Usart, M., Ott, M., Earp, J., de Freitas, S., & Arnab, S. (2012). Learning through playing: for or against each other? Promoting collaborative learning in digital game based learning. *European Conference on Information Systems.*

Romero-Ayuso, D., Cuerda, C., Morales, C., Tesoriero, R., Triviño-Juárez, J. M., Segura-Fragoso, A., & Gallud, J. A. (2021). Activities of Daily Living and Categorization Skills of Elderly with Cognitive Deficit: A Preliminary Study. *Brain Sciences*, 11(2), 213. Advance online publication. doi:10.3390/brainsci11020213 PMID:33578677

Romero-Ayuso, D., Toledano-González, A., Rodríguez-Martínez, M. del C., Arroyo-Castillo, P., Triviño-Juárez, J. M., González, P., & Ariza-Vega, P., Del Pino González, A., & Segura-Fragoso, A. (2021). Effectiveness of Virtual Reality-Based Interventions for Children and Adolescents with ADHD: A Systematic Review and Meta-Analysis. *Children (Basel, Switzerland), 8*(2), 70.

Romero, C., Ventura, S., & García, E. (2008). Data mining in course management systems: Moodle case study and tutorial. *Computers & Education*, 51(1), 368–384. doi:10.1016/j.compedu.2007.05.016

Romero, M., Usart, M., & Ott, M. (2014). Can Serious Games Contribute to Developing and Sustaining 21st Century Skills? *Games and Culture*, 10(2), 148–177. doi:10.1177/1555412014548919

Rooney, P. (2012). A Theoretical Framework for Serious Game Design: Exploring Pedagogy, Play and Fidelity and their Implications for the Design Process. *International Journal of Game-Based Learning*, 2(4), 41–60. doi:10.4018/ijgbl.2012100103

Roungas, B. (2016). A model-driven framework for educational game design. *International Journal of Serious Games*, 3(3), 19–37. doi:10.17083/ijsg.v3i3.126

Rouse, K. (2013). *Gamification in science education: The relationship of educational games to motivation and achievement*. The University Of Southern Mississippi.

Rubin, E., Prizant, B. M., Laurent, A. C., & Wetherby, A. M. (2013). Social communication, emotional regulation, and transactional support (SCERTS). In *Interventions for Autism Spectrum Disorders* (pp. 107–127). Springer.

Rubin, J., & Chasnell, D. (2008). *Handbook of usability testing: How to plan, design, and conduct effective tests* (2nd ed.). Wiley Publishing, Inc.

Ruipérez-Valiente, J. A., Cobos, R., Muñoz-Merino, P. J., Andujar, Á., & Kloos, C. D. (2017). Early prediction and variable importance of certificate accomplishment in a MOOC. Lecture Notes in Computer Science, 10254. doi:10.1007/978-3-319-59044-8_31

Ruipérez-Valiente, J. A. (2020). El Proceso de Implementación de Analiticas de Aprendizaje. *RIED. Revista Iberoamericana de Educación a Distancia*, *23*(2), 85–101. doi:10.5944/ried.23.2.26283

Ruiperez-Valiente, J. A., Gaydos, M., Rosenheck, L., Kim, Y. J., & Klopfer, E. (2020). Patterns of Engagement in an Educational Massively Multiplayer Online Game: A Multidimensional View. *IEEE Transactions on Learning Technologies*, *13*(4), 648–661. Advance online publication. doi:10.1109/TLT.2020.2968234

Ruiperez-Valiente, J. A., Gomez, M. J., Martinez, P. A., & Kim, Y. J. (2021). Ideating and Developing a Visualization Dashboard to Support Teachers Using Educational Games in the Classroom. *IEEE Access: Practical Innovations, Open Solutions*, *9*, 83467–83481. doi:10.1109/ACCESS.2021.3086703

Ruipérez-Valiente, J. A., & Kim, Y. J. (2020). Effects of solo vs. collaborative play in a digital learning game on geometry: Results from a K12 experiment. *Computers & Education*, *159*(September), 104008. Advance online publication. doi:10.1016/j.compedu.2020.104008

Ruipérez-Valiente, J. A., Muñoz-Merino, P. J., & Delgado Kloos, C. (2017). Detecting and Clustering Students by their Gamification Behavior with Badges: A Case Study in Engineering Education. *International Journal of Engineering Education*, *33*(2-B), 816–830.

Ruipérez-Valiente, J. A., Muñoz-Merino, P. J., & Kloos, C. D. (2018). Improving the prediction of learning outcomes in educational platforms including higher level interaction indicators. *Expert Systems: International Journal of Knowledge Engineering and Neural Networks*, *35*(6), e12298. Advance online publication. doi:10.1111/exsy.12298

Ruiperez-Valiente, J. A., Munoz-Merino, P. J., Kloos, C. D., Niemann, K., Scheffel, M., & Wolpers, M. (2016). Analyzing the Impact of Using Optional Activities in Self-Regulated Learning. *IEEE Transactions on Learning Technologies*, *9*(3), 231–243. Advance online publication. doi:10.1109/TLT.2016.2518172

Ruipérez-Valiente, J. A., Muñoz-Merino, P. J., Pijeira Díaz, H. J., Ruiz, J. S., & Kloos, C. D. (2017). Evaluation of a learning analytics application for open edX platform. *Computer Science and Information Systems*, *14*(1), 51–73. Advance online publication. doi:10.2298/CSIS160331043R

Rursch, J. A., Luse, A., & Jacobson, D. (2010). IT-adventures: A program to spark IT interest in high school students using inquiry-based learning with cyber defense, game design, and robotics. *IEEE Transactions on Education*, *53*(1), 71–79. doi:10.1109/TE.2009.2024080

Rusca, M., Huen, J., & Schwartz, K. (2012). Water management simulation games and the construction of knowledge. *Hydrology and Earth System Sciences*, *16*(8), 2749–2757. doi:10.5194/hess-16-2749-2012

Rusnak, P. J. (2008). *The Science of Gaming Consciousness: A Lesson for Teachers and Parents*. Canadian Society for the Study of Education.

Ryan, M. (2016). *Narrative as Virtual Reality 2: Revisiting immersion and interactivity in literature and electronic media*. Johns Hopkins University Press.

Ryan, R. M., & Deci, E. L. (2000). Intrinsic and extrinsic motivations: Classic definitions and new directions. *Contemporary Educational Psychology*, *25*(1), 54–67. doi:10.1006/ceps.1999.1020 PMID:10620381

Ryan, R. M., & Deci, E. L. (2000). Self-determination theory and the facilitation of intrinsic motivation, social development, and well-being. *The American Psychologist*, *55*(1), 68–78. doi:10.1037/0003-066X.55.1.68 PMID:11392867

Ryan, R. M., Rigby, C. S., & Przybylski, A. (2006). The motivational pull of video games: A self-determination theory approach. *Motivation and Emotion*, *30*(4), 344–360. doi:10.100711031-006-9051-8

Sailer, M., Hense, J. U., Mayr, S. K., & Mandl, H. (2017). How gamification motivates: An experimental study of the effects of specific game design elements on psychological need satisfaction. *Computers in Human Behavior*, *69*, 371–380. doi:10.1016/j.chb.2016.12.033

Sailer, M., & Homner, L. (2020). The Gamification of Learning: A Meta-analysis. *Educational Psychology Review*, *32*(1), 77–112. doi:10.100710648-019-09498-w

Sakai, A. F. (2021). *Learning Management System*. https://www.sakaiproject.org

Salant, B., & Benton, M. (2017). *Strengthening local education systems for newly arrived adults and children: Empowering cities through better use of EU instruments*. Migration Policy Institute Europe. https://ec.europa.eu/futurium/sites/futurium/files/mpieurope_urbanagenda_education.pdf

Salen, K., & Zimmerman, E. (2003). *Rules of Play: Game design fundamentals*. MIT Press.

Salen, K., & Zimmerman, E. (2004). *Rules of play: Game design fundamentals*. MIT press.

Salim, V. V. (2018). Development of a markerless control system for a human gait rehabilitation robot. Federal University of Uberlândia.

Samarasinghe, H. A. S. M., Weerasooriya, W. A. M. S., Weerasinghe, G. H. E., Ekanayaka, Y., Rajapakse, R., & Wijesinghe, D. P. D. (2017). Serious games design considerations for people with Alzheimer's disease in developing nations. *2017 IEEE 5th International Conference on Serious Games and Applications for Health, SeGAH 2017*. 10.1109/SeGAH.2017.7939301

Sanchez, E. (2011). Key criteria for Game Design. A Framework. MEET Project. European Commission.

Sanchez, A., Barreiro, J. M., & Maojo, V. (2000). Design of virtual reality systems for education: A cognitive approach. *Education and Information Technologies*, *5*(4), 345–362. doi:10.1023/A:1012061809603

Sanchez-Vives, M. V., & Slater, M. (2005). From presence to consciousness through virtual reality. *Nature Reviews. Neuroscience*, *6*(4), 332–339.

Sanmugam, M., Zaid, N. M., Abdullah, Z., Aris, B., Mohamed, H., & van der Meijden, H. (2016, December). The impacts of infusing game elements and gamification in learning. In *2016 IEEE 8th international conference on engineering education (ICEED)* (pp. 131-136). IEEE. 10.1109/ICEED.2016.7856058

Santos, L. H., Okamoto, K., Hiragi, S., Yamamoto, G., Sugiyama, O., Aoyama, T., & Kuroda, T. (2019). Pervasive game design to evaluate social interaction effects on levels of physical activity among older adults. *Journal of Rehabilitation and Assistive Technologies Engineering*, *6*. Advance online publication. doi:10.1177/2055668319844443 PMID:31285836

Santos, P., Ritz, M., Fuhrmann, C., Monroy, R., Schmedt, H., Tausch, R., Domajnko, M., Knuth, M., & Fellner, D. (2017). Acceleration of 3D Mass Digitization Process: Recent Advances and Challenges. In M. Ioannides, N. Magnenat-Thalmann, & G. Papagiannakis (Eds.), *Mixed Reality and Gamification for Cultural Heritage* (pp. 99–128). Springer. doi:10.1007/978-3-319-49607-8_4

Sapkowski, A. (2020). *The Witcher Saga*. Gollancz.

Sarkeesian, A. (2013). *Tropes vs women in video games*. https://feministfrequency.com/video-series/

Sarton, G. (1924). The new humanism. *Isis*, 9–42.

Sassoon, J., Maestri, A., & Polsinelli, P. (2019). *Games to be taken seriously. Gamification, storytelling and game design for innovative projects*. Franco Angeli.

Sauvé, L. (2010). Effective Educational Games. In D. Kaufman & L. Sauvé (Eds.), Educational Gameplay and Simulation Environments: Case Studies and Lessons Learned (pp. 27-50). Information Science Reference. doi:10.4018/978-1-61520-731-2.ch002

Savransky, M., Wilkie, A., & Rosengarten, M. (2017). The Lure of Possible Futures. In A. Wilkie, M. Savransky, & M. Rosengarten (Eds.), *Speculative Research* (pp. 1–17). Routledge. doi:10.4324/9781315541860-1

Sawesi, S., Rashrash, M., Phalakornkule, K., Carpenter, J. S., & Jones, J. F. (2016). The impact of information technology on patient engagement and health behavior change: A systematic review of the literature. *JMIR Medical Informatics*, *4*(1), e4514. doi:10.2196/medinform.4514 PMID:26795082

Schaie, K., & Willis, S. (2016). *Handbook of the Psychology of Aging* (8th ed.). Academic Press.

Schell, J. (2012). What Games are Good At [Paper presentation]. 9th Annual Games for Change Festival, New York, NY.

Schell, J. (2008). *The Art of Game Design: A book of lenses*. CRC press. doi:10.1201/9780080919171

Schell, J. (2019). *The Art of Game Design: A Book of Lenses* (3rd ed.). Taylor & Francis Ltd.

Schimanke, F., Mertens, R., & Vornberger, O. (2014). Spaced repetition learning games on mobile devices: Foundations and perspectives. *Interactive Technology and Smart Education*, *11*(3), 201–222. doi:10.1108/ITSE-07-2014-0017

Schrepp, M., Hinderks, A., & Thomaschewski, J. (2014). Applying the user experience questionnaire (UEQ) in different evaluation scenarios. *International Conference of Design, User Experience, and Usability*, 383–392. 10.1007/978-3-319-07668-3_37

Schroth, G. (1999). A review of belowground interactions in agroforestry, focussing on mechanisms and management options. *Agroforestry Systems*, *43*(1/3), 5–34. doi:10.1023/A:1026443018920

Schroth, G., & Sinclair, F. L. (2003). *Trees, crops and soil fertility concepts and research methods*. CABI Publishing.

Schuller, B. W., Dunwell, I., Weninger, F., & Paletta, L. (2013). Serious gaming for behavior change: The state of play. *IEEE Pervasive Computing*, *12*(3), 48–55. doi:10.1109/MPRV.2013.54

Schultz, W. (2004). Neural coding of basic reward terms of animal learning theory, game theory, microeconomics and behavioural ecology. *Current Opinion in Neurobiology*, *14*(2), 139–147. doi:10.1016/j.conb.2004.03.017 PMID:15082317

Scoresby, J., & Shelton, B. E. (2011). Visual perspectives within educational computer games: Effects on presence and flow within virtual immersive learning environments. *Instructional Science*, *39*(3), 227–254.

Scrum. (2021). *Scrum*. https://www.scrum.org/

Seaborn, K., & Fels, D. I. (2015). Gamification in theory and action: A survey. *International Journal of Human-Computer Studies*, *74*, 14–31. doi:10.1016/j.ijhcs.2014.09.006

Seligman, L. D., & Ollendick, T. H. (1998). Comorbidity of Anxiety and Depression in Children and Adolescents: An Integrative Review. *Clinical Child and Family Psychology Review*, *1*(2), 125–144. doi:10.1023/A:1021887712873 PMID:11324302

Sen, J., & Vaghasia, D. (n.d.). *Ridge to valley Approach in Watershed Experience of Teliamba Village of AKRSP, Netrang*. http://www.dscindia.org/dwnld.php?path=dXBsb2FkL3BkZi9wdWJsaWNhdGlvbnMv&filename=Ridgetovalleywatershed.pdf

Seo, J. H., Smith, B. M., Cook, M., Malone, E., Pine, M., Leal, S., Bai, Z., & Suh, J. (2017). Anatomy builder VR: Applying a constructive learning method in the virtual reality canine skeletal system. *International Conference on Applied Human Factors and Ergonomics*, 245–252. 10.1109/VR.2017.7892345

Seppo. (2021). Available at https://seppo.io/

Serrat, O. (2017). Design thinking. *Knowledge Solutions*, 129-134.

Settles, B., & Meeder, B. (2016). A trainable spaced repetition model for language learning. *54th Annual Meeting of the Association for Computational Linguistics*, 1848–1858. https://www.duolingo.com

Seymour, E., & Hewitt, N. M. (1997). *Talking about leaving: Why undergraduates leave the sciences*. Westview Press.

Shabani, K., Khatib, M., & Ebadi, S. (2010). Vygotsky's Zone of Proximal Development: Instructional Implications and Teachers' Professional Development. *English Language Teaching*, *3*(4), 237. doi:10.5539/elt.v3n4p237

Sharifzadeh, N., Kharrazi, H., Nazari, E., Tabesh, H., Khodabandeh, M. E., Heidari, S., & Tara, M. (2020). Health education serious games targeting health care providers, patients, and public health users: Scoping review. *JMIR Serious Games*, *8*(1), e13459. doi:10.2196/13459 PMID:32134391

Shaw, A. (2010). What Is Video Game Culture? Cultural Studies and Game Studies. *Games and Culture*, *5*(4), 403–424. doi:10.1177/1555412009360414

Shaw, M., Hodgkins, P., Caci, H., Young, S., Kahle, J., Woods, A. G., & Arnold, L. E. (2012). A systematic review and analysis of long-term outcomes in attention deficit hyperactivity disorder: Effects of treatment and non-treatment. *BMC Medicine*, *10*(1), 99. doi:10.1186/1741-7015-10-99 PMID:22947230

Shehabuddeen, N., Probert, D., Phaal, R., & Platts, K. (1999). *Representing and approaching complex management issues: part 1 - role and definition*. Centre for Technology Management (CTM).

Shen, C., Wang, H., & Ritterfeld, U. (2009). Serious Games and Seriously Fun Games: Can They Be One and the Same? In U. Ritterfeld, M. Cody, & P. Vorderer (Eds.), *Serious Games: Mechanisms and Effects* (1st ed., pp. 48–62). Routledge.

Shernoff, D. J., Csikszentmihalyi, M., Schneider, B., & Shernoff, E. S. (2014). Student Engagement in High School Classrooms from the Perspective of Flow Theory. In M. Csikszentmihalyi (Ed.), *Applications of Flow in Human Development and Education: The Collected Works of Mihaly Csikszentmihalyi* (pp. 475–494). Springer Netherlands. doi:10.1007/978-94-017-9094-9_24

Sherry, J. L., Lucas, K., Greenberg, B. S., & Lachlan, K. (2006). Video game uses and gratifications as predictors of use and game preference. In P. Vorderer & J. Bryant (Eds.), *Playing computer games: Motives, responses, and consequences* (pp. 213–224). Erlbaum.

Shim, G., & Jeong, B. (2018). Predicting suicidal ideation in college students with mental health screening questionnaires. *Psychiatry Investigation*, *15*(11), 1037–1045. doi:10.30773/pi.2018.08.21.3 PMID:30380820

Shu, H., Chen, X., Anderson, R. C., Wu, N., & Xuan, Y. (2003). Properties of school Chinese: Implications for learning to read. *Child Development*, *74*(1), 27–47. doi:10.1111/1467-8624.00519 PMID:12625434

Shum, S. B., Ferguson, R., & Martinez-Maldonado, R. (2019). Human-centred learning analytics. *Journal of Learning Analytics*, *6*(2), 1–9. doi:10.18608/jla.2019.62.1

Shute, V. J. (2005). Stealth Assessment in Computer-Based Games to Support Learning. In S. Tobias & J. D. Fletcher (Eds.), *Computer Games and Instruction* (pp. 503–524). Information Age Publishers.

Shute, V. J., D'Mello, S., Baker, R., Cho, K., Bosch, N., Ocumpaugh, J., Ventura, M., & Almeda, V. (2015). Modeling how incoming knowledge, persistence, affective states, and in-game progress influence student learning from an educational game. *Computers & Education*, *86*, 224–235. doi:10.1016/j.compedu.2015.08.001

Silva, F. G. (2020). Practical methodology for the design of educational serious games. *Information (Basel)*, *11*(1), 14. doi:10.3390/info11010014

Simon, H. A. (1990). Bounded rationality. *Utility and Probability*, 15-18.

Simon, H. A. (1979). Rational decision making in business organizations. *The American Economic Review*, *69*(4), 493–513.

Simon, H. A. (2013). *Administrative behavior* (4th ed.). Simon and Schuster.

Simonoff, E., Pickles, A., Charman, T., Chandler, S., Loucas, T., & Baird, G. (2008). Psychiatric disorders in children with autism spectrum disorders: Prevalence, comorbidity, and associated factors in a population-derived sample. *Journal of the American Academy of Child and Adolescent Psychiatry*, *47*(8), 921–929. doi:10.1097/CHI.0b013e318179964f PMID:18645422

Šimonová, I., & Bílek, M. (2012, April). On Individually Adapted ICT Applications in Computer-supported University Instruction. In DIVAI 2012 (p. 301). Academic Press.

SIMX. (2020). *Virtual Reality Medical Simulation*. https://www.simxvr.com/

Sinding-Larsen, H. (1924). *Akershus: bidrag til Akershus' slots bygningshistorie i de første 350 aar 1300 – 1650. Paa grundlag av den bygningsarkaeologiske undersøkelse 1905 – 1924* [Akershus: contribution to the history of the building of Akershus castle in the first 350 years 1300-1650. On the basis of the archaeological examination 1905-1924]. Eberh. B. Oppi Kunstforlag.

Singapore Land Authority. (2021, June 23). *Total Land Area of Singapore*. Data.Gov.Sg. https://data.gov.sg/dataset/total-land-area-of-singapore

Singh, H., & Singh, B. P. (2015). E-Training: An assessment tool to measure business effectiveness in a business organization. *2015 2nd International Conference on Computing for Sustainable Global Development (INDIACom)*, 1229-1231.

Sinkkonen, H. M., & Kyttälä, M. (2014). Experiences of Finnish teachers working with immigrant students. *European Journal of Special Needs Education*, *29*(2), 167–183. doi:10.1080/08856257.2014.891719

Siriaraya, P., Visch, V., Vermeeren, A., & Bas, M. (2018). A cookbook method for Persuasive Game Design. *International Journal of Serious Games*, *5*(1), 37–71. doi:10.17083/ijsg.v5i1.159

Sivak, S., Sivak, M., Isaacs, J., Laird, J., & McDonald, A. (2007). Managing the tradeoffs in the digital transformation of an educational board game to a computer-based simulation. *Proceedings of the 2007 ACM SIGGRAPH Symposium on Video Games*, 97–102. 10.1145/1274940.1274961

SketchUp. (2021, January 16). In *Wikipedia*. https://en.wikipedia.org/wiki/SketchUp

Slade, S., & Prinsloo, P. (2013). Learning Analytics: Ethical Issues and Dilemmas. *The American Behavioral Scientist*, *57*(10), 1510–1529. doi:10.1177/0002764213479366

Smart Nation and Digital Government Office. (2021, May 11). *Initiatives: Health*. Smart Nation Singapore. https://www.smartnation.gov.sg/what-is-smart-nation/initiatives

Smith, R. P. (2017, September 15). Fans of Minecraft Are Sure to Dig this Nationwide Museum Fest. *Smithsonianmag*. https://www.smithsonianmag.com/smithsonian-institution/minecraft-fans-dig-museum-fest-180964888/

Smith, P. K. (1982). Does play matter? Functional and evolutionary aspects of animal and human play. *Behavioral and Brain Sciences*, 5(1), 139155. doi:10.1017/S0140525X0001092X

Smith, T., Gildeh, N., & Holmes, C. (2007). The Montreal cognitive assessment: Validity and utility in a memory clinic setting. *Canadian Journal of Psychiatry*, 52(5), 329–332. doi:10.1177/070674370705200508 PMID:17542384

Snyder, E., & Hartig, J. R. (2013). Gamification of board review: A residency curricular innovation. *Medical Education*, 5(47), 524–525. doi:10.1111/medu.12190 PMID:23574079

Society for Learning Analytics Research (SoLAR). (2021). *What is Learning Analytics?* Retrieved from https://www.solaresearch.org/about/what-is-learning-analytics/

SOHA. (2021, July 26). Female gamers are on the rise. *Zestvine*. https://www.zestvine.com/female-gamers-are-on-the-rise-trends-stats/

Sonawane, K. (2017, November). Serious games market outlook: 2023. *Allied Market Research*. https://www.alliedmarketresearch.com/serious-games-market

Sousa, L., Oliveira, A. I., Marques, A. R., Morais, J., Mendes, M., Cardoso, R., Costa, S., & Capela, C. (2019). Global Geriatric Assessment at Internal Medicine: A More Appropriate Model in The Evaluation of Hospitalized Elderly Patients. *Revista da Sociedade Portuguesa de Medicina Interna*, 26(1), 40–46. doi:10.24950/rspmi/original/214/1/2019

Souza, J., & Chaves, E. (2005). O efeito do exercício de estimulação da memória em idosos saudáveis [The effect of memory stimulation exercise in healthy elderly]. *Revista da Escola de S. Paulo*, 39(1), 13–19.

Spencer, T. J. (2006). ADHD and comorbidity in childhood. *The Journal of Clinical Psychiatry*, 67, 27.

Sprint, G., & Cook, D. (2015, March). Enhancing the CS1 student experience with gamification. In *2015 IEEE integrated STEM education conference* (pp. 94-99). IEEE.

Squire, K. (2011). *Video Games and Learning: Teaching and Participatory Culture in the Digital Age. Technology, Education—Connections (the TEC Series)*. ERIC.

Squire, K. D. (2008). Video games and education: Designing learning systems for an interactive age. *Educational Technology*, 48(2), 17–26.

Sripada, C. S., Angstadt, M., Banks, S., Nathan, P. J., Liberzon, I., & Phan, K. L. (2009). Functional neuroimaging of mentalizing during the trust game in social anxiety disorder. *Neuroreport*, 20(11), 984–989.

Srisawasdi, N., & Panjaburee, P. (2019). Implementation of Game-transformed Inquiry-based Learning to Promote the Understanding of and Motivation to Learn Chemistry. *Journal of Science Education and Technology*, 28(2), 152–164. doi:10.100710956-018-9754-0

Stahel, W. R. (2010). The Preformance Economy (2nd ed.). Springer.

Stahel, W. R. (1982). The Product-Life Factor. In S. G. Orr (Ed.), *An Inquiry Into the Nature of Sustainable Societies: The Role of the Private Sector*. NARC.

Stallman, J. (2003). John Dewey's new humanism and liberal education for the 21st century. *Education and Culture*, 19(2), 18–22.

Stănescu, D. F., Ioniță, C., & Ioniță, A. M. (2020). Game-thinking in Personnel Recruitment and Selection: Advantages and Disadvantages. *Postmodern Openings/Deschideri Postmoderne, 11*(2), 267-276.

Stanziola, E., Ortiz, J. M., & Simón, M. (2014). UX in healthcare: lessons learned in a complex environment. In *Interaction South America (ISA 14): 6th Lationamerican Conference on Interaction Design*. Interaction Design Association; Asociación de Profesionales en Experiencia de Usuario; Internet Society; Universidad Católica Argentina. Available at: https://repositorio.uca.edu.ar/handle/123456789/7953

Stapleton, A. J. (2004). *Serious games: Serious opportunities. Australian Game Developers" Conference*. Academic Summit.

Starks, K. (2014). Cognitive behavioral game design: A unified model for designing serious games. *Frontiers in Psychology*, *5*, 28. doi:10.3389/fpsyg.2014.00028 PMID:24550858

Starkweather, J., & Stevenson, D. (2011). PMP® Certification as a Core Competency: Necessary But Not Sufficient. *Project Management Journal*, *42*(1), 32–41. doi:10.1002/pmj.20174

Steamcommunity. (2020, September 19). Playable female character. *Discussions: Medieval Dynasty*. https://steamcommunity.com/app/1129580/discussions/0/2942496178841957805/

Stein, M. B., Fuetsch, M., Müller, N., Höfler, M., Lieb, R., & Wittchen, H.-U. (2001). Social Anxiety Disorder and the Risk of Depression: A Prospective Community Study of Adolescents and Young Adults. *Archives of General Psychiatry*, *58*(3), 251–256.

Stein, M. B., & Stein, D. J. (2008). Social anxiety disorder. *Lancet*, *371*(9618), 1115–1125.

Stenros, J. (2017). The Game Definition Game: A Review. *Games and Culture*, *12*(6), 499–520. doi:10.1177/1555412016655679

Stephenson, A., McDonough, S. M., Murphy, M. H., Nugent, C. D., & Mair, J. L. (2017). Using computer, mobile and wearable technology enhanced interventions to reduce sedentary behaviour: A systematic review and meta-analysis. *The International Journal of Behavioral Nutrition and Physical Activity*, *14*(1), 1–17. doi:10.118612966-017-0561-4 PMID:28800736

Steptoe, A., Demakakos, P., de Oliveira, C., & Wardle, J. (2012). Distinctive biological correlates of positive psychological well-being in older men and women. *Psychosomatic Medicine*, *74*(5), 501–508. doi:10.1097/PSY.0b013e31824f82c8 PMID:22511728

Sterman, J. D. (1989). Modeling Managerial Behavior: Misperceptions of Feedback in a Dynamic Decision Making Experiment. *Management Science*, *35*(3), 321–339. doi:10.1287/mnsc.35.3.321

Stern, Y. (2012). Cognitive reserve in ageing and Alzheimer's disease. *Lancet Neurology*, *11*(11), 1006–1012. doi:10.1016/S1474-4422(12)70191-6 PMID:23079557

Stewart, I., & Wang, K. (2019). Simulations and Games in Management Education – The human costs of creating and participating in 'useful illusions'. *Proceedings of the British Academy of Management*.

Stewart, I., Denholm, J., & Blackwell, P. (2016). *Simulations in Project Management - Unexpected Events, Human Costs: Initiating an Autoethnographic Inquiry*. European Conference on Game Based Learning, Paisley, UK.

Stoll, J. (2021, Jan 13). Box-office revenue of the most successful films of all time. *Statista*. https://www.statista.com/statistics/262926/box-office-revenue-of-the-most-successful-films-of-all-time /

Stone City-Cold Stone Creamery, Inc. [Digital game]. (2003). Retrieved 17 07, 2021, from Persuasive games: https://persuasivegames.com/game/coldstone

Stop Disaster. (2018). *UNDRR, Producer, & playerthree*. Retrieved 2021, from Play and learn to STOP DISASTERS!: https://www.stopdisastersgame.org/

Streicher, A., & Smeddinck, J. D. (2016). *Personalized and Adaptive Serious Games*. doi:10.1007/978-3-319-46152-6_14

Strickland, D. (1997). Virtual reality for the treatment of autism. *Virtual Reality in Neuro-Psycho-Physiology, 44*, 81–86.

Strmečki, D., Bernik, A., & Radošević, D. (2016). Gamification in E-Learning: Introducing Gamified Design Elements into E-Learning Systems. *Journal of Computational Science, 11*(12), 1108–1117. doi:10.3844/jcssp.2015.1108.1117

Subramaniam, M., Abdin, E., Vaingankar, J. A., Shafie, S., Chua, B. Y., Sambasivam, R., Zhang, Y. J., Shahwan, S., Chang, S., Chua, H. C., Verma, S., James, L., Kwok, K. W., Heng, D., & Chong, S. A. (2019). Tracking the mental health of a nation: Prevalence and correlates of mental disorders in the second Singapore mental health study. *Epidemiology and Psychiatric Sciences, 29*, e29. doi:10.1017/S2045796019000179 PMID:30947763

Sugarman, J. (2018). A matter of design: English learner program models in K-12 education (Issue 2). Migration Policy Institute.

Sugarman, J. (2017). *Beyond teaching English: Supporting high school completion by immigrant and refugee students*. Migration Policy Institute.

Sultana, M., Bryant, D., Orange, J. B., Beedie, T., & Montero-Odasso, M. (2020). Effect of Wii Fit© exercise on balance of older adults with neurocognitive disorders: A meta-analysis. *Journal of Alzheimer's Disease, 75*(3), 817–826. doi:10.3233/JAD-191301 PMID:32310168

Sumtsova, O., Aikina, T., Bolsunovskaya, L., Phillips, C., Zubkova, O., & Mitchell, P. (2018). Collaborative learning at engineering universities: Benefits and challenges. *International Journal of Emerging Technologies in Learning, 13*(1), 160–177. doi:10.3991/ijet.v13i01.7811

Superior RPG Kit. (2019). *T-games*. https://www.unrealengine.com/marketplace/en-US/product/superior-rpg-kit

Susi, T., Johannesson, M., & Backlund, P. (2007). *Serious Games - An Overview*. School of Humanities and Informatics, University of Sköde, Sköde, Suécia.

Susi, T., Johannesson, M., & Backlund, P. (2007). *Serious games: An Overview*. Academic Press.

Susko, T. G. (2015). *MIT Skywalker: A novel robot for gait rehabilitation of stroke and cerebral palsy patients*. Academic Press.

Susko, T., Swaminathan, K., & Krebs, H. I. (2016). MIT-Skywalker: A Novel Gait Neurorehabilitation Robot for Stroke and Cerebral Palsy. *IEEE Transactions on Neural Systems and Rehabilitation Engineering, 24*(10), 1089–1099. doi:10.1109/TNSRE.2016.2533492 PMID:26929056

Svensson, E. (1962). *The medieval household: daily life in castles and farmsteads. Scandinavian examples in their European context*. Brepols.

Swinnen, E., Baeyens, J. P., Hens, G., Knaepen, K., Beckwe, D., Michielsen, M., Clijsen, R., & Kerckhofs, E. (2015). Body weight support during robot-assisted walking: Influence on the trunk and pelvis kinematics. *NeuroRehabilitation, 36*(1), 81–91. Advance online publication. doi:10.3233/NRE-141195 PMID:25547772

Swinnen, E., Baeyens, J. P., Knaepen, K., Michielsen, M., Clijsen, R., Beckwée, D., & Kerckhofs, E. (2015). Robot-assisted walking with the Lokomat: The influence of different levels of guidance force on thorax and pelvis kinematics. *Clinical Biomechanics (Bristol, Avon), 30*(3), 254–259. doi:10.1016/j.clinbiomech.2015.01.006 PMID:25662678

Swinnen, E., Baeyens, J.-P., Knaepen, K., Michielsen, M., Hens, G., Clijsen, R., Goossens, M., Buyl, R., Meeusen, R., & Kerckhofs, E. (2015). Walking with robot assistance: The influence of body weight support on the trunk and pelvis kinematics. *Disability and Rehabilitation. Assistive Technology, 10*(3), 252–257. doi:10.3109/17483107.2014.888487 PMID:24512196

Tachibana, Y., Miyazaki, C., Ota, E., Mori, R., Hwang, Y., Kobayashi, E., ... Kamio, Y. (2017). A systematic review and meta-analysis of comprehensive interventions for pre-school children with autism spectrum disorder (ASD). *PLoS One, 12*(12), e0186502.

Tajik-Parvinchi, D., Wright, L., & Schachar, R. (2014). Cognitive Rehabilitation for Attention Deficit/Hyperactivity Disorder (ADHD): Promises and Problems. *Journal of the Canadian Academy of Child and Adolescent Psychiatry, 23*(3), 207–217. PMID:25320614

Taladriz, C. C. (2021, April). Flipped mastery and gamification to teach Computer networks in a Cybersecurity Engineering Degree during COVID-19. In *2021 IEEE Global Engineering Education Conference (EDUCON)* (pp. 1624-1629). IEEE. 10.1109/EDUCON46332.2021.9453885

Tan, J. L., Goh, D. H.-L., Ang, R. P., & Huan, V. S. (2011). Child-centered interaction in the design of a game for social skills intervention. *Computers in Entertainment, 9*(1), 2:1-2:17. doi:10.1145/1953005.1953007

Tan, E. (2020). Play the City. In A. Gerber & U. Götz (Eds.), *Architectonics of Game Spaces* (pp. 265–276). Transcript Verlag., doi:10.14361/9783839448021-018

Tang, L., & Shi, P. (2021). Design and analysis of a gait rehabilitation cable robot with pairwise cable arrangement. *Journal of Mechanical Science and Technology, 35*(7), 3161–3170. Advance online publication. doi:10.100712206-021-0637-6

Tao, G., Garrett, B., Taverner, T., Cordingley, E., & Sun, C. (2021). Immersive virtual reality health games: A narrative review of game design. *Journal of Neuroengineering and Rehabilitation, 18*(1), 1–21.

Tate Gallery. (2012, January 4). *Tate's new art game for mobiles - Race Against Time. Press Release.* https://www.tate.org.uk/press/press-releases/tates-new-art-game-mobiles-race-against-time

Tate Gallery. (2013). *Digital transformation. July 2013 - February 2015.* https://www.tate.org.uk/about-us/projects/digital-transformation

Taylor, F. W. (1919). *Scientific management.* Harper & Brothers Publishers.

Taylor, M. J., & Griffin, M. (2015). The use of gaming technology for rehabilitation in people with multiple sclerosis. *Multiple sclerosis (Houndmills, Basingstoke, England), 21*(4), 355–371. doi:10.1177/1352458514563593 PMID:25533296

TECNALIA. (2021). *Arm Assist.* http://armassist.eu/

Teichner, G. (2016). *Attention-deficit/hyperactivity disorder in children and adolescents: A dsm-5 handbook for medical and mental health professionals.* Retrieved from https://ebookcentral.proquest.com

Teimouri, Y. (2018). Differential roles of shame and guilt in L2 learning: How bad is bad? *Modern Language Journal, 102*(4), 632–652. doi:10.1111/modl.12511

Terno, S. (2018). *Educational institution as a social institution: chaos or order?* Retrieved 07 20, 2021, from Prometheus: https://courses.prometheus.org.ua/assets/courseware/v1/228bd74b5c310bb220998b4fc174746b/asset-v1:Prometheus+CTFT102+2018_T3+type@asset+block/Лекція_3.2.pdf

Thakkar, S. R., & Joshi, H. D. (2016). E-Learning Systems: A Review. *Proceedings - IEEE 7th International Conference on Technology for Education*, 37–40. 10.1109/T4E.2015.6

The Black Death . (2016). [Video Game]. Small Impact Games & Syrin Studios/Green Man Loaded.

The Great War: 1914-1918 (1992). [Video Game]. Blue Byte Studio GmbH.

The Legend of Zelda . (1986). [Video Game] Nintendo.

The New York Public Library. (n.d.). *Find the Future: The Game.* http://exhibitions.nypl.org/100/digital_fun/play_the_game

The Plague . (2015). [Video Game]. Serious Games Interactive.

The Witcher 3: The Wild Hunt . (2020) [Video Game]. CD Projekt.

The Witcher. (2007-2020). [Video Game Series]. CD Projekt.

The World of Lexica. (n.d.). *Schell Games.* https://www.schellgames.com/games/the-world-of-lexica

Theodosiou, S. & Karasavvidis, I. (2015b). Serious games design: a mapping of the problems novice game designers experience in designing games. *Journal of e-Learning and Knowledge Society, 11*(3), 133-148.

Theodosiou, S., & Karasavvidis, I. (2015a). An Exploration of the Role of Feedback on Optimizing Teachers' Game Designs. *Bulletin of the IEEE Technical Committee on Learning Technology, 17*(4), 2.

Thomas, M. (2021). Cinematic forms and cultural heritage. In M. Breeze (Ed.), *Forms of the cinematic* (pp. 122–142). Bloomsbury. doi:10.5040/9781501361456.0015

Thomas, S. (2016). *Future Ready Learning. Reimagining the Role of Technology in Education. Office of Educational Technology, US Department of Education.*

Thomas, T. H., Sivakumar, V., Babichenko, D., Grieve, V. L. B., & Klem, M. (2020). Mapping Behavioral Health Serious Game Interventions for Adults With Chronic Illness: Scoping Review. *JMIR Serious Games, 8*(3), e18687. doi:10.2196/18687 PMID:32729836

Thompson-Bradley, O., Barrett, S., Patterson, C., & Craig, D. (2012). Examining the Neurocognitive Validity of Commercially Available, Smartphone-Based Puzzle Games. *Psychology (Irvine, Calif.), 3*(07), 525–526. doi:10.4236/psych.2012.37076

Thompson, S. J., Bender, K., Lantry, J., & Flynn, P. M. (2007). Treatment Engagement: Building Therapeutic Alliance in Home-Based Treatment with Adolescents and their Families. *Contemporary Family Therapy, 29*(1–2), 39–55. doi:10.100710591-007-9030-6 PMID:20556209

Tieri, G., Morone, G., Paolucci, S., & Iosa, M. (2018). Virtual reality in cognitive and motor rehabilitation: Facts, fiction and fallacies. *Expert Review of Medical Devices, 15*(2), 107–117. doi:10.1080/17434440.2018.1425613 PMID:29313388

Tobias, S., & Fletcher, J. D. (2007). What Research Has to Say About Designing Computer Games for Learning. *Educational Technology,* 20–29.

Tokarieva, A. v., Volkova, N. P., Harkusha, I. v., & Soloviev, V. N. (2019). *Educational digital games: models and implementation.* Освітній Вимір. doi:10.31812/educdim.v53i1.3872

Tolkien, J.R.R. (1954-55). *The Lord of the rings.* Allen and Unwin.

Tong, T., Chan, J. H., & Chignell, M. (2017). Serious games for dementia. *Proceedings of the 26th International Conference on World Wide Web Companion,* 1111–1115. 10.1145/3041021.3054930

Tong, T., Chignell, M., Tierney, M. C., & Lee, J. S. (2016). Test-Retest Reliability of a Serious Game for Delirium Screening in the Emergency Department. *Frontiers in Aging Neuroscience, 8,* 258. doi:10.3389/fnagi.2016.00258 PMID:27872590

Toplitz (2020). Introduction. *Medieval dynasty*. https://www.toplitz-productions.com/medieval-dynasty.html

Toppo, G. (2012). White House office studies benefits of video games. *USA Today*.

Toppo, G. (2013, June 18). Can a video game encourage kids to read the classics? *USA Today*. https://eu.usatoday.com/story/tech/gaming/2013/06/18/lexica-game-classic-books/2431337/

Tornero, J. P., & Tapio, V. (2010). *Media literacy and new humanism*. UNESCO Institute for Information Technologies in Education.

Tran, M. K. P., Robert, P., & Bremond, F. (2016). A Virtual Agent for enhancing performance and engagement of older people with dementia in Serious Games. *Workshop Artificial Compagnon-Affect-Interaction 2016*.

Travers, B. G., Mason, A. H., Mrotek, L. A., Ellertson, A., Dean, D. C. III, Engel, C., Gomez, A., Dadalko, O. I., & McLaughlin, K. (2018). Biofeedback-based, videogame balance training in autism. *Journal of Autism and Developmental Disorders*, 48(1), 163–175. doi:10.100710803-017-3310-2 PMID:28921103

Treskes, R. W., van der Velde, E. T., Barendse, R., & Bruining, N. (2016). Mobile health in cardiology: A review of currently available medical apps and equipment for remote monitoring. *Expert Review of Medical Devices*, 13(9), 823–830. doi:10.1080/17434440.2016.1218277 PMID:27477584

Tretinjak, M. F., Bednjanec, A., & Tretinjak, M. (2014, May). Application of modern teaching techniques in the educational process. In *2014 37th International Convention on Information and Communication Technology, Electronics and Microelectronics (MIPRO)* (pp. 628-632). IEEE. 10.1109/MIPRO.2014.6859643

Tripette, J., Murakami, H., Ryan, K. R., Ohta, Y., & Miyachi, M. (2017). The contribution of Nintendo Wii Fit series in the field of health: A systematic review and meta-analysis. *PeerJ*, 5, e3600. doi:10.7717/peerj.3600 PMID:28890847

Trujillo-Espinoza, C., Cardona-Reyes, H., & Guzmán-Mendoza, J. E. (2020). Model Proposed for the Production of User-Oriented Virtual Reality Scenarios for Training in the Driving of Unmanned Vehicles. *International Conference on Software Process Improvement*, 258–268.

Tsai, Y. S., & Gasevic, D. (2017). Learning analytics in higher education - Challenges and policies: A review of eight learning analytics policies. In *Seventh international learning analytics & knowledge conference* (pp. 233–242). doi:10.1145/3027385.3027400

Tsai, L. Y. (2014). Prevalence of Comorbid Psychiatric Disorders in Children and Adolescents with Autism Spectrum Disorder. *Journal of Experimental and Clinical Medicine (Taiwan)*, 6(6), 179–186. doi:10.1016/j.jecm.2014.10.005

Tschudi-Madsen, S., & Moberg, H. (1999). *Akershus: vårt riksklenodium 700 år* [Akershus: gem of our realm 700th anniversary]. Aschehaug.

Turcotte, I. (2019). Serious gaming for training non-technical skills in crisis management and emergency response. *Proceedings of the 16th International Conference on Information Systems for Crisis Response & Management (ISCRAM)*.

Tuti, T., Winters, N., Edgcombe, H., Muinga, N., Wanyama, C., English, M., & Paton, C. (2020). Evaluation of adaptive feedback in a smartphone-based game on health care providers' learning gain: Randomized controlled trial. *Journal of Medical Internet Research*, 22(7), e17100. doi:10.2196/17100 PMID:32628115

Udemy. (2021). *Online courses*. https://www.udemy.com/

Ultima Online . (1997). [Video Game]. Origin Systems. https://uo.com/

UNDDR. (2018). *Stop Disasters* [Online game]. UN Office for Disaster Risk Reduction. https://www.stopdisastersgame.org

Unity3D. (n.d.). *Unity Real-Time Development Platform | 3D, 3D VR & AR Engine*. Author.

University of Illinois Chicago. (2021). *Big Data and Wearable Health Monitors: Harnessing the Benefits and Overcoming Challenges*. https://healthinformatics.uic.edu/blog/big-data-and-wearable-health-monitors-harnessing-the-benefits-and-overcoming-challenges

Unreal Engine 4.26. (2021). [Software - game engine]. Epic Games. https://www.unrealengine.com/

UNWTO. (2017). Tourism and culture. *UNWTO General Assembly*. https://www.unwto.org/ethics-culture-and-social-responsibility

Upayanto, I. D., & Wuryandani, W. (2020). Utilizing virtual reality in learning for elementary schools during COVID 19 pandemic. *ISoLEC Proceedings, 4*(1), 26–30.

US Department of Education. (2016). Future ready learning. *2016 National Education Technology Plan*, 1–106.

Väätänen, A., & Leikas, J. (2009). Human-Centered Design and Exercise Games: Users' Experiences of a Fitness Adventure Prototype. *Design and Use of Serious Games, 37*, 33–47. Available at: http://en.scientificcommons.org/41680703

Vaishnavi, V., Kuechler, W., & Petter, S. (2004). *Design Science Research in Information Systems*. Retrieved Última atualização 30 de Junho de 2019, from http://www.desrist.org/design-research-in-information-systems/

Valenza, M. V., Gasparini, I., & Hounsell, M. da S. (2019). Serious Game Design for Children: A Set of Guidelines and their Validation. *Journal of Educational Technology & Society, 22*(3), 19–31.

Valladares-Rodríguez, S., Perez-Rodriguez, R., Facal, D., Fernández-Iglesias, M. J., Anido-Rifon, L., & Mouriño-Garcia, M. (2017). Design process and preliminary psychometric study of a video game to detect cognitive impairment in senior adults. *PeerJ, 5*, 5. doi:10.7717/peerj.3508 PMID:28674661

van der Oord, S., Ponsioen, A. J. G. B., Geurts, H. M., Brink, E. L. T., & Prins, P. J. M. (2014). A Pilot Study of the Efficacy of a Computerized Executive Functioning Remediation Training With Game Elements for Children With ADHD in an Outpatient Setting: Outcome on Parent- and Teacher-Rated Executive Functioning and ADHD Behavior. *Journal of Attention Disorders, 18*(8), 699–712. doi:10.1177/1087054712453167 PMID:22879577

Van der Veer, R., & Valsiner, J. (1991). *Understanding Vygotsky: A Quest for Synthesis*. Blackwell.

van der Zee, T., & Reich, J. (2018). Open Education Science. *AERA Open, 4*(3). doi:10.1177/2332858418787466

Van Staalduinen, J. P., & de Freitas, S. (2011). A Game-Based Learning Framework: Linking Game Design and Learning. In M. S. Khine (Ed.), *Learning to play: Exploring the future of education with video games* (pp. 29–53). Peter Lang.

van Steensel, F. J. A., Bögels, S. M., & Perrin, S. (2011). Anxiety Disorders in Children and Adolescents with Autistic Spectrum Disorders: A Meta-Analysis. *Clinical Child and Family Psychology Review, 14*(3), 302–317. doi:10.100710567-011-0097-0 PMID:21735077

Vannucchi, G., Masi, G., Toni, C., Dell'Osso, L., Erfurth, A., & Perugi, G. (2014). Bipolar disorder in adults with ' 'Asperger's Syndrome: A systematic review. *Journal of Affective Disorders, 168*, 151–160. doi:10.1016/j.jad.2014.06.042 PMID:25046741

Veeramachaneni, K., Reilly, U. O., & Taylor, C. (2014). *Towards feature engineering at scale for data from massive open online courses*. ArXiv Preprint ArXiv:1407.5238.

Velásquez, C. T. (2017). *Competency-Based Training and the Constructivist Approach to Teaching in Higher Education*. https://enlinea.santotomas.cl/blog-expertos/la-formacion-basada-competencias-enfoque-constructivista-ensenanza-la-educacion-superior/

Velázquez-Iturbide, J. Á., Robles-Martínez, G., Cobos, R., Echeverría, L., Claros, I., Fernández-Panadero, M. C., ... Delgado-Kloos, C. (2016, September). Project eMadrid: Learning methodologies, gamification and quality. In *2016 International Symposium on Computers in Education (SIIE)* (pp. 1-5). IEEE. 10.1109/SIIE.2016.7751874

Veldkamp, B. P., & Sluijter, C. (2019). *Theoretical and practical Advances in Computer-based Educational Measurement.* Academic Press.

Veneman, J. F., Kruidhof, R., Hekman, E. E. G., Ekkelenkamp, R., Van Asseldonk, E. H. F., & Van Der Kooij, H. (2007). Design and evaluation of the LOPES exoskeleton robot for interactive gait rehabilitation. *IEEE Transactions on Neural Systems and Rehabilitation Engineering, 15*(1), 379–386. doi:10.1109/TNSRE.2007.903919 PMID:17894270

Ventola, C. L. (2014). Mobile devices and apps for health care professionals: Uses and benefits. *P&T, 39*(5), 356. PMID:24883008

Ventura, M., Shute, V., & Zhao, W. (2013). The relationship between video game use and a performance-based measure of persistence. *Computers & Education, 60*(1), 52–58. doi:10.1016/j.compedu.2012.07.003

Vera, L., Herrera, G., & Vived, E. (2005). Virtual reality school for children with learning difficulties. *Proceedings of the 2005 ACM SIGCHI International Conference on Advances in Computer Entertainment Technology,* 338–341. 10.1145/1178477.1178541

Verbiest, F., Proesmans, M., & Van Goal, L. (2017). Autonomous Mapping of the Priscilla Catacombs. In M. Ioannides, N. Magnenat-Thalmann, & G. Papagiannakis (Eds.), *Mixed Reality and Gamification for Cultural Heritage* (pp. 75–98). Springer. doi:10.1007/978-3-319-49607-8_3

Vermunt, D. A., Negro, S. O., Verweij, P. A., Kuppens, D. V., & Hekkert, M. P. (2019). Exploring barriers to implementing different circular business models. *Journal of Cleaner Production, 222,* 891–902. doi:10.1016/j.jclepro.2019.03.052

Vermunt, J. D., Ilie, S., & Vignoles, A. (2018). Building the foundations for measuring learning gain in higher education: A conceptual framework and measurement instrument. *Higher Education Pedagogies, 3*(1), 266–301. doi:10.1080/23752696.2018.1484672

Verschueren, S., Buffel, C., & Vander Stichele, G. (2019). Developing theory-driven, evidence-based serious games for health: Framework based on research community insights. *JMIR Serious Games, 7*(2), e11565. doi:10.2196/11565 PMID:31045496

Viceconti, M., Zannoni, C., Baruffaldi, F., Pierotti, L., Toni, A., & Cappello, A. (2020). CT-scan data acquisition to generate biomechanical models of bone structures. *Computer Methods in Biomechanics and Biomedical Engineering, 2,* 279–287.

Videla Rodríguez, J. J., Sanjuán Pérez, A., Martínez Costa, S., & Seoane Nolasco, A. (2017). Usability and design for augmented reality learning interfaces. *Digital Education Review, 31,* 61–79. doi:10.1344/der.2017.31.61-79

Villegas, A. M., & Lucas, T. (2007, March). The culturally responsive teacher. *Educational Leadership.* https://www.ascd.org/el/articles/the-culturally-responsive-teacher

Virtual Songlines. (n.d.). www.virtualsonglines.org

Virvou, M., & Katsionis, G. (2008). On the usability and likeability of virtual reality games for education: The case of VR-ENGAGE. *Computers & Education, 50*(1), 154–178.

Visual Studio. (2021). *Microsoft Visual Studio.* https://visualstudio.microsoft.com/

Vonn, C. (2016, July 12). Pokémon Go Users Flock to Museums, Passing Picasso in Search of Pikachu. *Hyperallergic*. https://hyperallergic.com/310589/pokemon-go-users-flock-to-museums-passing-picasso-in-search-of-pikachu/

Vygotsky, L. S. (1981b). The Genesis of Higher Mental Functions (J.V. Wertsch, Ed. & Trans.). In The Concept of Activity in Soviet Psychology (pp. 144-188). M.E. Sharpe. (Originally published 1960)

Vygotsky, L. S. (1987). The Collected Works of L.S. Vygotsky. Vol. 1. Problems of General Psychology (Rieber, R.S. & Carton, A.S. Eds., N. Minick Trans.). Plenum Press.

Vygotsky, L. S. (1997). *The collected works of L.S. Vygotsky: Problems of the theory and history of psychology*. Springer US, Science & Business Media. doi:10.1007/978-1-4615-5893-4

Vygotsky, L. S. (2016). Play and Its Role in the Mental Development of the Child. *International Research in Early Childhood Education, 7*(2).

Vygotsky, L. (1978). Interaction between learning and development. *Readings on the Development of Children, 23*(3), 34–41.

Vygotsky, L. (1980). *Mind in Society: The Development of Higher Psychological Processes*. Harvard University Press. doi:10.2307/j.ctvjf9vz4

Vygotsky, L. S. (1978). *Mind in society: The development of higher psychological processes*. Harvard University Press.

Vygotsky, L. S. (1981a). The Instrumental Method in Psychology. In *The concept of activity in Soviet psychology* (J. V. Wertsch, Ed. & Trans.; pp. 134–143). M.E. Sharpe. Inc. (Original work published 1960)

Waldheim, C. (2006). Strategies of Indeterminacy in Recent Landscape Practice. *Public 33: Errata*, 80-86.

Walther, B.K. (2003). Playing and Gaming: Reflections and Classifications. Game Studies, volume 3, issue 1.

Wanat, G. (2020, June 19). Popularity of Netflix production *The Witcher* by region. *Statista*. https://www.statista.com/statistics/1085978/popularity-of-netflix-production-the-witcher-by-region/

Wang, C., & Huang, L. (2021). A Systematic Review of Serious Games for Collaborative Learning: Theoretical Framework, Game Mechanic and Efficiency Assessment. *International Journal of Emerging Technologies in Learning, 16*(6), 88. doi:10.3991/ijet.v16i06.18495

Wang, H., Shen, C., & Ritterfeld, U. (2009). Enjoyment of Digital Games What Makes Them "Seriously" Fun? Enjoyment: At the Heart of Digital Gaming. In U. Ritterfeld, M. Cody, & P. Vorderer (Eds.), *Serious games: Mechanisms and effects*. Routledge.

Wang, J. L., Sheng, J. R., & Wang, H. Z. (2019). The association between mobile game addiction and depression, social anxiety, and loneliness. *Frontiers in Public Health, 7*, 247.

Wang, Y., Nguyen, H., Harpstead, E., Stamper, J., & McLaren, B. M. (2019). How Does Order of Gameplay Impact Learning and Enjoyment in a Digital Learning Game? In S. Isotani, E. Millán, A. Ogan, P. Hastings, B. McLaren, & R. Luckin (Eds.), *Artificial Intelligence in Education* (pp. 518–531). Springer International Publishing. doi:10.1007/978-3-030-23204-7_43

Warthen, K., Boyce-Peacor, A., Jones, K., Love, T., & Mickey, B. (2020). Sex differences in the human reward system: Convergent behavioral, autonomic and neural evidence. *Social Cognitive and Affective Neuroscience, 15*(7), 789–801. doi:10.1093can/nsaa104 PMID:32734300

Watershed. (2014). *Playable City*. https://www.playablecity.com/

Watersheds and Drainage Basin. (2019, June 8). *Water Science School.* https://www.usgs.gov/special-topics/water-science-school/science/watersheds-and-drainage-basins

Watson, W. R., Mong, C. J., & Harris, C. A. (2011). A case study of the in-class use of a video game for teaching high school history. *Computers & Education, 56*(2), 466–474. doi:10.1016/j.compedu.2010.09.007

Watson, W., & Yang, S. (2016). Games in schools: Teachers' perceptions of barriers to game-based learning. *Journal of Interactive Learning Research, 27*(2), 153–170.

Wattanasoontorn, V., Boada, I., García, R., & Sbert, M. (2013). Serious games for health. *Entertainment Computing, 4*(4), 231–247. doi:10.1016/j.entcom.2013.09.002

Watt, K., & Smith, T. (2021). Based Game Design for Serious Games. *Simulation & Gaming.*

Ways of History. (2017). [Video Game]. Glyph Worlds.

Wegrzyn, S. C., Hearrington, D., Martin, T., & Randolph, A. B. (2012). Brain games as a potential nonpharmaceutical alternative for the treatment of ADHD. *Journal of Research on Technology in Education, 45*(2), 107–130.

Weinstock, L. S. (1999). Gender differences in the presentation and management of social anxiety disorder. *The Journal of Clinical Psychiatry, 60*(9), 9–13.

Weitlauf, A. S., McPheeters, M. L., Peters, B., Sathe, N., Travis, R., Aiello, R., . . . Warren, Z. (2014). Therapies for children with autism spectrum disorder: Behavioral interventions update. Comparative Effectiveness Review, 137.

Weizsäcker, E., & Wijkman, A. (2018). *Come On! Capitalism, Short-termism, Population and the Destruction of the Planet A Report to the Club of Rome, prepared for the Club of Rome's 50th Anniversary in 2018.* Springer Science+Business Media LLC.

Wen, D., Lan, X., Zhou, Y., Li, G., Hsu, S. H., & Jung, T. P. (2018). The study of evaluation and rehabilitation of patients with different cognitive impairment phases based on virtual reality and EEG. *Frontiers in Aging Neuroscience, 10,* 88. Advance online publication. doi:10.3389/fnagi.2018.00088 PMID:29666577

Werbach, K., & Hunter, D. (2012). For the win: how game thinking can revolutionize your business. Wharton Digital Press.

Werbach, K., & Hunter, D. (2012). *For the Win. How Game Thinking Can Revolutionize Your Business.* Wharton Digital Press.

Werbach, K., & Hunter, D. (2012). *For the Win: How Game Thinking can Revolutionize your Business.* Wharton Digital Press.

Werbach, K., & Hunter, D. (2015). *The gamification toolkit: dynamics, mechanics, and components for the win.* University of Pennsylvania Press.

Werning, J. P., & Spinler, S. (2020). Transition to circular economy on firm level: Barrier identification and prioritization along the value chain. *Journal of Cleaner Production, 245,* 118609. doi:10.1016/j.jclepro.2019.118609

Wertsch, J. V. (1991). *Voices of the Mind. A Socio-Cultural Approach to Mediated Action.* Harverster-Wheatsheaf.

Wertsch, J. V. (1998). *Mind as Action.* Oxford University Press.

Westera, W. (2019). Why and How Serious Games can Become Far More Effective: Accommodating Productive Learning Experiences, Learner Motivation and the Monitoring of Learning Gains. *Journal of Educational Technology & Society, 22*(1), 59–69.

West, L. R. (2015). Strava: Challenge yourself to greater heights in physical activity/cycling and running. *British Journal of Sports Medicine, 49*(15), 1024. doi:10.1136/bjsports-2015-094899 PMID:25964665

Whalen, K. A., Berlin, C., Ekberg, J., Barletta, I., & Hammersberg, P. (2018). 'All they do is win': Lessons learned from use of a serious game for Circular Economy education. *Resources, Conservation and Recycling, 135*(May), 335–345.

Whitton, N. (2011). Encouraging engagement in game-based learning. *International Journal of Game-Based Learning, 1*(1), 75–84. doi:10.4018/ijgbl.2011010106

WHO - World Health Organization. (2005). *Envelhecimento ativo: uma política de saúde* [Active aging: a health policy]. Author.

WHO - World Health Organization. (2015). *Relatório mundial de envelhecimento e saúde* [World Aging and Health Report]. https://sbgg.org.br//wp-content/uploads/2015/10/OMS-ENVELHECIMENTO-2015-port.pdf

Whyte, E. M., Smyth, J. M., & Scherf, K. S. (2015). Designing Serious Game Interventions for Individuals with Autism. *Journal of Autism and Developmental Disorders, 45*(12), 3820–3831.

Wiener, N. (1964, February 24). Machines Smarter than Men? Interview with Dr. Norbert Wiener, Noted Scientist. *U.S. News & World Report*, 84–86.

Wijman, T. (2021, May 6). *Newzoo*. https://newzoo.com/insights/articles/global-games-market-to-generate-175-8-billion-in-2021-despite-a-slight-decline-the-market-is-on-track-to-surpass-200-billion-in-2023/

Wikipedia. (2021). *The climate Fresk*. https://en.wikipedia.org/wiki/The_Climate_Fresk

Wikipedia. (n.d.). *Video game*. Available at: https://en.wikipedia.org/wiki/Video_game

Wiklund-Engblom, A., & Högväg, J. (2014). The quest for integrating data in mixed research: User experience research revisited. In M. Horsely, M. Elliot, B. A. Knight, & R. Reilly (Eds.), *Current trends in eye tracking research* (pp. 161–175). Springer. doi:10.1007/978-3-319-02868-2_12

Williams, A. D., & Andrews, G. (2013). The Effectiveness of Internet Cognitive Behavioural Therapy (iCBT) for Depression in Primary Care: A Quality Assurance Study. *PLoS One, 8*(2), e57447. doi:10.1371/journal.pone.0057447 PMID:23451231

Williams, L. W., Matson, J. L., Beighley, J. S., Rieske, R. D., & Adams, H. L. (2014). Comorbid symptoms in toddlers diagnosed with autism spectrum disorder with the DSM-IV-TR and the DSM-5 criteria. *Research in Autism Spectrum Disorders, 8*(3), 186–192. doi:10.1016/j.rasd.2013.11.007

Wittland, J., Brauner, P., & Ziefle, M. (2015). Serious Games for Cognitive Training in Ambient Assisted Living Environments – A Technology Acceptance Perspective. In *Human-Computer Interaction – INTERACT 2015* (pp. 453–471). Springer International Publishing. doi:10.1007/978-3-319-22701-6_34

Wolcott, M. D., McLaughlin, J. E., Hann, A., Miklavec, A., Beck Dallaghan, G. L., Rhoney, D. H., & Zomorodi, M. (2021). A review to characterise and map the growth mindset theory in health professions education. *Medical Education, 55*(4), 430–440. doi:10.1111/medu.14381 PMID:32955728

Wolf, M. J. P. (2019). *The Routledge companion to imaginary worlds*. Routledge.

Woo, B. S. C., Chang, W. C., Fung, D. S. S., Koh, J. B. K., Leong, J. S. F., Kee, C. H. Y., & Seah, C. K. F. (2004). Development and validation of a depression scale for Asian adolescents. *Journal of Adolescence, 27*(6), 677–689. doi:10.1016/j.adolescence.2003.12.004 PMID:15561310

Woo, B. S. C., Ng, T. P., Fung, D. S. S., Chan, Y. H., Lee, Y. P., Koh, J. B. K., & Cai, Y. (2007). Emotional and behavioural problems in Singaporean children based on parent, teacher and child reports. *Singapore Medical Journal*, *48*(12), 1100–1106. PMID:18043836

Wood, L. C., & Reiners, T. (2015). Gamification. In M. Khosrow-Pour (Ed.), *Encyclopedia of Information Science and Technology* (3rd ed., pp. 3039–3047). IGI Global. doi:10.4018/978-1-4666-5888-2.ch297

Woods, B., Aguirre, E., Spector, A. E., & Orrell, M. (2012). Cognitive stimulation to improve cognitive functioning in people with dementia. *Cochrane Database of Systematic Reviews*, *2*. Advance online publication. doi:10.1002/14651858. CD005562.pub2 PMID:22336813

Woods, B., Thorgrimsen, L., Spector, A., Royan, L., & Orrell, M. (2006). Improved quality of life and cognitive stimulation therapy in dementia. *Aging & Mental Health*, *10*(3), 219–226. doi:10.1080/13607860500431652 PMID:16777649

World Bank. (2019, April 9). *Singapore Overview* [Text/HTML]. World Bank. https://www.worldbank.org/en/country/singapore/overview

World Bank. (2021). *World Development Indicators*. The World Bank | Country Profile. https://databank.worldbank.org/views/reports/reportwidget.aspx?Report_Name=CountryProfile&Id=b450fd57&tbar=y&dd=y&inf=n&zm=n&country=SGP

World Health Organization. (2001). *The World Health Report 2001: Mental health: new understanding, new hope*. World Health Organisation.

World Trade Organisation. (2012). *Trade policy review—Singapore* (WT/TPR/S/267). World Trade Organisation. https://www.wto.org/english/tratop_e/tpr_e/tp367_e.htm

Wu, M., & Luo, J. (2019). Wearable technology applications in healthcare: A literature review. *On-Line Journal of Nursing Informatics*, *23*(3).

Wu, T., & Huang, Y. (2017). A mobile game-based English vocabulary practice system based on portfolio analysis. *Journal of Educational Technology & Society*, *20*(2), 265–277.

Wu, Y. (2020). The analysis of Elsa's growth from the perspective of ecofeminism. *Open Journal of Social Sciences*, *8*(6), 30–36. Advance online publication. doi:10.4236/jss.2020.86003

Wyckoff, M. H., Aziz, K., Escobedo, M. B., Kapadia, V. S., Kattwinkel, J., Perlman, J. M., Simon, W. M., Weiner, G. M., & Zaichkin, J. G. (2015). Part 13: Neonatal resuscitation. 2015 American Heart Association guidelines update for cardiopulmonary resuscitation and emergency cardiovascular care. *Circulation*, *132*(18, suppl 2), S543–S560. doi:10.1161/CIR.0000000000000267 PMID:26473001

Xavier, A. J., d'Orsi, E., de Oliveira, C. M., Orrell, M., Demakakos, P., Biddulph, J. P., & Marmot, M. G. (2014). English longitudinal study of aging: Can Internet/E-mail use reduce cognitive decline? *The Journals of Gerontology. Series A, Biological Sciences and Medical Sciences*, *69*(9), 1117–1121. doi:10.1093/gerona/glu105 PMID:25116923

Xexéo, G., Carmo, A., Acioli, A., Taucei, B., Dipolitto, C., Mangeli, E., & Azevedo, V. (2017). *O que são Jogos: Uma ntrodução ao Objeto de Estudo do LUDES*. Universidade Federal do Rio de Janeiro.

Xing, Y., & Hu, S. (2010). Following Construction Study of One Village One College Student Training Plan in Heilongjiang Province. *International Conference on e-Education, e-Business, e-Management and e-Learning*, 436–439. 10.1109/IC4E.2010.46

Xu, Z., Yu, B., & Wang, F. (2020). Artificial intelligence/machine learning solutions for mobile and wearable devices. *Digital Health: Mobile and Wearable Devices for Participatory Health Applications*, *55*.

Xu, F., & Buhalis, D. (2021). *Gamification for tourism*. Channel View Publications.

Xu, J., Lio, A., Dhaliwal, H., Andrei, S., Balakrishnan, S., Nagani, U., & Samadder, S. (2021). Psychological interventions of virtual gamification within academic intrinsic motivation: A systematic review. *Journal of Affective Disorders*, *293*, 444–465. doi:10.1016/j.jad.2021.06.070 PMID:34252688

Yamada-Rice, D., Mushtaq, F., Woodgate, A., Bosmans, D., Douthwaite, A., Douthwaite, I., Harris, W., Holt, R., Kleeman, D., Marsh, J., & others. (2017). *Children and virtual reality: Emerging possibilities and challenges*. Academic Press.

Yanev, V. (2019, May 2). Video Game Demographics - Who Plays. *Games*, *2020*. https://techjury.net/stats-about/video-game-demographics/#gref

Yang, S. (2010). Defining Exergames & Exergaming. *Proceedings of Meaningful Play*, 1–17. Available at: https://meaningfulplay.msu.edu/proceedings2010/mp2010_paper_63.pdf

Yang, J. C., Quadir, B., & Chen, N. S. (2016). Effects of the badge mechanism on self-efficacy and learning performance in a game-based english learning environment. *Journal of Educational Computing Research*, *54*(3), 371–394. doi:10.1177/0735633115620433

Yeh, S.-C., Tsai, C.-F., Fan, Y.-C., Liu, P.-C., & Rizzo, A. (2012). An innovative ADHD assessment system using virtual reality. *2012 IEEE-EMBS Conference on Biomedical Engineering and Sciences*, 78–83. 10.1109/IECBES.2012.6498026

Yeo, C. L., Ho, S. K. Y., Tagamolila, V. C., Arunachalam, S., Bharadwaj, S. S., Poon, W. B., Tan, M. G., Edison, P. E., Yip, W. Y., Haium, A. A. A., Jayagobi, P. A., Vora, S. J., Khurana, S. K., Allen, J. C., & Lustestica, E. I. (2020). Use of web-based game in neonatal resuscitation-is it effective? *BMC Medical Education*, *20*(1), 1–11. doi:10.118612909-020-02078-5 PMID:32456704

Ylvisaker, M., Robin, H., & Doug, J.-G. (2003). Rehabilitation of Children and Adults With Cognitive-Communication Disorders After Brain Injury (No. TR2003-00146). American Speech-Language-Hearing Association. doi:10.1044/policy.TR2003-00146

Yohannis, A., & Prabowo, Y. (2015, September). Sort attack: Visualization and gamification of sorting algorithm learning. In *2015 7th international conference on games and virtual worlds for serious applications (vs-games)* (pp. 1-8). IEEE.

Yokoi, T. (2021, March 3). Female gamers are on the rise – can the gaming industry keep up? *Forbes*. https://www.forbes.com/sites/tomokoyokoi/2021/03/04/female-gamers-are-on-the-rise-can-the-gaming-industry-catch-up/

Yonemura, K., Yajima, K., Komura, R., Sato, J., & Takeichi, Y. (2017, November). Practical security education on operational technology using gamification method. In *2017 7th IEEE International Conference on Control System, Computing and Engineering (ICCSCE)* (pp. 284-288). IEEE. 10.1109/ICCSCE.2017.8284420

York, J., & deHaan, J. W. (2018). A constructivist approach to game-based language learning: Student perceptions in a beginner-level EFL context. *International Journal of Game-Based Learning*, *8*(1), 19–40. doi:10.4018/IJGBL.2018010102

Young, M. F., Slota, S., Cutter, A. B., Jalette, G., Mullin, G., Lai, B., & Yukhymenko, M. (2012). Our princess is in another castle: A review of trends in serious gaming for education. *Review of Educational Research*, *82*(1), 61–89. doi:10.3102/0034654312436980

Young, S.-S.-C., & Wang, Y.-H. (2014). The game embedded call system to facilitate english vocabulary acquisition and pronunciation. *Journal of Educational Technology & Society*, *17*(3), 239–251.

Youtopia. (2021). Available at https://youtopia.com/

Yuan, Z., Bi, J., & Moriguichi, Y. (2006). The circular economy: A new development strategy in China. *Journal of Industrial Ecology, 10*(1–2), 4–8. doi:10.1162/108819806775545321

Yu-Che, H., & Yi-Ru, C. (2019). The Study of Virtual Reality Product Design in Education Learning. *Proceedings of the 2019 The 3rd International Conference on Digital Technology in Education*, 9–11. 10.1145/3369199.3369207

Yudintseva, A. (2015). Synthesis of research on video games for the four second language skills and vocabulary practice. *Open Journal of Social Sciences, 3*(11), 81–89. doi:10.4236/jss.2015.311011

Yuhanna, I., Alexander, A., & Kachik, A. (2020). Advantages and disadvantages of Online Learning. *Journal Educational Verkenning, 1*(2), 13–19. doi:10.48173/jev.v1i2.54

Yuill, N., & Hollis, V. (2011). A systematic review of cognitive stimulation therapy for older adults with mild to moderate dementia: An occupational therapy perspective. *Occupational Therapy International, 18*(4), 163–186. doi:10.1002/oti.315 PMID:21425381

Yunyongying, P. (2014). Gamification: Implications for curricular design. *Journal of Graduate Medical Education, 6*(3), 410–412.

Zabolotna, O. (2012). Holistic pedagogy as a theoretical source of alternative school education. *Psychological and Pedagogical Problems of Rural Schools*, (41), 224-230.

Zaboski, B. A., & Storch, E. A. (2018). Comorbid autism spectrum disorder and anxiety disorders: A brief review. *Future Neurology, 13*(1), 31–37. doi:10.2217/fnl-2017-0030 PMID:29379397

Zaichkin, J., Mccarney, L., & Weiner, G. (2016). NRP 7th Edition: Are You Prepared? Neonatal Network, 35(4), 184-191. doi:10.1891/0730-0832.35.4.184

Zain, N. H. M., Othman, Z., Noh, N. M., Teo, N. H. I., Zulkipli, N. H. B. N., & Yasin, A. M. (2020). GAMEBC model: Gamification in health awareness campaigns to drive behaviour change in defeating COVID-19 pandemic. *International Journal of Advanced Trends in Computer Science and Engineering, 9*(4).

Zainuddin, Z., Chu, S. K. W., Shujahat, M., & Perera, C. J. (2020). The impact of gamification on learning and instruction: A systematic review of empirical evidence. *Educational Research Review, 30*, 100326. doi:10.1016/j.edurev.2020.100326

Zemlock, D., Vinci-Booher, S., & James, K. H. (2018). Visual–motor symbol production facilitates letter recognition in young children. *Reading and Writing, 31*(6), 1255–1271. doi:10.100711145-018-9831-z

Zhang, G. X., & Li, L. M. (2010). Chinese language teaching in the UK: Present and future. *Language Learning Journal, 38*(1), 87–97. doi:10.1080/09571731003620689

Zhang, P. (2008). Motivational affordances: Reasons for ICT design and use. *Communications of the ACM, 51*(11), 145–147. doi:10.1145/1400214.1400244

Zhu, C. (2012). Student satisfaction, performance, and knowledge construction in online collaborative learning. *Journal of Educational Technology & Society, 15*(1), 127–136.

Zichermann, G., & Cunningham, C. (2011). *Gamification by Design: Implementing Game Mechanics in Web and Mobile Apps*. O'Reilly Media.

Zichermann, G., & Cunningham, C. (2011). *Gamification by design: Implementing game mechanics in web and mobile apps*. O'Reilly Media, Inc.

Zou, D., Ma, L., Yu, J., & Zhang, Z. (2015). Biological databases for human research. *Genomics, Proteomics & Bioinformatics, 13*(1), 55–63. doi:10.1016/j.gpb.2015.01.006 PMID:25712261

About the Contributors

Oscar Bernardes holds a Ph.D. in management, since 2013. He worked as management consultant for several years, in several organizations (social, profitable, and governmental). He is Invited Professor at Polytechnic Institute of Porto (P.Porto), Portugal, where he has been lecturing courses in the following areas: entrepreneurship, innovation, marketing and general management. His research interests include entrepreneurship, gamification, innovation, and marketing.

Vanessa Amorim is a Business and Economics Ph.D. student at the University of Aveiro - Portugal. She has a master's in Organizational Management - Specialization: Business Management and a Post-Graduation in Management Tools for Business Competitiveness from Institute Polytechnic of Porto - Portugal. Her main research interests are Innovation, Entrepreneurship, Marketing, and Business Management.

* * *

Emmanuel Acquah is an Associate Professor (Tenure-Track) in Minority Research at the Faculty of Education and Welfare Studies, Åbo Akademi University. His primary research interests are in advancing equity in the training and practice of educators of multicultural and multilingual learners. He has related interests in diversity, equity, and inclusion. He has published extensively in the areas of multicultural and multilingual education, adolescents' socio-emotional well-being and children's social interaction in the classroom. Acquah is the Director of the new International Master's Degree Programme in Education called Teaching and Learning at the Faculty of Education and Welfare Studies at the Åbo Akademi University. ORCID ID: orcid.org/0000-0003-3720-443X

Adnan Ahmad holds a BS (Hons), MS, and Ph.D in Computer Science from GCU, Pakistan, LUMS, Pakistan, and Massey University, New Zealand, respectively. He has around thirteen years of teaching and research experience at various educational and research institutes. More than 40 peer-reviewed articles in renowned conferences and journals are to his credit, including Trustcom, Computers & Security, ACM Transactions, and IEEE Communication Magazine. He is a reviewer for various IEEE, Elsevier, IET, and Springer journals and has been a part of TPC at several prestigious conferences. He has supervised five PhDs, twelve MS thesis students, and several startup projects. He has also co-authored a book on socio-technical design. He served as the founding in-charge of Center of Advance Research in Distributed Systems and Security (CARDS) research group at COMSATS University Islamabad, Pakistan. His research interests include Distributed Systems, Cyber Security, Software Engineering, and the Internet of

Things (IoT). Currently, he is performing his duties as an Assistant Professor at COMSATS University Islamabad, Lahore Campus, Pakistan.

Nadeem Khan has a B. Tech. in Electronics and Communications from the Govt. Engineering College in Ajmer; and a M. Tech. in Electronics and Communications from the National Institute of Technology in Jalandhar.

Meike Belter is a PhD candidate in Human Interface Technology at HIT Lab NZ, which is a part of the University of Canterbury. For her research, she is working on immersive Virtual Reality for children with ADHD in formal education. She has a background in technical communications, educational science, as well as media and entertainment management.

Anette Bengs currently holds a position as a project researcher at the Experience Lab, Faculty of Education and Welfare Studies at Åbo Akademi University. Her focus is on digital design research, methods, and processes. Her research interests include digital content and technology as facilitators of social inclusion and basic psychological need fulfillment across the lifespan and across cultures. She has been involved in several projects targeting the inclusion of multicultural target groups and she is currently coordinating the REDIT project, which is about the evidence-based development of a second language learning digital game for facilitating language learning and the inclusion of immigrants.

Sonali Beri has completed her Bachelor of Technology in Electronics and Communication in 2019. Furthermore, she has completed her Master of Technology in Electronics and Communication in 2021. The research topic for the MTech Thesis was based on serious games.

Kartheka Bojan received her MSc in Biomedical Engineering from the University of Nottingham in 2014, in the United Kingdom. She is highly innovative and has presented her ideas to NASA in 2010. She was hired as a Chief Medical Device Engineer at Nemaura Medical, where she developed a non-invasive Glucose Monitoring Device, with which the company went public. She holds patents on innovative medical diagnosis methods, digital therapies, and continuous monitoring systems. In 2018, she started her own company, BrainBerry Ltd., a Medtech company focusing on non-pharmacological interventions for dementia. This stems from her personal experience of accompanying her grandmother through a rough journey with Alzheimer's disease a decade ago. Her interest lies in the development of technologies to improve mental health. She is an entrepreneur in spirit and scientific in her head, approaching the problems of the healthcare system with great zeal.

Hector Cardona Reyes has a Ph.D. in computer science from the Universidad Juarez Autonoma de Tabasco. Dr. Cardona Reyes is a member of SNI I in Mexico. He is currently a Catedra Conacyt researcher at the Center for Mathematics Research (CIMAT), Zacatecas unit. He has experience in mobile applications, web engineering, video game design, and virtual reality. His research interests include Software Engineering, Human-Computer Interaction, virtual reality, and interactive systems-oriented health and education.

Aikaterini Christogianni completed a PhD in Experimental and Thermal Physiology at Loughborough University in the United Kingdom. She also received her MSc in Clinical Neuropsychology from the University of Groningen in the Netherlands. She has training in assessing, evaluating, and diagnosing neuropsychological diseases and disorders that impact cognitive, emotional, and behavioral functioning in patients. She is motivated to apply her neuropsychological knowledge in the fields of neuroscience and psychopathology, with a special interest in research ethics. She is working on projects that are developing unique technologies to radically improve the way mental health conditions and cognitive impairments are assessed, monitored, and treated. She shares the vision of research teams to transform the way mental health and cognitive deficit concerns are identified and stratified, paving the way for better understanding, treatment, and outcomes.

Mario Cortes-Cornax is a Computer Engineer and Computer Science PhD in Information Systems. He spent 18 months as a PosDoc at the Xerox research center in Grenoble (France). Since 2014, he has been an assistant professor at the University of Grenoble, attached to the Computer Science Laboratory (LIG). His research interests concern Information Systems, Business Process Management and Model Driven Engineering.

Van-Dat Cung is Professor in Computer Science and Operations Research at Grenoble INP, Graduate schools of Engineering and Management of Université Grenoble Alpes, and member of the laboratory G-SCOP. His research fields are (1) Logistics and Transport Systems Modeling and Optimization and (2) Sustainable Supply Chain Design and Management.

Maria Cutumisu is an Associate Professor, Department of Educational Psychology, Faculty of Education, University of Alberta.

Luciane Fadel holds a Ph.D. in Design from the University of Reading, UK (2007) and a Post-Doctorate in Narratives supervised by Jim Bizzocchi at Simon Fraser University, Canada. She is currently an assistant professor in the Design and New Media at the Federal University of Santa Catarina, Brazil. She researches the Poetics of Digital Media and Design for Experience on the following themes: interaction design, narratives, new media, and digital storytelling.

Paola Falcone holds a PhD in Marketing from Sapienza University of Rome, is Lecturer on contract at Sapienza University of Rome and formerly at Università Politecnica delle Marche. She is trainer in post-graduate and post-experience programs in marketing and communication, and consultant. Her professional experiences have included the organization of scientific events, research communication, content production, publications editing and scientific review. She is author of several contributions published in international volumes. Her research is primarily focused on intangible assets, relationship marketing, and digital marketing / communication applications.

Daniel Fung is a child and adolescent psychiatrist and the Chief Executive Officer of the Institute of Mental Health in Singapore. He is an Adjunct Associate Professor at the Yong Loo Lin School of Medicine at the National University of Singapore, the Lee Kong Chian School of Medicine at Nanyang Technological University, and the Duke-NUS Graduate Medical School, and teaches both undergraduate and postgraduate students. Dr. Fung is the President of the International Association for Child and Adolescent Psychiatry and Allied Professions and the President of the College of Psychiatrists at the Academy of Medicine, Singapore. His research interests are wide-ranging, and he leads multiple research projects and workgroups on various topics in mental health. He is currently working on several projects involving neurophysiological and psychological interventions in neurobehavioral disorders. He was previously involved in a longitudinal cohort study on the epidemiology of video games and gaming and their relationship to psychiatric disorders.

Lorella Gabriele is with the Physics Department at the University of Calabria, Rende, Italy. She is a post-doc fellow and lecturer and is interested in the following topics: psychology of programming, educational technologies and their use in a didactic context, learning, and techniques of Human-computer Interaction, communications systems and their use for educational purposes. She is an occasional referee for the journals Computers & Education, Scientific Research, and Essays, and a member of the Editorial Board of the Journal of Applied Research in Higher Education (JARHE). She worked on different national and international projects.

Simran Ghoman, MSc from the University of Alberta, is a current medical student at the University of Calgary Medical School.

Nicholas Goh received his B.Soc.Sci (Hons) in Psychology at the National University of Singapore in 2019. In the same year, he started work as a Research Assistant at the Department of Developmental Psychiatry, Institute of Mental Health (IMH), Singapore, and is currently an Assistant Psychologist at IMH. Nicholas has experience working clinically with children struggling with mood and anxiety disorders and conducting cognitive assessments for children and adolescents. He is also trained in administering the Autism Diagnostic Observation Schedule-2 (ADOS-2). Nicholas has been involved in various research projects at IMH relating to child mental health, including cognitive rehabilitation for autism, youth suicide, and sleep.

Tze Jui Goh is a Principal Clinical Psychologist with the Department of Developmental Psychiatry, Institute of Mental Health (IMH), Singapore. She has extensive clinical experience working directly with children, parents, and caregivers to address a wide range of issues. She also teaches students, supervises fellow professionals, and oversees the Internship Program in Child Mental Health. She is also a certified trainer in the Autism Diagnostic Interview and the Autism Diagnostic Observation Schedule. In 2011, Dr. Goh was awarded the National Medical Research Council Fellowship award by the Ministry of Health, Singapore. She is also a fellow with the Rehabilitation Research Institute of Singapore and a Donald J. Cohen Fellow with the International Association for Child Adolescent Psychiatry and Allied Professions. She received the Healthcare Manpower Development Plan Fellowship Award (Team) in 2017 for the United Kingdom, with the aim of developing services for Autism Spectrum Disorders.

Rogério S. Gonçalves received the mechanical engineering degree from the Federal University of Uberlandia in 2004, the master's degree in 2006, and the Ph.D. from the same university in 2009. In 2016, he was a visiting scientist at The Eric P. and Evelyn E. Newman Laboratory for Biomechanics and Human Rehabilitation at the Massachusetts Institute of Technology – MIT. He joined the School of Mechanical Engineering of Federal University of Uberlandia, Brazil, in 2008, where he is currently Professor. He is the president of RoboCup Brazil (2020/2021). He is the author or co-author of about 100 papers. His research interests include kinematics and dynamics of serial and parallel structures, stiffness, cable-driven parallel structures, mobile robots, biorobotics, rehabilitation robots, and humanoid robots.

Ana Maria Gonzaga graduated in 1987 at Escola Superior de Saúde do Instituto Politécnico do Porto, where she later was a lecturer for 12 years. Ana Maria is an occupational therapy specialist in the Psychogeriatric service and is also the coordinator of the occupational therapists at Hospital Magalhães Lemos. She has also been the coordinator of internships for occupational therapists. Ana Maria is the co-author of two articles published in scientific journals: - "A Percepção dos Avós acerca das suas Relações Intergeracionais", in co-authorship with Prof. Dra. Orlanda Maria Cruz, published in Infância e Educação – Investigação e Práticas – n° 1, January 2000. - "Comportamentos suicidários em pacientes com distúrbios de personalidade internados em Hospital de Dia", in co-authorship with fellow professionals at Hospital de Dia do Hospital de Magalhães Lemos, presented at 3ª Jornadas Comportamentos Suicidários, October 2000, published in Psiquiatria Clínica, Jan./Apr.2001, Vol.22, n°1, pp.131-136. Ana Maria is also the co-author of the book "Mente Ativa, Corpo Feliz", published in March 2021.

Muhammad Hamid received the M.Sc. degree in information technology and the M.Phil. and Ph.D. degrees in computer science. His Ph.D. dissertation focuses on increasing the software exports of Pakistan by overcoming the most recurring problems using Artificial Intelligence (AI). During his Ph.D., he did research work at the Department of Computer Science and Operations Research at the University of Montreal, Canada. He has over ten years of administrative, research, and teaching experience with the University of Veterinary and Animal Sciences, Lahore. He has authored a number of research papers in reputed journals and conferences. His research interests include software engineering, software project management, and AI.

Soufiane Kaddouri is an industrial engineer with a master's degree in operations management.

Ilias Karasavvidis is assistant professor of learning with ICT in the Department of Preschool Education at the University of Thessaly, Greece. He is the head of the Science and Technology Laboratory in the same department. He holds a PhD in Educational Technology from the University of Twente, a M.Ed in Educational Technology, and an Honors degree in Teacher Education from the University of Crete. He has authored several international and national publications that cover various topics related to supporting learning with technology. His current research interests include digital media, serious games design and development, machine learning, and preservice/in-service teacher ICT training.

Heidi T. Katz is a doctoral student at the Faculty of Education and Welfare Studies at Åbo Akademi University in Vaasa, Finland. Her research interests include racial equity, educational opportunity, student well-being, and inclusive schooling.

Nadeem Ahmed Khan has completed Bachelor of Technology from Rajasthan Technical University and Master of Technology from Dr B R Ambedkar National Institute of Technology Jalandhar. His research interests are Serious Gaming, Virtual Reality.

Arun Khosla is currently working as a Professor in the Department of Electronics and Communication Engineering at the Dr B R Ambedkar National Institute of Technology, Jalandhar, India. His research interests include assisted technologies, healthcare, gamification, artificial intelligence, machine learning, and entrepreneurship.

Asiye Kurt has received an MSc degree in Operations Management and a PhD degree in Industrial Engineering from the University of Grenoble Alpes. She is currently a post-doctoral researcher at the laboratory G-SCOP. Her primary research interest is Supply Chains in the context of the Circular Economy.

Maria do Céu Lamas is a Professor at the School of Health | IPP (ESS IPP), in the technical and scientific area of Clinical Analysis and Public Health. Member of the Center for Research in Health and Environment (CISA), ESS IPP, and collaborator of the Research Center in Technologies and Health Services (CINTESIS) - University of Porto (UP), Portugal, in the line of research on aging. She is the author and co-author of several scientific papers. She graduated in Clinical Analysis and Public Health and received a Master's in Hydrobiology from the Faculty of Sciences, UP, and is a doctoral student in Gerontology at the Institute of Biomedical Sciences Abel Salazar (ICBAS), UP, Portugal.

Richard Li is currently a research assistant professor in the Department of Computing at the Hong Kong Polytechnic University. He received the B.Sc. degree in computer science and technology from Nanjing University in 2008, and the M.Sc. (Distinction) and PhD degrees in computer science from the City University of Hong Kong in 2011 and 2018, respectively. Before joining the Department, he worked as a senior research associate at the Centre for Innovative Applications of Internet and Multimedia Technologies (AIMtech Centre), City University of Hong Kong, and then as a postdoc research fellow at the Human Interface Technology Lab New Zealand (HIT Lab NZ), University of Canterbury. As a Human-centered Computing researcher, Dr Li's research interest is in collaborating with talents with various backgrounds to design new technology-assisted solutions for supporting people in their daily lives. His research works, especially in using virtual reality for children with special education needs, have been widely covered by local and international newspapers. Academically, his research works were published in international journals such as Computers & Education, IEEE Transactions on Visualization and Computer Graphics, IEEE Transactions on Learning Technologies, and Journal of Computer Assisted Learning, as well as conference proceedings such as the proceedings of the IEEE Virtual Reality conference, the International Conference on Artificial Reality and Telexistance & Eurographics Symposium on Virtual Environments, Australian Conference on Human-Computer Interaction, and the International Conference on Web-based Learning. He also serves as the programme chair of the International Conference on Blended Learning.

Choon Guan Lim is a senior consultant psychiatrist and the deputy chief of department at the Department of Developmental Psychiatry, Institute of Mental Health (IMH), Singapore. He is also an Adjunct Associate Professor at Duke-NUS Graduate Medical School, Lee Kong Chian School of Medicine at Nanyang Technological University, and a senior clinical tutor at the Yong Loo Lin School of Medicine at the National University of Singapore. Dr. Lim is a senior editor on the editorial board of the Journal, Child and Adolescent Psychiatry and Mental Health. His research interests are in child mental health, Attention-Deficit Hyperactivity Disorder, and Autism. Currently, he is involved in several projects involving brain-computer interfaces and attention training programs.

Tetiana Luhova is a Ph.D. in Art History, assistant professor of Information Activity and Media Communications Department of Odessa Polytechnic National University (Ukraine), Deputy Dean of the Humanities Faculty. Basic higher education – teaching, and psychologist in educational institutions. Experience teaching activities in higher education - 17 years. Research interests: gamification of education, game-based learning, knowledge management, spirituality in digital culture, traditional and modern culture, serious games in higher education, and spiritual upbringing.

Heide Lukosch is an Associate Professor at the HIT Lab NZ, University of Canterbury, New Zealand. With her research, she aims to understand how immersive games, which have a specific purpose such as training and learning, and use immersive technologies such as virtual or augmented reality for this, have to be designed and used in order to achieve the intended effect. Heide investigates how realistic in terms of representation, social interaction, and experience these games have to be to be valid and engaging games. She applies games to domains such as education, logistics, safety and security, and disaster management. Heide works together with local and international academics, as well as with organizations and game developers, to answer her research questions and to support organizations with game-based solutions through the interplay with the games industry.

Fabien Mangione is an assistant professor at the G-SCOP Laboratory of Grenoble Alpes University. He works on operation management planning activities. It can be on the supply chain level with the integration of the new concepts as circular economy. But he also works on the production level for scheduling with the integration of the industry 4.0 technologies.

Rutab Marriam is currently pursuing her Ph.D. degree in Computer Sciences. She has published various research articles at well-reputed venues including ACM Transaction on Computing Education and Journal of Computing in Higher Education. Her research interests include Software Engineering, Cyber Security, and Social Media Analysis.

Richard McCurry has been deeply engaged with the problems encountered by Chinese learners, to address the perception that, despite being the world's most spoken language, it is impossible to learn as a second language. His work in this time has focused on developing a new pedagogy which engages with visual, aural, and cognitive achievements in Chinese for new learners. Through delivery of Newby Chinese to thousands of students over a number of years, this core pedagogy has developed in close association with a game-based learning system which is well informed by effectiveness and 'in the field' delivery criteria.

Elizabeta Mukaetova-Ladinska is currently an Academic Staff in the Neuroscience, Psychology, and Behaviour Department at Leicester University in the United Kingdom. She has done research to identify blood biomarkers to diagnose dementia, and as a clinician, she is working to improve the clinical diagnosis of early onset dementia. She is also collaborating with NHS service users and their carers with the aim of promoting quality of life in the ageing population. She has been collaborating with BrainBerry Ltd. on neurofeedback treatment projects to prevent and treat early dementia. Her areas of interest and expertise include clinical assessments in dementia patients, psychopharmacology and new drug approaches, mental health, and autism in adults and the elderly.

Pierluigi Muoio has a PhD in Educational Technology and is a lecturer at the University of Calabria. He has been involved in e-learning for several years and is an expert on the subject in the fields of didactics and experimental pedagogy. He deals with the design and implementation of online 2.0 learning environments and tools to be applied in formal, non-formal, and informal training contexts in order to improve the activities carried out in e-learning and blended learning modes. He is the author of several scientific publications in the fields of innovative teaching and educational research in general.

Ana-Gabriela Núñez is a Ph.D. in Computer Science. She received her Ph.D. in Computer Science from the Universitat Politècnica de València (2018), Spain. Her line of research has been related to Emergency Management since her master's degree in Software Engineering and Information Systems at the UPV. Currently, she is a researcher at the University of Cuenca in the Department of Computer Science (DCC), Cuenca-Ecuador.

Miguel Angel Ortiz Esparza is a research professor at the Universidad Autónoma de Aguascalientes (UAA) in Mexico. He received the degree of Doctor in Computer Science from the Universidad Juarez Autónoma Tabasco, México. His research topics are in the domains of Human-Computer Interaction, e-learning, Software Engineering and Educational Resources.

Roger Paez is a PhD architect, professor and researcher. Architect ETSAB, Barcelona (Hons.); MS AAD Columbia University, New York (GSAPP Honor Award for Excellence in Design); PhD UPC, Barcelona (Excellent Cum Laude); Certified PhD (AQU 2020). Professional experience in the studios of Alison+Peter Smithson and Enric Miralles. Founder of AiB (www.aib.cat), a studio devoted to contemporary architectural practice with a critical edge. Architectural design professor at ETSALS (URL), MEATS director at ELISAVA (UVic-UCC) (meats.elisava.net), guest professor at universities worldwide, including Columbia, Cornell, Harvard, IIT, Sci-ARC and USC in the USA; ETSAB, ETSAV, BAC, IaaC, UdP (Porto), ETSAM (Madrid), ENA (Paris), PJAIT (Warsaw), UMA (Umeå) and ETH (Zürich) in Europe. Member of the editorial board of Quaderns d'arquitectura i urbanisme, awarded the Jean Tschumi Prize. He is a research leader at ELISAVA Research, where he develops public and private research projects. He regularly publishes both scientific articles and books, notably Design Strategies for Temporary Intervention in Public Space (Elisava, 2013), Critical Prison Design (Actar, 2014), and Operative Mapping: Maps as Design Tools (Actar, 2019). He works at the intersection of design, architecture, and the city, focusing on temporality, experimentation, and social impact.

M. Carmen Penadés Gramaje received her degree and Ph.D. in Computer Science from the Universitat Politècnica de València (UPV), Spain, in 1994 and 2002, respectively. She is currently an Associate Professor in the Department of Computer Science (DSIC) at the UPV. Her current research interests include emergency management information systems, document engineering, public participation, software product lines, feature modeling, and business processes. She participated in National, European, and Ibero-American research projects. She is a member of the Software Engineering and Information Systems (ISSI) research group at ITI (Technological Center for Research, Development, and Innovation in Information and Communication Technologies).

Zoë Platt-Young is a designer and PhD researcher who works at the crossroads of design, technology, and social sciences.

Girish S. Pujar is currently working as a Senior Scientist (SG) in the Rural Development and Watershed Monitoring Division in the Remote Sensing Application Area of NRSC, ISRO, India. He joined the NRSC in March 1998. He is a forestry professional by training and holds bachelor's and master's degrees in Forestry. His doctoral study focused on object-based image analysis of high resolution images for assessing tree spread. Currently, he coordinates GIS Implementation of the MGNREGA (Mah. Gandhi National Rural Employment Guarantee Act) programme of the Govt. of India and Monitoring of Implementation of the Integrated Watershed Management Programme of the Dept. of Land Resources, Govt. of India, using Bhuvan (ISRO Web. GIS) Web Services. The focus of the work is on issues of image-based detection of activities, reporting the impact, communicating the analysis of the database, capacity building of state teams, and coordination of Web GIS activities. He has worked extensively in application of remote sensing for themes of rural development, forestry, environment. He contributed in key roles to nationally significant studies such as the Central Committee (of the Supreme Court) on assessing mining status in Bellary, KRN, India, the world's first large-scale Carbon Credit project by ITC (Indian Tobacco Co., Ltd.), and promoted Agroforestry and Biodiversity Characterization at the National level using a Geospatial approach. He is mentoring projects with national-level academic institutions on fine scale modeling of watershed intervention impacts and serious gamification of ridge to valley treatments in rural development interventions under MGNREGA.

Patricia Quiroz-Palma received her degree in Higher Education degree in systems engineering from the University "Eloy Alfaro" of Manabi (ULEAM), Equator, and the master's degree in engineering and software systems technologies from the Universitat Politècnica de València (UPV), Spain, where he is currently pursuing a Ph.D. degree in computer science. He is currently an Associate Professor with the Faculty of Computer Science (FACCI) at the University "Eloy Alfaro" of Manabi (ULEAM), Ecuador. His current research interests include software engineering and emergency management, especially stakeholder training. In the field of research, he has presented several papers at national and international conferences.

Sam Redfern has been developing video games since the 1980s and has published them on many platforms and consoles. In addition to his role as technical lead at Newby Chinese, he is also a lecturer in Computer Science, with a focus on software development and video game development. His current research is in the areas of game-based learning, artificial intelligence for games, and distributed multiuser systems. His PhD was in photogrammetry and image processing.

Lucas Rodrigues received a mechatronic engineering degree from the Federal University of Uberlandia in 2014, a master's degree in 2017, and is currently pursuing a Ph.D. at the same university. He is also a consultant engineer for the top players in the consumer goods industry. He collaborated on about 30 papers. His research interests include the kinematics and dynamics of serial and parallel structures, data analytics for experimental tests, machine learning and computational optimization, cable-driven parallel structures, and rehabilitation robots for the upper and lower limbs.

José A. Ruipérez-Valiente received the B.Eng. degree in telecommunications from Universidad Católica de San Antonio de Murcia, and the M.Eng. degree in telecommunications and the M.Sc. and Ph.D. degrees in telematics from Universidad Carlos III of Madrid while conducting research with Institute IMDEA Networks in the area of learning analytics and educational data mining. He was a postdoctoral associate at MIT. He has received more than 20 academic/research awards and fellowships, has published more than 90 scientific publications in high-impact venues, and participated in over 18 funded projects. He currently holds the prestigious Spanish Fellowship, Juan de la Cierva, at the University of Murcia.

Alia Samreen received her B.S. (Gold Medalist) in Computer Science from COMSATS University Islamabad, Vehari Campus, Pakistan in 2014 and her M.S. in Computer Science from COMSATS University Islamabad, Lahore Campus, Pakistan in 2017. She was pursuing her Ph.D. degree in Computer Sciences from COMSATS University Islamabad, Lahore Campus, Pakistan. Previously, she had served as a lecturer at the Government Degree College Vehari, Pakistan and the University of Management Technology, Lahore, Pakistan. Miss Samreen has published various research articles at well-reputed venues including ACM Transaction on Computing Education and IEEE access. Her research interests include Trust management, Cyber Security, and other online privacy issues.

Georg Schmölzer is an Associate Professor, Department of Pediatrics, Faculty of Medicine and Dentistry, University of Alberta.

Parampreet Singh, B. Tech. from Guru Nanak Dev Engineering College, Ludhiana. M. Tech. from NIT Jalandhar. Currently, pursuing a PhD from IIT Kanpur.

Fredrik Sten received a bachelor's degree in ethnography from the Åbo Akademi University in 2012, where the foundations of academia were introduced to him. He later received a master's degree in digital culture from the University of Bergen in 2015, where he studied technological development and its impact on society. He has since been engaged in creative digital development and design, earning a certificate in game development at the University of Applied Sciences in Oulu in 2016. He specialised in audio for video games and received a degree as a Master of Fine Arts in Audio and Music for Video Games from the University of Chichester in 2021, giving him a full range of experience in practical development and technical aspects of the design of video games. His latest work at the Experience Lab at the Åbo Akademi University in Vasa has involved ethnographic research, user tests in lab environments, and developing user research methods for a variety of case studies.

Ian Stewart is a Reader in Project Management Education at the University of Manchester. He is also Programme Director of the MSc Management of Projects group of programmes and Academic Lead of the Management of Projects Research Group. His research interests are around the human costs of experiential teaching & learning techniques in large-class cohorts. He enjoys developing games and simulations for teaching project management competencies.

Arthur Stofella has a master's degree in the Postgraduate Program in Engineering and Knowledge Management at the Federal University of Santa Catarina, focusing on knowledge media. He developed works using rapid prototyping techniques for undergraduate students and professors of the architecture and urbanism course at UFSC. He is interested in interaction and interface design, new media, and serious game development.

Maureen Thomas, dramatist, screenwriter, interactive story-architect, and director, became a professor at the Norwegian Film School in 2000, where she is Senior Artistic Researcher. In addition to her professional creative work, she has carried out practice-oriented research as a Senior Research Fellow at Churchill College, Cambridge; a Visiting Artist at the Media Lab, University of Art & Design, Helsinki; and a Senior Creative Research Fellow at the Interactive Institute Narrativity Studio, Malmø University. She is a former Head Tutor at the National Film & Television School and co-founding director of the Digital Studio at the Martin Centre, University of Cambridge. Maureen has a particular interest in medieval Scandinavian literature and culture, focusing on the tales of chivalry and King Arthur, which she studied at the University of Cambridge, University College, London, and the Institute for Icelandic Studies, Reykjavik.

Kun Wang is an Engineering Project Management Lecturer at the University of Manchester. Experienced in large-sized class teaching and project management, experiential learning design, and evolution. Research interests include project management pedagogy, sociology-technical research in project management, and project management professionalization.

Mattias Wingren is currently a PhD student at Åbo Akademi University, and a member of Experience Lab situated there. His research interests include psychology, user-centered design, and social robotics.

Furkh Zeshan is an Assistant Professor in the Department of Computer Science, COMSATS University Islamabad, Lahore Campus, Pakistan. He received his Ph.D. degree from the Department of Software Engineering, Universiti Teknologi Malaysia (UTM). His research interests include Service-Oriented Computing, Embedded and Real-Time Computing, Software Engineering, Software Project Management, Knowledge Management, and Self-Organizing Systems. He is a reviewer, technical committee, and editorial member of many reputed national and international conferences and journals.

Index

O

Open-Loop Activity 415, 419
open-loops 395, 397, 399, 415, 419
organizations 89, 164-167, 170-171, 174, 186, 311-313, 315, 320, 324-328, 393, 396

P

period drama 334-336
Pinyin 481-482, 485, 492
play 1-3, 6, 8-9, 13-15, 17-20, 22, 25-26, 30, 37, 48-49, 54, 61, 78, 84, 90, 92, 103, 122, 130, 137, 231, 248, 261, 263-265, 272, 275-277, 289-291, 294-295, 298, 304-305, 309, 312-316, 318-319, 323-324, 326, 330-333, 337-339, 344-345, 351-352, 358, 361, 363, 373, 375, 383, 393, 396-397, 411, 415, 421, 424-425, 433, 436, 445, 447-450, 466, 470, 474, 482, 492-493, 496-499, 518-522, 524, 534, 543, 549-550, 556-558, 564-565
playability 211, 270, 286, 559
Playful Environment 523
points 2, 4, 8, 13, 31-32, 45, 48-52, 54-55, 57, 61-64, 66-68, 83, 86, 88, 148, 169, 185, 202, 209-210, 229, 270, 312, 314, 316, 318, 321, 323, 327, 329, 333, 360, 363, 378, 380, 382, 384, 401, 456, 474-475, 480, 482, 503, 524, 539, 550-551, 557-558
preparatory education 553, 555-556, 568
professional training 1, 5, 376
project management 43-45, 47, 50, 54-55, 57-59, 326

Q

QuEP Maturity-Level 190

R

radical 77, 126, 473, 493, 497-500, 507, 518-519, 522-523
recruitment 233, 375-378, 380-381, 383-393
recycling 395, 397-398, 400, 402, 406-407, 411-413, 415, 419, 435
Refurbishment 397, 419
rehabilitation 41, 98, 114, 125-128, 132, 134-135, 149-154, 156-157, 161-162, 168, 191-199, 202, 205-206, 208, 210-212, 216-220, 241, 246, 252, 257-258, 270, 272, 278, 280-282, 284-285
remanufacturing 395, 397-398, 400, 402, 407, 411-412, 415, 419
repurposing 395, 397-399, 412, 415, 417, 419
RETAIN 3, 221, 223-237, 240, 292, 326, 396, 503

reuse 395, 397-398, 400, 402, 406-409, 411-413, 415, 417, 419, 517
reverse logistics 397, 400, 407, 409, 419
Reward-Based Gamification 62, 75
risk 3, 13, 23, 54, 87, 100, 126, 129-130, 136, 144-145, 147-148, 168, 173, 186, 190, 222, 241, 255, 258, 260-261, 299, 309, 323-325, 379, 399, 448-449, 513, 519, 522, 525, 551
Robotics 40, 90, 206, 212, 217-218
RPG 161, 270, 336, 352, 358, 361, 363, 367, 373-374

S

SAD 238-239, 241-242, 247-251
scientific concepts 288, 293-296, 300, 303-306, 310
second language learning 490, 545, 565, 567
sensation 1, 154, 193, 211
serious games 1-8, 11, 13-21, 23, 34-36, 41, 45, 57-58, 60, 70, 118-119, 125-126, 131-141, 150-161, 163-170, 173-174, 179, 182, 186-196, 199, 212, 216-219, 223, 229, 231, 233-237, 239-241, 248-249, 252-254, 256, 259-260, 262-266, 268-270, 274-280, 283, 285-286, 288, 307-313, 315-316, 318, 321-322, 324-331, 333, 335, 340, 368, 370, 372-373, 375-382, 384-389, 391-393, 396, 398-400, 415-418, 421, 424-425, 427-428, 442-450, 468, 471, 491, 493, 496-498, 517, 519-522, 541, 563
Serious Games Design 137, 307-310, 316, 321, 325, 416-417
simulation 5-8, 15-20, 45-46, 55, 58-59, 98, 100-101, 116-117, 133, 139, 149, 155, 166, 187, 189, 197, 221-225, 229-234, 236-237, 279, 300, 309, 319, 329, 336, 356, 371, 402-403, 405, 409, 414-416, 418, 428, 442-444, 493, 496, 498, 564
simulation-based education 222
simulations 5-7, 15-17, 19, 23, 37, 45, 59, 126, 165-166, 169-170, 190, 225, 232, 235, 243, 246, 319, 324, 403, 427, 539, 549
Situated Learning 550, 568
Skill-tree 352, 374
Snowcastle Games 334, 358, 361, 367
social anxiety disorder 238-239, 241, 247-248, 252, 254, 256, 258
Social Communication 242, 257, 286
social interaction 25, 127, 161, 249, 291-292, 305-306, 310, 315, 369, 376, 471, 492
sociocultural theory 288, 291, 296, 303, 305-306, 310, 567
Soft-Skills Serious Games 375, 384
soil erosion 422-423, 432, 436, 441, 446, 449, 454

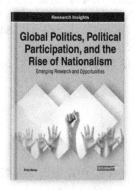

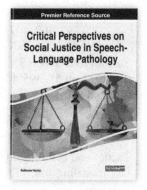

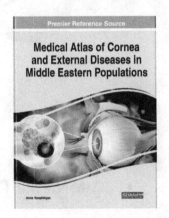

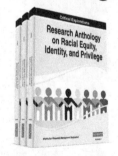
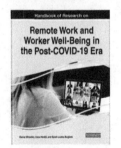

Printed in the United States
by Baker & Taylor Publisher Services

nted in the United States
r & Taylor Publisher Services